W9-CNJ-812

INTERNATIONAL PERSPECTIVE

TECHNOLOGY AND THE LAW

FIFTH EDITION

Canadian Business and the Law

FIFTH EDITION

Canadian Business and the Law

Dorothy DuPlessis
University of New Brunswick

Steven Enman
Acadia University

Shannon O'Byrne
University of Alberta

Philip King
Western University

NELSON EDUCATION

NELSON / EDUCATION

Canadian Business and the Law, Fifth Edition

by Dorothy DuPlessis, Steven Enman, Shannon O'Byrne, and Philip King

Vice President, Editorial Higher Education:
Anne Williams

Acquisitions Editor:
Alwynn Pinard

Marketing Manager:
Dave Stratton

Developmental Editor:
Suzanne Simpson Millar

Permissions Coordinator and Photo Researcher:
Julie Pratt

Senior Content Production Manager:
Natalia Denesiuk Harris

Production Service:
MPS Limited

Copy Editor:
Risa Vandersluis

Proofreader:
Tua Mondal

Indexer:
Maria Sosnowski

Manufacturing Manager:
Joanne McNeil

Design Director:
Ken Phipps

Managing Designer:
Franca Amore

Interior Design:
Martyn Schmoll

Interior Design Modifications:
Dianna Little

Cover Design:
Dianna Little

Cover Image:
Mark Hamblin/Getty Images

Compositor:
MPS Limited

Printer:
RR Donnelley

COPYRIGHT © 2014, 2011 by Nelson Education Ltd.

Printed and bound in the United States of America
2 3 4 5   17 16 15 14

For more information contact Nelson Education Ltd., 1120 Birchmount Road, Toronto, Ontario, M1K 5G4. Or you can visit our Internet site at http://www.nelson.com

ALL RIGHTS RESERVED. No part of this work covered by the copyright herein may be reproduced, transcribed, or used in any form or by any means—graphic, electronic, or mechanical, including photocopying, recording, taping, Web distribution, or information storage and retrieval systems—without the written permission of the publisher.

For permission to use material from this text or product, submit all requests online at www.cengage.com/permissions. Further questions about permissions can be emailed to permissionrequest@cengage.com

Every effort has been made to trace ownership of all copyrighted material and to secure permission from copyright holders. In the event of any question arising as to the use of any material, we will be pleased to make the necessary corrections in future printings.

Library and Archives Canada Cataloguing in Publication Data

Canadian business and the law / Dorothy DuPlessis ... [et al.]. — 5th ed.

Includes bibliographical references and index.
ISBN 978-0-17-650965-1

1. Commercial law—Canada—Textbooks. I. DuPlessis, Dorothy, 1955–

KE919.C36 2012   346.7107
C2012-907063-7   KF889.C36 2012

ISBN-13: 978-0-17-650965-1
ISBN-10: 0-17-650965-8

This book provides legal information of interest to those studying business law. It neither offers nor contains legal advice of any kind. If you have a personal legal question that requires legal advice, please consult a lawyer.

About the Authors

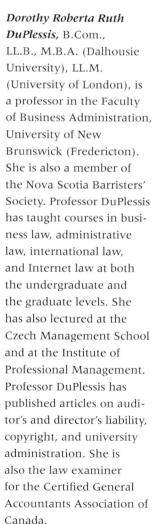

Dorothy Roberta Ruth DuPlessis, B.Com., LL.B., M.B.A. (Dalhousie University), LL.M. (University of London), is a professor in the Faculty of Business Administration, University of New Brunswick (Fredericton). She is also a member of the Nova Scotia Barristers' Society. Professor DuPlessis has taught courses in business law, administrative law, international law, and Internet law at both the undergraduate and the graduate levels. She has also lectured at the Czech Management School and at the Institute of Professional Management. Professor DuPlessis has published articles on auditor's and director's liability, copyright, and university administration. She is also the law examiner for the Certified General Accountants Association of Canada.

Steven Robert Enman, B.B.A. (Acadia University), LL.B. (Dalhousie University), LL.M. (Bristol University), was an associate professor in the Fred C. Manning School of Business Administration, Acadia University, when he retired in 2011. He was admitted to the bar of Nova Scotia in 1978, taught business law at Acadia for 32 years, and was director of the school for four years. Professor Enman is a retired member of the Nova Scotia Barristers' Society and a member of the Academy of Legal Studies in Business. He was the editor of two editions of *Canadian Business Law Cases*. He has presented papers at conferences dealing with privacy, unconscionable contracts, and commercial morality.

Shannon Kathleen O'Byrne, B.A. (University of Regina), M.A., LL.B., LL.M. (University of Alberta), is a professor in the Faculty of Law, University of Alberta, and a former Associate Dean of Graduate Studies and Research. She was admitted to the Law Society of Alberta in 1987 and is a past member of the board of directors of the Edmonton Bar Association. She is the recipient of the University of Alberta's highest teaching honour, the Rutherford Award for Excellence in Undergraduate Teaching, as well as the Faculty of Law's Teaching Excellence Award, named after the Hon. Mr. Justice Tevie Miller. Professor O'Byrne's articles have been cited with approval by courts across the country, including the Supreme Court of Canada.

Philip King, B.A. Philosophy (Western University), LL.B. (Western University), M.B.A. (Ivey Business School, Western University), teaches at Western Law, the Ivey Business School, and the Dan Program in Management and Organizational Studies, and practises corporate and commercial law in London, Ontario. Philip King has practised law since 1992, helping businesspeople achieve their goals by managing legal issues effectively. During that time, he has had the privilege of working with some of Canada's finest lawyers and businesspeople. While a student at Western, he was awarded the gold medal in the combined Law and M.B.A. program. Following graduation he worked at a major Canadian law firm on Bay Street in Toronto before returning to London, Ontario.

Brief Contents

Contents

Preface

In *Canadian Business and the Law,* Fifth Edition, legal knowledge is regarded as a business asset that builds competitive advantage for the individual and the organization alike. This text demonstrates how the law can protect persons and their property as well as resolve disputes. The text also shows that the law facilitates personal and commercial interactions. In short, the law provides both opportunities to be capitalized on and risks to be managed.

Canadian Business and the Law is written from the perspective that the law plays an integral role in all business decisions. Furthermore, it systematically advocates a risk management approach as the optimum way of dealing with legal considerations in the business world. A risk management model is introduced in Part 1 and applied in every subsequent part of the book. Topical coverage is organized as follows:

- **Part 1** establishes the rationale for students' study of business law. It accounts for what the law is, where it comes from, and how the law regulates business. It also establishes risk management as the recurring theme of the book and the study of business law.

- **Parts 2** and **3** recognize that the legal issues a businessperson is most likely to face are in the areas of contract law and tort law. Part 2, Contracts, and Part 3, Business Torts, provide a practical and contextualized analysis of these important areas. Here students acquire not only an essential legal grounding in contract and tort principles, but also the basic background for the specialized topics discussed later in the book. These two essential parts of the book are carefully written so that Contracts and Torts can be read and taught in whichever sequence is preferable to the user.

  The fundamentals of contract law are examined in depth in Part 2 to allow for application in context in later parts, which deal with topics such as agency, partnership, employment, and insurance. By applying the law to particular relationships, students gain insight into the kinds of contracts that will figure prominently in their professional lives.

In our experience, students best understand the law when it is related to core subject areas in the business curriculum, including finance, human resources, sales, and marketing. For this reason, the remaining parts of the book look at the functional areas of business and consider legal issues in relation to those activities.

- **Part 4** concerns the selection and use of the form of business.

- **Part 5** examines the creation, acquisition, use, and protection of property.

- **Part 6** analyzes the acquisition and use of human resources.

- **Part 7** focuses on the selling and marketing of goods and services.

- **Part 8** addresses financing the business activity.

- **Part 9** explores the transference of risk through the use of insurance.

Our work in *Canadian Business and the Law* focuses on meeting a number of objectives:

- Our most important aim is to explain the basic legal principles and concepts in a business context that is engaging and relevant for all readers.

- A second objective is to reinforce that all aspects of the legal environment necessitate active management. We offer a model for identifying, evaluating, and managing legal risk in Chapter 3. Examples of the model's application to business enterprises and a risk management orientation are reflected in the treatment of legal subjects throughout the text.

- A third objective is to convey legal information in contexts geared to the practical application of knowledge. A **Business Law in Practice** scenario opens each chapter with a business situation containing both legal and managerial implications. Questions posed by the opening scenario give students direction and purpose and encourage critical thinking as they read the chapter. As a means of testing the students' comprehension and analytical skills, the scenario is revisited later in the chapter with suggested responses to the opening questions.

    The practical application of legal knowledge is reinforced through boxes provided throughout the text entitled **Business Application of the Law.** These provide examples of the impact of the law on business enterprises. By illustrating how legal issues arise in the business environment and how these issues are managed, this feature helps students develop a concrete understanding of why the law matters in a business context.

- A fourth goal of the text is to recognize the importance of legal considerations inherent in the emergence of new technologies, internationalization and globalization of the economy, as well as ethical and environmental concerns, all of which cut across traditional legal subjects. Based on our contextualized approach to teaching and learning, these topics or unifying themes are integrated throughout the body of the text and through features entitled **Technology and the Law, International Perspective, Ethical Considerations,** and **Environmental Perspective.**

- A fifth goal is to provide a pedagogically effective framework for the presentation of judicial decisions. Our special Case format begins with a description of the business context surrounding the legal dispute in question, followed by a concise statement of the relevant facts that led to the legal conflict. Next, a statement of the legal issues is provided as a summary of how the court resolved the conflict. The feature concludes with several questions that students are asked to consider to deepen their understanding of the case under study. This feature focuses on context and relevance. Judicial rulings are summarized and supplemented with brief excerpts of judicial language.

    The **Landmark Case** and **Business and Legislation** features provide an account of pivotal case law and historical legislative initiatives, which can be essential to grasping contemporary law.

    Finally, an **Ethical Considerations** feature assists the student in assessing the sometimes uncomfortable compromises that the law forges between competing interests.

What's New in This Edition

New to this edition is enhanced coverage of the International, Environmental, Ethics, and Technology themes because of their importance to the modern business world. We have increased both the depth and breadth of coverage in these areas. As demonstrated in the chart on the inside front cover, the textbook organizes these four themes according to strands, or markers, to illustrate the range of topics that the text covers. The comprehensive chart is also designed to assist instructors in creating their lectures. At a glance, instructors can access the textbook's nearly 50 themed boxes and locate material according to the subject they wish to address, such as ethics in consumer relations or ethics in relation to employees.

To further enhance these themes, we have crafted a new Business Law in Practice chapter opener for Chapter 3 and Chapter 4 that explores the importance of environmental concerns, technology risks, and international issues in business decision making. Reflective of this approach, the chapters introduce new and revised materials on the management of a crisis, the role of lawyers in legal risk management, the use of alternative dispute resolution mechanisms, and class action law suits, for example.

We have continued to strengthen this text's emphasis on the pivotal role that the law plays in business decision making. This is accomplished by providing new and revised materials focusing on managing the risks inherent in legal requirements as well as identifying the protections and opportunities that law provides to business interests. Some of the major changes and additions to this edition in this regard are

- New cases. Many new cases have been added. Examples include *Tercon Contractors Ltd v British Columbia (Transportation and Highways)* 2010 SCC 4 (Chapter 9); *Jones v Tsige* 2012 ONCA 32 (Chapter 12); *Krawchuk v Scherbak*, 2011 ONCA 352, 332 DLR (4th) 310 (Chapter 13); *Canada (Attorney General) v Amazon.com Inc* 2011 FCA 328 (CanLII) (Chapter 18); *Covlin v Minhas*, 2009 ABCA 404 (Chapter 19); *Gill v Bucholtz*, 2009 BCCA 137 (Chapter 19); *Barrington v The Institute of Chartered Accountants of Ontario*, 2011 ONCA 409 (Chapter 22); and *SNS Industrial Products Limited v Bank of Montreal*, 2010 ONCA 500 (Chapter 25).

- New legislation. We have highlighted new and amended existing legislation relevant to business, including legislation affecting tanning beds (Chapter 1), tobacco (Chapter 2), apologies (Chapter 4), class action lawsuits (Chapter 4), SPAM (Chapter 6), franchises (Chapter 14), national securities regulation (Chapter 15), copyright (Chapter 18), workplace bullying (Chapter 20), consumer product safety (Chapter 23), identity theft (Chapter 25), and payday loans (Chapter 26).

- New real-world examples. This new edition discusses, for example, the killing of sled dogs owned by a business in British Columbia (Chapter 1); how companies such as Maple Leaf Foods and Toyota have managed a crisis (Chapter 3); whether a shop owner can chase down a shoplifter (Chapter 12); employees choosing to buy lottery tickets together (Chapter 14); how auditors have been put under greater scrutiny (Chapter 22); what that "no interest for 24 months!" will really cost (Chapter 26); and what happens when companies such as Blockbuster Video are no longer viable (Chapter 27).

- Updated and revised real-world examples from previous editions. Examples include insider-trading scandals in Canada (Chapter 15); to whom a baseball caught in the stands belongs (Chapter 17); the challenge against unpaid overtime (Chapter 20); testing for drugs or alcohol in the workplace (Chapter 20); and when performance claims for products are misleading (Chapter 23).

- New and updated chapter openings (**Business Law in Practice**).

- New and revised end-of-chapter material. We have added or replaced questions in the **Questions for Review, Questions for Critical Thinking,** and **Situations for Discussion** features.

Canadian Business and the Law, Fifth Edition, is offered as a modern resource for learning the fundamentals of business law from a business perspective. Rather than simply providing a summary of the law, it presents traditional business law topics in a manner that resonates with commercial reality. If you have any suggestions for improvements, additions, or clarifications, please let us know:

Dorothy DuPlessis   ddupless@unb.ca
Steven Enman   enman@acadiau.ca
Shannon O'Byrne   sobyrne@ualberta.ca
Philip King   king@pklaw.ca

The Teaching and Learning Package

Instructor Ancillaries

The **Nelson Education Teaching Advantage (NETA)** program delivers research-based instructor resources that promote student engagement and higher-order thinking to enable the success of Canadian students and educators.

Instructors today face many challenges. Resources are limited, time is scarce, and a new kind of student has emerged: one who is juggling school with work, has gaps in his or her basic knowledge, and is immersed in technology in a way that has led to a completely new style of learning. In response, Nelson Education has gathered a group of dedicated instructors to advise us on the creation of richer and more flexible ancillaries that respond to the needs of today's teaching environments. Whether your course is offered in-class, online, or both, Nelson is pleased to provide pedagogically driven, research-based resources to support you.

The members of our editorial advisory board have experience across a variety of disciplines and are recognized for their commitment to teaching. They include

Norman Althouse, Haskayne School of Business, University of Calgary
Brenda Chant-Smith, Department of Psychology, Trent University
Scott Follows, Manning School of Business Administration, Acadia University
Jon Houseman, Department of Biology, University of Ottawa
Glen Loppnow, Department of Chemistry, University of Alberta
Tanya Noel, Department of Biology, York University
Gary Poole, Senior Scholar, Centre for Health Education Scholarship, and Associate Director, School of Population and Public Health, University of British Columbia
Dan Pratt, Department of Educational Studies, University of British Columbia
Mercedes Rowinsky-Geurts, Department of Languages and Literatures, Wilfrid Laurier University

David DiBattista, *Department of Psychology, Brock University*
Roger Fisher, *PhD*

In consultation with the editorial advisory board, Nelson Education has completely rethought the structure, approaches, and formats of our key textbook and online-learning ancillaries. We've also increased our investment in editorial support for our ancillary and digital authors. The result is the Nelson Education Teaching Advantage and its key components: *NETA Engagement, NETA Assessment, NETA Presentation,* and *NETA Digital.* Each component includes one or more ancillaries prepared according to our best practices and may also be accompanied by documentation that explains the theory behind the practices.

NETA Engagement presents materials that help instructors deliver engaging content and activities to their classes. Instead of Instructor's Manuals that regurgitate chapter outlines and key terms from the text, NETA Enriched Instructor's Manuals (EIMs) provide genuine assistance to teachers. The EIMs answer questions like *What should students learn? Why should students care?* and *What are some common student misconceptions and stumbling blocks?* EIMs not only identify the topics that cause students the most difficulty, but also describe techniques and resources to help students master these concepts. Dr. Roger Fisher's *Instructor's Guide to Classroom Engagement (IGCE)* accompanies every Enriched Instructor's Manual. (Information about the NETA Enriched Instructor's Manual prepared for *Canadian Business and the Law* is included in the description of the IRCD below.)

NETA Assessment relates to testing. Under *NETA Assessment,* Nelson's authors create multiple-choice questions that reflect research-based best practices for constructing effective questions and testing not just recall but also higher-order thinking. Our guidelines were developed by David DiBattista, a 3M National Teaching Fellow whose recent research as a professor of psychology at Brock University has focused on multiple-choice testing. All Test Bank authors receive training at workshops conducted by Prof. DiBattista, as do the copyeditors assigned to each Test Bank. A copy of *Multiple Choice Tests: Getting Beyond Remembering,* Prof. DiBattista's guide to writing effective tests, is included with every Nelson Test Bank/Computerized Test Bank package. (Information about the NETA Test Bank prepared for *Canadian Business and the Law* is included in the description of the IRCD below.)

NETA Presentation has been developed to help instructors make the best use of PowerPoint® in their classrooms. With a clean and uncluttered design developed by Maureen Stone of StoneSoup Consulting, NETA Presentation features slides with improved readability, more multimedia and graphic materials, activities to use in class, and tips for instructors on the Notes page. A copy of *NETA Guidelines for Classroom Presentations* by Maureen Stone is included with each set of PowerPoint slides. (Information about the NETA PowerPoint® prepared for *Canadian Business and the Law* is included in the description of the IRCD below.)

NETA Digital is a framework based on Arthur Chickering and Zelda Gamson's seminal work "Seven Principles of Good Practice In Undergraduate Education" (*AAHE Bulletin,* 1987) and the follow-up work by Chickering and Stephen C. Ehrmann, "Implementing the Seven Principles: Technology as Lever" (*AAHE Bulletin,* 1996). This aspect of the NETA program guides the writing and development of our digital products to ensure that they appropriately reflect the core goals of contact, collaboration, multimodal learning, time on task, prompt feedback, active learning, and high expectations. The resulting focus on pedagogical utility, rather than technological wizardry, ensures that all of our technology supports better outcomes for students.

Instructor's Resource CD

Key instructor ancillaries are provided on the *Instructor's Resource CD* (ISBN 978-0-17-654182-8), giving instructors the ultimate tool for customizing lectures and presentations. (Downloadable web versions are also available at www.businesslaw5e.nelson.com.) The IRCD includes

- **NETA Engagement:** The Enriched Instructor's Manual was written by the authors of this text. It is organized according to the textbook chapters and addresses key educational concerns, such as teaching objectives and strategies, student activities, and detailed explanations of selected features from the text (such as boxes and figures), all of which address typical stumbling blocks student face and how to address them. Other features include answers to Questions for Review and Questions for Critical Thinking, and further discussion from the Situations for Discussion.

- **NETA Assessment:** The Test Bank, prepared by Panayota Papadeas of St. Clair College, includes more than 1,000 multiple-choice questions written according to NETA guidelines for effective construction and development of higher-order questions. Also included are more than 500 true/false questions and 260 essay questions. Test Bank files are provided in Word format for easy editing and in PDF format for convenient printing whatever your system.

  The Computerized Test Bank by ExamView® includes all the questions from the Test Bank. The easy-to-use ExamView software is compatible with Microsoft Windows and Mac OS. Create tests by selecting questions from the question bank, modifying these questions as desired, and adding new questions you write yourself. You can administer quizzes online and export tests to WebCT, Blackboard, and other formats.

- **NETA Presentation:** Microsoft® PowerPoint® lecture slides for every chapter, prepared by Lorrie Adams of Grant MacEwan University, include more than 400 slides, many featuring key figures, tables, and photographs from *Canadian Business and the Law.* NETA principles of clear design and engaging content have been incorporated throughout.

- **DayOne:** Day One—Prof InClass is a PowerPoint presentation that you can customize to orient your students to the class and their text at the beginning of the course.

- **TurningPoint®:** Another valuable resource for instructors is TurningPoint® classroom response software customized for *Canadian Business and the Law.* Now you can author, deliver, show, access, and grade, all in PowerPoint … with no toggling back and forth between screens! JoinIn on TurningPoint is the only classroom response software tool that gives you true PowerPoint integration. With JoinIn, you are no longer tied to your computer. You can walk about your classroom as you lecture, showing slides and collecting and displaying responses with ease. There is simply no easier or more effective way to turn your lecture hall into a personal, fully interactive experience for your students. If you can use PowerPoint, you can use JoinIn on TurningPoint! (Contact your Nelson publishing representative for details.)

CourseMate

Nelson Education's *Canadian Business and the Law* CourseMate brings course concepts to life with interactive learning and exam preparation tools that integrate with the printed textbook. Students activate their knowledge through quizzes, games, and flashcards, among other tools.

CourseMate provides immediate feedback that enables students to connect results to the work they have just produced, increasing their learning efficiency. It encourages contact between students and faculty: You can choose to monitor your students' level of engagement with CourseMate, correlating their efforts to their outcomes. You can even use CourseMate's quizzes to practise "Just in Time" teaching by tracking results in the Engagement Tracker and customizing your lesson plans to address their learning needs.

Watch student comprehension and engagement soar as your class engages with CourseMate. Ask your Nelson representative for a demo today.

Canadian Business and the Law, *Fifth Edition, DVD*
(ISBN 978-0-17-655518-4)

Enhance your classroom experience with the exciting and relevant videos. This DVD, prepared to accompany *Canadian Business and the Law,* is designed to enrich and support chapter concepts with CBC Videos that reflect chapter content.

Business Law Digital Video Library Printed Access Card
(ISBN 978-0-324-22327-9)

This dynamic online video library features more than 60 video clips that spark class discussion and clarify core legal principles. The library is organized into four series: Legal Conflicts in Business (including specific modern business and e-commerce scenarios), Ask the Instructor (presenting straightforward explanations of concepts for student review), Drama of the Law (featuring classic business scenarios that spark classroom participation), and LawFlix (containing clips from many popular films).

Student Ancillaries

CourseMate

The more you study, the better the results. Make the most of your study time by accessing everything you need to succeed in one place. *Canadian Business and the Law* CourseMate includes

- an interactive eBook, with highlighting, note taking, and search capabilities
- interactive learning tools such as
  - interactive quizzes
  - flashcards
  - videos
  - Student Study Guide
  - games
  - glossary
  - and more!

CourseMate provides students access to an interactive eBook and study tools in a dynamic, online learning environment. CourseMate comes automatically with every new copy of this textbook.

Acknowledgments

Canadian Business and the Law, Fifth Edition, was a team effort, and credit for the text must be widely shared. We would like to thank our student research assistants, Chantel Cabaj of the University of Alberta and Courtney Palmer of the University of New Brunswick.

In addition to the valued educators noted below, we extend our appreciation to our colleagues who made an important contribution by commenting on draft chapters in this or earlier editions. They include James McGinnis of Parlee McLaws; Tamara Buckwold, Ronald Hopp, Wayne Renke, David Percy, Gerald Gall, Lewis Klar, Moe Litman, Linda Reif, Barbara Billingsley, Erin Nelson, and Kathryn Arbuckle of the Faculty of Law, University of Alberta; James Gaa of the School of Business, University of Alberta; Michael Pratt of the Faculty of Law, Queen's University; Dion Legge of Macleod Dixon; and Darren Charters of the University of Waterloo.

We would like to acknowledge administrative support from the Faculty of Law at the University of Alberta, particularly from Sandra Teves, and the Fred C. Manning School of Business Administration at Acadia University, as well as research and administrative support from the University of New Brunswick.

We are grateful to Nelson Education's editorial, sales, and marketing team, including Amie Plourde, Alwynn Pinard, Suzanne Simpson Millar, and Dave Stratton for their insights and support throughout the development of this project.

Finally, our deep appreciation goes to those who were instrumental in the preparation of this text by providing direction through their insightful reviews provided for the fifth edition. They include

Lorrie Adams,
Grant MacEwan University

Asher Alkoby,
Ryerson University

Douglas Beatty,
Lambton College

Darren Charters,
University of Waterloo

Paul Ebbs,
Algonquin College

Ray Klapstein,
Dalhousie University

Gilles Levasseur,
University of Ottawa

Robert Malach,
University of Calgary

Darragh McManamon,
Memorial University of Newfoundland

Douglas Peterson,
University of Alberta

Jodilynn Pitcher,
Fanshawe College

Jim Silovs,
Mount Royal University

John Stroud-Drinkwater,
British Columbia Institute of Technology

Don Valeri,
Douglas College

By dedication of this book we thank our families for their sacrifice and support.

Dorothy's dedication is to Neil, Andrea, and Charles.

Steven's dedication is to Jennie, Michael, and Edward.

Shannon's dedication is to Jamie, Kerry, and Sean.

Philip's dedication is to the memory of his father, Leon M. King.

Integrated Pedagogical System

Basic legal principles and concepts are explained and reinforced through the use of extensive pedagogy designed to help students proceed and learn the material.

CHAPTER 1

Knowledge of Law as a Business Asset

Objectives

After studying this chapter, you should have an understanding of

- the role of law in guiding conduct
- the importance of legal knowledge in the business environment
- the challenges posed by business ethics and their relationship to legal requirements

Business Law in Practice

Louella Lambast has decided to open a gift store. She intends to offer a wide selection of ever-changing, low-priced giftware, including T-shirts, novelty toys, costume jewellery, comic books, video games, and household goods. She is tremendously excited about her new venture but cash poor. For this reason, Louella decides to do a lot of the work of setting up the store herself, including assembling a large glass display case. Louella also takes some immediate steps to make her store known by arranging for mass commercial emails to be sent out.

Louella's next decision is to stock all her product from an overseas supplier, including an array of T-shirts bearing the labels of a streetwear manufacturer known as FUBU (For You By. Us). Louella tells friends that although she has a pretty good idea that product supplied to her may end up being illegal "knockoffs"[1] of brand-name designers, she does not know that with 100 percent certainty. "I'm not legally responsible for what people like my supplier do, anyway," she determines. "Plus, business is a game; I'll handle any fallout as it arises."

Louella also imports some small table lamps. When the lamps arrive, she notices that they do not contain labels identifying them as certified safe by Underwriters Laboratories of Canada or another approved group. Underwriters Laboratories is an international, independent, not-for-profit organization whose mandate is to evaluate product safety. The UL mark means that the organization has tested samples of the product in question and concluded that requisite safety requirements have been met.[2] Because Louella is completely satisfied that the lamps pose no risk, she decides to attach some counterfeit labels on the lamps to reassure her customers.

1. For discussion of counterfeit products or "knockoffs," see Chapter 18.
2. Underwriters Laboratories of Canada, "ULC Home Page" (n.d.), UL Canada <http://www.ul.com/canada/eng/pages/>.

(Continued on the next page)

Chapter Objectives outline the learning goals of each chapter.

A **Business Law in Practice** scenario opens each chapter with a business situation containing both legal and managerial implications. A special section before the Chapter Summary called **Business Law in Practice Revisited** reviews the questions posed in the scenario with suggested responses.

The real-world application of legal knowledge is reinforced through the **Business Application of the Law** feature, which provides examples that illustrate how the law affects a business enterprise—such as the issues to consider when determining whether to pursue a legal conflict.

BUSINESS APPLICATION OF THE LAW

Fraud on the Public

For reasons of public safety, electrical products must be approved by Underwriters Laboratories (UL) or another approved group such as the Canadian Standards Association. In defiance of this requirement, San Francisco Gifts Ltd., also called San Diego Gifts, with stores across Canada, has admitted in court to attaching fake UL safety labels to table lamps as well as selling counterfeit brand-name products such as Tommy Hilfiger, Playboy, and West Coast Chopper, as reported by the press. The presiding judge in the case for copyright infringement was particularly concerned about the phony UL labels: "That is despicable," he stated. "We're talking about electrical appliances causing fires.... The exercise of getting cheap stuff somewhere else and dressing it up with false labels and false safety certificates causes me great pause.... Quite frankly, this should be described as nothing less than a despicable fraud on the public, bordering on a massive scale." San Francisco Gifts Ltd. and its sole shareholder were fined a total of $150 000 by the judge.

Critical Analysis: What are the alternatives to market regulation by government?

Sources: Gordon Kent, "Angry judge slams chain for fake labels on goods" *The Edmonton Journal* (31 December 2004) at A1, A14; and *R v San Francisco Gifts Ltd.,* [2004] A.J. No 1608 (Prov. Ct.).

New technologies, globalization, and the environment all have implications for many aspects of business law. Learn how in the **Technology and the Law, International Perspective,** and **Environmental Perspective** features.

TECHNOLOGY AND THE LAW

University of Ottawa Law Students Help Challenge Facebook

In 2008, the Canadian Internet Policy and Public Interest Clinic, staffed in part by law students from the University of Ottawa, filed a complaint with the Office of Privacy Commissioner of Canada against Facebook—a social networking site created by Mark Zuckerberg as a Harvard undergraduate—now boasting over 800 million active users worldwide. The Clinic claimed that Facebook did not comply with Canada's *Personal Information Protection and Electronic Documents Act (PIPEDA).*

PIPEDA is legislation passed by the federal government. It has a number of objectives, including the regulation of how the private business sector collects, uses, and discards personal information acquired from its customers. Such customer protection is essential because, as the Office of the Privacy Commissioner of Canada's website notes,

> When you do business with a company, you do more than simply exchange money for a product or service: Unless you pay in cash, you also leave behind a trail of personal information about yourself. Your name, address, credit card number and spending habits are all information of great value to somebody, whether that's a legitimate marketer or an identity thief.

PIPEDA sets national privacy standards that apply in most Canadian provinces, though Alberta, British Columbia, and Quebec have enacted their own largely comparable provincial regimes. However, even in these provinces, *PIPEDA* applies to industries governed by the federal government, such as banking. For more discussion on legislation generally, see Chapter 2.

A website maintained by the Office of the Privacy Commissioner of Canada (OPC) describes the obligations that commercial organizations owe to their customers under *PIPEDA*. In short, such organizations can only collect, use, or disclose personal information "by fair and lawful means" and only with the consumer's consent, and only for the purposes "that are stated and reasonable." The website also notes

that the private sector must protect this personal information "through appropriate security measures and to destroy it when it's no longer needed for the original purposes."

PIPEDA gives consumers the option of making a complaint to the Privacy Commissioner. The Privacy Commissioner is independent from government and is mandated to try to resolve such complaints. When the OPC looked into allegations against Facebook, it found that several of the complaints were well founded. For example, Facebook tools such as Superpose—which allow users to play computer games with each other—are created by outside software developers. Facebook was giving these outside developers more access to users' personal data than was necessary for those purposes. In response, the Commission recommended that Facebook "implement technological measures to restrict application developers' access only to the user information essential to run a specific application." Also an issue for the OPC was Facebook's account deletion policy. There were two options for users who wanted to leave Facebook: 1) to have their account *deleted* (meaning that all personal information removed from Facebook servers) and 2) to have their account *deactivated* (meaning that all personal information would remain on Facebook servers in case the member wished to return in the future). The OPC said that this distinction was not being made clear and in response, Facebook agreed to improve online description of the alternatives.

CASE ***Gilbert Steel Ltd v University Construction Ltd*, [1976] 12 OR (2d) 19 (CA)**

THE BUSINESS CONTEXT: A business may enter into a contract that suddenly becomes unfavourable because of changes in the market. If it secures a concession from the other side in response to these changes, without regard to legal requirements, the concession may prove to be unenforceable.

FACTUAL BACKGROUND: Gilbert Steel (Gilbert) and University Construction (University) were in a contract that required Gilbert to supply a set amount of fabricated steel at an agreed-upon price. When steel prices rose dramatically, Gilbert asked University if it would pay more for the steel. University agreed but later refused to pay the increase and sent only payment for the originally agreed-upon price. Gilbert sued for breach of contract.

THE LEGAL QUESTION: Is there consideration supporting University's promise (i.e., what is Gilbert doing in return for University's promise to pay more for the steel)?

RESOLUTION: There is no consideration from Gilbert for University's promise, and it is therefore unenforceable. Gilbert is doing only what it is already contractually obliged to do—namely, supply steel to University. Put another way, Gilbert has a pre-existing legal duty to provide the steel and, accordingly, is giving nothing "extra" to University to support University's promise to pay more. The promise is therefore unenforceable, even though University made the second promise in good faith, possibly with a full intention to pay the higher price. Gilbert's action for breach of contract therefore fails.

Gilbert should have contemplated a rise in the cost of steel when setting the original price and built into the contract a formula permitting an increase in the contract price. Alternatively, it could have provided something in return for the higher price, such as earlier delivery or any other benefit that University requested. A final option would have been to get University's promise under seal (see below).

CRITICAL ANALYSIS: Does this rule concerning performance of a pre-existing legal duty reflect the reasonable expectations of both the parties involved and the broader business community?

The **Special Case format** follows a standard analysis for every featured case and landmark case, beginning with an explanation of the BUSINESS CONTEXT that is at issue. Readers are then given the FACTUAL BACKGROUND of the case and presented with the LEGAL QUESTIONS before they read the court's actual RESOLUTION. Each case ends with questions for CRITICAL ANALYSIS. Each of these sections is clearly labelled for easy reference.

ETHICAL CONSIDERATIONS

The Subprime Mortgage Crisis

The United States' subprime mortgage crisis refers to the international financial collapse that was triggered when U.S. subprime borrowers (that is, borrowers with poor or "subprime" credit histories) defaulted on their mortgage obligations. A mortgage is the security or collateral that a borrower gives the lender at the time of borrowing money for a home purchase. If the borrower fails to pay off his or her loan, the creditor is entitled to sell the home and use the proceeds to pay off the borrower's debt. See Chapter 19 for more analysis of mortgages.

Because U.S. housing prices had been rising dramatically since the late 1990s, a home purchase was seen as a "risk-free" way of achieving financial security.[8] However, the housing bubble that fuelled subprime mortgages began to burst in 2006 and has since generated upheaval worldwide, including in Canada.[9] The fallout from mortgage foreclosures has caused the near collapse of major banking institutions,[10] the actual failure of several investment banks,[11] large declines in the stock market,[12] and an increase in homelessness because of personal foreclosure or landlord mortgage defaults that literally leave tenants out in the cold.[13] The multiple causes of the subprime crisis are still being uncovered but include corruption by mortgage lenders who would extend loans even to those who had absolutely no prospect of being able to repay.

Traditionally, lenders did have strong incentives to ensure the underlying creditworthiness of the borrower, since if the borrower could not pay back the loan, the lender risked taking a loss. However, "securitizing" the mortgage—essentially creating investment products backed by subprime mortgages—meant that the lender retained little to no risk in the event of borrower default. This risk belonged to purchasers of the investment product related to that mortgage.[14] As a result, many subprime lenders simply did not care about the borrower's financial fitness, and, on a related front, made no

© ISTOCKPHOTO.COM/BLUEFLAMES

What are the costs of foreclosure to the homeowner?

effort to ensure that borrowers understood the complex terms of the mortgage contracts they signed.[15] The goal was simply to place as many subprime mortgages as possible. While some borrowers themselves were fraudulent and over-reported their real incomes (taking out what are called "liar loans"[16]), other borrowers were honest but simply naive about their ability to repay. As Nicholas Retsinas, director of Harvard University's Joint Center for Housing Studies writes,

> As this [subprime] empire collapses, the people at the base—the waitress in Detroit, the laborer in Sacramento, the daycare worker in Boston—will lose not just the dream and security of a financial asset, but their homes.[17]

While government regulation is not a foolproof method of preventing economic problems or keeping honest but unqualified borrowers out of harm's way, it can be tremendously important. Financial reform legislation in the United States—called the *Dodd-Frank Wall Street Reform and Consumer Protection Act*[18]—has reduced incentives on lenders to place bad mortgages in part by requiring securitizers (those to

(Continued)

The **Ethical Considerations** feature assists the student in assessing the sometimes uncomfortable compromises that the law forges between competing interests.

CHAPTER 1: *Knowledge of Law as a Business Asset*

PART ONE

Chapter Study

Key Terms and Concepts

age of majority (p. 10)
arbitration (p. 12)
breach of contract (p. 8)
business ethics (p. 15)
business law (p. 4)
contract law (p. 10)
law (p. 5)
legal risk management plan (p. 15)
liability (p. 12)
litigation (p. 11)
mediation (p. 12)

Questions for Review

1. What is the function of law?
2. How does the law protect members of society?
3. How does the law facilitate business activity?
4. In what ways does law facilitate certainty in the marketplace?
5. Does the nature of the business relationship affect the enforcement of legal rights?
6. How does the law resolve disputes?
7. Does dispute resolution always involve going to court?
8. In what way is knowledge of the law a business asset?
9. How might a lack of knowledge of the law negatively impact a business?
10. Why should a business put in place a legal risk management plan?
11. What is the role of business ethics?
12. Why are business ethics important?
13. What is spam?
14. What is the purpose of regulating spam?

Questions for Critical Thinking

1. What is the relationship between ethics and law? Are ethical responsibilities the same as legal responsibilities?
2. When is a lawsuit the best response to a legal dispute? What is at risk?
3. Knowledge of the law is a business asset. How can you acquire this asset short of becoming a lawyer? How is ignorance of the law a liability?
4. There has been considerable concern about the safety of Tasers (electroshock weapons) and their possible role in the death of hundreds of people in North America. The danger associated with Tasers was most recently brought to light because of the death of Robert Dziekanski, a Polish immigrant who died at the Vancouver International Airport immediately after being tased by RCMP officers. According to the CEO of Taser International, however, there is "no other device with as much accountability" as a Taser and he maintains that Tasers actually save lives.[36] What is the role of the law in regulating the products sold in the marketplace and ensuring their safety or relative safety?
5. Adam Guerbuez, the spammer described in this chapter, was made subject to a judgment of almost a $1 billion dollars by an American court. Do you think this judgment is unreasonably large? Should the defendant's ability to pay be taken into consideration by the court? Why or why not?
6. In 2010, the New Brunswick government implemented new voluntary guidelines governing the indoor tanning industry, including that people under 18 should not be permitted to indoor tan. These guidelines would be voluntary to start with but that would change if indoor tanning operators ignored the guidelines at which point legislation would be brought in. Is this a good approach to regulating business? Why or why not?

36. Omar El Akkad, "Taser CEO grilled by public safety committee" *The Globe and Mail* (31 January 2008) online: The Globe and Mail [illegible]

NEL 19

End-of-chapter materials include **Key Terms and Concepts** with page references, **Questions for Review, Questions for Critical Thinking,** and **Situations for Discussion. Questions for Review** will help students to check their understanding of chapter topics; **Questions for Critical Thinking** and **Situations for Discussion** will let them apply the concepts they have learned to other business situations.

The **Landmark Case** and **Business and Legislation** features provide accounts of pivotal case law and historical legislative initiatives.

LANDMARK CASE ***Dickinson v Dodds*, [1876] 2 Ch D 463 (CA)**

THE HISTORICAL CONTEXT: This case is the leading decision—valid even today—on whether an offeror can renege on a commitment to hold an offer open for a specified period of time.

FACTUAL BACKGROUND: On Wednesday, June 10, Dodds delivered to Dickinson a written offer to sell his property to Dickinson for £800. The offer stated that it would be open for acceptance until 9 a.m. on Friday, June 12. On Thursday, Dickinson heard that Dodds had been offering or was agreeing to sell the property to Mr. Allan. That evening, Dickinson delivered an acceptance to the place where Dodds was staying, and at 7 a.m. on Friday morning—a full two hours before the deadline—he personally delivered an acceptance to Dodds. Dodds declined the acceptance, stating: "You are too late. I have sold the property." Dickinson sued Dodds, alleging there was a contract between them.

THE LEGAL QUESTION: To determine whether Dickinson's action should succeed, the court had to decide whether Dodds was entitled to revoke his offer prior to the deadline he had set. This decision was necessary because if the offer had been properly revoked, it was not capable of being accepted, and, accordingly, there could be no contract between the two men.

RESOLUTION: The court decided that what Dodds did was permissible: "[I]t is a perfectly clear rule of law . . . that, although it is said that the offer is to be left open until Friday morning at 9 o'clock, that did not bind Dodds. He was not in point of law bound to hold the offer over until 9 o'clock on Friday morning."

On this footing, a firm offer can be revoked at any time before acceptance because the offeree has not provided any consideration to support the offeror's implicit promise not to revoke before the deadline. More controversially, the court also held that Dodds' offer had been effectively revoked prior to acceptance because Dickinson learned in advance—from a presumably reliable source—that Dodds was selling the property to someone else.

CRITICAL ANALYSIS: Being guided primarily by legal principles is certainly an acceptable way of doing business. However, what might be the impact on your business reputation of going back on your word and revoking an offer sooner than you had promised you would? Do you think that the method used by Dodds for revocation (i.e., relying on the fact that Dickinson had learned that Dodds was selling to someone else) is the usual way of revoking an offer? What would be a more certain and reliable way of effecting revocation?

BUSINESS AND LEGISLATION

Regulating the Tanning Industry

At least two Canadian jurisdictions to date have banned anyone under the **age of majority** from using tanning beds. This is because tanning bed use is associated with very serious forms of skin cancer that can cause death. As reported by the CBC, the World Health Organization has classified the ultra violet rays from tanning beds as high cancer risks, ranking with tobacco smoke and mustard gas. This classification is based on research finding that the risk of skin melanoma increases "by 75 per cent if a person starts tanning before age 30."

In 2011, the Capital Regional District of Victoria passed a bylaw which bans tanning beds for those under the age of majority and imposes a fine of between $250 to $2000 for violations. Nova Scotia became the first province to do so via the *Tanning Beds Act*, SNS 2010, c 44. Tanning salon owners face business closure for up to two years and fines of up to $10 0000 for permitting those under the age of 19 to tan. In a press release, Maureen MacDonald, Minister for Health Promotion and Protection in Nova Scotia, explained: "We are taking a preventative approach to protect the health and safety of our youth. We know that excessive exposure to UV rays over the long term can have negative health effects, like skin cancer."

RIDO/SHUTTERSTOCK

Critical Analysis: Should the government try to protect young people from the dangers of tanning beds or should the matter be left up to the individual consumer? What is the role of government in such a context?

Sources: Capital Health "Proposed tanning bed legislation to protect youth" (24 November 2010) online:http://www.cdha.nshealth.ca/media-centre/news/proposed-tanning-bed-legislation-protect-youth; CBC staff "NB's voluntary tanning rules applauded" online: CBC News at http://www.cbc.ca/news/canada/new-brunswick/story/2011/01/17/nb-tanning-rules-959.html

Table of Cases

The boldface page locators denote pages on which the cases are developed in the text.

Table of Statutes

PART ONE

The Legal Environment of Business

This text deals with the importance of the law to business and, in Parts Two to Nine, presents fundamental legal principles in their relevant business contexts. The text contends that those engaged in business need to manage the legal environment as much as any other aspect of their business. Part One provides the basis for that management by introducing the foundations of business law and the concept of legal risk management. It emphasizes the importance of knowing the law, complying with the law, avoiding unexpected legal problems, and regarding law not as an obstacle, but as a way to facilitate commercial activity.

DMITRIY SHIRONOSOV/SHUTTERSTOCK

Knowledge of Law as a Business Asset

Objectives

After studying this chapter, you should have an understanding of

- the role of law in guiding conduct

- the importance of legal knowledge in the business environment

- the challenges posed by business ethics and their relationship to legal requirements

DAVID CHASEY/PHOTODISC

Business Law in Practice

Louella Lambast has decided to open a gift store. She intends to offer a wide selection of ever-changing, low-priced giftware, including T-shirts, novelty toys, costume jewellery, comic books, video games, and household goods. She is tremendously excited about her new venture but cash poor. For this reason, Louella decides to do a lot of the work of setting up the store herself, including assembling a large glass display case. Louella also takes some immediate steps to make her store known by arranging for mass commercial emails to be sent out.

Louella's next decision is to stock all her product from an overseas supplier, including an array of T-shirts bearing the labels of a streetwear manufacturer known as FUBU (For You By Us). Louella tells friends that although she has a pretty good idea that product supplied to her may end up being illegal "knockoffs"[1] of brand-name designers, she does not know that with 100 percent certainty. "I'm not legally responsible for what people like my supplier do, anyway," she determines. "Plus, business is a game; I'll handle any fallout as it arises."

Louella also imports some small table lamps. When the lamps arrive, she notices that they do not contain labels identifying them as certified safe by Underwriters Laboratories of Canada or another approved group. Underwriters Laboratories is an international, independent, not-for-profit organization whose mandate is to evaluate product safety. The UL mark means that the organization has tested samples of the product in question and concluded that requisite safety requirements have been met.[2] Because Louella is completely satisfied that the lamps pose no risk, she decides to attach some counterfeit labels on the lamps to reassure her customers.

---

1. For discussion of counterfeit products (ie "knockoffs") see Chapter 18.
2. Underwriters Laboratories of Canada, "ULC Home Page", online: UL Canada <http://www.ul.com/canada/eng/pages/>.

(Continued on the next page)

A few months later, Louella's world is falling apart. A customer suffers a head injury when the glass display case that Louella had improperly assembled suddenly collapses. A group of demonstrators has begun picketing Louella's business premises, protesting the violent kind of video games she sells. Underwriters Laboratories has learned that lamps in Louella's store contain counterfeit labels indicating that they have UL approval, and the police are now involved. Louella's lawyer has explained that she will likely face prosecution for distributing material infringing copyright as well as for violating the *Criminal Code of Canada*.

Just when it seems that things could not get worse, Louella receives a phone call from an American who has been inundated with her unsolicited commercial email. The individual is livid, advising Louella that she has sent unsolicited commercial email—otherwise known as spam—and is therefore in breach of American legislation that he calls the *CAN-SPAM Act*. The *Controlling the Assault of Non-Solicited Pornography and Marketing Act of 2003*[3] permits e-advertising only under certain circumstances. The law bans false or misleading headers (e.g., the email's "From" and "To" information) as well as deceptive subject lines. It requires the email to provide an opt-out mechanism, to identify commercial email as such, and to include the sender's valid physical address.[4] The American tells Louella that she could go to jail for five years and faces civil penalties of $16 000 per violation.[5] Since Louella's spam did not conform with the legislation, Louella is terrified that she will receive a large fine or possibly end up serving time in an American prison. Needless to say, Louella's business cannot survive this barrage of legal problems. Nor can her reputation.

1. How does the law affect Louella's business?
2. What are the purposes of the laws that affect Louella's business?
3. What has gone wrong in Louella's business and why?

Law in the Business Environment

The law impacts virtually every aspect of society, including the business environment. The law affects most business decisions—from development of the basic business idea through to its implementation, and all the attendant matters in between, including financing, hiring, production, marketing, and sales. As Louella starts her business, for example, she will be involved in a number of transactions and events with significant legal implications.

For instance, to get her business off the ground, Louella has to decide whether to form a corporation, operate as a sole proprietor, or find partners. She also has financing decisions to make: should she borrow money, use her own funds, or perhaps sell shares in her venture? Louella also needs to find a location for her store, whether by constructing a new building, purchasing an existing structure, or leasing premises from someone else. She

---

3. *Controlling the Assault of Non-Solicited Pornography and Marketing Act of 2003*, 15 USC §§ 7701-7713 (2003), online: Cornell Legal Information Institute http://www.law.cornell.edu/uscode/html/uscode15/usc_sup_01_15_10_103.html [*"CAN-SPAM Act"*].
4. See Bureau of Consumer Protection Business Center, "CAN-SPAM Act: A Compliance Guide for Business", online:Federal Trade Commission <http://www.ftc.gov/bcp/edu/pubs/business/ecommerce/bus61.shtm>.
5. *Ibid.*

requires furnishings, signage, and supplies. While her operation is starting out small, she may ultimately have to hire employees. Louella also has to market her business in order to build and maintain a customer base. All of these decisions have legal aspects, whether Louella recognizes that or not.

By understanding the role of law in the multitude of business decisions that people like Louella must make, an entrepreneur can maximize the protection that the law extends while avoiding its pitfalls. Put another way, knowledge of the law is a business asset that can assist owners and managers in reaching their goals and objectives. This is because **business law**

Business law
A set of established rules governing commercial relationships, including the enforcement of rights.

- defines general rules of commerce
- protects business ideas and more tangible forms of property
- provides mechanisms that permit businesspeople to select their desired degree of participation and exposure to risk in business ventures
- seeks to ensure that losses are borne by those who are responsible for them
- facilitates planning by ensuring compliance with commitments

Of course, a businessperson can function with little or no understanding of the law. This lack of knowledge, however, may result in failure to maximize opportunities or in losing out on them altogether. For example, a business that neglects to protect its intellectual property may have its ideas taken with impunity by a competitor; a business that ignores employment and human rights laws may be forced to reverse human resource decisions or pay compensation to wronged employees; and a business that fails to explore different modes of carrying out business may suffer unnecessary losses. Perhaps even more seriously, legal ignorance may result in the business or its owner being subjected to regulatory and judicial sanctions, including being fined, forced to pay penalties, or closed down altogether.

BUSINESS APPLICATION OF THE LAW

Fraud on the Public

For reasons of public safety, electrical products must be approved by Underwriters Laboratories (UL) or another approved group such as the Canadian Standards Association. In defiance of this requirement, San Francisco Gifts Ltd., also called San Diego Gifts, with stores across Canada, has admitted in court to attaching fake UL safety labels to table lamps as well as selling counterfeit brand-name products such as Tommy Hilfiger, Playboy, and West Coast Chopper, as reported by the press. The presiding judge in the case for copyright infringement was particularly concerned about the phony UL labels: "That is despicable," he stated. "We're talking about electrical appliances causing fires....The exercise of getting cheap stuff somewhere else and dressing it up with false labels and false safety certificates causes me great pause....Quite frankly, this should be described as nothing less than a despicable fraud on the public, bordering on a massive scale." San Francisco Gifts Ltd. and its sole shareholder were fined a total of $150 000 by the judge.

Critical Analysis: What are the alternatives to market regulation by government?

Sources: Gordon Kent, "Angry judge slams chain for fake labels on goods" *The Edmonton Journal* (31 December 2004) at A1, A14; and *R v San Francisco Gifts Ltd*, [2004] A.J. No 1608 (Prov. Ct.).

US SPAM Laws

Canadian Adam Guerbuez, pictured at right, scammed Facebook users into giving him their user names and passwords through 'phishing' schemes. That is, Guerbuez fraudulently sent out what looked to be a legitimate email so as to entice recipients to reveal personal information such as passwords or user names. He then inundated them with more than 4 million unsolicited advertising messages for marijuana and 'adult' products. In 2008, a California court determined that Guerbuez was in violation of American *CAN-SPAM* legislation and other laws. The court ordered Gerbetz to pay $873 million (US) to Facebook, in part based on assessing a per spam penalty multipled by the number of spam sent. In 2010, Justice Lucie Fournier of the Quebec Superior Court agreed to Facebook's request that its US judgment be recognized as valid in Canada, noting that: "[I]t was after the repeated and intentional actions of Guerbuez that the [American] judgment was rendered. It was not an arbitrary award." The judge also considered how Guerbuez would be treated under Canada's then-proposed anti-spamming legislation ("Bill C-27") and concluded that the outcome could be similar. Beyond this, both pieces of legislation shared the goal of deterring reprehensible online behaviour. She therefore rejected Guerbuez's argument that the award was so large and punitive that to enforce it in Quebec would be against "public order." Guerbuez applied to the Quebec Court of Appeal in 2011 for leave to appeal but this application was denied. Accordingly, Facebook can pursue Guerbuez's assets in Canada so as to help collect on its nearly billion dollar judgment.

As Paul Taylor writes for *Canadian Lawyer* magazine, Facebook has to sue spammers like Guerbuez in order to protect the positive experience of its users, retain customer loyalty, and protect legitimate ad revenue. As Taylor writes:

> ... [I]n a time when increasing value is placed on individual's privacy, that is the nature of statutory damages. The 4,366,386 messages Guerbuez sent infringed upon the privacy of users of the site and made it appear as though one's friends sent these messages....[D]eleting the message and moving on does not take away the feeling, and the fact, that one's privacy has been violated.

Guerbuez has also declared bankrupcy, started his own website, and appears to be enjoying the limelight, at least for

PAUL CHIASSON/THE CANADIAN PRESS

the time being. In a CBC interview with Mark Kelley, Guerbuez welcomed all the publicity surrounding his case, stating:

> This gets me out there. People know my name. People know what I do because I'm telling them what I do and they know I can get across to millions of people without paying a cent to do so. This is free publicity for me....This is wonderful....I don't know anybody who could afford this kind of publicity if they were paying for it to....I'm everywhere....If you type in the word 'Adam' [Guerbuez's first name], I'm the third suggested result on Google right now in the world. That is something that is amazing.

In the meantime, Facebook is being realistic about what it can recover from Guerbuez, noting on its Blog:

> Does Facebook expect to quickly collect $873 million and share the proceeds in some way with our users? Alas, no. It's unlikely that Guerbuez....could ever honour the judgment....(though we will certainly collect everything we can.) But we are confident that this award represents a powerful deterrent to anyone and everyone who would seek to abuse Facebook and its users.

Critical Analysis: Should American judgments be enforceable in Canada? Why or why not? What is objectionable about spamming? How is it different from marketing?

Sources: *Facebook Inc v Guerbuez*, 2010 QCCS 4649, aff'd 2011 QCCA 268; YouTube, "Adam Guerbuez on primetime TV show 'Connect'"online: YouTube <http://www.youtube.com/watch?v=_unvC5jP-5M>; Chloe Albanesius, "Judge Awards $873M Fine for Spamming Facebook" (24 November 2008), online: *PCMag* <http://www.pcmag.com/article2/0,2817,2335375,00.asp>; CBC News Staff, "Quebec spammer must pay Facebook $873M", *CBC News* (5 October 2010) online: CBC News <http://www.cbc.ca/news/canada/montreal/story/2010/10/05/quebec-court-upholds-facebook-spammer-ruling.html>; and Max Kelly, "Making Facebook Safe Against Spam" (24 November 2008), online: The Facebook Blog <http://blog.facebook.com/blog.php?post=40218392130>.

Rules and Principles

Broadly defined, the **law** is a set of rules and principles intended to guide conduct in society, primarily by protecting persons and their property, facilitating personal and commercial interactions, and providing mechanisms for dispute resolution.

Law

The set of rules and principles guiding conduct in society.

Protecting Persons and Their Property

Probably the most familiar purpose of the law is to provide protection. Those who violate the *Criminal Code of Canada*—such as by breaking into another person's house, assaulting someone, or committing a commercial fraud—are subject to criminal sanctions, such as fines or imprisonment.

As another example, businesses are legally required to adequately protect their customers' personal information due to the regime established by the *Personal Information Protection and Electronic Documents Act*. This is discussed in the following box.

TECHNOLOGY AND THE LAW

University of Ottawa Law Students Help Challenge Facebook

In 2008, the Canadian Internet Policy and Public Interest Clinic, staffed in part by law students from the University of Ottawa, filed a complaint with the Office of Privacy Commissioner of Canada against Facebook—a social networking site created by Mark Zuckerberg as a Harvard undergraduate—now boasting over 800 million active users worldwide. The Clinic claimed that Facebook did not comply with Canada's *Personal Information Protection and Electronic Documents Act* (*PIPEDA*).

PIPEDA is legislation passed by the federal government. It has a number of objectives, including the regulation of how the private business sector collects, uses, and discards personal information acquired from its customers. Such customer protection is essential because, as the Office of the Privacy Commissioner of Canada's website notes,

> When you do business with a company, you do more than simply exchange money for a product or service: Unless you pay in cash, you also leave behind a trail of personal information about yourself. Your name, address, credit card number and spending habits are all information of great value to somebody, whether that's a legitimate marketer or an identity thief.

PIPEDA sets national privacy standards that apply in most Canadian provinces, though Alberta, British Columbia, and Quebec have enacted their own largely comparable provincial regimes. However, even in these provinces, *PIPEDA* applies to industries governed by the federal government, such as banking. For more discussion on legislation generally, see Chapter 2.

A website maintained by the Office of the Privacy Commissioner of Canada (OPC) describes the obligations that commercial organizations owe to their customers under *PIPEDA*. In short, such organizations can only collect, use, or disclose personal information "by fair and lawful means" and only with the consumer's consent, and only for the purposes "that are stated and reasonable." The website also notes

JUSTIN SULLIVAN/GETTY IMAGES

that the private sector must protect this personal information "through appropriate security measures and to destroy it when it's no longer needed for the original purposes."

PIPEDA gives consumers the option of making a complaint to the Privacy Commissioner. The Privacy Commissioner is independent from government and is mandated to try to resolve such complaints. When the OPC looked into allegations against Facebook, it found that several of the complaints were well founded. For example, Facebook tools such as Superpose—which allow users to play computer games with each other—are created by outside software developers. Facebook was giving these outside developers more access to users' personal data than was necessary for those purposes. In response, the Commission recommended that Facebook "implement technological measures to restrict application developers' access only to the user information essential to run a specific application." Also an issue for the OPC was Facebook's account deletion policy. There were two options for users who wanted to leave Facebook: 1) to have their account *deleted* (meaning that all personal information removed from Facebook servers) and 2) to have their account *deactivated* (meaning that all personal information would remain on Facebook servers in case the member wished to return in the future). The OPC said that this distinction was not being made clear and in response, Facebook agreed to improve online description of the alternatives.

As a final example, the OPC found a problem with the default privacy settings of new members. Such settings allowed members' picture albums to be viewed by the general public, and—for all profiles listing an age of 18 or older—to be listed as a result for search engine queries. To address the issue, Facebook has agreed to create low, medium, and high privacy settings for its members' data as well as to enable its members to tailor their own security settings.

Canada is reportedly the first country to call Facebook to task for privacy violations.

Critical Analysis: In what way does PIPEDA protect people and their property? Do you think that the legislation puts too much responsibility on business?

Sources: Susan Delacourt, "Facebook gets poked by Canada over privacy", *The Star* (17 July 2009) online: The Star <http://www.thestar.com/News/Canada/article/667700>; Nicholas Carlson, "Facebook Has More Than 600 Million Users, Goldman Tells Clients", *Business Insider* (5 January 2011) online: Business Insider <http://www.businessinsider.com/s?q=Goldman+to+clients%3A+Facebook+has+600>; The Canadian Press, "University of Ottawa law students file privacy complaint against Facebook", *CBC News* (30 May 2008) online: CBC News <http://www.cbc.ca/news/story/2008/05/30/facebook-privacy.html>; Office of the Privacy Commission of Canada, "A Guide for Individuals: Your Guide to PIPEDA", online: Office of the Privacy Commission of Canada <http://www.priv.gc.ca/information/02_05_d_08_e.cfm>; Jacquie McNish, "Jennifer Stoddart: making your privacy her business", *The Globe and Mail* (11 December 2010) online: The Globe and Mail <http://www.theglobeandmail.com/report-on-business/careers/careers-leadership/the-lunch/article1833688.ece >; Karim Bardeesy, "Facebook makes friends with privacy czar", *The Globe and Mail* (28 August 2009) online: The Globe and Mail <http://www.theglobeandmail.com/news/technology/facebook-makes-friends-with-privacy-czar/article1267665/; and Peter Ruby and Victoria Petherbridge, "Facebook forced to amend privacy practices" *Lawyers Weekly* (2 October 2009) 9, 11; "Facebook Statistics" online: http://www.facebook.com/press/info.php?statistics

As another example of the role of law, business is required by law to treat humanely any animals in its care. Failure to do leads to prosecution under animal welfare statutes and even the *Criminal Code of Canada,* as discussed in the following box:

ETHICAL CONSIDERATIONS

Inhumane Killing of Sled Dogs in British Columbia

Howling Dog Tours Whistler Inc. ("Howling Dog") is a dog sledding business in the tourism industry which, in turn, is owned by Outdoor Adventures at Whistler Ltd. ("Outdoor Adventures"). In 2010, an employee and operator of Howling Dog, Robert Fawcett, inhumanely killed more than 50 sled dogs. The circumstances were horrific. Marcie Moriarty, general manager of cruelty investigation for the provincial Society for the Prevention of Cruelty to Animals ("SPCA") gave this summary of how the killings were conducted:

MARCEL JANCOVIC/SHUTTERSTOCK

> I won't use the term euthanized, [which] implies a humane death, and I can say that based on his [Fawcett's] description, at least a number of dogs did not have a humane death. His [Fawcett's] descriptions of using a shotgun, blowing off half of the dog's head while it ran off, a dog crawling out of a mass grave, it just made me shudder.

Outdoor Adventures denies that post-Olympic business had been falling off and that this was why the "cull" had been instigated. A jointly issued statement from Outdoor Adventures and Fawcett also asserted, among other matters, that the dogs in question were old and weak, that no specific instructions were given to Fawcett by Outdoor Adventures as to how to end the dogs' lives, and that "Mr. Fawcett was known to have very humanely euthanized dogs on previous occasions."

Fawcett experienced post-traumatic stress disorder as a result of the inhumane cull and successfully filed for compensation under B.C. worker's compensation regime.

The Howling Dog incident led to a provincially constituted task force which recommended changes to B.C.'s animal protection legislation. In response, the B.C. legislature has, among other matters, increased fines for violation to $75 000 and increased the maximum prison sentence to two years. The Province has also imposed a mandatory set of rules on sled dog operators called the *Sled Dog Code of Practice* (January 30, 2012).

The premier of B.C., Christy Clark, acknowledged that none of the legislative changes in place now would necessarily have prevented the Howling Dog incident. As reported by the *Globe and Mail,* Clark stated:

> The thing is that people will do bad things. That certainly happens not just to animals, but to other people, to property. But what we can do as a government and as a society is to try to put in place deterrents that are strong and will be enforced.

Clark also stated that the incident was a "terrible black eye" on British Columbia.

(Continued)

In the meantime and after an investigation, the SPCA recommended that criminal charges be brought against Fawcett. Crown Counsel did so and Fawcett has pled guilty. The relevant *Criminal Code* provision states:

445.1 (1) Every one commits an offence who

    (a) wilfully causes or, being the owner, wilfully permits to be caused unnecessary pain, suffering or injury to an animal or a bird;

    ....

  (2) Every one who commits an offence under subsection

  (1) is guilty of

    (a) an indictable offence and liable to imprisonment for a term of not more than five years; or

    (b) an offence punishable on summary conviction and liable to a fine not exceeding ten thousand dollars or to imprisonment for a term of not more than eighteen months or to both.

RSC, 1985, c C-46.

Critical Analysis: What is the role of business to ensure the ethical treatment of animals? Is it acceptable to kill sled dogs with a shotgun? What is the role of government to ensure the ethical treatment of animals?

Sources: CBC Newstaff, "Cruelty charges laid in BC sled dog slaughter" (20 April 2010) online: CBC News at http://www.cbc.ca/news/canada/british-columbia/story/2012/04/20/bc-sled-dog-slaughter-charge.html; Sunny Dhillon, "Crackdown on animal cruelty won't ban sled-dog culls", *The Globe and Mail* (5 April 2011) online: The Globe and Mail <http://www.theglobeandmail.com/news/national/british-columbia/bc-politics/crackdown-on-animal-cruelty-wont-ban-sled-dog-culls/article1971437/>; CBC News Staff, "Mass sled dog killing probed in B.C.", *CBCNews* (31 January 2011) online: CBC News <http://www.cbc.ca/news/canada/british-columbia/story/2011/01/31/bc-dog-mutilation.html>; Jeremy Hainsworth, "BC to enact tougher animal cruelty laws", *The Lawyers Weekly* (15 April 2011) 3; Allan Wotherspoon, "Review Decision R0119660" (25 January 2011) online: CBC News <http://www.cbc.ca/bc/news/bc-110131-worksafebc-whistler-dog-cull.pdf>; Province of British Columbia, "Sled Dog Task Force" (March 2011) online: Government of British Columbia <http://www.gov.bc.ca/agri/down/sleddog_taskforce_report_25mar11.pdf>; and Robert Matas, "Tourism Whistler suspends reservations over post-Olympic sled dog cull", *Newswire* (31 January 2011) online: Newswire <http://www.newswire.ca/en/releases/archive/February2011/02/c7576.html>.

The law protects members of society in two ways: (1) it sets rules with penalties in order to encourage compliance, and (2) it seeks to make those who break the law accountable for their misconduct.

The law also protects businesses by setting penalties and ensuring accountability. For example, if one business misappropriates another business' legally protected commercial idea, the law can step in and censure that conduct. As well, the law ensures that losses are paid for by the parties responsible for creating them. For example, if a law firm gives negligent advice to a client, that client can sue the firm for associated losses.

Louella's business intersects with the law in both of these ways. First, the law guards her business interests. For example, should a supplier fail to deliver a product to Louella, this is a **breach of contract** and she can sue for damages. If a competitor wrongfully injures Louella's business reputation, she can sue for defamation.[6] However, the law also protects those who deal with Louella's business. Louella must not discriminate in hiring practices. She must not disregard health and safety regulations governing the workplace. She must pay her creditors. Louella must not sell knockoffs of brand-name designers, nor is it a defence that she "did not know with 100 percent certainty" that the product supplied was counterfeit—she is responsible nonetheless.[7] Louella should respect the laws of other countries that may apply to her business operation. In sum, Louella is obliged to abide by the law on a variety of fronts, since failure to comply can have severe consequences, including financial penalties and criminal prosecution.

Government may also neglect or decide against regulating in a given area. This can have adverse consequences as when, for example, it provides an opportunity for unscrupulous market participants to act exploitatively.

Breach of contract
Failure to comply with a contractual promise.

---

6. Defamation is the public utterance of a false statement of fact or opinion that harms another's reputation. For further discussion, see Chapter 12.
7. Selling products that Louella "had a pretty good idea" were knockoffs could, among other illegalities, amount to criminal fraud under section 380 of the *Criminal Code*, RSC 1985, c C-46.

ETHICAL CONSIDERATIONS

The Subprime Mortgage Crisis

The United States' subprime mortgage crisis refers to the international financial collapse that was triggered when U.S. subprime borrowers (that is, borrowers with poor or "subprime" credit histories) defaulted on their mortgage obligations. A mortgage is the security or collateral that a borrower gives the lender at the time of borrowing money for a home purchase. If the borrower fails to pay off his or her loan, the creditor is entitled to sell the home and use the proceeds to pay off the borrower's debt. See Chapter 19 for more analysis of mortgages.

Because U.S. housing prices had been rising dramatically since the late 1990s, a home purchase was seen as a "risk-free" way of achieving financial security.[8] However, the housing bubble that fuelled subprime mortgages began to burst in 2006 and has since generated upheaval worldwide, including in Canada.[9] The fallout from mortgage foreclosures has caused the near collapse of major banking institutions,[10] the actual failure of several investment banks,[11] large declines in the stock market,[12] and an increase in homelessness because of personal foreclosure or landlord mortgage defaults that literally leave tenants out in the cold.[13] The multiple causes of the subprime crisis are still being uncovered but include corruption by mortgage lenders who would extend loans even to those who had absolutely no prospect of being able to repay.

Traditionally, lenders did have strong incentives to ensure the underlying creditworthiness of the borrower, since if the borrower could not pay back the loan, the lender risked taking a loss. However, "securitizing" the mortgage—essentially creating investment products backed by subprime mortgages—meant that the lender retained little to no risk in the event of borrower default. This risk belonged to purchasers of the investment product related to that mortgage.[14] As a result, many subprime lenders simply did not care about the borrower's financial fitness, and, on a related front, made no

What are the costs of foreclosure to the homeowner?

© ISTOCKPHOTO.COM/BLUEFLAMES

effort to ensure that borrowers understood the complex terms of the mortgage contracts they signed.[15] The goal was simply to place as many subprime mortgages as possible. While some borrowers themselves were fraudulent and over-reported their real incomes (taking out what are called "liar loans"[16]), other borrowers were honest but simply naive about their ability to repay. As Nicholas Retsinas, director of Harvard University's Joint Center for Housing Studies writes,

> As this [subprime] empire collapses, the people at the base—the waitress in Detroit, the laborer in Sacramento, the daycare worker in Boston—will lose not just the dream and security of a financial asset, but their homes.[17]

While government regulation is not a foolproof method of preventing economic problems or keeping honest but unqualified borrowers out of harm's way, it can be tremendously important. Financial reform legislation in the United States—called the *Dodd-Frank Wall Street Reform and Consumer Protection Act*[18]—has reduced incentives on lenders to place bad mortgages in part by requiring securitizers (those to

(Continued)

---

8. J Shiller, *The Subprime Solution: How Today's Global Financial Crisis Happened and What to Do about It* (Princeton, NJ: Princeton University Press, 2008) at 5.

9. For example, six of Canada's biggest lenders (excluding TD Bank) have absorbed write-downs of about C$4.7 billion caused by losses on investments related to U.S. subprime mortgages. See John Kiphoff, "Canadian Stocks Fall Most Since 2004 after CIBC's Share Sale", Bloomberg (15 January 2008) online: Bloomberg <http://www.bloomberg.com/apps/news?pid=newsarchive&sid=aDU0Yw976Sq0&refer=canada>.

10. NYSSCPA.org E-Zine Staff, "Bank Failures and Fed Bailouts Stun Wall Street, World Markets" (18 September 2008) online: NYSSPCA.org E-Zine <http://www.nysscpa.org/ezine/ETPArticles/ML91808.htm>.

11. Ibid.

12. Katalina M Bianco, *The Subprime Lending Crisis: Causes and Effects of the Mortgage Meltdown* (CCH: 2008) at 19 online: Wolters Kluwer Law & Business <http://business.cch.com/bankingfinance/focus/news/Subprime_WP_rev.pdf>.

13. *Ibid* at 20.

14. See, for example, Oren Bar-Gill, "The Law, Economics and Psychology of Subprime Mortgage Contracts" (2009) 94 Cornell L Rev 1073 at 1091.

15. *Ibid* at 1102-03.

16. See Vikas Bajaj, "Subprime mortgage lending: A cross-country blame game", *The New York Times* (8 May 2007) online: *New York Times* <http://www.nytimes.com/2007/05/08/business/worldbusiness/08iht-subprime.4.5623442.html>.

17. Nicolas P Retsinas, "Building Sandcastles: The Subprime Adventure", *Harvard Business School Working Knowledge* (12 September 2007) online: Harvard Business School <http://hbswk.hbs.edu/item/5771.html>.

18. *Dodd-Frank Wall Street Reform and Consumer Protection Act*, Pub L No 111-203, 124 Stat 1376 (2010).

whom the lenders would sell the mortgages in question) to retain a portion of the risk of mortgage default. Presumably, securitizers will be more careful about what mortgages they acquire going forward, giving lenders more reason to screen borrowers carefully. As well, the legislation requires that more disclosure be made available to the borrower, in plain, comprehensible language. As another example, the new legislation requires lenders to assess the borrower's underlying ability to repay.

All these measures should have the effect of keeping unqualified borrowers out of the housing market and sparing them the financial, emotional, and social consequences of foreclosure.

Critical Analysis: Even though the lenders may not have acted illegally at the time, do you think that they had any ethical responsibility to ensure that mortgage applicants were financially able to afford the loan in question? Do you think it is better for borrowers who overextend themselves to simply bear the consequences of their own actions? Is government to blame for not doing more to protect naïve borrowers?

Sources: Ronnie Cohen & Shannon O'Byrne, "Risk Allocation and Misplaced Emotion: The U.S.'s Subprime Crisis," (2011) 45 Real Property, Trust and Estate Law Journal 677.

BUSINESS AND LEGISLATION

Regulating the Tanning Industry

At least two Canadian jurisdictions to date have banned anyone under the **age of majority** from using tanning beds. This is because tanning bed use is associated with very serious forms of skin cancer that can cause death. As reported by the CBC, the World Health Organization has classified the ultra violet rays from tanning beds as high cancer risks, ranking with tobacco smoke and mustard gas. This classification is based on research finding that the risk of skin melanoma increases "by 75 per cent if a person starts tanning before age 30."

In 2011, the Capital Regional District of Victoria passed a bylaw which bans tanning beds for those under the age of majority and imposes a fine of between $250 to $2000 for violations. Nova Scotia became the first province to do so via the *Tanning Beds Act*, SNS 2010, c 44. Tanning salon owners face business closure for up to two years and fines of up to $10 000 for permitting those under the age of 19 to tan. In a press release, Maureen MacDonald, Minister for Health Promotion and Protection in Nova Scotia, explained: "We are taking a preventative approach to protect the health and safety of our youth. We know that excessive exposure to UV rays over the long term can have negative health effects, like skin cancer."

RIDO/SHUTTERSTOCK

Critical Analysis: Should the government try to protect young people from the dangers of tanning beds or should the matter be left up to the individual consumer? What is the role of government in such a context?

Sources: Capital Health "Proposed tanning bed legislation to protect youth" (24 November 2010) online:http://www.cdha.nshealth.ca/media-centre/news/proposed-tanning-bed-legislation-protect-youth; CBC staff "NB's voluntary tanning rules applauded" online: CBC News at http://www.cbc.ca/news/canada/new-brunswick/story/2011/01/17/nb-tanning-rules-959.html

Age of majority
The age at which a person becomes an adult for legal purposes. In Canada, this ranges from 18 to 19 years of age, depending on the province.

Contract law
Rules that make agreements binding and therefore facilitate planning and the enforcement of expectations.

Facilitating Interactions

The law facilitates personal interactions by providing rules concerning marriage, adoption, and the disposal of property upon the owner's death, to name a few examples. The law also facilitates commercial activity by providing rules governing the marketplace. The law of contract, for example, provides a way for parties to enter into binding agreements, thereby creating a measure of security and certainty in their business operations. **Contract law** allows business enterprises to plan for the future and to enforce their expectations.

Although the law addresses failed relations—as when one party does not meet its contractual obligations or gives negligent legal advice—it is not primarily about conflict.

Rather, the law functions to prevent disputes and to facilitate relationships. It provides certainty for Louella's commercial agreements and enables her to engage in transactions that might otherwise be unstructured and unpredictable.

Nor is the law primarily about rules that constrain commerce. Though the law does forbid certain activities—such as false advertising and operating without a business licence—its more significant role is facilitative. Legal rules provide definition and context to doing business. For example, assume that Louella wants to enter into a long-term relationship with a particularly reliable local supplier. Contract law allows her to accomplish this end by providing a mechanism through which Louella and the supplier can describe—and enforce—their commitments to each other. Therefore, Louella can agree in advance with her supplier on what kind of product is to be provided, how much, at what price, over what period of time, and when.

The creation of certainty in business relationships is one of the most important contributions that law can make to the commercial arena. While the necessity of creating certainty means that some anticipated contracts founder when it comes to formalizing their content, the law has not necessarily "failed." It more likely means that the businesspeople involved were not as close to being in agreement as they had initially assumed. Further discussions, perhaps through lawyers, have simply identified problems that, although hidden, were always there.

No contract can recite and provide for all contingencies; there will be some issues left unstated, but often the parties themselves find ways of overcoming these omissions. Generally, they will be guided by the need to achieve the original intent behind the contractual relationship, with the objective of dealing fairly with the unexpected or unaddressed event that has just occurred. In this way, the business relationship "fills in the blanks" in the contractual arrangement. If one or both of the parties involve the legal system, a judge will apply established rules governing contracts that lack the necessary specificity.

The influence of the law on the business environment does not have to be exacting and literal. In fact, parties to a business contract do not always observe their agreement to the letter, preferring to maintain their relationship rather than sue for breach of contract. For example, assume that Louella has a five-year contract with a reputable supplier of plastic bags customized to Louella's specifications. These bags are important to Louella's business since they hold her customers' retail purchases and are also part of her business' look. Owing to poor planning, the supplier will be unable to make its delivery on time and has advised Louella of the delay. Although she may be annoyed at the default, Louella stands to lose more than she would gain from suing, particularly if the supplier is otherwise reliable and the two have a solid working relationship. There is no good reason to risk this relationship and devote resources to **litigation**, that is, the process involved in suing someone. In this way, the contract between Louella and the supplier provides the legal backdrop to their relationship—by defining rights and obligations—but it is the business relationship that determines whether strict legal rights will be insisted upon. This is an important reality that affects how the law actually operates in the business environment.

Litigation
The process involved when one person sues another.

Providing Mechanisms for Dispute Resolution

Whether a conflict can or even should be resolved outside the formal legal system depends on the circumstances. If Louella hires an on-site manager who proves to be incompetent, it is in the interests of her enterprise to terminate the person's employment. While Louella may have a case to fire the employee outright, she might also consider offering a small severance package to reduce the possibility of being sued for wrongful dismissal.[19] This is a judgment call, but the time and money saved in avoiding a court battle may more than offset the cost of the severance package. Conversely, it may be that the employee has had his hand in the till and has stolen some of the business' daily receipts. Louella is in a different situation now. She not only must ensure that the employee leaves the company immediately but also will probably want to involve the police and try to recover what the employee has taken. In these kinds of circumstances, a full-blown legal conflict is much more likely and appropriate.

When one party fails to keep a contractual commitment, suing that person may seem to be the best and only response. This is particularly true when someone feels badly treated and believes that an essential principle is at stake in the conflict. However, the desire to stand up for this principle at all costs tends to betray a short-term perspective and should be resisted. Maintaining a good business relationship with the party in breach—or at least minimizing the financial costs of the dispute—is often much more important than proving yourself to be "right" in a court of law. Questions to ask include:

- Are legal proceedings absolutely necessary, at least right now?
- Is there a way to resolve the problem from a larger, relationship-preserving perspective, rather than from a strictly legal viewpoint?

Mediation
A process through which the parties to a dispute endeavour to reach a resolution with the assistance of a neutral person.

Arbitration
A process through which a neutral party makes a decision (usually binding) that resolves a dispute.

Liability
Legal responsibility for the event or loss that has occurred.

Solutions to a legal dispute exist at various levels of formality. The first logical step is for the parties to try to come to a resolution between themselves and produce, if necessary, a formalized settlement agreement. If this solution does not work, the legal system offers **mediation** and **arbitration** as ways of avoiding litigation. Thus, the law provides a number of mechanisms for settling disputes short of a courtroom battle.

Sometimes, however, one business will commence legal action against another and take the matter to court. Perhaps there had been no previous agreement between the parties to refer disputes to arbitration and they have no desire to do so now; perhaps one of the parties refuses to accept mediation; perhaps one of the parties is tremendously unfair and cannot be reasoned with; or perhaps the dispute has reached the point at which a court ruling is the only way to end the matter once and for all. It is essential to a workable business environment that the last-resort solution provided by the litigation process be available to the disputants. In this way, the **liability** of one business to another can be established.

---

19. For a discussion of wrongful dismissal, see Chapter 21.

How can parties resolve a business dispute without going to court?

ANDERSEN ROSS/PHOTODISC/JUPITER IMAGES

How and Why the Law Works

There are any number of ways to resolve a dispute, including trial by ordeal (as in the notorious Salem witch trials of 17th-century America); pistol duel (prevalent in France and England until the 19th century); and even modern-day drive-by shootings. What these methods lack, however, is accordance with modern ideas of what is just, fair, and reasonable.

Canada's legal system stands in opposition to such inequitable, arbitrary, and violent alternatives. While our legal system is far from perfect, it possesses essential improvements over its predecessors because it determines liability in accordance with certain principles and processes that are regarded as just.

For example, assume that Louella is suing a supplier for breach of contract for failure to deliver and the matter has now come before a judge. The Canadian legal system demands that both the process for determining liability and the rules or laws that are applied in that process are fair and free from bias. Though it is impossible for our legal system to completely reach such a standard, these are its laudable goals. Louella, as the party who has initiated the complaint of breach of contract, is obligated to prove her case. The judge, in turn, is obligated to be as objective as possible in determining whether Louella has proven her case. Part of the judge's job is to determine what the agreement between the parties actually was, as well as the law governing the matter. The judge must then apply this law as impartially as possible to the situation. In order that the outcome of Louella's dispute with the supplier be seen as just, the law that the judge ultimately relies on must also be fair and reasonable.

For instance, it is a rule of law that a party who suffers a breach of contract is entitled to be put in the position that she would have been in had the contract been fulfilled. If Louella can prove that as a result of the supplier's breach she lost business, for example, a court may well award her damages for loss of profit. The rationale behind the rule is simple: the supplier has broken his contractual promise. The supplier must therefore assume responsibility for any direct and foreseeable financial consequences Louella experiences as a result.

This man claimed to have been locked in a car trunk over a debt owed to his attackers. He was freed from the trunk by firefighters. How is this method of dispute resolution inconsistent with the values informing the Canadian justice system?

GLOBAL NEWS EDMONTON

The goals of the Canadian justice system are ambitious and often difficult to achieve. There are also obvious limitations to what the law can actually accomplish, even when it is most successful. Employment equity law will not end discrimination. Reform of bankruptcy law will not prevent business failures. More restrictive copyright laws will not stop unauthorized copying in everyday life. As noted earlier, the law can, however, offer itself as a mechanism for achieving the goals of protection, facilitation, and dispute resolution. For example, bankruptcy law is the vehicle for ensuring that all those affected by a failed business are treated fairly, reasonably, and according to a set of agreed-upon rules. The law is prepared to confront bigotry by providing remedies to those who are the targets. It provides rules for contract formation. And it provides a vast machinery for resolving conflict.

Knowledge of the Law as a Business Asset

Entrepreneurs like Louella can use the law to protect and advance their business interests. Conversely, they can cause themselves much anxiety, grief, and financial loss by ignoring the law.

For example, the law holds Louella responsible for the head injuries suffered by her customer because Louella was negligent in how she assembled the display case.[20] Louella also infringed copyright law and the *Criminal Code of Canada* in using the counterfeit UL labels.[21] Selling products that she "had a pretty good idea" were knockoffs could, among other illegalities, amount to criminal fraud under section 380 of the *Criminal Code of Canada*. As for her problems with the American anti-spamming legislation, Louella faces penalties that range from fines to imprisonment.[22]

---

20. For a discussion of the tort of negligence, see Chapter 11.
21. For a discussion of copyright, see Chapter 18.
22. See *CAN-SPAM Act supra* note 3.

Though the application of a foreign criminal statute is a fact-specific, complex inquiry, in practice it is unlikely that Louella will suffer any criminal sanctions under US law, provided she remains in Canada.[23] Nor does she appear to have assets in the US that would be at risk. However, if Louella faces a successful civil action in the US – as Facebook successfully sued Adam Guerbuez (see page 5) – and the judgment is recognized by a Canadian court as valid, then her assets are at risk. Setting these legal consequences aside, persistence in spamming will further damage her business reputation. Beyond this, such conduct will put Louella at risk of violating Canada's anti-spamming legislation when it comes on stream. See Chapter 6 for further discussion.

While Louella's negative experience with the law is exaggerated, it illustrates the point that knowing the law is a business asset. Had Louella taken the time to inform herself about the laws governing her operations—as well as about the consequences for failing to abide by them—her business experience presumably would have been much more positive and profitable.

An effective way to avoid Louella's negative business experience and enhance returns is to implement a **legal risk management plan**. This means identifying the legal risks associated with a business and implementing concrete measures for managing those risks. The objective is to identify and plan for risks *before* they occur rather than adopting the reactive mode that Louella favours.[24]

Legal risk management plan
A comprehensive action plan for dealing with the legal risks involved in operating a business.

Law and Business Ethics

From the perspective of reputation and profitability, it is not enough for a commercial enterprise simply to comply with the law. **Business ethics** also provide an increasingly important overlay. Business ethics concern moral principles and values that seek to determine right and wrong in the business world. On this basis, while it is ethical for a business to comply with the law, ethics may demand even more. Business ethics require entrepreneurs to conform to principles of commercial morality, fairness, and honesty. Entire books have been written about the ethical problems or dilemmas that a business might face.[25] However, from an introductory perspective, it is useful to consider how ethics impacts on business decisions from a number of vantage points:[26]

Business ethics
Moral principles and values that seek to determine right and wrong in the business world.

- *Business to Consumer:* How far should a company go in extolling the virtues of its product? When does sales talk become deception?

- *Business to Society:* To what lengths should a company go to enhance shareholder return? To reduce costs, should a business employ child labour in those countries where it is legal to do so? What if the child's income is essential to the family's survival?

- *Business to Employee:* Should a business monitor employee emails and Internet use on company computers?

- *Business to Business:* Short of lying or fraud, is it ethical to bluff during business negotiations? When does bluffing become a form of corruption?

23. For further analysis of the problems of enforcing anti-spamming legislation, see Christopher Scott Maravilla, "The Feasibility of a Law to Regulate Pornographic, Unsolicited, Commercial E-Mail" (2002) 4 Tul J Tech & Intell Prop 117.
24. See Chapter 3 for a risk management model.
25. See, for example, Robert Sexty, *Canadian Business and Society: Ethics and Responsibility,* 2d ed (Whitby, ON: McGraw-Hill Ryerson, 2011); Robert Larmer, *Ethics in the Workplace: Selected Readings in Business Ethics,* 2d ed (Belmont, CA: Wadsworth Thomson Learning, 2002).
26. These vantage points are derived from the work of Larmer, *supra* note 25.

As for Louella, many of her legal problems actually arise *because* of her unethical perspective and sole focus on "doing the deal" whatever the subsequent cost. On a related front, Louella does not take the law seriously. Both these attitudes can contribute to the demise of a business.

Louella seems consumed with short-sighted goals, causing her to violate overlapping legal and ethical norms. It is illegal and unethical to misrepresent a product as having passed a safety test when it has not, yet this is exactly what Louella does by using counterfeit UL labels on the imported lamps she retails. Similarly, it is illegal and unethical for Louella to sell knockoffs of FUBU merchandise; she is essentially misappropriating one company's reputation to increase her own sales. Even Louella's spamming has legal and ethical implications, since not only is she breaking American law, she is also arguably breaching ethical norms by commandeering the time and resources of the recipients without compensation.

Sometimes ethical standards are even stricter than legal ones, as Louella is learning. Though Louella may be free to sell any kind of legal product she sees fit—including extremely violent video games—her choices are not automatically sanitized as a result. Indeed, skirting ethical norms can lead to lost revenue, bad publicity, public demonstrations, and condemnation for contributing to social injustice.

Companies accused of breaching legal and ethical standards include Nike (for allegedly paying offshore workers subsistence wages) and Shell (for allegedly contributing to environmental degradation and human rights violations in Nigeria).[27] Shell has agreed to pay $15.5 million to settle a lawsuit that stated that Shell was complicit in the Nigerian government's 1995 execution of leader-activist Ken Saro-Wiwa and others. Shell contends that such allegations are false but that it agreed to the settlement on humanitarian grounds in order to "assist the process of reconciliation and peace" in the region.[28]

Business Law in Practice Revisited

1. How does the law affect Louella's business?

As Louella starts her business, she will be involved in a number of transactions and events with significant legal implications, including the following:

- **Business form.** Does Louella want to operate her business alone as a sole proprietor, would she prefer to work with partners, or is she interested in incorporating? Each business vehicle has its own set of rules, which Louella must find out about. For instance, the incorporation process is strictly dictated by federal and provincial law.[29]

- **Business name.** Louella must be sure to choose a name that is not confusingly similar to the name of another business. Even if she chooses such a name inadvertently, she will be subject to legal consequences, including being sued for damages by the individual or company that has built up goodwill in the name in question.[30]

27. For a rebuttal, see Shell Nigeria, "Home Page", online: Shell Nigeria <http://www.shell.com.ng/> and Nike Inc., "Corporate Responsibility Report: FY 07 08 09", online: Nikebiz <http://www.nikebiz.com/responsibility/reporting.html>.
28. See Shell Nigeria, Press Release, "Shell Settles Wiwa Case with Humanitarian Gesture," (8 June 2009) online: Shell Nigeria <http://www.shell.com.ng/home/content/nga/aboutshell/media_centre/news_and_media_releases/2009/saro_wiwa_case.html>. See also Andy Rowell, "Secret papers 'show how Shell targeted Nigeria oil protests'" *The Independent* (14 June 2009) online: The Independent Americas <http://www.independent.co.uk/news/world/americas/secret-papers-show-how-shell-targeted-nigeria-oil-protests-1704812.html>.
29. For a discussion of the incorporation process, see Chapter 15.
30. *Ibid*.

- **Financing considerations.** If Louella decides to borrow her operating capital from the bank, she must enter into a specialized form of contract known as a promissory note. In this contract, she promises to repay the loan, with interest, according to a schedule.[31] If Louella decides that she wants to raise money by selling shares, she will definitely have to incorporate a company. As well, should Louella's company end up selling shares to the public, it will have disclosure obligations under securities legislation.[32]

- **Property.** Louella must determine whether to buy, build, or lease premises for her business operation. Each option involves a unique set of laws.[33] Furthermore, many aspects of the property used in Louella's business are regulated through health legislation and fire regulations, to name two examples. Furthermore, if customers are injured on her premises, Louella may be held liable and be required to pay damages.

- **Services.** Louella may ultimately hire staff to run her business. She must become aware of the law concerning unjust dismissal and employment equity, as well as human rights legislation that prohibits discrimination.[34]

- **Marketing.** In promoting her store to the public, Louella must be sure to abide by laws prohibiting false and misleading advertising,[35] as well as trademark and copyright law, to name two examples.

- **Selling.** Louella must be sure to provide a reasonable level of service to her customers.

Just as Louella must devote resources to monitoring any staff that she might have, attending to proper bookkeeping, and keeping her loans in good standing, she also must spend time managing the legal elements of her business environment. Since the law affects Louella's business from a variety of perspectives, she is much better off accepting this responsibility from the outset, rather than fighting a rearguard action. Once she understands the law, Louella can take simple, proactive steps to ensure that she complies with it; just as importantly, she can plan for the future. A properly devised risk management plan is an invaluable tool to achieving this end.

2. What are the purposes of the laws that affect Louella's business?

One of the most important functions of law in the business environment is to facilitate planning, particularly—though not exclusively—through contract law. Business law also has a protective function in that it seeks to ensure that those who cause a loss are held financially responsible and otherwise accountable for their actions, including through the criminal justice system. Finally, the law provides a series of mechanisms and rules for dispute resolution, thereby making an essential contribution to certainty in the marketplace.

3. What has gone wrong in Louella's business and why?

The Business Law in Practice scenario provides a lengthy illustration of the kinds of penalties and liabilities Louella faces if she neglects to pay attention to the legal rules that govern her enterprise. Louella's ignorance of her legal obligations—combined with her lack of business ethics—will lead to the demise of her fledgling enterprise.

---

31. For a discussion of credit, see Chapter 26.
32. For a discussion of securities law, see Chapter 15.
33. For a discussion of real estate law, see Chapter 19.
34. For a discussion of employment law, see Chapters 20 and 21.
35. For a discussion of marketing law, see Chapters 23 and 24.

Chapter Summary

Law is involved in all aspects of business, whether the entrepreneur is aware of it or not. The law protects persons and their property, facilitates commercial interactions, particularly through contract law, and provides mechanisms for dispute resolution.

Though not perfect, the Canadian legal system has much to recommend it. The system strives for just outcomes by demanding that both the process for determining liability and the rules or laws that are applied in that process are fair, objective, and free from bias. No justice system, of course, can consistently accomplish all these goals.

Indeed, there are serious limitations to what the law can realistically achieve when a legal problem arises; thus, it is imperative that a business adopt a proactive approach in managing the legal aspects of its environment through a legal risk management plan. This chapter has emphasized the idea that knowledge of the law is an essential business asset. Informed owners and managers can protect their businesses by ensuring compliance with legal requirements. They can capitalize on the planning function of law to ensure the future of their business by entering into contracts. They also can seek enforcement of legal rules against those who do business or have other interactions with the enterprise. In this way, the property, contractual expectations, and profitability of the business are made more secure. Business ethics—while sometimes but not always coextensive with legal requirements—are also increasingly important to running a successful business.

Chapter Study

Key Terms and Concepts

age of majority (p. 10)

arbitration (p. 12)

breach of contract (p. 8)

business ethics (p. 15)

business law (p. 4)

contract law (p. 10)

law (p. 5)

legal risk management plan (p. 15)

liability (p. 12)

litigation (p. 11)

mediation (p. 12)

Questions for Review

1. What is the function of law?

2. How does the law protect members of society?

3. How does the law facilitate business activity?

4. In what ways does law facilitate certainty in the marketplace?

5. Does the nature of the business relationship affect the enforcement of legal rights?

6. How does the law resolve disputes?

7. Does dispute resolution always involve going to court?

8. In what way is knowledge of the law a business asset?

9. How might a lack of knowledge of the law negatively impact a business?

10. Why should a business put in place a legal risk management plan?

11. What is the role of business ethics?

12. Why are business ethics important?

13. What is spam?

14. What is the purpose of regulating spam?

Questions for Critical Thinking

1. What is the relationship between ethics and law? Are ethical responsibilities the same as legal responsibilities?

2. When is a lawsuit the best response to a legal dispute? What is at risk?

3. Knowledge of the law is a business asset. How can you acquire this asset short of becoming a lawyer? How is ignorance of the law a liability?

4. There has been considerable concern about the safety of Tasers (electroshock weapons) and their possible role in the death of hundreds of people in North America. The danger associated with Tasers was most recently brought to light because of the death of Robert Dziekanski, a Polish immigrant who died at the Vancouver International Airport immediately after being tased by RCMP officers. According to the CEO of Taser International, however, there is "no other device with as much accountability" as a Taser and he maintains that Tasers actually save lives.[36] What is the role of the law in regulating the products sold in the marketplace and ensuring their safety or relative safety?

5. Adam Guerbuez, the spammer described in this chapter, was made subject to a judgment of almost a $1 billion dollars by an American court. Do you think this judgment is unreasonably large? Should the defendant's ability to pay be taken into consideration by the court? Why or why not?

6. In 2010, the New Brunswick government implemented new voluntary guidelines governing the indoor tanning industry, including that people under 18 should not be permitted to indoor tan. These guidelines would be voluntary to start with but that would change if indoor tanning operators ignored the guidelines at which point legislation would be brought in. Is this a good approach to regulating business? Why or why not?

---

36. Omar El Akkad, "Taser CEO grilled by public safety committee" *The Globe and Mail* (31 January 2008) online: The Globe and Mail <http://portal.sre.gob.mx/canada/pdf/taserceo31.pdf>.

Situations for Discussion

1. Joe has recently opened a bar and adjoining restaurant, specializing in seafood. It is named "The Finny Friends" after a restaurant that Joe had visited in Toronto several years ago. In accordance with the law, Joe has a liquor licence from the provincial liquor-licensing authority that limits the seating capacity in the bar to 30. As Joe's bar becomes increasingly popular, he begins to regularly allow over 60 patrons in at one time. Eventually he is caught, and—having already received two warnings—his operation is closed down for 30 days. Joe is flabbergasted at the severity of the penalty. Soon thereafter, Joe is contacted by a lawyer for The Finny Friends restaurant in Toronto. The lawyer says that Joe has 48 hours to take down his restaurant awning and destroy anything else with the name The Finny Friends on it (including menus, invoices, placemats, napkins, and even match covers) or he will bring an application for a court order to that effect. To make matters worse, a health inspector is on Joe's doorstep saying that there have been several recent reports of food poisoning originating from Joe's restaurant. What has gone wrong in Joe's business and why?

2. The Privacy Commissioner's Annual Report (2011) criticized Staples Business Depot for not taking better steps to protect the privacy of customers who returned computers and USB hard drives. These returned items had undergone a "wipe and restore" process prior to resale but the Privacy Commission's audit found that sensitive data such as social insurance numbers and tax records had not been erased in all cases. What should Staples Business Depot do to ensure better compliance with privacy legislation? Would it be sufficient, for example, to ask customers to sign a form saying that they have wiped the returned electronic clean?

3. Assume that you have a major dispute with a business on the property next to yours over acceptable use of its land. You find that although zoning allows a small tool shop to operate on the property, the noise is too much for you. Your lawyer tells you that there may be a legal case for you to pursue, but it will be costly and the results are not guaranteed. What alternative approaches might address your problem more effectively?

4. Several provinces across Canada, including Ontario, Manitoba, and Saskatchewan, have proposed or passed legislation that prevents children from buying or renting video games that are expressly violent or sexual, as determined by a ratings board. Businesses found selling these games to minors face penalties that range from fines to having their licences revoked.[37] How effective do you think government regulation is in limiting children's access to violent video games? Are there better ways of achieving these types of goals? Is it the role of governments to provide legal consequences for the underage renting or purchase of violent video games?

5. Olivia owns a convenience store and has invested a lot of money in gambling machines for the store. Recently, the government passed a law banning the machines from the store immediately, although pubs are allowed to continue operating these machines. Is this law fair? Does it violate any of the common values associated with the law? Would it make a difference if the law applied only to new businesses? Would it make a difference if the government provided compensation to the convenience stores affected, or phased in the law to allow for a period of adjustment?

6. When her husband died of a heart attack in 2001 after taking the painkiller Vioxx, Carol Ernst sued the pharmaceutical manufacturer, Merck & Company. In 2005, a Texas jury awarded her $253.5 million after concluding that Vioxx had caused Mr. Ernst's death. In 2008, a Texas appeals court reversed Mrs. Ernst's victory. The court concluded that there was no evidence that Vioxx had in fact caused the death of Mr. Ernst[38] and, as a result, Mrs. Ernst has been left with no compensation whatsoever for her husband's death.

   According to news reports, Merck has taken an aggressive stance on lawsuits against it and spent more than $1 billion on legal fees to date.[39] Merck has observed that the plaintiffs are required to prove that

---

37. Based, in part, on Steve Lambert, "Manitoba video-game legislation remains in limbo", *The Globe and Mail* (6 January 2005) at A9; and CBC News, "Manitoba moves to rate violent video games", *CBC News* (29 April 2004) online: <http://www.cbc.ca/canada/story/2004/04/29/vids040429.html>.
38. Eric Strauss, "Merck wins Vioxx appeals in Texas, New Jersey", *The Star-Ledger* (30 May 2008) online: NJ.com <http://www.nj.com/business/index.ssf/2008/05/merck_wins_vioxx_appeals_in_te.html>.
39. Alex Berenson, "Plaintiffs Find Payday Elusive in Vioxx suits", *The New York Times* (21 August 2007) online: New York Times <http://www.nytimes.com/2007/08/21/business/21merck. html?_r51&scp51&sq5plaintiffs%20find%20payday%20elusive%20in%20Vioxx%20suits&st5cse&oref5slogin>.

Vioxx caused the heart attack in question. Given that heart attacks are the most common cause of death in the United States, Merck would have faced "an essentially unlimited pool of plaintiffs" without taking such a hard line, according to an American law professor.[40]

In 2007, a lawyer representing Mrs. Ernst stated to *The New York Times* that Merck should be amenable to settling at least some of the cases brought against it. He claimed that "Merck's goal is to manipulate the legal system to deprive justice to tens of thousands of people. ... Justice delayed is justice denied."[41]

Merck has taken steps to resolve some of the cases brought against it, however. In 2007, it entered into a $4.85 billion agreement, the goal of which is to bring to a conclusion a majority of the remaining Vioxx law suits.[42] According to press accounts, more than 44 000 plaintiffs involved in the most serious claims have enrolled in the proposed settlement.[43] Beyond this, a settlement of the Canadian Vioxx class action has been negotiated and is now subject to court approval.[44]

Do you agree with Merck's approach to the lawsuits that have been brought against it? What happens to people who want to sue Merck but cannot afford a lawyer?

For more study tools, visit
http://www.NELSONbrain.com.

40. *Ibid.*
41. *Ibid.*
42. Strauss, *supra* note 38.
43. *Ibid.*
44. Vioxx National Class Action Canada at http://vioxxnationalclassaction.ca/.

CHAPTER 2

The Canadian Legal System

Objectives

After studying this chapter, you should have an understanding of

- the impact of the Canadian legal system on business
- the role of constitutional law in protecting commercial rights and freedoms
- the government's law-making powers under sections 91 and 92 of the *Constitution Act, 1867*
- the executive's formal and political functions in regulating business
- the judiciary's role in assessing the constitutionality of legislation
- the classifications of law
- how administrative law affects business

The Right Honourable Beverley McLachlin, Chief Justice of the Supreme Court of Canada

© SUPREME COURT OF CANADA. PHOTO: ANDREW BALFOUR

Business Law in Practice

James McCrae owns a small convenience store in Nova Scotia which sells a variety of items, including cigarettes and other tobacco products. On what he regards to be a point of principle, McCrae refuses to comply with recent regulations passed under Nova Scotia's *Tobacco Access Act*.[1] These regulations prohibit the display of tobacco or tobacco products in retail outlets and specify how such products are to be stored. The law requires that tobacco not be visible to the public except at the moment of sale at the till.

McCrae is also aware that the tobacco industry pays retailers to display their goods and this is part of his income stream. One provincial department of health estimates that, in 2005, tobacco companies spent $100 million on point-of-purchase (POP) advertising in Canada alone.[2] The Canadian Cancer Society estimates that, via POP payments, retailers receive the equivalent of about 5 cents per cigarette package sold.[3]

Legislation like that of Nova Scotia is found in jurisdictions across the country. The idea behind such enactments is that the retail display of tobacco products (called power walls) 'normalizes' the consumption of tobacco and encourages smoking. As noted on the government of Nova Scotia's website:

"Power walls, or point-of-sale advertising, are large, visually appealing displays, located in most gas stations and local stores. Research has indicated these displays are particularly appealing to children and young adults. The legislation will force store owners

---

1. *Tobacco Access Act*, SNS 1993 c 14.
2. "Tobacco power walls banned in N.B. stores as of Jan. 1", CBC News (31 December 2008) online: CBC News <http://www.cbc.ca/news/canada/new-brunswick/story/2008/12/31/nb-powerwall-ban.html>.
3. See Canadian Cancer Society, "What the Tobacco Industry Says Versus the Facts", online: The New Brunswick Anti-Tobacco Coalition. <http://www.nbatc.ca/tatu/images/powerwalls/What_the_Tobacco_Industry_Says.pdf>.

(*Continued on the next page*)

to conceal cigarettes, and any other tobacco product. The removal of power walls will further restrict the advertising reach of tobacco companies."[4]

There is also evidence that anti-power wall legislation has helped reduce the number of young people who smoke or take up smoking. As the *Guardian* notes for example, "Those countries that have removed displays of tobacco have experienced falls in smoking prevalence among young people. In Iceland, there was a fall of 7.5% among people aged 15-16, while Canada saw a fall of 10% over five years among those aged 15–19."[5] The tobacco industry and smoking-rights groups, however, contend that such legislation is simply not defensible.[6]

From McCrae's perspective, Nova Scotia's legislation interferes with freedom of expression, as protected under the s. 2(b) of the *Canadian Charter of Rights and Freedoms* which states:

> 2. Everyone has the following fundamental freedoms. . . .
>
> (b) freedom of thought, belief, opinion and expression, including freedom of the press and other media of communication;[7]

McCrae's view is that displaying tobacco products is a protected form of expression.

McCrae is eventually charged under the *Tobacco Access Act* for displaying tobacco products out in the open. He wants his lawyer to have the charges thrown out on the basis that the *Tobacco Access Act* is unconstitutional, as contrary to s. 2 of the *Charter*, quoted above.

1. Is the Nova Scotia's *Tobacco Access Act* constitutional and hence enforceable?
2. Who assesses whether the legislation is permissible?
3. Are there any moral or ethical questions that arise from this scenario?

Introduction

The Canadian legal system is the machinery that comprises and regulates government. Government, in turn, is divided into three branches:

- The legislative branch creates law in the form of statutes and regulations.

- The executive branch formulates and implements **government policy** and law.

- The judicial branch adjudicates on disputes.

Constitutional law—which is the supreme law of Canada—is charged with ascertaining and enforcing limits on the exercise of power by the branches of government. It is also charged with upholding "the values of a nation."[8] These values are tied to the political philosophy known as **liberalism**. Briefly put, liberalism emphasizes individual freedom as

Government policy
The central ideas or principles that guide government in its work, including the kind of laws it passes.

Constitutional law
The supreme law of Canada that constrains and controls how the branches of government exercise power.

Liberalism
A political philosophy that emphasizes individual freedom as its key organizing value.

---

4. See Government of Nova Scotia, News Release, "Government Pulls the Plug on Tobacco Power Walls" (31 October 2006) online: Government of Nova Scotia News Releases <http://www.gov.ns.ca/news/details.asp?id=20061031002>.
5. Janet Atherton, "Keep it hidden", *The Guardian* (4 February 2009) online: The Guardian <http://www.guardian.co.uk/society/joepublic/2009/feb/04/children-smoking>.
6. For tobacco industry arguments and rebuttal, see Canadian Cancer Society, *supra* note 3.
7. *Canadian Charter of Rights and Freedoms*, s.2(b), Part I of the *Constitution Act, 1982*, being Schedule B to the *Canada Act 1982* (UK), 1982, c 11 [*Charter*].
8. Peter Hogg, *Constitutional Law of Canada*, vol. 1, loose-leaf (Scarborough, ON: Carswell, 2007) at 1–1. Note: Throughout this chapter, Hogg is cited to page number, not paragraph number.

its key organizing value. A related aspect is that any interference with freedom—including the freedom to display a legal product in one's business premises—must be justified according to the principles of constitutional law.

Canadian legal system
The machinery that comprises and governs the legislative, executive, and judicial branches of government.

The **Canadian legal system**—along with the constitutional law that governs it—can be an overwhelming and sometimes very technical area. Even so, some basic knowledge is essential for business owners and managers because

- the legislative branch of government passes laws that impact on business operations. For example, when government enacts a law, failure to comply can result in fines and other penalties, including closure of the business. Ignorance of a law means that business loses out on opportunities to influence government policy and to take advantage of favourable laws. And failure to challenge laws that are unconstitutional means that business is needlessly constrained.

- the executive branch implements and generates policy that may be directed at business. For this reason, companies such as General Motors of Canada Ltd. have a corporate and environmental affairs department that is charged with monitoring government policy as well as tracking and contributing to debates over public policy that could affect GM operations.[9] Smaller businesses may work to influence government on a more modest scale by monitoring issues in-house, hiring lobbyists, and working through industry associations.

- the judicial branch provides rulings that not only resolve existing legal conflicts but also impact on future disputes. For example, the Supreme Court of Canada's

When Ontario's tobacco display ban went into effect, some customers were unhappy, including Rene LaPointe. "It's just another law for the government to throw at us," says LaPointe. "They're treating the adults like children." Do you agree with his analysis?[10]

AP PHOTO/BOB JORDAN

---

9. Interview of Ms. Miriam Christie, Manager of Government Relations, Corporate and Environmental Affairs Department, General Motors of Canada Ltd. (10 March 2000).
10. "Smokers fume over tobacco display ban" *The Edmonton Journal* (1 June 2008) A8, see <http://www.canada.com/edmontonjournal/news/story.html?id=cb2b5095-4506-495a-8650-207f27169acb>.

determination of whether commercial expression is protected speech under the *Canadian Charter of Rights and Freedoms* has an impact on any number of industries, from cigarette producers to toy manufacturers.

McCrae's challenge to the *Tobacco Access Act,* mentioned in the chapter opener, involves all three of these branches. The legislative branch passed the law to which McCrae objects. The executive branch formulated and advanced the government policy that led to the legislation being enacted. And the judicial branch—by applying constitutional law—will determine whether McCrae's objections to the law are valid or not.

The Canadian Constitution

The Canadian Constitution is not contained in one document. Rather, it is located in a variety of places, both legislative and political, written and unwritten. While this means that the Constitution may sometimes not be specific, it also means that the Constitution can more easily grow to resolve questions or issues related to government.

The written elements of the Constitution include the *Constitution Act, 1867* (part of which divides legislative power between the federal and provincial governments) and the *Canadian Charter of Rights and Freedoms* (which identifies the rights and freedoms that are guaranteed in Canada). Additionally, relevant decisions by judges concerning constitutional law—discussed later in this chapter—also form part of the Constitution. Though these documents provide some of the framework and values informing Canada's system of government, other important constitutional features (known as constitutional conventions) are not mentioned at all.

Constitutional conventions are a "code of ethics that governs our political processes."[11] They are not binding the way that constitutional rules contained in legislation would be. They cannot be enforced in a court of law. Rather, they are in place because politicians historically have agreed to abide by them. One example relates to the office of prime minister. Nowhere in Canada's written Constitution is this important office even mentioned, yet no one doubts that the federal government is to be headed by such an officer. In this way, constitutional conventions come to the fore and provide some of the detail of governance.

The Canadian Constitution also attends to a number of other matters, including the admission of new provinces and territories to Canada,[12] provisions for amending the Constitution,[13] and autonomy from the United Kingdom Parliament.[14] Most significantly for our purposes, however, the Canadian Constitution provides for the three branches of government: legislative, executive, and judicial, discussed below.

The Legislative Branch of Government

The **legislative branch** of government creates a form of law known as **statute law** or legislation. A familiar example of statute law is the *Criminal Code of Canada,* which prohibits

Constitutional conventions
Important rules that are not enforceable by a court of law but that practically determine how a given power is exercised by government.

Legislative branch
The branch of government that creates statute law.

Statute law
Formal, written laws created or enacted by the legislative branch of government.

---

11. Bernard Funston & Eugene Meehan, *Canada's Constitutional Law in a Nutshell,* 3rd ed. (Toronto: Carswell, 2003) at 16.
12. As Hogg observes, *supra* note 8 at 2-12, s. 146 of the *Constitution Act, 1867* governs this matter. For a link to constitutional documents, including legislation creating provinces as they are admitted to Canada, see <http://laws.justice.gc.ca/en/Const/index.html> .
13. See Part V of the *Constitution Act, 1982,* being Schedule B to the *Canada Act 1982* (UK), 1982, c 11, and Hogg, *supra* note 8 at 4–11 to 4–12 and 4–15 to 4–43.
14. For further discussion of this point, see Hogg, *ibid.* at 3–1 to 3–14.

a variety of offences, such as assault, theft, and fraud. The *Tobacco Access Act* is also created by the legislative branch, this time at the provincial level.

In fact, three levels of government—the federal, provincial, and municipal levels—make legislation in Canada. Parliament, the federal legislative branch, is composed of the House of Commons and the Senate. For legislation to become law, it must first be passed by the House of Commons and then be approved by the Senate. Because the Senate assesses the work of the House of Commons, it has been called "the chamber of sober second thought."

Each province also has a law-making body. In British Columbia, for example, this is called the Legislative Assembly, while in Nova Scotia this is called the House of Assembly. At the provincial level, there is no Senate, or upper house.

Municipalities, which are created by provincial legislation, have legislative bodies often called city councils. Their powers are delegated to them by the province in which they are located. (See Figure 2.1 on page 27.)

Statute Law and Jurisdiction

Jurisdiction
The power that a given level of government has to enact laws.

As already noted, the Constitution—through the *Constitution Act, 1867*—dictates whether each level of government can make a given law or not. Expressed in legal language, each level of government has the **jurisdiction** to pass laws within its proper authority or sphere. Jurisdiction is divided in this way because Canada is a federal state, which means that governmental power is split between the central, national authority (the federal government), and regional authorities (the provincial governments). Additionally, the federal government empowers territorial governments to engage in a form of limited self-government. The provincial governments, in turn, empower municipal governments to legislate in specifically defined areas.

BUSINESS AND LEGISLATION

Constitution Act, 1867

The federal government has the power, or the jurisdiction, to make laws in those areas set out in section 91 of the *Constitution Act, 1867* (formerly known as the *British North America Act* or the *BNA Act*). Areas in which the federal government may enact laws include the following:

- interprovincial/international trade and commerce
- trade as a whole
- postal service
- navigation and shipping
- currency
- national defence
- criminal law
- banking
- all legislative areas not given to the provinces

(Note: This is a residual category in the sense that the federal government has all the law-making power not expressly given to the provinces. For example, it is the residual power that justifies federal legislation that creates federally incorporated companies.)

The provincial governments have jurisdiction to make laws in those areas set out in section 92 of the *Constitution Act, 1867*, including the following:

- hospitals
- property and civil rights within the province (e.g., the regulation of contracts)
- administration of justice (e.g., the court system)
- local matters (e.g., highway regulation)
- incorporation of provincial companies

Municipalities have no constitutionally recognized powers. They have only the law-making authority that is delegated to them by the provincial governments. The municipal governments have jurisdiction to make laws as permitted by the relevant provincial government, for example, in these areas:

- zoning
- subdivision
- taxation for the benefit of the municipality
- licensing

FIGURE 2.1

Law-Making Jurisdiction

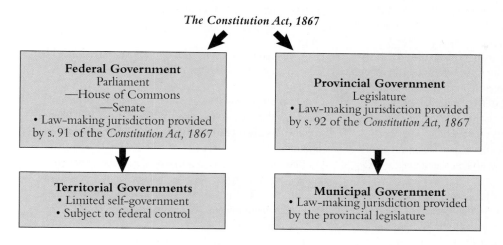

The Constitution specifies that the federal government has jurisdiction over criminal law, which includes the power to define new crimes, provide penalties for breaches of the criminal law, and pass laws with the purpose of protecting the public. Because criminal law falls under federal jurisdiction, there is a *Criminal Code of Canada* but there are no provincial criminal codes. In fact, if the legislature of Manitoba were to attempt to enact a law known as the *Criminal Code of Manitoba*, for example, this law would be unconstitutional because a provincial government does not have the power to pass such a law. No court would enforce the code because it would be contrary to the Constitution to do so. In short, the federal government has **exclusive jurisdiction** over criminal law.

Sometimes, the federal and provincial governments have shared or **concurrent jurisdiction.** This means that the area being regulated does not fall neatly into the federal or provincial jurisdiction but straddles them both. Public health is one such area, with both federal and provincial governments legislating in the area. The environment is another, as discussed in the following box.

Exclusive jurisdiction
Jurisdiction that one level of government holds entirely on its own and not on a shared basis with another level.

Concurrent jurisdiction
Jurisdiction that is shared between levels of government.

ENVIRONMENTAL PERSPECTIVE

Concurrent Jurisdiction Over the Environment
From a business perspective, one tremendously significant area of concurrent jurisdiction relates to the environment. Both the federal and provincial governments share jurisdiction but perhaps surprisingly, so do municipalities. This is because, as Shawn Denstedt and Daniel Kirby observe, municipalities are "traditionally responsible for water and sewage systems and noise issues, [and] in some cases now restrict or prohibit the use of pesticides and herbicides (even after their use has been

approved by the federal or applicable provincial government), require public disclosure regarding the use of toxic substances and often try to control the impact of development on the environment through their role as the primary authority for land-use planning."[15]

As Robert Warren, John Bulman & Carole McAffee Wallace note, federal jurisdiction over the environment centres on (a) protection of oceans and inland waterways; (b) fisheries protection; (c) the import and export of hazardous products;

(Continued)

15. Shawn Denstedt & Daniel Kirby with contributions by Rahda Curpen, "Doing Business in Canada: Environmental Law in Canada", (March 2009) online: Osler <http://www.osler.com/NewsResources/Details.aspx?id=1227>.

and (d) the interprovincial/international transportation of dangerous goods.[16] For example, the federally enacted legislation called the *Canadian Environmental Protection Act*[17] ("*CEPA*") sets out comprehensive rules governing toxic substances as they relate, from a business perspective, to "research and development through to production, marketing, use and disposal."[18] The goal of the legislation is to protect human health and the environment from the dangers of harmful and toxic substances.[19] On a related front, CEPA is important because, as Environment Canada notes, it "manages environmental and human health impacts of products of biotechnology, marine pollution, disposal at sea, vehicle, engine and equipment emissions, fuels, hazardous wastes, environmental emergencies and other sources of pollution."[20]

CEPA provides strong penalties for violation, including fines of up to $1 million a day for each day the offence continues, imprisonment for up to three years or both. Those convicted are also subject to paying clean-up costs, as relevant, or forfeit any profit earned as a result of failing to comply with the act.[21]

The *Criminal Code of Canada* is another example of federal law concerning the environment.[22] Charges can be laid under the *Criminal Code* when, for example, an environmental discharge causes bodily injury or death.[23]

Every province and territory in Canada has extensive environmental protection legislative regimes. In Ontario, for example, the most significant legislation on point is the *Environmental Protection Act*.[24] As summarized by Ontario's Ministry of the Environment, the Act:

• "prohibits the discharge of any contaminants into the environment which cause or are likely to cause negative effects—and in the case of some approved contaminants—requires that they must not exceed approved and regulated limits

• requires that any spills of pollutants be reported and cleaned up in a timely fashion."[25]

Court can impose fines and even jail time for violation of the Act with penalties varying according to the kind of offence committed as well as whether the violation was a first offense or not.[26]

Directors and officers also face personal liability for non-compliance with environmental protection legislation and are thereby exposed to potentially heavy fines and, in the extreme case, even imprisonment. For further discussion on this point, see Chapter 16.

Regulation and protection of the environment is complex in part because jurisdiction is spread amongst three levels of government. This makes it particularly important for businesses to know what legislation applies to the situation in question, to deploy risk management strategies to ensure that such legislation sees compliance, and to acquire environmental insurance as a backstop should the organization fail in its statutory obligations.

Critical Analysis: What are the advantages of concurrent jurisdiction over the environment? What are the disadvantages?

Paramountcy
A doctrine that provides that federal laws prevail when there are conflicting or inconsistent federal and provincial laws.

In areas of concurrent jurisdiction, what the provincial government cannot do is enact legislation that would create a conflict with federal legislation. That is, in an area of concurrent jurisdiction—such as health or the environment—the doctrine of **paramountcy** applies. This doctrine makes the federal legislation paramount or supreme and the provincial law inoperative, but only to the extent of the conflict. Though a significant doctrine, it is also a limited one. The judiciary has held that paramountcy generally applies only if there is an express contradiction between the two laws. If a person could simply obey the stricter law—and thereby comply with both pieces of legislation—then paramountcy would not apply. Both laws would operate fully.

---

16. Robert Warren, John Buhlman & Carole McAffee Wallace, "Environmental Protection Law in Ontario" (Spring 2009) online: WeirFoulds <http://www.weirfoulds.com/files/4130_WeirFoulds%20LLP-EnvironmentalLawProtectionOntario.pdf> at 2.
17. *Canadian Environmental Protection Act*, 1999 SC c 33 ["*CEPA*"].
18. Denstedt, *supra* note 15.
19. Environment Canada, "A Guide to Understanding the *Canadian Environmental Protection Act, 1999*" (December 2004) online: Environment Canada <http://www.ec.gc.ca/lcpe-cepa/default.asp?lang=En&n=E00B5BD8-1> [Environment Canada] at 2.
20. *Ibid.*
21. *Ibid.* at 29.
22. *Criminal Code*, RSC 1985, c C-46.
23. Warren, *supra* note 16 at 5.
24. *Environmental Protection Act*, RSO 1990, c E 19.
25. Ontario Ministry of Environment, "*Environmental Protection Act*", online: Ontario Ministry of Environment <http://www.ene.gov.on.ca/environment/en/legislation/environmental_protection_act/index.htm>. This website also states that, "The Act also governs commercial transactions involving contaminated land."
26. Warren, *supra* note 16.

INTERNATIONAL PERSPECTIVE

Antismoking Treaty

In response to the millions of deaths caused by tobacco every year, numerous countries, including Canada, have **ratified** a **treaty** known as the "Framework Convention on Tobacco Control." According to the World Health Organization,

> the treaty requires countries to impose restrictions on tobacco advertising, sponsorship and promotion; establish new packaging and labelling of tobacco products; establish clean indoor air controls; and strengthen legislation to clamp down on tobacco smuggling.

For example, countries would be required to adopt and implement rotating health warnings and messages on tobacco products, occupying at least 30 percent of the display areas. Canada ratified this treaty in 2004.

In 2005, World Health Organization officials reported that the tobacco industry was working hard to limit the number of countries participating in the treaty, including intense lobbying efforts in the United States. These efforts appear to have missed their mark. According to the World Health Organization, this Framework Convention on Tobacco Control is "one of the most rapidly embraced treaties in the United Nations system."

Critical Analysis: How might a treaty ratified by multiple countries be more effective in reducing tobacco consumption than if each country simply worked in isolation? What are the advantages of global cooperation? What are the disadvantages?

Sources: Stephanie Nebehay, "UN anti-smoking pact kicks in as cigarette firms fight back" *The Globe and Mail* (28 February 2005) at B7; World Health Organization, "An international treaty for tobacco control" (12 August 2003), online: World Health Organization <http://www.who.int/features/2003/08/en>; Health Canada News Release, "Canada ratifies the Framework Convention on Tobacco Control, the world's first public health treaty" (2 December 2004), online: Health Canada <http://www.hc-sc.gc.ca/ahc-asc/media/nr-cp/2004/2004_63_e.html>; World Health Organization, "Conference of the Parties to the WHO Framework Convention on Tobacco Control", online: World Health Organization <http://www.who.int/gb/fctc/PDF/cop1/FCTC_COP1_ID1-en.pdf>; and Melanie Wakefield & Jonathan Liberman, "Back to the Future: Tobacco Industry Interference, Evidence and the Framework Convention on Tobacco Control" *Tobacco Control* 17 (2008) at 145–46 (http://tobaccocontrol.bmj.com/cgi/content/full/17/3/145).

Business is affected by all levels of government, but it is most affected by the provincial and municipal governments. An important exception relates to businesses in banking, international or interprovincial transport, and communication (e.g., telephone and cable). These are areas of federal jurisdiction and, accordingly, such businesses are subject to federal law concerning licensing, labour, and occupational health and safety, to name several examples.

The regulation of business is generally a provincial matter because the provinces have jurisdiction over property and civil rights.[27] Municipalities have jurisdiction to legislate in a broad variety of matters, from levying appropriate taxes and regulating local zoning, parking, and subdivision to requiring the licensing of businesses and dogs. Municipal legislation takes the form of **bylaws**.

The Executive Branch of Government

The executive branch of government has a formal, ceremonial function, as well as a political one. From a formal or ceremonial perspective, for example, the executive branch supplies the head of the Canadian state, the Queen. The **formal executive** also has a significant role in the legislative process, since the executive branch of government, represented by the governor general (the Queen's federal representative) or lieutenant governor (the Queen's provincial representative), issues approval as the final step in creating statute law.

The **political executive** is of great relevance to businesses because it performs the day-to-day operations of government by formulating and executing government policy and administering all departments of government. It is also the level of government that businesses typically lobby in order to secure favourable or improved treatment under legislation or with respect to policy formation.

Ratify
To authorize or approve.

Treaty
An agreement between two or more states that is governed by international law.

Bylaws
Laws made by the municipal level of government.

Formal executive
The branch of government responsible for the ceremonial features of government.

Political executive
The branch of government responsible for day-to-day operations, including formulating and executing government policy, as well as administering all departments of government.

27. *Hogg, supra* note 8 at 21–3.

BUSINESS AND LEGISLATION

Tobacco Regulation by the Federal Government

Regulations are a form of legislation that is more precisely referred to as subordinate legislation. This is because regulations can be passed only if that power is accorded by the statute in question. That said, such power is routinely given. For example, the *Tobacco Act (Canada)* permits the Governor (General) in Council (i.e., the federal cabinet) to make regulations respecting information that must appear on cigarette packages. Cabinet exercised this power through the Tobacco Products Information Regulations which require that graphic health warnings and other information be placed on cigarette packages.

In 2011, new federal regulations came into force governing warnings to be placed on cigarette packages. Important features include

- "new graphic health warning messages covering 75 percent of the front and back of cigarette and little cigar packages;
- new health information messages that are enhanced with the use of colour and graphic elements;
- a pan-Canadian toll-free quitline number and web portal to inform tobacco users about the availability of

This image depicts Barb Tarbox, who died of lung cancer caused by smoking. She was so addicted to cigarettes that she continued smoking until her death. One of her final wishes was that her dying image appear on cigarette packages as a warning to others.[28] Are such images effective?

smoking cessation services, subject to provincial/territorial agreement; and

- easier-to-understand toxic emissions statements."

These regulations also provide a set of images to be included on cigarette packages, including the one depicted above.

Sources: *Tobacco Act*, SC 1997, c 13; Health Canada "Tobacco Products Labelling Regulations " http://www.hc-sc.gc.ca/hc-ps/tobac-tabac/legislation/reg/label-etiquette/index-eng.php

Cabinet
A body composed of all ministers heading government departments, as well as the prime minister or premier.

The chief executive of the federal government is the prime minister, while the chief executive of the provincial government is the premier. Other members of the political executive—both provincial and federal—include cabinet ministers, civil servants, and the agencies, commissions, and tribunals that perform governmental functions.

Regulations
Rules created by the political executive that have the force of law.

The **cabinet**—made up of all the ministers of the various government departments, as well as the prime minister or premier—also has a very significant law-making function. It is often the cabinet that passes **regulations** providing detail to what the statute in question has enacted. When the cabinet enacts regulations, it is known by its formal name: the lieutenant governor in council (provincially) and the governor general in council (federally).

The Judicial Branch of Government

Judiciary
A collective reference to judges.

It may seem surprising that the **judiciary** is a branch of government, given that the judiciary is supposed to be independent of government. Expressed more completely, however, the concept is this: the judiciary is to be independent from the legislative and executive branches of government.

Judges
Those appointed by federal and provincial governments to adjudicate on a variety of disputes, as well as to preside over criminal proceedings.

The judiciary is composed of **judges** who are appointed by both federal and provincial governments. These judges are required to adjudicate on a variety of matters, including divorce and the custody of children, civil disputes such as those arising from a will, breach of contract, car accidents, wrongful dismissal, and other wrongful acts causing damage or

28. "Family of Tarbox wants her deathbed image on cigarette packs" (08 December 2010) at <http://calgary.ctv.ca/servlet/an/local/CTVNews/20101207/CGY_smoke_warnings_101207/20101208/?hub=CalgaryHome>.

FIGURE 2.2

Courts Dealing with Commercial Disputes

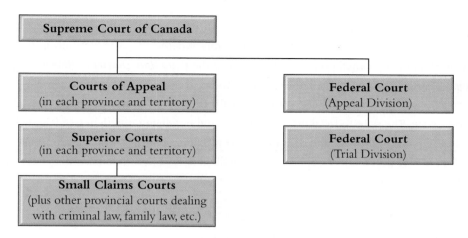

injury. Judges also preside over criminal proceedings. Businesses, however, predominantly rely on the courts to settle commercial disputes.

The System of Courts

Judges operate within a system of courts that vary somewhat from province to province. Despite these variations, each provincial and territorial system of courts has three basic levels: trial, intermediate appeal, and final appeal. Figure 2.2 above indicates the hierarchy of courts relevant to commercial disputes.

Trial courts are of two types: inferior and superior. **Inferior courts** are presided over by judges appointed by the provincial government. These courts are organized by type of case, such as criminal, family, and civil. The civil court—sometimes called **small claims court**—handles disputes involving smaller amounts of money. The amount varies from province to province: $25 000 is the limit in British Columbia, Nova Scotia, and Ontario[29] while $20 000 is the limit in Saskatchewan.[30] The process is designed to be simpler, quicker, and less expensive than mainstream litigation. Parties often appear in this court without a lawyer. **Superior courts**—whose judges are appointed by the federal government—have the jurisdiction to handle claims involving an unlimited monetary amount. In addition, they are the entry level for the more serious criminal matters. Here, the procedure is much more formal and technical, with parties usually being represented by lawyers.

Provincial courts of appeal hear appeals from these lower courts, and from there cases go to the **Supreme Court of Canada.** In most commercial cases, litigation tends to end in provincial courts of appeal because appeal to the Supreme Court of Canada is available only after permission or "leave" to appeal is granted by the Supreme Court itself. Ordinarily, the Supreme Court of Canada will hear only appeals that involve questions of national concern or significance.

Inferior court
A court with limited financial jurisdiction whose judges are appointed by the provincial government.

Small claims court
A court that deals with claims up to a specified amount.

Superior court
A court with unlimited financial jurisdiction whose judges are appointed by the federal government.

Supreme Court of Canada
The final court for appeals in the country.

---

29. See the Courts of Nova Scotia, "Nova Scotia Small Claims Court", online: The Courts of Nova Scotia <http://www.courts.ns.ca/SmallClaims/index_claims.htm>; The Ministry of the Attorney General of Ontario, "Small Claims Court", online: Ontario Ministry of the Attorney General <http://www.attorneygeneral.jus.gov.on.ca/english/courts/scc/>; and Small Claims BC, "A Provincial Court Pilot Project", online: Small Claims BC <http://www.smallclaimsbc.ca/>.
30. See Courts of Saskatchewan, "Provincial Court", online: Courts of Saskatchewan <http://www.sasklawcourts.ca/default.asp?pg=pc_newsmallclaimshome>.

Federal Court of Canada
The court that deals with some types of litigation involving the federal government.

Canadian Charter of Rights and Freedoms
A guarantee of specific rights and freedoms enshrined in the Constitution and enforceable by the judiciary.

The **Federal Court of Canada** has special authority to deal with certain cases in which one of the parties is the federal government or one of its agencies.

The Canadian Charter of Rights and Freedoms

An important responsibility for judges is determining whether a given law meets the requirements of the Canadian Constitution, including the ***Canadian Charter of Rights and Freedoms*** [*Charter*]. Created in 1982, the *Charter* is intended as a judicially enforceable guarantee that the government will act consistently with the values associated with a liberal democratic state. The right to freedom of expression and of religion, the right to a fair and speedy trial, equality rights, and the right to vote are all examples of *Charter* protections that reflect a set of constitutional values founded on individual freedom. Two protections that are particularly germane to business are contained in sections 2 and 15.

Fundamental Freedoms

2. Everyone has the following fundamental freedoms:

   a. freedom of conscience and religion;

   b. freedom of thought, belief, opinion and expression, including freedom of the press and other media of communication;

   c. freedom of peaceful assembly; and

   d. freedom of association.

Equality Rights

15. (1) Every individual is equal before and under the law and has the right to the equal protection and equal benefit of the law without discrimination and, in particular, without discrimination based on race, national or ethnic origin, colour, religion, sex, age or mental or physical disability.

The *Charter* is a powerful constitutional document because it provides protection from improper or oppressive government conduct—conduct that most often takes the form of legislation or policy. In short, section 32 of the *Charter* prohibits government and government alone from violating any of the rights or freedoms recited. By way of contrast, violation of rights in the private sector, such as through employment discrimination, is a matter for provincial and federal human rights codes and thus is addressed according to a separate set of rules.[31]

It is almost certainly the case that Nova's Scotia's *Tobacco Access* legislation violates section 2 of the *Charter*—freedom of expression. Indeed, the Supreme Court of Canada has already affirmed that commercial expression is protected under section 2, stating:

> [o]ver and above its intrinsic value as expression, commercial expression which, as has been pointed out, protects listeners as well as speakers, plays a significant role in enabling individuals to make informed economic choices, an important aspect of individual self-fulfillment and personal autonomy. The Court accordingly rejects the view that commercial expression serves no individual or societal value in a free and democratic society and for this reason is undeserving of any constitutional protection.[32]

---

31. For a discussion of human rights codes in an employment context, see Chapter 20.
32. *Ford v Quebec (Attorney General)*, [1988] 2 SCR 712 at 767.

But demonstrating a violation of section 2 does not automatically render legislation unconstitutional because the rights and freedoms guaranteed by the *Charter* are not absolute. On the contrary, the *Charter* acknowledges that the government is entitled to restrict freedom of expression—as well as any other right recited in the *Charter*—but only if it has balanced all relevant interests carefully and reasonably, as required by the very first section of the *Charter*.

1. The *Canadian Charter of Rights and Freedoms* guarantees the rights and freedoms set out in it subject only to such reasonable limits prescribed by law as can be demonstrably justified in a free and democratic society.

Section 1 requires the government to justify why it is infringing a right, as well as to demonstrate that in doing so, it is restricting the right in question in a reasonably measured, controlled, and appropriate way. If it is unable to do so, the legislation is struck down by the court, that is, it is declared to be of no force or effect. In essence, the Act is thrown out because it is unconstitutional. The court's authority to order such a powerful remedy is set out in sections 24 and 52 of the *Charter*.

A court assessing the constitutionality of Nova Scotia's *Tobacco Access Act*, for example, would first seek to determine what the government was trying to accomplish through the legislation. Here, the goal is clear, as section 2 of the legislation states:

Section 2: The purpose of this Act is to protect the health of Nova Scotians, and in particular young persons, by

(a) restricting their access to tobacco and tobacco products; and
(b) protecting them from inducements to use tobacco, in light of the risks associated with the use of tobacco.

This identified purpose helps to refute the argument that the Nova Scotia's *Tobacco Access Act* cannot be saved under s. 1. This is because any challenger to the legislation would be forced to rely on arguments similar to those rejected by the Supreme Court of Canada in *Canada (Attorney General) v JTI-Macdonald Corp.* [*JTI-Macdonald*].[33] To this extent, the arguments cannot succeed. In *JTI-Macdonald*, at issue was the constitutionality of the federal government's 1996 legislation known as the *Tobacco Act*, which prohibits most forms of tobacco advertising, including "lifestyle" advertising. The Act defines "lifestyle advertising" as "advertising that associates a product with, or evokes a positive or negative emotion about or image of, a way of life such as one that includes glamour, recreation, excitement, vitality, risk or daring."[34] The Supreme Court of Canada held, among other things, that though the *Tobacco Act*'s prohibition on lifestyle advertising violated the *Charter*'s guarantee of freedom of expression, this violation was justified under s. 1 because of Parliament's pressing and substantial purpose, namely to prevent young people from starting to smoke. By way of analogy, the Supreme Court of Canada's analysis in *JTI-Macdonald* suggests that Nova Scotia's legislation is also constitutional. That is, since

33. *Canada (Attorney General) v JTI-Macdonald Corp.*, 2007 SCC 30.
34. See *Tobacco Act*, SC 1997, c 13, s 22(4).

prevention of smoking in young people informs the core of Nova Scotia's Act, infringement on freedom of expression (in the form of a power wall ban) is likely also justifiable under s. 1. The fact that the tobacco industry has yet to bring a *Charter* challenge against power wall legislation anywhere in the country suggests, perhaps, that the industry does not like its chances of success either.

That said, an individual store owner has brought a *Charter* challenge against Nova Scotia's legislation, as discussed in the following box.

BUSINESS AND LEGISLATION

Store Owner Challenges: Nova Scotia's Tobacco Access Act

Robert Gee owns a store in Kentville, Nova Scotia, that focuses on tobacco sales. He was charged in 2009 with displaying tobacco products contrary to the *Tobacco Access Act*. Though Gee had been complying with some provisions in the Act, he had been refusing to cover up his tobacco products. Gee plans to take his case as far as the Supreme Court of Canada if necessary, stating in a press interview:

> I find it troubling that government is coming into my business and telling me what I can and can't do selling a legal product. It's to the point we can't show the product. If they [governmental authorities] don't want it, they should make it illegal.[35]

Gee is challenging the constitutionality of the *Tobacco Access Act* and, while the matter is still pending, has had some success to date. In 2010, a provincial court judge ruled that the *Tobacco Access Act* constitutes an infringement of a protected form of freedom of expression—namely product display.[36] In the court's words, the legislation restricted "communicative activity" with respect to the sale of tobacco products[37] thus running afoul of a *Charter* guarantee.

This judge's decision to date does not, of course, end the matter. Now that Gee has established breach of a *Charter* guarantee, it falls to government lawyers to prove, under s. 1 of the *Charter*, that this particular violation of freedom of expression is "demonstrably justified in a free and democratic society" as already discussed. If the governmental lawyers are successful in relying on s. 1, the legislation survives Gee's challenge and the question of whether Gee violated the Act itself

Robert Gee

KIRK STARRATT, KINGS COUNTY ADVERTISER, TC MEDIA

will go to trial. If the government lawyers fail, Gee's charges will be thrown out. In the meantime, this matter is still pending before the courts.

Critical Analysis: Do you support Gee's decision to fight the legislation?

---

35. Kirk Starratt, "Won't Give Up: Tobacco store owner vows to see legal batter through to bitter end", *Kings County News* (9 July 2009), online: Kings County News <http://www.kingscountynews.ca/Business/Retail-%26amp%3B-services/2009-07-09/article-590703/Wont-give-up/1>.
36. *R v Mader's Tobacco Store Ltd*, 2010 NSPC 52 [*Mader's Tobacco Store*].
37. *Mader's Tobacco Store, supra* note 36 at para 59.

Not all Canadians agree with the idea that the judiciary should have the power to strike down legislation as being unconstitutional. Some believe that it is undemocratic for the courts to have the right to eliminate or amend a law duly enacted by elected representatives. However, those who support the *Charter* argue that even a majority (the elected representatives who enacted the legislation) should not have the power to infringe on the rights of others. Put another way, a liberal democratic system of government is not just about majority rule, as suggested in the following statement from Madam Justice Wilson of the Supreme Court of Canada:

> The *Charter* is predicated on a particular conception of the place of the individual in society. An individual is not a totally independent entity disconnected from the society in which he or she lives. Neither, however, is the individual a mere cog in an impersonal machine in which his or her values, goals and aspirations are subordinated to those of the collectivity. The individual is a bit of both. The *Charter* reflects this reality by leaving a wide range of activities and decisions open to legitimate government control while at the same time placing limits on the proper scope of that control. Thus, the rights guaranteed in the *Charter* erect around each individual, metaphorically speaking, an invisible fence over which the state will not be allowed to trespass. The role of the courts is to map out, piece by piece, the parameters of the fence.[38]

Though the court has the power to assess the constitutionality of legislation—and to strike down the law, if need be—it is the legislative branch of government which has the last word in many cases. That is, the *Charter* permits the government to override or disregard a judicial decision that a given piece of legislation is unconstitutional or to pre-empt judicial involvement at the start. Section 33 of the *Charter* allows the government to enact legislation "notwithstanding" its unconstitutionality. While the government does not have this option with respect to all rights and freedoms guaranteed by the *Charter*, it does have this option for a great many of them, including the right to freedom of expression.[39]

There are, of course, political consequences to using section 33, as when the government of Alberta invoked this provision when it introduced Bill 26 on 10 March 1998. This bill would limit the right of recovery to $150 000 for those wrongfully sterilized under that province's *Sexual Sterilization Act*, which was repealed in 1972. As a result of public outcry that the government would deny sterilization victims their right to establish in court that they had suffered damages exceeding $150 000, the government quickly withdrew its proposed legislation.[40]

---

38. *R. v Morgentaler*, [1988] 1 SCR 30 at 164.
39. Section 33 of the *Charter* permits government to violate a large number of rights and freedoms, including freedom of conscience and religion; freedom of thought, belief, opinion, expression, and peaceful assembly; freedom of association; the right to life, liberty, and security of the person; the right to be free from unreasonable search and seizure; the right to be free from arbitrary detention and imprisonment; the right not to be subject to cruel or unusual punishment; the right against self-incrimination; and the right to equality.
40. Eoin Kenny, "Klein Government Drops Bill to Compensate Victims," (11 March 1998) online: QL (CP98). Eugenics is a discredited belief that, through selective breeding, the "quality" of the human race can be improved.

FIGURE 2.3

Sampling of Constitutional Challenges Brought by Business

Case	Nature of alleged Charter violation	Result
Siemens v Manitoba (Attorney General), [2003] 1 SCR 6	Provincial law permitting a ban on lottery terminals based on a local plebiscite is contrary to the right to life, liberty, and security of the person. Local businesses rely on such terminals as a source of revenue.	Action failed. The Supreme Court of Canada ruled that purely economic interests—such as being able to retain business income—are not encompassed in the *Charter*'s protection of life, liberty, and security of the person.
R v Big M Drug Mart, [1985] 1 SCR 295	Federal law that prohibited most commercial activity on Sunday is contrary to the right to freedom of religion.	Action succeeded. The Supreme Court of Canada ruled that the law was unconstitutional since its purpose was "to compel the observance of the Christian Sabbath."
R v Edwards Books and Art, [1986] 2 SCR 713	Provincial law prohibiting retail stores from opening on Sunday is contrary to the right to freedom of religion.	Action failed. The Supreme Court of Canada held that the law was valid. Though the law did violate freedom of religion (i.e., its *effect* placed a burden on those who observed a non-Sunday sabbath), the law was saved under s. 1. The court held that the valid secular purpose of the law—to provide a common day off for retail workers—was sufficiently important to justify limiting the right of freedom of religion.
Little Sisters Book and Art Emporium v Canada, [2000] 2 SCR 1120	The federal *Customs Tariff Act* that prohibits importation of "obscene" books and magazines violates the right to freedom of expression.	Mixed result. The Supreme Court of Canada held that the standard of obscenity was valid. However, the court identified discrimination in how the legislation was implemented since homosexual literature was disproportionately and without justification targeted by customs officials.
Ford v Quebec, [1988] 2 SCR 712	A Quebec law requiring advertisements and signage to be in French violates the right to freedom of expression.	Action succeeded. The Supreme Court of Canada ruled that freedom of expression includes "the freedom to express oneself in the language of one's choice." *(Note: This law was reenacted using s. 33.)*
Irwin Toy v Quebec, [1989] 1 SCR 927	A Quebec law prohibiting advertising directed at children under 13 years of age violates the right to freedom of expression.	Action failed. Though the law violated freedom of expression, it was saved under s. 1. The Supreme Court ruled that protection of children is important, hence justifying the limitation. As well, since the law permitted the advertisement of toys and breakfast cereals provided cartoons were not used, the ban was only partial in any event.
Rocket v Royal College of Dental Surgeons, [1990] 1 SCR 232	Ontario's *Health Disciplines Act* violates freedom of expression since it prohibits dentists from advertising their services, including office hours or languages spoken.	Action succeeded. The Supreme Court of Canada held that while maintaining high standards of professional conduct justified some kind of regulation, this act went too far in banning all advertising.
Slaight Communications v Davidson, [1989] 1 SCR 1038	Labour board order that an employer provide a reference letter to an unjustly dismissed employee violates the right to freedom of expression.	Mixed result. The Supreme Court of Canada held that if the letter were ordered to contain an opinion that the employer did not hold, that would be unconstitutional. Where the letter had only to contain "objective facts that are not in dispute," the order can be justified under s. 1.
Hunter v Southam, [1984] 2 SCR 145	Powers of search and seizure permitted by the *Combines Investigation Act* violates the right to be free from unreasonable search and seizure.	Action succeeded. The Supreme Court of Canada held that the act did not contain enough safeguards to determine when documents can be seized.
McKinney v University of Guelph, [1990] 3 SCR 229	Mandatory retirement policy of the university violates prohibition of discrimination on the basis of age.	Action failed. The *Charter* applies only to government or bodies that are not independent from government. Here, the university was classified as a private body. Additionally, the university could rely on the Ontario *Human Rights Code* (which applies to the private sector), which permitted mandatory retirement. Though this provision of the code contravened s. 15, the discrimination was demonstrably justified under s. 1.

Bill
Proposed legislation.

As noted earlier, the *Charter* governs the relationship between the person and the state, restraining government action that is, for example, discriminatory. By way of contrast, certain kinds of discrimination in the marketplace by one person against another are made illegal primarily by human rights codes as well as by related forms of legislation.[41]

---

41. For a discussion of human rights codes in relation to employment, see Chapter 20.

BUSINESS AND LEGISLATION

Gender-Based Pricing

Ontario Liberal MPP Lorenzo Berardinetti introduced to the Ontario Legislative Assembly proposed legislation (called **Bill** 9) to prohibit business from setting prices based on the gender of their customers. He became concerned about this issue when he went clothes shopping with his wife and noted that brand-name men's suits were priced at about one-third less than women's equivalent suits, even though the women's suits used less material. What follows is an excerpt from Bill 9:

Preamble

Throughout the course of our recent history, our Province has enacted a *Human Rights Code* and passed laws to eliminate injustices committed against people on the basis of gender, ethnic and religious persuasions and sexual orientation.

In spite of all of these efforts, a lot of work still needs to be done to eliminate systemic discriminatory practices that continue to this very day. One such practice is discriminatory pricing on the basis of gender.

In order to create a society where people are judged by the content of their character rather than their physical characteristics, practices such as these must be eliminated.

As a result, it is appropriate to prohibit gender-based discriminatory pricing.

Therefore, Her Majesty, by and with the advice and consent of the Legislative Assembly of the Province of Ontario, enacts as follows:

Definition

1. In this Act, "gender-based pricing" means the practice of charging a different price for the same goods or services on the basis of gender.

Prohibition against Gender Pricing

2. No person shall engage in gender-based pricing.

Limitation

(2) Nothing in subsection (1) prevents price differences that are based upon the cost, difficulty or effort of providing the goods or services.

A copy of the entire bill can be found at http://www.ontla.on.ca/web/bills/bills_detail.do?locale5en&Bil lID5272&isCurrent5false&ParlSessionID538%3A2 under Bill 9.

Berardinetti commented on the bill as follows: "It's a fairness issue and a human rights issue. It's to amend the *Human Rights Code*. We're not trying to put anyone out of business. We're just telling them to operate fairly."

The online publication *Business Edge* reported that Randy Bridge, then president of the Toronto-based Ontario Fabricare Association, which represents about 120 dry cleaners in the province, was not a fan of the legislation. Bridge provided the following explanation for why women's dry cleaning is more expensive than men's:

"The automated technology generally used in our industry is specifically designed for larger shirts, those usually worn by men," he said. "Women's sizes are normally smaller and thus require additional hands-on touch-ups."

Business Edge also reported the rebuttal to this argument given by Joanne Thomas Yaccato, author of *The 80% Minority: Reaching the Real World of Women Consumers*: "Bottom line: If the technology is there for men's apparel, it must be there for cleaning women's garments," she said.

Berardinetti's bill was based on California's gender-based price discrimination law. In 2005, the dating service Lavalife settled a U.S. class action, related to this legislation, which accused Lavalife of improperly discriminating against its male customers by charging them to use certain features of the service while not charging women to use similar or identical features. In a court-approved settlement, Lavalife agreed, among

Is there any justification for gender-based pricing?

COURTESY OF ERIN NEKERVIS.

(Continued)

other matters, to provide to the class members 33 minutes of free air time (to an aggregate maximum of $706 464) and to discontinue price differentials based on gender. *The Toronto Star* reported that the plaintiffs were also seeking recovery of legal fees and costs in the amount of approximately $180 000. Meanwhile, back in Canada, two Toronto-based online dating services were reportedly opposed to the Berardinetti bill, concerned about similar lawsuits. Lavalife and Quest even hired a Liberal lobbyist to stop the proposed Ontario legislation.

Like the vast majority of private member's bills, Berardinetti's bill failed to be passed into law,[42] and he has taken no steps to re-introduce the legislation since.

Critical Analysis: Should government regulate price when it is discriminatory or should that be left to the free market?

Do you think that hiring a lobbyist is a good risk management strategy?

Sources: Jack Kohane, "'Gender Tax' in Ontario's Crosshairs: Backbencher's Bill Would Eliminate Unequal Pricing" *Business Edge* 1 (26 May 2005), online: Business Edge News Magazine <http://www.businessedge.ca/article.cfm/newsID/9591.cfm>; 1 Cal Civ Code § 43, online: Find law <FindLaw at http://caselaw.lp.findlaw.com/cacodes/civ/43-53.html>; CTV.ca News Staff, "Ontario MPP seeks end to gender-based pricing" (16 March 2005), online: CTV News <http://www.ctv.ca/servlet/ArticleNews/story/CTVNews/1110908196485_106317396/?hub5Canada>; CBC News, "Ontario Bill Targets 'Gender-based Pricing'" (16 March 2005), online: CBC News <http://www.cbc.ca/canada/story/2005/03/15/haircuts-100-050315.html>; Robert Benzie, "Liberal lobbyist hired to halt gender bill: Lavalife, Quest say they will be forced to leave Ontario; Ex-McGuinty aide will fight for the two dating companies" *The Toronto Star* (13 March 2006) at A9; Press Release, "Dating Firms Fight Gender-Price Bill" (16 March 2006), online: Press Release <http://www.24-7pressrelease.com/view_press_release.php?rID512114>; and Christi Dabu, "For Canadian Women, That Haircut May Soon Get Cheaper" *Christian Science Monitor* (10 August 2005), online: The Christian Science Monitor <http://www.csmonitor.com/2005/0810/p12s02-woam.htm>.

Sources of Law

There are four sources of law in Canada: constitutional convention (discussed earlier), statute law (outlined in the preceding section), the royal prerogative, and the common law. (See Figure 2.4, below.)

Royal prerogative

Historical rights and privileges of the Crown, including the right to conduct foreign affairs and to declare war.

The **royal prerogative** has diminishing influence in the modern Canadian legal system. Briefly put, the royal prerogative refers to the historical rights and privileges of the Crown, including the right to conduct foreign affairs and to declare war.[43]

Common law

Rules that are formulated in judgments.

Common law, unlike statute law, is judge-made law. Common law is the end product of disputes that come before the judiciary. That is, when a judge gives a decision in determining the outcome of a given legal conflict, it is known as a judgment; judgments referred to cumulatively are called the common law.

Ordinarily, a judge does not just give a bald resolution to the dispute in question. Rather, the judge seeks to explain, justify, and account for whatever decision she has reached. In doing so, the court relies on decisions made by other judges in other cases that are relevant to the matter at hand. These cases are known as **precedent.**

Precedent

An earlier case used to resolve a current case because of its similarity.

The key principle of precedent can be summarized as "like cases should be treated alike." This means that judges should rule in a given case in a manner consistent with the way judges have adjudicated on or dealt with similar matters in the past. In short, the judge looks to the common law in order to resolve the matter at hand.

FIGURE 2.4

The Sources of Law

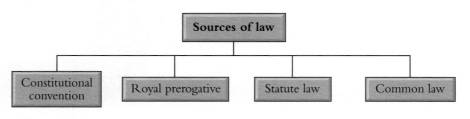

---

42. See Legislative Assembly of Ontario, "Bill and Lawmaking: Current Parliament", online: Legislative Assembly of Ontario <http://www.ontla.on.ca/web/bills/bills_detail.do?locale5en&BillID−5272&isCurrent −false&detailPage−bills_detail_status>.

43. *Hogg, supra* note 8 at 1-19 to 1-20.

There are a number of rules governing the application of precedent, including the following:

- A lower court must follow a relevant precedent created by a higher court within the same jurisdiction.

- Not all precedents are of equal value—the higher the court that created the precedent, the more valued the decision is.

- The Supreme Court of Canada—the highest court in Canada—is entitled to decide a case in any way it sees fit.

Should any challenge to Nova Scotia's *Tobacco Access Act* continue before the courts, the judges will rely on precedent in determining the question of constitutionality. If, for example, there is a Supreme Court of Canada decision on point, the Nova Scotia courts are required to follow it.

While the process of applying precedent is reasonably easy to describe, it is inevitably riddled with some ambiguity, uncertainty, and subjectivity. Although judges endeavour to be impartial, unbiased, and objective, such a standard is probably impossible to consistently achieve. Further, even reasonable people may differ in interpreting whether a given case from the common law applies to the dispute in question. This is not to imply that the study of law is futile or that the judicial application of precedent is without rhyme or reason. It is merely to suggest that the outcome in any case cannot be fully predicted.

Judges sometimes choose to apply another set of rules, known as rules of **equity**. Like common law, equity originated in England. The role of equity is to provide assistance to the deserving person who otherwise would not receive adequate help under the rules of common law. Equity focuses on what would be fair given the specific circumstances of the case, as opposed to what the strict rules of common law might dictate. In this way, equity seeks to soften the harsh or unfair result that the common law might otherwise cause. This is not to suggest that "anything goes, as long as it's fair." Equity itself is constrained by principles that limit when it can render assistance. For example, assume that a businessperson has transferred some real estate to her spouse in order to hide that asset from creditors. If the spouse later refuses to transfer that property back, the businessperson may be in some difficulty. Should the businessperson seek help from a judge on equitable grounds to get her property back, a court would have the discretion to refuse. This is because—according to an important equitable principle—equity assists only those with "clean hands." There is a good argument that the businessperson fails to meet this description.

Equity also provides its own set of remedies—rectification, *quantum meruit*, rescission, specific performance, and the injunction—which will be described in more detail in later parts of this text.

Judges are bound to apply relevant legislation enacted by the three levels of government even if the legislation has the effect of reversing a common law or judge-made rule. The only exception relates to the constitutionality of the legislation in question. If such legislation violates the division of powers between the levels of government or violates *Charter* provisions, a court may declare that it has no force or effect. Otherwise, statute law

Equity
Rules that focus on what would be fair given the specific circumstances of the case, as opposed to what the strict rules of common law might dictate.

trumps or otherwise has priority over the common law. Note too that the courts can make common law about statutes and how to interpret them.

Classifications of Law

The law can be organized according to various categories. It is important for a business-person to have a basic understanding of these classifications in order to better grasp the nature of the legal problem at issue. Such an understanding will also assist the business-person to better communicate with legal counsel.

Domestic versus International Law

Domestic law is the internal law of a given country and includes both statute and common law. Domestic law deals primarily with individuals and corporations and, to a lesser extent, the state.

International law governs relations between states and other entities with international legal status, such as the United Nations and the World Trade Organization. An important source of international law is treaty law. International law focuses mainly on states and international organizations.

Substantive versus Procedural Law

Substantive law refers to law that defines rights, duties, and liabilities. Substantive law was at issue in all the cases described in Figure 2.3 on page 36. They concerned the duty of the government to legislate in accordance with the *Charter* as well as the right of the plaintiff to challenge the government for failing to meet that standard.

Procedural law refers to the law governing the procedure to enforce rights, duties, and liabilities. For example, the fact that a trial judge's decision can be appealed to a higher court is a procedural matter.

Public versus Private Law

Public law describes all those areas of the law that relate to or regulate the relationship between persons and government at all levels. An important aspect of public law is its ability to constrain governmental power according to rules of fairness. Examples of public law are criminal law, tax law, constitutional law, and administrative law (see Figure 2.5).

Domestic law
The internal law of a given country, which includes both statute and case law.

International law
Law that governs relations between states and other entities with international legal status.

Substantive law
Law that defines rights, duties, and liabilities.

Procedural law
The law governing the procedure to enforce rights, duties, and liabilities.

Public law
Areas of the law that relate to or regulate the relationship between persons and government at all levels.

FIGURE 2.5

Examples of Public Law

Criminal law	Identifies behaviour that is seriously unacceptable. In the interests of maintaining order and security in relations between citizens, the government prosecutes those who transgress basic standards of conduct, and the courts provide sanctions for that conduct, including fines and imprisonment.
Tax law	Sets the rules for the collection of revenue for governmental operation.
Constitutional law	Sets the parameters on the exercise of power by government.
Administrative law	Governs all regulatory activity of the state.

FIGURE 2.6

Examples of Private Law

Contract law	Provides rules that make agreements between parties binding.
Tort law	Includes rules that address legal wrongs committed by one person against another, apart from a breach of contract. The wrongs may be intentional (as in an assault) or unintentional (as in a case of negligent driving).
Property law	Sets rules that define and protect property in all forms.
Company law	Provides rules concerning the rights, liabilities, and obligations of companies and other business vehicles.

Private law concerns dealings between persons. Many of the major topics in this text fall within private law, including contract law, tort law, property law, and company law (see Figure 2.6 above).

The distinction between public and private law is not absolute. Most of the law of property is private, even if the government is buying, selling, or leasing. However, should the government choose to exercise its executive right to expropriate land, for example, issues of public law would be involved.

Furthermore, a single set of circumstances can have two sets of consequences, one involving private law and the other involving public law. For example, where a personal injury arises from an assault, the Crown may decide to prosecute the perpetrator of the assault under the *Criminal Code*. This is the domain of public law. The victim, however, also has civil rights that can be enforced through tort law, which is the area of private law. Specifically, the victim of the assault can initiate an action in the courts to seek financial compensation for damages from the perpetrator.

Private law
Areas of law that concern dealings between persons.

Common Law versus Civil Law

While common law refers to judge-made law, it is also used in a totally different sense to describe the system of private law in place in all provinces except Quebec. A common law system is one that bases its private law on judicial decisions that—if relevant and binding—must be applied to the case at issue. The private law in nine Canadian provinces, as well as the territories, is governed by common law in this sense of the word.

Figure 2.7 on the next page shows the various classifications of law and how they are related.

The province of Quebec is, of course, bound by federal law such as the *Criminal Code*, but it has its own system of private law, which is governed by the **Civil Code of Quebec** [*Civil Code*]. Although there are many similarities between common law principles and what would be found in the *Civil Code*, conceptually there are significant differences between the two systems. One key difference is that judges in Quebec look to the *Civil Code* for general principles to be applied to the case at hand. They are not bound by how other judges have interpreted the *Code*, though practically speaking, these interpretations would be helpful and relevant.[44] Nor is a judge in a civil code system bound to apply a relevant provision of the *Code* if to do so would produce an unjust outcome.[45]

Civil Code of Quebec
The rules of private law that govern Quebec.

---

44. Gerald L Gall, *The Canadian Legal System*, 5th ed (Toronto: Carswell, 2004) at 31.
45. *Ibid*.

FIGURE 2.7

Divisions/Classifications of the Law

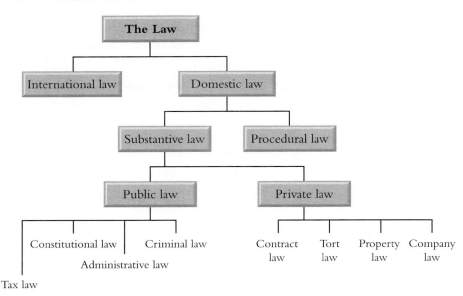

Source: From Gerald G. Gall, *The Canadian Legal System*, 5th edition (Toronto: Carswell, 2004). Adapted by permission of Carswell, a division of Thomson Reuters Canada Limited.

These various classifications can be applied to the legal problem faced by retailer in the chapter opener. The question of the validity of Nova Scotia's *Tobacco Access Act* concerns

- domestic law (not international law) because the *Tobacco Control Act* was passed by the government of Nova Scotia and does not in any way involve a foreign jurisdiction

- substantive law (not procedural law) because at issue is whether the law violates the right to freedom of expression

- public law (not private law) because at issue is a law that regulates the relationship between tobacco retailers and the government. More specifically, it involves constitutional law because the challenge will concern whether the government has exercised its law-making power appropriately

- common law (not Quebec civil law) because the dispute will be resolved by applying Nova Scotia's common law system, not the *Civil Code of Quebec*

The elements of constitutional law are summarized in Figure 2.8.

Administrative Law and Business

Administrative law
Rules created and applied by those having governmental powers.

Administrative law is one of the primary legal areas in which government and business interact. This area of law refers to rules created and applied by the various boards, agencies, commissions, tribunals, and individuals who exercise a governmental function as a result of legislation giving them that power. It also refers to rules of fairness that constrain how administrative bodies exercise their authority.

FIGURE 2.8

A Summary of Constitutional Law

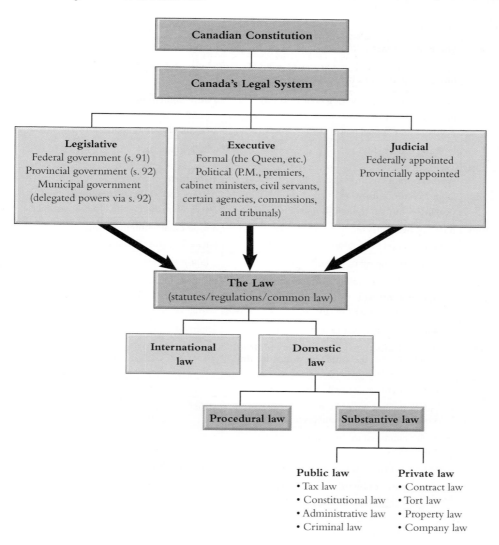

Administrative bodies have often been established on a needs basis to deal with particular problems or difficulties as they have arisen, rather than pursuant to some overall regulatory plan. This piecemeal nature can make the area somewhat perplexing at times.

The functions of administrative bodies and officials often vary, as well. In some instances, the body or individual carries out purely administrative functions, as when the Employment Insurance Commission processes a claim for benefits; sometimes the body also has judicial functions, such as when the Labour Relations Board settles a dispute between an employer and employee; sometimes the body exercises legislative functions, as when the Canadian Radio-television and Telecommunications Commission (CRTC) passes regulations concerning the amount of Canadian content on radio and TV; and sometimes the body has some combination of these functions. As a result, it is often difficult to summarize how businesses are subject to administrative regulation.

FIGURE 2.9

Administrative Bodies and Officials Affecting Business

Legend: F = federal; P = provincial; M = municipal

If you plan to . . .	you may interact with . . .	in regard to . . .
establish a business	regional and/or municipal licensing tribunal, minister, agency, or officer (M)	a business permit
construct new facilities or make exceptions to existing zoning regulations	development officer zoning board (M) building officer (M) development appeal board (M)	a development permit a building permit a denial of permit application
alter the interior or exterior of an existing building	building officer (M)	a building permit
hire employees	workers' compensation board (P) labour relations board (P) provincial human rights tribunal (P)	an accident or injury unions, collective agreements discriminatory practices in the workplace
manufacture, sell, or store food or drink	board of health (P, M) Canadian Food Inspection Agency (F)	a food establishment permit packaging and labelling requirements
sell alcohol	liquor control board or commission (P)	a liquor licence
manufacture, sell, or advertise products	Consumer Product Safety Commission (F) Competition Bureau (F) trade practices legislation (P)	product/item hazards fair advertising practices
import products	Canadian Food Inspection Agency (F)	approval
practise in architecture, pharmacy, law, dentistry, medicine, or accountancy	professional society (e.g., Law Society of British Columbia; Public Accountants Council for the Province of Ontario) (P)	a licence to practise the profession
sell real estate	Superintendent or Council of Real Estate (P)	a licence to sell
carry on a radio, television, or telecommunications business	Canadian Radio-television and Telecommunications Commission (F)	structure, scope, and content approval
sell financial products	securities commission, financial services commission (P)	licensing and procedural requirements
engage in interprovincial trucking	Canadian Transportation Agency (F)	a business licence
sell a particular agricultural product	product agency or board (e.g., Canadian Egg Marketing Agency; Canadian Wheat Board) (F)	a production and sales licence

Source: Researched and written by Catherine Bradley

Nonetheless, this area of law has a significant impact on business because so much commercial activity is regulated by these bodies—from licensing requests to zoning and subdivision applications and human rights complaints. (See Figure 2.9 for a summary of the administrative bodies and officials that affect business.)

Business Law in Practice Revisited

1. Is the Nova Scotia's *Tobacco Access Act* constitutional and hence enforceable?
As discussed in more detail in this chapter, it is likely that the legislation violates s. 2 of the *Charter* by forbidding the public display of tobacco products. However, since the purpose of the Act is to reduce smoking in young people, it is almost certainly demonstrably justified in a free and democratic society and is saved by s. 1. This means that the McCrae's challenge to the Act will ultimately fail.

2. Who assesses whether the legislation is permissible?

The judiciary makes this assessment. Under the Constitution, judges are mandated to hear challenges to the legal foundation of laws passed by all levels of government.

3. Are there any moral or ethical questions that arise from this scenario?

While cigarettes are a legal product, cigarettes cause death and serious illness. For this reason, there are moral and ethical issues for anyone associated with the tobacco industry. It would seem, in particular, that retailers would not want to do anything to encourage children or young people to smoke.

Chapter Summary

Canadian society is bound by a set of constitutional values, many of which insist on the importance of the individual and the right to freedom from unreasonable government interference. These values restrain how government operates at all levels—federally, provincially, and municipally. Constitutional law plays an important role in how government does its job by constraining how the three branches of government exercise power.

Each branch of government has its own work to do. The legislative branch creates statutes. The executive branch is responsible for the ceremonial features of government and for day-to-day operations, including formulating and executing government policy, as well as administering all departments of government. The judiciary has a significant role in scrutinizing the legislative and executive branches of government and can be an important resource for those who believe they have been unreasonably limited, such as in how they are permitted to carry out business, or unfairly treated by a governmental officer, board, or tribunal. The judiciary also adjudicates on private disputes.

The Constitution places mandatory limits on the power of the legislature to pass any law it sees fit. The court, as required by the Constitution, insists that the power of government be exercised in a manner that is

- within that body's "jurisdiction," as defined by the *Constitution Act, 1867*

- consistent with the values and principles contained within the *Charter*

The judiciary itself is bound by the rules of precedent to help ensure that any given legal dispute is resolved in a manner that is consistent with decisions in previous similar disputes. An important part of precedent involves the court system since only a higher court can bind a lower court. Judges also have discretion, accorded to them by the rules of equity, to ensure that each matter before them is justly resolved.

Canadian law is organized according to classifications reflecting the nature of the legal problem at issue: domestic/international; substantive/procedural; public/private; and common law/civil law. Administrative law provides protection by ensuring that a fair process accompanies any regulatory decisions that affect a business or any other activity.

Chapter Study

Key Terms and Concepts

administrative law (p. 42)

bill (p. 36)

bylaws (p. 29)

cabinet (p. 30)

Canadian Charter of Rights and Freedoms (p. 32)

Canadian legal system (p. 24)

Civil Code of Quebec (p. 41)

common law (p. 38)

concurrent jurisdiction (p. 27)

constitutional conventions (p. 25)

constitutional law (p. 23)

domestic law (p. 40)

equity (p. 39)

exclusive jurisdiction (p. 27)

Federal Court of Canada (p. 32)

formal executive (p. 29)

government policy (p. 23)

inferior court (p. 31)

international law (p. 40)

judges (p. 30)

judiciary (p. 30)

jurisdiction (p. 26)

legislative branch (p. 25)

liberalism (p. 23)

paramountcy (p. 28)

political executive (p. 29)

precedent (p. 38)

private law (p. 41)

procedural law (p. 40)

public law (p. 40)

ratify (p. 29)

regulations (p. 30)

royal prerogative (p. 38)

small claims court (p. 31)

statute law (p. 25)

substantive law (p. 40)

superior court (p. 31)

Supreme Court of Canada (p. 31)

treaty (p. 29)

Questions for Review

1. What is the key idea upon which the Canadian Constitution is based?

2. What does "jurisdiction" mean?

3. What is an example of a constitutional convention?

4. Which document determines whether a government has the jurisdiction to pass a law or not?

5. What is the doctrine of paramountcy?

6. Which level of government does paramountcy seem to favour?

7. How does the authority of a municipal government come into existence?

8. What is the difference between a regulation and a bylaw (or an ordinance)?

9. What is the executive branch of government?

10. How is the executive branch different from the legislative branch?

11. What is precedent? Why is a system of courts essential to its creation?

12. What are the two types of trial courts?

13. What is the common law? Who creates it?

14. What is the *Canadian Charter of Rights and Freedoms?*

15. What can a judge do if he determines that a piece of legislation is unconstitutional?

16. If a law is found to violate a person's freedom of expression pursuant to the *Charter*, is it automatically struck down? Is there something in the *Charter* that might allow the government to justify violating that person's freedom of expression?

17. What is the difference between public law and private law?

18. Which Canadian province operates under a civil law system?

19. What is the role of equity?

20. What is one important function of administrative law?

Questions for Critical Thinking

1. Canada has often been described as an over-governed state. What features of Canada's system of government contribute to this opinion? Do you agree?

2. There are several reasons traditionally offered for why commercial expression should be protected under s. 2 of the *Charter*. For example, such speech is seen as contributing to the 'marketplace of ideas' and, furthermore, it is hard to separate out commercial speech from other 'higher' forms of speech such as political and social.[46] Do you agree with these rationales?

3. Under a common law system, judges follow precedent when making decisions or resolving disputes. What are the advantages of following precedent? Describe a situation where it might be inappropriate to follow precedent.

4. Review Figure 2.3 on page 36. In your opinion, how has the *Charter* affected business activity?

5. Do you think that the *Charter* strikes a good balance between protecting the rights of individual citizens and allowing governments to legislate for the benefit of larger groups, or even all members of society? Is section 1 of the *Charter* necessary, or should an individual's fundamental rights and freedoms be absolute?

6. Dozens of administrative tribunals, such as the Labour Relations Board, the Canadian Radio-television and Telecommunications Commission, various human rights tribunals, and the Occupational Health and Safety Commission, have been established by both the federal and provincial governments. Why do you think administrative tribunals are such a predominant feature in Canada? Why have they been established?

Situations for Discussion

1. The government of Alberta has announced new regulations that include requirements that home inspection businesses be provincially licensed and carry $1 million in errors and omission insurance. Beyond this, the province has mandated educational standards for home inspectors with the goal of improving the quality of work done by the home inspection industry. Opposition Liberal MLA Hugh MacDonald endorses the regulations as a means of clamping down on

> some of these midnight home inspectors....If I'm making an important decision to purchase a home based on information I'm getting from a home inspector, that person should be licensed and have minimum credentials.[47]

Do you agree that government should regulate such an industry? What are the costs and benefits of such regulation to the consumer?

2. A brawl at a popular Halifax nightclub called the Dome resulted in 38 arrests and the suspension of the Dome's liquor licence. Governmental officials believe that one-dollar drinks offered by the Dome are one factor contributing to such violence. "This has blown into a cultural problem, and one of the issues we have identified is low-price, deep-discount drinks," said Barry Barnet, Nova Scotia's Minister of Health Promotion and Protection.[48] The Nova Scotia government says it hopes to develop recommendations to address problems associated with excess alcohol consumption.[49] From a risk management perspective, how should local bar owners approach governmental concern over bar violence?

3. Following legislative initiatives from California, the federal government of Canada announced its intentions to reduce greenhouse gas emissions from new vehicles which would "harmonize with the mandatory national standards of the United States beginning with the 2011 model year" according to a 2010 press release. Part of the goal, as previously stated by the federal government, is to harmonize Canada's climate change action with the U.S.'s regulatory environment so as to "protect the environment and ensure a level playing field for the automotive industry." In the past, industry has lobbied government to reject California-style regulation, saying that such regulation

---

46. Hogg, *supra* note 8 at 43-8.
47. Karen Kleiss, "Home buyers get more protection" *The Edmonton Journal* (14 May 2011).
48. Dakshana Bascaramurty, "Officials blame $1 drinks for Halifax brawl" *The Globe and Mail* (20 December 2007) A12.
49. *Ibid.* Note that NS now mandates minimum prices under NS Reg 448/2008.

could cause damage to both the auto industry and the economy at large. Environmental research groups suggest that manufacturers are merely exaggerating their projected costs. What is the role of government in regulating industry and protecting the environment, particularly when doing so drives up the cost of the product?[50]

4. The Federal government recently proposed legislation which would establish a national securities committee to replace the patchwork of provincially constituted securities commissions. Does the federal government have the jurisdiction to do so under s. 91 or does the jurisdiction fall to the provinces under s. 92?[51]

5. An accounting student is researching the deductibility of business expenses. She has found an amendment to the federal *Income Tax Act* that states that

certain expenses are not deductible. However, she has also found case law that states that the expenses are deductible. Which law prevails? What additional information do you require to answer this question?

6. Several provinces have passed legislation that restricts the sale of violent video games to children.[52] How could this legislation be challenged under the *Charter*? Explain. Are there any ethical considerations when contemplating such a challenge?

For more study tools, visit http://www.NELSONbrain.com.

---

50. Transport Canada, News Release, "Canada and the United States Announce Common Standards for Regulating GHG Emissions from New Vehicles" (1 April 2010), online: Transport Canada<http://www.ec.gc.ca/default.asp?lang=En&n=714D9AAE-1&news=B1DDFE4D-5147-46F9-BA97-BA1BDDC3B7A6> ; Transport Canada, News Release, "Canada's first motor vehicle fuel consumption regulations: Consultations begin" (17 January 2008) online: Transport Canada <http://www.tc.gc.ca/eng/mediaroom/releases-nat-2008-08-h006e-4909.htm> ; and Mike De Souza, "30% emission reduction by 2016" CanWest News Service (11 April 2008) online: CanWest News Service <http://www.canada.com/montrealgazette/features/greenlife/story.html?id5db37d100-7bd6-4495-be38-fe31eac66f07>.

51. See *Reference re Securities Act (Can.)* 2011 SCC 66.

52. Chris Metcalfe & Chris Bennett, "Commentary: Anti-violence legislation on video games passes easily under *Charter*" *The Lawyers Weekly* (9 March 2007) 8.

CHAPTER 3

Managing Legal Risks

Objectives

After studying this chapter, you should have an understanding of

- methods of managing the legal environment of business

- the development of a legal risk management plan

- the importance of anticipating and reacting to developments in the legal environment

- how to access and manage legal services

Business Law in Practice

Northland Mining Inc. ("Northland") is a nickel mining company located in northern Manitoba. With all its operations situated adjacent to a town of 10 000, Northland extracts 3000 tons of ore per day from underground mines. In addition to several mines, the Northland property contains an on-site processing facility, a large maintenance shop, a building devoted exclusively to office space, and a lake which is used to hold "tailings" or mining waste after nickel has been extracted. Northland discards about half of its tailings back into the ground with the remainder being deposited into this lake on a regular basis.

Most of the company's underground extraction process relies on a continuous mining machine which cuts ore from the mine walls. Upon extraction, the ore is hoisted to the surface where it is crushed, washed, and conveyed to the processing plant which, in turn, produces a nickel concentrate. Northland employees transport this concentrate by truck to the railway so that it can reach customers in eastern Canada and the United States. Most of the customers are stainless steel manufacturers.

Alex Tanguay, president of Northland, is pleased with the company's success to date and wonders if Northland should begin pursuing opportunities to operate mines in South America, including Peru. To help deliberations on this point, Alex asks Marie Gagnon, the Director of Insurance and Security for Northland, to undertake two related investigations. First, he requires a review of Northland's entire legal risk management plan. Second, he wants an assessment of the kinds of new legal risks Northland faces should it take some of its operations global. Alex wants an assurance that Northland has identified and managed all the major legal risks associated with its Canadian operations before it undertakes any new projects in foreign countries.

1. What is a legal risk management plan and how is it developed?

JOE GIBBONS/ST. JOHN'S TELEGRAM/THE CANADIAN PRESS

(Continued on the next page)

2. What are Northland's major legal risks from its Canadian operations? How should Northland manage these risks?

3. What are Northland's legal risks should it decide to operate in a foreign jurisdiction such as Peru? How should it manage these risks?

Assessing the Legal Environment

Many factors determine the success of a business organization. It must be able to analyze and evaluate its activities, forecast changes in the business environment, and react effectively to unexpected developments. Of central importance is the ability to strike the right balance between managing the present and planning for the future.

To meet its goal of producing a product or delivering a service at a profit, the business enterprise must have a set of functions and systems in place, including finance, marketing, and human resources. To ensure the smoothest possible operation of these systems, the business also needs to deal effectively with the legal environment. By doing so, the business will reduce the likelihood and impact of mistakes that are

- costly in terms of the expense of legal services and damage claims

- distracting in terms of time and effort

- harmful in terms of relationships and reputation in the industry

This chapter explores how a business can manage its interaction with the law and legal issues. It considers two basic approaches—preventive and reactive. The preventive approach requires a thorough evaluation of the risks associated with the business' activities in order to minimize their impact. The emphasis is on compliance with legal requirements and anticipation of changes in the legal environment. The reactive approach recognizes that legal problems may still materialize, so the firm needs a strategy in place to deal with such developments. These two approaches are combined in a management plan that reduces the impact of **legal risks** on the organization.

Legal risk
A business risk with legal implications.

Legal Risk Management Plan

Managing the intersection of law with an organization's activities requires completing a comprehensive assessment of legal risk exposure and developing a **legal risk management plan**. This process is often part of a broader exercise—called enterprise risk assessment—in which *all* risks within an organization, including those with legal implications, are assessed and managed. In essence, legal risk management attempts to identify and then manage threats that could generate negative legal consequences such as fines, penalties, compliance orders, license suspensions, and liability for the payment of money. This requires an understanding of what could happen, how it could happen, and how its impact could be most effectively managed.

Legal risk management plan
A comprehensive action plan for dealing with the legal risks involved in operating a business.

Large businesses like Northland may have a department headed by a senior manager with a title such as risk officer or compliance officer (or as in Marie's case, Director of Insurance and Security) to organize and oversee this process. In smaller organizations, the risk management function may be performed by the chief executive or delegate or even by someone outside the organization, such as an insurance agent or a risk management consultant. Lawyers may also be involved in the process in a variety of roles as determined by their familiarity with the legal risks of the business.

Regardless of where primary responsibility lies, risk management is not a task for any one individual since no single person within an organization has complete knowledge. Risk management involves the cooperation of managers and employees at every level. The challenge for those responsible for this function is to identify the players inside and outside the business who can help in the development of a useful plan. Those involved may use a variety of methods and approaches, such as surveying or interviewing managers and employees, forming workplace committees, or convening a panel of experts.

Creating a legal risk management plan is a four-step process:

- **Step One:** Identify the legal risks.

- **Step Two:** Evaluate the risks.

- **Step Three:** Devise a risk management plan.

- **Step Four:** Implement the plan.

Applying the Four-Step Process

Identify the Legal Risks

The most critical step in the development of a legal risk management plan is the identification of risk because a risk which is not identified cannot be managed. That said, it is probably not possible to identify all possible risks. The goal is to be reasonably certain that no significant risks have been overlooked. There are many methods that a business can use to identify its potential exposure to legal risks. For example, in applying Step One, a business may assess its functional areas, that is, the areas traditionally recognized in business school curricula (such as marketing and sales, human resources, finance and accounting, and information systems). It could also approach the problem by assessing its business decisions, its business relationships, or its operations and transactions. The approach or approaches used will vary depending on the nature of the business and the industry. A highly departmentalized company might choose to focus on evaluating the risks associated with its functional areas because relevant information is organized in this manner. A small consulting firm would not be organized by functional areas and therefore it, by way of contrast, would more likely focus on legal risks arising from its business relations, that is, client relationships. A utility company with varied sources of power generation (hydro, coal, oil, nuclear, and wind) and a transmission and distribution system would concentrate on its operations. This is because its major risks arise from operating procedures and systems relating to the production and delivery of power. There is no single method which is the correct one for any particular situation. The key is to be systematic so that major risks and threats are not overlooked.

Step One: Identify the legal risks

✓ Assess the organization's functional areas.

✓ Review the organization's business decisions.

✓ Examine the organization's business relationships.

✓ Analyze the organization's operations and transactions.

In reviewing how her predecessor identified legal risks at Northland, Marie concluded that his focus had been on the functional areas of business only. What follows is the list he assembled of activities and events that have possible legal consequences:

- *Marketing and sales:* aggressive marketing programs by Northland could result in fines and penalties under the *Competition Act*; the improper transportation of mine waste could result in prosecution under *The Dangerous Goods Handling and Transportation Act* of Manitoba; the sale of inferior nickel or the late delivery of nickel could result in customers suing for breach of contract;

- *Production:* processes used by Northland could harm the environment and result in prosecution under environmental legislation or civil actions by affected people; machine break-down could result in a loss of production and an inability to fulfill contracts resulting in lawsuits for breach of contract; members of the public could be injured on property resulting in liability under occupier's liability legislation;

- *Human resources:* injury to Northland workers could result in prosecution under occupational health and safety legislation; employee harassment could result in human rights investigations and penalties; improper terminations could result in actions for wrongful dismissal;

- *Finance and accounting:* harsh credit terms from suppliers may result in Northland being unable to pay debts as they fall due, thereby triggering legal action by creditors; aggressive accounting practices could result in an investigation by the securities commission.

Marie's predecessor correctly identified several important risks relating to production and human resources. Northland production processes do pose environmental hazards and, most certainly, Northland workers could be injured, harass others, and be wrongfully dismissed. However, the predecessor did not take his analysis far enough. For example, he failed to consider possible changes in the law that could negatively affect Northland's operations and he failed to identify risks that crossed functional lines. Most significant was a failure to identify technology-related risks, including those posed by hackers. This is a particularly important risk to identify since a successful breach by hackers might not only result in a disruption of Northland's operations but also the loss of customer and employee data. Such losses could result in lawsuits as well as penalties under privacy legislation. The following Technology and the Law box provides examples of the risks and costs associated with technology.

TECHNOLOGY AND THE LAW

The Risk and Costs of a Breach of Privacy

Privacy breaches are a common occurrence at many companies and agencies. In some instances, the breach is the result of a sophisticated computer hacker infiltrating systems to collect data. For example, in April and May 2011, hackers successfully infiltrated Sony Corporation's PlayStation Network and compromised the personal information of more than 100 million accounts.[1] In 2009, hackers broke into Heartland Payment Systems' networks and stole over 130 million credit and debit card numbers. In February 2008, a thief stole the personal information of 3.3 million Bell customers. Privacy breaches, however, are not limited to criminal behaviour by hackers. Many breaches are due to carelessness and security system flaws. In January 2007, the Canadian Imperial Bank of Commerce suffered the loss of a computer file in transit between offices; it contained data on 470 000 customers. In December 2007, a security flaw on Passport Canada's website allowed unauthorized access by the public to passport applicants' personal information, including driver's licence numbers, social insurance numbers, and birth dates. In January 2008, the Canadian Bar Association disclosed a security breach that had allowed unauthorized access to online orders and credit card information of its members.

The costs associated with security breaches can be huge. Sony reported that it had spent US$171 million for the 2012 fiscal year to cover costs related to the hacking of its PlayStation Network. Analysts estimate that the total costs to Sony could amount to more than US$1 billion. Costs associated with a privacy breach include:

- direct damage costs (e.g., decline in revenue related to the breach, extra expenses to restore assets)
- liability to others (e.g., compensation to affected clients from unauthorized access to personal information;

What steps can a business take to protect its sensitive data from hackers?

LAGUNA DESIGN/SCIENCE PHOTO LIBRARY

third-party costs, such as credit card issuers' charges to reissue credit cards)

- the cost of preparing a response plan (e.g., costs of public disclosure to clients, including letters and advertisements;[2] regulatory costs and fines; crisis management costs, including costs of establishing a call centre to handle inquiries; the cost of advice from legal and public relations professionals)

Critical Analysis: Most businesses depend on computer and network systems to conduct their businesses. While there are enormous benefits to conducting business over network systems, there is a downside. The loss or theft of data is one risk associated with computer technology. What are other computer technology or cyber risks faced by business? How can these risks be effectively managed?

Sources: James Brightman, "PlayStation Network Crisis May Cost Sony Billions", *Business Insider* (9 May 2011) online: Business Insider <http://www.businessinsider.com/playstation-network-crisis-may-cost-sony-billions-2011-5>; Janet McFarland, "Insurers Look to Cover Hacking Damage", *The Globe and Mail* (13 March 2008), B4.

At the same time, Marie also noted that risks that were not particularly relevant to Northland had somehow been put on the list. For example, the risk of an aggressive marketing campaign was identified yet Northland, as a miner of nickel, has no need to market its product at all, let alone aggressively.

Marie decided to use a combination of risk management approaches based on consultation with a broad spectrum of people in Northland, several risk management consultants in the mining industry, and the global mining and metals group of an international law firm. As a result of this better process, Marie developed a list of legal risks that was

---

1. See Chapter 11, pages 246–247, for a detailed account of the hacking of Sony's PlayStation Network.
2. In Canada, compulsory privacy breach reporting for the private sector exists only in Alberta. In other provinces and at the federal level, there is currently no express obligation for organizations to notify affected individuals or privacy regulators when breaches occur; however, good risk management may require notification.

much more reflective of the mining industry at large and included challenges posed by technology, the regulatory environment, and operating in a foreign country. This list is contained in the Figure 3.1 below.

FIGURE 3.1

Legal Risks at Northland

Whether Northland continues to operate only domestically or decides to expand internationally, it faces a number of legal risks, including:

Environmental: damage to the environment (including wildlife and fisheries) by tailings waste; harm to the property of adjacent landowners and contribution to climate change by plant emissions; impact on land surface and the water table by drilling and extraction; liability triggered by improper closure or remediation of mines;

Human resources: injury to workers due to pit failure, underground collapse, or large equipment failure; health risk to workers (noise-induced hearing loss, dermatitis due to contact with solutions containing nickel); injury to employees when transporting product; harassment and termination of employees;

Operational: breakdown of machinery and equipment; production of inferior or defective product; injury to visitors on property; damage to property or vehicles when product is in transit; injury to employees or members of the public when the product is in transit;

Regulatory: changes to regulatory, legislative, or compliance regimes (i.e., occupational health and safety, environmental, licensing requirements) impacting on operations; changes to laws in foreign jurisdictions affecting the viability of company; operations in foreign countries resulting in liability under Canadian law;

Financial: inability to meet obligations as they become due; incomplete or poorly performed contracts; extending credit to customers who do not pay their bills; errors in financial statements that mislead the public;

Technological: lack of security in electronic transaction; failure of computer systems and networks.

GREG TAYLOR/GETSTOCK.COM

What are the legal risks from mining operations?

The approach taken by Marie in identifying risk is superior to what her predecessor had devised. This is because rather than identifying and treating each risk individually, she has utilized a combination of approaches that assesses and addresses the risks from all sources. The focus is on the corporation's entire risk profile rather than risks emerging from individual departments.

This first step in developing a legal risk management program may seem to be unduly negative because it seeks to identify everything that could possibly go wrong in a business operation. The purpose of Step One, however, is to provide a realistic assessment of the potential legal dangers of doing business, with a view toward minimizing loss.

Evaluate the Risks

The techniques used in Step Two vary from a simple, subjective evaluation to a complex, statistical approach involving actuaries and other professionals. These techniques involve assessing both the probability and the severity of loss.

Step Two: Evaluate the risks

> ✓ Assess the probability of loss.
>
> ✓ Assess the severity of loss.

Most organizations have a wealth of information to assist in performing such assessments, including the organization's loss history, industry statistics on losses, and expert opinion from both within and outside the organization.

A high probability that a particular event will occur can be offset by a relatively low level of loss should the event actually occur. Events that are unlikely to occur also deserve close attention if the potential loss is high. In the Northland situation, employees may occasionally come into contact with solutions that contain nickel, despite the use of protective clothing and precautionary measures. However, the contact is unlikely to result in serious injuries that could jeopardize Northland's operations. However, if an employee is seriously injured or dies in a workplace accident, this can result in severe penalties. Other risks, such as environmental impairment or breach of contract, may have varying consequences depending on their severity. The expansion of Northland's operations into a foreign country such as Peru also poses risks. Although there are many multinational corporations operating in South America and there is the potential for profits, there are considerable risks for a company like Northland. The International Perspective box on page 59 explores risks that arise from international operations.

The international law firm advising Marie indicates that expansion into South America poses the risk of expropriation. Bolivia and Argentina have nationalized foreign operations and Peru could do likewise. Also, because mining has a tremendous impact on the natural environment, Northland because of its inexperience in operating abroad could run afoul of local legislation. Even if Northland obeys Peruvian laws, there is the risk that it could become the target of legal action by environmental activists in the Americas and beyond.

The point in evaluating risks is to recognize that not all risks are alike, nor should they be treated alike. Some risks crystallize into liability fairly often, but their financial and legal impact is relatively small. Other risks materialize infrequently, but when they do, their impact is severe. A business can use this assessment to determine priorities for risk management and as guidance in choosing how to manage a particular risk in Step Three.

Devise a Risk Management Plan

A business can follow a number of methods to manage its legal risk, including risk avoidance, risk reduction, risk transference, and risk retention. Choosing one or more approaches involves evaluating the risk matched with the organization's resources, financial or otherwise—in other words, doing a cost-benefit analysis.

Step Three: Devise a risk management plan

- ✓ Avoid or eliminate the risk.
- ✓ Reduce the risk.
- ✓ Transfer the risk.
- ✓ Retain the risk.

Risk avoidance
Ceasing a business activity because the legal risk is too great.

Risk Avoidance   Eliminating risk, or **risk avoidance**, is appropriate when the risk is simply too great or when the undesirable result of the activity, product, or service is greater than the advantages. In the Northland context, Marie has determined that the legal risks associated with expanding to a foreign jurisdiction like Peru are too high relative to the benefits. As indicated above, although there is potential for profits, there is considerable risk that the operations will result in liability.

Another example of risk avoidance relates to Northland's Canadian operations. The company can avoid potential liability under legislation that protects endangered species, such as the boreal woodland caribou, by operating in areas away from where these animals herd and graze. Similarly they can avoid First Nations' hunting and burial grounds by not locating operations near them.

Businesses often eliminate products and product lines, discontinue programs such as tours and job-shadowing, and stop activities as a way to avoid the associated risk.

Risk reduction
Implementing practices in a business to lower the probability of loss and its severity.

Risk Reduction   A business can undertake **risk reduction** in relation to most risks that cannot be avoided. This strategy involves introducing policies, practices, and procedures to reduce the probability of an event happening. For example, Northland cannot do business without extending credit to customers. The provision of credit inevitably involves the risk that some customers will not pay their accounts. To minimize that risk, Northland should have procedures in place (such as regular credit checks and taking collateral) for evaluating and periodically reassessing the creditworthiness of customers.

As another example, Northland can reduce potential liability under environmental legislation by improving its environmental performance. In can improve air quality by installing and upgrading equipment to voluntarily reduce emissions. It can construct facilities to treat all mine water to reduce the risk of contamination. It can also monitor and manage the tailings pond to ensure that waterfowl and other birds that nest in the grasses on the shores are protected.

To address the health and safety of employees, Northland could introduce a system that includes the reporting and auditing of workplace accidents as well as encouraging a culture of safety. A tracking system provides the information needed to determine the root cause of accidents and the appropriate corrective measures. The company may also provide personal protection equipment such as custom-molded hearing devices, and provide education on hygiene practices and their importance in reducing exposure to harmful chemicals.

To minimize the chance that members of the public will injure themselves by falling, Northland can pay extra attention to keeping its grounds clear of possible hazards. It can also limit access to its property through fencing and other barriers.

Risk Transference   This approach complements risk reduction by transferring the remaining risk to another by contract. Insurance, which is an integral part of most risk management plans, is discussed in detail in Chapter 28. Insurance is likely the best response to many of the risks faced by Northland. Injuries to members of the public will be covered by a comprehensive general liability policy. Motor vehicles owned by Northland will be covered by vehicle insurance. Damage to plant and equipment through events such as fires will be covered by property insurance. Northland may also consider environmental insurance policies to cover clean-up costs and impairment of the environment and cyber-insurance to cover the costs associated with technology failures. However, insurance can be costly, some risks (such as potential environmental liability) are difficult to insure against, and insurance provides coverage only to the extent and in the amount actually purchased. As well, insurance does not prevent loss or the adverse publicity resulting from a high-profile case, even if the insurance company honours the policy.

Although **risk transference** is usually thought of in terms of insurance, it can also involve protection such as limited or excluded responsibility that can be provided by contract (see Chapter 7).

Risk transference
Shifting the risk to someone else through a contract.

Northland produces a product and delivers it by truck to the railway. Many things can go wrong that may cause loss to the customer, resulting in a claim against the business. The product may be delivered late, it may fail to meet the customer's expectations, or it may be defective. One common approach to such risks is to negotiate for terms in the contract that limits the liability of the business for such claims. For example, Northland might negotiate for a clause in its customer contracts providing that in the event of a defect, Northland is liable only to pay the customer a specified portion of the purchase price in damages.

The challenge in such a contract is to create terms and conditions that achieve the business objective of risk transference that are acceptable to customers, clearly written, and legally enforceable if a dispute arises.

Risk Retention   Keeping or absorbing all or part of the risk within the organization is known as **risk retention**. This approach is appropriate when the cost of avoiding or transferring a risk is greater than the impact on the business if the risk materializes. In effect, the organization pays losses out of its own resources. The organization can do this in several ways:

Risk retention
Absorbing the loss if a legal risk materializes.

- **Self-insurance**. The organization can establish a funded reserve.

- **Insurance policy deductibles**. The organization can retain risks to a certain dollar amount.

- **Noninsurance**. The organization can charge losses as an expense item.

There has been a marked increase recently in the use of risk retention, owing in part to significant increases in insurance premiums in many industry sectors or even the refusal of insurance companies to cover certain risks such as terrorism or sexual abuse in volunteer organizations. There are also some risks that cannot be avoided or reduced to zero. These risks must be absorbed by the business. For example, Northland cannot avoid regulations relating to its operations. If occupational health and safety or waste disposal rules change, Northland may face significant expense, despite its best efforts to anticipate and adapt to the changes.

Another example concerns equipment. Despite training and instruction, accidents involving Northland's vehicles occur. Rather than fully insuring the vehicles, Northland may insure subject to a deductible of $2000 per vehicle. This means that Northland has accepted the first $2000 in risk of damage to vehicles and has transferred the remainder to the insurance company. The same concept applies to injuries on its property. Claims to the insurance company for injuries suffered by members of the public are subject to a deductible, meaning Northland is absorbing part of the risk.

The Ethical Considerations: Exploding Gas Tanks box below gives a classic example of risk management gone wrong.

Any plan devised in Step Three must be reasonable in terms of its cost and complexity. No plan can eliminate all risk. The goal is to be aware of risks and to make conscious

ETHICAL CONSIDERATIONS

Exploding Gas Tanks

In the 1970s, General Motors discovered that because the gas tank of its Chevrolet Malibu was placed behind the rear axle instead of in front of it, there was a risk that the gas would explode if the vehicle was hit from behind. To assess the risk, GM did a cost-benefit analysis that showed that based on the projected number of related accidents, it would cost $2.20 per auto to settle claims involving fatalities caused by exploding tanks versus $8.59 per car to fix the problem beforehand.

GM decided not to fix the problem and to retain the risk and cost of injuries caused by the defect. On Christmas Eve 1993, a mother, her four children, and a friend were driving in a 1979 Malibu when a drunk driver hit the rear of the Malibu at 80 to 110 km per hour. All six occupants in the car were injured. The children were trapped in the back seat and badly burned. Those injured sued GM, and in the course of the trial, the GM cost-benefit analysis was revealed. In its defence, GM argued that the speeding drunk driver was responsible for the crash and that most cars made in the 1970s had the gas tank in the same position as the Malibu.

The jury found GM responsible for the injuries and awarded the claimants a total of $4.9 billion—$107 million in compensation and $4.8 billion in punitive damages to

How can the risk of a defective product causing harm to consumers be managed by the manufacturer?

punish GM. The punitive damages were later reduced to $1.09 billion. Brian Panish, lead attorney for the victims, said, "Without the risk of juries holding companies accountable for their reprehensible conduct, GM and other automobile manufacturers would have little reason to put passengers' safety first."

Critical Analysis: Do you agree with Mr. Panish? How might this case affect GM's management of similar risks in future?

Source: Michael White, "Jury Orders GM to Pay Crash Victims $4.9-Billion (U.S.)", *The Globe and Mail* (10 July 1999) B3.

decisions about dealing with them. To assist in this process, managers may turn to legal professionals for balanced advice, either on a lawyer–client basis or through in-house counsel. However, the lawyer must know the business and the industry in which it functions in order to provide useful input.

INTERNATIONAL PERSPECTIVE

Managing Risks When Going Global

The emerging economies of countries in the former Soviet Union, Eastern Europe, Central and South America, Asia, and Africa provide tremendous opportunities for investment. Although the rewards from doing business in these countries can be great, so can the risks. Consider the following examples of legal difficulties faced by Canadian companies operating in foreign countries:

• From 2005 to 2009, a Canadian junior mining company, Khan Resources Inc., spent approximately $40 million on feasibility studies and exploration at the Dornod uranium mining site in Mongolia. Khan held a 70 percent interest in the site estimated to contain about US$2.5 billion in uranium. In 2009, Mongolia revoked Khan's licenses and announced a joint venture with Russian state-owned miner, ARMZ, to develop the site. Khan has sued ARMZ in Ontario claiming $700 million in damages for wrongly interfering with its Mongolian operations. It has also filed a claim in a Mongolian court challenging the legality of the revocation of the licenses and started an international arbitration action against the government of Mongolia for its "expropriatory and unlawful treatment."

• Canadian Barrick Gold Corp. is the world's top producer of gold. Its subsidiary, African Barrick Gold, operates the North Mara gold mine in Tanzania. Between the beginning of 2009 and mid-2010, 19 people were killed at the mine site. Most were villagers seeking the mine's waste rock, and most were killed by Tanzanian police controlling access to the mining site. The violence, along with environmental problems as well as land and compensation disputes, has resulted in an intense campaign by African, North American, and European activists against Barrick.

• Copper Mesa is a Canadian junior mining corporation that carries on mining exploration and development. Though a subsidiary, it obtained the rights to build a copper mine in Junin, Ecuador in 2004 and subsequently carried out preparatory work for the construction of a large-scale open pit mine. In 2008, Ecuador's Ministry of Mines and Petroleum terminated this right without compensation, allegedly for Copper Mesa's failure to consult with the community and to carry out a valid environmental impact assessment. In 2011, Copper Mesa was unsuccessfully sued[3] in Ontario by opponents of

Demonstration against Barrick Gold in Tanzania

ALLAN LISSNER

the mine who alleged that between 2005 and 2007, they had been subject to a campaign of intimidation and violence by security forces controlled by the mining company.

If businesses in foreign countries are to proceed and succeed, potential risks such as those described above need to be evaluated and managed. However, forecasting risk is extremely difficult. Furthermore, the scope of the loss if the risk materializes could be catastrophic. There are, however, steps that businesses can take to manage the risks associated with international operations:

• Consider business strategies that can mitigate risk. Through local partnerships, corporate social responsibility, and public relations campaigns, companies can reduce their exposure to actions such as expropriation, discriminatory regulation, and breaches of government contracts.

• Structure foreign investments to take full advantage of any foreign investment protection and promotion agreements or bilateral investment treaties that may be in place. Agreements and treaties can mitigate risk by providing guarantees against expropriation, unfair treatment, and other forms of host government misconduct.

• Determine the cost and availability of political risk insurance. Although coverage is often limited, it has the advantage of claiming against an insurer rather than the host government.

(Continued)

---

3. *Piedra v Copper Mesa Mining Corp* 2011 ONCA 191, 280 OAC 1.

• Negotiate for international arbitration and stabilization clauses in license agreements, concessions, and other contracts with host governments. An arbitration clause creates a neutral forum for the resolution of disputes and a stabilization clause provides some assurance against unexpected changes in the law governing the foreign investment.

Critical Analysis: How should the legal risk management model be adapted for conducting international business? Which of the four steps of the model are most important?

Sources: Jeff Gray, "Khan Resources stranded in the bitter Mongolian cold", *The Globe and Mail* (17 May 2011) online: The Globe and Mail <http://www.theglobeandmail.com/report-on-business/industry-news/the-law-page/khan-resources-stranded-in-the-bitter-mongolian-cold/article2025679/>; Brett Popplewell, "Copper Mesa sued for alleged assault", *thestar.com* (22 November 2009) online: thestar.com <http://www.thestar.com/news/canada/article/729148>; "Amid violence, Barrick sticks with Tanzanian gold mine", The *Globe and Mail* (29 September 2011) B1; Robert Wisner, "Limiting political risk in international projects", *The Lawyers Weekly* (28 March 2008) 12; and Cyndee Todgham Cherniak, "Reducing risk in international business", *The Lawyers Weekly* (11 July 2008) 13.

Implement the Plan

Once a business has devised a risk management plan, it must put the plan into action and assess its effectiveness on an ongoing basis.

Step Four: Implement the plan

✓ Carry out the plan.

✓ Monitor and revise the plan.

Responsibility for implementing the risk management plan must be clearly assigned. Much of this allocation may be obvious. For example, if the analysis has suggested a quality-control problem, the plan must identify those responsible for both monitoring quality and delivering the service or producing the product. It will not be enough, however, to simply advise the appropriate personnel of the problem. The employees must be educated as to why the problem requires correction and what techniques should be adopted to ensure that the problem is corrected. In addition, guidelines for carrying out the procedures should be collected in a manual for immediate reference. The document should include, as appropriate, a schedule of inspections of facilities, a formal system of ensuring that those inspections take place as scheduled, an accident-reporting system, and information on any insurance coverage in place. Such a manual can be a two-edged sword, however. If Northland is sued for injury or loss and it is shown that Northland neglected to follow its own policy on the matter, the claimant may have grounds for establishing liability.

The plan must be continually monitored and revised as necessary. Management should have a regular review process in place to determine whether the plan is working, and, if not, why. The frequency and severity of events anticipated in the plan will provide feedback on the plan's effectiveness. For example, as a result of the exploding gas tanks, GM will reconsider its retention of the risk in relation to the Malibu and the design of all of its vehicles.

The nature of the business conducted by a firm may change, requiring major reconsideration of the plan. For example, a meatpacking company might decide on a major strategic shift from fresh meat and poultry products to a broader range of processed and packaged meat products. The latter involve greater value added and higher profit margins. The company would need to determine that its previously sound risk management approach is appropriate for the changed business or ensure that it was adequately adapted and altered. Risks may frequently change and practices will need to be adapted, but a routine review process can help to ensure that the requisite adjustments are made.

The legal risk management model is summarized in Figure 3.2.

FIGURE 3.2

Summary of the Legal Risk Management Model

Step One: Identify the legal risks.
✓ Assess the organization's functional areas.
✓ Review the organization's business decisions.
✓ Examine the organization's business relationships.
✓ Analyze the organization's operations and transactions.

Step Two: Evaluate the risks.
✓ Assess the probability of loss.
✓ Assess the severity of loss.

Step Three: Devise a risk management plan.
✓ Avoid or eliminate the risk.
✓ Reduce the risk.
✓ Transfer the risk.
✓ Retain the risk.

Step Four: Implement the plan.
✓ Carry out the plan.
✓ Monitor and revise the plan.

A risk management plan need not be a lengthy or complicated document. The key is for managers like Marie to identify and evaluate legal risks and then rely on a cost-benefit analysis to devise an action plan in response. For example, the cost of installing fencing around Northland's mine site may outweigh the possible cost of members of the public falling and injuring themselves there. The cost of prevention is a certainty, while risks and the resulting losses may never materialize. Proper signage throughout the property may be a legally effective response, including No Trespassing signs and signs warning of dangers such as open pits. Figure 3.3 outlines a summary of a possible plan for Northland that Marie might develop with the management team by applying the risk management model. It addresses the risks identified in Figure 3.1 on page 54.

FIGURE 3.3

Summary of Northland's Risk Management Plan

Environmental risks:

Reduce: introduce practices to minimize impact of operations on the environment; install a new scrubber (a piece of equipment that captures and removes large particles like heavy metals from exhaust) to prevent pollutants from entering the atmosphere; upgrade waste water filtration system for tailings pond; ensure the clay liner in tailings pond remains intact

Avoid: decide not to expand operations into environmentally sensitive areas; decide not to operate in foreign country

Transfer: secure comprehensive general liability insurance that includes coverage for damage to third parties; purchase an all risks[4] property insurance policy with environmental coverage for mine site

Retain: agree to a deductible on all insurance policies based on cost of insurance, frequency of events, and ability to absorb losses

(Continued)

---

4. All risks insurance is a type of insurance coverage where any risk not specifically excluded is covered. For example, if a policy does not exclude flood coverage, then the property is covered in the event of a flood.

FIGURE 3.3

Summary of Northland's Risk Management Plan (continued)

Human resources risks:

Reduce: work towards establishing a culture of safety; establish a workplace health and safety management system including a safety committee; establish a reporting and audit system for workplace injuries; ensure that the mine safe room is equipped with first aide materials and water; review human resource policies relating to termination and harassment

Transfer: ensure registration under provincial Workers Compensation program; maintain the company in good standing under the program

Operational risks:

Reduce: train operators on equipment; introduce enhanced product control measures; permit visitors on property only under supervision; install fencing and other barriers to prevent access to dangerous areas

Transfer: purchase comprehensive general liability insurance for injuries to third parties, all risks property insurance for equipment and machinery break down and loss of inventory, business interruption for losses from a temporary shut-down, and auto insurance to cover injuries and damage to vehicle

Retain: agree to a deductible on all insurance policies based on cost of insurance, frequency of events, and ability to absorb losses

Regulatory risks:

Reduce: monitor political environment for potential changes to regulations; lobby and provide input to potential changes

Retain: ensure that Northland adheres to Canadian regulatory, legislative, and compliance regimes

Avoid: decide against operating in a foreign country

Financial risks:

Reduce: institute quality control measures to ensure full and complete performance of contracts; ensure compliance with accounting and reporting requirements through internal and external audit functions; conduct credit checks of customers prior to issuing credit

Transfer: negotiate for contractual provisions in contracts with customers reducing potential liability

Technological risks:

Reduce: hire an Information Technology firm specializing in security to install firewalls (software that protects against unauthorized access to computers and networks); store data off-site on a daily basis

Transfer: purchase all risks property insurance to cover damage to computers and cost of data recovery

To create this kind of plan, management needs to analyze business activities, develop practices to minimize risks, and know when to seek assistance outside the business, whether by securing insurance or retaining professionals for advice. All risks are generally dealt with through some combination of risk avoidance, reduction, transference, and retention.

Interacting with the Legal Environment

Reacting When Prevention Fails

Prevention of loss is the primary goal of a risk management plan, but some risks cannot be avoided. Disputes inevitably arise; products and services sometimes fail; the business climate, the attitude of government toward business, or the marketplace can change. The value of a risk management plan is that when a risk does materialize, the business already has in place an effective way of addressing it and can more readily assess when legal advice may be necessary.

In the case of Northland, despite measures to protect workers, an employee may be injured on the job site. In such a situation, details of the risk management plan should include guidelines as to how the employee is to be treated; what kind of investigation should take place; what kind of record is to be made of the incident; what follow-up is to be done to ensure that that this type of incident does not reoccur; and the process for accessing income from the workers' compensation plan.

In other situations, however, an event may occur that is not contemplated by the risk management plan or the consequences of an event are much greater than anticipated. For example, despite its best efforts, one of Northland's mines could cave in resulting in the loss of life. In this situation, the company would be in crisis management.

BUSINESS APPLICATION OF THE LAW

The Management of a Crisis

A crisis can come in many forms. Sometimes it is a minor or expected event that spirals out of control, or sometimes it is an unforeseen and unexpected event that an organization is ill-prepared to handle. One of the more famous crises affecting a company occurred in 1982 when seven people died after taking extra-strength Tylenol that was laced with cyanide. The manufacturer of Tylenol, Johnson & Johnson, responded quickly by pulling 31 million bottles of Tylenol off the shelves and stopping all production and advertising. The culprit was never found. Other more recent examples of the management of a crisis are British Petroleum dealing with the spilling of roughly 4.9 million barrels of oil from a blown-out well into the Gulf of Mexico, and Maple Leaf Foods responding to a wide-spread outbreak of listeriosis linked to the company's plant in Toronto, which resulted in 22 deaths. Most recently is the case of Toyota Motor Corp., which recalled 8.8 million cars because of unintended acceleration problems. The recall was precipitated by a single horrific car crash in California in August of 2009. The improper installation of all-weather floor mats from a sports utility vehicle into a loaner Lexis sedan by a dealer led to the vehicle's accelerator getting stuck. An off-duty highway patrol officer and three members of his family were killed in the ensuing crash.

Although these events are very different, all of the companies involved were able to effectively manage the crisis and restore their reputations. They were able to do so because of their reaction to the event and their communication strategy. The latter is particularly important for public companies in that statements made by company representatives have an impact on the market for their shares. The lessons from these events include:

• React quickly and in a positive fashion: Toyota, Maple Leaf Foods, and Johnson and Johnson immediately recalled products;

• Use a prominent spokesperson to tell the company's side of the story and, as appropriate, publically

apologize for the tragic event:[5] both Toyota's and Maple Leaf Foods' presidents publically apologized for the situation;

• Explain how the problem occurred and what the company is doing to fix it: Johnson & Johnson introduced tamper resistant bottles; Maple Leaf Foods improved its cleaning processes and inspection systems;

• Use appropriate messages in different media: the companies expressed concern for the victims and did not argue whether it was responsible; they used both traditional media such as television, radio, and newspaper advertisements and social media;

• Be open and consistent in acknowledging the problem and the company's role in the problem: the companies did not remain quiet or complacent nor did they offer vague, content-free, public statements.

Critical Analysis: How can the lessons learned from a crisis be incorporated into an organization's risk management plan?

Sources: Kim Bhasin, "9 PR Fiascos That Were Handled Brilliantly By Management", *Business Insider* (26 May 2011) online: Business Insider <http://www.businessinsider.com/pr-disasters-crisis-management-2011-5?op=1>; "7 lessons from Maple Leaf Foods' crisis communication", *Dave Fleet* (25 August 2008) online: Dave Fleet <http://davefleet.com/2008/08/7-lessons-from-maple-leaf-foods-crisis-communications/>; Christopher Guly, "Dealing with the storms", *In-House Counsel* (Spring 2010) 24.

Akio Toyoda of Toyoto Motors Corp.: "I am deeply sorry"

---

5. For discussion of the legal consequences of an apology in the context of apology legislation, see Chapter 4.

Managing Legal Services

The development of a risk management plan, the operationalization of the plan, and crisis management can involve accessing legal services. Lawyers may be part of the risk management team or consulted by the team at various stages of the process. They can help in identifying and assessing legal risks, suggesting options for the risk management plan and managing a crisis (see Business Application of the Law: The Role of Lawyers in Risk Management on page 65). Legal services may be provided in-house, as when the organization employs a lawyer or lawyers on a full-time basis, or they can be provided by outside legal counsel. The following sections provide an account of the issues involved in hiring outside legal counsel.

When to Seek Legal Advice

Knowing when to seek legal advice is central to successful management of legal services. Consulting lawyers too soon and too often is expensive and cumbersome. Consulting them infrequently to save money may be more expensive in the long run. Seeking advice at the appropriate time is preferable to waiting for problems to develop.

In Northland's case, legal advice is necessary to access the legal risks associated with operating in a foreign jurisdiction. It may also be necessary to understand regulatory matters. It may be more efficient for a lawyer to assess environmental requirements, waste disposal guidelines, occupational health and safety rules and the like than for a business to explore such issues on its own. Beyond this, even if a dispute is unlikely to go to court or a crisis is unlikely to materialize, legal advice is important in negotiations and exploring options.

It is important to clarify within the organization who should decide when a matter requires legal advice. If there is an internal law department, likely those in that department will make the decision, otherwise there must be clear guidelines as to who has the authority to seek outside counsel and when.

How to Choose a Lawyer

Lawyer
A person who is legally qualified to practise law.

Law firm
A partnership formed by lawyers.

A **lawyer** provides legal services, and the business should manage this service in the same way as any other service. The first step is to find the lawyer or **law firm** appropriate to the business' needs in terms of expertise, approach to dealing with clients and cost.

There are many sources available for identifying lawyers such as friends, relatives, and business associates. Local and provincial bar associations maintain lists of members by geographical area and preferred type of practice. *The Canadian Law List*[6] is a publication available in libraries and online that includes basic biographical information about most lawyers in private practice.

Some advice follows for choosing from among a group of lawyers or firms:

- Consult with business associates with similar legal problems and needs about the service they have received from any of the prospects.

---

6. See <http://www.canadianlawlist.com>.

- Consider meeting with each lawyer or with a representative of each firm to discuss the need of the business for legal advice in general or in relation to a particular legal problem. Lawyers have a strict professional duty to maintain the confidentiality of client affairs.

- Discuss alternative fee structures with the prospects. Lawyers are increasingly willing to provide a fee structure that suits the client, such as billing at an hourly rate, setting a standard fee for routine work, working on an annual retainer, or accepting a percentage fee. The client should expect itemized billing on a schedule that suits the business financial cycle.

- Evaluate the prospects according to a predetermined list of criteria such as expertise, availability, willingness to understand the business, and willingness to communicate.

The object of the exercise is to develop a productive, long-term relationship between the business and the legal advisor. For this reason, there is also a need to continually monitor and evaluate the relationship, primarily to ensure that the business is receiving the advice and assistance it needs at a cost it can afford.

BUSINESS APPLICATION OF THE LAW

The Role of Lawyers in Legal Risk Management

Legal risk management is the identification and management of risks that have or could have legal consequences for an organization. Lawyers can play a huge role in this function by offering:

- An understanding of the organization derived from providing advice on various aspects of the organization's functions;
- An expertise in law and legal analysis;
- An independence that comes from membership in a professional body.[7]

The specific role a lawyer plays depends, to a large extent, on whether the lawyer is outside or in-house legal counsel. Traditionally, outside counsel's role is more circumscribed as she is often only called when an event has occurred. In this situation the outside counsel's role is reactive as she is providing advice on a known event or transaction. The narrow, reactive role for outside counsel, however, is changing and increasingly outside counsel is moving into a preventative role in managing legal risk. For example, Simon A. Fish, general counsel of BMO Financial Group, states that managing risk is no longer an internal exercise. BMO is now bringing in outside counsel as part of the process. According to Fish:

In representing BMO, the firms are required to be mindful of the legal, regulatory, and reputational risks involved in any transaction or matter, and involve the senior members of the legal group in the assessment and management of such risks.

The role of in-house legal counsel in legal risk management has always been broad because an awareness of risks has always been central to the job. But this role too is changing as in-house legal counsel is increasingly seen as an integral part of the management team. Rather than simply being responsible for keeping an eye on legal matters and supervising the work of outside counsel, in-house counsel is often taking part in corporate strategic decision making. Sanjeeve Dhawan senior counsel at Hydro One states that "...companies are discovering that in-house counsel can transcend their traditional legal roles." By being part of the team that makes the organization's strategic decisions, in-house counsel is in an excellent position to ensure that legal risks are recognized and managed as part of the organization's overall strategy.

Critical Analysis: What skills and techniques do lawyers need to contribute effectively to the risk management process?

Sources: Christine Dobby, "A Game of Risk", *The Financial Post* (28 May 2011) FP7; Jeremy Hainsworth, "A novel risk-management plan", *Canadian Lawyer Magazine* (October 2012) online: Canadian Lawyer Magazine <http://www.canadianlaw-yermag.com/A-novel-risk-management-plan.html>.

---

7. Andrew M Whittaker, "Lawyers as Risk Managers", *Butterworths Journal of International Banking and Financial Law* (January 2003) 5.

Business Law in Practice Revisited

1. What is a legal risk management plan, and how is it developed?

A legal risk management plan is a plan that identifies the major legal risks of an organization; evaluates the probability of the risk materializing and the impact of the risks; develops strategies for managing the risks; and implements and monitors the strategies. The plan is developed by the appropriate executive or manager in consultation with internal and external personnel familiar with the legal risks of the organization.

2. What are the Northland's major legal risks from its Canadian operations? How should Northland manage these risks?

Northland's major legal risks from its Canadian operations are identified in Figure 3.1 on page 54. Once the major legal risks are identified, Marie and her team need to evaluate them by assessing the probability and the severity of each potential loss. They must then develop a risk management plan by deciding how to address each risk—by avoiding, reducing, transferring, retaining, or through some combination of those options. Figure 3.3 on pages 61–62 presents the outline of a plan that Marie might produce. Risk management is a continuous process, so Marie or others must monitor the plan to measure its effectiveness in dealing with risks and be prepared to recommend any necessary adjustments.

3. What are Northland's major legal risks should it decide to operate in a foreign jurisdiction such as Peru? How should it manage these risks?

The major legal risks to going global are identified in Figure 3.1 on page 54 and are also discussed in the International Perspective box on page 59. Risks include the possibility that Northland will commit environmental transgressions in Peru. Should this risk ensue, Northland will face adverse publicity, prosecution under environmental legislation, and civil suits by environmental activists and local residents affected by the breach. As well, there is a possibility that the Peruvian government prohibitively tightens legal rules thereby affecting the viability of Northland's operation or even nationalize it. As noted in the risk management plan in Figure 3.3 on pages 61–62, Marie recommended that Northland not expand operations to outside of Canada because the current risks are simply too large.

Chapter Summary

A business can manage its legal environment by assessing that environment, developing a risk management plan, reacting to changes in the legal environment, and managing its legal services.

It is crucial for a business to actively manage the legal risks arising from its activities in order to avoid and minimize legal claims and expenses. Legal risk management involves a four-step process: identifying legal risks, assessing those risks, devising a risk management plan, and implementing the plan. Risks can be identified through assessment of the functional areas of the business, the decisions made within the organization, and the internal and external relationships maintained by the business and its operations and transactions. However, it is important to also identify risks that might cross categories and maintain a flexible approach. The risks are then assessed in terms of how likely they are to occur and how severe the losses might be. There must be an action plan for dealing with each risk. Should the risk be avoided? If not, how can it be reduced or transferred to someone else? To what extent must the risk be retained? These strategies are not usually mutually exclusive and the management of most risks will involve some combination of them.

Management must assemble a knowledgeable team of employees and experts in order to make the plan work. A business also must monitor and revise its plan to ensure that it is current and effective. No risk management plan can anticipate and deal with all possible developments. A business must, therefore, be prepared to react in a coordinated and timely fashion to a crisis.

A business also needs to actively manage its legal services, whether it is employing outside lawyers or in-house counsel. This management involves identifying the legal services that are needed, carefully searching out an appropriate lawyer or law firm and maintaining a stable relationship with legal advisors.

Chapter Study

Key Terms and Concepts

law firm (p. 64)

lawyer (p. 64)

legal risk (p. 50)

legal risk management plan (p. 50)

risk avoidance (p. 56)

risk reduction (p. 56)

risk retention (p. 57)

risk transference (p. 57)

Questions for Review

1. What is meant by the preventive and reactive approaches to legal issues in a business?

2. What is the primary goal of a legal risk management plan?

3. How does a legal risk management plan relate to enterprise risk management?

4. What is the value of a legal risk management plan?

5. What steps are involved in the legal risk management model?

6. How can a business identify its legal risks?

7. What legal risks are posed by technology?

8. How is breach of privacy a legal risk? What are the costs associated with a privacy breach?

9. How can a business evaluate its legal risks? What is the purpose of evaluating legal risks?

10. What is the best strategy for managing legal risks?

11. What is an example of risk retention? When is this strategy most appropriate?

12. What is an example of risk avoidance? When is this strategy most appropriate?

13. What procedures are necessary to implement a risk management plan?

14. How can a business keep its risk management plan current and relevant?

15. What legal risks are involved in doing business internationally? How can these risks be managed?

16. How does the management of a legal crisis differ from managing legal risks?

17. When should a business seek legal advice?

18. What is the role of lawyers in legal risk management?

Questions for Critical Thinking

1. The active involvement and commitment of employees at all levels of an organization is crucial for successful risk management. Who is ultimately responsible for managing legal risks and legal services? What factors are relevant for assigning responsibility within an organization?

2. Risk avoidance is an appropriate strategy when the potential losses seriously outweigh the likely benefits. What factors should be considered on the cost and benefit sides of the analysis? At what point should a business decide to discontinue an activity rather than try to manage the risk involved? What are some examples of risk avoidance?

3. The pharmaceutical industry involves inherent risks. The drugs developed by corporations in the industry may not be as effective as research indicated and over time may produce unexpected, unintended, and serious side effects. How can pharmaceutical corporations use risk avoidance, risk reduction, risk transference, and risk retention in managing these risks?

4. Risk management is a continuous process that requires commitment, time, and expense. However, the benefits are often difficult to identify because they arise largely from prevention. How can a business decide whether the benefits of a risk management plan compensate for the time and expense involved in its design and implementation?

5. A common method of controlling the cost of legal services is to refrain from consulting a lawyer until a serious legal problem absolutely requires it. Another approach is to hire or retain lawyers on an ongoing basis to provide advice as business decisions are made. Which approach is the most expensive? What should a business consider in making that choice?

6. An article in *The Lawyers Weekly*, a leading legal publication, is entitled "Corporate counsel key to risk management."[8] Do you agree with that statement? How can lawyers contribute to risk management? Do you see any problems with outside or in-house lawyer involvement in risk management?

Situations for Discussion

1. Johann is the comptroller of Super Tech Inc., a highly aggressive firm in the high-tech industry that specializes in software development. Sarah, the CEO, prides herself on her ability to make fast decisions and doesn't worry about documenting her actions. Her favourite sayings are, "We can't spend all of our time writing things down," and "Why worry? That's why we have insurance and lawyers." This approach appears to have served her well, at least in the initial years of the business. Johann is concerned, however, because he is often faced with legal bills without having any knowledge of the issues involved. The firm's legal costs are steadily increasing. How should Johann present a recommendation to Sarah that Super Tech should develop a legal risk management plan?

2. If Sarah accepts Johann's recommendation, whom should he recruit for the risk management team? Should he be the leader of the team? How should he go about identifying the legal risks in the firm's business? Whom should he consult?

3. Johann's review has identified a particular problem with Super Tech's software designers. When used by customers, their designs are failing at a higher rate than the industry norm. The designers are unwilling to go back and correct problems because they prefer to develop new products and are under pressure to do so. Super Tech is faced with legal claims and lost customers. How should Johann evaluate and address this problem in the context of his risk management plan, taking into consideration the software designers and the company's profitability? Which of the four risk management strategies are appropriate?

4. Pascal is the manager of software development for Super Tech. He discovers that Bill, the lead software designer, has announced that he is leaving the company next week. Pascal finds that Bill has accepted a job with Super Tech's main competitor. Pascal fears that in his new job Bill will use technology developed while at the company and will disclose the identities of key customers. How could Pascal and Super Tech have identified and addressed this risk in advance? What should Pascal do now?

5. A routine review of Super Tech's accounts receivable discloses a recurring problem with collections from one important customer. What factors should Super Tech consider in its review of this account? How could a risk management plan help Super Tech in determining its course of action regarding this customer? Which steps of the process would be most important?

6. Siena Foods Ltd., located in Toronto, Ontario is a manufacturer and distributor of prepared meat products. In 2010, the Canadian Food Inspection Agency and Siena Foods issued a health hazard alert warning the public not to consume certain Siena brand ham as it may be contaminated with *Listeria monocytogenes*.[9] Food contamination is a major risk in the food processing business with potentially disastrous consequences for the company and its customers. How should Sienna manage this risk? What preventive and reactive action plans should be in place? To what extent can Siena rely on the Canadian Food Inspection Agency to manage the risk?

7. Anna, a customer in a Wendy's restaurant, claimed that she bit into a piece of a human finger while eating a bowl of chili. Anna filed a claim for damages. The event attracted wide media attention. Anna gave several interviews in which she graphically described the trauma that she experienced. The volume of business at all Wendy's outlets in the region plummeted. After several weeks, Wendy's accused the customer of deliberately placing the

---

8. Luigi Benetton, "Corporate Counsel Key to Risk Management", *The Lawyers Weekly* (20 February 2009) 20.
9. Canadian Food Inspection Agency, *Health Hazard Alert: Certain Siena brand prosciutto cotto cooked ham may contain* listeria moncytogenes, (11 March 2010) online: Canadian Food Inspection Agency <http://www.inspection.gc.ca/english/corpaffr/recarapp/2010/20100311be.shtml>.

finger fragment in the chili. When the finger was examined, it proved to be uncooked. Anna and her husband were eventually charged and convicted of several criminal offences. The finger came from a co-worker of Anna's husband, who had lost it in a workplace accident. Apparently Anna and her husband have a history of filing false injury claims.[10] Apply the legal risk management model to this situation. What plan should organizations such as Wendy's have in place to deal with this risk?

8. JetBlue is an American low-fare airline. In 2007, its operations collapsed after an ice storm hit the East Coast of the United States. The storm led to the cancellation of over 1000 flights in five days.

Other airlines were affected by the storm but were able to rebound within a day or two. JetBlue's problems dragged on for days. The main problem was JetBlue's communication system. A large portion of its pilots and flight attendants were not where they were needed and JetBlue lacked the means to locate them and direct them to where they were needed.[11] How could a risk management plan have addressed JetBlue's problems? How should JetBlue's crisis have been handled? Are there opportunities for an organization in responding to a crisis?

For more study tools, visit http://www.NELSONbrain.com.

---

10. Based, in part, on The Associated Press, "Finger-in-chili caper nets wife 9 years, hubby 12", *The Edmonton Journal* (19 January 2006) A3.
11. Jeff Bailey, "JetBlue's C.E.O. is 'mortified' after fliers are stranded", *The New York Times* (19 February 2007) online: NY Times <http://www.nytimes.com/2007/02/19/business/19jetblue.html?pagewanted=all>.

CHAPTER 4

Dispute Resolution

Objectives

After studying this chapter, you should have an understanding of

- how business activities may lead to legal disputes
- the options for resolving a legal dispute
- alternative dispute resolution methods
- the litigation process

Business Law in Practice

Marie Gagnon, referred to throughout Chapter 3, is the Director of Insurance and Security of Northland Mining Inc., a nickel mining company located in northern Manitoba. She has just returned from a well-deserved holiday in Mexico. For several weeks prior to her holiday, Marie was involved in revising Northland's legal risk management plan using the approach outlined in Chapter 3. The basic elements of the plan are presented in Figure 3.3 on pages 61–62. During Marie's absence, several events occurred that related to Northland's plan. Marie is reviewing the following incident reports:

- **The delinquent customer**. A customer failed to pay its account within the usual 30 days. When Northland investigated, it discovered that the customer was in serious financial difficulty.

- **The hacking attempt**. An environmental activist group opposed to mining attempted to "hack" into Northland's computer system. Although there was no loss of data, there was some minor damage to Northland's network and it had to be shut down for several hours.

- **The pollution incident**. A small amount of ash-laden dust from Northland's processing mill was blown onto a neighbouring farmer's land causing some damage to his crops and buildings. The farmer is irate and is threatening to bring legal action. He has told Northland that he intends to contact the media and environmental protection groups to let them know about what has happened to him.

- **The machine breakdown**. The conveyor belt on the continuous mining machine that cuts ore from the mine walls caught on fire. It will take at least three weeks for it to be fixed. Although Northland has insurance covering its losses, the insurance company is denying coverage.

1. How well does Northland's risk management plan deal with these incidents and how could its performance have improved?

2. How well does Northland deploy the various methods of dispute resolution in relation to the legal risks that did materialize?

© ROYALTY FREE/CORBIS/MAGMA

Introduction

As emphasized in Chapter 3, business organizations require a risk management plan to minimize the potentially adverse impact of the legal environment through prevention and a planned reaction to adverse events when they arise. Legal problems cannot always be avoided even when sound management practices are in place. This chapter focuses on the reactive aspect of risk management.

It is not in the best interest of a business to avoid all legal conflict at all costs. For example, if Northland is not being paid on a large account, it must risk a legal dispute or face the unpalatable alternative of a substantial writeoff. It could spell the end of Northland if management were simply to concede defeat any time a legal problem seemed to be developing. Businesses like Northland should seek, instead, to manage such disputes with the express goals of

- avoiding time-consuming and expensive litigation
- preserving desirable long-term commercial relationships

Business Activities and Legal Disputes

Business operations—both internal and external—involve numerous interactions that have potential legal consequences. Consider the following analysis of how the legal risk management plan anticipated and dealt with the events in the Business Law in Practice scenario.

The Delinquent Customer

The customer's refusal to pay its account may indicate that Northland has failed in its procedures for extending credit. Management should explore this possibility to prevent recurrences. In the meantime, Northland must decide if it should: give the customer an opportunity to recover financially before demanding payment; offer to accept less than the full amount; write off the debt altogether; or take steps to be paid on its account, such as selling the debt to a collection agency at a discount, suing for the debt, or filing a claim if the customer is involved in bankruptcy proceedings.

Setting guidelines for granting credit to customers does not guarantee that every debt will be collectible. If this debt is not large and the customer is in serious financial difficulty, coming up with a negotiated repayment plan or writing it off may be more practical than spending money to try to collect it. The debtor is certain to welcome such a compromise, and therefore no legal dispute will arise from this event.

The Hacking Attempt

The hacking attempt by an outside party—an environmental activist group—was anticipated by the plan. Northland, as part of its risk reduction strategy, had engaged the services of an information technology security firm to install firewalls. As a result, the damage to Northland's computer systems was minimal and there was no loss of data. The incident does highlight that hacking incidents can potentially be quite costly. If future hackers are able to breach the firewalls, Northland could incur extra expense associated with the recovery of data, liability for the loss of sensitive customer and employee data, and a loss of revenue resulting from an interruption of the computer system. Northland's investigation of the incident reveals that while it has an insurance program in place, it does not cover all of the possible costs associated with a breach of its computer system. Northland will analyze the costs of obtaining additional, specialized insurance coverage and, if it is warranted, revise its risk management plan accordingly.

The hacking attempt by the environmental activist group is unlikely to result in a legal dispute. Although Northland could potentially sue the group for trespass to its property, this course of action is premature in that Northland does not know the identity of any of the group members. Even if their identity were known, it is still unlikely that Northland would pursue a lawsuit as the damage to its system was minimal and the publicity associated with such an action may be unwelcomed.

The Pollution Incident

Northland's operations have resulted in the discharge of a small amount of pollutants into the environment. Northland must report the pollution incident to the relevant environmental regulatory agency. The agency may impose a fine, clean-up order, or some other administrative penalty depending on the nature, cause, and severity of the incident. This possibility was anticipated by the risk management plan and is unlikely to result in a legal dispute, providing the penalty is in accordance with the applicable environmental protection legislation. Northland has no viable option but to comply with properly enacted legislation.

Northland must also report the incident to its insurer. The insurance policy covering this event will require reporting within a short period of time—usually 5 to 10 days—otherwise the insurance coverage for the event is invalidated. An investigation by Northland reveals that the discharge of pollutants was due to a malfunction in the scrubber (a piece of equipment that captures and removes large particles like heavy metals from exhaust). When a new scrubber was being installed, the exhaust fan controlling the intake and discharge of exhaust stopped working. This, in turn, caused a build-up of ash and dust particles. The build-up was not noticed by the operator so when the scrubber was re-started, a huge dust cloud was released into the atmosphere. Luckily, the wind was blowing away from the adjacent town, but it blew the ash and dust particles onto a farmer's land. Although the pollution incident was anticipated by the risk management plan and Northland has insurance in place to cover the damage to the farmer, this incident may result in a legal dispute. The insurance company has indicated that the damage to the farmer—including the cost of washing his buildings and replacing a barn roof, as well as a reduced crop yield—comes in at less than $50 000. The farmer, however, insists that his damages amount to over $100 000. This matter is a legal dispute, since the farmer is refusing to accept compensation and is threatening to contact the media and environmental protection groups. The dispute with the farmer goes beyond the payment of money as Northland's relationship with a neighbour and its reputation in the community are also in jeopardy.

The pollution discharge incident highlights to Northland that any pollution into the environment can be problematic. In this particular incident, Northland was "lucky" in that the wind was not blowing towards the nearby town. Even though insurance coverage may cover all of the claims, Northland is likely to suffer the loss of goodwill and damage to its reputation. Northland's risk management plan may need revision to further reduce the possibility of a future discharge. For example, Northland may need to purchase a back-up fan or it may need enhanced operator training and re-start procedures.

The Equipment Breakdown

An investigation into the machine breakdown reveals that a bearing in the machine failed causing the ore conveyor belt to catch on fire. It will take at least three weeks to get and install a replacement belt. Northland's chief financial officer estimates that the breakdown will result in lost profits of $3 million dollars. The insurer has been notified of the event, but it is denying coverage. It is arguing that the bearing failure and the resultant losses were not due to a sudden and accidental event covered by the insurance policy, but was due to Northland's failure to properly maintain the equipment. Ordinary wear and tear and failure to maintain the equipment are not covered by the insurance policy. Beyond this, the insurance policy contained a provision requiring Northland to keep complete maintenance records on the machine's bearing or else coverage would be voided. The insurer is demanding those records. For its part, Northland argues that it properly maintained the equipment in accordance with the manufacturer's original specifications.

Although machine breakdown and resulting loss of profit was anticipated and managed by the purchase of insurance, this incident will result in a legal dispute. The amount of money involved is simply too large for Northland to write off.

As the foregoing analysis suggests, Northland's risk management plan predicted and planned for several events that did in fact occur. For various reasons, a legal dispute is unlikely to arise from them. Some events will not develop into legal disputes because the company has no other viable option but to live with what has happened. That is, Northland will likely write off the delinquent customer's bad debt as an anticipated cost of doing business; Northland will not throw away its resources on a lost cause. Similarly, Northland cannot launch a legal action over the hacking attempt because it does not know the identity of the hackers and, besides, there is little point in launching an action where the damage is minor and the resulting publicity is unwelcome. However, other events may result in legal conflict, including the problems with the disgruntled farmer and the intransigent insurance company.

Northland's challenge with these latter issues is to actively and effectively manage them—just as it would any other aspect of the business's environment. Managing disputes does not mean simply proceeding to court. There are many ways to resolve a dispute that do not involve litigation. See Figure 4.2 on page 91 for a summary of **alternative dispute resolution** methods. The most common are negotiation, mediation and arbitration.

Alternative dispute resolution (ADR)
A range of options for resolving disputes as an alternative to litigation.

Negotiation
A process of deliberation and discussion intended to reach a mutually acceptable resolution to a dispute.

Alternative Dispute Resolution
Negotiation

Negotiation is a problem-solving process in which parties discuss their differences and attempt to reach a mutually agreeable resolution. It is the most common alternative dispute resolution method because it is cost effective, usually quick, and allows parties to craft a solution that is suitable for their particular situation as opposed to having another party, such as a judge, impose a resolution. It also helps to preserve the relationship between the parties because it does not tend to be as confrontational as more formal methods of dispute resolution.

When to Negotiate   Negotiation can be used to resolve virtually any type of dispute. It can, for example, be used to resolve Northland's dispute with the farmer and the insurance company, provided they are willing to negotiate. In addition to situations where the parties agree to negotiate once a dispute arises, a provision in a contract may require the parties to attempt negotiation. It is increasingly common for parties to include in their contract a clause whereby they agree that during and after the conclusion of the contract, they will make efforts to resolve any disputes by negotiation. When negotiation is used, it can be employed at any stage of a dispute. It is, for example, common for a dispute to be resolved by negotiation on the eve of a trial or even midway through a trial.

Even through negotiation may be used to resolve most types of disputes, there are some situations where negotiation is not the proper way to proceed, even as a first step, such as when insurance covers the risk that is the subject of the dispute. In such circumstances, the business is required to allow the insurer to conduct settlement negotiations. Any attempt by the business to negotiate privately may jeopardize the coverage. In Northland's dispute with the farmer, insurance potentially covers the farmer's damage and the insurance company would normally negotiate a settlement. However, in this situation, the insurance company agreed to allow Northland to attempt to resolve the dispute because of its sensitive nature and its potential impact on Northland's reputation.

How to Negotiate   Negotiations are most often carried out by the parties to the dispute. However, in some cases it may be preferable to hire a lawyer, advocate, or counselor who has the expertise to help in the negotiations or who can negotiate on behalf of the parties. In Northland's case, because both disputes involve insurance issues, negotiations will most likely be carried out by the person responsible for acquiring the insurance, that is, Marie Gagnon, Director of Insurance and Security.

Regardless of who does the actual negotiating, the first step is to investigate the situation to determine the nature and extent of the dispute. The person responsible should contact the individuals involved in her own organization and the appropriate people on the other side of the dispute to clarify the situation. The process of negotiation is not governed by technical rules; it can operate in whatever way the parties wish to solve their problem. It is however important to get the negotiations off on the right foot. For example, Northland in negotiating with the disgruntled farmer should contact him immediately, assure him that it is concerned with his situation and will make every effort to remedy his loss. Northland may also decide to apologize to him for the damage. As the box below explains in more detail, several provinces including Manitoba[1] have passed "apology legislation" to permit an individual to show remorse without triggering adverse legal consequences.

---

1. *Apology Act*, SM 2007, c 25, CCSM c A98.

BUSINESS AND LEGISLATION

Saying Sorry

Research in the area of apologies suggests that they facilitate personal reconciliation and can assist in resolving legal disputes.[2] According to the Uniform Law Conference of Canada ("ULCC"), however, the traditional concern was that an apology in a legal context could prove dangerous. An apology might amount to an admission of liability that "could void an insurance policy, encourage a lawsuit, or result in a court holding the apologizer liable."[3] In response, several jurisdictions in Canada have passed broad apology legislation. As summarized by the ULCC, the apology legislation in British Columbia—which covers statements admitting or implying wrongdoing as well as expressions of regret or sympathy—provides that an apology:

- is not an admission of liability
- is not relevant when a judge makes a determination of liability
- cannot be used as evidence establishing liability
- cannot be used to void an insurance policy[4]

Businesses that operate across the country must be particularly cautious in issuing apologies, however, since not

Why do apologies de-escalate legal disputes?

every jurisdiction in Canada will provide adequate protection to the apologizer. For example, Quebec has no apology legislation at all and in New Brunswick, apology legislation only applies to shelter police officers.[5] As Mary Jane Stitt, a commercial litigation partner in Toronto, stated to *The Lawyers Weekly*, "If you are a Canadian business and you sell a product or service nationally and decide to make an apology, you will not be protected in every province. That is the downfall."

Critical Analysis: What are the pros and cons of an apology in face of a legal dispute?

With negotiation, the goal is to reach a resolution that is agreeable to all parties. That said, there is no guarantee that a settlement will be reached. Whether negotiations do succeed will depend on a number of factors, including the following:

- the willingness of the parties to compromise and negotiate in good faith
- the nature and significance of the dispute
- the priority the parties give to its resolution
- the effectiveness of those involved in the negotiations

If negotiations are successful and the parties reach a settlement, it is usual for them to enter into a settlement agreement or release so that the dispute cannot be resurrected or litigated in the future. It is also common to have a confidentiality clause as a part of the settlement or release. This prohibits the parties from revealing the terms of the settlement and prevents other persons from using the settlement to advance claims against the parties.

Northland entered into negotiations with the disgruntled farmer who was willing to talk once he understood that Northland was concerned about his situation. He agreed not to call the media or environmentalists pending a resolution of the dispute. As part of the negotiations, Northland explained how and why the pollution occurred and what it was doing to prevent a future incident. The farmer was adamant that his damage was over $100 000. However,

---

2. Russell J Getz, "Uniform Apology Act" Uniform Law Conference of Canada (Civil Law Section), 2007 at 2.
3. *Ibid* at 3–4.
4. *Ibid* at 13.
5. Donalee Moulton, "No spike in mea culpas from apology laws", *The Lawyers Weekly* (9 March 2012) 5.

BUSINESS APPLICATION OF THE LAW

The Finality of Out-of-Court Settlements

Settlement out of court through negotiation or other dispute resolution mechanisms is common. Dr. Julie Macfarlane, a professor in the Faculty of Law at the University of Windsor and author of *The New Lawyer: How Settlement Is Transforming the Practice of Law*, notes that figures out of the United States indicate that 98.2 percent of civil matters are settled before court. The rate is almost as high in Ontario at approximately 95 to 96 percent.

The trend towards settling out of court, as opposed to bringing a dispute before the courts, raises an important issue: is an out-of-court settlement final? For example, in 2008, Cameron and Tyler Winklevoss entered into a settlement with Facebook over their allegations against Mark Zuckerberg, the founder of Facebook. They alleged that they had hired Zuckerberg, their classmate at Harvard University, to work on their social networking site, ConnectU, but instead, he stole their idea and launched his own site. The dispute was settled for $20 million cash and $45 million in Facebook shares. In 2011, the Winklevoss twins attempted to have the settlement overturned on the basis that they had been misled during negotiations about the value of the shares they would receive as part of the settlement. They lost their attempt at both the US Circuit Court and the US Court of Appeals. Chief Judge Alex Kozinski wrote,

> The Winklevosses are not the first parties bested by a competitor who then seek to gain through litigation what they were unable to achieve in the marketplace. And the courts might have obliged, had the Winklevosses not settled their dispute and signed a release of all claims against Facebook. . . . For whatever reason, they now want to back out. Like the

Twin brothers Cameron and Tyler Winklevoss lost their legal effort to re-open a 2008 settlement with Facebook.

district court, we see no basis for allowing them to do so. At some point, litigation must come to an end. That point has now been reached.[6]

The result in the Winklevoss case illustrates that courts are very reluctant to reopen settlements. While there is always a possibility that a settlement may be reopened, this is unlikely absent evidence of fraud.

Critical Analysis: Why is settling out of court replacing going off to court? Is this a good trend? Why are courts reluctant to reopen settlements? What steps can be taken to reduce the possibility of litigation after a settlement?

Sources: Jessica Guynn, "Twins gamble $160M on Facebook suit", *Edmonton Journal* (1 March 2011) D1; Donalee Moulton, "Vanishing trials: Out-of-court settlements on the rise", *The Lawyers Weekly* (17 October 2008) 22; Will O' Hara, "Releases that don't stay final", *The Lawyers Weekly* (29 May 2009) 13; Nina Mandell, "Winklevoss twins, who claim Mark Zuckerberg stole their idea, lose appeal in federal court", *The Daily News* (11 April 2011) online: NY Daily News.com <http://articles.nydailynews.com/2011-04-11/news/29426547_1_winklevoss-twins-mark-zuckerberg-cameron-and-tyler-winklevoss>.

included in his estimate was structural improvement to his facilities (he wanted new siding on all buildings as opposed to having the siding cleaned) as well as depreciation on the barn's roof. After further discussion, the farmer agreed to abandon his claim for new siding when Northland agreed to pay for a new roof without consideration of depreciation. The parties settled for $75 000 and the farmer signed a release with a confidentiality clause.

When Negotiations End   In the majority of cases, such as the dispute with the farmer, parties reach settlement, often without the involvement of anyone else. Other times, an impasse is reached where neither party is prepared to compromise further.

Northland also negotiated with its insurance company, but the results were disappointing. The insurance company was not willing to compensate Northland for any losses. It continued to argue that the losses were due to poor maintenance, which was an exclusion (a provision that eliminates coverage for certain events or named perils) under the insurance policy.

---

6. *Facebook v Connectu, Inc*, No.08-16745 at 4911-4912 ((9th Cir Ct App, Apr 11, 2011) online: Unites States Courts for the Ninth Circuit <http://www.ca9.uscourts.gov/datastore/opinions/2011/04/11/08-16745.pdf>.

When an impasse such as this occurs, the business is faced with a difficult choice: concede and cut its losses or risk the expenditure of more time and money. Whether Northland should continue or abandon the legal conflict depends on its analysis of what is in the best interests of the organization in the long term. Any organization that is deciding whether to proceed with a legal conflict that could not be resolved through negotiation should consider the questions in Figure 4.1:

FIGURE 4.1

In Deciding Whether to Proceed or Not to Proceed with a Legal Dispute Consider the Following Questions:

- What further steps are available and how long will they take?
- Can the business devote the resources necessary to proceed with the dispute, in terms of both the commitment and the time of business personnel?
- Will a lengthy dispute affect the public profile and reputation of the business?
- Is the relationship with the other side valuable?
- Will that relationship be harmed, whatever the outcome?
- What is the likely cost in terms of legal fees and company time?
- Are there worthwhile principles at stake that go beyond the particular dispute?
- If the dispute goes to court, what are the chances of winning?
- If the court decides in favour of the business, does the other side have the assets to pay the claim?

If Northland decides to continue its dispute with the insurance company, it may end up having to sue. Alternatively, the parties may agree to either mediation or arbitration as a method to resolve the dispute.

Mediation

Mediator
A person who helps the parties resolve their dispute.

Mediation is an alternative dispute resolution (ADR) process whereby a neutral person, called a **mediator**, assists the parties in reaching a settlement of their dispute. It is a popular as a method for resolving disputes because, like negotiation, it:

- is less expensive and quicker than more formal dispute resolution methods;

- is private and confidential if the parties choose;[7]

- helps to preserve the relationship between the parties;

- can result in a resolution tailored to the needs of the parties.

When Mediation Is Used   Mediation, like negotiation, can be used to resolve most disputes. Whereas historically mediation was mainly used in family disputes and divorce issues, it is now commonly used to settle commercial disputes. It has been successfully used to resolve a wide range of business conflicts involving contract matters, personal injuries, employment matters, environmental protection, and the like. That said, some disputes are more amenable to mediation than others. Success is more likely if the parties are interested in considering each other's position with the goal of compromising and settling the dispute, and if they value the advantages of mediation. Northland and its insurer could agree to mediation to resolve their dispute over insurance coverage.

---

7. To ensure confidentiality in ADR proceedings, the parties should include a clause to that effect. Parties should not automatically assume that their deliberations and settlement are confidential. See: Anthony Daimsis, "Confidentiality in ADR", *The Lawyers Weekly* (11 February 2011) 9.

In addition to situations where the parties voluntarily agree to mediation, or where it is required pursuant to a clause in a contract, there are cases where it is imposed. For example, Ontario has a mandatory mediation program that requires many civil (non-criminal) cases[8] to be referred to mediation before a trial can be scheduled. These cases are referred to mediation very early in the litigation process.

How Mediation Works   Once the parties have agreed to mediation, they choose a neutral third party to act as mediator. There are no mandatory qualifications for ADR practitioners, but there are many training programs available through universities and the private sector. Mediators are often lawyers or retired judges, but anyone is eligible to become a full-time or part-time practitioner. The ADR Institute of Canada, a self-regulatory body for ADR professionals, maintains a national roster of mediators. Usually the mediation will happen with the parties meeting face-to-face, but it can also be conducted through videoconferencing and online[9] if it is appropriate for the parties and the type of dispute. Once the mediator has been chosen, she helps the parties clarify their interests and overcome obstacles to communication. The mediator does not work for either party and instead manages the process, organizes the discussion, clears up misunderstandings, and helps reduce tensions between the parties. The mediator does not, however, make or impose a solution on the parties—it is the parties that must reach a resolution voluntarily.

In the case of mandated mediation programs, the parties may choose a mediator, but if they are unable to agree, a mediator will be assigned to them from a roster of mediators. In mandated mediation, like voluntary mediation, the mediator does not impose a solution but merely assists the parties.

When Mediation Ends   Mediation, like negotiation, has a very high success rate. For example, it is considered to be successful in settling approximately 80 percent of the cases where it is used even after litigation has begun.[10] At the end of a successful mediation, the parties normally enter into a settlement agreement setting out the essential terms of their agreement. This will bring closure to the dispute and help prevent future litigation concerning the same matter. The settlement agreement is a contract and can be enforced in the same manner as any other contract. Ontario[11] and Nova Scotia[12] have also enacted legislation that allows parties who have settled a commercial dispute through mediation to register their agreement and have it enforced like a court judgment.

Mediation, however, is not uniformly successful. It does not always produce a resolution, so time and money may be invested only to have the matter proceed to litigation. Northland and its insurer initially agreed to mediation, but quickly realized that their dispute was not amenable to this resolution approach. This was because both parties were unwilling to compromise and both wanted a definitive decision on whether the insurance covered Northland's losses.

---

8. The mandated mediation program applies in Toronto, Ottawa, and Windsor to most non-family civil actions where the claim exceeds $50 000. See: Ontario, Rules of Civil Procedure, RRO 1990, Reg 194, r 24.1.
9. See: Luigi Benetton, "The benefits of video mediation", *The Lawyers Weekly* (10 December 2010) 9; Garry Oakes, "Your virtual day in court: How online dispute resolution is transforming the practice of ADR", *The Lawyers Weekly* (15 August 2008) 23.
10. Paul Jacobs, "Deal mediation: settling disputes before they arise", *The Lawyers Weekly* (18 September 2009) 10.
11. *Commercial Mediation Act*, 2010, SO 2010, c 16, Schedule 3.
12. *Commercial Mediation Act*, SNS 2005, c 36.

Arbitration

Arbitrator
A person who listens to the parties to a dispute and makes a ruling that is usually binding on the parties.

Arbitration is a method for resolving a dispute whereby a third person(s), called an **arbitrator**, appointed by the parties makes a decision. It is similar to litigation in that it usually involves a hearing where the parties or their representatives make submissions, and the resolution is outside the control of the parties. Arbitration has advantages in comparison to litigation. The parties control the process in that they choose the rules for conducting the arbitration including the degree of formality, privacy, and finality of the decision, the timing, and the decision-maker or arbitrator. Arbitration is advantageous because the parties have an opportunity to review the arbitrator's background prior to ceding decision-making power and can choose an arbitrator who has knowledge and expertise in their particular dispute. This option is not available in a court action. Arbitration is usually cheaper and faster than litigation and can lead to an overall sense of satisfaction. However, if the parties choose a process that has the same degree of formality as the litigation process, or if a party uses an absence of rules to engage in delay tactics, the arbitration can lead to costs and time periods similar to, or greater than, those experienced in a court action.

When Arbitration Is Used   Arbitration, like other forms of ADR, is theoretically capable of resolving any dispute. It works particularly well for most commercial and business disputes because the parties can select an arbitrator with relevant experience and keep commercially sensitive information private.

Arbitration is often chosen by the parties before a dispute arises through a term in a contract providing that disagreements arising from the contract are to proceed to arbitration. Most significant commercial contracts, whether domestic or international, have an arbitration clause. Increasingly, many contracts between providers, particularly online providers, of goods and consumers contain arbitration clauses.

BUSINESS APPLICATION OF THE LAW

Arbitration Clauses in Consumer Contracts

In 2003, Dell Computer published the wrong prices on its online order pages. Two models of handheld computers indicated prices of $89 and $118 rather than $379 and $549, respectively. Several hundred consumers attempted to buy computers at the erroneous prices but were unable to so. The consumers attempted a class action to force Dell to sell them the computers at the lower advertised prices. Dell argued that the consumers were not able to take the matter to court because of a clause in the online contract requiring all disputes to proceed to arbitration. The Supreme Court of Canada upheld Dell's argument. The consumers were left with their individual remedy of going to arbitration—presumably a very much inferior option. Since then, Alberta, Quebec, and Ontario have passed legislation explicitly prohibiting arbitration clauses in consumer contracts. In other provinces without such legislation, arbitration clauses are likely enforceable with a few exceptions.[13]

What are the advantages and disadvantages of arbitration clauses in consumer contracts?

Critical Analysis: Should arbitration clauses be prohibited in consumer contracts? Why or why not?

Sources: Luis Millan, "Customers can sue despite ADR clause", *The Lawyers Weekly* (1 April 2011) 1; *Dell Computer Corp v Union des consommateurs*, 2007 SCC 34, [2007] 2 SCR 801.

---

13. See *Seidel v Telus Communications Inc*, 2011 SCC 15, [2011] 1 SCR 531, where the Supreme Court of Canada held that in some cases, consumer protection legislation provisions may override an arbitration clause.

© CAN STOCK PHOTO INC. / LUCKYTOMMY7

In the absence of a clause, arbitration can be adopted at any point in a dispute if the parties agree. Northland and its insurer did not have an arbitration clause in their contract. They initially considered arbitration as a method of resolving their dispute but could not agree on an arbitrator. But more importantly, the insurance company wanted to establish a legal precedent. It wanted a judge's interpretation of the scope of the exclusion clauses in its insurance policy, a result not available with arbitration.

How Arbitration Is Used   Agreements to settle a dispute by arbitration are subject to arbitration legislation[14] in the relevant jurisdictions. These statutes oust the jurisdiction of the courts and provide general guidelines for the conduct of the arbitration. The agreement between the parties to submit their dispute to arbitration will normally specify the process for choosing an arbitrator and the rules of procedure.

The parties may agree on an arbitrator or they may have a third party choose an arbitrator. As mentioned above, there are no mandatory qualifications for ADR practitioners. Many of the same people who provide mediation services also provide arbitration services. The ADR Institute of Canada maintains a roster of arbitrators. The key is to retain the services of a qualified and skilled professional experienced in both the type of dispute and the dispute resolution process.

The parties decide on the rules for conducting the arbitration. They may establish their own rules, or incorporate rules set out in the arbitration statutes or developed by a recognized body such as the ADR Institute of Canada. The parties have great flexibility in specifying the degree of formality in the procedures. The rules, for example, will specify how the hearing is conducted, when and where it is conducted, how evidence can be presented, and timelines for its presentation.

When Arbitration Ends   At the end of the arbitration, the arbitrator renders a decision. The finality of the decision depends on what the parties have agreed to in their agreement to submit the dispute to arbitration. Usually the decision will be a final decision with little or no right of appeal. Alternatively, the parties may agree to preserve rights of appeal and may provide for an appeal process. For example, the parties may decide that the decision of an arbitrator may be appealed to a panel of arbitrators chosen by the parties.

The arbitration award, unless it is overturned or varied on appeal is **binding**, that is, it is enforceable by the courts. The arbitration Acts provide for the enforcement of the arbitral decision in much the same manner as a judgment of the court.

Binding
Final and enforceable in the courts.

INTERNATIONAL PERSPECTIVE

Arbitration Is the Norm in International Transactions

Litigation of a business dispute in a domestic transaction can be time-consuming, damaging, and expensive. If the dispute arises in an international transaction, problems are compounded by questions of which country's law applies, which country's courts will hear the case, and whether the courts of one country will recognize and enforce a judgment obtained in another country. There is no international court for the resolution of commercial disputes, nor is there a comprehensive international system for the enforcement of awards obtained in domestic courts of other countries.

(Continued)

---

14. See for example, *The Arbitration Act*, SM 1997, c 4, CCSM c A120. The general arbitration acts do not govern certain types of arbitration, most notably, arbitrations in labour relations are governed by specific legislation.

For these reasons, ADR mechanisms are extremely popular for settling international commercial disagreements. In international commercial contracts, arbitration has emerged as the favoured form of settlement, and arbitration clauses are the norm. In fact, it would be a rare situation where a significant international commercial contract did not have an arbitration clause in it. The arbitration process has been greatly enhanced by the adoption in many countries of standardized rules as well as by procedures and provisions for the reciprocal recognition and enforcement of the arbitral award. Canada, for example, has adopted the *New York Convention on the Recognition and Enforcement of Foreign Arbitral Awards*. This convention ensures international arbitration awards are enforceable in the over 140 countries that are signatories to it. Also, all jurisdictions in Canada have enacted international commercial arbitration legislation based on the United Nations Commission on International Trade Law (UNCITRAL) *Model Law on International Commercial Arbitration*. The legislation sets out the process for an international commercial arbitration as well as its review and enforcement.

Critical Analysis: Is arbitration of international disputes a positive development?

Source: Mary Jo Nicholson, *Legal Aspects of International Business: A Canadian Perspective*, 2d ed (Toronto: Emond Montgomery, 2007) at 361–71.

The Litigation Process

As already discussed, most of the legal risks that materialized for Northland—including the delinquent customer situation and the pollution incident—are likely to be resolved out of court. However, Northland's conflict with its insurer over the equipment failure may end up in litigation because alternative dispute resolution methods have failed. As the parties have been unable to find a compromise, they will now seek a court's answer to whether the continuous mining machine broke down because of an accidental event (which means Northland's losses would be covered by the insurance policy) or due to improper maintenance by Northland (which would not be covered).

Plaintiff
The party that initiates a lawsuit against another party.

Litigation arises when one party brings a legal action against another. In this case, Northland would be the **plaintiff** or claimant. It would sue (that is, initiate legal action, known as a lawsuit or litigation) the insurer (as **defendant**), claiming that the defendant breached the insurance contract when it refused to pay out Northland's loss under the policy.

Defendant
The party being sued.

Litigation should be deployed only when all other feasible methods have failed and the claim cannot realistically be abandoned. This is not just because litigation can harm commercial relationships and bring unwelcome publicity. Complicated litigation, in particular, is a drain on corporate resources, diverts operations from profitable business activities, and causes stress for those involved in the process. Beyond this, there is no guarantee of success in obtaining a favourable decision from the court or in collecting a judgment from the defendant. In short, litigation is generally slow, expensive, and unpredictable.

While litigation often involves just a single plaintiff against a single defendant, class actions are also possible, as the Business and Legislation box below discusses.

The legal foundation and outcome of a lawsuit are governed by legal rules contained in common law and statute law. Some of these rules are substantive because they address, in part, who should win the action and why. *How* the claim is carried through the civil justice system is dictated by the procedural rules—that is, the rules that mandate such matters as what documents are to be filed with the court, what the process leading up to the trial will be, and in what manner the trial will proceed.

Limitation period
The time period specified by legislation for commencing legal action.

There are crucial rules in each province which set specific time periods within which to commence legal action. **Limitation periods** vary widely, depending on the nature of the lawsuit and the province in which the litigation will occur. Alberta, for example, has a

BUSINESS AND LEGISLATION

Class Action Lawsuits

A **class action** is a proceeding brought by a representative plaintiff on behalf of, or for the benefit of, a class of persons having similar claims against the same defendant. The purpose of a class action is to improve access to justice by enabling claimants to combine their resources in a single action and to efficiently address cases of alleged mass wrong by eliminating the need for a large number of individual actions.

Until the 1990s, class actions were uncommon in Canada because of precedents that made it difficult to use this process. Beginning in 1992, all of the provinces,[15] with the exception of Prince Edward Island,[16] passed legislation to broaden the availability of class actions. Generally, the legislation enables a class action to be certified or approved by the court if:

- the pleadings disclose a cause of action;
- there is an identifiable class of two or more persons;
- the claims of the class raise issues that are common to all class members;
- the class proceeding is the preferable procedure for the resolution of the common issues; and
- there is a representative plaintiff who fairly and adequately represents the interests of the class and who does not have a conflicting interest with other class members.

The result of the legislation has been a complete transformation of the class action landscape in Canada. There has been a tremendous increase in not only the number of lawsuits launched and certified, but also in the amounts of money involved. The actions have been commenced in a wide variety of areas such as product liability, environmental contamination, securities, financial services, employment disputes, consumer protection, franchises, and pension plans. The actions have involved every conceivable claim.

GINO DONATO/ THE CANADIAN PRESS

What "class" might be harmed by these activities?

Some recent examples of settled class actions are:

- a class action against Money Mart for violating the *Criminal Code* provisions relating to high rates of interest charged to borrowers was settled for $100 million
- a class action against Eli Lilly (the manufacturer of Zyprexa) by individuals who became diabetic after taking the antipsychotic drug was settled for $17.6 million
- a class action by shareholders against Biovail for alleged misrepresentations relating to some of its key pharmaceutical products was settled for US$138 million.

The advent of the class action in Canada has not been without controversy. Some applaud class actions not only for making it less onerous for individuals to seek redress against large companies, but also for forcing companies to change behaviour in a positive way. Others complain the courts have been too lenient in allowing class actions to proceed and that it is usually just the lawyers who benefit.

Critical Analysis: Class action legislation has significantly increased the risk of a class action for business. How can a business address this risk in its legal risk management plan?

Sources: Luis Millan, "Class action conundrum", *The Lawyers Weekly* (23 April 2010) 24; Jacob Ziegel, "Class actions: the consumer's best friend?", *The Lawyers Weekly* (20 February 2009) 5; David Weiner, "Class action communications: the era of the public lawsuit has arrived", *The Lawyers Weekly* (2 May 2008) 27.

general limitation period of two years (meaning that the action must be commenced within two years of when the cause of action is discovered) and an ultimate limitation period of 10 years (commencing when the cause of action arises), whichever period expires first.[17] Ontario has a general limitation period of two years and an ultimate limitation period of 15 years,[18] as does New Brunswick.[19] Provinces such as Nova Scotia permit actions to proceed after the limitation has expired if there is a reasonable explanation for the delay,[20] but the general rule is that the right to sue is lost after the applicable period of time ends.

Class action
A lawsuit launched by one person who represents a class of persons having similar claims against the same defendant.

15. See, for example, *Class Proceedings Act,* 1992, SO 1992, c 6; and *Class Proceedings Act,* SNS 2007, c 28.
16. The PEI courts may still certify class actions under the common law.
17. *Limitations Act,* RSA 2000, c L-12, s 3.
18. *Limitations Act, 2002,* SO 2002, c 24, Schedule B, ss 4, 15.
19. *Limitation of Actions Act,* SNB 2009, c L-8.5, s 5.
20. *Limitation of Actions Act,* RSNS 1989, c 258, s 3.

The rationales for strict limitation periods include:

- providing a very strong incentive for plaintiffs to advance their claims within a reasonable period of time;

- preventing plaintiffs from advancing old claims in which evidence has been lost because time has passed;

- providing defendants with a time after which the threat or possibility of litigation comes to an end.[21]

Limitation period rules are an important reason why legal advice should be sought at an early stage in disputes, particularly where there are significant financial consequences. Lawyers in such cases must be aware of the relevant limitation period and ensure that litigation is commenced if settlement does not occur within that period.

Commercial litigation (which involves businesses suing businesses) is also known as private (or civil) litigation. The litigants bear the costs of bringing a matter through the judicial system and any recovery of compensation comes from the losing party. Government's only involvement in the process is through the provision of the administrative structure, the court facilities, the judges, and other court officials. There is no government funding for the private litigants themselves, with the limited exception of legal aid programs which assist in certain civil matters, such as divorce and custody lawsuits, but not in commercial disputes.

Every province and territory has its own system of courts and rules for civil litigation. In some cases, the amount of the claim determines the court in which the action would be commenced. When the plaintiff is suing for a relatively small amount of money, for example, the lawsuit can be processed in the local equivalent of a small claims court. The name of the court varies from province to province, with the monetary limit ranging from $10 000 all the way up to $25 000. The small claims process is designed to be simpler, quicker, and less expensive than mainstream litigation. Litigants do not need to hire a lawyer to assist them though some choose to do so, especially if the matter is complex.

Claims in excess of small claims limits must be pursued in the local equivalent of the superior court, which has unlimited monetary jurisdiction. Litigation in superior courts is governed by complicated rules of court determined by each province. Such litigation is ordinarily conducted by a lawyer in consultation with the client. While it is technically permissible for a business to attempt to meet the many formal requirements of superior court litigation without the benefit of legal advice, this is generally inadvisable. A litigant's need for what can often be costly legal advice raises the issue of accessibility to the justice system by those who cannot afford the services of a lawyer.

Stages of a Lawsuit

In superior courts, a lawsuit that goes through the full court process is comprised of four stages.

---

21. Pamela Pengelley, "Limitation Periods for Property Damage Losses in Canada", Res Ipsa Loquitur, (8 November 2009) online: Res Ipsa Loquitur, The Canadian Law Blog that Speaks for Itself <http://canadianlaw.wordpress.com/2009/11/08/limitation-periods-for-property-damage-losses-in-canada/>.

Pleadings

The first stage is known as **pleadings** and involves the exchange of the formal documents outlining the basis of the suit. The plaintiff initiates the action by preparing a document that contains the allegations supporting the **claim**. For example, in Northland's action against its insurer, the initial document would, among other matters, identify the insurance contract and the coverage provided. The claim would indicate that the equipment was insured under that contract of insurance, identify the accident which caused the loss, and state how much the loss was in a dollar amount. The claim would then also state that the insured had made demand for payment of the loss from the insurer under the policy and that the insurer had refused to do so, in breach of the policy. This initial document is a notice of the claim and is registered, or "filed," with the appropriate court office. It is then formally delivered to the party being sued (the defendant), through a process known as service. If the defendant has retained a lawyer, that lawyer may accept service of the documents on the defendant's behalf.

This first stage does not include evidence, but instead outlines the key points that the plaintiff needs to prove at trial in order to succeed. The defendant then has a short period of time (for example, 20 days in Ontario) in which to respond to the allegations. Failure by the defendant to respond within the allowed time is equivalent to admitting the claim. If the defendant has no defence to the claim, he or she may choose to allow the plaintiff to "win" the case. The plaintiff, in turn, simply explains to the judge that the defendant has conceded the case. The court gives a default judgment to the plaintiff, who is then free to move to the enforcement stage.

If there are matters in dispute, the defendant will likely seek legal advice and prepare a formal response to the claim, known as a **defence.** The lawyers may agree to allow the defendant longer than the minimum period in which to prepare the defence. In the Northland's example, the insurer would assert in its statement of defence that Northland's loss was not an insured loss. The statement of defence would state that the loss did not arise as a result of accident but as a result of poor maintenance.

Speaking more generally, the defendant also has the option of filing a **counterclaim** against the plaintiff in the appropriate case. For example, when a defendant is sued for allegedly causing a motor vehicle accident resulting in injury to the plaintiff, the defendant may turn the tables and file a counterclaim, alleging that it was actually the plaintiff who caused the accident and injury to the defendant.

Discovery

Once the basic claims and allegations have been made and clarified, the suit proceeds to the second stage, commonly known as **discovery.** Both parties must now reveal and demonstrate the facts that support their allegations. These facts are found in documents, in the oral testimony of those directly involved in the situation, and in expert reports. In this context, documents include electronic data (such as email archives and the contents of hard drives) and give rise to complicated issues of preservation and access. Electronic data is easier to access, organize, and distribute, but can be challenging to find and control. It has become important for firms to have comprehensive data retention policies in anticipation

Pleadings
The formal documents concerning the basis for a lawsuit.

Claim
The formal document that initiates litigation by setting out the plaintiff's allegations against the defendant.

Defence
The defendant's formal response to the plaintiff's allegations.

Counterclaim
A claim by the defendant against the plaintiff.

Discovery
The process of disclosing evidence to support the claims in a lawsuit.

of e-discovery. Computer technology can help track the numerous documents in complicated cases. In its litigation with the insurer, Northland would produce, among other documents, the maintenance records it kept regarding the continuous mining machine. Unfortunately for Northland, it was unable to locate some of the relevant maintenance records on the bearing.

The time frame for this stage is undefined and depends largely on the degree of complexity of the case. The purpose of this stage is to test the strength of the opposing positions, so that, based on a greater appreciation of the strengths and weaknesses of both sides of the case, the parties will be encouraged to reach a compromise. At this stage, initiatives in various provinces come into play for the purpose of clearing the backlogs in the courts and streamlining the litigation process. Generally, these initiatives require the parties involved in litigation to engage in a formal attempt to resolve their dispute before it actually goes to court. These attempts may require the parties to engage in a process of mediation, whereby a facilitator, who may be a judge, helps them reach a compromise and avoid a trial. In many jurisdictions, the parties can proceed to trial only when the mediation phase is completed. Besides these mandatory dispute resolution methods, the parties are required to participate in a settlement and pretrial conference, the purpose of which is to narrow the issues in dispute and make the actual trial as short as possible in the event that it does occur.

Trial and Decision

Trial
A formal hearing before a judge that results in a binding decision.

If no settlement is reached at the discovery stage, the plaintiff can proceed to **trial.** The timing will depend on the availability of the courts and on how long it takes the parties to prepare for the formalities of the trial. Most trials proceed with a single judge and no jury. Jury trials are available for commercial matters, but a jury trial can be opposed if, for example, the case is deemed too complex for a jury to understand.

Burden of proof
The obligation of the plaintiff to prove its case.

Evidence
Proof presented in court to support a claim.

At trial, the **burden of proof** falls on the plaintiff. The plaintiff must formally introduce **evidence**, according to established rules, to prove that its version of events is more likely true than not, known as "proving the case on the balance of probabilities." Expressed numerically, the plaintiff must prove that there is a better than 50 percent chance that the circumstances of the dispute are as it contends they are and that, furthermore, these circumstances entitle it to receive the remedy that it seeks. The defendant has the opportunity to challenge the plaintiff's witnesses and documents and to introduce its own account of events to oppose the claim. The judge must decide what happened between the parties and whether their claims are justified. This is not generally a straightforward task, as the parties typically have widely differing versions of events. Once the facts have been established, the judge is then in a position to consider and apply the relevant law.

The parties make submissions about the legal rules and precedents that support their desired conclusion. The judge then identifies and applies relevant legal rules to those factual findings to produce a decision. The decision may be given by the judge immediately at the end of the trial or reserved until a later time, to allow the judge some time for deliberation.

The trial between Northland and its insurer is likely to proceed before a judge without a jury unless one side feels that a jury might be more sympathetic to its position than a judge. In a commercial matter such as this, that is unlikely to be the case. Northland, as plaintiff, will present its evidence to support its claim that its insurer is bound to honour the insurance policy and more specifically, that the machine in question failed as a result of an accident. The insurer will produce evidence in opposition to the Northland claim, suggesting that deficient maintenance procedures were the cause. In this case, a crucial issue is what caused the Northland equipment to fail. Both sides will likely rely on experts' reports to support their opposing versions of events.

The judge's **decision** contains the judge's resolution of the case—who must pay how much to whom—supported by the appropriate justification based on the evidence and legal rules. Though most plaintiffs seek a monetary award, other remedies are available in exceptional circumstances, such as when the successful party requests an order from the court for the losing party to perform a specific act (e.g., transfer a piece of land) or cease some activity (e.g., trespassing on property).

Decision

The judgment of the court that specifies which party is successful and why.

In the Northland litigation, the pivotal issue of what caused the machinery to fail would be determined by the judge, in part, on the basis of his or her assessment of expert reports on point. Also important would be the judge's assessment of the credibility of the witnesses who, for example, had responsibility to maintain the machinery in question. As previously noted, Northland, as plaintiff, has the onus of proof and must demonstrate to the judge, on the balance of probabilities, that the machinery failed due to an accidental fire and not improper maintenance.

Any monetary award includes the basic amount of the claim plus interest, and, in the usual case, the legal **costs** of the successful party. Costs are awarded by the judge based on a predetermined scale, combined with the judge's view of the complexity of the case. An award of costs usually falls well short of fully compensating the winning party for all its legal expenses. They provide only a partial recovery for the successful litigant. In Alberta, for example, costs typically only cover up to about one third of the successful party's actual legal costs. In short, even successful litigation involves expense. The downside for the losing party is significant: in addition to the amount of the judgment and interest, it is likely to be required to pay "costs" to the winner, as well as pay its own legal expenses.

Costs

Legal expenses that a judge orders the loser to pay the winner.

In exceptional cases where the conduct of the losing party has been seriously objectionable, the court may award what are known as solicitor and client costs. This award reflects the actual legal expenses incurred by the successful party so that they are fully indemnified for their litigation expenses.

The dispute between Northland and its insurer was resolved by litigation, with Northland being mainly successful. To obtain coverage on the bearing, the policy required that Northland produce complete maintenance records. It was unable to do so and, therefore, the judge disallowed that portion of the claim. Fortunately for Northland, the requirement to produce complete maintenance records did not apply to the conveyor belt and attendant losses. The court awarded damages for these losses because it was satisfied that the fire was triggered by an accident, as claimed by Northland. Beyond this, Northland was awarded its costs.

ENVIRONMENTAL PERSPECTIVE

The Risks of Environmental Litigation

Businesses that emit toxins on a large scale— such as chemical manufacturing plants, petroleum processing, and metal refineries—face an increased risk of class actions in relation to the release of pollutants. As already noted, class actions permit affected individuals to advance a claim on a group basis, thereby accessing legal resources, including representation by lawyers, that they almost certainly could never afford as individuals working alone.

For example, in 2000, Ellen Smith became alarmed upon learning of high levels of nickel contamination in the soil on her property in Port Colborne, Ontario. The nickel particles had come from Inco Ltd.'s nickel refinery, which had operated in the area starting in 1918 and ending in 1984. She was not alone. Residents were concerned about possible health risks and decreased property values accompanying such contamination. In response, a class action against Inco was eventually certified, meaning that a judge approved of a claim against Inco going to trial, where the full matter concerning Inco's liability could be adjudicated upon. The class of claimants approved to proceed in this action included those who owned residential property in most of Port Colborne; approximately 7000 properties were involved.

Among other matters, the trial judge ruled that the nickel particles which Inco operations deposited in the surrounding soil constituted physical damage to the properties in question. He also ruled that potential public health concerns surrounding such deposits meant that the properties in question failed to appreciate in value as much as they otherwise would have. On this basis, the trial judge went on to award the plaintiffs $36 million in damages.

In October of 2011, however, the Ontario Court of Appeal overturned this award.[22] Among this court's conclusions was that the nickel deposits did not cause physical harm to the properties in question, but merely changed the chemical composition of the soil—like fertilizer would, for example. For the plaintiffs to win their case, according to the Court of Appeal, they would also have to show some detrimental effect either on the land itself or on its use by the owners. Harm to the land could be demonstrated if there was evidence of harm to the claimant's health or that the nickel "at least posed some realistic risk of actual harm to their health and wellbeing."[23] The fact that nickel particles in the land raised public concerns about potential

DEBORAH BAIC/THE GLOBE AND MAIL/THE CANADIAN PRESS

How does the risk of litigation make industry more accountable for the pollution it may cause?

health risk was not enough. And in a fatal blow, the Court of Appeal concluded that the plaintiff had failed to show that there was insufficient appreciation in the value of the property affected by the nickel deposits. The Court of Appeal dismissed the plaintiffs' action in its entirety and awarded Inco costs of $100 000.

The Supreme Court of Canada has recently ruled that it will not hear Smith's appeal.

Critical Analysis: What are the risks that litigants such as Smith take in commencing an action of this kind? Are these risks outweighed by the possible benefits?

Source: Tracy Glynn, "Canada's Largest Environmental Lawsuit", *The Dominion* (12 July 2010) online: The Dominion <http://www.dominionpaper.ca/articles/3545>.

---

22. *Smith v Inco Ltd*, 2011 ONCA 628, 107 OR (3d) 321.
23. *Ibid* at para 57.

Enforcement

The fourth and final stage of the litigation process is enforcement of the judgment awarded to the winning party. The winner of the suit must enforce the judgment with the assistance of the court. The judge issues a judgment for a certain amount of money which, in turn, can be enforced against the loser, now known as the **judgment debtor**. If the judgment debtor fails to voluntarily pay the judgment, court officials or other designated persons will assist in seizing and selling the assets of that debtor, which may include land, vehicles, equipment, inventory, accounts receivable, and other assets. Laws in every jurisdiction limit the extent to which the winning party can take assets when the losing party is a human being rather than a corporation, the point being to ensure that the individual is not left destitute.

Judgment debtor
The party ordered by the court to pay a specified amount to the winner of a lawsuit.

The winner recovers the judgment only to the extent that the loser's assets provide. There is no public fund from which these judgments are paid. Therefore, it is advisable for a prospective plaintiff to investigate the defendant's ability to pay before commencing the suit. A judgment in any amount is generally of little value if the proposed defendant has insufficient assets to pay, has a large number of other unpaid creditors, or is in bankruptcy proceedings.

A judgment is valid for a long period (up to 20 years depending on the jurisdiction) and can be extended.

Appeals

A party who does not wish to accept the trial decision may consider an **appeal** to the next court in the hierarchy. An appeal must be initiated within a specific period of time (such as 30 days). There are several reasons an appeal should be undertaken only after careful consideration. In addition to the time and commitment required to pursue an appeal, the chances of success are limited. An appeal is not a rehearing of the case, but merely an opportunity to argue that the trial decision contains significant errors in how the law was applied. It is normally not possible to dispute the conclusions regarding what events actually transpired between the parties (i.e., what the trial judge found the "facts" to be), but only to dispute the judge's understanding and application of the law. Appeal courts tend to confirm trial decisions unless serious errors have been demonstrated.

Appeal
The process of arguing to a higher court that a court decision is wrong.

Appeals at higher levels are normally conducted by a panel of at least three judges. Generally, no new evidence is presented. The lawyers representing the **appellant** (who makes the appeal) and the **respondent** (who defends the appeal) make written and oral submissions to the appeal judges, who then decide whether to confirm the original decision, vary it in some way, reverse the decision, or, in exceptional cases, order that another trial be conducted.

Appellant
The party who begins or files an appeal.

After the court of appeal rules, the unsuccessful party can consider a further appeal to the Supreme Court of Canada. The appellant must obtain leave from the Supreme Court to proceed with that appeal. The leave application is only successful if the case involves a matter of "public importance" or involves an "important issue of law."[24] As a result, the chance of an appeal making it all the way to the Supreme Court of Canada is very slight.

Respondent
The party against whom an appeal is filed.

Developments in litigation (in particular, contingency fees, punitive damages, and class actions) are addressed in the following comparison of the systems in Canada and the United States.

---

24. Role of the Court: Leave to Appeal, online: Supreme Court of Canada <http://www.scc-csc.gc.ca/court-cour/role/index-eng.asp>

INTERNATIONAL PERSPECTIVE

The Risks of Litigation in the United States

A significant risk for Canadian companies doing business in the U.S. marketplace is litigation with competitors, partners, suppliers, customers, and governments. The incidence and costs of litigation in the U.S. are significant[25] and high in relation to Canada. Differences between the American and Canadian civil ligation systems contribute to the greater litigation risks in the U.S. The key differences are as follows:

Costs: In Canada, the losing party in civil litigation pays a portion of the winner's legal costs. In the U.S., there is no general rule[26] that the losing party pays any of the winner's legal costs. The "loser pay" rule in Canada increases risk and discourages weak and questionable cases. In the U.S., there is no such disincentive.

Jury Trials: In the U.S., litigants have a constitutional right to a jury trial. In Canada, jury trials, except for defamation and personal injury cases, are rare. Some cases are prohibited by statute from being tried by a jury, and even where juries are permissible, courts have a broad discretion to deny a jury if the legal or factual issues are complex or if the defendant may be prejudiced. The use of juries increases costs such as the costs of retaining jury consultants and increases risk because of the unpredictability of juries. Juries are often unsympathetic to business and may award large damages against such defendants. This poses a significant risk for business.

Damage Awards: Damage awards in the U.S. are much larger than in Canada, thus the incentives to sue are greater. In the U.S., punitive damages (to punish the loser) are generally available whereas in Canada they are rarely awarded and when they are, they are much lower than in the U.S.[27] Although many states have passed legislation capping punitive damage awards, the awards can still be 10 times the compensatory damages. Also, in Canada damages for pain and suffering in personal injuries cases are capped;[28] there are no similar caps in the U.S. A further factor contributing to large damage awards in the U.S. are statutes in areas such as antitrust that provide triple damages.

Class Actions: Class action lawsuits are widely available in the U.S. and create incentives to sue. A single individual with a small claim is not a great risk, but when many individuals with small claims unite and pursue their claims as a group, the risk for business is huge. In Canada, as described earlier, class actions are becoming more accessible and widely used so the distinction between the two systems on this basis may be decreasing.

Contingency Fees: The use of **contingency fees** is more widespread in the U.S. A contingency fee is an arrangement between the lawyer and the client where the lawyer receives a percentage of the judgment if the case is won and receives nothing (or disbursements only) if the case is lost. Such arrangements increase risk for business because they improve accessibility to the legal system for claimants who might otherwise lack the resources to sue.

Discovery: In the U.S., discovery rules are far-reaching. This results in more time-consuming and expensive litigation. U.S. litigants have broad powers to obtain oral and documentary evidence whereas in Canada oral discovery can be restricted in the number of persons who can be examined and time limits for examination.

Critical Analysis: How can Canadian businesses manage the litigation risks of doing business in the U.S.?

Sources: Berkley Sells, "Litigation: Civil Litigation in Canada and in the United States - Part 1", *Inside Counsel* (14 April 2011) online: Inside Counsel <http://www.insidecounsel.com/2011/04/14/litigation-civil-litigation-in-canada-and-the-united-states->; Berkley Sells, "Litigation: Some Key Differences between Civil Litigation in Canada and the United States - Part 2", *Inside Counsel* (28 April 2011) online: Inside Counsel <http://www.insidecounsel.com/2011/04/28/litigation-some-key-differences-between-civil-litigation-in-canada-and-the-united-states-part-2->; Berkley Sells, "Litigation: Some Key Differences between Civil Litigation in Canada and the United States—Part 3", *Inside Counsel* (12 May 2011) online: Inside Counsel <http://www.insidecounsel.com/2011/05/12/litigation-some-key-differences-between-civil-liti>; Richard S Sanders, "Litigation is a risk of doing business in the United States", *The Lawyers Weekly* (6 February 2004) 15.

Contingency fee

A fee based on a percentage of the judgment awarded, and paid by the client to the lawyer only if the action is successful.

---

25. The U.S. has a uniquely costly civil justice system with costs as a percentage of gross domestic product far higher than those in the rest of the developed world. See: Marie Gryphon, "Greater Justice, Lower Cost: How a "Loser Pays" Rule Would Improve the American Legal System", (2008) 11 *Civil Justice Report, Manhattan Institute for Policy Research* online: Manhattan Institute for Policy Research <http://www.manhattan-institute.org/html/cjr_11.htm>.
26. In the U.S., costs are generally not recoverable unless specifically permitted by statute or contract. However, many states are moving towards a 'loser pay' system. See: Adele Nicholas, "Texas' 'loser pay' law mixed bag for business", *Inside Counsel* (1 August 2011) online: Inside Counsel <http://www.insidecounsel.com/2011/08/01/texas-loser-pays-law-mixed-bag-for-business>.
27. For additional discussion of punitive damages awards in the U.S., see Chapter 10.
28. The cap is currently approximately $325 000 and is indexed to inflation.

FIGURE 4.2

Forms of Dispute Resolution

	Negotiation	**Mediation**	**Arbitration**	**Litigation**
Who is involved	Parties and/or their representatives	Parties and a mediator	Parties, their lawyers (usually) and arbitrator(s)	Parties, lawyers, a judge and, occasionally, a jury
When it is used	By consent or contract	By consent or contract or by statute	By consent or contract or by statute	By one party suing the other
How it works	Parties decide	Mediator assists the parties	Arbitrator makes decision after submissions	Judge makes decision after trial
When it ends	If successful, settlement	If successful, settlement	Binding decision (usually)	Judgment by the Court
Advantages	Quick, cheap, controllable, private, helps preserve relationships, may produce final decision	Quick, cheaper than arbitration and litigation, controllable, private, helps preserve relationships, may produce final decision	Can be quicker and less costly than litigation, can be private, choice of process and arbitrator, decision may be binding	No agreement to proceed required, sets precedent, final decision
Disadvantages	Requires agreement to proceed, no precedent, may fail	May require agreement to proceed, no precedent, may fail	May require agreement, can be as slow and expensive as litigation, imposed decision, no precedent, may destroy relationships	Slow, expensive, stressful, imposed decision, no choice over process and decision-maker, public, usually destroys relationships

Business Law in Practice Revisited

1. How well does Northland's risk management plan deal with these incidents and how could its performance have improved?

Marie prepared a comprehensive risk management plan for Northland which is found in Chapter 3 at Figure 3.3. The plan was largely successful because it anticipated numerous events that might give rise to legal consequences and offered solutions on how and when to reduce, transfer or accept the risks associated with those events. Four risks materialized and the effectiveness of the plan in relation to these incidents is recounted in more detail on pages 72–74 of this chapter. To recap:

- The delinquent customer situation was anticipated, but not avoided. Northland should have properly investigated the customer's credit worthiness in advance, particularly given the size of the account. Northland requires an improved system for deciding when to grant credit to customers and must ensure that the new system is properly deployed by its staff going forward.

- The hacking attempt was particularly well anticipated by the risk management plan. Firewalls helped prevent data loss and even though the attack caused a temporary shutdown of Northland's network, there was no lasting damage. Northland also had obtained insurance to cover off legal risks associated with such attacks, but the insurance proved to be under-inclusive. Northland should investigate purchasing a more comprehensive policy to cover additional costs associated with breaches of its computer system. Its insurance program requires enhancement.

- The risk management anticipated the pollution incident, but did not adequately prevent its occurrence. Northland must improve procedures for replacing scrubbers to prevent a future incident, a matter its insurance company will certainly require in any event. Fortunately, the dispute with the farmer whose land was impacted by the pollution was nicely resolved. The farmer was compensated to his relative satisfaction and he signed a confidentiality agreement. Insurance covered the cost of the settlement.

- The equipment breakdown proved to be the most intractable problem for Northland and highlighted a problem with the implementation of the risk management plan. Even though the plan called for maintenance records on all equipment, the records were incomplete. As a result, Northland was unsuccessful in recovering all of its losses. Setting aside this deficiency, it is hard to see how the dispute with the insurer over the interpretation of the insurance policy could have been avoided. Northland worked hard to resolve the dispute through negotiation and mediation, but a compromise was unattainable. Some disputes – albeit the tiny minority – can only be resolved by litigation.

2. How well does Northland deploy the various methods of dispute resolution in relation to the legal risks that materialized?

Northland accessed a variety of dispute resolution methods as it sought to manage the legal risks that had materialized. With the exception of the hacking attempt, each one of the incidents required negotiation. Negotiation alone solved the problem with the disgruntled farmer, likely propelled by Northland's open approach and willingness to offer an apology. Also through negotiation, Northland learned that the delinquent customer could not pay its bill and has simply decided to write the debt off. This outcome, though perhaps disappointing, is based on facts surrounding the customer's financial status and is therefore realistic. There is no sense spending money needlessly by launching what would almost certainly be a pointless lawsuit. In both these instances, therefore, ADR proved highly effective for Northland.

Northland's dispute with its insurer over coverage related to the equipment breakdown went through the phases of negotiation and mediation. Because the parties became unwilling to compromise, these phases failed to produce a resolution. Arbitration was not required by the contract between Northland and its insurer, but the parties considered the possibility in any event. This option was ultimately rejected, however, when the insurer decided it wanted a judge's interpretation concerning a clause in the insurance policy. Only litigation could produce the result the insurer wanted. As noted, not every dispute can be effectively resolved through ADR.

All in, Marie's risk management plan and Northland's willing to access ADR proved to be a highly successful combination. The risk management plan prevented or reduced a great many legal risks from occurring, but when they did occur, Northland's response was largely effective. As a result, only one of the disputes discussed in this chapter will be resolved through the slow, costly, and uncertain process of litigation.

Chapter Summary

This chapter has explored a range of disputes in which a business such as Northland might become involved. A risk management plan that is well developed and carefully implemented can minimize the number of disputes that arise and provide guidance for dealing with those that do. Legal disputes should be approached with a view to achieving an acceptable resolution, rather than winning at all costs.

There are a wide variety of techniques for resolving disputes that avoid litigation altogether or enable the parties to minimize damage to the businesses and their commercial relationships. The parties can negotiate their own resolution, or, if that is not possible, they can involve another person as a mediator to assist them or as an arbitrator to make a decision for them. If the parties resort to litigation, they are involving themselves in a lengthy, costly, public, and risky process with strict procedural rules. The process has four stages—pleadings, discovery, trial, and decision. The winner must collect the amount awarded by the court. That amount usually does not include full recovery of the legal expenses incurred to win the lawsuit.

Chapter Study

Key Terms and Concepts

alternative dispute resolution (ADR) (p. 74)

appeal (p. 89)

appellant (p. 89)

arbitrator (p. 80)

binding (p. 81)

burden of proof (p. 86)

claim (p. 85)

class action (p. 83)

contingency fee (p. 90)

costs (p. 87)

counterclaim (p. 85)

decision (p. 87)

defence (p. 85)

defendant (p. 82)

discovery (p. 85)

evidence (p. 86)

judgment debtor (p. 89)

limitation period (p. 82)

mediator (p. 78)

negotiation (p. 74)

plaintiff (p. 82)

pleadings (p. 85)

respondent (p. 89)

trial (p. 86)

Questions for Review

1. What are some business law disputes that could arise from the operation of a fast-food restaurant?

2. What is the goal of negotiation in resolving legal problems?

3. What happens when negotiations fail?

4. What is the process for attempting to resolve disputes informally?

5. What issues should a business consider before deciding to proceed with a legal dispute rather than abandon it?

6. What is mediation? What are the advantages of mediation as a method of resolving a dispute?

7. What are the differences between mediation and arbitration?

8. Why is arbitration particularly attractive in international disputes?

9. What are the advantages of arbitration in comparison to litigation?

10. What are the major steps in the litigation process?

11. What happens during the "discovery" stage of litigation?

12. Why is settlement out of court more common and preferable than going to trial?

13. How does a class action differ from a normal lawsuit?

14. What is a limitation period?

15. To what extent does the winner of a lawsuit recover the expenses of the litigation?

16. How does the winner of a lawsuit enforce the judgment?

17. What factors should be considered before appealing a court decision?

18. What is a contingency fee?

Questions for Critical Thinking

1. How could management use the various options for dispute resolution to deal with the disputes you identified in Question for Review 1? Which might be suitable for negotiation? mediation? arbitration? litigation?

2. The Canadian system of litigation partially compensates the winning party for its legal expenses through an award of "costs," to be paid by the loser in addition to any damages awarded by the court. In the United States, it is usual for the parties to bear their own costs. Which rule is fairer? Does the awarding of costs encourage or discourage litigation?

3. Class actions are growing in popularity as a way for a large number of small consumer claims that might otherwise have been ignored to be brought against a corporation. For example, Canadian purchasers of iPods brought a class action against Apple Inc. for the lack of staying power in their batteries. Apple settled and the purchasers were credited $44.75 each. Who benefits from a successful class action lawsuit? Who loses from a successful class action lawsuit?

4. Most jurisdictions in Canada now have an element of mandatory ADR in their systems of litigation. For example, in British Columbia all civil litigation with a few exceptions is subject to mandatory mediation. What is the purpose of requiring ADR prior to litigation? Is it logical to make ADR mandatory rather than consensual? Are weaker litigants at the mercy of stronger parties?

5. Alternate dispute resolution has many positive features. It can be faster and cheaper than litigation. And unlike litigation, the process can be confidential and the parties can control the process, the timing, and the selection of the facilitator. Are there any downsides to the avoidance of litigation in favour of ADR in the resolution of disputes? When is litigation the most appropriate method of resolving a dispute?

6. Consumers are buying many items such as books, food, and clothing on the Internet. They are not always satisfied with every aspect of their purchases. Complaints concern delivery of the wrong items, failure of items to meet statements and descriptions made on business websites, late delivery, refusal of returns, and problems with warranties. Consumers sometimes have difficulty contacting sellers and getting them to deal effectively with complaints. How appropriate are established methods of dispute resolution to deal effectively with these complaints? Are new rules needed? Is a specialized process needed?

Situations for Discussion

1. Diane Blanchard is in charge of purchasing for Best Produce Ltd. (BP), a wholesale dealer in fruit and vegetables. She is informed by the receiving department that BP has just received a large shipment of tropical fruit from a supplier, Tropical Delights Ltd. (TD), which has been reliable in the past. Not only is the shipment significantly short, but also the quality is poor and about 20 percent of the delivered product cannot be used. Identify the informal steps Diane could take to address this problem.

2. Tropical Delights has a new sales manager, Brad Carpenter, who is unwilling to concede anything. TD insists on full payment of $50 000 for the shipment in situation 1 above. Diane thinks a reduction in price of $15 000 would be fair for BP. Diane consults the legal department of BP and is advised to consider mediation as a means of resolving this dispute. Diane is not optimistic about the prospect of successful mediation in view of her recent dealings with Brad, but she knows that BP needs TD as a supplier of exotic fruit and suspects that TD values her company as a customer. Suggest how Diane might use mediation in this situation. What critical factors should Diane consider in deciding whether to pursue this dispute further?

3. Mediation failed and TD was unwilling to consider arbitration. Diane was unable to find another reliable supplier of exotic fruit. Meanwhile, TD sued BP for $50 000. Diane's CEO is puzzled and upset about TD's attitude. He is about to refuse to ever buy anything again from TD and to fight the lawsuit. Sarah Rickard, the CEO of Tropical Delights, was not consulted about the decision to sue BP. When she became aware of the litigation, Sarah was upset about the prospect of losing BP as a customer. When she investigated further, she discovered that several TD customers were unhappy with the service provided by TD in recent months and were seeking other suppliers. What should Sarah do about the BP lawsuit and her other dissatisfied customers? What arguments could Diane use to persuade her CEO to contact Sarah? Can Diane use her experience with TD to improve her relationship with suppliers in future?

4. The Loewen Group, based in Burnaby, B.C., was one of the largest owners of funeral homes in North America. Throughout the 1980s and 1990s, the company pursued a strategy of growth through the aggressive acquisition of U.S. funeral homes. In 1990, Loewen purchased Wright & Ferguson, the largest funeral operation in Jackson, Mississippi. Shortly after the purchase, a dispute arose concerning an earlier contract involving Gulf Insurance. Gulf alleged that Loewen had breached this earlier contract and sued Loewen for damages of $107 million. In 1995, a Jackson jury awarded the plaintiff $100 million in compensation and $400 million in punitive damages. The award equalled almost half the value of Loewen's assets and almost 13 times its 1994 profit of $38.5 million. Loewen vowed to appeal. However, under Mississippi law, Loewen was required to post a bond of 125 percent of the award—$625 million—while appeals were pending. Rather than face several years of uncertainty, the

company agreed to a settlement worth about $175 million.[29] Despite the settlement, the litigation seriously undermined Loewen's equity value and credit rating. The company eventually went bankrupt. Shareholders who lost their equity filed claims under NAFTA, but were unsuccessful. What does this case illustrate about the risks of doing business internationally and the uncertainties of litigation? How could Loewen have tried to avoid these uncertainties?

5. A woman from British Columbia, Saliha Alnoor, recently sued Colgate-Palmolive, alleging that she was injured by a defective toothbrush. She stated that the toothbrush snapped as she was brushing her teeth, which injured her gums and caused them to bleed profusely. Alnoor claimed that she had endured permanent injury and sought damages, including $94 000 in anticipated treatments. Colgate denied any wrongdoing. Soon after the trial began, the judge made several rulings against Alnoor, who was self-represented. Alnoor later agreed to drop her claim in response to Colgate's offer to waive legal costs against her (estimated at about $30 000) if she did so. According to the *National Post*, Alnoor's brother stated as follows: "We spent $21,000 on lawyers and experts, but we have no regrets. Now we know how justice works. Now we are much wiser."[30] Do you agree with Colgate's approach to Alnoor's litigation? What are the risks Colgate faced from the litigation? What are Alnoor's risks?

6. In 1959, the Canadian-born Lord Beaverbrook, a newspaper baron and member of Sir Winston Churchill's World War II war cabinet, established an art gallery in Fredericton, New Brunswick. Situated on the banks of the St. John River, the Beaverbrook Art Gallery houses an impressive collection of over 3000 pieces of Canadian and British art as well as unique sample of works from international artists.

In 2004, two charitable foundations founded by Lord Beaverbrook claimed ownership of over 200 paintings and sculptures, arguing that the paintings had not been gifts to the gallery but were merely

on loan. More specifically, the United Kingdom Beaverbrook Foundation (Foundation "A") claimed ownership of 133 paintings valued at more than $200 million, including JMW Turner's *Fountain of Indolence* valued at $25 million and Lucien Freud's *Hotel Bedroom* valued at $5 million. The Canada Beaverbrook Foundation (Foundation "B") claimed ownership of another 83 pieces of art. Both Foundations launched lawsuits against the Gallery and its board of directors in Great Britain while the Gallery sued the Foundations in N.B.

In 2006, the Gallery and Foundation A agreed to arbitration. Lawsuits by Foundation B were set aside pending the outcome of the arbitration with Foundation A. The parties chose retired Supreme Court Justice Peter Cory as arbitrator and hearings were held in public in Fredericton and Toronto. In March 2007, Cory ruled that of the 133 works, 85 including the core of the collection belonged to the Gallery and the other 48 belonged to Foundation A. Cory also ordered Foundation A to pay $2.4 million in compensation for several paintings it removed from the gallery over the years and costs of $4.8 million. Foundation A appealed, as under the terms of the arbitration a disputant could appeal if it felt that the arbitrator's ruling contained legal errors or disregarded important rules of evidence.[31]

In September 2009, a three-person appeal panel composed of retired judges upheld Cory's ruling in its entirety. In July 2010, Foundation A filed an application in the Court of Queen's Bench of New Brunswick to appeal the panel's results on a point of law. Before a hearing on the application was held, the parties reached a confidential settlement. Each side is estimated to have spent more than $10 million in legal fees.[32] The dispute between Foundation B and the Gallery is still on-going. It has been reported that the parties are meeting with a mediator to resolve their dispute. Why do you think Foundation A (the UK Foundation) and the Gallery chose arbitration for their dispute? What were the advantages of arbitration for the parties? How well did the dispute resolution methods work for the Gallery and the Foundations?

29. Based, in part, on Adam Liptak, "Review of US Rulings by Nafta Tribunals Stir Worries", *The New York Times* (18 April 2004) online: The New York Times <http://www.nytimes.com/2004/04/18/politics/18COUR.html?ex=1397620800&en=13814425a12bc791&ei=5007&partner=USERLAND>.

30. Brian Hutchinson, "BC woman walks away smiling from foolish 'killer toothbrush' lawsuit", *National Post* (5 January 2012) online: National Post <http://fullcomment.nationalpost.com/2012/01/04/brian-hutchinson-b-c-woman-walks-away-smiling-from-foolish-killer-toothbrush-lawsuit/>; Keith Fraser, "Toothbrush suit dropped", *Edmonton Journal* (5 January 2012) A10.

31. James Adams, "Beaverbrook foes go at it again in $100-million battle", *The Globe and Mail* (20 September 2008) R4.

32. Marty Klinberg, "Lengthy Beaverbrook art dispute has drawn to a close", *New Brunswick Telegraph-Journal* (15 September 2010) online New Brunswick Telegraph-Journal <http://www.globalnews.ca/lengthy+beaverbrook+art+dispute+has+drawn+to+a+close/83952/story.html>.

7. In 1997, the Flynns hired Applewood Construction to build them an environmentally friendly home. The house was erected on a concrete slab. The Flynns moved into their new home and discovered within the first year that the concrete slab had cracked, causing considerable damage to the structure. The Flynns successfully sued Applewood for damages, but before they could collect, Applewood went out of business. In 2005, the Flynns sued Superior Foundation who had been hired by Applewood to pour the concrete slab.[33] What defence might Superior have against the Flynns' claim?

8. In 2008, several hundred people became ill and a number of them died as the result of an outbreak of the listeria bacteria. The illnesses were traced to the consumption of deli meats that were produced from a single processing plant operated by MegaMeats Inc. Those most affected by the bacteria were the elderly, the very young, and those who were already ill. Is this an appropriate situation for a class action lawsuit? What do the victims have in common? How are their claims different? What process must be followed? How should MegaMeats deal with these claims?

For more study tools, visit http://www.NELSONbrain.com.

---

33. Based, in part, on *Flynn v Superior Foundations Ltd*, 2008 NSSC 296, 269 NSR (2d) 279.

PART TWO

Contracts

Business relies on contract law—more than any other area of law—to facilitate commerce. Contract law provides a structure through which individuals and organizations are able to create legally binding, commercial commitments. Essentially, parties must keep their contractual promises or pay damages to the other side for breach.

A working knowledge of contract law is essential to anyone involved in business. This knowledge is crucial because the law advances commercial activities and can be used to build productive and cooperative business relationships. In fact, contract law forms the basis of many commercial relationships, including employment, credit, property, and insurance dealings, as well as the sale of goods and services.

ISTOCKPHOTO/THINKSTOCK

CHAPTER 5

An Introduction to Contracts

Objectives

After studying this chapter, you should have an understanding of

- the general concept of a contract
- the legal factors in the contractual relationship
- the business factors influencing the formation and performance of contracts

Business Law in Practice

Amritha Singh is a middle manager with Coasters Plus Ltd. (Coasters), a company that designs and manufactures roller coasters for amusement parks across North America. She has been appointed one of the project managers for the design and delivery of a special roller coaster for the Ultimate Park Ltd., an American customer. A major component of the project is the steel tracking, and one possible source is Trackers Canada Ltd. (Trackers). Amritha's supervisor has asked her to negotiate the necessary contract. This task causes Amritha some concern, since she has never been solely responsible for contractual negotiations before. She does know, however, that Coasters needs a reliable supplier that can deliver high-quality tracking for under $2 million, and in good time for installation at the Ultimate Park site.

1. How should Amritha approach her task of securing the necessary tracking?
2. How can the law facilitate Amritha's acquisition task?
3. What rules apply to a commercial relationship between a manufacturer (such as Coasters) and a supplier (such as Trackers), and how are disputes resolved?
4. What are the legal consequences to Coasters of assigning the negotiation task to Amritha?
5. What are the non-legal factors contributing to the proposed legal agreement?

ISTOCKPHOTO/THINKSTOCK

DAVID TOASE/PHOTODISC

Introduction to Contract Law

Amritha needs to extract a firm commitment from Trackers to ensure that Coasters receives the necessary tracking in a timely fashion at the agreed-upon price (see Figure 5.1 on page 102). The flip side of her task is to ensure that—should Trackers renege—Coasters can sue Trackers to recover any related financial loss. Simply put, Amritha needs to negotiate and secure a contract with Trackers on behalf of her company.

A **contract** is a deliberate and complete agreement between two or more competent persons, not necessarily in writing, supported by mutual consideration, to do some act voluntarily. By definition, a contract is enforceable in a court of law.

What follows is a brief synopsis of these elements, which are analyzed more comprehensively in subsequent chapters.

- **An agreement.** An agreement is composed of an offer to enter into a contract and an acceptance of that offer. This is a matter explored in Chapter 6. The promises contained in the agreement are known as terms. These are discussed in Chapter 7. The informing idea behind a contract is that there has been a "meeting of the minds"— that the parties have agreed on what their essential obligations are to each other.

- **Complete.** The agreement must be complete, that is, certain. Certainty is explored in Chapter 6.

- **Deliberate.** The agreement must be deliberate, that is, both parties must want to enter into a contractual relationship. This matter—formally known as an intention to create legal relations—is discussed in Chapter 6.

- **Voluntary.** The agreement must be freely chosen and not involve coercion or other forms of serious unfairness. This is explored in Chapter 8.

Contract

An agreement between two parties that is enforceable in a court of law.

- **Between two or more competent persons.** Those who enter into a contract are known as parties to the contract. There must be at least two parties to any contract, who must have legal capacity—a matter discussed in Chapter 8. As a general rule, only parties to a contract can sue and be sued on it. This matter is discussed in Chapter 9.

- **Supported by mutual consideration.** A contract involves a bargain or exchange between the parties. This means that each party must give something of value in exchange for receiving something of value from the other party. Expressed in legal terminology, a contract must be supported by mutual consideration. This is discussed in Chapter 6.

- **Not necessarily in writing.** As a general rule, even oral contracts are enforceable, though it is preferable for negotiators to get the contract in writing. That said, in most Canadian jurisdictions there are certain kinds of contracts—such as those involving an interest in land—that must be in writing in order to be enforceable. These exceptions are discussed in Chapter 8.

The genius of contract law is that once a contract is created, it permits both parties to rely on the terms they have negotiated and plan their business affairs accordingly. If a dispute arises between the two parties, there are various options for dispute resolution, outlined in Chapter 4. This includes taking the matter to court and suing for losses sustained. In short, contract law ensures that each party gets what it bargained for—namely, performance of the promises made to it or monetary compensation in its place. Chapter 9 discusses the termination and enforcement of contracts.

For the most part, the rules governing contracts are based on common law. The common law, as discussed in Chapter 2, refers to judge-made laws, as opposed to laws made by elected governments. This means that a judge resolving a contractual conflict is usually relying not on statute law to guide deliberations, but rather on what other judges have said in past cases that resemble the current case. As noted in Part One, these past cases are known as precedents because they contain a legal principle found in a past situation similar to the one being litigated. The judge will hear evidence from the two parties in support of their respective positions and then determine which common law rules of contract are applicable to the situation and what the outcome should be. Depending on the nature of the contract, legislation such as the *Sale of Goods Act* may also be relevant.

FIGURE 5.1

A Contract Contains Binding Promises

Through a contract:

Trackers
makes binding promises concerning price, quantity, and delivery of tracking to
➡ **Coasters**

Coasters
makes a binding promise to pay the purchase price to
➡ **Trackers**

Contracts are the legal cornerstone of any commercial operation. Through a contract, the business enterprise can sell a product or service, hire employees, rent office space, borrow money, purchase supplies, and enter into any other kind of binding agreement it chooses. In this way, contract law is facilitative: it allows participants to create their own rights and duties within a framework of rules that a judge will later enforce, if called upon to do so.

Contracts come in a wide variety. A contract for the purchase and sale of a box of pens from the corner store, for example, is casually conducted and instantly completed. The only document that will be produced is the sales receipt. Other contracts, such as for the purchase and sale of high-quality tracking for a commercial project, will require lengthy negotiations, considerable documentation, and time to perform. Some contracts are one-shot deals, in that the parties are unlikely to do business with each other again. Other contracts are part of a long-standing and valued commercial relationship, as one might find between supplier and retailer. Regardless of the context, however, every contract is subject to the same set of mandatory legal rules. This means that contract law principles will be applied by a judge to resolve a contractual dispute between the parties, whether the parties were aware of those principles or not.

Amritha's attention is currently focused on one transaction: her company's acquisition of tracking from a suitable supplier. Her goal should be to enter into a contract with a supplier like Trackers, because Coasters requires legally enforceable assurances that its supplier will fulfill its commitments. The alternative to a contract—in the form of a casual understanding—makes little business sense, even if Trackers is highly reputable and trustworthy, because cooperation and goodwill between parties can suddenly evaporate when an unforeseen conflict or problem arises. Personnel can change, memories may become selective and self-serving, and genuine differences of opinion may arise. At this point, Amritha's company needs the protection of a well-constructed contract—including the right to commence a lawsuit based upon it—not the vague assurances she may have received from Trackers personnel sometime in the past.

This is not to say that informal business arrangements never succeed, but only that there is no remedy in contract law should one of the parties fail to keep its word. This is a risk that a business should ordinarily not be prepared to run.

CASE | **Tal v Ontario Lottery Corporation/Lotto 6/49 OLG, 2011 ONSC 644**

BUSINESS CONTEXT: Lottery sales are big business in Canada, with over $7.7 billion in sales over 2010 alone.[1] This volume makes it particularly essential that clear rules governing the pay-out process are in place and contractually enforceable. Disappointed lottery ticket purchasers have sued lottery agencies, alleging breach of these rules, though not always with success, as this case illustrates.

FACTUAL BACKGROUND: The plaintiff, David Tal, is a 74-year-old retired business man. He held a winning 4/6 ticket in the October 1, 2008, draw of the Lotto 6/49 game in that he matched four out of the six numbers selected. The applicable prize pool for 4/6 winners was over $1.3 million but because 20 000 other players held a winning ticket, the amount was divided equally amongst them all, with a per-person pay-out of $66.90.

(Continued)

---

1. North American Association of State and Provincial Lotteries, "Lottery Sales and Profits", online: NASPL <http://www.naspl.org/index .cfm?fuseaction=content&menuid=17&pageid=1025>.

Mr. Tal, however, read the rules differently and took the position that he was entitled to the full amount of the prize pool. He sued for $3 182 667.81 in damages—the amount he claims the pool to be—plus $35.3 million in punitive damages. (Note that the law governing punitive damages is discussed in detail in Chapter 9.)

THE LEGAL QUESTION: What are the contractual rules governing the Lotto 6/49 game in this case? Which party has interpreted them correctly?

RESOLUTION: The court decided in favour of the lottery organization. It confirmed that the parties were in a contract that was formed as follows: the lottery organization made an offer to the public to play a lottery game governed by written rules that the plaintiff accepted by purchasing the ticket. The written rules therefore were part of the contract and governed this dispute.

The court went on to note that the lottery organization had properly applied those rules:

> Pursuant to the Winning Selections Reports prepared by the regional and provincial lottery organizations, there were 20,120 4/6 Winners nation-wide for the October 1 Draw, of whom 8,353 were located in Ontario. Pursuant to ss. 6 and 8 of the …Game Conditions, each of these 4/6 Winners was entitled to a share of the 4/6 Pool, which was calculated by dividing the dollar amount of the 4/6 Pool ($1,347,143.10) by the total number of 4/6 Winners (20,120). This amounted to a prize of $66.90 per 4/6 Winner (after being rounded down from $66.96 pursuant to s. 8 of the ILC Game Conditions).

The court rejected all the plaintiff's arguments to the contrary. For example, the plaintiff asserted an interpretation of the rules such that *every* 4/6 winner was entitled to the entire pool as opposed to merely sharing in it. This was rejected as contrary to the plain meaning of the rule in question as well as being commercially absurd. As the court stated:

> If all 20,120 of the 4/6 Winners were entitled to a prize of $1,347,143.10, over $26 <u>billion</u> in prizes

STEVE WHITE/THE CANADIAN PRESS

would have to be paid out to just the 4/6 Winners in that one Draw. This amount is more than 600 times higher than the total national ticket sales of approximately $42 million for the October 1 Draw. . . . [T]he regional and provincial lottery organizations would lose billions of dollars in virtually every Lotto 6/49 draw, making this lottery game completely unsustainable.

CRITICAL ANALYSIS: Do you think this case could have been settled out of court? Why or why not?

This chapter has thus far introduced the *legal* elements to a contract, but *business* factors also figure prominently in contractual relationships. The next section locates important legal factors in their business context. Without this context, the legal ingredients of a contract cannot be properly understood.

BUSINESS APPLICATION OF THE LAW

Concert Hall Cancels Alleged Contract with Maximum Fighting Inc.

The Francis Winspear Centre for Music ("Winspear"), through its foundation, is alleged to have entered into a contract to lease its premises to Maximum Fighting Inc. ("MFI"), a mixed martial arts promoter, for three Maximum Fighting Championship ("MFC") events in exchange for a rental fee. According to press accounts, the concert hall then cancelled the arrangement, saying that the booking had been made in error.

PERRY NELSON/QMI AGENCY

Ryan Jimmo, pictured above, won the MFC light heavyweight title in 2011 at the River Cree Resort and Casino in Alberta.

By way of explanation, a Winspear spokesperson said that the facility was designed for concerts, was not a "suitable venue" for MFC events, and offered an apology:

> It is regrettable that this unfortunate situation has occurred and the Winspear Centre has taken steps to ensure that it never happens again. The Winspear has extended its apology to representatives of MFC for what has transpired.

Mark Pavelich, president of MFC, responded by filing a $500 000 lawsuit against the foundation responsible for operating the Winspear Centre, alleging breach of contract. The claim seeks compensation for loss of profit, loss of sponsorship funds, out of pocket expenses—such as printing and advertising—as well as for embarrassment and damage to reputation.

Critical Analysis: Is there a contract between the Winspear Foundation and MFI and if so, what are the terms? Do you think that the Winspear foundation has a successful defence, namely that the booking itself was a 'mistake' and the music hall was not suitable for sporting events? How can these kind of disputes be best resolved?

Source: Elizabeth Withey, "No more fight night at Winspear Centre", *Edmonton Journal* (23 January 2010) D1, and Tony Blais "MMA promoter sues over cancelled match", *Edmonton Sun* (9 August 2010) online: Edmonton Sun <http://www.edmontonsun.com/news/edmonton/2010/08/09/14972086.html>.

Legal Factors in Their Business Context: Creating the Contract

Communication

Most contractual relationships begin with communication, which may originate in a number of ways—through informal contact between individuals in different businesses who recognize mutual needs, or perhaps through a general inquiry made to a supplier concerning price and availability of materials. Amritha may initiate contact with potential suppliers based on recommendations from others in her company who have purchasing experience, from colleagues in the industry, or from industry organizations. And, of course, Coasters may be approached periodically by tracking suppliers. Regardless of who makes the first move, Amritha will likely communicate with a number of businesses in order to determine who can give her company the most favourable terms.

Communication is not just about discussing possibilities with the other side, however. Communication—in the form of contractual negotiations—is automatically laden with legal meaning. It is therefore important for the businessperson to know when simple business communications crystallize into legal obligations.

ETHICAL CONSIDERATIONS

Is It Ethical to Bluff during Business Negotiations?

Albert Carr, in a well-known article published in the *Harvard Business Review*, argues that business is a game and therefore is not subject to the same ethical standards that govern one's private life. On this footing, it is perfectly acceptable for a businessperson to bluff during negotiations since it is merely strategic—just as it is in poker—and does not reflect on the morality of the bluffer. According to Carr:

> Most executives from time to time are almost compelled, in the interests of their companies or themselves, to practice some form of deception when negotiating with customers, dealers, labor unions, government officials, or even other departments of their companies. By conscious misstatements, concealment of pertinent facts, or exaggeration—in short, by bluffing—they seek to persuade others to agree with them. I think it is fair to say that if the individual executive refuses to bluff from time to time—if he feels obligated to tell the truth, the whole truth, and nothing but the truth—he is ignoring opportunities permitted under the rules and is at heavy disadvantages in his business dealings.

Carr goes on to argue that, like every poker player, a businessperson can be faced with a choice between certain loss or "bluffing within the legal rules of the game." The individual who wants to win and have a successful career "will bluff—and bluff hard."

Carr is not suggesting that businesspeople break the law to seek an advantage in business negotiations. He is, however, claiming that the morality of the businessperson who conceals, exaggerates, or misstates is simply not in question. Short of fraud or actionable misrepresentation, bending the truth a little is simply playing the game of business.

Critical Analysis: What are the dangers of Carr's approach to business ethics? What are the possible benefits?

Source: Albert Z Carr, "Is Business Bluffing Ethical?" (1968) 46: 1 Harvard Business Review 143.

First and foremost, contract law concerns itself with what the negotiators say and do, not with what they think or imagine. For example, if Amritha makes what looks like an offer to purchase tracking, the other side is entitled to accept that offer whether it was intended as one or not. This is because contract law is governed by the **objective standard test**. This test asks whether a reasonable person, observing the communication that has occurred between the negotiators, would conclude that an offer and acceptance had occurred. Assuming that all the other ingredients of a contract are in place, the parties are completely bound.

Objective standard test
The test based on how a "reasonable person" would view the matter.

Bargaining Power

The kind of contract a businessperson ends up creating is very much influenced by her bargaining power. The business reality is that negotiating parties rarely have equal bargaining power. It is almost invariably the case that one side will have more experience, knowledge,

DILBERT © SCOTT ADAMS. USED BY PERMISSION OF UNIVERSAL UCLICK. ALL RIGHTS RESERVED.

market leverage, or other advantages. The greater one's bargaining power, of course, the more favourable terms one will be able to secure.

The law, however, does not recognize or attach legal significance to this business reality. On the contrary, contract law is constructed on the basic assumption that those who negotiate and enter into contracts have **equal bargaining power,** meaning that they are capable of looking out for themselves and will work to maximize their own self-interest. As a result, courts are normally not entitled to assess the fairness or reasonableness of the contractual terms the business parties have chosen. Courts will generally assume that the parties had their eyes open, considered all the relevant factors, evaluated the risks, and were prepared to accept both the costs and benefits of the contract.

The law applies the principle of equality of bargaining power even though, in almost every situation, one party will have some distinct advantage over the other. The rationale is that parties should be able to rely on contractual commitments. Though one party may have agreed to a price she now considers too high or, in fact, may have made a bad deal, none of this is justification for securing the court's assistance and intervention. People are simply expected to take care of themselves.

Occasionally, however, circumstances favour one party over the other to such an extent that the court will come to the assistance of the weaker party and set the contract aside. Such judicial assistance is very much the exception, not the rule.

The fact that Amritha may have less bargaining power than the tracking supplier she contracts with does not generally affect the enforceability of their concluded contract. On the contrary, Amritha must be careful to protect her company's position and not enter into a bad bargain. Coasters is unlikely to succeed in having any contract set aside because Amritha was an inexperienced negotiator or because the supplier was a relatively bigger, more powerful company.

Legal Factors in Their Business Context: Performing or Enforcing the Contract
Business Relationships

Businesspeople regularly breach contracts. For example, a purchaser may fail to pay invoices on a timely basis. A supplier may deliver the wrong product, or the wrong amount of product, or a defective product. All these amount to breaches of contract. Whether the other side sues for breach of contract, however, is as much a business decision as it is a legal one.

Contract law is narrow in scope: its emphasis is often on a specific transaction, such as a single sale, and is not traditionally concerned with longer-term business relationships. Because contract law does not focus on the longer-term relationship, one may be misled into thinking that when faced with a legal wrong, the best response is a lawsuit. When the business context is considered, however, this approach reveals itself to be counter-productive in many circumstances. For example, if Coasters' supplier is late in delivering its tracking, the supplier is in breach of contract, and Coasters will be entitled to compensation for any resulting loss, such as that caused by late completion of the project for the Ultimate Park. However, if Coasters insists on that compensation, the relationship with that supplier may be irreparably harmed. Absorbing the loss in this instance—or splitting

Equal bargaining power
The legal assumption that parties to a contract are able to look out for their own interests.

PART TWO

the difference—may be a small price to pay in the long term, particularly if the supplier is otherwise reliable and Coasters is not interested in investing time and money in finding a replacement. Put another way, insisting on one's strict legal rights may not be the best business option.

The expense and uncertainty of litigation are also reasons to avoid a full-blown legal conflict.

BUSINESS APPLICATION OF THE LAW

Seeing the Big Picture

Even with a comprehensive contract in place defining the obligations and relationship between a customer and service provider, issues can arise because contracts can never be entirely black and white. There is an inevitable grey area. In dealing with a customer who seeks to expand or restrict a contract on a large project, for example, owners and managers can approach the question with a number of objectives in mind, including

- maintaining the project's profitability;
- treating the customer with respect while seeking a standard of reasonableness in return;
- ensuring that the work is completed on a safe and timely basis without incident;

- not approaching matters legalistically. Down the legal road, one faces intractable positions and an ultimate settlement based not on the "correct answer" but on how each side perceives its risk of losing the lawsuit. It is much more preferable to find practical ways of interpreting contracts to arrive at resolutions to issues;
- understanding that business relationships are long-term, and so is reputation.

Critical Analysis: Why is a contract an imperfect tool for defining the rights and obligations of a service provider and customer?

Source: Personal interview with Terry Freeman, CA, Managing Director of Northern Plains Investment Capital Ltd. and former Chief Financial Officer of Flint Energy Services Ltd.

Economic Reality

Though contract law exists to create legally binding commitments, it is not always the best economic decision for a party to keep that commitment. The law has some built-in flexibility, since it requires contractual obligations to be performed or compensation to be paid for non-performance. Accordingly, there may be situations where the cost of compensation is a perfectly acceptable price to pay for release from obligations. For example, a business whose production is committed to a one-year contract may be quite willing to pay what is necessary to be relieved of the one-year obligation if a more profitable, long-term deal becomes available for the same production. This idea is explained further in the Business Application of the Law box below.

BUSINESS APPLICATION OF THE LAW

Economic Breach

An economic breach occurs when one party calculates that it is more financially rewarding to breach the contract in question than to perform it. For instance, suppose hypothetically, that Trackers signs a contract to deliver tracking to Coasters for $2 million in two equal installments. After Trackers has delivered half the order, another business contacts Trackers and explains that, owing to an emergency, it desperately needs tracking to complete a major project. This new business offers Trackers $2 million to supply the same amount of tracking

still owed to Coasters—double the price that Trackers would receive from Coasters. Trackers has several options in response to this new request:

- *Option 1*: Complete delivery to Coasters as agreed and decline the new business' request.
- *Option 2*: Try to persuade Coasters to accept late delivery of the remainder of its order and offer a price break as an incentive.
- *Option 3*: Abandon the balance of Coasters' contract and fill the new business' order.

Each option has its own economic and legal consequences:

• *Option 1* respects the Coasters contract and maintains good relations with Coasters but concedes the extra profit and the potential relationship to be gained from filling the new business' order.

• *Option 2* has the potential to satisfy both customers and to gain from the new business (less some portion for Coasters as compensation).

• *Option 3* generates extra profit and a potential long-term relationship with the new business, but it destroys any relationship with Coasters and likely will lead to a claim for compensation from Coasters for its extra tracking cost and potential losses from late completion of the project. Before accepting the competitor's order, Trackers needs to assure itself that the extra profit generated from the new business will offset the damages it will have to pay to Coasters for breach of contract. Those damages could be quite high, depending on the circumstances, and difficult for Trackers to assess.

There is no question that Trackers has a legal obligation to Coasters, but that does not preclude Trackers from considering other opportunities. If Trackers chooses to breach the contract, there are also non-financial factors to be considered, such as future relations with Coasters, but in legal terms, a business that is prepared to pay damages for breach of contract can always refuse to perform its contractual obligations. Contract law provides compensation for breach, rather than punishment. There are no criminal consequences to breach of contract, and the law has traditionally refrained from making moral judgments about business activities.

Note: For further discussion of economic breach, see Richard Posner, *Economic Analysis of Law*, 8th ed (Wolters Kluwer Law & Business, 2010).

Reputation Management

A business that makes a practice of breaching contracts due to bad planning or to pursue an apparently more lucrative business opportunity will certainly be within its legal rights to breach and pay damages in lieu of performance. Such a business is also likely to acquire a reputation in the industry as an unreliable and undependable company. The long-term viability of a business organization is undoubtedly compromised if customers, suppliers, and employees grow reluctant to deal with it.

Similarly, a business that insists on strict observance of its legal rights may damage its reputation in the marketplace. Although a manufacturer may have a valid defence for having produced a defective product, for example, it may be better in the end to compensate the customer voluntarily rather than fight out a lawsuit. A lawsuit in the circumstances of this example may result in a serious blow to reputation and a public relations disaster.

Business Law in Practice Revisited

1. How should Amritha approach her task of securing the necessary tracking?
Given the size and expense of the proposed acquisition of tracking, Amritha should make it a priority to enter into a contract with a supplier such as Trackers. Nothing less than a contract will do, since Coasters must be able to exercise its legal right to sue, should Trackers fail to perform as promised.

2. How can the law facilitate Amritha's acquisition task?
Legal knowledge will help Amritha ensure that her negotiations produce an enforceable contract that meets her employer's needs and protects its interests. If Amritha does not know what a contract is, how it is formed, and what its legal significance might be, she is not competent to accomplish the task her employer has set for her.

3. What rules apply to a commercial relationship between a manufacturer (such as Coasters) and a supplier (such as Trackers), and how are disputes resolved?

The rules governing contracts are found in the common law (which develops through the decisions of the courts on a case-by-case basis), and to a lesser extent, in statute law. If a dispute arises between Coasters and Trackers, there are several options available for attempting to resolve the dispute, including mediation and arbitration. Litigation is a last resort and will bring the matter to court. A judge will evaluate the terms of the contract and the conduct of the parties, apply the relevant law, and then come to a determination.

4. What are the legal consequences to Coasters of assigning the negotiation task to Amritha?

Amritha is representing her employer in negotiations and therefore will need to appreciate at what point legal commitments are being made by both sides. Coasters should consider its relative bargaining position with available suppliers and ensure that Amritha has adequate support in her negotiations. Her inexperience and Coasters' size and expertise in contract negotiations will not relieve Coasters of its obligations. The contract itself will be between Coasters and the supplier (as the parties to the contract). They are the only parties able to enforce rights and the only parties that are subject to the obligations in the contract.

5. What are the non-legal factors contributing to the proposed legal agreement?

If Coasters has a good working relationship with companies that can supply the required tracking, those suppliers are the logical candidates for Amritha's project. Their business practices and reliability will be known to Coasters, and negotiating a contract with them is likely to be more efficient than with a new supplier. Even a significant price advantage from a new supplier may not justify endangering long-term relationships with others.

Although both parties are obligated by the terms of any contract they make, there may be developments in the market or in the situation relating to the operations of Coasters or Trackers. The request to Trackers from a competitor of Coasters for the supply of tracking is only one example of an event that may cause these companies to reconsider their business and legal relationship. They must weigh all factors, including long-term business dealings and their reputation in the industry, when faced with a decision about whether to honour the contract, seek adjustment, or consider breaching the contract.

Chapter Summary

Through an awareness of contract law, business organizations are better able to protect themselves when forming and enforcing contracts. Contracts generally are not required to be in a particular form, but clear agreement on all essential terms is necessary. Those involved in negotiating contracts should be aware of the legal impact of their communication with each other, and they should realize that they are largely responsible for protecting their own interests before agreeing to terms. Contract rules are understood best when assessed in the broader business context, which includes the impact that any given legal decision by a business may have on its reputation with other businesses, with its customers, and in the community at large. A business must also assess its legal options in light of the business relationship at issue, the need to generate a profit, the uncertainty of the marketplace, and the importance of conducting operations with a sense of commercial morality, honesty, and good faith.

Chapter Study

Key Terms and Concepts

contract (p. 101)

equal bargaining power (p. 107)

objective standard test (p. 106)

Questions for Review

1. What is a contract?

2. What are the elements of a contract according to the common law?

3. Must all contracts be in writing in order for them to be legally binding?

4. What are the purposes of contract law?

5. Is the matter of whether a contract exists judged according to a subjective standard or an objective one? Explain.

6. Contract law assumes that parties have equal bargaining power. What is the effect of this assumption?

7. How does the presence of a written contract assist in dispute resolution?

8. What is the role of public relations in contracts?

9. What is an economic breach?

10. Why might a business elect to not perform on a contract, and what are some of the consequences that may arise from this decision?

Questions for Critical Thinking

1. Is there a better way to resolve disputes about contracts than by applying common law rules in litigation?

2. Should the law insist that there be actual equal bargaining power between the parties before a contract can be formed? What would the dangers of such a rule be?

3. Why are the non-legal factors in a contractual relationship so important? Why is it important to place contract law in a business context?

4. Should negotiators follow a course of strict and absolute honesty in contractual negotiations? Why or why not?

5. How important is it to be aware of the law when negotiating a contract? Does it depend on who you negotiate with? Does it depend on the size and complexity of the contract in question?

6. How could relying on the notion of economic breach prove disastrous to a business?

Situations for Discussion

1. Trackers is a supplier of tracking, which is used by customers in a variety of applications. Trackers' business is booming, and its scheduling is tight for meeting delivery commitments. Trackers is contacted by a representative of Coasters, who inquires whether Trackers is capable of providing tracking for a special roller coaster in Florida and, if so, what price Trackers could offer and when could it deliver. Trackers knows that Coasters is a leader in the industry and would be a valuable customer. What factors should Trackers consider before responding to the Coasters inquiry? What are the risks and benefits of agreeing to fill Coasters' order?

2. Jason, the owner of a furniture store, is thinking about hiring an independent contractor to do deliveries for him.[2] If the independent contractor proves unreliable, Jason is, of course, entitled to sue to recover his losses. How else does inadequate performance by the independent contractor put Jason at risk and how can that risk be reduced?[3]

3. Melissa, an accounting student, interviews for a job with two firms. She really wants to work for Firm X but gets an offer of employment from Firm Y first and accepts it. A week later she receives an offer from Firm X, which she also accepts. She does so because she believes she is economically better off with firm X and will be able to "cancel" her acceptance with Firm Y.

   a. What is Melissa's legal situation now?

   b. Even assuming that she is better off economically by joining Firm X, what other costs does she face?

---

2. For a discussion regarding the difference between an employee and an independent contractor, see Chapter 20.

3. Based, in part, on *Total E-com Home Delivery Inc v Smith*, 2008 NSSC 37.

c. Do you think that Firm Y will sue Melissa for breach of contract because she has accepted an employment offer elsewhere?

d. What could Melissa have done to prevent this situation from occurring in the first place?

e. What should Melissa do now?

4. Samantha Jones entered into a contract with Jason Black to act as a contractor for a new house she is having built. She was anxious to have the house built as soon as possible, and upon receiving Jason's estimate that the work, including labour and materials, will cost $250 000, she immediately paid a $50 000 deposit. However, since receiving Samantha's deposit, Jason has been contacted by a developer who is willing to pay him a significant amount more to work on a new housing development, provided that he begin immediately. Jason does some calculations based on the current market. He decides that the amount the developer is offering is enough that he can afford to return the deposit, compensate Samantha for breaching the original contract, and still come out ahead on the development contract. He lets Samantha know that she will have to find a new contractor and begins work on the housing development. When he calls Samantha a few months later to offer her compensation, she informs him that she has finally been able to hire a new contractor, but that the estimate for the work has now doubled. In the intervening months, the costs of labour and materials have skyrocketed. The house that originally would have cost $250 000 will now cost her $500 000. Do you think that Jason should be responsible for the additional costs of building Samantha's house, even though they very much exceed his original estimates?

5. Mr. Leopold applied to his provincial government for a student loan and was advanced $13 500. The loan agreement obligated the government to advance further funds midway through the school year. Mr. Leopold stopped attending classes in September for medical reasons but did not advise his university's Student Services Office of this, contrary to a term in his loan agreement. He also used the funds for living expenses instead of for tuition, contrary to the loan agreement. The university determined that Mr. Leopold was not eligible for the second installment of his loan, and the government therefore refused to advance it. Mr. Leopold sued the government for breach of contract and sought damages in the amount of $1.5 million. Do you think Mr. Leopold's action should be successful? Why or why not?[4]

6. A 22-year-old Grande Prairie man was shocked to receive an $85 000 cellphone bill from Bell Canada. The reason for the high cost was that the customer had been using his cellphone as a modem for almost two months. In one month alone, he downloaded what amounted to 10 high-resolution movies, according to Bell. The customer contended that he did not realize what the cost would be to use the modem system and that Bell should have alerted him as his cellphone bill began to climb precipitously. Bell acknowledged that accessing the modem services is costly but also emphasized that to do so, customers are required to register online and must agree to contractual terms that show the higher fees. It also admitted that its newly implemented data-usage monitoring system failed to pick up the customer's high usage. In the meantime, Bell has offered to reduce the bill to approximately $4000, but the customer is refusing to pay even that sum. Who is right in this dispute and why? What additional information do you require to answer this question?[5]

For more study tools, visit http://www.NELSONbrain.com.

4. See *Wang v HMTQ (British Columbia)*, 2006 BCCA 566, leave to appeal to SCC refused, [2007] SCCA No 82.
5. See Jorge Barrera, "Grande Prairie cellphone user racks up $85,000 bill in 2 months" *The Edmonton Journal* (13 December 2007) at A1–2.

CHAPTER 6

Forming Contractual Relationships

Objectives

After studying this chapter, you should have an understanding of

- how negotiations lead to a contractual relationship

- how negotiations can be terminated

- the legal ingredients of a contract

- how contracts can be amended or changed

GOODLUZ/SHUTTERSTOCK

Business Law in Practice

Amritha, introduced in Chapter 5, began negotiations with Jason Hughes. Jason is a representative of Trackers, the steel tracking manufacturer willing to supply tracking to Coasters, Amritha's employer. Amritha provided Jason with the plans and specifications for the roller coaster, and they negotiated a number of points, including price, delivery dates, and tracking quality. A short time later, Jason offered to sell Coasters a total of 900 metres of track in accordance with the plans and specifications provided. Jason's offer contained, among other matters, the purchase price ($1.5 million), delivery date, terms of payment, insurance obligations concerning the track, and a series of warranties related to the quality and performance of the tracking to be supplied. There was also a clause, inserted at Amritha's express request, that required Trackers to pay $5000 to Coasters for every day it was late in delivering the tracking.

After reviewing the offer for several days, Amritha contacted Jason and said, "You drive a hard bargain, and there are aspects of your offer that I'm not entirely happy with. However, I accept your offer on behalf of my company. I'm looking forward to doing business with you."

Within a month, Trackers faced a 20 percent increase in manufacturing costs owing to an unexpected shortage in steel. Jason contacted Amritha to explain this development and worried aloud that without an agreement from Coasters to pay 20 percent more for the tracking, Trackers would be unable to make its delivery date. Amritha received instructions from her supervisor to agree to the increased purchase price in order to ensure timely delivery. Amritha communicated this news to Jason, who thanked her profusely for being so cooperative and understanding.

Jason kept his word and the tracking was delivered on time. However, Coasters has now determined that its profit margin on the American deal is lower than expected, and it is looking for ways to cut costs. Amritha

(Continued on the next page)

is told by her boss to let Jason know that Coasters would not be paying the 20 percent price increase and would remit payment only in the amount set out in the contract. Jason and Trackers are stunned by this development.

1. At what point did the negotiations between Jason and Amritha begin to have legal consequences?
2. In what ways could negotiations have been terminated prior to the formation of the contract?
3. Can Coasters commit itself to the price increase and then change its mind with no adverse consequences?
4. How could Trackers have avoided from the outset this situation related to cost increases?

The Contract

Chapter 5 emphasized that Coasters must enter into a contract with Trackers in order to secure the product that Coasters needs. This chapter accounts for several of the basic elements of a contract, namely that it is

- an agreement (i.e., composed of offer and acceptance)

- complete (i.e., certain)

- deliberate (i.e., intention to create legal relations is present)

- supported by mutual consideration

In short, this chapter sets out the legal ingredients that transform a simple agreement—which can be broken without legal consequences—into an enforceable contract.

An Agreement

Before a contract can be in place, the parties must be in agreement, that is, they have reached a consensus as to their rights and obligations. This agreement takes the form of offer and acceptance.

Offer
Definition of Offer

Offer
A promise to perform specified acts on certain terms.

An **offer** is a promise to enter into a contract, on specified terms, as soon as the offer is accepted. This happened in negotiations between Amritha and Jason when Jason committed to provide tracking to Coasters in the concrete terms noted: he named his price, terms of payments, delivery date, and other essential matters. At this point, negotiations have taken an important turn because Amritha is entitled to accept that offer, and, upon her doing so, Trackers is obligated to supply its product exactly as Jason proposed, assuming that the other ingredients of a contract are established.

Certainty of Offer

Only a complete offer can form the basis of a contract. This means that all essential terms must be set out or the contract will fail for uncertainty. An offer does not, however, have to meet the standard of perfect clarity and precision in how it is expressed. If the parties intend to have a contract, the courts will endeavour to interpret the alleged offer in as reasonable a fashion as possible and thereby resolve ambiguities.

An offer can achieve the requisite standard of certainty even if it leaves certain matters to be decided in the future. For example, Jason's offer could have made the final price for the tracking contingent on the market price, as determined by a given formula (for example, cost plus 15 percent). Though the price would not be set out in the offer, a workable way of determining price would have been established, and a contract could be entered into on that basis. A court will not speculate, however, on what the parties would have agreed to had they completed their negotiations.

Invitation to Treat

An offer is different from a communication that merely expresses a wish to do business. In law, the latter form of communication is called an invitation to treat and has no legal consequences. Whether a communication is an offer or an **invitation to treat** depends on the speaker's intention, objectively assessed. Subjective intent is of no legal relevance.

When Amritha provided Jason with plans for the roller coaster, she was not offering to buy tracking from Jason at that point but merely indicating her interest in receiving an offer from him. This was an invitation to treat. Similarly, if Jason had offered to sell tracking to Coasters during negotiations but provided no other detail, he would simply be demonstrating his wish to do business with Coasters. Such expressions of interest have no legal repercussions because they essentially have no content. Vague commitments to buy or sell tracking are invitations to treat and not offers because they fail to specify the terms or scope of the proposed arrangement.

To assist in the sometimes difficult task of classifying whether a communication is an offer or an invitation to treat, the common law has devised a number of rules. A rule of particular significance to business relates to the advertising and display of goods for sale in a store.

Enterprises such as retail outlets prosper by attracting customers to their premises. They do this through advertising their existence, as well as describing the products they sell and prices they charge, especially when those prices have been reduced. For practical reasons, these advertisements are generally not classified as offers.[1] If advertisements were offers, the store owner would be potentially liable for breach of contract if the store ran out of an advertised item that a customer wished to purchase. By classifying the advertisement as an invitation to treat, the law ensures that it is the customer who makes the offer to purchase the advertised goods. The owner is then in a position to simply refuse the offer if the product is no longer in supply. As a result of this refusal, no contract could arise.[2] In this way, the law seeks to facilitate commercial activity by permitting a businessperson to advertise goods or services without ordinarily running the risk of incurring unwanted contractual obligations.

Invitation to treat
An expression of willingness to do business.

---

1. An exception to this general rule occurs when the advertisement is so clear and definite that there is nothing left to negotiate. See *Lefkowitz v Great Minneapolis Surplus Store, Inc*, 86 NW 2d 689 (1957).
2. A store owner may have other legal problems if she runs out of an advertised sale product; for example, see the "bait and switch selling" provision of the *Competition Act*, RSC 1985, c C-34, s 74.04(2).

Similarly, the display of a product in the store is not an offer by the store to sell. The display is simply an indication that a product is available and can be purchased. In short, it is an invitation to treat and, by definition, is not capable of being accepted. In this way, the store maintains the option of refusing to complete the transaction at the cash register (see Figure 6.1).[3]

FIGURE 6.1
Legal Analysis of the Retail Purchase

Some contracts are only formed after protracted discussions. Other contracts, like the purchase of photocopying paper from an office supply store, are formed without any negotiations whatsoever. The customer simply takes the purchase to the cashier—thereby offering to purchase the item at its sticker price—and the cashier accepts the offer by receiving payment. Similarly, the **standard form contract** is entered into without any negotiations. Sales and rental businesses frequently require their customers (consumer and commercial) to consent to a standard set of terms that have been developed by the business over years of operation. Such contracts often heavily favour the business that created them and, because they are not usually subject to bargaining, are known colloquially as "take it or leave it" contracts. Examples include renting a car and borrowing money from the bank. Standard form contracts are not inherently objectionable, however, since they help reduce transaction costs and increase business volume, thereby potentially lowering price.[4]

Regardless of whether bargaining precedes the contract or not, the law expects people to take care of themselves. While there is provincial consumer protection legislation that may be of assistance in certain consumer transactions, the better course—particularly in a contract of some importance—is to read and understand the contract before signing it.

When negotiations are complicated, it is important for the parties to know when an offer has been made, since at that moment significant legal consequences arise, whether the parties intend them to or not. A fundamental rule is that a contract is formed only when

Standard form contract
A "take it or leave it" contract, where the customer agrees to a standard set of terms that favours the other side.

---

3. Note, however, that human rights legislation across the country prohibits a business owner from refusing to serve a customer on the basis of race, gender, and other discriminatory grounds.
4. For a discussion of the benefits of the standard form contract, see, for example, M J Trebilcock & D N Dewees, "Judicial Control of Standard Form Contracts" in Paul Burrows & Cento G Veljanovski, eds, *The Economic Approach to Law* (London: Butterworths, 1981).

a complete offer is unconditionally accepted by the other side. The key factor in deciding whether an offer has been made is this: if the purported offer is sufficiently comprehensive that it can be accepted without further elaboration or clarification, it is an offer in law. Jason's proposal to Amritha, outlined in the opening scenario, contains the requisite certainty and completeness. On this basis, the first building block to a contract between Trackers and Coasters is in place.

BUSINESS APPLICATION OF THE LAW

Spamming

Unsolicited bulk commercial email (sometimes called spam) is an annoyingly common way of advertising goods and services. Like traditional advertising, spam is likely to be classified as an invitation to treat, though if it contained enough specificity, it could constitute an offer. Though this remains an open question as there is no case law on point, courts almost certainly will approach the matter on a case-by-case basis.

The 2005 National Task Force on Spam reported that spam constituted an overwhelming majority of global email. According to this Canadian task force, such volume of spam causes a rash of problems, including wasting employee time, tying up Internet service providers, and causing injury to legitimate Internet marketers. Beyond this, and as the report states,

Why is spam objectionable?

[t]he new mutations of spam undermine consumer confidence in the Internet as a platform for commerce and communications. Because of this, the potential of information and communications technology to buttress productivity, and the ability of e-commerce to attract investment, create jobs and enrich our lives, is constrained not only by torrents of spam, but also by the deceptive, fraudulent and malicious activities that sometimes accompany it.[5]

Following many of the Report's recommendations, the Canadian Parliament passed Canada's new anti-spam legislation (known as "CASL" for short)—which will be likely be proclaimed in force sometime in 2013.[6] CASL is regarded as one of the strictest anti-spam regimes in the world and tightly regulates commercial electronic messages whether, for example, by email, instant messaging, social media, or SMS (short message service). Important features include:

• Prohibiting the sending of a commercial electronic message unless the recipient has consented to receiving it. This is known as an "opt-in" system.

• Requiring that the message be in a prescribed form. The message must identify the sender or person on whose behalf the sender is acting; set out contact information of the sender and, if different, the person on whose behalf the message is sent; and set out an unsubscribe mechanism.

• The person, when seeking express consent to send commercial electronic messages, must identify the purpose for which the consent is being sought, among other requirements.

The legislation also permits senders to rely on implied consent to receive commercial electronic messages but on a limited basis. Implied consent can be derived from having an existing business relationship with the intended recipient. This includes, for example, a business relationship arising from "the purchase or lease of a product, goods, [or] a service..." within two years prior to the message being sent, under s. 10.

• The legislation also prohibits the installation of computer program or program update on a computer

(Continued)

5. Industry Canada, "Stopping Spam: Creating a Stronger, Safer Internet: Report of the Task Force on Spam" (2005) online: Industry Canada <http://e-com.ic.gc.ca/epic/internet/inecic-ceac.nsf/en/h_gv00317e.html>. Spam is often used to promote illegal schemes as well as schemes that should be illegal, as the task force notes.
6. Alex Vorro, "Understanding Canada's anti-spam law" *Inside Counsel* (31 July 2012) online: http://www.insidecounsel.com/2012/07/31/understanding-canadas-anti-spam-law.

FUZZBONES/SHUTTERSTOCK

without the owner's express consent. The goal is to stop malware—short for malicious software—which refers to "any software designed to cause damage to a single computer, server, or computer network"[7]—but all computer programs are captured. The prohibition therefore impacts on all businesses that install or induce the installation of software, "including software for PCs as well as applications for devices such as smart phones, e-readers — or even those that operate websites."[8]

Businesses which outsource their marketing must ensure that whomever they have hired to do the work is compliant with the legislation. As Drew Hasselback notes in the *Financial Post*: "You can't outsource your marketing, then plead ignorance if your contract provider runs afoul of the law."[9]

The Act permits the defence of due diligence to protect the person who is trying to comply but nonetheless makes a mistake and runs afoul of the rules.

Penalties for non-compliance are up to $1 million for individuals and up to $10 million for organizations, per violation. Beyond this, the legislation gives a private right of action to any spam victim which will most usually be used to target major spammers, perhaps by way of class action.

Critical Analysis: Do you agree that anti-spam legislation should be part of Canada's strategy to combat spam? Why not leave the problem of spam to the marketplace to resolve?

Sources: See generally Government of Canada, "Legislative Summary of Bill C-28" at <http://www.parl.gc.ca/About/Parliament/LegislativeSummaries/bills_ls.asp?ls=c28&source=library_prb&Parl=40&Ses=3&Language=E>, and "Canada's antispam legislation" at <http://fightspam.gc.ca/eic/site/030.nsf/eng/home>.

Offeror
The person who makes an offer.

The person who makes an offer is known as the **offeror.** The person to whom an offer is made is known as the **offeree.** In the Business Law in Practice scenario, Jason is the offeror, and Amritha is the offeree.

Offeree
The person to whom an offer is made.

Termination of Offer

An offer can be accepted only if it is "alive," meaning that it is available to be accepted. If the offer has been legally terminated, no contract can come into existence, since one of its essential ingredients—the offer itself—is missing.

An offer can be terminated or "taken off the table" by any of the following events:

- revocation
- lapse
- rejection
- counteroffer
- death or insanity

Revocation

Revocation
The withdrawal of an offer.

The offeror can **revoke** his offer at any time before acceptance simply by notifying the offeree of its withdrawal. An offer that has been revoked does not exist anymore and therefore cannot be accepted.

In the opening scenario, there were several days between the communication of Trackers' offer and Amritha's acceptance of that offer. During this time, Jason would have been legally entitled to revoke his offer by simply advising Amritha of that fact. Amritha's alternatives would then be reduced, since she cannot accept an offer that has been revoked, nor can she make Trackers do business with her if it is no longer interested.

---

7. Robert Moir, "Defining Malware: FAQ" (2003) online: Microsoft TechNet <http://technet.microsoft.com/en-us/library/dd632948.aspx Microsoft Technet>.
8. David Elder, "Anti-spam law governs software—not just email", *Lawyers Weekly* (15 April 2011) 16.
9. Drew Hassleback, "Banishing spam: New crackdown to include all e-messages, experts say," *Financial Post* (6 January 2011) online: http://www2.canada.com/saskatoonstarphoenix/news/business/story.html?id=bdbbc88f-ec4e-4bea-ad1d-e05dff45f4d6&p=1

What factors will determine whether a contract will be the result of lengthy negotiations or will be easily and quickly concluded?

SPENCER PLATT/GETTY IMAGES

CASE — *Bigg v Boyd Gibbins Ltd*, [1971] 2 All ER 183 (CA)

THE BUSINESS CONTEXT: For the purpose of entering into a contract, parties may negotiate considerably. Difficulties arise when one party believes that a contract has been concluded while the other party disputes that conclusion.

FACTUAL BACKGROUND: Plaintiff and defendant negotiated extensively for the purchase and sale of real estate by the plaintiff to the defendant. The negotiation over this property—known as Shortgrove Hall—took the form of correspondence that the plaintiff/vendor claims culminated in a contract. The first legally important letter from the plaintiff stated:

> Thank you for your letter received last week. . . . As you are aware that I paid £25,000 for this property, your offer of £20,000 would appear to be at least a little optimistic. For a quick sale I would accept £26,000, so that my expense may be covered.

In response, the defendant wrote:

> I have just recently returned from my winter holiday and, turning this matter over in my mind now, would advise you that I accept your offer.

The plaintiff replied:

> I thank you for your letter ... accepting my price of £26,000 for the sale of Shortgrove Hall. I am putting the matter in the hands of my solicitors. . . . My wife and I are both pleased that you are purchasing the property.

The defendant denies a contract was formed, asserting that the parties had merely agreed on price.

THE LEGAL QUESTION: Is there a contract between the parties?

RESOLUTION: The court found for the plaintiff. There was a contract for the purchase and sale of Shortgrove Hall. To reach this conclusion, the court carefully analyzed the correspondence provided and acknowledged the defendant's argument that agreement on price does not necessarily mean that the parties have reached a full agreement. On these facts, however, a contract did exist. As the court concluded,

> The impression conveyed to my mind by these letters, and indeed the plain impression, is that the language used was intended to and did achieve the formation of ... [a] contract. As I have indicated, in the last letter stress was laid on the phrase "accepting my *price* [emphasis added] of £26,000 for the sale of Shortgrove Hall." I think, in the context of the letters that preceded that, it is to be read, as I have said, as "accepted my *offer* [emphasis added] to sell Shortgrove Hall at that price."

CRITICAL ANALYSIS: Who is the offeror and who is the offeree in this case? Do you agree with the court that a contract was in place? Should courts hold parties to the meaning of the exact words they use, or should words be interpreted in their larger context?

Revocation in the Context of a Firm Offer   As the following landmark case illustrates, the law permits offerors to revoke their offers despite a promise to leave the offer open for a set period of time (called a firm offer). In short, such a promise is enforceable only if the other party has purchased it or otherwise has given the offeror something in return for the commitment. Accordingly, if Jason had promised to leave his offer to sell tracking open for 30 days, but Amritha did not provide something in return for this promise—like the payment of a sum of money—she would have no legal recourse if Jason were to break his word and revoke his offer the next day.

LANDMARK CASE   *Dickinson v Dodds*, [1876] 2 Ch D 463 (CA)

THE HISTORICAL CONTEXT: This case is the leading decision—valid even today—on whether an offeror can renege on a commitment to hold an offer open for a specified period of time.

FACTUAL BACKGROUND: On Wednesday, June 10, Dodds delivered to Dickinson a written offer to sell his property to Dickinson for £800. The offer stated that it would be open for acceptance until 9 a.m. on Friday, June 12. On Thursday, Dickinson heard that Dodds had been offering or was agreeing to sell the property to Mr. Allan. That evening, Dickinson delivered an acceptance to the place where Dodds was staying, and at 7 a.m. on Friday morning—a full two hours before the deadline—he personally delivered an acceptance to Dodds. Dodds declined the acceptance, stating: "You are too late. I have sold the property." Dickinson sued Dodds, alleging there was a contract between them.

THE LEGAL QUESTION: To determine whether Dickinson's action should succeed, the court had to decide whether Dodds was entitled to revoke his offer prior to the deadline he had set. This decision was necessary because if the offer had been properly revoked, it was not capable of being accepted, and, accordingly, there could be no contract between the two men.

RESOLUTION: The court decided that what Dodds did was permissible: "[I]t is a perfectly clear rule of law . . . that, although it is said that the offer is to be left open until Friday morning at 9 o'clock, that did not bind Dodds. He was not in point of law bound to hold the offer over until 9 o'clock on Friday morning."

On this footing, a firm offer can be revoked at any time before acceptance because the offeree has not provided any consideration to support the offeror's implicit promise not to revoke before the deadline. More controversially, the court also held that Dodds' offer had been effectively revoked prior to acceptance because Dickinson learned in advance—from a presumably reliable source—that Dodds was selling the property to someone else.

CRITICAL ANALYSIS: Being guided primarily by legal principles is certainly an acceptable way of doing business. However, what might be the impact on your business reputation of going back on your word and revoking an offer sooner than you had promised you would? Do you think that the method used by Dodds for revocation (i.e., relying on the fact that Dickinson had learned that Dodds was selling to someone else) is the usual way of revoking an offer? What would be a more certain and reliable way of effecting revocation?

Option agreement
An agreement where, in exchange for payment, an offeror is obligated to keep an offer open for a specified time.

One way to avoid application of the rule in *Dickinson v Dodds* that firm offers can be revoked prior to their deadlines is for the parties to form an **option agreement**, whereby the offeree pays the offeror to keep the offer open for the specified time. An option agreement is a separate contract that may or may not lead to the acceptance of the offer and a resulting agreement of purchase and sale. Its purpose is simply to give the offeree a guaranteed period of time within which to deliberate whether to accept the offer or not. If the offeror withdraws the offer before the option agreement permits, he has committed a breach of contract, and the offeree can sue for damages.

Option agreements are commonly found in real estate developments—the developer will buy a number of options to purchase land from owners in the development area. The developer can choose whether to exercise the options and knows that during the option period, the owners are contractually bound to not withdraw their offers to sell at the specified price.

Dickinson v Dodds also demonstrates that an offer does not have to be directly revoked by the offeror—that revocation can take place through a reliable third-party source. This method of revocation, however, is both unusual and unreliable. Prudent business practice would have the offeror expressly revoking offers as necessary.

Revocation in the Context of a Tendering Contract   A specialized set of rules governs the tendering process. When an owner wishes to secure competitive bids to build a large project, for example, it typically calls for tenders. In response, contractors (also known as tenderers) submit tenders (or offers) that set out a price for the work to be done. If the ordinary rule of revocation applied, a contractor could simply withdraw its tender any time prior to acceptance and thus be positioned to avoid any commitments it would ultimately rather avoid. However, such latitude would undermine the tendering process and so the Supreme Court of Canada, in *R v Ron Engineering & Construction Ltd*,[10] devised a new legal structure for how tenders are to be understood. Instead of regarding the call for tenders as an invitation to treat, the Supreme Court of Canada said that the call for tenders could be construed an offer of a preliminary contract known as Contract A. While this is a fact specific matter, Contract A typically requires the tenderer and the owner to follow the rules governing the tender selection process, including a promise by the tenderer not to revoke its tender for a specified period of time. Everyone who submits a tender is accepting the offer of a Contract A to govern the relationship as well as offering to enter into Contract B, if chosen to do so. Contract B refers to the larger contract to perform the work in question. While there would be as many Contract A's as there were tenderers, only the successful tenderer would enter into a Contract B with the owner.

Should the tenderer seek to revoke its tender before the specified period of time has elapsed, it is likely a breach of Contract A and subject to legal action by the owner. As well, if the tenderer refuses to enter into Contact B when chosen to do so, it has committed another breach of Contract A.

Lapse

An offer **lapses** in one of two ways. It may contain a date upon which it expires. After this date, it is no longer "alive" and therefore cannot be accepted. If the offer contains no expiry date, it will remain open for a reasonable period of time, which, in turn, will depend on all the circumstances of the case, including the nature of the transaction at issue. For example, an offer to sell a piece of woodland that is sitting idle would probably remain open longer than an offer to sell a piece of property that is about to be commercially developed. A judge will bring as much precision as possible to the question of when an offer lapses, but the whole exercise is inherently speculative.

With this in mind, an offeror should consider specifying an expiry date for the offer and thereby avoid the debate altogether. For his part, the offeree should act promptly, because of the principle in *Dickinson v Dodds* permitting revocation prior to the expiry date, or at least keep in contact with the offeror to ensure that the status of the offer is known.

Lapse

The expiration of an offer after a specified or reasonable period.

---

10. [1981] 1 SCR 111.

Rejection

It is important for those involved in contractual negotiations to know that an offer is automatically terminated when it is **rejected** by the offeree. The offer can be accepted only if the offeror revives it by offering it anew or if the offeree presents it as his own offer, which can then be accepted or rejected by the original offeror. The risk in rejecting an offer is that it may never be renewed by the other side.

Rejection
The refusal to accept an offer.

Counteroffer

A **counteroffer** is a form of rejection. Through a counteroffer, the offeree is turning down the offer and proposing a new offer in its place. The distinction between an acceptance and a counteroffer is not always readily apparent. For example, suppose that a seller offers 100 widgets to the buyer at $10 per widget, and the buyer responds, "Great, I'll take 800." Or suppose a seller offers a car for $10 000, and the buyer says, "I'll take it. I'll give you $5000 today and the balance next week." In both situations, it looks like the buyer has accepted, but in law he or she has made a counteroffer. Any change to a term of an offer—including to price, quantity, time of delivery, or method of payment—is a counteroffer. Because a counteroffer is a rejection, the original offer is automatically terminated and can be accepted only if it is renewed by one of the parties. Whenever a party makes a counteroffer, he or she jeopardizes the chance of being able to accept the original offer.

Counteroffer
The rejection of one offer and proposal of a new one.

Death or Insanity

While the matter is not free from controversy, it would seem that an offer generally dies if the offeror or offeree dies. However, if the offer concerns a contract that would not require the affected party to personally perform it, a court may decide that the offer could be accepted notwithstanding that party's death.

Someone who makes an offer and then subsequently becomes insane would not be bound, as a general rule.

Acceptance
Definition of Acceptance

When an offer made by one party is unconditionally and unequivocally **accepted** by the other party, a contract is formed. To be effective, the acceptance must demonstrate an unqualified and complete willingness to enter into the contract on the precise terms proposed. If the purported acceptance does not mirror the offer by agreeing to all its content, it is a counteroffer and no contract has been formed.

Acceptance
An unqualified willingness to enter into a contract on the terms in the offer.

In the opening scenario, Amritha clearly accepted Jason's offer—she did not propose modifications or alterations to his proposal. While she expressed some reservations, saying that she was not entirely happy with the offer, this was not a rejection. Rather, she went on to fully and completely accept his offer. At this point, two of the building blocks of a contract between Coasters and Trackers are in place—namely, offer and acceptance.

Communication of Acceptance

In order to effect legal acceptance, the offeree must communicate—by words or by conduct—an unconditional assent to the offer in its entirety. This message of acceptance

© ROYALTY FREE/CORBIS/MAGMA

Why might a business decide to accept an offer by conduct instead of formally communicating acceptance to the other side? What are the risks of doing so?

can be conveyed in any number of ways: in person, in writing, by mail, by fax, by email, by telephone, and by other actions. In fact, any manner of communication that is reasonable in the circumstances ordinarily will do. However, the offer must be scrutinized to determine if it requires a specific method of communicating an acceptance. If it does, and by the terms of the offer that method of communication is mandatory, then the offeree must follow that method of communication in order to ensure legal acceptance. For example, if a company offers, by telephone, to sell a given item but specifies that acceptance must be in writing, then the offeree's calling back with a purported acceptance will be ineffective. In this case the offeror is entitled to insist on written acceptance before it is bound.

CASE	*Lowe (DJ) (1980) Ltd v Upper Clements Family Theme Park Ltd (1990), 95 NSR (2d) 397 (SCTD)*

THE BUSINESS CONTEXT: Businesses often have to act quickly to address a problem that has developed. In such circumstances, proper attention may not be given to the legal requirements of contract formation. This lack of focus can lead to disappointed expectations.

FACTUAL BACKGROUND: Mr. Bougie, construction manager of Upper Clements Family Theme Park, was under a tight construction schedule and needed a crane quickly to complete construction of a theme park. He discussed leasing a crane from Mr. Lowe's company, but the two men could not come to an

(Continued)

agreement. Lowe insisted that the crane be leased for a minimum period of two months, whereas Bougie did not want to commit to that length of a term, preferring to prorate[11] charges based on a monthly rental. The next day, however, Bougie delivered a letter to Lowe from Mr. Buxton, the general manager of the theme park, dated November 24, 1988. The letter summarized the parties' agreement and included this statement: "The Upper Clements Family Theme Park Limited agrees to pay the sum of $10 000 (ten thousand dollars) per month, prorated for partial months for crane hire." The letter concluded by asking Lowe to sign a copy of the letter if he was in agreement with this condition.

This letter did not, in fact, reflect the parties' agreement and was never signed by Lowe, but he did send a crane to the construction site. Lowe apparently believed that he and the theme park personnel could come to an agreement on price, and within two days of delivering the crane, approached Bougie with a draft agreement setting out a monthly rate for a two-month term. Bougie said that he had no authority to deal with the document, and it would have to wait for Buxton's return from an out-of-town trip. In the end, the theme park had the crane on-site for four days and then immediately returned it, along with payment of $1250. Lowe's company sued for the balance, claiming that it was owed a total of $20 000.

THE LEGAL QUESTION: Is there a contract between the parties? If so, did Buxton's terms on price prevail or did Lowe's?

RESOLUTION: The trial judge determined that there was a contract between the parties for the rental of the crane. Whether Buxton's letter was classified as an acceptance or a counteroffer, said the judge,

> it was the serious expression of an intention by the Theme Park to enter into a contract with the Lowe

company. . . . Having received that letter, Mr. Lowe had his company go ahead with delivery of the crane, knowing it was essential that the Theme Park have it at the earliest possible moment. Rather than risk losing the contract, Lowe accepted the offer by delivering the crane and acquiescing in the Theme Park's use of it.

In doing so Mr. Lowe was not intentionally capitulating to an unfavourable counteroffer. Based upon his experience in the industry and his previous dealings with the Theme Park, Mr. Lowe was taking a calculated risk that even though his company was entering into a contract, he could later negotiate more satisfactory terms. . . . His expectations were not unreasonable. However they were frustrated first by Mr. Buxton's absence and then by his own. . . . The two-month term [set forth in the draft lease that Lowe subsequently presented to Bougie] was not part of the contract that was entered into. The governing provision is in Mr. Buxton's letter of November 24th. . . . That is the provision of the counter-offer Mr. Lowe wished to avoid, but it is the one that governs. The Theme Park is entitled to return the crane for the monthly rental prorated for the partial month when it had possession of the crane. . . . The amount to be paid was calculated at $1250.00 by the Theme Park and previously tendered to the Plaintiff. I accept that calculation and award the Plaintiff damages.

CRITICAL ANALYSIS: How can a business avoid unwanted obligations when there is insufficient time to properly negotiate a contract? Is it reasonable for the judge to decide the case based on the terms of one letter?

Since entering a contract is about assent, the law determines that the offer is effective only when it has been communicated to the offeree. In this way, the offeree becomes aware of its terms and can respond. Similarly, the acceptance, if any, must be communicated to the offeror so that the offeror is aware of the unqualified acceptance. Acceptance is achieved expressly, as when the offeree accepts in person or sends a message through some medium to the offeror. Occasionally, however, acceptance can be indicated by conduct, as the case just above demonstrates.

It is also possible—though less than usual—for the offer to be expressed in such a way that no communication of acceptance is needed.

---

11. When a sum is prorated, it means that what is charged is determined in relation to a certain rate. In this example, the monthly rate is $10 000. Based on a 30-day month, the prorated daily charge would be $10 000 divided by 30, or $333.

LANDMARK CASE

Carlill v Carbolic Smoke Ball Co, [1893] 1 QB 256 (Eng CA)

THE HISTORICAL CONTEXT: This case was decided at a time when Victorian England was being inundated with quack cures. Examples of "miracle" cures included Epps Glycerine Jube Jubes and a product called Pepsolic, which claimed to prevent marriage breakups because it prevented indigestion. The ad for this product noted that indigestion "Causes Bad Temper, Irritability, Peppery Disposition, Domestic Quarrels, Separation and—the Divorce Court."[12]

FACTUAL BACKGROUND: This case considers the legal obligations that resulted from the advertisement placed by the Carbolic Smoke Ball Company in a London newspaper at the turn of the 19th century (see Figure 6.2).

FIGURE 6.2

Carbolic Smoke Ball Advertisement

£100 REWARD
WILL BE PAID BY THE
CARBOLIC SMOKE BALL CO.
To any person who contracts the increasing Epidemic,
INFLUENZA
Colds, or any diseases caused by taking cold,
AFTER HAVING USED the BALL
3 times daily for two weeks according to the printed
directions supplied with each Ball.
£1000
Is deposited with the ALLIANCE BANK, REGENT STREET,
showing our sincerity in the matter.
During the last epidemic of Influenza many of our
CARBOLIC SMOKE BALLS were sold as Preventives
against this Disease, and in no ascertained case was
the disease contracted by those using the
CARBOLIC SMOKE BALL.

Mrs. Carlill used the smoke ball as directed for two weeks but caught influenza anyway. When the company refused to pay her the advertised reward, she commenced an action for breach of contract.

THE LEGAL QUESTION: Was there a contract between the parties, even though Mrs. Carlill did not communicate her acceptance of the Carbolic Smoke Ball Company's offer?

RESOLUTION: While communication of acceptance is generally required, this is not always the case. Because the Carbolic Smoke Ball Company—the offeror—had chosen to dispense with the necessity of notice, it could not complain about Mrs. Carlill's failure to communicate acceptance now. In the end, the court found that Mrs. Carlill had accepted the company's offer of a reward by using the smoke ball as requested and that, upon becoming sick, she was contractually entitled to the £100.

CRITICAL ANALYSIS: This case is an example of an offer of a unilateral contract, though the court did not identify it as such. Through such an offer, the offeror promises to pay the offeree a sum of money if the offeree performs the requested act. For example, a company might offer a $200 reward to anyone who finds a missing laptop computer. Unlike the ordinary business contract, where both parties have obligations, in the unilateral contract only the offeror is bound because the offeree can perform the requested act—find the laptop—or not. He has no obligation even to try. If he does find the computer and returns it, the contract is complete, and the offeror is contractually required to pay. For obvious reasons, this kind of offer typically does not require people who decide to look for the computer to advise the company of their intention to do so. From the company's perspective, it is enough to hear from the person who actually finds the computer.

Ordinarily, however, communication of acceptance is expected and required. In practical terms, the offeror needs to be aware of the acceptance in order to appreciate that the contract exists and that performance of the obligations in it should proceed.

A problem arises if the offeree sends an acceptance that for some reason never reaches the offeror. Perhaps a letter gets lost in the mail, an email message goes astray, or a fax gets sent to the wrong number. Has there been acceptance or not? Normally, the answer would be that no acceptance has occurred until actually received. Put another way, acceptance is effective only when communicated—it is at this moment that a contract comes into existence.

---

12. AWB Simpson, "Quackery and Contract Law: The Case of the Carbolic Smoke Ball" (June 1985) 14:2 J Legal Stud 345 at 355-56. The historical information contained in this box draws heavily on Simpson's analysis.

PART TWO

A specific exception to this general rule is the "postbox rule," also called the "postal rule." If it is clear that the offeror intends the postbox rule to apply to her offer, then acceptance is effective at the time of mailing the acceptance, rather than the time of delivery. Even if the letter containing the acceptance is never delivered to the offeror, a contract has been formed. Since application of the postbox rule means that an offeror could end up being in a contract without even knowing it, that person is best advised to avoid application of the postbox rule by making it clear in the offer that actual communication or notice of acceptance is absolutely required.

When a court will apply the ordinary rule (which requires communication of acceptance) and when it will apply the postbox rule depends on the facts of the case. As Lord Wilberforce states, "No universal rule can cover all such cases; they must be resolved by reference to the intentions of the parties, by sound business practice and in some cases by a judgment where the risks should lie. . . ."[13] Courts have suggested that the postbox rule applies to telegrams but only where the offeror had impliedly constituted the telegraph company as his agent for the purpose of receiving the acceptance.[14] Otherwise, the ordinary rule applies and the acceptance by telegram is effective only upon receipt.[15] The postbox rule has also been applied where the acceptance was delivered by courier.[16]

That said, it is much more common for the courts to apply the ordinary rule—that acceptance is effective only when communicated. They have done so with respect to all forms of instantaneous communication, including the telephone, the telex, and the fax.[17]

The practical application of the rules governing offer and acceptance is affected by the requirement of proof that the necessary events occurred. Someone who seeks to enforce a contract that the other party denies exists must be able to prove that offer and acceptance occurred. While ideally this proof is created through documentary evidence, documents are not always available. In such circumstances, the individual seeking to rely on the contract must convince the court of its existence without the benefit of extraneous proof. Oral agreements are very difficult to prove without some independent verification or corroboration—by a witness to the negotiations, for example—of what was said. Beyond this, some contracts must be evidenced in writing to be enforceable.[18]

TECHNOLOGY AND THE LAW

Electronic Contracting

Electronic business—such as the sale of goods and services, the exchange of commercial information, and the payment of debts conducted over public and private computer networks—has grown tremendously over the last decade.

In an effort to facilitate the growth of electronic business, the Uniform Law Conference of Canada has adopted the *Uniform Electronic Commerce Act (UECA)*[19] based on the United Nations Commission on International Trade Law's (UNCITRAL) Model Law on Electronic Commerce.[20] The *UECA*, which is designed to remove barriers to electronic commerce, is intended to serve as the basis for provincial and federal electronic commerce legislation. The model law has three parts. The first sets out basic functional equivalency rules. To remove

---

13. *Brinkibon Ltd v Stahag Stahl Und Stahlwarenhandelsgesellschaft mbH*, [1983] 2 AC 34 (HL) [Brinkibon]; the rule in *Brinkibon* was adopted in Canada by *Eastern Power Ltd v Azienda Comunale Energia & Ambiente* (1999), 178 DLR (4th) 409 (Ont CA).
14. *Smith & Osberg Ltd v Hollenbeck*, [1938] 3 WWR 704 (BCSC).
15. *Società Gei A Responsabilità Limitata v Piscitelli*, [1988] CLD 679 (Ont Dist Ct).
16. *Nova Scotia v Weymouth Sea Products Ltd* (1983), 4 DLR (4th) 314 (NSCA) and *Fp Bourgault Ind. Cultivator Division Ltd v Nichols Tillage Tools Inc* (1988), 63 Sask R 204 (QB).
17. *Eastern Power Ltd v Azienda Comunale Energia* (1999), 178 DLR (4th) 409 (Ont CA), leave to appeal to SCC refused, [1999] SCCA No 542.
18. See Chapter 8 for further discussion.
19. Uniform Law Conference of Canada, "*Uniform Electronic Commerce Act*", online: ULCC<http://www.ulcc.ca/en/us/index.cfm?sec=1&sub=1u1>.
20. United Nations Commission on International Trade Law,"1996—UNCITRAL Model Law on Electronic Commerce with Guide to Enactment", online: UNCITRAL <http://www.uncitral.org/uncitral/en/uncitral_texts/electronic_commerce/1996Model.html>.

any doubts pertaining to the legal recognition of electronic contracts, the model legislation provides that a contract shall not be denied effect on the sole ground that it was entered into electronically.[21] Part 2 deals with special rules for the formation and operation of contracts, the effect of using automated transactions, corrections of errors when dealing with a computer, and the sending and receipt of computer messages. Part 3 makes special provision for the carriage of goods. Electronic commerce legislation is in place across the country based on this model.[22] Federally, electronic commerce legislation is in place to govern contracts with the Federal Crown.[23] In most cases the legislation is the same or similar to the *UECA*; however, important variations do exist.

The *UECA* and the legislation that it has spawned do not modify or change the general rules applicable to contracts. The formation of electronic contracts is governed by the same general rules as other contracts. There must be an offer, acceptance, and communication of the acceptance.

Offer: The *UECA* provides that an offer may be expressed electronically. The legislation does not, however, specify whether communication displayed on a website is an offer or an invitation to do business. Generally, advertisements in catalogues and goods displayed in a store are not viewed as offers on the basis that merchants have only a limited supply and therefore could not reasonably be making offers to everyone. Presumably, electronic catalogues, advertisements, and price lists would be subject to the same rule. However, if the website displaying goods or services for sale not only indicates the price but also indicates that the item is in stock then the online advertisement could conceivably be considered an offer.[24]

Acceptance: The *UECA* provides that acceptance of an offer can be made electronically. Thus an offer made electronically may be accepted electronically unless the party making the offer insists on some other means of communication. Case law has recognized that an offer made electronically can be accepted by clicking on an online icon or an "I agree" button.

CARL PENDLE/PHOTOGRAPHER'S CHOICE/ GETTY IMAGES

How does electronic business benefit from a standardized set of legislative rules?

In *Rudder v Microsoft*,[25] an Ontario court held that an online membership agreement became enforceable against the subscriber once the subscriber clicked on the "I agree" button.[26] The *UECA* also recognizes that an acceptance (as well as an offer) can be affected by an electronic agent.[27]

Communication of Acceptance: An acceptance of the offer must be communicated to the offeror to take effect. Where the acceptance is effective usually determines where the contract is formed and consequently what law applies to the transaction. In the absence of an agreement, an acceptance using an instantaneous means of communication (telephone, telex, facsimile) takes effect where the offeror receives the communication, whereas, generally speaking, acceptance using a non-instantaneous means of communication (such as the mail) can be effective on sending, that is, where the offeree is located. What then of communication by electronic means? Is this an instantaneous means of communication? Electronic mail is not quite like ordinary mail because, generally, it is significantly faster and it is often dependent on the actions of the recipient for arrival; it is not quite like a telephone because there is no direct line of communication between the parties and it is not always possible to verify whether the intended recipient has heard the message. Communications on the World Wide Web, however, can be interactive and in real time,

(Continued)

21. Uniform Law Conference of Canada, *supra* note 19, s 5.
22. Timothy Banks, Sonja Homenuck, and Greg Barker, "Electronic Delivery of Lease Documentation: Is E-Delivery Enforceable?" (2010) 11:2 Internet and E-Commerce Law in Canada 9 at 11 online: Law Society Library Newfoundland & Labrador Library <http://www.lslibrary.ca/userfiles/file/Internet%20and%20E-Commerce%20Law%20in%20Canada,%20Vol,%2011,%20No_%202,%20%20June%202010. pdf>. For general discussion, see Michael Geist, "Attachment 4," in International Telecommunication Union (ITU), eds, *A Handbook on Internet Protocol (IP)-Based Networks and Related Topics and Issues* online: ITU <http://www.itu.int/ITU-T/special-projects/ip-policy/final/Attach04.doc>. UNCITRAL e-commerce legislation in Canada includes the *Electronic Transactions Act*, SA 2001, c E-5.5 (Alberta); the *Electronic Transactions Act*, SBC 2001, c 10 (British Columbia); the *Electronic Commerce and Information Act*, CCSM 2000 c E55 plus other related legislative amendments (Manitoba); the *Electronic Transactions Act*, RSNB 2011, c 145 (New Brunswick); the *Electronic Commerce Act*, SNL 2001, c E-5.2 (Newfoundland); the *Electronic Commerce Act*, SNS 2000, c 26 (Nova Scotia); *the Electronic Commerce Act*, SO 2000, c17 (Ontario); the *Electronic Commerce Act*, RSPEI 1988, c E-4.1 (Prince Edward Island); the *Electronic Information and Documents Act*, SS 2000, c E-7.22 (Saskatchewan); *the Electronic Commerce Act*, RSY 2002, c 66 (Yukon); and *the Electronic Commerce Act*, SNu 2004, c 7 (Nunavut).
23. Banks, *supra* note 22.
24. Barry Sookman, *Computer, Internet and Electronic Commerce Law*, vol 2, loose-leaf (Toronto: Carswell, 1991) at 10–16.
25. (1999), 2 CPR (4th) 474 (Ont SCJ).
26. The enforceability of these types of contracts—known as click-wrap agreements—is discussed in Chapter 7.
27. According to the *UECA, supra* note 19, s19, an electronic agent is a computer program or electronic means used to initiate an action or to respond to electronic documents in whole or in part without review by an actual person at the time of the response or action. Electronic agents are discussed in Chapter 13.

therefore exhibiting characteristics of instantaneous means of communication.[28] The UECA has provisions specifying when a message is sent and when it is received, but it does not specify where an acceptance becomes effective. Therefore, unless electronic traders specify where acceptance becomes effective, the question of where an electronic contract is formed will be presumably decided on a case-by-case basis.

Critical Analysis: Legislation has removed some of the uncertainty about online contracting. However, questions still remain concerning whether communications on a website are an offer or invitation to do business and whether an electronic acceptance is effective on sending or receipt. What risks do these uncertainties pose for business? What steps can a business take to minimize these risks and avoid contractual disputes?

Developments in technology have created new methods of doing business that test the relevance and applicability of the older common law rules regarding offer and acceptance to which this chapter has already alluded.

Formalization

Even though the parties may have reached an agreement through offer and acceptance, this will not always produce an enforceable agreement. This is because a court will not enforce an agreement that the parties have decided will not be effective until the exact wording of the contract has been agreed upon and the contract has been written and signed. This kind of intention is signalled by phrases such as "this agreement is subject to formal contract." Unless and until the formal contract comes into existence, there are generally no enforceable obligations between the parties.

Consideration
The Nature of Consideration

Consideration
The price paid for a promise.

A contract is a set of commitments or promises. It therefore entails a bargain or an exchange between the parties. Each party must give up something of value in exchange for receiving something of value from the other contracting party. In the example of the agreement between Jason and Amritha, it is clear that there is **consideration** on both sides of the transaction: the buyer promises to pay the purchase price in exchange for the seller's promise to provide tracking of the specified quality and quantity. Seen from the other perspective, the seller promises to provide tracking of the specified quality and quantity in exchange for the buyer's promise to pay the purchase price (see Figure 6.3 on page 129). This bargain, or exchange of promises, is a classic example of the legal requirement of consideration.

Gratuitous promise
A promise for which no consideration is given.

Consideration is a key ingredient that distinguishes a legally enforceable promise from one that is not legally enforceable. If Trackers promises to provide tracking to Coasters at no charge and later changes its mind, Coasters cannot sue for breach of contract. Coasters has not given something back to Trackers in order to purchase Trackers' promise; accordingly, there is no contract in place, and any lawsuit by Coasters will fail. In law, Trackers has made a **gratuitous promise**—that is, a promise unsupported by consideration. Classically, the law has concluded that such a promise can be broken with legal impunity because it has not been "purchased," though, as discussed below, another view on the matter is emerging.[29] Certainly, if the parties have exchanged promises or something else of value, their obligations are contractual and therefore undoubtedly enforceable.

28. Sookman, *supra* note 24 at 10–7.
29. See discussion at notes 30–35 and surrounding text.

As the above examples illustrate, a "price" must be paid for a promise before a party can sue when it is broken. Most commonly, the price for a promise to supply goods or services takes the form of another promise—including a promise to pay an agreed-upon sum in the future—or immediate payment of money. However, the consideration need not be monetary. The only requirement is that something of value be given up by the party seeking to purchase the promise of another. Furthermore, that item of value may be conferred on a third party and still amount to consideration, provided it was conferred at the request of the other side. For example, if Jason requested that the purchase price of the tracking be paid to a creditor of Trackers, Coasters' agreement to do so would support Trackers' promise to supply the tracking.

FIGURE 6.3

Consideration as an Exchange of Promises

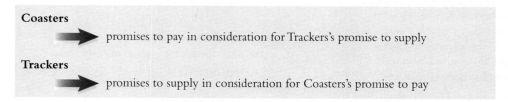

Coasters

➤ promises to pay in consideration for Trackers's promise to supply

Trackers

➤ promises to supply in consideration for Coasters's promise to pay

The requirement for consideration is strongly linked to the idea of freedom of bargaining. Although the law requires that consideration be present on both sides of the transaction, it is up to the parties to negotiate a deal that is mutually acceptable. They, not a judge, decide what constitutes a fair and reasonable price. Therefore, the adequacy of consideration is normally not open to challenge. If Amritha has agreed to pay a price for the tracking that turns out to be well above its market value, that is her choice. She cannot later go to a judge and ask that the price be lowered on that basis alone. The law will generally enforce a contract even where one party has agreed to pay too much because the parties are responsible for being fully informed of all aspects of the transaction and for evaluating the risks involved. If Amritha is concerned that she may end up paying too much for tracking, she should consult experts in the field and seek competing bids to help her establish a fair market price before accepting Jason's offer. Similarly, if one or both of the parties is concerned that the value of the goods or services contracted for may change between the time of agreement and the time of performance, a clause allowing the contract price to be adjusted for market fluctuations should be included in the contract. In short, parties are expected to take care of themselves and plan for contingencies.

Pre-Existing Legal Duty

Just as a contract can be viewed as a set of promises, it can also be viewed as a set of duties. The consideration for each party's duties is the other party's duties. Once those duties or promises have been finalized, the contract is concluded. If the parties agree to alter the contract in a way that benefits only one of them, the traditional perspective says that the alteration is unenforceable. In other words, a new promise needs new or fresh consideration. For example, if a contract provides that a project is to be completed on a particular date, a promise by the owner to pay an additional sum of money, say $2000, to ensure completion on that date is unenforceable. The promise to pay an additional $2000 is not supported by

Pre-existing legal duty
A legal obligation that a person already owes.

fresh consideration because completion on a particular date is already required under a contract. In short, it is a **pre-existing legal duty.** This is the view taken in the following case.

CASE

Gilbert Steel Ltd v University Construction Ltd, [1976] 12 OR (2d) 19 (CA)

THE BUSINESS CONTEXT: A business may enter into a contract that suddenly becomes unfavourable because of changes in the market. If it secures a concession from the other side in response to these changes, without regard to legal requirements, the concession may prove to be unenforceable.

FACTUAL BACKGROUND: Gilbert Steel (Gilbert) and University Construction (University) were in a contract that required Gilbert to supply a set amount of fabricated steel at an agreed-upon price. When steel prices rose dramatically, Gilbert asked University if it would pay more for the steel. University agreed but later refused to pay the increase and sent only payment for the originally agreed-upon price. Gilbert sued for breach of contract.

THE LEGAL QUESTION: Is there consideration supporting University's promise (i.e., what is Gilbert doing in return for University's promise to pay more for the steel)?

RESOLUTION: There is no consideration from Gilbert for University's promise, and it is therefore unenforceable. Gilbert

is doing only what it is already contractually obliged to do—namely, supply steel to University. Put another way, Gilbert has a pre-existing legal duty to provide the steel and, accordingly, is giving nothing "extra" to University to support University's promise to pay more. The promise is therefore unenforceable, even though University made the second promise in good faith, possibly with a full intention to pay the higher price. Gilbert's action for breach of contract therefore fails.

Gilbert should have contemplated a rise in the cost of steel when setting the original price and built into the contract a formula permitting an increase in the contract price. Alternatively, it could have provided something in return for the higher price, such as earlier delivery or any other benefit that University requested. A final option would have been to get University's promise under seal (see below).

CRITICAL ANALYSIS: Does this rule concerning performance of a pre-existing legal duty reflect the reasonable expectations of both the parties involved and the broader business community?

Variation of Contracts

The rule that performance of a pre-existing legal duty is not good consideration for a new promise also finds expression in the traditional rule that all variations of a contract must be supported by "fresh" consideration. As *Gilbert Steel Ltd v University Construction Ltd* illustrates, just as a contract needs to reflect a two-sided bargain, so must variations or changes to that contract. This is why University's promise to pay more for the steel is, under this traditional analysis, considered to be worthless without some corresponding concession from Gilbert.

More recently, however, the New Brunswick Court of Appeal (in *Greater Fredericton Airport Authority Inc v NAV Canada*[30]) has ruled that a contractual variation unsupported by consideration is enforceable—provided it is not otherwise procured by economic duress. As the court notes, among other matters:

> The reality is that existing contracts are frequently varied and modified by tacit agreement in order to respond to contingencies not anticipated or identified at the time the initial contract was negotiated. As a matter of commercial efficacy, it becomes necessary at times to adjust the parties' respective contractual obligations and the law must then protect their legitimate expectations that the modifications or variations will be adhered to and regarded as enforceable.[31]

The court expressed the view that the doctrine of consideration should not be frozen in time and that incremental change to the common law is important in order to advance modern

---

30. 2008 NBCA 28. For further discussion of duress, see Chapter 8.
31. *Supra* note 30 at para 28.

policy objectives.[32] Provided that the party who agrees to a gratuitous variation did not do so because of pressure that left no practical alternative and that the party therefore essentially "consented" to the variation, it is enforceable.[33] The idea is to respect the parties' legitimate expectations that the contractual modifications would be adhered to.[34]

This means that there are now two lines of authority in Canada regarding the enforceability of gratuitous contractual variations. In Ontario and jurisdictions following the *Gilbert Steel* approach, they are not enforceable. In New Brunswick and jurisdictions that choose to follow *Greater Fredericton Airport Authority* case, they can be. When consideration *is* present, of course, the difference between the two jurisdictions is no longer relevant—the variation is most certainly enforceable.

Note that when parties to a contract decide to terminate it and replace it with a new contract, there is no doubt that consideration is present in that both parties have given something back to the other. If only one side has given something up, however, then the contract has been varied (as opposed to being replaced) and the enforceability of the variation depends on what authority the court in question relies on—*Gilbert Steel* or *Greater Fredericton Airport Authority.*

When Trackers, through Jason, asked Amritha's company to pay more for the tracking, it was seeking a variation of the contract. Because Trackers did not provide anything new to Coasters in return, Coasters' commitment to pay an increased price was a gratuitous promise. On the traditional analysis, the fact that Trackers supplied the tracking on time does not count as consideration because Trackers had a pre-existing duty to do just that. On this basis, Coasters is not bound by its promise to pay more. Its only obligation is to pay the price recited in the contract that Amritha first negotiated. From a business perspective, however, its refusal to abide by its own promise will almost certainly destroy any possibility of Coasters and Trackers ever doing business together again. On the new analysis offered by the New Brunswick Court of Appeal in *Greater Fredericton Airport Authority*, it would seem that Coaster's commitment to pay an increased price *is* enforceable. This is because Trackers did not put Coasters under economic duress—there seems little doubt that the agreement to pay more was entirely voluntary and something to which Coasters consented.

Promises Enforceable without Consideration

Consideration is not always necessary for a contract or contractual variation to be enforceable. Important exceptions to the consideration requirement are promises under seal, promissory estoppel, and, in some jurisdictions, partial payment of a debt.

Promise under Seal

Before commercial negotiations became as commonplace and sophisticated as they are today, and before the rules of contract were fully developed, a practice originated to authenticate written agreements by putting hot wax beside the signature on a document and placing an imprint in the wax, unique to the person who signed. The use of a seal has

---

32. *Ibid* at paras 30–31, relying on *Williams v Roffey Bros & Nicholls (Contractors) Ltd*, [1990] 1 All ER 512 (CA)
33. *Supra* note 30. at para 55.
34. *Ibid* at para 28.

What is the purpose of placing a seal on a document?

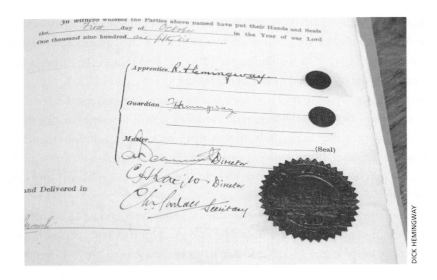

DICK HEMINGWAY

evolved so that today the seal takes the form of a red gummed circle or wafer attached to the document beside the signature of the party making the promise. The legal effect is the same, however. If the document containing the promise is signed and the seal affixed, the fact that there may not be consideration for the promise is irrelevant. The seal is taken as evidence of serious intent by the promisor and amounts to an acknowledgment that the promise is enforceable, even if it is gratuitous. Contracts of guarantee, for example, typically have seals attached.[35]

Promissory Estoppel

Without a seal, a gratuitous promise is traditionally not enforceable at common law, even if made with great deliberation, and regardless of the adverse consequences to the person who relied on the promise. In response to the harshness that this common law rule could sometimes generate, courts began to assist parties through the equitable doctrine of **promissory estoppel**.

Promissory estoppel
A doctrine whereby someone who relies on a gratuitous promise may be able to enforce it.

Promissory estoppel focuses on the idea of fairness, but since fairness is relatively subjective and courts are reluctant to stray too far from the doctrine of consideration, the party seeking to rely on the doctrine (Party A) must show that a number of distinct factors also exist in relation to the promise made by Party B, as listed below:

- Party B has, by words or conduct, made a promise or an assurance to Party A that was intended to affect their legal relationship and to be acted on.

- In reliance on the representation, Party A acted on it or in some way changed its position.[36]

- Party A's own conduct has been above reproach and, in this way, Party A is deserving of the court's assistance.

---

35. Guarantees are discussed in detail in Chapter 26.
36. *Maracle v Travellers Indemnity Co of Canada*, [1991] 2 SCR 50.

A final requirement is that promissory estoppel can be used only as a defence to legal claims made by the promise-breaker.[37]

Assume, for example, that Jason contacts Amritha one month before the delivery date specified in their contract. Jason tells her that Trackers is having minor production difficulties and there is a chance that the tracking will be delivered three days late. He asks Amritha if this will be a problem for Coasters. He also wants to know if Coasters will insist on enforcing the late delivery clause in their contract obligating Trackers to pay $5000 per day for every day it is late. After securing instructions from her supervisor, Amritha gets back to Jason and tells him not to worry: "Jason, it poses no problem for us if you are up to one week late, and no, we won't come after you for late charges. We just want our tracking in good time." In the end, the tracking is delivered three days late, and Coasters suddenly takes the position that it is owed $15 000.

Subject to the reach of *Greater Fredericton Airport Authority,* Coasters' promise not to rely on the late charges clause is unenforceable at common law because there is no consideration supporting it. Trackers is giving nothing back to Coasters in exchange for Coasters' promise to accept late delivery without complaint. For this reason, the common law would allow Coasters to go back on its word and collect the $15 000. However, there is an excellent chance that the doctrine of promissory estoppel would be applied by a judge to prevent this outcome because

- Coasters promised not to rely on its contractual right to collect late charges.

- Trackers relied on this promise and changed its position by scheduling production accordingly and taking no additional steps to speed up its schedule.

- Trackers' conduct throughout has been beyond reproach—it did not threaten Coasters or otherwise place undue pressure on it to accept late delivery.

- Trackers is using the doctrine to defend itself from a claim by Coasters for the late charges.

For these kinds of reasons, Coasters would be estopped from relying on the late charges clause, and its action for $15 000 would fail.

Promissory estoppel is a relatively complicated doctrine and cannot be fully detailed here. The foregoing analysis is offered only as an introductory account of how the doctrine might arise in a business context.

Partial Payment of a Debt

A common difficulty encountered by a business arises when the customer cannot pay its account but offers a smaller amount to settle the debt in full. Can the business agree to the customer's proposal, accept the smaller amount, and then sue for the balance? Put another way, does the compromise on a bill amount to a binding contract, or is it simply a gratuitous promise by the creditor to accept a lesser amount? The discussion under promissory

---

37. Most Canadian courts insist that promissory estoppel can be used only as a defence, though there is some case law to the contrary. See, for example, *Robichaud c Caisse Populaire de Pokemouche Itée* (1990), 69 DLR (4th) 589 (NBCA). See too criticism of the rule in *Greater Fredericton Airport Authority, supra* note 30 at para 29. Based on the traditional doctrine, promissory estoppel cannot be used by Trackers to enforce Coaster's promise to pay more for the tracking. Trackers cannot sue on the promise—it can use it only as a defence.

estoppel illustrates that equity may provide assistance to the debtor and enforce the creditor's promise. As well, the debtor may have recourse because she has provided consideration or because the new agreement is under seal. Finally, there may be a statute that makes the creditor's promise binding.

The common law rule that a creditor can go back on a promise to accept a lesser sum in full satisfaction of the debt has been reversed by legislation in several jurisdictions, including Ontario. Section 16 of Ontario's *Mercantile Law Amendment Act*, for example, essentially provides that once the lesser amount has been freely agreed upon and paid, the creditor cannot later claim the full amount.[38] A policy rationale for the legislation is to promote settlement of debts on a final basis.

For example, assume that Coasters has fallen on hard times and has been able to pay only $1.0 million on its account with Trackers. Therefore, $500 000 is outstanding. Trackers agrees to accept $300 000 from Coasters and write off the balance. At common law, Trackers can go back on its word and sue for the remaining $200 000 because its promise to accept a smaller sum is gratuitous. There is no consideration from Coasters supporting Trackers' promise to accept less than what is owed. Since Coasters has a preexisting legal duty to pay $500 000, paying $300 000 is not consideration for Trackers' promise to forgive the balance. Put another way, Coasters is not giving Trackers anything in return for Trackers' promise, except a $300 000 payment that it was obligated to make in any event.

In jurisdictions that have legislation making such agreements binding, the creditor cannot sue for the balance once she has received from the debtor the smaller amount promised. In jurisdictions without such legislation, the creditor's promise is not enforceable, under traditional analysis. The consideration rule remains in force so that in order for the promise to be enforced, the creditor must give the promise under seal or receive something in return for her promise to accept less (such as payment earlier than required).[39] Another alternative for the debtor seeking to enforce the creditor's promise is to rely on promissory estoppel, if circumstances permit.

A question arises in jurisdictions governed by legislation on point when the debtor has agreed to pay a lesser sum by installments over a period of time instead of all at once. What if the creditor changes her mind halfway through and seeks repayment of the entire amount owed? While case law is somewhat unclear on this point, it would seem that the legislation, as drafted, does not cover such a scenario and therefore the common law applies. In such a situation, the creditor may well be able to sue for the entire amount owing.[40]

---

38. The *Mercantile Law Amendment Act*, RSO 1990, c M.10, s 16 states, "Part performance of an obligation either before or after breach thereof when expressly accepted by the creditor or rendered in pursuance of an agreement for that purpose, though without any new consideration, shall be held to extinguish the obligation." Similar provisions are in effect in jurisdictions such as British Columbia (*Law and Equity Act*, RSBC 1996, c 253, s 43); Manitoba (*Mercantile Law Amendment Act*, CCSM c M120, s 6 as amended by the *Law Reform (Miscellaneous Amendments) Act*, SM 1992, c 32, s 10); Saskatchewan (*Queen's Bench Act*, SS 1998, c Q-1.01, s 64); and Alberta (*Judicature Act*, RSA 2000, c J-2, s 13).

39. The debtor in New Brunswick (where there is no legislation binding the creditor to a gratuitous promise to accept a lesser sum) may now have a new argument that the creditor is bound notwithstanding, due to the *Greater Fredericton Airport Authority* case, *supra* note 30. The conclusion would be that, absent duress, the creditor's gratuitous promise to accept a lesser sum should be enforceable, for the policy reasons given in that case. Note that such a parallel argument was unsuccessful in England (which likewise has no such legislation binding the creditor). The English Court of Appeal in *Selectmove* stated that the common law rule (which says that a promise to take a lesser sum is unenforceable absent consideration) should not be judicially reversed. It was up to Parliament to enact legislation to effect such a result, if it were so inclined. See *Re: Selectmove Ltd.* [1955] 2 All ER 531 (CA).

40. Christine Boyle & David Percy, eds, *Contracts: Cases and Commentaries*, 7th ed (Scarborough, ON: Carswell, 2004) at 216.

The varying status of how partially paid debts are handled across Canada illustrates two important aspects of contract law. First, provincial legislatures may intervene at any time to alter or override a common law rule governing contracts. Second, though largely uniform across the country, contract law is under provincial control and is therefore subject to important provincial variations.

Intention to Contract

The last important ingredient in a contract is the intention to contract. In order for one party to enforce the promise of another, the promise at issue must have been intended to be a contractual one, that is, one that would be enforceable by a court of law. Absent such an intention, there is no contract between the parties.

Business Agreements

Most agreements in the commercial world, such as the one between Trackers and Coasters, are quite obviously intended to be contractual. The common law recognizes this reality through the rule stating that in the marketplace, the intention to contract is *presumed*. Therefore, if Trackers ends up suing Coasters for breach of contract, it will not have to prove that the agreement between them was intended to be a contractual one. The law gives Trackers a presumption to this effect. The presumption is **rebuttable**, however. This means that while the court will assume that intention was present, Coasters can try to displace that presumption by proving a lack of intent to contract, judged objectively. Given the circumstances of its relationship with Trackers, Coasters faces an uphill battle on this point.

Rebuttable presumption
A legal presumption in favour of one party that the other side can seek to rebut or dislodge by leading evidence to the contrary.

Family Agreements

Agreements between family members are regarded differently in law because of the personal nature of the underlying relationship. In fact, the common law presumes that promises between family members are non-contractual. Therefore, people who want to enforce an alleged contract against their parents or siblings, for example, must demonstrate to a court that there was an intention to contract. If they cannot positively prove that intent, their action will fail.

Managing the Risks in Contract Formation

Negotiators such as Jason and Amritha face two main risks. The first is the risk of misunderstanding when statements and conduct have legal consequences. For example, if Amritha makes what objectively looks like an offer to Jason, he is entitled to accept it and a contract is thus formed. Amritha cannot then go back and unilaterally amend the terms of her offer. The second risk is failing to anticipate and plan for contingencies that might occur after the contract has been formed. For example, if Jason agrees to supply tracking at a set price and later faces a substantial increase in production costs, Trackers still must provide the tracking as agreed, even though this will cause enormous financial hardship to Trackers. Customizing contractual terms in order to accommodate future contingencies such as these is discussed further in Chapter 7.

Business Law in Practice Revisited

1. At what point did the negotiations between Jason and Amritha begin to have legal consequences?

When Jason made an offer to sell tracking on specific terms, his negotiations with Amritha took a legal turn. At this point, Amritha was in a position to accept Jason's offer and, if she did, Trackers would be obligated to supply tracking on precisely those terms.

2. In what ways could negotiations have been terminated prior to the formation of the contract?

Amritha could have ended her negotiations by rejecting Jason's offer and telling him that Coasters would be looking elsewhere for its tracking. Though Amritha is not legally obligated to reject an offer, it is helpful to do so to ensure clarity and to avoid misunderstandings and disappointed expectations later on. Amritha should also withdraw any offer she may have made on behalf of Coasters to prevent Jason from accepting it sometime down the road. While the doctrine of lapse will prevent Jason from accepting after a certain point in time, it is difficult to predict how long a court would consider the offer to be open. It is preferable to simply withdraw the offer and avoid the debate altogether.

3. Can Coasters commit itself to the price increase and then change its mind with no adverse consequences?

Trackers has a pre-existing legal duty to supply the tracking at the price stated in the contract. Since it has given Coasters nothing in return for Coasters' promise to pay more, the traditional view is that Coasters has no legal obligation to pay the increase. Put another way, the promise is gratuitous. Any change to a contract—known in law as a "variation"—must be supported by consideration or be under seal in order to be enforceable. There is, however, a significant consequence to Coasters' decision from a business perspective: its relationship with Trackers will be seriously harmed and possibly destroyed. If Coasters ever needs tracking again, it is unlikely that Trackers will agree to be its supplier.

A competing analysis is offered by the New Brunswick Court of Appeal: provided the variation is not the product of duress, a contractual variation is enforceable due to principles of commercial or business efficacy—the goal is to protect the parties' legitimate expectations that such a contractual variation would be respected and adhered to.

4. How could Trackers have avoided from the outset this situation related to cost increases?

Trackers should have negotiated a clause in the contract that included a formula for varying the price according to prevailing market conditions, as established by a third party, trade journal, or other source. Other possibilities include negotiating a "cost plus contract," meaning the contract price would comprise the tracking manufacturer's actual costs, plus a set percentage of profit. Another alternative would have been to charge a higher price to begin with to cover unexpected cost escalations.

If Trackers were unsuccessful in getting such price adjustment mechanisms into the contract, it would assume the full risk of unanticipated cost increases. If Coasters did subsequently agree to pay more for the steel, Trackers should provide consideration for that promise or get it under seal.

Chapter Summary

A contract comprises four essential elements: an offer, an acceptance, consideration, and an intention to contract. Before a contract can be formed, one party must make an offer on a complete set of certain terms. An offer can be terminated in a number of ways, including by revocation, lapse, rejection, counteroffer, death, or insanity. Assuming that an offer is on the table, the other party must unconditionally accept all the terms of the offer for the offer to be considered accepted. Each party must give something (called consideration) in exchange for the promise or performance of the other. The parties must intend their bargain to be a contractual one. If any one of these elements is missing, the relationship is non-contractual by definition.

There are occasions, however, when the law will enforce a promise that is not supported by consideration. In short, if the promise is under seal, meets the requirements of promissory estoppel, or is subject to a specialized statutory scheme, such as the partial payment of debt, it will be enforceable. As well, the New Brunswick Court of Appeal is willing to enforce gratuitous contractual variations provided there is no economic duress. Aside from these exceptions, a gratuitous promise is not binding, no matter how seriously it was intended and no matter how much the other party may have relied on it. This legal reality is particularly important when varying a term in an existing contract.

While the conditions for creating a legal agreement may seem stringent, they serve an important purpose. Contract law is about creating voluntary agreements and is therefore facilitative. In sum, it helps those in the marketplace to determine—in advance of litigation—the legal enforceability of commitments they have received, and thereby lets them do business more effectively.

Chapter Study

Key Terms and Concepts

acceptance (p. 122)

consideration (p. 128)

counteroffer (p. 122)

gratuitous promise (p. 128)

invitation to treat (p. 115)

lapse (p. 121)

offer (p. 114)

offeree (p. 118)

offeror (p. 118)

option agreement (p. 120)

pre-existing legal duty (p. 130)

promissory estoppel (p. 132)

rebuttable presumption (p. 135)

rejection (p. 122)

revocation (p. 118)

standard form contract (p. 116)

Questions for Review

1. What must an offer contain?

2. Is an advertisement an offer or an invitation to treat? Why?

3. Are oral contracts enforceable?

4. What is a standard form contract?

5. Explain why it might be a good idea to get a contract in writing.

6. Does the acceptance of an offer have to mirror it exactly, or are slight variations permissible?

7. What is the "postal rule"?

8. How is the postal rule different from the "ordinary rule" for acceptance?

9. When must an offeree communicate acceptance to the offeror in a specific form?

10. Why is a counteroffer a form of rejecting an offer?

11. When can an offeror revoke or withdraw an offer?

12. What is consideration?

13. What is an option agreement? How is the concept of consideration related to the enforceability of such an agreement?

14. What is a pre-existing legal duty?

15. Is a promise to pay more for performance of a pre-existing legal duty generally enforceable?

16. What is a gratuitous promise? Give an example.

17. Are the rules governing the formation of electronic contracts any different than those for written or oral contracts?

18. How does the relationship between the parties affect presumptions concerning their contractual intent?

19. What does Contract A refer to in a tendering context?

20. What does Contract B refer to in a tendering context?

Questions for Critical Thinking

1. The Ontario Court of Appeal in *Gilbert Steel* and the New Brunswick Court of Appeal in *Greater Fredericton Airport Authority* take opposite views on the enforceability of contractual variations unsupported by consideration. Which view do you prefer and why?

2. Based on information contained in the box Business Application of the Law: Spamming, what risk management steps should a business take in order to help ensure that any commercial email it sends out is compliant with Canada's new anti-spamming legislation?

3. Family members are presumed not to intend legal relations, while businesspeople are subject to the opposite presumption, namely that an intention to create legal relations is present. Why should the relationship between the parties affect the enforceability of their promises?

4. When the common law rules of contract were being formed by the judiciary, paper correspondence was the only form of distance communication. Are the traditional rules of contract formation appropriate for modern methods of communication?

5. What risks do negotiators face if they lack knowledge of the rules of contract?

6. Do you think that the doctrine of promissory estoppel serves a useful purpose? Would it not be easier if the law simply insisted that all contractual variations be supported by consideration?

Situations for Discussion

1. Mr. Gaff made the following written offer to Ms. Paulo:

   > MEMO FROM: J. Gaff
   >
   > TO: R. Paulo
   >
   > DATE: June 7, 2000
   >
   > I hereby agree to sell to R. Paulo my entire fleet of Rolls-Royce automobiles for the sum of $1 million. This offer is open until Friday, June 9, 2000, at 9:00 a.m.

   On Thursday, June 8, Gaff decided to sell the cars to his well-to-do neighbour instead. Paulo heard about the alleged sale later that same day and rushed over to Gaff's house, stating that she wished to accept Gaff's offer. Gaff smiled and said, "Sorry, you're too late. I've sold to someone else." Is Gaff obligated to keep the offer open until the specified time? What could Paulo have done to better protect her position?

2. An advertisement similar to the following appeared in a popular Canadian business magazine. What legal obligations does it create for Star?

   > ## At ★ Star ★ We try harder!!
   >
   > Any car rental company will reserve you a car.
   > Only ★ Star ★ tries harder to get you where you're going.

3. Jack and his sister Lisa inherited their parent's commercial building. Jack suggested to Lisa that he would be willing to buy her out for $50 000. Lisa thought about it for a minute and then quickly agreed. "A deal is a deal," said Lisa and shook hands with her brother. "There is no need for us to go to a lawyer and get a big fancy contract written up."

   If Lisa ever has to prove this contract in a court of law, what are the problems she faces?

4. On 30 October, Casgrain offered to purchase some farmland from Butler for $14 500, with possession in January. On 15 November, Butler made a counteroffer, by telegram, at $15 000. The telegram was delivered to Casgrain's home on 20 November but Casgrain was absent on a hunting trip. Casgrain's wife opened the letter and wrote back to Butler saying that her husband was away for 10 days and asking that he hold the deal open until Casgrain could consider the matter. Butler did not respond. On 10 December, Casgrain returned home and immediately wired Butler, purporting to accept Butler's offer of $15 000. The wire was received on 12 December. By this time, Butler had already sold the land to someone else. Has Casgrain accepted the offer in time or has it lapsed?[41]

5. Mr. and Mrs. Smith were regular participants in a lottery pool with their friends. Each Friday, the group would meet at the local pub and contribute to a pool of cash which would then be used to purchase lottery tickets. The group agreed that if a winning ticket were purchased, the amount would be shared amongst the participants. There was also discussion that if someone in the group did not come to the pub on the day in question, another person present would contribute on the missing person's behalf and get paid back later. On one Friday, the Smiths did not attend the pub nor, therefore, contribute to the pool of lottery cash but they trusted that their friends would contribute on their behalf. This did not happen. One of the tickets purchased turned out to be a winner. Mr. and Mrs. Smith say they are entitled to a share. The others in the group say that only those who actually paid into the pool for that winning ticket are entitled to a share of the prize. Which view do you think is correct and why?[42]

6. ABC Ltd. is owed $10 000 from Mr. Smith for home repair. Mr. Abbott, a senior officer with ABC Ltd., went to the Smith's home to secure payment and spoke with Smith. Abbott explained that without

---

41. Based, in part, on *Barrick v Clark*, [1951] SCR 177.
42. Based, in part, on *Clancy v Clough*, 2011 ABQB 439.

payment, ABC faced bankruptcy. In response, Smith began complaining about the poor quality of the work done (even though he knew the work was perfectly fine) and that he would only pay $4000. "Take it or leave, buster," he said. Abbott took his cheque and cashed it, feeling that he had no choice in the matter. He would now like to go after Mr. Smith for the balance. Can he do so?[43]

7. April manufactures leather chairs and sofas, and she is happy because she has just negotiated a contract with Bob's Fine Furnishings, Ltd., to supply them with her handmade furniture. The terms of the contract are that on the first Monday of every month, April is to send over 10 chairs and two sofas, and Bob's Fine Furnishings will pay her $7000. She is excited to learn that her furniture is so popular that Bob's Fine Furnishings has a waiting list of customers who have prepaid for their chairs, as her last shipment sold out in only a week. April is a little worried, however, as she has just received a phone call saying that her leather supplier will not be able to send her any leather for the next three months, due to a local shortage. Without the leather, she knows she cannot fill her order for Bob's Fine Furnishings by the first Monday of next month, much less for the two months after that. What could April have done when negotiating the contract with Bob's Fine Furnishings to help manage the risk of a situation like this? What should she do now that the contract is already in place?

8. Mr. M, living in British Columbia, and Ms. A, living in England, met online and struck up a relationship. Mr. M promised Ms. A that if she would come to live with him in Canada, with a view to marriage, he would pay off the balance on her mortgage on her home in England. Relying on this promise, Ms. A gave up her job and moved to Vancouver. The relationship proved to be an unhappy one particularly because Mr. M did not pay off Ms. A's mortgage though he did lend her $100 000. She applied that money to her mortgage but was soon thereafter evicted from M's home. Can Ms. A enforce Mr. M's promise to pay off her mortgage by relying on the doctrine of promissory estoppel? Is Ms. A's reliance on Mr. M's promise enough to make that promise enforceable?[44]

For more study tools, visit http://www.NELSONbrain.com.

---

43. Based, in part, on *D & C Builders v Rees*, [1965] 3 All ER 837 (CA).
44. Based, in part, on *M(N) v A(AT)*, 2003 BCCA 297.

CHAPTER 7

The Terms of a Contract

Objectives

After studying this chapter, you should have an understanding of

- the difference between implied and express terms

- how judges determine and interpret the content of a contract

- how a party can use terms as a business tool to protect itself from liability

FENG YU/SHUTTERSTOCK

Business Law in Practice

The dispute discussed in Chapter 6 between Coasters and Trackers over the purchase price was resolved reasonably amicably—the parties agreed to split the increased cost of the steel required to manufacture the tracking and thereby avoid the expense and disruption of litigation. All the tracking has been delivered, and the new purchase price has been paid. Jason not only is tremendously relieved but also wants to improve his performance as a negotiator, since matters did not proceed entirely smoothly. He is reviewing the Coasters–Trackers contract to determine whether it did, in fact, contain the terms Trackers needed to protect itself.

The contract between Coasters and Trackers covered a number of terms already discussed in the previous chapter, including price ($1.5 million); quantity (900 metres); delivery dates; and late-delivery charges ($5000 a day). Other significant clauses are excerpted below.

Excerpt from the contract between Trackers (the "Seller") and Coasters (the "Buyer") for the purchase and sale of tracking (the "Goods")

...

12. Warranties—Guarantees.

Seller warrants that the goods shall be free from defect in material, workmanship, and title and shall conform in all respects to the design specifications provided by Buyer and attached as Appendix A to this contract. Where no quality is specified, the quality shall be of the best quality.

If it appears within one year from the date of placing the goods into service for the purpose for which they were purchased that the Goods, or any part thereof, does not conform to these warranties, Buyer, at its election and within a reasonable time after its discovery, may notify Seller. If notified, Seller shall thereupon promptly correct such nonconformity at its sole expense.

...

13. Limitation of Seller's Liability.

Except as otherwise provided in this contract, Seller's liability shall extend to all damages proximately caused by the breach of any of the foregoing warranties or guarantees, but such liability shall in no event exceed unit price of defective Goods and in no event include loss of profit or loss of use.

...

(Continued on the next page)

> **14. Exemption of Seller's Liability.**
> Seller is exempted from all liability in respect to losses, damages, costs, or claims relating to design of Goods.
>
> …
>
> **20. Entire Contract.**
> This is the entire agreement between the parties, covering everything agreed upon or understood in connection with the subject matter of this transaction. There are no oral promises, conditions, representations, understandings, interpretations, or terms of any nature or kind, statutory or otherwise, as conditions or inducements to the execution hereof or in effect between the parties or upon which the parties are relying relating to this agreement or otherwise.

1. How is the scope of Trackers' and Coasters' obligations determined?
2. Are there any ambiguous or unclear terms in the contract?
3. Are there any additional terms that Jason should have tried to have included?
4. Does the contract relieve the parties from responsibility for inadequate performance?

The Content of a Contract

This chapter is about the content—or terms—of a contract and how the courts interpret those terms. The terms of a contract simply refer to promises made by one party to another by virtue of offer and acceptance. From a risk management perspective, a contract is a business tool that can be used to manage a business' exposure to liability—also the subject matter of this chapter.

Terms

Contractual terms can be express or implied.

Express Terms

Express term
A provision of a contract that states a promise explicitly.

An **express term** is a provision of the contract that states or makes explicit one party's promise to another. In the Coasters–Trackers contract, for example, a number of terms are express, including the price, quantity, and warranties associated with the tracking. It is important that the essential terms of a contract be expressed so that each party knows its obligations and the obligations of the other side. Parties negotiating a contract should be very careful not to make assumptions about any aspect of the transaction, as only terms, not assumptions, have legal weight.

Judicial Interpretation of Express Terms

Vague or Ambiguous Language   Even when a term is express, there may be problems interpreting what it means because the language is vague or ambiguous. Assuming that the existence of the contract is not in doubt, the court assigns as reasonable a meaning as possible to vague or ambiguous terms.[1] As well, if the contract has been drafted by one of the parties, any ambiguity in language will be construed against that party in favour of the other.[2] The policy rationale for this rule is that the drafter should bear the risk of unclear language.

---

1. Stephanie Ben-Ishai & David R Percy, eds, *Contracts: Cases and Commentaries*, 8th ed (Scarborough, ON: Carswell, 2009) at 113.
2. *Ibid* at 503.

The reference to "best quality" in clause 12 of the Coasters–Trackers contract is somewhat nebulous, as it introduces an express element of subjectivity: what, exactly, is "best quality"? If faced with such a question, a court would conclude that "best quality" refers to the highest quality available, which, in turn, is a matter that expert evidence would establish. A court would not set the contract aside for uncertainty because some meaning can be assigned to the phrase "best quality."

There is a point, however, at which language is so ambiguous that the contract cannot be understood. In such cases, the contract will fail for uncertainty, and none of the promises it contains will be enforceable.

It can be very difficult to predict how a court will interpret any given contract because **rules of construction**—that is, guiding principles for interpreting or "constructing" the terms of a contract—are often conflicting. For example, on the one hand, courts are required to enforce the contract as it is written and to rely primarily on the plain, ordinary meaning of the words that the parties have chosen. The court simply asks how a reasonable person would regard the term in question and can refer to dictionaries, legal reference materials, and cases that have considered such terms in the past. On the other hand, courts are to give effect to the parties' intentions. Both of these rules make sense standing alone, but they do not provide a solution to the situation in which the parties' intentions may be inadequately reflected in the written contract itself. Should the court apply the plain-meaning rule or give effect to the parties' intentions? Which rule should prevail?

| **Rules of construction** Guiding principles for interpreting or "constructing" the terms of a contract. |

In the Coasters–Trackers contract, Trackers promised to pay $5000 to Coasters for every day it was late in delivering the tracking. The intent of the parties, objectively assessed, may have been to motivate Trackers to do everything in its power to provide the tracking by the contractual delivery date. On this basis, if Trackers were late delivering because of a mechanical problem in its plant, the clause would apply. It would be more contentious to apply the clause if late delivery were caused by an event completely outside Trackers' control—such as a severe lightning strike disrupting electricity to its plant for several days. Trackers might advance the position that to apply the clause in such circumstances would be contrary to the parties' intentions.

In response, Coasters would ask that the court apply the plain-meaning rule and disregard evidence of the parties' intentions. On the basis of the plain-meaning rule, a court could easily conclude that the late-delivery clause speaks for itself and is unconditional: if Trackers delivers late, it has to pay $5000 per day. Whether a court would use the plain-meaning rule standing alone or allow the clause's plain meaning to be tempered with evidence of what the parties intended the term to mean is impossible to predict—another inherent risk of litigation.

Trackers could face further problems in convincing a court of its interpretation of the late-delivery clause based on the parties' intentions. Two possible sources of problems are the parol evidence rule and the fact that the Coasters–Trackers contract contains what is known as an entire contract clause. Both matters are discussed later in this chapter.

When parties fail to address an important aspect of their contractual relationship, the law may help to "fill in the blanks" through implied terms, discussed below. The assistance that implied terms can provide, however, is sporadic and cannot be relied on with any certainty.

Implied Terms

When an event arises that is not addressed in the contract through express terms, courts may be asked to imply a term in order to give effect to the parties' intentions. A judge will do so if he is satisfied that not all of the terms that the parties intended to include in the contract were in fact included. In the classic scenario, the plaintiff argues to include an **implied term** but the defendant asserts that no such term was intended. Since the plaintiff carries the burden of proof, she will lose unless she can demonstrate that the term exists based on the balance of probabilities (i.e., she needs to prove that it is more likely than not that the parties intended such a term to be included).

Implied term
A provision that is not expressly included in a contract but that is necessary to give effect to the parties' intention.

BUSINESS APPLICATION OF THE LAW

911 Emergency Access

In 2010, James Anderson of Yellowknife successfully commenced a Northwest Territories class action against Bell Mobility Inc. ("Bell"), a Canadian cellular phone service provider.[3] For years, Bell had been charging Anderson 75 cents a month for 911 Emergency access even though there actually is no 911 emergency access service in the NWT. Calling 911 anywhere in the NWT simply triggers a generic recording, directing the caller to hang up and dial the local police or fire station for assistance. Anderson alleges in his statement of claim that Bell breached an express or implied term of their contract that Bell would provide the services for which fees and monies are charged, namely live '911' service. Put another way, if Bell is going to charge for Emergency access, then that access must be available. If such service is not available—as when a simple 911 recording is offered—no charge should be levied. On behalf of himself and his class, Anderson claims damages of $6 million. Bell's defence is that though Anderson cannot access live 911 services where he lives, these services are available to him when he travels elsewhere in Canada. As well, Bell says it is only obligated to provide call-routing services. Whether local governments provide emergency dispatch is not its concern.

Anderson's lawyer estimates that Bell Mobility has been charging at least 50 000 northern customers such fees for years. Beyond certification in the NWT, the class action has recently been certified in Nunavut and Yukon. Given early success to date, the action will presumably be taken up by customers in other Canadian jurisdictions who believe that they too have been charged for a service by Bell that was never actually provided.

THE CANADIAN PRESS/FRED LUM/THE GLOBE AND MAIL

Anderson required certification because it would make no economic sense for him or anyone else to pursue such an action alone. This is because each Bell customer was, at worst, overcharged by only $9.00 a year. Who would bother suing over such a small amount?

The class action is expected to go to trial in 2012.

Critical Analysis: Who do you think should win this action?

Sources: Grant Robertson "Frustrated with no 911 services, customers fight back", Globe and Mail (11 April 2010) online: Globe and Mail <http://m.theglobeandmail.com/report-on-business/frustrated-with-no-911-service-customers-fight-back/article1530801/?service=mobile>; Landy Marr Kats LLP, "Class Actions", online: Landy Marr Kats LLP <http://www.thetorontolawyers.ca/class_actions.htm>; *CBC News*, "Lawsuit over Bell's 911 fees back in court", CBC News (13 April 2010) online: *CBC News* <http://www.cbc.ca/news/canada/north/story/2010/04/13/bell-911-lawsuit.html> and Josh Kerr, "Bell law suit spread to the Yukon", Yukon News (3 June 2011) online: *Yukon News* <http://www.yukon-news.com/news/23304/>.

---

3. By Order dated July 30, 2010, of the Supreme Court of the Northwest Territories, a civil action was certified as a class action in *Anderson v Bell Mobility Inc,* 2010 NWTSC 65. See also, Landy Marr Kats LLP, "Notice of Class Proceeding: To: Bell Mobility Customers", online: Landy Marr Kats LLP <http://www.thetorontolawyers.ca/PDFs/anderson_v_bell_notice_of_class_proceeding.pdf>. Note that Bell's application to strike the statement of claim was dismissed by an appellate court in *Anderson v Bell Mobility Inc,* 2009 NWTCA 03.

Courts will imply terms based on a number of grounds, such as those listed below.

Business Efficacy   Through the doctrine of business efficacy,[4] a judge is entitled to imply terms necessary to make the contract workable. For example, if Trackers promised to use a certain grade of tracking, "providing it is available," a court will almost certainly imply a promise by Trackers to put reasonable effort into trying to find that grade of tracking. Though Trackers has not expressly committed itself to make systematic efforts in this regard, business efficacy makes the obligation implicit.[5] Were it otherwise, the express term in relation to the quality of tracking would mean next to nothing.

A term that courts are increasingly willing to imply as part of commercial contracts is that of good faith, owing, in large part, to the influence of the following case.

LANDMARK CASE

Gateway Realty Ltd v Arton Holdings Ltd (1991), 106 NSR (2d) 180 (SC), aff'd (1992), 112 NSR (2d) 180 (CA)

THE BUSINESS CONTEXT: Businesspeople might assume that the only obligations they owe the other party are those recited in the contract between them. This assumption may prove to be unfounded, particularly in the situation where one party is in a position to adversely affect the interests of the other.

FACTUAL BACKGROUND: Gateway owned a shopping mall in which Zellers was the anchor tenant. The lease permitted Zellers to occupy the premises, leave them vacant, or assign them to a third party without any obligation to secure the consent of the landlord. After being approached by Arton, a competitor of Gateway, Zellers agreed to locate in Arton's mall. As part of this arrangement, Arton agreed to take an assignment of Zellers' lease with Gateway. As a result, a large part of Gateway's mall had been assigned to its competitor. Pursuant to a subsequent contract between Gateway and Arton, the companies agreed to use their best efforts to get a tenant for the space formerly occupied by Zellers. Arton, however, rejected all prospective tenants. Gateway then sued, alleging that Arton was in breach of contract for declining prospective tenants. From Gateway's perspective, Arton was simply trying to undermine the economic viability of the mall by letting a large portion of it remain unoccupied.

THE LEGAL QUESTION: Is there an implied obligation of good faith on Arton's part to take reasonable steps to sublet the premises?

RESOLUTION: The court found that Arton breached the express obligation to use its "best efforts" to find a tenant, as well as an implied term to act in good faith.

According to the court:

> The law requires that parties to a contract exercise their rights under that agreement honestly, fairly and in good faith. This standard is breached when a party acts in a bad faith manner in the performance of its rights and obligations under the contract. "Good faith" conduct is the guide to the manner in which the parties should pursue their mutual contractual objectives. Such conduct is breached when a party acts in "bad faith"—a conduct that is contrary to community standards of honesty, reasonableness or fairness.

The court went on to say:

> In most cases, bad faith can be said to occur when one party, without reasonable justification, acts in relation to the contract in a manner where the result would be to substantially nullify the bargained objective or benefit contracted for by the other, or to cause significant harm to the other, contrary to the original purpose and expectation of the parties.

CRITICAL ANALYSIS: The *Gateway* case has been followed or cited with approval by numerous Canadian courts, but the case has not yet been expressly considered by the Supreme Court of Canada. Other courts have determined that a good faith clause is not an automatic term of every contract and can be implied only when it is consistent with the parties' intentions. Should all parties to a commercial deal be bound by a duty to act in good faith, or should parties be expected to take care of themselves?

---

4. GHL Fridman, The *Law of Contract in Canada*, 5th ed (Toronto: Carswell, 2006) at 467.
5. For a case that follows this analysis, see *Dawson v Helicopter Exploration Co*, [1955] SCR 868.

Customs in the Trade of the Transaction   Relying on trade customs to imply a term is rarely successful, since it must be proved that the custom is so notorious that the contract in question must be presumed to contain such an implied term.[6] Though a party is occasionally successful in relying on custom in a trade, the more prudent course is to ensure that all important terms in a contract are expressly recited.

CASE

Glenko Enterprises Ltd v Ernie Keller Contractors Ltd, [1994] 10 WWR 641 (Man QB), aff'd [1996] 5 WWR 135 (Man CA)

THE BUSINESS CONTEXT: Unpaid accounts are an unfortunate reality of the business world. Even when the customer admits that the account is owed, disputes can arise on the rate of interest payable if the contract does not expressly address this matter.

FACTUAL BACKGROUND: Though a number of factual and legal matters were at play in this case, it is most germane to note that the subcontractor, Glenko Enterprises Ltd., worked on a project but was not paid by the project contractor (Ernie Keller Contractors Ltd.). The contractor admitted that it owed $123 862.75 but insisted that since no interest had been stipulated in the contract, no interest on the overdue account should be payable. The plaintiff stated that interest was owed at the rate of 1.5 percent per month or 18 percent per annum on accounts over 30 days for three reasons:

• There was an implied agreement that such interest was payable based on the term being contained in the invoices sent to the contractor.

• The contractor did not object to the term regarding interest and, on the contrary, continued to deal with the subcontractor.

• It is a common trade practice to be charged and to pay interest on overdue accounts. The contractor itself included such an interest provision in its own invoices.

THE LEGAL QUESTION: Since the contract between the contractor and subcontractor was silent on the point of interest, what interest, if any, would be payable? Could a term be implied based on trade custom?

RESOLUTION: Even though this matter was not extensively discussed at trial, the judge ruled that the contractor was aware of and followed an industry practice of charging interest on overdue accounts. This was largely because the contractor had itself included a provision for interest in its own invoices. The plaintiffs were therefore entitled to the interest as claimed.

CRITICAL ANALYSIS: Why should industry or trade practice be relevant to understanding the parties' contractual obligations? Would it not be simpler for a court to apply the contractual terms as stated and refuse to look outside that document? What are the risks of relying on industry practices as a way of implying terms into a contract?

Previous Dealings between the Parties   If parties have contracted in the past, it may be possible to imply that their current contract contains the same terms.[7] A risk management perspective would suggest, however, that the parties clarify the basis of their contractual relationship each time they do business with each other.

Statutory Requirements   An important source of terms implied by statute[8] is found in provincial sale-of-goods legislation, which is largely uniform across the country. This legislation provides that certain terms are a mandatory part of every contract for the sale of goods unless specifically excluded by the parties.[9] Specialized rules governing the sale of goods and the extent to which consumer transactions can exclude their application are discussed in more detail in Chapter 23.

---

6. Fridman, *supra* note 4 at 477.
7. *Ibid* at 475.
8. For discussion, *ibid* at 479.
9. For a discussion of sale of goods legislation, see Chapter 23 as well as GHL Fridman, *Sale of Goods in Canada*, 5th ed (Scarborough, ON: Carswell, 2004).

DILBERT © SCOTT ADAMS. USED BY PERMISSION OF UNIVERSAL UCLICK. ALL RIGHTS RESERVED.

PART TWO

If Trackers delivers too much tracking to Coasters under its contract, the Ontario *Sale of Goods Act*,[10] for example, would resolve the situation according to the following rule:

> 29. (2) Where the seller delivers to the buyer a quantity of goods larger than the seller contracted to sell, the buyer may accept the goods included in the contract and reject the rest, or may reject the whole, and if the buyer accepts the whole of the goods so delivered, the buyer shall pay for them at the contract rate.

DICK HEMINGWAY

How can a business avoid having terms implied into a contract?

10. *RSO* 1990, c S1.

In general, terms are not easily implied except in routine transactions or unless the *Sale of Goods Act* applies. It must be clear that both parties would have included the term in question, had they addressed the matter.

Similarly, courts ordinarily will not imply terms when the parties have agreed that their contract is complete as written. The clearest way parties can signal this intention is through an **entire contract clause** like the one in the Coasters–Trackers contract excerpted earlier in this chapter. The function of this clause is to require a court to determine the parties' obligations based only on what is recited in the contract itself.

Entire contract clause
A term in a contract in which the parties agree that their contract is complete as written.

BUSINESS APPLICATION OF THE LAW

A Request for Goods or Services: Implying a Promise to Pay

When someone requests the supply of goods or services, the law—be it through common law or by applicable legislation such as the *Sale of Goods Act*—will imply a promise to pay a reasonable price for those goods or services. The law draws this conclusion because, in a business situation, it is the intention of the parties that goods or services are not to be provided for free, but rather are to be purchased. Implying such a term reflects what can only be the reasonable expectation of the parties—especially that of the seller—and is needed to give purpose and effect to the rest of the contract.

If the goods or services have already been provided but there has been no agreement on price, a term must be implied to require payment. The obligation on the customer is not to pay whatever the supplier chooses to charge or whatever the customer is willing to pay, but to pay a reasonable amount, as determined by the judge. This is known as a **contractual quantum meruit**, which is Latin for "as much as is merited or deserved." Given the expense and uncertainty of judicial proceedings, it is in the interests of both parties to agree on the price, in advance, as an express term. The objective is to avoid the surprises and misunderstandings that may lead to a legal dispute.

Contractual *quantum meruit*
Awarding one party a reasonable sum for the goods or services provided under a contract.

The Parol Evidence Rule

Contracts can take three possible forms:

- entirely oral (i.e., the terms of the contract are based on a conversation);

- entirely written (i.e., the terms of the contract are contained in a written contract);

- both oral and written (i.e., some of the agreement is written down and other assurances are not). For example, if Jason gave Amritha an oral assurance that Trackers would provide expert advice on how to install the tracking as a service included in the contract price, their contract would be both oral and written.

Except in a few specialized instances discussed in Chapter 8, the form a contract takes does not affect its enforceability. So long as the party claiming that there is a contract can prove it—through witnesses, for example—the fact that the parties only "shook hands" on the deal is not an impediment. Nevertheless, from the perspective of proving the contract, a written contract is always best.

There is an important consequence to having a written contract. Such contracts may trigger the **parol evidence rule** when a court is asked to determine—according to the parties' intentions—what a contract means and includes. "Parol" means "oral" or "spoken" but in this context refers to any kind of evidence that is extrinsic to the written agreement. The rule forbids outside evidence as to the terms of a contract when the language of the

Parol evidence rule
A rule that limits the evidence a party can introduce concerning the contents of the contract.

written contract is clear and the document is intended to be the sole source of contractual content. In the example above, the parol evidence rule may prohibit Amritha from bringing forward evidence of Jason's oral promise to provide expert installation advice. For this reason, a businessperson must be careful not to rely on oral assurances made by the other party, because if the assurance is not in the contract, a court may decline to enforce it as a contractual term.

Entire contract clauses are used to ensure application of the parol evidence rule to the contract in question. As noted earlier, such clauses generally operate to prevent a party from arguing that the terms of the agreement were found not just in the written document, but also in oral form. Clause 20 of the Coasters–Trackers contract is an entire contract clause. Such a clause is intended to ensure that any oral commitment made by one side to the other that is not ultimately written into the contract simply dies.

The parol evidence rule emphasizes the sanctity of the written agreement and means that the parties should, before agreeing to a written contract, ensure provision of all terms important to them. Failure to do so may mean that the rule is invoked against the party that cannot support its interpretation of the contract without leading evidence "outside" the contract.

The parol evidence rule has itself become the subject of judicial consideration, which in turn has justifiably limited its operation. Indeed, there are several situations where evidence outside the contract is important and is considered:

- If there is an alleged problem going to the formation of the contract—because one party alleges fraud at the hands of the other or asserts that there has been a mistake, for example—a party may bring to the court evidence to establish that allegation. Chapter 8 considers problems going to the formation of a contract in more detail.

- If the contract is *intended* to be partly oral and partly in writing, the rule has no application. The rule applies only when the parties intended the document to be the whole contract.

- If the promise to be enforced is contained in a separate (collateral) agreement that happens to be oral, the rule does not apply. For example, an agreement to sell for a set price a building with all the equipment in it may not include the equipment if the written agreement fails to mention it. If there is a separate agreement and a separate price for the equipment, however, the fact that the agreement for the building says nothing about the equipment is likely not a concern. The difference in the two situations is in the matter of there being separate consideration for the building and the equipment. If there is only one agreement and one price, the rule likely applies to the detriment of the party seeking to enforce the purchase and sale of the equipment.

- If the language in the contract is ambiguous, evidence outside the written contract can be used to resolve the ambiguity.

The following case demonstrates how even an entire contract clause may not prevent a court from considering parol evidence.

CASE

Corey Developments Inc v Eastbridge Developments (Waterloo) Ltd (1997), 34 OR (3d) 73, aff'd (1999), 44 OR (3d) 95 (CA)

THE BUSINESS CONTEXT: The parol evidence rule in its absolute form may cause manifest injustice and defeat the true intentions of the parties. Thus, almost from its inception, it has been subject to many exceptions. In recent times, the rule has also received disapproval from various law reform commissions. As well, several provinces have abolished the rule altogether in consumer situations. Consumer protection legislation in these provinces means that oral pre-contractual statements are not necessarily superseded by written terms.

In commercial transactions, the parol evidence rule has generally prevented the introduction of extrinsic evidence in challenging the written document and establishing the existence of oral promises. This treatment of the parol evidence rule as an absolute bar in commercial transactions has come under attack, however.

FACTUAL BACKGROUND: Corey Developments Inc. signed an agreement of purchase and sale with Eastbridge Developments Ltd., which was controlled by Mr. Ghermezian, a well-known Alberta developer. Corey gave a deposit of $201 500 to Eastbridge. According to Corey, as the money was to be used by Eastbridge to fund the costs of obtaining subdivision approval, Ghermezian said he would give his personal guarantee for the return of the deposit if the agreement did not close. The agreement of purchase and sale, however, made no mention of the personal guarantee, and Ghermezian denied ever having made such a promise. Evidence, including various letters between the parties, established the existence of the promise. The agreement of purchase and sale, however, contained an entire contract clause indicating that the agreement was intended to be the whole agreement. Therefore, by strict application of the parol evidence rule, the judge could not admit the oral evidence of Corey or the other documentary evidence.

THE LEGAL QUESTION: Was Ghermezian's personal guarantee to return the deposit a part of the contract?

RESOLUTION: Justice MacDonald referred to *Gallen v Allstate Grain Ltd,*[11] in which Mr. Justice Lambert found that the parol evidence rule provided only a presumption that the written terms should govern and allowed the extrinsic evidence. Justice MacDonald went on to state, "The court must not allow the rule to be used to cause obvious injustice by providing a tool for one party to dupe another."

Applying the principle from *Gallen*, Justice MacDonald ruled that Ghermezian's personal guarantee was part of the contract between the parties, notwithstanding the entire contract clause and the parol evidence rule.

CRITICAL ANALYSIS: Is the *Corey* decision a welcome development? What are the justifications, if any, for abolishing the parol evidence rule in a commercial context?

Source: Jan Weir, "The death of the absolute parol rule", *The Lawyers Weekly* (6 February 1998) 3.

BUSINESS AND LEGISLATION

Evidence of Electronic Contracts

Those who seek to enforce a contract must be able to prove that the contract was formed and that its terms support the claim that is made. Traditionally, that proof takes the form of witness testimony and documents that are submitted to the court as evidence. Of course, in proving the contract, the parties will have to respect the parol evidence rule and other rules of evidence.

With the growth of electronic business, contracts are increasingly negotiated online and the terms are recorded electronically, without a paper version. This method of doing business creates difficulty if it becomes necessary to produce the "original" contract in court. In response, governments across Canada have begun to enact legislation addressing this point.

In 1997, the Uniform Law Conference of Canada proposed draft legislation—called the *Uniform Electronic Evidence Act*, or *UEEA* for short—to make the proof of electronic contracts subject to a uniform set of rules. This draft legislation has since been implemented in a number of jurisdictions. For example, Ontario implemented the *UEEA* by amending its *Evidence Act*. Section 34.1 of that Act, as amended, provides

Authentication:

> (4) The person seeking to introduce an electronic record has the burden of proving its authenticity by evidence capable of supporting a finding that the electronic record is what the person claims it to be.

---

11. (1984), 9 DLR (4th) 496 (BCCA).

Application of Best Evidence Rule:

(5) Subject to subsection (6) where the best evidence rule is applicable in respect of an electronic record, it is satisfied on proof of the integrity of the electronic records system by or in which the data was recorded or stored.

Beyond Ontario, other provinces and territories (including Alberta, Manitoba, Nova Scotia, PEI, Saskatchewan and the Yukon), as well as the federal government, have enacted legislation which mirrors, in whole or in part, the Uniform Conference of Canada's draft act.[12]

Using Contractual Terms to Manage Risk

The planning function of law permits a businessperson to use contractual terms as a buffer against future, uncertain events as well as a way of limiting liability.

Changed Circumstances

Numerous circumstances may arise that prevent a party from performing its contractual obligations or that make performance much more expensive than anticipated. The rule, however, is that the terms of a contract are settled at the time of acceptance. Therefore, if disaster strikes—such as when a plant burns, railways go on strike or are closed, trade regulations change, or an entire manufacturing process becomes obsolete—the obligations in a contract are enforceable, unless a clause to the contrary is included. Though the legal doctrine of "frustration" occasionally relieves parties from their obligations (see Chapter 9), it operates in very limited circumstances and cannot be counted on to provide an avenue of escape.

It is therefore particularly important in longer-term contracts that negotiators evaluate risks, speculate on possible changes in the business environment, and be wary of making

Why do well-drafted contracts anticipate events that can affect performance?

12. See, for example *Alberta Evidence Act*, RSA 2000, c A-18 ss 41.1-41.8; *Evidence Act*, RSNS 1989, c 154 ss 23A-23H (Nova Scotia); *Evidence Act*, RSO 1990, c E.23 ss 34.1(1)-34.1(11) (Ontario); *Electronic Evidence Act*, RSPEI, c E-4.3 (Prince Edward Island) and Manitoba *Evidence Act*, CCSM c E150 ss 51.1-51.8. For discussion of UEAA legislation in Canada, see Charles Morgan & Julien Saulgrain, *E-Mail Law* (Markham: LexisNexis, 2008) at 130–132.

inflexible commitments. Taking these precautions is essential because changed circumstances may render a contract extremely disadvantageous to one party. For example, the price for the tracking that Trackers needed to fill Coasters' order dramatically increased, making it very expensive for Trackers to complete its end of the bargain. Rather than run such a risk, Trackers could have negotiated for a term that would permit the contract price for the tracking to rise should the price of tracking increase. A contractual term could

- provide a formula setting the price of the goods supplied, in a manner that is tied to market value

- set the price according to the cost of materials, plus a specific percentage for profit

- allow the parties to reopen negotiations or terminate the contract altogether if specified events occur, such as a commodity price reaching a certain level

Instead of having to go to Coasters for some kind of accommodation, Trackers could have included a clause protecting its interests. Though the approach of voluntarily altering the agreement as the need arises can be successful, legally there is no obligation on either party to reach agreement. Furthermore, as discussed in Chapter 6, the voluntary agreement is unenforceable unless fresh consideration is given, a court is willing to apply the novel case of *Greater Fredericton Airport Authority Inc v NAV Canada*,[13] promissory estoppel applies, or the document is put under seal.

Parties must try to build some flexibility into their agreements, while avoiding creating a document that is so vague that they run the risk of having no contract at all. If in negotiations a customer such as Coasters refuses to accept a price-variation clause of any description, the supplier must then choose to risk an adverse change in market conditions, try to negotiate a higher price to compensate for possible market changes, or lose the order altogether.

Conditional Agreements

Conditional agreements are essential when one party wants to incur contractual obligations but only under certain circumstances. For example, a business enterprise may be interested in buying a warehouse, but only if it is able to secure financing from the bank. If the business simply agrees to purchase the warehouse without making its agreement conditional on securing financing, it will be obligated to complete the transaction even if the bank refuses the request for a loan. This outcome could have devastating financial consequences for the business in question. Conversely, if the business makes an offer to purchase the property subject to financing,[14] and that offer is accepted by the vendor, the business is obligated to complete only if and when the financing is approved.

From a risk management perspective, it is important that the law provide a mechanism not only for making the contractual obligation conditional on a certain event happening, but also for binding the parties in some way during the time set aside for that condition to occur. If the vendor of the warehouse was entitled to sell to someone else while the business enterprise was trying to secure necessary financing, the whole arrangement would be somewhat futile.

---

13. 2008 NBCA 28.
14. Such a clause must contain sufficient detail; otherwise, it will be unenforceable owing to uncertainty. For discussion of such clauses, see Gwilym Davies, "Some Thoughts on the Drafting of Conditions in Contracts for the Sale of Land" (1977) 15:2 Alta L Rev 422.

To bind the other side during the time set aside for the condition's fulfillment, the law provides two mechanisms: the condition subsequent and the condition precedent. **Conditions subsequent** will always bind the parties to a contract pending the fulfillment of the condition. The occurrence of a condition subsequent operates to terminate the contract between the parties—that is, it must, by definition, relate to an existing contract. For example, parties to an employment contract may agree that an employee is to work for an organization unless the employee's sales drop below a certain amount. This is a contract subject to a condition subsequent. If the condition occurs—that is, if the employee's sales fall below the threshold—the contract automatically comes to an end.

For the most part, **conditions precedent** work in the same way—that is, there is a contract between the parties.[15] However, unlike the condition subsequent situation, where parties perform their contractual obligations until the condition occurs, the condition precedent situation means that the parties' obligations to perform are not triggered pending fulfillment of the condition. That is, a contract exists between the parties, but the obligation to perform the contract is held in abeyance pending the occurrence of the event. Because there is a contract between the parties, the law is able to imply certain terms binding on the parties in the meantime. In the real estate situation, for example, a court would imply a term that the vendor must wait until the time for fulfilling the condition has passed before it can sell to someone else. Similarly, a court would imply a term on the purchaser to make good faith efforts to secure the necessary financing. Without a contract between the parties, these kinds of terms could not be implied, because without a contract, there are no terms whatsoever.[16]

Purchasers of real estate, for example, frequently rely on the conditional agreement by making the contractual obligation to buy and sell subject to

- rezoning

- subdivision approval

- annexation of the property by a municipality

- mortgage financing

- provision of adequate water and sanitary sewer services to the property

Conditional agreements might also arise in other contexts. For example, a business may be willing to commit to perform a contract provided it can

- access a certain source of supply

- engage people with the necessary expertise

- obtain a licence to use certain intellectual property

Conditional agreements would permit such an enterprise to contract with the other side but would provide an established reason to escape the obligation to perform.

Condition subsequent
An event or circumstance that, when it occurs, brings an existing contract to an end.

Condition precedent
An event or circumstance that, until it occurs, suspends the parties' obligations to perform their contractual obligations.

PART TWO

---

15. Not all conditions precedent operate within the context of a contract, however, and this is where the law can become somewhat confusing. As a rule, conditions precedent will bind the parties to a contract if the condition itself is reasonably certain and objective. Conditions that are tied to whim, fancy, or extreme subjectivity as in "I'll buy your house if I decide that I like it" do not bind the parties because they essentially have no objective content. These are known as illusory conditions precedent and leave the parties free to do as they please, since there is no contract between them. For obvious reasons, illusory conditions precedents are rare. For discussion and case law on this point, see Ben-Ishai & Percy, *supra* note 1 at 317–52.

16. It is beyond the scope of this text to discuss the issue of waiver of conditions precedent. For an assessment of this particularly thorny problem, see Gwilym Davies, "Conditional Contracts for the Sale of Land in Canada" (1977) 55:2 Can Bar Rev 289.

CASE	*Wiebe v Bobsien* (1984), 14 DLR (4th) 754 (BCSC), aff'd (1985), 20 DLR (4th) 475 (CA), leave to appeal to SCC refused (1985), 64 NR 394 (SCC)

THE BUSINESS CONTEXT: Because the purchase of real estate can involve a large expense, businesses and individuals alike often require time to either borrow the money necessary to make the purchase or divest themselves of an existing property, the proceeds of which can be applied to the contemplated purchase. Such a process can take weeks or months, during which time the freedom of the vendor to deal with other buyers or back out of the arrangement altogether can become an issue.

FACTUAL BACKGROUND: Dr. Wiebe made an offer to purchase a house owned by Mr. Bobsien. This offer was made conditional on Wiebe being able to sell his current residence on or before August 18, 1984. Wiebe's offer was accepted by Bobsien. However, on July 22, 1984, Bobsien changed his mind and informed Wiebe that their agreement was "cancelled." Wiebe did not accept this cancellation and on August 18 he informed Bobsien that he had obtained a buyer for his current house and that, since the condition had been fulfilled, the main transaction had to go through. Bobsien refused to complete the sale, saying that he had no contractual obligation to do so.

THE LEGAL QUESTION: Was there a contract between Wiebe and Bobsien such that Bobsien was obligated to wait until August 18 to see whether Wiebe could fulfill the condition?

RESOLUTION: According to the court, the condition precedent that Wiebe be able to sell his current residence merely suspended the obligation to perform the contract pending occurrence of that event. On this basis, Wiebe had a contractual obligation to take all reasonable steps to sell his house, and if he failed to take those reasonable steps, he would be in breach of contract and liable in damages to Bobsien. As for Bobsien, he was contractually bound to wait and see if Wiebe would be successful in selling his current residence and did not have the legal right to "cancel" the contract on July 22. Since Wiebe fulfilled the condition within the time provided in the contract, Bobsien was contractually bound to sell to him. Bobsien's failure to do so was a breach of contract.

CRITICAL ANALYSIS: Do conditions precedent introduce too much uncertainty into contracts?

Limitation of Liability Clause

When a party fails to meet its contractual obligations, it is liable for breach of contract and is responsible to the other side for any reasonably foreseeable damages the breach may have caused.[17] For example, in the Coasters–Trackers contract, a failure by Trackers to deliver adequate tracking may result in Coasters losing its contract with the American amusement park, the ultimate purchaser of the roller coaster (see Figure 7.1).

FIGURE 7.1

Trackers's Liability to Coasters

1. **Trackers ➡ ➡ ➡ ➡ Coasters**
   breaches contract by
   supplying substandard tracking
2. **Coasters ➡ ➡ ➡ ➡ American customer**
   breaches contract by
   failing to deliver tracking
3. **American customer finds an alternative supplier and terminates contract with Coasters.**
4. **Coasters loses $1 million in profit on contract with American customer.**

---

17. The classic test for foreseeability in contract, discussed further in Chapter 9, is stated in *Hadley v Baxendale* (1854), 9 ExCh 341: Where two parties have made a contract which one of them has broken, the damages which the other party ought to receive in respect of such breach of contract should be such as may fairly and reasonably be considered either arising naturally, i.e., ... such as may reasonably be supposed to have been in the contemplation of both parties, at the time they made the contract, as the probable result of the breach of it. Now, if the special circumstances under which the contract was made were communicated by the plaintiffs to the defendants, and thus known to both parties, the damages resulting from the breach of such a contract, which they would reasonably contemplate, would be the amount of injury which would ordinarily follow from a breach of contract under these special circumstances so known and communicated.

On the basis of this scenario, Coasters could recover from Trackers its loss of profit, particularly since Trackers knew very well that Coasters needed the tracking to fulfill contractual obligations to an American amusement park. However, since contracts are about consensus and choice, parties can agree to limit liability for breach to something less than would otherwise be recoverable. This is precisely what the parties to the Coasters–Trackers contract accomplished. Clause 13 of the contract (set out in the opening scenario) is a **limitation of liability clause**. It provides that Trackers' liability shall in no event exceed the unit price of the tracking, and in no event shall it include loss of profit. Therefore, by the clear words of the contract, any loss of profit that Coasters may suffer from Trackers' breach is not recoverable. Since the parties agreed to place such a limit on damages when they entered into the contract, Coasters is bound.

Limitation of liability clause
A term of a contract that limits liability for breach to something less than would otherwise be recoverable.

Exemption Clause (or Exclusion Clause)

Through an **exemption clause**, a party to a contract can identify events or circumstances causing loss for which it has no liability whatsoever. Clause 14 in the Coasters–Trackers contract achieves such an end, since it exempts Trackers from all liability in respect to losses, damages, costs, or claims relating to design of tracking. This means that if there is a problem with the design, Coasters cannot sue Trackers for any loss it might sustain to replace or alter the tracking, for example.

Exemption clause
A term of a contract that identifies events causing loss for which there is no liability.

LANDMARK CASE · *Tilden Rent-A-Car Co v Clendenning* (1978), 83 DLR (3d) 400 (Ont CA)

THE BUSINESS CONTEXT: A business may decide to use a standard form contract with its customers in order to save money. However, this may prove to be a false economy should the business fail to properly explain to the customer the consequences of the standard form contract in question. Such a business runs the risk of a court taking the customer's side and disallowing a term that would otherwise protect the business.

FACTUAL BACKGROUND: Mr. Clendenning rented a car from Tilden at the Vancouver airport. At the time of entering into the agreement, he was asked if he wanted additional insurance, which involved a higher fee but did provide full, nondeductible coverage. Thinking that this would protect him if the car were damaged in his possession, he agreed. As he was in a hurry, he signed the long and complicated rental agreement without reading it. An exemption clause, on the back of the agreement and in very small type, provided that the insurance would be inoperative if the driver had consumed any alcohol whatsoever at the time the damage occurred. Clendenning was unaware of the clause. When the

car was damaged—Clendenning drove into a pole after consuming some alcohol—Tilden sued to recover the full cost of repairing the vehicle.

THE LEGAL QUESTION: Can Clendenning rely on the clause providing him with full, nondeductible coverage, or is that clause inoperative because Clendenning had consumed some alcohol?

RESOLUTION: The Ontario Court of Appeal held that Clendenning's signature on the contract was not a true assent to the terms of the contract and, therefore, Tilden could not rely on the exemption clause denying insurance coverage to Clendenning. The clerk who had Clendenning sign knew that he had not read the contract and knew therefore that the contract did not represent his true intention. Given that the contract contained "stringent and onerous provisions," it was incumbent on Tilden to show that it took reasonable measures to draw these terms to Clendenning's attention. This did not occur and therefore Tilden could not rely on the exemption clause. The court went on to observe that since the trial judge

(Continued)

SUZANNE PLUNKETT/BLOOMBERG VIA GETTY IMAGES

What risks do lengthy contracts—as found in the car rental industry—pose to the consumer and to the business supplying the vehicle?

had accepted that Clendenning was capable of proper control of a motor vehicle at the time of the accident, and since Clendenning had paid the premium, he was not liable for any damage to the vehicle.

CRITICAL ANALYSIS: Courts may be less helpful to the customer in a non-consumer context, since parties are expected to look after their own interests. In a 1997 decision from the Ontario Court of Appeal, for example, the court emphasized that inadequate notice of the kind complained of in the *Tilden* case will not ordinarily be grounds for attacking an exemption clause in a commercial situation. The court affirmed the rule that a person will be assumed to have read and understood any contract that she signs.[18] Should consumer and commercial contracts be treated differently?

TECHNOLOGY AND THE LAW

Shrink-Wrap, Click-Wrap, and Browse-Wrap Agreements

Even when terms are written down, one party may claim not to have known that certain terms were actually part of the contract. As noted above, this can arise in the standard form contract, for example, when a customer of a car rental company signs a lengthy agreement without having read it. Questions of enforceability of terms also arise in the more modern context of shrink-wrap, click-wrap, and browse-wrap contracting practices.

Shrink-Wrap Agreements: A shrink-wrap agreement (also referred to as a shrink-wrap licence) is an agreement whose terms are enclosed with a product such as prepackaged software. Usually there is also a notice to the effect that opening the package constitutes agreement to the terms. The terms normally cover warranties, remedies, or other issues relating to the use of the product such as prohibiting the user from making copies.

At one time, the practice was to put the terms on the box containing the software disk and wrap the box tightly in cellophane so that the purchaser could see the terms before buying. Today, the common practice is to put the terms inside the box (i.e., sometimes in a printed manual or on the envelope containing the disk), to which reference is made on the outside of the box.

There is uncertainty in Canada as to whether shrink-wrap agreements are enforceable, particularly where the packaging fails to alert the purchaser that he will not have full rights to the product inside the box. In *North American Systemshops Ltd v King*,[19] a software program was distributed on a floppy disk that was contained inside a shrink-wrapped manual. A licence agreement—which restricted use of the program—was contained inside the packaging but was not visible at the time of purchase. The Alberta Court of Queen's Bench found that the licence enclosed in the program manual was not binding on the purchaser as the terms of the licence were not made known at the time of sale. As noted by the court:

---

18. See *Fraser Jewellers (1982) Ltd v Dominion Electric Protection Co et al* (1997), 34 OR (3d) 1 (CA). Note that *Abrams v Sprott Securities Ltd* (2003), 67 OR (3d) 368 (CA) distinguished *Fraser Jewellers* by narrowing the proposition in three ways: first, the *Fraser* proposition depends on the absence of misrepresentation by the party seeking to rely on the written agreement (the party seeking to rely on the clause had no legal obligation to draw it to the other party's attention); second, it depends on there being no special relationship between the parties; and finally, a person cannot rely by way of estoppel on a statement induced by his or her own misrepresentation.

19. (1989) 68 *Alta LR* (2d) 145 (QB).

In the case at bar, the plaintiff manifestly did not bring home to the defendants, or any of them, that there were restrictions on the purchase. Not one of the simple, cheap, obvious methods to do this [was] used by the plaintiff.[20]

Click-Wrap Agreements: A click-wrap is an agreement that appears on a user's computer screen when a user attempts to download software or purchase goods or services online. The user is instructed to review the terms prior to assenting by clicking an "I accept" button, a hyperlink, or an icon. Usually the user cannot proceed any further without agreeing to the terms.

In Canada, the validity of this method of contracting has been upheld. In *Rudder v Microsoft Corp*,[21] the plaintiffs brought a class action suit against Microsoft (MSN), alleging that MSN had breached the member service agreement. MSN applied for a permanent stay of proceedings based on a clause in the click-wrap agreement that indicated that all MSN service agreements are governed by the laws of the state of Washington and that all disputes arising out of the agreement would occur in that state's courts. The Ontario Superior Court granted the application. In response to the plaintiffs' argument that they did not receive adequate notice of the term, Mr. Justice Winkler said,

All of the terms of the Agreement are the same format. Although there are certain terms of the Agreement that are displayed entirely in upper-case letters, there are no physical differences which make a particular term of the agreement more difficult to read than any other term. In other words, there is no fine print as the term would be defined in a written document. The terms are set out in plain language, absent words that are commonly referred to as "legalese." Admittedly, the entire Agreement cannot be displayed at once on the computer screen, but that is not materially different from a multi-page written document which requires a party to turn the pages.[22]

Browse-Wrap Agreements: Also of recent interest has been the validity of browse-wrap agreements. Browse-wrap agreements are said to be formed on this basis: the user agrees that—by virtue of simply using the website—he or she is bound by the terms of use associated with the website and agrees that those terms are part of a binding contract between the parties. In short, a browse-wrap agreement is formed not because the user has clicked on an "I accept" button. Rather, the webpage presents a link or button that takes the user to the terms and conditions that apply to the transaction or the terms are found at the bottom of the website in question. This would seem to be a potentially risky way of attempting to create a contract, particularly as the common law requires that the person purporting to accept an offer do something affirmative or positive to signal assent.[23]

That said, the Quebec decision in *Canadian Real Estate Association ("CREA") v Sutton (Quebec) Real Estate Services*[24] recognized a browse-wrap form of acceptance. In this case, the realtor Sutton had been downloading listings from the Canadian Real Estate Association ("CREA")'s Multiple Listing Service website which was expressly contrary to the terms of use posted on the website. Sutton argued that any such breach was not actionable because it had done nothing to expressly consent to these terms of use, such as clicking on an "I agree" button. The Court disagreed, noting that the terms were posted on MLS website and could be accessed via hyperlink. Moreover, as Charles Morgan et al point out, Sutton itself had similar terms of use on its own website and therefore "should have known" that such terms would also govern CREA's MLS site.[25] Relying in part on the *CREA* case, the British Columbia Supreme Court also recently enforced a browse-wrap agreement, concluding that a contract had been formed between the plaintiff and defendant.[26] The court noted that the defendant had a clear opportunity to review the terms of use of the website and knew that acceptance would be deemed by continued use.

Note too that browse-wrap agreements have been deemed enforceable as they relate to *amending* an existing contract, but not consistently so. In *Kanitz v Rogers Cable Inc.*,[27] for example, a click-wrap agreement expressly allowed telecommunications company Rogers to amend its online service agreement with customers by simply posting such amendments on its website. The court agreed that the customer's continued use of the service after such amendments were posted amounted to acceptance of Rogers unilateral amendments. In short, the parties had agreed to a means of amending their contract which did not require an act of positive acceptance by the consumer.[28] By way of contrast, a court in Quebec held in 2005 that continued use of an online system (here, myPaySystems Services) was not good acceptance of a

(Continued)

---

20. *Ibid* at 155.
21. (1999), 47 CCLT (2d) 168 (Ont SCJ).
22. *Ibid* at 173.
23. Morgan & Saulgrain, *supra* note 12 at 10. In the U.S. decision of *Ticketmaster Corp v Tickets.com*, 2000 US Dist Lexis 4553 (Dist Ct, CD Cal 2000) for example, a California court found that without a positive gesture, such as clicking on an "I accept" button, there was no contract between the parties. Mere use was insufficient.
24. *Canadian Real Estate Association v Sutton (Quebec) Real Estate Services Inc*, [2003] JQ no 3606 (CS).
25. Morgan & Saulgrain, *supra* note 12 at 15.
26. *Century 21 Canada Ltd Partnership v Rogers Communications Inc*, 2011 B.C.J. No. 1679.
27. *Kanitz v Rogers Cable Inc*, (2002) 58 OR (3d) 299 (Sup Ct).
28. Morgan & Saulgrain, *supra* note 12 at 10–11.

contractual amendment requiring arbitration.[29] To side-step such controversy regarding enforceability, e-vendors should consider avoiding browse-wrap agreements altogether and require their customers to do something affirmative to signify assent—such as clicking on an icon[30] which says "I accept" or "I assent." This is particularly important in a consumer context where courts are more likely to be solicitous of the customer than in a business-to-business scenario.[31]

Hyperlinked terms: The Supreme Court of Canada in *Dell Computer Corp v Union des consommateurs*[32] has upheld the enforceability of contract terms introduced via hyperlink. The court decided that contractual terms are enforceable provided they are "reasonably accessible" and this accessibility can be provided by a hyperlinked document. That is, even though the terms may not be on the ordering page itself, it is sufficient that the terms are accessible via a hyperlink.[33]

Critical Analysis: The enforceability of terms in click-wrap agreements depends on notification prior to assent. What steps can a business take in preparing and presenting an agreement to ensure that the terms will be found to be enforceable? What steps could a business take to increase the chances that a shrink-wrap agreement is found enforceable? Do you think that browse-wrap agreements should be enforceable? Why or why not? As a businessperson, how confident would you be at this point concerning the enforceability of a browse-wrap contract in Canada?

Liquidated Damages Clause

Liquidated damages clause
A term of a contract that specifies how much one party must pay to the other in the event of breach.

A **liquidated damages clause** sets out—in advance—what one party must pay to the other in the event of breach. Through such clauses, the parties themselves decide before a breach has even happened what that breach would be worth by way of compensation. Provided that the clause is a genuine pre-estimate of the damages that the innocent party will suffer, it is enforceable.[34] The clause will not be enforceable, however, if it sets an exorbitant amount as a remedy for the innocent party. If so, the clause is a penalty clause—it intends to punish, not compensate—and a court will simply disregard it in assessing damages for the breach in question. As a general rule, contract law is only interested in compensating the innocent party, not punishing the party in breach. As noted in Chapter 6, Amritha had insisted on a contractual clause that Trackers pay $5000 to Coasters for every day it was late in delivering the tracking. Such a clause is enforceable only if it fits the definition of a liquidated damages clause. If it is simply a clause meant to scare or terrorize Coasters into timely performance because of the financial punishment it would face in the event of delay, the court will simply not enforce it.

These three kinds of clauses—the limitation of liability clause, the exemption clause, and the liquidated damages clause—illustrate the planning function of the law. Through such clauses, a business can manage the kind and extent of liability it faces.

Business Law in Practice Revisited

1. How is the scope of Trackers' and Coasters' obligations determined?

If the parties cannot resolve a dispute concerning obligations by themselves, a judge will determine whether there is a contract between the parties and, if so, what its

---

29. *Aspencer1.com Inc v Paysystems Corporation*, [2005] JQ no 1573 (CS).
30. For further discussion, see Derek Hill, "'Click-wrap' online contracts generally considered enforceable", *Law Times* (4 August 2008) 12.
31. *Ibid*
32. 2007 SCC 34.
33. Michael Geist, "*Dell* Case Sets Standard for Online Contracts", (31 July 2007) online: Michael Geist <http://www.michaelgeist.ca/content/view/2141/1/>.
34. See Harvey McGregor, *McGregor on Damages*, 18th ed (London: Sweet & Maxwell, 2009) at para 13-013.

content is. Every contract must cover certain essentials in order to be enforceable. If key terms are missing, the court may conclude that the parties were still at the point of negotiating and had not actually entered into a contract yet. The other possibility is that the court will imply a term that one or the other party finds unsatisfactory or contrary to expectations.

The Coasters–Trackers contract was complete because it contained all the terms that the circumstances of the case would identify to be essential, as well as some clauses that defined the relationship in more detail. For example, the contract identified the following terms:

Parties: Coasters and Trackers
Price: $1.5 million
Delivery dates: as specified
Product: tracking
Quantity: 900 metres
Quality: as per specifications and where no specifications, of the best quality
Guarantees: tracking to be free from defect for one year
Limitations on/exemptions of liability: liability not to exceed unit price; no liability for design defects; no liability for defects after one year
Insurance: vendor to insure tracking

2. Are there any ambiguous or unclear terms in the contract?

While certain aspects of the contract were somewhat ambiguous, such as the term specifying that the quality was to be of the best quality, a court would have been able to assign meaning to the term because there was a contract between the parties and expert evidence would have been available to establish what the phrase meant.

3. Are there any additional terms that Jason should have tried to have included?

Jason managed to negotiate a reasonably complete contract, as noted above. He included a number of clauses to limit the liability of Trackers, which was prudent, but he should have gone further and included a clause expressly eliminating application of the *Sale of Goods Act*. This term would have ensured that the Act would have no application in a contractual dispute with Coasters sometime down the road. It was wise from Trackers' perspective to include, as it did, an entire contract clause, as this would have helped forestall any arguments from Coasters that there were additional warranties or guarantees not expressly recited in the contract.

Jason probably should have included a price-variation clause to deal with the problems that arose when the price of steel rose dramatically. In addition, an arbitration or mediation clause might have proven useful to deal with conflicts, although, as it turns out, the parties negotiated their own resolution to the pricing dispute that arose.

4. Does the contract relieve the parties from responsibility for inadequate performance?

The contract limited Trackers' liability for defective tracking for one year and to an amount not exceeding the unit price. Trackers had no liability for problems in the design of the tracking.

Coasters' obligation to pay the purchase price was not qualified by the express terms of the contract. Of course, if Trackers had failed to deliver, Coasters would not have had to pay. If Trackers had delivered seriously defective goods, Coasters would have had the option to refuse delivery. If the defect had been less significant, Coasters probably would have remitted payment in a reduced amount, to reflect the track's lesser value or the cost of repairing the defects in the tracking. Clauses to this effect are not necessary and probably do not help in establishing certainty, in any event. Whether the tracking was seriously defective or only somewhat so would have been not a question of fact but a matter for debate, which no clause in a contract can resolve. If the parties cannot resolve that question informally, it will be determined by a judge in an action by Trackers against Coasters for the purchase price set out in the contract.

Chapter Summary

The nature, scope, and extent of the obligations of the parties to a contract are known as the terms of the contract. The terms may be express, as when they have been specifically mentioned and agreed upon by the parties, or they may be implied. Since the court has considerable discretion to imply a term or not, parties are best advised to make their agreement as clear and as explicit as possible.

How courts will resolve a contractual dispute over terms is an open question, as is any matter that proceeds to litigation. An important evidential rule that guides a judge is known as the parol evidence rule. It prevents the introduction of evidence that varies or adds to the terms of a written contract when the contract is clear and intended to be the sole source of the parties' obligations. Entire contract clauses are used to propel a court to apply the parol evidence rule in any given case.

An important planning function of contract law lies in the fact that it permits parties to manage the risk of future uncertainties. Additionally, it permits them to establish, in advance, the extent of responsibility for breach through limitation clauses and exemption clauses. Furthermore, parties can bargain for what will be payable in the event of breach. Such a term will be enforceable, provided the amount is a genuine pre-estimate of damages and not a penalty.

Courts may refuse to apply a clause that disadvantages a consumer if the business in question failed to take reasonable steps to ensure that the consumer was alerted to the clause in question in circumstances where it appears the consumer has not assented. Courts are less likely to assist the commercial or industrial customer, however, on the basis that sophisticated business interests should be left to take care of themselves.

Chapter Study

Key Terms and Concepts

condition precedent (p. 153)

condition subsequent (p. 153)

contractual *quantum meruit* **(p. 148)**

entire contract clause (p. 148)

exemption clause (p. 155)

express term (p. 142)

implied term (p. 144)

limitation of liability clause (p. 155)

liquidated damages clause (p. 158)

parol evidence rule (p. 148)

rules of construction (p. 143)

Questions for Review

1. What is the difference between an express and an implied term?

2. What are two major rules of construction used by the courts in interpreting a contract?

3. Who decides the content of a contract and on what basis?

4. What are four sources that the court can rely on to imply terms?

5. Why are express terms preferable to implied terms?

6. How does the doctrine of business efficacy affect the interpretation of implied terms?

7. How do the courts deal with ambiguities in the contract?

8. What is the expression used to describe an implied legal promise to pay a reasonable price for goods or services?

9. What are three ways that a party can control its exposure to liability for breach of contract?

10. What is a limitation of liability clause?

11. How is a limitation of liability clause different from an exemption clause?

12. Why are conditional agreements important?

13. What is the parol evidence rule?

14. What is a separate or collateral agreement?

15. What is an entire contract clause?

16. What assumptions do the courts make about how contract terms relate to changing circumstances?

17. What is the difference between a click-wrap agreement and a browse-wrap agreement?

18. What is a liquidated damages clause?

Questions for Critical Thinking

1. Entering a contract can create a great deal of risk for the parties. What are examples of these risks, and how can they be managed?

2. Do you think conditional contracts contribute to uncertainty in the marketplace since parties will not know their obligations pending the outcome of an event?

3. Courts are increasingly willing to imply into contracts a term requiring the parties to act in good faith. Is this a welcome development? Why or why not?

4. Why does contract law refuse to enforce a penalty clause? Why are penalty clauses inherently objectionable?

5. Do you agree that contracts should be interpreted based on an objective assessment of the parties' intentions? What would be the advantages and disadvantages of interpreting contacts based on evidence of what the parties subjectively intended?

6. Do you think the law is unreasonable to require business owners to point out to consumers any unexpected clauses in a standard form contract if it appears that the consumer has not assented? Should customers simply be required to take care of themselves and read the contract before signing it?

Situations for Discussion

1. Former U.S. administrative law judge Roy Pearson famously sued a local dry cleaner over a lost pair of pants. Among other things, he sought $2 million for mental distress and discomfort as well as $15 000 for a rental car he said he would need in order to drive to another dry cleaner outside his neighbourhood. Pearson claimed, for example, that the dry cleaner owners committed fraud by not living up to the sign in their window that stated "Satisfaction guaranteed." According to Pearson, this guarantee was

PART TWO

unconditional, he was by no means satisfied, and the defendants had thereby committed an unfair trade practice. How should a judge interpret the "satisfaction guaranteed" sign?[35]

2. Louise purchased a shrink-wrapped piece of software from a local software developer. She used the software properly but, much to her dismay, the product contained a virus that destroyed the hard drive of her computer. When Louise looked in the software packaging, she found a card that contained a number of terms of conditions, including a limitation of liability clause. Is this term a part of the contract, or can Louise argue that she is not bound by it? Explain.

3. Ms. Weir was engaged by Canada Post to deliver advertising flyers for a five-year term. She was entitled to payment on a per-piece basis. The contract provided that Canada Post could terminate the agreement on 60 days' notice if it changed its ad flyer distribution system and "alternatively, Canada Post may in its sole discretion terminate this agreement immediately on giving written notice to the Contractor." Payment per piece became costly for Canada Post, and two years later it instituted a new payment system based on packages (containing several pieces).[36] Is Canada Post entitled to terminate the contract with Ms. Weir? What evidence is relevant? Is it a contract at all when one party has so much discretion?

4. Kristin signed a user agreement with Hagel's Cable, Inc., upon installation of high-speed Internet service in her home. Included in the agreement was a provision that the agreement could be amended at any time, and that customers would be notified of changes on Hagel's website, by email, or through regular mail. Hagel's later added a clause to the agreement that any right to commence or participate in a class action suit was waived. The agreement, including the new clause, was posted on its customer support website, and a notice was posted on the main website that the agreement had been amended. Kristin has continued using the service since this time. However, she now wants to join a class action suit that is alleging a number of

breaches of the agreement.[37] Will the clause in the amended user's agreement prevent her from bringing such an action? Did she receive adequate notice of the amended term? Does the fact that the user agreement relates to Internet services make a difference in whether the notice was adequate? How is this situation similar to the *Rudder v. Microsoft Corp.* case discussed in this chapter?

5. Jason and Floë booked a two-week vacation in the Caribbean with The Nation's Vacations Inc. ("Nation"), having reviewed Nation's brochure regarding destinations there. The brochure also contained an exclusion of liability clause, which stated:

> Please review with care the terms and conditions below as they govern your purchase of travel services from Nation. Your booking with Nation constitutes acceptance of these Terms & Conditions.
>
> ...
>
> **LIABILITY**
>
> **Liability for suppliers:** Nation makes arrangements with third-party suppliers who provide travel services such as flights, accommodation, and car rentals. Nation endeavours to choose the most reputable suppliers but is not responsible for their acts and omissions. Disappointed customers must sue those third party suppliers directly for any loss or damages.
>
> ...
>
> Nation assumes **no responsibility** for any claim, loss, damage, cost or expense arising out of personal injury, accident or death, loss, damage, inconvenience, loss of enjoyment or upset caused by Nation's third party suppliers.

The brochure itself was designed to open to the page quoted above when flipping through the brochure from back to front. It was in easy-to-read font and with the emphasis indicated above. Though Jason and Floë had spent about 90 minutes reading over the brochure before booking their vacation package,

35. There are multiple Internet stories on point. See, for example, Dan Slater, "The Great American Pants Suit, R.I.P.", *The Wall Street Journal* (18 December 2008) online: Wall Street Journal Law Blog< http://blogs.wsj.com/law/2008/12/18/the-great-american-pants-suit-rip/>. For a basic statement of the facts of the claim, see Manning Sossamon, "The Facts of *Pearson v. Chung*", online: Manning Sossamon<http://www.manning-sossamon.com/pantfacts/>. For the trial judge's decision, see *Pearson v Chung*, 644 F Supp (2d) 23 (Dist Ct DC 2009) online: DC Courts <http://www.dccourts.gov/dccourts/docs/05CA4302PearsonFindings.pdf>. Following an unsuccessful appeal, it appears that Pearson has now abandoned his lawsuit, see Manning Sossamon, "The Facts of *Pearson v. Chung*", online: Manning Sossamon<http://www.manning-sossamon.com/pantfacts/>.
36. Based, in part, on *Weir v Canada Post Corp* (1995), 142 NSR (2d) 198 (SC).
37. Based, in part, on *Kanitz v Rogers Cable Inc,* (2002) 58 OR (3d) 299 (SC).

they say that they did not know about the exclusion clause. Moreover, Jason, a construction firm manager, says that he does not know even what an exclusion clause is, so reading it would have been pointless in any event.

When Jason and Floë arrived at the Caribbean resort, they were immediately disappointed. Though the resort was a 4-star resort as advertised by Nation, Jason and Floë say that when they went to eat dinner in the resort buffet restaurant, they found the conditions to be unhygienic because, among other matters, several small tropical birds were walking around on the floor of the restaurant, having gained access through open doors. At a later point, a cat strolled into the restaurant and, they say, defecated in the corner though the resort disputes this. Jason and Floë also claim that the bathroom in their suite was unhygienic and the staff were uniformly unfriendly, even hostile. Jason and Floë hotly refused management's offer of a free room upgrade and demanded to be flown home immediately. The resort made those arrangements. Jason and Floë left the next day. Jason and Floë have now sued Nation for breach of contract, seeking, among other matters, reimbursement for their flight to and from the resort as well as ground transportation and accommodation costs.[38] Nation says it delivered the requested travel services contracted for and in any event has successfully limited its liability through the exclusion clause. What do you think a judge will say?

6. Lunar Inc. had developed a mechanism that harnessed heat from the sun. What the company lacked, however, was a method for storing the heat until it was needed. Trays-R-Us had developed a unique tray that appeared to solve this problem, so the parties entered into negotiations. It was agreed that Trays would sell the trays to Lunar at a set unit price per tray for a term of one year. No particular sales volume for the year was agreed upon or guaranteed. After the trays were produced, however, Trays discovered that they leaked and were unable to hold any solar heat owing to a design flaw that could not be fixed. As a result, Trays refused to fill any orders for the trays placed by Lunar. Lunar sued for breach of contract, alleging that there was an implied term in the contract that Trays would make trays available to Lunar as required.[39] Does the business efficacy rule require that such a term be implied in the contact between Trays and Lunar? Do you think that such a term might have been left out on purpose? How can a business avoid having terms implied into a contract?

7. The decision of *Wiebe v Bobsien*, discussed earlier in this chapter, went on to appeal and at that level, the dissenting judge would have found for the vendor. According to the dissent, the conditional agreement was unenforceable because its scope was too uncertain. The dissent stated:

> I think this case falls in that category of incurable uncertainty. What term should be implied? A term requiring the purchaser to make all reasonable efforts to sell his house sounds alright.... [but] it leaves unresolved the question of whether he must sell at the price he can get, on the market, in the time allotted, or whether he is entitled to insist that the sale can only take place at a price he considers reasonable and is willing to accept.

> I think that what the parties usually intend by this type of clause is the second alternative. That is, that the purchaser is only committed to sell his own house if he gets the price he has in mind. The reason is that in the residential housing market the purchaser is likely to be unfamiliar with the market, but he is almost sure to know how much cash he has and what size of mortgage he can count on being able to service.

> ... The way to deal with this problem in the real estate market is for the form of subject clause to state the price and the essential terms upon which the purchaser must sell his own house. Then a court would have no trouble in implying a term that the purchaser must make all reasonable efforts to sell at that price and on those terms. And the court could assess whether the purchaser had made reasonable efforts to do so.

Do you think that the dissent is asking for too much precision and detail in a subject to clause. Why or why not?

---

38. Based, in part, on *Eltaib v Touram Ltd Partnership*, 2010 ONSC 834.
39. Based, in part, on *Solar U.S.A. Inc v Saskatchewan Minerals*, [1992] 3 WWR 15 (Sask QB).

8. Trackers is three days late in delivering the tracking to Coasters. Amritha now wants to rely on the clause in the contract that Trackers will pay $5000 for each day that the tracking is late, and she is claiming that Trackers owes Coasters $15 000. However, Trackers points out that Amritha has not been inconvenienced by the late delivery, because construction on the roller coaster had already been delayed by two weeks. It has been a week and a half since Trackers was able to deliver the tracking, and Coasters has still been unable to use it. Is Amritha entitled to rely on the clause and collect the $15 000? Do you need any additional information to make your decision?

For more study tools, visit http://www.NELSONbrain.com.

CHAPTER 8

Non-Enforcement of Contracts

Objectives

After studying this chapter, you should have an understanding of

- why enforcement of contracts is the norm

- the exceptional circumstances in which contracts are not enforced

- which contracts must be in writing and why

DAJAMANA IMAGES/JUPITER IMAGES

Business Law in Practice

Martha Smith bought a fitness club in downtown Toronto and renamed it "Martha's Gym." She invested $50 000 of her own money and financed the remainder through a business loan from the local bank. Martha tried to attract a large clientele to the facility, but the volume of business failed to meet her expectations. She began to run short of cash and fell behind in her monthly loan payments to the bank. Eventually, the bank called the loan, which had an outstanding balance of $20 000. The bank told Martha that unless she paid off the entire balance in two weeks, it would start seizing assets from the fitness club.

Martha convinced her elderly parents, Mr. and Mrs. Smith, to help her by borrowing $40 000 from the same bank. She explained that through such a cash infusion, she would be able to retire her own loan with the bank and use the balance as operating capital for her business. Martha assured her parents that the problems at the fitness club were temporary and that by hiring a new trainer, she would be able to quickly turn the business around.

Martha and her parents went to meet Kevin Jones, the branch manager, who had handled Mr. and Mrs. Smith's banking for over 35 years. Kevin said that he would give the Smiths an acceptable interest rate on the loan—namely, 8 percent—but insisted that the loan be secured by a mortgage on their home. Since the Smiths had no other means of paying back the loan and the house was their only asset, they were nervous about the proposal, which they did not fully understand. However, they did not want Martha to go through the humiliation of having her fitness equipment seized and sold at auction.

For his part, Kevin was tremendously relieved that the Smiths had come in to see him. Kevin was the one who had approved Martha's ill-fated business

(Continued on the next page)

loan in the first place, and he had failed to ensure that it was properly secured. He saw this as an opportunity to correct his own error and get Martha's loan off his books altogether.

Kevin had the mortgage documents prepared and strongly encouraged the Smiths to sign, saying that this would protect Martha's assets from seizure. He also told them that to a large extent, signing the mortgage was just a formality and that he was confident that nothing would come of it.

In the end, the Smiths decided to put their trust in Kevin that he would not let them enter into a contract that could bring about their financial ruin. They simply signed the mortgage. Immediately, $20 000 went to the bank to pay the outstanding balance on Martha's loan. The remaining $20 000 was paid directly to Martha (see Figure 8.1 below).

Martha's business continued to operate until the additional capital was completely expended. Its prospects failed to improve, as Martha was still unable to attract customers and the new trainer quit. Eventually, neither Martha nor her parents could make the payments on the mortgage, and the bank began to foreclose on the Smiths' home. Mr. and Mrs. Smith are in shock—they never believed that it would come to this.[1]

FIGURE 8.1

Martha's and Her Parents' Financial Arrangements with the Bank

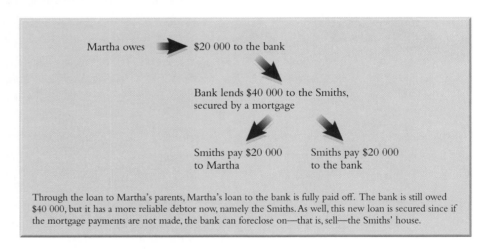

Martha owes ➡ $20 000 to the bank

Bank lends $40 000 to the Smiths, secured by a mortgage

Smiths pay $20 000 to Martha

Smiths pay $20 000 to the bank

Through the loan to Martha's parents, Martha's loan to the bank is fully paid off. The bank is still owed $40 000, but it has a more reliable debtor now, namely the Smiths. As well, this new loan is secured since if the mortgage payments are not made, the bank can foreclose on—that is, sell—the Smiths' house.

1. Did Kevin manipulate or pressure the Smiths into signing the mortgage? If so, what legal remedies do the Smiths have?
2. Did Mr. and Mrs. Smith enter into the contract on the basis of mistake or misrepresentation? If so, what legal remedies do they have?
3. How could Kevin have managed this transaction better?

1. This Business Law in Practice scenario is based on *Morrison v Coast Finance Ltd* (1965), 55 WWR 257 (BCCA); and *Lloyds Bank v Bundy,* [1974] 3 All ER 757 (CA).

The Importance of Enforcing Contracts

Once negotiators reach an agreement that appears to contain their consensus on the essential elements of a bargain, a contract is formed. The law then focuses on enforcing that agreement in order to preserve the integrity, reliability, and predictability of contractual relationships. Were it otherwise, the business world would be unable to predict with any certainty which agreements would be binding.

At the same time, the Canadian legal system recognizes the injustice of enforcing contracts without any provision for exceptional circumstances. Accordingly, the law endeavours to achieve a balance between two competing goals. On the one hand, it must prevent people from pulling out of deals because they have found better opportunities elsewhere or have failed to conduct diligent negotiations. On the other hand, it must remedy situations where an apparently valid contract fails to reflect the real agreement of both parties or is fundamentally unjust.

This chapter presents a number of legal doctrines—developed through common law and statute—that are exceptions to the general rule that a contract, once formed, is enforceable. It categorizes these doctrines on the basis of there being

- an unequal relationship between the two parties

- misrepresentation or important mistakes concerning the contract

- a defect within the contract itself

If the aggrieved party can bring itself within one of the doctrines discussed in this chapter, there are two possible outcomes. In certain circumstances, he may elect whether to keep the contract in force or have it brought to an end. Where this option is available, the contract is said to be **voidable**. For example, when someone signs a contract under duress, it is that person's choice whether to abide by the contract or seek to have it set aside by a judge. In other, more limited instances, the legal problem is so serious that the aggrieved party has no choice in the matter: a court must declare the contract to be null and void. In other words, because of some tremendously substantial defect—such as the illegality that underlies the "hit man" contract—the contract is considered never to have existed at all and, for that reason, to be of no force or effect. This is known as a **void contract**.

Voidable contract
A contract that, in certain circumstances, an aggrieved party can choose to keep in force or bring to an end.

Void contract
A contract involving a defect so substantial that it is of no force or effect.

Contracts Based on Unequal Relationships
Legal Capacity

In general, the law assumes that individuals and properly constituted organizations have the **legal capacity** to form contracts. Contract law also emphasizes the importance of consent and voluntariness. Because they may be unable to give true consent to their agreements, certain kinds of people—namely, children and those with mental incapacities—are given the benefit of special legal protection.

Legal capacity
The ability to make binding contracts.

Minors

The **age of majority** is the age at which a person is recognized as an adult for legal purposes. Those under the age of majority (minors or infants) are in a very different position concerning their ability to enter contracts than are those who have attained the age of majority. To protect minors from the enforcement of contracts that may not be in their best interests, the general rule is that minors are not obligated by the contracts they make.

Age of majority
The age at which a person becomes an adult for legal purposes.

However, since the goal of the law in this area is to protect the underaged, minors have the option to fulfill their contractual commitments and can enforce a contract against the other party should that party be in breach. In this way, contracts with a minor are usually voidable, at the option of the minor alone.[2]

The age of majority—which defines who is not a minor—is within provincial control and is set at 18 or 19 years of age, depending on the province.[3] For example, Ontario's *Age of Majority and Accountability Act*[4] sets the age of majority at 18.

Because minors may have to provide for their own welfare in certain circumstances, there are exceptions to the general common law rule of immunity from liability. Minors are obligated by contracts for essentials, known in law as "necessaries," and are required to pay a reasonable price for them. What amounts to a necessity in a given case is legally determined in relation to two questions:

1. Is the item being acquired necessary to this minor?[5]
2. Does this minor already have an adequate supply of the item?[6]

BUSINESS APPLICATION OF THE LAW

Dealing with Minors

Although there may be sound business reasons for entering into a contract with a minor, there is considerably more risk of non-performance and unenforceability than when contracting with an adult. If the contract is for any significant value, a contractor should consider either contracting with the parent or guardian instead of the minor, or requiring an adult to cosign or guarantee the performance of the minor.

In the employment context, in order for the employment contract to be enforceable against the minor, the employer must be able to prove that the minor is receiving a significant benefit. Otherwise, the minor can simply abandon the contract, at the minor's sole option.

While food, shelter, and clothing are the most common categories of necessaries, the two-step test must still be satisfied in order for the supplier to be able to enforce the specific contract. Suppliers should also be aware that even when the contract is one for necessaries, problems of enforcement can arise. Suppliers may be faced with the presumption that a minor who lives with a parent or guardian is already adequately provided for and has no outstanding needs.[7]

Contracts known as beneficial contracts of service are also binding if they are considered largely for the benefit of the minor. For example, an employment contract with a minor is enforceable if the employer can show that the contract involves a significant element of training and career development, such as one would expect in a program required to enter or progress through a trade or profession. Enforceability in this context means that the employer can be awarded damages for breach of contract.

---

2. It is beyond the scope of this chapter to discuss whether there is a category of void minors' contracts. For discussion see G.H.L. Fridman, *The Law of Contract in Canada*, 5th ed. (Toronto: Thomson Carswell, 2006) at 150 and following.
3. *Ibid* at 140.
4. RSO 1990, c A7.
5. Courts are entitled to consider the infant's socioeconomic status in determining the answer to this question. See, for example, *Ottenbreit v Daniels*, [1975] SJ No 98 (Dist Ct).
6. Fridman, *supra* note 2 at 142. This common law rule has been codified in sale of goods legislation in Canada. For example, s 4 of the Alberta legislation, RSA 2000, c S-2 states,

    4(2) When necessaries are sold and delivered to a minor or to a person who by reason of mental incapacity or drunkenness is incompetent to contract, the minor or person must pay a reasonable price for them. (3) In this section, "necessaries" means goods suitable to the condition in life of the minor or other person and to the minor's or person's actual requirements at the time of the sale and delivery.

7. See David Percy, "The Present Law of Infants' Contracts" (Edmonton: Institute of Law Research and Reform, 1975) at 5.

The common law generally provides that when a minor reaches the age of majority, there is no impact on contracts formed when underage. They remain unenforceable against the minor unless they involve necessaries or beneficial service contracts. Only if the person—now of legal age—expressly adopts or ratifies the agreement does it become enforceable. The one exception to this rule is where the agreement is of a permanent or continuous nature, such as a partnership agreement. In such a case, the minor, upon attaining the age of majority, must reject (repudiate) this obligation, even if it is for non-necessaries. If he fails to do so, liability will be imposed from the time the minor becomes of age.[8]

In all Canadian jurisdictions except British Columbia, the common law governs the contractual capacity of minors.[9] In British Columbia, a different set of rules applies, as set out in the *Infants Act*.[10] This legislation provides even more protection for the infant than is present at common law, since generally, even contracts for necessities and beneficial contracts of service are unenforceable at the election of the minor pursuant to this Act.[11] However, a court has a number of powers under the legislation and can order, for example, that compensation be paid by or to any of the parties to the contract.

Mental Incapacity

In order for a contract to be formed freely and voluntarily by both parties, both must be able to understand the nature and consequences of their agreement. If people were mentally impaired through illness or intoxication by alcohol or drugs, such that they were unable to understand the consequences of their actions, and the other party was aware of their state, they may be able to avoid the contract[12] at their option.[13] To the extent that the other party has unfairly exploited the party who is lacking capacity, there are additional grounds for attacking the contract's validity—namely, duress, undue influence, and unconscionability. All three are considered below.

The fact that Martha's parents are elderly does not, of itself, mean that they lack mental capacity to enter into financial transactions. Rather, before Martha's parents can avoid paying the mortgage on this ground, a court will have to be satisfied that their advanced age has affected their sanity or mental competence—an unlikely outcome on the facts of this scenario. They may be old and overly trusting, but not legally incompetent.

Duress

Contracts that are made as a result of one of the parties being threatened with physical harm are obviously not enforceable. The presence of this extreme form of duress indicates that the threatened party did not freely consent to the terms of the contract and, in fact, was the victim of a crime. Duress is now a broader concept and includes **economic duress**.

Economic duress
The threat of economic harm that coerces the will of the other party and results in a contract.

---

8. Fridman, *supra* note 2 at 144 and following.
9. *Ibid* at 141 and following.
10. See Part 3 of the *Infants Act*, RSBC 1996, c 223.
11. Fridman, *supra* note 2 at 157 describes the operation of B.C.'s *Infants Act* in the following terms:
    A contract by a minor, i.e., someone who was an infant at the time the contract was made, is unenforceable against him unless: (a) the contract is enforceable against him by some statute; (b) the minor affirms the contract on attaining majority; (c) it is wholly or partially performed by the minor after majority; or (d) was not repudiated by the minor within a year after majority. However, the minor can enforce the contract against the adult party as if the minor had been an adult at the time of contracting. In the case of an unenforceable contract, the minor or another party (if the minor has repudiated the contract or is in breach) can apply to a court for relief.
12. Ibid at 162–63; and Edwin Peel, *Treitel: The Law of Contract*, 12th ed (London: Sweet & Maxwell, 2007) at 588 and following.
13. Fridman, *supra* note 2 at 158–62.

In the more difficult cases—those more likely to arise in commercial dealings—economic duress takes the form of one party financially pressuring the other. For example, a company might threaten to break a contract that it knows is crucial to the other side unless the other side gives certain financial concessions or payments in return.[14] Under the traditional test, these concessions will be unenforceable if it is shown that the coercion went beyond ordinary commercial pressure to a force or a coercion of will that prevented the other side from giving true consent to the proposal.[15] Other courts have suggested that a party's lack of a "practical"[16] or "realistic"[17] alternative can count as evidence of economic duress in the proper case.

When duress is established, the contract is voidable at the option of the party who was subject to the duress.

There is no possibility that Martha's parents can rely on the doctrine of duress to avoid their obligations under the mortgage. Though the bank was going to seize Martha's fitness club equipment and offer it for public sale, this "threat" did not amount to duress. Certainly, her parents may have been very upset and worried by the situation, but this would not force them to borrow $40 000 from the bank. Furthermore, the bank is fully within its legal rights to seize property when a loan has fallen into arrears.

Undue Influence

Undue influence
Unfair manipulation that compromises someone's free will.

Since the basic premise of contract formation is that both parties have chosen to enter into the contract, surrounding circumstances that put in question the ability of one of the parties to exercise free will are of great concern. If these factors are sufficiently strong, then the contract is voidable at the option of the party whose free will was lost because of the undue influence of the other contracting party.

Undue influence traditionally operates in two circumstances:

- *Actual pressure.* Sometimes a transaction—commercial or otherwise—arises because one party has exerted unfair influence on the other. In such a case, the party who seeks relief from the contract must show that the influence existed, was exercised, and resulted in the agreement in question.[18] If an elderly person is pressured into signing over an estate to caregivers in return for care, such a transaction could be set aside for undue influence.

- *Presumed pressure.* Sometimes the relationship that already exists between the parties gives rise to a presumption that the ensuing agreement was brought about by one party's unfair manipulation of the other. For example, when the contract is formed between family members or between a lawyer and client or a doctor and patient, for example, the court is entitled to assume that undue influence has been exerted. Other kinds of relationships—as between a banker and a customer, for example—do not import this presumption. When the presumption is in place, however, it then falls to the more powerful party to prove that no undue influence was present.[19]

14. This was held to amount to duress in *North Ocean Shipping Co Ltd v Hyundai Construction Co Ltd*, [1978] 3 All ER 1170 (QB).
15. The traditional case in the area is *Pao On v Lau Yiu Long*, [1979] 3 All ER 65 (PC).
16. *NAV Canada v Greater Fredericton Airport Authority Inc*, 2008 NBCA 28.
17. *Stott v Merit Investment Corp* (1988), 63 OR (2d) 545 (CA).
18. Peel, *supra* note 12 at 447.
19. It is beyond the scope of this text to discuss whether it must also be proven that the contract was a "manifest disadvantage" to the party seeking to have it set aside. For discussion of this point, see Fridman, *supra* note 2 at 317–18 and following.

There is a chance that the elderly Mr. and Mrs. Smith would succeed in having the $40 000 mortgage set aside as having been procured by undue influence, either actual or presumed. The Smiths could argue that they entered into the mortgage with the bank only because the bank manager insistently preyed on their overwhelming need to help their daughter. If so, they could then win on the grounds of actual pressure. An argument could also be advanced on the grounds of presumed pressure. Though courts will not ordinarily presume that a bank has undue influence over its customers, the Smiths may succeed by proving that they placed themselves entirely in the hands of their long-standing bank manager and had received no qualified outside guidance.[20] It would then fall to the bank to show that the mortgage was freely and independently entered into by the Smiths.[21]

One way of proving that the contract was freely chosen is to arrange for the weaker party—such as the Smiths—to get independent legal advice concerning the transaction before it is entered into. The lawyer providing that advice will also produce what is called a "certificate of independent legal advice," which is then appended to the mortgage or other document in question. In the certificate, the lawyer attests that

- he or she has explained the proposed transaction to the weaker party

- the weaker party appears to understand the proposed transaction

- the weaker party is proceeding with the transaction on a free and informed basis

---

CASE

Bank of Montreal v Duguid (2000), 47 OR (3D) 737 (CA), leave to appeal to SCC granted, (2000) SCCB 2238; notice of discontinuance filed (2001) SCCB 1416

THE BUSINESS CONTEXT: When a bank lends money to a customer, it wants to ensure that, in the event of default, the customer has provided sufficient collateral to cover any shortfall. If the customer does not have satisfactory collateral, the bank may refuse to make the loan unless a third party either cosigns or guarantees the loan. This situation can pose serious risks for the third party, given its responsibility that loan payments must be made.

FACTUAL BACKGROUND: In 1989 Mr. Duguid and a business partner applied to the Bank of Montreal for a loan to finance their investment in a condominium project. The bank said that it would make the loan only if Mrs. Duguid would cosign it.

Mr. Duguid approached his wife, a real estate agent, who did sign the loan. Contrary to the bank's usual policy in such matters, its representative failed to recommend to Mrs. Duguid that she secure independent legal advice prior to signing. In short order, the loan went into default, Mr. Duguid declared bankruptcy, and the bank sued Mrs. Duguid for the amount outstanding on the loan, namely $87 000 plus interest.

THE LEGAL QUESTION: Did Mrs. Duguid cosign the loan as a result of her husband's undue influence?

RESOLUTION: Though the bank itself did not exert undue influence, any undue influence exerted by the husband would release the wife from her obligation under the loan if the bank knew or should have known about the undue influence and did nothing about it. Because Mr. Duguid was in a close, personal relationship with the other debtor—namely, his wife—the bank had a duty to make inquiries since the loan was clearly to the wife's disadvantage. If there were any undue influence, this failure by the bank would lead to the wife's loan being set aside.

A majority of the Ontario Court of Appeal said, however, that there was no undue influence. Only if the wife could demonstrate that she reposed "trust and confidence" in her husband concerning financial matters, would there be a presumption of undue influence. As a real estate agent, she knew the risks of her husband's investment, and there was no potential for domination. On this basis, undue influence could not be presumed. Even if it could be presumed, the bank had rebutted that

(Continued)

---

20. This argument is based on *Lloyds Bank Ltd v Bundy, supra* note 1.
21. Peel, *supra* note 12 at 457 and following.

presumption, given Mrs. Duguid's knowledgeable background. On this basis, the loan was enforceable against her.

The dissenting judge would have set the loan aside based on undue influence. The dissent said that while Mrs. Duguid did not repose trust and confidence in her husband in the classic sense, she did fear "destroying the relationship between herself and her husband" should she refuse to cosign. Her background as a real estate agent was simply irrelevant to this more emotional question. Given that Mrs. Duguid agreed to the loan during a low ebb in her marriage and that she signed in order to maintain "some level of tranquility" in the household, a presumption of

undue influence had been established. This presumption was not rebutted by the bank since it knew that the transaction was to the wife's disadvantage and that there was a substantial risk that her husband would pressure her to sign. Since the bank failed to advise her to get independent legal advice, Mrs. Duguid's loan should be set aside due to undue influence.

CRITICAL ANALYSIS: Do you think that the dissent was correct to assess Mrs. Duguid's emotional reasons for cosigning the loan? Or do you prefer the majority's focus on Mrs. Duguid's relatively sophisticated background as a real estate agent?

Unconscionability

Unconscionable contract
An unfair contract formed when one party takes advantage of the weakness of another.

Where one party stands in a position of being able to take advantage of someone and causes that person to enter into an unfair or improvident agreement, an **unconscionable contract** is the result. According to the Supreme Court of Canada, proof of unconscionability involves a two-step process:

- proof of inequality between the parties
- proof of an improvident bargain or proof of exploitation.[22]

If the transaction is sufficiently divergent from community standards of commercial morality, this is a "strong indication of exploitation."[23] At this point, the court will presume unconscionability. It then falls to the stronger party to show that the contract was, in fact, fair.

Inequality between the Parties

The required inequality may result because one party is unsophisticated, is poorly educated, lacks language facility, or has lower economic standing than the stronger party. Parties to a contract are never on strictly equal bargaining terms; therefore, disparity between them is, on its own, insufficient to upset a contract.

Since the Smiths are inexperienced and unsophisticated senior citizens who received no independent legal advice prior to signing the mortgage, this element could arguably be established, particularly if a court were sympathetic to their plight.

An Improvident Bargain

The party seeking to have the contract set aside must also be able to demonstrate that its terms greatly advantaged one party over the other. In short, there must be proof of substantial unfairness.

---

22. *Norberg v Wynrib*, [1992] 2 SCR 226 at 228 [*Norberg*]. Though this case involved non-commercial facts, courts have considered *Norberg's* analysis of unconscionability in a commercial context. See, for example, *Waxman v Waxman* (2002), 25 BLR (3d) 1 (Ont Sup Ct Jus), varied as to damages (2004), 44 BLR (3d) 165 (CA), leave to appeal refused, [2004] SCCA No 291, reconsideration allowed (2004), 6 BLR (4th) 167 (CA); *Floyd v Couture*, 2004 ABQB 238 and *Ellis v Friedland*, [2001] 2 WWR 130 (Alta QB), aff'd 2003 ABCA 60. Note that in *Norberg*, Justice Sopinka in dissent took the position that the doctrine of unconscionability had not yet been settled, at 233. Note too that recently, certain appellate courts have regarded unconscionability as involving a four-step test—see *Cain v Clarica Life Insurance Co.* 2005 ABCA 437 and *Titus v William F Cooke Enterprises*, 2007 ONCA 573 at para 38—and have adopted a four-step test as follows: 1. a grossly unfair and improvident transaction; 2. victim's lack of independent legal advice or other suitable advice; 3. overwhelming imbalance in bargaining power caused by victim's ignorance of business, illiteracy, ignorance of the language of the bargain, blindness, deafness, illness, senility, or similar disability; and 4. other party's knowingly taking advantage of this vulnerability.
23. *Norberg*, *supra* note 22.

Why should contracts that appear normal on the surface be subject to challenge on the basis of the relations between the parties or the surrounding circumstances?

LISA F. YOUNG/SHUTTERSTOCK

In the case of the Smiths' mortgage to the bank, the rate of interest was set at 8 percent and, from that perspective, was reasonable. However, there is a strong argument that the transaction was nonetheless a very unfair bargain for them. Through the mortgage, the Smiths put at risk their only substantial asset, for a loan they could never repay from their own resources. In fact, while the bank and Martha stood to gain enormously from the transaction, the Smiths stood to lose everything for absolutely no return.

People seeking to avoid a contract owing to mental incapacity, duress, undue influence, or unconscionability must do so as promptly as possible or risk losing their case.

CASE

Atlas Supply Co of Canada v Yarmouth Equipment (1991), 103 NSR (2d) 1 (CA), leave to appeal to SCC granted (1991) SCCB 3035; notice of discontinuance filed (1992) SCCB 897

THE BUSINESS CONTEXT: Businesses are expected to obtain necessary information and not agree to terms until they have an agreement they can live with. Sometimes, however, one party takes such extreme advantage of the other that the court agrees to intervene.

FACTUAL BACKGROUND: Atlas was a subsidiary of Esso that supplied parts and accessories to Esso auto service stations. Atlas decided to franchise its operations because its profits were declining. Mr. Murphy's company, Yarmouth Equipment, was

interested in purchasing the franchise for a particular area. Atlas prepared two sets of financial projections for the business in that area. The projections given to Murphy portrayed a viable operation. The other set showed that the franchise was not viable at all. Yarmouth bought the franchise in reliance on the optimistic written projections supplied to him as well as on other oral assurances. The contract Murphy signed with Atlas, however, contained an "entire agreement" clause stating, "Except as provided herein, there are no conditions, representations,

(Continued)

warranties, undertakings, inducements, promises or agreements." This would mean that the written projections and other oral assurances were not to form part of the contract. Another clause recited,

> The Franchisee [Murphy] further acknowledges that it has had an adequate opportunity to be advised by advisors of its own choosing regarding all pertinent aspects of the franchise business, Atlas and this agreement.

Murphy's operation failed and closed in less than a year. Murphy was called upon to pay a substantial sum under his personal guarantee of Yarmouth's debt to Atlas. In defence, Murphy argued that Atlas' positive income projection was a term of the contract and that Atlas was in breach of that term. On a related front, he argued that the exclusion clauses—which would suggest that Atlas' income projection formed no part of the contract—should not apply, given Atlas' unconscionable conduct. The trial judge found in Murphy's favour. Atlas appealed.

THE LEGAL QUESTION: Do Atlas' income projections constitute a contractual warranty or do the exclusion clauses prevent this conclusion? Is Murphy liable on his guarantee to Atlas?

RESOLUTION: The appeal court ruled 2 to 1 in favour of Murphy. Justice Matthews found that the agreement

was entered into on the one hand by a national company with international connections through its parent, Imperial Oil, and on the other by a small businessman who, though no neophyte, had little or no retail experience.

He concluded that it was unconscionable for Atlas to give Murphy misleading information while withholding contrary information. On this footing, he refused to allow Atlas to rely on the exclusion clauses. This meant that Atlas was in breach of its contractual warranty. The court also partially released Murphy from his guarantee to Atlas, given all the circumstances, including Atlas' unconscionable conduct.

The dissenting judge found that Murphy was a very experienced businessperson who was aware of the basis for the financial projections and was not compelled to agree to the terms, which were clearly expressed. He cautioned that the courts should be very reluctant to set aside business deals such as this one.

CRITICAL ANALYSIS: Should a large business with the advantage in information (such as Atlas) be allowed to take advantage of a small, relatively uninformed one (such as Yarmouth)? Which of the judges do you find to be the most persuasive?

BUSINESS AND LEGISLATION

Unconscionability

Many provinces have enacted legislation that relies on unconscionability as a standard against which to assess the fairness of a consumer transaction. For example, Ontario's *Consumer Protection Act* gives remedies—including damages and the right to have the contract set aside—to the consumer who has entered into a contract on the basis of an unfair practice, which includes unconscionable representations. In determining whether to assist the consumer, the court is directed by the legislation to consider whether the person making the representation knows or ought to have known that, for example,

- the consumer was not reasonably able to protect his interests because of his physical infirmity, ignorance, illiteracy, inability to understand the language, or similar factors

- the price grossly exceeded the price at which similar goods or services are readily available to like consumers
- there was no reasonable probability of payment of the obligation in full by the consumer[24]

Many jurisdictions also have legislation that applies when the cost of the loan is excessive. In such circumstances, the courts have a range of options open to them, including redrafting the loan agreement so that it is fair.[25]

Critical Analysis: Does such legislation fill a real need in commercial transactions? Does it unfairly restrict business?

---

24. *Consumer Protection Act, 2002*, SO *2002*, c 30, Sch A, s 15(2). See too the *Fair Trading Act*, RSA 2000, c F-2 (Alberta); the *Business Practices and Consumer Protection Act*, SBC 2004, c 2, (British Columbia); the *Business Practices Act*, CCSM c B-120 (Manitoba); the *Consumer Protection and Business Practices Act*, SNL 2009, c C-31.1; and the *Business Practices Act*, RSPEI 1988, c B-7 (Prince Edward Island).

25. For legislation concerning unconscionability, see, for example, the *Unconscionable Transactions Act*, RSA 2000, c U-2 (Alberta); the *Unconscionable Transactions Relief Act*, CCSM c U20 (Manitoba); the *Unconscionable Transactions Relief Act*, RSNB 2011, c 233 (New Brunswick); the *Unconscionable Transactions Relief Act*, RSNS 1989, c 481 (Nova Scotia); the *Unconscionable Transactions Relief Act*, SNL 2009, c C-31.1 (Newfoundland); the *Unconscionable Transactions Relief Act*, RSPEI 1988, c U-2 (Prince Edward Island); the *Unconscionable Transactions Relief Act*, RSS 1978, c U-1 (Saskatchewan); the *Business Practices and Consumer Protection Act*, SBC 2004, c 2 (British Columbia); and the *Unconscionable Transactions Relief Act*, RSO 1990, c U.2 (Ontario).

Misrepresentations and Important Mistakes
Misrepresentation of Relevant Facts

Parties involved in negotiating a contract are usually not obligated to volunteer information. The basic principle or rule is that both parties are to look out for their own interests and if they want information, they should ask for it.

Sometimes parties do owe a duty to disclose information without being prompted, however.[26] Consider the follow scenarios:

- *One party provides only partial information to the other side*. This may amount to a misrepresentation, since once information is offered, it must not be misleading or incomplete.

- *One party actively conceals the truth*. For example, if the vendor of a building takes steps to conceal a crack in the foundation, this must be disclosed or it will amount to a misrepresentation.

- *One party neglects to correct an earlier assertion that, when stated, was correct but now no longer is so*. If a physician selling his practice gives initial information regarding its value that later becomes inaccurate, the physician must go back and disclose this new fact to the prospective purchaser.

- *The parties are in a relationship requiring utmost good faith*. Insurance law provides an example of this. The person applying for insurance coverage has a duty to disclose all information that would be relevant to the insurer who is assessing the risk of accepting the application.[27]

- *A statute imposes a positive obligation to disclose information*. For example, and as discussed in Chapter 16, legislation requires directors of a corporation to disclose their interest in certain kinds of contracts involving the corporation they serve.[28]

The difference between a statement made in the contract and one that is made prior to entering into the contract is crucial in this area of law.[29] If the statement is made in the contract, it is a promise or a term of the contract. If it proves to be untrue, a breach of contract has occurred. However, if the statement is made prior to entering into the contract but is not a term, it still can have legal consequences. A statement that meets the conditions set out below is known in law as an actionable **misrepresentation**.

Contract law allows the party who has relied on a misrepresentation to have the contract cancelled. This cancellation is called **rescission** and involves putting the parties back into their pre-contractual positions. Because rescission is an equitable remedy, the court requires the person seeking such assistance to act promptly in bringing the complaint forward.

Misrepresentation
A false statement of fact that causes someone to enter a contract.

Rescission
The remedy that results in the parties being returned to their pre-contractual positions.

---

26. There are a number of areas in which a duty to disclose can arise. For discussion, see Shannon O'Byrne, "Culpable Silence: Liability for Non-Disclosure in the Contractual Arena" (1998) 30:2 Can Bus LJ 239.

27. The first four examples in this part of the text are based in case law and are taken from John McCamus, *The Law of Contracts* (Toronto: Irwin Law, 2005) at 332–33. For discussion of the insurance contract scenario, see Peel, *supra* note 12 at 430. Note that the common law duty to disclose information is also repeated in legislation governing insurance contracts. See for example, *Insurance Act*, RSO 1990, c I.8, s 148.

28. See, for example, discussion of the self-dealing contract in Chapter 16. Directors must disclose their interest in certain kinds of corporate contracts.

29. Consumer protection legislation in some jurisdictions, however, specifies that pre-contractual representations are part of the contract. The distinction between pre-contractual representations and terms of the contract, while important in the commercial context, is less important when a business deals with a consumer.

Where rescission is not possible, such as when one party has substantially altered the subject matter of the contract, the courts will endeavour to do what is practically just so that the innocent party receives some redress, including monetary compensation.[30]

Ingredients of an Actionable Misrepresentation

The law provides that a negotiating party must answer inquiries accurately and that any information volunteered must be correct. Whether or not a statement is a misrepresentation that allows the other party a remedy depends on its nature and effect. To count as a misrepresentation, it must be proven that the statement is

- false

- clear and unambiguous

- material to the contract; that is, it must be significant to the decision of whether or not to enter into the contract

- one that actually induces the aggrieved party to enter into the contract

- concerned with a fact and not an opinion, unless the speaker claims to have special knowledge or expertise in relation to an opinion

Categories of Actionable Misrepresentations

The law further divides misrepresentations into three categories:

- *Fraudulent misrepresentation*. The speaker has a deliberate intent to mislead or makes the statement recklessly without knowing or believing that it is true.

- *Negligent misrepresentation*. The speaker makes the statement carelessly or negligently.

- *Innocent misrepresentation*. The speaker has not been fraudulent or negligent, but has misrepresented a fact. By process of elimination, the misrepresentation is merely innocent.

When Kevin told the Smiths that signing the mortgage was a formality, this statement amounted to a misrepresentation, since a mortgage is in fact a legal instrument with far-reaching consequences, the most serious being that the bank could foreclose on the Smiths' house. If the Smiths can prove that they relied on that representation in deciding to sign the mortgage, they will probably succeed in establishing an actionable misrepresentation. Minimally, this statement was negligent, but, given the likely state of Kevin's banking knowledge, the statement might even be fraudulent.

When Kevin told the Smiths he was confident that nothing would come of their signing the mortgage, this was arguably an expression of opinion—not a statement of fact—and therefore not actionable. A court might find, however, that since Kevin is an expert in the area of mortgages and other banking matters, his statement was one of fact, and order a remedy on that basis. While a court would be unlikely to find this statement to be a fraudulent misrepresentation, given the sparse facts, it may well find it to be negligent.

---

30. See, for example, *Kupchak v Dayson Holdings Ltd*, [1965] 53 WWR 65 (BCCA).

Remedies for Misrepresentation

Besides entitling courts to rescind or set aside a contract, certain kinds of misrepresentations are torts, which provide for a remedy in damages. If the misrepresentation is fraudulent or negligently made, damages in tort can be awarded in addition to the remedy of rescission provided by contract law. Where the misrepresentation is neither fraudulent nor negligent, an action is still available to set the contract aside based on innocent misrepresentation (see Figure 8.2 below). Negligence and fraud (or deceit) are discussed further in Chapters 11 and 12.

Upon the Smiths demonstrating an innocent misrepresentation, the court can order that their contract with the bank be set aside. If the Smiths can go on to prove that the bank—through Kevin—is responsible for the tort of negligence or fraud, they are entitled to damages as well, though these are probably not large.

FIGURE 8.2

Remedies for Misrepresentation

Type of Misrepresentation		
	Fraudulent	*Negligent*	*Innocent*
Remedy	Rescission in contract Damages in tort	Rescission in contract Damages in tort	Rescission in contract

Given the cost of litigation—and the fact that the innocent party may fail to prove her case on the balance of probabilities that an actionable misrepresentation had been made—prevention is the best medicine. It is prudent to insist that important terms be an express part of a written contract, so as to achieve the goal of clarity between the parties. It is generally easier to prove breach of a written term than to establish that an oral statement made during contractual negotiations amounts to a misrepresentation in law. If the other party balks at reciting an important representation as an express, written term, the customer would be best advised to do business elsewhere.

Mistake

The doctrine of legal **mistake** is one of the most difficult aspects of contract law. In the course of its development by the courts, the law of mistake has become so complex and confusing that it presents a major challenge even to seasoned lawyers and judges. In practice, legal mistake is rarely proven, but when it is, the court is entitled to set the contract aside as a remedy.

Mistake
An error made by one or both parties that seriously undermines a contract.

The central point is that legal mistake is much narrower than the everyday idea of a mistake. A simple oversight or error by one negotiating party does not constitute a legal mistake and provides no basis for voiding a contract. As previously noted, negotiators are expected to look after themselves and to exercise appropriate caution before making legal commitments.

Compare the following two examples:

Example 1   Kerry intends to make an offer to sell her car for $11 000 and in error sends a written offer to Sean for $10 000. Sean accepts her offer.

Example 2   Kerry makes a written offer to sell her car for $1100 rather than $11 000, and Sean promptly accepts. There is no reason to believe that the car, worth approximately $11 000, should be sold at a substantially lower price. Moreover, there is nothing in the relationship that would suggest that Kerry would give Sean a break in price.

In both cases, Kerry has made a mistake according to the common understanding of that word. However, in all likelihood, only in Example 2 would this be interpreted at law as a mistake worthy of a remedy. The error Kerry has made in Example 1 is not one that would surprise Sean. This could be exactly the price for which Kerry intends to sell her car. In contrast, in Example 2, Sean could not reasonably expect that the price would be so low, especially if Kerry and Sean have had earlier discussions about the possible price range. Kerry has made an error, and any reasonable person in Sean's position would realize that. In the latter example, there can be no true agreement for $1100. The law will not permit Sean to "snap up" Kerry's offer in this way.

A legal mistake may also occur if both parties have made the same error (known as **common mistake**). If Kerry's car appears to be old and relatively worthless, and she and Sean negotiate on that basis for a relatively low price, their agreement is based on a common mistake if the car turns out to be a valuable antique. Only if the error is such that the car purchased is a totally different thing from what the parties thought it was will the contract be set aside on the basis of mistake. For example, if the difference is between low-grade transportation (what the parties thought the car was) and a classic car to be displayed and never driven (what the car actually is), a mistake in law could possibly be established. To the extent that the error is simply a mistaken assumption about the quality of the car (i.e., in terms of value), however, no legal mistake has occurred, and the purchaser is entitled to retain what may appear to be a windfall. Needless to say, such distinctions can be subtle.

Under the Business Law in Practice scenario, Martha's parents may have signed the mortgage under the mistaken belief that Martha's business problems were temporary and reversible. This is not a legal mistake, however, and there is no possibility that the mortgage would be set aside on the basis of this misapprehension.

Common mistake
Both parties to the agreement share the same fundamental mistake.

CASE   *R v Ron Engineering & Construction Ltd*, [1981] 1 SCR 111

THE BUSINESS CONTEXT: As noted in Chapter 6, owners commonly secure competitive bids to build large projects through a call for tenders. In response, contractors (also known as tenderers) submit tenders that set out a price for the work to be done. Though this is a fact-specific matter, the tendering rules can require the contractors to submit a tender deposit that is forfeited by the contractor who is chosen if he refuses to undertake the job. It is therefore important that the tender price is

accurately tabulated before the tender is submitted to the owner since it can be difficult to withdraw after the fact, at least not without risking the deposit.

FACTUAL BACKGROUND: Ron Engineering submitted a tender on a project for a price of $2 748 000 along with a certified cheque for $150 000 as the tendering rules required. The tendering rules—contained in the Information for Tenderers—stipulated that tenders could be withdrawn up to the official closing time, after which they would be irrevocable. The rules also provided that the deposit was forfeited by the successful contractor if the successful contractor refused to proceed with the project.

Tenders closed at 3:00 p.m. and soon thereafter, Ron Engineering realized that, due to a simple miscalculation, it had submitted a bid that was $750 000 less than it had intended to submit. Though this error was detected by Ron Engineering and explained to the owner within 72 minutes of closing, the owner insisted that Ron Engineering proceed with the project or forfeit its deposit.

THE LEGAL QUESTION: Does the law of mistake provide Ron Engineering with a route of escape, or is the company obligated to either perform or forfeit its deposit? Is it too late for Ron Engineering to withdraw its tender?

RESOLUTION: The Supreme Court of Canada ruled that tenderers in the position of Ron Engineering could not withdraw tenders after the official closing time. Upon submission of its tender, Ron was in a preliminary contract with the owner. This preliminary contract (known as Contract A) required the

owner to respect the rules on how to evaluate tenders and required tenderers not to withdraw their tenders after the official closing time. Only the successful tenderer would enter into the larger contract to perform the work in question (known as Contract B).

Ron Engineering unsuccessfully argued that the law of mistake prevented Contract A from ever coming into existence. According to the court, since Ron Engineering intended to submit the very tender submitted, including the named price, there was no mistake in any legal sense. Furthermore, even though the tender was $750 000 less than it should have been, this error was not so large as to suggest to the other side that there had been a miscalculation. Unless there was something seriously amiss with the tender—such as an entire page missing—Contract A would come into existence. Since no such circumstances existed here, Ron Engineering lost its deposit. The court insisted that such strictness was essential to protecting the integrity of the tendering process.

CRITICAL ANALYSIS: Is the law of mistake too harsh? What would the consequences be if a party could escape its contractual obligations simply because it had made a mathematical error?

CASE   *Miller Paving Ltd v B Gottardo Construction Ltd* (2007), 86 OR (3d) 161 (Ont CA)

THE BUSINESS CONTEXT: When a supplier provides product to its customer over time, there can be confusion as to whether all accounts have been rendered. When the supplier and customer sign mutual releases whereby they agree that no further monies are owing, they are generally bound even if an error has been made.

FACTUAL BACKGROUND: Miller was a supplier of aggregate material, which its customer, Gottardo, used as highway construction material. In December 2001, the parties signed an agreement or release in which Miller acknowledged it had been paid by Gottardo in full. The next month, however, Miller rendered a further invoice in the amount of $480 000 upon determining that one delivery had not yet been billed out.

THE LEGAL QUESTION: Does the release prevent Miller from collecting on this invoice, or should the release be set aside on the grounds of mistake?

RESOLUTION: The Court of Appeal concluded that the release was binding. There was a common mistake because both parties shared the same error—that all the material supplied by Miller had been paid for—and this error made the contract something essentially different from what it was thought to be. However,

the contract itself precluded Miller from relying on the defence of mistake. Therefore, Miller must live with the contract it struck. According to the court,

> [The "Memorandum of Release"] clearly provides that it is the supplier that "acknowledges and agrees that payment in full has been received for the materials supplied." Moreover, the billing practice here, as with most supply contracts, made it the responsibility of the supplier to determine what was owing for the material supplied and to then invoice for that amount. When the contract language is read in the context of this factual matrix, I conclude that the contract clearly allocates to Miller the risk that payment in full has not been received. I would therefore find that the December 20 agreement itself requires Miller to bear the consequence when that risk transpires, rather than allowing it to invoke the doctrine of common mistake.

CRITICAL ANALYSIS: Do you think that the outcome of this decision is too harsh on Miller? Should parties always be held to their contracts?

An argument that is often made, though seldom successfully, concerns signed documents. The signer may misunderstand the type or nature of the document. Perhaps the signer thinks he is signing a guarantee of a debt, but the document is actually a mortgage on his residence. Or the document is a transfer of land, and the signer thought he was signing an option to sell the property. The argument is "I never intended to sign this type of contract." In practice, this argument tends to succeed only when there is a good reason for the signer's failure to more closely examine the document before signing—as when the signer is poorly educated, illiterate, or otherwise dependent on the creator of the document (the other party) for an explanation of what it is. Simple carelessness in signing a document without attention to what it is or to what its consequences might be is not enough to avoid enforceability.[31]

Contracts Based on Defects
Illegality

Under the classical model of illegality, even a freely chosen contract will be unenforceable if it

- is contrary to a specific statute and/or

- violates public policy

These contracts are void and of no effect unless the court decides that the offending portions of the contract can be deleted, or severed, and the remaining portions saved. In such a case, only some of the contract will remain in effect and be enforceable. What a court will not do, however, is re-draft the offending portions to make them comply with the law.

Contracts that are illegal may or may not be criminal. In this context, an **illegal contract** is simply one that violates statute law or public policy.[32]

> **Illegal contract**
> A contract that cannot be enforced because it is contrary to legislation or public policy.

Illegal by Statute

Numerous kinds of contracts are made illegal by legislation. Examples include the following:

- The *Criminal Code*[33] forbids loans at a rate of interest considered "criminal"— defined as a rate exceeding 60 percent per year. The courts may or may not invalidate the entire transaction, depending on whether it is possible to sever the clauses dealing with the criminal rate of interest from the rest of the contract.

- The federal *Competition Act*[34] invalidates a range of commercial transactions that unduly restrict competition. For example, resale price maintenance contracts are prohibited because, through them, manufacturers attempt to influence retail prices in the stores by keeping them high. Entering into such contracts can lead to criminal sanctions.

- Ontario's *Real Estate and Business Brokers Act*[35] provides that an unlicensed realtor cannot maintain an action for services rendered.

Business enterprises should take care to meet their statutory and regulatory obligations lest they be faced with a challenge to the legality of a contract they have entered into.

---

31. For an exception to this statement see the discussion in Chapter 7 concerning *Tilden Rent-A-Car Co v Clendenning* (1978), 83 DLR (3d) 400 (Ont CA).
32. See Stephanie Ben-Ishai & David R Percy, eds, *Contracts: Cases and Commentaries*, 8th ed (Scarborough, ON: Carswell, 2009) at 729.
33. *Criminal Code*, RSC 1985, c C-46, s 347.
34. *Competition Act*, RSC 1985, c C-34.
35. *Real Estate and Business Brokers Act, 2002*, SO 2002, c 30, Sch C, s 9.

Increasingly, however, the consequences of statutory illegality depend on all the circumstances of the case.[36] As one leading text in this area of law states, "If every statutory illegality, however trivial in the course of performance of a contract, invalidated the agreement, the result would be an unjust and haphazard allocation of loss without regard to any rational principles."[37] This statement signals a more flexible perspective, which may fully eclipse the strict, traditional approach that says that illegal contracts are automatically unenforceable.

Contrary to Public Policy

At common law, contracts are contrary to **public policy** when they injure the public interest. For example, an employer may wish to restrict the activities of employees to prevent them from joining the competition or becoming the competition. Or someone wishing to acquire a business may want to ensure that the vendor cannot simply set up shop down the street and immediately begin competing with the new owner. The motivation for such clauses is understandable since both the employer and business acquirer, as the case may be, want to protect their own best interests. Clauses which restrict someone's business activities in this way are known as restrictive covenants or covenants in restraint of trade. If drafted too broadly, they are unenforceable as being contrary to public policy. In short, restrictive covenants may unduly interfere with the other side's ability to earn a livelihood, and they reduce competition within a sector.[38] In 2009, the Supreme Court of Canada in *Shafron v KRG Insurance Brokers* expressly reaffirmed that restrictive covenants in the sale of a business are subject to less scrutiny because the business owner is typically paid for goodwill.[39] In the employment context, by way of contrast, the employee receives no such recompense, and there is typically a power imbalance between employee and employer.[40]

Public policy
The community's common sense and common conscience.

INTERNATIONAL PERSPECTIVE

Paying Bribes to Foreign Officials

Canadian businesses may feel compelled to pay bribes in order to "grease wheels" overseas but they also face serious liability for doing so, not to mention damage to corporate reputation. In 2011, a Calgary-based oil and gas company, Niko Resources Ltd., entered a guilty plea under Canada's *Corruption of Foreign Public Officials Act*—for bribing a Bangladeshi official—and agreed to pay fines and penalties in the amount of approximately $9.5 million. This is the highest penalty ever assessed by a Canadian court in relation to corporate bribery of a foreign official. Niko also agreed to three years of probation and is required to improve its corporate culture during that time. Justice Scott Brooker, the judge hearing the matter, said that the Niko bribe was an "embarrassment to all Canadians" that "tarnishes the reputation of Alberta and of Canada."

In an agreed statement of facts, Niko acknowledged that it gave goods and services to Bangladeshi officials to induce such officials "to use their position to influence any acts or decisions" of the Bangladeshi government. More specifically, Niko's subsidiary company spent $190 984 to furnish Bangladesh's junior minister of energy with a Toyota Land Cruiser.

(Continued)

---

36. See *Still v Minister of National Revenue*, [1998] 1 FC 549 (CA), whose analysis was approved by the Supreme Court of Canada in *Transport North American Express Inc v New Solutions Financial Corp*, 2004 SCC 7.
37. SM Waddams, *The Law of Contracts*, 6th ed (Toronto: Canada Law Book, 2010) at 420.
38. *Doerner v Bliss and Laughlin Industries Inc*, [1980] 2 SCR 865 at 873.
39. *Shafron v KRG Insurance Brokers*, [2009] 1 SCR 157 at paras 20–21.
40. *Ibid* at paras 22–23.

© JIRI REZAC/ALAMY

What reputational damage does a bribery conviction create?

It also gave that same official approximately $5000 in travel "perks" and paid for the official's accommodation in Calgary and later in New York. When news of the bribes became public, Canada's then ambassador met with the president of Niko's subsidiary who stated that "these things are done all the time" and are "the cost of doing business in Bangladesh."

From 2005 forward, Niko was experiencing difficulties in Bangladesh due to an explosion at one of the company's northeastern natural gas fields. The junior minister receiving the bribes was to have influence over what the affected villagers in the region would receive from Niko by way of compensation. Niko acknowledges that the price it is paying for the misconduct is much more than merely financial. As Niko lawyer Kristine Robidoux stated:

> There's also the significant embarrassment that this has caused Niko, the reputational damage this will surely cause employees and shareholders, so, certainly, this is being taken very seriously by the company.

Note that Canada enacted the *Corruption of Foreign Public Officials Act* over a decade ago but has been criticized for doing little to enforce it. For example, a 2004 report by a working

group of the Organization for Economic Cooperation and Development said that Canada has failed to develop a "government-wide agenda for proactively addressing foreign bribery." In 2009, anti-corruption watchdog Transparency International described Canada as a "laggard" in this same arena but did call Niko's recent penalty a "great start," albeit paling in comparison to fines assessed in the United States for similar offenses.

An article in the *Lawyers Weekly* emphasizes the importance of enforcing the anti-corruption act as well educating judges and prosecutors so that bribery of foreign officials is regarded as a serious matter. This is especially important because "the corrosive effect of bribery still ultimately harms the poorest of people." Indeed, the World Bank notes on its Institutional Integrity website the tremendous toll that corruption (including bribery) has on those who are economically destitute because corruption erects barriers to economic and social development as well distorts the rule of law. According to the World Bank:

> The harmful effects of corruption are especially severe on the poor, who are hardest hit by economic decline, are most reliant on the provision of public services, and are least capable of paying the extra costs associated with bribery, fraud, and the misappropriation of economic privileges.

Critical Analysis: Do you agree with the penalty assessed to Niko? How do you think the bribery of public officials harms the poor of those countries?

Sources: Rebecca Penty & Dan Healing, "Niko bribery an 'embarrassment,' says judge; company fined $9.5 million", *Calgary Herald* (25 June 2011) online: Calgary Herald <http://www.calgaryherald.com/Niko+bribery+embarrassment+says +judge+company+fined+million/5001181/story.html#ixzz1Vru4hSAs>; Lauren Krugel, "Bangladesh bribes costly for Niko", *Chronical Herald* (25 Jun 2011) C3; James Klotz, "Canadian firms do pay bribes, they just aren't punished", *The Lawyers Weekly* (2 May 2008) 18; Karen MacGregor & Karen Howlet, "World Bank penalizes Canadian company", *The Globe and Mail* (24 July 2004) B2 online: Odious Debts <http://www.odiousdebts.org/odiousdebts/index.cfm? DSP=content&ContentID=11039>; and World Bank, "Anticorruption", online: World Bank <http://web.worldbank.org/WBSITE/EXTERNAL/TOPICS/ EXTPUBLICSECTORANDGOVERNANCE/EXTANTICORRUPTION/0,contentMDK:21540 659~menuPK:384461~pagePK:148956~piPK:216618~theSitePK:384455,00.html>.

Non-solicitation clause
A clause forbidding contact with the business' customers.

Non-competition clause
A clause forbidding competition for a certain period of time.

There are two main kinds of restrictive covenants that are found in this area. **A non-solicitation clause** simply forbids the employee (or business vendor) from contacting the business' customers. A **non-competition clause** forbids competition outright for a certain period of time and is therefore much more intrusive.

The following case explains how non-competition clauses should be assessed by the judiciary.

CASE
Elsley v J G Collins Insurance Agencies Limited, [1978] 2 SCR 916

THE BUSINESS CONTEXT: The purchaser of a business often wants to prevent the vendor from competing against him for a specified period of time in order to prevent the vendor from setting up a similar business across the street. If the purchaser hires the vendor to work at the business, the employment contract may also contain a non-competition covenant for a related reason.

FACTUAL BACKGROUND: Elsley and Collins entered into a purchase and sale agreement whereby Collins purchased Elsley's general insurance business. This agreement contained a non-competition covenant, which stipulated that Elsley was restricted from carrying on or engaging in the business of a general insurance company within a certain geographic area for a period of 10 years. By a separate employment agreement, Elsley worked as a manager for Collins. This agreement also contained a non-competition covenant covering the same geographic area, whereby Elsley could not compete with Collins for a period of five years after he ceased to work for Collins. After 17 years, Elsley resigned and opened his own general insurance business, which took some of Collins' customers.

THE LEGAL QUESTION: Is the non-competition covenant in Elsley's employment contract valid?

RESOLUTION: In finding the non-competition covenant to be valid, the court stated:

> A covenant in restraint of trade is enforceable only if it is reasonable between the parties and with reference to the public interest. As with many of the cases which come before the Courts, competing demands must be weighed. There is an important public interest in discouraging restraints of trade, and maintaining free and open competition unencumbered by the fetters of restrictive covenants. On the other hand, the courts have been disinclined to restrict the rights to contract, particularly when the right has been exercised by knowledgeable persons of equal bargaining power. In assessing the opposing interests the word one finds repeated throughout the cases is the word "reasonable." The test of reasonableness can be applied, however, only in the peculiar circumstances of the particular case.

According to the court, the assessment of non-competition clauses involves considering whether

- the employer has a proprietary interest that he is entitled to protect
- the temporal and geographic restrictions are reasonable
- the restrictions are reasonably necessary to protect the employer, given the nature of the business and the nature and character of the employment

Once the reasonableness of a restrictive covenant has been established, it is enforceable unless it runs contrary to the public interest.

In this case, the clause was reasonable and therefore fully enforceable. The plaintiff was entitled to an injunction and damages for breach of the clause.[41]

CRITICAL ANALYSIS: Do you agree that non-competition clauses in employment contracts should be less likely to be enforced than similar clauses in sale-of-business agreements? What are an employer's "proprietary interests"?

The Supreme Court of Canada has also confirmed that courts are not to re-draft overly broad non-competition clauses by "reading them down" until they become reasonable—that is, legal and enforceable.[42] Rather, such clauses are simply and utterly unenforceable. A central policy objective is to prevent employers from intentionally drafting broad clauses with the promise that the courts will simply reduce their scope as appropriate. This could lead to employees who never make it to court, being bound by an unreasonable non-competition clause.[43] The Court also agreed that judges may remove part of an impugned provision to "cure" it, but only sparingly and "only in cases where the part being removed is clearly severable, trivial and not part of the main purport of the restrictive covenant."[44] Finally, the Supreme Court also ruled that vaguely or ambiguously drafted clauses are also

---

41. For a recent example of how lower courts have relied on both *Shafron and Elsley*, see *Belron Canada Incorporated v TCG International Inc*, 2009 BCSC 596, aff'd 2009 BCCA 577.
42. *Supra* note 39 at paras 33, 36.
43. *Ibid* at para 40.
44. *Ibid* at para 36.

unenforceable, generally speaking, because it is difficult to prove that the clause is reasonable when its meaning is in fact unclear.[45]

Writing as a Requirement

As a general rule, contracts do not have to be in writing in order to be enforceable. A party to an oral contract must find other means to prove its existence, such as calling of witnesses. Sometimes, however, a contract must be evidenced in writing due to the *Statute of Frauds*.

The *Statute of Frauds* was imported to Canada from England. Except in Manitoba, where it has been completely repealed,[46] it applies to differing extents in all common law provinces.

The purpose of the *Statute of Frauds* is to prevent fraud and perjury by requiring written proof of certain kinds of contracts. The categories discussed below are the most relevant to business. A contract falling into these categories must have its essential terms contained in a document or documents signed by the party against whom the contract is to be enforced. Several documents can be combined to meet the requirement if each of the documents can be connected with the others. If the writing requirement cannot be met, however, the contract is generally unenforceable.

Contracts of Guarantee

Guarantee
A promise to pay the debt of someone else, should that person default on the obligation.

A **guarantee** is a promise to pay the debt of someone else, should that person default on the obligation. A guarantee must generally be evidenced in writing.[47]

The province of Alberta has gone even further than the *Statute of Frauds* by requiring additional formalities from non-corporate guarantors, including the requirement that the written guarantee be accompanied by a notary's certificate. In this certificate, the notary attests that the guarantor understands the consequences of entering into the guarantee and that the guarantee is freely given.[48]

Contracts Not to Be Performed within a Year

The rationale for requiring a written record for these kinds of contracts is the difficulty of proving promises that were possibly made in the distant past. Since the arbitrary cutoff of one year is bound to be unfair in some cases, the courts have been known to interpret the *Statute of Frauds* in such a way as to avoid an injustice.

The requirement of writing for this kind of contract has been repealed in several jurisdictions, such as Ontario,[49] British Columbia, and Manitoba.

Contracts Dealing with Land

Contracts concerning land—including leases and sales—generally must be evidenced in writing in order to be enforceable.[50] Nevertheless, in the interest of fairness, the courts

---

45. *Ibid.*
46. *An Act to Repeal the Statute of Frauds*, CCSM c F158.
47. This rule does not apply in Manitoba.
48. See the *Guarantees Acknowledgment Act*, RSA 2000, c G-11. British Columbia has extended the writing requirement to indemnities owing to the *Law and Equity Act*, RSBC 1996, c 253, s 59(6).
49. *Statute of Frauds*, RSO 1990, c S-19, s 4, amended by *Statute Law Amendment Act*, SO 1994, c 27, s 55.
50. Even in Manitoba—where the *Statute of Frauds* has been repealed—courts have been known to insist that contracts dealing with land be in writing, particularly when the offer is made in writing, as in *Jen-Den Investments Ltd v Northwest Farms Ltd*, [1978] 1 WWR 290 (Man CA). See too *Megill-Stephenson Co Ltd v Woo* (1989), 59 DLR (4th) 146 (Man CA).

have also created an exception to the absolute requirement for writing in the case of "part performance." If the person attempting to enforce an oral agreement for purchase and sale of land has performed acts in relation to the land that could be explained by the existence of an agreement, that performance may be accepted in place of a written agreement.[51]

TECHNOLOGY AND THE LAW

E-Signatures

Commercial contracts are generally enforceable, no matter what form they take, but there are important exceptions. For example, signature requirements exist in statutes such as the *Statute of Frauds*.

A traditional definition of a signature is a "physical, hand-written mark that authenticates a document." The courts, however, have been quite liberal in applying the signature requirement in a paper context and have, for example, accepted typewritten names and initials as well as formal signatures, whether legible or not.

In relation to e-contracts, many legislators across the country have offered guidance as to what fulfils a signature requirement. Ontario's *Electronic Commerce Act*, 2000, for example, provides that, with some exceptions, "a legal requirement that a document be signed is satisfied by an electronic signature." Section 1(1) defines an "electronic signature" as "electronic information that a person creates or adopts in order to sign a document and that is in, attached to, or associated with the document." Most Canadian jurisdictions have accepted electronic signatures according to statutory rules of varying strictness. The key notion is that the e-signature must be a reliable means of identifying the person and reliably associated with the document in question.

ED HONOWITZ/STONE/GETTY IMAGES

How does legislation governing e-signatures help create certainty in the marketplace?

Ontario courts have confirmed that an effective electronic signature need not be equivalent to a cursive signature. See *Newbridge Networks Corp (Re)*, [2000] OJ 1346 (Ont Sup Ct), which dealt with the e-signature question in the context of electronic voting. As Timothy Banks et al. summarize the matter for Ontario:

> the signature can be in any font and even take the form of a series of numbers of letters or both. It could be a picture or figure. What matters is that the signature can be used reliably to identify the maker of the signature.

Of course, some forms of electronic signatures are by nature more secure than others. For example, a "digital signature" is a specific type of electronic signature and is generally unique to a particular signer, capable of verification, and capable of indicating whether the record to which it is attached was changed after it was signed.

Federally, the validity of e-signatures is addressed in the *Personal Information Protection and Electronic Documents Act (PIPEDA)*, SC 2000, c 5, ss 31 and 43. *The Secure Electronic Signature Regulations*, SOR/2005-30, issued in 2005 pursuant to the *PIPEDA*, provide for a "secure electronic signature," much like the "digital signature" mentioned above, that is to be used for electronic documents that are originals, declarations, sealed, sworn, or witnessed. The secure electronic signature technologies must ensure that the signature is unique to the signer, the application of the signature was under the signer's sole control, the signer is identifiable, and the technologies can be used to determine if the document was changed after it was signed.

Critical Analysis: Are electronic signatures more or less reliable than the hand-written variety?

Sources: Timothy Banks, Sonja Homenuck, and Greg Barker, "Electronic Delivery of Lease Documentation: Is E-Delivery Enforceable?" (2010) 11:2 IECLC 9 at 14; Michael Erdle, "Legal Issues in Electronic Commerce" (1996) 12 CIPR 251; Alan M Gahtan et al, *Internet Law: A Practical Guide for Legal and Business Professionals* (Scarborough, ON: Carswell, 1998) at 313; Bradley J. Freedman, "Digital Signatures and Authentication Processes" (12 July 2004) online: Continuing Legal Education Society of British Columbia <http://www.cle.bc.ca/CLE/Analysis/Collection/04-54321-signatures>; and Michael Deturbide, "Canadian laws on e-contracting still leave many questions unanswered", *The Lawyers Weekly* (27 January 2006) 14, 16.

---

51. It is beyond the scope of this text to discuss the varying tests for part performance that exist at common law.

The mortgage given by the Smiths to the bank must comply with the *Statute of Frauds*, since it concerns an interest in land. That is, through the mortgage, the bank acquires the right to sell the land and apply the proceeds against the Smiths' loan, should they default on payments. The mortgage prepared by the bank appears to meet the requirements of the Statute *of Frauds* because the agreement is a written contract and has been signed by the Smiths.

Contracts for the Sale of Goods

All provinces have a version of the *Sale of Goods* Act, and most[52] contain a provision that contracts for the sale of goods above a specified amount must be in writing to be enforceable by the courts. The amount is generally set at between $30 and $50, not adjusted to reflect inflation. Thus, it would appear that most sales of goods are caught by the Act. Since written contracts are generally not produced for routine transactions, it is fortunate that sale of goods legislation also contains very broad exceptions that limit the application of the rule. For example, if partial payment is made by the buyer, or if the buyer accepts all or part of the goods, no written evidence is required for the contract to be enforceable.

BUSINESS AND LEGISLATION

Internet Contracts

Even where a contract is not caught by *Statute of Frauds* requirements such that it must be in writing, other legislation may nonetheless require the business in question to produce a written copy of the contract. That is, governments may decide it is in the best interests of consumers to give them additional protection and safeguards when entering into certain kinds of transactions.

Several provinces, including Manitoba, Alberta, Nova Scotia, Ontario, and British Columbia, have passed legislation reflecting the consumer protection measures of the *Internet Sales Contract Harmonization Template*. The template was released by the Consumer Measures Committee, and endorsed by all federal, provincial, and territorial ministers responsible for consumer affairs. The template and its various counterparts apply to consumer purchases of goods and services over the Internet and require sellers to clearly disclose certain information to the buyer before an online contract is formed. The information to be disclosed includes the seller's business name and address (including email address), a fair and accurate description of the goods and services, all costs (including taxes and shipping), delivery arrangements, and return policies.

All of this information must be accessible such that it can be printed and retained by the consumer, and it must be clearly and prominently displayed. Consumers must also be given an opportunity to accept or decline the terms of the agreement and to correct errors before the contract is formed.

Some provinces' legislation goes beyond the minimum requirements set out in the template. For example, *Ontario's Consumer Protection Act* requires a supplier to deliver to a consumer who has entered into an Internet agreement a copy of that agreement. If the supplier fails to do so within a specified time, the consumer may cancel the agreement and it becomes unenforceable.

By requiring that the supplier provide a written contract to the consumer, the consumer is better able to confirm what rights and liabilities exist under the contract. The consumer is also able to confirm whether the written agreement reflects the consumer's understanding of the contract.

Researched and written by Meredith Hagel.

Sources: Michael Deturbide, "Canadian laws on e-contracting still leave many questions unanswered", *The Lawyers Weekly* (27 January 2006)14,16; see also s 39(1) and s 40(2) of the *Consumer Protection Act, 2002*, SO 2002, c 30, Sch A.

Even without *Statute of Frauds* requirements, creating a record of an agreement is generally a prudent business decision. Personnel may change and memories may fade, and genuine disagreement as to the terms of a contract can result. Through a well-recorded written document, such disagreements—and perhaps the expense of litigation—can be avoided.

---

52. The exceptions include New Brunswick, Manitoba, Ontario, and British Columbia. See too GHL Fridman, *Sale of Goods in Canada*, 5th ed (Toronto: Carswell, 2005) at 43.

That said, businesses and individuals must strike a reasonable balance between the comfort of complete records and the time and effort required to produce them, particularly in small transactions.

Managing the Risks of Unenforceability

When contracts are entered into, a business runs the risk that they may ultimately be unenforceable. Since a contract is only as good as the process leading up to its formation, businesses should train their employees carefully in how to negotiate contracts. Matters to be concerned about include:

- Are the parties to the contract under any legal incapacities?

- Has one party taken unfair advantage of the other?

- Has one party misled the other?

- Has a substantial mistake been made?

- Is the contract contrary to legislation or in violation of public policy?

- Is the contract required to be in writing?

An affirmative response to any of the foregoing may signal a possible problem if suing becomes necessary. Securing a deal at any cost may end up producing no deal at all.

Business Law in Practice Revisited

1. Did Kevin manipulate or pressure the Smiths into signing the mortgage? If so, what legal remedies do the Smiths have?

While the Smiths have the capacity to contract and were not subject to duress by Kevin, the mortgage transaction is probably unconscionable. There was inequality between the parties—namely the bank and the Smiths—because the Smiths were inexperienced senior citizens who had received no prior independent legal advice. As well, the transaction was very unfair, since the Smiths were risking their only substantial asset for a loan they could never repay on their own. In short, only the bank and Martha would benefit from the transaction, while the Smiths stood to lose everything. On this basis, both of the steps necessary to establish unconscionability have been met, and a court will set the mortgage aside unless the bank can somehow show that the transaction was fair.

The mortgage transaction is also liable to be set aside at common law on the grounds that it was signed on the basis of undue influence. There is a good argument that the Smiths did not freely enter into the mortgage but did so only because Kevin preyed on their deep need to help their daughter. As well, it appears that the Smiths put their entire trust in Kevin, which is another basis for a court to find undue influence.

2. Did Mr. and Mrs. Smith enter into the contract on the basis of mistake or misrepresentation? If so, what legal remedies do they have?

The Smiths could argue that they did not understand what they were signing and that the whole thing was a "mistake." This may be true from their point of view, but they did sign the mortgage document. The law ordinarily expects people not to sign documents unless they understand them. Accordingly, the mortgage is unlikely to be set aside on the grounds of mistake.

There is a very strong argument, however, that Kevin misrepresented the nature of the transaction by telling the Smiths that signing the mortgage was just a formality and that likely nothing would come of it. While it could be argued that this statement was merely an opinion, this defence is unlikely to succeed since the words were spoken by a banker who should know better. While it also could be argued that the Smiths did not rely on Kevin's statement—in other words, that they knew very well that their house could be foreclosed upon if Martha failed to make the payments—a judge is much more likely to take the Smiths' side. There is an excellent chance that the mortgage would be set aside on the basis of Kevin's misrepresentation.

3. How could Kevin have managed this transaction better?

Since the essence of a contract is the free and voluntary adoption of obligations, Kevin should never have asked the Smiths to sign the mortgage until they had secured independent legal advice.

Furthermore, it would probably have been better for Kevin not to have been involved in the transaction at all, and instead to have sent the Smiths elsewhere. Most of the legal problems in this scenario arose because Kevin was trying to get a bad loan he had given to Martha off his books. This motivation may have interfered with his judgment in how to handle the Smiths from the outset.

Chapter Summary

There is a broad range of doctrines available to cancel all or part of a contract, but they apply only in relatively unusual or extreme circumstances. Moreover, courts are justifiably demanding in what parties must prove in order to be released from their obligations. Courts expect parties to negotiate carefully and deliberately to ensure that any commitment they make accurately reflects their intentions. If the deal merely turns out to be less desirable than expected, the doctrines in this chapter are unlikely to apply.

With limited exceptions, contracts made by minors are not enforceable against them. At common law, unless the contract is for a necessary, or amounts to a beneficial, contract of service, it is unenforceable at the election of the minor. In British Columbia, minors have even more protection through legislation. Persons suffering from a mental impairment also do not generally have the capacity to contract when they are incapable of understanding the transaction.

The doctrine of duress permits a court to set aside a contract when one of the parties was subjected to such coercion that true consent to the contract was never given. The doctrine of undue influence permits the same outcome if one party, short of issuing threats, has unfairly influenced or manipulated someone else into entering into a contract. Unconscionability also considers the unequal relationship between the two contracting parties. If both inequality between the parties and an improvident bargain can be established, the contract can be rescinded by the court. If the transaction is sufficiently divergent from community standards of conduct, this may signal the presence of exploitation and lead to a finding of unconscionability.

Misrepresentation concerns the parties' knowledge of the circumstances underlying a contract. If one party misrepresents a relevant fact and thereby induces the other side to enter into the contract, the innocent party can seek to have the contract set aside or rescinded. If the misrepresentation also counts as a tort, the innocent party is entitled to damages as well.

A party who has entered into a contract based on wrong information can try to have the contract set aside on the basis of mistake, but this strategy will rarely be successful because mistake is an exceedingly narrow legal doctrine.

Contracts that are illegal because they violate a statute or are at odds with public policy can also be rescinded. Courts are increasingly looking at all the circumstances surrounding the contract and will not automatically set them aside.

The *Statute of Frauds*, in its various forms, seeks to prevent fraud and perjury by requiring written proof of certain kinds of contracts. With the use of electronic and Internet contracts becoming more and more common, modern legislation also seeks to address the same types of problems in the new environment of technological commerce.

Chapter Study

Key Terms and Concepts

age of majority (p. 167)

common mistake (p. 178)

economic duress (p. 169)

guarantee (p. 184)

illegal contract (p. 180)

legal capacity (p. 167)

misrepresentation (p. 175)

mistake (p. 177)

non-competition clause (p. 182)

non-solicitation clause (p. 182)

public policy (p. 181)

rescission (p. 175)

unconscionable contract (p. 172)

undue influence (p. 170)

void contract (p. 167)

voidable contract (p. 167)

Questions for Review

1. Explain the difference between a void contract and a voidable contract.

2. Who has the legal capacity to form contracts?

3. What must be proven by someone seeking to avoid a contract based on mental impairment?

4. Describe the doctrine of undue influence.

5. What is duress? How does it relate to the idea of consent?

6. What is an unconscionable transaction?

7. Give an example of economic duress.

8. What is a misrepresentation?

9. How does the concept of a legal mistake differ from its ordinary meaning?

10. Name one statute that makes certain kinds of contracts illegal.

11. What is the role of public policy in contract enforcement?

12. How are non-competition covenants used in employment contracts?

13. How does the Statute of Frauds affect contracts?

14. What four types of contracts relevant to business law are required to be in writing?

15. How might the fact that a contract is electronic affect its enforceability?

16. Is an electronic contract subject to the same basic principles as a traditional contract?

17. Who is a minor?

18. Are contracts with minors binding?

Questions for Critical Thinking

1. Though contracts are generally enforceable, there are important doctrines that provide exceptions to this general rule. Do these exceptions undermine the notion of sanctity of contracts—the principle that once a contract is made, it should be enforced? Do these doctrines give the courts too much discretion to set aside a contract?

2. What factors should a business consider in developing a policy on documentation of commercial relationships? Should it insist that all contracts be in writing, or is more flexibility in order?

3. Which doctrines discussed in this chapter would be unlikely to arise in an online transaction? Why?

4. How can a business use a risk management plan in order to reduce the chances that it will enter into an unenforceable contract?

5. The law of mistake will rarely provide a defence for someone seeking to avoid a contract. Is the law of mistake too strict and inflexible? Why or why not?

6. Courts have shown flexibility in what they would accept as a traditional signature (including mere initials) or an e-signature (which can include someone simply typing his or her name). Do you think this flexibility opens the door to fraud? Why or why not?

Situations for Discussion

1. Through her lawyer, Ms. Tanya, a commercial landlord, sent a letter to her tenant, Ms. Desie, who ran

a bridal shop out of the premises. Tanya's lawyer demanded all back rent and stated that if the rent owed was not received by the deadline specified, Tanya would lock her tenant out of the business premises. Desie had no money to pay the back rent and therefore did not make the specified deadline. In fact Desie sent in no money at all. The landlord changed the locks. Soon thereafter, the parties later came together in settlement whereby Desie agreed to provide a promissory note in the amount owed in addition to Tanya's legal fees in relation to this matter.

Subsequently, Desie alleged that Tanya's lawyer had forced her to settle and sign the promissory note in question. Desie said that she felt that she had no choice but to sign because otherwise, she would not have been allowed back onto the rental premises. Desie says that the agreement should be unenforceable due to the lawyer's duress.[53] Did the conduct of the lawyer amount to duress? What constitutes duress?

2. Tim Donut Ltd. was founded by Tim Horton, a professional hockey player, in 1964. Ron Joyce, the company's first franchisee, became an equal partner with Horton in 1966. Tim Horton died in 1974, and his wife inherited his share of the business. In 1975 she sold that share to Joyce for $1 million. Mrs. Horton later claimed that, after the death of her husband, she became addicted to drugs and did not know what she was doing when she sold her share. She said she was unaware for days that she had sold her interest and remembered little from the day of the sale, other than sitting in an office and signing some papers. She subsequently sought to have the contract cancelled.

What doctrines in this chapter are relevant to the situation? What further information is needed to apply those doctrines? What major challenges to succeeding on her claim did Mrs. Horton face?

3. Ms. Stewart bought a business operating in rented space in a shopping mall. Shortly after she took over the business, the landlord pressured her to sign a lease that made her responsible for the arrears in rent of the previous tenant. The landlord secured Ms. Stewart's agreement by exerting tremendous pressure on her. For example, he called in the sheriff to execute a

distress for rent when, at that time, she was in arrears only for the month of January. The landlord told Ms. Stewart that if she did not pay the former tenant's arrears, "she would be the one to suffer." The landlord knew that Ms. Stewart was unsophisticated in business dealings and that she had signed the lease without seeking advice.[54] Is she obligated by the lease?

4. Leona was interested in purchasing property that she intended to use for her family's expanding brickyard business. She spoke with the owner, who had recently inherited the property from his elderly aunt. Leona asked if there were any restrictions on the land preventing it from being used as a brickyard. The owner replied, "Not that I am aware of." Though this was literally true, the owner failed to explain that he had never checked whether the land was subject to any restrictions. Leona purchased the land and has found out that it cannot be used as a brickyard. Can she have the contract rescinded based on misrepresentation? Why or why not?[55]

5. As part of her contract to work as a branch manager for ABC Ltd. (a foreign currency exchange company), Suzie was asked to agree to the following non-competition clause:

> That for a period of eighteen (18) months from the termination date of the Employee's employment with ABC Ltd., for whatever reason, he/she will not, for any reason, directly or indirectly as principal, agent, owner, partner, employee, consultant, advisor, shareholder, director or officer or otherwise howsoever, own, operate, be engaged in or connected with or interested in, or associated with, or advise, or anyway guarantee the debts or obligations of, or have any financial interest in or advance, lend money to, or permit his/her name or any part thereof to be used or employed in any activity, operation or business whether a proprietorship, partnership, joint venture, corporation, or other entity or otherwise carry on, engage in, in any manner whatsoever, any activity, business or operation which is the same as or in any manner competes with the Business of ABC Ltd. within the

53. Based on *Taber v Paris Boutique & Bridal Inc (cob Paris Boutique)*, 2010 ONCA 157.
54. Based, in part, on *Stewart v Canada Life Assurance Co* (1994), 132 NSR (2d) 324 (CA).
55. Based on *Nottingham Patent Brick and Tile Co v Butler* (1886), 16 QBD 778 (CA).

Country of Canada in any City or municipality in which ABC Ltd. operates or conducts business, in any manner.

Is this clause enforceable when measured again the factors identified by the SCC in *Elsley* (discussed earlier in this chapter)?[56]

6. Symphony & Rose was a developer and builder of high-rise condominium projects. A Symphony & Rose sales rep told Wendy and Sam that a penthouse apartment was still available in their current project. Wendy and Sam provided Symphony & Rose's real estate agent with information relevant to the purchase and delivered cheques for the various deposits. The agent told them that in a few days they would be required to sign an offer on Symphony & Rose's standard form. They thought they had a deal. A few days later, a senior representative of Symphony & Rose contacted Wendy and Sam to tell them that the penthouse had already been sold but 40 other units were currently still available.[57] Do Wendy and Sam have an enforceable agreement? Should they have done anything differently?

7. John Tonelli was an exceptionally talented young hockey player who, in 1973 at the age of 16, entered into a two-year contract with the Toronto Marlboros Major Junior A hockey club, a team in the Ontario Major Junior A Hockey League. The league had an agreement with the National Hockey League (NHL) that prevented the drafting of underage players and that called for the payment of certain fees once a player was drafted at the end of his junior career. However, a similar agreement could not be reached with the World Hockey Association (WHA). John—like all other junior hockey players of his time—was forced to sign a new contract as a condition of continuing to play in the junior league. This new contract essentially bound him to play three years longer than his earlier contract with the Toronto Marlboros; in addition, it imposed monetary penalties if he signed with a professional team within that time frame or within a period of three years after he ceased to be

eligible to play in the junior league. As soon as he turned 18 (the age of majority), John abandoned the contract with the Toronto Marlboros and signed with the Houston Aeros, a professional team. The Marlboros sued him for breach of contract.[58] Is John's contract enforceable against him? If yes, does this seem fair, and from whose point of view? If no, is it fair that John can sign a contract and then ignore his obligations under it?

8. Sam Moore, an alert and intelligent 52-year-old businessman, tried without success to purchase a piece of farmland from Louis Wells. When he heard that Louis' brother, James, was willing to sell his nearby farm, he went to see him at his nursing home to make an offer to purchase it. James was 62 years old and, unbeknownst to Sam, was suffering from brain damage. Sam offered to purchase the land for $7000. James signed an acceptance to the offer and received a deposit of $100, without receiving any independent advice on the transaction. The land in question was worth quite a bit more than $7000—in fact, the farmer who was leasing James' land at the time had offered to pay $14 000 to $15 000 for it just the year before. Since then, a trust company had been appointed under the *Mentally Incapacitated Persons Act* and had taken over the management of James' affairs. The trust company refused to transfer the farm to Sam, who decided to sue in order to enforce the contract he entered into with James.[59] Is the contract for the sale of the farm enforceable? If yes, does that seem like a just result? If not, what legal doctrine would likely be used to rescind it? If the contract is not enforceable, do you think that it is fair to Sam, who did not know about James' mental state? Or is it reasonable to expect him to make sure that the person he is contracting with is mentally capable of entering into a contract? What factors ought Sam to have taken into account?

For more study tools, visit http://www.NELSONbrain.com.

56. Based on *Globex Foreign Exchange Corp v Kelcher*, 2011 ABCA 240.
57. Based, in part, on *Bay Tower Homes v St Andrew's Land Corp* (1990), 10 RPR (2d) 193 (Ont HCJ).
58. Based, in part, on *Toronto Marlboro Major Junior 'A' Hockey Club v Tonelli* (1979), 96 DLR (3d) 135 (Ont CA).
59. Based, in part, on *Marshall v Canada Permanent Trust Co* (1968), 69 DLR (2d) 260 (Alta SC).

CHAPTER 9

Termination and Enforcement of Contracts

Objectives

After studying this chapter, you should have an understanding of

- the termination of a contract by performance

- the termination of a contract by agreement

- the termination of a contract by frustration

- the methods of enforcing contracts

- the concept of privity

- remedies for breach of contract

Business Law in Practice

Janet and Alphonso Owen entered into a contract with Charles Conlin to construct their family home in Vancouver, B.C. Conlin inspired a lot of confidence. He told the Owens that he understood the importance of building the family home with great care and attention. "It's where you're going to live, for goodness sake," he stated. "Your home is an extension of you. Don't worry about anything. My work is second to none." For her part, Janet was particularly excited about a see-through fireplace that would be installed in the centre portion of the proposed house. A see-through fireplace opens onto two rooms: in this case, the living room and dining room.

Pursuant to the contract, Conlin, known as the "Contractor," had a number of obligations, including the following:

...

12. The Contractor covenants to construct in accordance with the relevant sections of the British Columbia *Building Code*.

13. The Contractor covenants to construct in accordance with plans and specifications attached to this Contract.

...

20. The Contractor covenants to complete construction on or before 30 June 2009.

The plans and specifications were duly attached to the contract and included a provision for the see-through fireplace that Janet loved so much.

The Owens covenanted to pay a total of $500 000 and provide advances on a regular basis. Over time, the Owens advanced $300 000 to Conlin and looked forward to the day when they would be able to move in. Their excitement about their new home construction eventually turned to disappointment when Conlin failed to complete construction according to schedule. The Owens gave several extensions, but when Conlin missed the last deadline, the Owens went to talk to him at the job site. Upon arrival at the site, Alphonso noted that the house was only half-built

(Continued on the next page)

RYAN MCVAY/PHOTODISC/GETTY IMAGES

and did not even look structurally sound (the centre of the living room ceiling drooped in an alarming fashion). He asked Conlin for an explanation and a progress report. Conlin became absolutely enraged, stating, "You're complaining about things here just to grind me down on my price. Well, at least my wife isn't ugly like yours is." This was the last straw. The Owens ordered Conlin and his crew to leave the property. They took possession of the house and promptly changed the locks.

About two weeks later, the Owens' luck changed for the better. A well-known house-building expert, Mr. Holmstead, agreed to assist the Owens. The Owens hired Holmstead to fix the problems and finish the house.

In addition to creating structural problems, Conlin's employees had defectively constructed the see-through fireplace. When in use, it filled the entire living area with smoke due to the failure of the chimney to draw. Holmstead took the view that, in order for it to properly function as a fireplace, parts of it would have to be dismantled and rebuilt. When consulted on this, Conlin took the position that the problem could easily be solved by simply bricking in one side of the fireplace, since this would create the draw needed to carry the smoke up and out the chimney. "My solution will cost about $200," said Conlin. "Your so-called solution will cost at least $5000. It's insane." Notwithstanding, the Owens decided to have Holmstead rebuild the fireplace and deal with Conlin later.

All in all, the Owens paid $300 000 to Holmstead, who fixed and completed the house to high standards.

In the meantime, Janet has been suffering considerable distress. Her disappointment in Conlin's work became overwhelming, and every day seemed to get harder. Though not clinically depressed, Janet found herself bursting into tears and waking up in the middle of the night, worrying about the house.

1. Can the Owens demonstrate all the steps in an action for breach of contract against Conlin?
2. Are the Owens themselves in breach of contract for refusing to permit Conlin to complete the contract?
3. Did the Owens properly mitigate their damages?
4. What damages can the Owens receive?

What kind of issues can a construction contract raise in relation to the termination and enforcement of contracts?

MELISSA DOCKSTADER/SHUTTERSTOCK

Termination of Contracts: An Overview

When parties enter into a contract, there are several ways in which it can be brought to an end—known, in law, as "termination":

- *Through performance.* When both parties fulfill their contractual obligations to each other, they have performed the contract. This is generally the ideal way of concluding a contractual relationship.

- *Through agreement.* Parties are always free to voluntarily bring their contract to an end. Both parties could agree to simply walk away from their agreement, or one party could pay a sum to the other side by way of settlement in exchange for agreeing to end the contract.

- *Through frustration.* The doctrine of frustration applies when, after the formation of a contract, an important, unforeseen event occurs—such as the destruction of the subject matter of the contract or the death/incapacity of one of the contracting parties. The event must be one that makes performance functionally impossible or illegal.[1] When a contract is frustrated, it is brought to an end.

- *Through breach.* A breach of contract, when it is particularly serious, can release the innocent party from having to continue with the contract if that is his wish. Less significant breaches generally entitle such a party to damages only.

What follows is a discussion of these four methods of termination and an outline of the remedies available for breach of contract.

Termination through Performance

What amounts to termination by performance depends on the nature of the contract, as in the following examples:

- A contract to provide an audit of a corporation is performed when the audit is competently completed and the auditor's account for service rendered is paid in full.

- A contract to buy and sell a house is performed when the purchase price is paid and title to the property is transferred to the buyer.

- A contract to provide a custom-designed generator is complete when a generator conforming to contract specifications is delivered and the purchase price is paid.

In short, a contract is performed when all of its implied and express promises have been fulfilled. When a contract is terminated through performance, this does not necessarily mean the end of the commercial relationship between the parties, however. They may continue to do business with each other by means of new, continuing, and overlapping contracts.

Performance by Others

The law easily distinguishes between those who have the contractual obligation to perform and those who may actually do the necessary work. When a corporation enters into

---

1. Edwin Peel, *Treitel: The Law of Contract,* 12th ed (London: Sweet & Maxwell, 2007) at 924.

a contract to provide goods or services, for example, it must by necessity work through employees/agents. Even when the contracting party is an individual, employees may still have an important role. In both cases, the employee/agent is ordinarily not a party to the contract. Expressed in legal terms, such an employee/agent lacks privity of contract and therefore cannot sue or be sued on the contract, though there may be liability in tort. Privity is discussed in more detail later in this chapter. Agency is discussed in Chapter 13.

Vicarious performance
Performance of contractual obligations through others.

It is permissible to use employees to **vicariously perform** a contract in question, as long as personal performance by the particular contracting individual is not an express or implied term of a contract. For example, if a client engages an accountant and makes it clear that only that particular accountant is to do the work, performance through other accountants is not permitted. If there is no such term, the accountant is free to delegate the work to others in the firm while remaining contractually responsible for the timing and quality of the work.

In the case of Conlin and the Owens, there was nothing in the contract requiring Conlin to perform the contract unassisted. In fact, it would appear that the Owens fully understood that Conlin would use staff members to help him. For this reason, Conlin is not in breach of contract simply because he did not perform every aspect of the contract himself. He is, however, in breach of contract because his employees failed to properly perform aspects of the contract: the structural defects mean that the house was not built to Code and the fireplace was not constructed in accordance with plans and specifications since it could not draw air properly. The law holds Conlin responsible for his employees' incompetence.

Termination by Agreement
By Agreement between Parties

Parties may enter into an agreement that becomes unfavourable for one or both of them. In response, they may decide to

Novation
The substitution of parties in a contract or the replacement of one contract with another.

- *Enter into a whole new contract.* This is known as **novation**. Provided both parties benefit from this arrangement, the agreement will be enforceable by the court as a new contract. For example, if the Owens subsequently decide that they want to buy an entirely more luxurious home than they have contracted for from Conlin, they and Conlin are free to negotiate a new contract and cancel the old one.

- *Vary certain terms of the contract.* If the Owens decide that they would like upgraded bathroom fixtures installed instead of the ones provided for in the plans and specifications, they can seek a variation of contract. Traditionally, as discussed in Chapter 6, the party benefiting from the variation (the Owens) must provide consideration to the other side (Conlin). In a case like this, the typical consideration would be an increase in the contract price, reflecting the additional cost of acquiring and installing the upgraded bathroom fixtures. Note, however, and as discussed in Chapter 6, that the New Brunswick Court of Appeal[2] has shown a willingness to enforce contractual variations that are not supported by consideration in certain circumstances.

2. *NAV Canada v Greater Fredericton Airport Authority Inc*, 2008 NBCA 28.

- *End the contract.* The parties may decide to simply terminate the contract, with both parties agreeing not to enforce their rights or with one party paying the other to bring his obligations to an end.

- *Substitute a party.* The law permits a more limited form of novation whereby one party's rights and obligations are transferred to someone else. In short, a new party is substituted, and the old party simply drops out of the contract altogether. For example, if Conlin discovered that he had double-booked himself and could not in fact build the Owens' house, he might be able to recommend someone else who would "step into his contractual shoes." This new contractor not only would assume all of Conlin's obligations but also be entitled to payment by the Owens. However, everyone—the Owens, Conlin, and the new proposed contractor—must agree to this substitution in order for it to be effective. Of course, if the Owens are unhappy with Conlin's proposal, they are free to insist on performance by him and sue for breach of contract if he fails to perform.[3]

An agreement between the parties is almost always the best way of dealing with events that make the contract disadvantageous in some respect. By taking such a route, the parties are able to avoid the expense and uncertainty of litigation.

Transfer of Contractual Rights

A party who wants to end his involvement in a particular contract has the option—in certain circumstances—to transfer it to someone else. This transfer does not terminate the contract but does have the effect of eliminating the transferor's role in it. In short, while contractual duties or obligations cannot be transferred to someone else without agreement by the other side, contractual rights can be transferred without any such permission being required.

This means that Conlin cannot unilaterally transfer to another contractor his obligation to build the Owens' home. The Owens have contracted for performance by Conlin and his employees. They cannot be forced to deal with a new contractor altogether. However, Conlin can transfer his right to be paid for the building job to someone else.

In law, when one party transfers a contractual right to someone else, this is known as an **assignment** (see Figure 9.1 on page 198). The person who is now or will be entitled to payment from a contract is known as a creditor. The party who is obligated to make the payment is known as a debtor.

Assignment
The transfer of a right by an assignor to an assignee.

The law of assignment of rights permits the creditor (the assignor) to assign the right to collect to another person (the assignee) without the agreement of the debtor. However, to be effective, the debtor must have notice of the assignment so that she knows to pay the assignee rather than the creditor. The assignee is entitled to collect the debt despite not being involved in the creation of the contract that produced the debt. Conversely, after receiving notice of the assignment, the debtor can perform his obligation only by paying the assignee. If the same debt is assigned to more than one assignee, normally the assignee who first notifies the debtor

---

3. If they choose this route, the Owens still have a duty to mitigate, as discussed later in this chapter.

FIGURE 9.1

The Steps in Assignment

Step One: Creditor–Debtor Relationship
C (creditor) ⟷ D (debtor)
Contract is entered between C and D, whereby D owes money to C
for services rendered.

Step Two: Assignor–Assignee Relationship
C (assignor) ⟷ A (assignee)
Contract is entered between C and A, whereby C assigns the debt he
is owed by D.

Step Three: Assignee–Debtor Relationship
A (assignee) ⟷ D (debtor)
A gives notice to D.
D is now obligated to pay debt directly to A.

is entitled to payment.[4] Expressed in legal language, the rule is that the assignees who take in good faith rank in the order that they have given notice to the debtor. This means that a later assignee may end up collecting from the debtor ahead of an earlier assignee simply by being the first to give notice to the debtor. In the meantime, the disappointed assignees can sue the assignor for breach of the contract of assignment; however, doing so is usually pointless if the assignor has disappeared or has no resources to pay damages.

The advantage of an assignment for a creditor such as Conlin is that he can "sell" rights for cash now and let the assignee worry about collecting from the Owens. Of course, Conlin will pay a price for this advantage by accepting less than the face value of the debt from the assignee. This discount will reflect the cost of early receipt, as well as the risk that the debtor cannot or will not pay.

Additionally, the assignee's right to payment is no greater than the right possessed by the assignor. This means, for example, that if Conlin breaches his contract with the Owens and becomes entitled to less than the full contract price, Conlin's assignee is likewise entitled to less. The objective is to ensure that the debtor—in this case, the Owens—is not disadvantaged by the assignment.[5]

Termination by Frustration

Frustration

Termination of a contract by an unexpected event or change that makes performance functionally impossible or illegal.

When a significant, unexpected event or change occurs that makes performance of a contract functionally impossible or illegal, the contract between the parties may be **frustrated.** In such circumstances, both parties are excused from the contract and it comes to an end. Neither side is liable to the other for breach.

---

4. GHL Fridman, *The Law of Contract in Canada*, 5th ed (Toronto: Thomson Carswell, 2006) at 685.
5. *Ibid* at 686. Note that in certain jurisdictions, there is also legislation related to assignments. These are discussed by Fridman, *ibid* at 688 and following.

Unlike the doctrine of mistake—which relates to severely erroneous assumptions concerning existing or past circumstances surrounding a contract at its formation—frustration deals with events that occur after the contract has been formed. Like mistake, however, the defence of frustration is difficult to establish, given that the purpose of contract law is to enforce voluntarily chosen agreements.

The person claiming frustration must establish that the event or change in circumstances

- was dramatic and unforeseen

- was a matter that neither party had assumed the risk of occurring

- arose without being either party's fault

- makes performance of the contract functionally impossible or illegal[6]

All of these elements must be demonstrated.

Sometimes events that would amount to frustration are expressly dealt with in the contract through a *force majeure* or other clause. That is, rather than leaving it to a judge to decide whether the occurrence of a given event amounts to frustration, the parties contractually define for themselves—in advance—what events would frustrate the contract.

Many circumstances that may appear to frustrate a contract do not amount to frustration in law. For example, if Conlin finds that construction material has unexpectedly tripled in price, and thus he will suffer a substantial loss on the contract, this circumstance would not amount to frustration. It has become financially disadvantageous to perform the contract, but it is still possible to do so. Similarly, if Conlin contracts to provide a certain kind of building material and no other, and that material proves to be unavailable at any price, that part of the contract has not been frustrated either. Conlin has simply made a promise that he cannot keep and is in breach. As a final example, if Conlin is unable to perform the contract because he has fired all his employees at the last minute, the contract may have become impossible to perform, but owing only to Conlin's own conduct. Self-induced impossibility does not count as frustration in law.

In those rare cases in which a contract is terminated by frustration—as when the contract expressly states that the goods to be supplied must come from a particular source, which fails[7]—the consequences for the parties are often unsatisfactory. At the moment frustration occurs, any further obligations under the contract cease. If neither party has performed, they are left where they were before the contract was formed. If one party has begun to perform and incurred costs, there is no easy way to compensate that party, the reason being that, by definition, the contract has ended through the fault of neither party. Shifting the loss to the other would be no more just than leaving it where it lies. There are complicated and uneven developments in the common law and in the statutes of some provinces that attempt to address these problems, but these are beyond the scope of this book.[8]

---

6. *Ibid* at 643 and following.
7. *Howell v Coupland* (1876), 1 QBD 258 (CA).
8. For a discussion of statute law applying to frustration, see Fridman, *supra* note 4 at 672 and following.

Taylor v Caldwell (1863), 122 ER 309 (CA)

THE BUSINESS CONTEXT: A common situation giving rise to frustration occurs when the subject matter of the contract is destroyed, as discussed below.

FACTUAL BACKGROUND: Taylor rented from Caldwell the Surrey Gardens and Music Hall for four days to be used for a series of concerts. Prior to the scheduled concerts, the music hall was destroyed by a fire for which neither party could be faulted, and all of the concerts had to be cancelled. Taylor sued for his expenses related to advertising and other preparations, which were now wasted.

THE LEGAL QUESTION: Was Caldwell in breach of contract for failing to supply the music hall as promised?

RESOLUTION: Since the parties had not expressly or implicitly dealt with who would bear the risk of the music hall being destroyed by fire, the court had to decide whether the contract had been frustrated or not. It reasoned that the existence of the music hall was essential to performance of the contract, or, put another way, its destruction defeated the main purpose of the contract. On this basis, the contract had been frustrated, and Taylor's action failed.

CRITICAL ANALYSIS: Why did the court not simply decide that the owner of the music hall was liable when he failed to supply the promised venue, no matter how extenuating the circumstances?

INTERNATIONAL PERSPECTIVE

Force Majeure *Clauses*

The commercial objective of parties to a contract sometimes can be defeated by circumstances beyond their control. Unforeseen events, both natural and human-made, may occur that make performance onerous or even impossible. The risk of unforeseen events is particularly great in international transactions. Storms, earthquakes, and fires may destroy the subject matter of the contract. Wars, blockades, and embargoes may prevent the performance of the contract. Hyperinflation, currency devaluation, and changes in government regulation may create hardship for the parties to the contract.

Legal systems, for the most part, recognize that the occurrence of some unforeseen events may be a valid excuse for non-performance. This notion finds expression in various doctrines, such as commercial impracticality, impossibility, and frustration. The difficulty for traders is that, although legal systems recognize this kind of defence, there are varying rules governing when non-performance is excused without liability on the part of the non-performing party. It is difficult to predict precisely which events will release a party from contractual obligations. Additionally, exemption from performance is normally restricted to situations where it is impossible to perform—hardship or additional expense involved in

performance is usually not an excuse. For these reasons, it is common business practice both in domestic and international contracts to include *force majeure* clauses.

A *force majeure* clause deals with the risk of unforeseen events. It allows a party to delay or terminate a contract in the event of unexpected, disruptive events such as the following:

- fire, flood, tornado, or other natural disaster
- war, invasion, blockade, or other military action
- strike, labour slowdown, walkout, or other labour problems
- inconvertibility of currency, hyperinflation, currency devaluation, or other monetary changes
- rationing of raw materials, denial of import or export licences, or other governmental action

Critical Analysis: What is the problem with drafting a clause that is very simple, such as, "In the event of a *force majeure*, the affected party may terminate its obligations under the contract"? Similarly, what is the problem with drafting a very specific clause that lists the events that allow a party to terminate the contract?

Source: Mary Jo Nicholson, *Legal Aspects of International Business*, 2d ed (Toronto: Edmond Montgomery Publications, 2007) at 226–27.

Balance of probabilities
Proof that there is a better than 50 percent chance that the circumstances of the contract are as the plaintiff contends.

Enforcement of Contracts

When one party fails to perform its contractual obligations, it is in breach of contract and subject to a lawsuit. To succeed in its action for breach of contract, the plaintiff (the person who initiates the lawsuit) is obligated to demonstrate the following elements to the court's satisfaction, that is, on the **balance of probabilities**:

- *Privity of contract.* The plaintiff has to establish that there is a contract between the parties.

- *Breach of contract.* The plaintiff must prove that the other party (the defendant) has failed to keep one or more promises or terms of the contract.

- *Entitlement to a remedy.* The plaintiff must demonstrate that it is entitled to the remedy claimed or is otherwise deserving of the court's assistance.

As noted in Chapter 4, the balance of probabilities means that the plaintiff must prove there is a better than 50 percent chance that the circumstances of the contract are as it contends they are and, furthermore, that these circumstances entitle it to receive what is claimed.

Privity of Contract

Privity is a critical ingredient to enforcing a contract. It means that, generally speaking, only those who are parties to a contract can enforce the rights and obligations it contains.[9]

Because a strict application of the doctrine of privity can lead to serious injustices, courts have recently shown a willingness to allow third parties to rely on contractual clauses placed in the contract for their benefit. For example, a contract between a business and a customer may have an exclusion clause protecting employees from liability in the event that the customer suffers a loss. Under a classical approach to privity, employees would not be permitted to rely on such clauses as a defence to any action brought by a disgruntled customer because they are not parties to the contract—only their employer and the customer are. In the following case, however, the Supreme Court of Canada refused to apply privity in this way, choosing instead to create a limited exception to its application.

CASE — *London Drugs Ltd v Kuehne & Nagel International Ltd,* [1992] 3 SCR 299

THE BUSINESS CONTEXT: Businesses may try to protect their employees from being successfully sued by including clauses in their contracts with customers that shelter employees from liability.

FACTUAL BACKGROUND: Kuehne & Nagel International Ltd. (K&N) stored a variety of merchandise for London Drugs, including a large transformer. A term in the storage agreement limited K&N's liability on any one item to $40. Owing to the negligence of two K&N employees, the transformer was dropped while it was being moved and sustained over $33 000 of damage. London Drugs brought an action for the full amount of damages against both the employees and K&N. It was acknowledged that K&N's liability was limited to $40.

THE LEGAL QUESTION: Can the employees rely on the clause limiting liability to $40?

RESOLUTION: The trial judge agreed that the negligent employees could be sued by the customer. Expressed in more technical legal language, the court applied the rule that employees are liable for torts they commit in the course of carrying out the services their employer has contracted to provide. Because the K&N employees were negligent in their attempt to lift the transformer, they were liable for the full extent of London Drugs' damages. The employees could not rely on the clause limiting recovery to $40 because this clause was found in a contract to which they were not a party. Put another way, the employees lacked privity to the contract between London Drugs and K&N.

In response to the harshness that the strict doctrine of privity creates in this kind of situation, the Supreme Court

(Continued)

---

9. There are a number of ways in which someone who is not a party to a contract (called a third party) may acquire an enforceable benefit, but this chapter discusses only one of them, in the employment context.

of Canada created an exception to its application. As Justice Iacobucci explains,

> This court has recognized ... that in appropriate circumstances, courts have not only the power but the duty to make incremental changes to the common law to see that it reflects the emerging needs and values of our society. ... It is my view that the present appeal is an appropriate situation for making such an incremental change to the doctrine of privity of contract in order to allow the ... [employees] to benefit from the limitation of liability clause. ... I am of the view that employees may obtain such a benefit if the following requirements are satisfied: (1) the limitation of liability clause must, either expressly or impliedly, extend its benefit to the employees (or employee) seeking to rely on it; and (2) the employees (or employee) seeking the benefit of the limitation of liability clause must have been acting

in the course of their employment and must have been performing the very services provided for in the contract between their employer and the plaintiff (customer) when the loss occurred.

The court went on to hold that the employees could rely on the limitation of liability clause. This is because the clause in question did extend its protection to the employees and, when the transformer was damaged, it was due to the negligence of the employees while doing the very thing contracted for, as employees. Though the negligence of the employees caused London Drugs' damages in the amount of $33 955.41, it was entitled to recover only $40 from the employees.[10]

CRITICAL ANALYSIS: Do you agree with Justice Iacobucci's decision? Should employees be able to rely on a clause in a contract to which they are not parties? How could employees protect themselves if they were not permitted to rely on such a clause?

The Owens could easily establish a critical step in a successful breach of contract action against Conlin—namely, privity of contract. Conlin and the Owens entered into a contract whereby Conlin would supply certain goods and services to the Owens in exchange for payment.

The Owens may well have an action against Conlin's employees, but only for the tort of negligence (discussed in detail in Chapter 11). There is no action in contract against the employees, however, because there is no contract between them and the Owens. The contract is between only the Owens and Conlin.

Statutory Modifications of the Doctrine

The common law of privity has also been modified by statute in two important areas: consumer purchases and insurance. In certain jurisdictions such as Saskatchewan, consumer protection legislation provides that a lack of privity is no defence to an action brought under the act for breach of warranty brought against a manufacturer, for example.[11] Similarly, insurance legislation across the country permits the beneficiary under a life insurance contract to sue the insurer even though the beneficiary is not a party to the contract (i.e., even though the beneficiary lacks privity).

Breach of Contract

Classification of the Breach

Virtually every breach of contract gives the innocent party the right to a remedy. When determining what that remedy should be, the courts will first consider whether the term breached can be classified as a condition or a warranty.

---

10. Those who are not party to a contract containing exclusion clauses should not automatically assume that they can rely on those clauses notwithstanding the outcome in *London Drugs*. In *Haldane Products Inc v United Parcel Service* (1999), 103 OTC 306 (Sup Ct Just), for example, the plaintiff contracted with UPS to deliver industrial sewing needles to British Columbia. The contract contained a limitation of liability clause but there was no stipulation that anyone other than UPS employees would discharge UPS contractual obligations. UPS' subcontractor—who was transporting a UPS trailer containing the package—failed to deliver due to a fire in the trailer. The subcontractor was found liable for over $40 000 because the court refused to allow it to shelter under the exclusion clause in the UPS–Haldane contract.
11. The *Consumer Protection Act*, SS 1996, c C-30.1, s 55. See too *Consumer Product Warranty and Liability Act*, SNB 1978, c C-18.1, s 23.

A contractual term will be classified as a condition or warranty only if that is the parties' contractual intention. Courts will consider all the circumstances surrounding the contract, including the language chosen by the parties in the contract itself, in making this determination.

A **condition** is an important term that, if breached, gives the innocent party the right not only to sue for damages, but also to treat the contract as ended. This latter right means that, if she so chooses, the non-defaulting party can consider herself to be freed from the balance of the contract and to have no further obligations under it. For example, it is an implied term of the contract between the Owens and Conlin that Conlin will be reliable. His multiple breaches of contract and insulting behaviour strongly suggest that he will not properly perform the contract in the future. On this basis, it could be argued that Conlin has breached a condition of the agreement and the Owens are not obligated to continue in the contract with him.[12]

A term classified as a **warranty** is a promise of less significance or importance. When a warranty is breached, the innocent party is entitled to damages only. Viewed in isolation, Conlin's failure to build the fireplace properly is likely to be regarded as a breach of warranty, entitling the Owens to damages only.

Even after the parties' intentions have been assessed, some terms cannot easily be classified as warranties or conditions and are known in law as **innominate terms**. In such circumstances, the court must look at exactly what has happened in light of the breach before deciding whether the innocent party is entitled to repudiate the contract. For example, it is a term of the contract that the house be built to Code. It would be difficult to classify such a term as either a condition or a warranty of the contract. The contract is unclear on this point and the term is one that could be breached in large and small ways. If Conlin failed to install shingles on the roof that were Code approved, this is likely a breach of a warranty-like term, giving rise to a claim for damages only. On the other extreme, Conlin's failure to provide a structurally sound home would be a breach of a condition-like term, allowing the Owens to end the contract on the spot, as they have done. Provided that the plaintiffs can establish just one breach of condition or condition-like innominate term, they are entitled to end the contract.

Note, however, that if the Owens end the contract on the erroneous assumption that such a serious form of breach has occurred, they themselves will be in breach of contract and subject to a lawsuit by Conlin.

Parties are free to classify a term in advance within the contract itself by setting out the consequences of breach. The court will generally respect this classification if it has been done clearly.[13]

Exemption and Limitation of Liability Clause

As already noted, parties are free to include a clause in their contract that limits or excludes liability for breach. This is what the storage company did in the *London Drugs* case discussed earlier. Historically, courts have been reluctant to allow the party in breach to rely on such a clause when the breach in question was severe and undermined the whole foundation

Condition
An important term that, if breached, gives the innocent party the right to terminate the contract and claim damages.

Warranty
A minor term that, if breached, gives the innocent party the right to claim damages only.

Innominate term
A term that cannot easily be classified as either a condition or a warranty.

PART TWO

---

12. This analysis is based on John McCamus, *The Law of Contracts* (Toronto: Irwin Law, 2005) at 635 and cases cited therein.
13. *Wickman Machine Tool Sales Ltd v Schuler*, [1974] AC 235 (HL).

Fundamental breach
A breach of contract that affects the foundation of the contract.

of the contract. This is known as a **fundamental breach**. The argument is that such a breach automatically renders the entire contract (including the exclusion clauses) inoperative, and therefore the innocent party should be compensated. While such judicial concern might be helpful in a consumer contract, it is less welcome in a commercial context. The Supreme Court of Canada has finally resolved the issue by ruling in 2010 that the doctrine of fundamental breach in relation to exclusion clauses no longer forms any part of the law in Canada as discussed in the box below.

CASE

Tercon Contractors Ltd v British Columbia (Transportation and Highways) 2010 SCC 4

THE BUSINESS CONTEXT: Owners who put a project out to tender often include a contractual term to limit or even exclude liability so as to permit wide latitude in decision making and provide a defence in any action for breach of contract. Whether the clause will have its intended effect depends very much on the facts of the case.

FACTUAL BACKGROUND: Tercon, an unsuccessful bidder on a large highway project, sued the government of British Columbia because it chose an ineligible bidder for the job and even tried to hide that ineligiblity, contrary to the terms of Contract A.[14] Tercon also said that this breach of Contract A entitled it to damages in the amount of profit it would have earned had it been awarded Contract B.

By way of defence, the government relied on an exclusion clause (specifically called a 'no claims clause') that stated:

Except as expressly permitted … no Proponent [bidder] shall have any claim for any compensation of any kind whatsoever, as a result of participating … and by submitting a proposal each proponent shall be deemed to have agreed that it has no claim.

According to the government, the effect of exclusion clause was to make any breach of the contract not actionable. Note that, unlike in *Tilden Rent-a-Car v Glendenning*[15] (discussed in Chapter 7), which went to whether the exclusion clause was even part of the contract, the concern in *Tercon* was the effectiveness of an exclusion clause which was otherwise an uncontested part of the contract.

THE LEGAL QUESTION: Does the exclusion clause provide the government with a defence to Tercon's action?

RESOLUTION: The court was unanimous in holding that the concept of fundamental breach should no longer have any role

to play when a plaintiff seeks to escape the effect of an exclusion of liability clause. Instead, the outcome is determined by considering the answers to three issues or enquiries. As the court states:

The **first** issue … is whether as a matter of interpretation the exclusion clause even applies to the circumstances established in evidence. This will depend on the Court's assessment of the intention of the parties as expressed in the contract. If the exclusion clause does not apply, there is obviously no need to proceed further with this analysis. If the exclusion clause applies, the **second** issue is whether the exclusion clause was unconscionable at the time the contract was made, "as might arise from situations of unequal bargaining power between the parties" (Hunter, at p. 462). This second issue has to do with contract formation, not breach.

If the exclusion clause is held to be valid and applicable, the Court may undertake a **third** enquiry, namely whether the Court should nevertheless refuse to enforce the valid exclusion clause because of the existence of an overriding public policy, proof of which lies on the party seeking to avoid enforcement of the clause, that outweighs the very strong public interest in the enforcement of contracts. [emphasis added]

The court also confirmed that:

Conduct approaching serious criminality or egregious fraud are but examples of well-accepted and "substantially incontestable" considerations of public policy that may override the countervailing public policy that favours freedom of contract. Where this type of

---

14. For discussion in this text regarding the difference between Contract A and Contract B, see discussion of *R v Ron Engineering & Construction Ltd*, [1981] 1 SCR 111 in Chapter 6.
15. (1978), 83 DLR (3d) 400 (Ont CA).

misconduct is reflected in the breach of contract, all of the circumstances should be examined very carefully by the court.

On these facts, the Supreme Court of Canada agreed that that the government breached Contract A by choosing an ineligible bidder. A slim majority found in favour of the plaintiff because it concluded that the exclusion clause did not apply to the facts at hand. As the majority stated, clear language would be necessary to exclude damages resulting from the government permitting an ineligible bidder to participate and to exclude the government's implied duty to conduct itself fairly in relation to all bidders. As the majority stated: "I cannot conclude that

the parties, through the words found in this exclusion clause, intended to waive compensation for conduct like that of the Province in this case that strikes at the heart of the integrity and business efficacy of the tendering process which it undertook."

Because the clause did not apply to the breach in question, Tercon had won and it was not necessary for the majority to consider the other two issues. Instead, it affirmed the trial judge's decision awarding Tercon over $3 million for loss of profit.

CRITICAL ANALYSIS: Do you think that the Supreme Court of Canada's three issue analysis injects too much uncertainty into contract law? Should parties be bound by whatever clause they agree to?

ETHICAL CONSIDERATIONS

Is It Unethical to Breach a Contract?

Contract law generally does not punish a contract breaker but rather compensates the innocent party for any loss associated with the breach. According to famous jurist Oliver Wendell Holmes,

> The duty to keep a contract at common law means a prediction that you must pay damages if you do not keep it—and nothing else. . . . If you commit [to] a contract, you are liable to pay a compensatory sum unless the promised event comes to pass, and that is all the difference. But such a mode of looking at the matter stinks in the nostrils of those who think it advantageous to get as much ethics into the law as they can.

This is known as the "bad man" theory of breach and coincides with the concept of economic breach already discussed in Chapter 5. Economic breach means that the potential contract breaker measures the cost of breach against the anticipated gains. If the projected benefits exceed the probable costs, the breach is efficient. The difficulty with this strictly economic perspective on the question of breach is that it purposely ignores or marginalizes the ethical implications of breaking a promise.

What, then, is the role of ethics in the realm of contract law? It must have at least a limited role, according to Robert

Larmer, since morality is essential for a functioning business environment:

> [U]nless those in business recognize the obligation to keep promises and honour contracts, business could not exist. This is not to suggest that business people never break contracts, but if such behaviour ever became general, business would be impossible. Just as telling a lie is advantageous only if most people generally tell the truth, shady business practices are advantageous only if most business people recognize the existence of moral obligations. Immorality in business is essentially parasitic because it tends to destroy the moral environment which makes its very existence possible.

Critical Analysis: Should contract law start punishing more regularly those who breach contracts because such conduct amounts to a betrayal of trust and may lead to the market being undermined? Is it practical to ask the law to enforce a moral code or is Holmes' approach preferable? What non-legal penalties might a contract breaker face?

Sources: Robert Larmer, *Ethics in the Workplace: Selected Readings in Business Ethics*, 2d ed (Belmont, CA: Wadsworth Thomson Learning, 2002); and Oliver Wendell Holmes, "The Path of the Law" (1897) 10 Harv L Rev 457.

Timing of the Breach

A breach of contract can occur at the time specified for performance—as, for example, when one party fails to deliver machinery on the date recited in the contract. A breach can also occur in advance of the date named for performance—as, for example, when one party advises the other, in advance of the delivery date, that no delivery with be forthcoming. This is known as an **anticipatory breach**. Anticipatory breaches are actionable because each party to a contract is entitled to a continuous expectation that the other will

Anticipatory breach
A breach that occurs before the date for performance.

perform during the entire period between the date the contract is formed and the time for performance. This means that the innocent party can sue immediately for breach of contract and is not required to wait and see if the other party has a change of heart.

When the anticipatory breach is sufficiently serious, the innocent party is not just entitled to damages. She can also treat the contract as at an end. This option puts the innocent party in somewhat of a dilemma, since she will not know for sure whether the contract can legally be treated as at an end unless and until the matter is litigated—an event that will occur months or, more likely, years later.

Entitlement to a Remedy

Damages
Monetary compensation for breach of contract or other actionable wrong.

The final step in an action for breach of contract is for the plaintiff to satisfy a court that he is entitled to a remedy. In the usual case, **damages**—or monetary compensation—are awarded, but in specialized circumstances, a plaintiff is entitled to an equitable remedy.

The Measure of Damages

Expectation damages
Damages which provide the plaintiff with the monetary equivalent of contractual performance.

There are several ways of measuring the plaintiff's loss. The most common way is to award **expectation damages**, which provide the plaintiff with the monetary equivalent of performance.

Expressed in legal language, the plaintiffs, in this case the Owens, are entitled to compensation that puts them, as much as possible, in the financial position they would have been in had the defendant, Conlin, performed his obligations under the contract. Subject to the principles discussed in this chapter, the Owens should at least be able to recover from Conlin any amount to complete the house over and above what they had committed to pay Conlin. Though they paid Holmstead $300 000 to complete the job, they cannot recover that whole sum. Had the contract been properly performed by Conlin, the Owens would have spent $500 000 on their home. As it is, they had to spend $600 000. They are only entitled to recover the difference (i.e. $100 000) because the house promised by Conlin would not have come to them for free. The costs the Owens would have had to pay to Conlin for the house must be deducted in this case.

Punitive damages
An award to the plaintiff to punish the defendant for malicious, oppressive, and high-handed conduct.

Whether the context is a claim for pecuniary (tangible) or non-pecuniary (intangible) loss, the purpose of damages in contract law is to *compensate* a plaintiff. As the Supreme Court of Canada confirms in *Whiten v Pilot Insurance Co*, **punitive damages** are exceptional and are only awarded against the defendant for "malicious, oppressive and high-handed" misconduct that "offends the court's sense of decency."[16] In addition, the plaintiff must show that the defendant has committed an independent actionable wrong—for example, *two* breaches of contract. Though this requirement is long established, its rationale is less than clear.

Pecuniary and Non-Pecuniary Damages

As will be discussed in detail in Chapter 10, damages in tort can be pecuniary (for financial loss) and non-pecuniary (for loss of enjoyment, mental distress, and other emotional consequences). The same holds true in contract law, except that recovery for non-pecuniary damages

---

16. *Whiten v Pilot Insurance* Co, 2002 SCC 18 at para 36. For further discussion of the *Whiten* case, see Chapter 28.

is historically unusual. In law, a defendant is responsible only for the reasonably foreseeable damages sustained by the plaintiff and not for absolutely every adverse consequence experienced by the innocent party after the contract has been breached.[17] While pain and suffering or other emotional distress is reasonably foreseeable when one person negligently injures another in a car accident, it is not generally anticipated as being the consequence of a breach of contract.

Test for Remoteness   The kinds of damages recoverable in contract law are determined by the test for remoteness, which was established in the still-leading decision of *Hadley v Baxendale*.[18] That test states that the damages claimed are recoverable provided

- the damages could have been anticipated, having "arisen naturally" from the breach, or

- the damages—although perhaps difficult to anticipate in the ordinary case—are reasonably foreseeable because the unusual circumstances were communicated to the defendant at the time the contract was being formed

Any claim for damages in contract must pass one of the remoteness tests set out above; otherwise, it is simply not recoverable. The policy rationale of such a rule is the need to ensure that defendants do not face unlimited liability for the consequences of a breach and to allow them, by being informed of special circumstances, the option of turning down the job, charging a higher price to compensate for the increased risk, or perhaps, purchasing the necessary insurance.

BUSINESS APPLICATION OF THE LAW

Breach of Contract and Reasonable Foreseeability

Gabriella Nagy of Toronto is suing Rogers Wireless for $600 000 for breach of contract. She alleges that Rogers, at her husband's request, terminated her personal cell phone account and rebundled it with the family's TV, home phone, and Internet bill. The bill was then listed in her husband's name. Nagy's husband discovered that Nagy was having an extra-marital affair after reviewing her cell phone records, which showed that she had been calling one number with particular frequency. When the husband called that number, the man who answered said that he had recently ended a three-week affair with Gabriella Nagy. Nagy's husband immediately left her, and she fell into a depression and lost her job.

Critical Analysis: Has Rogers breached its contract with Nagy by bundling her cell phone account without her permission? Assuming this is breach of contract, are the nature of Nagy's damages reasonably foreseeable? What other problems might Nagy have in proving all the elements of her action for breach of contract?

Source: Linda Nguyen, "Woman sues Rogers for exposing her affair", *Edmonton Journal* (18 May 2010) online: Edmonton Journal <http://www2.canada.com /edmontonjournal/news/story.html?id=38f9f276-5c87-4ce3-8ebc-a1040907fd10>.

Gabriella Nagy, shown in disguise, is suing Rogers Wireless.

17. It is beyond the scope of this book to discuss whether the test for remoteness is stricter in contract than it is in tort.
18. (1854), 9 Exch 341.

Recovery of Non-Pecuniary Damages   As already noted, recovery for non-pecuniary damages—such as for mental distress—is traditionally viewed with suspicion in contract law. This traditional approach has been challenged, however, by the Supreme Court of Canada in the case discussed just below.

CASE

Fidler v Sun Life Assurance Company of Canada, 2006 SCC 30

THE BUSINESS CONTEXT: When a supplier of goods or services fails to meet contractual obligations, the customer may experience frustration and distress. Depending on the kind of contract involved, the customer may be entitled to damages for enduring such upset, thereby driving up the size of the damage award.

FACTUAL BACKGROUND: Ms. Fidler worked as a receptionist at a bank in British Columbia. She was covered by a long-term disability policy that would provide her with an assured income should she become ill and unable to work. Ms. Fidler began to receive benefits when she was diagnosed with chronic fatigue syndrome and fibromyalgia. The insurer later cut her off from payments, citing video surveillance that detailed activity proving that she could work. In face of medical evidence that Fidler could not, in fact, work, the insurer refused to reinstate her benefits. Fidler sued the insurer for breach of contract. Just before trial, the insurer agreed to reinstate benefits, leaving only a few issues to be determined at trial, including the one described below.

THE LEGAL QUESTION: Was the plaintiff entitled to recover damages for mental distress caused by the defendant's wrongful denial of benefits?

RESOLUTION: The Supreme Court of Canada rejected the traditional notion that damages for mental distress should be tightly controlled and exceptional. On the contrary, the court

should simply ask, "What did the contract promise?" and provide damages on that basis. More specifically, the plaintiff seeking recovery for mental distress must show

1. that the object of the contract was to secure a psychological benefit that brings mental distress upon breach within the reasonable contemplation of the parties [i.e., the test in *Hadley v Baxendale* cited above]; and
2. that the degree of mental suffering caused by the breach was of a degree sufficient to warrant compensation.

The court ruled that—as disability insurance contracts are to protect the holder from financial and emotional stress and insecurity—mental distress damages should be recoverable. On this basis, Fidler was able to bring herself with the first step of the test above. And because Fidler's distress was of a sufficient degree, she met the second part of the test. The court affirmed the trial judge's award of $20 000 for mental distress.

CRITICAL ANALYSIS: Do you agree that damages for mental distress should be recoverable? Do you think that a plaintiff who is left feeling angry or frustrated by a breach would pass the test for recovery stated in *Sun Life* or is something more pronounced required?

Based on this case, it would seem that Janet Owen has a particularly strong claim for mental distress damages. A contract to construct a home—given its personal nature—has as one of its objects the provision of a psychological benefit that brings mental distress upon breach within the reasonable contemplation of the parties. Second, since Janet has been very upset because of Conlin's breach and is even having trouble sleeping, it would seem that the degree of mental suffering caused by the breach is of a degree sufficient to warrant compensation.

Recovery of Pecuniary Damages   Those who have suffered a breach of contract can recover all their resulting pecuniary (or monetary) losses unless a clause is included that limits, excludes, or fixes liability at a set amount.[19] Recovery of pecuniary damages is possible in situations such as the following:

---

19. Liquidated damages clauses are discussed in Chapter 7.

- A purchaser of a warehouse with a leaky roof can recover the cost of repairing the roof provided the roof was warranted to be sound.

- A client who suffers a financial loss owing to negligent legal advice can recover those losses from the lawyer in question.

- A person whose goods are stolen while they are in storage can recover the cost of those items from the warehouse owner.

Similarly, because Conlin did not construct and complete the house properly, the Owens are entitled to recover additional damages that flow from that breach. This is discussed in the next section of the text.

Duty to Mitigate   Everyone who suffers a breach of contract has a **duty to mitigate**. This means that they must take reasonable steps to minimize losses that might arise from the breach, as in the following examples:

- A person who is fired from his job, in breach of contract, has a duty to mitigate by trying to find replacement employment.

- A landlord whose tenant breaches a lease by moving out before the expiry of its term has a duty to mitigate by trying to find a replacement tenant.

- A disappointed vendor whose purchaser fails to complete a real estate transaction has a duty to mitigate by trying to find a replacement purchaser.

Duty to mitigate
The obligation to take reasonable steps to minimize the losses resulting from a breach of contract or other wrong.

If the plaintiff fails to mitigate, its damage award will be reduced accordingly. For example, if the employee making $100 000 a year had one year left on his contract before he was wrongfully terminated, his damages would be $100 000. However, his duty to mitigate requires him to look for comparable employment. If he immediately does so and secures a job at $80 000, his damages drop to $20 000. If he fails to mitigate—by, for example, refusing such a job—a court will reduce his damages by $80 000, since that loss is more attributable to him than to his former employer.

By the same token, any reasonable costs associated with the mitigation are recoverable from the party in breach. An employee could, in addition to damages related to salary loss, also recover reasonable expenses related to the job search.

In the Owens' case, mitigation took the form of hiring Holmstead to finish and repair the house for $300 000. Assuming that this is reasonable, the Owens will be able to recover $100 000 from Conlin. This is because the Owens have had to pay an extra $100 000 for their house over and above what they had committed to pay Conlin. The calculation is based on the following analysis: The Owens were going to spend $500 000 on the house but have paid Conlon $300 000 and Holmstead $300 000 for a total of $600 000. Since this extra cost of $100 000 to obtain their bargain flows from Conlin's breach of contract, it is recoverable. Note that even the $5000 to rebuild the see-through fireplace (which is included in Holmstead's $300 000 bill) is recoverable. A court will almost certainly agree that the Owens are entitled to the price of rebuilding the fireplace even though this amount is much higher than Conlin's solution of simply bricking in one of the fireplace walls. In short, the Owens had contracted for a see-through fireplace and are entitled to it.

PART TWO

Should the court enforce contracts as they relate to aesthetics and matters of taste or should contractors be given the discretion to follow cheaper alternatives?

MEREDITH HEUER/PHOTONICA/GETTY IMAGES

Equitable Remedies

In those relatively rare situations in which damages would be an inadequate remedy for breach of contract, the court may exercise its discretion to grant one of the equitable remedies discussed below.

Specific Performance   An order by the court for the equitable remedy of specific performance means that instead of awarding compensation for failing to perform, the court orders the party who breached to do exactly what the contract obligated him to do. This remedy is available only when the item in question is unique and cannot be replaced by money. The classic situation for specific performance is a contract for the sale of land, where the particular piece of land covered by the contract is essential to the buyer's plans, perhaps as part of a major development project. Without the remaining piece, the project cannot proceed, so damages would fail to provide a complete remedy.

Because specific performance is an equitable remedy, a court can refuse to order it, at its discretion, as in the following circumstances:

- *Improper behaviour by the plaintiff.* Any improper motive or conduct on the part of the plaintiff may disqualify him from being granted such special assistance. Rules governing equity, like "he who seeks equity must do equity" or "she who comes to equity must come with clean hands," mean that only the deserving plaintiff will succeed.

- *Delay.* Failure by the plaintiff to bring a claim promptly can be grounds for denying the plaintiff an equitable remedy.[20]

---

20. For a discussion and excerpts of relevant case law concerning equitable remedies and defences thereto, see Stephanie Ben-Ishai and David R Percy, eds, *Contracts: Cases and Commentaries*, 8th ed (Toronto: Carswell, 2009) at 902 and following.

- *Impossibility.* A court will not order a defendant to do something that is impossible, such as convey land that the defendant does not own.[21]

- *Severe hardship.* If specific performance would cause a severe hardship to the parties, or to a third party, a court may refuse to order it.

- *Employment contracts.* A court will not, ordinarily, order specific performance of an employment contract, because being forced to work for someone else against the employee's wishes would interfere too much with the employee's personal freedom.

Injunction   If a contract contains promises not to engage in specified activities, disregarding those promises by engaging in the prohibited acts is a breach of contract. While an award of damages is of some help, additionally, the plaintiff would want a court order requiring the offender to refrain from continued violation of the contract. For example, if the vendor of a business agrees not to compete with the new owner and the relevant clauses are reasonable restrictions (see Chapter 8), damages alone are an inadequate remedy for breach because they fail to prevent the vendor from competing. Only an order to cease doing business will provide the buyer with a complete remedy.

Like an order of specific performance, an injunction is an equitable remedy and is subject to the court's discretion. However, it is commonly ordered to restrain a party from breaching a promise not to do something, as noted above. There are occasions where a court will not order an injunction, however, as when the plaintiff does not have "clean hands" (i.e., is undeserving) or delays in bringing the matter before the court.

Courts also have the jurisdiction to order an injunction for a limited period of time. This type of injunction, known as an **interlocutory injunction**, requires someone to stop doing something until the whole dispute can be resolved through a trial.

Interlocutory injunction
An order to refrain from doing something for a limited period of time.

Rescission   It may be appropriate, in some cases, to restore the parties to the situation they were in before the contract was formed, rather than use compensation to put the innocent party in the position it would have been in had the contract been completed. For example, many of the doctrines in Chapter 8 for avoiding contracts provide rescission as the contractual remedy.

As with other equitable remedies, there are bars to receiving rescission of a contract. For example, where parties cannot restore each other to their pre-contractual positions—because, perhaps, the subject matter of the contract has been altered—the court has the power to do what is practically just, including the power to order that the innocent party be compensated. Another bar to rescission is delay by the plaintiff in seeking the court's assistance.

Restitutionary Remedies

Sometimes a contractual claim fails not because the plaintiff is undeserving but because he cannot prove that an enforceable contract is in place. The law of restitution gives recourse to a plaintiff who has conferred benefits on the defendant in reliance on a contract that

---

21. See *Castle v Wilkinson* (1870), 5 LR Ch App 534.

cannot be enforced due, for example, to noncompliance with the *Statute of Frauds*.[22] For example, if the plaintiff has done work for the defendant pursuant to an unenforceable contract for the purchase of land, the plaintiff may end up being recompensed by the defendant, not under contract but pursuant to the law of restitution.

Restitution is a complex area of law but its main objective is clear—to remedy unjust enrichment. **Unjust enrichment** occurs when the defendant has undeservedly or unjustly secured a benefit at the plaintiff's expense. In such circumstances, the court will ordinarily order that the benefit be restored to the plaintiff or otherwise be accounted for by the defendant.

In response to an unjust enrichment, the court has several options, including ordering the defendant to

- pay a **restitutionary *quantum meruit***; that is, an amount that is reasonable given the benefit that the plaintiff has conferred.[23]

- pay compensation; that is, an allowance of money to put the plaintiff in as good a position as the plaintiff was in prior to conferring the benefit.[24]

Unjust enrichment
Occurs when one party has undeservedly or unjustly secured a benefit at the other party's expense.

Restitutionary *quantum meruit*
An amount that is reasonable given the benefit the plaintiff has conferred.

Managing Risk

There are several risks that a business faces when the time comes to perform a contract. It may be that the business cannot perform at all or that when it does perform, it does so deficiently. A business can attend to these possibilities proactively or reactively. From a proactive perspective, the business can negotiate for clauses to limit or exclude liability as well as for a *force majeure* clause, as appropriate. It may be, however, that the other side is unwilling to agree to such clauses. Another proactive strategy is to ensure that employees are competent and properly trained, since any mistakes they make in performance of the contract are attributable to the employer. The better the employees do, the more likely the contract will be performed without incident. Securing proper insurance can also be effective, a matter discussed in Chapter 28 in more detail.

Once the business is in breach of contract, however, matters are now in a reactive mode. The contract breaker is in an unenviable position, since it faces liability for all reasonable costs associated with its default. To reduce financial exposure and litigation expenses, the business should consider seeking mediation, arbitration, and other forms of compromise, including settlement offers, as alternatives to going to trial. Depending on the nature of the breach, the loss may be covered by insurance.

Those who contract for the provision of a product or service should undertake to ensure that the supplier is reputable and reliable. This way, legal conflict is perhaps avoided altogether.

When faced with a breach of contract, the innocent party must make a business decision—as much as a legal one—and decide how it should treat that failure. This decision involves evaluating the risks of losing in court; the remedies available, including the amount of damages; the likelihood of being able to negotiate a settlement; and whether there is a valuable business relationship to preserve.

---

22. See Chapter 8.
23. Contractual *quantum meruit* has already been discussed in Chapter 7.
24. GHL Fridman, "*Quantum Meruit*" (1999) 37 Alta L Rev 38.

Business Law in Practice Revisited

1. Can the Owens demonstrate all the steps in an action for breach of contract against Conlin?

The Owens can meet all the steps to succeed in an action for breach of contract. They can show privity of contract between themselves and Conlin. They can show that Conlin breached the contract in multiple ways, including by failing to build the house according to Code and not providing the fireplace contracted for. Finally, the Owens can show that they are entitled to a remedy. Both have suffered pecuniary loss and, in addition, Janet has suffered non-pecuniary damages in the form of mental distress.

2. Are the Owens themselves in breach of contract for refusing to permit Conlin to complete the contract?

Conlin's multiple breaches of contract and insulting behaviour strongly suggest that he will not properly perform the contract in the future. A court may well conclude that this amounts to a breach of a condition of the contract—namely that he will be reliable. If the Owens can prove a breach of condition, they have the right to end the contract. They are therefore not in breach of contract for refusing to permit him to complete.

The term that the house be built to Code may be hard to classify as a condition or warranty up-front since the parties' intentions are not clear and the term itself can be breached in large ways and small. On this basis, the court will look to how serious the structural defects are. If they are serious, the breach will be of a condition-like innominate term, also bringing with it the right to treat the contract as at an end.

3. Did the Owens properly mitigate their damages?

Assuming that there has been a breach of condition or condition-like innominate term, the Owens properly mitigated their loss in hiring Holmstead to repair and complete the home. This is also based on the assumption that the extra cost was reasonable.

4. What damages can the Owens receive?

The Owens stand a good chance of receiving considerable pecuniary and non-pecuniary damages.

Pecuniary Damages Because the Owens had to hire Holmstead to finish and repair the house for $300 000, they paid an extra $100 000 for their home. That is, the contract price with Conlin was $500 000. They have already paid Conlin $300 000 and will be paying Holmstead another $300 000. Assuming that Holmstead's fees were reasonable, the Owens will be able to recover $100 000 in pecuniary damages from Conlin.

Note that even the $5000 to rebuild the see-through fireplace (which is included in Holmstead's $300 000 bill) is probably recoverable even though a cheaper "solution" was offered by Conlin. The Owens contracted for a see-through fireplace and therefore Conlin's idea of simply bricking in one of the fireplace walls is not acceptable. Note that the recovery of $5000 is already included in the $100 000 discussed above. It cannot be claimed and recovered twice.

Non-Pecuniary Damages Janet Owens may also be able to recover damages for mental distress and suffering because Conlin's breach of contract caused her mental distress. A contract for home construction arguably has, as one of its objects, the provision of a psychological benefit, so the first step in *Fidler* is met. The second step is also met since

Janet has suffered mental distress to a degree sufficient to warrant compensation. She has experienced great upset and even has had trouble sleeping.

It is difficult to predict how much a court will award for non-pecuniary damages but, based on existing case law, it is unlikely to be a large sum given the extent of her upset.[25]

Chapter Summary

In the vast majority of situations, a contract terminates or ends when the parties fully perform their obligations. Less common are situations where the contract ends because the parties find it impossible or tremendously difficult to perform their obligations. In such cases, prudent business parties will have addressed such a possibility through a *force majeure* clause or equivalent.

A more usual and complicated situation, from a business perspective, occurs when one party breaches the contract by failing to perform or by performing inadequately.

There are several ways that a contract is terminated: by performance, by agreement, through frustration, and through breach.

When a contract is terminated by performance, the parties have fulfilled all their implied and express promises. The work necessary to achieve performance may be done by the parties personally or through their agents/employees, unless a term to the contrary is included.

Sometimes, parties terminate a contract by agreement. For example, the parties may agree to end the contract entirely or to replace it with a new one. Alternatively, the parties may vary certain terms of the contract or substitute a new party who, in turn, assumes rights and duties under the contract.

Contract law allows one party to assign his right under a contract but not the liabilities. The law of assignment permits the creditor to assign his right to collect under a contract to another (the assignee) without the agreement of the debtor. Once the assignee has given notice of the assignment to the debtor, the latter can perform the obligation only by paying the assignee.

The doctrine of frustration terminates a contract, but only in very limited circumstances. It must be shown that an unanticipated event or change in circumstances is so substantial that performance has become functionally impossible or illegal. Provided the risk of such an event has not been allocated to one party or the other, and provided the event did not arise through either party's fault, the contract has been frustrated.

When one party fails to perform its contractual obligations, it is in breach of contract and subject to a lawsuit. To succeed in its action for breach of contract, the innocent party must establish the existence of a contract, breach of contract, and entitlement to a remedy.

Privity means that, with limited exceptions, only those who are parties to a contract can enforce the rights and obligations it contains.

When a party to a contract fails to keep his promise, he has committed a breach of contract and is liable for such damages as would restore the innocent party to the position she would have been in had the contract been performed. These are known as expectation damages. If there is an exclusion or limitation of liability clause in the contract, the defendant's liability will be reduced or eliminated, depending on the circumstances.

---

25. For a discussion of quantum, see Shannon Kathleen O'Byrne, "Damages for Mental Distress and Other Intangible Loss in a Breach of Contract Action" (2005) 28:2 Dal LJ 311.

Damages in contract are ordinarily pecuniary, but in some circumstances, the innocent party is entitled to non-pecuniary damages for mental suffering and distress. As well, punitive damages are exceptionally available.

When one party suffers a breach of contract, she must take reasonable steps to mitigate. If the party fails to do so, the damage award will be reduced accordingly. By the same token, any reasonable costs associated with mitigation are also recoverable from the party in breach.

Contract law also offers equitable remedies, such as specific performance and injunction, when damages are an inadequate remedy. On occasion, the best solution is to rescind the contract—that is, return the parties to their pre-contractual positions.

The law of restitution also provides remedies in a contractual context because its main objective is to remedy unjust enrichment. Unjust enrichment occurs when the defendant has undeservedly or unjustly secured a benefit at the plaintiff's expense.

Whether the innocent party takes the contract breaker to court is as much a business decision as it is a legal one.

Chapter Study

Key Terms and Concepts

anticipatory breach (p. 205)

assignment (p. 197)

balance of probabilities (p. 200)

condition (p. 203)

damages (p. 206)

duty to mitigate (p. 209)

expectation damages (p. 206)

frustration (p. 198)

fundamental breach (p. 204)

innominate term (p. 203)

interlocutory injunction (p. 211)

novation (p. 196)

punitive damages (p. 206)

restitutionary *quantum meruit* (p. 212)

unjust enrichment (p. 212)

vicarious performance (p. 196)

warranty (p. 203)

Questions for Review

1. What are the four major ways that a contract can be terminated?

2. What is an assignment? What risks does the assignee of a contractual right assume?

3. What is privity of contract?

4. How is vicarious performance used by business?

5. How is a new contract created through novation?

6. When is a contract frustrated?

7. What is a *force majeure* clause?

8. What elements need to be established in a successful action for breach of contract?

9. How is the severity of a breach of contract evaluated?

10. What is the difference between a warranty and a condition?

11. What is the purpose of awarding damages for breach of contract?

12. When will a court award punitive damages for breach of contract?

13. When is a plaintiff entitled to damages for mental distress?

14. What is unjust enrichment?

15. What is restitutionary *quantum meruit*?

16. What is specific performance?

17. When will a court grant an injunction?

18. What is the remedy of rescission?

19. When can the innocent party treat the contract as at an end?

20. How can a plaintiff avoid the application of an exclusion of liability clause?

Questions for Critical Thinking

1. A contract is considered frustrated only in very unusual situations. Should the doctrine of frustration be applied more often? Would a broader application produce fairer results? What is the downside of such a change in commercial contracts?

2. Breach of a condition can signify the end of the contract while breach of warranty does not. Should courts be allowed to exercise discretionary power in determining whether an innominate term should have this same result? What should parties do if they wish to reduce the uncertainty as to how a given term will be classified?

3. The privity rule is one of the basic elements of contract law. Is it too restrictive? On the other hand, is there a danger in creating too many exceptions to the rule?

4. Contract law is intended to facilitate commercial activities and to enable businesses to conduct their affairs so that their legal obligations are certain. Do you think, after considering the material in the last five chapters, that contract law achieves its goals? Can you think of ways to improve the effectiveness of contract law?

5. The Supreme Court of Canada stated that mental distress damages for breach of contract can be awarded when an object of the contract was to secure a psychological benefit. What kinds of contracts can you think of that promise a psychological benefit?

6. Everyone who suffers a breach of contract still has a duty to mitigate his damages. Do you think it is fair to impose a positive duty on someone when a contract is breached through no fault of his own? How strict do you think courts should be in analyzing whether someone has fulfilled his duty to mitigate?

Situations for Discussion

1. Leonard purchased an unconstructed condominium in a large development. The contract stated that delivery of the completed condo was to be on a date set by the developer before February 1, 2010. Construction proceeded on schedule except on April 25, 2009, the whole development burned to the ground. After spending some time looking for the cause of the fire, the developer started the process of rebuilding in October 2009. It looks like the condo will be delivered about a year later than originally anticipated. Is Leonard bound by the contract under these circumstances? Does it matter if the fire was caused by the developer's negligence?[26]

2. John chartered a large ship from Rent-a-Boat Ltd. The duration of the charter was 24 months, and it was a term of the contract that Rent-a-Boat would provide a seaworthy ship and supply John with competent engine-room staff. Immediately, there were problems. For example, due to the ship's engine being old and its engine-room staff being inexperienced, the ship was in repair for the first 20 weeks of the charter. In week 18, John advised Rent-a-Boat that its breaches of contract permitted him to end the contract and sue for damages. Is John correct? What remedy is John entitled to and why?

3. Susan, a law professor, was in Israel when her cellphone was stolen from her home in Toronto. Upon her return, Rogers, the cellphone service provider, advised that $12 000 in calls had been made from that phone and she was responsible for payment. Susan replied that she would not pay, since those calls were unauthorized and had been made from her phone after it had been stolen. In response, Rogers, among other actions, cut off her young son's cellphone service. The son's phone had been acquired by Susan for safety reasons since he would be taking the subway, alone, to school for the first time starting in September. Susan was responsible for bills associated with her son's cellphone, but the cellphone was held under a separate contract.

A judge ultimately determined that Rogers was in breach of contract when it cut off her son's phone service, since it had no legal reason to do so. Among other heads of damage, the judge awarded Susan $612 in damages for "lost wages" because she had to drive her son to school while his cellphone was blocked. Do you think Susan's mitigation was reasonable? What else could she have done? Do you think that Rogers should appeal this decision? Why or why not?[27]

4. Atlantic Fertilizer (AF) operates a fertilizer plant in New Brunswick. AF made a major sale to the government of Togo in Africa and engaged Pearl Shipping (PS) to transport the fertilizer to Togo for a fee of $60 000. The contract between AF and PS specified that AF would deliver the cargo to PS for loading on its ship between 25 and 31 March and that AF would pay $1000 (in addition to the shipping charges) for each day after 31 March that the cargo was delayed. AF had difficulty in filling the large order in its plant and notified PS that delivery would be sometime after 31 March.[28]

PS is contemplating AF's message and deciding how it should react. Options under consideration are to wait for AF to deliver and add the $1000 daily charge to the bill, give AF a firm date by which it must deliver, or terminate the contract with AF and seek another cargo for its ship. Which options are legally available to PS? Which should PS choose?

5. ABC Ltd. was in a contract to supply 1000 widgets at $1 each to XYZ Ltd. by a specified date. Due to a mechanical failure at its factory, ABC Ltd. cannot fill the order on time and has advised XYZ Ltd. to expect delivery to be two months late. XYZ Ltd. planned to use the widgets as components in a machine that it had already contracted to sell for an anticipated profit of $30 000. It cannot wait the two months without jeopardizing that sale. What is XYZ Ltd. obligated to do now? What if the only other source for replacement widgets is from a manufacturer that is proposing to sell them at an exorbitant sum? What other costs can XYZ Ltd. seek to recover?

---

26. Based, in part, on *Fishman v Wilderness Ridge at Stewart Creek Inc*, 2010 ABCA 345.
27. Based, in part, on *Drummond v Rogers Wireless*, [2007] OJ No 1407; and John Jaffey, "Law prof wins punitive damages against Rogers in small claims", *The Lawyers Weekly* (27 April 2007) 7.
28. Based, in part, on *Armada Lines Ltd v Chaleur Fertilizers Ltd* (1994), 170 NR 372 (FCA), rev'd [1997] 2 SCR 617.

6. XYZ Ltd. entered into a contract with ABC Ltd. for the supply of resin which XYZ Ltd. needed in order to produce pipe necessary for a large pipeline. ABC Ltd. made the business decision to supply defective resin to XYZ Ltd. and drafted the contract between the parties to protect itself from liability in relation to that defect as follows:

> XYZ Ltd. assumes all responsibility and liability for loss or damage arising from the use of the resin supplied under this contract herein and acknowledges that ABC Ltd.'s liability is limited to the selling price of the resin.

Another clause stated:

> XYZ Ltd. to notify ABC Ltd. of any objection to the resin supplied within 30 days. Failure to provide such notice constitutes unqualified acceptance and waiver of all claims.

ABC Ltd. knew that the resin was dangerous and would allow natural gas to escape. In fact, this is exactly what happened. There was an explosion in the pipeline for which XYZ Ltd. supplied pipe and which XYZ Ltd. fixed at great cost. When it asked ABC Ltd. for help, ABC Ltd. refused to take any responsibility, pointing to the exclusion clauses. Due to negative publicity surrounding the gas pipe leaks, XYZ Ltd. lost both its reputation and financial viability. Assuming that the supply of defective was a breach of contract, do you think ABC Ltd. will be able to rely on the exclusion clauses above? On what basis?[29]

7. Imperial Brass Ltd. wanted to computerize all of its systems. Jacob Electric Systems Ltd. presented Imperial with a proposal that met Imperial's needs. In August, Imperial accepted the proposal, along with Jacob's "tentative" schedule for implementation, which led Imperial to expect a total computerized operation by mid-January, with the possibility of a 30-day extension. In October, it became clear that there were problems with the software being developed, and Imperial asked for corrections to be made. At the end of October, the hardware and two software programs were delivered to Imperial, and Imperial's employees attempted to begin to use the programs. Very little training was provided, however, and there were major problems with the computer screens freezing and data being lost. More programs were delivered in January, along with some operating instructions, but Imperial's employees were still unable to make any use of the programs they had. The programmer whom Jacob assigned to Imperial's contract, Mr. Sharma, continued to work on the remaining programs. In May, however, Jacob informed Imperial that Sharma would be leaving the company, and Imperial informed Jacob that if that were to happen, given the problems and delays the company had already experienced, Imperial would be forced to end the contract with Jacob's company.[30] Is the breach by Jacob's company serious enough to permit the innocent party, Imperial, to treat the contract as at an end?

8. Canadian Pacific Airlines (CP) agreed to safely transport the Newells' two pet dogs on a flight from Toronto to Mexico City. The Newells were concerned about the safety and welfare of their dogs, but CP's employees reassured them that the dogs would be safe in the cargo compartment of the aircraft and reported to them before they boarded that their dogs had been safely placed in the cargo area. When the flight arrived in Mexico City, one dog was dead and the other was comatose. The Newells sued CP for general damages to compensate them for "anguish, loss of enjoyment of life and sadness" that they allege resulted from the breach of contract.[31] Are the Newells entitled to anything other than compensation for their direct financial loss (i.e., the monetary value of the dogs)? If so, what would be an adequate amount to compensate for the mental distress suffered by the Newells?

For more study tools, visit http://www.NELSONbrain.com.

---

29. Based, in part, on *Plas Tex Canada Ltd v Dow Chemical of Canada Ltd*, 2004 ABCA 309.
30. Based, in part, on *Imperial Brass Ltd v Jacob Electric Systems Ltd (1989)*, 72 OR (2d) 17 (HCtJ).
31. Based, in part, on *Newell et al v Canadian Pacific Airlines Ltd* (1977), 14 OR (2d) 752 (Co Ct J).

PART THREE

Business Torts

Tort law provides remedies to persons who have suffered physical harm and/or economic loss because of the intentional or careless actions of another.

Business is exposed to tort risks on a variety of fronts. A paper mill may release toxins into a nearby river and ruin the water downstream. A customer may slip on the floor of a store and suffer serious injury. One business may intentionally seek to drive a competitor out of business by spreading lies. An accountant or lawyer may provide negligent advice that causes the client to lose money. Tort law provides a set of rules through which the innocent party can recover financial compensation for the loss sustained. The next three chapters consider the risk exposure of business in the context of tort law.

MARTIN HAAS/SHUTTERSTOCK

CHAPTER 10

Introduction to Tort Law

Objectives

After studying this chapter, you should have an understanding of

- the broad scope of tort law

- the differences between a civil action and a criminal action

- the purpose of tort remedies

- how business can manage its potential liability in tort

Business Law in Practice

Bar-Fly is a large bar operating in Eastern Canada. Though most of its staff members are trained to diffuse hostility and aggression among patrons, fights occasionally occur. At least one bouncer is on duty to handle such situations.

Sam, a university student, visits Bar-Fly one night with several of his friends. Though Sam and his friends stick to themselves, an altercation breaks out at the table beside them. It is soon quelled by Bar-Fly staff. Mike, one of the bouncers, then accuses Sam of starting the fight and demands that he leave. When Sam protests his innocence, Mike begins to gesture wildly very close to Sam's face. He then grabs Sam by his shirt collar and throws him from the premises with such force that Sam suffers serious spinal injuries. While all this is going on, one of Sam's friends slips in the men's room on spilt beer that had been accumulating for hours. He lands hard and breaks his arm.

1. What kind of tort action does Sam's friend have as a result of breaking his arm?
2. What potential legal actions result from the altercation between Sam and Mike?
3. Is Bar-Fly responsible for Mike's actions?
4. What risk management actions could Bar-Fly have taken to prevent this altercation and the fall in the men's room?

DICK HEMINGWAY

Defining Tort Law

The word **tort**[1] describes any harm or injury caused by one person to another—other than through breach of contract—and for which the law provides a remedy.[2] According to the Supreme Court of Canada, tort law provides a means whereby compensation, usually in the form of damages, may be paid for

> injuries suffered by a party as a result of the wrongful conduct of others. It may encompass damages for personal injury suffered, for example, in a motor vehicle accident or as a result of falling in dangerous premises. It can cover damages occasioned to property. It may include compensation for injury caused to the reputation of a business or a product. It may provide damages for injury to honour in cases of defamation and libel. A primary object of the law of tort is to provide compensation to persons who are injured as a result of the actions of others.[3]

Given this diversity, the law historically evolved so as to break torts down into distinct categories, each with its own discrete definition. What follows is a brief sampling:

- *Trespass to land*. **Trespass to land** involves wrongful interference with someone's possession of land.[4] Parking garage operators might rely on the tort of trespass when drivers leave their cars in the lot but fail to purchase the required ticket from the automated ticket dispenser. The driver is responsible for the tort of trespass because he has left the vehicle on the property without permission.

- *Deceit or fraud*. This tort is based on a false representation intentionally or recklessly made by one person to another that causes damage.[5] The tort of **deceit or fraud** occurs when, for example, a customer purchases a vehicle based on the vendor's intentional representation that the vehicle has a new engine when, in fact, it does not. The vendor has committed the tort of deceit because he made an untrue statement, which the purchaser relied on in deciding to make the purchase.

- *Negligence*. The tort of **negligence** compensates someone who has suffered loss or injury due to the unreasonable conduct of another.[6] It is one of the most common torts to arise in a business context. For example,

  - when a taxi driver is injured due to an unsafe lane change by another driver, he is the victim of the tort of negligence. The driver causing the injury is responsible for the tort of negligence because she has made the unsafe lane change and failed to show the care and attention that the circumstances required.

Tort
A harm caused by one person to another, other than through breach of contract, and for which the law provides a remedy.

Trespass to land
Wrongful interference with someone's possession of land.

Deceit or fraud
A false representation intentionally or recklessly made by one person to another that causes damage.

Negligence
Unreasonable conduct, including a careless act or omission, that causes harm to another.

PART THREE

---

1. The word "tort" is derived from the Latin word meaning "crooked" and the French word meaning "wrong." See Lewis Klar, *Tort Law*, 5th ed (Toronto: Thomson Carswell, 2012) at 1.
2. *Ibid*.
3. *Hall v Hebert*, [1993] 2 SCR 159 at para 58, per Cory J.
4. *Supra* note 1 at 110.
5. *Ibid* at 696 and following.
6. *Ibid* at 167.

- when lawyers, accountants, or other professionals give their clients incompetent advice that causes loss, they have committed not only a breach of contract but also the tort of negligence, more specifically known as professional negligence.

- when consumers purchase a defective product, they may have an action against the manufacturer for negligence if the product was improperly designed and/or produced. This area of law is known more specifically as product liability, but its foundations are in negligence.

- when a bar over-serves a customer, it may be found negligent if that intoxicated customer is injured or causes injury to others.

The law of torts will not automatically provide a remedy when someone has been physically or economically injured. One of the key objectives of tort law is to distinguish between a situation in which the loss suffered by an injured individual should remain uncompensated and one in which responsibility for the loss should be "shifted" to another party considered responsible for causing the loss, known as the **tort-feasor**. Tort law provides an evolving set of rules for making that determination.

Tort-feasor
Person who commits a tort.

To a large extent, tort law seeks to impose liability based on fault, as the following two examples illustrate:

Example 1   A truck driver falls asleep at the wheel. As a result, his rig crashes into a parked car, causing substantial property damage.

- The driver has committed the tort of negligence. His careless acts or omissions have caused harm or loss to another, namely the owner of the parked car. The owner can successfully sue in tort.

Example 2   A truck driver—with no previous history of health problems—suffers a heart attack while at the wheel. As a result, his rig crashes into a parked car, causing substantial property damage.

- Assuming that the driver's heart attack was not reasonably foreseeable or reasonably preventable, no tort has been committed by the driver. Though his rig caused property damage, it was not due to a careless act or omission.

It is important to note that liability in these examples will vary from province to province depending on the no-fault elements of the provincial *Insurance Act* as relating to auto insurance that may be in place. A pure no-fault system eliminates the ability to claim in tort. No-fault insurance is discussed further in Chapter 28.

A central function of tort law is to compensate an injured party when the injury is the result of someone else's blameworthy conduct. While one may feel sympathy for anyone who suffers damages, tort law does not provide a remedy in all circumstances.

As noted in Chapter 2, courts are governed by precedent when determining the law in any particular case. The nature of precedent is inherently historical, meaning that judges can reach back and rely on old cases as well as more recently decided ones. The case below, for example, was decided in 1948 but maintains the status of a reliable and useful precedent even today.

CASE   *Jones v Shafer Estate,* [1948] SCR 166

THE BUSINESS CONTEXT: Those who transport goods along the nation's highways may encounter serious mechanical problems while en route. When leaving the truck or other vehicle at the side of the road, they must be concerned about not putting other drivers in danger, but, at the same time, are not responsible for every untoward event that subsequently occurs.[7]

FACTUAL BACKGROUND: Jones was driving a Diamond T oil truck, loaded with gasoline, along a highway in Western Canada. He realized that one of his wheels was coming off, so he pulled to the side of the road, leaving ample room for other vehicles to get by his truck. Jones inspected the vehicle and saw that the outer bearing of his left wheel was gone and the brakes could not be used. Since it was impossible for him to move the truck until the next morning, he placed two oil-powered flares out on the road to alert other drivers. Jones then left. Several hours later, between 10:00 and 11:00 p.m., the flares were stolen by an unknown person. A police officer was called to the scene when notified by a passerby that a truck was parked on the side of the highway without warning flares or lights in place. The police officer broke into the truck, turned on the vehicle's marker lights, and also left.

The next morning, conditions were foggy and visibility was poor. Mr. Shafer, the deceased, was driving alone. He collided with Jones' broken-down truck and was killed. It appeared that there had been a head-on collision of Shafer's car and Jones' truck, which was still parked on the highway shoulder. Had the flares not been removed, they would have been burning at the time of the accident.

THE LEGAL QUESTION: Did Jones commit the tort of negligence?

RESOLUTION: The Supreme Court of Canada reversed both the trial and appellate judges, instead ruling that there had been no negligence. Jones' duty was not to guarantee that there could never be an accident associated with his parked truck but merely to exercise the care of a reasonable person in all the circumstances. As Justice Estey observed, Jones was not required, in this particular case, to anticipate that someone else would commit the "contemptible act" of stealing the flares he placed on the highway as a warning to others.

Another Justice of the Supreme Court of Canada, Justice Locke, criticized the trial judge's reasoning that Jones was liable in negligence since he could have done more to prevent the accident. As Justice Estey points out, "[T]his is hardly the true test in deciding the question of his liability: it was the duty of the defendant to take reasonable care under the circumstances to avoid acts or omissions which he could reasonably foresee would be likely to cause injury to person driving upon the highway." He went on to add, "That anyone would jeopardize the lives of people upon the highway by stealing articles of such slight intrinsic value is a contingency which, in my opinion … [Jones] could not reasonably have foreseen."

CRITICAL ANALYSIS: Can you think of any arguments as to how Jones may have been negligent? Should he have called the police when his truck broke down? Even if he had done so, would this have prevented the accident from happening, based on these facts?

What are the risks here and how can they be managed?

© ROYALTY FREE/CORBIS/MAGMA

---

7. The law of nuisance can also be triggered in such situations. Nuisance is discussed in Chapter 12.

How Torts Are Categorized

Intentional tort
A harmful act that is committed on purpose.

Torts can generally be categorized as falling into two main groups: torts committed intentionally and torts committed through negligence. The first, called **intentional torts**, are harmful acts that are committed on purpose. For example, when Bar-Fly's bouncer gestured wildly in Sam's face, he committed the tort of **assault**. Assault involves a threat of imminent physical harm without there being any actual physical contact. When the bouncer ejected Sam from the premises, he committed the tort of **battery**. Battery involves the intentional infliction of harmful or offensive physical contact.[8] Chapter 12 examines several kinds of business-related torts, most of which are intentional.

Assault
The threat of imminent physical harm.

Battery
Intentional infliction of harmful or offensive physical contact.

Torts committed through negligence comprise another large group. When someone is negligent, she is liable for damages even though she did not intentionally cause the event in question. For example, Bar-Fly has a responsibility to keep the floor of the men's room in a good and safe condition.[9] It did not intentionally cause Sam's friend to fall and break his arm, but its failure to maintain the floor properly brought about the injury. Under these circumstances, Sam's friend can sue Bar-Fly for negligence. The tort of negligence is assessed in more detail in Chapter 11.

This chapter discusses tort law from a more general perspective in order to lay the foundation for subsequent discussion.

Tort Law and Criminal Law

The same event can give rise to two distinct legal consequences: one in tort and one in criminal law. For example, since Sam has been seriously attacked by Mike the bouncer, section 268(1) of the *Criminal Code of Canada*[10] likely applies. That section states, "Everyone commits an offence of aggravated assault who wounds, maims, disfigures or endangers the life of the complainant." According to section 268(2), a person who commits aggravated assault "is guilty of an indictable offence and liable to imprisonment for a term not exceeding fourteen years."

Mike could be charged with aggravated assault by the police, and he could be sued by Sam in tort.

Put another way, Mike's behaviour and its consequences give rise to two separate legal actions. This is because, in addition to tort law, the *Criminal Code* prohibits one person from assaulting another, except in self-defence. There are important differences between tort claims and criminal prosecutions.

Purposes of the Actions

The purpose of a criminal prosecution is to censure behaviour—such as the assault that Sam experienced at the hands of Mike—and secure the punishment of a fine, imprisonment, or both. The action is brought because the Parliament of Canada has determined that anyone who violates the *Criminal Code* should be punished and deterred from such conduct in the future. Prosecution is considered to be critical to maintaining a rights-respecting society.

---

8. *Norberg v Wynrib* (1992), 12 CCLT (2d) 1 (SCC) at 16 defines battery as the "intentional infliction of unlawful force on another person."
9. This situation can also be treated under occupier's liability. See Chapter 12.
10. RSC 1985, c C-46.

In tort law, on the other hand, the objective is to compensate the victim for the harm suffered due to the culpability of another. It enforces the victim's private right to extract compensation from the party who has caused the loss.[11]

Commencing the Actions

In criminal law, the legal action is called a prosecution and is brought most often by Crown prosecutors employed by the federal or provincial governments. Rarely do the injured parties bring the prosecution, though it is technically possible for them to do so.[12] In a criminal action, Mike, the bouncer, would be known as the "accused" or "defendant" and Sam, the injured party, as the "complainant."

In tort law, the injured party brings the legal action. This means that Sam would sue in order to enforce his personal or private right to secure compensation for Mike's attack. His action is called a civil action because it is enforcing a right belonging to an individual. In a civil action, Sam is known as the "plaintiff" and Mike as the "defendant."

Proving the Actions

To secure a conviction under section 268(1) of the *Criminal Code*, the Crown must prove that force was applied, that it was intentional, and that the actions were so serious as to "wound, maim, disfigure or endanger" Sam's life. The Crown would have to establish that Sam was not the aggressor; that even if Sam were the aggressor, the response from Mike was not reasonable in light of Sam's actions; that Mike did indeed use excessive force; and that it was this force that caused Sam's injuries.

The Crown has the burden of proof in a criminal action. This means that the prosecutor must prove all the elements of the offence beyond a reasonable doubt based on "reason and common sense,"[13] not on "sympathy or prejudice."[14] Guilt must be a logical deduction from the evidence, and it is not sufficient that the jury or judge believed the accused "probably" committed the act.[15]

In tort, by way of contrast, the injured party, Sam, must prove that Mike is responsible for the assault and battery, on the balance of probabilities. Put another way, Sam must establish that it is more likely than not that assault and battery took place. Represented in numerical terms, Sam must convince the judge that there is a better than 50 percent chance that he was harmed by the defendant.

Given the different burdens, it is obviously easier to prove a civil case than a criminal case, and for good reason (see Figure 10.1 on page 226). Criminal convictions can result in depriving persons of their liberty. This has always been considered to be far more serious than requiring them to pay damages in a civil action. While the odds are high that the plaintiff will succeed in tort if the defendant has already been convicted under criminal

PART THREE

---

11. Note that, in Ontario, for example, victims of crime also have access to a fund that allows some compensation for their loss or suffering: *Compensation for Victims of Crime Act*, RSO 1990, c C-24. In Ontario there is also the *Victims' Bill of Rights*, 1995, SO 1995, c 6 and the *Prohibiting Profiting from Recounting Crimes Act*, SO 2002, c 2.
12. Private prosecutions—that is, those brought by the victim or anyone else who is not an agent of the Crown—are uncommon but permissible. See Law Reform Commission of Canada, *Private Prosecutions*, Working Paper No. 52 (Ottawa: Law Reform Commission of Canada, 1986) at 51–59.
13. *R v Lifchus*, [1997] 3 SCR 320 at para 30.
14. *Ibid* at para 31.
15. *Ibid* at para 39. See too Arbour J's decision in *Rhee v Rhee*, [2001] 3 SCR 364 at para 20.

law, this is not a certainty since the definitions of the individual torts and crimes are not always exactly the same. However, some courts have agreed that evidence of a conviction for conduct constituting a crime is relevant to establishing the existence of a related tort.[16]

FIGURE 10.1
Differences between Civil and Criminal Actions

Type of action	Commencing the action	Proving the action	Outcome
Assault and battery as torts	Sam files a claim against Mike based on the torts of assault and battery.	Sam must prove his case on the balance of probabilities.	A court orders Mike to pay Sam compensation for his injuries.
Aggravated assault as a crime	The Crown prosecutes Mike based on section 268(1) of the *Criminal Code*.	The Crown must prove its case beyond a reasonable doubt.	A court orders Mike to be fined, imprisoned, or both.

In a case with similarities to the scenario involving Mike and Sam,[17] a bouncer was convicted of aggravated assault and sentenced to 18 months, to be served in the community, and prohibited from owning a gun for 10 years. In addition, he was ordered by the judge to

- perform 240 hours of community service
- speak to bouncers about their responsibilities
- take anger-management courses
- pay a $1000 victim surcharge

The victim started a civil action against all parties involved, including the bar. The case was settled out of court for an undisclosed amount. The victim was provided with what is known as a "structured settlement." He receives an annuity that provides him with annual, tax-free benefits.

Liability in Tort
Primary and Vicarious Liability

There are two kinds of liability in tort law: primary and vicarious. Primary liability arises due to one's own personal wrongdoing. Mike the bouncer, for example, has primary liability for the torts of assault and battery because he is the individual who actually attacked Sam. **Vicarious liability**, by way of contrast, arises due to the relationship that someone has to the person who actually commits the tort. For example, the doctrine of vicarious liability makes an employer liable for the torts committed by its employees acting in the ordinary course or scope of employment.

Vicarious liability
The liability that an employer has for the tortious acts of an employee committed in the ordinary course or scope of employment.

---

16. *Simpson v Geswein*, [1995] 6 WWR 233 (Man. Q.B.). For a further discussion of this point, including relevant statute law, see Klar, *supra* note 1 at 41.
17. "Judge wants bar bouncer training" *Canadian Press* (19 January 1997) (QL).

Traditionally regarded, an employee's wrongful conduct is within the ordinary course or scope of employment if it is

- authorized by the employer; or

- is an unauthorized mode of doing something that is, in fact, authorized by the employer

It can be particularly difficult to distinguish between an unauthorized "mode" of performing an authorized act that attracts liability and an entirely independent "act" that does not. This problem is illustrated in the application of vicarious liability to sexual assaults and other intentional, as opposed to negligent, acts committed by employees.[18] To provide further context, the Supreme Court of Canada states in *Blackwater v Plint*:

> Vicarious liability may be imposed where there is a significant connection between the conduct authorized by the employer … and the wrong. Having created or enhanced the risk of the wrongful conduct, it is appropriate that the employer or operator of the enterprise be held responsible, even though the wrongful act may be contrary to its desires. … The fact that wrongful acts may occur is a cost of business.[19]

Applying the law to the Business Law in Practice scenario, the court must decide whether there is a "significant connection" between the conduct authorized by the employer and the wrong committed by the employee to justify making the employer vicariously liable. Since there is, in fact, a strong relationship between Mike's job as a bouncer and his assault and battery of Sam, Bar-Fly will almost certainly be vicariously liable for Mike's tortious conduct. By way of contrast, if Mike assaulted a friend whom he had invited to the Bar-Fly—after hours and without his employer's permission—the doctrine of vicarious liability is unlikely to have any application. Though it may seem unfair to make an employer responsible for a tort committed by its employees, the doctrine of vicarious liability has been justified on the following basis:

- employers have the ability to control employees and therefore should be liable for the employee's conduct

- the person who benefits from a business enterprise (the employer) should bear the associated costs[20]

- innocent plaintiffs have a better chance of being compensated[21]

- the employer should be given an incentive to try to prevent torts from occurring in the first place[22]

Vicarious liability is discussed further in Chapter 20.

Liability and Joint Tort-Feasors

When a person is injured due to the tortious conduct of more than one person, those culpable are known as **joint tort-feasors**. For example, if Sam were attacked by Mike and another employee, Mike and his coworker would have joint liability for Sam's injuries.

Joint tort-feasors
Two or more persons whom a court has held to be jointly responsible for the plaintiff's loss or injuries.

---

18. See, for example, the Supreme Court of Canada's analysis in *Bazley v Curry*, [1999] 2 SCR 534.
19. *Blackwater v Plint*, [2005] 3 SCR 3 at para 20, per McLachlin CJ.
20. Klar, *supra* note 1 at 673.
21. *Ibid.*
22. *Ibid* at 674.

Legislation passed across Canada states that if the negligence of more than one person is responsible for the loss, the victim or plaintiff can sue any or all of them, with recovery apportioned between the joint tort-feasors according to their level of responsibility. Notwithstanding the apportionment of liability *between* the joint tort-feasors, the plaintiff can recover 100 percent of the judgment from any of those defendants whom a court has held to be jointly responsible for the loss or injuries.[23]

Liability and Contributory Negligence

Tort victims may be at least partially responsible for their own injuries. If the defendant successfully argues that the plaintiff was responsible for at least a part of the loss—that is, the defendant uses the defence of **contributory negligence**—the amount of damages that the plaintiff is awarded is reduced by the proportion for which the plaintiff is responsible. Contributory negligence is a common defence used in lawsuits involving car accidents. If the plaintiff was not wearing a seat belt at the time of the accident, the defendant may well be able to establish that the injuries sustained were worse than they otherwise would have been. The court will then go on to decrease the plaintiff's damages award in proportion to the plaintiff's degree of contributory negligence. For example, if the plaintiff's damages are set at $100 000 and the court finds the plaintiff to have been 20 percent contributorily negligent—that is, responsible for 20 percent of the loss—the plaintiff's damages award will be reduced to $80 000.

Contributory negligence
A defence claiming that the plaintiff is at least partially responsible for the harm that has occurred.

Damages in Tort
The Purpose of Damages

The primary goal of a tort remedy is to compensate the victim for loss caused by the defendant. Generally, this is a monetary judgment. Less common alternatives are equitable remedies, such as an injunction—a court order requiring or prohibiting certain conduct. An injunction would be ordered if money would not suffice—for example, in the case of a recurring trespass where there is little economic harm, but the plaintiff simply wants the trespasser to stop coming onto the land in question. Financial compensation means the defendant is ordered by the court to pay a sum of money to the successful plaintiff. Such a remedy has obvious limitations. For example, where the plaintiff has suffered serious physical injuries, how can money truly compensate someone for the permanent loss of health? However, in personal injury cases there are no ready alternatives to financial compensation such as in the trespass example above.

Workers' compensation legislation
Legislation that provides no-fault compensation for injured employees in lieu of their right to sue in tort.

BUSINESS AND LEGISLATION

Workers' Compensation

Although tort law remains primarily a common law matter, it has also been modified by statute law. **Workers' compensation legislation,** for example, provides monetary compensation to employees for work-related injuries and illnesses. At the same time, it prohibits the employee from suing the employer for any negligence that might have caused the problem. In this way, the statute takes away the employee's common law right to sue but provides compensation no matter who is at fault.

---

23. For example, *Negligence Act,* RSO 1990, c N-1; *Contributory Negligence Act,* RSNB 2011, c C-131; *Contributory Negligence Act,* RSNS 1989, c 95; *Negligence Act,* RSBC 1996, c 333.

Tort law compensates not only for physical injury or loss but also for mental pain and suffering and other forms of emotional distress. These latter areas are approached with more caution by the judiciary, but are compensable if proven through psychiatric and other expert evidence.

Because any award or out-of-court settlement is final, a plaintiff's lawyer will not usually settle or bring the case to court until the full extent of damages is known.

Pecuniary and Non-Pecuniary Damages

Under Canadian law, the losses for which damages are awarded are categorized as being either pecuniary (that is, monetary) or non-pecuniary.

Non-pecuniary damages—sometimes called general damages—are damages that are awarded to compensate the plaintiff for

- pain and suffering

- loss of enjoyment of life

- loss of life expectancy

Non-pecuniary damages
Compensation for pain and suffering, loss of enjoyment of life, and loss of life expectancy.

Because Mike's attack on Sam caused him severe spinal injuries, Sam undoubtedly has suffered a considerable amount of general damages. These damages are non-pecuniary in the sense that they are not out-of-pocket, monetary losses, but they are nonetheless both real and devastating. The quality of Sam's life has been seriously diminished due to a loss of mobility and independence. His life expectancy has likely been reduced. A judge will award damages based on these facts, as well as on expert testimony as to how badly Sam has been injured. The more serious and permanent the injury is, the higher the general damages will be. Courts have developed precedents to assist in this process, and the Supreme Court of Canada has set a clear upper limit on what can be awarded for general damages.[24]

Pecuniary damages fall into three main categories:

- cost of future care

- loss of future income

- special damages (out-of-pocket expenses)

Pecuniary damages
Compensation for out-of-pocket expenses, loss of future income, and cost of future care.

Cost of Future Care

A plaintiff like Sam is entitled to an award sufficient to provide him with all the care and assistance his injury will necessitate. This can include the cost of a personal care attendant for the rest of his life, modifications to his living accommodations to increase accessibility, and the costs related to equipment and treatment of his condition. As in other areas of damages, what the plaintiff is ultimately awarded will be based on the testimony of experts, including occupation, rehabilitation, and medical experts.

---

24. *Andrews v Grand & Toy Alberta Ltd*, [1978] 2 SCR 299; *Arnold v Teno*, [1978] 2 SCR 287; and *Thornton v School Dist No 57 Bd of School Trustees*, [1978] 2 SCR 267. In *Andrews*, the Supreme Court of Canada placed a ceiling on recovery for general pain and suffering at $100 000. In 2011 dollars, this amounts to approximately $352 000.

PART THREE

Loss of Future Income

A judge will value the plaintiff's diminished earning capacity resulting from the injury. This calculation can be complex, involving the input of vocational experts, labour economists, accountants, and actuaries. Since Sam has suffered a serious injury as a result of Mike's attack and he is a young person, his loss of future income will likely be considerable.

Special Damages

These relate to out-of-pocket expenses resulting from the injury-causing event. These expenses may include any number of items, including ambulance costs, medication costs, housekeeping, and yard work. Sam should keep records and receipts of such costs and expenses in order to prove them in court. In some provinces medical costs must be claimed as special damages, although these will be repaid to the provincial health insurer under the insurance principle of subrogation.[25]

Dennis Schulz was catastrophically injured at a Bon Jovi concert. Schulz alleges that several people started fighting in the stands and one of them ended up falling on him from above, breaking his neck and resulting in quadriplegia. What kinds of damages should Schulz seek and why?[26]

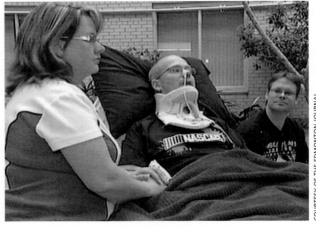

COURTESY OF THE EDMONTON JOURNAL

Punitive or Exemplary Damages

Punitive damages
An award to the plaintiff to punish the defendant for malicious, oppressive, and high-handed conduct.

Punitive damages—also known as exemplary damages—are an exception to the general rule that damages are intended only to compensate the plaintiff. Punitive damages are awarded to punish the defendant for malicious, oppressive, and high-handed conduct or where the defendant might otherwise profit from the behaviour.[27] If, for example, the bouncer or the bar refused to call an ambulance for the seriously injured Sam, punitive damages would almost certainly be awarded. The court would seek to punish such offensive conduct.

---

25. It is beyond the scope of this text to discuss the law governing health care expense subrogation.
26. Based on Ryan Cormier, "Man seeks $13M for injuries at Bon Jovi concert", *The Edmonton Journal* (23 November 2007) at B7.
27. *Supra* note 1 at 122.

BUSINESS APPLICATION OF THE LAW

Punitive Damages in the United States and Canada

The Canadian Press regularly reports instances of high punitive awards given by American juries to sympathetic plaintiffs in the United States. Most famously, Stella Liebeck of Albuquerque, New Mexico, was awarded nearly $3 million in punitive damages against McDonald's when she suffered serious burns upon opening a cup of coffee that she had placed between her legs. Due to severe scalding, she remained hospitalized for eight days. According to *The New York Times*, the jury was influenced by McDonald's knowledge that at least 700 of its customers had also been burned. *The Times* also reports what is less commonly known, namely that the plaintiff was found 20 percent contributorily negligent and that an out-of-court settlement reduced her damages award significantly.[28]

Jury trials are much less common in Canada than they are in the United States. This is at least one factor that keeps punitive damages lower, since judges may be less easily influenced to make large awards than members of the public who compose juries. Second, the spectre of "uncontrolled and uncontrollable awards of punitive damages in civil actions"[29] is a matter that the Supreme Court of Canada guards against by insisting on "proportionality" as the measure for punitive damages. Any punitive award must be rationally related to and be no more than necessary to punish the defendant, deter wrongdoers, or convey denunciation of the defendant's conduct. Moreover, the court has insisted that punitive damages should be exceptional, leaving criminal law as the main venue of punishment.

Recently, the United States Supreme Court in *Exxon v Baker*[30] reviewed the history of punitive damages in the United States. At issue was the appropriate amount of punitive damages the plaintiffs should receive as a result of damage caused by an Exxon supertanker grounding on a reef and spilling millions of gallons of oil into Prince William Sound, Alaska. The plaintiffs were commercial fishers, seafood producers, and others who relied on Prince William Sound to make their livings. What made the circumstances of the accident particularly egregious was that the captain, who had a history of drinking problems, "inexplicably left the bridge, leaving a tricky course correction to unlicensed

Should the defendant's ability to pay be a consideration in the awarding of punitive damages?

subordinates."[31] Expert evidence indicated that the captain was legally impaired at the time of the accident. At trial, the jury awarded $5 billion in punitive damages against Exxon, which was lowered to $2.5 billion by the appeals court. The U.S. Supreme Court lowered that amount even further, based on its view that punitive damages, in federal maritime law, should be limited to the same amount as the compensatory damages. Compensatory damages in this case were set at $507.5 million, and therefore an equivalent amount was awarded by way of punitive damages. In bolstering its analysis, the U.S. Supreme Court noted that some states have regulated punitive damages by legislation, such as, for example, limiting them to a 3:1 ratio of punitive damages to compensatory damages,[32] with Nebraska going so far as to ban punitive awards altogether.[33] The Supreme Court's view was that, contrary to myth, there have been no "mass-produced runaway awards" in the United States.[34] However, the court acknowledged that "punitive damages overall are higher and more frequent in the U.S. than anywhere else"[35] and, more importantly, expressed concern about the "stark

(Continued)

---

28. Anthony Ramirez, "For McDonald's, British justice is a different cup of tea", *The New York Times* (7 April 2002) at 7. In *Bogle v McDonald's Restaurants Ltd*, [2002] EWHC 490 (QB), an English court was much less sympathetic to a similar claim by plaintiffs who had been burnt by hot beverages at McDonald's outlets in the United Kingdom. According to that judge, "Persons generally expect tea or coffee purchased to be consumed on the premises to be hot. ... Persons generally know that if a hot drink is spilled onto someone, a serious scalding injury can result. ... [T]he allegations ... that McDonald's are legally liable for these unfortunate injuries have not been made out".
29. *Whiten v Pilot Insurance Co* (2002), 209 DLR (4th) 257 (SCC). This case is summarized in Chapter 28.
30. 554 US (2008).
31. *Ibid* at 1 per headnote summary.
32. *Ibid* at 37.
33. *Ibid* at 21.
34. *Ibid* at 24.
35. *Ibid* at 22.

unpredictability of punitive awards"[36] in the United States. Setting a 1:1 ratio would alleviate that problem. The court was fortified in its selection of a 1:1 ratio by studies indicating that most awards of punitive damages put the median ratio at less than 1:1. In the court's words, "we consider that a 1:1 ratio, which is above the median award, is a fair upper limit in such maritime cases."[37]

Critical Analysis: Do you think that Canada should follow the approach taken by the U.S. Supreme Court or do you prefer the flexibility of the Canadian approach? Would it be a good idea just to set a fixed dollar amount as a maximum and not worry about ratios or word descriptors?

How can businesses avoid being ordered to pay punitive damages?

Aggravated Damages

Aggravated damages
Compensation for intangible injuries such as distress and humiliation caused by the defendant's reprehensible conduct.

Aggravated damages compensate the plaintiff for intangible injuries such as distress and humiliation caused by the defendant's reprehensible conduct.[38] For example, when store detectives unlawfully restrain a customer, they have committed the tort of false imprisonment. If, in restraining the customer, they treat the person in a humiliating or degrading fashion, a court may well award aggravated damages to compensate the plaintiff for the mental distress the whole experience caused.

Tort Law and Contract

Sometimes the same set of facts can give rise to liability in tort and in contract. For example, when Mike attacked Sam, he committed a tort. Mike's tortious conduct is attributed to his employer by way of vicarious liability and, by that same fact, *also* places Bar-Fly in breach of its contract with Sam. That is, it would be an implied term in the contract for the purchase of beverages that Bar-Fly would provide a reasonably safe environment for their consumption. When Sam was attacked by Mike the bouncer, this term was breached.

Overlapping liability in contract and tort is also common when a professional—such as an accountant, lawyer, or banker—gives advice to a client. If that advice is incompetent, the professional is in breach of contract *and* has committed the tort of negligence. This matter is explored further in Chapters 11 and 22.

Managing Tort Risk

Chapters 3 and 4 discussed extensively the issues of risk management and dispute resolution. Businesses are exposed to a wide variety of risks related to tort actions, particularly in the area of negligence. In addition, they are vulnerable because of the doctrine of vicarious liability.

---

36. *Ibid at* 26.
37. *Ibid at* 40.
38. *Vorvis v Insurance Corporation of British Columbia,* [1989] 1 SCR 1085.

No business can eliminate all risk. It must, however, assume active measures to minimize it. This is because ignoring tort risk can result in

- incurring the costs of a tort that could have been avoided, including lawyers' fees, management time devoted to defending the claim, and the amount of the actual judgment awarded to the successful plaintiff

- losing insurance coverage because of a poor claims history

- losing a hard-earned business reputation

Risk management strategies that business operations such as Bar-Fly might deploy are set out in Business Law in Practice Revisited.

Business Law in Practice Revisited

1. What kind of tort action does Sam's friend have as a result of breaking his arm?
Sam's friend has an action in negligence against Bar-Fly for failing to take reasonable steps to ensure that the washroom floor was free of hazards. He likely also has an action for breach of contract due to this same failure.

2. What potential legal actions result from the altercation between Sam and Mike?
Mike could be prosecuted for a criminal offence, perhaps that of aggravated assault. If successful this could lead to a fine, imprisonment, or both. Mike can also be sued by Sam, who will be seeking compensation by way of civil action—here a complaint based on the torts of assault and battery—for the damages he has suffered.

3. Is Bar-Fly responsible for Mike's actions?
Sam will claim that Bar-Fly is responsible for Mike's actions based on the principle of vicarious liability. Since Mike is an employee of Bar-Fly and it appears that there is a significant connection between Mike's job and the tort he committed, Bar-Fly will probably be responsible for Mike's tortious actions.

4. What risk management actions could Bar-Fly have taken to prevent this altercation and the fall in the men's room?
Bar-Fly's risk of liability in tort can be reduced through a risk management plan. Possibilities include

- reducing risk by hiring employees with care and instituting training programs to help them perform their jobs well. Employees should be hired for their good judgment and interpersonal skills and not simply their brawn. They should be instructed as to both the parameters of acceptable behaviour and how to address patrons. Employees should learn what they are entitled to do and when they have to call in the police, as much for their own safety as for that of patrons. It may be appropriate to have employees working in pairs to ensure they have backup and are able to monitor each other's behaviour and well-being.

- reducing risk by setting up a system of checks so that floor surfaces in the bar remain free of hazards.

- transferring risk by purchasing insurance to cover the business' liability to patrons who are injured on its premises.

Chapter Summary

Tort law has a significant impact on business enterprises, particularly in the area of negligence. Tort law permits someone who has been injured or suffered a loss to sue the responsible person for damages. The objective of a damages award is to compensate the plaintiff, though punitive damages are sometimes available if the defendant's conduct has been particularly egregious. Aggravated damages are also available to compensate the person who suffers intangible injuries such as distress or humiliation caused by the defendant's reprehensible conduct. Less commonly, the injured party will seek an injunction or other form of equitable remedy, as in a trespass-to-land scenario.

Criminal law also affects a business, though to a lesser degree. As the purpose of a criminal law is to punish the offender—through fines and imprisonment—distinct procedures are in place to help ensure that only guilty people are convicted. For example, in a criminal prosecution the Crown must prove its case beyond a reasonable doubt. By way of contrast, the plaintiff in a tort action need only demonstrate his case on the balance of probabilities.

Liability in tort can be primary and vicarious. Primary liability arises due to one's own personal wrongdoing. Vicarious liability arises due to the relationship one has with the actual tort-feasor, as in an employer–employee context. Since a business may have several employees, its exposure in this area can be considerable.

When a person is injured due to the tortious conduct of more than one person, those culpable are known as joint tort-feasors. A court can apportion liability between them, but the victim or plaintiff can recover 100 percent of the judgment from any one of them.

When a tort victim is at least partially responsible for his own injuries, he has been contributorily negligent. The amount that the plaintiff is awarded will be reduced by the proportion for which he is responsible.

Sometimes, the same set of facts can give rise to liability in tort and in contract, particularly in the context of a professional advice giver such as a lawyer or an accountant.

The best response a business can have to its potential liability in tort is to establish a risk management plan that reduces, eliminates, or transfers risk.

Chapter Study

Key Terms and Concepts

aggravated damages (p. 232)

assault (p. 224)

battery (p. 224)

contributory negligence (p. 228)

deceit or fraud (p. 221)

intentional tort (p. 224)

joint tort-feasors (p. 227)

negligence (p. 221)

non-pecuniary damages (p. 229)

pecuniary damages (p. 229)

punitive damages (p. 230)

tort (p. 221)

tort-feasor (p. 222)

trespass to land (p. 221)

vicarious liability (p. 226)

workers' compensation legislation (p. 228)

Questions for Review

1. What does the term "tort" mean?

2. Give an example of a tort.

3. What are the two main categories into which torts are organized?

4. What is the difference between the tort of assault and the tort of battery?

5. The goals of tort and criminal law are quite distinct, even when they stem from the same event. Explain the differences.

6. What is a joint tort-feasor?

7. What does burden of proof mean?

8. How does the burden of proof differ between a criminal case and a tort action?

9. What is the difference in the way tort and criminal actions are initiated?

10. What is the purpose of damages in tort?

11. Under what circumstances might an injunction be awarded in tort?

12. Vicarious liability is an essential feature of modern tort law. What is it?

13. What might be a defence to a claim for vicarious liability?

14. How does contributory negligence affect the amount of damages a plaintiff may receive?

15. Explain the difference between pecuniary and non-pecuniary damages.

16. How are pecuniary damages typically calculated?

17. What are punitive damages? How are they different from aggravated damages?

18. When is overlapping liability in tort and contract common?

Questions for Critical Thinking

1. What are the justifications for the basic legal principle that the standard of proof is higher in a criminal matter than in a civil one?

2. Punitive damages are somewhat controversial even in jurisdictions where they are relatively common. At the same time, there are circumstances in which a person's tortious actions have been particularly callous and calculating, yet the actual loss suffered by the plaintiff is not extensive in monetary terms. In these latter cases, what are the compelling reasons for allowing the plaintiff additional recovery over and above the actual loss? Should the compensation principle of tort law be compromised in this way?

3. The concept of vicarious liability developed in the business world, where the company is out to make a profit and its activities are for the most part directed to generating profit. Is it appropriate to apply a test developed in this context to a charitable organization? What are the pros and cons for holding organizations liable for the conduct of their employees?

4. Does the idea of contributory negligence reflect the major aims and purposes of tort law? Does it make sense to reduce the amount of damages available to a plaintiff, when he may not have suffered the loss to the same extent, or at all, but for the negligence of someone else?

5. Without permission, Angela borrows Jacob's car. Has Angela committed a crime? Do you think that her conduct might be tortious as well?

6. Aggravated damages compensate the plaintiff for distress and humiliation. Do you think this opens tort law to abuse by plaintiffs who may misrepresent or exaggerate how the defendant's conduct made them feel?

Situations for Discussion

1. It was Susan's turn to drive her three classmates to university, this time for the final exam in the business law course. Unfortunately she had left home late, and by the time she had picked up everyone else, they were in serious danger of arriving at least 10 minutes after the exam began. The weather was not good and the roads were obviously slippery—there were cars off to the side of the road in a number of locations. Susan's friends urged her to speed up, which she did, although as a relatively inexperienced driver she was uncomfortable handling the car under these conditions. As she approached a major intersection, the light turned amber and Susan braked. When the car began to slide, Susan instinctively braked harder, causing the car to go out of control and enter the intersection, where it slid straight into the path of a car proceeding on a green light from the cross street. In the subsequent collision, one of the passengers in Susan's car, Jean-Guy, was seriously injured.

   The police arrived and, after investigating the case, charged Susan with dangerous driving under the *Criminal Code*. In time it became clear that Jean-Guy's injuries had resulted not only in short-term harm—for example, because he could not sit his exam, he fell behind one term in his program—but also in permanent damage. In particular, his right arm and wrist were shattered and, being right-handed, he has and will continue to have limited manual dexterity. He was planning a career in IT and finds that these injuries severely affect his ability to perform basic tasks. For which categories of damages will Jean-Guy seek compensation?

2. Discuss the relationship between criminal and civil law in relation to Situation 1. How will each case be proven and by whom?

3. Reginald Smith, an employee of UR Safe Ltd., a security company, broke into a branch of a bank that was a customer of UR Safe Ltd. Smith did so when he was not on shift with UR Safe Ltd., and by using keys he had stolen from his employer. Using these keys, Smith gained access to the ATM room in the bank, but could not figure out how to open the ATM combination lock. He was close to giving up when he noticed that the bank kept an ATM instruction manual on a shelf right beside the ATM in the ATM room. Smith read the manual and on that basis was able to open the safe. Is UR Safe Ltd. vicariously liable for Smith's tortious conduct?[39]

4. Albert was walking home from his nightshift at 3:30 a.m. The road was very dark, and Albert was wearing a red jacket, blue pants, black shoes, and a green cap. Albert walked along the edge of the road but on the wrong side, such that his back was to oncoming traffic. Albert heard a vehicle approaching behind him but decided not to look or even move. Unfortunately, Albert was hit by the vehicle, a delivery van; the driver was taking newspapers to a local drop-off point so that carriers could then deliver them to homes on their routes. Albert was seriously injured.

   Albert has two witnesses. The first is a police officer who arrived on the scene and administered a breathalyzer test to the van driver. The van driver was not impaired. Albert's second witness is an individual who lives in a house directly across the road from the accident scene. This witness heard the impact of the accident and ran outside to help. This witness' evidence only related to the position of the plaintiff's body and the location of the defendant's delivery van.

   Will Albert be able to establish negligence as against the driver of the van? Why or why not?[40]

5. The plaintiff hired the defendant to renovate the wooden wharf that the plaintiff owned in British Columbia. The wharf was part of the plaintiff's grain-loading facility in Vancouver Harbour. During this renovation process, the wharf was seriously damaged by fire. The fire was started by molten slag from an oxy-acetylene torch operated by the defendant's employee. The defendant's employee did not minimize the fire hazard created by the torch. Among other deficiencies, the defendant's employees failed to wet the combustible surfaces before using the torch and failed to keep

---

39. Based, in part on *Royal Bank of Canada v Intercon Security Ltd* (2005), 143 ACWS (3d) 608 (Ont SJ).
40. Based on *Anderson v Short* (1986), 62 Nfld & PEIR 232 (Nfld. S.C. T.D.).

a proper fire watch during cutting operations so that any slag that landed could then be doused with water. When it came time to fight the fire, the defendant's employee ran into difficulties because the plaintiff had not provided a fire protection system anywhere near the wharf in question, not even a fire extinguisher. The plaintiff claims damages in the amount of $1 million. Assuming that the defendant's employee has been negligent in how he used the torch, what would a possible defence of the defendant be? Should the plaintiff recover all its damages or only a portion thereof? Is the defendant responsible for the tort of its employee? Why or why not?[41]

6. Louise arrived for a two week vacation at a Mexican resort. She spent the day at the beach and, upon returning to her room, found a bottle in the fridge containing a clear liquid. Louise assumed the liquid was water and started to drink from the bottle. It turns out that a member of the cleaning staff had inadvertently a bottle of caustic cleaning solution in the fridge in Louise's room and this is what Louise had drunk. Louise suffered extensive injury and required emergency surgery to remove some of her esophagus. Louise wants to sue the cleaning staff member who had left cleaning solution in Louise's fridge. Will this action be successful? Does the cleaning staff member have any defences?[42]

For more study tools, visit http://www.NELSONbrain.com.

---

41. Based, in part, on *Alberta Wheat Pool v Northwest Pile Driving Ltd* (1998), 80 ACWS (3d) 692. (B.C.S.C.), reversed in part (2000), 80 BCLR (3d) 153 (CA).
42. Based on news story by Elise Stolte, "Woman sues Mexican resort over caustic cleaning fluid left in fridge", *Edmonton Journal* (20 February 2011) at A5.

PART THREE

CHAPTER 11

The Tort of Negligence

Objectives

After studying this chapter, you should have an understanding of

- the conduct that the law of negligence addresses

- the principles of the law of negligence

- the defences in a negligence action

- the common kinds of negligence actions that businesses face

- the difference between negligence and strict liability

Business Law in Practice

Meat Products Ltd. ("Meat") is an Ontario-based food-processing and distribution company. It supplies deli meat and related products throughout Canada and parts of the United States. It seems that several consumers have recently died or been sickened as a result of consuming products manufactured by Meat. A bacteria known as *Listeria monocytogenes* has somehow infected meat processed there.

The CEO quickly instituted a recall of all Meat products, closed the production plant, and ordered that it be tested for Listeria. This was a crucial step, since technicians found *Listeria* deep inside the machinery of several meat-slicing machines. These germs somehow survived the company's cleaning and sanitizing protocols.

The CEO's worst fears were confirmed when tests demonstrated that several of Meat's products had tested positive for *Listeria monocytogenes*.

Prior to the recall, Jennifer Jones consumed a deli product made by Meat and became seriously ill with listeriosis. Jennifer missed several months of work, and as soon as she felt better, she spoke to a lawyer. As a result, Meat has now been made the subject of a class action. The firm Jennifer contacted is acting on her behalf as well as on behalf of other members of that class of persons who contracted listeriosis after having consumed contaminated food produced by Meat. The claim for damages is in the amount of $100 million.[1]

1. What tort may Meat have committed and what do the plaintiffs have to prove in order to establish that tort?
2. What defences does Meat have to this action?
3. What additional risks does a class action create for Meat?
4. How could Meat have better managed its risk of tort liability in this case?

1. Based, in part, on press accounts of the *Listeria* outbreak at Maple Leaf Foods Inc's Bartor Road plant. For stories on point, see CBC News Staff, "Class action lawsuit launched over listeria outbreak", *CBC News Canada* (26 August 2008) online: CBC News< http://www.cbc.ca/news/canada/british-columbia/story/2008/08/26/bc-listeria-class-action-lawsuit.html>; CBC News Staff, "$27 M settlement reached in Maple Leaf listeriosis suits", *CBC News Canada* (2 February 2009) online: CBC News <http://www.cbc.ca/news/story/2009/02/02/maple.html>.

DAVID BUFFINGTON/PHOTODISC

The Law of Negligence

What Is Negligence?

Chapter 10 defined the tort of negligence as a careless act that causes harm to another. The law understands carelessness as a failure to show **reasonable care**, that is, the care that a reasonable person would have shown in a similar situation.

Negligence is a very common tort action in the commercial world because it covers a broad range of harmful conduct. For example, a negligence action can be brought by someone

- who has been injured by the dangerous driving of a delivery truck driver

- who has suffered loss by relying on poor advice provided by an accountant, lawyer, architect, or engineer

- whose furniture has been damaged in transit by a moving company

The plaintiff need not show that the defendant intended to cause the damage or that there were deliberate acts that gave rise to the damage. Instead, the tort of negligence makes the defendant liable for failing to act reasonably—for driving too fast, for giving unprofessional advice, or for not taking proper care of furniture entrusted to it.

In the Business Law in Practice scenario above, the class action plaintiff, Jennifer, can only succeed in her action in negligence against Meat if she can show that Meat failed to use reasonable care in the manufacture of the meat product she consumed and that it caused her illness.

Negligence law—like tort law in general—seeks to compensate victims for their loss or injury. It provides this compensation after applying rules that determine who is liable to compensate another, on what basis, and for how much. Without such limiting rules, business and professional people might be reluctant to produce goods and services because the risk of liability in negligence would be unknowable. Those goods and services that did reach the market would be relatively more expensive since the price would need to reflect the increased risk flowing from widespread liability.

With these kinds of factors in mind, the courts have the task of balancing competing interests. They must compensate victims of negligence, but without discouraging legitimate activity and without making the legal standards a business must meet unreasonably exacting.

Steps to a Negligence Action

The rules that govern when a plaintiff like Jennifer will succeed in a negligence action are set out in a series of classic steps, as summarized in Figure 11.1.

The steps in a tort action, by design, lack a certain specificity. Their purpose is to describe general standards or markers that help a court assess whether the defendant in any given case has been negligent.

Reasonable care
The care a reasonable person would exhibit in a similar situation.

PART THREE

FIGURE 11.1

Steps to Negligence Action

Step 1: Does the defendant owe the plaintiff a duty of care? If yes, proceed to the next step.

Step 2: Did the defendant breach the standard of care? If yes, proceed to the next step.

Step 3: Did the defendant's careless act (or omission) cause the plaintiff's injury? If yes, proceed to the next step.

Step 4: Was the injury suffered by the plaintiff too remote? If not, the plaintiff has proven negligence.

Duty of care
The responsibility owed to avoid carelessness that causes harm to others.

Neighbour
Anyone who might reasonably be affected by the defendant's conduct.

Step 1: Does the Defendant Owe the Plaintiff a Duty of Care?

The defendant Meat will be liable to Jennifer if it owes Jennifer what is known in law as a **duty of care**. A defendant owes a duty of care to anyone who might reasonably be affected by the defendant's conduct. This is known as the **neighbour** principle, as formulated by the House of Lords in the classic case of *Donoghue v Stevenson* just below.

LANDMARK CASE | *Donoghue v Stevenson* [1932] AC 562 (HL)

THE BUSINESS CONTEXT: Before large-scale production, most goods were sold directly from producer/artisan to consumer. By the 20th century, a multistage distribution chain was the norm, comprising several distinct transactions or contracts—from manufacturer, to supplier, to retailer, to the ultimate consumer.

FACTUAL BACKGROUND: A customer bought some ice cream and an opaque bottle of ginger beer for her friend, Donoghue. Some of the ginger beer was poured over the ice cream and some was drunk by Donoghue. When the remainder of the beer was being poured into a tumbler, a decomposed snail was discovered in the contents. Donoghue became ill and subsequently sued the manufacturer for damages, based on negligence.

THE LEGAL QUESTION: At this time, the extent of the manufacturer's duty of care was severely constricted: the manufacturer was responsible only to those with whom it had a contractual arrangement. Most consumer "victims" were prevented by this limited responsibility from recovering from the manufacturer. There was almost certainly a retailer in the transaction and no direct contractual relationship between the manufacturer and consumer.

RESOLUTION: Lord Atkin, for the majority, wrote the following classic statement when discussing how to determine to whom a duty of care is owed in negligence:

> The rule that you are to love your neighbour becomes in law, you must not injure your neighbour, and the lawyer's question, Who is my neighbour? receives a restricted reply. You must take reasonable care to avoid acts or omissions which you can reasonably foresee would be likely to injure your neighbour. Who, then, in law, is my neighbour? The answer seems to be—persons who are so closely and directly affected by my act that I ought reasonably to have them in contemplation as being so affected when I am directing my mind to the acts or omissions which are called in question.

CRITICAL ANALYSIS: Is it reasonable to make manufacturers liable for their products to end users? Would it be enough, simply, to make the retailer liable for breach of contract and leave the manufacturer out of the equation?

Since *Donoghue*, courts have continued to refine the test for whether a duty of care is owed. As formulated by the Supreme Court of Canada, a court must first ask whether the case at bar presents a novel situation or not. If the case is comparable to an already-decided case in which a duty of care was recognized, the first stage described below can be skipped and the plaintiff can proceed directly to the second stage. If the case at issue is novel, then the court is required to assess the issue of duty in the following way:[2]

Stage 1   Is there a ***prima facie*** duty of care? In order to answer this larger question, the court must consider several smaller ones, namely:

Prima facie
At first sight or on first appearances.

    a. *Is the harm that occurred a reasonably foreseeable consequence of the defendant's act?* Reasonable foreseeability considers whether the defendant should objectively have anticipated that his or her act or omission would cause harm to the plaintiff.

If the answer to this question of reasonable foreseeability is yes, proceed to the next question.

    b. *Is there a relationship of sufficient proximity between the parties such that it would not be unjust or unfair to impose a duty of care on the defendant?* Proximity considers whether the specific circumstances of the parties' relationship are such that the defendant is under an obligation to be mindful of the plaintiff's "legitimate interests" in conducting his or her affairs.

If the answer to this question is yes, proceed to Stage 2.

Stage 2   Are there residual policy considerations outside the relationship of the parties that may negate the imposition of a duty of care? This stage of the inquiry no longer considers the relationship between the parties but asks the question more generally, to determine whether imposing a duty in these kinds of circumstances "would ... [be] unwise."[3]

There is no doubt that a business like Meat owes a duty of care to the consumer.[4] Under Stage 1, it is reasonably foreseeable that careless acts or omissions by a manufacturer of food products could cause harm to the consumer due to food contamination, including contamination by *Listeria*. It is also clear that the relationship between the manufacturer and the end user is a relationship of sufficient proximity to establish a duty of care. There is nothing in the specific relationship between Meat and the plaintiff-consumers to negate or reduce that duty.

On this basis, a *prima facie* duty of care is established. Under Stage 2, it is necessary to determine whether there are any more general considerations that ought to eliminate or reduce that duty. The objective of this is to ensure that businesses and other defendants are not made liable to an unreasonably broad, unknowable, and indeterminate extent. In practice, considerations that eliminate or reduce a defendant's duty of care are more likely to arise in the area of pure economic loss—such as loss of profit—than in cases of physical harm such as Jennifer has suffered. Concerns regarding economic loss recovery are prevalent in the context of negligent misstatement, a tort that is discussed later in this chapter.

In Meat's case, a judge would almost certainly not find any reason under Stage 2 that would eliminate or reduce Meat's duty of care to consumers. This conclusion flows from the nature of Meat's business—manufacturers like Meat want people like Jennifer

---

2. The approach is based, in part, on *Odhavji Estate v Woodhouse*, 2003 SCC 69 at paras 47–51.
3. *Ibid.* at para 51.
4. See, for example, *376599 Alberta Inc v Tanshaw Products Inc*, 2005 ABQB 300 at para 146.

to purchase its product. If consumers are sickened or even die as a result of the product being contaminated, what possible reason could there be to suggest that Meat should not owe a duty of care to them? Though Meat stands to be liable to a great number of consumers, this is the nature of its chosen business and the fact that its product is intended to reach a large number of the public. Furthermore, the class of those who could successfully sue Meat will be composed of those who have consumed product from the contaminated plant only and hence is not an unlimited or indeterminate class.

Having established that Meat owes a duty of care to the ultimate consumer of its product, it is necessary to move to the next steps in establishing a successful action in negligence.

Step 2: Did the Defendant Breach the Standard of Care?

Reasonable person
The standard used to judge whether a person's conduct in a particular situation is negligent.

In general, the defendant's conduct is judged according to the standards of behaviour that would be observed by the reasonable person in society. In law, a **reasonable person** is regarded as being an ordinary person of normal intelligence who uses ordinary prudence to guide his conduct. The law does not demand that the reasonable person be perfect.

Where the defendant exercises specialized skills, the standard of the reasonable person described above is not applied. Professionals such as doctors, accountants, engineers, and lawyers must meet a higher or specialized standard of care because the level of expertise of the average member of society is simply inadequate as a measure of competence. In cases involving specialized tasks, courts introduce the standard of the "reasonable" person with that specialized training—the reasonable electronics engineer, or the reasonable heart surgeon, for example. To determine just what the standard is on the facts before it, the court will hear from expert witnesses who, in turn, will present evidence of what that standard is.

Where the activity or product poses a high risk, the law imposes a higher standard of care. The policy reason for this higher standard is to encourage competence and caution in light of the very serious harm that could result if the task were poorly performed.

In assessing whether Meat breached its duty of care, a court will apply a higher standard because of the dire consequences should Meat's products be contaminated and the specialized knowledge that goes into their production. Of crucial relevance would be how sanitation at the defendant's plant measured up to standards in the industry and whether there were any failures in Meat's hygiene protocol. Practically speaking, Meat will be held to a very high standard given the nature of their products and the tremendous amount of harm those products might cause were something to go wrong in the manufacturing process.

Causation
The relationship that exists between the defendant's conduct and the plaintiff's loss or injury.

Step 3: Did the Defendant's Careless Act (or Omission) Cause the Plaintiff's Injury?

While the legal test for **causation** is sometimes debated, courts generally ask the following question: Would the harm not have occurred *but for* the defendant's actions?[5]

---

5. Lewis Klar, *Tort Law*, 5th ed (Toronto: Thomson Carswell, 2012) at 448. See, too, *Clements v Clements* 2012 SCC 32.

Whether any failure by Meat to use reasonable care in the production process caused Jennifer and others in the plaintiff class to sicken and even die is a matter to be established through expert evidence. Given that *Listeria* was found in Meat's premises and in its some of its products, including the kind consumed by Jennifer, causation appears to be in place.

CASE   *Kauffman v Toronto Transit Commission* [1960] SCR 251

THE BUSINESS CONTEXT: Even when a customer is injured on business premises, it may be that the injury was not caused by a negligent act or omission by the business itself but occurred for other reasons. If so, the business would have a complete defence to any claim brought against it by the injured party.

FACTUAL BACKGROUND: Mrs. Kauffman was riding up the escalator owned by the Toronto Transit Commission (TTC). The escalator was equipped with a metal-clad handrail instead of the rubber type, which presumably would have been less slippery. Several youths, riding the same escalator just above Kauffman, began pushing each other around. They ultimately fell on Kauffman, knocking her over and severely injuring her. Kauffman sued the TTC for damages, claiming that it had been negligent in installing an untested handrail made of metal. Furthermore, she argued that the defendant had failed to supply proper supervision of those using the escalators and was therefore liable.

THE LEGAL QUESTION: Did the TTC cause Kauffman's loss?

RESOLUTION: The Supreme Court of Canada ruled that the TTC did not cause the loss suffered by Kauffman. The cause of the fall was the wrongful and grossly negligent conduct of the youths who fell on her. The nature of the grip on the handrail—though not as effective as a rubber grip—did not contribute to the accident. As one of the judges observed,

> It is impossible to seriously suggest that when the weight of three men amounting to approximately 450 lbs. was projected suddenly from above against this elderly lady she would not have fallen backwards, whatever the nature of the grip on the handrail.

Furthermore, the court determined that the defendant did not owe a duty to supply supervision of those using the escalator. While it was required to use all due, proper, and

What steps could the owner of the escalator take to reduce accidents?

reasonable care, it was not an insurer of the safety of those using the escalators.

CRITICAL ANALYSIS: Do you agree with the court's analysis? Should not a business be liable whenever one of its customers is hurt?

DICK HEMINGWAY

Step 4: Was the Injury Suffered by the Plaintiff Too Remote?

At this point in the test for negligence, a court asks, "Even if there is an obligation to take reasonable care and it was breached, how far will the legal liability of the defendant stretch?"[6] The idea is that there must be some limit on the defendant's responsibility for the consequences of his negligence.

---

6. *Ibid* at 487.

PART THREE

Jennifer was sickened by listeriosis due to bacterial contamination in the meat she consumed. This injury is not too remote and is clearly a reasonably foreseeable consequence of Meat's negligence.

By way of contrast, consider the following case, where the concept of **remoteness of damage**—that is, the absence of a sufficiently close relationship between the defendant's action and the plaintiff's loss—is illustrated.

Remoteness of damage
The absence of a sufficiently close relationship between the defendant's action and the plaintiff's injury.

CASE   *Spagnolo v Margesson's Sports Ltd* (1983), 145 DLR (3d) 381 (Ont CA)

THE BUSINESS CONTEXT: A business owner's negligence can have very broad consequences in that not just immediate customers may suffer loss or injury.

FACTUAL BACKGROUND: A customer's car was stolen from a parking lot due to the negligence of the parking lot owner in keeping the keys safely secured. Six days later, the thief was in an accident with the plaintiff while driving the stolen car.

THE LEGAL QUESTION: Is the parking lot owner responsible for the plaintiff's injury, or is the loss too remote?

RESOLUTION: The court held that damage to the plaintiff was not a reasonably foreseeable consequence of the parking lot owner's negligence, particularly given that the accident occurred so long after the theft. The court also noted that the term "reasonably foreseeable" lacks a precise meaning and that it contains "more policy than fact."

CRITICAL ANALYSIS: What if the plaintiff were injured as the thief was fleeing the parking lot in the stolen vehicle? Would this change the outcome?

In assessing Meat's responsibility, a court need only be satisfied that the injury Jennifer suffered was foreseeable. It is not necessary, in addition, to foresee the full extent of the injury of any given type.

The principle that only the type of the injury must be foreseeable also finds expression in the **thin skull rule**. This rule protects the plaintiff who has an inherent weakness or "thin skull" that makes a given injury more serious than one might otherwise reasonably anticipate. The rule states that such a plaintiff is still entitled to recovery for the full extent of the injury. For example, if Jennifer's recovery from listeriosis takes a longer period of time than would normally be anticipated because she has an impaired immune system, her damages will not be reduced for that reason. Though the condition impairing the immune system is reasonably rare, Meat cannot use this fact to escape liability to fully compensate Jennifer.

Thin skull rule
The principle that a defendant is liable for the full extent of a plaintiff's injury even where a prior vulnerability makes the harm more serious than it otherwise might be.

CASE   *Mustapha v Culligan of Canada Ltd* 2008 SCC 27

THE BUSINESS CONTEXT: Manufacturers and suppliers who provide a product to the consumer are responsible for the quality of that product. Even with the best quality-control measures in place, a defective product can slip through the system.

FACTUAL BACKGROUND: Mustapha was a customer of Culligan, a manufacturer and supplier of drinking water. Mustapha used Culligan's services because cleanliness and proper sanitation were tremendously important to him.

As Mustapha was replacing a large, empty water bottle with a new, unopened one, he noticed that the new bottle contained a dead fly. Mustapha became obsessed with the dead fly and its "revolting implications" for his family's health and well-being. At trial, Justice Brockenshire awarded $80 000 for Mustapha's emotional upset although he found the claim to be "objectively bizarre." He also awarded $237 600 for past and future economic loss. According to the trial judge, it was clearly foreseeable that supplying contaminated water would cause the plaintiff and others like him to suffer nervous shock. The Court of Appeal reversed the decision, and leave to appeal to the Supreme Court was granted.

THE LEGAL QUESTION: Was Mustapha's reaction a reasonably foreseeable consequence?

RESOLUTION: The Supreme Court of Canada agreed that Culligan owed a duty of care to Mustapha to provide clean water and that it breached the standard of care by supplying water containing a dead fly. As well, this breach was the factual cause of the serious psychological damages Mustapha suffered, which included a major depressive disorder. The problem with Mustapha's case was that his extreme reaction to a relatively insignificant event was not a reasonably foreseeable consequence of the fly incident. Only if mental injury would occur in a person of ordinary mental fortitude could recovery for such damages flow. Here, the plaintiff could not show that mental injury would occur in the ordinary person faced with a dead fly in an unopened bottle of water. On this basis, the plaintiff's action failed. Note that if mental injury would occur in a person of ordinary mental fortitude, then the thin skull rule applies and the defendant must take the plaintiff as it finds him. In such a case, even an extreme reaction would be compensable.

ROB GURDEBEKE/THE WINDSOR STAR

Mr. Mustapha, shown above, had his case litigated all the way to the Supreme Court of Canada.

CRITICAL ANALYSIS: Do you agree with the Supreme Court of Canada's resolution of this case? Do you think that Mustapha's action in contract might succeed even though the tort action failed?

Based on analysis in this chapter thus far, Jennifer should be entitled to recover for damages related to consuming Meat's contaminated product. This would include the right to recover loss of income during her convalescence and, if her ability to work in the future is compromised, the amount of lost future income attributable to her reduced ability. These damages are recoverable because Jennifer is entitled therefore to be put in the position she would have been in had the tort not occurred.

What tort law traditionally is reluctant to permit is recovery for **pure economic loss**, that is, loss that is only financial and involves no personal injury or property damage to the plaintiff. When a person not in a contractual relationship causes someone else to suffer a financial detriment only, such a loss is generally not recoverable. One explanation is that the rule prevents defendants from being overwhelmed with liability.[7] A related explanation is that to permit recovery of damages in such cases would cause too much litigation in the courts. It is only in a relatively few areas, such as negligent misstatement (discussed later in this chapter), that a plaintiff can recover for pure economic loss.

Pure economic loss
Financial loss that results from a negligent act where there has been no accompanying property or personal injury damage to the person claiming the loss.

---

7. For a general discussion of these points, see *ibid* at 230.

The law requires the plaintiff to prove *each and every step* in a negligence action. It is not enough to establish some of the steps or even most of them. In short, the plaintiff must show that the defendant owed a duty of care and breached the standard of care associated with that duty. Provided that the breach in question caused the plaintiff's loss and that the loss was not too remote, the plaintiff has won the negligence action.

TECHNOLOGY AND THE LAW

Business' Liability in Contract and Tort for the Consequences of Online Hacking

Companies regularly conduct their business online, acquiring consumers' personal information during transactions. However, they also run the risk of hackers stealing this highly sensitive data. Successful attacks not only expose the company to legal action by affected customers, they also compromise corporate reputation.

On April 21, 2011, Sony Corporation ("Sony") reported an outage of its online gaming service, PlayStation Network, and cloud-music service, Qriocity. Sony did not explain the cause of the outage until April 26, 2011, when it announced that their servers had been hacked. All told, the attack had successfully stolen personal information from up to 100 million accounts, including credit card information. The outage continued for almost a month while Sony worked to improve network security. During this downtime, Sony offered many freebies to consumers as compensation, including provision of free downloadable content (such as video games) plus credits. Sony's response to assist some customers has included offering free identity theft insurance as well as access to fraud investigators.

While no one has admitted to instigating the attacks, Sony alleges that Anonymous—a collective of loosely allied individuals dedicated to "hacktivism"—may be to blame. (According to Search Security.com, a hacktivist "uses the same tools and techniques as a hacker but does so in order to disrupt services and bring attention to a political or social cause.") The attack was seemingly launched in response to a series of corporate decisions taken by Sony, beginning with changes Sony made to what was permitted to run on its PlayStation console. That is, while Sony had originally permitted open source operating systems such as Linux to run on its console, it reversed this policy on the basis that security was being compromised—such programs could also be used to run "pirated" games, for example. Sony therefore released a "patch" eliminating PlayStation 3 compatibility with the suspect programs. In response, then 21-year-old George Hotz from Glen Rock, New Jersey "jailbreaked" or interfered with the system, restoring pre-patch functionality on his own console. Hotz then published on his website instructions on how he successfully jailbreaked Sony presumably so that others would have the option of doing

Jailbreaker George Hotz, pictured above, found a way to interfere with Sony's PlayStation console.

the same with their own consoles. In response, Sony sued Hotz and secured a subpoena (or court order) against Hotz's hosting company to compel production of the IP addresses of those who visited Hotz's website containing the jailbreaking instructions. Sony suspects this forceful legal response angered Anonymous for which reason it disrupted online services and compromised the security of customer data.

A branch of Anonymous, AnonOps, has denied responsibility for the main attack but appears to have admitted to subsequent attacks. For a YouTube posting, apparently by Anonymous regarding Sony's legal steps, see:
<http://www.youtube.com/watch?v=2Tm7UKo4lBc>

To date, there appears to be no instance of the information stolen from Sony having been sold or otherwise deployed to effect identity theft of any Sony customer.

As a result of the hacking incident, Sony is the subject of at least two class action suits, one initiated in the United States and another proposed in Canada. The statement of claim filed in California action alleges, among other matters, that the impugned "breach of security was caused by SONY's negligence in data security, including its failure to maintain a proper firewall and computer security system, failure to properly encrypt data, its unauthorized storage and retention of data. ...." Furthermore, the statement of claim alleges that Sony was in breach of contract for failing to "properly

CARMINE GALASSO/MCT/LANDOV

maintain Plaintiffs'. . . . data and provide uninterrupted PSN [PlayStation Network]." For the entire Statement of claim in this matter, see: <http://www.techfirm.com/storage/JohnsvSony-Complaint-FINAL.pdf>

According to a press release issued by Canadian law firm McPhadden Samac Tuovi LLP, it has filed a proposed class action in Canada seeking over $1 billion in damages, including the anticipated cost of credit monitoring services and fraud insurance for two years for the affected class.

In the meantime, jailbreaker George Hotz was hired by Facebook as a software engineer but has since quit. And Sony has taken steps to block future class actions by requiring customers to agree to a binding arbitration clause when they accept the next mandatory system update. Sony permits opting out of the arbitration clause but not electronically. The customer's opt-out must arrive at Sony's legal department by letter only.

Critical Analysis: What will the plaintiffs have to show to succeed in a tort action against Sony? What will the plaintiffs have to show to succeed in a contract action? What are Sony's defences? Assuming that no case of identity theft or other fraud comes to light, do the plaintiffs have any damages? If so, what are these damages?

Sources: Researched and written by Sean McGinnis. See <http://blog.us.playstation.com/2011/04/26/update-on-playstation-network-and-qriocity/>; Chris Lander, "Serious Business: Anonymous Takes On Scientology (and Doesn't Afraid of Anything)", *Baltimore City Paper* (2 April 2008) online: Baltimore City Paper < http://www2.citypaper.com/columns/story.asp?id=15543>; Mark Hachman, "The Sony Hack: When it Started, and When It Will End", *PCMag* (7 May 2010) online: PCMag <http://www.pcmag.com/slideshow/story/264153/the-sony-hack-when-it-started-and-when-it-will-end/9>; Tim Hornyak, "Friday Poll: Is Sony's compensation enough?", *CNet News* (13 May 2011) online: CNet News <http://news.cnet.com/friday-poll-is-sonys-compensation-enough/8301-17938_105-20062620-1.html#ixzz1SZpS1sMw>; Ben Berkowitz & Paritosh Bansal, "LulzSec hackers to disband after Sony, CIA security breaches" The Globe and Mail (25 June 2011) online: The Globe and Mail < http://www.theglobeandmail.com/news/technology/tech-news/lulzsec-hackers-to-disband-after-sony-cia-security-breaches/article2076124/>; Christopher Williams, "PlayStation hack: Sony blames Anonymous hacktivists", *The Telegraph* (5 May 2011) online: The Telegraph <http://www.telegraph.co.uk/technology/sony/8494177/PlayStation-hack-Sony-blames-Anonymous-hacktivists.html>; Ellis Hamburger, "Facebook Just Hired George Hotz, The Famous PlayStation Hacker Sued by Sony", *Business Insider* (27 June 2011) online: Business Insider <http://www.businessinsider.com/facebook-just-hired-george-hotz-2011-6>; McPhadden Samac Tuovi LLP, Press Release, "Canadian Sony PlayStation Network Class Action" (2 May 2011) online: McPhadden Samac Tuovi LLP <http://www.mcst.ca/LinkClick.aspx?fileticket=RIXFlfrf51k%3D&tabid=405>; Scott Grill, "Sony updates PSN user agreement to block class action lawsuits", (15 September 2011), online: *The Examiner* <http://www.examiner.com/console-gaming-in-national/sony-update-psn-user-agreement-to-block-class-action-lawsuits>.

Defences to a Negligence Action

Though a court may find the defendant to have been negligent, the plaintiff is not automatically entitled to recover all of her damages. The defendant may raise defences against the plaintiff in order to place at least some of the responsibility for the loss on that party. This section explores two such defences: the defence of contributory negligence and the defence of *volenti non fit injuria*—that the plaintiff has voluntarily agreed to assume the risk in question.

Contributory Negligence

The defence of contributory negligence was introduced in Chapter 10. It refers to unreasonable conduct by the plaintiff that contributed—or partially caused—the injuries that were suffered.[8] This defence recognizes that, in many instances, both the defendant and the plaintiff may have been negligent. If the plaintiff is found to have been part author of his own misfortune, then, as noted in Chapter 10, provincial legislation[9] will then come into play. It provides that responsibility for the tortious event must be apportioned between or among the respective parties. Through this mechanism, the plaintiff's damages award is then reduced in proportion to his own negligence.

Voluntary Assumption of Risk

When the court makes a finding of *volenti non fit injuria* or **voluntary assumption of risk**, it is concluding that the plaintiff consented to accept the risk inherent in the event that gave rise to the loss. *Volenti non fit injuria* is therefore a complete defence to the lawsuit, and the plaintiff will be awarded nothing by a judge even though the defendant had been negligent.

Voluntary assumption of risk
The defence that no liability exists as the plaintiff agreed to accept the risk inherent in the activity.

---

8. *Ibid* at 509.
9. *Ibid* at 512. Each common law province has contributory negligence legislation, which has replaced the common law.

To succeed on this defence, the defendant must show that the plaintiff—knowing of the virtually certain risk of harm—released his right to sue for injuries incurred as a result of any negligence on the defendant's part.[10] In short, both parties must understand that the defendant has assumed no legal responsibility to take care of the plaintiff and that the plaintiff does not expect him to.[11] Since this test is not easy to meet, *volenti non fit injuria* is a very rare defence.

CASE   *Crocker v Sundance Northwest Resorts Ltd* **[1988] 1 SCR 1186**

THE BUSINESS CONTEXT: When a business sponsors promotional events, it runs the risk of being held legally responsible for any injuries that might occur.

FACTUAL BACKGROUND: Crocker entered an inner-tube race at an event put on by Sundance, the operators of a ski slope. He decided to do so having seen a video of the event held in the previous year. Like other participants, Crocker was required to sign a waiver—that is, a commitment not to sue the promoters for any loss or injury associated with participating in the event. Crocker signed the waiver without reading it or knowing what it involved.

It was obvious to the manager of the facility that Crocker had been drinking. In fact, on Crocker's second trip down the hill, the manager advised him not to proceed with the race. Crocker did not listen. On his way down the hill, Crocker fell off the tube, broke his neck, and was rendered quadriplegic. Crocker sued.

THE LEGAL QUESTION: Was Sundance negligent? Did Crocker voluntarily assume the risk (i.e., could Sundance rely on the defence of *volenti non fit injuria*)? Was Crocker contributorily negligent?

RESOLUTION: The Supreme Court of Canada ruled that Sundance owed a duty of care to the participants because it had set up an "inherently dangerous competition in order to promote its resort and improve its financial future." It was therefore obligated to take all reasonable care to prevent Crocker—who was clearly drunk—from competing in the event at all. Management's suggestion to Crocker that he not continue with the race was insufficient to meet the standard of care associated with the duty. On the contrary, Sundance allowed and even assisted a visibly intoxicated person to participate in a dangerous event it had organized. Sundance was therefore liable for the resulting damages.

The court rejected Sundance's defence of *volenti non fit injuria*. The court stated that while Crocker's participation in the event could be regarded as an assumption of the *physical* risks involved, even this was a questionable conclusion given that Crocker was inebriated. But leaving this aside, Crocker had certainly not consented to the *legal* risk. As the court observed, "Sliding down a hill in an oversized inner tube cannot be viewed as constituting per se a waiver of Crocker's legal rights against Sundance." Even though Crocker had signed a waiver, this had no legal effect since he had not read the waiver nor did Sundance have any reasonable grounds for concluding that the signed waiver expressed Crocker's true intention. The defence of *volenti non fit injuria* therefore failed.

The trial judge's finding that Crocker was 25 percent contributorily negligent for his own injuries had not been appealed to the Supreme Court and therefore was not disturbed. Crocker was awarded 75 percent of his damages because his voluntary intoxication had contributed to the accident.

CRITICAL ANALYSIS: Was Crocker treated too harshly by the court in deducting 25 percent from his award for contributory negligence? Was Crocker treated too leniently given that Sundance's defence of *volenti non fit injuria* failed?

Negligent Misstatement
(or Negligent Misrepresentation)

Negligent misstatement or negligent misrepresentation
An incorrect statement made carelessly.

When negligence takes the form of words, the tort is known as a **negligent misstatement or negligent misrepresentation**. The plaintiff's loss does not arise due to the defendant's physical actions but due to the defendant's careless oral or written statements. If the plaintiff relied in a reasonable manner on those careless words and suffered damages as a result,

---

10. *Dubé v Labar*, [1986] 1 SCR 649 at 658.
11. *Ibid.*

those losses are recoverable subject to one large proviso. The plaintiff must first show that the defendant owed a duty of care based on there being a special relationship between the parties.[12] In the box below, the Supreme Court of Canada demonstrates how courts are to analyze the "duty" question in relation to negligent misstatement.

From a business perspective, it is **professionals**—such as accountants, lawyers, and engineers—who are most likely to commit the tort of negligent misstatement by giving bad advice or providing the client with an incompetent report. The professional who gives poor advice to his client not only faces liability for the tort of negligent misstatement but also is in breach of his contract with the client. That is, providing incompetent advice is both a tort and a breach of contract. This is a matter discussed more fully in Chapter 22.[13]

When professionals are sued by their clients, they are clearly not faced with an unduly broad scope of liability. If a professional takes someone on as a client and performs her service negligently, a lawsuit is perfectly justifiable. The justification is considerably less strong when the professional gives incompetent advice or provides a negligent report that is relied upon by a **third party** (that is, someone other than the client). Should that third party have an action in negligence? Keep in mind that in many cases, the professional has had no dealings with that third party and may not even know that third party exists until she is sued. Courts are concerned that the professional could face an unreasonable level of liability. In fact, they have stated that such defendants should not be exposed to liability "in an indeterminate amount for an indeterminate time to an indeterminate class."[14]

Also tied up in the analysis of professional liability is the idea that, generally speaking, professionals cause pure economic loss as opposed to physical loss or injury. When the loss is merely economic—that is, purely monetary—the law is simply less solicitous of the victim. From tort law's perspective, monetary loss is simply not as worthy of compensation as is property damage or personal injury.

For more discussion on professional liability, see Chapter 22.

Professional
Someone engaged in an occupation requiring the exercise of special knowledge, education, and skill.

Third party
One who is not a party to an agreement.

CASE   *Hercules Managements Ltd v Ernst & Young* [1997] 2 SCR 165

THE BUSINESS CONTEXT: Accountants are regularly hired by corporations to prepare the audited financial statements that many corporations are required to present to shareholders at their annual general meeting. The audit reports—though prepared for the corporate client—are in fact reviewed by a variety of people from directors and officers, to shareholders, to prospective investors around the world.

FACTUAL BACKGROUND: Ernst & Young prepared audited financial statements for two companies. These financial statements were the result of incompetent work by the auditors.

Shareholders in the two companies claimed that they relied on the financial statements in deciding to invest further in the companies. These shareholders lost hundreds of thousands of dollars when the companies failed to perform.

THE LEGAL QUESTION: Do the auditors owe a duty of care to the shareholders such that they are responsible to the shareholders for negligent misstatement?

RESOLUTION: As a first step, the court agreed that the defendants owed the shareholders a *prima facie* duty of care because there existed between them a neighbour relationship

(Continued)

---

12. See *Queen v Cognos Inc*, [1993] 1 SCR 87 at 109–110.
13. As Chapter 22 discusses, such conduct can also be a breach of fiduciary duty.
14. *Ultramares Corp v Touche Niven & Co*, (1931), 255 NY 170 (USCA).

(or relationship of proximity). The auditors would have realized that the shareholders would look at the audited financial statements and, furthermore, such reliance by the shareholders would be reasonable. At the second step, however, the court ruled that there were policy reasons that limited or eliminated the *prima facie* duty of care the accountants otherwise owed. While there were no concerns about indeterminate liability in the sense that the defendants had knowledge of the plaintiffs, the concern arose in another context. That is, the accountants prepared the financial statements for the corporate client to be used at the annual general meeting of the shareholders. It was not prepared for the purpose of

helping shareholders decide whether or not to invest further in the companies. As soon as the plaintiffs used the financial statements for other than their intended purpose, they put the accountants at risk of indeterminate liability. On the policy basis, the *prima facie* duty of care owed by the accountants to the shareholders was eliminated. The shareholders' action failed.

CRITICAL ANALYSIS: Do you agree with the court's formulation that the *sole* purpose for which financial statements are produced is for the annual general meeting? Are accountants being too sheltered by the courts? Why did the shareholders simply not sue the accountants for breach of contract?

Negligence and Product Liability

Product liability
Liability relating to the design, manufacture, or sale of the product.

The law imposes a standard of care on manufacturers in relation to the design, manufacture, or sale of their products. This area of law is known generically as **product liability**. The Business Law in Practice scenario under discussion at the beginning of this chapter is a product liability case because Meat breached the standard of care it owed consumers by producing contaminated meat.

Product liability cases often involve contract law as well. Besides being able to sue Meat in negligence, Jennifer has an action for breach of contract against the retailer who provided her with the contaminated product. The retailer is in breach of contract because it supplied Jennifer with a product that was not fit to be sold. Jennifer does not, of course, have a contract action against the manufacturer, since there is no contract between them.

Jennifer's contract action against the retailer will probably be more straightforward than her negligence action against Meat. This is because liability for breaching a contractual term is strict. Since the retailer's promise to supply a non-contaminated product is not qualified in any way, there is no defence for breaching that promise. It is no defence to the contract action for the retailer to prove that it purchased from a reputable supplier, for example, or that there was no way of telling that the product was contaminated. To succeed in negligence against the manufacturer, however, Jennifer has to demonstrate all the steps in the action, as outlined earlier in this chapter.

Because of the nature of product liability, Jennifer has two defendants she can sue and would be well advised to proceed against both of them. Having two defendants increases the chances that Jennifer will be able to collect at least something on any judgment in her favour. For example, if the retailer is out of business by the time the matter goes to trial, Jennifer will still have the manufacturer left as a source of payment of damages and vice versa.

The nature of product liability in foreign jurisdictions is discussed at the end of this chapter. Chapters 23 and 24 offer further discussion of liability relating to the manufacture, distribution, and sale of products.

Why should retailers be responsible for defective products?

© PHOTOZOO/DREAMSTIME.COM

Negligence and the Service of Alcohol

Commercial establishments serving alcohol owe a duty of care to impaired patrons to assist them or prevent them from being injured.[15] Similarly, these establishments can be liable to members of the public who are injured by the conduct of one of their drunken customers,[16] most notably through drunk driving. An important rationale for this duty is that clubs, bars, and taverns benefit economically from serving drinks to their patrons. It stands to reason that such commercial establishments should also have some positive obligation to

---

15. See Klar, *supra* note 5 at 200.
16. See, for example, the discussion in *Stewart v Pettie*, [1995] 1 SCR 131.

the inebriated patron and to others put at risk by that patron.[17] This economic relationship between the commercial host and patron provides an important rationale for extending the law of negligence in this way.

CASE   *McIntyre v Grigg* (2006) 274 DLR (4th) 28 (Ont CA)

BUSINESS CONTEXT: Owners of nightclubs and other drinking establishments must actively manage the risk that a patron will become impaired and then drive a vehicle. Not only might patrons injure themselves or others, but also the owner may be found liable for those injuries and be subject to a large damages claim.

FACTUAL CONTEXT: Andrea McIntyre, a McMaster University student, was walking with several friends, on her way back home from "The Downstairs John," owned and operated by commercial host, McMaster Students Union. As McIntyre was walking along the side of the curb of the sidewalk, she was struck by the defendant's vehicle. The defendant—a Hamilton Tiger-Cats football player named Andrew Grigg—had run a stop sign, and then made a wide right-hand turn while speeding. Next, his vehicle sheared off a lamp post and struck McIntyre, causing severe physical and psychological injury. Just previous to the accident, Grigg had been drinking at The Downstairs John as well as at other venues earlier that evening.

McIntyre sued Grigg as well as the McMaster Students Union.

THE LEGAL QUESTION: Does the Students Union—a commercial host—have any liability for the injuries suffered by McIntyre?

RESOLUTION: The Court of Appeal quoted the following portion of the trial judge's charge to the jury as properly stating the law regarding commercial host liability:

> At common law commercial vendors of alcohol owe a general duty of care to persons who might reasonably be expected to come into contact with an intoxicated person and to whom the patron may pose some risk.

That duty of care arises if there is some foreseeable risk of harm to the patron or to the third party. . . .

Common law and statutory law therefore impose a duty on taverns to its patrons and others to ensure that the tavern does not serve alcohol which would either intoxicate or increase the patron's intoxication. They do not escape liability simply because a patron does not exhibit any visible signs of intoxication if in the circumstances the tavern knew or ought to have known that the patron was becoming intoxicated.

The jury accepted that Grigg was showing signs of intoxication. Even though the majority of witnesses said that Grigg did not appear to be drunk at The Downstairs John, one witness at the accident scene said he did exhibit such signs. As well, Grigg's blood alcohol level two hours after the accident measured nearly three times the legal limit. Expert evidence established that, on this basis alone, he may have been served up to eighteen drinks at The Downstairs John. Accordingly, there was sufficient evidence that Grigg would have been visibly impaired.

The Court of Appeal rejected McMaster Students Union's appeal of the jury's findings. In the result, McIntyre received $250 000 for pain and suffering as well as a sizeable amount representing loss of future income. Grigg was held 70 percent liable and the Students Union held 30 percent liable. Grigg was also ordered to pay an additional sum in punitive damages.

CRITICAL ANALYSIS: Do you agree that bars should be held responsible when their patrons cause injury to themselves or others?

The Negligence Standard versus Strict Liability

Strict liability
The principle that liability will be imposed irrespective of proof of negligence.

Strict liability in tort makes the defendant liable for the plaintiff's loss even though the defendant was not negligent and, by definition, had exercised reasonable care.[18] Given that Canadian tort law is founded on a fault-based system, the scope of strict liability is necessarily limited.[19] These exceptions are largely confined to liability for fires, for dangerous animals, and for the escape of dangerous substances.[20]

---

17. See Klar, *supra* note 5 at 200.
18. Klar, *supra* note 5 at 643.
19. *Ibid.*
20. *Ibid* at 644. This is the *Rylands v Fletcher* tort. The tort is "no fault," and the mere fact that the dangerous substance escapes from one's non-natural use of land is enough to make the defendant tortiously liable, even if the escape was not due to negligence/lack of due care. What constitutes non-natural use is a matter of debate beyond the scope of this text. For discussion, see Klar, *ibid* at 620 and following.

Another reason strict liability is so unusual is because the law of negligence has expanded to provide a remedy to most victims of accidents who merit compensation.[21]

Though strict liability[22] makes only rare appearances in the law of torts, it would be wrong to conclude that businesses rarely face strict liability. As already noted, there are significant areas where liability is strict, including

- *Liability in contract.* When a business makes a contractual promise that it breaches or fails to perform, that business is liable for breach of contract. The absence of negligence is no defence.

- *Vicarious liability.* As already discussed in Chapter 10, vicarious liability is a form of strict liability. An employer is *automatically responsible* for the torts of his employee when, for example, there is a significant connection between what the employer was asking the employee to do and the employee's tort.

A third relevant instance of strict liability is described in the following box.

INTERNATIONAL PERSPECTIVE

Strict Liability

Some of Canada's major trading partners, such as members of the European Union (EU) and areas in the United States, use a strict liability rather than a fault-based standard in defective-product liability cases.

For example, all EU member states are subject to a directive requiring that manufacturers be strictly liable for their defective products. The directive provides that a product is defective when it does not provide the safety that a person is entitled to expect, taking into consideration all the circumstances. Relevant considerations include the presentation of the product, expectation of use, and the time the product was put into circulation. The directive also provides for a "state of the art" defence by stating that a product will not be considered defective for the sole reason that a better product is subsequently put on the market.

The effect of a strict liability standard is that manufacturers can be held liable for unsafe products even if they were not negligent in any way and exercised due care. This is markedly different from the result under a fault-based standard. In the latter case, if the manufacturer takes due care at all stages of product production—in designing the product, in selecting a production process, in assembling and testing, and in packaging and labelling—there is no liability regardless of defects. Strict liability, on the other hand, is imposed irrespective of fault.[23]

Critical Analysis: Which approach to liability do you prefer and why?

Business Law in Practice Revisited

1. What tort may Meat have committed and what do the plaintiffs have to prove in order to establish that tort?

Meat may have committed the tort of negligence. Jennifer must establish that she is owed a duty of care by Meat. This will be straightforward, as manufacturers like Meat

---

21. *Ibid* at 643–644.

22. Note that strict liability in the context of tort law is different from strict liability in the context of regulatory offences. Governments enact regulatory statutes—creating regulatory offences—in order to protect the public interest. According to the leading case of *R v City of Sault Ste Marie*, [1978], 2 SCR 1299, regulatory statutes such as environmental protection legislation contemplate three classes of offences, one of which is known as a *strict liability offence*. In this context, strict liability does not mean that an offence is created to which there is no defence. For strict liability offences in the regulatory context, a person charged can raise the defence of due diligence. That is, if such a person can show that he took all reasonable care, there will be no liability.

23. EC, Council Directive 85/374/EEC of 25 July 1985 on the approximation of the laws, regulations, and administrative provisions of the Member States concerning liability for defective products, as amended, [1985] OJ. 210/29. For further discussion, see, for example, Helen Delaney & Rene van de Zande, eds. *A Guide to the EU Directive Concerning Liability for Defective Products (Product Liability Directive)* (Gaithersburg, MD: U.S. Department of Commerce, 2001) online: NIST Global Standards Information Europe <http://gsi.nist.gov/global/docs/EUGuide_ProductLiability.pdf>; Europa, "Summaries of EU Legislation: Defective Products: Liability", online: Europa <http://europa.eu/legislation_summaries/consumers/consumer_safety/l32012_en.htm>.

PART THREE

owe a duty of care to consumers of their product. That is, Jennifer is clearly Meat's neighbour because it is reasonably foreseeable that a negligent act or omission by Meat in the manufacturing process would cause harm to Jennifer and there is a relationship of sufficient proximity between them. Jennifer is thereby owed a *prima facie* duty of care under Stage 1 as discussed in this chapter. There are no policy considerations under Stage 2 to reduce or eliminate this duty. Next, Jennifer will have to establish that Meat breached the standard of care by failing to have an adequate sanitation and hygiene system such that *Listeria* could not be introduced into the meat via the manufacturing process. In terms of causation, Jennifer must prove that "but for" eating the contaminated meat she would not have become sick. Finally, Jennifer will have to establish that her injury is not too remote. This will also be straightforward, as it is entirely foreseeable that someone who consumes meat contaminated by the bacteria *Listeria monocytogenes* would contract listeriosis.

2. What defences does Meat have to this action?

Meat will have difficulty establishing a defence given the facts as recited. It can insist that the plaintiff prove her case, since not everyone who becomes ill after having eaten deli meat has necessarily contracted listeriosis. There could be other reasons why someone has fallen ill, such as viruses. However, if Jennifer's lawyer has done a proper job preparing her case, it may prove difficult to defend.

3. What additional risks does a class action create for Meat?

As noted in Chapter 4, a class action is a lawsuit launched by one or more persons representing a larger group whose members have similar claims against the same defendant. Class actions allow claims to be brought by a group of people that could not economically be brought by the individual acting alone.[24] This means that individuals who otherwise might not have sued can join the class action and receive their fair portion of the damages awarded.

4. How could Meat have better managed its risk of tort liability in this case?

Meat is producing a consumer good that can pose a serious risk to health should the product be contaminated. In the unlikely case that Meat did not have a risk management plan, then devising one according to the principles discussed in Chapter 3 would be very important. Meat almost certainly maintains third-party liability insurance so that, in the event of Jennifer succeeding in her action, Meat can use insurance proceeds to pay out on any damage award. Insurance, which is discussed further in Chapter 28, is a central element in any risk management plan. Meat has already instituted a review process to see why the *Listeria* outbreak occurred. This is an essential step and one which Meat's insurer will insist upon in any event.

There is no doubt that once the contamination problem at Meat's manufacturing plant became known, Meat did an excellent job of managing the risk of future illness and death by initiating a recall and taking immediate steps to determine the cause of the outbreak.[25]

---

24. See David Morritt, "Product Liability: Class Actions Raise the Risks" Osler (1 September 2003) online: Osler <http://www.osler.com/resources.aspx?id58320>.
25. Maple Leaf Foods has been praised for its response. See Robert Todd, "A 'case study' in effective crisis management", *Law Times* (29 September 2008) at 5 but see Steve Rennie, "More hygiene issues cited at Maple Leaf plant", *Globe and Mail* (9 November 2009) at A10.

Maple Leaf Foods, who is involved in a situation not unlike that of Meat Ltd., has taken several steps to continuously improve its operation. These can be seen as forming the basis of its risk management plan going forward. For example, Maple Leaf has announced the establishment of a Food Safety Advisory Council. This council, which will guide Maple Leaf, is made of leading experts in the area of food safety, microbiology, and public health. As well, Maple Leaf has created the position of Chief Food Safety Officer, who will establish best practices to enhance food safety. The Maple Leaf plant that was the source of the *Listeria* outbreak has undergone six complete sanitization cycles; the slicing equipment has been torn apart, deep cleaned, tested, and reassembled. More stringent sanitation systems are now in place as well as other operational improvements. For a detailed account, see "Maple Leaf Foods Safety Pledge."[26] And beyond this, the class actions against Maple Leaf Foods have been settled.[27]

Chapter Summary

Donoghue v Stevenson is the foundation of modern negligence law. Negligence law is an inherently flexible, growing legal area. It seeks to provide a remedy to the plaintiff who has suffered a loss or injury due to the culpable though unintentional conduct of the defendant.

The four steps to a negligence action describe general standards or markers that help a court assess whether the defendant in any given case has been negligent.

One of the most common defences to a negligence claim is that of contributory negligence. The plaintiff's damages award will be reduced in proportion to her own culpability in causing the loss, for example, by failing to wear a seat belt or drinking to the point of impairment.

A less common defence is to allege that the plaintiff voluntarily assumed the risk. This defence is rarely established since the defendant must prove that the plaintiff consented not only to the *physical risk* of harm but also agreed to accept the *legal* risk of not being able to sue the defendant for resulting loss or injury.

Negligent misstatement or negligent misrepresentation holds the defendant responsible for negligence taking written or oral form. Professionals such as accountants and lawyers are most likely to commit this kind of tort. Courts guard against the professional facing liability in "an indeterminate amount for an indeterminate time to an indeterminate class." This sheltering of the professional is also partially justifiable in light of the fact that a professional's negligent misstatement is likely to cause only pure economic loss as opposed to personal injury or property loss. Tort law has been historically less concerned when the plaintiff's loss is purely monetary.

Business is also affected by product liability. Product liability involves both negligence law and the law of contract. The manufacturer of a poorly produced or designed product will face an action in negligence by the disappointed purchaser. The retailer will face a

PART THREE

---

26. Maple Leaf Foods, "Maple Leaf Foods Safety Pledge" online: Maple Leaf Foods <http://www.mapleleaf.ca/en/market/food-safety/food-safety-at-maple-leaf/food-safety-pledge/>.
27. Maple Leaf states on its website that the settlement "provides that the defendants will pay between $25 and 27 million in full and final settlement of all claims, applicable taxes, class counsel fees and expenses, subrogation claims by provincial health insurers, trustee fees and expenses, arbitration fees and expenses and claim administration fees and expenses." See: <http://www.mapleleafclaim.com/claim.php?locale=en_CA>

breach of contract action by that same person and—if the retailer was also negligent—an action in negligence as well.

Another area of liability for business relates to the service of alcohol. Commercial servers of alcohol, such as bars, taverns, and restaurants, owe a duty of care to protect against the foreseeable risks of intoxication.

Strict liability is a liability imposed even where the defendant has not been negligent. This is a rare phenomenon in tort law, but there are other areas of law in which strict liability is common. The two most important areas relate to liability for breach of contract and vicarious liability for the torts of one's employees. As well, some of Canada's major trading partners, including the EU and parts of the United States, use strict liability rather than a fault-based standard in defective-product liability cases.

Chapter Study

Key Terms and Concepts

causation (p. 242)

duty of care (p. 240)

negligent misstatement or negligent
   misrepresentation (p. 248)

neighbour (p. 240)

prima facie (p. 241)

product liability (p. 250)

professional (p. 249)

pure economic loss (p. 245)

reasonable care (p. 239)

reasonable person (p. 242)

remoteness of damage (p. 244)

strict liability (p. 252)

thin skull rule (p. 244)

third party (p. 249)

voluntary assumption of risk (p. 247)

Questions for Review

1. What competing interests must a court balance in deciding a negligence action?

2. What are the four steps in a negligence action?

3. Before *Donoghue v Stevenson*, what defence could most manufacturers of goods raise when faced with a claim for negligence brought by an injured user of those goods?

4. How does the foreseeability test help in defining the neighbour principle in negligence?

5. What is the standard of care in negligence?

6. How is causation usually determined in negligence?

7. Does the normal standard of care vary in any specific circumstances? Explain.

8. Does tort law generally allow recovery for pure economic loss?

9. What does contributory negligence mean and what are the consequences of it being found to exist?

10. What is the consequence of a *volenti non fit injuria* finding?

11. Given an example of when the defence of *volenti non fit injuria* might be applied.

12. What kinds of plaintiffs will be likely to succeed in an action for negligent misstatement against a professional?

13. Why was there no duty of care owed in *Hercules Managements v Ernst & Young*?

14. What area of law other than tort law do product liability actions often involve? Why are actions in that area often more straightforward than in tort law?

15. What is the thin skull rule? Give an example of when it would apply. How does the thin skull rule protect the plaintiff?

16. Is the commercial host liable if one of its patrons is injured because of the patron's own impaired driving? Explain.

17. Why is strict liability rare in Canada's tort regime?

18. Name two areas where strict liability is common.

Questions for Critical Thinking

1. The principles of *volenti non fit injuria* have been restricted to allow the defence to apply only in limited circumstances. Are these circumstances too limited? For example, should the person getting into the car with an impaired driver still be allowed to recover in negligence? Is there not sufficient public knowledge of the dangers of impaired driving for people to understand the risk they assume? What about those who deliberately choose not to wear a seat belt? Why should they potentially recover?

2. From time to time, it has been proposed that the principles of strict liability be applied to product liability in Canada as they are in certain other jurisdictions. What are the pros and cons of applying this concept in Canada? What changes would result for producers of goods and services, as well as for consumers? Are there inherent risks that might arise for society as a whole if strict liability were imposed in certain industries?

3. One of the areas in which liability for negligence is expanding is in the case of those serving alcohol both as a business and at office parties. Think of the contexts in which businesses might be exposed to these

risks either because they make their money from selling alcohol or because they are conducting a social event. To what extent should the business be held liable for negative outcomes of the excessive consumption of liquor?

4. It is relatively new for courts to allow recovery for pure economic loss in negligence, that is, loss unrelated to any physical loss. Some would argue that extending negligence in this regard potentially places an unfair burden on some occupations and service providers. In our society, people should accept that there are some losses for which recovery cannot be obtained. What are the pros and cons of allowing recovery for purely economic loss?

5. The application of the "thin skull rule" often places a considerable burden on a defendant who is found liable in negligence, above and beyond what would normally be "reasonably foreseeable." Is it fair that the negligent party should assume the burden of these extra costs? Does the thin skull rule make sense when considered alongside the rule about remoteness of damage?

6. In the *Mustapha* case described in this chapter, the plaintiff could not recover for his distress at seeing a dead fly in an unopened bottle of water because such a mental injury would not occur in a person of ordinary mental fortitude. Do you think such an approach unfairly favours the water supplier over the customer?

Situations for Discussion

1. Sue regularly hosts social events for her employees at which alcohol is served. Sue's lawyer says that she faces liability should a drunken employee get behind the wheel and become injured in a car accident. This is because the employer maintains a duty to provide the employee with a safe working environment even in such circumstances.[28] What steps can Sue take to manage the risk of alcohol related liability when hosting a social event?

2. Kurt, an avid skier, wanted to clear some wet snow and ice from his chair on the chairlift as it moved toward him from the boarding ramp. He was unable to sit down in time and simply grabbed onto the chair,

which began to ascend the mountain. Kurt realized that the longer he held on, the higher the fall would be, so he quickly let go and fell about three metres into an embankment, injuring his right leg. Kurt sued the owner of the ski hill and its employee, the ski-lift operator who failed to stop the chair as soon as she could see that Kurt had not loaded properly.[29] On what basis is the ski-lift operator liable? Do you think any judgment Kurt might receive should be reduced? Why?

3. Klutz won a contest sponsored by a radio station, entitling him to play in a twilight golf tournament. He went to the radio station and signed a form releasing the station from any liability connected with the tournament. The event was held at the Dark Side Country Club, beginning at 11 p.m. Klutz attended a pre-tournament instructional meeting and was told that his team was to tee off on the second hole. While the team headed for that spot, Klutz hurried to his car to get his clubs and golf shoes. As he sprinted down the path to the parking lot, he ran into one of a series of black iron posts embedded in the asphalt path at the point where the walkway and parking lot met. Klutz somersaulted several times, ending up on the driveway with banged knees and a badly bruised elbow. He played seven holes of golf, but could not carry on. Prior to the accident, he was a self-employed upholsterer. Following the accident, he was unable to work for three months. After that his production was down 20 percent. His ability to participate in household and leisure activities was also reduced.[30]

    Apply the principles of tort law to this situation. Suggest a result. What further information would be useful?

4. Burger Heaven (BH) is a large chain of restaurants specializing in burgers and fries. In response to customer demand, BH added coffee to its menu. The temperature of the coffee and the style of container and lids were part of BH operating standards to be followed by all restaurant operators and staff. BH restaurants provide counter and drive-through service. Sandra bought coffee at the drive-through for herself and her husband, Morley. Sandra passed both cups of coffee to Morley. The car hit a big bump and the coffee spilled in Morley's lap, burning him severely.

---

28. Klar, *supra* note 5 at 216.
29. Based, in part, on *Kralik v Mount Seymour Resorts Ltd*, 2008 BCCA 97.
30. Based, in part, on *Poluk v City of Edmonton* (1996), 191 AR 301 (QB).

What should BH do about this particular incident? Is Morley likely to be successful in any claim for negligence? What defences might BH raise? How can BH manage the risk of a similar incident occurring in the future? Can any preventive steps be taken?

5. Mr. Worton purchased a slide for the family's four-foot-deep aboveground backyard pool from Jacuzzi Canada Inc. A Jacuzzi Canada employee told Mr. Worton that installing this kind of slide with his pool would be "ok" and "not a problem." He was not advised that there was any risk at all in doing so. Worton installed the slide according to the instructions. Unfortunately, Carla, his 15-year-old, was seriously injured when she went down the slide headfirst and as a result is now paralyzed.[31] Carla had been instructed by her parents only to go down the slide feet first, but on this occasion, she failed to follow this rule. Carla's parents have sued Jacuzzi on her behalf. Is there negligence? Did this negligence cause Carla's accident?

6. Ellen attended a skin care clinic to receive laser removal of unwanted hair. The technician performed the entire treatment without first conducting a full patch test and failed to stop the treatment when Ellen complained of pain. As a result, Ellen sustained facial and neck scarring. She was left with permanently lighter skin below the lasered skin and was very concerned that others would think she had leprosy. She was very traumatized and unable to work for at least a month. She also requires ongoing psychological care.[32] What steps must Ellen establish in order to demonstrate a negligence claim? What kind of damages should she seek and on what basis?

7. Big Pizza, a province-wide pizza chain, has a new promotional campaign. The chain guarantees that all pizzas will be delivered within 30 minutes or they will be free. While this promise is readily kept in small cities and towns, it places considerable stress on franchises in large urban areas. Franchisees are required by their franchise agreement to pass on this stress to drivers by fining them half of the cost of any pizza not delivered within the requisite time. To overcome this threat, drivers often are forced to drive well above the speed limit. One driver, attempting to meet the deadline, fails to notice another vehicle in its path and collides with it, seriously injuring the passengers in that vehicle.

Assuming that the issue of negligence by the driver is clear-cut and that the driver is an employee, can the injured persons claim damages from the franchisee for the actions of the employee? Why or why not? Is there any argument that Big Pizza has itself been negligent? Present arguments for both sides of the case, and determine whether liability will be upheld.[33]

8. The Bridge Engineering Company contracted to build a bridge between a suburb and the downtown of a medium-sized town. For years the two communities were joined by a one-lane bridge, and this new four-lane bridge was a major improvement. Indeed, as a result of the new bridge, a local contractor began building a new housing project of 30 homes. Just before the first home sales were made, a major defect was discovered in the bridge design that meant that the bridge would be unusable for at least two years. Residents would be forced to use a lengthy detour that added approximately 30 minutes to the average drive between the suburb and downtown, where the majority of the residents worked. The market for the new housing project immediately collapsed, and the contractor was unable to sell any houses. The contractor is considering litigation but realizes that he has no claim in contract against the engineering company. Are there any alternatives? Explain.

For more study tools, visit http://www.NELSONbrain.com.

31. Based, in part, on *Walford (Litigation guardian of) v Jacuzzi Canada Inc*, 2007 ONCA 729.
32. Based, in part, on *Ayana v Skin Klinic*, (2009) 68 CCLT (3d) 21.
33. Based on Michael Friscolanti, "Pizza Pizza sued for big money money" Macleans.ca (28 November 2007), online: Macleans <http://www.macleans.ca/canada/national/article.jsp?content=20071128_73882_73882>.

PART THREE

CHAPTER 12

Other Torts

Objectives

After studying this chapter, you should have an understanding of

- the range of torts that are relevant to business organizations

- how torts arise from the use of property

- how torts arise from business operations

- how a business can manage the risk of liability in tort

PRIVATE PROPERTY

NO TRESPASSING

TRESPASSERS WILL BE PROSECUTED

DARREN PRICE

Business Law in Practice

Ron Smithson owns and operates a small manufacturing business in St. John's, Newfoundland and Labrador. The business supplies specially crafted items for gift stores, specialty boutiques, and craft shops. Ron sells mostly through trade shows, although online sales are beginning to account for a sizable part of his business. He also has a small factory outlet. Ron conducts business in a two-storey building that he owns in a historic part of the city. The basement houses a manufacturing facility consisting of pottery wheels, kilns, and a decorating and glazing studio. The main floor is used for warehousing and storage, packing, and shipping. The second floor, with the exception of a small unit devoted to the factory outlet, is leased to a number of other small businesses.

Ron has had a successful year, although there are two situations that have the potential to jeopardize the bottom line:

- Julie Osbourne, a local resident, suffered serious injuries on Ron's premises. Julie had planned to visit the factory outlet to purchase some gifts for visitors. To access the store, she had to use the elevator. As she travelled between floors, the steel plate covering the indicator lights above the elevator door became unhinged and fell, hitting her on the head, neck, and shoulders. Apparently, the plate fell off because the elevator maintenance company, Elevator XL Services, which had been hired by Ron to maintain all features of the elevator, had run out of plate clips to keep the plate itself in place. It instructed its employee to use a broken clip for the time being rather than leave the steel plate off altogether. Ron knew that a broken clip had been used on the steel plate but had also been assured by the elevator maintenance company that a proper clip would be installed on the very next business day.

(Continued on the next page)

- While visiting a trade show on the mainland, Ron saw a replica of his best-selling figurine, "Old Man of the Sea." The replica was dressed in the same fisher garb as Ron's figurine, was decorated with the same colours, and had the same style of packaging and labelling. The only differences were that the replica was made with cheap plastic and that it was named "Man of the Sea." Ron is concerned about the impact that sales of this competing figurine will have on his business.[1]

1. What potential legal actions does Julie have against Ron's business?
2. What is the responsibility of Elevator XL Services?
3. Does Ron have any recourse against the manufacturer of the replica figurine?
4. How can Ron manage the risk his business faces of potential tort liabilities?

Introduction

Business activity—whether it involves generating electricity, cutting hair, filing tax returns, or selling automobiles—involves interactions that may ultimately have a negative impact on others and their property. Consider these examples:

- A customer in a grocery store slips on a lettuce leaf and falls, breaking his ankle.

- A store detective detains a shopper, assuming incorrectly, that the shopper has stolen merchandise.

- A salesperson intentionally overstates an important quality of a product because she wants to close a sale.

- A golf course adversely affects an adjacent landowner because players continually drive balls into her yard.

In each of these examples, the business may have interfered with a legitimate interest of another and could, as a result, be subject to a tort action.

The laws that make a business liable for its tortious conduct also operate to protect that same business when it is the victim of a tort. Consider these examples:

- A newspaper columnist maligns the environmental record of a business.

- Vandals continually spray-paint graffiti on factory walls.

- A competitor entices a skilled employee to break his employment contract and join the competitor's business.

- A new business creates a logo that is remarkably similar to that of an existing business in the same market.

Tort actions relevant to businesses can be conveniently divided between those that arise because a business occupies a property and those that arise because of actual business operations.

---

1. Based, in part, on *Sawler v Franklyn Enterprises Ltd* (1992), 117 NSR (2d) 316, 324 APR 316 (TD).

PART THREE

Torts and Property Use

Tort actions may arise in relation to property in a number of ways, most commonly when the occupier of the property harms others. An **occupier** is generally defined as someone who has some degree of control over land or buildings on that land.[2] An enterprise conducting business on property is an occupier, whether it is the owner, a tenant, or a temporary provider of a service. Following from this definition, it is entirely possible to have more than one occupier of land or a building.

Ron, as owner and user of the building, is an occupier. His tenants on the second floor are occupiers of that space. Elevator XL Services Ltd. was hired to service and maintain the elevator. As such, Elevator XL Services had control of the elevator at a critical time and can also be classified as an occupier, although for a much more fleeting moment. The main tort actions in relation to occupation of property relate to occupiers' liability, nuisance, and trespass.

Occupier
Someone who has some degree of control over land or buildings on that land.

Occupiers' Liability

Occupiers' liability describes the liability that occupiers have to anyone who enters onto their land or property. This area of the law varies by jurisdiction. For example, Newfoundland, Quebec, and Saskatchewan retain the common law while other provinces have occupiers' liability legislation.[3] In New Brunswick, statute has abolished occupiers' liability as a specialized category altogether.[4]

Liability at Common Law

The liability of the occupier for mishaps on property is not determined by the ordinary principles of negligence. Rather, liability is determined by classifying the visitor as a trespasser, licensee, invitee, or contractual entrant. Each class is owed a different standard of care, with the trespasser being owed the lowest standard and the contractual entrant being owed the highest. This area of law is often criticized for the difficult distinctions between the different classes of visitors, the blurring of duties owed between the various classes, and the severity of the result when the visitor is classified as a trespasser.

A **contractual entrant** is someone who has contracted and paid for the right to enter the premises.[5] Visitors to the premises who have bought tickets to see a pottery exhibit would be contractual entrants. The duty owed to this class (in the absence of a contract specifying the duty) is a warranty that "the premises are as safe as reasonable care and skill on the part of anyone can make them."[6]

Contractual entrant
Any person who has paid (contracted) for the right to enter the premises.

An **invitee** is someone whose presence on the property is of benefit to the occupier, such as store customers and delivery or service personnel. The occupier owes a slightly lower duty to the invitee than to the contractual entrant. He must warn the invitee of any "unusual danger, [of] which he knows or ought to know."[7] There is no requirement

Invitee
Any person who comes onto the property to provide the occupier with a benefit.

---

2. Lewis Klar, *Tort Law*, 5th ed (Toronto: Thomson Reuters, 2012) at 610 [Klar].
3. *Occupiers' Liability* Act, RSA 2000, c O-4; *Occupiers' Liability Act*, RSBC 1996, c 337; *Occupiers' Liability Act*, RSM 1987, c O-8; *Occupiers' Liability Act*, RSO 1990, c O-2; *Occupiers' Liability Act*, SNS 1996, c 27; and *Occupiers' Liability Act*, RSPEI 1988, c O-2. See also Klar, *supra* note 2 at 610.
4. See Law *Reform Act*, RSNB 2011, c 184, s 2.
5. Klar, *supra* note 2 at 616.
6. *Ibid* at 624, footnotes omitted.
7. *Indermaur v Dames* (1866), LR 1 CP 274 at 288; aff'd (1867), LR CP 314 (Ex Ch) cited by Klar, *ibid* at 622.

to warn of usual or common danger that "ordinary reasonable persons can be expected to know and appreciate."[8]

Julie is clearly an invitee, and the improperly fastened steel plate would be classified as an "unusual danger." She is therefore entitled to hold the owner and elevator maintenance company liable for injuries suffered as a result of that unusual danger.

A **licensee** is someone who has been permitted by the occupier to enter for the benefit of the licensee.[9] If Ron allowed people accessing an adjacent business to take a shortcut through his building, those users would be licensees. A licensee might also include guests invited to someone's property for a social occasion.

The general rule is that occupiers are responsible to licensees for any unusual danger of which they are aware or that they have reason to know about. The latter part of the rule is a recent addition and tends to blur the distinction between the duty owed an invitee and the duty owed a licensee.[10] Since there is no strong rationale for distinguishing between a licensee and an invitee to begin with, this blurring is entirely justifiable.

A **trespasser** is someone who "goes on the land without invitation of any sort and whose presence is either unknown to the occupier, or if known, is practically objected to."[11] A burglar clearly fits the definition of a trespasser.

An occupier still owes some responsibility to a trespasser. In particular, the occupier will be liable for any act done with the deliberate intention of doing harm to the trespasser, or an act done with reckless disregard for the presence of the trespasser.[12] Though the trespasser is not owed a common law duty of care as described in *Donoghue v Stevenson*,[13] the occupier does owe him "at least the duty of acting with common humanity towards him."[14]

Though a trespasser is owed a very low duty, courts have often mitigated the harshness of this result, particularly when the trespasser is a child. For example, courts have at times re-classified the trespasser as a licensee, interpreted the duty owed the trespasser very generously, and even brought the children's claims under the ordinary law of negligence.[15]

> **Licensee**
> Any person whose presence is not a benefit to the occupier but to which the occupier has no objection.

> **Trespasser**
> Any person who is not invited onto the property and whose presence is either unknown to the occupier or is objected to by the occupier.

Liability under Occupiers' Liability Legislation

Alberta, British Columbia, Manitoba, Nova Scotia, Ontario, and Prince Edward Island have enacted occupiers' liability legislation.[16] Although there are differences in the legislation from one jurisdiction to the next, there is also considerable common ground. One objective of the legislation is to simplify the common law. As the Supreme Court of Canada confirmed in the context of Ontario's *Occupiers' Liability Act*, the legislative purpose was "to replace the somewhat obtuse common law of occupiers' liability by

---

8. *McErlean v Sarel* (1987), 61 OR (2d) 396 at 418, 22 OAC 186 (CA), leave to appeal to SCC refused (1988), 63 OR (2d) x (note) (SCC) cited by Klar, *ibid* at 623.
9. Klar, *supra* note 2 at 614.
10. *Mitchell v Canadian National Railway* Co [1975] 1 SCR 592, [1974] SCJ No 67.
11. *Robert Addie & Sons v Dumbreck*, [1929] AC 358 at 371 (HL) [Robert Addie], cited by Klar, *supra* note 2 at 591.
12. Robert Addie, *ibid* at 365.
13. [1932] AC 562 (HL).
14. *British Railways Board v Herrington*, [1972] AC 877 (HL), quoted with approval by the Supreme Court of Canada in *Veinot v Kerr-Addison Mines Ltd*, [1975] 2 SCR 311, 51 DLR (3d) 533.
15. Klar, *supra* note 2 at 618–621.
16. *Supra* note 3.

a generalized duty of care based on the 'neighbour' principle set down in *Donoghue v Stevenson*."[17]

Indeed, legislation across the country provides for a high duty of care—equivalent to the negligence standard—to be owed to entrants who are on the property with express or implied permission (at common law, contractual entrants, invitees, and licensees). Responsibility to trespassers differs among the various statutes. In general, however, an occupier must not create deliberate harm or danger,[18] and, in Alberta, the responsibilities increase where the trespassers are children.[19]

If Ron's business were located in Ontario, where occupiers' liability legislation is in place, the court would likely still find both the elevator company and Ron liable to Julie. This is because under section 3 of the Act, an occupier owes a statutory duty of care as "in all the circumstances of the case is reasonable to see that persons entering on the premises, and the property brought on the premises by those persons are reasonably safe while on the premises." Specifically, a court would find that the elevator company ought to have foreseen that harm could occur as a result of a defective clip. Likewise, since Ron was aware of the use of the defective clip and was prepared to allow the elevator to remain in service, he too is liable.

In the context of Ron's business, the outcomes using either statutory or common law applications are, for all intents and purposes, the same. Nonetheless, it remains important to apply the correct principles to the specific provincial context, as responsibilities can vary at times.

BUSINESS APPLICATION OF THE LAW

Slip and Fall

Businesses face liability for the tort of negligence as well as under occupiers' liability legislation (as applicable) for what is known by lawyers as a "slip and fall." *In Heard v Canada Safeway Ltd*[20], for example, the plaintiff was awarded damages for injuries she sustained while shopping in the dairy section of Safeway. The plaintiff fell when she inadvertently walked through spilt yoghurt, which the store had neglected to clean up properly. The court concluded that Safeway had failed to take reasonable care for the safety of the plaintiff, contrary to Alberta's *Occupier's Liability Act*, RSA 2000 c O-4.

According to Ontario lawyer Stacey Stevens, slip and fall awards can top $50 000 in the most serious instances.

Critical Analysis: What risk management strategies can a business put in place to reduce the chances of a customer slipping and falling?

What main defences does a retailer have should a customer sue for a slip and fall?

Source: Kirk Makin, "Walker's slip-and-fall a lawyer's pick-me-up", *The Globe and Mail* (15 February 2008) A7.

---

17. *Waldick v Malcolm*, [1991] 2 SCR 456 at 466, 83 DLR (4th) 144 [*Waldick*] quoting with approval the appellate judge from (1989), 70 OR (2d) 717 (CA). Note however that in Alberta, for example, separate categories for trespassers and child trespassers are retained. As well, in some jurisdictions, snowmobilers are treated according to specialized rules. See Klar, *supra* note 2 at 606.
18. Klar, *ibid* at 639.
19. Klar, *ibid* at 638.
20. 2008 ABQB 439, [2009] AWLD 388.

HENRIK SORENSEN/THE IMAGE BANK/GETTY IMAGES

PART THREE

CASE

St Prix-Alexander v Home Depot of Canada Inc, [2008] OJ No 25, 162 ACWS (3d) 854 (Sup Ct)

THE BUSINESS CONTEXT: It is not uncommon for customers to be injured while on a business' premises, such as in a retail store. Such injuries can trigger liability for the business owner that can be very costly.

FACTUAL BACKGROUND: Deanna St. Prix-Alexander was shopping with her husband at a Home Depot store in Ottawa. While she stood in the store looking at a product display, an employee accidently hit her in the back of the head with a heavy box containing a pedestal sink. St. Prix-Alexander was seriously injured.

THE LEGAL QUESTION: Is the employee liable for negligence and liable under occupiers' liability legislation? Is Home Depot vicariously liable as employer?

RESOLUTION: According to the court, the Home Depot employee was negligent because he did not bring the box safely to the ground and he failed to keep a proper lookout for customers in the area. Under Ontario's *Occupiers' Liability Act*, the occupier must take reasonable care for the safety of people on the premises. The employee failed in this duty. Home Depot is also liable for the plaintiff's injuries due to vicarious liability based on the employment relationship.

The plaintiff was awarded over $400 000. Among other matters, this figure was to compensate her for pain and suffering as well as the impact the injury would have on her future earning capacity.

CRITICAL ANALYSIS: Do you think the employee should be responsible for the results of his momentary inattention?

ETHICAL CONSIDERATIONS

The Risk of Spectator Injury at NHL Games: Does Legal Analysis Answer the Ethical Questions?

When spectators are injured by pucks at sporting events, they might sue for breach of contract, in negligence, or pursuant to occupiers' liability—whether at common law or by legislation. Under occupiers' liability legislation in Ontario, for example, the argument would be that the club and facility owner failed in their duty to take reasonable care under section 3 of the Act. The argument in contract would be that the hockey club failed to provide the spectator with a reasonably safe environment, in breach of an implied term or promise to do so. The argument in tort would be that this same deficiency amounted to negligence. In short, whether by contract, tort, or statute, the hockey club and/or facility owner must ensure that the premises are reasonably safe.

One defence to an action based on occupiers' liability would be to show that the spectator assumed the risk that the premises were not safe. Under section 4 of the *Ontario Occupiers' Liability Act*, the club and facility owner's duty to take reasonable care does not apply to risks willingly assumed by the person who enters.[21] According to the Supreme Court of Canada, this kind of provision codifies the common law of *volenti non fit injuria* already discussed in Chapter 11.[22] *Volenti non fit injuria* requires the defendant to show that the plaintiff assumed both the physical and legal risks involved.

AP PHOTO/DAVID KOHL

Brittanie Cecil's funeral was held in May 2002.

From a contractual perspective, the argument of breach of contract would likely be met by the club because the ticket doubtless contains an exemption clause. Such a clause—discussed in Chapter 7—would seek to exclude liability for any injury caused by hockey pucks or other objects. Even if such a clause were absent, the club could point out that there was no promise of absolute safety. It would be sufficient under the contract that the seat provided was reasonably safe.

And yet another defence would be to argue that the plaintiff failed to properly watch for pucks and was therefore contributorily negligent.

(Continued)

---

21. Note that even under the circumstances where risk is willingly assumed, the occupier still owes a duty not to create a danger with reckless disregard (s 4).
22. See *Waldick*, *supra* note 17 at para 40.

Setting aside the possibility that the club's legal defence might well fail,[23] what kind of ethical resonance does it have in the context of a serious injury or fatality? Whatever the standard of safety in an NHL rink must be from a *legal* perspective, is it good enough from an *ethical* one?

In March 2002, Brittanie Cecil, a young spectator, died after being hit by a puck at a National Hockey League game. In light of this tragedy, the NHL's board of governors ordered that safety netting be installed at all league rinks. The board also ordered that the Plexiglas inside the bluelines be raised to a minimum of five feet (1.52 metres). "It's the right thing to do," said Oilers president Patrick LaForge.

Critical Analysis: If the NHL can make the ice arenas safer, is the NHL legally or morally obligated to do so—even though fatalities are extraordinarily rare and some fans will complain that such measures obscure their view of the ice? Does it affect the analysis whether the safety measures are more or less expensive? Should ethics be part of a business' risk management plan? If so, to what extent?

Sources: Jim Matheson, "'Right thing to do': NHL arenas now get safety nets", *The Edmonton Journal* (21 June 2002); John Heinzl, "Protective mesh at hockey rinks would save lives", *The Globe and Mail* (21 March 2002); and *Hagerman v City of Niagara Falls* (1980), 29 OR (2d) 609, 114 DLR (3d) 184 (H Ct J).

The Tort of Nuisance

Nuisance

Any activity on an occupier's property that unreasonably and substantially interferes with the neighbour's rights to enjoyment of the neighbour's own property.

The tort of **nuisance**[24] addresses conflicts between neighbours stemming from land use. It concerns intentional or unintentional actions taken on one neighbour's land that cause harm of some sort on another's, as in these examples:

- Noise from a steel fabricator's 800-ton press seriously interrupts the neighbours' sleep.

- Ashes and unpleasant odours escaping from a rendering company are carried onto neighbouring properties because of dated technology.

The focus of nuisance is on one's right to enjoy the benefits of land/property uninterrupted by the actions of neighbours. The general test is whether the impugned activity has resulted in "an unreasonable and substantial interference with the use and enjoyment of land."[25] For example, Ron may vent his kilns and the decorating and glazing operation in the direction of the window his neighbour must routinely leave open in the summer for cool air. Conversely, the restaurant/bar in the building next door may begin hiring bands that play so loudly that Ron's tenants are threatening to leave.

How can locating houses and factories adjacent to each other lead to claims in nuisance?

DICK HEMINGWAY

23. It may be that a judge would now find that flying pucks are dangers that the club should have reasonably anticipated. See Michael Hirshfeld, "Do spectator safety standards miss the net?", *The Lawyers Weekly* (7 June 2002)(QL).
24. As Klar, *supra* note 2 at 747, indicates, there are two distinct causes of actions in nuisance: public nuisance and private nuisance. Since public nuisance plays only a "peripheral role in contemporary law," this text will focus only on private nuisance.
25. *Ibid* at 759.

In striking a balance between the respective parties, courts have developed the following guidelines:

- Intrusions must be significant and unreasonable.

- Nuisance typically does not arise where the intrusion is only temporary. For example, construction and demolition may be unpleasant, but are likely to be considered temporary and will not lead to a remedy in nuisance.

- Not all interests are protected by the tort of nuisance. For example, the right to sunlight is an unprotected interest as far as the law of nuisance is concerned.

- In nuisance actions, courts will consider tradeoffs in interest. When the noise in question is reasonable and for the public good, the action in nuisance will fail.[26]

Trespass

The tort of **trespass to land** protects a person's possession of land from "wrongful interference."[27]

Trespass arises in several ways:

- A person comes onto the property without the occupier's express or implied permission.

- A person comes onto the property with the occupier's express or implied consent but is subsequently asked to leave.[28] Any person who refuses to leave becomes a trespasser.

- A person leaves an object on the property without the occupier's express or implied permission.

The tort of trespass is important for resolving boundary/title disputes and, more generally, for protecting property rights. It also protects privacy rights and the right to "peaceful use of land."[29] For these kinds of reasons, trespass is actionable without proof of harm or damage. In the exceptional case where the occupier suffers monetary damages due to another's trespass, however, those damages are recoverable. More commonly, the plaintiff will seek an injunction requiring the trespasser to stop trespassing. Provincial legislation in several jurisdictions also provides for fines against the trespasser.[30]

Trespass to land
Wrongful interference with someone's possession of land.

PART THREE

---

26. *Mandrake Management Consultants Ltd v Toronto Transit Commission*, [1993] OJ No 995, 62 OAC 202.
27. *Supra* note 2 at 90.
28. It should be noted that there are statutory restrictions on a businessperson's common law right to do business with whom she or he sees fit. Alberta human rights legislation (the *Alberta Human Rights Act*, RSA 2000, c A-25.5, for example, prohibits discrimination by those who offer goods or services that are customarily available to the public. This means that if a businessperson refused to serve a customer because of that customer's ethnicity or gender, for example, and that customer refused to leave, a trespass has occurred. However, the businessperson would also be subject to a penalty for violating human rights legislation.
29. *Supra* note 2 at 110.
30. Several jurisdictions have enacted legislation that permits trespassers to be fined. See, for example, *Trespass to Premises Act*, RSA 2000, c T-7 and *Petty Trespass Act*, RSA 2000, c P-11, *Trespass Act*, RSBC 1996, c 462; *Petty Trespass Act*, RSNL 1990, c P-11; *Trespass Act*, SNB 1983, c T-11.2; *Petty Trespass Act*, RSM 1987, c P-50; *Trespass to Property Act*, RSO 1990, c T.21. Note too that the Ontario legislation, for example, also provides for damages to be awarded against the trespasser.

ENVIRONMENTAL PERSPECTIVE

Tort Actions Relating to the Environment

At common law, there are four main torts that may provide remedies for environmental damage: the tort of negligence; the tort of trespass; actions based on *Rylands v Fletcher* [31] and the tort of nuisance. These avenues of redress are all somewhat hit and miss given their highly specific requirements.

To successfully sue in negligence, the plaintiff must establish all the steps of a tort action (discussed in Chapter 11), including that the environmental damage was caused by the defendant's *carelessness*. To succeed in trespass, the plaintiff must show direct intrusion of pollutants generated by the defendant and which came on to the plaintiff's land without permission or authorization. [32] The tort in *Rylands v Fletcher* does not require the plaintiff to show that the defendant was careless but rather that something from the defendant's land (such as water or gas) escaped onto the plaintiff's land due to the defendant's dangerous and non-natural use of his land. Much less drastically, the tort of nuisance requires proof that the defendant's pollutants amounted to an unreasonable and substantial interference with the plaintiff's rights to enjoyment of his or her own property. The plaintiff in all these kinds of actions would seek damages for associated losses and, in the right circumstances, an injunction to prevent future occurrences.

In response to the limitations of an exclusively private law response to environmental degradation as well as to facilitate tradeoffs in land use, governments began to enact environmental legislation of an increasingly sophisticated and complex nature. Such legislation seeks to balance economic development with a degree of "acceptable" environmental damage.

MICHAEL MIHIN/SHUTTERSTOCK

In what ways could storing chemical waste in oil drums generate torts in relation to adjoining landowners?

In addition, municipal and land-use planning laws have put further constraints on the kind of activity that can occur on the land affected. (For discussion of environmental legislation in Canada, see Chapter 2.)

Though legislation has therefore displaced some of the importance of common law actions from an environmental perspective, nuisance and other tort actions can be nonetheless regarded as Canada's original environmental law. Until the advent of legislation, they were the only way of controlling adverse neighbouring land use.

Critical Analysis: What are the advantages of regulation of the environment via environmental protection legislation as opposed to by private action?

Sources: Klar, *supra* note 2; Chris Watson, "Using Nuisance and Other Common Law Torts to Protect Water, Land, and Air", (Vancouver: Pacific Business & Law Institute, 2007); Interview of Professor Elaine Hughes, Faculty of Law, University of Alberta (2002).

Torts from Business Operations

Business operations involve a broad range of activities from which tort actions can arise. A useful way of categorizing these torts is to consider separately torts involving customers or clients and those more likely to involve competitors.

Torts Involving Customers

Chapter 11 considered the most important tort arising in this context: negligence. Product liability, motor vehicle accidents, alcohol-related liability, and negligent misrepresentations are all examples of negligence affecting the business/consumer relationship.

In this section additional torts will be considered.

---

31. [1868] UKHL 1, (1868) LR 3 HL.
32. *Smith v Inco Ltd*, 2010 ONSC 3790 at para 37, [2010] OJ No 2864, rev'd on other grounds 2011 ONCA 628, [2011] OJ No 4386.

Assault and Battery

The torts of assault and battery (introduced in Chapter 10) are not common in a business or professional context, although they may occur. For example, security personnel may commit the torts of assault and battery when seeking to apprehend a suspected shoplifter or eject a patron. An assault is the threat of imminent physical harm by disturbing someone's sense of security. Battery is the actual physical contact or violation of that bodily security. The contact need not cause actual harm,[33] though it must be harmful or offensive. Where the torts of assault or battery are proven, the most common remedy is damages.

Note that section 494 of Canada's *Criminal Code* (RSC 1985, c C-46) provides a defence to these kind of torts. For discussion, see the next section below.

False Imprisonment

False imprisonment occurs most often in retail selling. It arises where any person detains another without lawful justification.

False imprisonment occurs when the victim is prevented from going where he has a lawful right to be.[34] The tort includes physically restraining that person or coercing them to stay by psychological means.

The tort of false imprisonment presents retailers in particular with a real challenge. To defend against the tort of false imprisonment (as well as the torts of assault and battery), the retailer and/or its employees must show legal authority to detain, typically under section 494 of Canada's *Criminal Code*.[35] This is called the defence of **legal authority** (or citizen's arrest).

While there is some legal controversy on this matter,[36] the bulk of the case law requires the following be established for the legal authority defence:

- reasonable grounds to detain the person, and

- proof that a crime such as theft or fraud (or other indictable offence) was committed

A suspicion that someone committed a crime is not a justification under statute law for the restraint. Furthermore, when store personnel detain a customer in reliance on section 494, the *Criminal Code* requires them to "forthwith deliver the person to a police officer." This means that they must immediately call the police. Beyond this, the store owner or his employees can only use as much force as is necessary under the circumstances under s 25 of the *Criminal Code*. Otherwise, they face liability in tort and under the *Criminal Code*.

False imprisonment
Unlawful detention or physical restraint or coercion by psychological means.

Legal authority
The authority by law to detain under section 494 of the *Criminal Code*.

---

33. Klar, *supra* note 2 at 47.
34. *Ibid* at 59.
35. Under section 494(1) of the *Criminal Code*, Any one may arrest without warrant
    (a) a person whom he finds committing an indictable offence; or
    (b) a person who, on reasonable grounds he believes
        (i) has committed a criminal offence, and
        (ii) is escaping from and freshly pursued by persons who have lawful authority to arrest that person.
36. As *Kovacs v Ontario Jockey Club*, [1995] OJ No 2181, 126 DLR (4th) 576 notes, there are two lines of authority on this point.

CASE — *R v Chen*, 2010 ONCJ 641, [2010] OJ No 5741

BUSINESS CONTEXT: The retail industry loses a considerable amount of inventory to shoplifters every year. In its latest report, the Retail Council of Canada (in 2007) estimated that store theft and costs related to those thefts amounted to about $3.6 billion annually. The CBC reports on another study showing that 1 in 11 North Americans have shoplifted. Though the problem of inventory shrinkage is therefore rampant, store owners and employees who encounter shoplifters must be careful not to violate the *Criminal Code* or commit the torts of false imprisonment, assault, and battery (discussed in the previous section of this chapter.)

FACTS: David Chen, owner of Lucky Moose Food Mart in Toronto, and some of his employees were charged with assault and forcible confinement (under the *Criminal Code*) after they chased down a shoplifter, tied him up, and held him in a delivery van to await the arrival of the police. The shoplifter, convicted thief Anthony Bennett, had arrived at Chen's store earlier that same day. Surveillance cameras showed him loading up his bicycle with stolen product. As reported in the press, Bennett testified during Chen's trial that he had stolen plants from Chen's store and decided to return to the store one hour later to steal some more. This same media account notes that, during that return trip to the store, Chen asked Bennett to pay for the plants he had previously taken. Bennett refused, cursed Chen with a racist epithet, and then ran away. It was at this point that Chen and his employees gave chase, eventually confining Bennett to a van.

According to Crown prosecutor Eugene McDermott, in a statement to the media:

> Of course shopkeepers are entitled to protect their property. Of course they are entitled to arrest people in the terms of Article 494 [the justification or citizen's arrest provisions of the *Criminal Code*.] But that's not what happened in this case. He [Chen] seized a person off the streets, tied him up and threw him in the back of a van. Once again, nobody calls the police. There are a number of points that beggar belief.

By way of contrast, Chen's lawyer argued that tying up the shoplifter Bennett and holding him in the van was similar to department store personnel bringing a shoplifter to a back room to wait for the police.

LEGAL QUESTION: Are Chen and his employees guilty of forcible confinement and assault?

RESOLUTION: The court concluded that Chen was entitled to make a citizen's arrest under s 494 because he had found Bennett committing a theft on the video tape. Section 494 of the *Criminal Code* states: "Anyone may arrest without warrant: A person whom he finds committing an indictable offense." That Chen purported to arrest Bennett one hour later—when Bennett brazenly

Prime Minister Harper visited Mr. Chen at his store several months after Chen's acquittal.

returned to steal more product from the Lucky Moose—was perfectly fine said the court, because he regarded the original theft and Bennett's subsequent return as "one transaction."

An important related issue was whether Chen had brought himself within section 25 of the *Criminal Code* which provides that in making a citizen's arrest, one is only entitled to use "much force as is necessary" for that purpose. According to Chen's evidence, he had to tie up Bennett because Bennett was kicking and punching. He did not want to let Bennett go, but instead wanted to get back to his store so he could call the police. Bennett gave an entirely different account of events, suggesting, in the court's words, that "he stood by meekly as they [Chen and his employees] laid a beating on him." Based on this and other incongruities, the court expressed concern about the credibility of the evidence offered by Mr. Bennett, Mr. Chen, and his employees.

The court ultimately entered a verdict of not guilty against the accuseds because, according to the judge:

> It is impossible for me to say that I am satisfied on the material evidence before me that I know what happened that day. It follows therefore that the only conclusion that I can come to is that I have a reasonable doubt. All such doubts must always be resolved in the favour of the defence.

In the meantime, Chen has advised the media that he will no longer attempt a citizen's arrest: "I [will] just take the picture and call the police," he said.

CRITICAL ANALYSIS: Do you think the *Criminal Code* provides enough protection to a business owner trying to deal with a shoplifter? Note that government of Canada has recently enacted an amendment to the citizen's arrest provisions under 494(2)of the *Criminal Code* that states: "The owner or a person

© NATIONAL POST/AARON LYNETT

in lawful possession of property … may arrest a person without a warrant if they find them committing a criminal offence on or in relation to that property and (a) they make the arrest at that time or (b) they make the arrest **within a reasonable time after the offence** is committed and they believe on reasonable grounds that it is not feasible in the circumstances for a peace officer to make the arrest." [emphasis added.] Is this amendment to the *Criminal Code* necessary?

Sources: Sarah Hampson, "The Thrill of the Steal: Shoplifting is retail therapy of another kind", *The Globe and Mail* (18 July 2011) online: The Globe and Mail: <http://m.theglobeandmail.com/life/relationships/news-and-views/sarah -hampson/the-thrill-of-the-steal-shoplifting-is-retail-therapy-of-another-kind /article2098874/?service=mobile>; "A History of Shoplifting on The Current", *CBC Books* (5 August 2011) online: CBC Books <http://www.cbc.ca/books/2011 /08/a-history-of-shoplifting-on-the-current.html>; Peter Kuitenbrouwer, "Grocers to the defence", *National Post* (26 October 2010) A3 and Peter Kuitenbrouwer, "Steven Harper Pays a Visit to Lucky Moose, David Chen", *National Post* (17 February 2011) online: National Post <http://news.nationalpost.com/2011 /02/17/stephen-harper-pays-a-visit-to-david-chen/>.

Deceit

The tort of **deceit** arises out of misrepresentations, causing loss, that are made either fraudulently or with reckless disregard for their truth. When deceit arises in a contractual context, one of the remedies available is release from the contract (see Chapter 8) in addition to any other damages in tort that the plaintiff can establish. Though the tort of deceit is not confined to the contractual area, this is where it is most commonly found from a business perspective.

Deceit

A false representation intentionally or recklessly made by one person to another that causes damage.

Business-to-Business Torts

Passing Off

The tort of **passing off** occurs when one person represents her goods or services as being those of another. While it may be common to think of the tort in terms of the "dirty tricks" some businesses might adopt to compete unfairly with others, the tort can also be committed inadvertently or innocently.

The tort of passing off arises, for example, when a business name is used that is so similar to an existing business name that the public is misled into thinking that the businesses are somehow related. It also may occur where a competing company markets a product that is similar in presentation or overall look to a product already established on the market.

Passing off

Presenting another's goods or services as one's own.

CASE	***Ciba-Geigy Canada Ltd v Apotex Inc*, [1992] 3 SCR 120, [1992] SCJ No 83**

BUSINESS CONTEXT: Manufacturers of a product generally become concerned if a competitor starts to copy the look or "getup" of its product. This is because consumers will assume that the goods of the competitor are actually those of the original manufacturer.

FACTS: The plaintiff, Ciba-Geigy Canada Ltd., manufactured and sold the drug metoprolol tartrate in Canada. The defendants later began to manufacture and sell the same drug in Canada. The parties' products were officially designated as "interchangeable," meaning that the pharmacist could, in filling a prescription, give the defendant's product in place of the plaintiff's product provided the prescription did not contain a "no substitution" notation.

The plaintiff brought an action in passing off against the defendants (Apotex and Novopharm) on the basis that the defendants were copying the plaintiff's "getup" in relation to the size, shape, and colour of the pills. The plaintiff claimed that this was creating confusion that the Apotex/Novopharm product was actually a Ciba-Geigy product and sued for passing off.

THE LEGAL QUESTION: What must the plaintiff prove in order to succeed in its action for passing off? More specifically, the issue in this aspect of the litigation was as follows: in seeking to prove that there is confusion caused by the defendants, is the plaintiff limited to showing confusion in the mind of professionals (such as doctors and pharmacists) or can it also rely on confusion in the mind of the ultimate consumer (i.e., the patient)?

(Continued)

RESOLUTION: The Supreme Court of Canada confirmed "that competing laboratories must avoid manufacturing and marketing drugs with such a similar getup that it sows confusion in the customer's mind." The court also confirmed that there are three steps to proving the tort of passing off:

1. the existence of goodwill[37] (e.g., in this case, the plaintiff must show that there is goodwill in respect of the "look" or distinctiveness of the product)[38]
2. deception of the public due to a misrepresentation by the defendant (the misrepresentation may be intentional but it also includes negligent or careless misrepresentation), and
3. actual or potential damage to the plaintiff

Under step two, the plaintiff must show that the competing product is likely to create a risk of confusion in the public mind. On this latter point, the Supreme Court was clear that the plaintiff is not limited to showing confusion in the mind of professionals. Confusion in the mind of the patient who uses the product may also be included.

CRITICAL ANALYSIS: Do you think it is right that a manufacturer should receive legal protection for the features of its product, including colour?

Based on the Supreme Court of Canada's analysis above, Ron will need to establish the following in order to prove passing off:

1. *Goodwill or a reputation is attached to his product.* Ron's "Old Man of the Sea" product already has a well-established and valuable reputation among the relevant buying public. In other words, he holds goodwill in the product, and that goodwill, or ability to attract buyers, flows either from the look of the product or from its name, or from both.

2. *A misrepresentation—express or implied—by the maker of the cheap replica has led or is likely to lead members of the public into believing that it is Ron's product or a product authorized by Ron.* Whether the competitor actually intended to confuse the public does not matter. Given the similarity in appearance and name of the two figurines, the competitor will make many of its sales by falsely associating itself with the established reputation of Ron's "Old Man of the Sea" product. Ron could prove his point by commissioning a survey of the relevant sector of the buying public.

3. *He has or will likely suffer damages.* Ron must show that he has lost sales, or is likely to lose sales, because of the replica product.

While the award of damages is one remedy for a passing-off action, businesses claiming they are being harmed in this way will often seek an injunction forbidding the defendant from continuing the deceptive copying. In the case of *Walt Disney Productions v Triple Five Corp*,[39] for example, Walt Disney Productions secured a permanent injunction prohibiting the use of the name Fantasyland at West Edmonton Mall's amusement park.[40]

The *Trade-marks Act*[41] contains a statutory form of action that bears a strong resemblance to the tort of passing off. Such legislation will be considered more thoroughly in Chapter 18. Where the legislation is not relevant, as in the *Walt Disney Productions v Triple Five case*, the plaintiff is entitled to pursue its action for passing off at common law.

---

37. Goodwill refers to the reputation of the business and its expectation of patronage in the future.
38. This means that the product has a "secondary meaning" in the mind of the public.
39. *Walt Disney Productions v Triple Five Corp* (1994), 17 Alta LR (3d) 225, 149 AR 112 (CA).
40. *Ibid.*
41. RSC 1985, c T-13, s 7.

Interference with Contractual Relations

The tort of **interference with contractual relations** is known by a variety of names, including interference with contract, inducement of breach of contract, and procuring a breach of contract.[42] It has its origins in the relationship of master and servant. The common law made it actionable if one master attempted to "poach" the servant of another. In legal terms, the "poacher" was seen as enticing the servant to break his existing contract of employment, which, in turn, caused economic harm to the master. Over time, this tort extended beyond master/servant relations to any form of contractual relationship.

The tort prohibits a variety of conduct, including conduct whereby the defendant directly induces another to breach her contract with the plaintiff.

In Ron's business, the tort of interference with contractual relations could be important in at least two different contexts:

- Ron employs a skilled potter who makes the "Old Man of the Sea" product. The potter has a three-year employment contract. A competitor approaches the potter in the second year of the contract and encourages the potter to work for him with promises of higher wages and better conditions. The competitor's conduct is tortious because he knew about the contract and acted with the objective of convincing the potter to join him. Since this could happen only if the potter were to breach his contract with Ron, the tort has been made out.

- Ron's largest and most lucrative supply contract is with one of the leading tourism organizations in Nova Scotia. The owner of the competing business making "Man of the Sea" products approaches the tourism organization and suggests that if it breaks the contract with Ron and buys from her, she can offer them a much better deal.

In both cases, then, Ron could likely make out the tort of interference with contractual relations. While he will sue for damages, he may also seek an injunction to prevent a breach of contract occurring if he finds out in time. A court would never order the potter to work for Ron—courts will not award specific performance with contracts of personal service—but it can order damages against the potter for breach of contract and damages and/or an injunction against the competitor for the tort of interference with contractual relations.

An example of a successful tort action is *Ernst & Young v Stuart*.[43] A partner left the accounting firm of Ernst & Young to join the firm of Arthur Andersen. In so doing, the partner violated a term of the partnership agreement requiring one year's notice of intention to retire from the partnership. Ernst & Young sued both the partner and the new firm, the latter for interfering with contractual relations. Both actions were successful.

Interference with contractual relations Incitement to break the contractual obligations of another.

---

42. P Burns, "Tort Injury to Economic Interests: Some Facets of Legal Response" (1980) 58 Can Bar Rev 103 cited by Klar, *supra* note 2 at 708, his note 80.
43. [1997] BCJ No 524, 88 BCAC 182.

Defamation

The tort of **defamation** seeks to "protect the reputation of individuals against unfounded and unjustified attacks."[44] Though all jurisdictions in Canada have legislation modifying the common law of defamation to some extent, the fundamentals of the common law action remain.[45]

Common terms for defamation are slander (typically for the oral form) and libel (usually the print form). These terms are not always consistently applied but regardless, both slander and libel can simply be called defamation.[46] The key ingredients to the tort, as recently confirmed by the Supreme Court of Canada, are as follows:

- The defendant's words were defamatory in that they would "tend to lower the plaintiff's reputation in the eyes of a reasonable person."
- The statement did in fact refer to the plaintiff.
- The words were communicated to at least one other person beyond the plaintiff.[47]

The plaintiff will then succeed if the defendant is unable to establish a defence to the action. For example, if the defendant can show that the impugned statement is substantially true, he has a complete defence of **justification**.[48]

From a business perspective, a potential defamation scenario occurs when an employer provides a reference for an ex-employee. If the letter contains a defamatory statement that is true, the employer may have the defence of justification described above. Other defences in this scenario include **qualified privilege**. That is, if the employer's statement is relevant, made without malice, and communicated only to a party who has a legitimate interest in receiving it, the defence is established.

Another defence is **fair comment**. This defence permits a person to offer commentary on "matters of public interest" despite the commentary being defamatory.[49] The defence of fair comment requires the defendant to show that the comment (a) concerned a matter of public interest, (b) was factually based, and (c) expressed a view that could honestly be held by anyone.[50] The defence will then succeed unless the plaintiff can show the defendant was motivated by express malice.[51] In *Sara's Pyrohy Hut v Brooker*,[52] for example, a broadcast journalist raised fair comment as a defence to a restaurant review containing defamatory content. The court agreed that the defence had been made out, noting that "opinions, even if adverse, may be expressed so long as the facts are not distorted or invented. Here . . . the review was an expression of opinion without malice, even though some of [the] opinions were unfavourable."[53]

Responsible communication on matters of public interest is a defence recently recognized by the Supreme Court of Canada. It will apply to members of the traditional media where (1) the publication is on a matter of "public interest" and (2) the publisher was diligent in trying

Defamation
The public utterance of a false statement of fact or opinion that harms another's reputation.

Justification
A defence to defamation based on the defamatory statement being substantially true.

Qualified privilege
A defence to defamation based on the defamatory statement being relevant, without malice, and communicated only to a party who has a legitimate interest in receiving it.

Fair comment
A defence to defamation that is established when the plaintiff cannot show malice and the defendant can show that the comment concerned a matter of public interest, was factually based, and expressed a view that could honestly be held by anyone.

Responsible communication on matters of public interest
Defence that applies where some facts are incorrectly reported but (1) the publication is on a matter of "public interest" and (2) the publisher was diligent in trying to verify the allegation.

---

44. *Supra* note 2 at 781.
45. *Ibid* at 782.
46. The distinction between libel and slander has been abolished by statute in a number of provinces.
47. *Grant v Torstar Corp*, 2009 SCC 61 at para 28, [2009] 3 SCR 640 [*Grant*].
48. *Ibid* at para 32
49. Klar, *supra* note 2 at 824 and *Grant supra* note 47 at para 31.
50. Klar, *supra* note 2 at 824.
51. *Ibid*.
52. *Sara's Pyrohy Hut v Brooker* (1993), 141 AR 42, 8 Alta LR (3d) 113 (CA).
53. *Ibid*.

to verify the allegation.[54] The defence can also presumably be invoked by bloggers, Twitterers, and others who publish on the Web[55] because the Supreme Court agreed that the defence should be available to anyone "who publishes material of public interest in any medium."[56]

The Supreme Court of Canada offered an extensive list of factors which help determine whether the defence is available, including whether the publication sought the plaintiff's reaction or input, the steps taken by the publisher verify the story, and the importance of the subject matter from a public perspective.

If the plaintiff in a defamation action can prove actual monetary loss as a result of the defendant's defamation, this loss is recoverable. The law recognizes, however, that much of the damage suffered is intangible. Therefore, the court is permitted to assess damages from an alternate perspective. This includes considering the seriousness of the defamation, how widely the defamation was published, the malice of the defendant, and the extent of the damages that have been caused.[57] Where the defendant's conduct has been particularly reprehensible and oppressive, a court is entitled to award punitive damages, as the box below illustrates.

Absolute privilege is another defence to defamation which applies in the very limited context of parliamentary or judicial proceedings.[58] The notion is that freedom of expression is so vital in such venues that no successful defamation action can be brought.[59]

Absolute privilege
A defence to defamation in relation to parliamentary or judicial proceedings.

PART THREE

TECHNOLOGY AND THE LAW

E-Torts: Defamation on the Internet

A growing objective for business is to guard against defamation via electronic media. The danger of emails, in particular, is that once they are sent they cannot be retrieved, yet they can be instantaneously transmitted to an enormous audience. There is likely no email user who has not hit the Send key and then realized too late he was transmitting to unintended recipients. Since the legal process allows for the discovery or tracing of electronic words to their author, electronic defamation can most certainly be established even long after a defamatory message has apparently been deleted.

Defamation can also occur on websites found via the Internet. In a decision from the Ontario Superior Court, damages were awarded to the plaintiff—Mr. Reichmann—for just this form of defamation. Reichmann sued because the defendants had defamed him as part of an extortion campaign. They told Reichmann that if he failed to pay them a large sum of money, they would publish statements on the Internet that he had lied and cheated an innocent man of his inheritance. When Reichmann refused to pay, the defendants distributed cards to Reichmann's neighbours alerting them to a website containing these false allegations. Given the egregious circumstances—including the fact that Internet publication instantly communicates information worldwide—the court awarded a total of $400 000 in damages, including $100 000 in punitive damages.

More recently, the Supreme Court of Canada has held that merely providing a hyperlink to a site which contains defamatory material is not actionable. While someone who repeats defamatory words first uttered by someone else is liable for defamation because the second speaker has "published" the words of the first, the Supreme Court concluded that supplying hyperlinks does not amount to publication. As the court noted:

> Only when a hyperlinker presents content from the hyperlinked material in a way that actually repeats the defamatory content, should that content be considered to be "published" by the hyperlinker. Such an approach promotes expression and respects the realities of the Internet, while creating little or no limitations to a plaintiff's ability to vindicate his or her reputation.

Critical Analysis: How can a business protect its reputation from attack on the Internet?

Sources: *Crookes v Newton*, 2011 SCC 47, [2011] SCJ No 47; *Reichmann v Berlin*, [2002] OJ No 2732, [2002] OTC 464 (Sup Ct); and Bradley J Freedman, "Ontario Court Orders $400,000 in Damages for Internet Defamation", (25 July 2002) online: The Continuing Legal Education Society of British Columbia <http://www.cle.bc.ca/CLE /Stay+Current/Collection/2002/7/02-onthcj-reichmann>. See also <http://cle.bc.ca>

---

54. *Grant, supra* note 47 at para 126.
55. Jeffrey Vicq, "New defamation defences benefit the Twitiverse", *Lawyers Weekly* (12 February 2010)(QL).
56. Grant, *supra* note 47 at para 96.
57. Klar, *supra* note 2 at 835.
58. Klar, *supra* note 2 at 804.
59. *Ibid.*

Injurious Falsehood or Product Defamation

Injurious or malicious falsehood
The utterance of a false statement about another's goods or services that is harmful to the reputation of those goods or services.

Injurious or malicious falsehood concerns false statements made not about a person but about the goods or services provided by that person. Sometimes the distinction between injurious falsehood and defamation is subtle; for example, if the statement is made that a particular company routinely provides shoddy maintenance, is this a negative reflection on the quality of the people doing the work or on the company's services? In such a situation, the complainant would sue for both defamation and injurious falsehood.

Injurious falsehood requires the plaintiff to establish that the statement about the goods or services was false and was published (or uttered) with malice or improper motive. It is not necessary to prove that the defendant intended to injure the plaintiff. A reckless disregard for the truth or falsity of the statement is sufficient.

Injurious falsehood can be particularly problematic in the context of comparative and negative advertising, as the case below shows.

CASE | *Mead Johnson Canada v Ross Pediatrics*, 31 OR (3d) 237, [1996] OJ No 3869 (Gen Div)

THE BUSINESS CONTEXT: It is relatively common for sellers to engage in comparative advertising. Should the seller cross the line and commit the tort of injurious falsehood, it can be subject to legal action, including for an injunction to prevent the continued distribution of the impugned material.

FACTUAL BACKGROUND: Ross began selling a new infant formula, Similac Advance, using promotional materials that included many representations to which Mead, the maker of a competing infant formula, Enfalac, objected.

Mead representatives obtained samples of the professional brochure and some of the consumer materials. Research Management Group conducted market studies for Mead, which suggested that 81 to 91 percent of new parents, having seen the promotional materials, would choose the new product.

Mead argued that the Similac Advance materials were false and misleading in claiming that Similac was superior to other formulas, was similar to breast milk, and was clinically proven to strengthen infants' immune systems. Ross argued that Mead and

Enfalac were not identified by the Ross promotional materials. No injurious falsehood could be established where there was no identification of the injured party.

THE LEGAL QUESTION: Has Ross Pediatrics committed the tort of injurious falsehood?

RESOLUTION: While it was true that Enfalac was not identified in the brochure materials, Enfalac was identified as a target in the materials distributed to the Ross sales force. It was also true that Enfalac, being the other major competitor in this marketplace, would be identified by implication. On this basis, the court held that all of Ross' competitors, including Mead, might have a cause of action if the representations were false and misleading.

CRITICAL ANALYSIS: Many companies engage in comparative advertising. What could Ross have done that would have avoided any suggestion of injurious falsehood? If the injunction continued, what would be the business implications for Ross? What recommendations might you have for senior management in order to avoid a similar episode in the future?

BUSINESS APPLICATION OF THE LAW

Protection of Privacy

The common law protects privacy interests in a variety of ways. The tort of defamation protects reputation. The torts of trespass and nuisance protect the right to enjoy one's property. The torts of assault, battery, and false imprisonment protect the person's right to dignity.[60]

Beyond this, the Ontario Court of Appeal has recently recognized a new tort which permits a person to sue for invasion of privacy. In *Jones v Tsige*,[61] the appellate court ruled that when the defendant electronically accessed the plaintiff's personal banking records (on at least 174 occasions), she had also committed a tort. This new tort helps to recognize that

---

60. For more analysis, see Klar, *supra* note 2 at 86 and following
61. 2012 ONCA 32.

technological change, in the judge's words, "poses a novel threat to a right of privacy that has been protected for hundreds of years by the common law under various guises and that, since 1982 and the *Charter*, has been recognized as a right that is integral to our social and political order."[62] Most importantly, such a tort responds to "facts that cry out for a remedy" given that the defendant's actions were "deliberate, prolonged and shocking."[63] To succeed in establishing this new tort—also called the "intrusion upon seclusion" tort—the plaintiff must prove as follows: (1) that the defendant's conduct was intentional; (2) that the defendant invaded the plaintiff's private affairs without lawful justification; and (3) that a reasonable person would regard such conduct as "highly offensive causing distress, humiliation or anguish."[64] More specifically, victims will have a legal remedy when someone wrongfully accesses their "financial or health records, sexual practices and orientation, employment, diary or private correspondence."[65] In *Tsige*, the plaintiff was awarded $10 000 in damages,[66] with the court suggesting a ceiling in this kind of case of $20 000.[67]

Government has also sought to protect privacy through legislation that deals with the collection, use, and disclosure of personal information by organizations in the course of commercial activities.[68] In addition, certain provincial governments have passed legislation that creates the tort of breach of privacy.[69] British Columbia's *Privacy Act*,[70] for example, states:

1. (1) It is a tort, actionable without proof of damage, for a person, willfully and without a claim of right, to violate the privacy of another.

   (2) The nature and degree of privacy to which a person is entitled in a situation or in relation to a matter is that which is reasonable in the circumstances, giving due regard to the lawful interests of others.

   (3) In determining whether the act or conduct of a person is a violation of another's privacy, regard must be given to the nature, incidence and occasion of the act or conduct and to any domestic or other relationship between the parties.

   (4) Without limiting subsections (1) to (3), privacy may be violated by eavesdropping or surveillance, whether or not accomplished by trespass.

In *Hollinsworth v BCTV*,[71] the plaintiff successfully relied on this statute to bring his action against Look International Enterprises for releasing to BCTV a videotape showing the plaintiff undergoing an operation to have a hairpiece surgically attached to his head. Since Look International Enterprises had done so without the plaintiff's knowledge and consent, this amounted to a willful invasion of privacy, a clear violation of the statute. In response, the court awarded the plaintiff $15 000 in damages. Likewise, when a landlord secretly set up a video camera which captured on film everyone who entered the plaintiff's apartment, the court found that the *Privacy Act* had been violated and awarded $3 500 to the plaintiff. See *Heckert v 5470 Investments Ltd*.[72]

Critical Analysis: Does the new tort of intrusion upon seclusion improve the law? Do you think that the $20 000 ceiling on damage awards set by the court in *Tsige* is too low?

Managing the Risk of Diverse Commercial Torts

Each of the torts discussed in this chapter exposes a business to liability. A risk management analysis should address the fundamental problems that may arise, always taking into account that business activities are usually engaged in by employees in the course of employment. As discussed in Chapter 10, an employer is responsible under the doctrine of vicarious liability for the torts of its employees.

An occupier's liability risk management plan would ask the following questions:

- Are there dangers on the property? Are adequate warnings and protections given to visitors?

- Are there known trespassers, in particular children, who come onto the property?

---

62. *Ibid* at para 68.
63. *Ibid* at para 69.
64. *Ibid* at para 71.
65. *Ibid* at para 73.
66. *Ibid* at para 92.
67. *Ibid* at 87.
68. For discussion of the *Personal Information Protection and Electronic Documents Act*, 2000 SC 2000, c 5 ("PIPEDA"), see Chapters 1, 8, 12, 20, and 24.
69. See, for example, *Privacy Act*, RSBC 1996, c 373; *Privacy Act*, RSS 1978, c P-24; *Privacy Act*, CCSM c P-125; and *Privacy Act* RSNL 1990, c P-22. See too Quebec's *Charter of Human Rights and Freedoms*, RSQ c C-12, s 5, which provides that "[e]very person has a right to respect for his private life." See also Klar, *supra* note 2 at 87 and following.
70. *Privacy Act*, RSBC 1996, c 373.
71. 113 BCAC 304, [1998] BCJ No 2451.
72. 2008 BCSC 1298, [2008] BCJ No 1854.

- What could be done to eliminate or reduce the risk flowing from the dangers?

- Has the occupier complied with all legislative obligations? Examples include provincial legislation concerning workers' health and safety, as well as municipal bylaws providing for snow and ice removal.

- Is adequate insurance in place?

Although the classification of entrants under the common law of occupiers' liability may be a useful exercise after an incident occurs (it helps determine liability), from a risk management perspective the process is not particularly helpful since the business that occupies property cannot easily predict what class of entrant will be injured on its property. Maintaining safe premises as a preventive measure is much better than having to debate, after the fact, what class of entrant the injured plaintiff is and what standard is owed.

For each additional tort discussed in this chapter, a similar list of questions could be generated. For example, if the business designs and creates consumer goods:

- Do staff understand that they cannot innovate by copying others?

- Is a program in place to review new product ideas, including all aspects of design, to ensure there is no passing off?

- Is a climate in place that allows a manager to step in and say, "This cannot be done because I believe we have crossed the line"?

Tort law evolves to reflect changing social values. What at one time might have been acceptable behaviour may no longer be considered appropriate. This can be seen, for example, in the changing approach to the environmental effects of commercial activities. When a business is assessing its tort exposure, it cannot assume that existing legal rules will apply in perpetuity. Also, it must consider how it can influence public opinion and social values, as those will determine the bounds of future tort liability.

Business Law in Practice Revisited

1. What potential legal actions does Julie have against Ron's business?

Ron is an occupier of the building. As such, he is responsible to different classes of people who come onto his property both lawfully and unlawfully. The extent of the responsibility varies depending on why the person is on the premises and whether the premises are in a common law or statutory jurisdiction.

In Newfoundland and Labrador, common law principles apply. Julie is clearly an invitee and, as such, Ron owes a duty to warn of "any unusual danger [of] which he knows or ought to know." In this case, it appears he was aware of the inadequate, temporary repair job on the elevator, and therefore had the requisite knowledge.

If these events occurred in a jurisdiction where statute law has replaced the common law of occupier's liability, the responsibility to Julie, a person on the property legitimately, would be very similar to that of the tort of negligence. In all likelihood Ron would still be liable.

2. What is the responsibility of Elevator XL Services?

Elevator XL Services is an occupier, since it had control over the elevator in order to conduct the repairs. This was also the time when the harm occurred. Following the same analysis as used in question 1 above, Elevator XL Services will be liable to Julie under both common and statute law. Julie was on the property lawfully and, at common law, was an invitee.

3. Does Ron have any recourse against the manufacturer of the replica figurine?

Ron can take action based on the tort of passing off. He can claim that the actions of the competitor meet the conditions of the tort of passing off, and as such he will either seek an injunction to stop any further action by the competitor, or damages, or both. He will need to prove that his "Old Man of the Sea" figurine existed prior to the "Man of the Sea" product, that it had an established reputation that was of value, that the products' names and appearances are similar enough to result in confusion in the minds of the potential purchasers, and that the confusion has resulted or will result in loss of sales or harm to Ron's business. It is sufficient that the defendant's conduct compromises Ron's control over his own business reputation.

4. How can Ron manage the risk his business faces of potential tort liabilities?

Ron, as owner/occupier of the premises, should do a safety audit of all parts of the building to ensure that neither his tenants nor his visitors (lawful or otherwise) could be harmed by any hazards. Ron should consider all aspects of his business operations, including the building itself, obvious hazards such as the kiln, maintenance of elevators, clearing of sidewalks, hiring and training of all employees, and insurance coverage.

In terms of Ron's products, Ron should

- monitor the activity of competitors and potential competitors to ensure that there is no inappropriate copying of his designs

- ensure that the glazes and materials he uses are lead-free and otherwise harmless

- hire staff who know how to treat customers well and are trained as to their obligations should they have to handle shoplifters

Chapter Summary

While negligence is the most common tort a business will encounter, various other commercially relevant torts merit analysis. These torts can be categorized and assessed according to whether they would arise because the business is an occupier of property or because it provides a product or service. Furthermore, torts that could be committed against a competitor can be grouped separately from those more likely to involve a consumer. Though these distinctions are not definitive, they provide a useful way of organizing the variety of torts that affect the commercial world.

As an occupier, a business must be sure to keep its property safe so that people coming on-site are not injured, otherwise it faces occupiers' liability according to a regime that classifies the entrant in question under common law or by statute. To avoid committing the tort of nuisance, a business must not unreasonably and substantially interfere with the right of its neighbours to enjoy their property. The law governing trespass gives occupiers a right to exert control over who comes onto their premises, subject to human rights codes.

Torts arising from business operations in relation to customers are false imprisonment, assault and battery, and deceit. Through these torts, the law seeks to ensure people's right to move about as they please, to have their bodily integrity respected, and not to be misled about the quality of a product or service.

Torts more likely to be committed against a competitor include passing off, interference with contractual relations, defamation, and injurious falsehood or product defamation. These torts endeavour to protect a business' property and its own reputation.

Given the diverse and wide-ranging nature of a business' potential liability in tort, preventing torts from ever occurring should be one of management's top priorities.

Chapter Study

Key Terms and Concepts

absolute privilege (p. 275)

contractual entrant (p. 262)

deceit (p. 271)

defamation (p. 274)

fair comment (p. 274)

false imprisonment (p. 269)

injurious or malicious falsehood (p. 276)

**interference with contractual
relations (p. 273)**

invitee (p. 262)

justification (p. 274)

legal authority (p. 269)

licensee (p. 263)

nuisance (p. 266)

occupier (p. 262)

passing off (p. 271)

qualified privilege (p. 274)

**responsible communication on matters
of public interest (p. 274)**

trespass to land (p. 267)

trespasser (p. 263)

Questions for Review

1. How does the law define the occupier of a property?

2. Who is an occupier?

3. What are the four different classes of visitors in the law of occupiers' liability?

4. What is the standard of care owed to each of the four classes of visitors?

5. What is the major change made by legislation in many provinces of Canada to the common law of occupiers' liability?

6. What is a nuisance in tort law?

7. The courts have developed pragmatic rules for resolving inherent conflicts that arise in applying the tort of nuisance. Give two examples of these rules.

8. Under what conditions can trespass arise?

9. What are the limitations to the ability of a store detective to detain a customer who is suspected of shoplifting?

10. Describe how a false imprisonment claim might arise, other than by a person being physically restrained.

11. How can a business manage the risk of retail theft and fraud?

12. Identify what must be established to prove deceit.

13. What is "passing off," and what practices was this tort created to prevent?

14. Describe a situation that might amount to the tort of interference with contractual relations.

15. What is defamation, and what are the defences to this tort?

16. When is a court entitled to award punitive damages for the tort of defamation?

17. What is injurious falsehood?

18. What is the tort of intrusion upon seclusion?

Questions for Critical Thinking

1. One of the controversial aspects of occupiers' liability and its more recent statutory form arises out of the rights afforded trespassers. One possible change to the law would be to eliminate all rights. What would be the consequences of this approach? Are there some trespassers that you would feel uncomfortable leaving without protection?

2. What can businesses do to manage the risk of slip-and-fall incidents?

3. The tort of false imprisonment places serious limitations on any action the retailer can take to detain suspected shoplifters. What are the pros and cons of these limitations? Are they fair? What are the countervailing interests at stake? How can retailers reduce the risks associated with apprehending suspected shoplifters?

4. The common law states that someone is liable for defamation just for *repeating* or passing on defamatory words he or she heard from someone else. This is called publication. Do you think that publication should be actionable? Why or why not?

5. The tort of interference with contractual relations has its origins in the ancient master/servant relationship. Today, however, there is greater recognition of mobility rights, and those in business are generally used to competing in an aggressive marketplace. Given that the aggrieved party has the right to sue for breach of contract, should this tort be retained? What rights might not be protected if the tort of interference with contractual relations were to be abolished? Are these important?

6. A major aim of the tort of defamation is to seek to "protect the reputation of individuals against unfounded and unjustified attacks." However, it is relatively easy for a plaintiff to make out the tort, as it basically encompasses any statement that presents another in an uncomplimentary light. The major burden of the action then shifts to the person who made or published the statement to provide a defence. Do you think that the tort of defamation is too easily proven? Is it unfair to place such a heavy burden on someone to defend the statements they make, especially given that freedom of speech is such an important principle in Canada?

Situations for Discussion

1. A convenience store owner has suffered several burglaries in the past few months. He is very concerned, as he believes this trend means he will likely lose his livelihood. He elects to arm himself with a shotgun for self-protection: the most recent break-in was by armed thieves. One evening, three thieves enter the premises. He shouts at them to leave as they approach the till, and he brings out his shotgun. The thieves immediately start running from the store. The store owner shoots one of them as he is leaving. Has the injured thief any right to compensation? How could the owner have better managed the risk of theft and burglary?

2. Mr. Favo slipped and fell on a small patch of ice outside a popular car wash. Mr. Favo was late for an appointment and was walking somewhat faster than usual just prior to taking the tumble. Ms. Daby, owner of the car wash, was proud of the 10-year safety record she had established up until this point. She attributes this safety record to being acutely aware of the problems ice causes in winter when wet vehicles exit the car wash, leaving puddles in their wake. On a related front, Daby also held frequent staff meetings in order to emphasize how important it was to prevent ice formation and to salt the sidewalk according to a very strict schedule. The supervisor on shift when Favo fell was adamant that the area had been salted prior to the incident. He also conducted an inspection of the area immediately after the fall and found only a very small patch of ice had been missed. Is Daby liable? Is Favo contributorily negligent?[73]

3. Great Food Restaurant serves a very popular buffet style menu in central Saskatchewan. During one dinner service, a patron became ill and vomited on one of the buffet tables. A supervisor and employee tended to the situation by removing most of the food from the buffet itself, wiping up with a cloth soaked in a weak bleach solution and mopping the floor. They then replaced the food in the buffet and carried on business. Several people who subsequently ate at the restaurant became ill with the Norwalk virus, a highly contagious pathogen that is easily spread if not deactivated with a sufficiently strong disinfecting solution. A small local newspaper ran a story about the incident, with the headline "Vomit serves up virus at buffet." The article suggested that the illnesses were caused by "eating from a buffet that a customer had vomited on." It also quoted a health officer who said the virus was likely spread by contact with contaminated surfaces and "may not have involved the buffet food at all." There was no time to speak to Great Food Restaurant before the story had to go to press. Had the newspaper done so, it would have learned from the manager his view that the illnesses were not caused by the restaurant food. Great Food Restaurant has since suffered a large drop in business and wants to sue the newspaper for defamation. Will its action be successful?[74]

4. The Kumars are long-time residents of an older neighbourhood of a major city. They inherited their home from Mrs. Kumar's parents. Their own family is now grown up and gone, and Mr. and Mrs. Kumar enjoy the pleasures of their quiet and beautifully

---

73. Based on *Foley v Imperial Oil Ltd*, 2010 BCSC 797, 11 BCLR (5th) 125 aff'd 2011 BCCA 262, 307 BCAC 34.
74. Based on part on *PG Restaurant Ltd (COB Mama Panda Restaurant) v Northern Interior Regional Health Board*, 2005 BCCA 210, 211 BCAC 219; rehearing refused (2005), 41 BCLR (4th) 55 (CA); leave to appeal to SCC refused [2005] SCCA No 270.

maintained back garden—that is, they did until the past few months. The neighbours on one side of the Kumars sold their property about a year ago, and the new owners have shown the Kumars their plans for the property. The plans involve demolishing the home and building a much larger house very close to the boundaries of the property. Because the building will be three storeys high and because of its size and location, all afternoon sun will effectively be blocked from the Kumars' garden. Moreover, they will lose their privacy. The Kumars are distraught. They are also very concerned about the noise and disruption from the demolition and construction. Lastly, they have noticed that large and noisy air-conditioning and heating units will be placed adjacent to their property, right beside their bedroom wall. Assuming that all these changes are within the local planning rules, what are the Kumars' rights? What factors should the Kumars consider before launching a legal action?

5. The Happy Bar operates in Fergus, Ontario. The bar routinely attracts large numbers of students from the local universities. Because of its location, students have to drive at least 20 kilometres to get to the bar. The owners of the bar are acutely aware of their responsibilities both to ensure that no underage students drink and to make certain that any intoxicated patrons leave the bar in a vehicle driven by a designated driver. On peak nights the bar brings in additional staff to ensure compliance with its policies. On one Saturday night, a regular staff member calls in sick, but recommends his friend, who is a law and security student at the local community college. He assures the manager that this friend is familiar with the appropriate practices and guidelines and is fully responsible. The friend is hired for the night and appears to the manager to be capable. Around 11:30 p.m., a group of young people become particularly rowdy, and one moves toward the door, car keys in hand and shouting to her friends to get into the car quickly so they can find a "really good party." The new staff member is the only employee nearby and able to intervene. He rushes to the young woman, pins her arms behind her with one hand, and puts a chokehold around her neck. He demands she throw down her keys. Unfortunately, the woman suffers from epilepsy. This action precipitates a seizure, and in the course of the seizure, perhaps in part because of the amount of alcohol consumed, the woman chokes. She is unconscious for 10 minutes and suffers serious brain damage. Discuss the tort principles that arise in this case. Who will be sued and for what? What are the merits of the case?

6. Mandrake Ltd. owns and occupies an office building. Mandrake complains about the noise and vibration coming from the nearby subway system of the Toronto Transit Commission.[75] Will Mandrake be successful in an action for nuisance? In particular, would the ordinary and reasonable resident of that locality view the disturbance as a substantial interference with the enjoyment of land? What factors will a court consider in determining whether there is nuisance or not? At what point should legitimate activities be curtailed because of the unavoidable consequences to other nearby businesses?

7. Beginning in 1955, Disney started opening outdoor amusement parks around the world and now owns a number of parks, including those in California, Florida, Europe, and Japan. Each amusement park contains various theme parks, one of which is called Fantasyland. In 1981, Triple Five opened an indoor amusement park in the West Edmonton Mall, also called Fantasyland.[76] Has Triple Five committed the tort of passing off? What would a court take into account in determining whether the tort has occurred? If the tort is made out, do you think it is legitimate to give Disney a monopoly over the word "Fantasyland" in association with all amusement parks?

8. Mr. Bahner was hosting a dinner for friends at a restaurant in the Bayshore Inn, Vancouver. The group ordered one bottle of wine and, at 11:30 p.m., the waiter asked if they would like another, to which they agreed. There was still wine in the first bottle however. At 11:50 p.m., Bahner was told by the waiter that, due to a law in force in British Columbia at the time, all the wine on the table had to be consumed

75. Based, in part, on *Mandrake Management Consultants Ltd v Toronto Transit Commission*, [1993] OJ No 995, 62 OAC 202.
76. Based, in part, on *Walt Disney Productions v Triple Five Corp* (1994), 17 Alta LR (3d) 225, 149 AR 112 (CA).

before midnight. The plaintiff considered this to be impossible without resulting in drunkenness and therefore asked if they could simply take the second bottle away with them at the end of the evening. Bahner was advised by the waiter that this, too, was against the law. The plaintiff paid for the dinner itself and the first bottle of wine but refused to pay for the second, saying he would just leave it on the table. The second bottle was open but had been otherwise left untouched. In response, the hotel manager called a security guard. Bahner and his guests stood up and tried to leave. The security guard blocked the main restaurant exit, saying, "You cannot leave." When

Bahner again refused to pay, the security guard called the police. Since Bahner was not being permitted to leave the restaurant, he sat down at a table nearer the door and waited with his guests. He was then arrested and spent the night in jail before he was released. Does Mr. Bahner have a successful action for false imprisonment against the restaurant owner? Why or why not? How could such an unfortunate situation have been avoided to begin with?[77]

For more study tools, visit http://www.NELSONbrain.com.

77. Based on *Bahner v Marwest Hotel Co*, [1969] BCJ No 440, 6 DLR (3d) 322 (SC) aff'd [1970] BCJ No 617, 12 DLR (3d) 646 (CA).

PART FOUR

Structuring Business Activity

Entrepreneurs with services or products ready for market need to select a business vehicle—or ownership structure—through which to offer them. This choice, essentially limited to three basic forms, has broad legal consequences because each kind of business vehicle comes with a specific set of rights and liabilities.

- A *sole proprietorship* refers to an individual carrying on business alone. The actual business activity may be conducted by others, such as agents or employees, but ownership remains the responsibility of one person.

- A *partnership* involves two or more persons sharing ownership responsibilities either equally or in some proportion among the partners.

- A *corporation* is a separate legal entity that is owned by one or more shareholders.

Regardless of its form, the business will almost certainly rely on agency and employment relationships for its day-to-day operations. An agency relationship involves the business relying on someone else to act on its behalf. In law, the actions of the agent are often treated as the actions of the business itself.

JAMES THEW/SHUTTERSTOCK

CHAPTER 13

The Agency Relationship

Objectives

After studying this chapter, you should have an understanding of

- the agency relationship and its relevance to business

- how an agency relationship comes into being

- agency duties and liabilities

- how the agency relationship ends

ROB MELNYCHUK/DIGITAL VISION/JUPITER IMAGES

Business Law in Practice

Sonny Chu is a university student majoring in entrepreneurship and international business. Two years ago, while on a student exchange program in China, Sonny came up with an idea for an Internet business. In China, Sonny had been able to purchase tailor-made silk suits for $250 to $400. The equivalent suits cost $1500 to $1800 in Canada. Sonny believed that he could offer the tailor-made silk suits to Canadians at close to the same price that he had paid for the suits if he could solve the difficulty of having customers taking their own suit measurements.

Back in Canada, Sonny worked with a design student, and together they were able to develop a simplified method of taking suit measurements. With this problem solved, Sonny set up a website for his business called "This Suits Me." The website featured several suit styles, a range of silk fabric swatches, and instructions for taking measurements. Customers could easily order suits by clicking on the style and fabric and sending in their measurements by following the simplified instructions provided.[1]

To handle the China end of the business, Sonny employed Dong Lee, a student he had met on the exchange trip. Dong had been born in China and is very familiar with the fabric industry, as both his mother and father are dressmakers. His job for Sonny involves purchasing silk fabric, engaging the services of Chinese tailors, and delivering the customers' selections and measurements to the tailors. The arrangement proved to be very profitable, and, within six months of establishing the website, Sonny was meeting all of his the sales targets. However, a couple of recent developments threaten the success of Sonny's business:

- Dong agreed to pay $100 000 to a Chinese supplier for several bolts of silk fabric. Although the fabric is beautiful and will make wonderful suits, Sonny believes

1. The idea for this business is based on Canwest New Service, "Suit Yourself: Expert Offers Tips for Men" (5 March 2008), online: Canada.com <http://www.canada.com/story_print.html?id=8353c3a9-7552-4bb9-a689-0f9b53d8d020&>.

(Continued on the next page)

that Dong has agreed to pay too much for the fabric and, further, he does not think that his business can afford the purchase at this time. Sonny wants to cancel or renegotiate the contract. He is also very angry with Dong because Sonny had expressly told Dong that he could not enter into any contracts on his behalf in excess of $25 000 without getting his permission first.

- Sonny has also discovered that Dong has been purchasing fabric and engaging tailors on behalf of some of Sonny's competitors. When confronted with this information, Dong stated that he did not see any problem with his actions as he had not signed any exclusive representation contract with Sonny.

1. What is the nature of the legal relationship between Sonny and Dong?
2. Is Sonny bound by the expensive fabric contract Dong entered into with the Chinese supplier?
3. Has Dong breached any duty owed to Sonny by representing other businesses in China?

The Nature of Agency

Agency is the relationship between two persons that permits one person, the **agent**, to affect the legal relationships of another, known in law as the **principal**.[2] These legal relationships are as binding on the principal as if that person had directly entered them herself.

Agency is about one person representing another in such a way as to affect the latter's relationships with the outside world. In business, agency is a common relationship, as is shown in the following examples:

- A sports agent negotiates a multimillion-dollar deal on behalf of a hockey player.

- An insurance agent sells fire and theft insurance on behalf of several insurance companies.

- A travel agent sells tickets, cruises, and vacation packages on behalf of carriers and hotels.

- A booking agent negotiates fees and dates on behalf of entertainers.

- A stockbroker buys and sells shares on behalf of individuals and companies.

In each case, the agent is acting for someone else (the principal) and is doing business on that person's behalf. This kind of relationship is essential to the success of the principal, who may not necessarily have the expertise to handle the given matter—as may be the case

Agency
A relationship that exists when one party represents another party in the formation of legal relations.

Agent
A person who is authorized to act on behalf of another.

Principal
A person who has permitted another to act on her behalf.

PART FOUR

---

2. GHL Fridman, *Canadian Agency Law* (Markham, ON: LexisNexis, 2009) at 4.

with an athlete or an investor—or who cannot manage and promote his business single-handedly. For this latter reason, insurance companies, hotels, carriers, and entertainers rely on agents regularly.

In the Business Law in Practice scenario at the beginning of this chapter, Dong was needed for just these kinds of reasons. He was familiar with China and had connections in that part of the world; Sonny also required his assistance because Sonny could not run his business alone. Consequently, Dong became Sonny's agent.

Many of the examples of agency given so far are familiar because they involve businesses engaging external specialists or experts to act on their behalf in various transactions. The scope of agency, however, is considerably broader than these examples would suggest.

In fact, in almost every business transaction, at least one of the parties is acting as an agent. A corporation enters into a contract through the agency of one of its directors or employees. A partnership is likewise bound to a contract through the agency of one of its partners or a firm employee. Even in a sole proprietorship, the owner may hire others, such as office managers and sales clerks, to carry out critical tasks on the owner's behalf. In short, the agency relationship—which formally recognizes the delegation of authority from one party to another—is a cornerstone of business activity. It is a relationship that makes it possible for businesses to conduct a wide array of transactions.

Agency Defined

Agency relationships, like contractual relationships in general, operate for the most part with few difficulties—agents simply represent principals in transactions with others. This is not to say, however, that problems cannot occur. The fact that parties use agents instead of dealing with each other face to face can result in complications and questions. There are two key relationships at play in an agency situation. The first is the relationship between the agent and the principal (see Figure 13.1).

FIGURE 13.1

The Agent–Principal Relationship

This aspect of agency raises numerous questions, such as the following:

- How does A become an agent? When is one person considered to be an agent for another?

- What is the authority of A? What types of transactions can A enter on behalf of P?

- What are A's duties?

- What are P's obligations?

The second relationship in agency is between the principal and the party with whom the agent does business (see Figure 13.2). Such parties are known as **outsiders** because they are "outside" the agency relationship between principal and agent. The outsider is also sometimes called the third party.[3]

Outsider
The party with whom the agent does business on behalf of the principal.

FIGURE 13.2

The Outsider–Principal Relationship

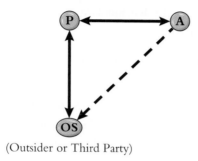

(Outsider or Third Party)

This relationship raises questions, including

- When is the principal liable to the outsider?
- When is the agent himself liable to the outsider?

The complications resulting from these relationships have necessitated rules of law to regulate and resolve them. These rules are known as the **law of agency**, which, in turn, is derived largely from tort and contract law. There is very little legislation pertaining to agency as such, other than special statutes that govern the duties and responsibilities of specific kinds of agents.[4]

Law of agency
The law governing the relationship where one party, the agent, acts on behalf of another, the principal.

The remainder of this chapter will explore how the common law of agency has dealt with the kinds of questions and problems posed above.

Creation of Agency

Agency relationships are created in a variety of ways. Most often, particularly in a business context, the relationship arises by contract between the parties. At other times, the relationship arises by conduct. The parties do not specifically agree to an agency relationship, but by words or actions, outsiders are led to believe the relationship is one of agency.

PART FOUR

---

3. The principal and agent are the first and second parties.
4. For example, insurance brokers, mortgage brokers, and mercantile and real estate agents are regulated by legislation that provides for their registration, their training, the regulation of their conduct, and so forth. See, for example, *Real Estate and Business Brokers Act, 2002*, SO 2002, c 30, Schedule C.

Agency by Agreement

An agency relationship created by contract normally involves the principal authorizing an agent to act on her behalf and the agent agreeing to do so in return for some fee or other remuneration. This often occurs through a contract created expressly and only for that single purpose, as illustrated in this example:

- A retired public figure who wishes to earn income by speaking about his experiences in office may engage an agent to contact organizations, negotiate fees, and book engagements on his behalf. In return, the public figure will pay the agent a certain sum, perhaps a percentage of his fee. Similarly, Sonny hired Dong to purchase fabric and employ tailors in China.

In other situations, the agency relationship may arise as part of another, broader contract:

- An employment contract may provide for a person to be paid a salary in return for carrying out certain duties including entering into contracts on behalf of the employer. For example, a sales clerk, besides greeting and assisting customers and stocking shelves, would have the authority to enter into sales transactions—at least at the sticker price—on behalf of his employer.

Of course, not all employees are agents for the businesses that employ them. A clerk/typist is not normally an agent, but, if asked to take money from petty cash and purchase a gift for a departing employee, then in this situation and for this purpose, the clerk/typist is an agent for the employer.

The Concept of Authority

The authority of the agent is a key aspect of the agency relationship. It determines whether there is a contract between the principal and the outsider. When an agent acts within the scope of the agent's authority and negotiates a contract for the principal, the principal is bound by the contract, whether the principal likes it or not. However, even when the agent has acted outside the scope of her authority in entering into the contract—that is, by exceeding the powers she has been given—the contract may still bind the principal.

The principal will be obligated by the contract when the agent has actual authority or when the agent has apparent authority.

Actual Authority

Actual authority
The power of an agent that derives from either express or implied agreement.

An agent's **actual authority** can be both express and implied. Express authority is the written or oral authority granted by the principal to the agent and is an authority that the agent actually has. Implied authority is also an authority that the agent actually has, but it is present by implication only. An agent will have implied authority when that authority

- is inferred from the position the agent occupies

- is reasonably necessary to carry out or otherwise implement the agent's express authority

- arises by virtue of a well-recognized custom in a particular trade, industry, or profession

Like other contracts, then, the agency contract can contain implied terms concerning the nature and extent of the agent's authority. It is important to remember that these terms are not any less "real" than express terms. They just exist in another, less tangible form.

In the Business Law in Practice scenario, it is clear that Sonny's agent, Dong, has the actual authority to engage tailors and to buy fabric up to $25 000 per contract. Above that amount, he is required to secure Sonny's approval before proceeding. What kind of implied authority might Dong have? This is always a fact-specific inquiry, but since Dong is empowered to purchase fabric and engage tailors, he almost certainly has the power to arrange for the transportation of the finished product to Canada. This, in turn, would also include the power to acquire insurance to cover any loss or damage to the suits while in transit. For this reason, transportation and insurance contracts will be binding on Sonny.

In a similar vein, the manager of a business may have aspects of his authority expressly recited in his employment contract or job description. To the extent that these documents are not exhaustive on the subject, other components of his authority exist due to the nature of his position and as a result of what is reasonably necessary to manage the business. For example, if he were the general manager of an automotive dealership, he presumably would have the implied power to purchase merchandise, order office supplies, arrange for appropriate advertising of the business, and hire and fire employees. A manager of another kind of business—a fast-food outlet or a convenience store—would have less implied power.

The nature of the authority given to the agent is inherently flexible and easily customized. For example, it can be

- very broad or very narrow

- for only one transaction or for several

- for a short, long, or indefinite period of time

- very formal, as in the case of a power of attorney, or very informal, in that it is included in the job description of an employee or merely consists of oral instructions

Dong has entered into a contract on behalf of Sonny. Was the contract binding on Sonny? This contract was not concluded within Dong's actual authority, as Sonny had limited Dong's authority to contracts of $25 000. Dong acted outside his actual authority, but nevertheless, Sonny will be bound by the contract if Dong has the apparent authority to enter into contracts over that monetary limit.

BUSINESS APPLICATION OF THE LAW

A Power of Attorney

A power of attorney is a written document in which one person gives authority to another person to act on her behalf. The person receiving the power is most often referred to as the "attorney," "agent," or "donee." The person giving the power is usually called the "donor" or "principal."

The rules regulating power of attorney vary considerably among provinces. Variations exist in such matters as who may witness a power of attorney, who is excluded from acting as an attorney, whether the power of attorney must be registered, the forms that must be used to execute a power of attorney, and, most importantly, the kinds of power of attorney that are available.

Typically, however, the kinds available are as follows:

• *a general power of attorney*: the agent has full authority to exercise all the principal's rights in relation to her property and financial affairs—for example, cash or deposit cheques; pay bills; withdraw money from bank accounts; make payments on loans; purchase, sell, or deal with stocks or bonds; collect rents, profits, or commissions; manage, buy, and sell real estate; and conduct business operations.

• *a specific power of attorney*: the agent has the authority to act for the principal only in relation to certain matters or in certain specified circumstances—for example, sell a car, cash a pension cheque, or accept an offer for the purchase of property.

• *a personal care power of attorney*: the agent has authority to act for the principal in relation to personal matters such as housing and health.

A power of attorney may be non-continuing, meaning that it is automatically revoked if the principal becomes incapacitated (e.g., by death, mental incapacity, or bankruptcy), or it may be continuing or enduring, that is, the power of attorney continues to operate when the donor becomes incapacitated and unable to manage her business.[5] A variation of the enduring power of attorney, available in some provinces, is the "springing power of attorney," which "springs" to life when an event specified in the power of attorney has taken place.[6]

A power of attorney can be a useful tool for conducting business in the event of health problems or other circumstances that would prevent people from managing their own business affairs. However, it also presents an obvious potential for abuse. An attorney with unlimited power over a donor's affairs can easily take advantage of the situation.

Critical Analysis: How may a businessperson manage the risk that her power of attorney may be misused?

Apparent Authority

Apparent authority
The power that an agent appears to have to an outsider because of conduct or statements of the principal.

Sometimes called ostensible authority, **apparent authority** is the authority that a third party or outsider would reasonably believe the agent has, given the conduct of the principal. For example, as Dong is acting as Sonny's purchasing agent, it would be reasonable for the outsider to infer that he had the usual authority of someone in such a position. It would not be reasonable to expect fabric suppliers to guess that Dong's authority to contract on Sonny's behalf had been limited to contracts for less than $25 000. Sonny is using Dong's services as his buying agent without telling outsiders that his authority is in any way limited. He must bear the risk of Dong exceeding the monetary limit he has privately set for him.

In sum, so long as an agent is acting within his apparent authority, the principal will be bound by the transaction unless the third party knew or ought reasonably to have known of the limitation on the agent's authority.

---

5. At common law, a power of attorney ended on the principal becoming incapacitated; however, all provinces have passed legislative provisions allowing for a continuing or enduring power of attorney.
6. In British Columbia, representation agreements that allow a person to appoint a representative to cover all areas of his life including financial, legal, health, and personal care are intended to replace the enduring power of attorney, which applies only to financial, property, and legal matters. See *Representation Agreement Act*, RSBC 1996, c 405, (Supp).

CASE   *Doiron v Devon Capital Corp*, 2003 ABCA 336, 20 Alta LR (4th) 11

THE BUSINESS CONTEXT: Actual authority exists when a principal expressly confers authority on the agent. Apparent or ostensible authority arises when the principal represents that an "agent" is authorized to act on his behalf or allows a third party to believe that the "agent" has been authorized to act on his behalf. The doctrine of apparent authority is particularly relevant when an investment adviser, financial planner, insurance broker, or the like, misappropriates client funds, leaving the client looking for a solvent defendant.

FACTUAL BACKGROUND: In 1998 Glennis and Elliot Doiron sold their home in Calgary and decided to invest the net proceeds of $60 000 for a short term until they required the money for a down payment on their new home. They contacted William Demmers for investment advice, as he had previously placed their life insurance and RRSPs with Manulife Financial and was known to them as a Manulife investment advisor. The Doirons were unaware that Demmers had a non-exclusive agency agreement (called a producer's agreement) with Manulife, which provided that he could not bind Manulife without written authorization.

The Doirons gave Demmers a cheque for $60 000 and Demmers filled in the payee as Devon Capital Corporation. The Doirons believed that they were investing in a Manulife product or one guaranteed by Manulife because they believed that Demmers was a Manulife employee and sold only Manulife products. When the investment became due, the Doirons received a cheque from Devon, which was dishonoured. It turned out that Devon was a sham, and the Doirons lost their entire investment.

THE LEGAL QUESTION: Is Manulife liable for the investment losses of the Doirons?

RESOLUTION: A principal is liable for the acts of an agent as long as the agent is acting within the scope of his or her actual or ostensible (apparent) authority. Demmers was not an agent of Manulife in the transaction with the Doirons and had no actual authority to bind Manulife as the guarantor of investments in Devon. However, the doctrine of ostensible authority gives an agent authority to bind a principal to agreements made with third parties when the principal represents to the third party that the agent has authority to enter into a contract and the third party relies on the representation. The representation may be express or implied. Manulife had cloaked Demmers with ostensible authority by providing him with business cards, stationery, and other Manulife paraphernalia and encouraging him to use it, and by allowing him to be contacted through the Manulife main switchboard. Also, Manulife had a co-op advertising program in which it ran advertisements in newspapers that included photographs of "producers" (i.e., salespeople like Demmers) and the Manulife logo.

Although Demmers did not represent that the Devon investment was a Manulife product, the Doirons were entitled to assume that that they were investing in Manulife because they had instructed Demmers to invest in a low-risk Manulife product, Demmers provided no written information regarding the investment before accepting their money, and Demmers did not tell them that Devon was not a Manulife product or was unconnected with Manulife. Therefore, given that Demmers purported to contract on behalf of Manulife and the ostensible authority conveyed by Manulife to Demmers, Manulife was bound by the contract.

CRITICAL ANALYSIS: How can companies like Manulife minimize the risk of liability for the actions of its "producers" (i.e., salespeople)? How can companies gain the benefits that accrue from representation without incurring the risk of liability?

Agency by Estoppel

In the preceding section, one of the risks of agency was illustrated: an agent may exceed his actual authority but act within his apparent authority and thereby bind a principal to a contract against his wishes. Sonny is bound to pay for the expensive fabric even though the contract is for an amount above Dong's authority. This is because the contract was within Dong's apparent authority and the fabric supplier was unaware of the limitation on Dong's authority. This is an application of what is known in law as **agency by estoppel.** The relationship between Sonny and Dong has been broadened or extended, not through their mutual consent but by conduct. Sonny is not entitled to deny Dong's apparent authority unless he actually informs the outsider in advance that Dong's authority is limited.

A less common situation in which an agency relationship can be created by estoppel involves one in which the principal indicates that another is his agent when, in fact, no agency relationship exists. For example, suppose that the owner of a business—in a burst of effusiveness—introduces a prospective employee to a customer, saying, "I want you to meet

Agency by estoppel
An agency relationship created when the principal acts such that third parties reasonably conclude that an agency relationship exists.

Terrence, my new vice president of marketing." It would be usual and reasonable for the customer to infer that Terrence has the authority to act on behalf of the owner with respect to selling, promotions, and advertising. Suppose, however, that ultimately Terrence is not hired and, unfortunately, the owner forgets all about having introduced him as the new vice president of marketing. Terrence—now sorely disappointed and wishing to extract some revenge—contacts the customer and enters into a transaction with him, pretending to act on behalf of the owner. Is the owner liable? Assuming the contract is marketing or sales-related and assuming the customer was unaware of the truth, then the owner probably will be liable. In such a situation, the principal's actions (introducing his "new vice president of marketing") create the appearance of an agency relationship. The principal will therefore be estopped from denying the relationship and be bound by the contract with the customer. Put another way, the principal is not permitted to avoid the contract by claiming—albeit truthfully—that no agency relationship existed, because the principal gave every appearance that one did.

Is it fair to place all responsibility on the owner like this? The difficulty is that someone—either the owner of the business or the customer—will end up being adversely affected by Terrence's conduct. That is, either the owner will be stuck with a contract that she never wanted or the customer will be denied the benefit of a contract that he negotiated in good faith. Between these two competing claims, the law sides with the customer through estoppel. In theory, at least, the owner can sue Terrence for misrepresenting himself as an agent, but this can be of little value if Terrence has few assets.

A third situation in which agency by estoppel may operate to bind a principal is that in which an agency relationship has been terminated or an agent's authority has been curtailed. In both situations, the agent had at one time the actual authority to bind the principal, but now the authority has been taken away or reduced.

The situations described in this section illustrate several of the risks associated with agency. The onus is on the principals to inform outsiders when a person ceases to be their agent; otherwise the principals continue to be liable for the agent's actions. Similarly, the principals have a responsibility to inform outsiders of any limitation on their agent's usual authority; otherwise the principals run the risk of being bound if the agent exceeds his actual authority but acts within his apparent authority. A principal can inform outsiders by contacting them by letter, telephone, or other means; by taking out advertisements in trade publications and newspapers; by clearly indicating on company forms what constitutes necessary approvals; and by otherwise indicating that only properly documented transactions will be binding.

CASE

Rockland Industries Inc v Amerada Minerals Corporation of Canada, [1980] 2 SCR 2, rev'g (1978), 14 AR 97 (Alta CA)

THE BUSINESS CONTEXT: This case concerns an agent whose authority has been reduced. The same general principles will apply where the agency relationship has been completely severed.

FACTUAL BACKGROUND: Rockland was a textile manufacturer that also engaged in the purchase and resale of sulphur. Amerada was a producer of natural gas. One of the by-products of the gas-processing procedure is sulphur. Mr. Kurtz was the manager of Amerada's petrochemical products with responsibility for domestic and foreign sales and the marketing of petrochemicals, including sulphur. He reported to Mr. Deverin, a senior vice president and a member of the executive operating committee.

After protracted negotiations between Amerada, represented by Kurtz, and representatives of Rockland, an agreement was reached for the sale by Amerada to Rockland of 50 000 tons of sulphur at $8 per ton. This agreement was concluded by telephone on 5 September 1974. In the meantime, on 3 September 1974, Deverin had informed Kurtz that he would need to get the approval of the executive operating committee for the sale to Rockland. In other words, Kurtz no longer had the authority to conclude the sale on behalf of Amerada.

The agreement, concluded on 5 September, was not performed by Amerada, and Rockland sued for breach of contract. Amerada argued that there was no contract between the parties, as Kurtz did not have the authority to act on Amerada's behalf.

THE LEGAL QUESTION: Was Amerada bound by the contract negotiated by Kurtz?

RESOLUTION: The court determined that Kurtz had actual authority to act on behalf of Amerada in negotiating and entering the contract with Rockland up until 3 September. At that time his actual authority was curtailed. This limitation on Kurtz's authority, however, was not communicated to Rockland. The court held that the onus was on Amerada to notify Rockland of the limitation—it was not up to Rockland to inquire as to Kurtz's authority. Amerada, by permitting Kurtz to act in its business by conducting negotiations, had represented to Rockland that he had permission to act. In short, there was a representation of authority by Amerada on which Rockland relied.

CRITICAL ANALYSIS: How could Amerada have prevented this situation?

Agency by Ratification

Agency by ratification occurs when a person represents himself as another's agent even though he is not, and when the purported principal adopts the acts of the agent. For example, suppose Ahmed is keenly interested in obtaining a franchise for a certain fast-food restaurant, and his friend Frank is aware of this interest. An opportunity comes on the market, but Frank cannot reach Ahmed to tell him about it. Feeling pretty sure of himself, Frank goes ahead and purchases the franchise on Ahmed's behalf although he does not have any authority to do so. Though Frank acted with good intentions, Ahmed has no responsibilities unless he chooses to adopt the contract. When and if he does adopt the transaction, an agency relationship will be created between Frank and him. The result is that Ahmed's rights and duties under the franchise contract are identical to what they would have been had Frank been properly authorized to act as Ahmed's agent all along.

In both agency by estoppel and agency by ratification, the agent has no authority to do what he does. What distinguishes the two doctrines is whether the principal has conducted himself in a misleading way. Agency by estoppel forces the principal to be bound by the unauthorized contract because the principal has represented someone as his agent and must live with the consequences when that agent purports to act on his behalf. Under agency by ratification, the agent is perhaps equally out of line but not due to any fault of or misrepresentation by the principal. For this reason, the law does not force the principal to adopt the contract, but rather permits him to make that decision for himself, according to his own best interests.

> **Agency by ratification**
> An agency relationship created when one party adopts a contract entered into on his behalf by another who at the time acted without authority.

BUSINESS APPLICATION OF THE LAW

Real Estate Agents

The real estate agent is one of the most familiar and common types of agents. Most sales of property, especially those involving residential property, involve the services of a real estate agent. The real estate agent, however, is somewhat of an anomaly in agency law. Unlike most other agents, usually a real estate agent has no authority to make a binding contract of sale on behalf of his principal, the homeowner. Normally the agreement between the owner of property and the real estate agent—often taking the form of a standard listing agreement—does not confer any authority on the agent to enter a contract on behalf of the property owner. The real estate agent's role is usually limited to listing and advertising the property, showing the property to prospective purchasers,

(Continued)

and introducing and bringing together the parties. In short, a real estate agent usually does not have the actual authority to contract on behalf of the principal. As well, a real estate agent does not have the apparent authority to enter a contract on behalf of a homeowner. A principal could, of course, grant actual authority to a real estate agent to enter a contract on her behalf. However, such a grant of authority, to be effective, would need to be conferred by very clear, express, and unequivocal language.[7]

The case of real estate agents illustrates an important point. The term "agent" is often used very loosely to refer to anyone who represents another, and it is not always restricted to relationships where the agent enters into contracts on behalf of the principal. It is always necessary to look at the essence of a relationship rather than merely relying on what the parties call themselves. Just as agents are not always agents in the strict legal sense, so too, there may be an agency relationship even though the parties have not labelled it as such.

Critical Analysis: How is the authority of a real estate agent determined?

Does a real estate agent act for the vendor or the purchaser of property?

It should be noted that a principal cannot ratify every contract that his "agent" enters. A principal can only ratify a contract if

- he does so within a reasonable time
- the principal had the capacity to create the contract at the time the agent entered into it and at the time of ratification, and
- the agent identified the principal at the time of entering the contract

A principal's ratification may be express or implied. For example, if a principal accepts a benefit under the contract, the principal will be bound by the contract.

Figure 13.3 summarizes the points contained in the preceding sections.

FIGURE 13.3

Summary of Creation of Agency and Agent's Authority

	How Created	*Agent's Authority*
Agency by Agreement	P, expressly or impliedly, appoints X as an A	Actual: Express and/ or Implied Apparent
Agency by Estoppel	*Representation of Authority* P represents to OS that X has authority to act as an A even though no actual authority given	Apparent
	Extension of Existing Authority P represents to OS that A has authority in excess of actual authority given	Actual Apparent
	Termination or Reduction of Authority P terminates or reduces A's authority but does not give notice to OS	Apparent
Agency by Ratification	P adopts actions of X, and X retroactively becomes an A	No authority until P adopts X's actions

---

7. William F Foster, *Real Estate Agency Law in Canada*, 2d ed (Toronto: Carswell, 1994) at 99.

Duties in the Agency Relationship
Duties of the Agent

An agency relationship created by contract imposes on an agent certain duties to perform. If the agent fails to perform these duties, he is in breach of the contract. An agent is required to perform in accordance with the principal's instructions. In the event that the principal has not given any instructions as to how the performance is to be carried out, performance must meet the standard of the particular trade or industry. For example, a real estate agent's duties would normally include appraising property, estimating the revenue and expenses of property the principal wishes to acquire, checking the dimensions of property, advising the principal of the financial implications of transactions, and ensuring that properties the principal wishes to acquire do not contravene bylaws or other municipal regulations, among other matters.[8]

Normally, it is expected that the agent will personally perform the obligations. However, there may be an express or implied provision for delegation—that is, the agent may be permitted to "download" responsibility for performance onto someone else. For example, it may be that Sonny and Dong have an understanding that Dong can have members of his extended family contact fabric suppliers in remote regions of China.

An agent also owes a **fiduciary duty** to the principal. This duty requires the agent to show what the law describes as "utmost good faith to the principal." This duty is often expressed as a "profit rule"—a **fiduciary** must not personally profit by virtue of her position—and a "conflict rule"—a fiduciary must not place herself in a position where her own interests conflict with the interests of the principal. It is a breach of his fiduciary duty for Dong to act as a buyer for both Sonny and his competitors. This is because Dong may be tempted to put the interests of the competitors above the interests of Sonny.

Fiduciary duty

A duty imposed on a person who has a special relationship of trust with another.

Fiduciary

A person who has a duty of good faith toward another because of their relationship.

BUSINESS APPLICATION OF THE LAW

Duties of the Insurance Agent

An insurance agent owes a principal a duty of care in the performance of his responsibilities. The content of that duty varies according to the agreement between the principal and the agent and the surrounding circumstances. For example, if a business engages an insurance agent or broker[9] to obtain insurance coverage, the insurance agent or broker has strict duties to provide information and advice to ensure that the business has the coverage it requires.

In *Fine's Flowers Ltd v General Accident Assurance Co of Canada*,[10] Fine's Flowers instructed an insurance agent to obtain "full coverage" for its greenhouse operation. The agent obtained insurance to cover a number of risks but failed to obtain "wear and tear" coverage. Fine's Flowers lost all of its plants in a frost when the heating pumps failed to operate—the cause of the malfunction was "wear and tear." The court held

What are the duties of an insurance agent?

(Continued)

RYAN MCVAY/PHOTODISC/GETTY IMAGES

PART FOUR

8. *Ibid* at 218–19.
9. The distinction between an agent and a broker is discussed in Chapter 28.
10. (1977), 17 OR (2d) 529, 81 DLR (3d) 139 (Ont CA).

that the insurance agent was responsible for Fine's Flowers losses because the agent's undertaking to obtain "full coverage" created an obligation to ensure that Fine's Flowers was covered for all foreseeable and normal risks. The agent had a duty to advise Fine's Flowers what risks were not covered so that it could take steps to protect its business against those uninsured risks.

As a result of *Fine's Flowers*, an agent who has been instructed to obtain "full coverage" has onerous standards to meet to fulfill her duty of care. At a minimum, the agent must

- identify all of the client's foreseeable risks
- take all reasonable steps to determine if the market provides coverage for the risks identified

- provide information to the client about the coverage available
- procure the coverage if it is available
- advise the client if the coverage is unavailable so that the client can take other measures to reduce the risk

Critical Analysis: An agent or broker may face a broad array of duties and be subject to onerous liability for breach of these duties. How can an agent manage her exposure to the risk of liability?

Source: Najma Rashid, "You and Your Insurance Broker," *Howard Yegendorf & Associates News* (31 January 2005), online: Howard Yegendorf & Associates <http://www.yegendorf.com/news.asp?nID=110>.

The content of the fiduciary duty will vary with the circumstances. However, as a general rule, an agent has the duty to

- make full disclosure of all material information that may affect the principal's position (e.g., Dong must disclose to Sonny any good deals or bargains on fabrics that he discovers)

- avoid any conflict of interest that affects the interests of the principal (e.g., Dong must not go on a buying trip for Sonny and acquire clothes for a store that he is secretly running on the side)

- avoid acting for two principals in the same transaction (e.g., Dong must not represent both Sonny and a fabric seller in a sales transaction)

- avoid using the principal's property, money, or information to secure personal gain (e.g., Dong must avoid using contacts that he has gained through acting as Sonny's agent to set up his own business, and he must not sell or use Sonny's customer lists and records for personal gain)

- avoid accepting or making a secret commission or profit (e.g., Dong must avoid taking payments from fabric suppliers for doing business with them)

There is not, however, an absolute prohibition against conflicts such as acting for two principals or using the principal's property. The agent simply must not do any of these activities secretly, and he must obtain the fully informed consent of the principal prior to the event.

A fiduciary duty is not unique to the relationship between a principal and an agent. This duty is present, as a matter of course, in many other relationships found in business such as the relationships between

- lawyers and their clients

- accountants and their clients

- partners

- directors and senior officers of a corporation and the corporation

- senior employees and employers

The categories of fiduciary relationships are not closed. A fiduciary relationship can exist outside the settled categories and has been found to exist, in some circumstances, in other relationships such as the relationship between financial advisors (e.g., bankers, stockbrokers, and investment counsellors) and their clients. A fiduciary duty can arise in any relationship where the facts indicate sufficient elements of power and influence on the part of one party and reliance, vulnerability, and trust on the part of the other.[11] This is not to say that all "power-dependency" relationships are fiduciary. In addition to the discretionary power to unilaterally affect the vulnerable party's legal or practical interests, there must be an express or implied undertaking to act with loyalty.[12] For example, the relationship between an investor and a broker will not normally give rise to a fiduciary duty where the broker is simply a conduit of information and merely takes orders. However, where the client reposes trust and confidence in the broker and relies on the broker's advice in making business decisions, and the broker has undertaken to act in the client's best interests, the relationship may be elevated to a fiduciary relationship.

CASE — *Raso v Dionigi* (1993), 12 OR (3d) 580, 100 DLR (4th) 459 (Ont CA)

THE BUSINESS CONTEXT: As a general rule, an agent is precluded from acting for both the vendor and the purchaser in the same transaction. There is, however, an exception to the rule. An agent may act for both and not be in breach of fiduciary duties if full and fair disclosure of all material facts has been made to the principals prior to any transaction.

FACTUAL BACKGROUND: Raffaela Sirianni and her husband wanted to invest in income-producing property. They informed her brother-in-law, Guerino Sirianni, who was a real estate agent, that they were prepared to invest $250 000 to $300 000. He located a sixplex owned by Mr. and Mrs. Dionigi. The sixplex was not for sale; however, Sirianni actively prevailed upon the Dionigis to sign a listing agreement. Eventually they did sign an agreement with Sirianni's employer, a real estate agency. The listing price was $299 900. Sirianni presented an offer of $270 000 on behalf of "R. Raso in trust." Raso is the maiden name of Raffaela Sirianni. Sirianni never told the Dionigis that the purchasers were his brother and sister-in-law. The Dionigis made a counteroffer of $290 000, but this was not accepted. Sirianni persisted, and the Dionigis ultimately accepted an offer of $285 000. A few days later, the Dionigis became aware of the purchasers' relationship with the agent, and they refused to complete the action. Raffaela Sirianni sued for specific performance of the contract, and Sirianni and the real estate agency sued for their commission.

THE LEGAL QUESTION: Did Sirianni owe a fiduciary duty to the Dionigis? If so, did he breach the duty? Would a breach preclude him from claiming a commission?

RESOLUTION: Sirianni was not a mere middleman in the sense of introducing the parties; rather, he took an active role in the transaction. A real estate agent who acts for both sides of a transaction has a fiduciary duty to both his principals to disclose all material facts with respect to the transaction. Sirianni breached his fiduciary duty to the Dionigis by failing to disclose that the purchasers were his brother and sister-in-law and by failing to advise of the amount of money that the purchasers had available to purchase the property. A fiduciary who breaches his duty of disclosure of material facts is not entitled to prove that the transaction would have concluded had disclosure been made. In other words, it is immaterial whether the transaction is fair, and it is irrelevant whether the principal would still have entered the transaction if disclosure had been made.

Where an agent has breached a fiduciary duty in this manner, the agent is precluded from claiming any commission. It also follows that the purchasers are not entitled to specific performance, as they not only had knowledge of the agent's breach but also actively participated in the scheme.

CRITICAL ANALYSIS: What are the distinguishing features of a fiduciary relationship? What consequences flow from the designation of a relationship as a fiduciary one? If Guerino Sirianni had disclosed to the Dionigis just how much money Mr. and Mrs. Sirianni had available to purchase the property, would this disclosure have been a breach of his fiduciary duty to the Siriannis? What does this tell you about the perils of acting for both parties to a transaction?

---

11. *Hodgkinson v Simms*, [1994] 3 SCR 377, 117 DLR (4th) 161. For a summary of this case, see Chapter 22.
12. *Galambos v Perez*, 2009 SCC 48, [2009] 3 SCR 247.

PART FOUR

Because professional relationships can be easily categorized as fiduciary, it is incumbent on those who offer their services to others to understand the indicia of the fiduciary relationship. In addition, it is noteworthy that where fiduciary duties are found to exist, the innocent party can look to a wider range of remedies than found in contract or tort. The whole range of equitable remedies is available, and with the spectre of these remedies, it is important for businesspeople to comprehend not only when a fiduciary relationship exists but also the full scope of the duties.

Duties of the Principal

A principal's duties usually are not as onerous as an agent's and normally are set out in the contract creating the agency relationship. Such contracts usually obligate the principal to

- pay the agent a specified fee or percentage for services rendered unless the parties have agreed that the agent would work for free

- assist the agent in the manner described in the contract

- reimburse the agent for reasonable expenses associated with carrying out his agency duties

- indemnify against losses incurred in carrying out the agency business

In the example involving Sonny and his buying agent, Dong, it may be that Dong has had to travel to various parts of China to make necessary purchases. In the absence of any agreement to the contrary, Sonny would be required to reimburse Dong for his travel expenses. This is a cost that rightfully belongs to Sonny since Dong incurred it on a buying trip that Sonny instigated and sent him on. Similarly, Sonny has an obligation—either express or implied—to reimburse Dong for meals, hotel, and other reasonable expenses associated with the buying trip.

Insurance broker
One who provides advice and assistance to those acquiring insurance.

ETHICAL CONSIDERATIONS

Compensation of Life Insurance Brokers

Until the early 1990s, most major life insurance companies sold their products through in-house sales agents. Now the majority of life insurance policies are sold through independent **insurance brokers**. An insurance broker is an intermediary who represents several insurance companies and at the same time, provides clients with advice on the best insurance product for their needs.

Insurance companies provide a number of incentives to get brokers to direct business to them. An upfront commission is paid when the sale is made. The commission is a percentage of the cost of the insurance and can vary depending on the type of life insurance, company policy, and the province. Life insurance has always been considered a tough sell, therefore the upfront commission is high, often amounting to 30 to 70 percent of the price paid for the insurance. This commission may be the only compensation received by the insurance broker. However, the broker may also receive a contingent commission based on the volume of business done with the insurance company, or based on the loyalty of the customer directed to the insurance company. The greater the profitability and size of the business directed to the insurance company and the longer the retention of the broker's entire portfolio of business with the insurance company, the more likely the broker receives a contingency commission. Finally, the insurance company may reward brokers with perks such as deluxe trips to exotic locales for themselves and their spouses. These perks are often characterized as "educational" as they are an opportunity for insurance companies to provide brokers with information about insurance products, but usually only a few hours during a week-long trip is set aside for this purpose.

Critical Analysis: Do you see any problems with the incentives provided to insurance brokers by insurance companies?

Sources: Grant Robertson & Tara Perkins, "What your insurance broker doesn't want you to know", *The Globe and Mail* (21 December 2010) online: The Globe and Mail <http://www.theglobeandmail.com/report-on-business/what-your-insurance-broker-doesnt-want-you-to-know/article1846513/> ; Craig Harris, "Commission Controversy Calling for Clarity on Broker Compensation", *Canadian Underwriter* (October 2004) online: Canadianunderwriter.ca <http://www.canadianunderwriter.ca/news/commission-controversy-calling-for-clarity-on-broker-compensation/1000190679/>

Contract Liability in the Agency Relationship
Liability of the Principal to the Outsider

The most significant result of an agency relationship is that, when an agent enters into a contract on behalf of a principal with a third party, it is the principal, not the agent, who ordinarily is liable on the contract. To a large extent, discussion of this point is simply the flip side of a discussion regarding an agent's actual and apparent authority. Put another way, the principal's liability to the third party depends on the nature of the agent's authority.

As we have already seen under the discussion of an agent's authority above, Sonny is liable on the expensive fabric contract even though Dong exceeded his actual authority. Dong went over the monetary limit his principal had placed on him, but the doctrine of apparent authority applies. The outsider did not know about the limitation on Dong's authority, so on this basis, Sonny is bound.

Liability of the Agent to the Outsider

An agent who acts without authority and contracts with an outsider is liable to the third party for breach of **warranty of authority**. In this situation, there is no contract between either the principal and the outsider or the agent and the outsider.[13]

For example, Sonny would not be bound by a contract Dong enters into on his behalf to purchase a private jet. He could adopt, that is, ratify, such a contract, but otherwise he is not bound because such a contract is not within Dong's actual or apparent authority. Dong may be sued by the vendor of the jet because he wrongly claimed to have the authority to act on Sonny's behalf in the purchase of a jet.

An agent may also be bound when he contracts on his own behalf to be a party to the contract along with his principal.[14]

For example, if Dong negotiated the contract such that both he and his principal were ordering the fabric and promising to pay for it, then he has as much liability to the outsider as Sonny. They are both parties to the contract—Dong is contracting on his own behalf as well as on Sonny's behalf.

Liability of an Undisclosed Principal

An agent may incur liability when he contracts on behalf of an **undisclosed principal.** A principal is said to be "undisclosed" when the third party does not know that she is

Warranty of authority
A representation of authority by a person who purports to be an agent.

Undisclosed principal
A principal whose identity is unknown to a third party who has no knowledge that the agent is acting in an agency capacity.

PART FOUR

---

13. *Supra* note 2 at 154–56.
14. Peter Watts & FMB Reynolds, *Bowstead & Reynolds on Agency*, 19th ed (London: Sweet & Maxwell, 2010) at 546.

dealing with an agent at all and assumes that the party she is dealing with is acting only on his own behalf. From the perspective of the outsider, there is no principal waiting in the background.

When the agent is acting for an undisclosed principal, the general rule is that the principal is still liable on the contract so long as the agent is acting within his authority.[15] The agent has no liability, however.

For example, assume that, in negotiations with outsiders, Dong represents himself neither as an agent nor as a principal and that he could be acting in either capacity. In such circumstances, Sonny will generally be liable on the contract, but not Dong. This is a simple application of the general rule stated above.

The general rule, however, has been subject to qualification that may operate to render the agent liable on the contract in certain circumstances.[16] One such qualification relates to representations made by the agent.

Suppose that for the purposes of buying some special fabric, Sonny wishes to keep his identity a secret. He thinks that Dong, his purchasing agent, will get a better price if the seller (the outsider) is unaware of his identity.[17]

If Dong pretends to be the principal—representing to the outsider that he is actually the owner or proprietor of the suit business—and does not disclose the existence of Sonny, his principal, then Dong runs the risk of being personally liable on the contract that is concluded. For example, if the written contract expressly indicates that Dong is the principal, the parol evidence rule[18] may operate to prevent the admission of evidence of an undisclosed principal.[19] In such circumstances, Dong is liable.

A variation on the undisclosed principal is the unnamed principal.[20] If Dong tells the seller that he is acting for a principal but that he is not at liberty to reveal that person's identity, Sonny will be liable on any contract he enters into with the seller. In such circumstances, Dong himself has no liability on the contract because the outsider was fully aware of his status. The outsider did not know the identity of his principal but decided to enter into a contract anyway. If the outsider did not want to deal with an unnamed principal, the outsider could simply have refused to enter the contract in the first place.

Liability of the Agent to the Principal

When an agent exceeds his authority, the principal can sue the agent for breach of their contract—assuming that there is such a contract in place.

Because Dong exceeded his authority in purchasing the fabric, Sonny could sue him for breach of their agency or employment agreement.

Figure 13.4 summarizes the points contained in the preceding sections.

---

15. *Supra* note 2 at 157–58. This rule has been subject to heavy criticism as being inconsistent with the general principles of contract law.
16. *Supra* note 2 at 160–65.
17. This is a not uncommon practice in the real estate industry, particularly when a developer wishes to purchase several tracts of land.
18. The parol evidence rule is discussed in Chapter 7.
19. *Supra* note 2 at 160–62. The law is unsettled in this area: it is unclear when the law will permit evidence of an undisclosed principal.
20. *Supra* note 14 at 33. As Bowstead notes, terminology in this area is not consistently employed by the judiciary and legal writers.

FIGURE 13.4

Summary of Contract Liability in Agency

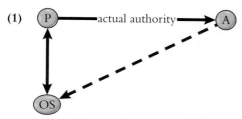

(1)

A acts within actual authority.
P is liable to outsider.

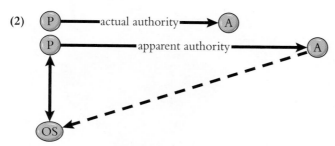

(2)

A exceeds actual authority but acts within apparent authority.
P is liable to OS unless OS knew or ought to have known of any
limitation on A's authority.
A is liable to P for breaching authority.

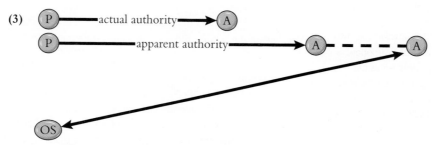

(3)

A exceeds both actual and apparent authority.
A is liable to OS for breach of warranty of authority.

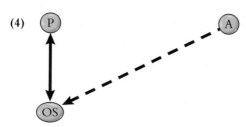

(4)

A acts without P's authority.
P is liable to OS if P adopts contract.

PART FOUR

CASE | *Krawchuk v Scherbak*, 2011 ONCA 352, 332 DLR (4th) 310

THE BUSINESS CONTEXT: In the early 1990's, the Ontario Real Estate Association (OREA) created a seller's disclosure form, the Seller Property Information Statement (SPIS)[21] to be used in residential real estate transactions. Although the form is voluntary (some local real estate boards, however, will not list property without the SPIS form), the OREA strongly encourages its use. The form, with 49 questions about the condition of a home, is controversial. Its proponents argue that it protects the public and real estate agents. Others argue that the form is too complex, requiring sellers to accurately answer questions of a technical and legal nature.

FACTUAL BACKGROUND: In 2004, Timothy and Cherese Scherbak listed their house for sale with real estate agent Wendy Weddell of Re/Max Sudbury Inc. The house, built on a peat bog, had experienced significant settling over the years. The floors were sloped and the foundation showed signs of cracking and repair. In addition, in the basement, there was a pit covered with a steel plate. The sewage from the house flowed into the pit and then drained into the municipal sewage system. The Scherbaks, with the assistance of Weddell, completed a SPIS form. In response to the question: "Are you aware of any structural problem?" they disclosed the following: "NW corner settled – to the best of our knowledge the house has settled. No further problems in 17 years." In response to the question, "Are you aware of any problems with the plumbing system?" the answer was, "No."

Zoriana Krawchuk, a first-time buyer, attended an open house conducted by Weddell. She retained Weddell as her agent (with the consent of all parties) and purchased the house for $110 100. After moving in, she discovered that the foundation walls were sinking into the ground, resulting in the failure of proper support for the floor joists and the building above. Consequently, the house had to be lifted off the foundation, the foundation had to be replaced and the house placed on the new foundation. This work also caused significant cracking to the interior walls. The cost of the remedial work, including the cost to address plumbing problems was $191 414.94—almost double what Krawchuk had paid for the house. She sued the Scherbaks, Weddell, and Re/Max Sudbury for misrepresentation in failing to disclose the defects in the house and Weddell and Re/Max for negligence for failing to insure that she got a home inspection.

At trial, the court found the Scherbaks liable for negligent misrepresentation. Even though the SPIS form stated that representations in the SPIS were not warranties, the Scherbaks were making representations about the property that were meant to be disclosed to buyers and it would be reasonable for buyers to rely on these representations. In these circumstances,

DEVINDER SANGHA/AGEFOTOSTOCK.COM

What are the risks for the agent in a real estate transaction?

there existed a special relationship between the Scherbaks and Krawchuk that gave rise to a duty of care. The Scherbaks had breached the duty of care by not fully disclosing the extent of the structural problems. They knew the problems were not restricted to the northwest corner and were more serious than disclosed. Also, they breached the duty of care by failing to disclose that they regularly experienced problems with their plumbing, including sewer backups once or twice per year.

The court dismissed the claim against Weddell and Re/Max. The court stated that Weddell had merely relayed information told to her by the Scherbaks, had no reason to doubt the veracity of their representations, and had no obligation to inquire about information relevant to the condition of the house. Further, the trial judge rejected the argument that she breached her duty of care by failing to recommend professional advice on structural problems, as Krawchuk knew and accepted the risk of not having a satisfactory inspection. Krawchuk and the Scherbaks appealed.

THE LEGAL QUESTIONS: Are the Scherbaks liable for negligent misrepresentation? Are Weddell and Re/Max liable for negligent misrepresentation and were they negligent in their representation of Krawchuk?

---

21. A copy of the SPIS may be obtained from local real estate boards. It is also available at www.michaelbate.com/SPIS.pdf

RESOLUTION: The Court of Appeal upheld the trial court decision with respect to the liability of the Scherbaks for negligent misrepresentation. However, it reversed the trial judge's decision on the liability of the real estate agents and held them equally liable with the Scherbaks for Krawchuk's damages. The Court of Appeal referred to the Real Estate Council of Ontario's Code of Ethics which states that an agent is required to "discover and verify the pertinent facts relating to the property ..." and an agent "'shall encourage the parties to a transaction to seek appropriate outside professional advice when appropriate." Applying these principles, the court held that Weddell had breached her duty of care in that she should have done more to protect her client. Given her awareness of the settling problems, she should have inquired into the sellers' disclosure that the foundation issues were resolved years earlier. She also should have recommended, in the strongest terms, that Krawchuk get an independent inspection either before submitting an offer, or by making the offer conditional on a satisfactory inspection. "The failure to do either was an egregious lapse."

CRITICAL ANALYSIS: Do you think this case creates any new duties of real estate agents?

Tort Liability in the Agency Relationship

As a general rule, an agent is personally liable for any torts that she commits. The fact that she may have been acting on behalf of another is no defence in a tort action.[22]

The principal is liable for any tort committed by the agent while the agent is acting within the scope of the agent's authority.[23] Put another way, a principal is vicariously liable for an agent's actions so long as the agent is acting within express, implied, or apparent authority.[24]

For example, assume that Dong is given the responsibility for selling Sonny's inventory of returned suits to discount outlets. Suppose that Dong represents to a discount house that some of these suits are from a famous designer's latest collection and, based on this representation, the discount house purchases a large number of suits. In this situation, Dong has committed the tort of deceit by representing the suits as suits from a famous designer when in fact they are Sonny's old stock. Dong is personally liable for committing a tort. Sonny is also liable for Dong's actions since they were committed within the scope of his authority.

Termination of Agency Agreements

An agency agreement can come to an end in a number of ways:

- The parties may agree to bring their relationship to an end. For example, Sonny and Dong may simply agree to end their relationship.

- One party may give notice of termination to the other.[25]

- An agency relationship can cease by operation of the law. Most commonly this occurs due to the death, dissolution (in the case of a corporate agent and/or principal), insanity, or bankruptcy of one of the parties.

When an agency agreement is terminated by the parties, the principal should give notice to third parties so that customers do not assume that the relationship is continuing.

---

22. *Supra* note 2 at 193.
23. *Supra* note 2 at 187.
24. The question of vicarious liability arising from agency principles overlaps with the application of the doctrine in relation to the acts of employees and independent contractors. For example, a principal is liable for the acts of an agent only if the agent was acting within his actual and apparent authority; however, if the agent has the status of an employee, the employer is liable if the act was committed in the course of employment. Therefore, whereas a principal may not be liable for the agent's acts because they were outside the agent's authority, the employer may be liable for the agent's acts if the agent was an employee acting within the scope of his employment. The liability of employers for the actions of employees and independent contractors is explored in Chapter 20.
25. As Dong is Sonny's employee, the rules of notice in employment relationships are applicable. These rules are discussed in Chapter 21.

In the absence of such notice, the principal may face liability to outsiders, based on his agent's apparent authority.

Business Law in Practice Revisited

1. What is the nature of the legal relationship between Sonny and Dong?
Dong is an employee of Sonny's business. He was granted the power to purchase fabric and engage tailors in China on Sonny's behalf. Therefore, he is considered in law to be an agent, and the relationship between Sonny and Dong comprises both employment and agency.

2. Is Sonny bound by the expensive fabric contract Dong entered into with the Chinese supplier?
Much of this chapter has been devoted to Sonny's liability on the contracts Dong made on his behalf. Agency law states that the principal, Sonny, is one party to the contract, and that the other party is the outsider, the fabric supplier. The agent, Dong, is merely the means by which the parties enter the contract. Sonny would not be liable for Dong's purchase if the supplier knew or ought to have known that Dong was not authorized to make the purchases he did. But a manufacturer is not expected to know or suspect that Dong was limited to entering into contracts not exceeding $25 000. Sonny is bound, but he can hold Dong liable for breaching his agency agreement in that he exceeded his authority. As noted, however, this will not relieve Sonny of his liability to the fabric supplier, and it is probably not an attractive course of action, as Dong may not have the means of satisfying the debt. As well, suing one's agent can create a lot of adverse publicity.

3. Has Dong breached any duty owed to Sonny by representing other businesses in China?
Dong is an agent for Sonny, the principal. An agent automatically owes a fiduciary duty to his principal. There is no requirement that the duty be specified in the agency agreement or in an exclusive representation contract. The fiduciary duty requires Dong to avoid conflicts of interest unless he has fully disclosed his conflict to Sonny and Sonny has agreed to the conflict. By acting for competitors without Sonny's consent, Dong is in a conflict of interest and in breach of his fiduciary duty.

Chapter Summary

This chapter introduced one of the cornerstone relationships in business. Agency is a relationship that allows one person's actions to be attributable to another. In this way, agency permits one party to represent and bind another in contractual matters. Thus a business may use agents in many facets of its operations, such as buying, selling, leasing, and hiring. As a practical matter, without the advantage of agency relationships, business could not be conducted on any significant scale.

The agency relationship most commonly comes into existence when a principal grants authority to the agent to act on her behalf. The law, however, recognizes an agency relationship when the principal represents to another that she is represented by an agent—agency by estoppel—or when the principal adopts a contract made on her behalf by someone who is not her agent—agency by ratification. In this area, it is the substance of the relationship that is important, not what parties call their relationship. An agent's authority to act on behalf of a principal varies. An agent may have actual authority. This is the authority that he is actually given by the principal or that is implied from his position. Alternatively, an agent may have apparent authority. This is the authority that a third party would reasonably believe the agent to have based on the principal's representations. The scope of an agent's apparent authority is fact-specific and therefore varies with the circumstances.

An agent has both express and implied duties to his principal. Most importantly, an agent has a fiduciary duty to act in the best interests of the principal. The principal also has express and implied duties, particularly the duty to compensate the agent for services rendered and for costs associated with the agency relationship.

Agency operates in such a way that the principal is generally liable on contracts entered into by the agent on her behalf. A contract is formed between the principal and the outsider, and the agent drops out of the transaction. Though there are a number of potential problems, the agency relationship generally functions well and according to plan. However, it is possible that agency can operate in ways not desired. For example, the principal may be liable on contracts not desired, as when the agent negotiates a poor contract or exceeds his actual authority but not his apparent authority. So too, a principal may be liable for torts committed by an agent. Thus, ironically, the same person who can help a business grow and prosper can lead that same enterprise to financial loss. The key point is that agency, like other aspects of a business, needs to be managed and monitored: businesspeople must choose an agent wisely, instruct him carefully, and review his work regularly.

PART FOUR

Chapter Study

Key Terms and Concepts

actual authority (p. 290)

agency (p. 287)

agency by estoppel (p. 293)

agency by ratification (p. 295)

agent (p. 287)

apparent authority (p. 292)

fiduciary (p. 297)

fiduciary duty (p. 297)

insurance broker (p. 300)

law of agency (p. 289)

outsider (p. 289)

principal (p. 287)

undisclosed principal (p. 301)

warranty of authority (p. 301)

Questions for Review

1. What is agency? Give an example.

2. Why would a business use an agent to act on its behalf?

3. How is an agency relationship entered into?

4. What is the difference between the actual and apparent authority of an agent?

5. When will an agent have implied authority?

6. What is a power of attorney? What is the risk involved with using a power of attorney?

7. What is meant by agency by estoppel? How does agency by estoppel arise?

8. How is an agency by ratification created?

9. Is a principal permitted to ratify any contract entered into by an "agent?" Explain.

10. Is a real estate agent a typical agent? Explain.

11. What are the duties of the agent?

12. What are the duties of the principal?

13. Do all business advisors owe fiduciary duties? Explain.

14. When can an agent be personally liable on a contract entered into on behalf of a principal?

15. Describe how an agent can be liable to the principal.

16. When is a principal liable for torts committed by an agent? How can a principal reduce his liability for torts committed by an agent?

17. What is an undisclosed principal?

18. How may an agency relationship be terminated?

Questions for Critical Thinking

1. In the insurance industry, the agent acts primarily for the insurance company, which is the principal. Typically, the insurance agent also advises the client on the needed coverage and the meaning of the insurance policy. Do you see any potential problems with this situation?

2. Is it reasonable to hold principals responsible for contracts formed with only apparent authority? What are the tradeoffs?

3. The rise in electronic transactions has resulted in more homes being bought and sold without the use of a real estate agent. As in the travel industry, increasing Internet access and user savvy has empowered property buyers to do their own research and make their own deals. How does foregoing the services of a real estate agent affect recourse if things go bad for the purchaser?

4. In the Ethical Considerations box (pages 300–301), it was noted that life insurance brokers may receive a variety of compensation from insurance companies for the business that they direct to them. In the standard disclosure letter given to consumers at the time of purchasing a life insurance policy, there is usually a line stating that some companies may provide compensation to the insurance broker such as travel incentives or educational opportunities, in addition to commissions. Does disclosure in this manner address the criticism that such travel incentives and educational opportunities amount to a conflict of interest?

5. The application of fiduciary duty to those who are brought within its scope is to impose a high standard of morality. Is this to be applauded? Are there any concerns?

6. The agency relationship creates considerable risks for the principal. What is the nature of these risks in both contract and tort? How can these risks be managed? Does the agency relationship create risks for the agent? Explain.

Situations for Discussion

1. Kerry is interested in selling her convenience store for approximately $250 000 to $300 000. As Kerry is unfamiliar with the commercial real estate market in Red Deer, she engages a real estate agent, Patrick. The engagement is a standard listing agreement. Patrick shows the building to a young couple, Paul and Rick, who seem to be quite interested. In fact, they make an offer in writing to purchase the building for $250 000. They also indicate that they need a reply immediately. Patrick calls Kerry but is unable to reach her. Patrick is in a quandary, but knowing that Paul and Rick's offer is in Kerry's range, albeit at the bottom of it, Patrick accepts the offer on Kerry's behalf (he signs the written offer). Upon learning of Patrick's actions, Kerry is quite upset and wonders whether she must sell the building to Paul and Rick. Advise Kerry.

2. RCD Ltd. sells household appliances, including washers, dryers, dishwashers, stoves, and refrigerators. Most of RCD's customers are developers of apartment buildings and condominium complexes. RCD's sales representative is Alastair Du. He is authorized to make contracts with buyers provided the value of each contract does not exceed $100 000. Alastair ignored the restriction on his authority and concluded a contract to sell 50 sets of washers and dryers to BES Developers at a price of $500 000. BES placed its order on RCD's application form, which states that contracts over $100 000 require written approval of RCD's vice president of sales, and Alastair on behalf of RCD accepted the order. RCD delivered the 50 sets of washer and dryers, and received payment from BES. Within a month of delivery of the washers and dryers, BES complained that the washers vibrate excessively and the dryers overheat, and they have caused damage to the apartments in which they were installed. RCD claimed to be protected from any liability for the faulty machines because Alastair had no authority to bind RDC to this contract. Does RDC's argument constitute a valid legal defence to a claim against RDS by BES? Explain.

3. Atlantic Life Ltd. is a life insurance company. The corporation hired Toby Ryan as its representative in Newfoundland. Toby was provided with Atlantic Life business cards and brochures, along with a company car with the Atlantic Life logo on it. A clause in the contract between the parties provided

   > The representative will not without the prior approval of the Company incur any liability or debt on behalf of the Company, accept insurance or other risks, revive polices, waive forfeitures, extend the time of payment of any premium or waive premium payment in cash, or make, alter, or discharge any contract and will not make any expenditure on behalf of the Company.

   Toby negotiated on behalf of Atlantic Life the sale of a life insurance policy to Sadie Clements, insuring her life for $500 000. Shortly thereafter, Sadie died and her beneficiaries claimed benefits under the policy. Atlantic Life refuses to pay on the basis that Toby did not obtain approval of Atlantic for the sale of the insurance policy.[26] Does Atlantic Life have to pay the benefits? If it does, how could it have prevented this situation?

4. Imam Daud Malik, a community organizer had connections and influence with Sudanese politicians and government officials. He was interested in using these connections to promote relations between Islamic states and American Muslims. Through mutual acquaintances, Malik met Khan, the president of State Petroleum Corp. Khan, along with other investors had incorporated State Petroleum to pursue the acquisition of oil concessions in Sudan. At the request of Khan, Malik assisted State in its efforts. There was no contract in place regarding Malik's services. A short time later, State entered into an agreement with the government of Sudan for the acquisitions of oil concessions valued at $18 million. Malik claimed compensation from State for his services, but State refused to pay.[27] Is Malik entitled to compensation from State? Explain. If he is entitled, what factors are important in determining the amount of compensation?

26. Based on *Schwartz v Maritime Life Assurance Co* (1997), 149 Nfld & PEIR 234, [1997] NJ 77 (Nfld CA), leave to appeal to SCC refused, [1997] SCCA 362.
27. Based on *Malik (Representative Ad litem of) v State Petroleum Corp*, 2009 BCCA 505, 98 BCLR (4th) 92.

PART FOUR

5. Mollie Morrow was a real estate agent working for Commercial Properties. She was approached by Shane Jacobs to find a commercial building in downtown Halifax. She did some investigating and found a suitable property owned by Haldane Properties (HP). She approached the owners about selling, and they agreed to pay a commission of 2 percent if she acted as their agent in the sale of the building. After considerable negotiations, the sale was concluded for $6 million. Unknown to HP, Mollie had agreed to pay half of her commission to Shane. When HP learned about this it refused to pay the commission. Mollie argued that HP had received what it wanted out of the deal; she had made a sacrifice by giving up part of her commission; and her sacrifice ensured that the deal went through. In short, her actions helped, not harmed, HP. Is Mollie entitled to the commission?[28]

6. Hamilton Utility Inc. appointed Juan Abrams as one of its corporate officers. Juan rented cars from Quality Cars Ltd., a car rental business. The rental agreements named Juan as renter, and he signed the agreements describing himself as company secretary of Hamilton Utility. Juan, however, used the cars for personal purposes and not for company business. Hamilton refused to pay the charges, as Juan had not been given any authority to enter contracts on its behalf.[29] Is Hamilton liable to pay the car rental charges? Explain. What would be the result if Hamilton appointed Juan to a secretarial position?

7. Paul, an 88-year-old widower, rented out a house he owned in Toronto to Aaron. Using a forged power of attorney and posing as Paul's non-existent grandson, Aaron had the property listed for sale on the Multiple Listing Service. A short time later, Peggy entered into an Agreement of Purchase and Sale for the property. The purchase price was $450 000. The Agreement stated that the seller was Paul and that Aaron was acting pursuant to a power of attorney. Aaron's lawyer, Carter, who was unaware that the power of attorney was a forgery, sent a copy of it to Peggy's lawyer. Peggy financed most of the purchase price through a mortgage with HSBC that was title insured by Stewart Title Guaranty Company. On closing HSBC advanced the mortgage money to Sally, the lawyer acting on behalf of both Peggy and HSBC. She deposited the cheque into her trust account and drew a cheque in favour of Paul for $429 861.06, the balance of the purchase price. Aaron forged Paul's signature, deposited the cheque into an account at the Korean Exchange Bank of Canada and then disappeared with the money.[30] The fraud in this real estate transaction was made possible by a bogus power of attorney. Who should bear the loss in this case—Paul, Peggy, Carter, Sally, HSBC, Stewart Title, or the Korean Exchange Bank of Canada? How could this fraud have been prevented?

8. Ty Sharim has been employed as an agent for Farley's Game and Fishing Lodge Inc. for the past 10 years. Farley's runs an exclusive hunting and fishing camp in northern Ontario. Ty's contractual duties include advertising the camp and soliciting customers at fish and gun shows and conventions in North America and elsewhere. One weekend while on a fishing trip with his family, Ty came across a small fishing camp that was for sale. As Ty has always dreamed of owning and operating his own business, he is thinking of putting in an offer on the camp. Is Ty entitled to put in an offer to purchase the camp or must he inform Farley's of the camp? Would answer differ if Ty terminated his relationship with Farley's before offering to buy the camp?

For more study tools, visit http://www.NELSONbrain.com.

28. Based on *Ocean City Realty Ltd v A & M Holdings Ltd et al*, 36 DLR (4th) 94, [1987] BCJ 593 (BCCA).
29. Based on *Panorama Developments (Guildford) Ltd v Fidelis Furnishing Fabrics Ltd*, [1971] 2 QB 711 (CA).
30. Based on *Reviczky v Meleknia*, 88 OR (3d) 699, 287 DLR (4th) 193 (Ont Sup Ct).

CHAPTER 14

Business Forms and Arrangements

Objectives

After studying this chapter, you should have an understanding of

- the characteristics of the major forms of business organizations

- the advantages and disadvantages of the major forms of business organizations

- the legal consequences of a partnership

- methods of arranging business activity

Business Law in Practice

Adam Lane is young, energetic, smart, and largely broke. In fact, Adam has only two assets of any real value: a recently completed degree in computer science and a 1974 vintage Corvette worth over $15 000. The vehicle was a gift from his father. On the liability side, Adam has student loans totalling over $10 000.

Adam has spent the past few summers experimenting and thinks that he has come up with an improved voice-recognition system for computers. He wants to contract out the manufacture of his product and set up an organization for its distribution and sale. He already has a name in mind: "I-know-that-it's-you Enterprises," or IK Enterprises for short.

Adam's father, Cameron Lane, is retired and reasonably well off. He has $100 000 that he is willing to invest in IK Enterprises, but he does not wish to risk his position and that of Adam's young brother by having any greater commitment to the business.

Adam has also found Diane Levesque, a manufacturer's agent for many products, who is willing to advise Adam on setting up IK Enterprises and to assist in marketing the product. Diane is willing to invest $20 000 and to devote some of her time and expertise to the new business. The bank, under a program for young entrepreneurs, is also willing to lend some start-up capital.

1. What forms of business organization are available for carrying on Adam's business?
2. What are the major considerations in choosing a particular form?
3. Which form is best for Adam's business?

COURTESY OF CANADIAN TIRE CORPORATION

Forms of Business Organization

Choosing how to own a business is a critical decision because it determines in large part who

- is financially liable for the business

- shares in business profits and other assets

- makes and is accountable for management decisions

The Sole Proprietorship

Sole proprietorship
An unincorporated business organization that has only one owner.

The **sole proprietorship** is the oldest form of business organization and the one most often used by small business. It is a particularly popular choice for the home-based enterprise. From a legal perspective, it also represents the simplest form of business organization because there is no legislation pertaining to the sole proprietorship as such. A discussion of the legal consequences of this form of business is really a discussion of the rights and liabilities of an individual.

Financial Liability

The financial consequences to Adam should he conduct his computer business as a sole proprietorship are both straightforward and significant: any obligation of the business is Adam's personal obligation. Consider the following examples:

- *The bank loan.* If Adam decides to borrow start-up capital from the bank, it is Adam who promises to repay the loan, not his business. This is because a sole proprietorship, unlike a corporation, is not legally capable of borrowing money on its own. Adam is the business. Adam is the debtor and is responsible for the debt.

Suppose that IK Enterprises, Adam's sole proprietorship, begins to falter and the loan cannot be repaid. The bank will take the appropriate legal steps—discussed in more detail in Chapter 26—to recover as much as it can on the loan. All of Adam's business and personal assets are subject to the debts of the business. Also, any judgment against him can be kept alive indefinitely unless he declares bankruptcy, in which case, most judgments against him will be discharged. However, Adam's personal credit rating will be adversely affected, now and in the future. This may make it next to impossible to ever start another venture that would depend on Adam's creditworthiness.

- *The breach of contract.* If at some point IK Enterprises supplies defective computers to a customer, Adam, not IK Enterprises, is in breach of contract. This is because, as noted above, IK Enterprises cannot enter into a contract. As in the preceding example, Adam is the one who will be sued, and it is Adam's assets that are at risk.

Unlimited liability
Unrestricted legal responsibility for obligations.

In short, a sole proprietor has what is known in law as **unlimited liability**. Regardless of what the owner has invested in his business, his personal assets—and not just the business assets—may be seized to pay the outstanding debts of the business. Unfortunately, these debts can far exceed anything anticipated when the business was started.

Profit Sharing

The sole proprietor not only bears the risk of failure, but also enjoys this advantage: all the profits after taxes accrue to the sole proprietor alone. If IK Enterprises is a runaway success, Adam reaps all the benefits. The profit motive can be a strong incentive for the sole proprietor to seek to ensure the success of the business.

Decision Making

The sole proprietor, having no partners and no board of directors to report to, can make business decisions very quickly and independently. She has a lot of personal freedom to do exactly as she pleases concerning all aspects of the business, even if it means deciding to discontinue business activities altogether. Should the owner die, the business is terminated—in other words, the proprietorship has a limited life span.

There are, of course, disadvantages to working alone in this way: few people are good at everything, yet the sole proprietor is responsible for every aspect of the business, from buying and selling to financing and advertising. Another serious consideration is that the sole proprietor's absence through illness or incapacity can adversely affect the business because so much of the enterprise revolves around this one individual. Though the sole proprietor may hire employees, they have limited opportunities for advancement, since by definition a sole proprietorship is a one-person show. As a result, these workers may not be particularly motivated or able to provide a high level of commitment.

Sources of Capital

A major difficulty with "going it alone" is that the sole proprietor has limited access to capital. Since the proprietor has no business partners, he is limited to his own assets and to whatever credit he can draw on to finance the operation. Usually this is less than what would be available if more than one person was involved, as in a partnership, for example.

Taxation

Because a sole proprietorship is not a legal entity separate from the owner, there are no formal or specialized tax rules governing it. Profits and losses are simply reported on the owner's personal income tax return. This may be favourable or unfavourable depending on the taxpayer's circumstances, including whether the owner's marginal tax rate is higher or lower than the applicable corporate tax rate.

Transferability

A sole proprietorship cannot be transferred or sold to another because it has no legal status. There is, in effect, nothing to transfer. However, the assets associated with the proprietorship—such as inventory—are transferable.

PART FOUR

Regulations

The legal requirements for establishing and conducting this form of business organization are minimal—one simply commences business activity. There is no general need to incur legal fees to create the business vehicle. In short, doing business through the sole proprietorship is simple and inexpensive.

This is not to say that sole proprietorships are unregulated. They are subject to the same general legislation as any other business form. One important requirement is the registration or licensing of the business. Requirements vary from province to province, but generally persons who offer specialized services to the public must be licensed to practise their particular skill. Thus, lawyers, doctors, dentists, and electricians, for example, are required to follow provincial legislation governing their activity before providing services. Some businesses, such as those involving interprovincial trucking, require a federal licence to operate. Other types of business, such as door-to-door selling and the transportation of goods, are subject to specialized rules. The fees associated with licensing and registration are generally not substantial.

In addition to the regulations put in place by the federal and provincial governments, municipalities often impose their own registration or licensing requirements. For example, taxi businesses frequently require municipal licences to operate within municipal boundaries.

A sole proprietor who wishes to use a name other than her own for conducting the business must register the name at the local registry office or other government office designated by the province, where such records are kept and made available to the public.[1] The objective is to enable a person who deals with such a business to determine the identity of the proprietor of the business. Failure to register may result in a fine or other penalty and the inability to sue for an obligation incurred in connection with the business except with leave of the court.[2]

Aside from these requirements, the sole proprietor is subject to laws of general application. Local zoning bylaws may require sole proprietors to locate in certain areas, provincial tax laws may require them to obtain a permit to act as a collector of sales tax, and health legislation may require them to maintain a high degree of cleanliness where food service or processing is involved. As well, a sole proprietor who hires employees must comply with all applicable legislation, such as that regulating employment standards, employment insurance, workers' compensation, and occupational health and safety.

A sole proprietor (unlike a public corporation) is not required to publish the business' financial statements. Success or failure in the business is a private matter, restricted to the proprietor, the business' accountant, the Canada Revenue Agency, and perhaps the local bank manager.

The pros and cons of the sole proprietorship are summarized in Figure 14.1.

---

1. The use of trade or business names is discussed in Chapter 18.
2. See, for example, *Business Names Act*, RSO 1990, c B-17, s 7.

FIGURE 14.1

Pros and Cons of the Sole Proprietorship

Pros	Cons
Simplicity: There are few licensing and registration requirements. The sole proprietor just starts doing business and is free to discontinue business activities at any time.	**Unlimited personal liability:** The sole proprietor carries the risk of the business failing and losing both business and personal assets.
Speed and independence: Since the sole proprietor has no partners and is not answerable to a board of directors, he can make decisions quickly and independently.	**Working alone:** The sole proprietor is responsible for all aspects of the business operation. Though a sole proprietor can hire employees, it is difficult to retain high-calibre people because of the limited opportunities available to them in a sole proprietorship.
Profit motive: Any after-tax profit or other assets that accrue go entirely to the sole proprietor.	**Limited access to capital:** The capital available to the business is limited to the assets of the proprietor and the extent of her credit.
Lower costs: The fees for provincial and municipal licences are relatively small, varying according to the nature and size of the business and the municipality in which it is located. Generally, there is no need to incur legal fees.	**Limited life span:** The owner's death terminates the business. The proprietorship cannot be transferred.
Tax benefits: Profits and losses are reported on the owner's personal income tax return. This may be favourable or unfavourable, depending on the taxpayer's circumstances.	**Tax disadvantages:** See tax benefits.

The Partnership

When two or more persons want to pool their resources and carry on business together, one of the most common options is to form a **partnership** (a second common option is to create a corporation as discussed below[3]). A partnership is much like a sole proprietorship in that neither has a legal personality—or legal existence—separate from the people who comprise them. There are no special steps to create a partnership. It is simply the legal relationship that automatically arises when two or more people do business together with the objective of making a profit.

Partnership

A business carried on by two or more persons with the intention of making a profit.

The rules governing partnerships come from three sources: partnership legislation (in place in every province), contract law, and agency law. Later in the chapter, these sources will be analyzed in some depth. What follows is a general account of the basic principles that govern partnerships.

Financial Liability

If Adam, Cameron, and Diane decide to join forces and bring Adam's product to market through a partnership, each has unlimited liability for partnership debts and other obligations. Consider the following examples:

- *The bank loan.* If the partners borrow start-up money from the bank (say $100 000 plus interest) and fail to repay it, Cameron, Adam, and Diane are liable for the full amount outstanding. This is because—like a sole proprietorship but

---

3. There can be restrictions on professionals, such as accountants and lawyers, incorporating companies. See Chapter 22 for detail.

unlike a corporation—a partnership is not legally capable of borrowing money on its own. The partners are the partnership. The partners are the debtors and are responsible for the debt.

A very important feature of partnership law is that each partner is fully responsible for all the debts and obligations of the partnership and not just for some appropriate proportion. Accordingly, the bank can proceed against the partner with the most assets—perhaps Adam's father, Cameron—and collect from that one individual the entire amount owing on the debt. In law, this is known as **joint liability**.[4] The liability is considered to be joint because responsibility is not in relation to the partner's share in the partnership; rather, each one of the partners has full and complete exposure on each and every obligation incurred. If the bank proceeds only against Cameron for repayment of the bank loan, however, Cameron is entitled to be reimbursed by his partners for their share of the debt. Of course, if the other partners have no assets, Cameron will end up bearing the partnership debts himself.

Joint liability
Liability shared by two or more parties where each is personally liable for the full amount of the obligation.

- *The breach of contract.* If the partnership supplies defective computers to a customer, each of the partners is liable for the entire amount of the damages. The contract is between the customer, on the one hand, and all the partners, on the other.

The key point from a liability perspective is that each partner's personal assets can be seized and sold through the judicial process if the partnership assets are insufficient to satisfy partnership obligations. This legal reality should give Adam's father, Cameron, particular cause for concern. Since Cameron wants to limit his financial exposure to $100 000—in part because he has a young son whom he supports—Cameron will probably not find the partnership to be a feasible business vehicle through which to bring Adam's product to market. This is because a partnership, like a sole proprietorship, puts all of Cameron's assets at risk, not just his capital contribution. Adam and Diane also have cause for concern. Although they may have less at risk, they still need to consider the impact of a judgment on their assets and their future.

Profit Sharing

It is the partners themselves who decide how profits and other firm assets are to be divided. If they fail to agree on this point, partnership legislation requires them to share profits equally.[5]

Adam, Cameron, and Diane may decide to divide the partnership into unequal interests because the contribution of each partner varies. Since Adam has come up with the product and presumably will be working full-time at the business, the partners may decide

---

4. See, for example, *Partnership Act*, RSNB 1973, c P-4, s 10: every partner in a firm is liable jointly with the other partners for all debts and obligations of the firm while he is a partner.
5. *Ibid*, s 25(a): "The interests of partners in the partnership property and their rights and duties in relation to the partnership shall be determined, subject to any agreement express or implied between the partners, by the following rules: all partners are entitled to share equally in the capital and profits of the business, and must contribute equally towards the losses whether of capital or otherwise sustained by the firm."

that he should hold a majority interest in the firm, for example, 60 percent. Diane will be contributing her expertise as well as some cash, so she may end up with 30 percent. Since Cameron is unlikely to have much involvement in the day-to-day operations and primarily will be contributing capital, his interest in the firm may be set at 10 percent. The point is that the relationship among the partners themselves—including profit sharing—is something they are free to define in any way they see fit.

Decision Making

Because a partnership comprises two or more persons pooling their resources, the management base is potentially strong. Adam's product knowledge, Diane's marketing savvy, and Cameron's general life experience will all assist in making IK Enterprises a viable operation. If one of the partners becomes sick or otherwise unable to devote sufficient attention to the business, the other partners are in place to carry on.

The downside is that managing the business will require consultation among the partners, and they may not always achieve consensus. A dispute or disagreement between the partners can be extremely disruptive. Even though the partners may have agreed in advance—through a partnership agreement—on a method of dispute resolution, such clauses can be subject to varying interpretations and can be the source of ill feeling among the partners.

Just as there is the danger of disagreement, there is also the danger of divided authority, which may impede decision making. Although the partners may have determined that they will have authority in different areas, instances are bound to arise in which responsibility overlaps. This too can result in conflict and delayed decision making.

Sources of Capital

Because a partnership is composed of two or more persons, it provides more sources of capital than the sole proprietorship. The partnership looks to each partner for a capital contribution and can rely on the creditworthiness of each one to secure financing from other sources, including the bank.

Taxation

The partnership is not a separate legal entity, and therefore any income from the partnership business is allocated to the partners—on the basis of their interest in the partnership—and they must, in turn, include it on their individual tax returns.[6]

Transferability

The partnership does not provide for the ready transfer of interest from one owner to another. Partners do not individually own or have a share in specific partnership property. Each partner has an interest in all partnership property, from the photocopier to the filing cabinets to its intellectual property.

---

6. J Anthony VanDuzer, *The Law of Partnerships and Corporations*, 3d ed (Toronto: Irwin Law, 2009) at 12.

PART FOUR

Agency and the Partnership Act

Partnership law is based in large part on contract law, agency law, and provincial partnership legislation, known in every jurisdiction as the *Partnership Act*.[7] The legislation in place in the common law provinces provides mandatory rules with respect to

- when a partnership exists

- what the relationship of partners is to outsiders

These acts have optional rules (i.e., the rules are subject to an agreement to the contrary) with respect to

- the relationship of partners to one another

- how and why a partnership ends

Some of these partnership concepts have already been introduced to give a sketch of how partnerships operate relative to other business vehicles. The following section describes partnerships from a more technical and detailed perspective.

When a Partnership Exists   According to the *Partnership Act*, a partnership exists when two or more people "carry on business in common with a view towards profit." The definition excludes charitable and not-for-profit endeavours. It does not, however, exclude unprofitable ventures that otherwise meet the definition of partnership so long as an intention to make a profit is present.

The statutory definition of partnership covers people who expressly intend to be partners as well as people who may not necessarily intend to be partners but act as if they were. That is, a person who conducts himself as if he were a partner—by sharing in profits, by managing the business, by contributing capital to establish a business—is a partner in the eyes of the law. Such a person, therefore, has all the rights and liabilities of a partner.

The *Partnership Act* also sets out a number of circumstances that point toward there being a partnership but not conclusively so.[8] For example, if two or more persons own property together, this does not of itself make them partners. However, if in addition to owning property together, the persons share profits associated with that property and restrict their ability to sell unilaterally their interest in the property, a court is likely to conclude that a partnership exists.[9] This would likely be the result even though the parties have indicated in their written agreement that their relationship is not a "partnership."[10] The court will look to the essence of the relationship rather than the labels used by the parties.

This means, for example, that if Cameron wants to take an active part in the management of the business and share in the profits yet simultaneously avoid the joint, unlimited personal liability that goes with partnership, he is unlikely to succeed. If the business runs into

---

7. Legislation is virtually identical across the common law provinces.
8. *Supra* note 4 at s 3. The legislation provides that a number of situations do not by themselves create a partnership. A relationship is not necessarily a "partnership" in the following situations: the parties jointly own property; one party receives repayment of a debt out of profits; an employment contract where remuneration varies with profits; a loan where the lender's compensation is to be a share of profits; an annuity paid out of profits to a spouse or child of a deceased partner; and receipt of a share of profits of a business paid to a vendor as consideration for the sale of a business.
9. For a discussion of the difference between partnership and mere co-ownership, see *AE LePage Ltd v Kamex Developments Ltd* (1977), 16 OR (2d) 193, 78 DLR (3d) 223 (CA), aff'd [1979] 2 SCR 155, 105 DLR (3d) 84 (SCC).
10. *Lansing Building Supply (Ontario) Ltd v Ierullo* (1989), 71 OR (2d) 173 (Dist Ct).

financial difficulties, creditors can come after Cameron for the liabilities, even if Cameron has a document—signed by Diane and Adam—stating that Cameron is not a partner. In classifying Cameron's status, what matters is what Cameron actually does in relation to the business, not what a document says.

BUSINESS APPLICATION OF THE LAW

The Lottery Partnership?

Nineteen employees of Bell Canada won a $50 million Lotto Max prize on New Year's Eve. A short time later, nine of their colleagues whose names were not on the group form, and who had not contributed to the purchase of the winning ticket claimed a share of the prize. The nine claimants allege that they had been part of a group of lottery players at the Bell Toronto office that constituted a partnership. They claim that the rules of their partnership provided that each of the partners would contribute an agreed-upon weekly amount towards the purchase of lottery tickets, and that partners who failed to contribute on a specific occasion due to a temporary absence for any reason, would be permitted and expected to make their required payment at a later time. They further claim that the 19 winners withdrew from the partnership and formed their own group without any notice, either written or oral, of the unilateral dissolution or termination of the partnership arrangement.

In an out-of-court agreement, the parties decided that the money would be divided into 30 equal shares, that the 19 winners would be paid their shares and the remainder held in trust pending the outcome of litigation.

Critical Analysis: What do the nine claimants need to prove to establish a partnership with the 19 winners? If the

Is the relationship between the members of a group of lottery players a partnership?

relationship between them is one of partnership, have the winners breached any partnership duties? If the relationship is a partnership, how can the partnership be terminated?

Source: Anna Mehler Paperny, "Nine Bell employees sue 19 co-workers over $50-million lottery jackpot", *The Globe and Mail* (22 May 2011) online: The Globe and Mail <http://www.theglobeandmail.com/news/national/toronto/nine-bell-employees-sue-colleagues-over-50-million-lotto-max-win/article1913556/>.

The Relationship of Partners to One Another If Adam, Cameron, and Diane become partners, the *Partnership Act* provides that they also become one another's agents as well as the agents of the firm in matters relating to the partnership's business. This is significant because it imports the law concerning agency discussed in Chapter 13. It also means that the partners owe fiduciary duties to one another, which require a partner to put the interests of her partners above her own interests.

Accordingly, Adam cannot set up a secret business that competes with the partnership he has formed with Diane and Cameron. He cannot tell a client of the firm to buy its computer equipment from him "on the side" and then proceed to pocket the profits, or use the firm photocopier at night to run a duplicating service without his partners' permission. In short, the law does not allow a partner to make personal profit from the partnership property, to compete against the partnership, or to use a partnership opportunity for exclusive personal gain. Adam is required by law to put the interests of the partnership ahead of his own.

PART FOUR

Persons who wish to be associated in partnership should have a partnership agreement, preferably one drafted by a lawyer; Figure 14.2 summarizes the issues that the agreement should address. The partnership agreement provides the parties with significant freedom to define their relationship. For example, a partnership agreement can provide for the division of profits among Cameron, Adam, and Diane in any proportion they see fit. If there is no agreement, the *Partnership Act* will dictate that Cameron, Adam, and Diane will share in profits equally—a result that may be neither wanted nor intended.

As already noted, if the partners do not have a contract or if they have a contract that is silent on some points, the *Partnership Act* of the province in which the partners are residing will govern the relationship.

FIGURE 14.2
Partnership Agreement Checklist

A partnership has been described as a "marriage without love" because many of the concerns that partners face are similar to the ones faced by spouses—sharing of work, financial matters, authority to make decisions, and resolution of disputes. And just as many marriages end in divorce, so too many partnerships fail. Just as a marriage contract cannot save a bad marriage, a partnership agreement cannot guarantee a successful partnership. An agreement can, however, help in avoiding costly litigation and personal animosity if a "divorce" proves necessary.

A partnership agreement should address the following issues:

Creation of the partnership—name and address of partners, partnership name, term of partnership, if any, description of firm's business

Capital contribution—description of contribution by each partner, how shortfalls are handled, how the accounts are managed

Decision making—description of the partners' duties, any limits on authority, dispute resolution mechanism

Profit distribution—description of how profits are to be shared, how and when they are to be distributed, rights of withdrawal

Changes to partnership—rules for changing the relationship, admission of new partners, retirement of partners, option to purchase partner's interest, valuation of interests

Dissolution of partnership—description of events that could trigger dissolution, how dissolution will be handled, valuation of assets

A partnership agreement should also be reviewed and updated periodically to reflect changes in circumstances.

Relationship of Partners to Outsiders   While partners are free to enter into a partnership agreement in order to set out the rights and obligations between them, this will not modify the relationship between partners and outsiders, which is governed specifically by the *Partnership Act* and generally by partnership law, including agency law.

First and foremost, a partner is an agent of the firm. She acts for herself as well as for her partners, who from the perspective of the agency relationship are her principals. For this reason, the firm is responsible for contracts she enters into with actual or apparent authority. For example, assume that Diane purchases a BlackBerry to be used for partnership business and enters into a long-term contract for wireless communication services. Assume further that Cameron and Adam are appalled, since it is not clear that a BlackBerry is needed at this point, let alone for an extended period of time. They are still bound, however, because Diane—as a partner and therefore as their agent—has the apparent authority to enter into contracts for wireless communication access for the purpose of the partnership. Between the disappointed principals (Cameron and Adam) and the wireless communication company that had no idea that Diane was entering into a contract unpopular with her partners, the law protects the wireless communication company. This is because Diane's partners are in a better position to monitor and restrict her ability to do business on behalf of the firm, even to the point of voting her out of the partnership altogether. They must, therefore, absorb the risk of her "going astray."

BUSINESS AND LEGISLATION

The Partnership Act: The Relations between Partners

All of the common law provinces have a *Partnership Act* modelled on the British Act of the same name.

These Acts are substantially similar from province to province and have been subject to little change since their original enactments.

The Acts have both mandatory and optional provisions. The mandatory provisions relate to the relationship between partners and outsiders. The optional rules with respect to the relationship between partners can therefore be varied by agreement.

In each province, the *Partnership Act* provides for the following optional rules:

1. All partners are to share equally in the capital and profits of the business and must contribute equally to the losses.
2. Property acquired for the partnership shall be used exclusively for the partnership and not for the private purposes of individual partners. Property purchased with partnership money is deemed to be partnership property.
3. A partner shall be indemnified by the other partners for any liability incurred on behalf of the partnership. This means that all partners are liable for partnership liabilities and that a partner who pays a debt is entitled to reimbursement from her partners.
4. A payment made by a partner for the purposes of the partnership in excess of his agreed subscription shall earn interest.
5. Each partner may take part in the management of the business.
6. No partner is entitled to remuneration for acting in the partnership business.
7. No new member shall be admitted to the partnership without the consent of all the partners.
8. Disputes regarding the partnership business may be decided by a majority, but the nature of the partnership may not be changed without the consent of all the members.
9. Partnership books shall be kept at the partnership's place of business, and all partners shall have access to them.
10. No simple majority may expel any partner.

Source: *Partnership Act*, RSNB 1973, c P-4, ss 21(1), 25, 26.

Indeed, because the relationship between partners is based on agreement, Diane's authority to enter into contracts on behalf of the firm can be restricted. The parties can enter into an agreement whereby Diane promises not to enter into any long-term contract without first securing her partners' approval. Diane will presumably respect and abide by this restriction. However, should she enter into a contract that exceeds her actual authority, the firm will still be bound unless the outsider knows or should know that her authority has been limited in this way. The firm is obligated by virtue of the doctrine of apparent authority.

The *Partnership Act* and agency law also make partners responsible for one another's mistakes. For example, if Adam gives poor advice to a client as to its computer systems needs and is sued for the tort of negligence, all the partners, not just Adam, are liable for any damages that result. This is because Adam was acting in the course of firm business and incurred a liability by committing a tort. He and his partners have **joint and several liability**.[11]

Joint and several liability Individual and collective liability for a debt. Each liable party is individually responsible for the entire debt as well as being collectively liable for the entire debt.

---

11. See, for example, *Partnership Act*, RSNB 1973, c P-4, s 13, which provides that every partner is liable jointly with co-partners and also severally for wrongful acts or omissions of a partner acting within the course of employment. The differences between joint liability and joint and several liability are subtle. They mainly affect the procedures for maintaining the right to sue a partner who was not originally included in a legal action. Except to this extent, the differences simply do not matter. Regardless of whether liability is joint or joint and several, partners are both individually and to the extent of the partnership assets accountable to third parties.

Each partner is individually as well as collectively responsible for the entire obligation. This means that the client can recover all of the damages from any partner or he can recover some of the damages from each. A partner who pays the debt may, however, have a right of contribution from the other partners.

CASE

Strother v 3464920 Canada Inc, 2007 SCC 24, [2007] 2 SCR 177

THE BUSINESS CONTEXT: This decision clarifies the fiduciary duties owed by law firms to their clients. It also explores the liability of a law firm for the actions of one lawyer.

FACTUAL BACKGROUND: In the early 1990s, Monarch Entertainment Inc. (now a numbered company, 3464920 Canada Inc.) retained Davis & Company, a Vancouver-based law firm. Robert Strother, a partner specializing in taxation, was responsible for a crucial aspect of Monarch's business—setting up tax-sheltered syndication deals to finance film productions. Effective October 1996, the retainer agreement between Davis and Monarch expressly prohibited Davis from acting for clients other than Monarch in relation to these tax schemes. Near the end of 1997, the federal government implemented new rules that appeared to effectively shut down the tax shelters. Strother informed Monarch that he had no "technical fix," and, acting on this advice, Monarch abandoned its tax-shelter business. The agreement prohibiting Davis from acting for competitors ended in December 1997; however Monarch continued as a firm client. Throughout 1998 and 1999, Davis did legal work for Monarch on outstanding matters related to the tax schemes as well as unrelated general corporate work. In early 1998, Strother was approached by a former employee of Monarch, Paul Darc, who presented "a way around" the new rules. Strother agreed to prepare a tax ruling request in return for a share in the profits of the venture (called Sentinel Hill). Strother did not inform Monarch of his new client nor did he inform Monarch that there might be a way around the new rules. Strother obtained a favourable tax ruling that allowed Sentinel Hill to sell tax-sheltered limited partnerships to finance film productions. Strother informed Davis' management committee about his possible conflict of interest with respect to acting for Monarch and Darc/Sentinel and was told that he would not be permitted to own any interest in Sentinel. In early 1999, Strother left Davis and joined Darc as a 50 percent shareholder of Sentinel Hill. The venture was extremely successful, and during the period from 1998 to June 2001, Strother earned more than $32 million from it. When Monarch discovered the Sentinel Hill tax ruling, it sued both Strother and Davis for breach of fiduciary duty. At trial, Strother and Davis were successful in arguing that any obligation to keep Monarch advised of tax shelters ended when the retainer agreement ended near the end of 1997. The Court of Appeal, however, held that Strother was in breach of his fiduciary duty to Monarch and ordered him to disgorge his estimated $32 million profit from his involvement with Sentinel Hill. It also ordered Davis to disgorge the profits that it earned in legal fees from acting for Sentinel and to return to Monarch all fees it paid during the time Davis acted for both Sentinel and Monarch. Strother and Davis appealed.

THE LEGAL QUESTION: Had Strother breached his fiduciary obligations to Monarch by accepting Darc/Sentinel as a new client and accepting a financial interest in Sentinel? Had Davis breached its fiduciary obligations to Monarch by accepting Darc/Sentinel as a client? If the issues are resolved in favour of Monarch, what remedies lie against Strother and/or Davis?

RESOLUTION: In a 5–4 decision, the court held that Strother breached his fiduciary duty when he acquired a financial interest in a competitor of Monarch's and when he failed to advise Monarch how it could take advantage of a tax ruling. When a lawyer is retained by a client, the scope of his retainer will be governed by contract, which will determine the services he is to perform. However, this relationship is overlaid with fiduciary duties that may include obligations beyond what the parties expressed in their written retainer.

The fiduciary duty includes the duty of loyalty, of which an element is the avoidance of conflicts of interest. Strother was free to take on Darc and Sentinel as clients once the exclusivity arrangement with Monarch expired at the end of 1997. However, Strother was not free to take a personal financial interest in the Darc/Sentinel venture. The difficulty is not that Sentinel and Monarch were competitors but that Strother aligned his personal interest with Darc/Sentinel's interest. Strother's personal interest was in conflict with his duty to Monarch. Taking a direct and significant interest in the potential profits of Monarch's competitor created a substantial risk that his representation of Monarch would be materially and adversely affected by consideration of his own interests.

With regard to the obligations of Davis, the court stated that Davis was free to take on Darc and Sentinel as new clients. Conflict of interest guidelines do not generally preclude a firm from acting concurrently for different clients who are in the same line of business or who compete with each other for business. Commercial conflicts between clients do not present a conflict problem if they do not impair a lawyer's ability to properly represent the legal interests of both clients. As Davis was not aware of Strother's personal financial interest in Sentinel and as the managing partner had forbidden Strother from taking an interest in Sentinel, it was not acting in a conflict of interest. Davis cannot be held to have breached a fiduciary duty on the basis of facts of which its partners are ignorant.

Strother was ordered to remit to Monarch the personal profit gained directly from his involvement in Sentinel and indirectly through his earnings as a Davis partner on account of billings to Monarch for the period of 1 January 1998 to 31 March 1999, when Strother resigned from Davis. (This amount is estimated to be about $1 million). As Davis had not committed any breach of fiduciary duty to Monarch, its only liability was under s 12 of the *Partnership Act*, which deems partners liable for any wrongful act or omission of any partner acting in the ordinary course of the business of the firm. While the acceptance of personal financial benefits is not in the ordinary course of the firm's business, the wrongful act was "so connected" with Davis' ordinary business that it was not possible to hold that Strother was off "on a frolic of his own."

CRITICAL ANALYSIS: What are the implications of this decision for the Canadian legal profession and other professions such as those providing financial advisory services? This case represents a big win for Davis & Company because under the earlier appeal court ruling, it would have had to remit to Monarch several million dollars in fees that it earned from Strother's tax-shelter business. Under the Supreme Court of Canada ruling, it will only have to pay if Strother defaults, which is unlikely. How should partnerships like Davis & Company manage the risk of liability for the actions of one of their partners? In other words, what more could the Davis partners have done to keep Strother out of trouble?

How and Why a Partnership Ends   The *Partnership Act* provides for the termination of a partnership under certain circumstances:

- if entered into for a fixed term, by the expiration of the term

- if entered into for a single venture or undertaking, by the termination of that venture or undertaking

- by any partner giving notice to the others of her intention to dissolve the partnership

- following the death, insanity, or bankruptcy of a partner

Nevertheless, these provisions may be varied by agreement.[12] For example, many partnership agreements do in fact provide for the continuation of the business by the remaining partners even if the particular partnership entity is dissolved. For example, large professional partnerships—such as accounting firms and law firms—have partners joining or leaving every year. Their carefully drafted agreements generally call for an immediate transfer of all assets and liabilities from the old partnership to the new one.

On dissolution of a partnership, partnership legislation provides a process for dealing with partnership property. It must be applied in payment of the debts and liabilities of the partnership first and then to payment of what is due the partners. In the event that the partnership property is insufficient to satisfy all of the firm's obligations, partners must individually contribute to the obligations in proportion to their entitlement to profits or in another agreed-upon proportion.

After all of the firm's debts are satisfied, any excess is applied, in the following order, to

1. repayment of loans made to the firm by partners

2. repayment of capital contributed by the partners

3. payment of any surplus to partners according to their respective rights to profits[13]

---

12. See Figure 14.2, Partnership Agreement Checklist, on page 320.
13. These provisions may be varied by agreement.

Regulations

As with sole proprietorships, there are no legal requirements for the establishment and conduct of a partnership. The partners simply begin their business activity. While a lawyer may be required to assist in the preparation of a partnership agreement, doing business through a partnership is reasonably simple and inexpensive.

The pros and cons of partnership are summarized in Figure 14.3.

FIGURE 14.3

Pros and Cons of the Partnership

Pros	Cons
Simplicity: There are few licensing and registration requirements for partnerships.	**Unlimited personal liability:** Each partner carries the entire risk of the business failing. If it does, both the partnership assets and each partner's personal assets are at risk.
Lower costs: The fees for provincial and municipal licences tend to be small. However, a lawyer may be required to assist in drafting the partnership agreement.	**Loss of speed and independence:** The partners must work together, and a consensus is not always achievable.
Greater access to capital: The capital available to the business includes the assets of each partner and the extent of each partner's credit.	**Limitations on transferability:** The partner's interest in the partnership is not freely transferable.
Profit motive: Any after-tax profits or other assets accrue to the partners, according to their partnership interest.	**Profit sharing:** The partners must share profits equally or according to their partnership agreement.
Tax benefits: Profits and losses are reported on each partner's personal income tax return, according to that person's share in the partnership. This may be favourable or unfavourable, depending on the taxpayer's circumstances.	**Tax disadvantages:** See tax benefits.

Partnerships are bound by all rules of general application, including the obligation to comply with laws concerning licensing, employment, tax collection, and public health, for example. Additionally, most provinces require the filing of a declaration of partnership[14] that contains information on the partners, the partnership name, and the duration of the partnership. Failure to file a declaration is not fatal, but it can impede legal actions filed in the name of the partnership and can result in fines.[15]

BUSINESS APPLICATION OF THE LAW

Managing Partnership Risks

The risks associated with the partnership form of doing business are not insignificant. First, each partner is the agent of the partnership, meaning that each of the partners may bind the partnership when acting in the usual course of the partnership business. Second, each partner is fully liable for partnership obligations, meaning that all his personal assets may be seized to satisfy them. In addition, a partner who leaves a partnership may be liable for partnership debts incurred after he leaves if creditors are unaware of the partner's departure. Partners have both legal and practical methods of addressing liability concerns. The partnership agreement may expressly limit and control a partner's ability to bind the partnership. For example, the agreement may provide that all

---

14. Ontario, British Columbia, Alberta, and New Brunswick require filing a declaration only when the partnerships involve mining, trading, and manufacturing.

15. There are variations in this area from province to province.

expenditures above a certain amount require the approval of a majority of partners. Such a measure will not be effective against third parties who are unaware of the restrictions. It will, however, provide a basis for a contractual claim by the partners against the partner who exceeded his authority.

From a practical perspective, partnership risks can also be reduced by

- choosing partners with care (partner only with people who can be trusted)
- educating partners on their authority and limits, and the consequences of exceeding them

- monitoring the activities of partners to help prevent partners from overreaching their authority or entering unwanted transactions
- notifying clients and customers of the departure of partners so that the partnership cannot be held liable for debts contracted by the departed partners
- insuring against liabilities that might result from a partner's wrongdoing

Critical Analysis: How do the partnership variations discussed below reduce the risks associated with a general partnership?

Partnership Variations

There are two variations of the partnership: the limited partnership and the limited liability partnership.

Limited Partnership

A **limited partnership** is a partnership in which at least one partner has unlimited liability while others have limited liability. General partners have unlimited liability, whereas the limited partners have a liability limited to the amount that they have contributed to the partnership capital.

Limited partnership
A partnership in which the liability of some partners is limited to their capital contribution.

This vehicle has been used mostly as an investment device. Limited partners put money into a business, in such sectors as entertainment (e.g., Cineplex Entertainment), publishing (e.g., Canwest), or real estate (e.g., Century 21 Canada), in return for tax breaks and profits. The general partner manages the investment for a fee and carries the responsibility—assuming that the limited partners have not made guarantees or commitments beyond their investment.

This type of business entity cannot be created informally. A limited partnership requires a written agreement that must be registered with the appropriate provincial body. Without this filing, the limited partnership does not exist. The registration of the agreement is also important because it provides public notice of the capital contribution of the limited partners and identifies the general partners. This, in effect, allows members of the public to decide whether they want to do business with the limited partnership.

General partners have substantially the same rights and powers as partners in ordinary partnerships; limited partners have more narrowly defined rights. They have the right to share in profits and the right to have their contribution returned on dissolution, but they cannot take part in the management of the partnership. If they do, they lose their status of limited partners and become general partners. This is a significant consequence, since it puts all their assets, not just the amount of their capital contribution, at risk should the enterprise fail. Furthermore, what constitutes partaking in management is difficult to define and can be a contentious issue. In the end, the question is resolved by courts assessing the extent and the nature of the limited partner's involvement and deciding whether, on the balance, the limited partner should lose protected status.

Because Cameron wishes to protect his assets, he might want to suggest that Adam's product be marketed through a limited partnership. The advantage is that Cameron's losses as a limited partner will be restricted to his capital investment. For example, creditors will not be able to come after his personal assets. The disadvantage is that Cameron must not take part in management or he risks unlimited personal liability.

Limited Liability Partnership

Limited liability partnership (LLP)

A partnership in which the partners have unlimited liability for their own malpractice but limited liability for other partners' malpractice.

A **limited liability partnership (LLP)** is a variation on the partnership form of business. It is designed to address concerns of professionals who are not permitted to use incorporation as a means of achieving limited liability.[16] All of the provinces and territories with the exceptions of Prince Edward Island, Yukon, and Nunavut have amended their partnership Acts to allow for this variety of partnership.

An LLP has the characteristics of a general partnership, but with specific limitations on the liability of partners. The limitation on liability (the liability shield) varies depending on the jurisdiction.[17] Some jurisdictions (Alberta, Manitoba, Quebec, and Nova Scotia) provide a partial shield that protects a partner from liabilities arising from the negligent or wrongful acts of her partners or employees (so long as she is innocent or uninvolved in their negligence or wrongful acts), but continues to hold the partners liable for all other obligations of the partnership. Partners continue to be personally liable for their own acts and omissions, and the partnership assets continue to be available with respect to the acts and omissions of all partners.

In other jurisdictions (Saskatchewan, New Brunswick, British Columbia, Ontario, Newfoundland and Labrador, and the Northwest Territories), the legislation provides a full shield that not only protects a partner from the negligent or wrongful acts of her partners or employees (so long as she is innocent or uninvolved in their negligence or wrongful acts), but also protects the partners from the contractual obligations of the partnership, such as accounts payable and general debts. The liability shield means that partners' personal assets cannot be seized to satisfy these claims. Partners, however, continue to have liability for their own negligence,[18] and partnership assets continue to be available to satisfy claims against partners.

The LLP may be used for the purpose of practising a profession (for example, accounting or law), provided the statute governing the profession expressly permits its members to practise using this vehicle.[19] An LLP must include the words "limited liability partnership," its abbreviation "LLP," or the French equivalents in the partnership name, and it must be registered as a limited liability partnership. Also, the legislation may require professionals to have liability insurance to help ensure victims will be compensated for losses from wrongful acts.

---

16. Alberta Law Reform Institute, Limited Liability Partnerships, Final Report No 77 (Edmonton: Alberta Law Reform Institute, 1999) at 5.
17. There are considerable differences in the application of the liability shield in each jurisdiction.
18. A partner may also be liable for the negligent acts and omissions of a person who is under her direct supervision and control, depending on the applicable law in each jurisdiction.
19. British Columbia does not restrict the use of the limited liability partnership to "eligible professions."

BLOOMBERG/GETTY IMAGES

Most large accounting and law firms have registered as limited liability partnerships. What are the advantages of changing from a general partnership to an LLP?

The Corporation

The corporation is the most important form of business organization today. Chapters 15 and 16 explore the corporation in detail, including its formation, operation, and termination. The purpose of this section is to provide a brief account of the corporation for the purpose of contrasting it with the other business vehicles already discussed.

Financial Liability

The corporation is the safest vehicle that Adam, Cameron, and Diane could choose to conduct their business because a corporation is a distinct legal entity in law and is therefore capable of assuming its own obligations. Adam, Cameron, and Diane can participate in the profits of the corporation as **shareholders** and manage its operations as **directors**.

Consider the following examples:

- *The bank loan.* If Adam, Cameron, and Diane form a corporation, the corporation has the legal capacity to borrow the necessary start-up capital. This means that the corporation promises to repay the loan with interest, making the corporation, and no other entity, the debtor.

If the corporation cannot repay the loan, the bank will take the necessary steps to recover as much as it can from the corporation to make up the full amount owing. The bank will be in a position to seize anything owned by the corporation. However, the bank will not be able to seize assets belonging to Adam, Cameron, and Diane. Even though they have a close relationship to the corporation as its three shareholders, they did not promise to repay the loan. That commitment came from the corporation alone. Put another way, the corporation, not the shareholders, is the debtor.

There is an important proviso to this analysis, which concerns guarantees.[20] When a corporation does not have an established track record of creditworthiness and perhaps holds few assets, the bank will seek personal guarantees from those involved in the corporation,

Shareholder
A person who has an ownership interest in a corporation.

Director
A person elected by shareholders to manage a corporation.

PART FOUR

---

20. See Chapter 26 for a discussion of guarantees.

such as the shareholders. There is a very strong possibility that when Diane, Cameron, and Adam approach the bank for a loan to the corporation, the bank will agree only if the three provide personal guarantees. A personal guarantee means that if the corporation fails to meet its obligation to the bank, Diane, Cameron, and Adam will be held responsible for that default. Then, as with a partnership or sole proprietorship, all their personal assets will be at risk. At such a point, it becomes irrelevant that a corporation is a separate legal entity capable of assuming its own obligations. Diane, Cameron, and Adam would have no more protection than if they had proceeded by way of a partnership.

- *The breach of contract*. If the corporation supplies defective computers to a customer, it is the corporation and no other entity that is in breach of contract. It is the corporation that will be sued, and it is the corporate assets that are at risk.[21]

Again, recall the discussion of guarantees. Any entity that deals with a corporation may demand the personal guarantee of the corporation's shareholders or directors.

Limited liability
Responsibility for obligations restricted to the amount of investment.

The key characteristic of a corporation is that it provides **limited liability** to its shareholders. That is, should the corporation's financial health take a bad turn, the shareholder's loss is limited to what she paid to purchase shares in the corporation. Unless, in addition, the shareholder provided a personal guarantee, she has absolutely no liability for the corporation's obligations, however they were incurred.[22]

Profit Sharing

Profits of the corporation are distributed to shareholders through dividends. That is, shareholders are paid a return on their investment in the corporation, but only if there is profit, and only if the directors declare a **dividend**.

Dividend
A division of profits payable to shareholders.

The corporate form of business organization is inherently flexible from an investment perspective, because it permits varying degrees of ownership and various means for sharing profits.

Decision Making

The corporation is managed by a board of directors, which in turn is elected by the shareholders.

In addition, officers—that is, high-ranking corporate employees—can be hired by the board to assist in running the corporation. This provides a broad management base that allows the corporation to benefit from specialized and top-level expertise. However, it can also result in layers of authority that can delay decision making.

Sources of Capital

A corporation can get its capital in two ways: it can borrow, or its directors can issue shares. The purchase price of the shares is an important and potentially large source of capital for the corporation. A share represents an equity position in the corporation and provides the shareholder with the chance of making a profit through the declaration of dividends, which it is hoped will be greater than the interest rate the shareholder would have received had he simply lent the money. The disadvantage is that if the corporation fails, the shareholder

---

21. Of course, if an employee of the corporation misrepresented the product or committed a tort of some description, that employee would be liable. This is a matter distinct from the contractual liability of the corporation. See Chapter 16.
22. Only in rare situations, such as fraud on the creditors, will the courts hold the shareholders personally responsible for the corporation's actions. See Chapter 16.

is left with nothing while the creditor technically retains the right to be repaid. However, if the corporation is insolvent, that right is of little value.

Because the principle of limited liability protects investors against unlimited losses, the corporation is well suited to raise large amounts of capital.

Corporations that offer their shares to the public must publish information concerning their finances; this makes the corporation subject to greater outside scrutiny than the partnership or sole proprietorship.

Taxation

Because it is a separate legal entity, a corporation pays its own taxes. In other words, the income of the corporation is subject to taxation quite apart from the taxation of its owners. A shareholder of a corporation will be taxed if she earns a salary from the corporation, receives a dividend from it, or realizes a capital gain from the sale of her shares. Advantages in the form of reduced or deferred taxes may sometimes be gained through the appropriate splitting of distributions to shareholders between dividend and salary payments. For example, Cameron could take a salary from the corporation and his younger son could receive income through dividends. This may produce a more favourable tax treatment than if Cameron took both a salary and dividend payments himself. The ultimate effect of this kind of income splitting depends on a variety of factors, including the corporate tax rate and the marginal tax rate of the shareholder and employee. It is significant that the partnership and sole proprietorship enjoy no such options, since all income from the business is taxed at personal rates.

Transferability

The fact that a corporation has a separate legal identity often allows for easy transference of an ownership interest represented by shares. A shareholder can sell or bequeath his shares with no interference from corporate creditors because the shareholder has no liability for corporate debts. The shares belong to him and he can do what he wants with them. Transferability is, however, subject to restrictions in the corporation's incorporating documents and may also be restricted by a shareholders' agreement.

Perpetual Existence

Because the corporation exists independently of its shareholders, the death or bankruptcy of one or more shareholders does not affect the existence of the corporation. The corporation continues in existence perpetually unless it is dissolved, either by order of a court for failure to comply with statutory regulations or through a voluntary surrender of its legal status to the government.

Regulations

Like sole proprietorships and partnerships, a corporation must comply with laws of general application.

Most significantly, however, the corporation comes into existence only if proper documents are submitted to the government and it issues, in return, a certificate of incorporation. Thus, it is almost always more expensive to organize a corporation than a sole proprietorship or partnership because there are legal bills and additional filing fees to pay. As well, there are extensive rules contained in corporation statutes that govern many corporate decisions and result in the need for considerable record keeping. These extra requirements and expenses, however, can be more than offset by the protection provided to investors by the principle of limited liability.

The pros and cons of the corporation are summarized in Figure 14.4, and a comparison of the major forms of business organization can be found in Figure 14.5.

FIGURE 14.4

Pros and Cons of the Corporation

Pros	Cons
Limited liability: Because it is a separate legal entity, a corporation can assume its own liabilities. The shareholder stands to lose the amount he invested in the corporation, but no more.	**Higher costs:** Creating a corporation incurs filing fees and legal costs.
Flexibility: A corporation permits differing degrees of ownership and sharing in profits.	**Public disclosure:** When a corporation offers shares to the public, the corporation must comply with strict disclosure and reporting requirements.
Greater access to capital: Limited liability makes the corporation a very suitable vehicle through which to raise capital.	**Greater regulation:** Corporation statutes govern many decisions, limiting management options and requiring specific kinds of record keeping.
Continuous existence: The life span of a corporation is not tied to its shareholders.	**Dissolution:** Ending a corporation's life can be complicated.
Tax benefits: Though this is a fact-specific issue, a corporation can facilitate greater tax planning, for example, by permitting income splitting.	**Tax disadvantages:** A corporation may be subject to double taxation, depending on the circumstances. This is a fact-specific issue.
Transferability: Ownership in a corporation is more easily transferable through shares.	**Possible loss of control:** A corporation has diminished control because it issues shares with voting rights.
Potentially broad management base: A corporation is managed by directors and officers, who can provide a level of specialized expertise to the corporation.	**Potential bureaucracy:** The many levels of authority in a corporation may impede decision making.

FIGURE 14.5

A Comparison of Major Forms of Business Organization*

Characteristic	Sole Proprietorship	Partnership	Corporation
Creation	• at will of owner	• by agreement or conduct of the parties	• by incorporation documents
Duration	• limited by life of owner	• terminated by agreement, death	• perpetual unless dissolved
Liability of owners	• unlimited	• unlimited	• limited
Taxation	• net income taxed at personal rate	• net income taxed at personal rate	• income taxed to the corporation; dividends and salary taxed to shareholders
Transferability	• only assets may be transferred	• transferable by agreement	• transferable unless incorporating documents restrict transferability
Management	• owner manages	• all partners manage equally unless otherwise specified in agreement	• shareholders elect a board to manage the affairs of the corporation; officers can also be hired

*These are the legal differences between the major business forms. In practice, however, there are ways of minimizing the consequences of these differences. Whether one form of business organization or another is chosen will depend on individual circumstances. As with all other legal concerns, legal, accounting, and management advice should be sought in order to make an informed decision.

Business Arrangements

The preceding section introduced the basic forms of business organizations. Subject to some specialized exceptions, such as real estate investment trusts and mutual funds, every business will use one of these forms.

There are additional ways to carry on the business activity itself. These ways are not distinct business organizations but are, for the lack of a more accurate term, arrangements. These arrangements do not have any strict legal meaning as such; most commonly they refer to some sort of contractual commitment between two or more business organizations. These relationships are important from a legal perspective because they involve agency principles and fiduciary duties in addition to contractual obligations.

Adam, for example, may not be able to raise the capital necessary to manufacture and sell his product. He may then decide to license rights to his product or he may enter an arrangement with another business to sell his product. Adam's business may be very successful, and he may want to expand his business. One option is to grow internally by opening new branches, expanding existing branches, and hiring new employees. He may, however, for many reasons decide to enter an arrangement with another entity. Adam may want to capitalize on the goodwill he has developed in his business, or another organization may more easily be able to penetrate a market, or he may simply feel that he does not have the time and expertise needed to handle an internal expansion. The following section explores the range of options open to entrepreneurs like Adam.

The Franchise

A **franchise** is a contractual arrangement between a manufacturer, wholesaler, or service organization (franchisor) and an independent business (franchisee), who buys the right to own and operate one or more units of the franchise system. Franchise organizations are normally based on some unique product, service, or method of doing business; on a trade name or patent; or on goodwill that the franchisor has developed.

Franchise
An agreement whereby an owner of a trademark or trade name permits another to sell a product or service under that trademark or name.

Almost every kind of business has been franchised—motels, fast-food restaurants, dental centres, hair salons, maid services, and fitness centres, to name a few. Some familiar examples are Pizza Hut, 7-Eleven, McDonald's, Subway, Molly Maid, Magicuts, and Curves. Adam, too, could potentially franchise his business if it is successful.

Franchising involves a contract between the franchisor and the franchisee. Wide variations exist in franchise agreements, but generally they cover arrangements regarding such matters as how the business is to be run, where supplies may or must be purchased, royalty levels to be paid to the franchisor for sharing its business operation plan and other benefits, and charges for management, advertising, and other corporate services. The agreement negotiated depends on the relative bargaining power of the parties and the issues brought to the table. Usually, however, the franchisor, having a great deal more information about the business, is in the better position to negotiate an advantageous agreement or to insist on the use of a standard form contract.[23]

PART FOUR

---

23. See Chapter 6 for a discussion of the role of bargaining power and standard form contracts.

What legal factors are important to the success of a franchise?

© JULIE PRATT

The Franchise Relationship

The relationship between a franchisor and a franchisee is one of contract. The contractual relationship is governed by the general principles of contract. In Alberta,[24] Ontario,[25] Prince Edward Island,[26] New Brunswick,[27] and Manitoba,[28] the general principles are augmented by specific franchise legislation. The legislation is designed to provide protection for franchisees.

BUSINESS AND LEGISLATION

New Brunswick's Franchise Legislation

Following the lead of Alberta, Ontario, and Prince Edward Island, New Brunswick became the fourth Canadian province to enact franchise legislation. Manitoba has also passed a franchise Act that came into force on October 1, 2012. The legislation in all provinces has largely similar concepts, but there are important differences in format and in some details. The basic elements of the N.B. statute are a definition of franchise, disclosure requirements of the franchisor, a duty of good faith and fair dealing on all parties to the franchise agreement, a right of association for the franchisee, and a dispute resolution mechanism.

Definition of Franchise: The definition of franchise is very broad and captures both the "business format" franchise, such as a fast-food outlet, and "business opportunities"

arrangements, such as vending machines.[29] The definition captures not only traditional franchise operations but also distributorships and other arrangements that have not been traditionally thought of as franchises.

Disclosure Requirements: Franchisors are required to deliver a disclosure document to prospective franchisees 14 days prior to the franchisee entering into binding agreements or paying money.[30] The disclosure requirements set out in the regulations require the franchisor to disclose all material facts relating to the franchise. The disclosure document must contain (among other information) the business background of the franchisor, its finances, its bankruptcy and solvency history, the franchisee's expected costs of establishing the franchise, and contact particulars for both current and former franchisees.

24. *Franchises Act*, RSA 2000, c F-23. Alberta's legislation was first enacted in 1971 and substantially revised in 1995.
25. *Arthur Wishart Act (Franchise Disclosure), 2000*, SO 2000, c 3.
26. *Franchises Act*, SPEI 2005, c 36, RSPEI 1998, c F-14.1.
27. *Franchises Act*, SNB 2007, c F-23.5.
28. The *Franchises Act*, CCSM c F156.
29. There are some exemptions such as some ongoing commercial relationships and wholesale purchase arrangements.
30. There are a number of exemptions from the disclosure requirements under the legislation. For example, there is an exemption from providing financial statements for larger franchisors.

Franchisees have the right to rescind or cancel the franchise agreement within certain time periods if the disclosure document is late or does not meet the requirements of the Act (60 days), or if they do not receive it at all (2 years). In such cases, they are entitled to receive everything they paid for the franchise, as well as compensation for any losses incurred. In addition, the franchisee has a right of action for damages where it suffers a loss because of a misrepresentation contained in the disclosure document or as a result of a franchisor's failure to comply with its disclosure obligations.

Fair Dealing and Good Faith: Parties to a franchise agreement have a duty of fair dealing in the performance and enforcement of the agreement. The duty of fair dealing includes a duty to act in good faith and in accordance with reasonable commercial standards. This means, in effect, that

both the franchisor and the franchisee have at least the obligation to consider the interests of the other in making decisions and exercising discretion. The Act also establishes a right to sue for the breach of that duty.

Right of Association: Franchisees have the right to associate with one another and form or join an organization of franchisees. Franchisors may not interfere, either directly or indirectly, with the exercise of this right. The franchisee has a right of action for damages for contravention of this section.

Dispute Resolution: The Act, unlike its counterparts in other provinces, provides a framework for the resolution of franchise disputes. Parties are required to follow the formal mediation process outlined in the Act and accompanying regulations.

Critical Analysis: What are the advantages of franchise legislation? What are the problems, if any, with franchise legislation?

The relationship between a franchisor and a franchisee does not normally create fiduciary obligations.[31] However, the legislation imposes on the parties a duty of good faith and fair dealing in the performance and enforcement of the franchise agreement. The courts have also adopted this concept at common law.

CASE

Shelanu Inc v Print Three Franchising Corporation (2003), 64 OR (3d) 533, 226 DLR (4th) 577 (CA)

THE BUSINESS CONTEXT: Franchise legislation specifies that the parties to a franchise agreement owe each other a duty of fair dealing, which includes the duty to act in good faith and in accordance with reasonable commercial standards. The following case[32] confirms the applicability of the duty of fair dealing to franchise relationships at common law and explores the scope of that duty.

FACTUAL BACKGROUND: In 1987, BCD Print Inc., a corporation owned by Brian Deslauriers, purchased a print store franchise from Print Three Corporation. In 1989, Deslauriers and his wife purchased Shelanu Inc., which operated two Print Three stores. In 1990, Print Three set up a new business, Le Print Express, composed of small print outlets targeted at individuals and small businesses. Print Three franchises targeted a commercial and higher-volume clientele. In 1991, Shelanu, with the concurrence of Print Three, closed one of its stores. In 1995, Print Three and BCD orally agreed that BCD could close its store and combine its operations with the remaining Shelanu store (this would mean that by reporting its sales as a single franchise, Shelanu would be entitled to a higher royalty rebate). Also around this time, a dispute arose between Print Three and some of its franchisees, including Shelanu, about the expenditure of

advertising fees on the Air Miles advertising program (some franchisees were opposed to spending all the advertising fees on a program where not all the benefits would be capable of being used for their businesses). The relationship between Print Three and Shelanu deteriorated, and Print Three denied the termination of the BCD store and continued to treat the operation as two stores for royalty purposes. Shelanu brought an action alleging that Print Three stores had failed to make royalty payments in accordance with the oral agreement, had unilaterally changed the terms of the Air Miles program (rather than distributing unused Air Miles to the franchisees for their benefit, Print Three took control of Air Miles not distributed to customers), and had established another system of retail printing stores that competed with its existing franchises.

THE LEGAL QUESTION: Do the parties to a franchise agreement owe each other a duty of good faith? If so, has Print Three breached the duty?

RESOLUTION: The Court of Appeal upheld the trial court's recognition of the existence of a common law duty of good faith in franchise agreements. The court determined that a duty of good faith applies to franchise relationships because franchisees do not usually have equal bargaining power; franchise agreements are not

(Continued)

---

31. *Jirna Ltd v Mister Donut of Canada Ltd*, [1975] 1 SCR 2, 40 DLR (3d) 303.
32. This case was decided pursuant to the common law. The Court of Appeal held that Ontario's franchise legislation did not apply because the conduct complained of occurred prior to the legislation coming into force. Also note that this summary deals only with the good faith issue.

freely negotiated but are drawn up by the franchisor and imposed on the franchisee, and the franchisor remains in a dominant position throughout the relationship. The court also opined that the franchise relationship is not a fiduciary relationship. The duty of good faith requires that a franchisor give due consideration to the franchise's interests in exercising its powers and discretions, but it is not required to favour a franchisee's interests over its own. The court upheld the trial judge's finding that there had been a breach of the duty of good faith with respect to the payment of royalty rebates and acting unreasonably with respect to the Air Miles program but found that Print Three did not breach its duty of good faith by establishing Le Print Express. The business was found not to compete directly with the Print Three franchisees and there was no evidence that it caused a loss of income to Shelanu.

CRITICAL ANALYSIS: The decision in *Shelanu* limits the duty of good faith to particular classes of contractual relationships. Should the courts explicitly extend the duty of good faith to all contracts? Why or why not?

What are some specific ways franchisors can comply with the duty of good faith?

COURTESY OF DARCY SAGE

Joint Venture

Joint venture
A grouping of two or more businesses to undertake a particular project.

A **joint venture** is an association of business entities—corporations, individuals, or partnerships—that unite for the purpose of carrying on a business venture. Normally the parties agree to share profits and losses and management of the project. The key feature of a joint venture is that it is usually limited to a specific project or to a specific period of time. For example, several oil and gas companies may join for offshore exploration in a certain region, or a steel fabricator may combine with a construction company to refurbish a nuclear plant. Adam could conceivably enter into a joint venture with another entity for the purposes of marketing and selling his product to a particular event such as an international trade show.

The joint venture itself can take a variety of forms. The joint venture may be a partnership, in which case all the legal consequences associated with a partnership apply. It may also be what is known as an equity joint venture. This is when the parties incorporate a separate corporation for the project and each party holds shares in that corporation, in which case the consequences of incorporation apply. For example, Rogers Communications and Bell Canada formed Inukshuk Internet Inc. to build and operate a national wireless network. A joint venture may also simply be a contractual arrangement between the parties. In such a case, the contract may spell out the nature of the relationship between the parties. Also, the law can impose duties on the parties beyond those specified in the contract.[33] Most significantly, parties to a joint venture can be held to owe fiduciary duties to one another in relation to the activities of the joint venture.

---

33. *Supra* note 6 at 20.

LEFT: MARIO BEAUREGARD/THE CANADIAN PRESS;
RIGHT: FRANCIS VACHON/THE CANADIAN PRESS

What are the legal risks with joint ventures?

Strategic Alliance

A **strategic alliance** is a cooperative arrangement among businesses. It is an arrangement that may involve joint research, technology sharing, or joint use of production, for example.[34] CGI Canada, an information technology and business process services company has an alliance with Workday Inc., a specialist in solutions for human resources, payroll, and financial management systems. Adam could form a strategic alliance with another entity to do joint research into applications of his voice-recognition product.

Like a joint venture, a strategic alliance does not have a precise legal meaning. The underlying relationship between the parties is normally contractual. The contract or a series of contracts will spell out the parties' rights and obligations including whether or not they are agents for each other. Whether the parties to a strategic alliance owe fiduciary obligations to each other is unclear.

> **Strategic alliance**
> An arrangement whereby two or more businesses agree to cooperate for some purpose.

Distributorship or Dealership

A product or service **distributorship** is very much like a franchise. A contract is entered into whereby a manufacturer agrees to provide products and the distributor or dealer agrees to carry products or perform services prescribed by the manufacturer. This kind of arrangement is often encountered in the automotive and computer industries. Rather than selling his product himself, Adam could engage a distributor or dealer to sell his products.

The relationship between the parties is governed by the contract. There are no fiduciary obligations owed by the parties to each other beyond those spelled out in the contract. As well, a distributorship does not normally involve an agency relationship. In fact, the contract may specify that the distributorship is not an agency.

> **Distributorship**
> A contractual relationship where one business agrees to sell another's products.

PART FOUR

---

34. The term "strategic alliance" is sometimes used to include joint ventures. There is little precision in terminology in this area. The key point is that terms usually describe a contractual arrangement between two or more parties.

INTERNATIONAL PERSPECTIVE

Going Global

Strategic alliances are one of the leading business strategies of the 21st century. They take many forms: from simple market exchanges or cross-licensing agreements to complex cooperative-manufacturing arrangements or joint-equity ventures. Strategic alliances can help firms lower costs, exploit each other's specialized skills, fund costly research and development efforts, and expand into foreign markets. Using a strategic alliance to access a foreign market usually involves "partnering" with a "local" to take advantage of his familiarity with the social, cultural, legal, and other conditions in the market. There can also be a host of other advantages to this business arrangement, including sharing costs and risks with the local partner, avoiding import restrictions and other trade barriers, and meeting the host country's requirements for local ownership.

Critical Analysis: What are the risks associated with using a strategic alliance to access a foreign market? Why would a country require that a foreign business have local participation? Can you think of any legal reasons?

Sales Agency

Sales agency
An agreement in which a manufacturer or distributor allows another to sell products on its behalf.

A **sales agency** relationship is usually an arrangement whereby a manufacturer or distributor contracts with an agent to sell goods or services supplied by the manufacturer or distributor on a principal/agent basis.[35] The agent is not the actual vendor but acts on behalf of a principal, who is the owner of the goods or services. As this relationship is one of agency, fiduciary obligations are owed. This arrangement is often encountered in the travel and insurance industries.

Product Licensing

Product licensing
An arrangement whereby the owner of a trademark or other proprietary right grants to another the right to manufacture or distribute products associated with the trademark or other proprietary right.

In this arrangement, the licensee is granted the right to manufacture and distribute products associated with the licensor's trademarks or other proprietary rights, usually within a defined geographic area. Licensing is common for many consumer goods such as clothing, sporting goods, and merchandise connected to the entertainment industry. Anne of Green Gables (images of Anne, Green Gables, and related trademarks), for example, is licensed to almost 100 businesses.[36] Assuming Adam obtains rights such as a patent for his product, he could license these rights to another. Rather than doing the manufacturing and selling himself, he could license the rights in return for royalties. The relationship between the parties is contractual, and the agreement usually covers such matters as the granting of rights, the obligations of the parties, the term of the agreement, and fees and royalties. This arrangement is explored in more depth in Chapter 18.

Business Law in Practice Revisited

1. What forms of business organization are available for carrying on Adam's business?
Adam may carry on his business as a sole proprietorship, in partnership with others, or through a corporation.

2. What are the major considerations in choosing a particular form?
Adam's father, Cameron, is willing to invest in the business but is unwilling to accept risk beyond his investment. This consideration eliminates an ordinary partnership, as it would expose him to additional risk. A limited partnership is a possibility. However,

---

35. See Chapter 13 for a discussion of the duties and liabilities of agents.
36. Anne of Green Gables Licensing Authority Inc, *Licensed Products*, online: Innovation PEI <http://www.innovationpei.com/ann_list.php3>.

Cameron would not be able to partake in the management of the organization. If he did, he could lose his limited liability status. As Adam is young and presumably inexperienced, he might want to be able to seek the assistance of his father. A sole proprietorship exposes only Adam to unlimited liability; however, if Cameron participates in profits and management, there is a risk of an "unintended" partnership. Thus, it would seem that the most viable alternative is a corporation, with Cameron investing his money in shares. This alternative limits his exposure to risk and allows for his potential participation in profits.

Diane is interested in taking a role in the management of the venture, as well as in investing a sum of money. These considerations could be accommodated within a partnership agreement, although it may be difficult to agree on the valuation of her time and expertise, as she will not be working full-time on the project. As well, she may be averse to the risks associated with a partnership. The other option is a corporation, with Diane investing in shares. This would allow her to participate in profits as a means of compensation for her services. A contractual arrangement to compensate her for her services may not be viable, as Adam probably does not have the means to pay her.

3. Which form is best for Adam's business?
For the reasons given above, a corporation may be the most appropriate, but the success of Adam's business is not dependent on the form chosen. Much more important is the viability of his idea and his ability to bring it to fruition.

Chapter Summary

Most businesses are carried on using one of the basic forms—sole proprietorship, partnership (or one of its variations), or corporation. These forms have varying characteristics, most notably with respect to the exposure to liability. Sole proprietorships and partnerships expose their owners to personal liability for the business' obligations. A corporation, on the other hand, has the attraction of limited liability for the owners—their liability is limited to the amount of their investment. This characteristic, however, can be neutralized. For example, a sole proprietor can escape the effects of unlimited liability by transferring assets to a relative prior to commencing business. As well, the advantage of limited liability in the corporate form can become meaningless if creditors insist on a personal guarantee from the owners of the corporation.

Each form has other advantages and disadvantages. The form chosen for a business enterprise depends on an evaluation of numerous factors such as investors' aversion to risk, their desire to earn profits, and their wish to participate in decision making. In short, the best form for a particular situation depends on all the circumstances.

A partnership is the form most often found in the professions. This is due, in part, to prohibitions against some professionals incorporating. A partnership subjects the partners to unlimited liability. The other defining feature of a partnership is agency—a partner is an agent for other partners and for the partnership. The effects of agency between the partners can be modified by a partnership agreement; however, the effects of agency in relation to outsiders cannot, and are governed by the *Partnership Act*.

PART FOUR

A business may also at some point enter into an arrangement with another entity for carrying out business activities. The various arrangements are all based on a contract negotiated between the parties. Regardless of the arrangement entered into, the business still needs to be carried on using one of the basic business forms.

It is important to remember that it is the viability of the business itself that is critical, not necessarily the form of the business or the particular arrangements made. Put another way, a business does not succeed because it chooses a franchise arrangement over a distributorship. The key to a successful business is having a solid business plan that is well executed.

Chapter Study

Key Terms and Concepts

director (p. 327)

distributorship (p. 335)

dividend (p. 328)

franchise (p. 331)

joint and several liability (p. 321)

joint liability (p. 316)

joint venture (p. 334)

limited liability (p. 328)

limited liability partnership (LLP) (p. 326)

limited partnership (p. 325)

partnership (p. 315)

product licensing (p. 336)

sales agency (p. 336)

shareholder (p. 327)

sole proprietorship (p. 312)

strategic alliance (p. 335)

unlimited liability (p. 312)

Questions for Review

1. Define sole proprietorship, partnership, and corporation.

2. What are the advantages and disadvantages of a sole proprietorship?

3. How is a sole proprietorship created?

4. What are the advantages and disadvantages of a partnership?

5. How can a partnership come into existence?

6. Does the sharing of profits result in the creation of a partnership? Explain.

7. How can a partnership come to an end?

8. How can the risks of the partnership form be managed?

9. What is the difference between a general and a limited partner?

10. Explain the difference between a limited partnership and a limited liability partnership.

11. What are the advantages and disadvantages of the corporate form?

12. How is a corporation created?

13. What is the difference between a business form and a business arrangement?

14. What is the basis of a franchise? What is the relationship between parties to a franchise agreement?

15. How does franchise legislation change the relationship between a franchisor and a franchisee?

16. Is a joint venture a partnership? Explain.

17. What is the difference between a joint venture and a strategic alliance?

18. Is a distributor an agent? Explain.

Questions for Critical Thinking

1. Many people think of franchising as a quick and easy way to start their own business. Indeed, some buyers have experienced almost instant success, but far more have experienced dismal failure. It is estimated that about 20 percent of all franchises fail within the first three to five years. The key to success is often the choice of franchise and the franchise package or contractual arrangement. What should the franchise contract contain? What issues should it address?

2. Many of Canada's high profile franchise operations—Midas, Shoppers Drug Mart, General Motors, Tim Hortons and Quiznos, for examples—have been involved in litigation.[37] Why are franchising companies a magnet for litigation, particularly class action litigation? Do you think that franchise legislation tends to facilitate or hinder lawsuits by franchisees against franchisors?

3. The limited liability partnership is a response to concerns about professionals' exposure to liability for their partners' malpractice. What is the nature of the liability created by the partnership form? How does the creation of an LLP address this liability concern? Is it appropriate that accountants and lawyers, for

---

37. Jeff Grey, "Revolt of the franchisees", *The Globe and Mail* (18 January 2011) online: WikidFranchise < http://www.wikidfranchise.org/20110118-revolt-of>.

PART FOUR

example, enjoy limited liability? Is there a downside for a law or accounting firm to converting to an LLP?

4. What are the circumstances in which a partnership may be found to exist? What steps can be taken to avoid a finding of partnership? How can the consequences of being found a partner be minimized?

5. In *Shelanu v Print Three*, the Ontario Court of Appeal held that franchisors owe a duty of good faith to franchisees. What factors led the court to this conclusion? In what other contractual relationships might one party owe the other party a duty of good faith? What does "good faith" mean? How can franchisors comply with good faith obligations?

6. The three basic business forms are sole proprietorship, partnership, and corporation. How is each formed? How is each owned? How does each form allocate the risk associated with doing business?

Situations for Discussion

1. Michael Wright, Kyle Wright, and William Wright are farmers. Michael and Kyle are brothers, and William is their father. All three farmers have cattle ranches, and William has a grain operation. Each farmer keeps his own books of account, prepares his own income tax return, and maintains his own bank account. With regard to the cattle operations, each farmer has his own herd of cattle, which he individually markets. The cattle are fed and pastured together without regard to the source of the feed, and the farmers share machinery and labour. Some of the land is registered to the men individually, and some is registered in the names of all three farmers. With regard to the grain operations, William is responsible for all aspects including crop rotation, seed selection, and fertilizer purchases. Michael and Kyle are not involved in the grain cultivation and do not receive any gross or net profit from the grain operation. They are, however, allowed to share in the crops by way of cattle feed.[38] Are Michael, Kyle, and William partners? What factors do the courts consider in determining whether a partnership exists? What are the consequences of a finding that there is a partnership relationship?

2. Edie, Alma, and Tim established a restaurant called EATs. Edie, a retired teacher, invested $20 000 in the venture, and Alma and Tim each invested $10 000. Edie, Alma, and Tim do not have a formal agreement concerning the allocation of responsibilities, but they each take turns doing the cooking. The serving and cleanup tasks are done by staff. One day, while Edie was doing the cooking, Juan got food poisoning from his meal. Juan intends to sue EATs, Edie, Alma, and Tim for damages of $100 000. If Juan is successful, how will the damages be allocated among the parties? If the restaurant were incorporated under EATs Inc. and Edie owned 50 percent of the shares, Alma owned 25 percent, and Tim owned 25 percent, how would the damages be allocated? What do these two situations illustrate about risk?

3. Anson is a partner in the accounting firm Morris, Benton. According to the partnership agreement, Anson is entitled to 25 percent of the profits of the firm. Anson's partners recently contracted for the supply of a computer system at a cost of $50 000 for use in the firm's business. Anson strongly objected to the purchase of the system and voted against acquiring it, but the contract was approved by a majority vote of the partners, and his objections were ignored. Anson is so upset, he is thinking about resigning from the firm. Could the computer supplier hold Anson personally liable for any of the debt? If so, is there anything that Anson could do to avoid liability?

4. Review *Strother v 3464920 Canada Inc.* on pages 322–323. At the time of the dispute between Monarch, Strother, and Davis & Company, Davis operated as a general partnership. It became possible for a British Columbia law firm to become a limited liability partnership (LLP) only in 2005. At that time, Davis, along with many other B.C. firms, became an LLP. Assume that Davis was an LLP at the time of the dispute with Monarch. How would being a member of an LLP affect Strother's personal liability to Monarch? How would Davis being an LLP affect the liability of the other partners? How might the LLP structure affect the relationship between a law firm and its clients? How might the LLP structure affect the relationship between lawyers within a law firm?

5. Jody Ingalls is a recent university graduate with a BSc in kinesiology. As she was having difficulty finding a job, Jody decided that she could create her own job by opening a fitness club. As luck would have it, she saw

---

38. Based, in part, on *Redfern Farm Services Ltd v Wright*, 2006 MBQB 4, 200 Man R (2d) 129.

an advertisement in a Halifax newspaper featuring franchise opportunities in the fitness industry. Jody responded to the ad and the franchise owner showed her the financial statements for a "Fit for Life" fitness franchise in a Halifax suburb. The income statements indicated that the franchise had made $100 000 per year for the past several years. Jody was extremely excited and agreed to lease it for $50 000 per year for a five-year period. She signed the contract and started carrying on the business. Jody worked 12-hour days for a year but was not able to make a profit, and now she wants out of her contract. Can Jody get out of the agreement? Explain. Would your answer be different if the franchise was located on New Brunswick? Explain. What are the legal risks associated with "purchasing" a franchise? How can the risks be managed?

6. Ragini and Rajiv were co-owners of a number of properties located in the suburbs of Surrey. They had acquired the properties for resale and planned to subdivide and sell them for a profit over the next few years. One property, known as "the Corner" was too small to meet the legal requirements for subdivision. Ragini and Rajiv hoped that they would be able to acquire adjacent property so that their subdivision plans could proceed. Rajiv did all of the work in the investigation of the surrounding properties while Ragini stayed in the background. She had recently been "down-sized" out of her job and spent most of her time looking for alternate employment. Rajiv, through his investigative skills learned that Ming, the owner of an adjacent property would be willing to sell his property for the right price. Rajiv, also knew that Ragini, because of her job loss would not be able to raise her share of the purchase price. He, therefore, purchased Ming's property on his own behalf. Shortly thereafter, he offered to buy out Ragini's interest in "the Corner" for $15 000 more than the fair market value. Ragini accepted the offer. Rajiv consolidated "the Corner" and Ming's former property, subdivided them, and sold them for a $250 000 profit. When Ragini learned of Rajiv's purchase of Ming's property and the sale of the subdivided lots, she was very upset. Rajiv simply pointed out that she did not have the money or the means to share in the purchase of Ming's property, and he had paid a premium price for her interest in "the Corner." Besides, he argued, it was his investigative skills and hard work, not hers that led to the profit on the subdivision sale. What is the nature of the relationship between Ragini and Rajiv? Does Rajiv have any legal liability in these circumstances? Explain.

7. Thomas, a young entrepreneur, started a construction business. Ari, who owned and operated a radio station, agreed to run some advertisements for him. Unfortunately, Thomas was unable to pay Ari for the services. In the hopes of making the business profitable so that he could get payment under the broadcasting contract, Ari, without remuneration, assisted Thomas in his business. In fact, on behalf of Thomas, Ari signed a contract with Lopez for plumbing and heating supplies. When payment for the supplies was not forthcoming, Lopez sued Ari, claiming that Ari was Thomas' partner and therefore was responsible for the debt. Ari claimed that when he signed the contract, he was acting as Thomas' agent.[39] What difference does it make whether Ari is considered to be Thomas' agent or his partner? What factors are important in determining the nature of a relationship between individuals?

8. In *2038724 Ontario Ltd v Quizno's Canada Restaurant Corp*,[40] the franchisees brought a national class action against Quiznos and its designated supplier, Gordon Food Services over alleged overcharging on supplies. The defendants opposed certification primarily on the grounds that damages were not common among franchisees and would have to be established individually. Despite the defendants' arguments and a "class action waiver" clause in the franchise agreement purporting to prevent the franchisees from initiating or being part of any action, the Ontario Court of Appeal affirmed the certification of the class action. In certifying the class action lawsuit against the franchisor, the court strongly endorsed class actions as a means of resolving franchise disputes. What is it about franchising disputes that makes them suitable for resolution by class action? Why do you think the "class action waiver" failed to protect the franchisors from class action litigation?

For more study tools, visit http://www.NELSONbrain.com.

39. Based, in part, on *Lampert Plumbing* (Danforth) Ltd v Agathos, [1972] 3 OR 11, 27 DLR (3d) 284 (Co Ct).
40. 2010 ONCA 466, 100 OR (3d) 721; See also David Sterns, "Appeal rulings clear the path for franchise class actions", *The Lawyers Weekly* (3 September 2010) 12.

PART FOUR

CHAPTER 15

The Corporate Form: Organizational Matters

Objectives

After studying this chapter, you should have an understanding of

- a corporation as a legal person

- the distinction between federal and provincial incorporation

- the share structure of a corporation

- the selection of a corporation's name

- how a corporation is created

- how a corporation is financed

- how securities are regulated

COREL

Business Law in Practice

Adam (introduced in Chapter 14) is still young, energetic, and smart but not quite as broke. He has developed a prototype of his voice-recognition system for computers, and received glowing industry feedback at a recent trade show. Market studies have indicated that there is significant demand for a product such as his. Diane, who has been instrumental in assisting him in developing a business plan, has made a definite commitment to help develop a detailed marketing strategy. A lending institution has responded favourably to his business plan and has suggested that Adam incorporate a company. Adam thinks that the best approach is to start with a small local company. However, as the product has great national and international sales potential, he projects a fairly rapid expansion.

Adam has made an appointment with a lawyer to assist him with incorporating a company. He plans to hold half the shares in the company as he will be the manager of the business. Half of the shares will be held by Diane to compensate her for her advice and expertise in marketing. Adam's father, Cameron, is committed to investing $100 000 in the company. Adam wants Cameron to simply lend the money to the company, as he thinks that this is the only way to protect Cameron from unlimited liability should the business venture fail.

The other matter he has been considering concerns financing—the company will need more than $100 000 for its initial operations. "Simple," says Adam. "If the bank will not lend me enough money, I will sell some shares to a bunch of friends."

1. How is a corporation formed, and what factors should Adam consider in forming a corporation?
2. Does Adam appear to understand the concept of limited liability adequately?
3. What other financing options are available, in addition to Cameron lending money to the corporation?
4. What factors should Adam consider in seeking to raise money by selling shares?

The Corporation Defined

The corporation[1] is the predominant business vehicle in modern commerce because it is a separate legal entity. For this reason, it is able to remedy many of the shortcomings associated with the other prevalent business forms—the sole proprietorship and the partnership.

The notion that the corporation possesses a legal identity separate and distinct from its owners has fundamental repercussions. It means that the corporation alone is responsible for its own debts and other liabilities. Should the corporation fail to make good on its obligations, the shareholders are not responsible for the default. The most that they stand to lose is the purchase price of their shares.

If Adam decides to run his computer business as a sole proprietorship, he is gambling his personal assets if the venture proves to be a financial disaster. Yet if he decides to run the identical business through a corporation, none of Adam's assets are at risk.

The law recognizes this different outcome as being perfectly legitimate and eminently just. As indicated in Chapter 14, the key question is this: who has incurred the obligation in question? Liability falls on that entity—be it an individual or a corporation—and that entity alone. Put another way, the creditor must decide with whom she is doing business and live with the consequences of that decision.

The concept of a corporation being a separate legal entity is complex.[2] It was established in 1897 in a case that remains at the centre of modern corporation law.

Since *Salomon v Salomon Ltd* (see Landmark Case below), the separate legal existence of the corporation has not been seriously challenged. Corporations, with few exceptions, continue to be treated as entities separate from their shareholders. The cornerstone of corporation law—limited liability—is secure.

LANDMARK CASE

Salomon v Salomon Ltd, [1897] AC 22 (HL)

THE HISTORICAL CONTEXT: When *Salomon* was decided, the corporate form was just coming into wider usage. At the time, it was unclear whether companies with few shareholders would be recognized as separate legal entities.

FACTUAL BACKGROUND: Aron Salomon carried on a profitable shoe-manufacturing business for many years as a sole proprietor. He decided to form an incorporated company—Aron Salomon and Company, Limited—as the vehicle through which to run his business. *The Companies Act*, which set out the rules

for creating a company, required that a company have a minimum of seven shareholders. Therefore, Aron took one share and members of his family took the remaining six shares.

Aron became the managing director. Practically speaking, Aron Salomon and Company, Limited, was a "one-person company," since Aron entirely controlled the company. Put another way, the other participants in the company had no involvement in operations: any decision the company took was only because Aron wanted it to follow that particular course of action.

(Continued)

PART FOUR

---

1. In British Columbia, a corporation is usually called a "company." Although, strictly speaking, the terms are not synonymous, they are used interchangeably in this text.
2. Most of the distinguishing characteristics of a corporation—limited liability for shareholders, perpetual existence, separation of ownership and management, ease of transferring ownership, and separate taxation—are a consequence of a corporation being a legal entity distinct from its shareholders. The characteristics of a corporation are discussed in Chapter 14.

Next, Aron Salomon and Company, Limited, agreed to purchase the assets of Aron's sole proprietorship. As the corporation had little cash, Aron was issued 20 000 shares and a mortgage secured by the shoe-business assets. In this way, Aron became a highly protected creditor of his own company.

The business suffered financial problems due to a series of strikes and the loss of government contracts. The company became insolvent, and a trustee was appointed to deal with its creditors and close down the business. Many creditors of Aron Salomon and Company, Limited, lined up for payment, but there were insufficient assets to satisfy them. In response, the trustee in bankruptcy took the position that Aron was personally responsible for all his company's debts.

THE LEGAL QUESTION: Was Aron liable for the debts of Aron Salomon and Company, Limited? Was Aron a legitimate creditor of the company?

RESOLUTION: A corporation—large or small—is a separate legal entity and, as such, is totally responsible for its own obligations. Indeed, one of the main reasons for creating a company is to limit liability in the event of bankruptcy. The court rejected the argument that there was something essentially improper about an individual conducting his business through a one-person corporation to secure the protection of limited liability. If a number of persons can limit their liability in this way, then why shouldn't a single person be able to do the same thing? After all, it should not make any difference to a creditor whether one or several shareholders limit their liability.

The House of Lords also confirmed that there is nothing wrong with a shareholder being a creditor of the corporation, even when that shareholder essentially controls the company in question. Furthermore, the creditors had chosen to deal with Aron's company—not with Aron, the individual—and had chosen to do so on an unsecured basis. They, in turn, would have to live with the adverse outcome of that business decision.

CRITICAL ANALYSIS: Do you think that the court went too far in giving independent existence to the corporation, especially when the interests of Aron and his company were virtually identical? Should the shareholder of a one-person company be entitled to limited liability? How could the creditors, other than Aron, have better protected themselves in this situation?

Stakeholders in the Corporation

Stakeholder
One who has an interest in a corporation.

The corporation has a legal existence and, as such, is treated in law as a person. That said, the corporation is an artificial entity whose activities are controlled entirely by human beings. A corporation not only comes into being through the actions of humans, but also can make decisions, formulate policy, and enter contracts only through the actions of humans. These individuals, or groups of individuals, are often referred to as the internal **stakeholders** of the corporation. In short, internal stakeholders are those who have either a direct or indirect role in governing the corporation and determining its mission and how it will be achieved. Shareholders are those persons who have invested in the corporation by buying shares in return for a potential share of the corporate profits and other benefits. Shareholders do not have any direct authority to manage the corporation. However, they do have the power to elect the board of directors and therefore can have a strong influence on the direction of the corporation. The board of directors is charged with management functions—including policy development—and is answerable to the shareholders since, should it perform poorly, the board runs the risk of being voted out of office. Corporate officers, such as the president, secretary, and treasurer, are another important internal group. They are hired by the board of directors and are charged with managing the day-to-day operations of the corporation.

Not surprisingly, the internal stakeholders may come into conflict with one another, as well as with the corporation itself. The bulk of corporation law seeks to regulate the relationships among the corporation's internal stakeholders. Chapter 16 will provide a more detailed account of internal stakeholders. They are introduced here to establish some of the basic vocabulary associated with the corporate form, as well as to identify its central players.

The internal stakeholders are not the only stakeholders. The corporation has a tremendous impact on much of society. External stakeholders are people who have dealings with or are affected by the corporation but do not have an explicit role in governing the corporation. Examples are government, the general public, employees, customers, and creditors. These groups, although external in the sense that they are generally not involved in corporate governance, nonetheless have an interest in the corporation, and their interests receive recognition in some circumstances. The relationship between the corporation and its external stakeholders is explored briefly in Chapter 16.

Pre-Incorporation Issues

Assuming Adam decides to do business through a corporation, he must make a number of decisions prior to preparing and filing incorporation documents. He must decide

- whether to incorporate federally or provincially
- what type of shares will be available and to whom
- what to name the corporation

These decisions will be influenced by a host of factors, such as the kind of business Adam intends to operate, where he intends to operate, how he intends to manage the corporation, how he wishes to accommodate future growth, and in the case of a corporate name, its availability.

Provincial and Federal Incorporation

Adam has the choice between incorporating federally and incorporating provincially. He has this choice because jurisdiction over the incorporation of companies is divided between the federal government and the provincial governments. Both levels of government have passed legislation that provides for the incorporation of companies. These acts embody different models or prototypes as to how the corporation comes into existence.[3] Although the way in which the corporation is created varies, the different methods of incorporation have much in common. All methods allow for the creation of an entity that is recognized as a legal person, is owned by shareholders who enjoy limited liability for the debts of the entity,[4] and is managed by directors who owe fiduciary duties to the entity.

When, then, should a business incorporate federally, and when would it be best advised to incorporate provincially? There is no hard-and-fast answer to this question. Federally incorporated corporations have a right to carry on business in each province, whereas provincially incorporated corporations have the right to carry on business only in the province in which they are incorporated. This difference has little practical significance, because each province has straightforward licensing procedures through which corporations incorporated in other provinces can do business in that province.[5]

3. The different models currently in use are articles of incorporation, memorandum of association, and letters patent. The federal government, Alberta, Manitoba, New Brunswick, Newfoundland, Ontario, and Saskatchewan follow the articles of incorporation model. See *Canada Business Corporations Act*, RSC 1985, c C-44; *Business Corporations Act*, RSA 2000, c B-9; *Corporations Act*, RSM 1987, CCSM c C-225; *Business Corporations Act*, SNB 1981, c B-9.1; *Business Corporations Act*, RSN 1990, c C-36; *Business Corporations Act*, RSO 1990, c B-16; and *Business Corporations Act*, RSS 1978, c B-10. Nova Scotia follows the memorandum of association model. See *Companies Act*, RSNS 1989, c 81. Prince Edward Island and Quebec follow the letters patent model. See *Companies Act*, RSPEI 1988, c C-14 and *Companies Act*, RSQ 1977, c C-38. British Columbia has features of both the articles of association and the memorandum of association models. See *Business Corporations Act*, SBC 2002, c 57.
4. Nova Scotia, Alberta, and British Columbia also provide for unlimited liability corporations.
5. Peter Hogg, *Constitutional Law of Canada*, vol. 1, loose-leaf (Scarborough, ON: Carswell, 2008) at 23–27.

PART FOUR

For corporations that intend to operate in more than two provinces, federal incorporation may result in lower administrative costs. For corporations that intend to operate in only one or two provinces, provincial incorporation usually results in lower administrative costs.[6] Since Adam intends to operate nationally and even internationally, he should seriously consider incorporating under federal legislation.

Shares and Shareholders

Share structure

The shares that a corporation is permitted to issue by its constitution.

As part of the preparation for incorporation, Adam must decide on a **share structure** for the corporation. This entails deciding on the class or classes of shares that the corporation will be authorized to issue, what rights and privileges attach to each class, and the number of each authorized for issuance. Adam must also consider how the shares will be available and to whom they will be available.

Classes of Shares A share represents an ownership interest in the issuing corporation. It is, however, a unique kind of ownership interest. It does not give the owner or holder any right to use the assets of the corporation or any right to directly control or manage the corporation. It does, however, give the owner those rights that specifically attach to the share.

A corporation may simply have one type or class of shares with all the basic shareholder rights attached to it. In this case, the share must include the right to

- vote for the election of directors

- receive dividends declared by the directors

- share in the proceeds on dissolution of the corporation, after the creditors have been paid

A one-person corporation with no plans or aspirations for growth may choose this option. However, to ensure that the corporation has the flexibility to meet future needs, it is prudent to establish different classes at the outset. Though different classes could be created when the need arises, this would require an amendment to the corporation's constitution—a potentially costly and complicated procedure.

There are many possibilities for creating shares with diverse rights (see Figure 15.1 on page 347) so long as the basic rights mentioned above are distributed to one or more classes. For example, if Adam's father simply wants to be a passive investor in Adam's business, shares without voting rights could be created to meet his needs. If he wants some qualified assurance of the return of his share capital when and if IK Enterprises winds downs, then shares with preference rights on dissolution could be created. The possibilities are almost limitless; however, careful consideration must be given to how management and financial rights are distributed among classes of shares. These issues are explored further in Chapter 16.

Adam may limit the number of shares of each class that can be issued by stating a maximum number, or he can simply leave matters open-ended by indicating that the number is "unlimited."

---

6. Kevin Patrick McGuinness, *Canadian Business Corporations Law*, 2d ed (Markham, ON: LexisNexis, 2007) at 178.

FIGURE 15.1

Creating Classes of Shares

A class of share may include a combination of various rights and privileges. Examples of typical rights that may attach to a class of shares include the following:

- Voting rights: the right to vote for election of directors
- Financial rights: the right to receive dividends when declared by directors or the right to receive fixed dividends on a regular basis
- Preference rights: the right to receive dividends before dividends may be paid to any other class of shareholders and/or the right, on dissolution, to receive investment before any payments are made to any other class of shareholder
- Cumulative rights: the right to have a dividend not paid in a particular year added to the amount payable the following year
- Redemption rights: the right to have the corporation buy back the shares at a set price

Availability of Shares A corporation may issue shares to the general public. This type of corporation is usually referred to as a **widely held** or public **corporation**.[7] A corporation that issues shares to the public is subject to regulation pursuant to the relevant **securities legislation** in those provinces in which the securities are issued or traded. Securities legislation, discussed in more detail below, imposes registration and disclosure requirements on the issuers of the shares.

A corporation that does not issue its shares to the general public is usually known as a **closely held** or private **corporation**.[8] The vast majority of Canadian corporations, including some very large enterprises, such as McCain Foods and the Irving companies in New Brunswick, N.M. Paterson and Son Ltd. in Manitoba, and Holt Renfrew in Ontario, fall within this category. These corporations are generally exempt from most of the obligations of securities regulation so long as they meet the definition of a private corporation. For example, in Ontario, the *Securities Act*[9] provides that a corporation qualifies as a private corporation if it has the following provisions in its incorporating documents:

- a restriction on the transfer of shares
- a limit (with certain exceptions) on the number of shareholders in the corporation to no more than 50
- a prohibition on any invitation to the public to subscribe for the corporation's shares

An added advantage of private corporation status is the potential for a lower rate of income tax. *The Income Tax Act*[10] provides that a Canadian-controlled private corporation is entitled to a lower tax rate on its first $500 000 of business income earned in Canada in its fiscal year. In effect, a qualifying corporation pays about half the normal corporate income tax rate of approximately 50 percent on this income.

Widely held corporation
A corporation whose shares are normally traded on a stock exchange.

Securities legislation
Laws designed to regulate transactions involving shares and bonds of a corporation.

Closely held corporation
A corporation that does not sell its shares to the public.

PART FOUR

---

7. The term "widely held" is used interchangeably with "public" to denote a corporation that offers its shares for sale to the public. In some jurisdictions, the terms "offering" or "reporting" are also used.
8. The term "closely held" is used interchangeably with "private" to denote a corporation that does not offer its shares for sale to the public. In some jurisdictions, the terms "non-offering" or "non-reporting" are also used.
9. RSO 1990, c S-5, ss 1(1), 35 (2) (10), 73 (1) (a).
10. RSC 1985, c 1 (5th Supp), s 125.

What are the advantages of a private corporation?

FRED LUM/THE GLOBE AND MAIL/THE CANADIAN PRESS

BUSINESS APPLICATION OF THE LAW

The Trials of Lord Black of Crossharbour

In 2005, U.S. prosecutors charged Lord Black with 17 offences relating to the Chicago-based publishing company Hollinger International, now known as the Sun-Times Media Group. Black was convicted of one count of obstruction of justice and three counts of fraud.[11] He was found not guilty of nine other charges. He was sentenced to six-and-a-half years in prison, ordered to forfeit US$6.1 million (the estimated amount of the fraud) and fined $125 000. Through various legal challenges, his convictions were reduced to two and his sentence to 42 months. Black served most of his sentence at Coleman Federal Correction Complex, a low-security prison in Florida and was released in May 2012.

The Rise of a Newspaper Baron: Conrad Black was born in Montreal in 1944. He was the son of a prominent businessman who managed Canadian Breweries, a division of Argus Corporation. During the late 1960s and the early 1970s, Black, along with friend and business partner David Radler, entered the newspaper industry by acquiring several small Canadian regional newspapers. In 1976, Black's father died, leaving Black and his brother a 22.4 percent interest in Ravelston Corp., which owned a 61 percent voting control of Argus, whose holdings included Hollinger Mines. By 1978, Black managed to gain control over Ravelston and thereby

ASSOCIATED PRESS/CHARLES REX AROBASGT

"I have always tried to take success like a gentleman and disappointment like a man" —Conrad Black

gained control of Argus. Over the next few years, Argus sold most of its assets and reinvested the proceeds in newspapers. In 1985 Hollinger Mines, through amalgamation with various other Argus holdings, became Hollinger Inc. It continued to be controlled by Ravelston, Black's private holding company. In 1986, American Publishing, a subsidiary of Hollinger Inc., was formed in Delaware to acquire newspapers. In 1993, it went public and was renamed Hollinger International. During the 1980s and 1990s, Hollinger International (and its predecessor,

---

11. Specifically, Black was convicted on one count of mail fraud and two counts of mail and wire fraud pursuant to federal statutes. These laws date back to the 1800s and are popular for going after corporate crime because they can be interpreted broadly to include the honest services theory. Under this theory, executives, for example, can be convicted of fraud for any scheme or plan involving a breach of the obligation to provide honest services to their employers.

American Publishing) gained control of London's *Daily Telegraph*, the *Chicago Sun-Times*, the Southam newspaper chain, the *Financial Post, Saturday Night*, and many small-town U.S. dailies. By the late 1990s, Black's newspaper holdings through his companies comprised the world's third-largest newspaper group. It was publishing over 500 newspapers with a total daily circulation of nearly five million and was boasting revenues of more than $3 billion annually. It was during this period that Black renounced his Canadian citizenship and was inducted into the British House of Lords as Lord Black of Crossharbour.

The Downfall: By 2000, however, the enterprises were heavily in debt and Hollinger International sold most of the Canadian newspapers to CanWest Global Communications for $3.2 billion. As part of the deal, Black, Radler, and three other executives received $80 million in non-competition payments. A New York investment firm with an 18 percent stake in Hollinger International was outraged by the payments and insisted that Hollinger International investigate these and other payments to Black and his associates. Hollinger International created a special committee to review the payments, and Black resigned as CEO of Hollinger International after the committee reported US$32.15 million in unauthorized payments had been made to Black, Radler, and other officers. In 2004, Hollinger International ousted Black as its chairman and launched a US$200 million lawsuit against him, Radler, and others seeking the return of management fees and other payments. Several months after the launch of the lawsuit, the Breeden Report (named after its author, Richard Breeden, a former SEC chief who was named special monitor of Hollinger International) was released. In the report, Black and his associates were accused of having run a "corporate kleptocracy" at Hollinger International. Black was accused of pillaging hundreds of millions of dollars from Hollinger International, violating his fiduciary obligations, and ignoring corporate governance principles.

In the wake of the Breeden Report, several lawsuits were brought against Black and his associates, including a criminal action by the U.S. Attorney's office in Chicago. They charged Black with mail fraud, wire fraud, racketeering, obstruction of justice, and money laundering.

The Criminal Trial: In March 2007, the trial of the *United States of America v Lord Black et al* proceeded in front of a jury in Chicago. The key allegations against Black and the other defendants were that they abused their power to fraudulently divert millions of dollars to themselves. Specifically, the non-competition payments were frauds designed to allow Black and his codefendants to transfer tax-free money (non-competition payments were tax exempt in Canada at that time)

to their own pockets rather than to Hollinger International. The defence argued that non-competition payments are routine in the newspaper business and that all the payments were legal, disclosed to Hollinger International auditors, and authorized by Hollinger International's board of directors. The star witness for the prosecution was David Radler, who earlier had entered a plea bargain with the prosecution. He pleaded guilty to one fraud-related count connected to the non-competition payments and received a 29-month jail sentence in return for his testimony. After a 15-week trial, more than 40 witnesses, about 700 documents, and more than two weeks of jury deliberations, Black was convicted of three counts of fraud related to the non-competition payments and one count of obstruction of justice in connection to the removal of 13 boxes of documents from his Toronto office. He began serving his sentence in March 2008. In June 2008, the Seventh Circuit Court of Appeals affirmed the conviction.

In 2009, in a surprise move, the U.S. Supreme Court reviewed Black's fraud convictions. At the centre of the appeal was the application of the honest services[12] theory in fraud statutes. The honest services theory was originally enacted to target corrupt politicians but in recent years, prosecutors have used it in corporate fraud cases, including *Enron*. The Supreme Court redefined honest services so that it could only be applied to cases involving bribes and kickbacks and ordered the Illinois appeal court to reconsider Black's conviction. In 2011, the appeal court vacated two fraud convictions and reduced his sentence.

The saga of Lord Black raises interesting questions about how Black and his associates were able to defraud Hollinger International. Some of the answers may lie in the corporate governance structure of Hollinger International.

Corporate Structure: Hollinger International (renamed Sun-Times Media Group) was, at the time of the wrongdoings outlined above, controlled by Hollinger Inc., a publicly traded holding company. Hollinger Inc. was, in turn, controlled by Ravelston. Hollinger Inc. was able to control Hollinger International through what is known as a dual-class structure—different classes of shares have different voting rights. Hollinger Inc. owned all of Hollinger International's Class B shares, which gave it 30 percent of the equity but 73 percent of the votes. The multiple-voting share structure allowed Hollinger Inc. to control the fate of Hollinger International while holding a fraction of the equity. This structure has been a favourite of Canadian corporate empire builders and remains entrenched despite criticism from shareholder activists. The structure, in essence, allowed Black to call the shots and to select Hollinger International's board of directors. Indeed, the board was largely filled with prominent, outside directors, hand-selected by Black

(Continued)

---

12. *Ibid.*

and with whom he had a social, political, or business relationship. Apparently the "Black Board" functioned like a social club or public policy association, with extremely short meetings followed by a good lunch and a discussion of world affairs—actual operating results or corporate performance were rarely discussed. The board was often given false or misleading information, but it did not do much on its own about excessive management fees and non-compete payments. It took no steps and asked no questions.

Critical Analysis: How did the share structure of the Hollinger companies contribute to the alleged abuse of the corporate form of carrying on business? Are there any lessons to be learned from the Conrad Black case?

Sources: Gordon A Paris, Chairman, *Report of Investigation by the Special Committee of the Board of Directors of Hollinger International Inc* (30 August 2004) at <http://www.sec.gov/Archives/edgar/data/868512/000095012304010413 /y01437exv99w2.htm>; Steven Skurka, *Tilted: The Trial of Conrad Black* (Toronto: Dundurn Press, 2008); Paul Waldie, "Black calls ruling 'immensely gratifying'" *The Globe and Mail* (25 June 2010) at B1; and Mitch Potter, "Judge orders Black back to jail, Amiel collapses" *The Saturday Star* (25 June 2011) at A1.

Who May Own Shares   A share is a piece of property and is freely transferable unless there is a restriction in place. In widely held corporations, shares are almost always freely transferable; otherwise the shares will not be accepted for listing on a stock exchange. In closely held corporations where shares are generally issued to family or friends, the shareholders have a strong interest in having control over who the other shareholders are. It is therefore common to have a provision in the incorporating documents that shares cannot be transferred without the agreement of the directors or a majority of the shareholders of the corporation. At the same time, shareholders require some flexibility in being able to transfer their shares; thus it is common to include "a right of first refusal" for directors or shareholders. When a right of first refusal is in place, it means that the shareholder wishing to sell must first offer her shares to the directors (or shareholders, as the case may be) at the same price she has negotiated with the outsider. This gives the insiders one last chance to acquire the shares for themselves instead of having to welcome a new investor to the company.

As an alternative to having a restriction in the corporation's constitution, the shareholders could have an agreement that covers transferring. Shareholders agreements are discussed in Chapter 16.

A Corporate Name

All jurisdictions require a company to be identified by a name or designated number. The selection and use of corporate names is subject to regulation by trademark law,[13] tort law,[14] and corporation law.

The basic requirements for a name are as follows:

- It must be distinctive (different from other existing names in the same field).

- It must not cause confusion with any existing name or trademark.

- It must include a legal element (e.g., Limited or Ltd., Incorporated or Inc., or Corporation or Corp., or the French equivalents). The purpose of the word is to distinguish a corporation from a partnership and a sole proprietorship and to signal to the public the fact of limited liability.

- It must not include any unacceptable terms (e.g., it must not suggest a connection that does not exist, falsely describe the business, or be obscene or scandalous).

---

13. See Chapter 18.
14. The tort of passing off.

On choosing a corporate name, entrepreneurs like Adam are advised to be particularly careful. If the corporate registry inadvertently approves a name that is confusingly similar to the name of another business, Adam can be sued for trademark infringement and the tort of passing off.[15] He will be liable for any damages that the other business has suffered and, perhaps even more problematically, be ordered to change the name of his corporation. This will require Adam to re-establish a corporate identity and reputation in the marketplace, as well as replace letterhead, invoices, business signs, and anything else bearing his former corporate name. This is obviously costly. Paws Pet Food & Accessories Ltd v Paws & Shop Inc illustrates how such a dispute can arise.

CASE   *Paws Pet Food & Accessories Ltd v Paws & Shop Inc* (1992), 6 Alta LR (3d) 22 (QB)

THE BUSINESS CONTEXT: A name is an important and valuable asset to a business. It helps distinguish one business from another.

FACTUAL BACKGROUND: Paws Pet Food & Accessories Ltd. (Paws Pet Food) was incorporated in 1987 under the Alberta Business Corporations Act. Three years later, Paws & Shop Inc. (Paws & Shop) was created under the same piece of legislation. Both corporations operated in Calgary, and both were in the business of retailing pet food and accessories. Paws Pet Food took the position that the registrar should not have allowed the second company to incorporate under a name that was so confusingly similar to its own. It went to court for an order directing the second company to change its name.

THE LEGAL QUESTION: Is Paws & Shop Inc.—the second company—confusingly similar to Paws Pet Food & Accessories?

RESOLUTION: The court decided that the registrar had made an error in permitting the second corporation to incorporate under the name of Paws & Shop. There was evidence that customers of Paws Pet Food mistakenly believed that it was associated or affiliated with Paws & Shop. The registration of Paws & Shop was therefore contrary to the Alberta Business Corporations Act and related regulations because it was leading to public confusion. On this basis, Paws & Shop was forced to change its name.

CRITICAL ANALYSIS: This case illustrates that there is no inherent protection in the fact that the registrar has approved a corporate name for use. A judge can overrule the registrar and, furthermore, since the tort of passing off can be committed unintentionally, a company with a name that is confusingly similar to that of another company can end up paying damages even though the registrar had approved the name to begin with. Is this fair? Who should bear the risk of a mistake being made—the business itself or the taxpayers?

Assuming that Adam wants to incorporate federally, he will have to send his proposed name—IK Enterprises Ltd.—to the federal corporate registry for approval. He will also have to have a Newly Upgraded Automated Name Search, or **NUANS, Report**. This document lists those business names and trademarks—if any—that are similar to the name being proposed. A NUANS Report is prepared using a database containing existing and reserved business names, as well as trademarks. If some other business is using the name IK Enterprises Ltd. or a name similar to it—such as IK Investments Inc.—the NUANS Report would presumably contain such information. In that case, Adam should avoid the name and come up with an alternative name for his fledgling business.

NUANS Report

A document that shows the result of a search for business names.

PART FOUR

---

15. This is because Adam would be representing to the public—either intentionally or not—that there is a relationship between his business and the other business when no such relationship exists.

It is common for a company's legislation to permit a corporation to be assigned a numbered name. Under the federal legislation, for example, the corporation can be issued a designating number, followed by the word "Canada" and then a legal element—such as "Limited" or "Incorporated." A numbered company is useful when a corporation must be created quickly, when the incorporators are having difficulty coming up with a suitable name, or when there is a wish to create a **shelf company**. Shelf companies are often incorporated by law firms for the future use of their clients. The company does not engage in any active business. It simply sits "on the shelf" until a firm's client needs it.

Shelf company
A company that does not engage in active business.

The Process of Incorporation

All Canadian jurisdictions follow a similar procedure for the creation of a corporation, though precise requirements do vary. Assuming that Adam wants to incorporate federally, he must submit the following to the federal corporate registry in Ottawa:[16]

- articles of incorporation[17]
- notice of registered office
- notice of directors
- Newly Upgraded Automated Name Search (NUANS) Report
- the filing fee, payable to the Receiver General for Canada

Articles of incorporation
The document that defines the basic characteristics of corporations incorporated in Newfoundland, New Brunswick, Ontario, Manitoba, Saskatchewan, Alberta, and the federal jurisdiction.

Incorporator
The person who sets the incorporation process in motion.

The **articles of incorporation** set out the basic features of the corporation—name, place of the corporation's registered office, class and number of shares authorized to be issued, any restrictions on the transferring of shares, the number of directors, any restrictions on the business that can be carried on, and any other provisions that an **incorporator** requires to customize the corporation to meet his needs. For example, incorporators may include provisions that require directors to own at least one share in the corporation, provisions prescribing how shareholders will fill a vacancy in the board of directors, or provisions that limit the number of shareholders to a certain number. The name or names of the incorporators must also be included in the articles of incorporation.

The Notice of Registered Office form is very brief because it has only one purpose: to provide a public record of the corporation's official address. This is the address that those having dealings with the company can use to communicate with the corporation, particularly with respect to formal matters, including lawsuits.

The Notice of Directors form contains the names and residential addresses of the directors and must correspond with the number of directors given in the articles of incorporation.

The completed forms, along with the requisite fee, are then submitted to the appropriate government office—the Corporations Directorate of Industry Canada. If the forms are in order, the directorate will issue a "birth certificate" for the corporation, known as the certificate of incorporation.

---

16. Federal incorporation is available online by accessing the Corporations Canada Online Filing Centre website at <http://www.ic.gc.ca/cgi-bin/sc_mrksv/corpdir/corpFiling/register.cgi?lang=e>.
17. The term "articles of incorporation" is also used in Alberta, Manitoba, New Brunswick, Newfoundland and Labrador, Ontario, and Saskatchewan. The equivalent term in Nova Scotia is "memorandum of association"; in Prince Edward Island and Quebec, it is "letters patent"; and in British Columbia it is "notice of articles."

Provincial incorporation legislation has its own requirements, which are parallel but are not necessarily identical to the requirements and procedures under the *Canada Business Corporations Act*.

BUSINESS AND LEGISLATION

Unlimited Liability Corporations

Unlimited liability corporations (ULCs) are corporations whose shareholders or former shareholders are, in certain circumstances, jointly and severally liable for the debts and liabilities of the corporation. Nova Scotia, Alberta, and British Columbia have amended their companies Acts to permit a company to incorporate as an ULC.

The ULC is used by American investors in Canadian ventures because of significant advantages under U.S. tax law for U.S. residents. This is because although ULCs are generally subject to taxation in Canada on the same basis as any other Canadian corporation, under U.S. tax law they are treated for many purposes as a partnership. This treatment allows for the "flow-through" of certain income and expenses to U.S. shareholders,

thus avoiding some of the double taxation that would otherwise exist. The U.S. owner of the ULC is allowed to consolidate the ULC's foreign income and losses and to claim a U.S. foreign tax credit for any Canadian income tax paid by the ULC.

The problem of exposing shareholders of ULCs to unlimited liability can be addressed by interposing an appropriate limited liability entity between the U.S. shareholders and the ULC.

Critical Analysis: Why would governments amend their corporation's legislation to allow for the incorporation of ULCs?

Sources: Linda Parsons, "Unlimited liability companies suffer setbacks under tax treaty", *The Lawyers Weekly* (7 March 2008) at 9; and Don R Sommerfeldt, "Alberta Unlimited Liability Corporations: New Kid on the Block", *Tax Notes International* (11 April 2005) at 141.

Organizing the Corporation

Following incorporation, the first directors will ordinarily undertake a number of tasks. Under federal legislation, for example, the directors are required to call an organizational meeting to

- make **bylaws**[18]

- adopt forms of share certificates and corporate records

- authorize the issue of shares and other securities

- appoint officers

- appoint an auditor to hold office until the first annual meeting of shareholders

- make banking arrangements

- transact any other business[19]

Bylaws
Rules specifying the day-to-day operating procedures of a corporation.

Federal legislation also specifies that the directors named in the articles of incorporation hold office until the first meeting of the shareholders. That meeting must be called within 18 months of incorporation.[20] At that first meeting, shareholders elect the permanent directors, who hold office for the specified term.[21] The directors carry on the management of the corporation until the next annual meeting, at which time they report to the shareholders on the corporation's performance.

---

18. Bylaws is the term used in the articles of incorporation and letters patent jurisdiction. In Nova Scotia, "articles of association"—the very general equivalent of bylaws—is the term used, and in British Columbia the term is "articles."
19. *Canada Business Corporations Act*, RSC 1985, c C-44, s 104.
20. *Ibid* at s 133(a).
21. *Ibid* at s 106(3).

Financing the Corporation

Adam needs to finance his company to have the funds to operate. He has two basic means of doing so: IK Enterprises Ltd. can borrow money (debt financing) or issue shares (equity financing).

Debt Financing

A corporation may raise money by borrowing. The company may obtain a loan from shareholders, family or friends of shareholders, lending institutions, or, in some cases, the government. If it is borrowing a substantial sum of money on a long-term basis, the corporation may issue **bonds** or **debentures**. The terms "bond" and "debenture" are often used interchangeably and refer to a corporate IOU, which is either secured or unsecured. Note that the word "bond" is sometimes used to describe a secured debt, and debenture to refer to an unsecured debt, but the only way to know what is actually involved is to read the debt instrument itself.

A bond or debenture does not represent any ownership interest in the corporation, and the holder does not have any right to participate in the management of the corporation.[22] However, these debts are often secured by a charge on the assets of the corporation. This means that if the debt is not repaid, the assets can be sold to repay the debt and the bondholder has a better chance of recovering his investment. Bonds and debentures—like shares—may have any number of features and are freely transferable, creating a secondary market for their purchase and sale.

The advantage of raising cash by issuing bonds is that Adam does not have to relinquish formal control. That is, he can raise money to run his operation without having to give management rights to his lenders. On the other hand, there is a requirement that the interest on the bonds be paid regardless of whether a profit is earned. In fact, if the interest is not paid on the debt, the corporation faces bankruptcy unless it can reach a new agreement with the bondholders.

Equity Financing

Shares are frequently used to raise money for the use of the corporation. This is done by issuing shares to investors in exchange for a purchase price.

Shares provide a flexible means of raising capital for a corporation because they can be created with different bundles of rights attached to them to appeal to different investors. Shares can be attractive to investors because, unlike debt, where the return is usually limited to a fixed amount, shares provide an opportunity to benefit from the corporation's growth. If the corporation prospers, the value of the shares will increase. Shares are advantageous to the issuer in that the money raised by selling shares does not have to be repaid in the way a loan must. On the other hand, the sale of shares may mean the relinquishing of management rights. Although it is possible to raise capital through the sale of shares that do not have any voting rights attached, investors may be interested only in shares that give them a say in the control and operation of the corporation.

Shares and bonds represent two very different ways of raising money for corporate activities. There are, however, many combinations of these two types of **securities**. Much depends

Bond
A document evidencing a debt owed by the corporation, often used to refer to a secured debt.

Debenture
A document evidencing a debt owed by the corporation, often used to refer to an unsecured debt.

Securities
Shares and bonds issued by a corporation.

---

22. It is possible, however, for bondholders to obtain management rights if the company defaults on the loan. This depends on the terms of issuance.

on the features that investors are interested in purchasing. Most businesses, particularly large ones, use some combination of these various methods of raising funds, maintaining a reasonable balance between them. Furthermore, shares and bonds can come with **conversion rights**. A convertible bondholder, for example, is entitled to convert his debt interest into shares and thereby assume an equity position in the company instead of being a creditor.

Conversion right
The right to convert one type of security into another type.

Figure 15.2 shows a comparison of the preceding points regarding securities.

FIGURE 15.2
Securities Compared

	Shareholder	*Bondholder*
Status of holder	Investor/owner	Investor/creditor
Participation in management	Elects directors (if voting rights); approves major activities	Does not participate (except in special circumstances)
Rights to income	Dividends, if declared	Interest payments
Security for the holder on insolvency of the corporation	Entitled to share in proceeds after all creditors paid	Entitled to payment from proceeds before general creditors, if secured, and before shareholders

The issuance of securities including bonds, debentures, and shares to the general public is governed by securities legislation. This means that the issuer must follow a complicated and potentially costly procedure. Securities legislation seeks to ensure that the potential purchasers know what they are getting into before they make any decision.

BUSINESS APPLICATION OF THE LAW

Securities Class Actions

The exposure of corporate Canada to securities class action lawsuits may be growing. According to a recently published study by National Economic Research Associates Inc., eight new securities class actions were filed during 2010, involving total claims of more than $870 million. There were settlements in six cases with defendants paying a total of almost $80 million. At the end of 2010, there was a record 28 active Canadian securities class actions representing approximately $15.9 billion in outstanding claims.

In two outstanding cases, *Silver v IMAX*,[23] where the plaintiffs allege that the entertainment company misrepresented 2005 financial results, and *Dobbie v Arctic Glacier Income Fund*,[24] where it is alleged that the company misrepresented itself as a good corporate citizen, a judge has given the class actions leave to continue to trial. The judge in each case determined that the plaintiffs met the requirement that the proposed class action had a reasonable chance of success.

Who bears the cost of class action lawsuits?

Critical Analysis: What do you think is the purpose of the leave requirement? What factors may account for the increase in Canadian securities class action lawsuits?

Source: Mark L Berenblut, Bradley A Heys & Tara K Singh, "Trends in Canadian securities class actions: 2010 update," *NERA Economic Consulting* (31 January 2011) at www.securitieslitigationTrends.com.

23. 2011 ONSC 1035.
24. 2011 ONSC 25.

Securities Legislation

All provinces have enacted securities acts.[25] In very general terms, the aim of all securities legislation is to

- provide the mechanism for the transfer of securities
- ensure that all investors have the ability to access adequate information in order to make informed decisions
- ensure that the system is such that the public has confidence in the marketplace
- regulate those engaged in the trading of securities
- remove or punish those participants not complying with established rules

With these objectives at the forefront, all securities regimes have three basic requirements: registration, disclosure, and insider-trading restrictions.

BUSINESS AND LEGISLATION

A National Securities Regulator

Canada is the only major, industrialized economy without a centralized, national body regulating securities. Instead, there are 13 different provincial and territorial securities regulators, with a corresponding multiplicity of statues, regulations, policies, and interpretations.

Beginning in 1964 with the Royal Commission on Banking and Finance (the Porter Commission), there have been numerous calls for a national securities regulatory commission. Most recently, the report of the federally commissioned "Expert panel on Securities Regulation" (Hockin Report, 2009) concluded that the global financial crisis increased the need for such a body. In its wake, the Federal Finance Minister, despite the vehement opposition of several provinces, unveiled draft legislation establishing a single national securities regulatory body, the Canadian Securities Regulatory Authority.

The draft legislation was submitted to the courts for an opinion on its constitutionality. The federal government argued

that its jurisdiction over trade and commerce in s 91(2) of the *Constitution Act, 1867* authorizes it to regulate the securities industry. The opposing provinces argued that their jurisdiction over property and civil rights in s 92(13) gives them authority.[26] The Supreme Court of Canada[27] unanimously held that the Act as drafted was not constitutional. The Court concluded that while legislation aimed at imposing minimum standards throughout the country and preserving the integrity of the financial markets might relate to trade as a whole, the proposed Act went beyond such matters. The Act was aimed at regulating all aspects of trading in securities, a matter that was within provincial jurisdiction.

Critical Analysis: What are the policy arguments in favour of a single securities regulator for all of Canada? What are the policy arguments against a single regulator?

Sources: Karen Howlett and Janet McFarland, "Fight brewing over securities watchdog plan", *The Globe and Mail* (15 July 2010) at B4 ; Christopher Guly, "Quebec, Alberta take on feds over national securities regulator", *The Lawyers Weekly* (16 July 2010) at 9.

Registration

Any company intending to sell securities to the public in a given province must be registered to do so with the relevant provincial securities commission. Furthermore, all persons engaged in advising on and selling securities to the public must be registered with the relevant securities commission. The definitions of those covered by the various statutes vary between provinces but generally extend to advisors, underwriters, dealers, salespeople, brokers, and securities issuers.

---

25. The *Canada Business Corporations Act* also contains provisions that regulate securities that are issued or traded by CBCA corporations.
26. See Chapter 2 for a discussion of sections 91 and 92 of the *Constitution Act*, 1867.
27. *Reference Re Securities Act*, 2011 SCC 66.

Disclosure

The company must comply with disclosure or **prospectus** provisions set forth in the securities legislation. With limited exceptions, this means that any sale or distribution of a security—in this case, meaning either debt (bonds) or equity (shares)—must be preceded by a prospectus that is accepted and approved by the appropriate securities commission. A prospectus is the statement by the issuing company of prescribed information. The list of information required to be in the prospectus is lengthy and ranges from financial information to biographical information about the directors. The overriding requirement is for "full, true, and plain" disclosure of all material facts, that is, facts that are likely to affect the price of the securities. The legislation assumes that prospective investors will rely on the prospectus in making investment decisions.

Prospectus
The document a corporation must publish when offering securities to the public.

The issuer of securities has an obligation to continue to keep the public informed of its activities. In general terms, this means that it must notify the public of any material change in its affairs, first by issuing a press release and second by filing a report with the securities commission within 10 days of the change. A material change is defined as one that is likely to have a significant effect on the market value of the securities and is not known to the public in general.

BUSINESS AND LEGISLATION

Ontario's Securities Act *and Secondary Market Liability*

In 2004, Ontario amended its *Securities Act* [28] to provide a new statutory right of action for misrepresentations contained in secondary market disclosures. Since then, all other provinces have introduced secondary civil liability regimes modelled on Ontario's. The objective of these regimes is to create a meaningful civil remedy for secondary market investors and to facilitate class action lawsuits.

Prior to the amendments, securities legislation provided only a statutory cause of action to investors who purchased securities in the primary market (i.e., purchased pursuant to a prospectus, offering memorandum, or securities exchange takeover bid circular). Investors in the secondary market [29] (i.e., purchasing or selling from third parties) had to rely on a common law action for fraudulent or negligent misrepresentation. This meant that the secondary market purchasers had to establish that they relied on the defendants' misrepresentations in making their investment decisions. This requirement made it next to impossible to have a class action certified because of the individual issues of reliance. The amendments create the statutory cause of action "without regard to whether" the purchaser or seller relied on the alleged misrepresentation. In other words, the investor is deemed to have relied on the

Bre-X share certificate

disclosures and does not have to prove that she relied detrimentally on the misrepresentation. This amendment facilitates the certification of class actions by removing the issue of proof of individual class member reliance.

The key provisions of the amendments are as follows:

• *Cause of action.* Secondary market investors have a right to sue where they bought or sold securities during a period where there was an uncorrected misrepresentation made by or on behalf of an issuer in a document released

(Continued)

28. RSO 1990, c S-5, Part XXIII.1, s 138.3 (1).
29. It is estimated that secondary market trading accounts for more than 90 percent of all equity trading in Canada.

PART FOUR

by the company or in a public oral statement. The right to sue is also available where there was a failure to make timely disclosure of a material change in the issuer's business.

• *Defendants*. The class of people that may be liable for a company's misrepresentation or failure to disclose is broad and includes the reporting issuer; its directors, officers, influential persons (including controlling shareholders, promoters, and insiders), and experts (including auditors and lawyers).

• *Defences*. There are a number of defences available to defendants, including reasonable investigation (defendant had conducted a reasonable investigation and had no reason to believe the document or oral statement contained a misrepresentation), plaintiff's knowledge (defendant proves that the plaintiff knew there was a misrepresentation of failure to disclose at the relevant time), no involvement, and reasonable reliance on experts.

• *Damages*. There is a complex formula for calculating damages, but generally a person who is found liable will be responsible for the losses the investor suffers (the difference between the price paid or received for a security and the average price in the 10-day period following the disclosure or public correction). If more than one person is liable, each defendant will be responsible only for the proportionate share of damages that corresponds to his responsibility unless he knowingly participated in the misrepresentation or failure to disclose. Also, liability for damage awards is capped except when a defendant knowingly participates in the misrepresentation or failure to disclose. Liability for individual defendants is the greater of $25 000 and 50 percent of their compensation from the issuer in the prior 12 months. The liability limits for corporate defendants are the greater of 5 percent of capitalization and $1 million.

Critical Analysis: How do the amendments enhance investor protection? Do the amendments do enough for investors?

Insider-Trading Restrictions

Insider trading
Transactions in securities of a corporation by or on behalf of an insider on the basis of relevant material information concerning the corporation that is not known to the general public.

The objective of **insider-trading** provisions is to ensure that trading in securities takes place only on the basis of information available to the public at large. Securities legislation achieves this aim in two primary ways: first, it requires **insiders** to report any trading that they have engaged in, and second, it prohibits trading by certain insiders—such as directors, senior officers, employees, and the corporation itself—on the basis of information not publicly available.

The reason insiders must report any trade is simple: if someone in this capacity is either buying or selling large blocks of securities, this is critical information for the investing public. Even small trades can be relevant. Insiders are prohibited not only from trading on material information not publicly disclosed but also from passing on this information to a third party or **tippee**. This person is similarly prohibited from trading on such information.

Insider
A person whose relationship with the issuer of securities is such that he is likely to have access to relevant material information concerning the issuer that is not known to the public.

Tippee
A person who acquires material information about an issuer of securities from an insider.

Those who engage in insider trading are subject to both criminal and civil liability under securities legislation and under corporation legislation.[30] In addition, the federal government has amended the *Criminal Code* to create improper insider trading and tipping offences. The insider trading offence carries a penalty of up to 10 years in prison and the tipping offence is punishable by up to five years in prison.[31]

In considering whether to offer securities to the public through a stock exchange, Adam has a number of factors to consider. Although selling securities is a means of obtaining funds from a wide group of investors, it entails public disclosure of information that would otherwise not be known to competitors, and certainly requires costly compliance with regulations.[32]

---

30. *Supra* note 19 at s 131(4). Note that under recent amendments the definition of insider has been expanded to catch more transactions.
31. *Criminal Code*, RSC, 1995, c C-46, Part X, ss 382.1 (1) (2).
32. Edmund MA Kwaw, *The Law of Corporate Finance in Canada* (Toronto: Butterworths, 1997) at 121–22.

BUSINESS APPLICATION OF THE LAW

Insider-Trading Scandals in Canada

In 2009, Stan Grmovsek pleaded guilty to illegal insider trading, criminal fraud and money laundering contrary to the *Criminal Code*. In 2010, he was sentenced to 39 months in prison, ordered to disgorge the proceeds from his unlawful conduct, and prohibited from buying and selling securities.[33] Grmovsek and his co-accused, Gil Cornblum, who met as students at Osgoode law school, used insider information to generate US$9 million from 1994 to 2008. Cornblum, who had worked for several law firms and was a partner with Dorsey & Whitney LLP, a Minnesota-based global law firm, passed on confidential information about clients' pending mergers and acquisitions to Grmovsek. He, in turn, used the information to buy and sell shares primarily in off-shore accounts. Cornblum committed suicide the day before he was scheduled to plead guilty to criminal charges. The case involving Grmovsek is the first criminal insider conviction since the *Criminal Code* was amended to provide for illegal insider trading. It is also the longest prison term ever imposed in Canada for insider trading.

In 2005, former RBC Dominion Securities Inc. investment banker Andrew Rankin was found guilty in Ontario provincial court of 10 counts of tipping a friend, Daniel Duic, about pending corporate deals. Duic used the tips to make a net profit of over $4.5 million in stock trades between February 2001 and February 2002. Insider-trading charges against Duic were dropped in return for his testimony against Rankin and the payment of a

John Felderhof

$1.9 million fine. Rankin was acquitted of 10 counts of the more serious offence of insider trading because he was apparently not aware of his friend's deals and he did not directly profit from them. Rankin was sentenced to six months in jail. However, in November 2006, the Ontario Superior Court, citing contradictory evidence (inconsistencies in Duic's evidence) and errors by the trial judge, overturned Rankin's conviction and ordered a new trial. The Court of Appeal for Ontario dismissed the Ontario Securities Commission (OSC)'s application for an appeal. A week before the new criminal trial was to begin, the OSC agreed to withdraw criminal charges in return for an admission by Rankin that he engaged in illegal tipping. Rankin also agreed to a payment of $250 000 toward OSC's investigation costs, a lifetime ban from working in the securities industry or serving as a director or officer of a public company, and a 10-year ban on trading on securities in Ontario.

In 1997, John Felderhof, the chief geologist of Bre-X Minerals pleaded not guilty in criminal court to eight violations of the Ontario *Securities Act*, including four based on insider trading. The Ontario Securities Commission (OSC) alleged that Felderhof sold $84 million of Bre-X stock in 1996 while having information about the company that had not been publicly disclosed. He sold nearly 3.6 million shares seven months before the Bre-X's reported gold find was exposed as a fraud. The trial, which began in 2000, was marred by numerous delays including a three-and-a-half-year adjournment for an unsuccessful attempt by the OSC to have the presiding judge removed from the trial.[34] Closing arguments were heard in August 2006, and a decision was rendered in August 2007. Felderhof, the only person who was ever charged in the biggest gold-mining scandal in Canadian history, made a court appearance in March 2005 but never testified. He was found not guilty of all charges. The OSC did not prove beyond a reasonable doubt that Felderhof had knowledge of the fraud (the salting of mineral samples) at the time that he sold $84 million of Bre-X shares.

Critical Analysis: There have been very few successful insider-trading prosecutions in Canada. What factors make prosecutions difficult?

Andrew Rankin

33. Ontario Securities Commission at <http://www.osc.gov.on.ca/static/_/AnnualReports/2010/report_effect_enforce.html>
34. *R v Felderhof* (2003), 68 OR (3d) 481 (CA).

PART FOUR

Business Law in Practice Revisited

1. How is a corporation formed, and what factors should Adam consider in forming a corporation?

A corporation is formed by an incorporator or incorporators making an application to the appropriate government body. The choice of the corporate form requires the consideration of a number of issues, including the cost of incorporation and where the corporation will conduct its business. Adam wishes to start small but foresees rapid expansion nationally and internationally; thus a federal incorporation would probably be the logical choice.

Adam also needs to consider such factors as whether the name he has chosen is already in use, what sort of capital structure he will employ, and how the corporation will be capitalized. In particular, Adam needs to recognize that his proposed share structure—half the shares to himself and half to Diane—may result in shareholder deadlock.

2. Does Adam appear to understand the concept of limited liability adequately?

Adam appears to be under a misconception concerning the nature of limited liability. He suggests that Cameron lend the money to the company as this will protect Cameron from unlimited liability. In fact, Cameron would be protected from unlimited liability both as a creditor and as a shareholder. A shareholder is not, except in rare situations, responsible for the debts of the corporation beyond the original investment. Thus, whether Cameron invests in debt or shares has little effect on the liability issue.

3. What other financing options are available, in addition to Cameron lending money to the corporation?

Cameron could invest as a shareholder, but a loan would give him priority over shareholders in the event of dissolution; however, a loan provides little opportunity to participate in profits unless the interest rate is tied to the profitability of the corporation. Shares offer profit opportunities but have greater risks of loss of investment should the company fail. Cameron's investment—whether in shares or debt—can be tailored to address Cameron's desire to participate in profits while avoiding risk.

4. What factors should Adam consider in seeking to raise money by selling shares?

In attempting to raise money by issuing shares, Adam needs to consider a number of factors. Most importantly, both public and private sales involve a consideration from a financial perspective as to whether there is a market for the corporation's shares. As well, any issuance or sale of shares involves an assessment of the impact on the control of the corporation. Sales on the public market also involve requirements as specified by the relevant securities legislation. These requirements can be significant and costly.

Chapter Summary

The corporate form is prevalent and widespread. The characteristic that distinguishes it from the other basic forms for carrying on business is its separate legal status. This means that the owners are not liable for the debts and obligations of the corporation. It also means that those who are dealing with a corporation need to understand that the owner's risk is limited. Thus, if security is important, they should demand a personal guarantee.

A corporation may be incorporated federally or provincially. There are few distinct advantages of incorporating in one jurisdiction versus another. Prior to commencing the incorporation process, incorporators must decide on a share structure, that is, the classes and number of shares authorized for issuance. The share structure may be simple or complex depending on the needs of the investors.

The actual process of establishing a corporation is relatively simple, and essentially the same format is followed in all jurisdictions. It is a matter of completing and filing the correct forms with the appropriate government body. That said, the incorporation process is not without risks, such as the risk of choosing a name that is similar to that of another business. This risk can be substantially reduced by obtaining legal advice.

A corporation can be financed by equity or debt. Equity represents what the shareholders have invested in the corporation in return for shares. Debt consists of loans that have been made to the corporation. The issuance of shares and debt instruments such as bonds to the public is strictly regulated by securities laws.

PART FOUR

Chapter Study

Key Terms and Concepts

Questions for Review

1. What does limited liability mean?

2. Who are the corporation's internal stakeholders? Who are the corporation's external stakeholders?

3. When should a business incorporate federally, and when should it incorporate provincially?

4. What basic rights must attach to at least one class of shares?

5. A class of shares may include a combination of various rights and privileges. Name three examples of typical rights that may attach to a class of shares.

6. What is the difference between a widely held and a closely held corporation?

7. How can a corporation qualify as a private corporation in Ontario? What are the advantages of a corporation qualifying as a private corporation?

8. Are shares freely transferable? Explain.

9. What are the basic requirements for a corporate name?

10. What is a NUANS Report, and what is its purpose?

11. What is a shelf company, and what is its purpose?

12. Describe the process for incorporating a company.

13. Compare shares to bonds. Which is the more advantageous method of raising money?

14. What are the objectives of securities legislation? How are the objectives achieved?

15. All securities acts have been amended to provide a new statutory right of action for misrepresentations contained in secondary market disclosures. What is the difference between the primary market and the secondary market for securities? What is the new statutory right of action for purchasers in the secondary market? Explain.

16. What is meant by insider trading? Insider? Tippee?

17. Is all insider trading prohibited? Explain.

18. What is a prospectus? What is its purpose?

Questions for Critical Thinking

1. *Salomon v Salomon* stands for the proposition that the corporation has a separate existence from its shareholders. This means that creditors of a corporation do not have recourse against the shareholders' assets. Is this fair? Is it fair that creditors of a sole proprietorship seek the sole proprietor's personal assets? What is the justification for the difference in treatment?

2. As noted on pages 357–358, all provinces have adopted legislation that provides a right of action for investors in the secondary market who suffer damages from misleading disclosures. It is expected that these provisions will greatly facilitate class actions. There are, however some significant differences in the various regimes with respect to class actions. For example, Ontario's legislation provides that the winning party, including the winning party in a class action, is entitled to costs. There is no equivalent provision in the B.C. legislation and, under the B.C. *Class Proceedings Act*, costs generally cannot be awarded against the losing party in a class action. Which rule do you prefer—loser pays costs or loser does not pay costs in class actions? What is the likely effect on litigation of having a costs distinction?

3. Dual-class share structures are prevalent in Canada. There are roughly 80 companies listed on the Toronto Stock Exchange that use some form of dual-class, multiple-voting share structure. Included in this group are Bombardier Inc., Canadian Tire Corp., Power Corp., Rogers Communications Inc., Shaw Communications Inc., Tech Resources Ltd., and Telus Corp.[35] Why do you think dual-class structures have emerged in Canada?

4. The Internet has had a tremendous impact on the securities industry—it has spawned online brokerages, has emerged as the primary source of information for investors, and is the means by which businesses can distribute prospectuses, financial statements, news releases, and the like. It also poses considerable challenges as its global, invisible nature increases the likelihood of fraud. Because scam artists can anonymously and cheaply communicate with a vast number of people, they can readily spread rumours that result in the manipulation of market prices, trade in securities without being registered to do so, and distribute securities in nonexistent entities. What is the rationale for regulating trade in securities? Do you think the rationale changes when the commercial activity is conducted over the Internet?

5. The Supreme Court of Canada ruled that the federal government's draft legislation for the creation of a single national securities regulatory body was unconstitutional. One of the strongest arguments for the establishment of a single national securities regulatory is the need for effective enforcement of securities market conduct. How does a single national body, as opposed to 13 provincial and territorial bodies, improve enforcement?[36]

6. The acquittal of John Felderhof, the former chief geologist for Bre-X Minerals, and the settlement with Andrew Rankin, the former RBC Dominion Securities managing director (see page 359), represent serious setbacks for Canada's largest securities regulator and raise important questions about securities regulation in Canada. Based on the Felderhof and Rankin cases, what are some of the difficulties with securities regulation in Canada?

Situations for Discussion

1. In *Silver v IMAX Corp*, shareholders in a class action[37] against IMAX Corporation and certain directors and officers are seeking $500 million in damages and an additional $100 million in punitives. The shareholders allege that IMAX misrepresented its 2005 earnings revenue in press releases and other disclosures for the period 9 March 2006 to 9 August 2006. It is alleged that 2005 revenues were overstated because IMAX recognized revenues from theatres that had yet to open and that this overstatement artificially inflated the trading price of IMAX securities. On 9 March, IMAX shares traded on the Toronto Stock Exchange (TSX) at $11.94. On 9 August, IMAX issued a press release stating that the U.S. Securities and Exchange Commission had made an informal inquiry about the company's timing of revenue recognition. On 10 August, the price of IMAX shares dropped to $6.44 on the TSX.[38] What will the plaintiffs have to prove at trial to be successful? How do the secondary market liability amendments in securities legislation assist the plaintiffs? If the plaintiffs are successful, how will damages be calculated?

2. Steering Clear Ltd. is a manufacturer of an expensive automatic helmsman that is used to navigate ocean cruisers. Perry Jones ordered such a helmsman on behalf of a company called Cruisin' Ltd. The helmsman was supplied, but Cruisin' Ltd. did not pay its account. Because of this delinquency, Steering Clear Ltd. decided to investigate the background of Cruisin' Ltd. and discovered that it has a grand total of two issued shares—one held by Perry and the other by his wife. Perry has advised Steering Clear that the debtor company has only $5 in the bank and may have to go out of business soon. Steering Clear wants to sue Perry personally for the debt.[39] Will Steering Clear be successful? On what basis? What is the largest obstacle facing Steering Clear's potential action against Perry? What should Steering Clear have done differently from a business perspective?

35. Janet McFarland, "Stronach move not expected to bury culture of dual-class ownership" *The Globe and Mail* (25 May 2010) at <http://www.theglobeandmail.com/globe-investor/stronach-move-not-expected-to-bury-culture>.
36. Poonam Puri, "The case keeps growing for a national securities regulator", *The Lawyers Weekly* (3 December 2010) at 5.
37. The class action was certified in 2009 and the Superior Court of Ontario has denied permission for IMAX Corporation to appeal the certification. See: *Silver v IMAX*, 2011 ONSC 1035.
38. John Jaffey, "Class action lawsuit to test new shareholder rights law", *The Lawyers Weekly* (22 September 2006) at 1. The class action was certified in 2009 and the Superior Court of Ontario has denied permission for IMAX Corporation to appeal the certification. See: *Silver v IMAX*, 2011 ONSC 1035.
39. Based on *Henry Browne & Sons Ltd v Smith*, [1964] 2 Lloyd's Rep 477 (QB).

PART FOUR

3. Sophie Smith has an opportunity to open a designer shoe store in a new mall. She believes that the shoe store will be quite lucrative because of the mall's location adjacent to a condominium development catering to young professionals. To exploit favourable tax laws, Sophie has decided to incorporate a company, and to save money she is going to do it herself. She knows that she will need a name for her corporation. Some of names that she is considering are Shoe Store Inc., Princess Sophie's Shoes Ltd., DownTown Shoes Inc., Sophie Smith Ltd., Nu Shuz Inc., Sophie Smith Clothing and Apparel Inc. and, simply, Sophie's Shoes. Are there any problems with the names that Sophie is considering for her corporation? Explain. Assume that Sophie has XZONIC Shoes Inc. approved as the corporation's name. What rights does registration of a corporate name give Sophie?

4. Dr. Jody Rice set up a veterinary hospital in Annapolis Royal, Nova Scotia. She registered the name Annapolis Royal Veterinary Hospital and received a certificate of registration, verifying approval of the name. Several months later, Dr Rice received a letter from the registry office directing her to change her business' name because of a complaint from Dr. Mike McGowan of Annapolis Animal Hospital Inc. Is Dr. Rice required to change the name of her business?[40] Explain.

5. Globex Foreign Exchange Corporation (Globex) is an Edmonton-based currency trader. It entered into a contract with 3077860 Nova Scotia Limited (Numberco) for the purchase by Numberco of nearly 1.2 million British pounds. Carl Launt is the sole director and shareholder of Numberco. He funded Numberco with a deposit of $124 676 Canadian dollars to effect the trade with Globex. Numberco failed to pay for the rest of the funds purchased and Globex incurred a loss of nearly $90 000 when it resold the currency. Globex commenced an action for breach of contract against Globex and discovered that it was a defunct company with no assets.[41] Is there any legal basis for holding Launt responsible for the unpaid debt of Numberco owed to Globex? Could Globex successfully argue that Numberco was Launt's agent? How could Globex have better protected itself in this situation?

6. In 2010, Frank Stronach relinquished control of auto parts giant Magna International. Since 1978 Magna has had a dual-class, multiple-vote share structure. Through this structure, Stronach was able to control the company despite owning just 0.6 percent of its 113 million shares because his 720 000 Class B share each carried 300 votes, while the remaining 112 million Class A shares had one vote each. In return for cancelling the Class B shares, the Stronach family trust received US$300 million in cash and 9 million new Class A shares. In addition, Stronach received a four-year consulting contract and a 27 percent stake in Magna's electric car business. It is estimated that the deal was worth $1 billion—an 1800 percent premium on the value of Stronach's shares. Seventy-five percent of the Class A shareholders voted for the deal and subsequently the Ontario Superior Court[42] approved the deal. Market reaction to the deal was also favourable—on the day following the announcement of the deal, Magna shares closed up 14 percent on the Toronto Stock Exchange.[43] What are the problems with dual-class share structures? What are the advantages? Do you think the deal to eliminate the dual-class structure at Magna was fair?

7. In June 2003, Sam Waksal, the cofounder and former CEO of ImClone was sentenced to seven years in prison and fined $4 million on charges of insider trading. He was found guilty of leaking confidential information to family and friends in the days leading up to the release of a federal ruling that rejected the company's Erbitux cancer drug. Among the friends said to have been tipped was Martha Stewart. She sold nearly 4000 shares of ImClone on the day prior to the regulator's announcement. The sale saved her about US$51 000. Stewart pleaded not guilty to charges of insider trading, conspiracy, obstruction of justice, and making false statements to investigators. She argued that she had an agreement with her stockbroker to sell the shares if

---

40. Bruce Erskine, "Veterinarian doggone mad", *The Chronicle Herald* (2 March 2006) at C1.
41. *Globex Foreign Exchange Corporation v Launt*, 2010 NSSC 229.
42. *Magna International Inc,(Re)* [2010] OJ No 3454.
43. Tony Van Alphen, "Vote would loosen Stronach's grip on Magna" *the star.com* (7 May 2010) at <http://www.thestar.com/business/companies/magna/article/805365—vote-could-loosen-str>; Michael McKiernan, "$1-billion Magna deal's fairness scrutinized", *Canadian Lawyer Magazine* (21 March 2011) at <http://www.canadianlawyermag.com/$1-billion-magna-deals-fairness-scrutinized.html>.

the price went below $60. The prosecution said Stewart had misled investigators by saying she did not recall if her stockbroker had called on the day she sold her shares. The presiding judge dropped the insider-trading charge and a jury convicted her of conspiracy, obstruction of justice, and making false statements to investigators. Stewart was sentenced to five months in prison, five months of house arrest, two years' probation, and a fine of $30 000. In January 2006, a federal appeals court in New York upheld her conviction. Was Martha Stewart an insider in relation to ImClone? What are the problems with insider trading? Should insiders be prohibited from trading in shares? Why is it difficult to prove improper insider trading?

8. Alimentation Couche-Tard Inc. is the Canadian leader in the convenience store industry. At 8:30 a.m. on 6 October 2003, Couche-Tard publicly announced a deal to purchase the 2013-store Circle K chain. Completion of the deal would make Couche-Tard the fourth largest convenience store operators in North America. When trading opened on the Toronto Stock Exchange at 9:30 a.m., the company's Class B stock was up 40 cents at $17.50. The price steadily gained all day and closed at $21, for a gain of $3.90. Within five minutes of the opening, Roger Longré, a Couche-Tard director, bought 1500 shares and by 10:30 he had bought a further 2500. At the end of the day, he had a one-day gain, on paper, of $11 372.[44] Did Longré breach any legal requirements? Did he breach any ethical requirements? Should insiders be prohibited from trading prior to earning announcements and after major announcements? Should insiders be required to clear all proposed trades in the company's securities with a designated in-house trading monitor?

For more study tools, visit http://www.NELSONbrain.com.

---

44. "Insider trading: A special report", *The Globe and Mail* (18 December 2003) at B6–7.

CHAPTER 16

The Corporate Form: Operational Matters

Objectives

After studying this chapter, you should have an understanding of

- the liabilities of a corporation
- the duties and liabilities of corporate directors and officers
- the rights and liabilities of shareholders and creditors
- how the corporation is terminated

JACOBS STOCK PHOTOGRAPHY/PHOTODISC/GETTY IMAGES

Business Law in Practice

IK Enterprises Ltd., incorporated under the *Canada Business Corporations Act*, has been in operation for a little over a year. Adam owns 50 percent of the common shares and Diane the remaining 50 percent. Adam's father, Cameron, was issued 100 preferred shares. Adam and Diane are directors and officers of the corporation, and Cameron is an officer, although not a director. He is the president of the corporation.

The company has done reasonably well with the marketing and selling of its enhanced voice-recognition system for computers. Although demand was less than anticipated, sales exceeded $500 000 for the first year of operations. There is, however, a major problem confronting the company.

Diane has recently come across a software program that translates computer output into French, Spanish, and German, which she thinks would be quite compatible with the company's present product. She is interested in buying the rights to the translation product for IK Enterprises. Adam, however, is not interested in expansion and wants to concentrate on a limited product line. Diane is contemplating forming another company to exploit this opportunity if the disagreement between her and Adam cannot be resolved. Cameron does not want to get involved in the dispute at all because he has much more immediate concerns.

Cameron believes that IK Enterprises is plagued by lax standards in its day-to-day operations. From Cameron's perspective, this is what Adam and Diane should focus their attention on. For example, Cameron has discovered that IK Enterprises has not been deducting and remitting income tax on salary paid to certain employees. Cameron not only finds this unacceptable from an accounting perspective, but also worries about IK Enterprises' liability and fears that he may have personal liability for this "oversight."

(Continued on the next page)

1. Is IK Enterprises liable for the failure to deduct and remit income tax? Does Cameron, as an officer of IK Enterprises, have any personal liability for the failure to deduct and remit the taxes?
2. What obligations do Cameron, Diane, and Adam have as corporate officers and directors?
3. How can the disagreement between Adam and Diane be resolved?
4. Are there any problems with Diane forming her own company to take advantage of the translation product opportunity?
5. What are Cameron's rights as a shareholder if he does not like how Diane and Adam are managing the company?

Corporate Liability

A corporation is a legal person in the eyes of the law. The corollary is that the corporation is responsible for its own actions. The responsibility of the corporation is, however, complicated by the necessity of corporations acting through human agents. The law has developed rules regarding how a corporation can be said to have committed a tort, committed a crime or regulatory offence, or entered a contract. These rules are particularly important to stakeholders such as Cameron, because they determine the legal consequences of corporate behaviour. A summary of the rules regarding liability for corporate conduct can be found in Figure 16.3 on page 392.

Liability in Tort

A corporation can experience two distinct kinds of liability in tort: primary liability and vicarious liability.

A corporation has primary liability for a tort when, in law, it is regarded as the entity that actually committed the tort in question. The idea of a corporation having primary liability is inherently problematic since a corporation, as noted above, can work only through human agents. How can a corporation commit a tort when it does not have a mind of its own and does not have a physical existence?

The courts have overcome this hurdle by developing what is known as the **identification theory** of corporate liability.[1] A corporation has liability—and could therefore be described as directly "at fault"—when the person committing the wrong was the corporation's "directing mind and will."

The theory seeks to determine which person or persons are the directing mind of the corporation. When that person (or persons) commits a tort related to the business enterprise, this conduct is identified with or attributed to the corporation itself. The liability of the corporation is thereby made direct—not vicarious—because in law, the conduct of the directing mind is the conduct of the corporation.

Identification theory
A theory specifying that a corporation is liable when the person committing the wrong is the corporation's directing mind.

PART FOUR

---

1. *Lennard's Carrying Co v Asiatic Petroleum Co,* [1915] AC 705.

Generally, it is the highly placed corporate officers who are classified as "directing" minds, while low-level employees are not. Whether a mid-range employee would be a directing mind is a more complicated and fact-specific inquiry. A corporation may have more than one directing mind. Each may be responsible for a different aspect of the corporation's business. For example, the vice president for marketing may be the corporation's directing mind in relation to the marketing function, whereas the vice president for finance may be the directing mind in relation to finance.

A corporation has vicarious liability[2] when the tort has been committed by an agent or employee who is not a directing mind of the corporation. The law of vicarious liability does not distinguish between the natural employer/principal—that is, a living, breathing human being—and the artificial employer/principal—that is, a corporation. Instead, the same principle applies to both.

Liability in Contract

While there is no reason the identification theory could not be used as a way of assessing a corporation's liability in contract, the courts generally have not followed this approach. Instead, agency law largely determines when a corporation is liable on a contract and when it is not.

A corporation is bound by the actions of the agent only if the agent is acting within his actual or apparent authority. For example, if Diane were to enter a contract on behalf of IK Enterprises to purchase the rights to translation software, IK Enterprises would be bound to the contract so long as Diane had the actual or apparent authority to enter the contract. Historically, an agent's apparent authority could be limited by filing with the incorporation documents a specific limitation of the agent's authority. As these documents were publicly filed, outsiders were deemed to have notice of them and to have read their contents. This was known as the doctrine of constructive notice and produced commercial inconvenience, since the only way that an outsider could fully protect herself would be to go down to the registry office and review what the company had filed there. The doctrine has been abolished,[3] meaning that outsiders can now generally rely on the apparent authority of agents. In such a case, the corporation would be liable on the contract.

To avoid personal liability, the person signing a document on behalf of a corporation should ensure that the document contains a clause clearly indicating that the person is signing on behalf of the corporation and is not signing in her personal capacity. This precaution is equally important in the case of pre-incorporation contracts.

Pre-incorporation contracts are contracts that have been entered into by the company's promoters[4] on behalf of the corporation before it has even been created. Such contracts are governed by federal and provincial corporate law statutes, which permit the company to adopt the contract—something that was impossible to do at common law. When adoption occurs, the corporation assumes liability on the contract. The promoter can avoid liability so long as the pre-incorporation contract expressly indicates that the promoter was acting on

---

2. Vicarious liability is discussed in Chapters 10 and 20.
3. See, for example, *Canada Business Corporations Act*, RSC 1985, c C-44, s 17.
4. A promoter is someone who participates in setting up a corporation.

behalf of the corporation.[5] Pre-incorporation contracts can be problematic if they do not indicate clearly who is intended to be liable[6] and if the corporation fails to come into existence.

From a risk management perspective, people would probably do well to avoid pre-incorporation contracts altogether. Although such contracts are sometimes necessary to take advantage of a valuable business opportunity that just cannot wait, it is usually possible to find a corporate vehicle quickly—such as through the purchase of a shelf company. In this way, the corporation is immediately in place and can enter the contemplated contract directly.

Criminal and Regulatory Liability

Criminal Liability

The criminal liability of a corporation poses the same conceptual problems as tort liability. As Baron Thurlow, L.C., observed in the 18th century, "Did you ever expect a corporation to have a conscience, when it has no soul to be damned and no body to be kicked?"

The judiciary solved this problem by adapting the identification theory to the criminal law scenario. The theory maintains that a corporation has committed a crime if the person who committed the crime was a directing mind of the corporation and he committed it in the course of his duties and did so mostly for the benefit of the corporation.[7] A directing mind of a corporation is an individual who exercises decision-making authority in matters of corporate policy. This approach to corporate criminal liability proved to be problematic because of the difficulty in proving beyond a reasonable doubt that the directing mind behaved in a criminal manner. This problem was highlighted by the lack of criminal convictions in the1992 Westray mine explosion in Nova Scotia.[8] In response to the Westray public inquiry's findings, the federal government amended the *Criminal Code*.[9] The amendments increased the scope of potential criminal liability of corporations[10] by expanding the range of individuals whose actions can trigger liability, by broadening corporate responsibility for all criminal offences, and by increasing the penalties.

Prior to the amendments, a corporation could be liable for a criminal offence only if the directing mind of the corporation committed the offence. The amendments expand the range of individuals whose actions can trigger liability of the corporation to senior officers. These are individuals who play an important role in the establishment of the organization's policies or are responsible for managing an important aspect of the organizations' activities. The definition focuses on the function of the individual, rather than any particular title.

The amendments also address both crimes requiring proof of knowledge or intent and crimes requiring proof of negligence. For offences that require intent,[11] an organization will

---

5. *Supra* note 3, s 14(4): "Exemption from personal liability—If expressly so provided in the written contract, a person who purported to act in the name of or on behalf of the corporation before it came into existence is not ... bound by the contract."
6. The legislative provisions protecting the promoter from personal liability have been strictly construed by the courts. For example, in *Landmark Inns of Canada Ltd v Horeak* (1982), 18 Sask R 30, 2 WWR 377 (QB), the court held that merely naming the yet-to-be incorporated corporation as a party to the contract was insufficient to relieve the promoter of personal liability. The contract must also contain an express provision that specifically relieves him of liability.
7. A corporation is not liable for an offence committed by a "directing mind" that is totally unrelated to her corporate position. For example, a corporation is not liable for a break and enter committed by the president on her way home from the office.
8. On 9 May 1992, 26 miners died in an underground methane explosion at the Westray coal mine in Plymouth, Nova Scotia. The employees of the mine were working in unsafe conditions that were known to the corporation yet criminal proceedings against the corporation and the mine's managers were unsuccessful.
9. RSC 1985, c C-46.
10. The amendments extended criminal liability to "organizations," which includes corporations, companies, partnerships, trade unions, and any association of persons that was created for a common purpose, has a structure, and holds itself out as an association of persons.
11. Most crimes in the *Criminal Code* fall within this category; examples include fraud, theft, and bribery.

be criminally liable if a senior officer, while acting in the scope of his or her authority and intending at least in part to benefit the organization, either actively engages in unsafe conduct, directs representatives[12] to do it, or knows about the unsafe conduct but does nothing or not enough to put a stop to it, and death or injury results. The effect of the changes is that it is no longer necessary that the intent and the guilty act of a criminal offence reside in the same person. Also, senior officers are now under a positive obligation to act when they have knowledge that an offence has been or will be committed; failure to act will result in corporate criminal liability. For offences based on negligence,[13] an organization can be convicted if any representative providing services for the organization causes injury or death by unsafe conduct and the senior officer or officers in charge of the activities of the representative departs markedly from the reasonable standard of care necessary to prevent the incident. These changes broaden negligence offences by allowing the combined conduct of two individuals, who individually may not be acting in a manner that is careless or reckless, to constitute the necessary elements of the crime in order to hold the corporation responsible.

The amendments provide for stiffer penalties and corporate probation orders. A less serious summary conviction offence carries a fine of up to $100 000 (an increase from $25 000) and fines for more serious indictable offences remain with no prescribed limits. The legislation also enumerates factors that the courts must consider when setting fines, including moral blameworthiness (i.e., the economic advantage gained by the organization by committing the crime), public interest (i.e., the cost of investigation and prosecution, the need to keep the organization in business), and the prospects of rehabilitation (remedial steps directed to preventing the likelihood of a subsequent offence). A corporate probation order may involve conditions such as providing restitution to victims, publishing the offence in the media, and implementing policies and procedures. Its purpose is to allow the court to oversee and regulate an organization's efforts to reform.

BUSINESS APPLICATION OF THE LAW

Death in the Workplace

On Christmas Eve 2009, four construction workers who were repairing concrete balconies at an apartment building died when their swing stage scaffolding broke and they plummeted 13 storeys to the ground. A fifth worker suffered severe leg and spinal injuries and a sixth worker, who had attached himself to a lifeline, was uninjured. Following an investigation, Toronto police charged Metron Construction Corporation, two directors including the President, and a project manager with four counts of criminal negligence causing death and one count of criminal negligence causing bodily harm. In June 2012, Metron pleaded guilty to one count of criminal negligence causing death and was fined $200 000. Criminal charges against the President were dropped. However, he was convicted of breaching the province's

CARLOS OSORIO/GETSTOCK.COM

What is an appropriate punishment for a corporation convicted of criminal negligence causing death?

---

12. A representative includes everyone working or affiliated with an organization, such as a director, partner, employee, agent, or contractor.
13. Examples of negligence-based crimes include storing a firearm in a careless manner, operating a motor vehicle in a manner dangerous to the public, and showing wanton and reckless disregard for the lives or safety of others.

Occupational Health and *Safety Act* and was fined $90 000. In addition, Metron and the President were ordered to pay a victim surcharge totally $52 500. Criminal charges against the other individuals are still pending.

This is the first Ontario case where a corporation has been convicted of criminal negligence causing death since the 2004 amendments to the *Criminal Code* broadened the scope of potential criminal liability of corporations. The only previous conviction post amendments occurred in Quebec in 2008. Transpavé Inc., a Quebec corporation, was charged with criminal negligence causing death after 23-year-old Steve L'Ecuyer was crushed to death by heavy machinery at a plant in Saint-Eustache, Quebec. Investigations by Quebec's Health and Safety Board and provincial police found that the company had allowed L'Ecuyer to operate the machine with its motion detector safety mechanism deactivated. They also determined that he was not properly trained to operate the machinery. Transpavé pleaded guilty and was fined $110 000.[14]

Critical Analysis: Do the penalties in these cases send a clear message to businesses of the importance of ensuring worker safety?

Postscript: Ontario's Ministry of the Attorney General is appealing the $200 000 fine against Metron Construction.

Sources: "Deadly scaffold leads to #340K in penalties", *CBC News* (13 July 2012) online: CBC News <http://www.cbc.ca/news/canada/toronto/story/2012/07/13/toronto-metron-fine.html> ; "Toronto scaffold death bring criminal charges", *CBC News* (13 October 2010) online: *CBC News* <http://www.cbc.ca/news/canada/toronto/story/2010/10/13/toronto-scaffolding-charges.html>; Luis Millan, "Company fined $110,000 for death of employee", *The Lawyers Weekly* (28 March 2008) 1.

Regulatory Offences

In addition to criminal liability under the *Criminal Code*, a corporation faces liability pursuant to a wide range of statutory enactments related to taxation, human rights, pay equity, employment standards, consumer protection, unfair or anticompetitive business practices, occupational health and safety, and environmental protection, to name a few. The relevant legislation often imposes penalties on the corporation, and sometimes on its directors and officers, including civil liability for damages.

The offences alluded to above are known as regulatory offences. They have a criminal aspect because they involve some kind of punishable conduct that is contrary to the public interest, such as polluting streams.

Owing to the large number of **regulatory offences** affecting business, as well as the expense and public relations problems associated with their commission, corporations have become increasingly concerned with assessing and managing their exposure. Although it is difficult to gauge the extent to which corporate liability in this area has increased, there have been dramatic examples of corporations being subjected to regulatory penalties. Consider, for example, the following:

Regulatory offence
An offence contrary to the public interest.

- In 2011, Bell Canada agreed to pay an administrative monetary penalty of $10 million, after a Competition Bureau investigation concluded that it was making misleading representations about the prices offered for its services.[15]

- In 2010, Syncrude Canada Ltd. was fined $3 million after being found guilty of the deaths of 1,606 birds on its tailings ponds. It had been charged under the *Alberta Environmental Protection and Enhancement Act* for storing a hazardous substance in a manner enabling it to contaminate wildlife, and under the federal *Migratory Bird Convention Act* for depositing substances harmful to migratory birds in areas that they frequent.[16]

---

14. *R v Transpavé Inc*, 2008 QCCQ 1598 (CanLII).
15. Competition Bureau Canada, Media Release, "Competition bureau reaches agreement with Bell Canada requiring bell to pay $10 million for misleading advertising" (Ottawa: Competition Bureau, 28 June 2011) online: Competition Bureau <http://www.competitionbureau.gc.ca/eic/site/cb-bc.nsf/eng/03388.html>.
16. Josh Wingrove, "$3-million fine a drop in the barrel for Syncrude", *The Globe and Mail* (23 October 2010) A20.

PART FOUR

- In 2011, Wabush Mines was fined $80 000 after it pleaded guilty to two charges under the Newfoundland's *Occupational Health and Safety Act*. An employee suffered broken bones in the ankle and foot in an incident at the company's Labrador operation.[17]

- In 2010, Panasonic Corporation and Embraco North America Inc. were each fined $1.5 million for price-fixing contrary to the *Competition Act*.[18]

IK Enterprises' operations may be affected by many legislative provisions. For example, the *Income Tax Act*[19] requires that every person paying salary, wages, or other remuneration withhold a prescribed amount of income tax. IK Enterprises is a person paying salary so it comes within the provisions of the legislation. Its failure to deduct and remit income taxes can trigger penalties including, for a first offence, a fine of 10 percent of the amount owing. Liability under this taxation legislation is strict,[20] and defences are therefore rare.[21]

What factors should the courts consider when fining a corporation that causes the death of wildlife?

STOCKBYTE/THINKSTOCK

Directors and Officers

The directors, who are elected by shareholders, manage or supervise the management of the business and the affairs of the corporation.[22] In addition to this general authority, directors have specific powers and obligations set out in legislation. For example, directors can

17. "Labrador mine fined $80 000 for two safety violations", *The Canadian Press* (26 July 2011) online: levittsafety <http://www.levitt-safety.com/training/2011/07/labrador-mine-fined-80000-for-two-safety-violations/>.
18. Competition Bureau Canada, *Panasonic Corporation pleads guilty to price-fixing conspiracy*, (Ottawa: Competition Bureau, 3 November 2010) online: Competition Bureau Canada <http://www.competitionbureau.gc.ca/eic/site/cb-bc.nsf/eng/03310.html>.
19. RSC 1985, c 1 (5th Supp), s 153(1).
20. The vast majority of regulatory offences are strict liability offences. This means that the accused may avoid liability if he can show that he acted with due diligence or took all reasonable care. Few offences impose absolute liability, that is, liability is imposed for doing the act, and it is not open to the accused to show he was without fault.
21. Vern Krishna, "Directors' liability for corporate taxes", *The Lawyers Weekly* (14 July 2000) 5.
22. This general power may be circumscribed by the bylaws or by a unanimous shareholder agreement.

declare dividends, call shareholder meetings, adopt bylaws, and issue shares. Directors are, however, not usually in a position to carry out the actual management themselves; generally they are authorized to appoint officers to carry out many of their duties and exercise most of their powers.[23] This power of delegation does not, however, relieve the directors of ultimate responsibility for the management of the corporation.

BUSINESS APPLICATION OF THE LAW

Corporate Governance Reforms

Corporate scandals at companies such as Enron and WorldCom in the United States and Hollinger in Canada have shaken investor confidence in the competence and integrity of management. They have also prompted shareholders to demand better accountability from public companies. In response, the United States passed the *Sarbanes-Oxley Act* in 2002. The Act introduced far-reaching provisions to strengthen accountability of corporate officers, improve corporate disclosure, enhance auditing standards, and limit conflicts of interests.

Following the American lead, Canada has also gradually introduced corporate and securities law reform. The Canadian Securities Administrators[24] have introduced a series of national policies, including rules requiring CEO/CFO certification of annual and quarterly reports, rules relating to new standards and an expanded role for the audit committee, rules establishing the Canadian Public Accountability Board to oversee the auditing profession, and rules dealing with the disclosure by Canadian public corporations of their governance practices.[25]

Regulation of corporate governance is not new. In 1995, the Toronto Stock Exchange (TSE) commissioned a report to examine corporate governance in Canada.[26] Also known as the Dey Report, it made 14 recommendations for the reform of corporate governance in public companies. Included were recommendations that a majority of the board be composed of directors who were independent of management and free of any interest that could interfere with their ability to act in the best interests of the corporation; that every board adopt a structure such as having a chair who was independent of management, to allow the board to act independently of management; and that the audit committee be composed of outside directors. The TSE adopted the non-mandatory best practices and required listed companies to

annually disclose their practices for comparison with the TSE standards. Since then, there have been other reports on corporate governance in Canada[27] and further amendments to the TSE guidelines. The Canadian Securities Administrators (CSA) rules are similar to the TSE guidelines. Effective from 30 June 2005, the Canadian Securities Commissions adopted the CSA polices on corporate governance ("best practices")[28] and the disclosure of corporate governance practices.[29]

The corporate governance "best practices" include the following:

- that a board have a majority of *independent* directors, that the chair of the board be independent, and that independent directors hold regularly scheduled meetings

- that a board adopt a *written mandate* that explicitly acknowledges responsibility for the stewardship of the company; the written mandate should include expectations and responsibilities of directors and measures to receive feedback from shareholders

- that a board develop clear *position descriptions* for the chair of the board and all committee chairs

- that a board ensure that new directors undertake a comprehensive orientation and provide continuing board *education* for all board members

- that a board adopt a written *code of business conduct and ethics* and monitor compliance with that code

- that a board have *nominating and compensation committees*, both comprising independent directors, and both of whose written charters clearly set out the committee's purpose, responsibilities, operations, and member qualifications

- that each board and committee member be *regularly assessed* as to his *effectiveness*

(Continued)

PART FOUR

---

23. Note that some matters, such as declaring dividends and approving the annual financial statements, may not be delegated.
24. A body composed of the 13 provincial and territorial securities regulators, whose role is to coordinate and harmonize securities regulation policy across Canada.
25. The CSA rules are called multilateral instruments (MIs) and national instruments (NLs). These provisions have been adopted by all jurisdictions in Canada with the exception of British Columbia, which has not adopted the rules with respect to the CEO/CFO board certification and audit committees. Most provisions are now in force.
26. Peter Dey, *Where Were the Directors? Guidelines for Improved Corporate Governance in Canada,* (Toronto: Toronto Stock Exchange, 1994).
27. Joint Committee on Corporate Governance, *Beyond Compliance: Building a Governance Culture, Final* (Toronto: Toronto Stock Exchange, Canadian Venture Exchange, Canadian Institute of Chartered Accountants, 2001).
28. National Instrument 58-201 *Corporate Governance Guidelines.*
29. National Policy 58-101 *Disclosure of Corporate Governance Practices.*

The corporate governance guidelines are not mandatory; rather, publicly traded companies are encouraged to consider them in developing their own corporate governance practices. However, companies are required to describe their adopted corporate governance practices and, where the adopted practice is different than the "best practice," explain how what is being done satisfies the objectives of the "best practice."

Critical Analysis: Are there any problems with having a majority of a board of directors composed of independent directors? Should good governance practices be mandated or can the market be relied on to impose good governance practices?

Duties of Directors and Officers

In exercising their management function, directors and officers have obligations contained in two broad categories: a fiduciary duty and a duty of competence.

The Fiduciary Duty

This duty requires directors and officers to act honestly and in good faith with a view to the best interests of the corporation. They cannot allow themselves to favour one particular group of shareholders, for example, because their duty is not to that group but rather to the corporation as a whole. One of the central principles informing fiduciary duties in corporate law can be summarized as follows: directors and officers must not allow their personal interest to conflict with their duty to the corporation. Not surprisingly, then, the fiduciary principle arises in multiple circumstances, two of which are explored below.

Self-dealing contract
A contract in which a fiduciary has a conflict of interest.

The Self-Dealing Contract   To understand how a **self-dealing contract** works, assume the following scenario. IK Enterprises requires some office furniture, which Adam just so happens to be in a position to supply. He has several reasonably nice executive desks stored in his basement and is willing to sell them to the corporation. Adam is now in a conflict-of-interest situation.

As director of IK Enterprises Ltd., Adam is obligated to try to buy the furniture at as low a price as possible. As vendor of the furniture, however, Adam may be motivated by self-interest to sell the furniture at as high a price as possible. In this way, his duty to the corporation and his self-interest may collide because Adam is on both sides of the contract. (See Figure 16.1.)

FIGURE 16.1
Self-Dealing Contract

Adam (the corporate director) ➡ buys from ➡ Adam (the individual)

In law, Adam is said to be in a self-dealing contract: he is dealing with himself in the purchase and sale of the office furniture.

Many jurisdictions have enacted procedures through which self-dealing contracts are permissible. The idea is to ensure that the corporation is not "ripped off" and, at the same time, to avoid a blanket prohibition on self-dealing contracts since some of them could be beneficial to the company. Under the *Canada Business Corporations Act*, for example, Adam's contract to sell furniture to his own company will be enforceable provided that

- Adam discloses the contract to the corporation in writing

- Adam does not participate in any vote of the directors approving the contract

- the contract is fair and reasonable to the corporation[30]

Failure to follow these statutory provisions gives the corporation the right to ask a court for a remedy, including that the contract be set aside or "cancelled" on any terms the court sees fit.

Corporate Opportunities Another area in which conflicts of interest frequently arise concerns **corporate opportunities.** Directors and officers are often required to assess any number of projects in which their corporation could become involved. These projects are known in law as "corporate opportunities"—they are opportunities to do business that the company can pursue or decline. If the directors and officers were permitted to take up any of these opportunities for themselves, problems very much like the ones present in the self-dealing contract scenario would arise.

Corporate opportunity
A business opportunity in which the corporation has an interest.

Assume that IK Enterprises has been approached by an Ontario company that is in the business of educating executives in the latest technology available for the workplace. That company would like to work with IK Enterprises to create a course on voice-recognition systems, the revenue potential of which appears to be very high. Adam is in a conflict-of-interest situation. As a director, he is required to assess the corporate opportunity on its own merits. As an individual, however, because he is interested in the contract for himself, he is motivated by self-interest. Put another way, if Adam were permitted to pursue the opportunity himself, he would be tempted—in his capacity as director—to turn down the project, not because it was in the best interests of the corporation to do so but because he wanted to present the course himself.

Given her fiduciary duty as a director, Diane must proceed cautiously if she is still determined to pursue the translation product opportunity. Provided that Diane secures Adam's and Cameron's fully informed consent, perhaps in the form of a directors' resolution and a shareholders' resolution, there is no obvious legal impediment to her proceeding to develop the translation product. She is being aboveboard and acting fairly *vis-à-vis* IK Enterprises. Since IK Enterprises does not want to pursue the opportunity, it would be highly unlikely that a court would decide that Diane was in breach of her fiduciary duty to IK Enterprises by taking the opportunity for herself.

---

30. *Supra* note 3, s 120.

LANDMARK CASE

Canadian Aero Service Ltd v O'Malley, [1974] SCR 592, 40 DLR (3d) 371

THE HISTORICAL CONTEXT: The Supreme Court's decision in this case is the leading analysis of the principles underlying the corporate opportunity doctrine in Canada. The case is also important because of the court's recognition that officers may owe fiduciary duties to the corporation and a director or officer may be precluded from appropriating a business opportunity even after she resigns.

FACTUAL BACKGROUND: On behalf of their company, Canadian Aero Service Ltd. (Canaero), the president and executive vice president had been negotiating to win an aerial mapping contract in Guyana. Subsequently, both officers left Canaero and set up their own company, Terra Surveys Limited. Terra began to pursue the very same line of work as Canaero and successfully bid on the aerial mapping contract in Guyana. Canaero brought an action against Terra and its former executives for improperly taking Canaero's corporate opportunity.

THE LEGAL QUESTION: Were the former executives in breach of their fiduciary duty to Canaero? Did the fact that the two had resigned and then, some time later, acquired the opportunity for themselves mean that there was no liability?

RESOLUTION: The former executives were held liable to account to Canaero for the profits they made under the contract. They had breached their fiduciary duties by taking something that belonged to the corporation. In determining whether the appropriation of an opportunity is a breach of fiduciary duty, the court suggested an examination of factors such as these:

- the position or office held by the directors and officers (the higher they are in the organization, the higher their duty)
- the nature of the corporate opportunity (how clearly was the opportunity identified by the corporation and how close was the corporation to acquiring the opportunity?)
- the director's or managerial officer's relation to the opportunity (was the opportunity one that the fiduciary worked on or had responsibility for?)
- the amount of knowledge the directors and officers possessed and the circumstances in which it was obtained
- the time between when the opportunity arose and when the officers took the opportunity for themselves
- the circumstances under which the employment relationship between the officers and the company terminated (was termination due to retirement, resignation, or discharge?)

Because the former officers violated their fiduciary duty, any profit gained—even if it was not at the expense of their former company—had to be given to the company. That they had resigned before pursuing the opportunity did not change the analysis.

CRITICAL ANALYSIS: When do you think a director of a corporation should be able to take advantage of a business opportunity? In other words, when is a business opportunity her own and when does it belong to the company she serves as director?

ETHICAL CONSIDERATIONS

Corporate Social Responsibility and Directors' Duties

Corporate Social Responsibility (CSR) is a term without a precise definition. It is used generally to encompass a business' policies and practices in relation to such issues as investment in community outreach, the creation and maintenance of employment, consumer protection, environmental sustainability, and the like. In short, CSR is about companies moving beyond mere compliance with laws to integrating social responsibility into their decision-making processes. Examples of CSR are Loblaw's efforts to divert millions of plastic bags from landfill sites, CIBC sponsoring "The Run for the Cure" to help the battle against breast cancer, Bombardier's practice of stripping and salvaging components of jets for reuse, and Edelman Canada's participation in a program that gives a little bit of money and a whole

Should governments pass legislation requiring corporate social responsibility?

© iSTOCKPHOTO.COM/CHRISTINE GLADE

lot of manpower to organizations that serve children and youth.

The concept of CSR is underpinned by the notion that business is accountable to a wide range of stakeholders, including employees, suppliers, customers, government, non-governmental organizations, and the community. CSR, however, is not enshrined in the legal system.[31] Corporate legislation gives little recognition to stakeholders, such as employees and the community within which the business is located, who may have an interest in corporate decisions. For example, directors, who are charged with the responsibility of managing a corporation, have a duty to act honestly and in good faith with a view to the best interests of the corporation. This fiduciary duty is owed to the corporation—not to stakeholders. The Supreme Court of Canada in *Peoples Department Stores v Wise*[32] stated, "At all times, directors and officers owe their fiduciary obligation to the corporation. The interests of the corporation are not to be confused with the interests of the creditors or those of any other stakeholders." The court also stated, "We accept as an accurate statement of the law that in determining whether they are acting with a view to the best interests of the corporation it may be legitimate, given all the circumstances of a given case, for the board of directors to consider *inter alia* the interests of shareholders, employees, suppliers, creditors, consumers, governments, and the environment." In essence, the court stated that directors may consider the interests of various stakeholders—but they are not bound to consider their interests. In *BCE v 1976 Debentureholders*,[33] the Supreme Court of Canada opined that the directors are to resolve conflicts between the interests of different stakeholders in accordance with their fiduciary duty to act in the best interests of the corporation, having regard to all relevant considerations, including the need to treat the affected stakeholders fairly, commensurate with the corporation's duties as a "responsible corporate citizen." The Court did not elaborate on the nature of the corporation's duties as a responsible corporate citizen.

Critical Analysis: Do you think the Supreme Court of Canada's language in BCE is signalling a shift towards a legal model that requires directors to consider the interests of all stakeholders in decision making? Regardless of legal requirements, CSR is becoming increasingly important to business. What factors are pushing business toward CSR? What can business gain from being socially responsible? What are the risks?

The Duty of Competence

This duty requires directors and officers to exercise the care, diligence, and skill that a reasonably prudent person would exercise in comparable circumstances. Put more informally, directors and officers must meet a general standard of competence.

At one time, directors had very minimal obligations to act with care in exercising their responsibilities. In *Re City Equitable Fire Insurance Co*,[34] for example, the court held that "a director need not exhibit in the performance of his duties a greater degree of skill than may reasonably be expected from a person of his knowledge and experience." This meant that if the director were ill-informed and foolish, then little could be expected of her; she was required only to display the competence of an ill-informed and foolish person. The unfortunate outcome at common law was that the less qualified a director was for office, the less time and attention she devoted to her duties, and the greater the reliance she placed on others, the lower was the standard that she was required to meet in managing the business affairs of the company.

---

31. The most recent attempt of legislating corporate social responsibility, a private member's bill requiring Canadian mining firms to respect environmental and human rights standards abroad was defeated. See: Bill Curry, "Ethical mining bill defeated after fierce lobbying", *The Globe and Mail* (28 October 2010) online: BNN <http://www.bnn.ca/News/2010/10/28/Ethical-mining-bill-defeated-after-fierce-lobbying.aspx>.
32. 2004 SCC 68, 3 SCR 461.
33. 2008 SCC 69, 3 SCR 560.
34. [1925] 1 Ch 407 at 428.

Recognizing that the common law standard of care was unduly low, legislatures have codified and upgraded what is expected of directors. The present standard contained in corporation legislation requires directors and officers to display the care, diligence, and skill that a reasonably prudent person would exercise in comparable circumstances. This is an objective standard, and, while directors are not expected to be perfect, they are to act prudently and on a reasonably informed basis.

CASE

Peoples Department Stores Inc (Trustee of) v Wise (2004), 2004 SCC 68, 3 SCR 461

THE BUSINESS CONTEXT: The *Canada Business Corporations Act* imposes a duty on directors and officers to act honestly and in good faith with a view to the best interests of the corporation (the fiduciary duty) and to exercise the care, diligence, and skill that a reasonably prudent person would exercise in comparable circumstances (a duty of care).[35] There have been questions about whether the duties of directors extend to creditors, particularly when the corporation is financially troubled.

FACTUAL BACKGROUND: Lionel, Ralph, and Harold Wise were majority shareholders and directors of Wise Stores Inc., a publicly traded company operating about 50 junior department stores in Quebec with annual sales of $100 million. In 1992, Wise Inc. acquired all of the shares of Peoples Department Stores Inc. from Marks & Spencer for $27 million. Peoples owned 81 stores and generated sales of $160 million annually. The Wise brothers became the sole directors of Peoples. The joint operation of Wise and Peoples did not function smoothly. In an effort to help the sagging fortunes of the companies, the Wise brothers implemented a joint inventory purchasing policy on the recommendation of the companies' vice president of administration and finance. The result of the policy was that Peoples purchased and paid for most of Wise Inc.'s inventory, subject to reimbursement by Wise Inc. Peoples ended up extending large amounts of trade credit to Wise, and by June 1994 Wise owed more than $18 million to Peoples. The financial situations of both companies continued to deteriorate and both ended up bankrupt in January 1995. After the sale of the assets and the payment of secured creditors, approximately $21.5 million in trade debt went unpaid. The Peoples' trustee in bankruptcy, representing the interests of the unpaid creditors, sued the Wise brothers, alleging that in implementing the joint inventory procurement program, they breached their duties as directors of Peoples.

THE LEGAL QUESTION: Did the Wise brothers as directors of Peoples owe duties to the creditors of Peoples? If so, did they breach these duties?

RESOLUTION: In a unanimous decision, the Supreme Court of Canada held that the Wise brothers did not owe a fiduciary duty to the creditors. While directors are entitled to have regard to the interests of various stakeholders—shareholders, employees, suppliers, creditors, consumers, government, and the environment—they owe their fiduciary duty only to the corporation. The directors' fiduciary duty does not change when the corporation is in the "vicinity of insolvency." The court further noted that stakeholders, like creditors, have other avenues of potential relief. The creditors can use the oppression remedy to protect their interests from the prejudicial conduct of directors.

The Court also held that creditors can pursue an action based on breach of the duty of care as the identity of the beneficiaries of this duty was "more open ended" and "obviously" included creditors (this marks the first time that the Supreme Court has extended the duty of care beyond the corporation). The Court stated that the duty of care is to be judged objectively. In analyzing whether particular conduct met the standard of care, the Court will consider the factual circumstances as well as the socioeconomic conditions. The Supreme Court (also for the first time) endorsed the "business judgment rule" in assessing whether directors have fulfilled the duty of care. The rule holds that the Court will not second-guess business judgments that are made honestly and on the basis of reasonable information. The Wise brothers did not breach their duty of care to creditors, as the inventory policy was a reasonable effort to address inventory management problems.

CRITICAL ANALYSIS: Is the decision in *Peoples v Wise* good news for directors of corporations? Is it good news for creditors?

---

35. Most provincial corporate statutes provide for similar duties.

Liabilities of Directors and Officers

Directors and officers are exposed to a broad range of liabilities relating to the business of the corporation, including liability in torts and contracts, and liability by statutory offences.

This section will discuss such liabilities in relation to directors, while recognizing that the same analysis usually also applies to officers.[36]

Liability in Tort and Contract

When a director is acting on behalf of a corporation and commits a tort, his actions may be attributed to the corporation itself by virtue of the identification theory. Similarly, when the director enters into a contract, as agent for his corporation, his actions make the corporation the other party to that contract and the director slips out of the equation altogether. There are times, however, when a director has personal liability for a tort he may have committed or a contract he may have entered into.

Liability in Tort Traditionally, courts have been reluctant to say that a director is automatically liable just because he commits a tort on company time. The idea is to permit the director to conduct company business without risking personal, unlimited liability at every turn. Think of it this way: if Adam were personally liable for any tort he committed during the course of his business day, there would really be no benefit in incorporating IK Enterprises from his perspective as a director. His liability would be the same whether he was running his business through a corporation or as a sole proprietorship, and the principle in *Salomon v Salomon* would fall by the wayside.

In line with this approach, some courts have ruled that directors are not personally liable provided that they were acting in furtherance of their duties to the corporation and their conduct was justifiable.[37] Nevertheless, case law from Ontario seems to take a step back from such a perspective. It appears to suggest that directors and officers will almost always be responsible for their own tortious conduct even if they were acting in the best interests of the corporation.[38] With this in mind, prudent directors will take care not to commit torts and will thereby avoid having to establish what the law concerning the matter is in their jurisdiction.

Most certainly, where the director's conduct is extreme, she will be found liable for committing a tort regardless of the approach taken by the court in question. For example, assume that Adam is meeting in his office with a customer who has not paid his bill to IK Enterprises Ltd. Things get a little out of hand and Adam bars the door for several hours, saying to the customer, "You're not getting out of here until you write a cheque for what you owe us." On these facts, Adam would face personal liability no matter what the legal test applied might be.

---

36. For example, particular legislation may impose liability on directors but not officers of the corporation.
37. *McFadden v 481782 Ontario Ltd,* (1984), 47 OR (2d) 134, 27 BLR 173 (HC).
38. See, for example, *ADGA Systems International Ltd v Valcom Ltd* (1999), 43 OR (3d) 101, 168 DLR (4th) 351 (CA), leave to appeal to SCC refused, [1999] SCCA No 124. Also see Edward M Iacobucci, "Unfinished Business: An Analysis of Stones Unturned in *ADGA Systems International v Valcom Ltd*", (2001) 35 Can Bus LJ 39; Janis Sarra, "The Corporate Veil Lifted: Director and Officer Liability to Third Parties" (2001) 35 Can Bus LJ 55; and Christopher C Nicholls, "Liability of Corporate Officers and Directors to Third Parties" (2001) 35 Can Bus LJ 1.

Liability in Contract   The director does not generally attract liability for the corporation's contracts—the principles of agency operate in such a way that the corporation is liable to the outsider and the director who has acted as agent for the corporation drops out of the transaction.

Nonetheless, a director faces personal liability on a contract if the facts indicate that the director intended to assume personal liability, as when

- the director contracts on his own behalf, as well as on behalf of the company

- the director guarantees the contractual performance of the company

Liability by Statute

In addition to the exposure that directors face for breaching their general management duties, dozens of pieces of legislation place obligations on them (see Figure 16.2 on page 382 for examples of the range of legislation affecting directors). These statutes impose potentially serious penalties for failure to comply, including fines of up to $1 million and imprisonment for up to two years.[39]

For example, the failure of IK Enterprises to withhold and remit income taxes can result in the directors being personally liable for the corporation's failure unless the directors can demonstrate that they acted in a reasonable and diligent manner.[40] Thus Adam and Diane, as directors of IK Enterprises, face personal liability for IK Enterprises' failure. Interestingly the *Income Tax Act* does not impose personal liability on officers—like Cameron—for this particular failure. While Cameron owes duties as a corporate officer under the *Canada Business Corporations Act,* at common law, and under his employment contract, he does not have any direct personal liability for his company's failure to remit under the *Income Tax Act.* It is important to check the provisions of legislation to determine who may be potentially liable.

ENVIRONMENTAL PERSPECTIVE

The Liability of Directors and Officers

In January 2005, General Chemical Canada closed its plant in Amherstburg, Ontario, leaving behind a badly contaminated lagoon, several environmental Orders issued by the Ministry of the Environment (MOE), and estimated clean-up costs of over $60 million. As the company was on the verge of bankruptcy and unlikely to be in a position to pay the clean-up costs, the MOE issued clean-up orders against General Chemical's U.S. parent company and a number of directors and officers of both companies. The directors and officers appealed the MOE clean-up orders but ultimately agreed to pay more than

$10 million to settle the case against them. This case highlights the potential liability of directors and officers for a corporation's environmental transgressions.

Both the *Canadian Environmental Protection Act, 1999*[41] (CEPA) and provincial environmental statutes have specific provisions imposing personal liability on directors and officers for the corporation's commission of an environmental offence.[42] In addition, directors and officers are subject to liability for a corporation's wrong doing on the grounds that they aided or abetted the corporation. They may also be named in a variety of administrative orders issued by government agencies

---

39. See, for example, the federal *Hazardous Products Act,* RSC 1985, c H-3.
40. *Supra* note 25, s 227.1 (1)(3).
41. SC 1999, c 33, s 280.
42. Only New Brunswick's environmental legislation does not specifically address the liability of officers and directors.

for the prevention, control or clean up of environmental contamination.

Specific Offences: The *CEPA* specifies that where a corporation commits an offence, any officer, director or agent who directed, authorized, assented to, acquiesced in, or participated in the commission of the offence, regardless of whether the corporation has been prosecuted or convicted is guilty of the offence. In addition to this provision that imposes liability on the basis of participation, the legislation also imposes on directors and officers a duty to take all reasonable care to ensure that the corporation complies with the Act, its regulations and environmental orders.[43]

Directors and officers have also been singled out in provincial legislation for personal liability in relation to corporate environmental practices. In Ontario, for example, the legislation imposes on directors and officers a positive duty to take all reasonable care to prevent the corporation from causing an unlawful discharge, contravening administrative orders, and contravening obligations with respect to approvals, notification of unlawful discharges, and hazardous waste management.[44] Failure to carry out that duty is an offence.

Defences: Environmental offences are generally of a strict liability[45] nature meaning directors and officers have available the defence of due diligence. A defendant is entitled to acquittal if he can show that he had "exercised all reasonable care by establishing a proper system to prevent commission of the offence and by taking reasonable steps to ensure the effective operation of the prevention system."[46] The defence of reasonable care and due diligence does not mean superhuman efforts, but it does mean a high standard of awareness and decisive, prompt and continuing action.[47]

Penalties: Convictions for environmental offences can result in range of penalties, including fines and/ or imprisonment. For

THE WINDSOR STAR

General Chemical Plant in Amherstberg, Ontario

example, individuals convicted under Manitoba's Environment Act are subject to a fine of up to $50 000 for a first offence or a term of imprisonment up to six months, or both.[48] Penalties are doubled for a second offence. Under the CEPA, directors and officers are subject to fines ranging from a minimum of $5 000 to a maximum of $1 million and prison terms up to three years, or both for the most serious offences.[49] In addition to these penalties, directors and officers face personal liability for the cost of preventative or remedial measures when they are named in an administrative order.

Critical Analysis: What can directors do to protect against environmental liability? What factors do you think are important in assessing whether directors and officers have been diligent?

Sources: Dianne Saxe, "General Chemical directors settle personal claim" (9 October 2009), online: Environmental Law and Litiation <http://envirolaw.com /general-chemical-directors-settle/>; Jamie Benidickson, *Environmental Law*, 3d ed (Toronto: Irwin Law, 2009) at 190-198.

Avoiding Liability

Directors have onerous duties to the corporation, and no one should agree to become a director without a sound understanding of the obligations involved. Willingness, enthusiasm, and ability are not enough: "the job may well require a considerable and unforeseen time commitment with ultimately limited compensation and considerable exposure of one's own personal assets."[50]

43. *Supra* note 41, s 280(2).
44. *Environment Enforcement Statute Amendment Act*, 1986, SO 1986, c 68, s 17.
45. Offences are generally categorized as absolute or strict liability. An absolute liability offence is one where the prosecution need only prove the physical elements of the offence and the blameworthiness or negligence of the defendant is immaterial. There are few defences available for these offences. A strict liability offence requires the same proof but unlike absolute liability offence, the defence due diligence is available. Most regulatory offences, including environmental offences are strict liability.
46. *R v Sault Ste Marie (City)*, [1978] 2 SCR 1299, 85 DLR (3d) 161.
47. *R v Courtaulds Fibres Canada* (1992), 9 CELR (NS) 304, 76 CCC (3d) 68 (Ont Div Ct). For general principles of a director's due diligence see: *R v Bata Industries Ltd*, [1992] OJ No 667, 7 CELR (NS) 245 (Ont Div Ct).
48. *Environment Act*, CCSM c E125, s 33.
49. *Supra* note 41, s 272.
50. David Ross, "Director's Obligations" in *Fiduciary Obligations—1995* (Vancouver: Continuing Legal Education Society of BC, 1995) 5.1.01.

PART FOUR

The exposure to risk suggests that a risk management plan as discussed in Chapter 3 is warranted. The basis for such a plan is provided in the Business Application of the Law box below.

FIGURE 16.2

Directors' Statutory Liabilities: A Sampling

Statutory Breach	Type of Statute	Nature of Penalty
Failure to pay employee wages	Federal and provincial incorporation statutes	Liability for wages
Directing, authorizing, or permitting the release of a toxic substance into the environment	Federal and provincial environmental protection statute	Fines and/or imprisonment
Failure to remit required taxes	Provincial and federal revenue acts	Liability for amount outstanding and interest or penalties
Failure to maintain health and safety standards	Provincial workplace health and safety legislation	Fines and/or imprisonment
Insider trading—using confidential information in buying and selling shares	Provincial securities acts, Federal and provincial incorporation statutes	Fines and/or imprisonment
Engaging in anticompetitive behaviour	Federal Competition Act	Criminal and civil liabilities
Paying a dividend when company is insolvent	Federal and provincial incorporation statutes	Personal repayment
Misrepresentation in a prospectus	Provincial securities legislation	Damages
Improperly transporting dangerous goods	Federal and provincial transportation of dangerous goods legislation	Fines and/or imprisonment

Indemnification
The corporate practice of paying the litigation expenses of officers and directors for lawsuits related to corporate affairs.

BUSINESS APPLICATION OF THE LAW

Avoiding the Risk of Personal Liability

Directors can reduce their exposure to personal liability by exercising care, diligence, and skill in the performance of their duties.

Directors can meet the statutory standard of care by being attentive, active, and informed. In this regard, directors should

- regularly attend directors' meetings
- read all relevant materials
- ask questions and speak up at meetings
- keep personal notes of meetings and review minutes of meetings
- make all their decisions informed decisions
- do what is necessary to learn about matters affecting the company
- identify possible problems within the company
- stay apprised of and alert to the corporation's financial and other affairs
- ensure that they receive reliable professional advice

Directors may also protect themselves by ensuring that an **indemnification** agreement with their company is in place. The purpose of such an agreement is to ensure that the corporation pays any costs or expenses that a director faces as a result of being sued because he is a director.

Directors should also ensure that the corporation carries adequate insurance. Directors' and officers' liability (D&O) insurance[51] provides coverage to the director who has a judgment or other claim against him. Directors should carefully review the policy's exclusion clauses to ensure that maximum protection is provided.

Source: Alex L MacFarlane & Alexandra North, "Canada: Directors' and Officers' Liability in the Shadow of Insolvency", *Mondaq Corporate/Company Law* (11 April 2011) online: Mondaq <http://mondaq.com/canada/article.asp?articleid=128316>.

---

51. See Chapter 28 for discussion of D&O insurance.

Shareholders and Creditors

Shareholders

A shareholder is someone who invests in a company by buying shares. As soon as IK Enterprises was created, for example, the company—through the directors—issued shares in the company to Adam, Cameron, and Diane. Another way of becoming a shareholder is by buying the shares from an existing shareholder or receiving the shares as a gift.

Regardless of how the shares are obtained, the shareholder has few responsibilities with respect to the corporation. Unlike directors and officers, the shareholder has no duty to act in the best interests of the corporation.[52] She can freely compete with the corporation in which she holds a share. She is not obligated to attend shareholder meetings, cast her vote, read the corporation's financial reports, or take any interest whatsoever in the progress of the corporation. And, of course, she is not generally liable for the debts and obligations of the corporation because of the principle in *Salomon*.

There are exceptions to this immunity, however, as the following section explores.

Shareholder Liability

Owners of the corporation are occasionally held responsible for debts and liabilities incurred by the corporation. In other words, the corporation is not considered a separate entity from its shareholders. This is known as piercing or **lifting the corporate veil**. Due to the *Salomon* principle, courts are generally reluctant to lift the corporate veil except when they are satisfied that a company is a "mere facade" concealing the true facts.[53] It must be shown that there is complete domination and control by the person or entity sought to be made liable, and that the corporate form must have been used as a shield for conduct akin to fraud that deprives claimants of their rights.[54]

For example, in *Big Bend Hotel Ltd v Security Mutual Casualty Co*[55] the court ignored the separate existence of the corporation when the corporation was being used to hide the identity of the person behind the corporation. Vincent Kumar purchased insurance for his company, Big Bend Ltd., which owned a hotel. The hotel burned down, but the insurance company refused to pay because Kumar had failed to disclose on the application for insurance that he had been president and sole shareholder of another corporation whose hotel had burned down less than three years earlier. The court held that the insurance company should be able to disregard the separate existence of the corporation and treat the policy as if it had been applied for by Kumar himself.

Also, in *Wildman v Wildman*,[56] the Ontario Court of Appeal ignored the principle of a corporation as a separate entity and held a husband's corporation liable for spousal and child support. The court opined that the corporation as a separate legal entity was not an absolute principle and the principle should not be used to defeat the enforcement of family

Lifting the corporate veil
Determining that the corporation is not a separate legal entity from its shareholders.

PART FOUR

---

52. There is an exception in some jurisdictions where an obligation can be imposed on shareholders if they hold enough shares to be classified as insiders, in which case they must not use insider information to their own benefit.
53. Kevin Patrick McGuiness, *Canadian Business Corporations Law*, 2d ed (Markham, ON: LexisNexis, 2007) at 49–60 points out a number of other situations where the veil will be lifted, including when it is required by statute, contract, or other documents, and when it can be established that the company is the agent of its controllers or shareholders.
54. *Gregorio v Intrans-Corp* (1994), 18 OR (3d) 527 (CA).
55. 19 BCLR 102, [1980] ILR 1-1217 (SC).
56. (2006), 82 OR (3d) 401, 215 OAC 239.

law orders. The Court allowed the wife to look to the corporation to satisfy the obligations of the principal and sole shareholder—the husband.

CASE

Le Car GmbH v Dusty Roads Holding Ltd, 2004 NSSC 75, 222 NSR (2d) 279

THE BUSINESS CONTEXT: A corporation is an entity separate from its shareholders, and the courts will not readily ignore the corporate form and hold shareholders liable for the conduct of the corporation. The most common basis for doing so is objectionable conduct amounting to fraud.

FACTUAL BACKGROUND: In 1995, Le Car GmbH, a German company that imported automobiles manufactured in other countries for sale in Germany entered into an agreement with Dusty Roads Holdings Inc., a company owned and operated by David Daley. Le Car wanted to acquire for resale in Germany new Mexican-built Volkswagen Golfs that could be sold at a lower price than comparable German-made models. Because there were obstacles to direct dealings between Le Car and Mexican interests and because Dusty Roads and Daley had contacts in Mexico who could supply the cars, a deal was made whereby Dusty Roads engaged a supplier in Mexico to provide and ship vehicles to Le Car in Germany. The oral arrangements between the parties provided that Le Car would advise Dusty Roads of the number and model of cars it wanted and Daley would contact the supplier. Le Car paid the amount specified by Daley plus a $100 commission for each car for Dusty Roads. Le Car did not pay the Mexican supplier directly but transferred the money to Dusty Roads, which paid the Mexican supplier. When Le Car placed an order, it was expected to pay Dusty Roads 25 percent of the purchase price. A 1995 shipment of 105 cars went smoothly. A 1996 order for 170 cars was not completed. When only 121 cars were delivered, Le Car sued Dusty Roads and Daley for outstanding deposits and damages for failure to deliver. Daley claimed Dusty Roads was entitled to keep the deposits.

THE LEGAL QUESTION: Were Dusty Roads and Daley liable for breach of contract?

RESOLUTION: The court found that the deposits were refundable as there was no evidence that they were non-refundable. The court also held that Le Car was entitled to recover damages from Dusty Roads for breach of contract. The key issue was whether liability could be imposed on Daley. The court determined that a 25 percent deposit was not required by the Mexican supplier and Dusty Roads did not relay the entire deposit to the Mexican supplier. Dusty Roads was required only to relay a 20 percent deposit, and it had retained the extra 5 percent to cover any deficiencies, expenses, or unpaid commissions. Daley also altered documents received from Mexico before relaying them to Le Car to remove references to the 20 percent. The court held that Daley's conduct with reference to the "additional deposit" warranted piercing the corporate veil and imposing liability on him. He misrepresented the use of the additional deposit and deceived Le Car by inducing it to provide an advance payment of 25 percent. Daley was therefore responsible for excess deposits on the entire order of 170 cars (US$87 000). The remaining damages (US$189 000) relating to the overpayment for undelivered cars was the responsibility of Dusty Roads, as these losses were not the result of any misconduct by Daley.

CRITICAL ANALYSIS: Despite the success of Le Car in having the court "pierce the corporate veil," courts are generally reluctant to do so. Can you think of situations where it would be appropriate to lift the corporate veil?

Shareholder Rights

Shareholder rights fall into three broad categories: the right to vote, the right to information, and financial rights. How directors decide to allocate these rights when issuing different classes of shares is largely up to them, as there are few requirements in this area. One kind of share can have all three rights, while another kind of share may have only one of these rights. All that is normally required, in this regard, is that the voting and financial rights referred to above be allocated to at least one class of shares; however, all those rights are not required to be attached to only one particular class.

The idea behind having different classes of shares is to permit different levels of participation in the corporation. As noted earlier, if Cameron does not want much of a role in the company, he may be content with nonvoting shares. These are often called **preferred shares.**[57] Voting shares are usually called **common shares.** Although nonvoting shares are normally called preferred and voting shares are normally called common, this is not always the case. The only way to know for certain what rights are attached to shares is to review the share certificate itself, as well as the articles of incorporation.

Preferred share
A share or stock that has a preference in the distribution of dividends and the proceeds on dissolution.

Right to Vote   Corporation legislation requires that there be at least one class of voting shareholders in a corporation. The most significant voting right traditionally attached to common shares is the right to vote for the board of directors. Note that the number of votes that a particular shareholder may cast depends on the number of shares he holds. If Adam holds 1000 common shares, he has 1000 votes. If he holds a majority of the shares, he will be in a position to elect at least a majority of the board of directors and therefore control the company.

Common share
A share that generally has a right to vote, share in dividends, and share in proceeds on dissolution.

As well, voting shareholders have the right to approve or disapprove of directors' actions since the last general meeting. This is because the right to vote brings with it other rights, including the right to

- hold a shareholder general meeting each year
- be given notice of the meeting
- attend the meeting
- ask questions
- introduce motions

A shareholder who cannot attend a meeting can exercise her voting power through a **proxy.** This means granting formal permission to someone else to vote her shares on her behalf. The use of a proxy is important, particularly in large corporations when there is a dispute between competing groups of shareholders. Whichever group does the best job of soliciting proxies is most likely to carry the day. Nonvoting shareholders—usually preferred shareholders—have the right to vote in certain specialized matters. Under the *Canada Business Corporations Act*, for example, Cameron—as the holder of preferred shares in IK Enterprises Ltd.—would have the right to vote on any proposal to sell all the corporation's assets.[58] The rationale is that even nonvoting shareholders should have a say when such a fundamental change in corporate direction is being put forward.

Proxy
A person who is authorized to exercise a shareholder's voting rights.

Right to Information   Shareholders have the right to certain fundamental information concerning the corporation. This includes the right to

- inspect the annual financial statement for the corporation
- apply to the court to have an inspector appointed to look into the affairs of the corporation if it can be shown that there is a serious concern about mismanagement

---

57. They are called preferred shares because ordinarily the holders of preferred shares get priority—or have a "preference"—on taking a slice of the corporation's assets if it is liquidated.
58. *Supra* note 3, s 189(3).

- inspect certain records, including minute books, the register of share transfers, incorporating documents, bylaws and special resolutions, and the registry of shareholders and directors
- know whether directors have been purchasing shares of the corporation. This is to permit shareholders to determine whether directors have been using confidential information to make personal profits.[59]

Financial Rights Shareholders generally buy shares with the hope or expectation that the corporation will prosper and generate financial rewards, in terms of either capital gains or income for them. In this respect, one of the fundamental rights of the shareholder is the right to receive any dividend declared by the corporation. The shareholder has no right to have dividends just because the corporation has earned large profits, since the declaration of dividends is within the discretion of the board of directors. However, if the shareholders can show that the directors are abusing their discretion, they can consider bringing an oppression action, which is discussed later in this chapter.

Once dividends are declared, directors are bound to pay them in order of preference assigned to the classes of shares. As well, there cannot be any discrimination among shareholders belonging to the same class. If Diane and Cameron both own the same class of shares, it is illegal for the directors to declare that Diane gets a certain dividend but Cameron does not.

Shareholders have a right to share in the assets of a corporation on dissolution after creditors are paid. Again, the right is dependent on the priorities of each class of shares. Preferred shareholders are often given the right to be first in line for corporate assets once all the creditors have been paid.

Pre-emptive right
A shareholder's right to maintain a proportionate share of ownership by purchasing a proportionate share of any new stock issue.

Additionally, shareholders may have what are known as **pre-emptive rights**. When this right exists, it requires the corporation to offer existing shareholders the chance to purchase a new issue of shares before these shares are offered to outsiders. This gives existing shareholders a chance to maintain their level of control or power in the corporation. For example, assume that Adam has 1000 common shares in IK Enterprises Ltd., and because of other entrepreneurial interests, he has unwisely resigned as a director in the company for the time being. Diane is the only corporate director left. Assume further that she resolves to issue 2000 common shares to Cameron. This issue would transform Adam's position from being an equal shareholder—with Diane—of common shares to being in the minority, but his pre-emptive right would allow him to maintain his proportional interest in the company if he could afford to purchase further shares.

Shareholder Remedies

A shareholder, such as Cameron, who is dissatisfied with a corporation's performance or management has a number of remedies available to him.

---

59. See, for example, *Securities Act*, RSO 1990, c S-5, ss 106–9.

Selling the Shares   Often the simplest and least costly remedy for a shareholder who is dissatisfied with the operation or performance of a corporation is to simply sell his shares.

This, of course, is an easily viable remedy only in the widely held or public corporation, where shares are traded on the stock exchange and there are no restrictions on their transferability.

The situation is quite different in the closely held or private corporation. In this case, there are usually restrictions on the transference of shares and—even where the restrictions are minimal—it may be difficult to find someone willing to buy such shares. Historically, this reality put the minority shareholder in the unenviable position of having little input into the operation of the corporation and no easy way to extricate his investment. In response, both the common law and the legislatures developed a number of remedies to protect a minority shareholder from abuse by the majority. The most important are the appraisal remedy, the derivative action, and the oppression remedy.[60]

Exercising Dissent and Appraisal Rights   In situations where shareholders, by a two-thirds majority vote, approve a fundamental change to the corporation, a dissenting shareholder may elect to have her shares bought by the corporation.[61] This **dissent and appraisal right** is limited to specific actions such as changes to the restrictions on share transfers or restrictions on the business a corporation may carry on; the amalgamation or merger with another corporation; or the sale, lease, or exchange of substantially all of the corporation's assets. The procedure for obtaining the remedy is complex, and the dissenter must strictly follow the prescribed steps.

Dissent and appraisal right
The right of shareholders who dissent from certain fundamental changes to the corporation to have their shares purchased by the corporation at a fair price.

Bringing a Derivative Action   Because of their managerial control, directors are well placed to rob the very corporation that they are charged with serving. For example, they could take a corporate opportunity and develop it for their own personal gain, they could vote that the corporation sell corporate assets to one of them at a price ridiculously below market, or they could vote themselves outrageously high compensation packages. What can a minority shareholder do when the directors are breaching their duty to the corporation and causing it injury?

At common law, courts permitted minority shareholders to take action on behalf of the corporation against the directors, but the system was far from adequate. In response, corporate law statutes have created what is called the statutory **derivative action**.[62] This permits a shareholder to obtain leave from the court to bring an action on behalf of the corporation, where he can establish that

- directors will not bring an action

- he is acting in good faith

- it appears to be in the interests of the corporation that the action proceed

Derivative action
A suit by a shareholder on behalf of the corporation to enforce a corporate cause of action.

PART FOUR

---

60. Other remedies include winding up, which involves dissolution of the corporation and the return of surplus assets to the shareholders. The use of this remedy is therefore uncommon.
61. See, for example, *Canada Business Corporations Act, supra* note 3, s 190.
62. For a discussion of the jurisdictions that provide for such an action, see Bruce Welling, *Corporate Law in Canada: The Governing Principles*, 3d ed (London, ON: Scribblers, 2006) at 509ff.

This action means that directors cannot treat the corporation as their own personal fiefdom with impunity. They owe strict duties to the corporation. Even if they breach those duties with the support of the majority of the shareholders, the minority has recourse to the courts and can secure any number of remedies on behalf of the corporation. By virtue of the derivative action, if the directors have stolen a corporate opportunity, they can be forced by the court to account for that profit. If they have disposed of corporate assets at below market value, the court can order them to account for the difference between what the asset is actually worth and what was paid for it. If they have voted to overpay themselves, the court can order them to return their ill-gotten gains. The court even has the power to remove the directors from office and replace them. In fact, the legislation empowers the court to make any order it sees fit.

Bringing an Oppression Action   The most widely used remedy by shareholders in Canada is called the **oppression remedy.** A shareholder who has been treated unfairly or "oppressively" may apply to a court for relief. Conduct that the courts have found to be oppressive usually falls into the following categories:

> **Oppression remedy**
> A statutory remedy available to shareholders and other stakeholders to protect their corporate interests.

- lack of a valid corporate purpose for a transaction

- lack of good faith on the part of the directors of the corporation

- discrimination between shareholders with the effect of benefiting the majority shareholder to the exclusion or the detriment of the minority shareholder

- lack of adequate and proper disclosure of material information to minority shareholders

- conflict of interest between the interests of the corporation and the personal interests of one or more directors[63]

The court is entitled to make such an order as it deems just and appropriate, including ordering the corporation to purchase the complainant's shares, ordering the improper conduct to cease, and, in extreme circumstances, ordering the company to be dissolved. The remedy is extremely flexible and has few attendant technicalities. Unlike a derivative action, which is brought on behalf of the corporation, the oppression remedy is a personal action, which can be brought by shareholders and specified stakeholders—security holders, creditors, directors, or officers.

Like all litigation, however, the process in securing a shareholder remedy is time consuming, costly, and unpredictable. Furthermore, the courts historically have been less than enthusiastic about getting involved in the internal affairs of corporations. Put another way, it is often a heavy and onerous burden to convince the court that the majority is in the wrong and has been oppressive.

As a way of avoiding litigation, shareholders may decide to enter into an agreement at the very beginning of their association in order to deal with potentially contentious areas and to streamline the procedure leading to the resolution of any conflict. Depending on

---

63. Shelly Obal & Julie Walsh, *Corporate Governance in Canada: A Guide to the Responsibilities of Corporate Directors in Canada*, 4th ed (Toronto: Osler, Hoskin & Harcourt, 2005) at 15.

the jurisdiction, there are two possibilities in this regard: a shareholders' agreement and a unanimous shareholders' agreement (also called a USA). Of course, such agreements do not guarantee that litigation will be avoided, since the meaning and enforceability of these agreements can themselves become the subject matter of litigation.

CASE

BCE Inc v 1976 Debentureholders, 2008 SCC 69, [2008] 3 SCR 560

THE BUSINESS CONTEXT: The following decision provides clarification of the duties of directors in the context of change-of-control transactions and in situations where stakeholder interests are in conflict. It also provides guidance on the application of the oppression remedy.

FACTUAL BACKGROUND: In June 2007, BCE Inc. announced an agreement with a consortium of investors led by the Ontario Teachers' Pension Plan Board. The agreement proposed the acquisition of all outstanding shares of BCE by a $52 billion highly leveraged plan of arrangement under the *Canada Business Corporations Act* (CBCA). The purchase price of CDN$42.75 per common share would provide a 40 percent premium for BCE's common shareholders but would require Bell Canada Inc., BCE's wholly owned subsidiary, to provide guarantees of approximately $30 billion to support Teachers' borrowings. These guarantees would result in the loss of investment-grade status of Bell Canada's outstanding debentures and a reduction in their trading value. The debentureholders opposed the transaction on the basis that it was oppressive.

THE LEGAL QUESTION: Did the directors of BCE act in an oppressive manner toward the debentureholders of Bell Canada by approving the sale of BCE?

RESOLUTION: The trial court dismissed all of the bondholders' claims and approved the plan. The Court of Appeal reversed the decision, holding that BCE had failed to establish that the plan was fair and reasonable. The Supreme Court of Canada, in a unanimous decision, reversed the Court of Appeal's decision and allowed the transaction to proceed.

Oppression remedy: The *CBCA* provides a remedy to a wide range of stakeholders whose legal and equitable interests have been affected by oppressive acts of a corporation or its directors. The remedy gives a broad jurisdiction to enforce not only just what is legal but also what is fair in the circumstances. What is just and equitable is judged by the reasonable expectations of the stakeholders in the context. In assessing a claim for oppression, the court must determine whether the evidence supports the reasonable expectation of the stakeholder and whether the reasonable expectation of the stakeholder was violated by oppressive conduct. To determine whether a reasonable

expectation exists, courts must consider the following factors: general commercial practice; the nature of the corporation; the relationship between the parties; past practice; steps the claimant could take to protect itself; representations and agreements; and the resolution of conflicting interests between corporate stakeholders (see below for the court's discussion of this factor). For the second question, a claimant must show that the failure to meet reasonable expectations was the result of unfair conduct.

The debenture holders argued that they had a reasonable expectation that BCE would protect their economic interests by putting forward a plan that maintains the investment-grade trading value of their debentures. In the alternative, they argued that they had a reasonable expectation that the directors would consider their economic interests in maintaining the trading value of their debentures. The Supreme Court of Canada concluded that the debentureholders could not have reasonably expected that the directors of BCE would protect Bell Canada's investment-grade credit rating or the value of the debentures. The court noted that any statements by Bell Canada suggesting a commitment to retain investment-grade ratings were accompanied by warnings precluding such expectations. The Court did find that the debentureholders had a reasonable expectation that the BCE directors would consider their interests in the proposed transaction. However, the directors had considered the interests of debentureholders but reasonably concluded that while the contractual terms of the debentures would be honoured, no further commitments could be made.

Directors' Fiduciary Duties in Resolving Competing Stakeholder Interests: In the context of a conflict between the interests of different corporate stakeholders (in this case, between shareholders and debentureholders), the Supreme Court of Canada restated its holding in *Peoples v Wise* that the directors' fiduciary duty is to act in the best interests of the corporation. It stated that "the fiduciary duty of the directors is a broad, contextual concept. It is not confined to short-term profit or share value. Where the corporation is an ongoing concern, it looks to the long-term interests of the corporation. The content of this duty varies with the situation at hand." The duty to act in the best interests of the corporation requires directors to consider the interests of all stakeholders and to

(Continued)

PART FOUR

treat individual stakeholders equitably and fairly. There are no absolute rules. "In each case, the question is whether, in all the circumstances, the directors acted in the best interests of the corporation, having regard to all relevant considerations, including, but not confined to, the need to treat affected stakeholders in a fair manner, commensurate with the corporation's duties as a responsible corporate citizen." The directors may look at the interests of shareholders, employees, creditors, consumers, governments, and the environment to inform their decision making, but in doing so, there is no principle that one set of interests must prevail over another. Thus the court conclusively rejected the "shareholder primacy" model according to which the directors' duty in a change-of-control situation is to maximize shareholder value. Instead, the directors should use business judgment to determine what is in the best interests of the corporation in the particular situation. In this regard, a court should give appropriate deference to the business judgment of directors, so long as the directors' decision is in the range of reasonable alternatives.

CRITICAL ANALYSIS: The Supreme Court's decision rejects the view that directors have a duty to maximize shareholder value in the context of change-of-control transactions in favour of a director's duty to treat all affected stakeholders fairly, commensurate with the corporation's duties as a responsible citizen. Does this holding make it easier or harder for stakeholders to challenge directors' decisions?

POSTSCRIPT: The transaction did not proceed, as a solvency opinion that was required as a condition precedent to the agreement could not be obtained. Auditor KPMG said BCE would have been forced into bankruptcy by the debt burden it would have acquired.

Shareholders' agreement
An agreement that defines the relationship among people who have an ownership interest in a corporation.

Asserting a Remedy under a Shareholders' Agreement or a USA **Shareholders' agreements** are common, particularly in small, closely held corporations. They serve a multitude of purposes, but in particular they allow shareholders to define their relationship in a manner that is different than that provided by the governing statute. Such agreements may address, for example, how the corporation is to be managed, how shares will be transferred, and how disputes will be resolved.

Unanimous shareholders' agreement (USA)
An agreement among all shareholders that restricts the powers of the directors to manage the corporation.

A **unanimous shareholders' agreement (USA)** is a specialized kind of shareholders' agreement among all shareholders that restricts, in whole or in part, the powers of the directors to manage the corporation. The purpose of a USA is to ensure that control over matters dealt within the USA remains with the shareholders. When shareholders, through a USA, take management powers away from directors, those directors are relieved of their duties and liabilities to the same extent. This means that if the shareholders improperly manage the corporation, they may be successfully sued for negligence or breach of fiduciary duty, for example.

The objective of a shareholders' agreement is to comprehensively set out—by agreement and in advance of any conflict—what the shareholders' expectations are, how the company is to be managed, and how disputes will be addressed. Shareholders' agreements seek to confront the reality that disagreements are inevitable and can be resolved according to mechanisms set up during the "honeymoon" phase of a business relationship.

Diane, Cameron, and Adam most definitely need a shareholders' agreement for the reasons given above.

BUSINESS APPLICATION OF THE LAW

Managing Risk through Shareholders' Agreements

A shareholders' agreement allows the shareholders to define their relationship, now and in the future. It should, as well, provide mechanisms and procedures that can be employed when the relationship encounters difficulties, along with means for undoing the relationship if the need to do so arises. An agreement must be tailored to meet the requirements of the particular situation and should address the following issues:

1. *Management of the company.* Who will be responsible for management? What will their rights and obligations be? How will they be appointed or elected or hired? How will they be paid?

2. *Protection for the minority shareholder.* How will the minority be protected from domination by the majority? How will representation on the board of directors be achieved? How will fundamental issues, such as dividends, sale of assets, and the like, be handled?

3. *Control over who the other shareholders will be.* What are the qualifications needed for being a shareholder? What happens in the event of a shareholder's death, retirement, disability, or simple loss of interest in the company?

4. *Provision of a market for shares.*[64] What are the circumstances that require a shareholder to sell her shares? What happens if a shareholder dies? Who will buy the shares and for how much? How will the purchase be funded?

5. *Capital contribution.* What happens if the corporation needs more cash? Who will provide it, and how much? How will payment be compelled?

6. *Buy-sell arrangements in the event of a dispute.* What (e.g., death, retirement, insolvency) triggers a sale? How will the shares be valued? What method will be chosen for their valuation (i.e., independent third party, formula, value fixed in advance and updated annually)?

7. *Mechanism for terminating the agreement.* How can the agreement be terminated? Can it be terminated on notice? How much notice?

Critical Analysis: When should the shareholders of a corporation consider entering into a shareholders' agreement?

Source: James W Carr, "Shareholder Agreements" in *Advising the Business Client* (Edmonton: The Legal Education Society of Alberta, 1995) at 14–16.

Creditor Protection

A corporation is responsible for its own liabilities, including its debts. As such, the shareholders/owners may be tempted to strip the entity of its assets in an attempt to defeat creditors, but doing so would be illegal. For example, if IK Enterprises Ltd. falls on hard financial times, Adam cannot clean out the entire computer inventory and bring it home with him to sell later. This is because the inventory belongs to the corporation, not to Adam, and the corporation's creditors have a prior claim on such property.

To help prevent abuses by shareholders, a number of legislative provisions have been enacted. For example, section 42 of the *Canada Business Corporations Act* forbids the corporation to pay a dividend to shareholders if doing so would jeopardize its ability to pay its own debts as they fall due (the liquidity test). The same section forbids such a dividend if that would make the company insolvent—that is, leave it without enough assets to cover its liabilities.[65] Directors who consent to a dividend under such circumstances are personally liable to restore to the corporation any amounts so paid.

---

64. Common mechanisms in shareholders' agreements for selling shares include a right of first refusal and a shotgun clause. A right of first refusal involves a shareholder offering to sell shares to other shareholders; if they refuse to purchase, then, for a limited time, the shareholder may sell to someone else for the same price. A shotgun clause involves a shareholder offering to sell shares at a certain price to another shareholder, who must either buy all the shares at that price or sell all his shares at the same price.
65. Insolvency is discussed in Chapter 27.

The Supreme Court of Canada has also indicated that duty of care imposed on directors by s 122 (1) (b) of the CBCA is owed not only just to the corporation but also to the creditors.[66] As well, the same court stated that creditors can avail themselves of the oppression remedy as a means of protecting themselves from the prejudicial conduct of directors.

FIGURE 16.3

Summary of Liability for Corporate Conduct

	Liability in Tort Law	*Liability in Contract Law*	*Liability in Criminal Law*	*Liability for Regulatory Offences*
Corporation	Identification Theory: The corporation is liable when a directing mind commits the tort in the course of carrying out her duties. Vicarious Liability: A corporation is vicariously liable for the torts of employees (who are not directing minds) committed in the course of employment.	Agency Theory: The corporation is liable so long as the agent was acting within actual or apparent authority.	Identification Theory: The corporation is liable if a senior officer of the corporation committed the offence at least partially in the interests of the corporation. A senior officer is someone who plays an important role in the establishment of the corporation's policies or is responsible for managing an important aspect of the corporation's activities.	The legislation specifies liability but generally the corporation is liable when a person engages in the prohibited behaviour on behalf of the corporation.
Directors/Officers	Law unclear and jurisdiction-specific. While formerly liable only for more extreme conduct, possibly liable for virtually any tort committed in the course of carrying out duties.	Agency Theory: No liability unless intended to assume liability.	Personally liable for the commission of criminal offences.	Statutes may impose liability on directors, officers, or both for a corporation's conduct.
Shareholders	Generally not liable for corporation's torts unless corporate veil lifted.	Generally not liable for corporation's contracts unless corporate veil lifted.	No liability for corporation's crimes.	No liability imposed on shareholders by statute.

Termination of the Corporation

Winding up
The process of dissolving a corporation.

When and if the time comes for IK Enterprises to shut down, it can be dissolved in several ways. In most jurisdictions, provisions in the companies act or a separate **winding up** act set out a process. The steps involved can be somewhat complicated, so in many instances it is more feasible simply to let the company lapse. This is particularly the case with a small, closely-held corporation. The principals may simply neglect to file their annual report or follow other reporting requirements; this will ultimately result in the company being struck from the corporate register.

A court has the authority to order a company to be terminated when a shareholder has been wrongfully treated and this is the only way to do justice between the parties. As well, a corporation whose debts exceed its assets may eventually go bankrupt. The result of bankruptcy is usually the dissolution of the corporation.

---

66. *Peoples Department Stores Inc (Trustee of) v Wise*, 2004 SCC 68, [2004] 3 SCR 461.

Business Law in Practice Revisited

1. Is IK Enterprises liable for the failure to deduct and remit income tax? Does Cameron, as an officer of IK Enterprises, have any personal liability for the failure to deduct and remit the taxes?

The *Income Tax Act* imposes liability on a person for failure to withhold and remit income taxes, and as IK Enterprises is considered to be a person, it is liable for this failure. Additionally, the Act imposes liability on the directors of the corporation for the corporation's failure to withhold and remit taxes. Therefore, unless they have a valid defence, Adam and Diane are exposed to liability. The Act, however, does not impose liability on officers; therefore, Cameron is not exposed to personal liability on this front.

2. What obligations do Cameron, Diane, and Adam have as corporate officers and directors?

As corporate officers and directors, Cameron, Diane, and Adam are obliged to competently manage the corporation and to act in the best interests of the corporation. This means, in effect, that they must not only apply their skills and knowledge to the operations of the corporation but also put the corporation's interests above their own personal interests.

3. How can the disagreement between Adam and Diane be resolved?

The dispute between Adam and Diane is problematic. Each owns 50 percent of the common shares of the corporation, and thus each has an equal voice in the management of the corporation. Their situation is the classic one of shareholder deadlock. In hindsight, the potential for deadlock should have been addressed in the decision to issue shares, or in a shareholders' agreement, or both. An agreement could have provided for a mechanism such as Cameron or an independent person casting a deciding vote. In the absence of an agreement, the parties could still agree to pursue an alternative dispute resolution mechanism. If one party is unwilling, there is little that can be done to resolve the dispute, short of litigation.

4. Are there any problems with Diane forming her own company to take advantage of the translation product opportunity?

If Diane decides to incorporate a company to pursue the translation product opportunity, she needs to be mindful of her fiduciary obligations to IK Enterprises. The law is somewhat unclear as to when a director may pursue an opportunity that came to her as a result of her position as director. However, as the company has rejected the opportunity, it would seem that Diane in the circumstances (she was in favour of IK Enterprises pursuing the opportunity) is free to take it up on her own, particularly upon securing the informed consent of both Adam and Cameron.

5. What are Cameron's rights as a shareholder if he does not like how Diane and Adam are managing the company?

Cameron could simply sell his shares, if he is permitted to do so and if he can find a buyer. Corporation legislation also provides for shareholder remedies; however, the

PART FOUR

remedies are not usually available simply because a shareholder dislikes how the corporation is being managed. There must be something more, such as oppressive conduct by the directors. Even if oppression can be proved, litigation can be costly and time consuming. Again, this issue should have been considered in advance and a remedy or alternative course of action should have been built into a shareholder agreement.

Chapter Summary

Of particular concern to anyone launching a corporation is the potential liability, both civil and criminal, that the corporation and its stakeholders are exposed to. A corporation, as a distinct legal entity, may be liable in tort, in contract, and for criminal and regulatory offences. Likewise, directors and officers also may be liable both in criminal and civil law for actions relating to the business of the corporation.

Directors and officers who are charged with the management of the corporation owe duties of competence and fiduciary duties to the corporation, and they may be liable to the corporation for breach of these duties.

Shareholders generally face few liabilities with respect to the actions of the corporation. There are, however, limited exceptions to this general rule—most importantly when the corporate form is being used to commit a fraud. Shareholders do, however, have certain statutory rights with respect to the operations of the corporation—the right to vote, the right to information, and financial rights. They also have remedies to enforce their rights. Shareholders can enter into agreements that define their relationships with one another and that provide mechanisms for resolving disputes and means for protecting their interests.

Creditors receive some specific protection under corporate law provisions. Also, the Supreme Court of Canada has also indicated that directors owe creditors a duty of care and creditors can avail themselves of the oppression remedy. Creditors can also negotiate for other rights.[67]

A corporation can enjoy perpetual existence; however, it can also be dissolved. The most common methods of dissolution are winding-up procedures and simply letting the corporation lapse.

---

67. See Chapter 26 for a discussion of creditors' rights.

Chapter Study

Key Terms and Concepts

common share (p. 385)

corporate opportunity (p. 375)

derivative action (p. 387)

dissent and appraisal right (p. 387)

identification theory (p. 367)

indemnification (p. 382)

lifting the corporate veil (p. 383)

oppression remedy (p. 388)

pre-emptive right (p. 386)

preferred share (p. 385)

proxy (p. 385)

regulatory offence (p. 371)

self-dealing contract (p. 374)

shareholders' agreement (p. 390)

unanimous shareholders' agreement (USA) (p. 390)

winding up (p. 392)

Questions for Review

1. How can a corporation be liable in tort law? Explain.

2. How does a corporation enter a contract? Explain.

3. How is the criminal liability of a corporation determined?

4. When is a director personally liable for committing a tort?

5. To whom do directors owe duties?

6. What is a self-dealing contract?

7. What are the duties of directors and officers?

8. Do directors owe duties to the corporation's creditors? Explain.

9. Is a director liable for a corporation's contracts? Explain.

10. How may a director avoid personal liability when carrying out her corporate duties?

11. What is meant by the term "lifting the corporate veil"? When will courts "lift the corporate veil"?

12. What three main rights do shareholders have?

13. What rights to dividends do shareholders have?

14. When is the dissent and appraisal remedy appropriate?

15. What is the difference between a derivative action and an oppression action?

16. When is a shareholder agreement appropriate? What issues should a shareholder's agreement address?

17. What protection do creditors have from shareholders stripping the corporation of its assets?

18. How is a corporation terminated?

Questions for Critical Thinking

1. What are the arguments for prosecuting, convicting, and punishing corporations? Does holding corporations criminally responsible serve any social purpose? What are the arguments against prosecuting, convicting, and punishing corporations?

2. The Canadian Democracy and Corporate Accountability Commission, an independent body designed to investigate corporate influence has recommended that corporation laws should be amended to allow directors, at their discretion, to take into consideration the effect of their actions on the corporation's employees, customers, suppliers, and creditors as well as the effects of their actions on the community in which the corporation resides.[68] How does the Supreme Court of Canada's decision in *BCE* account for stakeholders' interests? What is the problem with directors owing duties to all stakeholders?

3. There are literally dozens of statutes that impose personal liability on directors, and in many cases, officers. Directors and officers face liability, for example, under securities, environmental, employment, tax, and bankruptcy and insolvency legislation. Why do you think this has occurred? What are the problems associated with holding directors to higher standards? How can directors protect themselves in an increasingly litigious environment?

---

68. Canadian Democracy and Corporate Accountability Commission, *The New Balance Sheet: Corporate Profits and Responsibility in the 21st Century* (January 2002).

4. In *BCE*, the Supreme Court of Canada made it clear that the decisions of directors are to be given great weight. Provided directors follow the proper process and have regard to the interests of all stakeholders affected by their decisions, their balancing of conflicting stakeholder interests in determining the best interests of the corporation will be treated as a matter of business judgment not to be overturned by the courts unless it falls outside the range of reasonableness. What is meant by business judgment? The Supreme Court of Canada confirms the importance of process in directors' decision making. What are the key elements of that process? In other words, what steps can directors take to lessen the chances of a court second-guessing their decisions?

5. Although not required by securities or corporate law, a number of Canadian companies have held shareholder advisory votes on executive compensation (say on pay). Do you think shareholders should have a say on pay? What are the issues with shareholders deciding executive pay?

6. In 2010, Syncrude Canada Ltd. received the largest fine in Alberta history for the violation of environmental legislation that resulted in the death of 1,606 birds (see page 371). Prosecutors hailed the $3-million fine as precedent-setting and sending a clear message that the province will react to protect the environment. Critics of the fine, however, complained that the fine was a mere "drop in the barrel" for Syncrude and would not solve the problem of toxic tailings ponds and dead birds. They pointed out that the fine represents about a half a day's profit for the oil sands company.[69] Do you agree with the position of the prosecutors or the critics? Is fining corporations the best way to deal with environmental transgressions? Why or why not?

Situations for Discussion

1. Jerome Neeson is a shareholder in Gourmet Chefs Inc., a company that owns and operates a test kitchen in a large metropolitan area. The company is involved in a number of businesses, including catering at high-end business functions, giving cooking lessons, and developing new recipes. Gourmet Chefs recently added to its staff a top chef who was trained at Le Cordon Bleu cooking school in France. Jerome anticipated that the company's profits would increase in the future, and he was very happy with the direction that the company was moving. He was therefore very surprised to receive notice of a shareholders' meeting, where the directors proposed to sell the company's test kitchen. Jerome is opposed to the sale and does not want to be involved with Gourmet Chefs if the sale is completed. Advise Jerome.

2. Alicia, the president and CEO of a computer software company, broke into the offices of a competitor late one night in order to see what kinds of products they were in the process of designing. She was caught in the act by the police, who brought to her attention the following provision from the Criminal Code:

   s 348 (1) Every one who

   breaks and enters a place with intent to commit an indictable offence therein ... is guilty of an offence

   Has Alicia's computer software company committed the crime of break and enter?

3. Lennie purchased a quantity of pressure-treated lumber from GoodWood Building Ltd. (GoodWood) last April. Lennie used the wood to build a deck around the front of his house. By the fall, however, he found that the wood was starting to rot, and it appeared that the stain used to treat the wood was peeling away. When Lennie tried to contact GoodWood, he discovered that the store had closed and the company was insolvent. Lennie managed to locate the salesman who sold him the wood, and he agreed that the wood appeared to be defective. He also told Lennie that the wood had been imported from Thailand so a lawsuit against the manufacturer would probably be long and expensive. He suggested that Lennie bring an action against the directors and shareholders of GoodWood. The shareholders and directors are Jim, Tim, and Tom. What are Lennie's chances of success against the shareholders and directors? Does your answer change if GoodWood is an unincorporated business in which Tim, Jim, and Tom are the owners and managers? What are Lennie's chances of success against them in this circumstance?

---

69. *Supra* note 22.

4. The board of directors of Gismos & Widgets Inc., a manufacturer of computer components, has embraced the "green shift." It takes great pride in its decisions that have benefited both the corporation and the environment. Examples of their environmentally friendly decisions include replacing all light bulbs with lower wattage bulbs, replacing old delivery vehicles with low-emission vehicles, installing solar panels on the rooftop, and instituting a recycling program for obsolete computers. Recently, a member of the board suggested that Gismos & Widgets purchase a large tract of land and have it preserved as a sanctuary for migrating birds. Other members of the board are in agreement, but a group of shareholder activists have gotten wind of the idea and have threatened to sue the directors. If the board approves the purchase, on what potential basis could the shareholders sue? Are they likely to be successful? Explain.

5. Ryan and Sean are shareholders and directors of Springfield Meadows Ltd. (Springfield), a company that has developed land for a large trailer park. Springfield has 20 other shareholders. Ryan and Sean are approached by Louise, who wants to create a company whose business will be to lease trailers. Ryan and Sean are interested in participating as directors and shareholders in this new company, since this would be a good way to fill up some of the vacant sites at Springfield's trailer park. The new company is a big success, and Sean and Ryan receive impressively high dividends on a regular basis. Eventually, the other shareholders in Springfield learn about Sean and Ryan's new company and sue them for breach of their fiduciary duty. The shareholders contend that Sean and Ryan should have developed the opportunity to get into the trailer-leasing business for the benefit of Springfield and should not have taken that opportunity for themselves. Are Sean and Ryan in breach of their duty to act in the best interest of Springfield?

6. Peter sold his barbershop business to Andy for $25 000. As part of the agreement of purchase and sale, Peter agreed to a restrictive covenant that prohibited him from providing barbering services in an area within a 10-mile radius of his former shop for a period of one year. Within a month of the sale, Peter incorporated a company and commenced cutting hair in violation of the restrictive covenant.[70] Can Andy do anything about this situation? Should he do anything?

7. In *Allen v Aspen Group Resources Corporation*,[71] a class action lawsuit was certified against a Yukon oil-and-gas firm for alleged misrepresentations and omissions in a takeover circular. Included among the defendants are WeirFoulds LLP, a prominent Toronto based law firm that acted on behalf of Aspen and advised it in connection with the takeover bid, and one of the firm's partners, Wayne Egan. Egan acted as legal counsel for Aspen and had been a member of its board of directors. The plaintiffs argue that Egan's liability for both for his work as a lawyer and in his capacity as a director extends to WeirFoulds. What are the problems with professionals, such as lawyers and accountants, serving as directors for corporate clients? What are the advantages for the professional? What are the advantages for the corporation?

8. Liquor Barn Income Fund, owner of Liquor Depot, is suing its former chief executive officer (CEO) and chief operating officer (COO) for allegedly buying liquor stores through intermediary companies and reselling them to Liquor Barn. It is alleged that the defendants, between late 2006 and May 2007, bought nine liquor stores on Vancouver Island and one in Alberta and sold them to Liquor Barn at inflated prices. For example, court records show that the Days Inn liquor store in Victoria was bought for $720 000 and resold to Liquor Barn for $2.4 million, and the Grove Liquor Shoppe in Spruce Grove was bought for $948 617 and resold for $1.6 million.[72] Assume the allegations are proved to be true. What duties have the CEO and COO violated? What should they have done differently?

For more study tools, visit http://www.NELSONbrain.com.

70. Based on *Gilford Motors Co v Horne*, [1933] Ch 935 (CA).
71. (2009) 81 CPC (6th) 298, 67 BLR (4th) 99 (Ont Sup Ct).
72. David Finlayson, "Scheme by top managers to defraud Liquor Barn alleged in lawsuit", *The Edmonton Journal* (11 December 2008) online: Edmonton Journal <http://www.edmonton-journal.com/story_print.html?id=1060693&sponsor=>.

PART FOUR

PART FIVE

Property

Property consists of rights and interests in anything of value that can be owned. The law of property provides for the protection of those rights and interests.

Real property refers to land and anything attached to it. All other forms of property are included under personal property, which consists of tangible and intangible items. Tangible personal property has a physical substance from which it derives its value. Examples are trucks and appliances, which are sometimes called goods or chattels.

Intangible personal property derives its value from legal rights rather than its physical form. Examples are the right to enforce a contract and copyright in a published work. A business is likely to own an interest in many different forms of property that are important to its operation and value. An appreciation of the distinctions is useful for applying the rules that govern ownership and possession of the various forms, and for understanding the legal options for using property and generating value from it.

GALYNA ANDRUSHKO/SHUTTERSTOCK

CHAPTER 17

Personal Property

Objectives

After studying this chapter, you should have an understanding of

- the different forms of property

- how ownership and possession of property are acquired

- the obligations and rights associated with property

- the nature of the bailment relationship

- various types of bailment for reward

Business Law in Practice

Atlantic Storage Ltd. (ASL) operates a large warehouse facility in Moncton, New Brunswick, where it provides storage and safekeeping of customers' property. For the past 20 years, the customers were commercial enterprises who entrusted a wide variety of property to ASL for storage, including surplus equipment, inventory, and supplies; seasonal inventory and displays; and business records and files. ASL has recently decided to share in the sharp growth in the self-storage industry by expanding its facility to allow commercial and individual customers to rent lockers for storage of their property.

ASL owns the land on which the warehouse facility is located. ASL is situated in a suburban industrial park and has space for the warehouse and self-storage lockers, parking for customers and employees, and a vehicle garage. Because storage requirements vary according to the needs of business customers, the warehouse is divided into sections that can provide variations in storage conditions such as temperature and humidity. The building also contains extensive dividers, containers, and shelving. ASL leases five delivery vehicles and three forklifts from local equipment dealers. Other property of ASL includes accounts receivable, bank accounts, investments, and customer records. Of considerable value is the goodwill associated with the ASL business name, which has been recognized and respected in the community for 20 years. The ASL name and logo are registered trademarks.

Several problems have troubled ASL management recently. Some commercial customers have complained about improper storage of their property, resulting in damage from such causes as dampness or excessive heat. Self-storage customers expect unlimited access to their lockers, privacy regarding contents, and absolute security. Although ASL contracts are clear that ASL accepts no responsibility for damage to customers' property and customers are urged to obtain their own insurance coverage, ASL

(Continued on the next page)

has been involved in several disputes with customers about responsibility for loss. Self-storage customers also more frequently stop paying rental fees and abandon their property.

1. What types of property are used in ASL's business?
2. How did ASL acquire these various items of property?
3. What are ASL's rights in relation to property?
4. What obligations does ASL have in terms of property?

The Context of Personal Property
Description

Real property (see Chapter 19) refers to land, whatever is permanently attached to it, and the associated legal rights. ASL, as the owner of the land on which its business is located, also owns the building and any items such as light fixtures and the walls that divide the warehouse into sections. **Personal property** includes everything other than what is included under real property. Personal property falls into two major categories—tangible and intangible.

Tangible property refers to property that is concrete or material. In its business ASL uses trucks, forklifts, furniture, office supplies, and other portable items that are not attached to land or a building. In law, these kinds of personal property are known as "chattels."

Intangible property derives its value from legal rights, rather than concrete, physical qualities. Examples of intangible property are insurance policies, accounts receivable, bank accounts, and customer records, as well as the various forms of intellectual property. Internet domain names have recently been recognized as a form of property.[1] For example, the value of the fire insurance that ASL may have on its warehouse is not based on the piece of paper itself, which describes the terms of the insurance coverage. Rather, the value inherent in the fire insurance is the right that the policy creates, namely, the *right* to be compensated in the event that a fire destroys the warehouse. ASL's registered trademarks are a form of intellectual property (see Chapter 18) protected by legislation. In law, these kinds of property are known as "choses in action." Seen in this light, intangible property is no less real or significant than tangible property—in fact, it drives much of our modern economy.

Acquisition of Ownership

Ownership of property is acquired by a business in a variety of ways:

- Land is acquired through purchase or lease.

- The ownership of goods is acquired by purchasing or manufacturing them.[2]

- Insurance coverage is bought by paying premiums and is described in the insurance policy which gives the customer the right to recover losses in specified circumstances.[3]

Personal property
All property, other than land and what is attached to it.

Tangible property
Personal property which is mobile, the value of which comes from its physical form.

Intangible property
Personal property, the value of which comes from legal rights.

---

1. *Tucows.com Co v Lojas Renner SA*, 2011 ONCA 548, leave to appeal to SCC requested.
2. See the sale of goods in Chapter 23. Ownership can also be created by gift or inheritance.
3. See Chapter 28.

- Accounts receivable are created by delivering goods or services to customers, who agree to pay at a later date. The supplier acquires the right to collect the accounts, which can be sold to other businesses.[4]

- Certain kinds of intellectual property, such as copyright, are owned as a result of being created. Ownership of other forms—such as a trademark—is established through use, or registration, or both. Intellectual property can also be bought from other owners.[5]

There is no comprehensive system for publicly registering title to personal property as there is with real property, although there are some specialized registries for items such as motor vehicles, patents, and trademarks. One reason for the difference concerns the mobility of personal property. There is little utility in having a provincial registration system for most personal property when goods are so easily transported to another province. In addition, the value of individual items of personal property may not justify the cost of administering a registration system or the cost to owners of registering.

Interests in chattels are registered, however, when that property is used as security in its purchase on credit or later as collateral for a loan. Registration is considered economical because it protects the creditor's rights to the pledged property.[6]

Possession without Ownership

One party may gain possession of the property of another, often with the intent that possession ultimately be returned to the owner. Such an arrangement involves possession without ownership. There are several examples in the ASL scenario that are common in a business environment:

- ASL has chosen to lease trucks and forklifts rather than buy them.

- ASL's customers are using its facilities to store their property temporarily. There is no intention for ASL to become the owner of the stored property.

- ASL could lease its warehouse space from the owner of real property or in turn lease to another business a portion of the space that it owns.

- ASL could grant a licence to a business in another location to use its name and logo.

What most often drives the temporary split of ownership and possession is that it meets the business needs of both parties in each situation. For instance, by leasing, ASL gets the benefit of using vehicles and equipment without a large capital outlay. By storing equipment with ASL, customers get the benefit of a valuable service without having to purchase or lease a building themselves for that purpose.

Obligations Arising from Ownership and Possession

The owner of property bears ultimate responsibility for its protection. The law requires that someone other than the owner who has possession of property must take reasonable care of it and pay applicable charges for use of the property. Similarly, when a business such as ASL is providing a service to the owner, such as storage or repair, the service must be performed as agreed and reasonable care must be taken of the property until it is returned

---

4. Known as assignments of contractual rights (see Chapter 9).
5. See Chapter 18.
6. This system of registration is governed by legislation in each province and is discussed in Chapter 26.

to the owner. ASL must take good care of the leased equipment. ASL must return its customers' property in the same basic condition in which it was delivered.

This requirement to take reasonable care applies whether the arrangement is contractual or not.

If the chattels in ASL's possession have been lost, damaged, mishandled, or exposed to water, smoke, fire, or any number of other hazards, ASL is in breach of its obligation to take reasonable care. It will have to pay damages to the owners by way of compensation. Damages will be awarded in the amount necessary to restore the customer to the position it would have been in had the contract been properly performed.

Since the owner of property is the one who ordinarily bears the risk of loss from its damage or destruction, the owner may take steps to shift the risk to another business by such means as an insurance contract. When such a contract is in place, the insurance company agrees to reimburse the insured for its loss in return for payment of premiums.

Where property is in possession of someone who is not the owner, the question of who will purchase insurance should be addressed, since there is no utility in both parties insuring the same property. For example, ASL and its customers should agree on which of them is responsible if a customer's property is damaged or lost while in ASL's facilities. Whoever bears the risk of loss should place the insurance policy. In the same manner, the lease agreement between ASL and the equipment dealer should specify who is responsible for damage to the vehicles. That party, in turn, should insure the property.

Rights Arising from Ownership and Possession

The owner of property who is also in possession is entitled to deal with it essentially as she sees fit. Her options include:

- selling the property and transferring ownership and possession to the buyer

- leasing the property to another business with the intent of regaining possession or selling it when the lease expires

- using the property as security for a loan, thereby giving the lender the right to seize or sell the property if the borrower defaults on the loan

- transferring possession of chattels to another business for storage, repair, or transport with the corresponding right to regain possession

The possessor of property has the right to keep the property for the period of time provided for in the agreement with the property's owner. For example, ASL has possession of the trucks and forklifts for the duration of time set forth in the lease document. In terms of storage of customers' property, ASL has the right to be paid the agreed storage charges and generally is not required to relinquish possession until those charges are paid.

Personal Property Issues

Many legal problems relating to tangible personal property arise from its basic nature. Goods or chattels are by definition portable and therefore more difficult to track than real estate. Proof of ownership and valuation can be a challenge, as the following Business Application of the Law demonstrates.

PART FIVE

BUSINESS APPLICATION OF THE LAW

Million-Dollar Baseball

On 7 October 2001, at Pacific Bell Park in San Francisco, Barry Bonds hit his 73rd home run of the 2001 baseball season to break the single season home-run record. Alex Popov was a spectator in the right-field stands. When Bonds' home run sailed over the fence, the ball landed in Popov's glove. He was immediately hit from all sides by other spectators. The ball popped out of his glove and Popov was knocked down. When the scuffle ended, Patrick Hayashi had the ball. Popov had scratches, bruises, a bloody nose, and broken eyeglasses. Popov sued Hayashi, and the ball was held by the court pending the outcome of the litigation. While the lawsuit was underway, the ball could not be sold, and Popov posted a bond in case the record was broken; if that happened, the value of the ball would be much less than the current estimate of several million dollars.

The baseball itself gives no indication of its value or whose property it is. A normal baseball is worth less than $10. The Barry Bonds record ball is worth as much as someone is willing to pay. Difficult issues arise:

- how to prove that this ball is the real ball hit by Bonds
- how to ensure continuing authentication of the Bonds ball
- how to decide who has rights to the ball

Potential claimants included Hayashi, Popov, Barry Bonds, the pitcher, the team, the owners of the ballpark, and Major League Baseball.

There is no well-established set of rules to decide ownership of this sort of property, so many arguments can be made for resolving the dispute:

- Popov "caught" it, so he should get to keep it.
- Popov was assaulted by other spectators (including Hayashi), so they should not benefit from their criminal acts.
- Hayashi ended up with the ball. In a situation such as this, possession is the important factor.
- The rules of baseball should apply: the ball is not caught until the fielder or spectator with a glove has control.
- An umpire should decide after watching the replay.
- Use the common law that applies to hunting: the person whose harpoon first entered the whale or whose arrow first pierced the bird gets the carcass.

Judge McCarthy ultimately ruled that when the ball left the playing field, it became "intentionally abandoned property" and that the legal claims of Popov and Hayashi "are of equal quality and they are equally entitled to the ball. The ball must be sold and [the proceeds] divided equally between the parties."

When Bonds broke the career home-run record in 2007, Matt Murphy, a 21-year-old student and construction worker, emerged from a scrum in the crowd with the ball. He sold it in

Barry Bonds as a player

FRANK GUNN/THE CANADIAN PRESS

Barry Bonds sentenced on obstruction of justice conviction

JUSTIN SULLIVAN/GETTY IMAGES

an online auction for $752 467. The value of Bonds' memorabilia may be affected by his conviction in 2011 for obstruction of justice regarding his testimony in a 2003 grand jury investigation into performance-enhancing drug use by elite athletes. He was sentenced to house arrest, probation, community service, and a fine. His conviction is under appeal.

Critical Analysis: How do these examples help to resolve uncertainty about ownership and valuation of tangible personal property?

Sources: Martin Fletcher, "Million dollar baseball", *The Times [of London]* (12 December 2001) T2, 4; Larry Millson, "Bonds' HR ball cut in half", *The Globe and Mail* (19 December 2002) S1; Marcus Wohlsen, "Public to decide fate of Bonds' ball", *The Chronicle Herald* (18 September 2007) online: The Chronicle Herald<http://thechronicleherald.ca/> ; and Jason Turbow, "Bonds avoids prison time for giving evasive testimony", *The New York Times* (16 December 2011) online: The New York Times <http://www.nytimes.com/2011/12/17/sports/baseball/bonds-gets-probation-and-avoids-prison.html?nl=todaysheadlines&emc=tha27>.

Principles of Bailment
Overview

There are two key aspects of involvement with personal property—ownership and possession. Quite often the two aspects reside in the same party. For example, ASL owns and possesses the dividers and containers in its warehouse. However, it is also common for one person to be in possession of property owned by someone else. For example, ASL is only in possession of its leased equipment—the equipment is owned by the dealer. Similarly, it is only in possession of its commercial customers' property, which it holds for safekeeping in exchange for a fee. The property that ASL stores is owned by ASL customers, who are entitled to retrieve their property at any time, so long as they have paid their fees.

A **bailment** is a temporary transfer of possession of personal property from the owner, known as a **bailor**, to another party, known as a **bailee**. Ownership remains with the bailor. Possession, however, is transferred to the bailee. This is what distinguishes bailment from a contract of purchase and sale.

There are many examples of bailment in commercial transactions, including the following:

- the short-term rental of a vehicle[7]
- the long-term lease of a vehicle (e.g., ASL's leasing of trucks and forklifts)
- the delivery of property for repair
- the transport of property by a commercial carrier
- the storage of property in a warehouse (e.g., the main business of ASL)
- the shipping of an envelope by courier

Bailments are also common in the consumer context, as shown in these examples:

- leaving clothing at a dry cleaning shop
- depositing cars at a garage for servicing
- storing furniture
- borrowing library books

Any transaction that meets the definition of bailment—whether commercial, consumer, or simply personal—is covered by the general discussion in this section. To identify the rights and obligations relating to bailments, two basic questions need to be answered.

Is Payment Involved?

Most commercial bailments are based on a contract requiring payment for the use of the property or as compensation for storage or another service. These are known as **bailments for value**.

Possession of property may also be transferred without payment by virtue of a loan or a free service. This would occur when, for example, a prospective buyer takes a vehicle for a

Bailment
Temporary transfer of possession of personal property from one person to another.

Bailor
The owner of property who transfers possession in a bailment.

Bailee
The person who receives possession in a bailment.

Bailment for value
Bailment involving payment for use of property or a service.

---

7. See *Tilden Rent-A-Car Co v Clendenning* (1978), 18 OR (2d) 601 (CA) in Chapter 7.

test drive or someone parks his car in his neighbour's garage for the winter. Because there is no compensation involved in such arrangements, such instances are known as **gratuitous bailments** in the sense of being free or "without reward."

Gratuitous bailment
Bailment that involves no payment.

For Whose Benefit Is the Bailment?

The question of who benefits from a gratuitous bailment is particularly important, since the answer helps later in the chapter to determine the bailee's responsibility for the property. Gratuitous bailments can benefit the bailor or the bailee. When someone stores his car in his neighbour's garage for the winter at no charge, for example, the bailee—the person who owns the garage—derives no advantage from the relationship, while the bailor—the person who owns the car—now has protection for his vehicle from harsh weather. It is the bailor, therefore, who gains from the bailment.

Conversely, when a person borrows his neighbour's lawnmower, the owner of the lawnmower—the bailor—is simply doing a favour and does not derive any tangible benefit from the bailment. The borrower—the bailee—can now cut his grass without having to buy or lease a lawnmower from someone else and is therefore the party who profits from the relationship.

Bailments that benefit both the bailor and the bailee are most common in the commercial world and usually involve bailments for value—that is, bailments in which one of the parties is paid for the provision of a service or other benefit. For example, the owner of the vehicles and forklifts leased by ASL benefits from the relationship since it is paid by ASL. ASL also benefits since it gains possession of delivery vehicles and forklifts. Similarly, ASL benefits from storing the property of its customers since it is paid to provide the service. ASL's customers benefit because their property is stored and protected by ASL.

The Contract of Bailment

In bailments for value, the contract between the bailor and the bailee is central. The parties are free to negotiate the details of their own agreement. A contract for services will normally include a description of these aspects:

- the services to be provided by the bailee

- the price to be paid by the bailor and payment terms

- the extent to which the bailee is liable for damage or loss

- the remedies of the parties for failure to perform

In a storage contract, for example, the focus is on the bailee's liability for loss to the chattels in question and the bailee's remedies for collecting storage charges. Because a warehouse operator deals with the property of many customers in similar circumstances and is under pressure to keep prices competitive, a business such as ASL is likely to have a standard form agreement that all customers are expected to sign. The main object from ASL's perspective is to minimize its responsibility for damage caused to property in its possession, in order to keep costs down. At the same time, it is important for ASL to maintain a good reputation in the industry. Limiting liability through standard form agreements is common in the storage industry, as in the following clauses:

(a) The responsibility of a warehouseman in the absence of written provisions is the reasonable care and diligence required by the law.

(b) The warehouseman's liability on any one package is limited to $40 unless the holder has declared in writing a valuation in excess of $40 and paid the additional charge specified to cover warehouse liability.[8]

© RAMIN TALAIE/CORBIS

Who is responsible for property damaged during delivery? Who is responsible for damage to a leased truck?

While clause (b) may seem unfair—after all, if the **warehouseman's** negligence causes more than $40 in damage, should it not have to pay the full tab?—its function is to signal which party should buy insurance on the item being stored, the bailor or the bailee. In this case, the onus is on the bailor (as the owner who is limited to a claim for $40) to purchase insurance, since the item being stored is likely worth much more than that amount.

The other focus of a bailment contract is on the remedies that the bailee can use to obtain payment from delinquent customers. For example, the contract may provide that ASL is entitled to retain possession of the chattel until payment is received and may also give ASL the right to sell the chattel in order to apply the proceeds to the outstanding account. Of course, ASL's prime interest is timely payment from customers. It is interested in the right to keep customers' property only as a backup remedy.

The terms of ASL's bailment agreement for the leasing of vehicles are likely to be written by the owner of the vehicles, called the lessor, who is interested in protecting its property while that property is in ASL's possession. This is accomplished by inserting a clause in the contract making ASL responsible for any damage and by imposing limits on the extent to which ASL can use the vehicles (such as distance for the trucks and time for the forklifts). Again, insurance should be purchased to cover loss or damage, in this case by ASL. The owner of the vehicles should consider making it a term of the contract that it be named in the insurance policy as the party who is paid in event of loss.

Warehouseman
A bailee who stores personal property.

---

8. See *London Drugs Ltd v Kuehne & Nagel International Ltd*, [1992] 3 SCR 2 in Chapter 9.

PART FIVE

Liability of Bailees

Liability issues arise when some mishap occurs in relation to the property while it is in the possession of the bailee.[9] For example, the property of ASL's customers might be lost, damaged, or destroyed while in ASL's warehouse; employees might drop valuable equipment while moving it around; a forklift might run into items in its path; property could be stolen from the warehouse; there might be damage from water or a fire in the warehouse; if the property is perishable, it could spoil if not properly stored. Ideally, the contract between ASL and its customers will specify the extent of ASL's liability for these events. ASL is likely to transfer risks to customers by placing significant limits on its legal liability through exclusion or limitation of liability clauses as described above. If there is no formal agreement, the common law rules of bailment will apply.

The obligations of bailees to care for the goods of their bailors have evolved through various stages. Initially, bailees were 100 percent liable for the return of bailed chattels as well as for any damage, whether the bailee caused the damage or not and even where the bailee exercised reasonable or even extreme diligence. There are still remnants of this strict regime. Common **carriers** such as railways, as well as **innkeepers**, are caught by this old law; however, statutes have lessened and in some instances displaced the strict obligations of the early common law.

Later, the burden of the bailee to care for the goods of the bailor was determined by the concept of "benefit of the relationship." If a bailment benefited the bailor exclusively, the bailee was required to exercise slight care and was liable only for "gross neglect." If the bailment benefited the bailee exclusively, the bailee was required to exercise great care and was liable for even "slight negligence." If there was reciprocal benefit, the bailee was required to exercise ordinary diligence and was liable for "ordinary neglect."

Today, bailees are expected to exercise reasonable care in all circumstances, which include:

- *who benefits from the bailment*. If the bailment is gratuitous and for the benefit of the bailor, the standard of care is very low. If the bailment is gratuitous and for the benefit of the bailee, the standard is very high.

- *the nature and value of the property*. The bailee's standard is higher for more valuable property and should be appropriate for the type of property. This means that the bailee must show greater care when storing perishables as opposed to commodities such as wood products.

- *whether payment is involved*. A bailee for reward must show greater care than a gratuitous bailee.

- *the terms of the contract*. The contract may raise or lower the standard of care owed by the bailee.

Carrier
A bailee who transports personal property.

Innkeeper
Someone who offers lodging to the public.

9. The work of Professor Moe Litman of the Faculty of Law, University of Alberta, in this section is gratefully acknowledged.

- *the limits on liability*. The contract may set the standard at ordinary care and diligence but limit the amount of damages for which the bailee may be held liable.

- *special regulations for the type of bailment that may set out the standard of care*. Contracts to transport goods, for example, are subject to standard statutory terms.

- *special circumstances in the transaction*. Where the bailee is instructed by the bailor as to the value of the goods or special storage requirements, for example, this increases the standard of care that the bailee must meet.

- *the expertise of the bailee*. A bailee who specializes in a certain type of bailment (such as storage) is expected to take greater care than an ordinary person.

Bailees may not escape their responsibilities by turning over a bailed chattel to employees. If the chattel is damaged, lost, or stolen as a result of employees' negligence, the employer as bailee is vicariously liable so long as the employees were acting within the ordinary course or scope of their employment, that is, the employees were engaged in the performance of their assigned duties. In addition, bailees are liable for the intentional wrongdoing of their employees. A bailee who entrusts bailed goods to an employee is personally (not vicariously) liable for the theft of the goods by the employee. Another basis of liability of a bailee for theft by an employee is the law of negligence. The employer has a duty to hire honest, responsible people. Accordingly, failure to engage in proper hiring practices may result in liability for the employer.

Liability of Bailors

In contractual bailments, bailors warrant that the goods used by their bailees are fit for the purpose for which they were bailed.[10] If the goods are unfit and a bailee is injured while using a bailed chattel, the bailor may be liable. For example, if an ASL employee is hurt when the wheel falls off the forklift he is operating, the lessor will face liability.[11] This high obligation on the bailor can be reduced in the contract between the parties, however. In any event, insurance is likely to be in place to take care of the loss.

Remedies

Remedies for failure to perform obligations arising in a bailment relationship occur in two contexts:

- when a bailee is attempting to recover a fee for services performed in relation to the property

- when a bailor is trying to recover for damage or loss to the property while it was in the bailee's possession. This, in turn, usually involves two issues: (1) has the bailee met the relevant standard of care, and (2) does the agreement cancel or limit the bailee's liability? The following case illustrates these two issues.

---

10. *Ibid*.
11. In *Matheson v Watt* (1956), 19 WWR 424 (BCCA), the owner of a roller-skating rink was held liable for injuries sustained by the plaintiff when a wheel came off the roller skate the plaintiff had leased from the rink.

CASE

Melrose v Halloway Holdings Ltd, 2004 CanLII 50135 (ONSC)

THE BUSINESS CONTEXT: This case illustrates the risk that a storage company faces in exercising its rights to recover storage fees as well as the risk that the user of a storage locker takes in leaving valuable property in the locker. The primacy of legislation over contracts is also explored.

FACTUAL BACKGROUND: Robert Melrose (RM) rented storage locker 1415 from Halloway Holdings Ltd. (HH) in September, 2001. Teri Melrose (TM), RM's wife, was listed on the rental agreement as an "authorized user" of the locker. According to TM, most of the tools, furniture, and household goods in locker 1415 were hers. In November, RM rented another locker (13130) from HH. Both lease agreements exempted HH from "… loss or damage, however caused …"; stated that failure to pay rent might result in the goods stored being sold; and stated that the price obtained for the goods was deemed to be the best possible price. In March 2002, the Melroses separated. They cleared out locker 13130, moved TM's property to locker 1415, and provided a new address for RM. The locker rental fell into arrears. HH sent several notices to RM at his old address. No notice was sent to TM before the property was sold to an auction house for $800 in November. TM claimed the value of her property from HH, which she alleges was $60 000.

THE LEGAL QUESTION: Was TM protected by the *Repair and Storage Liens Act*, (*RSLA*)?[12] Was the sale of the property proper? Did the locker rental contract affect the rights provided in the *RSLA*? If not, what is the quantum of damages?

RESOLUTION: TM was found to be a person from whom property was received for storage and for which payment was made. Therefore, she was protected by the Act and entitled to her rights, even though she had no written contract with HH. HH was required to follow the statutory requirements and also owed her a common law duty of care as a bailee for value to treat the property as a prudent owner would do.

The sale by HH to the auction house did not conform to the requirements of the *RSLA* because notice was not sent to RM's last known address as required, was never sent to TM as required, and the notice sent to RM's old address was deficient in several respects. It lacked a specific description of the goods, the details of payment, and how payment could be made before the sale. In terms of the actual sale, there was no publicity, no attempt to ascertain the value of the property, and a huge gap between the sale price and the value alleged by TM.

The attempt by HH to have renters contract out of the provisions of the *RSLA* failed because the contract language was legalistic and in small print on the reverse of the agreement. There was no evidence that the terms were brought to RM's attention and even if they had been, that he would have fully understood their significance. In addition,

> [HH] disposed of the goods in a fashion so cavalier and lacking in the care that one might reasonably expect a bailee to exercise in relation to goods over which it holds a lien that, in my view, it can fairly be said that [HH's] conduct amounted to a fundamental breach of the contract of bailment.

In the alternative, Justice Clark found the offending terms to be unfair and unreasonable and therefore unconscionable. Regarding the quantum of damages, he ordered a trial to determine the contents of the locker, their fair market value, and any related damages.

CRITICAL ANALYSIS: Should there be a subsequent trial to determine damages? How could the participants in this transaction have better managed the risks arising from the locker rental? What changes in its business should HH make as a result of this case?

BUSINESS APPLICATION OF THE LAW

Defining Liability in Contracts of Bailment

As demonstrated by the exclusion of liability in the *Halloway* case above and the limit of $40 in the *London Drugs* case in Chapter 9, a key aspect of a bailment contract is often limitation of the liability that the common law rules of bailment create. The terms of these contracts are normally written by the businesses whose livelihood is based on the bailment relationship.

For example, in a bailment for services such as the ASL storage business, ASL as bailee will create the standard form agreement. In a leasing contract, the lessor as bailor will write the contract.

In the *London Drugs* case, the enforceability of the $40 clause between the customer and the warehouse company was not challenged. However, such clauses are vulnerable and can be challenged in various ways:

---

12. RSO 1990, c R.25.

• Failure to bring the standard terms to the attention of the customer. See the *Halloway* case above and the *Tilden* case in Chapter 7 for examples.

• Failure of the language in the clause to exclude liability in the circumstances. See the *Carling O'Keefe* case later in this chapter for the meaning of "package."

• Serious defect affecting the formation or performance of the contract such as fundamental breach or unconscionability. See the *Halloway* case above and the *Tercon Contractors* case in Chapter 9.

Exemption and limitation clauses are also regulated by statute:

• In the United Kingdom, bailors in rental agreements cannot exclude or restrict liability for failure of the goods to correspond with their description or in respect to their quality or fitness for a particular purpose. The statute requires that other terms limiting or excluding liability be "reasonable."[13]

• *The European Union Directive on Unfair Terms in Consumer Contracts*[14] prohibits the enforcement of terms (defined as "unfair") if they are not individually negotiated and if contrary to the requirement of good faith, would cause a significant imbalance in the parties' rights and obligations, to the detriment of the consumer.

• New Brunswick consumer protection legislation[15] applies to consumer sales that include leases. Clauses that limit liability will not be enforced unless they are considered to be "fair and reasonable."

• Industry-specific legislation may set the terms. See the *Carling O'Keefe* case below.

The courts are inclined to apply differing standards to commercial and consumer contracts. This is an important consideration for ASL since it serves both types of customers. ASL may presume that a business customer is more likely to understand contract terms and intend to be obligated by them than a consumer. Courts may also consider the contract price in relation to potential losses in deciding whether it is reasonable to enforce a limitation.[16]

Critical Analysis: Do these contract terms indicate that some businesses are exploiting customers who are less knowledgeable, less aware, or weaker, or do these clauses illustrate effective risk management? Are courts and legislatures justified in injecting ethical standards into business by applying standards such as "unfair," "unreasonable," and "unconscionable"?

Types of Bailment for Reward

The general principles of bailment described above differ to some extent when applied to the following types of bailment for reward. (See Figure 17.2 on page 417 for a summary of the following sections.)

The Lease

There are important legal distinctions between buying and leasing property. The most obvious one is that a lessee of property is not the owner and that it has possession subject to any limitations in the lease. In addition, because a lease is not a sale, it is not covered by the large number of terms implied through legislation governing the sale of goods.[17] However, there is a common law–implied term that leased property will be reasonably fit for its intended use. For example, it would be implied that the forklifts leased by ASL are suitable for the tasks normally performed with forklifts. The lessee must take reasonable care of the property while that property is in its possession and return it in the state that would be expected, subject to the normal wear and tear involved in its use. Of course, it is more prudent to address these issues of suitability, quality, and responsibility expressly in the lease agreement.

---

13. *Unfair Contract Terms Act* 1977 (UK), c 50, ss 1, 3.
14. *EC, Council Directive 93/13/EEC of 5 April 1993 on unfair terms in consumer contracts*, [1993] OJ L 95/29, 21.4.93.
15. *Consumer Product Warranty and Liability Act*, SNB 1978, c C-18.1.
16. See *Fraser Jewellers (1982) Ltd v Dominion Electric Protection Co* (1997), 148 DLR (4th) 496 (ON CA).
17. See Chapter 23.

Chattel lease
A contract where a lessee pays for the use of a lessor's tangible personal property.

There is no legislation dealing with commercial **chattel leases**,[18] so the rules come mainly from the general law of contract. The parties negotiate their own agreement as they see fit. These are some of the issues addressed in a typical lease:

- the risk that the lessee will remove the property from the district or province

- limits on the use of the property by the lessee in terms of the type and extent of work done with the equipment

- suitability of the equipment for its intended or typical uses

- responsibility for maintenance

- responsibility for damage

- the state in which the property must be returned at the end of the lease

- the period of time for which the lease runs

- the amount and schedule of payments

- termination of the lease

- remedies for breach by either party

Operating lease
A lease where the property is returned to the lessor when the term is up.

The short-term lease or rental of property is an attractive way for a business to acquire the use of equipment for a particular task or period of time. It makes little sense to purchase something that is not needed for a long period, unless, of course, the rental charges approach the cost of buying. At the end of a short-term rental, the property is returned to the owner (the lessor). This is known as an **operating lease**. Examples of this type of lease are the crane rental, which was the subject of the *DJ Lowe* case in Chapter 6,[19] and the car rental agreement discussed in the *Tilden* case in Chapter 7.[20] Lowe needed the crane only for a few days. A customer normally rents a car for a short time, such as a day, a weekend, or a week.

Leasing is also a means to acquire property needed on a permanent basis and is an alternative to purchasing. For example, the trucks and forklifts leased by ASL are needed as part of the ongoing operation, and ASL has made the financial decision to lease rather than buy. The lease is a means of financing ASL's acquisition of the equipment, through payment of rent over a defined period of time. ASL may lease the equipment directly from the dealer, in which case the dealer remains the owner and the lessor (see Figure 17.1 A). In a more complicated version of the transaction, the dealer sells the equipment to a financial company that in turn leases it to ASL (see Figure 17.1 B). Both variations are known as **financing leases**, but they involve quite different rights and obligations. A feature of both is the possibility that ASL may buy the equipment at the end of the lease, rather than return it to the lessor.

Financing lease
A lease that enables the lessee to finance the acquisition of tangible personal property.

---

18. Consumer protection legislation in most provinces now regulates consumer leases to varying degrees. See, for example, *Consumer Product Warranty and Liability Act*, SNB 1978, c C-18.1 (New Brunswick); *Consumer Protection Act, 2002*, SO 2002, c 30, Schedule A (Ontario).
19. *Lowe (DJ) (1980) Ltd v Upper Clements Family Theme Park Ltd* (1990), 95 NSR (2d) 397 (SC(TD)).
20. *Supra* note 7.

FIGURE 17.1

Forms of a Chattel Lease

A. Two-party leasing arrangement

Result: One contract—ASL has remedies against the dealer for problems with the property.

B. Three-party leasing arrangement

Result: Two contracts—dealer sells to financier, who leases to ASL. ASL has no contract with the dealer.

The contractual arrangements are more complicated if the lessor is a financial company rather than the original owner. In such a transaction there are two contracts—one of the sale between the dealer and the financier, and the other the lease between the financier and the lessee. The only parties to the contract for the purchase are the dealer and the financier. The dealer is not a party to the lease and therefore has no obligations to the lessee connected with it. If the lessee has relied on statements or assurances from the dealer in deciding to lease the property from the financier, it is difficult to hold the financier responsible for those statements.

ASL should know who the lessor is and ensure that the lease adequately protects it if the arrangement fails to go as planned. For example, ASL should ensure that its obligation to make payments is tied to the suitability and performance of the equipment. ASL's current concern about increased repair costs may be addressed by the lease terms. This is normally the case if ASL is leasing from the dealer, but if the lessor is a finance company, the lease will likely protect the financier from the normal rights that a buyer would have in a sale. Each type of transaction involves different risks to be managed.

Storage

This type of bailment forms the core of ASL's business—storage of commercial customers' property. Customers entrust their property to ASL and have limited means for monitoring ASL's treatment of their property. As a result, the law imposes a high level of accountability on ASL for its treatment of customers' property. Of particular importance are any limits on what ASL can do with the property in terms of the type of storage or the possibility of moving it to other locations. For example, ASL must keep items that would be harmed by cold temperatures in an adequately heated space. ASL may need permission from customers to store property in any facilities other than its own. Customers expect their property to be returned in the same condition in which it was delivered, unlike in the

PART FIVE

case of ASL's leased vehicles, where the intent is for ASL to use them. If the property is lost, damaged, or destroyed, customers will look to ASL for compensation. The main concern from ASL's perspective is payment of the storage fees by customers and its ability to collect.

ASL's general responsibility toward its customers' property is to treat it as a "skilled storekeeper" would deal with its own property.[21] This imposes a standard of reasonableness that includes responsibility for all foreseeable risks. Because the standard is high and the potential losses are high, ASL is likely to limit its liability to its customers in its standard form agreements with them. A typical limitation clause is the one shown on page 407, where the contract limits the bailee's liability to $40.

The circumstances of the self-storage contracts are much different in the sense that customers essentially rent the storage space and control the contents and their access to them. ASL is naturally reluctant to accept the same degree of responsibility that it might toward commercial customers whose property ASL more actively controls.

The remedies of a storage bailee, or warehouseman, are contained in legislation in each province.[22] The bailee has a lien over the property until the owner pays the storage fees. This means that ASL can keep its customers' property until payment is complete. If payment is not forthcoming, ASL also has the right to sell the property and apply the proceeds to the outstanding charges. Any surplus proceeds of the sale go to the owner. The legislation contains safeguards for the owner in that notice of the intended sale must be given and the bailee must deal with the property in a reasonable manner—for example, not sell valuable property for the amount of a relatively small storage bill. These limitations are of particular concern to ASL in self-storage situations, where ASL may have limited knowledge of the property that is stored. See the *Halloway* case on page 410 for discussion of these limits.

These rights and responsibilities relating to a storage bailment apply only if the arrangement meets the definition of a bailment—there must be a transfer of possession and control from the owner to another person. Otherwise, the responsibility for the property is much less and the remedies for collection are less effective. For example, leaving a vehicle in a parking lot and paying a parking fee does not amount to a bailment unless the keys are delivered to an attendant, thereby transferring control of the vehicle. If the owner keeps the keys, the parking lot is not in control of the vehicle and the transaction is likely one for the use of the parking space, with minimal responsibility for what is in the space.[23] Operators of parking lots commonly issue tickets that are meant to define the relationship (use of space rather than bailment) and either exclude liability completely or limit it to a small amount. As with any standard form contract, the customer must receive adequate notice of onerous and unexpected terms. ASL's relationship with its self-storage consumers could be similarly characterized, since ASL has access to the storage space only in exceptional circumstances, such as non-payment of fees or emergency.

---

21. See *Punch v Savoy's Jewellers Ltd* (1986), 54 OR (2d) 383 (CA).
22. See, for example, *Warehouse Lien Act*, RSBC 1996, c 480; *Warehouser's Lien Act*, RSNL 1990, c W-2; *Repair and Storage Liens Act*, RSO 1990, c R-25.
23. Bruce H Ziff, *Principles of Property Law*, 5th ed (Toronto: Carswell, 2010) at 321-22.

Repairs

When the owner of property takes it to a repair shop, the main purpose of the transaction is the repair of the property. If the property is left at the shop, a storage bailment, which is incidental to the main purpose of the arrangement, is also created. At the appointed time for pickup, the owner—the bailor—expects to receive the property in a good state of repair and otherwise in the condition in which it was delivered. The bailee must provide reasonable safekeeping for the property and complete the repairs in a workmanlike manner, as a reasonably competent repairer of that sort of property would.

From a business perspective, it makes sense to agree on a price in advance, but if the parties do not agree on the price for storage and repairs at the outset, the repairer's compensation will be a reasonable amount for the service provided. The repairer cannot charge more than is reasonable, nor can the owner refuse to pay anything, just because no price was agreed in advance.

Most provinces have legislation[24] giving the bailee a **lien** against the property for the value of the repairs as long as the bailee has possession of the property.[25] As with the storage situation, the bailee also has the right to sell the property (subject to procedural requirements) to recover the repair charges.

Lien
The right to retain possession of personal property until payment for service is received.

Transportation

Bailees who receive property and transport it according to the owner's instructions are called carriers. There are several categories of carriers, each with different obligations toward the property. The most relevant in business are common carriers—those who represent themselves to the public as carriers for reward, meaning they are prepared to transport any property for any owner so long as their facilities permit and they are paid for the service. Common carriers are held to a very high standard of care regarding the property they carry. If property is lost or damaged while in their possession, it is presumed that the carrier is liable. The owner is not required to prove fault by the carrier, mainly because it is difficult for the owner to know what happened to the property during the transport. Carriers are required to account for their treatment of the property and justify the application of one of the limited legal defences, which mainly relate to circumstances within the control of the owner or beyond the control of the carrier. For example, if the owner fails to pack fragile goods adequately or the goods are destroyed in a natural disaster, the carrier could be excused from liability.

As a result of this heavy responsibility based on legislation and the common law, carriers normally include provisions in their standard form agreements with customers that the carriers' liability will be severely limited should mishap occur with the property. These clauses typically limit liability to a low dollar amount. Customers are protected by legislation covering each form of transport—rail, road, sea, and air. Clauses used in contracts

---

24. See, for example, *Mechanics' Lien Act*, RSNL 1990, c M-3; *Builders' Lien Act*, RSNS 1989, c 277; *Repairers' Lien Act*, RSBC 1996, c 404; *Repair and Storage Liens Act*, RSO 1990, c R-25.
25. Some legislation also allows for non-possessory liens based on an acknowledgment of the debt. See *Repair and Storage Liens Act*, RSO 1990, c R-25.

PART FIVE

on international or interprovincial routes must be approved by the Canadian Transport Commission. The case below illustrates potential problems with the transport of goods.

Carriers do not have the same legislative remedies as those who repair or store property. Carriers have a common law lien against the property for transport charges, but enjoy no corresponding right to sell the property if the owner fails to pay.

CASE

Carling O'Keefe Breweries of Canada Ltd v CN Marine Inc, [1990] 1 FC 483 (CA)

THE BUSINESS CONTEXT: Deciding who is responsible for damaged goods and for how much requires a full investigation of the events that occurred and a detailed examination of the terms of the contract, any legislation, and applicable international rules.

FACTUAL BACKGROUND: Carling engaged CN to ship 4240 cases of beer from St. John's to Goose Bay. CN arranged shipping aboard a ship owned by Labrador Shipping. The beer was placed in three large containers and stowed on the deck of the ship with the edges of the containers protruding over the sides of the ship. The containers were washed overboard in heavy seas. Carling claimed the value of the beer ($32 000) from CN and the owners of the ship. The ship's owners became insolvent, leaving CN as the defendant able to pay a judgment. CN argued that it was acting only as agent for the ship's owners and therefore had no liability, and that in any event its liability should be limited to $500 per container (a total of $1500) by virtue of the applicable federal legislation.

THE LEGAL QUESTION: Did the contract relieve CN from liability as a carrier and limit damages to $500 for each container? Did the $500 limit apply to each of the three large shipping containers or to each of the 4240 cases of beer?

RESOLUTION: The contract was governed by federal legislation (the *Carriage of Goods by Water Act*), which incorporated the *Hague Rules* (an international convention providing for standardized terms in such transactions). The *Hague Rules* prevented a carrier from avoiding liability for improper storage of goods and also limited claims to $500 "per package." The court found that CN was the carrier (not just the agent of the ship's owners) because it had signed the contract in its personal capacity (becoming a "carrier" as defined in the *Hague Rules*) and because it had acted as a carrier in the loading and stowage of the cargo on board the vessel.

In terms of the number of "packages" on which Carling O'Keefe could recover up to $500, the court looked to the intention of the parties as revealed by the language of the documents, what they said, and what they did. The shipping documents listed 4240 packages. It was also noted that "it is common knowledge that beer is shipped in cases." On this basis, Carling recovered its full loss from CN.

CRITICAL ANALYSIS: Is the adoption of international rules an effective way to manage risk? How could CN have limited its liability to $1500 instead of $32 000? How could Carling have controlled its risk?

Transportation of goods involves many parties, contracts, and risks. What are some potential legal problems arising from this scene?

Lodging

Those who offer lodging to the public are known as innkeepers. At common law, their responsibility for guests' property is similar to that of common carriers. They must take great care of guests' property and are responsible for loss or theft. There is an important practical distinction in the degree of control between carriers and innkeepers. Carriers have total control of the property when it is delivered for shipment, while guests share control over their property through their occupation of rooms.

Innkeepers are permitted by legislation[26] to limit their liability to a specific amount ($40 to $150, depending on the province) if they post the legislated limits in the establishment. Their protection is lost if the loss to property is due to a negligent or deliberate act of the innkeeper (or the inn's employees) or if the property has been deposited with the inn for safekeeping.

FIGURE 17.2

Summary of Bailment

Type of bailment	Lease	Storage	Repair	Transport	Lodging
Specialized designation for the bailor	Lessor	Customer	Customer	Shipper	Guest
Specialized designation for the bailee	Lessee	Warehouse	Repairer	Carrier	Innkeeper
Bailee's standard of care	Reasonable	Reasonable	Reasonable	High	High
Liability normally limited	Wear and tear	Contract	Contract	Contract	Legislation
Who gets paid for a service	Bailor	Bailee	Bailee	Bailee	Bailee
Remedies for non-payment	Possession, damages	Lien, sale	Lien, sale	Lien	Lien
Applicable legislation	No	Yes	Yes	No	Yes
Examples	SD3, 6	*Halloway* case BLIP	SD 4	*Carling* case SD 8	QCT 3

Risk Management

The risks relating to personal property concern proof and protection of ownership, rights to possession, and the preservation of economic value. With tangible property, the major concern is with responsibility for loss or damage to the property. In bailments for value, an additional risk is the failure of the customer to pay for services such as storage or repair.

Businesses subject to these risks can use the risk management model to minimize their impact on the success of the business. For example, ASL can decline to accept items for storage that are particularly susceptible to loss or unsuitable for ASL's facilities, thereby avoiding such risks. ASL will strive to reduce the remaining risks through well-developed and administered procedures within its storage facilities. In bailment transactions, the transfer of risk is prominent. Carefully negotiated contracts will indicate who bears the loss in a variety of circumstances. The contract will assign the loss and thereby indicate which party should seek to transfer its risk through appropriate insurance policies. As in most business situations, the risks that cannot be avoided, reduced, or transferred will be retained.

---

26. See, for example, *Innkeepers' Act*, RSO 1990, c I-7; *Hotel Keepers Act*, CCSM c H150.

Business Law in Practice Revisited

1. What types of property are used in ASL's business?

ASL uses real property (its land, warehouse, and anything permanently attached to the land and warehouse), tangible personal property (shelving, dividers, vehicles, customers' property), and intangible personal property (trademarks, accounts receivable). A typical business would use a similar range of property, including examples of the major classifications of property.

2. How did ASL acquire these various items of property?

ASL acquired its property by purchase (land, warehouse furnishings), lease (vehicles), bailment (customers' property), creation and use (business name), and dealing with customers (accounts receivable, customer records).

3. What are ASL's rights in relation to property?

ASL's rights depend to a large extent on whether it is the owner or merely in possession of each type of property. For example, as owner of the land, ASL has total control subject to any contracts or statutory restrictions (see Chapter 19). For property it does not own, but of which it has temporary possession, ASL has more limited rights. For example, ASL has the right (according to legislation) to hold customers' property until they pay the agreed storage fees. If customers don't pay, ASL can sell their property to recover the outstanding fees. It is important to emphasize these rights in their agreements with customers.

4. What obligations does ASL have in terms of property?

For property it does not own, ASL's obligations arise from the nature of the transactions involving the property and the terms of the applicable contracts and legislation. For example, ASL has a duty to treat customers' property as a reasonably competent warehouse proprietor would treat its own property, subject to the protection for ASL contained in its standard form customer contracts. For example, where a customer's stored documents suffered water damage, ASL needs to improve its treatment of this type of property. This protection will relate to ASL's conduct and its level of liability in dollar terms. This duty is complicated in self-storage, since ASL is not aware of the contents of lockers. Customers should be advised about the types of property that are suitable for ASL's facilities. In addition, ASL must take reasonable care of the leased vehicles subject to normal wear and tear. The leases will likely set out ASL's obligations, including responsibility for repairs, in considerable detail.

Chapter Summary

Property can be divided into real and personal. There are two categories of personal property: tangible, which includes goods or chattels, and intangible, which includes various contractual and statutory rights.

Ownership is acquired by purchase or manufacture (goods); creation, registration, or purchase (intellectual property); or trading (accounts receivable). Possession can be acquired along with ownership or through a bailment.

The owner of property has full responsibility for it and bears the risk of loss. The owner also has the right to deal with the property in whatever way he chooses.

A bailment is the temporary transfer of possession with no change in ownership. A commercial bailment (bailment for value) benefits both the bailor (owner) and bailee (possessor). Key issues in bailment are the standard of care that the bailee must observe in relation to the property and the remedies that the parties have for recovering fees. Standard form contracts are a common feature of bailments.

The most common types of bailments are leasing, storage, repairs, transportation, and lodging. Each has somewhat different rules for liability and remedies.

PART FIVE

Chapter Study

Key Terms and Concepts

bailee (p. 405)

bailment (p. 405)

bailment for value (p. 405)

bailor (p. 405)

carrier (p. 408)

chattel lease (p. 412)

financing lease (p. 412)

gratuitous bailment (p. 406)

innkeeper (p. 408)

intangible property (p. 401)

lien (p. 415)

operating lease (p. 412)

personal property (p. 401)

tangible property (p. 401)

warehouseman (p. 407)

Questions for Review

1. How is personal property different from real property?

2. What are some examples of personal property?

3. How is tangible property different from intangible property?

4. Who bears the risk of loss to personal property?

5. How is ownership of personal property acquired?

6. What can the owner of personal property do with it?

7. When is the owner of personal property not in possession of it?

8. What is a bailment?

9. What are some examples of bailments?

10. How do commercial bailments and consumer bailments differ?

11. How can a bailee for value collect fees?

12. What is the liability of a bailee for damage to the goods?

13. How can a bailee limit the liability for damage to the goods?

14. When are contractual limits on damages not enforced?

15. What are the major differences among the types of bailment for reward?

16. What is the difference between an operating lease and a financing lease?

17. What role does insurance play in bailment?

18. What risks relate to personal property?

Questions for Critical Thinking

1. Personal property in the form of chattels is portable. Proving and tracking ownership and possession are challenging. Should we establish a comprehensive system of registering all chattels as we do for motor vehicles? How would such a system help in verifying and tracking? Would the benefits justify the expense?

2. Intangible personal property includes legal rights, which may be contained in legal documents such as a lease or a loan agreement. Are these rights as difficult to control as chattels? Should those documents be available for examination in a public registry?

3. Legislation governing innkeepers' liability for their guests' property was developed to deal with an environment when guests were to a large extent at the mercy of innkeepers with regard to the safety of their property. Is this the case today where most hotels are professionally owned and managed? Are guests still at risk?

4. The standard of care in a bailment depends on the type of bailment and the particular circumstances of the transaction. Therefore, the obligations of the bailor and bailee may be difficult to define in a contract in advance of a dispute. Would legislation be an easier way to set the standard?

5. The self-storage industry is growing rapidly as business and individuals need extra space to store their excess property. Does the rental of a storage locker fit the definition of bailment? Are there specific issues in this type of transaction that require a different set of rules from those in place for other bailment-type situations?

6. Commercial bailees generally try to minimize their liability in a standard form contract. They justify these low limits as a means of controlling risk and keeping their prices competitive. Is there a market opportunity

for more generous liability terms? For example, could a storage business increase market share by accepting a greater risk of liability than its competitors and charging a higher price?

Situations for Discussion

1. Clancy's Cars Ltd. engaged Railco Ltd. to transport several motor vehicles from Montreal to Halifax. The vehicles were to be delivered to Clancy's on Wednesday, but they were delayed. On Saturday, an employee of Railco informed Clancy's that the vehicles had arrived at Railco's facilities in Halifax and would be delivered to Clancy's on Monday. Over the weekend, a violent wind and rain storm hit Halifax. Although the vehicles were parked in an area for safekeeping, they were severely damaged in the storm. When Clancy's claimed damages, Railco argued that the storm was so severe it was an "act of God."[27] Who is responsible for the damage to the vehicles?

2. Black was looking to buy a quality used luxury vehicle. He found a 2010 Audi at Dexter's Audi that met his needs. He examined the car on several occasions and took it for a couple of test drives. Discussions with Dexter's salesperson White were productive, and Black and White were close to making a deal. Black wanted to have the car inspected by an expert mechanic before finally agreeing to buy it, so he asked to have the car over a long weekend so he could drive it further and complete the inspection. White agreed, but required Black to sign a draft agreement and pay a deposit on the purchase price. Black signed the document "subject to satisfactory inspection." Black took the car, but before the inspection could be done, he encountered a deer on the highway. He swerved to avoid the deer, lost control, went off the road, and hit a tree at high speed. Black was not injured but the car was demolished.[28] Was this a bailment situation? Who is responsible for the vehicle?

3. Ying leased a machine to haul large logs in her lumbering business. The lease required Ying to keep the machine in good repair and fully insured, and to return it at the end of the lease in its original condition, subject to "normal wear and tear." The machine never worked very well. Ying ran up large repair bills and began to suspect the machine was not heavy enough for the needs of her business. When she contacted the leasing company, she was reminded that the lessor had made no promises about performance of the equipment. Ying is thinking about stopping her lease payments and insurance premiums and leasing a heavier machine from another dealer. She needs that heavier machine to maintain profitable levels of production. What factors should she consider? What would you advise her to do? Would your opinion be different if Ying had instead leased a truck for her personal use?

4. Ying took her logging machine in for repairs. A week later she got a call from the shop to tell her that the machine was fixed and the bill was $4500. Ying had left strict instructions with the shop that she must approve all work before it was done. What rules of contract determine whether Ying is obligated to pay the bill? If she refuses, what are the shop's remedies? What safeguards and risks are involved in those remedies for Ying? Would the result be different for a consumer contract?[29]

5. Roach owned a truck with a large crane attached. Roach took the truck to Vern's Auto to have the crane removed with the intention of mounting it on another vehicle in the future. Vern's allowed Roach to leave the crane in its yard, assuring him it would be safe. A few months later, Roach decided to sell the crane. When he went to get the crane, it was gone. Vern's had no idea what had happened to it, and because the company had charged nothing for storing the crane, it was not interested in finding out.[30] Is Vern's responsible for the missing crane? What are the determining factors? What information is missing? What steps should Roach and Vern's have taken to safeguard the crane?

6. Ace Towing leased a truck from City Motors. TGI was anxious to sell Ace a new truck and offered to buy out the lease from City Motors if Ace would buy a new truck from TGI. The deal was completed and the leased truck was delivered to TGI without any examination of its condition. TGI discovered that the truck's engine required significant repairs.[31] Who is responsible for payment of the engine repairs?

---

27. Based, in part, on *Carroll Pontiac Buick Ltd v Searail Cargo Surveys Ltd*, 2005 NSSM 12.
28. Based on *Black v Dexter's Autohaus*, 2008 NSSC 274.
29. Based, in part, on *Gary Auto Repair v Velk*, 2010 ONSC 3183.
30. Based on *Lowe (DJ) (1980) Ltd v Roach* (1994), 131 NSR (2d) 268 (SC), aff'd (1995), 138 NSR (2d) 79 (CA).
31. Based on *T G Industries Ltd v Ace Towing Ltd*, 2007 NSSM 89, rev'd 2008 NSSC 65.

7. Horst is a collector of hockey memorabilia. He is particularly interested in hockey sticks that have been autographed by well-known players in the National Hockey League. When Horst checked on eBay, he found many autographed hockey sticks for sale, including several signed by his favourite players. He is prepared to pay the going rate, but wants to be sure that the autographs are authentic and that the current owners acquired the sticks legitimately. Horst has heard of organizations that purport to authenticate autographs, but has also heard of many "fake" autographs that were authenticated. What legal issues should Horst consider? How should he manage the risks facing him?

8. Canfor hired B.C. Rail to transport wood pulp from the interior of British Columbia to a shipping terminal for eventual delivery to a customer in Scotland. The contract between Canfor and B.C. Rail specified that the railcars would be clean and the pulp delivered free from contamination. Canfor insisted on wood-lined boxcars and also routinely inspected and swept out the cars before loading bales of pulp. When the pulp arrived in Scotland, it was contaminated with wood splinters and rejected by the customer. Canfor had to compensate its customer and pay for transporting the pulp back to B.C.[32] Can Canfor recover its losses from B.C. Rail? Explain.

For more study tools, visit http://www.NELSONbrain.com.

32. Based on *B.C. Rail Ltd v Canadian Forest Products Ltd*, 2005 BCCA 369.

CHAPTER 18

Intellectual Property

OBJECTIVES

After studying this chapter, you should have an understanding of

- the nature of intellectual property
- the rights that attach to intellectual property
- how intellectual property is acquired
- how to protect the intellectual property assets of an organization

COREL

Business Law in Practice

Since graduating from university three years ago, Estelle Perez has been employed in the engineering department of ELEX Technologies Inc., a small manufacturer of electronic products including sensors, mobile phones, and wireless routers. Estelle's main responsibility has been to devise better and more efficient production methods. Although she likes her job with ELEX, Estelle's ultimate goal is to start a company that would focus on her real passion, namely invention and design. Driven by this ambition, Estelle spends virtually every evening and weekend experimenting with her own highly innovative product ideas.

Though ELEX is a successful company, it faces many challenges. For example, last year alone, as much as 15 percent of its products malfunctioned and were returned by customers, resulting in lost sales and profits. ELEX confirmed that product breakdown was being caused by electrostatic discharge (ESD) during shipping, a huge problem for electronic manufacturers across the board. Estelle concluded that the main industry solution relied upon by ELEX, that of using plastic packaging to reduce ESD, had been neither efficient (witness ELEX's failure rate) nor environmentally friendly (because all that plastic simply ended up in landfills). Estelle has come up with a seemingly optimal solution. She has designed protective packaging made of recyclable conductive paper, which has the ability to absorb the damaging effects of static electricity.[1] Estelle's design called for the static protection to be woven into the fibre of the paper, which could, in turn, be converted into boxes, bags, and envelopes. She has even figured out how to add colour options to the packaging, thereby providing customization opportunities to suit the commercial customer's individual marketing requirements.

---

1. The idea for this Business Law in Practice is based on patented technology developed by Yonghao Ni, a professor and director of University of New Brunswick's Limerick Pulp and Paper Research Centre. See www.knowcharge.com.

(Continued on the next page)

Estelle believes in her new product and would like to quit her job with ELEX in order to work full time on it. However, she also worries about her lack of experience on the business side of product development and how she could ever keep her invention a secret while exploring the possibility of funding. As well, and assuming the product is successful, Estelle is concerned that she will be required to share the proceeds of her invention with ELEX.

Estelle knows that the future of her anticipated new product will depend, in part, on marketing and she has already come up with a catchy name for her product—"Chargeless." She does not think anyone else is using that name except a financial services company that deploys it as part of their slogan "We charge less." As her name has a different spelling and is in an entirely different business sector, Estelle concludes that she will be OK in using "Chargeless" as her product moniker.

1. Is Estelle's idea a patentable invention?
2. Who owns the rights to Estelle's invention—Estelle or ELEX?
3. How can Estelle protect her idea while she seeks funding from potential lenders and investors?
4. Is Estelle entitled to use the name "Chargeless" for her product, and should she do anything to protect the name?

Introduction

Intellectual property
The results of the creative process, such as ideas, the expression of ideas, formulas, schemes, trademarks, and the like; also refers to the protection attached to ideas through patent, copyright, trademark, industrial design, and other similar laws.

Intellectual property is a term often used to describe the results of intellectual or creative processes.[2] Put another way, the term is used for describing ideas or ways of expressing ideas. Some common business examples of intellectual property are:

- recipes and formulas for making products

- manufacturing processes

- methods of extracting minerals

- advertising jingles

- business and marketing plans

- the distinctive name given to a product or service

Estelle's method of weaving static protection into the fibre of paper, and the name for her product are also examples.

The term "intellectual property"[3] is also used to describe the "bundle of rights" that people have regarding their ideas or the ways in which they are expressed. These rights are rewards or incentives for creating and developing ideas. There are differing rights in intellectual property as the law gives varying types of protection to its many forms. The main categories of intellectual property laws are patents, trademarks, copyrights, industrial designs, and confidential (business) information.[4] (See Figure 18.1 on page 447 for a

---

2. The suggestions of Professor Wayne Renke of the Faculty of Law, University of Alberta, and Professor Peter Lown, director of the Alberta Law Reform Institute, in reviewing an earlier draft of this chapter are gratefully acknowledged.
3. The term "intellectual property" is used to refer to both intangibles—such as ideas and their expression, formulas, schemes, trademarks, and the like—and rights that may attach to these intangibles. However, not all intellectual property can be technically called "property," as the basis for protection is not always "property" principles but principles of contract and tort as well as specific statutory provisions.
4. The term "confidential information" includes a broad range of information, such as government secrets and private personal information. In this text, the term "confidential business information" is used to distinguish information of a commercial nature from other types of information.

comparison of these forms). There are other laws, however, that provide protection for specific types of intellectual property. For example, there are laws that protect plant varieties,[5] integrated circuit topographies,[6] and personality rights.[7]

Intellectual property is a necessary and critical asset in many industries, as illustrated in these examples:

- Patents protect inventions and are essential to businesses in the pharmaceutical, electronics, chemical, and manufacturing industries, as patents may be used to exclude others from using new technology.

- Industrial designs protect the appearance of useful articles against copying and are relevant to businesses that offer goods to consumers.

- Trademarks serve to distinguish the goods or services of one provider from those of another and are essential to all businesses that sell goods or services to the public.

- Copyright prevents the copying of certain works and is the basis for businesses involved in art, publishing, music, communications, and software, as copyright provides the basis for a saleable product.

- The law governing confidentiality is the means of protecting such information as marketing plans, customer lists, databases, and price lists, and is crucial to all businesses.[8]

Intellectual property offers both opportunities and challenges to business. Businesses can gain a competitive advantage by developing new products, innovative business methods, and creative brand names. Also, they can exploit these things by assigning or licensing their use to other businesses. However, the development of various technologies, such as photocopiers, tape recorders, video cameras, and computers, has made it easier for others to "take" intellectual property.[9]

This chapter explores the creation, acquisition, and protection of intellectual property.

Creation of Intellectual Property Rights

Estelle's intellectual property comprises the method for weaving static protection into the fibre, the name of her product, and any written materials such as drawings, plans, and brochures. Various aspects of her intellectual property may qualify for protection under different legal regimes.

Patents

Estelle's method for protecting electronic products may qualify for **patent** protection. A patent is a statutory right[10] that provides protection for inventions.

Patent
A monopoly to make, use, or sell an invention.

---

5. *Plant Breeders' Rights Act*, SC 1990, c 20. This Act provides 18-year patent-like protection for distinct new plant varieties.
6. *Integrated Circuit Topography Act*, SC 1990, c 37. This act provides 10-year protection for layout designs embedded in semiconductor chips or circuit boards (e.g., microchips).
7. Personality rights, or the right not to have one's name or likeness appropriated for another's gain, are protected under tort actions, trademark legislation, and privacy legislation, such as British Columbia's *Privacy Act*, RSBC 1996, c 373.
8. Sheldon Burshtein, "Executives remain unaware of the value of intellectual property assets", *The Lawyers Weekly* (27 June 1997) 23.
9. In recognition of the difficulties in policing copyright infringement of music, there is a levy on blank tapes. See *Copyright Act*, RSC 1985, c C-42 s 82 (1): Every person who, for the purpose of trade, manufactures a blank audio recording medium in Canada or imports a blank audio recording medium into Canada (a) is liable, subject to subsection (2) and section 86, to pay a levy to the collecting body on selling or otherwise disposing of those blank audio recording media in Canada.
10. The federal government has jurisdiction to make laws concerning patents, copyrights, and trademarks. See *Constitution Act, 1867*, s 91.

Patents Defined

The *Patent Act*[11] defines an invention as "any new and useful art, process, machine, manufacture or composition of matter or any new and useful improvement[12] in any art, process, machine, manufacture or composition of matter." The definition is very broad and encompasses a number of different kinds of inventions such as

- processes or methods (e.g., a pay-per-use billing system, a system for applying a selective herbicide to improve crop yield, a method of cleaning carpets)

- machines or apparatuses (e.g., computer hardware, a hay rake, a vacuum cleaner)

- products or compositions of matter (e.g., pharmaceuticals, chemical compounds, microorganisms)

Estelle's invention may qualify for patent protection as a new and improved method for protecting electronic products from electrostatic discharge.

Substances intended for food or medicine, as well as the processes for producing them are patentable. The question of whether new life forms created as the result of genetic engineering should be patentable has been the subject of much controversy.

CASE | ***Monsanto v Schmeiser*, 2004 SCC 34, [2004] 1 SCR 902**

THE BUSINESS CONTEXT: In 2002, in *Harvard College v Canada (Commissioner of Patents)*,[13] the Supreme Court of Canada held by a narrow 5-to-4 margin that higher life forms are not patentable. Although the process for genetically modifying cells was held to be patentable, the end result, a mouse susceptible to cancer, was not. The decision was a large disappointment to many in the biotechnology industry, as Canada's major trading partners, including the United States, Europe, Australia, and Japan, permit such patents. The decision also created uncertainty as to the scope of protection afforded to biotechnology-related inventions.

FACTUAL BACKGROUND: Percy Schmeiser is a Saskatchewan farmer who grows canola. Monsanto is a multinational firm specializing in biotechnologies used in agriculture. In the 1990s, Monsanto introduced Roundup Ready canola, a variety of canola containing genetically modified genes and cells patented by Monsanto. Roundup Ready canola is resistant to Roundup, a pesticide, which means that the canola plants can be sprayed with Roundup to kill weeds but not harm the crop. Monsanto licensed its Roundup Ready canola to farmers for a fee, provided the farmers purchased the canola seeds from an authorized Monsanto agent.

Schmeiser did not purchase Roundup Ready canola seeds nor did he obtain a licence from Monsanto. By chance, he discovered some Roundup Ready canola growing on his property. It is unclear how the canola got onto his property, but it is possible that the seeds blew there from a neighbour's land. Schmeiser collected and cultivated the seeds and most of his 1998 canola crop comprised Roundup Ready canola. Once his activities were detected, Monsanto sued him for patent infringement.

THE LEGAL QUESTION: Had Schmeiser, by collecting and planting the seeds and harvesting and selling the plants, infringed Monsanto's patents relating to genetically modified canola?

RESOLUTION: By a narrow 5-to-4 margin, the Supreme Court of Canada held that Monsanto's patents were valid and that Schmeiser had infringed them. Schmeiser had argued that he had not "used" the invention by growing canola plants because the plants are not covered by Monsanto's patents, only the plant cells containing the modified gene. The majority disagreed. The court held that the plants were composed of modified plant cells containing the modified genes, and therefore growing the modified plants constituted use of the invention. The majority used the following analogy: "If an infringing use were alleged in

---

11. RSC 1985, c P-4, s 2. The *Patent Act* was substantially amended in 1987, RSC 1987, c 33 (3rd Supp) and became effective 1 October 1989. Patents issued prior to this date remain subject to the earlier law. Substantial amendments, notably in respect to pharmaceuticals, were also effected by the *Intellectual Property Law Improvement Act*, SC 1993, c 15.
12. Ninety percent of all patents are for improvements to existing patented inventions. See Canadian Intellectual Property Office, *A Guide to Patents* (Gatineau, QC) online: Canadian Intellectual Property Office <http://www.ic.gc.ca/eic/site/cipointernet-internetopic.nsf/vwapj /GuideBrevet-PatentGuide-eng.pdf/$FILE/GuideBrevet-PatentGuide-eng.pdf>.
13. 2002 SCC 76, [2002] 4 SCR 45.

© AGSTOCK IMAGES/CORBIS

What are the benefits of granting patents for life forms?

building a structure with patented Lego blocks, it would be no bar to a finding of infringement that only the blocks were used and not the whole structure." In essence, the court confirmed the patentability of cells and genes, and held that the rights in patented genes and cells extend to plants containing them.

CRITICAL ANALYSIS: Are there any concerns with manipulating genes in order to obtain better weed control or higher yields? How does this decision support the Canadian biotechnology industry?

POSTSCRIPT: In 2005, more of the genetically modified canola appeared on Percy and Louise Schmeiser's farm. They pulled it out themselves and sent Monsanto a bill for $600. Monsanto agreed to pay provided the Schmeisers signed a release stating they would never talk about the agreement. The Schmeisers refused and sued in small-claims court. In 2008, the case settled with Monsanto paying the Schmeisers $660 but without the Schmeisers signing an agreement stopping them from talking about the terms of the settlement.

Source: Matt Hartley, "Grain farmer claims moral victory in seed battle", *The Globe and Mail* (20 March 2008) A3.

Exclusions from Patent Protection

There are also exclusions or exceptions to what may be patented. The most common are the following:

- *Things that receive exclusive protection under other areas of the law.* For example, computer programs (i.e., software) are not patentable, as they receive protection under copyright law. They could, however, receive patent protection as part of a broader patent, as, for example, a computerized method of controlling the operation of a plant.[14]

- *Things that do not meet the definition of a patent.* For example, scientific principles, natural phenomena, and abstract theorems are "discoveries" as opposed to inventions and are therefore not patentable. A practical application of a theory could, however, qualify for protection.

- *Things that are, for policy reasons, not patentable.* For example, methods of medical or surgical treatment are not patentable; neither are illicit objects. Also, historically, business methods such as franchising arrangements, accounting methods, insurance schemes, tax loopholes, and protocols for interacting with customers have not been patentable.[15] However, the Canadian Intellectual Property Office guidelines state that business methods[16] are not automatically excluded from patent protection, and a number of business methods patents have been issued in Canada. The following case is the first legal decision in Canada upholding the validity of a business methods patent.

---

14. David Vaver, *Intellectual Property Law: Copyrights, Patents, Trademarks*, 2d ed (Toronto: Irwin Law, 2011) at 314.
15. Business-methods patents have been allowed in the United States. See *State Street Bank & Trust v Signature Financial Group*, 149 F (3d) 1368 (Fed Cir 1998). However, in 2010, the U.S. Supreme Court made it much more difficult to obtain such patents. See *In re Bilski*, 545 F (3d) 943 (Fed Cir 2008) aff'd sub nom *Bilski v Kappos*, 561 US _ (2010).
16. Canadian Intellectual Property Office, *Manual of Patent Office Practice*, (Ottawa: 1998 last update Dec 2010) at s 12.04.04 online: Canadian Intellectual Property Office <http://www.cipo.ic.gc.ca/epic/site/cipointernet-internetopic.nsf/en/h_wr00720e.html>.

PART FIVE

CASE — *Canada (Attorney General) v Amazon.com Inc* 2011 FCA 328 (CanLII)

BUSINESS CONTEXT: In both Canada and the United States, there has been much debate about the patentability of methods of conducting business.[17] The following decision provides some clarity on the law in Canada and brings it more in line with the law in the United States.

FACTUAL BACKGROUND: In 1998, Amazon.com applied for a patent for an invention entitled "Method and system for placing a purchase order via a communications network." The invention is a system that allows a purchaser to reduce the number of interactions when ordering over the Internet. A purchaser can visit a website, enter her user and payment information and then be given an identifier that can be stored as a cookie on her computer. On a subsequent visit to the website, a server will be able to recognize the customer's computer with the identifying cookie and retrieve the user and payment information. By using this system, a customer could purchase an item with a single click of the mouse. The Canadian Intellectual Property Office rejected Amazon's "one-click" patent application on the basis that "a claimed invention which in form or in substance amounts to a business method is excluded from patentability" or alternatively, the claimed subject matter did not fall within the meaning of "art" in the *Patent Act*. Amazon.com appealed to the Federal Court.

LEGAL QUESTION: Is a business method patentable?

RESOLUTION: The Federal Court held that there is no authority in Canadian law to exclude business methods from patentability. A business method can be patentable under appropriate circumstances. To be patentable, an invention must fall within one of the categories of art, process, machine, manufacture, or composition of matter. The category for business methods is "art." Relying on the Supreme Court of Canada's decision in *Shell Oil*

Co v Commissioner of Patents,[18] the court stated that to be a patentable art, the subject matter of the claim (a) must not be a disembodied idea but have a method of practical application; (b) must be a new and inventive method of applying skill and knowledge; and (c) must have a commercially useful result. The court applied the test and held Amazon's one-click application to be patentable. The Commissioner of Patents appealed.

The Federal Court of Appeal largely affirmed the lower court's legal analysis. However, the Court granted the Commissioner's appeal and ordered that the one-click application be sent back to the Canadian Intellectual Property Office for re-evaluation. The court ruled that the lower court had insufficient evidence to determine whether the one-click application constitutes patentable subject-matter.

CRITICAL ANALYSIS: This decision affirms that there is no legal rationale for excluding business methods from patent protection. What will be the likely impact of this decision on business sectors such as insurance, banking, financial services, and securities?

POSTSCRIPT: The Canadian Intellectual Property Office ultimately allowed Amazon's patent application.

MIRCEA BEZERGHEANU/SHUTTERSTOCK

Requirements for Patentability

Not all inventions, however wonderful, are patentable. A patent will be granted only for an invention that is new, useful, and unobvious.

New The invention must be new or novel. An invention, however, need not be absolutely new.[19] It is "new" if it has not been disclosed publicly. This means that any public disclosure, public use, or sale of the invention prior to filing for a patent renders the invention "old" and unpatentable.[20] For example, displaying the new product at a trade show, distributing

---

17. Alan Macek, "Courts wrestle with business method patents", *The Lawyers Weekly* (1 October 2010) 13.
18. [1982] 2 SCR 536, 67 CPR (2d) 1.
19. *Supra* note 14 at 320.
20. Also of relevance to the issue of novelty are applications for patents filed in other countries. Canada is a signatory to both the *Paris Convention for the Protection of Industrial Property* and the *Patent Cooperation Treaty.* An applicant, by filing in a member country, can claim this date in other countries so long as the corresponding applications are filed within one year. This means that the earlier date becomes the disclosure date for purposes of establishing novelty.

marketing brochures that describe or display the product, or advertising the product in a way that reveals the invention[21] is a disclosure and a bar to obtaining a patent.

There is, however, a one-year grace period. If the inventor or someone who derived knowledge from the inventor makes a disclosure within the year preceding the filing of the application, this will not operate as public disclosure.

Estelle needs to determine whether her new and improved method of protecting electronic products from electrostatic discharge has been disclosed to the public in some manner. She can have a patent agent search relevant literature so that an opinion can be formed as to whether her invention is novel.

Useful   An invention must solve some practical problem, and it must actually work—that is, it must do what it purports to do. An invention that does not work is useless and unpatentable. The invention must have industrial value, although it need not be commercially successful. The invention must have practical use as opposed to being a mere scientific curiosity. For example, a perpetual motion machine[22] lacks utility, as it does not have a practical use. Estelle's product meets the requirement of usefulness as it solves an identifiable, industry problem and it apparently works.

Unobvious   The third requirement relates to "inventiveness." It means that there must be some ingenuity or inventive step involved in the invention.[23] Changes to something that would be obvious to someone skilled in the art to which the invention pertains would not be patentable. For example, simply using a different material for making a product would not be patentable, as it does not involve an inventive step.

The test is difficult to apply in practice because it involves ascertaining the state of the art or knowledge prior to the invention and analyzing whether the invention was merely the obvious, next step in the state of the knowledge or instead involves an inventive step.

The question of whether Estelle's new method is unobvious can be answered only by asking someone knowledgeable in the field of electrostatic discharge (ESD). The patent agent who searches the literature to determine whether an invention is novel will also express an opinion on whether the invention is obvious. That said, the industry's problems with ESD is indicative that Estelle's invention is unobvious and involves an inventive step.

Patent Protection and Application

Patent protection, unlike some other intellectual property rights, does not arise automatically. An application for a patent must be filed with the Canadian Intellectual Property Office.[24] Timing of the application is a critical concern because the patent regime is based on a first-to-file system.[25] This means, for example, that if more than one person has independently invented the same process, method, or machine, the Canadian Intellectual Property Office gives priority to the first person to file the application.

---

21. Ronald Dimock, *Canadian Marketing Law* (Toronto: Richard DeBoo, 1991) at 3–4.
22. *Supra* note 14 at 340.
23. See *Apotex Inc v Sanof Synthelabo Canada Inc*, 2008 SCC 61, [2008] 3 SCR 265 for the test for 'obviousness.'
24. The Canadian Intellectual Property Office's patent database can be accessed at <http://brevets-patents.ic.gc.ca/opic-cipo/cpd/eng/introduction.html>.
25. Until 1989, Canada's patent regime was based on a first-to-invent system.

PART FIVE

The inventor is generally the first owner of the invention and thus the person entitled to apply for a patent. The *Patent Act* does not contain specific provisions for the ownership of inventions created by employees in the course of employment; generally, however, an employee will be the owner unless (1) the employee was specifically hired to produce the invention and makes the invention in the course of employment, or (2) there is an express or implied agreement that precludes the employee from claiming ownership of inventions relating to and developed in the course of employment.[26] As Estelle has not been employed to produce a method to protect electronic products, and as she invented the method on her own time, she is the "inventor" and entitled to apply for a patent. Assuming she has not signed an agreement to the contrary, she has no obligation to share the invention and its proceeds with her employer. Employers should consider whether employment contracts, as well as contracts with consultants, address the ownership of all intellectual property including inventions produced in the course of employment.

Patent agent
A professional trained in patent law and practice who can assist in the preparation of a patent application.

The preparation of a patent application is a highly complex matter and is normally done by a **patent agent,** who has particular expertise in this area. The application has two main parts: one part describes how the product is made or the best way to perform the process or method. This is known as the **specifications.** The other part is known as the **claims.**[27] These are the sequentially numbered, single-sentence definitions of the invention. This part in effect defines the exclusive rights enjoyed by the patent holder. In short, the specifications tell the reader how to put the invention into practice after the patent expires. The claims tell the reader what he cannot do prior to the expiry of the patent.

Specifications
The description of an invention contained in a patent.

Claims
The exclusive rights of the patent holder.

The application is examined[28] by the Canadian Intellectual Property Office to ensure that the invention has not already been invented and that the application complies with the *Patent Act*. If the application is successful, a patent is issued upon the payment of the required fee. The word "patented" and the patent number may be put on all manufactured goods. Marking is not mandatory, but it is legally useful, as it notifies others of the existence of a right and reduces the number of "innocent" infringers. Often manufacturers will put the term "patent pending" or "patent applied for" on their products before the patent is issued. This warns others that a patent may eventually be issued for these products and they could be liable to pay damages for infringing the patent once the patent is granted. A patent gives the inventor the right to exclude others from making, selling, or using the invention to which the patent relates for a period of 20 years from the date of filing the application so long as the appropriate maintenance fees[29] are paid.

---

26. *Supra* note 14 at 368-69.
27. For an approach for interpreting and defining claims in patents, see *Free World Trust v Électro Santé Inc*, 2000 SCC 66, [2000] 2 SCR 1024; *Whirlpool Corp v Maytag Corp*, 2000 SCC 68, [2000] 2 SCR 1116; *Whirlpool Corp v Camco Inc*, 2000 SCC 67, [2000] 2 SCR 1067.
28. *Supra* note 11, s 35(1). An application for a patent is not automatically examined. The applicant must specifically request that an examination be done. Requests must be made within five years of filing the application, or the application will be deemed abandoned. The delay for requesting an examination gives the applicant a period of time to test the market for the invention.
29. Annual maintenance fees vary depending on how long a patent has been issued and whether the holder of the patent is a small or large entity. The amount paid by a large entity is usually double that paid by a small entity.

Patents are national in nature in that they exist only in the country in which the applications are made and granted.[30] The rights under a Canadian patent do not apply elsewhere. For example, an owner of a Canadian patent cannot stop the use or sale of the invention in the United States, unless the owner also has a U.S. patent.

Estelle's method of weaving static protection into the fibre of paper qualifies for patent protection if the method is considered to be new, useful, and unobvious. If it is patentable, she will need to apply for a patent and pay the requisite fee. The patent process requires her to disclose her discovery to the world; in return, she receives a monopoly over the invention for 20 years. The patent process is costly and time consuming, so Estelle needs to evaluate the costs and benefits of pursuing this route.

INTERNATIONAL PERSPECTIVE

i4i Sues Microsoft in the United States

Infrastructures for Information (i4i) Inc. is a small, Toronto-based software company that assists companies in converting complex information into database form. In 1994 Michel Vulpe, i4i founder, and his partner and co-inventor, Loudon Owen, filed a patent in the United States for a "Method and system for manipulating the architecture and the content of a document separately from each other." In essence, the patent covers technology to open documents using extensible mark-up language (XML). I4i developed a product based on this patent and established a sizeable client base, particularly among pharmaceutical companies.

In 2007 i4i sued Microsoft in Tyler, Texas, claiming it had infringed its patent. In 2009 a Texas jury, after a six-day trial, ordered Microsoft to pay US$200 million to i4i. The jury found that Microsoft Word 2003 and 2007 used XML that infringed i4i's patent. Following the jury's decision, a judge for the U.S. District Court for the Eastern District of Texas issued an injunction banning U.S. sales of Word 2003, Word 2007, and future versions of the software that use i4i's technology without a license, and increased the damages to approximately $290 million.

Microsoft removed the contested features from its software and appealed the decision on the basis that its products did not infringe i4i's patent and that i4i's patent was invalid. After several unsuccessful appeals in the lower courts, the Supreme Court of the United States agreed to hear the case. What began as a simple patent infringement case ended up as a case with much wider significance. Microsoft, rather than arguing the infringement or validity issue, argued for a change to the standard of evidence needed to prove a patent invalid. It argued that the standard should be on a "preponderance of the evidence" not a "clear and convincing" standard, as the clear and convincing standard insulated dubious patents

Michel Vulpe and Loudon Owen

FRANK GUNN/THE CANADIAN PRESS

from legal challenge and stifled innovation. The lower standard would make "bad" patents easier to invalidate and thereby promote innovation and competition. Microsoft believed that there was technology prior to i4i's patent that called it into question and that they believed had not been considered by the Patent and Trademark Office when it granted i4i's patent. Joining Microsoft in its fight were several of the biggest firms in the technology sector, including Google, Yahoo, Apple, Verizon, and Facebook. Supporting i4i's position were pharmaceutical giants Eli Lilly and Bayer, as well as other large corporations such as General Electric and Proctor and Gamble, several venture capitalists, universities, and the U.S. government.

In a unanimous decision,[31] the Supreme Court rejected Microsoft's argument to lower the evidentiary requirement

(Continued)

---

30. There is no such thing as an international patent. International treaties, however, have simplified the procedures for obtaining patents in different countries.
31. *Microsoft Corp v i4i Limited Partnership*, 564 US _ (2011) (USSC).

to invalidate a patent and upheld the $290 million damage award. The court held that the "clear and convincing" standard was the correct one and any decision to shift the standard for patent invalidity rests with Congress, not the courts. The case preserves the status quo in that there is a strong presumption of patent validity that is difficult to overcome. Loudon Owen, i4i's chairman, said in a statement to CBC, "The unanimous decision has very clearly confirmed the current state of the law and it has added a great deal of certainty to the business community."

Critical Analysis: Do you agree with Microsoft's argument that weakening the U.S. patent system will encourage innovation? Or do you think weakening the patent system would discourage innovation? Why do you think i4i sued Microsoft in Tyler, Texas?

Sources: Omar El Akkad, "Top court to review i4i's patent win", *The Globe and Mail* (30 November 2010) B5; Omar El Akkad, "Microsoft, i4i head to top court for final round in legal battle", *The Globe and Mail* (18 April 2011) B1; Arnold Ceballos, "i4i wins patent battle against Microsoft in top US court", *The Lawyers Weekly* (24 June 2011) 1; "Canada's i4i wins patent battle with Microsoft", *CBC News* (9 June 2011) online: CBC News <http://www.cbc.ca/news/technology/story/2011/06/09/technology-microsoft-i4i-patent.html>.

Industrial Designs

The *Industrial Design Act*[32] provides protection for the appearance of mass-produced (i.e., numbering more than 50) useful articles or objects.[33]

Industrial Designs Defined

Industrial design
The visual features of shape, configuration, pattern, ornamentation, or any combination of these applied to a finished article of manufacture.

The term "**industrial design**" is not defined in the Act. An industrial design is usually taken to mean a feature of shape, configuration, pattern, or ornament, or any combination of these, that in a finished article appeals to and is judged solely by the eye.[34] Put another way, an industrial design protects the shapes or ornamental aspects of a product but does not protect the functional aspect.

Typical examples of industrial designs are the shape and ornamentations applied to toys, vehicles, furniture, and household utensils, and the patterns applied to wallpaper or fabric. Also, the electronic or computer-generated icons displayed on computer monitors, cellular telephones, radio pagers, home appliances, and the like may be registered as industrial designs.[35]

What features of consumer goods may be protected by industrial design legislation?

RYAN MCVAY/PHOTODISC

---

32. RSC 1985, c I-9.
33. Works that qualify as industrial designs may also qualify for protection under the *Copyright Act*. To address the overlap, copyright protection is not given to designs applied to useful articles that are produced in quantities of more than 50. See *Copyright Act*, RSC 1985, c C-42, s 64(2), as am by *An Act to Amend the Copyright Act and Other Acts in Consequence Thereof*, SC 1988, c 65.
34. Martin PJ Kratz, *Canada's Intellectual Property Law in a Nutshell*, 2d ed (Scarborough, ON: Carswell, 2010) at 125.
35. Wing T Yan, "Screen display icons protectable as industrial designs", *The Lawyers Weekly* (17 November 2000) 14.

Requirements for Registration

To be registered, an industrial design must be original and novel. The originality standard is lower than the standard of inventiveness found in patents. A high degree of ingenuity or creativity is not necessary. The design may be entirely new, or it may be an old design that had not previously been applied for the purpose of ornamenting the article in question.

An industrial design must be novel. Disclosure or use of the industrial design or of articles displaying, bearing, or embodying the industrial design is a bar to registration unless it was within the year prior to filing the application.[36]

Registration Process and Protection

As with patents, industrial design protection does not arise automatically. An application, usually drafted by a patent agent, must be submitted to the Canadian Intellectual Property Office.

The owner of the rights in the design is entitled to make the application. The designer is the owner unless the design was ordered and paid for by another. The application normally consists of a written description and a graphic depiction, photograph, or drawing. If the application meets the requirements of the act, a certificate of registration will be issued.

The registration gives the owner the exclusive right to make, import, or sell any article in respect to which the design is registered. As well, the owner of the design can stop competitors from manufacturing and selling a design that looks confusingly similar. An industrial design registration lasts for 10 years.

It is not mandatory to mark the design to indicate that it is registered; however, doing so will enhance the owner's rights in a successful infringement action. If the product is marked, a court may award monetary damages for infringement. If there is no marking, the court is limited to awarding an injunction. The proper marking is a capital D inside a circle (Ⓓ), set next to the name of the design owner.

Trademarks

Estelle's intellectual property also includes the name of her product—Chargeless. This aspect of her intellectual property may qualify for protection under trademark law.

Trademark Defined

A **trademark**[37] is a word, symbol, design, or any combination of these used to distinguish a person's products or services from those of others. Its function is to indicate the source or origin of the goods or services.

Theoretically, a trademark could be anything, but it is usually one of the following:

- a word (e.g., Exxon, Xerox, Lego, Billabong)

- words (e.g., The Body Shop, The Pink Panther, Shake 'n Bake)

Trademark
A word, symbol, design, or any combination of these used to distinguish the source of goods or services.

---

36. *Supra* note 34 at 68. International conventions also apply to the application for industrial designs. Foreign applications filed up to six months before the Canadian filing may have priority to obtain a patent.

37. In addition to the type of trademark used by a business to identify goods or services, another category of trademark is the certification mark. This mark is used to indicate that a product or service conforms to a particular standard. For example, the "Woolmark" is a certification mark used by the Wool Bureau of Canada to identify garments made from pure new wool, and the Canadian Standards Association uses "CSA Approved" to indicate products of a certain standard. Certification marks are not owned by producers; thus, they are not used to distinguish one producer from another. Instead, the mark certifies that a product meets a defined standard.

- a slogan (e.g., "Just Do It," "Mr. Christie, You Make Good Cookies")

- a design (e.g., McDonald's golden arches, Disney's cartoon characters)

- a series of letters (e.g., ABC for a laundry detergent, BMW for a car)

- numbers (e.g., 6/49 for lottery services, 900 service for telephone operations)

- a symbol (e.g., a series of Chinese characters, Nike's "swoosh")

- a **distinguishing guise** (e.g., Coca-Cola bottle, Perrier bottle)

- any combination of the above (e.g., the words London Fog with a depiction of Big Ben for a brand of clothing)

Distinguishing guise
A shaping of wares or their container, or a mode of wrapping or packaging wares.

A colour is not registrable as a trademark, but colour[38] (such as pink for insulation) may be claimed as part of a trademark. Smells or odours have not been registered as trademarks in Canada; sounds, however, are registrable.[39]

Trade Names

Trade name
The name under which a sole proprietorship, a partnership, or a corporation does business.

Closely related to trademarks are **trade names**, which also receive protection under trademark law. A trade name is the name under which a business is carried on. It may be the name of a corporation, a partnership, or a sole proprietorship. An important connection between trade names and trademarks is that the adoption of a trademark may prevent the use of an identical or similar trade name, and vice versa—that is, the adoption of a trade name can prevent the adoption of a trademark. For example, if Estelle calls her business Chargeless, then her adoption of this as a trade name prevents others from using the name or a similar one as a trademark in the same line of business.

Common Law Trademarks

Trademarks may be registered or unregistered. If unregistered, they are often referred to as common law trademarks. Whether registered or unregistered, trademarks receive protection under both the common law and the *Trade-marks Act*.[40]

A common law trademark comes into existence when a business simply adopts and uses it. If Estelle simply starts using Chargeless to describe her product, then she has a common law trademark. Such a trademark is considered to be part of the goodwill of a company, and rights attach to it in much the same manner as they do to registered trademarks. Infringement of the trademark by a competitor using the same or similar trademark can be addressed through the tort of passing off.

The rights that attach to common law trademarks, however, tend to be more restrictive, and there are certain advantages associated with registration. A common law trademark has rights only in the geographic areas in which it has been used and in areas into which the

---

38. *Supra* note 14 at 469. The validity of registering smells as trademarks is uncertain.
39. Following a Federal Court order setting aside the Registrar of Trade-marks' refusal to grant Metro-Goldwyn-Mayer Lion Corp.'s trademark application for the sound of a lion roaring, the Canadian Intellectual Property Office published a notice indicating that it will accept applications for the registration of sound marks. See "Trade-mark consisting of a sound" *CIPO*, March 28, 2012 at <http://www.ic.gc.ca/eic/site/cipointernet-internetopic.nsf/eng/wr03439.html>.
40. RSC 1985, c T-13.

reputation of the owner has spread. For example, Estelle can prevent others from using her trademark or a similar one only in the areas where her reputation is known. A registered trademark enjoys protection throughout the country. Registration is also advantageous in that it creates a presumption of ownership and validity.

Trademarks and Domain Names

A **domain name** is essentially an Internet address. It consists of two or more elements divided into a hierarchical field separated by a "dot." To the right of the dot is an abbreviation describing the root identifier or a top-level domain (TLD). A TLD is either generic (such as .com, .org, or .net) or country-specific (such as .ca for Canada or .uk for the United Kingdom). To the left of the dot is the second-level domain, which is usually a business name, trademark, or other identifier. For example, in Nelson.com, "com" is the TLD and "Nelson" is the second-level domain.

Domain names are controlled by various organizations that act as registrars. Generic domain names such as .com, .org, .net, and .biz are controlled by the Internet Corporation for Assigned Names and Numbers (ICANN), a U.S. nonprofit corporation.[41] The country-specific domain names are assigned by national authorities. For example, in Canada, the Canadian Internet Registration Authority (CIRA)[42] is responsible for maintaining Canada's Internet domain names. The registrars issue names for a fee on a first-come, first-served basis.

Domain names come into conflict with trademarks when a domain name is issued that includes another's trademark. Sometime this occurs when two parties both have a legitimate interest in the trademark. For example, businesses such as Imperial Tobacco, Imperial Oil, and Imperial Margarine would all have a legitimate interest in a domain name containing "Imperial." These disputes can be settled through litigation using the general law on the adoption and use of trademarks. Often, however, domain names are registered for illegitimate purposes, such as for the purpose of selling it to the trademark owner, or as a means of advertising the registrant's own services or products, or to redirect traffic to the registrant's own website, or to prevent the trademark owner from using it. These activities are generally known as "**cyber-squatting.**" In such cases, a complainant may negotiate the purchase of the domain name, institute court proceedings for trademark infringement, or use the dispute resolution procedures set up by the domain name provider. Both ICANN[43] and CIRA provide a quick and cheap dispute resolution system to deal with bad-faith registration. To be successful, a complainant must prove that the domain name is identical or confusingly similar to the complainant's trademark, that the registrant has no legitimate interest in the domain name, and that the name is being used in bad faith by the registrant.[44] If the complainant is successful, the registrar can cancel the domain registration or transfer it to the trademark owner.

Domain name
The unique address of a website.

Cyber-squatting
The bad-faith practice of registering trademarks or trade names of others as domain names for the purpose of selling the domain name to the rightful owner or preventing the rightful owner from obtaining the domain name.

41. For more information, see <http://www.icann.org>. The organization recently approved several hundred new top-level domain names such as .hotel, .bank, and .sport.
42. For more information, see< http://www.cira.ca>.
43. The dispute resolution policy is available at < http://www.icann.org/en/dndr/udrp/policy.htm>.
44. Also, to succeed under the CIRA dispute resolution procedure, the complainant must satisfy a Canadian presence requirement.

Requirements for Registration

To register a trademark, an applicant must demonstrate that he has title to the trademark (this requirement is sometimes simply referred to as use), that the trademark is distinctive or capable of becoming distinctive, and that the trademark is registrable.

Title   An applicant may register only a trademark that he owns. Ownership or title is not established by inventing or selecting a mark. It comes from

- use of the trademark

- filing an application to register a proposed trademark

- making it known in Canada

A trademark is deemed to be in "use" in Canada if the trademark is on the goods or the packaging at the time of any transfer in the ordinary course of business. With respect to services, a trademark is deemed to be in use if it is used or displayed in the performance or advertising of the services. A distinguishing guise is registrable only on this basis.

A trademark can be registered if it is not yet in use, as long as the registrant proposes to use it as a trademark in Canada. Estelle may make an application to register "Chargeless" as a proposed trademark.

An application to register can be made on the basis that the mark, although not in use in Canada, is nonetheless well known in Canada. An applicant would need to demonstrate that the mark is, in fact, well known in Canada, that knowledge of the mark arose from advertisements that circulated in Canada, and that the applicant used the mark in another country.[45]

Distinctiveness   The second general requirement goes to the heart of trademark law. The mark must be distinctive—in other words, it must actually distinguish the goods or services in association with which it is used. Invented words like "Lego," "Exxon," and "Kodak" are distinctive and are ideal candidates, particularly with respect to applications based on proposed use. Other, more descriptive words, such as "pleasant," "sudsy," and "shiny" do not have the same quality of distinctiveness. They may gain this quality only through use in business and advertising.

Registrability   The *Trade-marks Act* specifies that a mark must be "registrable." To be registrable, the trademark must *not* be

- primarily the name or surname of an individual who is living or has died within the preceding 30 years (e.g., "Smith" or "Joe Enman")

- descriptive[46] of the character or quality of the wares or services, or their place of origin (e.g., "sweet" for apples, "Ontario wines" for wines from Ontario, or "shredded wheat" for cereal[47])

---

45. The foreign country must have been a country that is a member of the *Paris Convention* or the World Trade Organization.
46. Note that descriptive words can be used as part of a trademark so long as the applicant includes a disclaimer that he does not claim exclusive rights to the descriptive words.
47. *Canadian Shredded Wheat Co Ltd v Kellogg Co of Canada Ltd*, [1938] 2 DLR 145, 55 RPC 125 (PC).

- deceptively misdescriptive of the character or quality of the wares or services, or their place of origin (e.g., "sugar sweet" for candy that is artificially sweetened, or "all-silk" for a cotton blouse)

- the name in any language of any ware or service in connection with which it is used or proposed to be used (e.g., "avion" for airplanes, "wurst" for sausages)

- confusing with regard to another registered trademark (e.g., "Mego" for children's plastic building blocks; "Devlon" for hair care products)

- an official[48] or prohibited[49] mark

BUSINESS APPLICATION OF THE LAW

Whisky Name Dispute

Glenora Distillers International Ltd., based in Glenville, near Glenora Falls on Cape Breton Island, Nova Scotia, produces a single malt whisky, which it calls Glen Breton. The Scotch Whisky Association of Scotland opposed the word "glen" in the whisky's name on the grounds that it confuses consumers into thinking the whisky is from Scotland.

The Trade-marks Opposition Board (TMOB) ruled against the Scotch Whisky Association on the grounds that it failed to prove its claim of market confusion. The association appealed to the Federal Court, which agreed with its claim that the use of the word "glen" created confusion in the marketplace. The association filed more than 30 instances of Glen Breton being described as Scotch whisky in retail outlets, newspaper articles, price lists, menus, and websites. Glenora had argued that it was careful not to use the word Scotch in connection with its whisky and that it packaged the whisky as Canadian—on the label is a large red maple leaf and the words "Canada's Only Single Malt Whisky." There are no tartans, bagpipes, or highland dancers. Glenora also argued that the word "glen" is commonplace on Cape Breton; it can be found in 42 place names. Justice Harrington of the Federal Court, however, indicated that the name caused confusion with Scotch whisky, particularly the single malts named The Glenlivet, Glenfiddich, and Glenmorangie.

The Federal Court of Appeal reversed the decision and ordered the registrar to allow Glenora's trademark application. It stated that the word "glen" standing alone had never been used as a trademark in Canada for any product. The word "glen" was a common word forming part of numerous

COURTESY OF THE GLENORA DISTILLERY

When is a mark distinctive for purposes of trademark law?

registered trademarks. At best, "glen" was a weakly distinctive component of those trademarks and could not be segmented to form a mark on its own. The Supreme Court of Canada refused to hear an appeal.

Critical Analysis: Which arguments do you find the most compelling—those of the distillers of Glen Breton or those of the Scotch Whisky Association? What other legal strategy could the Scotch Whisky Association have used to protect its rights?

Sources: Bruce Erskine, "Glen, Canadian whisky don't mix", *The Chronicle Herald* (8 April 2008) C1; Adrian Humphreys, "Stiff ruling for N.S. distillery", *National Post* (8 April 2008) online: Free Republic <http://www.freerepublic.com/focus/f-news/1998884/posts>; *Glenora Distillers International Ltd v Scotch Whisky Association*, 2009 FCA 16, [2010] 1 FCR 195 and Susan Krashinsky, "Scotch snobs shudder as Glen Breton toasts win", *The Globe and Mail* (12 June 2009) B14.

---

48. Public authorities have the right to adopt an official mark and use that mark with respect to its wares or services. For example, The Official Island Store is an official mark of Gateway Village Development Inc. of Prince Edward Island.

49. Prohibited marks include marks that are likely to be mistaken for symbols or emblems of government, royalty, armed forces, or the Royal Canadian Mounted Police; the Red Cross, the Red Crescent, or the United Nations; flags and symbols of other countries; and symbols of public institutions. Also prohibited are scandalous, immoral, and obscene words, and anything that suggests a connection with a living or recently deceased individual.

Estelle's product name "Chargeless" may be registrable depending on the above factors. Although another business is using "charge less" in their slogan, this would not prevent the registration of Estelle's name, as "charge less" is not being used as a trademark, and it is being used in an entirely different business. A key concern, however, will be whether the same or a similar trademark has been registered in the same industry and whether the mark is considered sufficiently distinctive.

CASE — *Mattel v 3894207 Canada Inc*, 2006 SCC 22, [2006] 1 SCR 772

THE BUSINESS CONTEXT: A famous trademark—such as Coca-Cola or Walt Disney—has the power to attract legions of consumers. The extent to which Canadian trademark law protects famous marks from use by others is unclear. The following case explores the scope of protection accorded to famous and well-known marks.[50]

FACTUAL BACKGROUND: In 1992, a Quebec restaurateur opened the first of four Montreal-area licensed BBQ restaurants named "Barbie's." When the restaurateur tried to register "Barbie & Design" as a trademark for use across the country in the restaurant, takeout, catering, and banquet business, Mattel Inc., the maker of the Barbie doll, protested. Mattel had registered "Barbie" and "Barbie's" as trademarks in Canada for doll-related products more than 30 years previously. In 2002, the Trade-marks Opposition Board of the Canadian Intellectual Property Office accepted the restaurant's argument that its use of "Barbie" would not create consumer confusion with Mattel's dolls. Both the Federal Court and the Federal Court of Appeal upheld the Board's decision.

THE LEGAL QUESTION: Does the monopoly protection extended by the *Trade-marks Act* to Mattel's Barbie trademark prevent others from registering similar marks in connection with non-doll-related goods and services?

RESOLUTION: Under the *Trade-marks Act*, registration of a trademark is not permissible if the trademark could reasonably be confused with a previously registered trademark. Mattel contended that allowing adult-oriented bars or grills to register "Barbie" would create confusion in the minds of the public who might think that the restaurants are linked to the doll. The restaurant responded that most Canadians would know that the term "Barbie" here refers to the barbecue, as in "Throw some burgers on the barbie!" In a unanimous decision, the Supreme Court found that there was no likelihood of confusion in the marketplace between the doll and the restaurant. The court's decision was based upon the facts and evidence that included the absence of any instances of actual confusion. In other words,

How much protection should be given to famous trademarks?

COURTESY OF JOHN MORSTAD

the evidence showed that Mattel's Barbie mark was famous only when used in association with dolls and doll accessories.

Importantly, the court went on to make it clear, however, that a difference between goods or services associated with trademarks is only one factor to be considered in determining the likelihood of confusion. All surrounding circumstances, including the distinctiveness of the marks; the length of time the marks were used; the nature of the wares, services, or businesses; the nature of the trade; and the degree of resemblance must all be considered, and different factors will be given different weight in different situations. The court also suggested that some marks (e.g., Walt Disney) are so famous that they can transcend product lines. Thus, while fame does not by itself provide absolute protection for a trademark, it may in some instances result in the trademark having a broader scope of protection. The question of whether a famous mark is entitled to broader protection will depend on the facts.

CRITICAL ANALYSIS: Although Mattel lost its appeal, the very fact-driven nature of the decision leaves the door open to a different outcome for other well-known trademarks. Should the scope of protection afforded a trademark extend beyond the goods or services in relation to which it is registered? Would this provide too much protection to trademark owners?

---

50. In a companion decision, *Veuve Clicquot Ponsardin c Boutiques Cliquot Ltée*, 2006 SCC 23, [2006] 1 SCR 824, the Supreme Court held that the French champagne maker Veuve Clicquot Ponsardin could not prevent the use of the mark Cliquot in relation to women's clothing shops in Quebec and Eastern Ontario.

Registration Process and Protection

The first person who uses or makes a trademark known in Canada is entitled to trademark registration. In the absence of use, the first to file a trademark application is entitled to registration.[51]

Prior to applying for registration, a trademark agent usually does a search of the trademarks office database[52] to ensure that the trademark or a similar one is not already registered. Federal and provincial business name registries and other sources such as trade journals, telephone directories, and specialty magazines are also consulted to determine whether there are common law rights.

The application must comply with all the provisions of the Act. In particular, applicants must provide a comprehensive list of products or services associated with the trademark. An examiner reviews the application, and if it is acceptable the trademarks office advertises the trademark in the trademark journal. Any interested members of the public can object to the registration on the grounds that they have a better title to the trademark than the applicant, that the trademark is not distinctive, or that the trademark does not meet the requirements of registrability. If, on the other hand, there is no opposition or the opposition is overcome, the registration will be issued on payment of the appropriate fee.

A trademark registration gives the owner the exclusive right to use the trademark in association with the wares and services specified in the registration. It also provides a right to prevent others from using a confusingly similar trademark. A trademark owner should clearly indicate its ownership of a trademark with the following marks:

® for registered trademarks

™ for unregistered trademarks

Registration provides protection across Canada for a period of 15 years. The registration can be renewed for additional 15-year terms as long as the renewal fee is paid and the trademark continues in use.

Copyright

Estelle's intellectual property may also include promotional brochures, business plans, drawings, and other written material. All such works may qualify for **copyright** protection.

Copyright is governed almost entirely by the *Copyright Act*.[53] Copyright is intended to provide a right of exploitation to authors of certain works. As its name suggests, copyright is intended to prevent the copying of works. In other words, subject to certain exemptions, only the author (or the owner of the copyright) has the right to copy a work. Others are not entitled to copy the work unless they fall within one of the exemption categories or have the author's permission to make a copy. This "right to copy" or "copyright," however, does not protect the author's underlying ideas or facts. For example, no one has copyright in the life story of Ken Thomson or K.C. Irving, but once the story is written, copyright resides in the expression of the life story.

Copyright
The right to prevent others from copying or modifying certain works.

---

51. Canada is a signatory to the *Paris Convention*, which means that applicants from member countries have reciprocal rights with respect to filing in member countries. The date of filing in a convention country becomes the Canadian filing date, so long as the Canadian application is filed within six months of the date of the first filing in a convention country.
52. The Canadian Intellectual Property Office's trademark database can be accessed at <http://www.ic.gc.ca/app/opic-cipo/trdmrks/srch/bscSrch.do?lang=eng>.
53. RSC 1985, c C-42.

PART FIVE

Copyright Defined

Copyright applies to both traditional and non-traditional works. Copyright applies to every original literary, dramatic, musical, and artistic work, such as the following:

- *literary works*—books, pamphlets, compilations, translations, and computer programs
- *dramatic works*—any piece for recitation, choreographic works, scenic arrangements, and cinematography productions such as plays, operas, mime, films, videos, and screenplays
- *musical works*—any combination of melody and harmony, including sheet music
- *artistic work*—paintings, drawings, maps, charts, plans, photographs, engravings, sculptures, works of artistic craftsmanship, and architectural works of art

In essence, copyright extends to almost anything written, composed, drawn, or shaped. Items not protected include facts, names, slogans, short phrases, and most titles. The examples of works included in each category are non-exhaustive, which means the categories can encompass new technologies and new forms of expression. Copyright also applies to nontraditional works such as sound recordings, performances, and broadcasts.[54]

There are many business examples of these various kinds of works. In fact, whole industries are founded on works of this nature, particularly the entertainment and publishing industries. Businesses that are not so directly affected still create many works that may attract copyright protection, such as advertising copy, photographs, manuals, memorandums, plans, sketches, and computer programs, to name a few common examples.

Requirements for Protection

To attract copyright protection, a work must meet requirements of originality and fixation.[55] Originality means that the work must "originate" from the author, not be copied from another, and involve the exercise of skill and judgment. In *CCH Canadian Ltd v Law Society of Upper Canada*,[56] the Supreme Court of Canada held that the headnotes (a short summary of a case and key words) of a legal decision are "original" works; however, the edited version of a court decision is not original because it involves only minor changes and additions—a mere mechanical exercise too trivial to warrant copyright protection.

The requirement of fixation[57] means that the work must be expressed in some fixed form, such as paper or diskette. Works such as speeches, luncheon addresses, and lectures that do not exist in a fixed form do not attract copyright. The fixation requirement exists to separate unprotectable ideas from protectable expression and to provide a means of comparison for judging whether copyright has been infringed.

---

54. *Ibid*, ss 15, 18, 21.
55. The nationality requirement is no longer very important, as Canada has implemented the *Agreement on Trade-Related Aspects of Intellectual Property Rights (TRIPS)*. This agreement means that virtually every work qualifies for protection, regardless of the author's nationality.
56. 2004 SCC 13, [2004] 1 SCR 339.
57. The fixation requirement is expressly found in the *Copyright Act* only for dramatic works and computer programs. The requirement in relation to other works has developed through the common law.

Registration Process and Protection

Copyright protection arises automatically on the creation of a work. There is an optional registration process that has an evidentiary advantage in that registration provides a presumption of ownership. The owner of a copyright may mark a work; however, there is no requirement to do so to enforce copyright in Canada. The mark can, however, enhance international protection of the work. The following is the typical form of a copyright notice:

© year of publication; name of owner

Under the *Copyright Act*, the author[58] of a work is the copyright owner unless there is an agreement to the contrary. The major exception is for works created in the course of employment, in which case the employer is the owner. A further exception relates to photographs, engravings, and portraits that are ordered and paid for by another; in the absence of an agreement to the contrary, the customer is the first owner of the copyright.

Copyright protection is generally for the life of the author or composer plus 50 years.[59]

Rights under Copyright

Copyright gives certain rights to the owner of the copyright (the rights may vary somewhat depending on the type of work). These rights include:

- *reproduction*—the right to reproduce the work or a substantial part of it in any material form
- *public performance*—the right to perform the work or a substantial part of it
- *publication*—the right, if the work is unpublished, to publish the work
- *translation*—the right to produce, reproduce, perform, or publish any translation of the work
- *adaptation*—the right to convert works into other formats (e.g., a book into a movie)
- *mechanical reproduction*—the right to make sound recordings or cinematographic recordings
- *cinematographic presentation*—the right to reproduce, adapt, and publicly present the work by filming or videotaping
- *communication*—the right to communicate the work to the public by telecommunication
- *exhibition*—the right to present in public, for purposes other than sale or hire, an artistic work[60]
- *rental*—the right to rent out sound recordings and computer programs
- *authorization*—the right to "authorize" any of the other rights

Copyright is infringed when anyone does, without the consent of the owner, anything only the owner can do. This includes, for example, copying *all or a substantial part* of a work.

---

58. Copyright law recognizes the concept of joint authorship; however, the contribution of a copyrightable work to a project does not in and of itself create joint authorship. The parties must intend to be joint authors. See *Neudorf v Nettwerk Productions*, [2000] 3 WWR 522, 71 BCLR (3d) 290 (SC).

59. For some works, such as sound recordings, the term of protection is 50 years.

60. This applies only to works created after 7 June 1988 and does not apply to charts, maps, and plans.

The question of what is substantial is vexing. It is generally thought that *substantial* has both a qualitative and a quantitative aspect. The test seems to be whether the part that is taken is a key or distinctive part.[61]

It is also infringement for anyone to authorize doing anything that only the copyright owner is allowed to do. Authorization means to "sanction, approve and countenance."[62] A person does not, however, authorize infringement by merely providing the means that could be used to infringe copyright. For example, the provision of photocopiers does not constitute authorization of the use of the copiers to infringe copyright, particularly in the case where the provider has little control over the user.

The enforcement of rights has been problematic, particularly the collection of fees and royalties for the use of copyrighted works. These problems have been addressed by provisions in the *Copyright Act* for the establishment of collectives that negotiate agreements with users on royalties and use. For example, Access Copyright (The Canadian Copyright Licensing Agency, formerly known as CanCopy), represents numerous publishers and authors and negotiates agreements with institutions such as universities, libraries, and copy shops, providing for the payment of royalties for photocopying from books. Similar collectives such as the Society of Composers, Authors and Music Publishers of Canada (SOCAN) operate in the music industry.

ETHICAL CONSIDERATIONS

The Business of Counterfeit Goods

The sale of counterfeit and pirated goods is big business. Phony Prada shoes, Chanel sunglasses, Louis Vuitton hand bags, Gucci scarves, North Face ski wear, and Canada Goose parkas can be purchased in street markets, boutiques, and malls in many parts of Canada. Counterfeit goods, however, are not limited to high end designer goods but increasingly less expensive items like toothpaste, medications, printer cartridges, batteries, toys, sporting goods, and car parts are being counterfeited, mass-produced, and sold. The exact cost to economies of counterfeit and pirated goods is not known but the estimates are staggering. A study by Frontier Economics for the International Chamber of Commerce released in 2010 estimated that the total global and economic and social impacts of counterfeit and pirated products to be US$775 billion per year based on 2008 data.[63] The figure is estimated to double to US$1.7 trillion by 2015. According to a 2009 report from the Canadian Intellectual Property Council, counterfeiting and piracy costs the Canadian economy $22 billion annually in lost tax revenue, investment and innovation.[64]

Whose interests are harmed by the manufacturer and sale of counterfeit goods?

Most of the knock-offs and fakes come from China and other parts of Asia and most enter Canada through the port of Vancouver. Some of the fakes, however, are produced in Canada. The CBC reports that Canada has become a leader in producing pirated DVDs for worldwide distribution.[65]

---

61. *Supra* note 14 at 185–86.
62. *Supra* note 56.
63. International Chamber of Commerce, Press Release, "Impacts of counterfeiting and piracy to reach US$1.7 trillion by 2015" (2 February 2010) online: International Chamber of Commerce <http://www.iccwbo.org/uploadedFiles/Press%20Release_Impacts_of_counter-feiting_and_piracy.pdf>.
64. The Canadian Intellectual Property Rights Council, "A Time for Change: Towards a New Era for Intellectual Property Rights in Canada" online: Canadian Intellectual Property Council <http://www.ipcouncil.ca/uploads/ATimeForChange.pdf>.
65. "Counterfeit goods", *CBC News* (6 March 2007) online: CBC News <http://www.cbc.ca/news/background/consumers/counterfeit.html>.

The prevalence of pirated goods leaving and entering Canada has not gone unnoticed. Each year the United States Trade Representative (USTR) publishes a report identifying the countries that inadequately protect intellectual property rights. Canada has become a fixture on their "watch list" and in 2009 was moved to the "priority watch list." Among the USTR's concerns was Canada's need to improve its intellectual property enforcement systems so effective action can be taken against counterfeit and pirated products in Canada.

Luxury brands such as Louis Vuitton and Burberry, however, have not waited for government action but are fighting back. They have created their own civil enforcement divisions and have hired private investigators to ferret out producers and distributors of knock-offs. In the latest in a series of investigations and court actions, Louis Vuitton and Burberry sued two Vancouver based companies and one Toronto company for copyright and trademark infringement. The companies were involved in a large scale operation manufacturing

and importing fake goods into Canada. In *Louis Vuitton Malletier SA v Singga Enterprises (Canada) Inc*,[66] the Federal Court awarded $1.9 million in damages for trademark and copyright infringement and a further $0.5 million in punitive damages. This is the largest counterfeiting award imposed in Canada to date.

Critical Analysis: What are the legal, ethical, and economic problems posed by the manufacture and sale of counterfeit goods? Why do some people view counterfeiting to be a victimless crime? Do you agree with that view?

Sources: "Vancouver: Canada's Counterfeit Capital", *The Vancouver Sun* (23 June 2007) online: canada.com <http://www.canada.com/vancouversun /story.html?id=3a272710-2f5e-42d9-ba86-5b814f796c1f&k=34717>; John Cotter & Tara James, "Canada lands on U.S. trade rep's priority watch list", *The Lawyers Weekly* (7 August 2009) 11; Michael Manson, John Cotter & Mark Schonfeld, "Counterfeiting and piracy reach epidemic proportions", *The Lawyers Weekly* (13 August 2010) 12; "Burberry, Louis Vuitton sue companies over knock-offs", *Canadian Press* (9 March 2011) online: CTV News <http://www.ctv.ca/CTVNews /TopStories/20110309/burberry-court-110309/> ; Jeff Gray, "Fake purses, real money", *The Globe and Mail* (6 July 2011) B7.

Moral Rights

The author of a work has what are known as **moral rights**. Moral rights exist independently of copyright and provide authors with some control over how their works are used and exploited. Moral rights include the following:

Moral rights
The author's rights to have work properly attributed and not prejudicially modified or associated with products.

- *Paternity.* The author has the right to be associated with the work as its author by name or under a pseudonym and the right to remain anonymous if reasonable in the circumstances.

- *Integrity.* The author has the right to object to dealings or uses of the work if they are prejudicial to the author's reputation or honour.

- *Association.* The author has the right to object to the work being used in association with a product, service, cause, or institution.

CASE | *Snow v The Eaton Centre Ltd* (1982), 70 CPR (2d) 105 (Ont HC)

THE BUSINESS CONTEXT: Many works that receive copyright protection are created for the purpose of making a profit through a sale. However, the sale of a work does not extinguish all of the author's or creator's rights.

FACTUAL BACKGROUND: Michael Snow created a sculpture of geese known as *Flight Stop*, which was sold to the owners of the Eaton Centre in Toronto. In connection with a Christmas display, the Eaton Centre attached red ribbons to the necks of the 60 geese forming the sculpture. Snow claimed that his naturalistic composition had been made to look ridiculous by the addition. In short, he alleged that his moral rights in the sculpture had been infringed.

VICTOR LAST/GEOGRAPHICAL VISUAL AIDS

Michael Snow's Flight Stop

(Continued)

66. [2011] FC No 908.

PART FIVE

THE LEGAL QUESTION: Were the acts of the Eaton Centre a distortion or modification of Snow's work that would be prejudicial to his honour and reputation?

RESOLUTION: The court held that the ribbons distorted and modified Snow's work and that Snow's concern that this was prejudicial to his honour and reputation was reasonable in the

circumstances. The Eaton Centre was required to remove the ribbons.

CRITICAL ANALYSIS: Since the Eaton Centre paid for the sculpture, why should it not be able to do as it wants with the sculpture? Would the outcome have been the same if the sculpture had been sent to the dump or otherwise destroyed?

Exemptions

There are a large number of exceptions or defences under the *Copyright Act*. Many—among them the exemption for home copying;[67] libraries, museums, and archives; people with disabilities; and educational institutions—apply to specific situations and have little business application. The exemptions that are particularly relevant to business are the following:

Fair dealing
A defence to copyright infringement that permits the copying of works for limited purposes.

- *Fair dealing.* The **fair dealing** exemption permits the copying of works for the purposes of private study, research, criticism, or review. The test for fair dealing involves a two-step analysis. First, the copying must be for one of the enumerated purposes. In *CCH Canadian Ltd v Law Society of Upper Canada*,[68] the Supreme Court ruled that research must be given a large and liberal interpretation and not be limited to non-commercial or private research. Further, research is not limited to creative purposes but can include consumer research for the purpose of purchasing goods or services.[69] Second, the dealing must also be fair. In assessing whether the dealing is fair, the following factors are considered:

  - the purposes of the dealing

  - the character of the dealing

  - the amount of the dealing

  - alternatives to the dealing

  - the nature of the work

  - the effect of the dealing on the work[70]

- *Computer software.* The exemption relating to computer programs is quite specific. It permits the owner of the program to make a copy for adaptation for use on another computer and a copy for backup purposes.

BUSINESS AND LEGISLATION

Amending the Copyright Act

Since 2005, the federal government has introduced four bills to revise the *Copyright Act*. The first three died on the order table when Parliament was dissolved or prorogued. The fourth,

Bill C-11, *An Act to Amend the Copyright Act* received Royal Assent on June 29, 2012 (it will come into force at a later date). The Act represents the first substantial amendments to the *Copyright Act* since 1997. Highlights of the reforms include

---

67. *Supra* note 53, s 80 exempts the copying of musical works by an individual for private use from copyright infringement. In return, copyright collectives can collect levies on blank audio media in order to compensate the rights holders.
68. *Supra* note 56.
69. *Society of Composers, Authors and Music Publishers of Canada v Bell Canada* 2012 SCC 36.
70. The Supreme Court of Canada endorsed these factors in *Alberta v Access Copyright* 2012 SCC 37.

- *Technical protection measures:* prohibitions against the removal or tampering with digital locks built into music, DVDs, and other media and technical products;
  - *Reproduction for private purposes:* provisions that allow individuals to make copies of music and other copyrighted material for private purposes if the original copy is not an infringing copy, is legally owned, and technological protection measures are not circumvented;
  - *Anti-piracy provisions:* provision making it an infringement for any person to provide a service that is designed primarily for the purpose of enabling acts of copyright infringement over the Internet (e.g. per-to-peer distribution);
  - *"Notice and notice" system for claimed infringement:* provisions for limited liability of Internet service providers (ISP) for copyright infringement of their subscribers; copyright owners are entitled to send notice of infringement

to an ISP, who must send it to the alleged infringer; ISPs are required to retain records related to identity of infringer, which the copyright owner can obtain through a court order;
  - *Fair dealing and education exceptions:* extension of the existing fair dealing exemption to include fair dealing for purposes of education, parody, and satire; and exemptions for educational institutions and the use of digital technology for education;
  - *Time-shifting provisions:* permission to make a copy of radio and television programs or a web stream for the purpose of viewing or listening at a later time;
  - *Statutory damages:* the maximum damages is changed from $20 000 to $5000 for non-commercial infringement.

Critical Analysis: Are the amendments anti-consumer or good for business?

Confidential Business Information

There is no specific statutory protection for **confidential business information**[71] and therefore no statutory definition for the term. Generally, however, the term refers to information that is used in a business or commercial context and is private or secret.

The general categories of business information that is used or is capable of being used in business are these:

- strategic business information (e.g., customer lists, price lists, bookkeeping methods, presentation programs, advertising campaigns)

- products (e.g., recipes, formulas)

- compilations (e.g., databases)

- technological secrets (e.g., scientific processes, know-how)

Requirements for Protection

A key requirement for protection is the secrecy or confidentiality of the information. A number of factors are considered in ascertaining whether the information is "confidential":

- *Economic value as a result of not being generally known.* The information must have some commercial value to the company or its competitors. An indication of the commercial value of the information may be the efforts by others to obtain it. The value of the information derives in large measure from the fact that it is not known by some or is not generally known.

- *Subject to efforts to keep it secret.* There must be efforts to keep the information secret. Thus, if a company is careless about information or fails to take steps to protect the confidentiality of information, the information may indeed lose its status of "confidential."

Confidential business information
Information that provides a business advantage as a result of the fact that it is kept secret.

---

71. The term "trade secret" is also sometimes used either interchangeably with "confidential business information" or as a subset of "confidential information." The terms are used interchangeably in this text.

PART FIVE

- *Not generally known in the industry.* Information does not have to be absolutely confidential; it can be a compilation of readily available information from various sources. As well, information can be known by some and still maintain its status. In this regard, the extent to which the information is known within the company, as well as outside the company, is relevant.

Process and Scope of Protection

Confidential business information may be protected forever so long as the information is not disclosed to the general public. Recipes for well-known products such as Coca-Cola Classic, Hostess Twinkies, Mrs. Field's Chocolate Chip Cookies, Listerine, and Kentucky Fried Chicken have been "secret" for many years. There are no application procedures for protection. Information receives protection through claims for breach of express terms, for breach of confidence, or through implied obligations.

Parties may have express obligations to keep information confidential. Non-disclosure agreements require recipients of information to respect its confidentiality by agreeing not to discuss, disclose, or use it. Estelle could require potential lenders and investors to sign a confidentiality agreement prior to discussing her invention with them. In the absence of an express provision regarding confidence, an obligation of confidence may be implied in a contract or arise by virtue of a fiduciary relationship. This is the case in the employment context, particularly in industries in which there is a lot of confidential information and the importance of confidentiality is stressed.

Finally, an obligation of confidence can exist when information was conveyed in circumstances suggesting a relationship of confidence. The following case is a leading decision on receipt of confidential information in circumstances of confidentiality.

LANDMARK CASE — *LAC Minerals Ltd v International Corona Resources Ltd,* [1989] 2 SCR 574, 61 DLR (4th) 14

THE HISTORICAL CONTEXT: In the negotiations preceding a contract, the parties may divulge a great deal of information, some of which is sensitive and confidential. This is often necessary in order to reach contractual consensus. This case explores the obligations of the recipient of the information to the revealer of the information, in the absence of a contract of confidentiality.

FACTUAL BACKGROUND: Corona was the owner of a group of mining claims that it was exploring. Being a junior company, it was eager to attract investors and had publicized certain information about its property. LAC Minerals, a major mining corporation, became interested, and a site visit was arranged. The LAC geologists were shown core samples and sections, and the parties discussed the geology of Corona's site as well as the property to the west, known as the Williams property. Another meeting was held a couple of days later in Toronto, during

which it was again mentioned that Corona was attempting to purchase the Williams property. No mention was made of confidentiality. Following this meeting, there were further discussions and an exchange of joint venture ideas, as well as a full presentation by Corona of its results and its interest in the Williams property. A short time after these meetings, negotiations between LAC and Corona broke down. Subsequently, LAC made an offer to purchase the Williams property. The offer was accepted, and LAC proceeded to develop the property on its own. It turned out to be the biggest gold mine in Canada, and LAC made huge profits. Corona sued for breach of confidence and breach of fiduciary duty.

THE LEGAL QUESTION: Was LAC liable for breach of confidence or breach of fiduciary duty?

RESOLUTION: The Supreme Court of Canada unanimously found LAC liable on the grounds of breach of confidence. The court confirmed that there are three elements that must be established to impose liability on this ground:

- The information conveyed was confidential.
- It was communicated in circumstances in which a duty of confidence arises.
- It was misused by the party to whom it was communicated.

Although some of the information conveyed by Corona was not confidential, clearly most of it was, and LAC used it to acquire the Williams property. The court said the information was communicated with the mutual understanding that the parties were working toward a joint venture or some other arrangement. A reasonable person in the position of LAC would know that the information was being given in confidence. LAC used the information to its gain and at the expense of Corona. Although the court did not go so far as to find a breach of a fiduciary duty, there was a violation of confidence.

CRITICAL ANALYSIS: What is the importance of this case for business? How can a business determine whether information is confidential? Would it have been easier for Corona simply to have had LAC sign an express confidentiality agreement at the outset?

Limitations on Protection

Confidential business information loses the protection of the law when the information is no longer secret, either because the information has been divulged or because the information has been discovered by independent development using publicly available information, or by reverse engineering (i.e., finding the secret or confidential information by examining or dissecting a product). For example, if Estelle keeps her method a secret, and at the same time manufactures and sells products using the method she will not be able to prevent others, who discover the method through reverse engineering from using it.

Information is also no longer confidential when it becomes part of the employee's personal knowledge, skill, or expertise (i.e., trade information). In distinguishing between information that is "confidential" and trade information, the courts attempt to strike a balance between the employee's right to use the skills, knowledge, and experience gained during the course of employment and the employer's right to protect its information.

FIGURE 18.1

A Comparison of Major Forms of Intellectual Property

	Patents	Industrial designs	Trademarks	Copyrights	Confidential business information[1]
Subject matter	Inventions	Shape, configuration, pattern, ornamentation	Word, symbol, design	Literary, dramatic, musical, and artistic works; sound recordings, performances, broadcasts	Business information (e.g., technology, product recipes, databases)
Requirements	New, useful, unobvious	Original, novel	Title, distinctiveness, registrable	Original, fixed	Economic value, efforts to keep secret, generally not known
Protects against	Use, sale, manufacture	Use, sale, manufacture	Use	Copying, modifying	Disclosure, use
Term of protection	20 years	10 years	15 + 15 + 15 + years	Life + 50 years	Indefinite (until disclosure)
First owner[2]	Inventor	Designer	First person to use or apply	Author	Creator
Application process	Mandatory	Mandatory	Mandatory[3]	Optional	Not applicable
Example	Microwave oven	Design on the outside of oven	Name of the oven	User's manual	Ideas for improvement

1. The term "confidential business information" is used interchangeably with "trade secrets."
2. Ownership rights are subject to contracts that may specify other owners. This is particularly the case in employment.
3. Registration is required for protection under the *Trade-marks Act*. Unregistered trademarks receive protection under the common law.

PART FIVE

Acquisition and Protection of Intellectual Property

Intellectual property rights can be extremely valuable to a business. Intellectual property is often created within the business in much the same manner as Estelle invented her method of protecting electronic products and chose her product name. The process of doing so can be time consuming and costly. This suggests that an effective intellectual property program should be put in place to ensure that intellectual assets are valid, enforceable, and effectively exploited. Such a program should include the identification of all intellectual property assets; the determination of the nature, scope, and validity of the assets; and the evaluation of any potential risks and opportunities.

Assignments and Licences

Assignment
The transfer of a right by an assignor to an assignee.

Licence
Consent given by the owner of rights to someone to do something that only the owner can do.

Although intellectual property may be created in-house, it is also possible to purchase or receive an **assignment** of intellectual property rights or to receive a **licence** to use the intellectual property. By the same token, it is possible for a business to exploit its rights by assigning them or licensing their use. An assignment involves a change of ownership from the assignor to the assignee. As a general rule, all intellectual property rights are assignable in whole or in part. An exception to the general rule is that moral rights cannot be assigned, although they may be waived.

A business may also obtain a licence to use another's intellectual property. A licence is consent or permission to use the right on the terms specified in the licence. All intellectual property rights are capable of being licensed. This approach may be a viable way for Estelle to exploit her invention.

The process of getting an assignment or licence of intellectual property is not always easy. The process is often complicated by technological developments. Consider, for example, multimedia works that integrate text, graphics, still images, sounds, music, animation, or video, and with which the user can interact. The product involves various forms of media working together and may rely on literally thousands of sources, including copyrighted text, images, and music, for its content. The developer of the multimedia work has to ensure that all the relevant rights to these copyrighted works have been obtained, either through ownership or some form of licence or other permission.

Intellectual rights are often subject to compulsory licensing. For example, the Canadian Intellectual Property Office may order a patent holder to grant a licence if the exclusive rights under the patent are deemed to be "abused." Examples of abuses are refusal by the patent holder to grant a licence on reasonable terms, thereby prejudicing trade or industry, and failure by the patent holder to meet local demand for a patented article.

Protection of Intellectual Property

Intellectual property is an asset in the same manner as other business assets. Just as an organization takes measures to protect its buildings, land, equipment, and personnel, so too must it take steps to protect its intellectual property. It is not sufficient for Estelle to simply "create" intellectual property rights. Her rights require continuous monitoring and protection.

Use

Intellectual property rights are subject to loss if they are not properly used and maintained, as is shown in the following examples:

- A patent may be considered abused if, among other things, insufficient quantities of the patented item are produced to meet demand in Canada. As a result, a licence to use the patent may be granted to another, or the patent may even be revoked.

- Industrial design rights may be substantially reduced if the goods are not properly marked. A defence of innocent infringement is available unless proper notice (i.e., Ⓓ) is used on articles or their containers. The defence has the effect of limiting the owner's remedy for infringement to injunctive relief.

- A trademark can be subject to attacks for nonuse or abandonment if it is not used continuously in association with the goods or services for which it is registered. A trademark may also be lost if it loses its distinctiveness, as when it slips into everyday usage. For example, nylon, kleenex, zipper, escalator, cellophane, and dry ice, once trademarks, lost their distinctiveness and thus their status as trademarks by falling into everyday usage and becoming generic terms.

- Confidential business information is lost once it is disclosed. A business needs to be particularly vigilant in protecting confidential business information. A business can implement a program for maintaining security that includes restricting access to confidential information, implementing physical security measures (e.g., labelling documents "secret" or "confidential," locking areas where the information is kept, and changing computer passwords), and using confidentiality agreements that require others to maintain confidences.

BUSINESS APPLICATION OF THE LAW

Corporate Espionage at Coca-Cola

In July 2006, three people, including Joya Williamson, an employee of Coca-Cola Co., were charged with stealing confidential information, including a sample of a new drink from Coca-Cola. A person identifying himself as "Dirk" wrote PepsiCo, claiming to be a high-level employee with Coca-Cola. He asked for $10 000 for trade secrets and $75 000 for a new product sample. PepsiCo informed Coca-Cola, which contacted the FBI. An undercover agent paid $30 000 for the documents, marked "classified and confidential," and the sample. He promised the balance after the sample was tested. The agent offered Dirk $1.5 million for other trade secrets. The suspects were arrested on the day that the exchange was to occur. The information and sample came from Williamson, an executive assistant to a high-level Coca-Cola executive at the company's Atlanta headquarters. Video surveillance showed her at her desk going through multiple files and stuffing documents into her bags.

How does the law provide protection for trade secrets?

After a seven-day federal trial, Williamson was found guilty of conspiracy to steal and sell Coca-Cola's trade secrets. She was sentenced to eight years in prison with three years of supervised probation after release and ordered to pay

(Continued)

PART FIVE

$40 000 in restitution. Her sentence was affirmed on appeal.[72] Her co-conspirators pleaded guilty. One was sentenced to five years in prison. The other was given a lesser sentence of two years because he helped the government arrest Williamson. Both were ordered to pay $40 000 restitution, serve three years of supervised probation after release, and perform community service.

Critical Analysis: What steps should companies like Coca-Cola take to protect confidential business information?

Sources: Kathleen Day, "3 accused in theft of Coke secrets", The Washington Post (6 July 2006) D1; Amy S Clark, "Two Plead Guilty in Coca-Cola Spy Case", (23 October 2006) online: CBS News <http://www.cbsnews.com/stories/2006/10/23/business/main2115712.shtml>; and "Former Coke Employee Guilty in Conspiracy to Steal, Sell Coca Cola Secrets", The New York Times (2 February 2007) online: The New York Times <http://www.nytimes.com/2007/02/02/business/worldbusiness/02iht-coke.4451443.html>.

Litigation

At some point it may be necessary to engage in litigation in order to protect intellectual property rights. Intellectual property litigation is complex and expensive, often requiring the services of experts.

In many intellectual property infringement cases, it is common for the plaintiff to seek an injunction before trial to prevent the infringer from continuing to damage the business of the plaintiff. An injunction is granted if the applicant can demonstrate that there is a serious issue to be tried, irreparable harm may be caused, and the balance of convenience favours the applicant. In addition, because infringers may flee and destroy evidence, the law provides for the seizure of property before judgment. An **Anton Pillar order** allows the plaintiff to access the defendant's premises to inspect and seize evidence of infringement.

Anton Pillar order
A pretrial order allowing the seizure of material, including material that infringes intellectual property rights.

The most common intellectual property actions are as follows:

- *Patent infringement.* Infringement is not defined in the *Patent Act*, but it is generally taken to mean an unlicensed intrusion on the patent holder's rights (i.e., making, selling, using, or constructing something that comes within the scope of the patent claims). There is no requirement to show that the infringer intended to infringe on the patent, nor is it a requirement that the infringer's action come within the precise language of the claims. As long as the infringer is taking the substance of the invention, that will suffice. A successful action for patent infringement may result in the infringer having to pay damages or turn profits over to the patent holder, also known as the patentee. The patentee may also be entitled to an injunction prior to trial or after trial to prevent further infringement, and a "delivering-up" of the infringing product.

- *Copyright infringement.* Copyright is infringed whenever anyone, without the consent of the owner of the copyright, does anything that only the owner has the right to do. As noted above, this could involve various activities—copying, publishing, performing, translating, and the like. The copyright owner has a full range of remedies. An owner may also elect statutory damages of up to $20 000 instead of damages and profits.[73] As well, the infringer is subject to criminal sanctions of fines up to $1 million and/or five years in jail.

---

72. *United States v Williams*, 2998 WL 731993 (11th Cir, 2008).
73. When the amendments to the *Copyright Act* come into force, the statutory damages will change. See Business and Legislation: Amending the the Copyright Act, page 444.

- *Industrial design infringement.* The *Industrial Design Act* prohibits anyone from applying a registered industrial design to the ornamentation of any article without the permission of the owner. The prohibition also includes applying a confusingly similar design. The traditional remedies for infringement are an injunction to restrain further use of the design, damages, and an accounting of profits made by the defendant in using the design. The Act also provides for nominal criminal sanctions.

- *Trademark infringement.* Infringement of trademark is protected by both the *Trademarks Act* and the tort of passing off. The action can be brought against a trader who misrepresents the source of goods or services so as to deceive the public. This may be done by using the same or a similar trademark. Remedies for trademark infringement include injunctions, damages or an accounting of profits, and the destruction or delivery of the offending goods or the means to produce them, as well as criminal sanctions.

- *Confidential business information.* There is no statutory cause of action related to the misappropriation of confidential business information. There are, however, common law actions for breach of express and implied terms and breach of confidence, as discussed above. It must be shown that the information was confidential, that the information was disclosed under circumstances of confidence, and that the recipient misused the information to the detriment of the owner. Remedies available include injunctions, damages, an accounting, and/or a declaration of the entitlement to the information.

INTERNATIONAL PERSPECTIVE

Protecting Intellectual Property Abroad

It is difficult to protect intellectual property in a domestic setting; however, it is even more difficult to protect it in an international setting as, unlike tangible property, intellectual property is not bound by borders or geography. Protection is not just a question of designing and implementing rules for protection. There are very different perspectives on whether intellectual property should receive protection. Developing countries have little incentive to provide protection, as they need intellectual property in order to grow and prosper. Developed countries have a somewhat different perspective, as they consider intellectual property a valuable investment and worthy of protection.

Canada is a signatory to a number of treaties that give a measure of international protection to intellectual property rights. The major international conventions are these:

- *Paris Convention for the Protection of Industrial Property.* This convention provides national treatment and foreign filing priorities for patents, trademarks, and industrial designs.

- *Patent Cooperation Treaty.* This treaty is designed to facilitate the acquisition of patent protection in multiple countries around the world. Benefits are available only to nationals of contracting states.

- *Berne Convention.* This convention, which applies to literary and artistic works, provides for automatic copyright protection to nationals of member states without any requirement for formalities.

- *Universal Copyright Convention.* This convention provides national treatment for foreign copyrighted works provided the copyright symbol, the name of the copyright owner, and the date of publication are on the work.

- *Agreement on Trade-Related Aspects of Intellectual Property* (TRIPS). This is an agreement of the World Trade Organization (WTO) that establishes certain minimum standards of intellectual property protection for patents, trademarks, and copyrights. The agreement provides that a country should treat foreign nationals no less favourably than its own nationals with respect to intellectual property rights. Developing countries have a transition period for implementing it.

Canada has also signed but not yet ratified two Internet treaties: the *World Intellectual Property Organization's (WIPO's)*

(Continued)

Copyright Treaty (WCT) and *Performances and Phonograms Treaty* (WPPT). Both treaties respond to challenges posed by digital technology and are designed to update the Berne and Rome conventions.

The broad intent of the international agreements is to provide protection for foreign intellectual property. For example, works that have copyright protection in Canada have protection in countries that are signatories to the Berne Convention. By the same token, an author who is a citizen of a convention country receives copyright protection in Canada.

Critical Analysis: What is the justification for providing protection for foreign intellectual property? When intellectual property protection is extended in this manner, whose interests are curtailed?

Business Law in Practice Revisited

1. How can Estelle protect her invention?

Estelle's method for weaving static protection into the fibre of paper qualifies as an invention under the *Patent Act.* It is patentable if she can demonstrate that it is new, useful, and unobvious. Although there are presently methods of protecting products from electrostatic discharge, Estelle's method is new and an improvement over these methods. The very serious problems experienced by the electronic products industry indicate that Estelle's invention is useful and probably "unobvious." The cost of patenting is expensive but as the potential for the product is great, the investment is most likely to be worthwhile.

Keeping the method confidential or a trade secret is not really a feasible option for Estelle. Although secrecy does not cost anything in terms of filing fees, and secrecy can last forever, it hinders Estelle's ability to capitalize on her invention. As soon as she manufactures and sells a product utilizing her invention, other manufacturers, through the process of reverse engineering may be able to discover her "secrets." In such a case, nothing prevents them from copying and using Estelle's invention.

2. Who owns the rights to Estelle's invention—Estelle or ELEX?

Estelle owns the rights to her invention. Although Estelle is employed as an engineer for a manufacturer of electronic products, she is entitled to ownership of her invention as she was not hired to invent a method of protecting products from electrostatic discharge, and she made the discovery on her own time. Only if she had signed an agreement regarding the ownership of inventions, would she be required to transfer the patent (assuming a patent is granted) to her employer.

3. How can Estelle protect her idea while she seeks funding from potential lenders and investors?

Estelle can protect her idea while she seeks funding from potential investors and lenders by having them sign a confidentiality agreement. In the absence of an agreement, there may also be an implied obligation to keep the information confidential as the information would be conveyed in circumstances that suggest confidentiality.

4. Is Estelle entitled to use the name "Chargeless" for her product, and should she do anything to protect the name?

Estelle may start using the name "Chargeless" for her product so long as no one else has registered or is using the same or similar name in the same line of business. By simply using a name and not registering it, however, she runs the risk of someone else adopting the same or similar name in another part of the country. A common law (unregistered) trademark only provides protection in the area where a person's reputation has spread.

Estelle should register her name as a trademark to obtain national protection. To do so, she must meet requirements of use, distinctiveness, and registrability. Although another company in the financial services is using "charge less" as part of its slogan, this should not pose a problem because the use is in an entirely different industry. Estelle will have to have a trademark agent determine whether the name is in use as a trademark in the same industry and if it sufficiently distinctive.

Chapter Summary

The term "intellectual property" is used to describe the results of an intellectual or creative process. The term is also used to describe the rights people have or acquire in ideas and in the ways they express those ideas. The main categories of intellectual property rights are patents, industrial designs, trademarks, copyrights, and confidential information. The rights that attach to each category vary but generally encompass the right to use and the right to exclude others from using.

There is considerable overlap between the various categories of intellectual property. It is possible for more than one area of intellectual property law to protect different aspects of a single product or process. As well, there may be alternatives for protecting a single product. For example, an invention may qualify for patent protection, or the invention can be kept secret through the mechanism of a trade secret. Patent protection provides a monopoly for a period of time, but the price of the monopoly is the requirement to disclose the invention. A trade secret is just that—a secret. Once disclosure occurs, there is no protection. The ornamentation of a product subject to patent protection may receive industrial design protection.

Businesses acquire intellectual property in a number of ways. A lot of intellectual property is created in-house by employees, but it can also be bought or acquired through a licensing agreement.

Intellectual property, like other business assets, must be protected. An effective intellectual property policy should encompass its acquisition and proper use. Failure to acquire and maintain intellectual property rights may result in missed opportunities and losses for the business. In some cases, intellectual property rights ultimately may need to be protected by bringing legal action against infringers.

Chapter Study

Key Terms and Concepts

Anton Pillar order (p. 450)

assignment (p. 448)

claims (p. 430)

confidential business information (p. 445)

copyright (p. 439)

cyber-squatting (p. 435)

distinguishing guise (p. 434)

domain name (p. 435)

fair dealing (p. 444)

industrial design (p. 432)

intellectual property (p. 424)

licence (p. 448)

moral rights (p. 443)

patent (p. 425)

patent agent (p. 430)

specifications (p. 430)

trade name (p. 434)

trademark (p. 433)

Questions for Review

1. What is intellectual property?

2. What are the major forms of intellectual property rights?

3. What is a patent? Give an example.

4. Are life forms patentable in Canada? Explain.

5. Are computer programs patentable in Canada? Explain.

6. What are the three requirements for patentability?

7. What is the difference between specifications and claims in a patent application?

8. How long does patent protection last?

9. What is an industrial design? What are the requirements for industrial design registration? How long does an industrial design registration last?

10. What is the advantage of marking an industrial design to indicate that the design is registered?

11. What is the purpose of a trademark?

12. What is the relationship between trademarks and trade names?

13. Must trademarks be registered to receive legal protection? Explain.

14. What is meant by the term "cyber-squatting?"

15. Who owns the copyright in a book? How long does copyright last?

16. What are the moral rights of an author? Give an example.

17. One of the exemptions under the *Copyright Act* is fair dealing. What is fair dealing?

18. What are the requirements for the protection of confidential business information?

19. What is the difference between an intellectual property assignment and a licence?

20. Give an example of how intellectual property rights may be lost if they are not properly used.

21. How is injunctive relief used in intellectual property disputes?

22. What are the penalties for copyright infringement?

Questions for Critical Thinking

1. In *Monsanto v Schmeiser* (page 427), the Supreme Court of Canada ruled that the building blocks of life are patentable. Schmeiser was found guilty of patent infringement for saving and planting canola seeds containing Monsanto's engineered gene. In *Hoffman v Monsanto*,[74] a group of organic farmers in Saskatchewan launched a class action against Monsanto and Bayer Crop Science for contaminating their crops with genetically modified organisms. The Saskatchewan courts refused to certify the action, and the Supreme Court of Canada[75] refused leave to appeal. The Supreme Court's denial of leave leaves open the question of whether biotech companies are liable for damages caused by their

---

74. 2005 SKQB 225, 264 Sask R 1 aff'd 2007 SKCA 47, 293 Sask R 89.
75. [2007] SCCA No 347.

transgenic products. The farmers were seeking damages in tort against the biotech companies for failing to control the dispersal of their products and for failing to prevent them from doing economic and environmental damage. If the case had been heard by the Supreme Court of Canada, it would have provided an answer to the question of what is the proper balance between the property rights granted to Monsanto and Bayer and the obligation to mitigate the negative effects of the exercise of those rights.[76] Who should bear the social, economic, and environmental risks of biotechnological innovation? Who should have the responsibility of allocating the economic and environmental risks of biotechnological innovation?

2. When a major sporting event—the Grey Cup game, the Stanley Cup playoffs, the Olympics—occurs in a city, local businesses like to show their support of the home players. Often they decorate their businesses with the team logo, put signs of support in their display windows or develop products named after their heroes. The official sponsors of an event who have paid for the right to be a sponsor are often not happy. They do not like to see other businesses capitalizing on the goodwill associated with the event without paying. For example, during the 2011 Stanley Cup playoffs, a Vancouver Honda dealership received a cease and desist letter from the National Hockey League after it displayed "Go Canucks Go!" above the words "honk if you're a fan" and the Canucks stick-and-rink logo.[77] Do the actions of the dealership amount to trademark infringement? What intellectual property issues are raised when businesses try to benefit from the popularity and excitement of sporting events without paying for the right to be a sponsor? What is the risk to an organization in protecting its trademarks and sponsorship arrangements from violations?

3. Websites on the Internet offer powerful marketing opportunities for businesses. However, the websites, and the domain names that identify them, also present opportunities for others to take unfair advantage of the goodwill that a business has worked hard to establish. "Cyber-squatters" do this by registering domain names that include a business' trademark. How can a business, short of litigation, protect its portfolio of trademarks from cyber-squatters?

4. Beginning in 1998, the United States Patent and Trademark Office has allowed patents for all manner of business methods, including, for example, Amazon's one-click method for purchasing goods on the Internet; Priceline's name-your-own price reverse-auction process; and Mattel's system that allows its customers to order personalized toys. Patents have even been granted for reserving office bathrooms, for enticing customers to order more food at fast-service restaurants and for the process of obtaining a patent. The Federal Court of Appeal's decision in *Canada v Amazon* (see page 428) opens the door to similar patents being granted in Canada. Are business-method patents good for Canadian business? Some business-method patents have been criticized because they have covered subject matter that is old or obvious. What are other criticisms of allowing patents for business methods?

5. A "patent troll" is a person or company that holds patents for the sole purpose of extracting licence revenue or suing infringers. The troll does not make, use, or sell new products or technologies, but waits until a company has invested in, developed, and commercialized an idea and then it pounces—offering a licence in return for cash. The target company is often left with only two options: pay up or litigate.[78] How can companies manage the risk posed by patent trolls?

6. On June 29, 2012, *An Act to Amend the Copyright Act* received Royal Assent. Dominating the debate over the amendments have been the use of digital locks or technological protection measures (TPMs). These are basically electronic locks embedded into devices such as DVDs, computer software, and video games to prevent copying. The Act introduces provisions against tampering with or removing TPMs and provides penalties for circumvention. What is the purpose of TPMs? Does the use of TPMs coupled with penalties for circumventing strike the right balance between the rights of creators and the rights of users?

---

76. Jeremy de Beer & Heather McLeod-Killmurray, "Commentary: The SCC should step up to the environmental plate", *The Lawyers Weekly* (5 October 2007) 7.

77. Sunny Dhillon, "Local businesses embrace Canucks-logos and all", *The Globe and Mail* (6 June 2011) online: The Globe and Mail < http://m.theglobeandmail.com/news/british-columbia/local-businesses-embrace-canucks---logos-and-all/article582434/?service=mobile >; David Spratley, "Team spirit —or IP infringement?", *The Lawyers Weekly* (1 July 2011) 10.

78. Sarah Chapin Columbia & Stacy L Blasberg, "Beware Patent Trolls", *Risk Management Magazine* 53 (April 2006) 22.

Situations for Discussion

1. Meredith opened a restaurant called Checkers in St. John's, Newfoundland and Labrador. After about six months, she received a phone call informing her that "Checkers" is the name of a restaurant in Vancouver, British Columbia, and that she must immediately cease using the same name. Must she comply? Why or why not? How can Meredith obtain rights to the name?

2. Duncan, a small town on Vancouver Island, is known as the "City of Totems." Almost 80 totem poles can be found spread throughout the city, both in its downtown core and on the Trans-Canada Highway. In 2007, the city council created a copyright policy to govern the use of images of the totem poles. The policy states that the city holds the copyright policy on the totem collection, that the use of the totem images requires approval from the city, and that the city reserves the right to levy a copyright charge.[79] On what basis could Duncan claim to own copyright in the various totem poles located in the town? If Duncan owns copyright in the totem poles, could people be prevented from taking pictures of the totem poles? Is existing copyright law suitable for the protection of Aboriginal cultural property, such as traditional legends, stories, songs, and knowledge?

3. Anne recently returned from a holiday in Ottawa. While there, she visited the National Gallery and was most impressed by a landscape painting by one of the Group of Seven artists. Anne believes that the scene depicted in the painting would provide a wonderful design for her housewares business. She would like to use it for wallpaper, dishes, and kitchen bric-a-brac. Does her plan have any implications in terms of intellectual property? Explain.

4. Tabatha Pelkey had worked at Physical Fitness Equipment Sales Ltd. as its manager for six years; she left following a pay dispute with the owner. A few weeks later, she opened her own store just 18 blocks from Physical's site. She sold the same exercise equipment to the same market and featured an almost identical sign. Her business was instantly successful and had a serious negative impact on Physical's operations.[80] Could Physical successfully sue Pelkey for breach of confidence? What would Physical need to prove to be successful? How could Physical have protected itself from competition from Pelkey?

5. Mechanical engineer Vladislav Ircha was hired by Seanix Technology Inc. in March 2005 to design chassis and cases for computers. For the first few months, Ircha spent most of his time meeting with a subcontractor who was developing a case for Seanix's newest motherboard. Ircha soon realized, however, that the subcontractor's design was flawed, so he began working on a design of his own. Lacking proper design facilities at Seanix's office, he did most of the work at home and was able to produce a completed mockup of a new "swing-out" case in early 2006. Ircha's design was so impressive that the president of Seanix offered him a 30 percent salary increase and a bonus for a European vacation. Ircha, however, refused the president's offer, left the company, and claimed rights in the case. Seanix brought action for rights in the case. What legal issue(s) must be resolved?[81] Outline the law that governs them. How could Seanix have prevented this dispute?

6. Coco Sharpe is a software developer specializing in online games and puzzles. He has developed a revolutionary new poker game aimed at enhancing the skills of would-be poker players. Coco believes that he can make a lot of money selling the game online. Coco calls his game Coco Cardsharp, and he has received a registered trademark for the name. However, when Coco applies to register the domain name, he discovers that www.cococardsharp.com is registered to Janet Rollins. When contacted by Coco, Janet claims that she knows nothing about Coco's game but that she is willing to sell the rights in the domain name to Coca for $50 000. What are Coco's options? How should Coco attempt to settle the dispute with Janet? What are the advantages and disadvantages of pursuing online dispute resolution? What are the advantages and disadvantages of pursuing litigation?

7. In 1969, Cynthia and Frederick Brick opened a high-end furniture store in Winnipeg. They operated the store under the name, Brick's Fine Furniture. In 1988, Brick Warehouse Corp., a national chain of lower priced furniture sent the Bricks a letter demanding

---

79. David Spratley, "Copyright law offers poor protection for Aboriginal cultural property", *The Lawyers Weekly* (23 November 2007) 8.
80. Based on *Physique Health Club Ltd v Carlsen* (1996), 193 AR 196, 141 DLR (4th) 64 (CA), leave to appeal dismissed, [1997] SCC No 40.
81. Based, in part, on *Seanix Technology Inc v Ircha* (1998), 53 BCLR (3d) 257, 78 CPR (3d) 443 (SC).

that they stop using "Brick" as part of their business name. In 1977, Brick Warehouse had filed a number of trademark applications, which included the word "Brick." The Bricks had not registered the word "Brick" as a trademark. As they had used the same name for over 20 years, they refused to comply with Brick Warehouse's demand. The furniture chain sued and after a protracted legal battle that cost the Bricks $178 000 in legal fees, the case settled. The parties agreed to co-exist in Winnipeg.[82] What legal arguments were available to the Bricks? How could the Bricks have prevented this dispute?

8. For the past 15 years, Chuck Morrow has owned and operated Chuck's Grill House in Burnaby, British Columbia. His restaurant offers a selection of beef dishes including prime rib, steaks, burgers, and ribs.

The most popular dish on the menu is Chuck's BBQ Ribs. The ribs are cured and smoked (using a secret method invented by Chuck), slow-roasted, and then finished on a grill. Chuck has recently developed a new and improved method of curing and smoking ribs using flavoured wood chips, and he wants to protect it so that others cannot use it. Chuck may be able to protect his new and improved method of curing and smoking ribs from being used by others through a patent or by keeping his recipe a trade secret. What are the requirements for patent protection? What are the advantages and disadvantages of patents versus trade secrets? What factors should be considered in making a choice between secrecy and patenting?

For more study tools, visit http://www.NELSONbrain.com.

82. Eric Swetsky, "Trademark law is a sleeping tiger", *In-House Counsel* (Fall 2010) 8; John Shmuel, "Tips on challenging the heavyweights", *Edmonton Journal* (18 May 2010) F4.

CHAPTER 19

Real Property

Objectives

After studying this chapter, you should have an understanding of

- the nature and ownership of real property

- the various ways to acquire and transfer ownership

- how a mortgage works

- the rights and duties of landlords and tenants

© SUSAN VAN ETTEN/PHOTOEDIT

Business Law in Practice

Ashley Bishop has operated a furniture store in Halifax, Nova Scotia, for a number of years. The store has been successful to the point where it has outgrown its current leased space. Ashley has recently discovered a strip mall for sale in what she considers to be an ideal location for her store. A business colleague, Andrew Doncaster, is interested in joining Ashley in the strip-mall venture. They will incorporate Alpha Developments Ltd. (Alpha) to purchase and operate the mall. Half of the space is currently occupied by a number of businesses leasing space from the current owner. The plan is for Ashley's store to occupy most of the vacant space and to find new tenants for the balance of the vacant space. The listing price for the mall is $2 million. Ashley and Andrew can raise $800 000 and plan to borrow the remainder. Before she and Andrew proceed further, Ashley wants to know how she can escape from her lease with her current landlord. She also wants to understand the implications of buying the mall, obtaining the necessary financing, and dealing with current and future tenants.

1. What are the legal issues for Ashley in the planned purchase of the mall?
2. What are the risks in borrowing 60 percent of the purchase price of the mall?
3. What does Ashley need to know about the rights and obligations of her current lease and leases for the mall?

Ownership

The legal concept of **real property** refers to land or real estate.[1] When people own real property, they own a defined piece of land that includes not only the surface of the land but also everything above and below it—expressed in law as "the earth beneath and the air above." In practice, however, these broad ownership rights are limited by legal rules facilitating air travel above the surface and mining and oil drilling below the surface, to name a few examples. The term "real estate" also includes structures on the land, such as fences and buildings, as well as anything attached to those structures. Items so attached are known as **fixtures** and include heating ducts, lights, and plumbing.[2]

Land has always been a valuable commodity, and therefore the rules governing real property have deep historical roots. The value of land results from two key attributes. First, land is permanent and immovable, so it is easier to track and control than other, more portable forms of property, such as vehicles and furniture. Second, although land can be adapted for different purposes, the total quantity is finite. The value is determined by the market for a particular type and location of land.

Real property is largely governed by common law, and traditionally, the law is devoted to protecting rights to property, such as determining who owns a piece of land when more than one person is making a claim for it. Nowadays, however, public policy—in the areas of conservation and environmental protection, for example—means that statutes and administrative law are increasingly significant factors.

Interests in Land

The highest and most comprehensive level of ownership of land possible under our system of law is known as a **fee simple**.[3] An owner in fee simple essentially owns the land (subject to the limits described below) and can dispose of it in any way she sees fit. Ownership of land need not, however, be concentrated in one person or remain with that person in an uninterrupted fashion. In fact, ownership of land is easily divisible.

Division of Ownership

One piece of land can be owned by several people at once. For instance, rather than incorporating a new entity to buy the mall, Ashley and Andrew could choose to buy the mall themselves and share ownership. As co-owners they would each have an undivided interest in the entire building. Each owns a portion of the whole, but their respective shares cannot be singled out or identified in any distinct way.

Though Ashley and Andrew are the owners of the real estate, they are called tenants in this context. In ordinary usage, a tenant generally refers to someone who leases space rather than owns it outright; however, the legal use of the word "tenant" is much broader and includes someone who has any kind of right or title in land.

In the time leading up to purchase, Ashley and Andrew can negotiate either **tenancy in common** or joint tenancy. If they choose to be tenants in common, they each have an undivided interest in the land, meaning they can deal with their own interest in any way

Real property
Land or real estate, including buildings, fixtures, and the associated legal rights.

Fixtures
Tangible personal property that is attached to land, buildings, or other fixtures.

Fee simple
The legal interest in real property that is closest to full ownership.

Tenancy in common
Co-ownership whereby each owner of an undivided interest can dispose of that interest.

---

1. Bruce H Ziff, *Principles of Property Law,* 5th ed (Toronto: Carswell, 2010) at 74.
2. Bryan A Garner, ed, *Black's Law Dictionary,* 9th ed (St. Paul, MN: West, 2009) at 713.
3. *Supra* note 1 at 168.

PART FIVE

they see fit and without having to consult the other co-owner.[4] In a related fashion, if one of the tenants in common dies, that tenant's undivided interest in the real estate forms part of his personal estate and goes to his heirs.

Joint tenancy
Co-ownership whereby the survivor inherits the undivided interest of the deceased.

A **joint tenancy** is also a form of undivided co-ownership but is distinguished by the right of survivorship. Should one of the joint tenants die, his undivided interest goes directly and automatically to the other joint tenants.[5] The heirs of the deceased co-owner would have no claim on the land co-owned with the other. Both forms of co-ownership require cooperation among the owners in order to use or sell the property.

Division of Ownership in Time

Ownership in land can also be divided in time. The most common example is a lease. Since Alpha is buying a building that has more space than Alpha needs at the moment, it will seek tenants to use the extra space for a time. Through the mechanism of a lease, the owner—or landlord—gives a tenant possession of the building (or a portion thereof, depending on the agreement) for a period of time in exchange for rent. When the lease terminates at the end of the defined period, the landlord resumes control.

Limits on Ownership

There are numerous restrictions on land use imposed by statute law and common law, including the following:

- Municipal governments have the authority to control land use through planning schemes and zoning regulations. For example, if an area of a town is zoned for residential use, it is normally not available for commercial development.

- Environmental regulations affect the use of land by limiting or prohibiting the discharge of harmful substances.

- The common law of nuisance limits any use of land that unduly interferes with other owners' enjoyment of their land. A landowner who produces smoke or noise is subject to being sued for the tort of nuisance.[6]

- Family law may designate property as matrimonial—to be shared by both spouses—despite ownership registered in the name of one spouse. Both spouses must agree to the disposition of such property.

- Many government agencies have the authority to expropriate land for particular purposes. For example, if a new highway is to be built, the government can assume ownership of the portions of land along the route after providing compensation to the owners according to specified procedures.

- In a similar fashion, government agencies can make use of privately owned land for a particular purpose, such as a pipeline.

---

4. The parties can, of course, enter into a contract whereby they agree not to deal with their respective interests freely but to offer the other a right of first refusal, for example.
5. Many domestic couples own property as joint tenants because of this right of survivorship.
6. See Chapter 12.

- Ownership of land in a foreign country can be limited by that country's governmental policy. For example, foreign governments may nationalize whole industries without compensation to landowners from other countries. Foreign governments may also impose limits on the quantity of land that can be owned by nonresidents.

Other limits on ownership result from contracts made by the landowner. In short, the landowner has the option to "sell" part or all of his rights to the land in exchange for a payment of money or other benefit. For example, the landowner may do the following:

- Grant an adjoining landowner the right to use a portion of his land for a particular purpose. For instance, a landowner may give a neighbour the right to drive across his land to access her own or give a cellphone company the right to erect a tower. In law, these are known as **easements.**

> **Easement**
> The right to use the land of another for a particular purpose only.

- Grant a lease to a tenant, thereby giving the tenant the right to occupy the land for the specified period in exchange for rent.

- Grant an oil, gas, or mineral lease to occupy a portion of the land, access that portion, and remove materials.[7]

- Grant a mortgage on the land as security for a loan. This makes ownership subject to repayment according to the agreed terms of the loan. The right of the lender to be repaid takes priority, and the "owner" then holds the land "subject to the mortgage."

- Make the land subject to a **restrictive covenant**. Covenants are legally enforceable promises contained in the document transferring ownership. For example, title documents to lots of land in a housing development may contain covenants that prohibit or restrict certain activities (such as cutting trees or erecting storage sheds) for the purpose of preserving the character of the development and thereby enhancing its value.

> **Restrictive covenant**
> A restriction on the use of land as specified in the title document.

These various limits on ownership create a significant risk for businesspeople. Anyone contemplating the acquisition of any interest in land needs to do a thorough investigation of potential restrictions that could affect the rights to the particular piece of land. Otherwise, a buyer may end up owning land that cannot be used for its intended purpose.

Registration of Ownership

The provinces have constitutional jurisdiction over property rights.[8] A key aspect of this jurisdiction is the documentation and recording of interests in land. The value of land justifies a system in which those with an ownership interest are able to record or register their interests in a public fashion. The purposes of this type of system are twofold: first, to enable owners to give notice of the land they own and the extent of their ownership; and second, to enable anyone contemplating the acquisition of an interest in land to investigate the state of ownership in order to verify its status.

---

7. The law governing oil, gas, and mineral rights is complex. For example, in Alberta the government owns the rights and negotiates the leases.
8. *Constitution Act, 1982*, s 92(13): "property and civil rights in the province."

Because of the provincial control, the systems of registration vary from province to province, though historically there were only two general types.

A Registry System

The **registry system**, which originated in the eastern provinces,[9] provides the facilities for recording documents and the maintenance of the registrations. The public has access to the records and can examine or search the records to evaluate the state of ownership of a particular piece of land. This process is known as "searching the title." The main purpose of the search is to verify the seller's ownership by investigating the "chain of title" in order to confirm that no one has a conflicting claim to all or part of the land in question. Also required is an evaluation of the results of the search to decide whether the title is "clear" or not. If there are title defects, the parties will seek to fix those defects. For example, if Alpha has negotiated to purchase the strip mall but a search reveals that there is an unregistered title document (known as a deed) in the chain, it may be possible to register the missing deed and perfect the registered record—that is, cure the defect in the current owner's registration. If the defect cannot be cured, Alpha may still decide to proceed with the deal but extract a price concession from the vendor. For example, if the search reveals a small encroachment on the property by an adjoining owner, Alpha may decide to proceed with the transaction at a reduced purchase price. If the defect is fundamental, the deal may collapse.

The administrators of a registry system take no responsibility for the validity of the documents that are filed and express no opinion on the state of the title of a particular piece of property. Lawyers retained by the buyer of property are responsible for the search and the evaluation of the results. Law clerks or **paralegals** retained by the lawyer may do the actual search. If title problems emerge later, those who searched the title bear the potential liability.

The Land Titles System

The other system, which originated in the western provinces,[10] is the **land titles system**. The administrators of this system assume a much more active role, in that they evaluate each document presented for registration and maintain a record of the documents relating to each piece of property. They are also responsible for the accuracy of the information they provide, and they maintain an insurance fund to compensate those who suffer loss because of their errors. A person wishing to know the state of the title to a piece of land need only consult the certificate of title and is not ordinarily required to do a historical search. The certificate contains a legal description of the property and identifies the nature of and owners of the various interests in the land. Because the certificate itself is authoritative proof of title, there is less potential for competing claims. The greater certainty and reliability of the land titles system has caused several provinces that used the registry system, such as Ontario, New Brunswick, and Nova Scotia, to move toward the land titles system.

The sequence of registration is crucial to both systems. If there are conflicting claims to the same piece of land, the person who registered his interest first has priority, regardless of which transaction was completed first. So long as the one who registers first is not engaged

Registry system
The system of land registration whereby the records are available to be examined and evaluated by interested parties.

Paralegal
One who performs legal work under the supervision of a practising lawyer.

Land titles system
The system of land registration whereby the administrators guarantee the title to land.

---

9. Nova Scotia, New Brunswick, Prince Edward Island, Newfoundland, and parts of Ontario and Manitoba.
10. Saskatchewan, Alberta, British Columbia, and parts of Manitoba and Ontario.

in fraud, has no knowledge of the earlier transaction, and has paid valuable consideration for the land in question, that person's interest in and claim to the land is fully protected. The party who registers second has no claim to the land but may have actions against those who assisted in the failed transaction or who made representations concerning the status of title. This feature of registration is especially problematic in view of the recent increase in fraudulent mortgage activity, resulting in a conflict between an innocent landowner and an innocent bank.[11]

TECHNOLOGY AND THE LAW

Electronic Developments Affecting Interests in Land

Technology has produced increased efficiency, accessibility, and communication in real estate law, especially in the registration of interests in land. All provinces, whether they are operating under the registry system, the land titles system, or in transition, are aggressively using technology to improve their systems of land registration.

There are several technology-based improvements that have been implemented to varying degrees in all provinces:

- *Conversion of paper records to electronic records:* The savings in storage costs are huge.
- *Creation of a central database in the province:* This is a vast improvement over a system where each county or district had its own separate registry of records.
- *Improved access:* For purposes of filing documents and searching the records, the central database can be accessed from any of the county or district offices and remotely from law offices and other locations with access to the system.

Nova Scotia provides an example of the combination of two conversions—from registry to land titles and from paper to electronic. Each lot of land in the province was assigned a parcel identifier number. The title for each parcel will eventually be certified and registered under the new system, eliminating the previous need for a historical search every time the parcel is transferred. As a second stage, parties are able to file documents and conduct searches online.

There are some real and potential drawbacks to these major conversions. The cost of converting existing paper records to an electronic database is enormous, resulting in conversion over several years. There is a need for appropriate software for accessing and using the electronic systems. These systems are subject to the usual weaknesses of electronic databases—ensuring adequate capacity; controlling access; protection from viruses, crashes, and hacking; and the need for adequate backups. These risks also apply to developments in real estate transactions. Many property listings are now posted online by owners and agents. Connectivity software now enables lawyers, lenders, title insurers, and land registries to communicate directly. Electronic funds transfers facilitate payments among buyers, sellers, lawyers, and lenders. This development poses additional challenges in terms of verification of identity and electronic signatures.

Critical Analysis: Electronic systems are more vulnerable than paper systems in terms of issues such as documentation and security. Do the advantages in cost and efficiency compensate for these weaknesses? Who is responsible for the integrity of the electronic systems?

Sources: Dave Bilinsky, "Land registration systems in throes of change across Canada", *The Lawyers Weekly* (19 March 2004) 9; Christopher Guly, "A paperless world cuts both ways for property practitioners", *The Lawyers Weekly* (17 October 2008) 1; and Steven Pearlstein, "The next generation of conveyancing", *The Lawyers Weekly* (7 October 2011) 9.

Acquisition of Ownership

There are several ways to acquire an interest in land. Alpha plans to buy land with a building already in place, but it could buy land on which to build its own structure. Either purchase is likely to require financing, probably in the form of a loan from a financial institution secured by a mortgage on the property being purchased. As an alternative to buying, Ashley could lease larger premises as a tenant. By doing so, Alpha gains possession of the land for the term of the lease, but acquires no permanent ownership of the property.

---

11. See Robert Todd, "Bank didn't take proper steps", *Law Times* (28 January 2008) 1 and *Gill v Bucholtz*, 2009 BCCA 137 presented later in this chapter.

The Purchasing Transaction

Buying land is a buyer-beware situation, expressed in law as *caveat emptor*. It is up to the buyer (also known as the purchaser) to investigate and evaluate the property in both financial and legal terms. The risks are significant and require careful management. The seller (known as the vendor) must not mislead the buyer but generally is under no obligation to disclose information about the property, even when that information might cause the buyer to hesitate. There are legal and ethical complications to this general rule, however.

In legal language, "misleading" means misrepresentation, whether innocent or fraudulent (see Chapter 8). Misrepresentations may be oral or written false statements, but may also take the form of active attempts to hide defects in the property being sold. Silence and half-truths that imply something other than the truth may also be misrepresentation. There is a positive duty to disclose significant latent defects (not easily visible) that are known to the seller, especially if the defects cause the property to be dangerous or uninhabitable. Where there is a misrepresentation, the seller cannot justify it by claiming that the buyer could have discovered the truth through investigation. However, the buyer must show that the misrepresentation is material—an important factor in the decision to buy.[12] Examples of misrepresentations in commercial transactions relate to revenue potential, uses permitted by zoning regulations, permission to subdivide, and adequacy of water supply.[13]

An important development in residential real estate transactions is the use of a property condition disclosure statement, which requires the seller to provide detailed information on many aspects of the property. This statement can then be incorporated into the agreement of purchase and sale and thereby eliminate much of the uncertainty surrounding potential defects. However, there remains some obligation of the buyer to verify the statements made. See the *Krawchuk v Scherbak* case[14] in Chapter 13 where the sellers and their real estate agent were found liable for negligent misrepresentation in the disclosure statement concerning the sinking of the house foundation which led to cracking of the walls and major plumbing problems.

Ashley and Andrew have already identified the property that Alpha will buy, but Alpha should have its legal advisor involved from the outset to identify, among other matters, the contractual significance of communication and documents used by Alpha and the current owner. The technical nature of real estate transactions makes the use of professional advice a practical necessity.

Participants in the Transaction

The main participants in a real estate transaction are the buyer and the seller. In a commercial deal, such as the one Alpha is contemplating, the parties to the contract of purchase and sale are likely to be corporations. Individuals from both corporations will be chosen to coordinate the deal and conclude the contract. In addition, each party may have a real estate agent, a property appraiser, a land surveyor, an engineer, and a lawyer providing expert advice and guidance. The seller, for example, will likely have engaged a real estate

---

12. See Luis Millan, "SCC clarifies real estate disclosure standards", *The Lawyers Weekly* (1 July 2011) 13 commenting on *Sharbern Holding Inc v Vancouver Airport Centre*, 2011 SCC 23.
13. See Paul M Perell and Bruce H Engell, *Remedies and the Sale of Land*, 2d ed (Toronto: Butterworths, 1998) at 97.
14. 2011 ONCA 352, 332 DLR (4th) 310.

agent to find suitable buyers. For its part, Alpha might have engaged an agent to identify suitable properties. The lawyers on both sides will advise on the main agreement between the buyer and the seller. Appraisers may be hired to formally value the property, based on the structure and the current market. Surveyors may be retained to determine the physical boundaries of the property. Engineers may be retained to provide an expert report on the structural integrity of the building in question. Consultants may be involved to check for any environmental hazards.

From a legal point of view, Alpha's transaction is a complicated set of contracts revolving around the main contract for the transfer and sale of the property. Alpha must decide which professionals it requires and be clear regarding what services and advice each will provide. For example, a lawyer will normally do the investigation of title but is likely not in a position to place a value on the land.

In registry systems, lawyers have responsibility for evaluating the reliability of the title of the property their clients are buying. Lawyers search the title and give an opinion on its validity to clients and to the land registry if the property is in transition to the new system. They have professional liability insurance to cover negligence in providing this advice on title to property. In fact, a significant portion of claims made against lawyers arise from such situations. The cost of this insurance is reflected in the fees charged to clients in property transactions. In land titles systems, the administrators of the system accept responsibility for defects in title.

Title insurance is also an importance factor in real estate transactions. The use of title insurance diverts some of the responsibility, work, and related fees from lawyers.[15] However, when clients choose to use title insurance along with a lawyer, part of the lawyer's duty is to explain the impact of the title insurance policy.[16] Insurance companies offer protection to property buyers against problems with the title to the property, such as boundary encroachments, zoning problems, survey defects, liens, and fraudulent transfers or mortgages. A title search is preventive in that it identifies problems before the transaction closes. Title insurance provides compensation if a problem is discovered later.

In addition to the buyer, the seller, and professionals, others are less directly involved, as illustrated in the following examples:

- If the property is currently mortgaged, that obligation must be discharged by the vendor, assumed by the purchaser, or otherwise addressed in the financial adjustments between the parties.

- If Alpha needs a loan to finance its purchase, a bank or some other lender must be brought into the transaction. Alpha will be required to grant the bank a mortgage on the property for the amount borrowed plus interest.

- Since much of the strip mall is currently occupied by tenants, Alpha's ownership is subject to the rights of those tenants, depending on the jurisdiction involved and the length of the lease.

---

15. The legal profession resisted the advent of title insurance. For example, the New Brunswick bar unsuccessfully attempted to require a lawyer to be involved in mortgage refinancing. See Cristin Schmitz, "Law society rule invalid due to 'improper purpose'", *The Lawyers Weekly* (29 May 2009) 1.
16. See Raymond Leclair, "Title insurance does not replace legal expertise", *The Lawyers Weekly* (7 October 2011) 9.

Stages in the Transaction

There are three stages in the transaction that will result in the transfer of the land to Alpha: the agreement of purchase and sale, the investigation, and the closing.

Agreement of Purchase and Sale

Of prime importance is the agreement of purchase and sale between Alpha and the seller. Though the content of this agreement is entirely as negotiated between the parties, normal elements would include provision for Alpha to conduct a full investigation of the property and the opportunity to bring matters of concern to the seller. This agreement can also be made conditional, for example, "subject to a satisfactory engineer's report" or "subject to financing." If Alpha makes good-faith efforts to secure financing but is unable to find a willing lender, it can terminate the agreement with the vendor because the condition of being able to secure financing has not been fulfilled.[17]

What stages of a real estate transaction have occurred before these signs appeared?

DAVID COOPER/GETSTOCK.COM

Alpha's agreement with the seller must contain all requirements or terms of importance to Alpha, such as those listed below. As with any contract, once this one is signed, it is difficult to change without the agreement of both parties.[18] An important legal requirement that affects this contract is that it must be in writing and signed by the parties.[19] This eliminates attempts to incorporate into the agreement items that may have been discussed but on which no formal agreement has been reached.

The contents of the agreement of purchase and sale depend on the nature of the property and the value of the transaction. The basic terms are these:

- the precise names of the parties
- precise identification and description of the property, including reference to the registered title and sufficient detail so as to leave no doubt as to location, size, and boundaries

---

17. For discussion of conditions precedent and conditional agreements, see Chapter 7.
18. See the law of mistake in Chapter 8.
19. See the discussion of the *Statute of Frauds in* Chapter 8.

- the purchase price, deposit, and method of payment

- a statement of any conditions on which the agreement depends (such as financing, zoning, or environmental inspection)

- a list and description of exactly what is included in the price (e.g., equipment, fixtures)

- the date for closing and a list of what each party must deliver on that date

- a statement of who is responsible for what during the period between signing and closing

- any warranties relating to such matters as supply of water or soil contamination that continue after the closing

Normally, Alpha would submit an offer to buy, and the seller would accept it or respond to it with a counteroffer, which Alpha would then accept or vary, and so on until they both agreed unconditionally on all the terms. Only then would a contract exist.[20]

The Investigation

The second stage consists of the investigation by the buyer and the seller's response to any problems the buyer may raise.

The buyer must thoroughly investigate all aspects of the property during the search period allowed in the contract. Normally, Alpha's lawyer will conduct various searches on Alpha's behalf.

Title to the Property   Since this property is located in Nova Scotia, a **title search** in the local registry of deeds[21] may be needed. If this property has not been converted to the new system, the search normally goes back 40 years to ensure clear title. Any problems that can be fixed, such as an unregistered deed, will be remedied. If there is a more serious problem (e.g., someone else owns part of the land), Alpha will have the option to renegotiate terms or pull out of the deal. The search will also reveal registered restrictions on use of the land such as restrictive covenants or easements. If the land has previously been converted to the new system in Nova Scotia or if it were located in a land titles province, the search will not be necessary; Alpha can rely on the certificate of title from the land titles office.

Title search
Investigation of the registered ownership of land in a registry system.

Legal Claims against the Seller   Searches should be done to establish what legal claims exist against the seller of the property in question. For example, judgments registered against the seller are valid for a number of years; the exact duration varies from jurisdiction to jurisdiction. Such a judgment can form the basis of a claim against any land owned by the seller—a matter that a prospective purchaser would want to know about. Alpha would not want to own a piece of land subject to such a claim because it would have a less than clear title.

Verification of Boundaries   Alpha will retain a surveyor to confirm that the boundaries described in the registered title fit the physical boundaries of the land. For example, if the title provides for 1000 metres of road frontage but the surveyor finds only 800 metres, there is a problem to be addressed.

---

20. See Chapter 6.
21. *Registry Act*, RSO 1990, c R-20; *Registry Act*, RSNS 1989, c 392. See also *Land Registration Act*, SNS 2001, c 6.

Physical Examination   Alpha must confirm that the property is in the state it is expecting according to the agreement. Alpha must confirm the space occupied by the tenants currently in the mall. Alpha must also confirm the building's structural integrity, as provided for in the engineer's report. Excessive dampness and mould are also significant defects.

Environmental Audit   Alpha must ensure that there are no lingering or hidden environmental hazards. For example, if the property was used at some time as a gas station, Alpha must ensure that there is neither leaked fuel in the ground nor abandoned underground tanks that might leak (see the Environmental Perspective box below).

Taxes   Alpha must be sure that the municipal property taxes and any other local charges related to the property are paid up to date. If they are not, they will be deducted from the total due to the seller at closing.

Local Bylaws   Alpha must verify that the property can be used for its desired purpose. If Alpha were buying land on which to build or using an existing building for a new purpose, it must be especially careful that the zoning regulations permit that activity.

Any problems revealed by the various searches and investigations will be addressed according to the terms of the agreement. They will be fixed, or they will result in the renegotiation or termination of the agreement.

ENVIRONMENTAL PERSPECTIVE

Responsibility for Contaminated Land

The permanence of land facilitates the tracking of ownership because land cannot be moved or hidden. One of the negative features of this permanence concerns the long-term effects of commercial activities that may be harmful to the land itself and the surrounding community. In terms of pollution to the ground from toxic substances or the escape of harmful vapours from contaminants, the legal issue is liability for cleanup and for resulting harm to the environment and public health. Awarding damages for contamination is problematic since cleanup costs may well exceed the value of the land. Scientific advances have altered the public view of some activities; commercial activities that were once acceptable may not be any longer. The difficult issue is how to allocate responsibility for the harm already caused. There is a huge risk in buying property with a long history of use for industrial purposes (i.e., how should such "tainted" property be valued, and should the buyer purchase it or not?). A purchaser could face a large bill to clean up contamination caused by previous owners.

Liability for contaminated land has become such a barrier to development that all three levels of government are taking measures to encourage redevelopment of brownfields, the term for "abandoned, idle or under-utilized industrial or commercial facilities where expansion or redevelopment is complicated by real or perceived environmental contamination." For example, Ontario legislation[22] provides limited immunity from certain cleanup orders after a site has been restored to specific standards and a Record of Site Condition has been filed. Municipalities are considering property tax relief for redevelopers. Environmental insurance is also available in such situations. Developers must decide between complete remediation and a risk management plan that implements protective measures to contain harmful substances.

In the absence of these initiatives, the "polluter pays" principle is well established. The Supreme Court[23] has confirmed the right of a provincial regulatory authority to order further cleanup of a contaminated site that had been sold, cleaned up, and developed, only to exhibit subsequent effects of the earlier pollution. Results depend on the decisions of administrative tribunals. The broad social issue is how to balance the need to encourage development and commercial activity with the need to control and prohibit dangerous activities.

Critical Analysis: Who should bear the cost of environmental protection: the businesses that generate profits or the public sector? What are the risks in encouraging redevelopment of land that may be contaminated?

Sources: Pamela Young, "Time (or money) heals urban wounds", *The Globe and Mail* (15 May 2007) B12; and Dianne Saxe, "Tribunal spurns 'polluter pays' principle", *The Lawyers Weekly* (22 January 2010) 14.

22. *Environmental Protection Act*, RSO 1990, c E-19, Part XV.1 (known as the *Brownfields Act*). But see Elaine Wiltshire, "Critics sound alarm over brownfields regulation", *The Lawyers Weekly* (26 February 2010) 11 for concern about higher standards.
23. *Imperial Oil Ltd v Quebec (Minister of the Environment)*, 2003 SCC 58, [2003] 2 SCR 624.

The Closing

The third stage, the **closing**, occurs after all price adjustments have been made. At this point final payment is made and a formal transfer of ownership occurs.

If any difficulties found during the various searches can be remedied and Alpha is able to get its mortgage, the closing will proceed after the price is adjusted for such items as prepaid taxes (added to the price) or rent already received from tenants (deducted). Alpha will then make the final payment, and the seller will deliver the title document along with keys and other means of access to the property. Alpha will then immediately register its title at the local registry office to ensure that no competing claims intervene to disrupt its ownership. If electronic registration is available, this risk is eliminated. At the moment of closing, Alpha becomes responsible for the property. Alpha must therefore arrange for insurance coverage to be transferred at that time as well.

Figure 19.1 summarizes the stages of a real estate transaction.

Closing
The final stage of a real estate transaction when final documentation and payment are exchanged.

FIGURE 19.1

Summary of a Real Estate Transaction

Seller	*Buyer*
• decides to sell a piece of land	• decides to buy land
• determines the value of the land, possibly through a professional appraisal	• engages an agent to find suitable land
• engages a real estate agent to find a buyer and signs a listing agreement	• engages an appraiser to value the seller's land
• engages a lawyer to advise on the legal requirements	• engages a lawyer to advise on the legal requirements
• engages a surveyor to confirm boundaries	

Seller and Buyer	
• negotiate, possibly with the assistance of their agents and lawyers	
• reach agreement on all terms and conclude a formal written agreement	

Seller	*Buyer*
• addresses any problems discovered through the buyer's investigation	• investigates all aspects of the property, including the seller's title and any outstanding claims
	• confirms the boundaries of the land by retaining a land surveyor
	• arranges for financing
	• has an engineer assess the structural soundness of the building
	• has a consultant investigate environmental soundness

Seller and Buyer (and/or their lawyers)	
• attend the closing	

Seller	*Buyer*
• delivers the title document	• makes final payment
• delivers the keys to the property	• registers the title document
	• arranges for insurance
	• moves in

Incomplete Transactions

A deal may fall through for a number of reasons, some of which the agreement will anticipate. For example, if there is a title problem that cannot be fixed or the buyer is unable to arrange financing pursuant to a conditional agreement, the buyer normally has the right to bow out of the deal. In other situations, the buyer or the seller may find a better deal and simply refuse to complete the transaction as required by the agreement. Refusal to complete for a reason not contemplated by the agreement is a breach of contract and entitles the party not in breach to a remedy. If the buyer backs out, for example, the seller can keep the buyer's deposit. To claim further damages, the seller must try to mitigate by finding a replacement buyer. In such circumstances, the seller may experience costs in finding a new buyer and may end up selling the property for less than the defaulting buyer had agreed to. In such circumstances, the seller is entitled to recover the difference between these two prices from the defaulting buyer by way of damages for breach of contract. For example, if the defaulting buyer had agreed to buy the property for $200 000 and the seller is able to find a buyer for the property but only at $150 000, the defaulting buyer is liable to pay damages to the seller in the amount of $50 000.

If the seller refuses to complete, the buyer is entitled to the extra expense in acquiring a similar property. If monetary compensation is not adequate, the buyer can claim for specific performance—a special remedy for situations in which the subject of the contract is unique and the buyer cannot be compensated with anything less than the property itself.[24] In contrast, if the contract involves the purchase of goods (e.g., a computer) or services (e.g., office renovations) and the supplier fails to deliver, the customer can find another source and be fully compensated by an award for the extra cost. The following case contains a claim for specific performance.

CASE

Covlin v Minhas, 2009 ABCA 404

THE BUSINESS CONTEXT: This case illustrates the legal process for buying and selling land and the complications that result if the transaction is not completed as planned.

FACTUAL BACKGROUND: In December 2004 Verna Covlin agreed to buy a residential property in Edmonton near the University of Alberta campus. She paid a deposit of $10 000 and agreed to pay the balance of $177 000 on the closing date of 17 January 2005. The agreement also required that the vendor bear the risk of loss or damage up to closing, that closing documents (including the transfer document) be delivered to the buyer in advance of closing, and that if either party failed to complete the transaction then the other could pursue all available remedies. Covlin along with her husband owned six other properties in the immediate area. She intended to renovate the property and rent it to students in the short term, but planned a major residential

and commercial development in the longer term. Before closing, a water pipe burst and caused damage eventually agreed to be $10 000. Covlin learned of the water damage only at closing. She agreed to close when the damage was assessed and rectified. The vendor refused to proceed. Covlin sued for specific performance or damages in lieu of $163 000 for the increase in market value since the closing date and $248 000 for loss of development value.

THE LEGAL QUESTION: Did the vendors breach the agreement? If so, is Covlin entitled to specific performance? If not, what damages should be awarded?

RESOLUTION: The trial judge found that the vendors were in default. No duly executed transfer document was ever delivered. Covlin was at all times ready, willing, and able to perform. Regarding specific performance, he noted:

---

24. See Chapter 9.

... *Semelhago v Paramadevan*, 1996 CanLII 209 (SCC), [1996] 2 SCR 415 is the seminal decision with respect to specific performance in real estate transactions. Prior to *Semelhago*, specific performance for breach of a real estate contract was granted as a matter of course. However, in *Semelhago* Sopinka J. . . . stated:

"While at one time the common law regarded every piece of real estate to be unique, with the progress of modern real estate development this is no longer the case. Residential, business and industrial properties are all mass produced much in the same way as other consumer products. If a deal falls through for one property, another is frequently, though not always readily available."

Nevertheless, in the case before him, Justice Lutz concluded:

While the Plaintiff could arguably develop six lots instead of seven, the addition of the seventh property provides her with an opportunity that cannot be reasonably duplicated. She cannot simply go out and purchase another property that would have the same value to her as the subject property. The Plaintiff is not merely engaged in a speculative lawsuit for profit. The land in question is of particular and unique value to the Plaintiff, and for that reason damages are not an appropriate remedy in this case.

Covlin was awarded specific performance plus $10 000 for the water damage. On appeal, the trial decision was upheld. The property was unique because it formed an integral part of a larger plan for redevelopment.

CRITICAL ANALYSIS: Could Covlin have negotiated terms in the agreement to prevent this dispute? This property was considered unique because it was part of a development scheme. What other aspects of land might make it unique?

The Real Estate Mortgage
How a Mortgage Works

Alpha requires further financing to purchase the land and has decided to borrow the needed $1 200 000. In this chapter, a mortgage on the land itself is discussed.[25] Alpha will approach potential lenders—usually banks or other financial institutions, but possibly private lenders. Assuming that Alpha has a good working relationship with its own bank and is creditworthy, the bank is likely to be the lender, provided that the parties can agree on such matters as the rate of interest and a repayment schedule.

A mortgage transaction has two aspects. First, a **mortgage** is a contract for the extension of credit and is a debt owed by Alpha to its bank. The lender advances the principal sum to the borrower, who promises to repay the principal plus interest over the specified period. Alpha as a corporate borrower will likely be required to provide personal guarantees as well, probably from Ashley and Andrew.[26] Second, the mortgage transaction also involves the bank taking a security interest in the land purchased by Alpha. To attain this security protection, the bank must register the mortgage document, thereby giving notice to all creditors of Alpha—as well as anyone considering purchasing the property from Alpha—that the bank has first claim against the land. Registration gives the bank secured status, which will protect its claim against the land even if the borrower becomes bankrupt.

Any claims already registered against the land have priority over the new mortgage and will affect the bank's decision to grant the loan. The bank's mortgage does not forbid Alpha from attempting to borrow more money in the future using this land as security, but those subsequent lenders will be aware that the already registered mortgage forms a prior claim. Each subsequent mortgage against the same land involves significantly greater risk for the lender.

Mortgage
A credit arrangement where title to land is security for the loan.

---

25. See corporate financing in Chapter 15 and personal property security in Chapter 26.
26. See Chapter 26.

PART FIVE

Under the land titles system, registration of the mortgage creates a legal charge on the land. The registered mortgage amounts to a claim—or lien—on the land until repayment is complete. In provinces under the registry system, in contrast, the mortgage actually transfers ownership of the land to the lender for the duration of the lending period. The bank becomes the legal owner, but Alpha remains the equitable owner. This means that Alpha has the **equity of redemption**—the right to have legal ownership restored to it upon repayment.

Although the effect of the mortgage on ownership varies according to the land registration system in place in the particular province, the practical effect on the use of the land is the same. Alpha is the borrower, known as the **mortgagor**. Alpha remains the occupier of the land, so there is no apparent change in control of the land. The bank as the lender is known as the **mortgagee**. As long as Alpha makes the required payments on the loan, the bank is content to allow Alpha to carry on normal business activities on the land.

Equity of redemption
The right to regain legal title to mortgaged land upon repayment of the debt.

Mortgagor
The party who borrows the money and signs the mortgage promising to repay the loan.

Mortgagee
The party who lends the money and receives the signed mortgage as security for repayment.

Terms of the Mortgage

The focus of the mortgage is on preserving the value of the land in question. This protection is achieved by preventing the borrower from doing anything with the land that would lower its value and by giving the lender maximum flexibility in dealing with the borrower. For example, if the mortgagor does not adequately insure the property, the mortgagee (the bank) has the right to secure proper insurance and hold the borrower responsible for the cost. Recently the risk of fraud has become a major concern for lenders. They have developed practices to verify the identity of borrowers and to ensure that the necessary documentation is authentic. Provincial law societies also have regulations to guide lawyers in new client identification and verification. The following case deals with fraud.

CASE — *Gill v Bucholtz*, 2009 BCCA 137

THE BUSINESS CONTEXT: This case demonstrates the technical nature of the land registration system and the particular challenge of fraudulent mortgage activity.

FACTUAL BACKGROUND: In 2005 an unidentified fraudster forged the signature of A.S. Gill on a transfer of land to G. Gill. The fraudster and G. Gill were working together. G. Gill granted a mortgage to the Bucholtzes who advanced $40 000 to G. Gill and registered the mortgage. G. Gill then gave a second mortgage to a numbered company who advanced $55 000 and attempted to register the mortgage. The attempt failed because A.S. Gill filed an objection. At trial A.S. Gill regained title to the land, but subject to the two mortgages.

THE LEGAL QUESTION: Are the mortgages a valid charge against the land? Who should suffer the loss from the fraud— the innocent owner or the innocent mortgagees?

RESOLUTION: The mortgagees argued that they acquired the mortgages from G. Gill who was the registered owner of the land. They had no notice of G. Gill's fraudulent title and confirmed her identity. A.S. Gill argued that the mortgagees were in the best position to detect the fraud and, in any event, the mortgages were ineffective because G. Gill had no valid interest to give. The outcome depended on the court's interpretation of several sections of the *Land Titles Act (LTA)*.[27] The rights of a registered owner are subject to exceptions, one of which is the right of the true owner to show fraud. In addition, a void instrument includes a mortgage from one who has title by fraud and does not convey any rights to the fraudulent holder.

CRITICAL ANALYSIS: The court's finding based on the *LTA* favoured the true owner of the land. Is this a reasonable result? Who is in the best position to absorb such losses?

27. RSBC 1996, c 250, ss 23(2)(i), 25.1(1).

Historically, the bank would not grant the loan unless it was confident of Alpha's ability to repay. As a precaution, however, the amount of the loan was likely to be less than the current value of the land, for two reasons. First, the mortgage is a long-term arrangement, so the bank will consider the possibility of developments in Alpha's business or the market that might diminish the value of the security. Second, if Alpha defaults and the bank needs to use the security to recover its money, it is unlikely that the land will produce its full market value in a quick sale. A serious drop in the market could result in negative equity for the owner—that is, the amount owed on the mortgage could be more than the value of the property. This traditional approach was significantly altered in recent years (mainly in the United States) with the growth of subprime mortgages, which were granted to consumer borrowers with limited ability to pay on the assumption of a continually rising real estate market. Borrowers were often enticed with low interest rates at the beginning of the mortgage term. As property values declined, the default rate became alarming, which contributed to widespread disaster in the financial sector.

The mortgage document is normally prepared by the lender. Though each bank has its own standard form of mortgage, all of them include the following as basic terms:

- amount of the loan (known as the principal)
- interest rate
- date of renegotiation of the interest rate
- period of repayment over which the loan is amortized
- schedule of payments
- provision for payment of property taxes
- provision for full insurance coverage on the property, with the proceeds to be paid directly to the lender
- borrower's obligation to keep the property in a good state of repair and refrain from any activity that would decrease its value
- complete legal description of the land
- provision for early repayment (possible penalty)
- acceleration clause, which provides that on default of payment by the borrower, the whole amount of the loan becomes due
- remedies of the lender on default
- discharge (release) of the mortgage at the end of the term when the full loan is repaid

Of particular interest are the clauses dealing with taxes and insurance. The bank needs to be sure the taxes are paid because the appropriate municipal or provincial authorities have the right to sell the property to recover any unpaid taxes levied against the property. The land would then be owned by the purchaser at the tax sale and would not be available to the bank.

The bank's interest in insurance is twofold. First, the bank needs full coverage on the property so that if a fire occurs, the proceeds from the insurance will essentially replace the portion of the security destroyed by the fire. In addition, the bank needs direct access to those insurance proceeds. If paid to the borrower as the insured party, the money is more difficult for the bank to recover than the property would have been before the fire. As a result, the mortgage will contain a term assigning the insurance proceeds to the lender.

Life of a Mortgage

If the mortgage transaction proceeds as intended by both the borrower and the lender, the borrower will repay the loan as the mortgage requires and the lender's claim or charge against the land will cease. The lender will provide a document to release, or discharge, the mortgage. When this document is registered, it provides public notice that the borrower's obligations have been satisfied. However, since a mortgage is a long-term arrangement, many events can occur that result in some change to the liability, such as the following:

- Alpha may choose to pay off the mortgage before it is due. The mortgagee will likely anticipate this possibility in the mortgage document and require Alpha to pay a "penalty" or extra charge. This is to compensate the bank for interest it loses until it finds another borrower for the money lent to Alpha.[28]

- If the mall property that Alpha buys contains unused land, Alpha may choose to sell some of the excess. Since the mortgage forms a claim on all the land, Alpha needs to negotiate with the bank for a release of the piece to be sold. Only when this partial release is registered can Alpha transfer clear title to that piece.

- Alpha may need to renegotiate the mortgage for further financing. If the value of the land is well above the amount of the outstanding loan, the land could be used as security for an additional amount. This is a separate issue from the periodic renegotiation of the interest rate on the original loan. For example, the repayment period for the loan may be amortized—or spread out—over 25 years, with the interest rate adjusted every five years.[29] Such interest rate adjustments following a low introductory rate have contributed to the subprime mortgage crisis.

- The lending bank may assign its outstanding mortgages to another financial entity. Alpha must then make its payments to the new entity. This could be a routine business decision or the result of a corporate takeover or reorganization. These assignments on a mass scale resulted in bundling of high-risk mortgages to form new security instruments which figured prominently in the subprime crisis.

---

28. See new rules regarding mortgage prepayment information for consumers at Department of Finance Canada, *Code of Conduct for Federally Regulated Financial Institutions* (4 March 2012), online: <http://www.fin.gc.ca/n12/data/12-025_3-eng.asp>.
29. The federal government has tightened the rules for residential mortgages. See Department of Finance Canada, "Harper government takes further action to strengthen Canada's housing market", (21 June 2012), online: < http://www.fin.gc.ca/n12/12-070-eng.asp>.

- Alpha may decide to sell all of the land. This requires that Alpha pay out the mortgage fully or negotiate with the buyer to take over or "assume" the mortgage if the terms are attractive. For example, if Alpha has a lower interest rate than the current market rate, the lower rate could be used as a selling point by Alpha. This "assumption" requires the agreement of the bank and likely entails a significant risk for Alpha. When a mortgage is assumed, the original borrower—Alpha—remains liable for payment. Hence, if the new buyer defaults under the terms of the mortgage, the bank can claim the balance owing from Alpha.[30]

- Alpha's business may suffer to the point where cash flow no longer allows for payments to the bank. This is the situation that the bank most fears and that the mortgage is primarily designed to address in terms of remedies.

Mortgagee's Remedies

The bank is likely to give Alpha some leeway in payment, especially if the bank is hopeful that Alpha's business may recover. If this fails, the bank will proceed to exercise its legal remedies pursuant to the mortgage and applicable legislation. The rights of the lender and the procedures to be followed vary from province to province,[31] but all involve a combination of four remedies—suing the borrower, taking possession of the land, selling the land or having it sold, and **foreclosure.**

Foreclosure refers to the lender's right to terminate the borrower's interest in the property. It is the end of the process that allows the lender to realize the value of the land by selling it directly pursuant to a power of sale or through a court-supervised sale. Whichever procedure applies, the objective is to allow the lender to maximize the proceeds from the property to be applied against the outstanding loan. Most provinces[32] also permit the lender to proceed against the borrower for the shortfall—known as the **deficiency**—between the outstanding amount and the proceeds from sale of the property.

At any point before the foreclosure process is complete, ownership of the land can be regained if the borrower is able to repay the loan (assuming of course that another source of financing becomes available). If Alpha cannot repay the loan, it loses the land and may be left owing a substantial debt. The bank is left with a bad debt and the knowledge that the decision to lend the money was flawed. If there is more than one mortgage registered against the land, the remedies of the various mortgagees are more complicated. What remains clear is that each mortgagee's rights and remedies are determined in strict order of registration of the mortgages. As a result, mortgagees beyond the first are likely to recover less than those that registered ahead of them.

Foreclosure
The mortgagee's remedy to terminate the mortgagor's interest in the land.

Deficiency
The shortfall between the outstanding mortgage balance and the proceeds from sale of the land.

---

30. However, see *Citadel General Assurance Co v laboni* (2004), 241 DLR (4th) 128 (Ont CA) where the original mortgagors were not held responsible after they had sold their equity of redemption and the mortgage had been renewed without notice to them.
31. Sale by the court is preferred in Alberta, Saskatchewan, and part of Manitoba and is the only remedy in Nova Scotia. Otherwise, sale and foreclosure by the mortgagee is allowed.
32. In Alberta, Saskatchewan, and British Columbia, the mortgagee cannot personally sue individual borrowers and can sue only corporations that have waived their statutory protection.

The Real Estate Lease
The Landlord–Tenant Relationship

Ashley is currently in a landlord–tenant relationship because she is leasing her store space. Ashley is the **tenant**. The owner of the building that she occupies is the **landlord**. Since Alpha is intending to buy a partially leased mall, it will become an owner and landlord and will enter into further leases for the space not needed for Ashley's store.

A **lease** is a contract between a landlord and a tenant. It records the rights and obligations of both parties. It is also an interest in land. Leases are of two general types—commercial and residential. The two types are significantly different in terms of the ability of the parties to negotiate their own terms, the rights and obligations in the lease, remedies, and enforcement mechanisms.

Residential leases are heavily regulated by provincial legislation[33] that

- prescribes the form and content of the lease
- limits the amount of security deposits that can be required of residential tenants
- defines the rights and obligations of the landlord and tenant, including tenant's security of tenure
- requires the landlord to maintain the premises
- provides remedies for breach of the terms of the lease
- provides the procedures for resolving disputes

Commercial leases are relatively unregulated.[34] The terms are negotiated solely by the landlord and tenant. They are free to agree on the format and content of the lease. If Alpha were the owner of an apartment complex and a commercial mall, the apartment lease would be under the residential regime and the mall lease governed by commercial rules. The discussion that follows is geared mainly to commercial situations.

A lease is a means of dividing ownership of property for a time. Its key feature is the idea of **exclusive possession**, which means the tenant has a high level of control over and responsibility for the premises during the term of the lease. This concept of exclusive possession is doubly important because first, it is the main factor in deciding whether a lease has been created to begin with and, second, it is the major consequence of the creation of a lease. For example, a five-year lease means that the tenant has the right to occupy and control the property for the full five years and cannot be legally evicted from the land unless the lease is violated by that tenant in a major way, even if the land is sold to another owner. If Alpha, as landlord, enters into a long-term lease with a tenant and later wrongfully terminates that lease, Alpha is in breach of contract and must pay damages to the tenant. Alpha may also be subject to an order for specific performance or an injunction preventing the eviction of the tenant.

As with any contract, the parties need to appreciate the point at which they have achieved sufficient consensus to form a legal relationship. Each party wants terms

Tenant
The party in possession of land that is leased.

Landlord
The owner of land who grants possession to the tenant.

Lease
A contract that transfers possession of land from the landlord to the tenant in exchange for the payment of rent; also refers to the tenant's interest in land.

Exclusive possession
The tenant's right to control land during the term of a lease.

---

33. See, for example, *Residential Tenancies Act*, RSNS 1989, c 401; *Residential Tenancies Act*, 2006, SO 2006, c 17; and *Residential Tenancies Act*, CCSM c R119.
34. But see legislation such as *Commercial Tenancies Act*, RSO 1990, c L.7; *Tenancies and Distress for Rent Act*, RSNS 1989, c 464; and *Overholding Tenants Act*, RSNS 1989, c 329 that deals with such issues as forfeiture, re-entry and distress in commercial tenancies.

acceptable to it and wants to obligate the other party to them. At the same time, the parties want to avoid unintentional obligations. An offer to lease or an agreement to lease becomes enforceable only if it contains all the key terms (identification of the parties, the premises to be occupied, the term, the rent, and the intent to grant exclusive possession to the tenant) and has been accepted by the other party.

In a commercial context, a number of factors will determine the lease content, including the relative bargaining positions of the parties and the nature of the market for the property in question. If suitable space is scarce, the landlord has the advantage and can largely dictate terms, especially the amount of rent. If there is a glut of property and the tenant is in no hurry to move from its current premises, the tenant may be able to negotiate concessions from the landlord.

Terms of the Lease

The complexity of the lease depends on the value, nature, and size of the property. A lease for an office tower is lengthy and complicated because there are many issues to address and a great deal is at stake. Conversely, a lease of a garage to store surplus equipment could be quite simple.

These are some basic terms in every commercial lease:

- identification of the parties

- description of the premises

- permitted alteration of the space by the tenant and what happens to the alteration when the lease ends

- ownership of improvements to the space

- calculation of rent (e.g., based on the amount of space and/or a percentage of gross sales)

- responsibility for repairs and maintenance to the leased space and any common areas

- security and damage deposits

- permitted uses of the space by the tenant

- tenant's hours of operation

- limits on the landlord's ability to lease other space to the tenant's competitors

- time period of the lease (generally three to five years)

- provisions for renegotiation, renewal, or termination

- provisions for assignment and subletting

- remedies for either party if the other fails to comply with the lease

- what happens in case of events such as fire or flood that damage the leased property and adjacent property owned by the landlord or others

- protection of the landlord in the event of the tenant's bankruptcy

- dispute resolution process

Parties in a commercial lease are free to negotiate their terms. What are some key terms in the lease of this building?

PLANETSD LLC/SHUTTERSTOCK

Rights and Obligations

The rights and obligations contained in a commercial lease are formally known as covenants and consist largely of whatever the parties negotiate in the lease. Commercial leases vary significantly and must be reviewed closely in order to understand the rights and obligations of the parties. However, some covenants arise from the tenant's exclusive possession and corresponding responsibility:

- The tenant is responsible for repairs unless the lease imposes some obligation on the landlord.

- The tenant is entitled to exclusive and quiet possession of the premises for the full term. In return, the tenant must pay rent and observe the terms of the lease.

- The tenant cannot withhold rent, even if the landlord fails to meet a requirement in the lease. The tenant's remedy is to claim compensation from the landlord while continuing to pay rent.

- The tenant cannot terminate the lease and move out unless the landlord's breach of the lease has made the premises uninhabitable for normal purposes.

- Ordinarily, the tenant can assign the lease or sublet the property to another tenant.[35] Assigning the lease transfers full rights (and the related obligations) for the remainder of the term. A sublease, in contrast, is an arrangement whereby the tenant permits someone else to occupy the leased premises for part of the time remaining in the lease. The original tenant remains fully liable under the lease but has rights against the subtenant—should the subtenant fail to pay the sub-rent, for example. It is common for the lease to require the landlord's consent for both of these arrangements. Such leases normally also provide that the landlord's consent may not be unreasonably withheld.[36]

---

35. See *Gateway Realty Ltd v Arton Holdings Ltd* (1992), 112 NSR (2d) 180 in Chapter 7.
36. *Supra* note 1 at 294–299.

The landlord's basic obligations are to refrain from interfering with the tenant's use or enjoyment of the property and to provide any benefits or services promised in the lease. The landlord's goal is that the tenant pay rent, use the premises for acceptable purposes, and cause no damage to the property. The major risk for landlords is that the tenants may get into financial difficulties. Thus, remedies for landlords focus on collecting unpaid rent and evicting tenants for defaulting on payment or for other serious breaches.[37] Unlike the usual contract situation, a commercial landlord has no obligation to mitigate damages if the tenant abandons the premises. Commercial landlords also have the remedy of **distress**: if a landlord follows proper procedures, she can seize the property of the tenant located in the leased premises, sell the property, and apply the proceeds to the unpaid rent.[38] The following case deals with a dispute about the terms of a commercial lease.

Distress
The right of a commercial landlord to seize the tenant's personal property for non-payment of rent.

CASE   *Goodman Rosen Inc v Sobeys Groups Inc, 2003 NSCA 87*

THE BUSINESS CONTEXT: This case illustrates the importance of the terms of a commercial lease, especially regarding the permitted activities of a tenant over the period of a long-term lease.

FACTUAL BACKGROUND: Sobeys signed a 25-year lease for space in a shopping mall in which to operate a supermarket. A clause in the lease stated, "[T]he Lessee shall use the Leased premises only for the purposes of the business of the retail sale of a complete line of food products, as well as general retail merchandising, as carried on by the rest of the majority of its stores." The lease also contained a covenant by the landlord not to permit any part of the mall to be used for the purpose of carrying on the business of the sale of food in any form. This non-competition covenant was a fundamental term of the lease that, if breached, would entitle Sobeys to terminate the lease. Shortly after Sobeys opened its store in the mall, Shoppers Drug Mart leased space for 20 years in which to operate a pharmacy. Shortly before the expiry of its lease, Sobeys opened a pharmacy within its supermarket as part of a corporate strategy to include a pharmacy in all of its stores. The landlord claimed that Sobeys' pharmacy was a violation of the lease and demanded that it be closed.

THE LEGAL QUESTION: Does the Sobeys' pharmacy violate the lease? If so, what remedy is available to the landlord?

RESOLUTION: The court interpreted the clause in question to allow the retail sale of goods, but not the sale of services. The

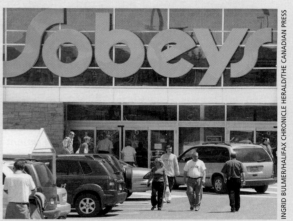

How can shopping mall leases deal with potential competition among tenants?

INGRID BULMER/HALIFAX CHRONICLE HERALD/THE CANADIAN PRESS

professional services offered by a pharmacy are outside the meaning of "general retail merchandising." The court also found that pharmacies were not yet part of the majority of Sobeys' stores and therefore not permitted on that basis. The court granted an injunction to the landlord ordering Sobeys to cease the operation of its pharmacy.

CRITICAL ANALYSIS: How can the language of a long-term lease provide for developments in retail operations? What is likely to happen at the end of Sobeys' 25-year lease?

---

37. Landlords may be flexible during economic downturns. See Annie Gagnon-Larocque and Cameron Whyte, "When a struggling tenant is better than no tenant", *The Lawyers Weekly* (9 October 2009) 13.
38. *Supra* note 1 at 283.

PART FIVE

Termination of the Lease

The parties may be able to terminate their relationship if the terms of the lease are not followed. Normally, the lease runs its natural course and ends when the agreed period for the tenant's occupation expires.

There are two types of leases in terms of time. One identifies the exact duration of the lease. If Ashley's lease of her current space was for a fixed term of five years, which is about to expire, the lease will automatically end on the specified date. Similarly, the Sobeys' lease in the case above will end when the 25-year term expires. Neither party is required to give any notice or obligated to negotiate a renewal or extension. Therefore the landlord should realize that Ashley is free to move, and she should realize that she has no right to stay beyond the specified date. If Ashley's current lease is not near its end, she will need to negotiate an early termination.

Periodic tenancy
A lease that is automatically renewed unless one party gives proper notice to terminate.

The other type is known as a **periodic tenancy** and automatically renews itself unless one party gives the required notice before the current term expires. For example, if Ashley has a lease from year to year, that lease will automatically be renewed for another full year unless either Ashley or the landlord gives sufficient notice (likely about three months).

Which type of tenancy has been created depends on the actions and agreement of the parties. If they have not clearly indicated their intentions in the lease, a court will classify the lease based on their actions and other circumstances of the case. To avoid uncertainty, the parties should deal with termination in detail in the lease so that there is no doubt about the length, renewals, or the need for notice to terminate.

A lease as an interest in land is, in theory, not affected by the sale of the property by the landlord. The tenant is entitled to stay until the end of the lease, with the new owner as landlord. However, long-term leases must be registered in some provinces, and in any event should be registered to give those who are investigating title clear notice of their existence.

When Alpha buys the mall, it will inherit the existing leases for the duration of their remaining term. When deciding how much space to use for Ashley's store and therefore how much extra space to lease to new tenants, Alpha must be aware of the rigidity of long-term leases. Alpha could consider finding tenants who are prepared to enter a short-term tenancy or a periodic tenancy from month to month. This would permit Alpha to regain full possession of the premises if the need arose. The disadvantage is that this may make the property less attractive to tenants unless their needs are short-term ones as well.

Disposition of Property

The owner of the fee simple in real property has total control over the disposition of ownership in that property. The options are as follows:

- Use the land as security for a loan by granting a mortgage. The owner remains in possession of the land and retains control, subject to the obligation to repay the debt and abide by the terms of the mortgage.

- Lease all or part of the land to tenants. The owner gives up possession for a defined period of time but retains ownership. At the end of the lease, possession reverts to the owner.

- Transfer the land to family or others by gift or through a will on death. There are various legal options available to the owner in terms of dividing ownership (such as a joint tenancy).

- Sell all or part of the land. This is a complete transfer of the fee simple in the portion of land sold. Full ownership rights are transferred to the purchaser, who becomes the registered owner.

Risk Management

The major risk relating to real property is the complexity of the law. This chapter provides an overview of the key aspects of the law and avoids many of the complexities that are beyond the scope of a basic text such as this one. A businessperson entering a transaction to buy, lease, or mortgage land needs to obtain competent legal advice to guide her through the complications and ensure that her interests are adequately protected. Real property is largely a buyer-beware proposition, in that those involved are expected to do their own thorough investigations before committing to a real estate transaction. Risk reduction is crucial.

Key commitments relate to contracts for the purchase or sale of land, the lease, or the mortgage. The language is complex, and it is crucial for those involved to understand the language in some detail as well as the broader implications of the transactions. A buyer of land must ensure that the agreement contains all terms of importance. A landlord and tenant need to understand the degree of control that the lease provides for the tenant. One who signs a mortgage should understand the far-reaching rights enjoyed by the lender in the event of default.

In many situations, the bargaining power of the businessperson may be limited by financial need, the challenges of dealing with large institutions, or the fluctuations of the market. The ability to avoid, reduce, or transfer risk may be limited. What cannot be bargained can at least be understood with the help of expert advice.

Business Law in Practice Revisited

1. What are the legal issues for Ashley in the planned purchase of the mall?

The major legal challenge in the purchase of the mall is the need to ensure that the agreement of purchase and sale is negotiated with legal assistance so that it provides adequate protection for Alpha, Ashley, and Andrew. They must realize that they have full responsibility to verify all aspects of the property, such as the title, zoning, and environmental condition, before proceeding to finalize the purchase.

2. What are the risks in borrowing 60 percent of the purchase price of the mall?

Ashley and Andrew need to appreciate the significance of signing a mortgage on behalf of Alpha (and perhaps as guarantors) for such a significant portion of the purchase price of the mall. They must be justifiably confident that the location and revenue from the mall will be ample to meet the mortgage payments. If Alpha defaults and they are unable to renegotiate more favourable terms, Alpha will lose ownership and possession of the mall.

3. What does Ashley need to know about the rights and obligations of her current lease and leases for the mall?
Ashley needs to understand the need to negotiate with her landlord for termination of her current lease. She and Andrew must understand that as purchasers of the mall through Alpha, they are obliged to honour the leases with the current tenants. They also need to appreciate the nature of the commitment to additional tenants for the space that will not be used for Ashley's store. Mall leases are complicated arrangements, so they need legal advice in drafting and negotiating.

Chapter Summary

Real property is permanent and immovable, and the total quantity is fixed. The focus of the law is on the land itself rather than the buildings or fixtures attached to it. Ownership is called the fee simple and includes everything on, above, and below the land, subject to a wide variety of limits on use. The owner of land can transfer and divide ownership in a number of ways. Registration of any interest in land is required to preserve priority over other claimants. There were two systems of registration in Canada—registry and land titles—although all provinces are moving toward an electronic land titles system. The most common ways to acquire ownership are to purchase the fee simple through a real estate transaction or to become a tenant through a lease. In buying land, there is considerable risk involved, which can be managed through investigation of all aspects of the land.

A mortgage is security for a loan that emphasizes the preservation of the value of the property. A mortgage gives the lender the right to sell the land or have it sold if the loan is not repaid.

The landlord transfers to the tenant the right of exclusive possession of the land for the term of the lease. In return, the landlord is entitled to rent and has the right to regain possession at the end of the lease or earlier if the tenant defaults. The lease will end when a specified term expires or when one party gives the required notice to the other.

The holder of the fee simple can dispose of her interest as she chooses: lease the land temporarily, sell it, or give it away while she is alive or in her will upon death.

Chapter Study

Key Terms and Concepts

closing (p. 469)

deficiency (p. 475)

distress (p. 479)

easement (p. 461)

equity of redemption (p. 472)

exclusive possession (p. 476)

fee simple (p. 459)

fixtures (p. 459)

foreclosure (p. 475)

joint tenancy (p. 460)

landlord (p. 476)

land titles system (p. 462)

lease (p. 476)

mortgage (p. 471)

mortgagee (p. 472)

mortgagor (p. 472)

paralegal (p. 462)

periodic tenancy (p. 480)

real property (p. 459)

registry system (p. 462)

restrictive covenant (p. 461)

tenancy in common (p. 459)

tenant (p. 476)

title search (p. 467)

Questions for Review

1. What are the unique features of land as a form of property?

2. What is a fee simple?

3. What are the limits on an owner's use of his land?

4. How does a joint tenancy operate?

5. How can ownership of land be divided by time?

6. What is the purpose of registering title to land?

7. What is a restrictive covenant relating to land?

8. What are the benefits of an electronic registration system?

9. What are the three stages in a transaction for the purchase and sale of land?

10. What should a buyer of land investigate?

11. What is clear title?

12. What happens at the closing of a property transaction?

13. What are the key features of a mortgage?

14. What are a lender's remedies if the borrower fails to make mortgage payments?

15. What are the essential terms in a lease?

16. What is the remedy of distress?

17. What is a periodic tenancy?

18. How can the owner of land dispose of his interest?

Questions for Critical Thinking

1. Land registration determines property rights strictly according to the order of registration, unless there has been fraudulent activity. Should the system allow for late registration in exceptional circumstances, such as when a buyer either fails to consult a lawyer or the lawyer neglects to register the documents? Can you think of other exceptional circumstances?

2. Identity theft and mortgage fraud are occurring more frequently. Property owners discover mortgages registered against their property about which they know nothing. The perpetrator of the fraud has fled with the money, leaving the property owner and the lender to absorb the loss. How can this problem be effectively prevented? Is it up to property owners, the banks, or the lawyers who facilitate the transactions?

3. Real property law originated as a means of protecting rights or resolving disputes between conflicting individual rights to property. Increasingly, broader uses of land in the public interest are coming into conflict with individual owners' rights. Some examples are wind turbines that produce noise; cellphone towers that are unsightly and may emit radiation; and oil or natural gas pipelines that entail environmental risks. What factors may help to resolve this friction between the public interest and individual ownership rights?

4. In most cases, a lender has more expertise and experience in credit transactions than the borrower. Do the

PART FIVE

rules of contracts and mortgages allow the mortgagee (lender) too much protection at the expense of the mortgagor (borrower)? Should the lender bear some responsibility for a decision to lend that turns out to be a bad one? Does it matter that the mortgage is subprime and the borrower has been enticed and persuaded by the lender to borrow the money?

5. The format and content of residential leases is largely dictated by legislation, while commercial leases are entirely negotiated by the parties, resulting in lengthy and complex documents. The difference is largely based on the assumption that commercial tenants can take care of themselves while residential tenants are vulnerable to exploitation by landlords. Is this a valid assumption? Should there be more similarity in the processes that create the two types of leases?

6. Covenants in commercial leases generally limit the landlord's ability to rent space to tenants whose businesses compete with those of existing tenants. In shopping malls, the anchor tenants have more bargaining power than smaller stores, so can better protect their business. In times of real estate downturn, small stores may fail at a higher rate. The covenants may limit the landlord's ability to fill the vacant space. What are the implications of this situation? Are there remedies to better promote the full use of mall space?

Situations for Discussion

1. The Mellicks owned a farm that the Haywards were interested in buying. During negotiations, the Mellicks told the Haywards that the farm contained a total of 94 acres, with 65 acres under cultivation. The offer to buy described the farm as containing 94 acres but made no mention of acres under cultivation. The agreement contained a clause indicating that there were no conditions, representations, or agreements other than those expressly contained in the offer. The deal closed, and several months later, the Haywards discovered that there were only 51.7 acres of land under cultivation.[39] Were the Haywards entitled to 65 acres under cultivation?

2. Campbell's business is in financial difficulty. Technology is advancing quicker than Campbell can

move. She is faced with a gradual reduction in business operations and a related need for less space. She has 20 years left in the lease of her business premises but cannot afford to pay the monthly rent. How should Campbell approach her landlord? What are her legal options? Is the situation different if Campbell owns her business premises subject to a mortgage on which she cannot make the payments? How should she approach her banker? What are her legal options?

3. Bayshore Trust granted a loan to Assam based on a mortgage for $210 000 with interest at 14 percent for a one-year term. The monthly payment was $2540. At the end of the term, Bayshore renewed the mortgage for another year at 14.5 percent. During that year, Assam defaulted and Bayshore sued Assam, who argued that Bayshore induced him into a state of financial disaster by granting a mortgage with monthly payments he could not possibly make. Assam alleged that Bayshore should never have lent him such a large sum of money. At the time of the mortgage, Assam's annual income was $28 000.[40] Who should decide whether a lender such as Assam can make payments on a loan? Should Bayshore be required to do anything more than protect its own interest in the mortgage? Would the outcome be different in today's subprime mortgage environment than when this case came to court in 1992?

4. Jeanette bought a small office building with a 25 percent cash payment and a 75 percent mortgage. The total price was $400 000, and her monthly mortgage payment was $3000. The location of the building was not convenient for tenants and their customers. Jeanette's major tenant defaulted on its lease and left. Jeanette sued for unpaid rent, but the lawsuit is dragging on. She was unable to keep up her payments on the mortgage, and the bank foreclosed. The building was eventually sold for $200 000. Because the outstanding balance on the mortgage was $280 000, the bank is now suing Jeanette for the $80 000 shortfall plus its legal expenses. Jeanette believes that the property was worth much more than $200 000, and she wants to attack the bank's conduct of the sale and avoid the claim against her.[41] Has the bank acted properly? Could Jeanette have decreased her risk?

---

39. Based on *Hayward v Mellick* (1984), 26 BLR 156 (Ont CA).
40. Based on *Bayshore Trust Company v Assam*, [1992] OJ No 715 (Gen Div).
41. Based, in part, on *Meridian Credit Union Ltd v Hancock*, [2009] OJ No 4609 (Sup Ct J).

5. Shoker engaged a real estate agent to find a property suitable for use as a trucking terminal. The agent found a property which was zoned "highway commercial." Its permitted uses included a retail store, car and truck sales agency, commercial garage, parking lot, and restaurant. Shoker signed an agreement to buy the property, which contained two conditions— the buyer would confirm the zoning with the municipality and the buyer would exercise due diligence to ensure that the property was suitable for his intended use. The agreement did not specify a trucking terminal as the intended use. Shoker discovered that the zoning would not permit the operation of a trucking terminal. He gave notice to terminate the agreement. The seller alleged breach of contract and kept the deposit of $50 000.[42] Is the agreement enforceable by the seller? How could the agreement have been more clearly written?

6. Bresson bought a piece of land for commercial development for $3 million. He was assured that it contained an unlimited supply of water from an existing well. When construction began, it was discovered that the water was unusable due to contamination in the soil caused by leakage of gasoline from underground tanks located on the adjacent property.[43] What investigation should Bresson have done before the deal closed? Was the seller obligated to disclose the state of the land? Is the owner of the adjacent property responsible?

7. Perkins leased space for two stores from Plazacorp. A few years ago, an awning across the front of the stores was removed, causing rain water to seep into one of the stores and damage carpets and inventory. Plazacorp fixed the leak after repeated complaints by Perkins over a period of time. The second store was affected by sewage backups that originated in the common area of the property. In an attempt to prompt Plazacorp to remedy these situations, Perkins ceased paying rent. When Plazacorp sued for the rent arrears, Perkins counterclaimed for the cost of damage and repairs to the two stores.[44] Was Perkins entitled to stop paying rent? Is Perkins' counterclaim valid? On what does the answer depend?

8. Greenwood rented office space to Evergreen for five years with an option for renewal of three or five years. In the second year of the lease, Greenwood informed Evergreen that it could not comply with its obligations under the lease beyond the end of the current year; Greenwood planned to demolish the building and erect a 21-storey office tower. Greenwood offered Evergreen preferential treatment in the new building when it was completed. Evergreen refused to move, claiming that the current building had architectural value and should be preserved. The lease did not include clauses dealing with demolition or the landlord's right to resume possession during the term of the lease.[45] How does this situation illustrate rights of ownership and landlord–tenant relations? How could the dispute be resolved?

For more study tools, visit http://www.NELSONbrain.com.

---

42. Based on *Shoker v Orchard Garden Markets Ltd* (2007), 62 RPR (4th) 81 (Ont Sup Ct J).
43. Based on *Bresson v Ward*, (1987) 79 NSR (2d) 156 (Co Ct) and *Edwards v Boulderwood Development* (1984), 64 NSR (2d) 395 (CA).
44. Based on *Plazacorp Retail Properties Ltd v Perkins Health and Safety Ltd*, 2007 NSSM 30.
45. Based on *Evergreen Building Ltd v IBI Leaseholds Ltd*, 2005 BCCA 583. See also Chris Atchison, "Tenants halt the wrecking ball's swing", *The Globe and Mail* (18 July 2011), online: The Globe and Mail <http://www.theglobeandmail.com/report-on-business/industry-news/property-report/tenants-halt-the-wrecking-balls-swing/article2101098/>.

Employment and Professional Relationships

Employment and professional relationships are essential components of business. Without the skills, knowledge, and experience of others, businesses would be unable to function and compete effectively. Most businesses require a wide range of services, including managerial, clerical, administrative, and professional services, which they acquire by hiring employees or by contracting for the services as needed.

The employment of others, whether through the employment relationship or through an independent service contract, has been affected by significant social change: the entry of women in large numbers into the workforce; recognition of the disadvantaged position of minorities; greater awareness of the needs of people with disabilities; heightened public concern for the fair treatment of workers; adaptation to technological developments; and concern for job security. Not surprisingly, there has been much legal intervention to address these developments. In addition to the common law, a vast array of federal and provincial legislation affects all aspects of employment.

YURI ARCURS/SHUTTERSTOCK

CHAPTER 20

The Employment Relationship

Objectives

After studying this chapter, you should have an understanding of

- the basic elements of the employment relationship

- the ways in which the law affects recruitment practices

- the content of a typical employment contract

- the legal issues relating to the terms and conditions of employment

Business Law in Practice

Hiram Dupuis owns and operates an independent weekly newspaper in southern Ontario. The newspaper has a circulation of 250 000 and focuses on mainly community news and human interest stories.

Several months ago Hiram engaged the services of Jeong Nash to write a column as well as feature stories on the local sports scene. Hiram refers to all of the reporters as independent contractors and permits them to accept writing assignments from other newspapers as long as the assignments do not conflict with obligations to Hiram's newspaper. Hiram pays Jeong on the basis of a fee per published word, as well as a base monthly salary of $3000. Hiram provides Jeong with office space and a computer and gives Jeong the freedom to pursue whatever stories she likes as long as they have a sports angle.

Recently Hiram learned that Jeong sent an email message to a local sports celebrity requesting an interview. When the hockey player declined the request, Jeong sent him a nasty reply. In addition, Jeong posted possibly defamatory remarks about the hockey player on a website dedicated to hockey.

1. Is Jeong an employee or an independent contractor?
2. Why is the distinction between an employee and an independent contractor important?
3. Is Hiram responsible for Jeong's conduct?

RYAN MCVAY/PHOTODISC

Employment Law

The employment relationship is a critical component of business activity. Engaging the services of others provide the means by which a business can carry out its mission. Employment, however, is much more than an engine of business. It is a relationship that provides a livelihood for a large portion of society. Given the importance of this relationship to both the employer and the employee, it is not surprising that there is a vast body of law regulating employment.

Employment law in all Canadian jurisdictions, with the exception of Quebec, is rooted in the traditions of the English common law, with an overlay of legislation. Both the federal and provincial governments have jurisdiction to pass employment legislation, and both levels have been active in this area.

The federal government has jurisdiction to make laws that affect employees of the federal government and federally regulated industries, such as the banking, airline, broadcasting, railway, and shipping industries. It is estimated that about 10 percent of all employees are subject to federal regulation. The provincial governments have jurisdiction to make laws that affect all other employees, including provincial employees. For example, as the newspaper industry is not federally regulated, employees of newspapers come under provincial jurisdiction. An employee is subject to either federal or provincial jurisdiction, and it is not unusual for employees working in close proximity to be subject to different employment legislation.

Both levels of government have enacted human rights legislation and an array of employee welfare legislation, such as employment standards, occupational health and safety standards, and workers' compensation. In addition to legislation of general application, governments have passed legislation that affects employees in specific jobs. Public sector employees, such as police officers, teachers, medical personnel, and civil servants, are commonly affected by specific legislation.

Employees may also be unionized, in which case labour relations legislation is applicable to the employment relationship. The federal government and all of the provinces have enacted labour or industrial relations statutes that facilitate the unionization process.

This chapter focuses on laws that affect the employment process in the private, non-unionized sector, as the majority of employees fall within this category. At the end of the chapter, a note is provided on differences in the union environment.

The Employment Relationship

The **employment relationship** involves a contract whereby one party, the employer, provides remuneration to another, the employee, in return for work or services.[1] Not everyone who works for another or provides services to another is an employee, however. In some situations, those who provide services are considered agents[2] or **independent contractors**.[3]

Employment relationship
A contractual relationship whereby an employer provides remuneration to an employee in exchange for work or services.

Independent contractor
A person who is in a working relationship that does not meet the criteria of employment.

---

1. The historical terms for employer and employee are "master" and "servant."
2. The law affecting agents is discussed in Chapter 13.
3. The Ontario Court of Appeal in *McKee v Reid's Heritage Homes Limited*, 2009 ONCA 916, 256 OAC 376 (CanLII) suggests that there is a third category, 'dependent contractor.' This is when a person is not an employee but a relationship of economic dependency exists usually as a result of the contractor working exclusively or nearly exclusively for another. Workers classified as dependent contractors will be owed reasonable notice on termination.

Usually, doctors and lawyers, for example, provide services in the capacity of independent contractors, rather than as employees of their patients/clients.

With the advent of "downsizing" and "right-sizing," people who traditionally worked as employees are increasingly working as independent contractors. The benefits for independent contractors are tax savings, flexibility, and independence in arranging a work schedule. An employer may prefer to engage independent contractors because the relationship offers simplicity and fewer financial and legal obligations.

Employee versus Independent Contractor

The distinction between an employee and an independent contractor is not always readily apparent. It is common to think of independent contractors as being short-term and temporary, while employees are long-term and permanent. In practice, this might be the case, but it is not a distinction based in law. Historically, the courts have used a variety of tests to distinguish between the two relationships, including the following:

- *The degree of control exercised over the individual by the employer*. The more direction and supervision provided by the employer, the more likely that the relationship is employment. Hiram exercises little control over how Jeong carries out her work and permits her to pursue other assignments; this is indicative of an employer and independent contractor relationship.

- *The ownership of tools, chance of profit, and the risk of loss from performance of the requested service*.[4] Sharing profits and losses and the ownership of tools are indicative of an independent contractor. On this basis, it appears as if Jeong is an employee, because she does not own her own tools or share in the profits or losses of the business.

- *The degree of integration*. The nature of the work being performed is considered in relation to the business itself. The question is whether the work being performed is "integral" to the business, or is "adjunct" to the normal work of the business.[5] The more the work is integrated into the company's activities, the more likely it is that the individual is an employee. For example, Jeong's work is integral to the operation of a newspaper; based on this fact, she would appear to be an employee.

The Supreme Court of Canada in the following case has indicated that there is no one conclusive test that can be universally applied. The nature of a relationship is a question of fact and will vary with the situation.

---

4. *Montreal (City of) v Montreal Locomotive Works Ltd*, [1947] 1 DLR 161, [1946] 2 WWR 746 (PC).
5. *Co-operators Insurance Association v Kearney*, [1965] SCR 106, 48 DLR (2d) 1.

CASE

671122 Ontario Ltd v Sagaz Industries Canada Inc, 2001 SCC 59, [2001] 2 SCR 983

THE BUSINESS CONTEXT: Changes in the workplace—corporate restructuring, globalization, and employee mobilization—have resulted in a shift away from traditional employment relationships. However, as relationships have grown more flexible, they have also grown more complex, and the question of whether a relationship is that of an employer and employee or that of an employer and independent contractor is receiving increased attention.

FACTUAL BACKGROUND: A design company sold seat covers to Canadian Tire. However, it lost its contract with Canadian Tire to Sagaz because of the actions of American Independent Marketing (AIM), hired by Sagaz to assist in securing Canadian Tire business. AIM and its employee bribed an employee of Canadian Tire in order to induce Canadian Tire to buy from Sagaz. As a result, the design company lost a substantial amount of money and went into steep decline.

THE LEGAL QUESTION: Was Sagaz vicariously liable for the bribery scheme perpetrated by AIM?

RESOLUTION: Vicarious liability is a theory that holds one person responsible for the misconduct of another because of the relationship between them. The most common relationship that attracts vicarious liability is the relationship between employers and employees. The relationship between employers and independent contractors, subject to limited exceptions, does not give rise to a claim for vicarious liability.

There is no one conclusive test that can be universally applied to determine whether a person is an employee or an independent contractor. What must always occur is a search for the total relationship of the parties. The central question is whether the person who has been engaged to perform the services is performing them as a person in business on his own account.

The contract designated AIM as an "independent contractor," but this classification is not always determinative for the purposes of vicarious liability. However, as AIM was in business on its own account, it is an independent contractor. This conclusion is supported by the following factors: AIM paid all of its own costs of conducting its business; AIM was free to carry on other activities and to represent other suppliers; Sagaz did not specify how much time AIM was to devote to representing Sagaz; AIM worked on commission on the sales of Sagaz's products; and AIM controlled how the work was to be done.

CRITICAL ANALYSIS: The determination of whether a worker is an employee or an independent contractor is critical, as employee status is the gateway to most employment protection under both the common law and employment-related legislation. What factors indicate the presence of an employer and employee relationship?

Implications of an Employment Relationship

Employees have certain statutory rights and benefits, such as paid holidays and paid overtime, which are not conferred on independent contractors. Employers have certain obligations with respect to employees, namely deduction of income taxes and employment insurance premiums, the payment of Canada (or Quebec) Pension Plan premiums, the provision of paid vacations, and the like, which they do not have with respect to independent contractors. The consequences of incorrectly characterizing a work relationship as an independent contractor arrangement can include retroactive responsibility for paying benefits as well as liability for penalties and interest charges.

Establishing the employment relationship is important to certain legal principles. For example, an employee can initiate an action for wrongful dismissal, but this avenue is not available to an independent contractor. An employer is responsible for the tort of an employee committed in the ordinary course of employment, whereas an employer is not usually responsible for the torts of an independent contractor committed in the course of carrying out the contract.[6] An independent contractor, however, may be an agent for the employer, in which case the employer can be vicariously liable for the acts of the agent under traditional agency principles.

---

6. The distinction between an employee and independent contractor for purposes of vicarious liability is increasingly being called into question. For example, in *Thiessen v Mutual Life Assurance*, 2002 BCCA 501, 6 BCLR (4th) 1 leave to appeal to SCC refused, [2002] SCCA No 454, the BC Court of Appeal imposed vicarious liability on an insurance company for the misconduct of a sales representative who was characterized as an independent contractor, not an employee.

Risks in Hiring

The hiring of workers is critical to business. Hiring well can be a boon to a business, and hiring poorly can result in low productivity and possibly a costly termination. From a business perspective, hiring the candidate who is best suited for the job results in the optimal use of resources. From a legal perspective, hiring well can reduce the risks associated with the employment relationship, in particular those associated with vicarious liability and negligent hiring.

Vicarious Liability

As previously stated, an employer is liable for the torts of an employee that are committed in the ordinary course or scope of employment. An employee's wrongful conduct is within the ordinary course or scope of employment if authorized by the employer. Thus, an employer is liable when an employee commits a wrong while carrying out assigned duties or authorized tasks. An employee's wrongful act is also within the ordinary course or scope of employment if it is an unauthorized mode of doing something that is authorized by the employer. Because the distinction between an unauthorized "mode" of performing an authorized act and an entirely independent act is difficult to discern, particularly in the case of intentional torts, the courts will consider whether the tortious conduct of the employee is significantly related or connected to conduct authorized by the employer. In other words, the employer will be vicariously liable if there is a significant connection between the wrongful acts of the employee and the creation or enhancement of the risk of the wrongful act by the employer. For example, when Jeong posted the possibly defamatory statement on the website, she was not carrying out assigned duties or authorized tasks; therefore, her employer will be liable for her acts only if there is a significant connection between her possibly wrongful conduct and the creation or enhancement of the risk of the wrongful conduct by the employer. Although the possibly defamatory statements are connected to conduct authorized by the employer—Jeong was authorized by her employer to write feature stories on the local sports scene—it is entirely possible that Jeong acted outside the employment relationship in that she was responding in a personal capacity to a perceived affront. An employer is not responsible for wrongs that occur completely outside the employment relationship.

As noted in Chapter 10, the justifications for holding employers responsible for their employees' actions include the following:

- Employers have the ability to control employees and therefore should be liable for the employee's conduct.

- Employers benefit from the work of the employees and therefore should be responsible for liability incurred by employees.

- Employers are usually in a better position than employees to pay damages. Imposing liability on employers helps ensure that an innocent victim is compensated.

- Employers have an incentive to try to prevent torts from occurring in the first place.

The imposition of vicarious liability does not relieve the employee of liability. Both the employer and employee may be liable to the plaintiff. The employee may also be liable to the employer for breach of the employment contract; however, it is rare for an employer to pursue an action against an employee because of the inability of the employee to pay damages and the negative publicity associated with a legal action.

Negligent Hiring

Another potential risk for employers in the hiring process is in the area of "negligent hiring." An employer has a duty to use skill and care in hiring employees (the extent of the duty will vary according to the position the candidate is to fill).[7] Therefore, if an employee injures another employee or causes harm to a third party, there may be an action against the employer for being negligent in having hired that employee. This action differs from vicarious liability, which holds the employee strictly liable for the actions of the employee as long as the actions are sufficiently related to the employment. With vicarious liability, there is no requirement to prove that the employer was at fault. Negligent hiring, on the other hand, requires the plaintiff to prove that the employer was careless in, for example, hiring, training, or supervising.

The Hiring Process

The hiring process involves a number of steps. In hiring employees, employers would normally

- develop job descriptions
- advertise the positions
- have candidates complete an application form or submit a résumé
- short-list candidates
- check backgrounds or references
- interview selected applicants

All aspects of employment are affected by human rights legislation, and in some cases, by employment equity legislation. The legislation may affect the kind of advertising done, the form the application takes, the questions that are asked in the interview, and the decision as to who will ultimately be hired.

Human Rights Requirements

The federal, provincial, and territorial governments have enacted human rights legislation[8] whose objective is to provide equal access to employment opportunities for all. To this end, discrimination in employment is prohibited. The acts also provide for the establishment of **human rights commissions**, which are charged with administering the legislation and investigating and hearing complaints.

Human rights commission
An administrative body that oversees the implementation and enforcement of human rights legislation.

---

7. Stacey Ball, *Canadian Employment Law*, loose-leaf (Aurora, ON: Canada Law Book, 2011) at 20.66.1.
8. See, for example, *Canadian Human Rights Act*, RSC 1985, c H-6 [*Canadian Human Rights Act*].

Prohibited Grounds of Discrimination

Human rights legislation does not prohibit all discrimination in employment, but only discrimination on certain prohibited grounds. There are variations from jurisdiction to jurisdiction as to what these prohibited grounds are, but generally the grounds are similar (see Figure 20.1).

FIGURE 20.1

Prohibited Grounds of Discrimination

The following are prohibited grounds of discrimination under all Canadian legislation:

✘ marital status

✘ race

✘ colour

✘ physical or mental disability

✘ religion or creed

✘ sex

✘ age

Examples of other common grounds that are expressly included in some jurisdictions are national or ethnic origin, family status, social condition, sexual orientation, criminal record, ancestry, place of origin, language and linguistic origin, and political beliefs.

If a particular ground of discrimination is not included in the human rights legislation, the exclusion may be challenged as a violation of the equality provisions of the *Canadian Charter of Rights and Freedoms*. If the challenge is successful, the courts may "read in" the ground. For example, alcohol dependency is included in physical disability; pregnancy[9] and sexual orientation[10] are included in sex.

ETHICAL CONSIDERATIONS

Genetic Screening in the Workplace

Advances in research have made it possible to identify the genetic basis for diseases such as Huntington's, Alzheimer's, cystic fibrosis, sickle cell anemia, and some types of cancers. Technologies such as DNA tests may, in some cases, identify those who will almost certainly be affected by genetic disease. In many cases, however, testing may only indicate whether there is a susceptibility to or an increased likelihood of developing a disease. This is because the majority of diseases do not result solely from genetic predisposition but from the interaction of genes with environmental factors such as lifestyle, diet, and exposure to toxins. For example, people with the sickle cell trait may be at an increased risk for sickle cell anemia if exposed to carbon monoxide or cyanide.

Because of the interaction between genes and environmental factors, genetic screening in the workplace is advocated by some on the basis that it benefits the employee, the employer, and society. With the information gained through genetic testing,

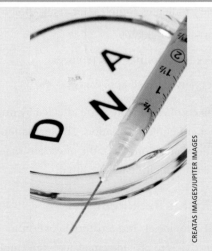

CREATAS IMAGES/JUPITER IMAGES

Under what circumstances is it ethically permissible for an employer to offer genetic testing to employees?

---

9. See Ball, *supra* note 7 at 33.72.

10. For example, in Newfoundland, sexual orientation was "read in" in *Newfoundland (Human Rights Commission) v Newfoundland (Minister of Employment and Labour Relations)* (1995), 127 DLR (4th) 694, 134 Nfld & PEI R 66, (Nfld SCTD). The Supreme Court of Canada decided, in *Vriend v Alberta*, [1998] 1 SCR 493, 156 DLR (4th) 385 that sexual orientation is a prohibited ground of discrimination in all jurisdictions.

CHAPTER 13: THE AGENCY RELATIONSHIP

Agency
: A relationship that exists when one party represents another party in the formation of legal relations.

Agent
: A person who is authorized to act on behalf of another.

Principal
: A person who has permitted another to act on her behalf.

Outsider
: The party with whom the agent does business on behalf of the principal.

Law of Agency
: The law governing the relationship where one party (the agent) acts on behalf of another (the principal).

Actual Authority
: The power of an agent that derives from either express or implied agreement.

Express
: Written or oral authority granted by the principal to the agent.

Implied
: Authority that is inferred from the position the agent occupies, is reasonable necessary to carry out or otherwise implement the agents express authority, arises by virtue of a well-organized custom in a particular trade, industry, or profession.

Apparent Authority
: The power that an agent appears to have to an outsider because of conduct or statements of the principal.

Agency by Estoppel
: An agency relationship created when the principal acts such that third parties reasonably conclude that an agency relationship exists. This forces the principal to be bound by the unauthorized contract. Even if agent is terminated, principal is still bound if they do not notify the other party.

Agency by ratification
: An agency relationship created when one party adopts a contract entered into on his behalf by another who at the time acted without authority. The principal does not have to adopt the contract, but is allowed to make that decision.

Principal can only ratify if:

- He does so within a reasonable time
- The principal had the capacity to create the contract at the time the agent entered into iit and at the time of ratification
- The agent identified the principal at the time of entering the contract.

Fiduciary Duty
: A duty imposed on a person who has a special relationship of trust with another.

Fiduciary
: A person who has a duty of good faith toward another because of their relationship.

Profit Rule
: A fiduciary must not personally profit by virtue of her position

Conflict Rule
: A fiduciary must not place herself in a position where her own interests conflict with the interests of the principal.

Agent has a duty to:

- Make full disclosure of all material information that may affect the principal's position

- Avoid any conflict of interest that affects the interests of the principal
- Avoid acting for two principals in the same transaction
- Avoid using the principal's property, money, or information to secure personal gain.
- Avoid accepting or making a secret commission or profit

Principal's duty:

- Pay the agent a specified fee or percentage for services rendered unless the parties have agreed that the agent would work for free
- Assist the agent in the manner described in the contract
- Reimburse the agent for reasonable expenses associated with carrying out his agency duties
- Indemnify against losses incurred in carrying out the agency business

Liability of Agents:

Warranty of authority	A representation of authority by a person who purports to be an agent. Eg. Agent for fabric buys a jet, not part of being an agent, therefore is liable.
Undisclosed principal	A principal whose identity is unknown to a third party who has no knowledge that the agent is acting in an agency capacity. AKA outsider thinks they are dealing with the principal when they are actually dealing with the agent. Principal is liable if contract within agents authority.

Vicarious Liability still applies for principals and agents as long as the agent is acting within express, implied, or apparent authority.

Termination of Agency Agreements:

- Parties agree to bring their relationship to an end
- One party may give notice of termination to the other
- An agency relationship may cease by operation of the law. (death, dissolution, insanity, bankruptcy)
- **remember to give notices of termination to third parties to avoid apparent authority

CHAPTER 22: Proffessional Responsibilities

Professional   Someone engaged in an occupation, usually governed by a professional body, requiring the exercise of specialized knowledge, education, and skill.

Proof of Negligent Misrepresentation:
- There must be a duty of care based on a special relationship between the professional and the recipient of the advice.
- The representation must be untrue, inaccurate, or misleading.
- The professional must have been negligent in making t representation.
- The recipient must have reasonably relied on the misrepresentation.

- The reliance must have resulted in damages to the recipient.

In Professional Negligence, there is a risk of imposing liability "in an indeterminate amount for an indeterminate time to an indeterminate class".

Professional Fiduciary responsibilities:

- Avoid any conflict of interest between the client's affairs and those of the professional or the firm
- Refrain from using the relationship for personal profit beyond charging a reasonable fee for services provided
- Disclose all relevant information to the client
- Act honestly, in good faith and with due care
- Maintain confidentiality of client information

Duty of confidentiality	The obligation of a professional not to disclose any information provided by ht client without the client's consent
Privilege	The professional's right not to divulge a client's confidential information to third parties.

CHAPTER 14: BUSINESS FORMS AND ARRANGEMENT

Sole Proprietorship
- An unincorporated business organization that has only one owner. It has no legal status.
- Unlimited Liability: owner has unrestricted legal responsibility for obligations.
- Profits are all the owners
- Owner can make decisions quickly and independently
- Sources of Capital are low
- Ownership cannot be transferred
- Taxes: profits included on individuals tax returns
- Few legal requirements although usually licensing fees are needed

Partnership

- A business carried on by two or more persons with the intention of making a profit.
- Joint Liability: Liability shard by 2 or more parties where each is personally liable for the full amount of the obligation.
- Joint and several Liability: Individual and collective liability for a debt. Each liable party is individually responsible for the entire debt as well as being collectively liable for the entire debt.
- Profit sharing is split how the owners see fit.
- Decision making may be impeded by divided authority
- Provides more sources of capital because there are more people than sole proprietorship
- Taxes: profits included on individuals tax returns
- Not transferable
- Legislation defines when a partnership exists and what the relationship of partners is to one another.

- Become each other's agents and have fiduciary duties to one another
- Partnerships ends if :
- Only entered for a fixed term, by the expiration of the term
- Entered into for a single venture or undertaking, by the termination of that venture or undertaking
- By any partner giving notice to the others of her intention to dissolve the partnership
- Following the death, insanity or bankruptcy of a partner

Limited Partnership

- A partnership in which the liability of some partners is limited to their capital contribution
- General Partners still have unlimited liability
- Must be registered and have a written agreement
- General partners have rights and powers. Limited partners have narrowly defined rights.
- Limited partners have right to profits but not management

Limited Liability Partnership (LLP)

- A partnership in which the partners have unlimited liability for their own malpractice but limited liability for other partner's malpractice
- Partial Shield protects from wrongful acts of partners or employees but still liable for obligations of partnership
- Full Shield protects from others negligence and contractual obligations. Still have liability for your own negligence

Partnership Act:

1. All partners are to share equally in the capital and profits of the business and must contribute equally to the losses.
2. Property acquired for the partnership shall be used exclusively for the partnership and not for the private purposes of individual partners. Property purchased with partnership money is deemed partnership property.
3. A partner shall be indemnified by the other partners for any liability incurred on behalf of the partnership. This means that all partners are liable for partnership liabilities and that a partner who pays a debt is entitled to reimbursement from her partners.
4. A payment made by a partner for the purposes of the partnership in excess of his agreed subscription shall earn interest.
5. Each partner may take part in the management of the business.
6. No partner is entitled to remuneration for acting in the partnership business.
7. No new member shall be admitted to the partnership without the consent of all the partners.
8. Disputes regarding the partnership business may be decided by a majority but the nature of the partnership may not be changed without the consent of all the members.
9. Partnership books shall be kept at the partnership's place of business, and all partners shall have access to them.
10. No simple majority may expel any partner.

Corporation

- Has a distinct legal entity in law and can assume its own obligations
- Shareholders: a person who has an ownership interest in a corporation
- Director: a person elected by shareholders to manage a corporation
- Limited Liability: responsibility for obligations restricted to the amount of investment
- Get profits through Dividends: a division of profits payable to shareholders
- Board of Directors (elected by shareholders) makes decisions
- Capital comes from borrowing (debt) or issuing shares (equity)
- Corporation is taxed at corporate rates
- Easy transference of ownership
- Corporation has perpetual existence
- Must submit proper documents to the government to become a corporation

Franchise

- An agreement whereby an owner of a trademark or trade name permits another to sell a product or service under that trademark or name.
- Franchisor is the organization, franchisee is the independent business
- Franchise agreements state how business is to be run, where supplies are purchased, royalty fees, advertisement, and other corporate services
- No fiduciary duty

Joint Venture

- A grouping of two or more businesses to undertake a particular project
- Usually share profits/losses and management
- Usually limited to a specific project or period of time
- Similar to a partnership legally
- Parties can be held to owe fiduciary duties to one another in relation to the project activities

Strategic Alliance

- An arrangement whereby 2 or more business agree to cooperate for some purpose
- Usually a contractual relationship that defines rights and obligations of parties
- Unclear if fiduciary duties

Distributorship or Dealership

- A contractual relationship where one business agrees to sell another's products
- Relationship is governed by contract, and no fiduciary duties beyond what is in the contract
- Usually no agency relationship

Sales Agency

- An agreement in which a manufacturer or distributor allows another to sell products on its behalf
- Because an agent, fiduciary responsibilities are owed

Product Licensing

- An arrangement whereby the owner of a trademark or other proprietary right grants to another the right to manufacture or distribute products associated with the trademark or other proprietary right.

CHAPTER 15: THE CORPORATE FORM: ORGANZATIONAL MATTERS

Stakeholder   One who has interest in a corporation

Internal   Internal stakeholders are those who have either a direct or indirect role in governing the corporation and determining its mission and how it will be achieved. Eg. Shareholder.

External   External stakeholders are people who have dealings with or are affected by the corporation by do not have an explicit role in governing the corporation. Eg. Government, general public, creditors, customers, employees.

Salomon Vs Salomon Case

- A corporation is a separate legal existence and to be treated as entities separate from their shareholders
- Proving Limited Liability is secure

Decisions prior to incorporation:

- Whether to incorporate federally or provincially -> How/where he intends to operate
    o Depending on the geographical range changes value of low admin costs
- What type of shares will be available and to whom -> How he intends to manage and accommodate future growth
    o Class or classes of shares the corp. will be authorized to issue
    o Rights and privileges attach to each class
        ▪ Vote for the election of directors
        ▪ Receive dividends declared by the directors
        ▪ Share in the proceeds on dissolution of the corp., after creditors have been paid
    o Number of each authorized for issuance
- What to name the corporation -> availability

Avaliability of Shares

Widley Held Corporation   Shares are normally traded on a stock exchange (Public).

Securities Legislation   Laws designed to regulate transactions involving shares and bonds of a corp.

Closely Held Corporation   Doesn't sell shares publicly (Private).

Private   Has a restriction on the transfer of shares, a limit on the # of shareholders in the corp. to no more than 50, a prohibition on any invitation to the public to subscribe for the corporation's shares.

Corporate name requirements:

- Must be distinctive
- Not cause confusion to an existing name or trademark
  - NUANS Report is a document that shows the result of a search for business names
- Must include a legal element (Ltd., Inc., Corp.)
- Must not include any unacceptable terms

Shelf Company   A company that doesn't engage in active business.

Documents needed to Federally Incorporate:

- Articles of incorporation
  - Document that defines the basic characteristics of the corporations.
- Notice of registered office
- Notice of directors
- Newly Upgraded Automated Name Search (NUANS) Report
- The filing fee, payable to the Receiver General for Canada

Incorporated, now have to call an organizational meeting:

- Make bylaws (rules specifying day-to-day operating procedures of the corporation)
- Adopt forms of share certificates and corporation records
- Authorize the issue of shares and other securities
- Appoint officers, an auditor to hold office until the first annual meeting of shareholders
- Make banking arrangements transact any other business

Financing the Corporation - Debt:

- Bond – a document evidencing a debt owed by the corp., often used to refer to a secured debt.
- Debenture – a document evidencing a debt owed by the corporation, often used to refer to an unsecured debt
- Usually secured by assets, debt is to repaid whether profit or not
- Plus is that it does not diminished control

Financing the Corporation – Equity:

- Shares do not have to be paid back
- Shares may mean relinquishing owner rights
- Securities – shares and bonds issued by a corporation
- Conversion right – the right to convert one type of security into another type

Securities Legislation:

- Provide the mechanism for the transfer of securities
- Ensure that all investors have the ability to access adequate information in order to make informed decisions
- Ensure that the system is such that the public has confidence in the marketplace
- Regulate those engaged in the trading of securities
- Remove or punish those participants not complying with established rules

Registration	Any company intending to sell securities to the public or engaged in advising on and selling securities must be registered with the relevant provincial securities commission.
Prospectus	The document of a corporation must publish when offering securities to the public.
Insider Trading	Transactions in securities of a corporation y or on behalf of an insider on the basis of relevant material information concerning the corporation that is not known to the general public.
Insider	A person whose relationship with the issuer of securities is such that he is likely to have access to relevant material information concerning the issuer that is not known to the public.
Tippee	S person who acquires material information about an issuer of securities from an insider.

CHAPTER 16: THE CORPORATE FORM: OPERATIONAL MATTERS

Liability in Tort

Primary Liability	When it is regarded that the entity committed the tort.
Identification Theory	Theory specifying that a corporation is liable when the person committing the wrong is the corporation's directing mind.
Vicarious Liability	Tort has been committed by an agent or employee who is not a directing mind of the corporation.

Liability in Contract	Usually the same rules for agency (actual/apparent contract)
Criminal and Regulatory Liability	The corporation can be charged for criminal / regulatory offences and those who are key or directing minds can be held responsible for actions performed on behalf of the company.
Regulatory Offence	An offence contrary to the public interest.
Directors	Elected by shareholders, they manage management and affairs of the corporation. Eg. Declare dividends, call shareholder meetings, adopt bylaws.
Officers	Carryout the actual management.
Fiduciary Duties	Directors and officers must act honestly and in good faith with the view to the best interests of the corporation.
Self-Dealing Conflict	A contract in which a fiduciary has a conflict of interest. Eg. Director selling furniture to the company. Director should think what is best for company but also wants to sell the furniture at a good price.
Corporate Opportunities	A business opportunity in which the corporation has an interest.

CASE: Canadian Aero Service LTD vs O'Malley
- Canadian Aero Service was negotiation a contract
- 2 directors left the company, set up a similar business and bid for the same contract

- Directors got the contract, CAS sued the directors for taking their corporate opportunities and that they had a fiduciary duty to CAS to act their CAS's best interest.
- Directors were liable to CAS for any profits they made off the contract

6 Factors if the Opportunity is a Breach of Fiduciary Duty
1. The position or office held by the directors and officers (higher in the firm, higher the duty)
2. The nature of the corporate opportunity (how clearly was the opportunity identified by the corporation and how close was the corporation to acquiring the opportunity)
3. The director's or managerial officer's relation to the opportunity (was the opportunity one that the fiduciary worked on or had responsibility for?)
4. The amount of knowledge the directors and officers possessed and the circumstances in which it was obtained
5. The time between when the opportunity arose and when the officers took the opportunity for themselves.
6. The circumstances under which the employment relationship between the officers and the company terminated (was termination due to retirement, resignation, or discharge?)

Duty of Competence	Directors and Officers must meet a general standard of competence; exercising care, diligence, and skill of a reasonably prudent person in such circumstances.
Corporate Social Responsibility	Business' policies and practices in relation to such issues as investment in community outreach, the creation and maintenance of employment, consumer protection, environmental sustainability, etc.

Liabilities of Directors and Officers

Liability in Tort	Directors are personally liable even if they were acting in furtherance of their duties to the corporation and if their conduct was unjustifiable.
Liability in Contract	Director is personally liable if he contracts on his own behalf, as well as on behalf of the company, or guarantees the contractual performance of the company.
Liability by Statue	Breaching their general managerial duties. Eg. Failure to withhold and remit income taxes.

Director's Statutory Liabilities: A Sampling		
Statutory Breach	Type of Statute	Nature of Penalty
Failure to pay employee wages	Federal and provincial incorporation statutes	Liability for wages
Directing, authorizing, or permitting the release of a toxic substance into the environment	Federal and provincial environmental protection statute	Fines and/or imprisonment
Failure to remit required taxes	Provincial and federal revenue acts	Liability for amount outstanding and interest or penalties
Failure to maintain health and safety standards	Provincial workplace health and safety legislation	Fines and/or imprisonment

Insider trading – using confidential info to buy/sell shares	Provincial securities acts, Federal and provincial incorporation statutes	Fines and/or imprisonment
Engaging in anticompetitive behaviour	Federal Competition Act	Criminal and civil liabilities
Paying a divided when company is insolvent	Federal and provincial incorporation statues	Personal Repayment
Misrepresentation in a prospectus	Provincial securities legislation	Damages
Improperly transporting dangerous goods	Federal and provincial transportation of dangerous goods legislation	Fines and/or imprisonment

Lifting the Corporate Veil   Determining that the corporation is not a separate legal entity from its shareholders.

Shareholders have the right to Vote and the right to Information (inspect annual Financial Statements)

Pre-emptive Right   A shareholder's right to maintain a proportionate share of ownership by purchasing a proportionate share of any new stock issue.

Shareholder Remedies:

- Sell shares
- Exercise dissent and appraisal rights: get their shares purchased by the company at a fair price.
- Bringing a Derivative Action (against company):
  - A suit by a shareholder on behalf of the corporation to enforce a corporate course of action.
  - Must establish that directors will not bring an action, you are acting in good faith, and the action is in the interests of the corporation.
- Bringing an Oppression Action (personal action):
  - A statutory remedy available to shareholders and other stakeholders to protect their corporate interests.
  - Conduct of Oppression
    - Lack of valid corporate purpose for a transaction
    - Lack of good faith on the part of the directors
    - Discrimination between shareholders with the effect of benefitting the majority shareholder to the exclusion or the detriment of the minority shareholder.
    - Lack of adequate and proper disclosure of material information to minority shareholders.
    - Conflict of Interest between the interests of the corporation and the personal interests of one or more directors.

Shareholders' agreement   An agreement that defines the relationship among people who have an ownership interest in a corporation.

Unanimous shareholders' agreement   An agreement among all shareholders that restricts the powers of the directors to manage the corporation.

Shareholder Agreement Should address:

1. Management of the company.
   a. Who will be responsible for management? Wat will their rights and obligations be? How will they be appointed or elected or hired? How will they be paid?
2. Protection for the minority shareholder.
   a. How will the minority be protected from domination by the majority? How will representation on the board of directors be achieved? How will fundamental issues such as dividends, sale of assets, and the like, be handled?
3. Control over who the other shareholders will be.
   a. What are the qualifications needed for being a shareholder? What happens in the event of a shareholder's death, retirement, disability, or simple loss of interest in the company?
4. Provision of a market for shares.
   a. What are the circumstances that require a shareholder to sell her shares? What happens if a shareholder dies? Who will buy the shares and for how much? How will the purchase be funded?
5. Capital contribution.
   a. What happens if the corporation needs more cash? Who will provide it, and how much? How will payment be compelled?
6. Buy-Sell arrangements in the event of a dispute.
   a. What (death, retirement, insolvency), triggers a sale? How will the shares be valued? What method will be chosen for their valuation?
7. Mechanism for terminating the agreement.
   a. How can the agreement be terminated? Can it be terminated on notice? How much notice?

CHAPTER 26: THE LEGAL ASPECTS OF CREDIT

Secured Credit	A debt where the creditor has an interest in the debtor's property to secure payment.
Unsecured Credit	A debt where the creditor has only a contractual right to be repaid.
Real Property	Land
Personal Property	Anything other than land
Letter of Credit	A written promise by a buyer's bank to a seller's bank to pay the seller when specified conditions are met. Used for international transactions when goods may take time to deliver.
Events of Default	Failure by the debtor to make required payments on a loan or to fulfill its other obligations under the credit agreement.

Methods to reduce Risk in Credit Transactions

1. Not lend money to people who will not pay it back
2. Change the structure of a transaction so it's not a credit arrangement (suppliers lease goods).

3. Creditors insist on security or collateral (property in which a creditor takes an interest as security for a borrower's promise to repay a loan.
4. Get assurances from others that the debt will be paid.
5. Put restrictions on the debtor, like being above a certain financial ratio

Letter of Commitment   Document provided by a lender to a borrower and sets out the terms of a loan.

- Amount of the loan and how it will be disbursed
- Rate of interest, and whether it is floating or fixed
- Repayment terms, including the amount and frequency of payments
- Term of the loan and conditions for renewal (if the entire loan will not be paid out during the term)
- Conditions that must be satisfied before the loan is made (eg. Guarantees, appraisals)
- Security or collateral required by the lender
- Requirements for maintenance of the borrower's financial position
- Events that constitute default and the lender's remedies
- Fees to be paid by the borrower

General security agreement   Where debtor's personal property assets are used as collateral.

After-acquired property   Collateral that includes personal property acquired by the debtor during the term of the loan.

Personal Property Security Act (PPSA)   Legislation where it registers a security interest. It gives notice to the world that you have an interest in that asset as a security, so if someone buys the asset they are now liable to pay the loan back with the asset.

Security interest   An interest in personal property that is intended to secure payment or performance of an obligation

Environmental Risk   If using land as a security, you will be responsible for the environment. If contaminated then the bank will not lend you money because they would become responsible for the cleanup of the property if contaminated. Same with houses.

Receiver   A person appointed by the secured party or by the court to seize, and usually sell, collateral.

Remedies

- If unsecured and not paid you can sue under contract and get damages and collect money.
- If secured you seize the asset you have security in
- If the asset does not generate enough money to pay off loan then the secured creditor becomes an unsecured creditor.
- Acceleration Clause: if you default on one payment, all payments become due.

CHAPTER 25: BUSINESS AND BANKING

Canada – Banking is under federal jurisdiction, therefore very stable.

U.S – Banks are regulated state-by-state, therefore smaller and less stable.

Bank-Customer Relationship

- Customer's money is on deposit with the bank
- Bank is the debtor and customer is the creditor
- Unique because bank (debtor) has all the power
- If providing financial advice -> have a fiduciary law
- If providing insurance advice -> contract law

Duties of the Banks:

- Honour payment instructions and repay deposits
- Collect payments for the customer
- Provide account information to the customer on a regular basis
- Maintain secrecy of the customer's affairs.

Customer's Duties:

- Take reasonable steps to provide documentation as to who is authorized to give instructions to the bank, in order to prevent fraud and forgery
- Keep authorizations current
- Notify the bank of any suspicious problem
- Provide safeguards for electronic communication

Money Laundering   The false reporting of income from criminal activity as income from legitimate business. Legislation where banks have to report suspicious transactions and large cross-border currency transfers.

Methods of Payment Cash, cheque, credit card, debit card/e-transfer.

Negotiable Instrument A written contract containing an unconditional promise or order to pay a specific sum on demand or on a specified date to a specific person or bearer. Eg. Cheque, promissory note, bills of exchange.

Promissory Note   A written promise to another person to pay a specified amount

Bill of exchange   A written order to a person to pay a specified amount to another person.

Requirements for negotiable instruments:

- Must be a self-contained obligation
- Must be in written form and signed by the person making the promise
- Must specify an amount and date
- Obligation must be unconditional

Implications of creating a cheque:

- Made an unconditional promise to pay a specified sum to the supplier or holder (person in possession of the cheque).

Implications of Accepting a Cheque:

- Risk of not having money in bank to transfer cheque money
- If cheque bounces bank may deduct value of worthless cheque off own account
- To prevent this have a certified cheque where a bank guarantees payment of a cheque
- Bank removes money from customer's account and holds it on reserve until cheque is presented ensuring payment.
- This prevents stop payment where a person writes a cheque then orders the bank not to pay it.

Endorsement and Transfer of Negotiable Terms:

Endorsement in blank	Endorsing a cheque by signing it without any special instructions.
Restrictive Endorsements	Signing a cheque for deposit only to a particular bank account.
Special Endorsement	Signing a cheque and making it payable to a specific person.

Case: SNS Industrial Products Limited VS Bank of Montreal

- Forged cheques were made taking Sanfillippo's money from his account
- Is the bank responsible for detecting the forgeries?
- The bank remained responsible for honouring a forged cheque.

CHAPTER 27: BANKRUPTCY AND INSOLVENCY

Informal steps:

- Try and convince creditors to make concessions in terms of payment
- Get creditors to meet with you or a facilitator to negotiate the terms

Trustee in Bankruptcy	The person who has legal responsibility under the BIA for administering bankruptcies and proposals.
Estate	The collective term for the assets of a bankrupt individual or corporation.
Insolvent	Unable to meet financial obligations as they become due or having insufficient assets, if liquidated, to meet financial obligations.
Bankruptcy	A legal mechanism whereby the assets of an insolvent person are transferred to a trustee, liquidated, and the net proceeds are distributed to creditors in a manner determined by the BIA.
Proposal	A procedure governed by the BIA that allows a debtor to restructure its debt in order to avoid bankruptcy.

Types of Proposals:

- Division I proposals are available to individuals and corporations with no limit on the total amount of debt that is owed

- Division II proposals are available to individuals with total debts less than $250 000 (not including mortgages). Also known as "Consumer proposals".

Secured Creditor   Can choose to seize the asset to pay down the debt owed, or appoint a receiver to take control of the business

Unsecured Creditor   Can sue the debtor and try to obtain judgement.

Purpose of BIA during Bankruptcy:

- To preserve the assets of the bankrupt for the benefit of creditors
- To ensure a fair and equitable distribution of the assets to creditors
- In the case of personal bankruptcies; to allow the debtor a fresh start

Methods to Become Bankrupt:

Assignment in Bankruptcy   The debtor's voluntary assignment to the trustee in bankruptcy of legal title to the debtor's property for the benefit of creditors.

Bankruptcy Order   An order of the court resulting in a person being declared bankrupt. Will be granted if creditors are owed >$1000 and committed to an *Act of Bankruptcy* (a list of specified acts that the debtor must commit before the court will grant a bankruptcy order).

If creditors reject a proposal then will become bankrupt.

The Bankruptcy Process

Trustee:

- Secure the business premises and storage facilities
- Conduct a detailed examination of assets
- Prepare the appropriate statements
- Ensure that assets are adequately protected including insurance coverage
- Establish appropriate books and accounts
- Sell any perishable goods immediately

CHAPTER 20: Employment Relationship

Employment Relationship   A contractual relationship whereby an employer provides remuneration to an employee in exchange for work or services.

Independent Contractor   A person who is in a working relationship that does not meet the criteria of employment.

Employee Vs Independent contractor

- The degree of control exercised over the individual by the employer
- The ownership of tools, chance of profit, and the risk of loss from performance of the requested service.
- The degree of integration

- If employee, the employer must provide paid holidays and deduction of income taxes and payment of insurance a CPP premiums.

Employers are Vicarious Liable because:

- Employers have the ability to control employees and therefore should be liable for the employee's conduct
- The person who benefits from a business enterprise should bear the associated costs
- Innocent plaintiffs have a better chance of being compensated
- The employer should be given an incentive to try to prevent torts from occurring in the first place.

Negligent Hiring Employer was careless in hiring, training, or supervising.

Discrimination The act of treating someone differently on the basis of a prohibited ground.

Prohibited grounds of discrimination:	Penalties of eliminating discriminatory practices
<ul><li>Marital status</li><li>Race</li><li>Colour</li><li>Physical or mental disability</li><li>Religion or creed</li><li>Sex</li><li>Age</li></ul>	<ul><li>Order employer to stop practices</li><li>Hire a particular individual</li><li>pay monetary compensation</li><li>write a letter of apology</li><li>reinstate an employee</li><li>institute an affirmative action plan</li><li>indirectly cause unwelcome publicity, time and money, and an unsettled work environment</li></ul>

Adverse effects of discrimination	Discrimination that occurs as a result of a rule that appears neutral but in its effects is discriminatory.
Systemic discrimination	Discrimination that results from the combined effects of many rules, practices, and policies.
BFOR	Bona Fide Occupational Requirement. A defense that excuses discrimination on a prohibited ground when it is done in good faith and for a legitimate business reason.
Duty to accommodate	the duty of an employer to modify work rules, practices, and requirements to meet the needs of individuals who would otherwise by subjected to unlawful discrimination.
Employment equity legislation	Laws designated to improve the status of certain designated groups.
Fixed or definite term contract	A contract for a specified period of time, which automatically ends on the expiry date.
Indefinite- term contract	A contract for no fixed period, which can end on giving reasonable notice.

Expressed Terms	have been actually agreed upon by the parties and are included in the contract or incorporated by reference.
Implied terms	these that have not been specifically agreed upon by the parties but are what the courts believe the parties would have agreed to had they sat down and negotiated the point.
Employment Standards Legislation	Laws that specify minimum standards in the workplace.

- Hours of work and overtime
- Minimum wage
- Vacations and vacation pay
- Termination and severance
- Statutory (paid) holidays
- Bereavement and sick leave
- Maternity and parental leave

Unions:

Collective Bargaining	A mechanism by which parties enter a collective agreement or contract.
Collective Agreement	The employment agreement reached between the union and employer setting out the bargaining unit employees terms and conditions of employment.

CHAPTER 21: Termination of Employees

Dismissal for *Just Cause*	Employee conduct that amounts to a fundamental breach of the employment contract. Employee is guilty of one of: serous misconduct, habitual neglect of duty, incompetence, conduct incompatible with duties or prejudicial to the employer's business, and willful disobedience in a matter of substance.
Serious Misconduct	Intentional, harmful conduct of the employee that permits the employer to dismiss without notice. May be a series of small infractions or one large misconduct.
Progressive discipline policy	A system that follows a sequence of employee discipline from less to more severe punishment. Employer has a duty to warn the employee and give them an opportunity to improve their performance.
Condonation	Employer behaviour that indicates to the employee that misconduct is being overlooked (and is okay).
Habitual Neglect of Duty	Persistent failure to perform employment duties. Eg. Absenteeism. Important factors are if there were warnings, if there was an excuse, and how critical of a time did it occur.
Incompetence	Lack of ability, knowledge, or qualification to perform employment obligations (that employee claimed to possess). If below a fair and reasonable performance standard after warnings and an opportunity to improve.

Conduct Incompatible	Personal behaviour that is irreconcilable with employment duties or prejudicial to the employers business. Eg. Accepting lavish gifts from clients, and conduct outside of working hours.
Willful Disobedience	Deliberate failure to carry out lawful and reasonable orders. Employer need to establish that instructions given were not ambiguous and therefore had no reasonable excuse for disobeying. Factors are if employee was provoked, upset, or in a moment of temporary anger.

Dismissal with Notice

Reasonable Notice	A period of time for an employee to find alternative employment prior to dismissal.

Factors to determine reasonable notice:

- Character of employment
  - How high status position
- Length of service
- Age
- Availability of similar employment
- Economic climate

Constructive Dismissal	Employer conduct that amounts to a breach of a fundamental term of the employment contract. Eg Moving him to a lower position in the company with a lower pay.
Fundamental Changes	A term that is considered to be essential to the contract. Changing salary, benefits, job function, responsibility, power/reporting structures.
Bad Behaviour	Employer's conduct creates intolerable working conditions. Eg. Harassment, or fraud from employer.

Bad Faith in Manner of Dismissal:

- Refusing to provide a deserved letter of reference
- Terminating while on disability leave
- Failing to communicate a termination decision in a timely manner
- Communicating false accusations to potential employers

Duty to Mitigate	Requires employees to take reasonable steps to find comparable employment.

Termination Settlement

- Employee should be given a period of time to consider the termination settlement
- Should always get a lawyer to look at it

Severance Pay	An amount owed to a terminated employee under employment standards legislation.
Release	A written or oral statement discharging another from an existing duty.

Grievance process   A procedure for resolving disputes contained in union contracts.

CHAPTER 28: Insurance

Insurance Policy   A contract of insurance

Insurer   A company that sells insurance coverage

Insured   One who buys insurance coverage

Premium   The price paid for insurance coverage

3 Kinds of Insurance:

- Life and disability insurance
- Property insurance
- Liability insurance

Deductible   The part of a loss for which the insured is responsible. Higher deductible, lower the premium

Duty to Disclose   The obligation of the insured to provide to the insurer all information that relates to the risk being insured. If not disclosed insurer may choose not to honour the policy.

Insurable Interest   A financial stake in what is being insured.

Indemnity   The obligation on the insurer to make good on the loss. Insured is not to profit from the event, but to come out even.

Subrogation   The right of the insurer to recover the amount paid on a claim from a third party that caused the loss.

Forfeiture Rule   A rule that provides that a criminal should not be permitted to profit from a crime.

Rider   A clause altering or adding coverage to a standard insurance policy.

Endorsement   Written evidence of a change to an existing insurance policy.

Auto Insurance: Third-Party Liability   Coverage against liability for the injury or death of someone else caused by the operation of the insured vehicle.

Collision Coverage   Compensation for loss or damage to the insured automobile itself.

Occupier's Liability Insurance   A building owner and occupier is liable for injuries suffered to people on its premises if the injuries are due to a failure to ensure premises are safe. Insurance compensates the injured person.

Comprehensive General Liability Insurance   Compenate for property damages, personal injury, loss of profit, related losses suffered by a their party when company is responsible for such losses.

Errors and Omissions Insurance	Insurer promises to pay all sums that company is legally obligated to pay as damages resulting from the performance of their professional services. Eg. Losses resulting from negligent advice.
Property Insurance	Can ensure the replacement value for the property or the property's actual cash value (lower).
Business Interruption Loss insurance	Earnings Insurance provides compensation to a business for loss of earnings from the time of a loss until it re-opens. Profit model provides compensation from the date of the loss to the time the business returns to normal profitability or until a certain period expires (12 months).
Key-Person Life Insurance	A business's type of life insurance that gives rights of other shareholder's to buy deceased shares.
Insurance Adjuster	The person who investigates and evaluates insurance claims. Eg. Checks if the fire was actually accidental.

Suing the Insurance People

Broker	If broker was not good and the company ended up with the wrong coverage then the broker could be faced with Negligence and be required to reimburse the company for any of its underinsured or uninsured losses or liabilities.
Insurance Company	If company is not receiving the coverage they expected they can sue for Breach of Contract. If the insurer did not properly investigate a claim they may breach Duty of Good Faith.

Case: Whiten vs Pilot Insurance

- Insurance company accused Whiten family of burning their house down, despite what the adjuster and fire chief concluded.
- Refused to provide payments to Whiten family
- Pressured experts and withheld information to prove arson defense
- High Punitive damages for lack of Duty of good faith

CHAPTER 19: Real Property

Real Property	Land or real estate, including buildings, fixtures, and the associated legal rights.
Fixtures	Tangible personal property that is attached to land, buildings, or other fixtures.
Fee Simple	The legal interest in real property that is closest to full ownership.
Tenancy in Common	Co-ownership whereby each owner of an undivided interest can dispose of that interest. If one person dies, the land goes to their heir and not the other owner.

Joint Tenancy	Co-ownership whereby the survivor inherits the undivided interest of the deceased.
Ownership in Time	Eg. Lease where the landlord give a tenant possession of the building for a period of time in exchange for rent, and once that period ends the landlord resumes control.

Limits of Ownership

- Municipal governments with zoning bylaws
- Environmental regulations
- Tort of Nuisance for land that interferes with other owner's enjoyment of their land.
- Family Law where both spouses own the house despite whose registered
- Government has the right to expropriate land, make private, or limit non-residences ownership
- Easement – the right to use the land of another for a particular purpose only
- Lease to a tenant
- Surface Rights and Mineral Rights, where you may buy the right to just the surface and a company can buy the rights to the minerals in the ground. People loose the right to use their property although company has to pay compensation for any damages.
- Mortgage on land as a security loan
- Restrictive Covenant – a restriction on the use of land as specified in the title document
- First Nations lands give joint venture to work on land

Titles Search	Investigation of the registered ownership of land in a registry system. Show who owns the land and any restrictions on it.
Registry System	The system of land registration whereby the records are available to be examined and evaluated by interested parties. Have to do a big historical search and count back 40 years from last person, and then your lawyer has to go through every transaction from the last 40 years and verify all transactions.
Land Titles System	The system of land registration whereby the administrators guarantee the title to land. Guarantees that the last registered person owns the property.

Who has claim to Property

- First person to register has claim and is fully protected
- Unless person was engaged in fraud, has knowledge of an earlier transaction, or hasn't paid valuable consideration for the land
- Second person who registers has no claim but can sue those who assisted in the transaction

Purchasing Transaction

- Caveat emptor or "Buyer beware" law that means it is the responsibility of the buyer to investigate and evaluate the property in financial and legal terms.
- Seller can't mislead buyer but has no obligation to disclose information about property
- Mislead are misrepresentations such as half-truths or active attempts to hide defects
- Eg. Revenue potential, zoning regulations, adequate water supply

- Covlin wanted to buy some property to rent out to students and make commercial development long term
- Water pipe burst before closing
- Covlin agreed to close deal once damage was assessed
- Vendor refused to proceed
- Vendor was sued for breach of contract

CHAPTER 18: Intellectual Property

Intellectual Property	The results of the creative process, such as ideas, the expression of ideas, formulas, schemes, trademarks, and the like; also refers to the protection attached to ideas through patent copyright, trademark, industrial design, and other similar ideas.
Patent	A monopoly to make, use, or sell an invention. Patents exist per country and rights do not apply elsewhere.
Industrial Design	The visual features of shape, configuration, pattern, ornamentation, or any combination of these applied to a finished article of manufacture.
Trademark	A word, symbol, design or any combination of these used to distinguish the source of goods or services. Can be registered or unregistered. Unregistered have rights only to a certain geographic area, registered is though out the country. Trademarks continue for as long as they are in use.
Tradename	The name under which a company does business. Can prevent others from using a confusingly similar name.
Distinguishing guise	Shaping of wares or the container, or a mode of wrapping or packaging wares.
Domain name	The unique address of a website.
Cyber Squatting	The bad-faith practice of registering trade names as domain names for the purpose of selling the website to the rightful owner or preventing the rightful owner from obtaining the name.
Copyright	The right to prevent others from copying or modifying certain works. Applies to literary, dramatic, musical, artistic works; sound recordings, performances, broadcasts. Does not protect author's underlying ideas or facts.
Fair Dealing	A defence to copyright infringement that permits copying of works for limited purposes of private study, research, criticism, or review.
Computer Software	Allowed to copy for adaption for use on another computer and a copy for backup purposes.

Confidential Business Information   Information that provides a business advantage as a result of the fact that it is kept a secret. Eg. Customer lists, recipes.

Case: LAC Minerals vs International Corona Resources Ltd.

- Corona negotiation a contract to a property for mining, and had to divulge confidential information in order to reach a contractual consensus
- This information was told to a LAC Minerals
- LAC bought the same property based on the confidential information
- Corona sued LAC on breach of confidence

A Comparison of Major Forms of Intellectual Property					
	Patents	Industrial Designs	Trademarks	Copyrights	Confidential Business Information
Subject Matter	Inventions	Shape, configuration, pattern, ornamentation	Word, symbol, design	Literary, dramatic, musical, and artistic works; sound recordings, performances, broadcasts	Business information (eg. Technology, product recipes, databases)
Requirements	New, useful, unobvious	Original, novel	Title, distinctiveness, registrable	Original, fixed	Economic value, efforts to keep secret, generally not known
Protects against	Use, sale, manufacture	Use, sales, manufacture	Use	Copying, modifying	Disclosure, use
Term of Protection	20 years	10 years	15 + 15 + 15 + years	Life + 50 years	Indefinite (until disclosure)
First owner	Inventor	Designer	First person to use or apply	Author	Creator
Application Process	Mandatory	Mandatory	Mandatory	Optional	Not applicable
Example	Microwave Oven	Design on the outside of oven	Name of the oven	User's manual	Ideas for improvement

employees could avoid work environments that are hazardous to their health and thereby avoid the physical, emotional, and financial costs associated with getting a particular disease. Employers could benefit through reduced workers' compensation costs, higher productivity, and lower absenteeism and turnover costs. As well, they could experience a decrease in health insurance costs and legal liability for occupational disease. Society could also benefit through reduced health care and other costs such as social assistance for those contracting diseases.

Critical Analysis: What are the arguments against genetic screening in the workplace? Should human rights legislation[11] be amended to prevent discrimination on the basis of genetic characteristics?

Sources: Claire Andre & Manuel Velasquez, "Read my genes: Genetic screening in the workplace", online: Santa Clara University <http://www.scu.edu/ethics/publications/iie/v4n2/genes.html>; Donalee Moulton, "Genetic profiling of employees may become part of the job", The Lawyers Weekly (5 March 2010) 12; Chris MacDonald & Bryn Williams-Jones, "Ethics and genetics: Susceptibility testing in the workplace", Journal of Business Ethics 35 (2002) 235–241.

Discrimination Defined

The human rights Acts prohibit **discrimination** but do not generally define the term.[12] It usually means the act of treating someone differently on the basis of a prohibited ground. For example, to post an advertisement that says "Wanted: Malay workers for Malaysian restaurant" would be an act of discrimination, because it discriminates on the basis of national or ethnic origin. On the other hand, it is not discrimination to require job applicants to meet certain educational or training requirements.

Not only is direct or explicit discrimination prohibited, but **adverse effects** and **systemic discrimination** are also prohibited. Adverse effects discrimination involves the application of a rule that appears to be neutral but has discriminatory effects.[13] For example, a rule that requires all workers to wear hardhats or to work every second Saturday appears to be neutral, but its effect may be to discriminate against those whose religion requires them to wear a turban or to refrain from work on Saturdays. Systemic discrimination refers to the combined effects of many rules, practices, and policies that lead to a discriminatory outcome.[14] For example, if a workforce is overwhelmingly dominated by male workers, this may mean that there is systemic discrimination.

Defences to Discrimination

There are situations where it is permissible to discriminate on one of the prohibited grounds. The most common defence to an allegation of discrimination is a *bona fide* **occupational requirement (BFOR)**; other defences include approved affirmative action or equity plans, and group insurance and pension plans. A BFOR is a discriminatory practice that is justified on the basis that it was adopted in good faith and for a legitimate business purpose. For example, a requirement that a person have a valid driver's licence discriminates against some persons with physical disabilities, but a valid driver's licence is a BFOR for the job of truck driver. Similarly, the requirement of wearing a hardhat discriminates against those whose religion requires them to wear a turban, but the hardhat requirement may be a BFOR for those working in construction. BFORs have been subject to much controversy, as there is little consensus on what constitutes legitimate, meaningful qualifications or requirements

Discrimination
The act of treating someone differently on the basis of a prohibited ground.

Adverse effects discrimination
Discrimination that occurs as a result of a rule that appears neutral but in its effects is discriminatory.

Systemic discrimination
Discrimination that results from the combined effects of many rules, practices, and policies.

Bona fide **occupational requirement (BFOR)**
A defence that excuses discrimination on a prohibited ground when it is done in good faith and for a legitimate business reason.

---

11. In 2008, President Bush signed into law the *Genetic Information Nondiscrimination Act*, which prohibits U.S. insurance companies and employers from discriminating on the basis of information derived from genetic tests. See "Breaking news: GINA becomes law May 2008" *Human Genome Project Information*, (16 September 2008) online: Genomics.energy.gov <http://www.ornl.gov/sci/techresources/Human_Genome/elsi/legislat.shtml>.
12. Only the Manitoba, Nova Scotia, Quebec, and Yukon acts offer statutory definitions of discrimination.
13. *Ontario (Human Rights Commission) v Simpson-Sears Ltd*, [1985] 2 SCR 536, 23 DLR (4th) 321 (SCC).
14. *Action Travail des Femmes v CNR Co*, [1987] 1 SCR 1114, 40 DLR (4th) 193 sub nom *Canadian National Railway Co v Canada (Canadian Human Rights Commission)*, [1985] 1 FC 96, 20 DLR (4th) 668 (FCA).

for job applicants. The Supreme Court of Canada in the *Meiorin* case described below set out a three-step test for determining whether a discriminatory standard qualifies as a BFOR.

CASE

British Columbia (Public Service Employee Relations Commission) v BCGEU (The Meiorin Case), [1999] 3 SCR 3, [1999] SCJ No 46

THE BUSINESS CONTEXT: Employers often implement physical performance standards or requirements for particular jobs. Standards are easy to apply and appear to be an objective or neutral basis for evaluating employees.

FACTUAL BACKGROUND: The province of British Columbia established a number of fitness standards for forest fire fighters. Among the standards, which included sit-up, pull-up, and push-up components, was an aerobic standard. The aerobic standard required a firefighter to run 2.5 km in 11 minutes. Tawney Meiorin, a three-year veteran of the service, was terminated from her job because she could not meet the standard. She needed an extra 49.4 seconds. Meiorin complained to the B.C. Human Rights Commission.

THE LEGAL QUESTION: Did the aerobic standard discriminate on the basis of sex?

RESOLUTION: The court held that the standard on its face was discriminatory, owing to physiological differences between males and females. Most women have a lower aerobic capacity than most men and cannot increase their aerobic capacity enough with training to meet the aerobic standard.

To justify the standard as a BFOR, the employer would have to show all of the following:

• the standard was adopted for a purpose rationally connected to the performance of the job

• the standard was adopted in an honest and good-faith belief that it was necessary to fulfill a legitimate, work-related purpose

• the standard was reasonably necessary to the accomplishment of that purpose. To show that a standard was reasonably necessary, it must be demonstrated that it is impossible to accommodate individuals affected by the discriminatory standard without imposing undue hardship upon the employer.

Applying the approach, the court concluded that passing the aerobic standard was not reasonably necessary to the safe

Tawney Meiorin with lawyer John Brewin

and efficient operation of the work of a forest fire fighter. The government had not established that it would experience undue hardship if a different standard were used. In other words, the employer failed to establish that the aerobic standard was reasonably necessary to identify those who are unable to perform the tasks of a forest fire fighter safely and efficiently.

CRITICAL ANALYSIS: The onus of proving that a standard, requirement, or qualification is a BFOR lies with the employer. What issues will the employer have to address in order to establish a BFOR?

Duty to accommodate
The duty of an employer to modify work rules, practices, and requirements to meet the needs of individuals who would otherwise be subjected to unlawful discrimination.

The test in *Meiorin* incorporates a **duty to accommodate** the special needs of those who are negatively affected by a requirement, up to the point of undue hardship for the employer. In effect, this means that employers, when designing standards, requirements, and the like, must consider the need for individual accommodation. This does not mean that the employer must change working conditions in a fundamental way. Rather it means that the employer has a duty, if it can do so without undue hardship, to arrange the employee's workplace or duties to enable the employee to do his or her work.

FRED CHARTRAND/THE CANADIAN PRESS

It remains an open question as to what constitutes undue hardship and how far an employer must go to accommodate special needs. The Supreme Court of Canada[15] has indicated that undue hardship does not require the employer to show that it is impossible to accommodate the employee. The court, however, declined to set strict guidelines as to what constitutes undue hardship, since every employee's condition and every workplace is unique. Factors such as the size of the organization, its financial resources, the nature of operations, the cost of the accommodation measures, the risk the accommodation measures will pose to the health and safety of the employee and his colleagues and the public, and the effect of the accommodation measure on other employees and the productivity of the organization have all been taken into consideration by courts in assessing the scope of the employer's duty.[16]

Penalties

Failure to avoid or eliminate discriminatory practices can result in a complaint to a human rights commission. This, in turn, can result in a board of inquiry investigating the complaint. If the board finds the complaint to be valid, it can order that the employer stop its practices, hire a particular individual, pay monetary compensation, write a letter of apology, reinstate an employee, or institute an affirmative action plan. Regardless of the outcome, a complaint may result in unwelcome publicity, expenditures of time and money to answer the complaint, and an unsettled work environment. To reduce the risk of a human rights complaint, an employer needs to review all aspects of the employment process. The following box provides some examples of ways to reduce the risks.

BUSINESS APPLICATION OF THE LAW

Avoiding Discrimination in Hiring Practices

A human rights complaint can be a costly and embarrassing situation for a company. Each step of the hiring process should be reviewed to ensure that the company is not discriminating.

Job Description: Do develop a list of job-related duties and responsibilities.

Don't describe job openings in terms of prohibited grounds (e.g., busboy, hostess, policeman, waitress).

Advertisements: Do advertise for qualifications related to ability to do the job.

Don't advertise for qualifications unrelated to ability to do the job (e.g., single, Canadian-born, young, tall, slim).

Application Forms: Do solicit information that is related to the applicant's ability to do the job.

Don't ask for information that suggests prohibited grounds are being considered; for example, age, sex, photograph, or title (Miss, Ms., Mr., Mrs.).

Interview: Do ask questions related to the applicant's suitability for the job.

Don't ask questions related to prohibited grounds (e.g., Are you planning to start a family? Do you have any physical disabilities (unless the requirement to not have the disability is a *bona fide* occupational requirement)? Have you ever been treated for a mental illness? How old are you? What church do you attend? What is your mother tongue? Have you ever received income assistance?).

An employer should provide human rights training for supervisors and other employees and develop policies prohibiting discrimination. Employees need to be made aware of the policies.

Critical Analysis: Why should employers be so constrained in the hiring process?

Source: "Pre-employment Inquiries", Alberta Human Rights and Citizenship Commission at <http://www.albertahumanrights.ab.ca/preEmplInq.pdf>.

---

15. *Hydro-Québec v Syndicat des employées de techniques professionnelles et de bureau d'Hydro-Québec*, 2008 SCC 43, [2008] 2 SCR 561 (CanLII).
16. *Ontario's Human Rights Code*, RSO 1990, c H-19, s 17(2) restricts the criteria to the cost, outside sources of funding, and health and safety requirements.

Employment Equity

Employment equity may also affect hiring decisions. Employment equity attempts to achieve equality in the workplace by giving underrepresented groups special consideration in hiring. Human rights legislation prohibits discrimination; **employment equity legislation** requires employers to take positive steps to make the workplace more equitable.

Employment equity legislation

Laws designed to improve the status of certain designated groups.

The federal *Employment Equity Act*[17] targets the underrepresentation of women, Aboriginal peoples, people with disabilities, and visible minorities in the workforce. The Act, which is administered by the Canadian Human Rights Commission,[18] applies to businesses that have 100 or more employees and that are under the regulation of the federal government. It requires employers to

- consult with employee representatives regarding the implementation of employment equity
- identify and eliminate barriers to the employment of the designated groups
- institute policies and practices and make reasonable efforts at accommodation to ensure that the designated groups have a degree of representation in proportion to the workforce from which the employer can reasonably be expected to draw employees
- prepare a plan that sets out the goals to be achieved and a timetable for implementation

There has been much debate about whether such programs are a form of reverse discrimination. The equality provisions of the *Charter of Rights and Freedoms* specifically permit such programs; however, the programs are not insulated from claims of discrimination. The Supreme Court of Canada has stressed that government programs targeted at disadvantaged groups are not immune from challenges of being "underinclusive" or claims that they contravene the right of equality.[19]

None of the provincial jurisdictions has legislation in this area. However, many employers have their own voluntary employment equity programs. As well, the federal government has a non-legislated federal contractors program. This program seeks to ensure that all contractors who have 100 or more employees and are bidding on federal contracts worth more than $200 000 achieve and maintain a fair and representative workforce.

Formation of the Employment Contract

During the negotiations leading to an offer of employment, a lot of information is exchanged. In many cases, disputes have arisen upon termination, based on representations in the negotiations leading up to the offer. There may have been pre-hiring promises,

---

17. SC 1995, c 44.
18. For information on the Employment Equity Branch of the Commission see < http://www.chrc-ccdp.ca/employment_equity/default-en.asp>.
19. *Lovelace v Ontario*, 2000 SCC 37, [2000] 1 SCR 950.

or representations made concerning the nature of the employment that did not materialize. On termination, the employee may be able to allege breach of oral promises, as *Queen v Cognos* illustrates.

CASE | *Queen v Cognos Inc*, [1993] 1 SCR 87, 99 DLR (4th) 626

THE BUSINESS CONTEXT: A company seeking to attract the most qualified candidate may sometimes oversell itself or the job. Promises and representations are often freely made.

FACTUAL BACKGROUND: Douglas Queen was hired by Cognos to help develop an accounting software package. Queen was told by an employee of Cognos that the project would run for a number of years and would be well funded. Based on these representations and a signed employment contract, Queen quit a secure job in Calgary and moved to Ottawa. About two weeks later, the company shifted funding into a different product. Queen was kept on for 18 months, during which time he had a number of fill-in jobs. After being dismissed, he brought an action against Cognos for negligent misrepresentation. He claimed that he would not have accepted the position had it not been for the representations about the scope and viability of the job.

THE LEGAL QUESTION: Does an interviewer owe a duty of care to a prospective employee?

RESOLUTION: The Supreme Court of Canada held that an interviewer has a duty to take reasonable care to avoid making misleading statements. Here, the interviewer failed by misrepresenting the security of the job. Although the contract Queen signed had a disclaimer that allowed the company to reassign or dismiss him, the disclaimer did not save the company from liability for making false promises about the job. Cognos was required to pay damages for Queen's loss of income, loss on the sale of his house in Calgary and the purchase of his house in Ottawa, emotional stress, and expenses incurred in finding a new job.

CRITICAL ANALYSIS: Promises and representations led to legal consequences for Cognos when the promises and representations failed to materialize. What if the promises and representations had been made by a recruiting firm rather than an employee of Cognos? What if the promises and representations had been made by an employee of Cognos that was not authorized to make them?

Offer of Employment

After employers have recruited job applicants, interviewed them, and checked their references, the next step is usually an offer of employment. The offer normally comes from the employer to the employee, but there is no legal requirement that it must.

Like offers in other types of contracts, the offer must be reasonably certain to constitute an "offer" in law. Thus, the statement, "We would like you to work for us" is not considered an offer, as it does not define the job, remuneration, or any of the other terms of employment. The offer, however, need not be in a particular form or in writing. As long as the statements are reasonably complete and certain, casual comments may be considered offers. Once made, the offer is capable of acceptance until it is terminated. Therefore, an offer of employment made to two candidates could result in two acceptances and two employment contracts for the one job. Offers should have time limits so that there are no problems with ascertaining when the offer expires.

Prior to making an offer, the employer should determine whether the candidate has any obligations to her most recent employer. These obligations may impede her ability to perform the job and could result in legal action against the new employer, such as in the following ways:

- *Inducing breach of contract.* If the newly hired employee breaks an existing employment contract in order to accept an offer, the former employer may sue the new employer for the tort of "inducing a breach of contract."[20]

---

20. The tort of inducing breach of contract is discussed in Chapter 12.

- *Restrictive covenants.* It is also not uncommon for employment contracts to contain restrictive covenants limiting the former employee's ability to compete against the former employer. The contract may seek to restrict the solicitation of customers and employees or the use of confidential information, for example. These restrictions are particularly common in industries in which businesses are highly dependent on customer contacts or skilled employees and there is a lot of confidential information and trade secrets.[21]

- *Fiduciary obligations.* A potential employee may also be considered to be in a "fiduciary" relationship with his former employer. Whether or not an employee is a fiduciary will be determined by the position held by the employee, the employee's duties and responsibilities, the nature of the business, and the organizational structure. Generally, only senior employees are considered to be in this relationship, but there is support for broadening the scope of the definition to include any "key" employee.[22] An employee may be in a fiduciary relationship with his employer without realizing it.[23] A finding of a fiduciary relationship may mean that such employees are prohibited from soliciting customers of their former employer and prohibited from taking advantage of business opportunities discovered through the former employer.[24]

CASE

RBC Dominion Securities Inc v Merrill Lynch Canada Inc, 2008 SCC 54, [2008] 3 SCR 79

THE BUSINESS CONTEXT: The following case clarifies the duties that departed employees owe their employer upon termination. It emphasizes that an employer, when recruiting from a competitor, must consider the express and implied duties that employees owe to their former employer.

FACTUAL BACKGROUND: The branch manager of the Cranbrook, B.C., office of RBC Dominion Securities orchestrated the departure of almost all of the investment advisors and assistants working under his supervision to join a competitor, Merrill Lynch. The employees did not give notice of their departure, and in the weeks preceding their exodus, they surreptitiously copied client records and transferred them to Merrill Lynch, which used the records to solicit RBC's clients. None of the employees had non-solicitation or non-competition clauses in their contracts. As a result of their actions, the RBC office lost approximately 85 percent of the client accounts serviced by the departed employees. RBC sued its former branch manager, its former investment advisors, and Merrill Lynch and its manager

for damages. RBC based its action on the employees' failure to give notice, their solicitation of business away from the firm while in its employ, their unlawful removal of records, their alleged breach of an implied duty to compete fairly following their employment, and on Merrill Lynch's conduct in inducing these events.

THE LEGAL QUESTIONS: Do employees have a duty not to compete post-employment? Do employees have a duty to give reasonable notice prior to resigning from their employment? To what extent are employees bound by duties of good faith and confidentiality?

RESOLUTION: The following is a summary of the court's findings.

Duty not to compete: Once the contract of employment is terminated by either the employer or employee, the employee's duty not to compete is at an end, in the absence of any written contractual provisions or a finding that the employee was a

---

21. See Chapter 8 for a detailed discussion of restrictive covenants in employment and other contracts.
22. *Canadian Aero Service Ltd v O'Malley,* [1974] SCR 592, 40 DLR (3d) 371; see also *Imperial Sheet Metal Ltd v Landry,* 2006 NBQB 303, 308 NBR (2d) 42.
23. *See Adler Firestopping Ltd v Rea,* 2008 ABQB 95, [2008] AWLD 1436 where the Alberta Court of Appeal found that a senior employee who acted as a general manager, even though the title was not officially given to him and who was involved in discussions regarding business operations, was a fiduciary.
24. Confidential business information is discussed in Chapter 18.

fiduciary. None of the former employees were deemed fiducia-ries. Although some had some managerial duties, they did not occupy senior positions at RBC. They were primarily investment advisors.

Failure to give notice: The written employment contracts between RBC and their former employees did not contain terms requiring the employees to give advance notice. The employees, however, breached the implied duty to give reasonable notice of resignation, which was in this case held to be two-and-a-half weeks. A total of $40 000 was awarded based on the profits these investment advisors would have contributed during the notice period.

Duty of good faith: The RBC manager who orchestrated the mass exodus was also determined not to be a fiduciary. Although he was responsible for the day-to-day operations of the branch, he was not in a position to affect the economic interests of RBC at either the national or local level. He, however, was determined to have breached the implied duty of good faith owed by him to his then-current employer. He breached his duty by failing to make efforts to retain employees under his supervision and by orchestrating the mass departure. Damages of $1.5 million were awarded against him based on an estimate of lost profits to the Cranbrook branch over a five-year period.

Misuse of confidential information: Punitive damages were awarded against Merrill Lynch ($250 000), Merrill Lynch's branch manager ($10 000), the RBC manager ($10 000) and each of RBC's former investment advisers ($5000) on the basis of conversion relating to the removal and copying of RBC client records. Employees owe a duty of confidentiality to their employers and although the duty does not necessarily extend to preventing

© RICHARD WINTLE

What duties do employees owe their employers?

departing employees from taking client information, it does extend to the wrongful copying of confidential information.

CRITICAL ANALYSIS: Based on this decision, what are the duties of departing employees? What are the implications of this decision for businesses where competition by former employees is a concern?

The Employment Contract

The employment relationship is contractual. The contract may be for a specified period of time, in which case the contract is known as a **fixed-** or **definite-term contract**. The contract, however, need not specify any period of time. Contracts such as these are known as **indefinite-term contracts**. The distinction is particularly important with respect to termination.[25] Historically, most employment contracts were indefinite, but term contracts are becoming more common. The contract may be oral or in writing,[26] but most commonly it is written.

Express and Implied Terms

Whether it is oral or written, the contract may include express terms and implied terms.[27] Express terms are those that have been actually agreed upon by the parties. They are included in the contract or incorporated by reference. Benefits packages, job descriptions,

Fixed- or definite-term contract
A contract for a specified period of time, which automatically ends on the expiry date.

Indefinite-term contract
A contract for no fixed period, which can end on giving reasonable notice.

---

25. For example, if an employee's contract is classified as indefinite-term, the employee is entitled to the common law protection of reasonable notice of termination. By contrast, if the contract is classified as fixed-term, then the contract ends when the fixed term expires, without the requirement of notice.
26. Writing requirements are discussed in Chapter 8.
27. Implied terms in contracts are discussed in Chapter 7.

and company rules and policies are often in separate documents and included by reference. Implied terms are those that have not been specifically agreed upon by the parties but are what the courts believe the parties would have agreed to, had they sat down and negotiated the point. Employment is an area where traditionally there have been a great many implied terms. For example, if the parties do not specify the duration of the contract, it is implied that the contract is for an indefinite period of time. Therefore, the contract does not come to an end until one of the parties gives notice of termination. This term leads to another implied term that the notice of termination must be reasonable.[28]

Content of the Contract

Most employers and employees now see the need to introduce certainty into the employment relationship by putting their relationship into writing.

Besides the advantage of certainty, a written employment contract offers other advantages, including a forum for negotiating terms and conditions that are tailored to the situation—notice periods, restrictive covenants, and limitation of pre-contractual promises, to name a few (see Figure 20.2 below). Written terms will override terms that are implied at law.

FIGURE 20.2

Essential Content of an Employment Contract

An employment contract should contain the following information:
✓ names of the parties
✓ date on which the contract begins
✓ position and description of the work to be performed
✓ compensation (i.e., salary, wages, bonuses)
✓ benefits (i.e., vacation, vacation pay, health and dental plans, pensions, etc.)
✓ probation period, if any
✓ duration of the contract, if any
✓ evaluation and discipline procedures
✓ company policies or reference to employee policy manual
✓ termination provisions (i.e., cause for dismissal, notice of termination, severance package)
✓ recital of management rights (i.e., employer has a right to make changes to job duties and responsibilities)
✓ confidentiality clause, if appropriate
✓ ownership of intellectual property, if appropriate
✓ restrictive covenants, if any
✓ "entire agreement" clause (i.e., the written contract contains the whole agreement)

Terms and Conditions

The ability of an employer and an employee to negotiate their contract has been abrogated to some extent by legislation designed to protect the employee. The terms of the employment contract are affected by legislation, and so are the conditions of employment.

---

28. Notice and termination are discussed in Chapter 21.

Employee Welfare Issues

Employment Standards

All the provinces and territories, as well as the federal government, have **employment standards legislation** (also sometimes called labour standards legislation) that sets out minimum standards in the workplace. An employer may provide greater benefits than those provided for in the legislation but not lesser. In short, any contractual provisions that provide lesser benefits than those set out in the legislation are not enforceable.

There are variations in the legislation from jurisdiction to jurisdiction. Most, however, cover the same general categories of benefits. A sampling of typical standards follows:

- *Hours of work and overtime*. Hours of work that an employee can be asked to work vary from 40 to 48. Overtime is usually paid at one-and-a-half times the employee's regular wages. In some provinces, it is paid at one-and-a-half times the minimum wage.

Employment standards legislation
Laws that specify minimum standards in the workplace.

BUSINESS APPLICATION OF THE LAW

Unpaid Overtime

Employment standards legislation in all jurisdictions requires employers to pay overtime to non-management employees after varying number of hours worked. In the federal jurisdiction, employers must pay employees who have worked more than eight hours in a day and 40 hours in a week.

In 2007, 10 000 employees (current and former) of the Canadian Imperial Bank of Commerce (CIBC) launched a $600 million class action lawsuit against their employer. The suit alleges that frontline employees regularly work overtime for which they do not get paid. The representative plaintiff in the suit is 34-year-old Dara Fresco, a personal banker and teller at a Toronto branch of the bank. She has worked for the bank for over 10 years and at the time of launching the lawsuit was paid an annual salary of $30 715. She calculates that she is owed $50 000 for unpaid overtime over the past decade and is required to work an average of two to five hours a week in unpaid overtime. Shortly after the CIBC employees launched their suit, a similar lawsuit was filed by Cindy Fulawka on behalf of 5000 current and former employees of the Bank of Nova Scotia (Scotiabank). They are seeking $350 million in damages for unpaid overtime. Other overtime class actions lawsuits have been launched against Canadian National Railway Co (CNR) and KPMG LLP. The case against KPMG, however, has been settled out of court for $10 million.

In 2012, the Ontario Court of Appeal overturned[29] lower court rulings denying the CIBC certification and upheld[30] the lower court's certification of the Scotiabank case. Certification

Dara Fresco and lawyer Louis Sokolov

of the CNR case, which involves allegations that class members were misclassified as managers exempt from the provisions of the Canada Labour Code requiring payment for overtime worked, was denied.[31] The Court of Appeal held that the misclassification could only be determined on an individual basis, and therefore the case lacked commonality. In the bank cases, the Court held that although there may be individual issues relating to damages (whether an individual worked overtime and how much), there was commonality as to the issue of liability (whether there was a systemic breach of contract by the banks).

The ruling in the CIBC and Scotiabank cases allows them to proceed to trial unless the banks seek leave to appeal the certification decision to the Supreme Court of Canada.

(Continued)

---

29. *Fresco v Canadian Imperial Bank of Commerce*, 2012 ONCA 444.
30. *Fulawka v Bank of Nova Scotia*, 2012 ONCA 443.
31. *McCracken v Canadian National Railway*, 2012 ONCA 445.

Critical Analysis: Managers and supervisors are not entitled to receive overtime pay under employment standards legislation. What is the distinction between a manager/supervisor and an employee entitled to overtime? If the class action lawsuits are ultimately successful, what will be the likely impact on employees working overtime? What should employers do to assess their exposure to similar class action lawsuits?

Sources: Shannon Kari, "Bank employee actions certified", *The Lawyers Weekly* (6 July 2012) 1.; Julius Melnitzer, "Overtime class actions: an endless maze of rulings and appeals", *The Law Times* (26 September 2010) online: Law Times <http://www.lawtimesnews.com/201009077484/Headline-News/Overtime-class-actions-an-endless-maze-of-rulings-and-appeals>; Virginia Galt & Janet McFarland, "CIBC faces massive overtime lawsuit", *The Globe and Mail* (6 June 2007) A1; Jacquie McNish, "Scotiabank hit with overtime suit", *The Globe and Mail* (11 December 2007) B14

- *Minimum wage.* The minimum wage is usually set on an hourly basis. For example, in New Brunswick,[32] the minimum wage is $10.00 per hour.

- *Vacations and vacation pay.* The length of paid vacation that an employee is entitled to usually depends on the amount of service. For example, in Alberta,[33] an employee is entitled to two weeks after one year of employment, and three weeks after five years.

- *Termination and severance.* The legislation normally provides for notice and severance pay. For example, in British Columbia,[34] an employee is entitled to one week's notice after three months, two weeks' notice after 12 months, three weeks' notice after three years, and one additional week for each additional year of employment, to a maximum of eight weeks.

- *Statutory (paid) holidays.* Every jurisdiction requires that employers pay employees for specific public holidays. For example, in Newfoundland and Labrador,[35] employees are entitled to New Year's Day, Good Friday, Memorial Day (July 1), Labour Day, Christmas Day, and Remembrance Day.

- *Bereavement and sick leave.* All jurisdictions have provisions for leaves, either paid or unpaid, for various reasons. For example, the federal jurisdiction[36] provides for 12 weeks of sick leave after three months of employment.

- *Maternity and parental leave.* Every jurisdiction provides for pregnancy leave after a minimum amount of service. For example, in Manitoba,[37] an eligible person is entitled to 17 weeks' maternity leave after seven months of service. Most provinces provide parental leave for eligible persons.

Other typical standards include equal pay for equal work, prohibitions against sexual harassment, prohibitions against the employment of children, and various leave provisions such as for court duty and family emergencies.

32. NB Reg 2011-54.
33. *Employment Standards Code*, RSA 2000, c E-9, s 34.
34. *Employment Standards Act*, RSBC 1996, c 113, s 63 (3).
35. *Labour Standards Act*, RSN 1990, c L-2, s 14(1).
36. *Canada Labour Code*, RSC 1985, c L-2, s 239(1).
37. *The Employment Standards Code*, SM 1998, c 29, ss 53, 54(1), 58(1).

Certain employees, such as doctors, lawyers, farmers, domestic workers, construction workers, and information technology professionals, may not be covered by the legislation or may be exempt from certain provisions, such as hours of work, minimum wages, and overtime pay.

The legislation also provides a mechanism for enforcing employment standards. In Ontario, for example, employment standards officers, employed by the Employment Standards Branch, investigate complaints, carry on general investigations, and, when necessary, issue orders requiring compliance with provisions of the *Employment Standards Act.*

INTERNATIONAL PERSPECTIVE

Labour Standards in Chinese Factory Manufacturing Microsoft Products

The National Labour Committee (NLC), a U.S. advocacy group for the rights of workers, reports that KYE—a factory in China that makes computer mice and Xbox controllers for Microsoft—is employing teenage workers and paying them the equivalent of 58 cents an hour. The report, produced after a three-year investigation, states that the mostly female workers, many 16 and 17 years old, were working 15-hour shifts, sometimes with 1 000 workers crammed into a workshop measuring 32 square metres. The work is monotonous and workers are not allowed to talk or listen to music during working hours. One worker reported that her job consisted entirely of sticking self-adhesive rubber feet to the bottom of computer mice. The pace of work is frantic as workers race to complete mandatory production goals. Failure to reach goals can result in fines for the entire production line. The workers sleep on site, in factory dormitories with 14 workers to a room. They eat substandard meals from the factory cafeteria and "shower" with a sponge and a bucket. However, it is not the working and living conditions that affect the workers the most. It is the militaristic management and sleep deprivation. One worker told the NLC: "We are like prisoners. It seems we live only to work. We do not work to live. We do not live a life, only work."

Microsoft is not the only company to outsource manufacturing to KYE, but according to the NLC it accounts for about 30 percent of the factory's work. Microsoft said in a statement that it was taking the claims seriously and was sending independent auditors to the factory.

Critical Analysis: What are the risks for North American companies in having their products manufactured abroad using "sweatshop" labour?

INSTITUTE FOR GLOBAL LABOUR AND HUMAN RIGHTS

Should North American employment standards apply to workers manufacturing products for North American companies?

Sources: Charles Kernaghan, "China's Youth Meet Microsoft", *Institute for Global Labour and Human Rights* (13 April 2010) online: Institute for Global Labour and Human Rights <http://www.globallabourrights.org/reports?id=0034>; Brian Tobey, "Working to ensure the fair treatment of workers in our manufacturing and supply chain", *The Official Microsoft Blog* (15 April 2010) online: The Offcial Microsoft Blog <http://blogs.technet.com/b/microsoft_blog/archive/2010/04/15/working-to-ensure-the-fair-treatment-of-workers-in-our-manufacturing-and-supply-chain.aspx>; "Microsoft 'using slave labour', *The Edmonton Journal* (17 April 2010) A13.

Safety and Compensation

Workers' compensation legislation is designed to address accidents and injuries in the workplace. It provides for a type of no-fault insurance scheme. Employers are required to pay into a fund, and workers who have job-related injuries, accidents, or illnesses are compensated from the fund, regardless of fault. Compensation covers lost wages, medical aid, and rehabilitation. The scheme prevents a civil suit by the employee against the employer relating to a workplace injury or accident. Not all employees, accidents, or illnesses are covered by the legislation, however. Illness must be job related, which is not always easy to determine, particularly as the causes of many illnesses are unclear and the illnesses themselves can take decades to develop.

All jurisdictions have enacted comprehensive occupational health and safety legislation that generally applies to all sectors of the economy. In addition to general provisions, there are industry-specific provisions and hazard-oriented provisions. The purpose of the legislation is to protect workers in the workplace by giving them a right to participate in safety issues, a right to know about hazards in the workplace, and a right to refuse to work in unsafe conditions.

Also, the *Criminal Code of Canada*[38] has been amended to impose a new legal duty on organizations and individuals to protect the health and safety of workers.[39]

Employee Economic Safety

Two legislative schemes in the area of employee economic safety are employment insurance and the Canada and Quebec pension plans.

The *Employment Insurance Act*[40] is federal legislation that applies to both the federally and provincially regulated sectors. The basic concept of employment insurance is that the employer and employee contribute to a fund that provides insurance against loss of income. The plan provides benefits for unemployment, maternity and parental leave, and sickness, as well as some retirement benefits. A limited number of employees are not covered by the scheme. The most common exclusions are casual workers, some part-time workers, and those employed in agriculture.

The *Canada Pension Plan*[41] (in Quebec, the Quebec Pension Plan) is an insurance plan designed to provide pensions or financial assistance in the case of retirement, disability, or death. Both the employer and the employee contribute to the plan.

Workplace Discrimination

Discrimination on certain grounds is prohibited in all aspects of employment, including promotions and terminations. One aspect of discrimination that has received a great deal of attention is workplace harassment, including sexual and racial harassment that occurs in the workplace.

---

38. RSC 1985, c C-46, s 217.1 provides "Everyone who undertakes, or has the authority, to direct how another person does work or performs a task is under a legal duty to take reasonable steps to prevent bodily harm to that person, or any other person, arising from that work or task."
39. See Chapter 16 for further discussion.
40. SC 1996, c 23. The Act was formerly known as the *Unemployment Insurance* Act but was re-named in 1996 as part of a general reform package. It covers provincial sectors as a result of a specific amendment to the Constitution.
41. RSC 1985, c C-8.

Workplace Harassment

Harassment is any unwanted physical or verbal behaviour that offends or humiliates the victim and detrimentally affects the work environment or leads to adverse job-related consequences for the victim. Such conduct can take many forms, including threats; intimidation; verbal abuse; unwelcome remarks or jokes about race, religion, sex, disability, or age; the display of sexist, racist, or other offensive pictures; sexually suggestive remarks or gestures; unnecessary physical contact, such as touching, patting, pinching, or punching; and physical assault, including sexual assault.[42]

Prohibitions against harassment in the workplace are found in an array of legislative provisions. Human rights legislation, in both the federal and provincial jurisdictions, prohibits harassment. For example, the *Canadian Human Rights Act* section 14(1)[43] provides "It is a discriminatory practice ... (c) in matters related to employment, to harass an individual on a prohibited ground of discrimination." Employment standards legislation also often protects employees from harassment, particularly sexual harassment, and the *Criminal Code* protects people from physical and sexual assault. In addition, most jurisdictions have a provision in their Occupational Health and Safety legislation that requires employers to take all reasonable precautions to protect the health and safety of employees. Some provinces have addressed the workplace harassment problem more directly (see the Business and Legislation: Workplace Bullying and Violence box on page 508).

An anti-harassment policy addresses inappropriate behaviour in the workplace. What should the policy contain?

FUSE/JUPITER IMAGES

The prohibition against harassment in human rights legislation extends not only to employers but also to their employees. The employer is vicariously liable for any violations

---

42. See the Canadian Human Rights Commission website at <http://www.chrc-ccdp.ca/discrimination/what_is_it-en.asp>.
43. *Supra* note 8.

of human rights legislation committed by its employees.[44] Several jurisdictions modify this position by providing for a due diligence defence. For example, the Manitoba legislation[45] provides that an employer is responsible for any act of harassment committed by an employee or an agent of the employer in the course of employment unless it is established that the employer did not consent to the act and took all reasonable steps to prevent the act from being committed and, subsequently, took all reasonable steps to mitigate or avoid its consequences.

In order to fulfill their responsibilities under human rights legislation, it is incumbent on employers to develop and implement a workplace harassment policy. Although employers may still be liable for harassment, whether they knew of it or not, the penalties will be less or nonexistent for employers that not only respond quickly and effectively to instances of harassment but also take action to prevent the wrongful conduct from occurring in the first place.

BUSINESS AND LEGISLATION

Workplace Bullying and Violence

In 2005, Lori Dupont, a nurse was stabbed to death at the Hotel-Dieu Grace Hospital in Windsor, Ontario by her former boyfriend and co-worker, Dr. Marc Daniel. Although the hospital was aware of repeated and escalating harassment by Daniel, an anaesthesiologist, it failed to take steps to discipline him. Partly, in response to this tragic case of workplace violence, the government of Ontario introduced amendments[46] *to the Occupational Health and Safety Act*[47] to address workplace violence and harassment.

The amendments, which came into effect in June 2010, provide expansive definitions and a new right for employees. "Workplace harassment" is defined as engaging in a course of vexatious comment or conduct against a worker in a workplace that is known or ought reasonably to be known to be unwelcome. "Workplace violence" is defined to include threats of physical violence, attempts to exercise physical force, and the actual exercise of force. The definitions are such that the conduct can come from not only a fellow employee but also customers, suppliers, clients, patients or the general public. Workers are entitled to refuse work where they have reason to believe that they are likely to be the target of workplace

violence (the same right does not apply to workplace harassment).

The legislation places new, proactive obligations on employers. They are required to conduct a risk assessment for violence and harassment in the workplace. Following the assessment, they must develop policies to address the risks identified and provide training in respect to the policies. In addition, employers are required to take every reasonable precaution to address domestic violence in the workplace and they must disclose information about a person with a history of violent behaviour, where it is likely that a worker will be exposed to the person through the course of their work and that exposure creates a risk of physical injury.

The *Act* provides for fines of up to $500 000 for companies and up to $25 000 or 12 months imprisonment for individuals for violations.

Critical Analysis: Human rights legislation prohibits harassment, so why are specific workplace anti-harassment and anti-violence rules needed?

Sources: Wallace Immen, "Keeping the bullies and brutes at bay", *The Globe and Mail* (12 June 2010) B16; Michael McKiernan, "Few ready for Bill 168", *Law Times News* (13 June 2010) online: Law Times <http://www.lawtimesnews.com>.

Pay Equity

Discrimination in pay scales between men and women has led to legislation designed to ensure that female and male employees receive the same compensation for performing the same or substantially similar work. All jurisdictions provide for some type of equal pay in their

---

44. *Robichaud v The Queen*, [1987] 2 SCR 84, 40 DLR (4th) 577. The decision makes it clear that, subject to statutory provisions to the contrary, vicarious liability applies to human rights law.
45. *Human Rights Code*, SM 1987–88, c 45, s 10.
46. *Occupational Health & Safety Amendment Act* (*Violence and Harassment in the Workplace*) 2009, SO 2009 c 23.
47. RSO 1990 c O.1.

human rights legislation.[48] In addition, some jurisdictions have equality of pay provisions in their employment standards law, and some have enacted specific **pay equity** statutes.[49]

Pay equity provisions are designed to redress systemic discrimination in compensation for work performed. They require an employer to evaluate the work performed by employees in order to divide the workforce into job classes. The classes can then be considered to determine whether they are male or female dominated. Next, employers must value each of the job classes in terms of duties, responsibilities, and required qualifications; compare like classes; and endeavour to compensate each female job class with a wage rate comparable to the male job class performing work of equal value. This procedure, however, has been difficult to administer and apply. For example, a pay equity dispute between female postal workers and Canada Post took 28 years to resolve. It ended when the Supreme Court of Canada upheld a decision of the Canadian Human Rights Commission that awarded the workers $150 million.[50]

> **Pay equity**
> Provisions designed to ensure that female and male employees receive the same compensation for performing similar or substantially similar work.

Drug and Alcohol Testing

Employers have a legitimate interest in having a safe workplace. Sometimes they have attempted to achieve this goal through drug and alcohol testing of their employees. Such testing, however, is contentious as it is *prima facie* discriminatory. Employers can nevertheless justify discriminatory rules if they can meet the three-part test in *Meiorin*.

BUSINESS APPLICATION OF THE LAW

Drug and Alcohol Testing in the Workplace

Drug and alcohol testing in the workplace is a contentious issue. In the wake of disasters such as the Hinton train derailment and the sinking of the *Exxon Valdez*, and pressure from third parties who want testing as a condition of doing business, employers have sought to implement mandatory drug- and alcohol-testing policies. Employees have often resisted on the grounds that testing infringes their human and privacy rights.

It is generally accepted that, in most cases, an employer may test an employee for alcohol and drug use where there is a reasonable suspicion that the employee is under the influence or where a serious incident has occurred. The situation with respect to pre-employment and random drug and alcohol testing is less clear. Challenges to these programs have received mixed results from the courts.

In 2000, the Ontario Court of Appeal in *Entrop v Imperial Oil Limited*[51] struck down Imperial Oil's pre-employment and

What is the legal argument against drug and alcohol testing in the workplace?

random drug-testing policies for safety-sensitive jobs. The court determined that drug testing is discriminatory but can be justified as a *bona fide* occupational requirement. Imperial

(Continued)

---

48. For example, the *Canadian Human Rights Act*, *supra* note 8 at s 11 specifies that it is discriminatory to establish or maintain different wage rates for men and women doing work of equal value in the same establishment.
49. The provinces of Manitoba, New Brunswick, Nova Scotia, Prince Edward Island, Ontario, and Quebec have specific pay equity legislation. Ontario and Quebec are the only provinces in which the legislation applies to the private sector. The other provinces limit the legislation's application to the public sector. See *Pay Equity Act*, RSO 1990, c P-7 and *Pay Equity* Act, RSQ c E-12.001.
50. Kathryn May, "After 28-year pay-equity fight, female postal workers awarded $150-million", *National Post* (17 November 2011) online: National Post <http://news.nationalpost.com/2011/11/17/after-28-year-pay-equity-fight-female-postal-workers-awarded-150-million/>.
51. (2000), 50 OR (3d) 18, 84 Alta LR (4th) 205 (CA).

Oil, however, could not justify its drug test as a *bona fide* occupational requirement because the test could only detect past drug use; it could not detect whether a person is impaired and unable to do his or her job now or in the future. In other words, the test could not detect actual impairment at the time of testing and therefore could not be justified as reasonably necessary to accomplish the employer's goal of a safe workplace free of impairment. The court did uphold random breathalyzer tests for alcohol in safety-sensitive positions, as these tests do measure present impairment.

In 2007, the Alberta Court of Appeal in *Alberta (Human Rights and Citizenship Commission) v Kellogg, Brown & Root*,[52] held that pre-employment drug testing at a safety-sensitive Syncrude oil sands project was justified. The Court expressly declined to follow *Entrop* and held that pre-employment drug testing in safety-sensitive positions was not discriminatory, at least with respect to casual drug users. The court recognized that this workplace was dangerous and the testing program was necessary to ensure that employees were not compounding the risks by being impaired by drugs and alcohol.

The court did not consider the issue of random drug and alcohol testing during employment.

In 2011, the New Brunswick Court of Appeal *in Irving Pulp & Paper Ltd v Communications, Energy and Paperworkers Union of Canada, Local 30*,[53] upheld the employer's random alcohol testing policy of employees in safety sensitive positions. The Court found that because the pulp and paper mill was an inherently dangerous workplace, the breathalyzer test was minimally intrusive and the test was only applied to those in safety sensitive positions, the testing policy was reasonable. The Court restricted its decision to random alcohol testing, noting that drug testing was more problematic as it cannot measure present impairment.

The law respecting drug and alcohol testing in the workplace has developed somewhat differently across Canada. This may change as the Supreme Court of Canada has agreed to hear an appeal in the *Irving* case.[54]

Critical Analysis: Which court do you think strikes the right balance between workplace safety and protection of employee rights?

Workplace Privacy

Privacy, particularly since technological developments have made it easier to "watch" or monitor employees, is a concern in the workplace. Issues centre on collecting and disseminating information about employees, watching and searching employees, and monitoring employees' electronic communications.

Collection and Dissemination of Information

Employers have the ability to collect and store, in hard copy or electronically, a great deal of employee data—performance reviews, work activity reports, medical records, disciplinary reports, credit ratings, and letters of recommendation. Employees, however, have rights to control the collection and use of information.

A wide array of legislation in the public sector, at both the federal and provincial levels, gives individuals the right to control personal information. For example, the federal *Privacy Act*[55] regulates the collection and use of personal information held by the federal government. The Act gives individuals the right to see information and to request corrections if it is inaccurate. Similar provincial legislation applies to information held by provincial governments. *The Personal Information Protection and Electronic Documents Act*[56] (*PIPEDA*) extends these rights to the private sector. *PIPEDA* applies to employee information in federal works, undertakings, and businesses. *PIPEDA* does not, however, apply to employee information in

52. 2007 ABCA 426, 289 DLR (4th) 95 leave to appeal to SCC dismissed 29 May 2008.
53. 2011 NBCA 58, 2011 CLLC 220-043.
54. *Communications, Energy and Paperworkers Union of Canada, Local 30 v Irving Pulp & Paper, Limited* 2012 CanLII 14844 (SCC).
55. RSC 1985, c P-21.
56. SC 2000, c 5.

the provincial private sector. This information is regulated by similar provincial legislation. To date, Quebec[57], Alberta,[58] and British Columbia[59] have enacted similar legislation.[60]

The basic principle of *PIPEDA* and its provincial counterparts is that personal information should not be collected, used, or disclosed without the prior knowledge and consent of the individual concerned. *PIPEDA* defines "personal information" as information about an identifiable individual, but does not include the name, title, business address, or telephone number of an employee of an organization. Therefore, to collect all other types of employee information the employer requires the consent of the employee. The Alberta and British Columbia legislation contain an exception. For example, the Alberta legislation allows employers to access the personal information reasonably necessary to administer the employment relationship without obtaining consent.

To meet their obligations under *PIPEDA* and similar provincial legislation, employers are required to

- identify and document the limited purposes for which personal information is collected, prior to collecting the information

- communicate the identified purposes to the individual prior to obtaining the individual's consent

- collect, use, and disclose the personal information only for the identified purposes

- obtain the express consent of individuals for "sensitive" information such as health records and financial information (implied consent may be sufficient for less sensitive information)

- maintain responsibility for personal information under its possession or custody

- designate a personal information supervisor

- maintain the accuracy of personal information held by the organization

- retain information only as long as required for the purposes identified

- adopt security safeguards to protect personal information from loss and unauthorized use

- provide access and the right to amend inaccurate information to each individual

Penalties for breach of the Act include making public an organization's personal information policies, fines ranging from $10 000 to $100 000, and court orders to correct practices and to pay damages to the complainant.

Surveillance and Searches

The surveillance of employees with video cameras or closed-circuit television is sometimes used to prevent, detect, or investigate fraud, theft, and harassment. The appropriateness of surveillance has been challenged pursuant to *PIPEDA*.

---

57. *An Act Respecting the Protection of Personal Information in the Private Sector,* RSQ c P-39.1.
58. *Personal Information Protection Act,* SA 2003, c P-6.5.
59. *Personal Information Protection Act,* SBC 2003, c 63.
60. Ontario, Alberta, Saskatchewan, and Manitoba have passed specific legislation to deal with the collection, use, and disclosure of personal information by health care providers and other health care organizations.

TECHNOLOGY AND THE LAW

The Monitoring of Employees and Privacy

Video cameras, Global Positioning Systems (GPS) tracking, and smartphones have made it possible for employers to closely monitor employees and their activities. Employers justify the use of technology on the basis of concerns about safety and security, productivity and efficiency, misappropriation of confidential or proprietary information, theft and other illegal activities, and liability.

The surveillance and monitoring of employees, however, may infringe the privacy rights of employees. Privacy protections for employees emanate from several sources: the terms of a collective agreement, the tort of invasion of privacy, and privacy legislation. Employees in the federally-regulated sectors may challenge employer's practices pursuant to *PIPEDA* and employees in some provinces may challenge pursuant to privacy legislation governing the private sector.

Whether a specific monitoring practice is permissible or an invasion of privacy depends on a host of factors including the method of surveillance, the purpose of surveillance, whether the surveillance was done openly, and the employee's reasonable expectation of privacy. The business interests of the employer are balanced against the employee's privacy rights and a determination is made as to whether the monitoring is reasonable in light of the balance.

The use of surveillance equipment was considered in *Eastmond v Canadian Pacific Railway*.[61] An employee made a complaint pursuant to *PIPEDA* that Canadian Pacific Railway's (CPR) installation of six digital recording surveillance cameras focused on door entrances and exits was unacceptable. He argued that they were installed without union consent, there was no security problem that justified this invasion of privacy, and they could be used to monitor employees' work performance. CPR responded that the installation was necessary to reduce vandalism and deter theft, to reduce its potential liability for property damage, and to provide security for staff. In assessing the employee's complaint, the court adopted the following test: (1) Is the measure necessary to the specific needs? (2) Is it likely to be effective in meeting that need? (3) Is the loss of privacy proportionate to the benefit gained? and (4)

When are employers justified in spying on their employees?

Is there a less privacy-invasive way of achieving the same end? The court held that CPR's purpose of video data collection—deterrence of theft, vandalism, and trespassing; security of employees; and investigation of reported incidents—was appropriate. The collection of information was done openly, and it was not limited to CPR employees in that it captured members of the public, contractors, suppliers, and trespassers. The collection was not intended to measure employee performance, and the images were kept under lock and key and were not viewed unless an incident was reported. Finally, the court concluded that there was no alternate way for CPR to achieve the same result in a less invasive way. The court also held that the employee's consent was not required for the collection of this information because of the exception in *PIPEDA*, which permits the collection of personal information without consent for purposes relating to an investigation where collection with consent would jeopardize the accuracy or availability of information.

Critical Analysis: In this case, the video surveillance was justified on the basis of a safety and security concern. Do you think video camera surveillance could be justified on the basis of the employer's interest in managing the productivity of employees?

Intrusive searches of employees or their belongings are carefully scrutinized by the courts. An employer would need to have some particularly compelling reason, such as bomb threats being issued or thefts occurring, to undertake such practices. Additionally, the employer would need to demonstrate that all other alternatives for dealing with the threats had been exhausted. Employees should be informed in advance of any policy in this regard, and any searches would need to be conducted in a systematic and non-arbitrary manner; otherwise, the employer may be vulnerable to charges of discrimination.

---

61. 2004 FC 852, 254 FTR 169.

Monitoring of Communications

Many employees, particularly those who work in an office, have access to email and the Internet, as well as traditional means of communication—telephone and facsimile. Employers have a legitimate interest in ensuring that employees are not spending excessive amounts of time on personal communication and are using company equipment for legitimate uses. Employees, on the other hand, have a legitimate expectation that their private and personal communications will not be monitored or intercepted. Currently, there is no comprehensive law in Canada prohibiting employers from monitoring their employees' email and Internet activities.

The *Criminal Code*[62] provides that it is an offence to intercept a private communication. The section, however, does not apply to communications that are not private or to interception that is consented to by one of the parties. A communication is private if the parties have an expectation that it will not be intercepted. There is judicial authority for the notion that email via the Internet ought to carry a reasonable expectation of privacy, although it is not to be accorded the same level of privacy protection as first-class mail.[63] However, the manner in which the technology is managed may serve to diminish the user's expectation of privacy. For example, a comprehensive technology-use policy, which addresses the employer's monitoring activities, may make it clear that an employee has no reasonable expectation of privacy in the use of the employer's communication tools.

The *PIPEDA* and provincial privacy legislation may affect the employer's ability to monitor electronic communications. Although the legislation does not expressly address this issue, it requires that all organizations including businesses, in order to collect, use, and retain personal information, get the consent of the individual concerned. This suggests that in order to monitor and view the content of communications, employers will require the consent of employees. Presumably, an employer could require such consent as a condition of employment.

The Union Context

Discussion in this chapter thus far has focused on the hiring and employment of non-unionized employees. It has also focused on private sector as opposed to public sector employees, as there is often specific legislation that affects public sector employees' employment.

In a unionized environment, many of the same employment issues that arise in a non-union environment are also relevant—recruiting, terms and conditions of employment, and so on. However, negotiating and entering into an employment contract is a much different process.

Both the federal and provincial governments have enacted labour or industrial relations legislation that guarantees the right of employees to join trade unions. The Acts apply to most employees, but certain employees—namely, managers and those in specific occupations, such as domestic workers and farm hands—are excluded. The legislative enactments provide for a **certification** process, by which the union is recognized as the bargaining agent for a group of employees. An employer, however, can voluntarily recognize the union as the bargaining agent for the employees without a certification process. The certification

Certification
The process by which a union is recognized as a bargaining agent for a group of employees.

---

62. RSC 1985, c C-46, s 184.
63. See *R v Weir*, 1998 ABQB 56, 59 Alta LR (3d) 319.

Labour relations board
A body that administers labour relations legislation.

Collective bargaining
A mechanism by which parties enter a collective agreement or contract.

Collective agreement
The employment agreement reached between the union and employer setting out the bargaining unit employees' terms and conditions of employment.

process is basically a method by which the **labour relations board** approves the union as the employees' representative upon the union being able to show that a majority of the employees in the bargaining unit want the union to represent them.

The legislation provides a mechanism known as **collective bargaining**, by which the parties enter a collective agreement or contract. The contract applies to all employees in the bargaining unit, regardless of whether they voted for the union representation. The union and the employer have a duty to bargain in good faith—that is, they must make a substantive effort to negotiate the agreement. The collective agreement, like an individual employment contract, sets out the terms and conditions of employment. The two types of contracts cover many of the same issues, such as wages, benefits, and the like, but a **collective agreement** is usually far more comprehensive. As well, a union bargaining on behalf of many employees generally has far more bargaining power than a single individual negotiating with an employer (although some highly skilled or specialized employees do have a lot of individual bargaining power). During the term of the collective agreement, there can be no legal strikes by the employees or lockouts by the employer.

In return, the legislation provides a process involving grievance and arbitration procedures for resolving disputes. These procedures are discussed in Chapter 21.

Business Law in Practice Revisited

1. Is Jeong an employee or an independent contractor?

The distinction between an employee and an independent contractor is not always readily apparent. The label that the parties apply to their relationship is not conclusive, as the nature of the relationship is a question of fact. The courts have developed a number of tests to make the determination. Some factors, such as the lack of control, suggest that Jeong is an independent contractor. Other factors, such as the employer providing a computer, the method of payment, and the degree of integration, suggest that Jeong is an employee. In the final analysis, as Jeong does not appear to be in business for herself, it is likely that the courts will consider her an employee.

2. Why is the distinction between an employee and an independent contractor important?

The distinction is important because an employer is responsible for torts committed by an employee in the course of employment, whereas the employer is not generally responsible for the torts of an independent contractor. In addition, the distinction is critical because common law, as well as statutory rights and obligations, in most cases apply only to employees and not to independent contractors.

3. Is Hiram responsible for Jeong's conduct?

If Jeong is considered an employee, then Hiram is responsible for the torts committed by Jeong in the course of employment. Hiram is not responsible for the torts committed by Jeong outside the course of her employment. Although the posting of the possibly defamatory statement on the hockey website is related to her work, it is likely that her actions will be considered to be outside the scope of employment because it appears that she was responding in a personal capacity to a perceived affront. Assuming this is the case, Hiram is not responsible.

Chapter Summary

The employment relationship is one of the most fundamental relationships in business. The cornerstone of this relationship is a contract, either individual or collective, whereby one party provides services to another in return for remuneration. However, not everyone who provides services to another through a contract is an "employee." The distinction is crucial because common law, as well as statutory rights and obligations, in most cases applies only to employees and not to independent contractors.

The hiring process has a number of phases—advertising, application submission, interviewing, and reference checking. Legal issues such as discrimination and employment equity apply to each of these steps and provide the opportunity for potential liability for the unwary employer. Most of the costly mistakes made by employers who end up as the subject of a human rights investigation or the recipient of a wrongful dismissal suit can be avoided. Organizations need to be proactive by designing and implementing policies, practices, and procedures to address the legal issues at all stages of the employment relationship.

A well-drafted employment contract sets out the terms and conditions of employment. It describes the employment relationship and, at a minimum, sets out the job to be performed and the remuneration to be provided. The employment contract can be advantageous for both the employer and employee, as it contributes to certainty and clarity in the relationship.

The ability to freely negotiate an employment contract has been somewhat curtailed by a host of legislation designed to protect employees. This protection is provided not only with respect to the terms of employment, such as wages, vacation, and hours of work, but also with respect to the conditions of employment. There is a vast array of legislation affecting employee welfare, discrimination in the workplace, and privacy.

When a union is in place, negotiating and entering into an employment contract takes place through a process known as collective bargaining. The collective agreement that emerges from negotiations applies to all employees, regardless of whether they voted for union representation.

Chapter Study

Key Terms and Concepts

adverse effects discrimination (p. 495)

***bona fide* occupational requirement (BFOR) (p. 495)**

certification (p. 513)

collective agreement (p. 514)

collective bargaining (p. 514)

discrimination (p. 495)

duty to accommodate (p. 496)

employment equity legislation (p. 498)

employment relationship (p. 489)

employment standards legislation (p. 503)

fixed- or definite-term contract (p. 501)

human rights commission (p. 493)

indefinite-term contract (p. 501)

independent contractor (p. 489)

labour relations board (p. 514)

pay equity (p. 509)

systemic discrimination (p. 495)

Questions for Review

1. Which level of government has jurisdiction to make laws in the area of employment?

2. What are the tests for determining the difference between an employee and an independent contractor? Why is it important to distinguish between an employee and an independent contractor?

3. Define vicarious liability and negligent hiring. How do they differ?

4. The human rights Acts attempt to prohibit discrimination in employment. What is meant by "discrimination"?

5. What is the difference between systemic and adverse effects discrimination?

6. What is a *bona fide* occupational requirement? Give an example.

7. What is the "duty to accommodate"?

8. What is the purpose of the federal *Employment Equity Act?*

9. Do employees have fiduciary obligations? Explain.

10. Do employment contracts need to be in writing to be enforceable? What are the advantages of a written employment contract? Can you think of any disadvantages?

11. What is the purpose of employment standards legislation? Give an example of an employment standard.

12. Explain how the freedom to contract in employment has been affected by legislation, and give examples.

13. What is the purpose of workers' compensation legislation?

14. Would displaying a picture of a nude person be an example of sexual harassment in the workplace? Explain.

15. What is the purpose of pay equity?

16. Is alcohol and drug testing in the workplace permissible? Explain.

17. Do employees have a right to privacy? Explain.

18. Describe how unionized employees enter into employment contracts.

Questions for Critical Thinking

1. A recent article in *The Globe and Mail* reports that headhunters are having difficulty getting references for ex-employees from employers.[64] Mark Reidl, the president of Acchuman, a Toronto-based executive search firm states, "I've been in the business for 16 years, doing background checks, and companies just aren't giving references anymore. They don't say anything and, if they do, they certainly aren't looking to give me the goods." Why do you think employers are reluctant to give references? Are there any legal reasons for not providing reference information? Are there any legal concerns with an employer not providing a reference for a former employee? Are there any legal concerns with a prospective employer asking the former employer for reference information?

2. An advertisement that reads "Wanted: Vietnamese waiters for a Vietnamese restaurant" is discriminatory.

---

64. David Hutton, "Job reference chill grows icier", *The Globe and Mail* (18 June 2008) C1.

On what basis does the advertisement discriminate? Could or should ethnicity qualify as a *bona fide* occupational requirement? Would it make any difference where the restaurant was located?

3. The distinction between an independent contractor and an employee is not always clear. What steps can be taken by an employer who wishes to engage independent contractors in order to ensure that its workers will be classified as independent contractors? What are the risks associated with having "independent contractors" classified as employees?

4. Mandatory retirement has been abolished in the federal sector and most of the provinces and territories. It is discriminatory under human rights legislation, although exceptions are generally permitted for *bona fide* occupational requirements and *bona fide* retirement or pension plans. Is ending mandatory retirement good for business? What are the advantages and disadvantages of mandatory retirement policies? How might employers require their employees to retire at age 65 without breaching applicable human rights laws?

5. An employer has a duty to accommodate the special needs of a physically or mentally disabled employee unless the accommodation causes undue hardship. What is the duty to accommodate? What are some examples of accommodation? What is undue hardship? What are some factors to consider in determining undue hardship? What are some factors not to consider in determining undue hardship? Is accommodation "special treatment"? Is it fair that one person gets "special treatment" over another?

6. In the wake of evolving methods of communication (emailing, text messaging, and blogging) and methods of surveillance (closed-circuit cameras and software for monitoring Internet and email use), privacy in the workplace is an area of growing contention. On one side is the employer's right to monitor its workforce and on the other is the employee's right of privacy with respect to technology use. One of the ways to strike an appropriate balance between these competing interests is a computer-use policy. What are the benefits of such a policy? What should such a policy contain?

Situations for Discussion

1. In 2001, Cindy Choung became British Columbia's first accredited Chinese-language court interpreter. Interpreters are called by court services (a branch of the government) when needed and are selected from a list in rotation. They are paid an hourly rate, plus expenses. All travel arrangements are made by and paid for by court services. There is no guarantee of a minimum amount of work, and there is no prohibition against working for other agencies. Court services make no deductions for income tax, employment insurance, or pension plans. A code of professional conduct implemented by court services governs how interpreters are to translate and to dress in court. It also sets out rules of confidentiality and prohibits interpreters from assigning their work to another interpreter.

   In 2004 the court services' executive director received complaints about Cindy's work and decided to remove her name from the list of interpreters. Cindy is considering bringing an action for wrongful dismissal.[65] Is she entitled to bring such an action? What does she need to prove? Explain.

2. Silvia Cabrera is an account executive at a major bank. Over the past six months she has noticed that the performance of one of her loans officer, Jorge Rodriquez has been declining. Jorge had always been an excellent employee who maintained great relationships with colleagues, performed his work on time, and rarely missed a day of work. However, in the past six months, he has had frequent absences from work, has had difficulty meeting deadlines, and is moody and distracted. When asked if he was having any problems, Jorge simply replied, "It's personal."

   Last week, Silvia happened to be delivering some important bank documents to Jorge's office when she thought she saw some pornographic images on Jorge's computer before he switched screens to some graphs and tables. Silvia was not 100 percent sure of what she saw, so she did not say anything to Jorge. She decided to speak to the branch manger about her concerns.

   The branch manager was quite taken aback and would like to search Jorge's computer, his email account, and his Internet usage.[66] Can the branch

---

65. Based on *Truong v British Columbia*, 1999 BCCA 513, 67 BCLR (3d) 234.
66. Source: Karen Sargeant, "Big brother is watching you", *The Lawyers Weekly* (28 September 2008) 9.

manager legally perform such a search? Discuss. Would it be appropriate and legal for the bank to install computer-surveillance technologies that target the use of information sources on all employees' computers?

3. Tom Mason was hired as a technical salesperson for Chem-Trend Limited Partnership, a chemical manufacturer that sold industrial chemicals worldwide. At the time of hiring, he signed a standard form contract that contained both a confidentiality clause and a non-competition clause. The confidentiality clause prohibited him from using or disclosing any trade secrets or confidential information after the termination of his employment. The non-competition clause prohibited him from engaging in any business or activity that could be deemed in competition with Chem-Trend for a period of one year following termination of his employment, regardless of whether he had been fired or quit. This prohibition included providing services or products to any business entity that was a client of Chem-Trend during the course of his employment.

Seventeen years later, Chem-Trend terminated Mason's employment. At the time of his termination, his sales territory spanned all of Canada and several U.S. states. As a result, he was familiar with some of Chem-Trend's clients that operated worldwide, and he had acquired extensive knowledge of Chem-Trend's products, operations, customers and pricing.[67] Given this situation, are the confidentiality and non-competition clauses enforceable against Mason? What factors are relevant in determining the enforceability of the non-competition clause? How could Mason and Chem-Trend have better protected their interests?

4. a. Bill Reyno owns and operates a bottle-recycling plant. He has recently experienced a rash of thefts and break-ins and wants to hire a night watchman or security guard. Bill wants someone large and feisty in case there are any problems. What steps should Bill take in hiring someone to fill the position?

   b. Jon Blondin applied for the position. When he showed up for the interview, he seemed to be a little "unstable." In fact, Bill thought he might have been drinking, but he was not sure. Other than this concern, Jon seemed to be perfect for the job. Bill would like Jon to take a drug and alcohol test. Is it permissible for Bill to make this request?

5. In January 2005, the Canadian Imperial Bank of Commerce (CIBC) launched a lawsuit against a number of its former employees and Genuity Capital Markets. CIBC is seeking damages in excess of $10 million. CIBC alleges a variety of transgressions, including the theft of client information and the solicitation of its employees. CIBC alleges that the former CEO of CIBC World Markets (CIBC terminated the CEO's employment in February 2004) and others set up a competitor, Genuity Capital, while still employed with CIBC. In less than a year, a total of over 20 senior employees of CIBC left to join Genuity. The allegations are supported by copies of numerous BlackBerry messages exchanged by the defendants in the summer of 2004. Since CIBC filed its suit, the defendants have counterclaimed for $14 million, alleging that the bank breached the privacy of the defendants by going through their email. Further, the former CEO has stated that he was not restricted by any agreement from competing with CIBC.[68] Assuming that the former CEO was not restricted by any agreement from competing with CIBC, does that exonerate him from liability? What can companies like CIBC do to avoid similar situations? What steps can an employer take to minimize the risks associated with the loss of employees and intellectual assets such as client lists, business strategies, and the like?

6. Melissa Antidormi was a successful 41-year-old working as a sales manager with BEA Systems Inc., a California-based software firm, when she left to join Blue Pumpkin Software Inc. At the time of her departure, her base salary was $90 000, and she was on target to earn approximately $300 000 in sales commissions. For 19 months, Blue Pumpkin had pursued her to lead its expansion into Canada and Latin America. She initially declined the offer as she had no interest in leaving her job at BEA Systems. However, Blue Pumpkin was persistent in selling their vision of a "New Canadian Team." Blue Pumpkin flew Antidormi to California, where the CEO indicated

---

67. *Mason v Chem-Trend Limited Partnership*, 2011 ONCA 344, 106 OR (3d) 72.
68. Patricia Best, "CIBC head invokes history in Genuity war", *The Globe and Mail* (6 December 2006) B2; Andrew Willis, "CIBC sues 6 former employees", *The Globe and Mail* (6 January 2005) B1; and Marjo Johne, "How to Cover Your Assets," *The Bay Street Bull*, August 2005 online: e2r Solutions <http://www.e2rsolutions.com/Libraries/Documents/05_08_The_Bay_Street_Bull.sflb.ashx>.

that Melissa's new position would provide a long-term opportunity. With promises of better pay, greater responsibilities, and job security, she joined Blue Pumpkin. Six months later, Melissa was terminated when the company changed its business plans to concentrate on the U.S. market. The company offered her two weeks of severance; she sued for wrongful dismissal. After a two-year legal battle, the Ontario Superior Court awarded her $320 000—the equivalent of one year's salary, commission, and bonuses—plus her legal costs. The court ruled that Melissa deserved 10 months' notice because Blue Pumpkin had misrepresented certain facts—in particular, the job security that she would enjoy as long as she performed well.[69] How can employees protect against false promises and misrepresentations? How can employers protect against false promises and inflated expectations?

7. Jordan Wimmer, a blonde, 29-year-old financier employed by Nomos Capital Partners Ltd. is suing her supervisor because he allegedly sent her emails calling her a "dumb blonde" and "decorative." She is also claiming that he sent the following joke to her and her colleagues: "A blonde asks her boyfriend for help assembling a jigsaw puzzle. She struggles to match the pieces to the picture of a rooster on the box. Eventually the boyfriend calms her down and says 'Let's just put all the cornflakes back in the box.'"[70] What is the legal basis for Wimmer's lawsuit? What does she have to prove to be successful? Assuming the allegations are true, is she likely to be successful? Is Nomos Capital responsible for the supervisor's actions? How should companies deal with issues of "jokes" in the workplace?

8. In May 2006, WestJet Airlines apologized to rival Air Canada and agreed to pay it $5.5 million for investigation and legal fees plus donate $10 million to children's charities to settle a lawsuit. In 2004, Air Canada had sued WestJet and several of its executives, in Ontario Superior Court, for $220 million. It was alleged that a former Air Canada employee, now employed by WestJet, passed on confidential, proprietary information to WestJet.

Apparently the former Air Canada employee, who continued to have access to an Air Canada website for the limited purpose of booking personal travel, gave his password to a WestJet executive. WestJet accessed Air Canada's website approximately a quarter of a million times and created automated technology to download and analyze passenger load and booking information. Air Canada claimed that, by obtaining this confidential information, WestJet was able to compile computer-generated reports for its own strategic planning, routing, and pricing decisions. WestJet countered with accusations that Air Canada hired private investigators to sift through an executive's garbage and then had a U.S. firm digitally reconstruct shredded documents.[71]

What obligations did WestJet have to Air Canada as a result of the decision to hire one of its former employees? Were WestJet's actions wrong, or was it just taking advantage of lax security?

For more study tools, visit http://www.NELSONbrain.com.

69. *Antidormi v Blue Pumpkin Software Inc*, 35 CCEL (3d) 247, 2004 CLLC 210-008 (Ont Sup Ct).
70. Dave McGinn, "Office blonde jokes no laughing matter", *The Globe and Mail* (24 November 2009) L3.
71. Craig Wong, "WestJet accused of spying", *The Globe and Mail* (7 April 2004) G1; Richard Blackwell, "Dogfight ends, war continues", *The Globe and Mail* (30 May 2006) B1.

CHAPTER 21

Terminating the Employment Relationship

Objectives

After studying this chapter, you should have an understanding of

- how the employment relationship ends

- the differences among dismissals for just cause, dismissals with notice, constructive dismissals, and wrongful dismissals

- the issues arising from a wrongful dismissal suit

- the components of a termination settlement

PHOTODISC

Business Law in Practice

Hiram Dupuis, the owner and operator of an independent newspaper in southern Ontario, is reviewing his options in light of a dramatic drop in circulation. In recent years, the newspaper industry has changed significantly due the merger of several large dailies and the advent of online sources of news. Hiram believes that there is still a role for the weekly community newspaper, but in order to survive he will have to downsize his workforce. He has come to the conclusion that Jeong Nash will have to go. Jeong, a staff reporter, is 32 years old and has been with the newspaper for a couple of years, but her stories are often controversial and Hiram has had to defend her on a couple of occasions. Most recently, a story she wrote about an aging basketball player has upset a number of advertisers, and they are threatening to take their business elsewhere.

The other change that Hiram is contemplating is the merger of two of the newspaper's departments—Community Homes & Gardens and Living in Our Community. The managers of the departments are 58-year-old Stella Blanchard, who has been with the newspaper for 25 years, and 37-year-old Josiah Rutgers, who has been with the newspaper for five years. As Stella is the older, more senior employee, Hiram wants to make her the manager of the new department. Josiah will retain his title and the same salary. The only difference is that, after the merger, he will report to Stella rather than to Hiram. The restructuring of the newspaper will give Hiram an opportunity to terminate the general manager, 56-year-old Levi Cameron. Although he has been with the newspaper for 15 years, he has, over the years, committed a number of infractions. He often tells off-colour jokes and sometimes makes comments about the appearance and dress of female colleagues. Recently, Hiram discovered inappropriate content on Levi's computer.

1. Is Hiram justified in terminating Jeong Nash and Levi Cameron?

2. Is Hiram entitled to change Josiah Rutgers' position?

3. What course of action would you advise Hiram to pursue?

Ending the Relationship

In many instances, the employment relationship ends in an amicable fashion. An employee resigns to pursue other interests, retires, or simply leaves at the end of a fixed-term employment contract.

The employment relationship can also come to an end through less pleasant means, as when the employer

- summarily dismisses, or fires, an employee
- gives the employee notice of termination
- acts in such a manner that the employment relationship becomes untenable

It is an implied term of an employment contract that an employer may terminate the employment relationship without any notice if there is "just cause." This implied term is subject to collective agreements and individual employment contracts, which may specify the terms for ending the employment relationship. The term is also subject to legislation that may give to certain employees, such as teachers, police officers, and firefighters, special rights in the case of dismissal.

It is also an implied term that an employer may terminate the employment contract by giving the employee reasonable notice of the termination. In this case the employer is not required to have a reason or cause for the termination. The implied term is also subject to collective agreements and individual employment contracts that provide for notice periods and rights on dismissal. As well, provincial and federal employment standards legislation provides for notice periods and procedures on dismissal. The periods of notice provided by the legislation are only minimum periods, and often employees are entitled to more notice.

This area of the law has become increasingly important for employers, owing to the courts' recognition of the importance of work in people's lives. It has been the subject of much litigation over the last couple of decades and thus has seen profound changes.

Dismissals for Just Cause

When there is **just cause**, an employer may dismiss an employee without notice. Just cause for dismissal means, in effect, that the employee has breached a fundamental term of the employment contract.

Just cause
Employee conduct that amounts to a fundamental breach of the employment contract.

Just cause exists when the employee is guilty of one or more of the following:

- serious misconduct
- habitual neglect of duty
- incompetence
- conduct incompatible with duties or prejudicial to the employer's business
- willful disobedience in a matter of substance[1]

---

1. *R v Arthurs, Ex parte Port Arthur Shipbuilding Co*, [1967] 2 OR 49, 62 DLR (2d) 342 (CA), reversed on other grounds, *Port Arthur Shipbuilding Co v Arthurs*, [1969] SCR 85, 70 DLR (2d) 693.

The grounds for dismissal with cause are easy to articulate but difficult to apply in practice, because whether an employee's conduct justifies dismissal is a question of fact that requires an assessment of the context and circumstances of the conduct. It is impossible to specify all of the conduct that may constitute just cause; however, it is possible to make some general comments about the various categories.

Is using the company computer for personal use grounds for dismissal?

CIG-TECHNOLOGY/GETSTOCK.COM

Serious Misconduct

A minor infraction by an employee is insufficient to justify dismissal, although the cumulative effect of many minor instances may be sufficient. The cumulative effect must be such that there is a serious impact on the employment relationship. For example, Levi's telling of an off-colour joke would not be sufficient grounds for dismissal. However, if the telling of the joke is combined with a number of other incidents, such as making inappropriate comments and having inappropriate content on his computer, then the cumulative effect of the incidents may be considered **serious misconduct**.

Serious misconduct
Intentional, harmful conduct of the employee that permits the employer to dismiss without notice.

If Hiram wants to terminate on the basis of an accumulation of a number of minor incidents, he has a duty to warn the employee and give an opportunity to improve performance. This duty is particularly important in situations where there is a **progressive discipline policy** in place. This is a system whereby the employer applies discipline for relatively minor infractions on a progressive basis. Each step in the progression carries a more serious penalty, until the last step—dismissal—is reached. The warning may be oral[2] or in writing and should be clear and understood by the employee. The employee should be advised not just about the unacceptable conduct, but also about the consequences of failure to improve.

Progressive discipline policy
A system that follows a sequence of employee discipline from less to more severe punishment.

A single act of misconduct can justify dismissal if it is sufficiently serious. For example, a single act of dishonesty can be sufficient grounds for dismissal, as when an employee steals a large sum of money from the employer. However, an act of dishonesty, in and of itself, is not necessarily sufficient to warrant just cause for dismissal. The nature and context of any dishonesty must be considered.[3] Other examples of conduct that may constitute

---

2. Warnings, especially oral warnings, need to be documented so that an employer can establish that the duty to warn was fulfilled.
3. *McKinley v BC Tel*, 2001 SCC 38, [2001] 2 SCR 161.

serious misconduct include lying to an employer, forging signatures and documents, and cheating. What constitutes serious misconduct may also be affected by workforce policies. For example, having an affair with a co-worker does not constitute just cause for dismissal unless the employer can prove that the conduct negatively affected the business or the employer has a policy against office romance.

An important principle with respect to any of the grounds for dismissal is **condonation**. Condonation occurs when an employer indicates through words or actions that behaviour constituting grounds for dismissal is being overlooked. For example, an employer who is aware of the harassing activities of an employee and who ignores or tolerates the activities will have difficulty arguing just cause for termination. Condonation occurs only if the employer is fully aware of the wrongful behaviour.

Condonation
Employer behaviour that indicates to the employee that misconduct is being overlooked.

Habitual Neglect of Duty

An employee may be terminated with cause for chronic absenteeism and lateness that are considered **habitual neglect of duty**. The absenteeism must be without the employer's permission or authorization and be more than an occasional absence. Important to this ground is whether warnings were issued, whether there was any excuse for the absence, and whether the absence occurred at a critical time for the employer.

Habitual neglect of duty
Persistent failure to perform employment duties.

BUSINESS APPLICATION OF THE LAW

The 16-Cent Firing

Nicole Lilliman, a three-year employee of a Tim Hortons franchise in London, Ontario, was caught on a surveillance videotape giving a 16-cent Timbit to a cranky baby. Two days later, she was called into the office by three managers and fired for theft. The termination papers stated "terminated for giving baby product without paying." Lilliman was hastily reinstated when the story went public and threatened to become a public relations nightmare. A spokesperson for Tim Hortons blamed the incidence on an overzealous manager at a store that had a policy against giving away food. Head office apologized to Lilliman, paid her for the lost days of work, and gave her a job at a Tim Hortons store close to where she was previously employed.

Critical Analysis: The cost of one Timbit is 16 cents. What were the costs to Tim Hortons for the firing of an employee for giving one away for free? What is the problem with "freebies"? How should Tim Hortons revamp its policies to prevent similar public relations disasters?

Should giving away free food be just cause for dismissing an employee?

COURTESY OF DARCY SAGE

Sources: Tavia Grant, "Tims eats humble pie to avert PR catastrophe", *The Globe and Mail* (9 May 2008) B1; Carly Weeks, "Cost of one Timbit: 16c", *The Globe and Mail* (12 May 2008) L1; and Gregory Bonnell, "Tim Hortons red-faced over free Timbit firing", *The Canadian Press* (8 May 2008) online: The Canadian Press <http:// conoe ca/CNEWS/WeirdNews/2008/05/08/5507571-cp.html>.

It is more difficult to establish lateness than absenteeism as grounds for dismissal. The courts will consider whether the employee had a valid excuse, whether there were warnings concerning lateness, and whether the time was ever made up, as well as related factors.

Incompetence

To dismiss on the ground of **incompetence**, the employer must be more than merely dissatisfied with an employee's work. There must be actual incompetence. The substandard

Incompetence
Lack of ability, knowledge, or qualification to perform employment obligations.

level of performance must be evident after the employee has been given a warning and an opportunity to improve. An employer must establish fair and reasonable performance standards against which to measure performance. An employee can raise a number of issues to explain poor performance—inadequate training, insufficient volume of business, inexperience, and condonation of performance problems.

A single act of incompetence is rarely grounds for dismissal, unless it shows a complete lack of skills that an employee claimed to have possessed.

Conduct Incompatible

Conduct incompatible
Personal behaviour that is irreconcilable with employment duties or prejudicial to the employer's business.

An employer may be justified in terminating with cause for **conduct incompatible** with the employee's duties or prejudicial to the employer's business—for example, accepting lavish and inappropriate gifts from the employer's clients. The conduct complained of is not limited to conduct on the job—it can also apply to conduct outside working hours. For example, a school board was deemed justified in dismissing a school superintendent who was convicted of a petty fraud outside the performance of his duties.[4]

TECHNOLOGY AND THE LAW

The Facebook Firings

Facebook, Twitter, blogs, and other social media are increasingly becoming part of the workplace. Employees are blogging, tweeting and accessing social networking websites, and often, the conversation is work. Inappropriate social networking—whether done at work or outside of the workplace—can, however, be just cause for dismissal. Employers have the right to terminate employees whose posting comments expose confidential information or have an impact on the employer's reputation or work environment.

In *Lougheed Imports Ltd (West Coast Mazda) v United Food and Commercial Workers International Union, Local 1518*,[5] the British Columbia Labour Relations Board upheld an employer's termination of two employees for posting inappropriate work-related comments on their personal Facebook profiles. The two employees, who worked at West Coast Mazda in Pitt Meadows, B.C., had been involved in the successful unionization of the workforce. During the unionization drive, they posted various derogatory and offensive comments in the statuses of their Facebook accounts. They openly called supervisors and managers offensive and insulting names and posted comments such as "don't spend your money at West Coast Mazda as they are crooks out to hose you and the shop ripped off a bunch of people I know." The comments increased in number and became increasingly angry once the union was certified. Among their 477 friends on Facebook were managers and

THOMAS COEX/AFP/GETTY IMAGES

When are the social media activities of employees grounds for dismissal?

co-workers, who were able to view every comment that was posted. When the comments included references to stabbing and TV's vigilante killer, Dexter, and homophobic slurs and threats, they were fired. The labour board found that despite the fact that the comments were off-site during non-work hours, they contributed to a hostile work environment and constituted insubordination.

Critical Analysis: Do you think the outcome might have been different if the comments had been made to a few friends on a password-protected blog or if their privacy settings on Facebook only included a few friends? How can employers reduce the risk of their legitimate business interests being harmed by the social media activities of their employees?

---

4. *Cherniwchan v County of Two Hills No. 21* (1982), 21 Alta LR (2d) 353, 38 AR 125 (QB).
5. 2010 CanLII 62482 (BC LRB).

Closely related to incompatible conduct is the ground for dismissal related to an employee's conflict of interest. For example, if an employee were to run a business that was in direct competition with the employer's business, it could be a breach of the employee's duty of loyalty and good faith to the employer.[6]

Willful Disobedience

An employer is entitled to expect an employee to carry out lawful and reasonable orders. Failure to do so is considered **willful disobedience**. A single act of disobedience would not ordinarily constitute grounds for dismissal, unless that act was very serious, such as not attending an important meeting or refusing to follow important safety rules. To rely on this ground, the employer would have to establish that the instructions or directions given to the employee were unambiguous and that the employee had no reasonable excuse for disobeying. Less serious instances of disobedience may justify dismissal when combined with other types of misconduct, such as insolence and insubordination.

Willful disobedience
Deliberate failure to carry out lawful and reasonable orders.

JOHN CUMMING/DIGITAL VISION/JUPITER IMAGES

Should an office romance be just cause for dismissal?

An employer is entitled to expect an employee to carry out orders without extended debate and with respect. Whether an employer is justified in terminating an employee who fails to meet this standard depends on a number of factors, such as whether the employee was provoked, whether the employee was upset, and whether it was a moment of temporary anger.

Other Causes

In addition to the grounds discussed thus far, there can be other bases for termination without notice. Most may fit within the general category of misconduct; examples include harassment (including sexual harassment), disruption of corporate culture, consumption of alcohol or drugs in the workplace, and drug abuse.

---

6. Stacey Ball, *Canadian Employment Law*, loose-leaf (Aurora: Canada Law Book, 2011) at 11–24.

However, each situation needs to be analyzed on its facts and examined in relation to whether the

- conduct was a single act

- conduct was condoned in some manner

- employee had a disability

- employee had been warned about conduct and the consequences of failure to improve

---

CASE — *McKinley v BC Tel*, 2001 SCC 38, [2001] 2 SCR 161

THE BUSINESS CONTEXT: Employers often argue that a single act of dishonest conduct by an employee gives rise to just cause for dismissal. Employees contend that any act, including dishonesty, should be judged on its context and its entirety.

FACTUAL BACKGROUND: Martin McKinley, 48, was a chartered accountant who worked 17 years for BC Tel. He held various positions with the company, and in 1991 was promoted to controller. In May 1993, he began to experience high blood pressure, and in May of the following year, on the advice of his physician, he took a leave of absence. By July, his supervisor raised the issue of termination. McKinley indicated that he wished to return to work in a position that carried less responsibility. However, alternative positions were never offered to him, and in August his employment was terminated. BC Tel claimed that it had just cause to dismiss McKinley as he had been dishonest about his medical condition and treatments available for it. He had failed to clearly disclose that his doctor told him he could return to work if he took a beta-blocker, a medication with various side effects.

THE LEGAL QUESTION: Does an employee's dishonest conduct, in and of itself, give rise to just cause for dismissal?

RESOLUTION: The court noted that there were two approaches that have been adopted in various Canadian jurisdictions.

One approach dictates that any dishonesty by an employee, however minor, is automatically considered just cause for dismissal. The other approach requires a determination of whether the nature and degree of the dishonesty warrants dismissal in the context of the entire employment relationship. The court adopted the "contextual" approach and restored the trial court's finding that McKinley had been wrongly dismissed. In other words, McKinley's conduct did not merit just cause for dismissal. The court did note, however, that in cases involving serious fraud, theft, or misappropriation, either approach would ultimately lead to a finding of just cause.

The court also went on to say that although less serious dishonesty may not merit firing without notice, "that is not to say that there cannot be lesser sanctions for less serious conduct. For example, an employer may be justified in docking an employee's pay for any loss incurred by a minor misuse of company property." The court indicated that this was one of several disciplinary measures that an employer might take in these circumstances.

CRITICAL ANALYSIS: Given that not all dishonesty is just cause, how big a lie must an employee tell before he can be fired for just cause? For example, could an employer fire an employee who left work early, saying he had a headache, and then went to the mall to shop?

Non-cause and Near Cause

There are many potential reasons or situations that may constitute just cause for dismissal. However, it is important to note that what might seem to be a good reason for terminating an employee is not necessarily just cause. For example, Hiram's newspaper has suffered economic setbacks, and although this is a good reason to scale back its workforce, it is not "just cause" for termination. Similarly, Jeong is a difficult employee, but although this may be a good reason to terminate her employment, again, it is not "just cause."

In the absence of just cause, the employer who wishes to terminate an employee is required to give notice or pay in lieu of notice. The period of notice will either be the term agreed upon in the employment contract, the period specified in employment standards legislation, or **reasonable notice**. What constitutes "reasonable" notice is to be determined in relation to factors such as age, length of service, availability of employment, and the status of the employee.

Reasonable notice
A period of time for an employee to find alternative employment prior to dismissal.

In some situations, an employer may have an employee who is neither particularly good nor bad. Is an employer entitled to give the "so-so" employee a lesser period of notice? In *Dowling v Halifax (City of)*,[7] a long-serving stationary engineer who would have been entitled to about 24 months' notice of termination had the notice period reduced to six months by the employer because of inappropriate conduct—favouring one contractor over another and making work difficult for the competing contractor. The Supreme Court flatly refused to accept any argument by the employer that the reduction was justified because of near cause and sent the matter back to the trial judge for an assessment of reasonable notice. Thus, either an employer has just cause to dismiss an employee and the employee is not entitled to any notice, or the employer does not have just cause to dismiss and the employee is entitled to the full period of reasonable notice. There is no halfway position.

However, the Supreme Court of Canada in *McKinley* indicates that conduct that does not merit dismissal without notice can be addressed by lesser sanctions. The court gives the example of an employer docking an employee's pay for dishonest conduct that does not warrant firing. This approach may open the door to employers giving forms of discipline such as suspensions for "near cause" conduct.

Risks in Just Cause Dismissals

Since an employee is not entitled to any compensation when dismissed for cause, the employee is more likely to bring a suit against the employer. An employer should carefully consider all of the potential costs of dismissing for cause and consider a termination settlement.

An employer who determines that dismissal for cause is justified can reduce the risks considerably by ensuring that sound policies and procedures for dismissal with just cause are established and practiced.

Dismissal with Notice

An employee who has been hired for an indefinite period of time may be dismissed at any time and without cause as long as the employer gives notice of the termination (or pay in lieu of notice).[8] While indefinite-term employment contracts are the norm in most industries, many individuals do work for fixed periods of time.[9] For those employees, their contracts end without any notice when the term expires. Termination of a fixed-term contract prior to its expiry is a breach of contract.

The period of notice required to terminate an indefinite-term employment contract is, as noted above, either the period agreed upon in the employment contract, the period specified in employment standards legislation, or reasonable notice. In many cases the parties do not agree in the employment contract on a period of notice, and even in cases when they do, the courts do not always uphold the provisions. This is particularly the case when the agreed-upon notice is considerably less than what would be implied by the courts as

---

7. [1998] 1 SCR 22, 222 NR 1.
8. Note that employers cannot give effective notice or payment in lieu of notice to someone who is unable to work, since an employee who is disabled or on pregnancy or parental leave cannot take advantage of the notice period to look for other work.
9. Note that a series of fixed-term contracts may be interpreted as a contract for an indefinite term. For example, in *Ceccol v Ontario Gymnastic Federation*, 55 OR (3d) 614, [2001] OJ No 3488 (CA), the Ontario Court of Appeal held that a series of 15 one-year contracts was an indefinite-term contract and therefore the employee was entitled to reasonable notice of termination.

reasonable notice. The courts may justify ignoring the contractual provisions on the basis that the circumstances of the employment contract have changed or that the contract was unfair and unconscionable. It is therefore often the case that employees are entitled to reasonable notice despite the contractual terms that provide for lesser periods of notice. The period of notice provided in employment standards legislation is a minimum period only[10] and does not override the reasonable notice common law obligation. Many employees are entitled to considerably more than the statutory period of notice. As Hiram is unlikely to establish just cause for terminating Jeong and possibly Levi, the better course of action is to give reasonable notice.

Reasonable Notice Periods

In theory, notice is a period of time to enable the soon-to-be terminated employee to find alternative employment. In determining how much notice, the primary factors to be considered are those set out in *Bardal v Globe & Mail Ltd*:[11]

- character of employment

- length of service

- age

- availability of similar employment

Character of Employment

This factor refers to whether the employee was at a high-status position in the organization. Generally, a senior, high-level, or management employee is entitled to more notice than a junior, non-management employee. For example, Levi occupies a higher position at the newspaper than Jeong, so on this basis Levi is entitled to more notice than Jeong. The rationale behind this factor is the assumption that it takes a higher-level employee a longer period of time to find alternative employment than it does a lower-level employee. In recent years, however, this distinction has been called into question. Mr. Justice McPherson in *Cronk v Canadian General Insurance*[12] noted that those who are better educated or professionally trained are more likely to obtain other employment after dismissal than individuals with fewer skills. His decision to grant a 55-year-old clerical worker with 35 years' experience 20 months' reasonable notice, however, was reduced to 12 months on appeal.[13] Nevertheless, the case is important because it signals a willingness on the part of the judiciary to re-examine the notice factors. Also, the Court of Appeal decision in *Cronk* has been severely criticized as being repugnant to modern social values in contemporary Canada, and subsequent courts have taken a narrow approach to the decision in order not to reduce notice periods. These cases have held that all of the factors in *Bardal* must be appropriately weighted, and an inappropriate weight should not be given to "character of employment."[14]

---

10. Typically, employment standards legislation provides one week of notice for each year of service up to a maximum of eight weeks, whereas reasonable notice for middle-level employees is, on average, more like one month of notice for each year of service up to a maximum of 24 months.

11. [1960] OWN 253, 24 DLR (2d) 140 (Ont HC). These factors were endorsed by the Supreme Court of Canada in *Machtinger v HOJ Industries Ltd*, [1992] 1 SCR 986, 91 DLR (4th) 491.

12. (1994), 19 OR (3d) 515, 6 CCEL (2d) 15 (Gen Div).

13. (1995), 25 OR (3d) 505, 85 OAC 54 (CA).

14. *Supra* note 6 at 9–24.

Length of Service

A longer-term employee is entitled to more notice than a shorter-term employee. On this basis Levi, with 15 years' service, is entitled to more notice than Jeong, with a mere two years' service. The rationale is that a long-serving employee does not have the same degree or breadth of experience as an employee who has had several shorter-term jobs. In essence, a long-serving employee has a smaller range of comparable re-employment prospects.

Reasonable notice is not calculated by a rule of thumb of one month of notice for every year of service.[15] Short-term employees, in particular, have often received notice periods well above the one-month per year of service benchmark.

Age

Older employees, particularly those over 50 years of age, are entitled to more notice than younger employees because they have more difficulty in finding employment. Many employers are unwilling to hire older persons. Levi, at 56 years of age, is entitled to more notice than 32-year-old Jeong.

Younger employees in their 20s and 30s are generally entitled only to short periods of notice despite high rates of unemployment among youth.

FUSE/JUPITER IMAGES

Why are older employees generally entitled to more notice than younger employees?

Availability of Similar Employment

The more employment opportunities available, the shorter the period of notice to which the employee will be entitled. The availability of employment opportunities may be gauged by expert opinion of job openings, advertisements, and other indicators of market conditions. From a practical perspective, the availability of job opportunities will be affected by an employee's experience, training, and qualifications.

---

15. *Supra* note 6 at 9–14.

Developments in Notice

Although the factors in *Bardal v Globe & Mail* remain of prime importance in determining reasonable notice, they are not an exhaustive list. Other factors that tend to lengthen notice are

- a high degree of specialization
- inducement to join an organization
- company policy
- custom and industry practice
- personal characteristics
- economic climate[16]

Risks in Dismissal with Notice

The calculation of reasonable notice is a task fraught with uncertainty. Although the factors used in the calculation are well known, the weight to be given to each is uncertain; the only certainty is that each factor must be appropriately weighted. Most courts list the factors and then state a period of notice without indicating whether one factor has been given more weight than another. Notice periods have generally increased, and there have even been cases where the notice period has exceeded two years.[17] This development suggests that there is not a general cap on notice, although in most provinces it is recognized that the maximum range for reasonable notice is between 18 and 24 months.[18]

How much notice would Levi and Jeong be entitled to? Levi is a 56-year-old management employee with 15 years' experience and unknown employment opportunities. He would be entitled to approximately 16 to 18 months' notice. Jeong is a 32-year-old staff reporter with two years' experience and unknown employment opportunities. She would probably be entitled to notice of one to two months.

Constructive Dismissal

An employer has no entitlement to make a fundamental change to the employment contract without the employee's consent. The employee may accept the change and create a new employment contract or refuse to accept the change, quit, and sue for what is called **constructive dismissal**. The dismissal is not express—the employer has not said to the employee, "You're fired"—but changing a key aspect of the employment contract may be equivalent to dismissal.

Constructive dismissal
Employer conduct that amounts to a breach of a fundamental term of the employment contract.

Fundamental term
A term that is considered to be essential to the contract.

Fundamental Changes

For constructive dismissal to arise, the employer must make a significant change to a **fundamental term** of the contract without the employee's consent. A minor change

---

16. See generally Ellen Mole & Marion J Stendon, *The Wrongful Dismissal Handbook*, 3d ed (Markham, Ontario: LexisNexis, 2004) at 255–281.
17. See, for example, *Baranowski v Binks Manufacturing Co* (2000), 49 CCEL (2d) 170, 93 ACWS (3d) 1033 (Ont SCJ), where the court awarded 30 months' notice; and *UPM-Kymmene Miramichi Inc v Walsh*, 2003 NBCA 32, 257 NBR (2d) 331 where the court awarded 28 months' notice.
18. *Supra* note 6 at 9.

will not generally trigger a constructive dismissal, although the cumulative effect of many minor changes may do so. As well, the employment contract may reserve for the employer the right to make certain unilateral changes without triggering a constructive dismissal. For example, geographical transfers are often provided for in the contract.

CASE — **Farber v Royal Trust Co, [1997] 1 SCR 846, 145 DLR (4th) 1**

THE BUSINESS CONTEXT: In the 1980s, it was common to see whole industries restructure and downsize. Many employees lost their jobs; others saw their jobs changed.

FACTUAL BACKGROUND: In June 1984, as part of a major restructuring of its real estate arm in Quebec, Royal Trust decided to eliminate all but one of its regional manager positions.[19] At the time, David Farber, 44, was the highly regarded regional manager for western Quebec. He had been with the company for 18 years and had received many promotions. As regional manager, he supervised 400 real estate agents and administered 21 offices, whose real estate sales exceeded $16 million in 1983. He had a base salary of $48 800, but with commissions and benefits, his earnings were $150 000 in 1983.

Royal Trust offered him the manager's job at one of the company's least profitable branches in Quebec—a position he had been promoted from eight years previously. The branch employed 20 real estate agents and had sales of $616 000 in 1983. As well, the company proposed to eliminate his base salary and pay him by commission only. Farber estimated that his income would be reduced by half. He tried to negotiate with the company, but to no avail. He was told to appear at the new branch on a certain date; if he did not, he would be deemed to have resigned. Farber did not show up for work and sued.

THE LEGAL QUESTION: Had Farber been constructively dismissed from his job?

RESOLUTION: Farber lost both at trial and on appeal largely owing to the admission of evidence showing that sales at the new branch were very good in 1984 and that Farber would have earned about the same as he had earned in 1983. The trial judge, in particular, thought that Royal Trust's offer was reasonable and adequate, both in terms of money and prestige, and that Farber should have accepted it.

The Supreme Court of Canada overturned the decision and awarded Farber damages equivalent to one year's pay. The court held that where an employer decides unilaterally to make substantial changes to the essential terms of an employee's contract and the employee does not agree to the changes and leaves his job, the employee has not resigned, but has been dismissed. This is a constructive dismissal. The test for determining whether a substantial change is made is an objective one; the basic question is whether at the time of the change the reasonable person would believe that essential terms of the employment contract were being changed. Subsequent evidence of what actually happened is irrelevant—the critical time for assessment is the time the changes were made. The change to Farber's employment was substantial, since it amounted to a demotion with less income.

The court also noted that an employer can make changes to an employee's position, but the extent of the changes depends on what the parties agreed to at the time of entering into the contract. Constructive dismissal does not have to involve bad faith on the part of the employer. There need be no intent on the employer's part to force the employee out. In other words, sound business reasons for making changes are not a defence in a constructive dismissal suit.

CRITICAL ANALYSIS: Do you think the doctrine of constructive dismissal unduly affects a company's ability to manage its affairs?

Generally, the changes that are considered to be fundamental are adverse changes to salary or benefits, job function, responsibility, and the power/reporting structures, although other changes may be considered fundamental, depending on the circumstances. It is negative changes that trigger constructive dismissal, as employees normally readily accept positive changes. Hiram's contemplated merger of two departments with the result that Josiah reports to Stella rather than Hiram may trigger a constructive dismissal. Even though Josiah may have the same job title and may be earning the same money, changing the reporting structure is, in effect, a demotion.

---

19. Although this case arose in Quebec and was decided pursuant to the civil law, the court noted that the doctrine of constructive dismissal, a creature of the common law, is now also part of the civil law. The case therefore has application to Canadian jurisdictions outside Quebec.

"Bad" Behaviour

Although most constructive dismissal cases involve demotions and pay cuts, the doctrine is not limited to these kinds of factors. Unacceptable or unethical practices by an employer may amount to constructive dismissal. For example, the BC Supreme Court awarded constructive dismissal damages to an employee who quit when he discovered that his boss was sending out fraudulent bills.[20] Humiliating or abusive behaviour, such as shouting and swearing, and threats of dismissal can also constitute constructive dismissal.[21]

In *Shah v Xerox Canada Ltd*,[22] the Ontario Court of Appeal upheld an employee's claim of constructive dismissal where the employer's conduct, which included unjustified criticisms and unfair performance appraisals, created intolerable working conditions. The court indicated that it is unnecessary that an employee establish that the employer breached a specific term of the employment contract. It is sufficient that the employee prove a poisoned or intolerable work environment.

In *Carscallen v FRI Corporation*,[23] a marketing executive was suspended without pay after a botched trade show and a heated exchange with her boss. The court held that, unless a specific term in the contract of employment permitted suspension without pay, it is considered to be constructive dismissal.

Risks in Constructive Dismissal

Before making changes that affect an employee's job, employers need to consider the nature of the change, whether the change is likely to be acceptable to the employee, why the change is being made, and whether there are any contractual provisions that permit the contemplated changes. An employer could also provide a "try-out" period during which the employee can assess the changes prior to being required to accept them. These actions can help minimize the risk of triggering a constructive dismissal. Employers should also have procedures and systems in place for dealing with incidents or complaints of "bad" behaviour.

Wrongful Dismissal Suit

A wrongful dismissal suit may arise in several situations, such as when an employee has been dismissed for cause and the employee claims there was no just cause, or when an employee is given notice of dismissal and the employee claims the notice was inadequate. Wrongful dismissal can also arise from a constructive dismissal. An employee is not obligated to go to a court to claim wrongful dismissal; she may proceed by making a claim to an employment standards tribunal. This action would limit an employee's compensation to an amount equivalent to the statutory period of notice. It is the route most often used by low-level employees, as they are often entitled to no more than the statutory notice and this method is considerably less expensive.

---

20. *Nethery v Lindsey Morden Claim Services Ltd*, 1999 BCCA 340, 127 BCAC 237.
21. See *Lloyd v Imperial Parking Ltd* (1996), 192 AR 190, 46 Alta LR (3d) 220 (QB).
22. 131 OAC 44, [2000] OJ No 849 (CA).
23. 2006 CLLC 210-037, 52 CCEL (3d) 161 (Ont CA).

ETHICAL CONSIDERATIONS

Whistleblowers and the Law

The term "whistleblowers" is often used to describe employees who "blow the whistle" or report wrongdoing involving their employers. Employees who disclose irregularities and fraud are sometimes greeted as heroes; often, however, they are viewed as rats or cranks and subjected to acts of retaliation and termination from their employment.

Take, for example, Linda Merk, the office manager and bookkeeper for Iron Workers Local 771 in Regina, Saskatchewan. She complained of irregular payment practices by the local's president and the business manager. She alleged that they had misused a union credit card and were triple-claiming some expenses. She reported the wrongdoing to her direct supervisor, then to the board of trustees that reviews the monthly bills, then to the auditor who did the annual statement of the union, and then to the director of the international union. She was fired.

Merk invoked s 74 of Saskatchewan's *Labour Standards Act*,[24] which states, in part, that "no employer shall discharge or threaten to discharge an employee because the employee has reported or proposed to report to a lawful authority any activity that is likely to result in an offence." She won the first successful private prosecution under a whistleblower law in Canada. However, the union was later acquitted by a split Saskatchewan Court of Appeal. It held that the law did not protect her because she complained to her bosses, who were not a "lawful authority." The Supreme Court of Canada disagreed, stating that "[T]he plain meaning of 'lawful authority' includes those who exercise authority in both the private and public interest." This includes individuals within the employer organization who exercise lawful authority over the employees complained about or over the activity that may result in an offence. Merk was ultimately reinstated to her job and awarded $250 000

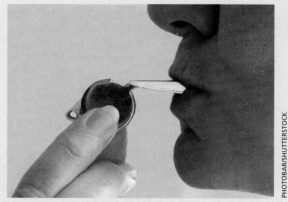

What protection, if any, should be given whistleblowers in the workplace?

PHOTOBAR/SHUTTERSTOCK

in compensation. The union was fined $2000 for a first offence under the legislation.

Whistleblowers also receive protection under the *Criminal Code* when they report wrongdoing that is an offence contrary to any provincial or federal act or regulation. Section 425.1 makes it a criminal offence to retaliate against any employee that reports unlawful conduct on the part of the employer or by directors, officers, or other employees of the employer.

Critical Analysis: Does whistle-blowing by an employee conflict with the employee's duty of loyalty and good faith to the employer? How should an employee's duty of loyalty and good faith be reconciled with the public's interest in exposing corporate wrongdoing? How can employees be encouraged to disclose corporate wrongdoing?

Sources: Deanna Driver, "Can a whistleblower return to work for business as usual?", *The Lawyers Weekly* (16 February 2007) 7; Deanna Driver, "Whistleblower reinstated to her job in Saskatchewan", *The Lawyers Weekly* (24 February 2006) 1; and *Merk v International Assn of Bridge, Structural, Ornamental and Reinforcing Iron Workers, Local 771*, 2005 SCC 70, [2005] 3 SCR 425.

Specific performance or reinstatement is rarely an option in the non-unionized sector.[25] The common law does not provide for this remedy, on the rationale that after a termination the employment relationship is usually irreparably damaged.

Manner of Dismissal

An employer who conducts a dismissal "in bad faith" or in an unfair manner may be vulnerable to additional damages beyond those required for reasonable notice.

---

24. RSS 1978, c L-1.
25. Human rights legislation, however, provides for reinstatement.

CASE   *Wallace v United Grain Growers*, [1997] 3 SCR 701, [1997] SCJ No 94

THE BUSINESS CONTEXT: Termination of employment can be a traumatic event for the employee. When such an event is handled in bad faith, it can be especially devastating.

FACTUAL BACKGROUND: Jack Wallace, 59, had been a marketing manager for United Grain Growers for 14 years when he was terminated without explanation. Prior to his employment with United, he had worked for a competitor for 25 years. When he was originally approached by United, he was disinclined to leave his stable job. However, he was assured that if he performed satisfactorily he could work until retirement. In fact, he was United's top sales representative in each year prior to his abrupt termination. He sued for wrongful dismissal, whereupon the company alleged that it had cause to fire him. The company claimed that he was insubordinate and failed to carry out his duties. This allegation was abandoned at trial. The termination of employment and the allegations of cause created emotional difficulties for Wallace. He was forced to seek psychiatric help, was unable to find another job, and eventually declared bankruptcy.

THE LEGAL QUESTION: How much notice was Wallace entitled to?

RESOLUTION: The Supreme Court awarded Wallace 24 months' notice—14 months for reasonable notice based on age, length of service, and limited prospects for re-employment, and another 10 months for United's bad-faith conduct in the manner of dismissal.

The court stated that the end of the employment relationship is a very traumatic time for an employee—a time when the employee is most vulnerable and in need of protection. To ensure that the employee receives protection, employers ought to be held to an obligation of good faith and fair dealing in the manner of the dismissal. Mr. Justice Iacobucci wrote:

> The obligation of good faith and fair dealing is incapable of precise definition. However, at a minimum, I believe that in the course of dismissal employers ought to be candid, reasonable, honest and forthright with their employees and should refrain from engaging in conduct which is unfair or in bad faith by being for example, untruthful, misleading, or unduly insensitive.

The court found several examples of bad faith on the part of United—the abrupt manner of dismissal after complimenting him on his work only days before; unfounded allegations of cause, which were maintained until the day of the trial; and the conscious decision of United to play "hardball" with Wallace. The finding of bad faith extended the notice period. The extension compensated for intangible injuries such as humiliation, embarrassment, and loss of self-esteem as well as tangible injuries to the employee's prospects for future employment.

CRITICAL ANALYSIS: The Supreme Court decision requires an employer to pay extra damages when unfounded allegations are made in the termination process or the employer otherwise treats the dismissed employee in a reprehensible fashion. Should employees be required to pay damages when they make unfounded, damaging, or irresponsible claims in the termination process?

The *Wallace* decision introduced the standard of good faith and fair dealing into the workplace. In addition to the instance of alleging cause when there is none, the Supreme Court gave several examples of bad faith:

- refusing to provide a deserved letter of reference
- terminating while on disability leave
- failing to communicate a termination decision in a timely manner
- communicating false allegations to potential employers

Since *Wallace* the courts have found a breach of the duty of good faith and fair dealing in numerous circumstances—failing to conduct a proper investigation prior to dismissal, neglecting to give an employee an opportunity to explain her version of events, conducting the termination insensitively, withholding statutory severance unless the employee signs a release, being insensitive in timing the termination, escorting an employee out the door, and making it difficult for an employee to find new employment.[26] Also, *Wallace* damages have not been limited to acts of the employer at the time of termination but may also involve pre- and post-termination conduct.[27]

The *Wallace* factor has resulted in courts increasing or "bumping up" the notice period to compensate for bad-faith termination. The Supreme Court of Canada, however, has called into question this approach and has changed the way in which damages related to the manner of dismissal are awarded. In *Honda v Keays* (see page 536), the court stated that damages for the manner of dismissal must be based on the losses employees actually suffer and are no longer to be awarded by arbitrarily extending the notice period. If an employee can prove that the manner of dismissal caused mental distress, the damages should be awarded through an award that reflects the actual damage, not an arbitrary extension of the notice period.

Wrongful Dismissal Damages

Once a court determines how many months' notice a successful claimant is entitled to, the general approach is to multiply this number by the salary and the benefits that the employee was entitled to for each month. In addition, the claimant may be entitled to other special damages for out-of-pocket losses associated with the termination. From the total, a deduction may be made for any money earned (income from a new job) or received (employment insurance) during the notice period. As well, a deduction may be made for a failure to mitigate damages by promptly seeking replacement employment. Figure 21.1 illustrates a typical damage award in a successful wrongful dismissal case.

FIGURE 21.1

A Sample Damage Award for Wrongful Dismissal

Millyard Systems Manager, 53 years old, 20 years of service, $84 000 annual salary

Base salary: ($7, 075.83 × 18 months[28])	$127 364.94
Bonus: ($910 × 18)	16 380
Commissions ($1500 × 18)	27 000
Employee share purchase plan ($140 × 18)	2 520
Health care spending account ($25 × 18)	450
Medical services plan ($90 × 18)	1 620
Extended medical and dental coverage ($99 × 18)	1 782
Long-term disability ($172.12 × 18)	3 098.16
Car allowance (includes a component for ongoing lease commitments)	15 600
Total damages	$195 815.10

Source: *Jamieson v Finning International Inc*, 2009 BCSC 861, [2009] BCWLD 5513.

A claimant may also be entitled to other types of damages, such as aggravated and punitive damages. Aggravated damages are designed to compensate the victim and they focus on the employee's losses. Punitive damages are designed to punish the wrong-doer and

---

26. Bill Rogers, "The *'Wallace'* Factor': Where's the Top?", *The Lawyers Weekly* (2 April 1999) 7.
27. *Supra* note 6 at 22.59.
28. The damages were based on a 19-month notice period, with a one month deduction for the possibility of mitigation earnings, as the decision was handed down well in advance of the expiry of the notice period.

they focus on the employer's conduct. Aggravated and punitive damages will be awarded only where the damages arise from a separate, actionable wrong, such as deceit, breach of fiduciary duty, abuse of power, or defamation. These damages, particularly punitive damages are generally awarded only in very exceptional circumstances.

CASE — *Honda Canada Inc v Keays*, 2008 SCC 39, [2008] 2 SCR 362

THE BUSINESS CONTEXT: When an employee carries a white cane, wears a hearing aid, or sits in a wheelchair, an employer's duty to accommodate is obvious. When an employee has a "hidden" disability—depression, mental illness, chronic fatigue syndrome—the employer has no less an obligation to accommodate.

FACTUAL BACKGROUND: Kevin Keays began working at Honda's Alliston, Ontario, assembly plant in 1986. After 20 months on the production line, he moved to the Quality Engineering Department, where he became a specialist in implementing design changes in cars. His health deteriorated, and in 1996 he began receiving disability payments. Two years later the payments were terminated when the insurance company concluded that his claim could not be supported by "objective medical evidence." He returned to work, although his doctor had diagnosed him as suffering from chronic fatigue syndrome. Keays continued to experience work absences, and when he claimed that a disability caused his absences, Honda put him on a program that required him to produce a doctor's note every time he was absent. When Keays' absences exceeded his doctor's estimates, he was directed to the company doctor, who expressed reservations about his condition and suggested that he should be sent back to the production line. When Honda subsequently requested him to see an independent medical specialist, Keays refused to go unless the company clearly stated the purpose of the second medical assessment. The company refused and terminated Keays for insubordination. Keays was advised of his termination by a co-worker who phoned him at home to tell him that his dismissal had been announced to the department.

THE LEGAL QUESTION: Was Keays wrongfully terminated from his employment? If so, what is the appropriate remedy?

RESOLUTION: The trial court found that Keays had been wrongfully dismissed, and it awarded 15 months' salary in lieu of notice. The court concluded that Honda's request for Keays to see the independent medical specialist was not made in good faith but was made as a prelude to terminating him to avoid having to accommodate his disability. Keays, because of previous difficulties with his employer over his absences, had a reasonable basis for believing that Honda would continue to

When are employers required to pay punitive damages in wrongful dismissal cases?

DAVID HARTLEY/REX FEATURES/THE CANADIAN PRESS

refuse to recognize the legitimacy of his disability. Therefore, Keays had good cause for his failure to follow the employer's direction. Honda's reaction to Keays' alleged insubordination was disproportionate. It was not just cause for dismissing Keays. The court also awarded an additional nine months of *Wallace* damages for the manner of dismissal and $500 000 in punitive damages for the discriminatory and highhanded treatment of Keays by Honda.

The Ontario Court of Appeal upheld the 15-month notice period and the nine-month *Wallace* extension, but reduced the punitive damages to $100 000 on the basis that the trial judge relied on findings of fact that were not supported by the evidence and because the award did not meet the requirement of proportionality. In particular, the appeal court stated that the trial judge's finding that Honda's outrageous conduct had persisted over a period of five years was a gross distortion of the circumstances. The misconduct for which Honda was responsible took place over a seven-month period. Also, while the appeal court acknowledged the gravity of some of Honda's conduct, it could not be characterized as "malicious."

The Supreme Court of Canada agreed that 15 months was an appropriate period of notice for Keays' almost 14 years of service but eliminated the nine-month *Wallace* extension and the award of punitive damages.

With respect to the elimination of the nine-month *Wallace* extension, the court stated that damages for a bad-faith dismissal are available only if the employee can prove that the manner of dismissal actually caused mental distress and the distress suffered by the employee was in the contemplation of the parties at the time of entering the employment contract (the normal distress and hurt feelings resulting from dismissal are not compensable as it is not within the contemplation of the parties that these would be compensated). In other words, in order to receive damages for mental distress, the employee must show that the employer's behaviour in termination was particularly egregious and its effect on the employee caused more harm than the normal impact of termination. The court also stated that awarding damages for bad-faith dismissal by an arbitrary increase to the period of reasonable notice is no longer the appropriate method. Damages are to be awarded through an award that reflects the actual damages. The Supreme Court concluded that Honda's conduct was "in no way an egregious display of bad faith justifying an award of damages for conduct in dismissal."

With respect to punitive damages, the court stated they must be awarded only in "exceptional cases" where the employer's bad faith acts "are so malicious and outrageous that they are deserving of punishment on their own." They are only recoverable if the conduct gives rise to an independent "actionable wrong." The court overturned the lower court's finding that a breach of human rights legislation can serve as an independent actionable wrong. Human rights claims are to be dealt with by human rights tribunals, not the courts.

CRITICAL ANALYSIS: What does this decision mean for employers?

Duty to Mitigate

Employees who have been terminated or constructively dismissed have a duty to mitigate their damages. The duty, however, does not arise in all circumstances. The Ontario Court of Appeal in a recent decision[29] held that when an employment contract stipulates the specific notice period to which an employee will be entitled on termination, and is silent on the duty to mitigate, the dismissed employee is not under an obligation to mitigate her damages. In other words, the employer is required to make all the payments specified in the contract without a deduction for failure to mitigate or for income earned from alternative employment during the notice period.

When the duty arises, it requires that an employee takes reasonable steps to find comparable employment. What is required of an employee depends on the nature of the job, on the job market, and on the way that a job would normally be obtained in that market (e.g., by searching newspaper advertisements, registering at a human resource centre, searching the Internet, or engaging the services of an employment agency).

The duty requires the employee to look for comparable or similar employment. It does not require an employee to take or look for a lower-level job. Nor does it usually require an employee to take a lower position with the same employer, since working at the same place after a dismissal may be untenable.[30]

Whether the duty to mitigate requires an employee to move to look for employment depends on a host of factors, including age of employee, family situation, attachment to the community, prospects of employment in the present area, and the housing market. A failure to mitigate will result in a deduction from the damages awarded. The amount of the reduction varies and depends on the circumstances.

---

29. *Bowes v Goss Power Products Ltd*. 2012 ONCA 446 (CanLII).
30. See *Farquhar v Butler Brothers Supplies Ltd*, 23 BCLR (2d) 89, [1988] 3 WWR 347 (CA).

Terminated employees have a duty to mitigate their damages. What does this duty entail?

CHUCK STOODY/THE CANADIAN PRESS

Developments in Wrongful Dismissal Suits

In addition to wrongful dismissal suits, some employees have turned to other avenues to procure relief. In some situations the dismissed employee can sue for defamation. The advantage of this route is that damages for defamation are usually significantly higher than those for breach of the employment contract, as the amount of damages is not limited by the notice period. As well, the courts are more willing to award punitive damages pursuant to a defamation claim. A further claim that can be made by an employee is intentional infliction of mental suffering.[31]

Regardless of the action taken by a dismissed employee, litigation is an expensive process. It is a particularly expensive proposition in cases where an employee may not be entitled to a large sum of money in compensation if successful, even though there is legitimate cause of action. However, the availability of contingency fee arrangements, the class action suit, and alternative dispute mechanisms is changing these dynamics somewhat and making it feasible for a group of ill-treated employees to pursue small claims.

Termination Settlements

The costs associated with a wrongful dismissal suit can be high. Therefore, it may be incumbent on an employer to offer a termination settlement or severance package rather than dismiss for just cause.

Negotiation of the Settlement

Severance pay
An amount owed to a terminated employee under employment standards legislation.

The package offered should contain all monies due to the employee at the time of termination including statutory entitlements such as **severance pay**. The package may also include other items such as pension benefits, medical or dental coverage, disability insurance, tax-sheltered income, stock options, and financial or career counselling. An employer should also consider providing a factual letter of reference to assist the employee. An employee should be given a period of time (one to two weeks) to consider the termination settlement and should be encouraged to seek independent advice on the fairness of the offer.

---

31. The Ontario Court of Appeal has awarded damages for such a claim in the employment context. See *Prinzo v Baycrest Centre for Geriatric Care* (2002), 60 OR (3d) 474, 161 OAC 302 (CA).

The termination settlement may help the departed employee feel better about the termination. A fair offer and settlement may also help keep remaining employees motivated. A fair settlement may ultimately avoid a lawsuit and be less costly in the long run. It also helps maintain a positive corporate image.

The Release

When an employee accepts a termination package, it is customary to have the employee sign a **release**. The release normally indicates that the employee has been dismissed and paid a sum of money in return for giving up any right of action against the employer. The release form may include a stipulation that the employee will not pursue an action for wrongful dismissal, as well as a statement that the employee has not been discriminated against, and therefore will not pursue a claim under human rights legislation. It may also contain provisions to keep the settlement confidential and restrictions preventing the employee from competing against the former employer.

A release will normally be binding on the employee, provided that the settlement was fair and reasonable, the release was clear and unambiguous, and the employee had ample time to consider the package and obtain independent advice. On the other hand, a release will likely be unenforceable if the termination package was "unconscionable" and the employee did not obtain independent advice.

Release
A written or oral statement discharging another from an existing duty.

The Union Context

The provisions of a collective agreement will vary depending on the nature of the industry involved and the issues the parties bring to the negotiating table. The agreement will provide for a process for settling disputes arising from the agreement. This procedure is usually the only route a unionized employee has to challenge an employer's dismissal decision.[32] The final step in the procedure is arbitration, which is binding on the parties. Unlike the situation in the non-unionized sector, courts do not make the final decision.

In addition, most agreements will have specific provisions relating to termination.

Grievance and Arbitration

Regardless of the individual content of collective agreements, disputes about their interpretation, administration, or application are required to be submitted to a **grievance process**. The grievance procedure will vary widely from organization to organization. Some procedures involve only a couple of steps; others have several. All usually have time limits attached to the steps, and most begin with an informal consultation. The final step in almost all jurisdictions is third-party binding arbitration.[33] This step arises when the dispute cannot be resolved by less formal means and all the other steps in the grievance process have failed.

The arbitration itself usually involves either a single arbitrator or a three-person panel that conducts a hearing of the grievance and renders a decision. The arbitrator may dismiss the grievance; order compensation for breach of the collective agreement; order reinstatement of

Grievance process
A procedure for resolving disputes contained in union contracts.

---

32. The existence of a collective agreement that applies to an employee and provides for final settlement of disputes bars a wrongful dismissal action. *Supra* note 16 at 128.
33. Saskatchewan is the exception.

the employee without loss of seniority and with back wages and benefits; or, in most jurisdictions, fashion a remedy somewhere between dismissal and full reinstatement. The arbitration award can be filed with the court and enforced in the same manner as a judicial decision.

Seniority

Most collective agreements contain an extensive clause dealing with seniority (the length of time the employee has been with the company). These clauses usually provide that an employer cannot promote, demote, transfer, lay off (usually defined as temporary suspension of the employment relationship), or recall without giving some consideration to the seniority of the employee. These clauses do not, however, affect the employer's ability to terminate the employment relationship (usually referred to as "discharge" in labour law).

Discipline and Discharge

The general rule in the union context is that an employer may not discipline or discharge an employee without justification or just cause.

The discipline and discharge of employees is the largest category of grievances carried to arbitration. In assessing whether the penalty imposed by the employer was appropriate in the circumstances, the arbitrator will look for evidence of progressive discipline. In other words, discipline should progress from warnings to suspensions and only finally to discharge. In upholding a particular penalty imposed by an employer, the arbitrator will consider many factors, including the following:

- the record and service of the employee

- provocation

- any special economic hardship imposed on the employee by the penalty

- the seriousness of the offence

- premeditation

- uniform enforcement of policies and rules

- circumstances negating intent

- condonation

The arbitrator has the authority to mitigate or soften the severity of the penalty imposed by the employer. In other words, the arbitrator may substitute his judgment for that of management (unless the collective agreement mandates a specific penalty for the infraction).

Business Law in Practice Revisited

1. Is Hiram justified in terminating Jeong Nash and Levi Cameron?

A dramatic drop in circulation that results in a genuine lack of work is a good reason for terminating employees, but it is not legal or just cause, which deprives employees of reasonable notice. Jeong's controversial stories do not amount to incompetence or misconduct, particularly in view of Hiram's apparent condonation. The cumulative effect of Levi's infractions—off-colour jokes, sexist comments, and inappropriate material on his computer—may constitute misconduct. However, prior to dismissal, the employer must consider the following questions: Was Levi's behaviour contrary to a company policy? Was Levi aware of the company policy? Was Levi given a warning about his behaviour? Did he understand that failure to improve could lead to termination? That said, a single incidence of bad conduct may be sufficient grounds for dismissal without notice. For example, if Levi downloaded truly offensive material onto his work computer, that could amount to grounds for dismissal.

2. Is Hiram entitled to change Josiah Rutgers' position?

The merger of two departments resulting in a change to the reporting structure may trigger a constructive dismissal. Although Josiah would receive the same pay and have the same title, reporting to Stella rather than Hiram is an obvious demotion. Hiram may want to consider whether Josiah is likely to accept the change and whether there are sufficient benefits to the change that, in the overall context, he will not view the change negatively. Also, Hiram may want to offer Josiah a period of time to try out the change to see if he likes it. An employer is entitled to make some changes without triggering a dismissal; Hiram should check Josiah's employment contract to see what is permissible.

3. What course of action would you advise Hiram to pursue?

As it is highly unlikely that Hiram has grounds to dismiss Jeong and, possibly, Levi, he needs to consider what a reasonable settlement would be. Levi is an older, long-serving, high-level employee, so he is probably entitled to notice somewhere in the 16- to 18-month range. For Jeong, a younger, shorter-term, low-level employee, reasonable notice would probably be somewhere in the one- to two-month range. The amount of notice for both employees is affected in either direction by the availability of alternative employment. Hiram should seek legal advice on this issue, as this area of the law is somewhat unpredictable and subject to rapid change.

Hiram should know that the proposed change in Josiah's position may trigger a constructive dismissal. He needs to consider whether Josiah is likely to view the change negatively. If that is likely, Hiram needs to reconsider the change or terminate Josiah's employment with reasonable notice. As a younger, short-term, middle-level employee, Josiah is likely entitled to notice in the two- to four-month range—depending, again, on alternative employment opportunities.

Hiram should carefully choose the manner of dismissal. The amount of damages payable to employees in the event of a wrongful dismissal action could be severely affected by any bad-faith conduct on his part, such as alleging cause when there is none, escorting the employee out the door, refusing to provide a fair reference, or otherwise acting in bad faith.

Chapter Summary

Employment ends when an employee resigns or retires, or when the employer dismisses, gives notice, or otherwise terminates the relationship. An employer may, subject to contractual provisions, summarily terminate an employee if just cause exists. What constitutes just cause is a question of fact, but it must involve a situation where the employee has breached a fundamental term of the employment contract. In the absence of just cause, an employer must give notice of termination (or pay in lieu of notice). Notice is either what is specified in the employment contract or employment legislation, or reasonable notice. The latter is determined by reference to the employee's age, position within the organization, and length of service, and by the availability of alternative employment. When the employer breaches a fundamental term of the employment contract (i.e., demotes or cuts pay), the employee may treat the breach as a constructive dismissal. The termination of employment by the employer is often a traumatic event in the life of the employee. Courts have increasingly put an onus on the employer to act fairly and decently toward the terminated employee. In the event of a successful wrongful dismissal suit, an employer may be required to compensate for unfair and harsh conduct in the termination process. Wrongful dismissal suits can be costly, time consuming, and embarrassing. An employer may want to reduce the risks by considering a termination settlement that provides a measure of compensation to an employee. It may be much cheaper in the long run.

Chapter Study

Key Terms and Concepts

condonation (p. 523)

conduct incompatible (p. 524)

constructive dismissal (p. 530)

fundamental term (p. 530)

grievance process (p. 539)

habitual neglect of duty (p. 523)

incompetence (p. 523)

just cause (p. 521)

progressive discipline policy (p. 522)

reasonable notice (p. 526)

release (p. 539)

serious misconduct (p. 522)

severance pay (p. 538)

willful disobedience (p. 525)

Questions for Review

1. In what circumstances may an employee be terminated?

2. What is meant by "just cause"?

3. What is a progressive discipline policy? How does a progressive discipline policy affect the termination of employees?

4. When does incompetence amount to just cause for dismissal?

5. An employer may dismiss an employee for cause when the employee's conduct is prejudicial to the employer's business. Give an example of conduct that is prejudicial to the employer's business.

6. In the absence of just cause, how much notice of termination must an employee be given?

7. In the absence of just cause, how much notice must a superior-performing employee be given?

8. How is reasonable notice calculated?

9. In the calculation of reasonable notice, which factor is the most important? Explain.

10. In general, a longer-term employee is entitled to more notice than a shorter-term employee. What is the rationale for this distinction?

11. What is constructive dismissal? Give an example.

12. How can a wrongful dismissal suit arise? Name three ways.

13. Why is the manner of termination important?

14. When is a successful litigant entitled to punitive damages? Explain.

15. What is the duty to mitigate? When does it arise?

16. What should a termination settlement contain?

17. How does the process for termination differ between the union and nonunion sectors?

18. What is the grievance process? When is it used?

Questions for Critical Thinking

1. On occasion, employers and employees have argued for a rule of thumb in calculating reasonable notice. Most frequently they have argued for a "month-per-year-of-service" rule. Courts have generally rejected such an approach. What are the advantages of such a rule? How is such a rule defective?

2. Mandatory retirement has been abolished in almost all Canadian jurisdictions. This will result in more people working past the traditional retirement ages of 60 to 65. When there was mandatory retirement, employers often ignored performance issues with older employees because they would soon retire. With the abolition of mandatory retirement, employers will have to deal with aging workers who may not be able to keep up with the evolving demands of their occupations or companies. How should employers manage this challenge? What is the risk for employers who require older employees to acquire new skills?

3. The introduction of technologies such as fax machines, email, and the Internet into the workplace has greatly increased the possibility of employees using company property for personal use. It is a new spin on the old nuisance of employees making personal phone calls at work—but with greatly magnified consequences. Use of technologies by employees

ranges from occasional online shopping ventures to hours spent surfing the Internet and the use of a company computer to run a personal business. Should excessive Internet use be grounds for dismissal? Under what circumstances? Other than to prevent lost productivity, why would an employer want to control an employee's Internet use?

4. The Supreme Court of Canada[34] has indicated that in some circumstances, it is necessary for a dismissed employee to mitigate her damages by returning to work for the same employer. In what circumstances do you think a terminated employee should be required to return to work for her ex-employer? Do you see any problems for the terminated employee and the employer with the employee returning to work?

5. In *Honda v Keays*, the Supreme Court of Canada stated that if an employee can prove the manner of dismissal caused mental stress that was in the contemplation of the parties (mental distress over and above the normal impact of termination), the damages should be awarded through an award that reflects the actual damages, not through an arbitrary extension of the notice period. Is this approach beneficial to employees? Explain.

6. Employees have been disciplined and, in some cases, terminated for just cause when their use of social media has adversely affected the employer's legitimate interests. A social media policy may reduce the risk of harm to the employer's business interests, and the risk of penalties to the employee for her social media conduct. How can an employee's use of social media harm the employer's business interests? How should a social media policy be developed within business? What should a social media policy contain?

Situations for Discussion

1. Rhianne Dolman was an insurance adjuster who had worked for Dillman Adjusters for eight years. Her annual salary with Dillman was $60 000. Groger Adjusters persuaded Rhianne to work for it at a salary of $75 000 per year. Rhianne agreed and signed an employment contract. Several days later, Groger asked her to sign a non-solicitation agreement. Rhianne agreed.

Three months later, Rhianne was having lunch with some colleagues when Rhianne asked one of them if he would be interested in opening an adjusting business to compete with Groger. She also asked another employee if, hypothetically, he would like to work for her someday in the adjusting business. The conversation was overheard by another employee of Groger, who informed senior management. Rhianne's employment was terminated immediately.[35] Did Groger have just cause to terminate Rhianne? What is the effect of the non-solicitation clause? If Groger does not have just cause to terminate Rhianne, to how much notice is she entitled?

2. In 2007, Paul Wolfowitz, president of the World Bank, was forced to resign in wake of revelations that he had secured a new pay package for bank employee Shaha Riza, who happened to be his girlfriend. When Wolfowitz took over as president in 2005, he arranged to have Riza transferred to the U.S. State Department from her position as a Middle East expert. The move was a promotion, and her salary rose to $193 590 from $133 000.[36]

Love in the workplace is an exceedingly common occurrence, with half of Americans regularly reporting in surveys that they have been involved in an office romance. What are the risks of office romances for employees? What are the risks for employers? Should companies have policies regarding workplace romances? If so, what should such a policy contain?

3. Margaret Brien, 51, was terminated from her job as office manager at Niagara Motors Limited, a car dealership, after 23 years. Her termination came as a complete surprise to her as she had never been disciplined and had not received any warnings about her performance. At the time of her termination, the dealership told Brien that she was being terminated because her position was being eliminated. This was not correct. The dealership had secretly advertised her position and required Brien to train her replacement after her dismissal. She was offered eight weeks' pay in lieu of notice and 23 weeks of severance if she signed a

34. *Evans v Teamsters Local Union No 31*, 2008 SCC 20, [2008] 1 SCR 661.
35. Based on *Alishah v JD Collins Fire Protection Co*, [2006] OJ No 4634, 55 CCEL (3d) 116 (SC).
36. Virginia Galt, "Cupid's in the office. You might want to think twice", *The Globe and Mail* (12 May 2007) B19.

release. Brien sued for wrongful dismissal. In response, the dealership alleged that Brien performed her duties incompetently and unprofessionally and that it had just cause for her termination. The dealership also refused to provide Brien with a letter of reference or to assist her in any way with her job search. Brien successfully sued Niagara Motors for wrongful dismissal.[37] What would be reasonable notice in this situation? What factors will the court consider in an award for damages? How would the award of damages differ pre-*Honda v Keays* versus post-*Honda v Keays*?

4. Randal Martin joined International Maple Leaf Springs Water Corp. of Vancouver, B.C., in July 1994. He was hired to assist with the construction of a bottling plant at a spring near Chilliwack, B.C., and to develop markets in North America and Asia. He had been running a similar operation in Saskatchewan but left on the assurance that the B.C. company was viable and would be able to finance the new plant and fund the marketing initiatives. By March 1995, Martin had settled contracts with six companies and was close to three more, including a major deal with an American brewery that wanted to use its own brand name on Maple Leaf's products.

   In April 1995, the company fired Martin, accusing him of dishonesty and of coming to work drunk. Maple Leaf alleged that Martin was dishonest in registering trade names belonging to the company. Martin had registered the trade names personally, as the company did not have the funds to do this itself. The president of Maple Leaf knew about Martin registering the trade names and knew that the trade names would be transferred to the company as soon as Martin was repaid. There was no evidence of Martin's coming to work drunk. Martin successfully sued for wrongful dismissal.[38] What would be reasonable notice in this situation? What factors would the courts consider in awarding a period of notice?

5. Clyde Peters worked as a senior systems analyst for 17 years at NJ Industries. He had a good work record and a positive image throughout the company. Recently, he came under the supervision of the new controller, John Baxter, who quickly found himself dissatisfied with Peters' performance. Baxter believes that Peters

failed to properly implement the company's new computerized financial system. As well, he feels that Peters has failed to design a strategic plan for his department.

   These two matters have caused considerable problems between the two. Baxter is considering recommending Peters' termination.[39] How should the problem be resolved? Do grounds for termination exist?

6. Sandra Sigouin had worked at a Montreal branch of the National Bank for 20 years before being promoted to the position of special loans administrative officer. She was given the post even though she lacked the proper qualifications and training. The new job went badly. Sigouin made many mistakes, and the bank warned her in writing that if she did not improve she would be terminated. She asked to take courses, and promised to improve but no further training was provided. A few months later, she was fired for incompetence after failing to renew a letter of credit. The mistake cost the bank $850 000.[40] What should Seguin do? Do you think the bank had grounds to terminate Seguin for just cause? Do you think the bank acted fairly? Should an employer be permitted to promote an employee to his level of incompetence and then fire him for incompetence? What are the risks for an employer that uses such a tactic?

7. Philip Kelly was a materials manager for Linamar Corporation. He supervised approximately 10 to 12 employees, some reporting to him directly and some indirectly. He was required to instruct his staff on a regular basis and had disciplinary authority over them. In addition, he was a member of the plant operating committee, which was a management committee. As such, he was regularly involved with management issues with his peers and other divisions of the company. In addition to his responsibilities within the company, Kelly was also responsible for contact with suppliers and customers of the company. He had worked at five different divisions of the company and was well known throughout the organization.

   On 21 January 2003, Kelly was charged with possession of child pornography as a result of an investigation into a Texas child-pornography ring. By that time, he had been an employee with the company for 14 years, had a good employment record, and was

37. *Brien v Niagara Motors Limited*, 2009 ONCA 887, 78 CCEL (3d) 10.
38. Based on *Martin v International Maple Leaf Springs Water Corp*, [1998] BCJ No 1663, 38 CCEL (2d) 128 (SC).
39. Based on *Russell v Nova Scotia Power Inc* (1996), 150 NSR (2d) 271, 436 APR 271 (SC).
40. Paul Waldie, "Federal Court rules against placing employees in a Catch-22 situation", *The Globe and Mail* (17 April 2008) A3; and Wallace Immen, "Peter Principle meets legal principles", *The Globe and Mail* (18 April 2008) C2.

earning $64 000 per year. Two days later, Linamar dismissed Kelly for cause.[41] Does Linamar have just cause for dismissal? Who has the onus to prove just cause? What is the standard of proof? What factors will the court consider in determining whether just cause exists?

8. Terry Schimp, 25, worked as a bartender for RCR Catering and Pubs. Although he was occasionally tardy, sometimes missed a staff meeting, and a few times was short on his cash, he was considered a productive employee. At the end of a private function that RCR was catering, one of Schimp's supervisors noticed an open water bottle on his bar. He took a drink and discovered that it was vodka, not water. Suspecting that Schimp had stolen the vodka, the supervisor immediately fired Schimp. He was

escorted off the premises in front of about 50 other staff members, and he was banned for six months from returning to the hotel premises where RCR's offices were located. Schimp was extremely upset, but within a month he was able to get a new job with the same hourly rate of pay, only without tips. He sued for wrongful dismissal. At trial he was awarded $30 000 in damages. On appeal, the damages were reduced to $10 000, of which approximately $7000 was compensation for the humiliation and degradation he suffered.[42] Aside from the damages award, what costs did RCR incur as a result of this situation? How should RCR have acted differently?

For more study tools, visit http://www.NELSONbrain.com.

---

41. Based on *Kelly v Linamar Corporation*, [2005] OJ No 4899, 2006 CLLC 210-003.
42. Based on *Schimp v RCR Catering Ltd*, 2004 NSCA 29, 221 NSR (2d) 379.

CHAPTER 22

Professional Services

Objectives

After studying this chapter, you should have an understanding of

- how business uses the services of professionals

- the legal responsibilities of professionals to their clients and others who rely on their work

- the role of professional bodies

© ISTOCKPHOTO.COM/MARCUS CLACKSON PHOTOGRAPHY

Business Law in Practice

Ted Dalmo is the CEO of Dalmo Technology Ltd. (DT), a well-established business that supplies components to large telecommunications companies. Early in 2011, Ted and his management team (which included chief financial officer Sandra Roberts, a professional accountant) decided to explore a major expansion of the business in order to take advantage of growth in the industry. DT engaged DRC Consultants Ltd. to do a feasibility study of the expansion plans. Ted indicated to DRC that the projected profitability of the expanded business would need to be favourable in order to attract lenders and investors.

DRC's report indicated that, based on DT's plans and projections, the expansion should produce sufficient cash flow to repay lenders and generate profits for a healthy return on equity for investors. DT was able to borrow from the Provincial Bank and sell shares in the company to a group of local investors. A few months after the expansion got under way, one of DT's major customers moved to another supplier, putting DT's revenue projections in jeopardy. In addition, when DT's accounting firm, Asher & Breem did its next audit, it was revealed that revenue was inflated because of premature recognition of revenue from sales. The bank and the investors became nervous. They began to question DT's future and exert pressure on Ted for better financial performance. Ted met with Sandra and told her that, to survive the current crisis and keep the business going, the company would continue to recognize revenue as soon as possible and that Sandra as the CFO should seek additional means of improving the bottom line.

Sandra was concerned about Ted's demands. In her opinion, current practices at DT were pushing the limit of what is acceptable under generally accepted accounting principles. She was reluctant to explore further changes in reporting practices for the sole reason of improving DT's bottom line. Sandra consulted Bill Caton, DT's in-house legal counsel, regarding her legal and ethical position. To receive an independent opinion, Bill engaged DT's outside law firm, Holland & Hunt. The firm advised

(Continued on the next page)

Bill and Sandra to leave it to the auditors. DT continued to operate and its situation worsened. Within a year, the company was bankrupt.

1. Did the professionals fulfill their obligations to DT?
2. Can creditors and investors in DT recover their losses from the professionals?
3. Did the professionals act consistently with their obligations to their professional bodies?

Businesses and Professional Services

This chapter balances the two different perspectives of professionals and business. The main focus is for students going into business careers to understand the professions and the various duties of their members. This enables businesspeople to structure their relationships with professionals and develop realistic expectations of professional services. The other focus is for students who will become members of professions and therefore need some understanding of the workings of professional bodies. Knowledge of these workings is also useful for business clients who engage professionals in order to maximize the utility of their services and manage their related risks.

Relationships and Obligations

Professional
Someone engaged in an occupation, usually governed by a professional body, requiring the exercise of specialized knowledge, education, and skill.

Businesses depend on **professional** services, which can be either supplied in-house or contracted out to private firms. Most mid-sized or large businesses have professionals on staff. For example, DT employs a professional accountant, Sandra, as its CFO, and a practising lawyer, Bill, as its in-house legal counsel. Other professional services, such as those of an engineer, architect, or consultant are hired on an *ad hoc* or project basis.

Whether the professional is an employee or an independent supplier of a service, that person owes responsibilities to the business. Professionals who are employees are governed by the basic principles of employment law. Relationships with external professional service providers are defined by contract law. In addition, the professional–client relationship is a special relationship of trust and loyalty that goes beyond the protection normally provided by contract. Professionals are held to higher standards than other service providers.

The legal or ethical obligations that employed professionals owe the business vary according to the capacity in which they are hired. For example, some employed professionals perform purely managerial functions, so they become non-practising members of the relevant professional body. Other employees choose to retain their professional status and are hired in this capacity. Corporate counsel are practising members of the provincial bar who are hired for their professional expertise. The chief financial officer may hold one or more of the three professional accounting designations and be a member of the relevant provincial bodies.

In principle, the legal obligations of employed professionals are the same as those who work in private practices outside the firm. They are in a fiduciary relationship with their employer, where elements of trust, confidence, and reliance on the professionals' skill, knowledge, and advice exist. They can be liable for negligence, and their employers can be vicariously liable for their actions.

Ethical Obligations

Professionals' ethical obligations are especially important to employers. Managers value the services of, for example, in-house lawyers, because of the independence and ethical training they bring to the task. Professionals retaining membership in their profession continue to be bound by the rules of professional conduct and codes of ethics of their professional bodies. These obligations bring a level of independence that distinguishes a professional employee from a manager. Both owe ethical obligations to their employers, but professionals have additional obligations imposed by their governing bodies.

Ethical conflicts or dilemmas tend to arise when the business is under stress. Ted pressured Sandra to adopt aggressive accounting practices that she believed were counter to her professional obligations. The motive appeared honourable—to "save the company." However, the accounting profession had good reasons for establishing the rules governing Sandra. If she violates these rules, she is breaching her own professional responsibilities and risking sanctions (up to and including expulsion from the profession). Moreover, she will be placing DT at further risk, since outsiders reviewing the conduct will hold DT responsible for any harm that results.

Hiring Professionals In-House

Deciding whether to acquire professional services on a contract basis from outside firms or to hire full-time professionals as employees is difficult. If the cost of external professional services for a business becomes significant, the business will likely consider the employment option. It is important to approach this decision systematically and consider all factors, quantitative and qualitative. What level of experience is required of an in-house professional? Is there a need for specialization, and will there still be a need to hire externally from time to time? In-house professionals should provide enhanced value through their knowledge of the organization, their skill in managing external services, and their ability to contribute to the development and implementation of risk management programs.[1] DT decided at some point to hire an accountant as CFO and a lawyer as counsel. However, outside services are still required, such as the audit from Asher & Breem and independent legal opinions from Holland & Hunt. DT should regularly evaluate the cost-effectiveness of these arrangements.[2]

Responsibilities of Professionals to Clients and Others Who Rely on Their Work

Professionals owe a range of responsibilities to their clients, many of which are identical to those of all service providers. The consulting firm, DRC, the accounting firm, Asher & Breem, and the law firm, Holland & Hunt, all owe contractual responsibilities to DT. Likewise, professionals owe tort duties—in particular, those arising from negligence. Finally, beyond contract and tort duties, professionals owe fiduciary responsibilities to their clients.

---

1. See Christopher Guly, "Dealing with the storms", *In-House Counsel* (Spring 2010) 24 for examples of how legal counsel can be involved in all stages of crisis management.
2. See "Managing Legal Services" on page 64 in Chapter 3.

Responsibilities in Contract

Professional responsibilities in any given engagement are defined, in part, by contract. The nature of the service to be provided, the timeliness of the delivery of the service, and the way in which fees for service will be billed are established by the terms of the contract between the professional and the client. The legal rules governing the contract are those described in Part Two of this text.

Retainer

An advance payment requested by a professional from a client to fund services to be provided to the client.

In practice, contractual terms are often presented by the professional, and only a well-prepared client might think to negotiate additional or alternative provisions. Clients are often unaware of provisions in the contract dealing with how work will be billed and how and when **retainers** will be required. Clients should treat their contracts with professionals in the same careful and questioning manner as other contracts for goods and services.

Both the professional and the client must comply with the terms of the contract negotiated. The most contentious issues in practice tend to be those relating to quality of service and the fee. If a client is dissatisfied, most professional associations have mechanisms for providing advice and investigating fee and quality-of-service disputes. Lawyer–client bills are subject to special provisions.[3] Clients may submit lawyers' bills to taxing officers for review. The officer determines whether the sum charged was fair and reasonable in the circumstances.

BUSINESS APPLICATION OF THE LAW

Professional Service Contracts

Prior to engaging a professional's services, a client needs to address the key terms of the contract. Of particular importance are the following:

• How will fees be charged—by the hour, as a flat fee for the particular task, as a percentage of the value of the transaction, or on a contingency-fee basis?[4] Although the flat-fee and percentage approaches appear more certain, the client must be satisfied that the charges are appropriate for the nature of the service. Hourly rates can, with proper monitoring, provide control over costs. Clients may even seek to link fees to subjective factors such as the professional's demonstrated understanding of the client's affairs, responsiveness, predictive accuracy, and effectiveness. Particularly in the legal profession, there is a move toward value-based alternative fee arrangements rather than billable hours.[5] The project management approach to billing is another option.[6] Professionals generally are increasingly receptive to alternative fee structures and terms of payment that fit the client's business structure and practices.

• What expertise is required for the work? Does the professional fully understand the client's business needs?

• Do both parties understand the nature of the work to be performed and the likely results? Are the client's expectations appropriate and reflected in the agreement?

• When is the project to be completed? How will changes to the schedule be addressed?

• How frequently will the professional contact the client? The relationship should provide for reasonable consultation and input from the client. The advent of email, cellphones, and other forms of instant communication has created heightened expectation by clients in terms of ongoing communication.

• How will disputes about the engagement be handled? The agreement should contain a process acceptable to both parties.

• How will risk be allocated? The agreement should provide for unforeseen developments during the course of the contract.

If a contract price is not stated, the principle of *quantum meruit* applies—the professional provides an appropriate level of service, and the client pays a reasonable amount for that service. For small tasks performed by a familiar service provider, this situation is satisfactory because fee disputes are unlikely and there is little at risk. However, for larger engagements or contracts with a new service provider, such an arrangement leaves too many issues unresolved.

Critical Analysis: What are the risks if a formal professional service contract is not in place?

---

3. For example, see the *Legal Profession Act*, SBC 1998, c 9, ss 69–74.
4. See Chapter 4 for discussion of contingency fees.
5. See Christopher Guly, "Alternative billing on the verge?", *The Lawyers Weekly* (7 October 2011) 21.
6. See Luis Millan, "Project management", *The Lawyers Weekly* (11 February 2011) 20.

Responsibilities in Tort

General Responsibility

Professionals have duties in tort equivalent to those of other service providers. While they can be responsible for a range of torts, negligence is most common. The professional must perform services in accordance with the standards of a reasonably competent member of that profession. Liability for negligence was introduced in Chapter 11. In order for a professional to be liable for negligence, the basic elements of a negligence action must be present:

- The professional owes the claimant a duty of care.

- The professional has breached the standard of care.

- The professional's conduct has caused the claimant's loss.

- The claimant's loss is not too remote from the professional's actions.

In the context of professional services, negligence usually consists of careless or negligent advice, characterized in legal terms as negligent misstatement or negligent misrepresentation. The four elements of negligence listed above have been adapted into five requirements for proof of negligent misrepresentation[7]:

- There must be a duty of care based on a special relationship between the professional and the recipient of the advice.

- The representation must be untrue, inaccurate, or misleading.

- The professional must have been negligent in making the representation.

- The recipient must have reasonably relied on the misrepresentation.

- The reliance must have resulted in damages to the recipient.

These elements involve particular challenges in terms of defining the scope of a professional's special relationship, professional performance standards, and types of losses that can be claimed by recipients. The most difficult cases are those in which professionals give careless advice (misrepresentations) with negative economic consequences for claimants who are third parties (not clients). For example, DT's auditors and consultants have produced reports on which DT's bank and investors have relied. Those users will claim compensation for their losses resulting from DT's bankruptcy. Why should this be any different from any other form of negligence liability? What is the difference between a negligently prepared appraisal or audit and a negligently manufactured widget? In cases of professional negligence, there is a risk of imposing liability "in an indeterminate amount for an indeterminate time to an indeterminate class."[8]

The remainder of this section will focus on this difficult issue in professional responsibility—the extent of the professional's duty of care.

---

7. See *Queen v Cognos Inc*, [1993] 1 SCR 87 (summarized in Chapter 20), confirmed in *Sharbern Holding Inc v Vancouver Airport Centre*, 2011 SCC 23.

8. This remains the best-known statement of this problem and comes from a U.S. case: *Ultramares Corp v Touche Niven & Co* (1931), 255 NY 170 (Ct App).

Who is responsible for the losses and injuries resulting from this disaster?

ROBERT YAGER

Responsibility to Third Parties

Traditionally, the courts denied the claims of third parties (i.e., non-clients) who had relied on a professional's negligent misstatements. They refused to extend the duty of care beyond the client. Underlying these decisions was the public policy concern of maintaining the economic viability of those professions in the business of giving advice. For example, while a property appraiser can manage the risk exposure to the client, extending such risk to all subsequent purchasers of property may be economically oppressive. If all existing and potential investors could sue for negligence as a result of depending on a negligently prepared audit opinion for a public company, the delivery of audit services might no longer be economically feasible. Nonetheless, denying claims against the professionals in such situations does not necessarily leave the user without remedy. The purchaser of contaminated land can sue the vendor. Audit failures typically are uncovered because of some significant failure in the company itself. Shareholders can pursue their rights in company law and also sue the directors. The professions have been attractive targets for plaintiffs principally because they have the "deep pockets" otherwise lacking in these contexts. In the event of business failures (such as DT in the Business Law in Practice above), they may be the only persons left with the economic resources to meet claims.

The potential for third-party claims for economic loss resulting from negligent misrepresentations was first recognized in Britain in 1964.[9] In Canada, *Haig v Bamford*[10] was the key case in which the court found that auditors owed a duty of care where they had actual knowledge of the limited group that would use and rely on their statements. From the auditor's perspective of risk management, imposing liability in this context did not extend liability beyond that of most other providers of goods and services. The existence of the limited group of investors who might use the audit opinion was known at the time of the engagement.

The difficult question remaining after *Haig v Bamford* was whether liability should extend beyond this relatively narrow scope. Of critical importance was the question of whether liability would also exist in situations where third parties were neither known nor limited in number. Specifically, would a court apply the neighbor principle from *Donoghue v Stevenson*[11] in cases of negligent misrepresentation resulting in economic loss? In the context of auditing, would investors in a public company be entitled to make claims if the audit opinion they relied on for their investment decision was negligently prepared?

These issues were eventually addressed by the Supreme Court of Canada in *Hercules Managements Ltd v Ernst & Young.*[12] This case is summarized and discussed in detail under "Negligent Misstatement (or Negligent Misrepresentation)" on page 248 in Chapter 11. (Readers should consult that material before proceeding further in this chapter.) In this case, shareholder investors in a company brought action against the auditing firm Ernst & Young based on inaccurate financial statements produced as the result of an incompetent audit. To decide whether the auditors owed the investors a duty of care, the court applied a two-step test and found that in the case of an audit, it is reasonably foreseeable that a large number of persons will use and rely on the statements. Applying the first stage of the test, a duty of care exists. However, in applying the second step and evaluating possible policy considerations, the court examined the limited purpose of the audited financial statements as set out in the relevant legislation—"to assist the collectivity of shareholders of the audited companies in their task of overseeing management."

Because the shareholders were using the audited statements for investment decisions and not the statutory purpose of the audit, they were owed no duty of care. The court held that to decide otherwise "would be to expose auditors to the possibility of indeterminate liability, since such a finding would imply that auditors owe a duty of care to any known class of potential plaintiffs regardless of the purpose to which they put the auditors' reports." In terms of the five requirements for negligent misrepresentation (listed on page 551), the absence of a special relationship necessary to create a duty of care nullified the need to consider the other four requirements. The only remedy investor plaintiffs have is the indirect right to bring a derivative action on behalf of the company (see Chapter 16).

---

9. *Hedley Byrne & Co v Heller & Partners,* [1964] AC 465 (HL (Eng)). In fact, an exclusion clause protected the Heller Bank.
10. [1977] 1 SCR 466.
11. [1932] AC 562 (HL (Eng)) in Chapter 11.
12. [1997] 2 SCR 165.

In the Business Law in Practice scenario, DT, Provincial Bank, and the investors may consider suing DRC Consultants, Asher & Breem, and Holland & Hunt for negligence. The five requirements for negligent misrepresentation will apply as follows:

- All three firms owe their client (DT) a duty of care using the two-step test, but the firms owe Provincial Bank and the investors as third-party claimants a duty only under certain circumstances. The key is whether policy considerations exist that would limit the duty of care as defined by the neighbour principle. This will depend on the stated purpose of the consulting and the audit. In this situation, the audit was not mandated by legislation, and therefore it is not relevant to apply that aspect of the *Hercules case*. Determining the stated purpose will call for an interpretation of what Ted told Asher & Breem at the time the engagement contract for auditing was formed. Since DRC was told that its consulting report would be important for financing purposes, the limited group of third-party users would be owed a duty of care. If Ted failed to be this explicit, then a court, applying a policy analysis, would not likely find that a duty of care was owed. The law firm, on the other hand, is unlikely to be held responsible to anyone other than its client. There was no indication that anyone other than DT and those acting on its behalf would rely on the law firm's opinion.

- The claimants must prove that the firms provided untrue, inaccurate, or misleading reports.

- Whether the firms were negligent will depend on whether they breached the standard of care in their respective professions. Professional testimony as to generally accepted auditing standards and standards of competency in the legal and consulting professions will be crucial in resolving this issue. With regard to auditing standards, for example, International Standards on Auditing were adopted as Canadian Auditing Standards in 2010 and now constitute generally accepted auditing standards (GAAS) for financial statement audits. In 2011, International Financial Reporting Standards were adopted as Canadian generally accepted accounting principles (GAAP).[13]

- The claimants must be able to establish the requisite reliance and resulting losses. Did the claimants, for example, actually use the consulting report, the audited financial statements, and the legal opinion? If so, did they reasonably rely on them to make their decision, and did that reliance cause the loss?

Although the *Hercules* decision severely restricted auditors' duty of care to third-party investors, the second stage of the duty test invites analysis on a case by case basis.[14] In addition, regulatory changes since the Enron collapse have focused to a large extent on the quality and reliability of audits. They are discussed in the following box on the next page.

---

13. See The Chartered Accountants of Canada, "Canadian Standards in Transition", online: Chartered Accountants of Canada <http://www.cica.ca/transition/index.aspx>.

14. See for example *Widdrington (Estate of) v Wightman*, 2011 QCCS 1788 where auditors were held liable to investors based on Quebec law. The court also examined the common law and focused on the auditors' knowledge of users of the audits and the various purposes for which they were prepared.

BUSINESS APPLICATION OF THE LAW

Greater Accountability for Auditors

Accounting firms and auditors, in particular, have long been subject to claims for compensation by clients and investors who allege they have suffered loss due to negligent work by members of the firm. These claims have normally been considered on a case-by-case basis. *Haig v Bamford* and *Hercules Managements* are two examples discussed earlier in this chapter. The prevention of such claims is a key part of risk management by the firms. The rise of class actions by investors against auditors and directors of companies has raised the stakes, but normally no single case threatens the survival of the firm.

The Enron affair was a disaster on many fronts, but particularly for the accounting profession. Prior to the Enron collapse in 2002, Arthur Andersen, the firm providing auditing and consulting services to Enron, was one of the Big Five firms in the profession. Following investigation after the collapse, the firm was charged with the criminal offence of obstruction of justice based on alleged concealment and destruction of key documents. A jury found Arthur Andersen guilty. The firm's reputation was destroyed and it dissolved, leaving only four key firms in the profession. In 2005, the conviction was overturned by the U.S. Supreme Court, but long before this decision, the damage was done—the firm was ruined as the result of difficulties with one client.

The potential disappearance of another major firm was avoided in a later case, this one involving KPMG. In 1997, the firm began offering clients what became "questionable" tax shelters. Over the next seven years, shelters produced $11 billion in "losses" that saved clients $2.5 billion in taxes and generated $124 million in fees for KPMG. The firm came under increasing scrutiny by law enforcement authorities and in 2005 agreed to a settlement to forestall criminal charges that could have consigned the firm to the same fate as that of Arthur Andersen. The firm acknowledged wrongdoing, agreed to pay $456 million, accepted an outside monitor of its operations and restrictions on its tax practice. The firm has survived.

Since Enron, regulators have tended to focus on auditors and senior managers of companies in their aggressive reaction to this serious lack of confidence. In the United States, the *Sarbanes-Oxley Act* of 2002 established the Public Company Accounting Oversight Board to set auditing standards and oversee the accounting profession, in particular the audit of public companies. Auditors must assess the internal controls of their clients and report any material weaknesses. Senior management must certify the audit results. In addition, the Act assigns the Securities and Exchange Commission responsibility for regulating lawyers' conduct and requiring them to report apparent malfeasance within their corporate clients. Another major piece of legislation, the *Dodd-Frank Act*, was passed in 2010 as a major overhaul of financial regulation in response to the 2008 financial crisis.

In Canada, the accounting profession established the Canadian Public Accountability Board with authority to oversee

How can a firm such as KPMG improve its public accountability through prudent management of its legal risks?

MARK RENDERS/GETTY IMAGES

auditing firms through periodic inspections dealing with particular audit files, training programs in the firms, standards for accepting new clients, and employee compensation. The board is financed by public audit firms that are required to register as members. In 2011, the board found deficiencies in a quarter of the files it examined in the Big Four firms and in 47 percent of the files of ten smaller firms. When the board finds problems, it can go to the auditors directly, to the directors of the audited company, or ultimately to the jurisdiction's securities commission.

These regulatory regimes have generated a backlash. The changes have been criticized for the level of intervention and detail, and the ensuing cost of compliance for companies. It is suggested that this encourages clients and auditors to seek legitimate means of circumventing the regulations. There is also concern that fewer accounting firms are willing to perform audits of public companies. Whether the new regimes are accomplishing their goal of greater accountability is under discussion.

Critical Analysis: How does the risk of litigation affect the viability of professional firms? In terms of standards and accountability, can business and the professions develop their own solutions, or is more legislation inevitable?

Sources: Kurt Eichenwald, "Reversal of Andersen conviction not a declaration of innocence", *The New York Times* (1 June 2005), online: New York Times <http://www.nytimes.com/2005/06/01/business/01assess.html?scp=1&sq=Reversal%20of%20Andersen%20conviction%20not%20a%20declaration%20of%20innocence&st=cse>; Jonathan D Glater, "Settlement seen on tax shelters by audit firm", *The New York Times* (27 August 2005), online: New York Times <http://www.nytimes.com/2005/08/27/business/27kpmg.html?scp=1&sq=Settlement%20seen%20on%20tax%20shelters%20by%20audit%20firm&st=cse>; Janet McFarland, "Audit firms show little progress, weaknesses persist: report", *The Globe and Mail* (3 April 2012), online: Globe and Mail <http://www.theglobeandmail.com/globe-investor/audit-firms-show-little-progress-weaknesses-persist-report/article2390440>/; Eric Dash, "Feasting on Paperwork", *The New York Times* (8 September 2011), online: *New York Times* <http://www.nytimes.com/2011/09/09/business/dodd-frank-paperwork-a-bonanza-for-consultants-and-lawyers.html?pagewanted=all>; Public Company Accounting Oversight Board, online: PCAOB <www.pcaobus.org>; and Canadian Public Accountability Board, online: CPAB-CCRC <http://www.cpab-ccrc.ca>.

Fiduciary Responsibilities

The term "fiduciary" was introduced in Chapter 13, and further discussed in Chapters 14, 16, and 20. Agents owe fiduciary responsibilities to their principals; directors owe fiduciary responsibilities to the corporation; partners owe fiduciary responsibilities to one another; and senior or key employees owe fiduciary responsibilities to their employers. The essence of the professional–client relationship is also fiduciary. Professionals act in a fiduciary capacity and are deemed by law to owe duties of loyalty, trust, and confidence that go beyond those contractual or tort responsibilities owed by the nonprofessional service provider.

A fiduciary must act primarily in the interest of the person to whom a responsibility is owed. This is a broad and overriding concept captured by the notions of loyalty and trust. It is also expressed in terms of specific obligations. The professional as fiduciary must

- avoid any conflict of interest between the client's affairs and those of the professional or the firm
- refrain from using the relationship for personal profit beyond charging a reasonable fee for services provided
- disclose all relevant information to the client
- act honestly, in good faith, and with due care
- maintain confidentiality of client information

CASE · Hodgkinson v Simms, [1994] 3 SCR 377

THE BUSINESS CONTEXT: Professionals sometimes blur their professional and business activities, raising questions of where the boundaries of the fiduciary obligations begin and end.

FACTUAL BACKGROUND: In 1980, Hodgkinson hired Simms, a chartered accountant, for independent advice about tax shelters. Simms recommended investment in multi-unit residential buildings (MURBs). Their relationship and Hodgkinson's confidence in Simms were such that Hodgkinson did not ask many questions regarding the investments. He trusted Simms to do the necessary analysis and believed that if Simms recommended a project, it was a good investment. Hodgkinson made substantial investments in four MURBs recommended by Simms. In 1981, the real estate market in British Columbia collapsed, and Hodgkinson lost most of his investment. His claim against Simms was based on breach of fiduciary duty. Specifically, by not advising Hodgkinson that he had a personal stake in the MURBs (the developers were also Simms' clients and, in addition to fees, Simms received a bonus for MURBs sold), Simms failed to provide the independent advice for which he was hired and thus breached his fiduciary duties to Hodgkinson.

THE LEGAL QUESTION: Did Simms owe a fiduciary responsibility to Hodgkinson? If so, did his actions amount to breach of that responsibility and what are the consequences of the breach?

RESOLUTION: Justice La Forest examined the nature of the relationship between Simms and Hodgkinson and found that a fiduciary duty was owed, based on "the elements of trust and confidence and reliance on skill and knowledge and advice." He also discussed the relationship between fiduciary responsibilities and the rules of the respective professions, stating that the rules of the accounting profession of which Simms was a member required that "all real and apparent conflicts of interest be fully disclosed to clients, particularly in the area of tax-related investment advice. The basis of this requirement is the maintenance of the independence and honesty which is the linchpin of the profession's credibility with the public."

Therefore, the fiduciary duties imposed by courts should be at least as stringent as those of a self-regulating profession. Simms had been in a clear conflict of interest. The court accepted Hodgkinson's evidence that he never would have purchased the MURBs had he been aware of Simms' interest in selling them. The breach of fiduciary obligation was deemed to be so serious that the court was prepared to place all risk of market failure on Simms and compensated Hodgkinson accordingly.

CRITICAL ANALYSIS: It could be argued that Hodgkinson's losses were caused by the failure of the real estate market in British Columbia. What is the justification for transferring the losses to Simms simply because he assisted in the selection of the particular MURBs? What is the message for professionals? For clients?

The fiduciary must comply with the *spirit* of the obligation and not merely the letter. The case on page 556 illustrates the fiduciary obligation of an accountant. See the *Strother* case[15] on page 322 in Chapter 14 for discussion of a law firm's fiduciary duty to its clients.

The fiduciary obligation to give independent advice free from self-interest has a distinct meaning in the case of the audit. The auditor, besides acting without self-interest, must also act independently of any interest of the company, since she is fulfilling a public function—namely, providing assurance to shareholders (and, indirectly, to the financial markets, in the case of publicly listed companies) that the financial statements have been prepared according to established guidelines. Audit firms are prohibited from involvement in their clients' business and are increasingly limited in their ability to provide services other than the audit to their audit clients.[16]

Professionals owe a **duty of confidentiality** to their clients because of both fiduciary principles and professional rules of conduct.[17] For example, a rule of conduct for professional engineers is the following:

> Engineers, geoscientists, and members-in-training shall … not disclose information concerning the business affairs or technical processes of clients or employers without their consent.[18]

Related to confidentiality is the concept of professional-client **privilege**. When Bill seeks legal advice on behalf of DT, Holland & Hunt must not divulge the contents of that consultation to others. The basis for this principle is the overriding need of clients in specific circumstances to be able to put their entire trust in their professional advisor. The only advice to which privilege attaches is legal advice. Privilege may extend to the advice given by other professionals only when they prepare documentation at a lawyer's request and solely as part of the lawyer's advice to the client.

Duty of confidentiality
The obligation of a professional not to disclose any information provided by the client without the client's consent.

Privilege
The professional's right not to divulge a client's confidential information to third parties.

Professionals' Risk Management Practices

How professionals manage risk exposure arising from their responsibilities has a direct impact on the businesses that hire them. Clients need to be aware of the risk management strategies of professionals and plan their affairs accordingly. Three ways in which professionals can manage risk are through contracts, incorporation or limited liability partnerships, and insurance.

Professional Service Contracts

As discussed earlier, these contracts are a vehicle for defining the parameters of the work that professionals are engaged to do. Both parties benefit from a clear and careful agreement that includes all essential terms and clarifies expectations.

---

15. *Strother v 3464920 Canada Inc*, 2007 SCC 24.
16. See "Independence Standards – Harmonized Rule of Professional Conduct 204", online: Chartered Accountants of Canada <http://www.cica.ca/about-the-profession/protecting-the-public-interest/conduct-204-harmonized-rules/item45429.pdf>.
17. In very limited circumstances, confidentiality must be violated, such as when a patient tells her doctor that she plans to seriously harm herself or others.
18. Association of Professional Engineers and Geoscientists of New Brunswick, *Engineering and Geoscience Professions Act: By-Laws and Code of Ethics* 2011, s 4, online: Engineers & Geoscientists New Brunswick <http://www.apegnb.com/site/media/APEGNB/2011_By_Laws.pdf>.

Incorporation and Limited Liability Partnerships

Historically, businesses have managed risk through corporations with limited liability for shareholders, while professional service providers have been required to assume liability personally. There are now other models for managing professional liability.

Some professions may incorporate. Generally, professions may incorporate only if they are specifically permitted to do so by the legislation governing the particular profession in that province.[19] Even where incorporation is allowed, it typically does not protect the professional from the liability of greatest concern—namely, personal liability for negligence. For example, where accountants have been able to incorporate, the act establishing the right to practise specifies that the personal liability of the accountant for negligence will not be affected by the limited liability of the shareholders, directors, or officers of the corporation.[20] From the client's perspective, the individual professional generally remains personally liable for negligent work, and the assets of the professional organization (the corporation) can be claimed.

Partnerships may register as limited liability partnerships (LLPs) (see Chapter 14). The impetus for allowing this business form came from the large professional partnerships that considered it unfair, for example, that a partner in Vancouver should be responsible for the negligence of a partner in Ontario. LLPs have been introduced by amendments to the provincial *Partnership Acts*. Whether or not individual professions allow members to form LLPs is determined by the provincial legislation governing that profession.[21] LLPs protect individual partners from personal responsibility arising from negligence claims that are brought against the partnership in general or other partners in the firm. Individual partners remain liable for their own negligence. Likewise, the firm itself retains liability, and the firm's assets (and insurance) can be used to compensate for losses.

A new aspect of law firm organization coming under discussion is whether firms should be able to seek outside investors in order to expand and compete more widely. Greater competition may improve the public's access to legal services, but there is concern that the fiduciary relationship between lawyers and clients may be clouded by obligations to investors.[22]

From the perspective of the client or user who is suing, the concern is whether there will be compensation, which in turn depends on the availability of insurance.

Insurance

Errors and omissions insurance is described in Chapter 28. It is a condition of practice in most professions that members carry this professional liability insurance. For the claimant, guarantees of insurance coverage are essential. Insurance claims, however, can be a challenge for claimants. Professional insurers, such as the Canadian Medical Protection Association, are highly specialized and expert at defending claims. If the loss is significant,

---

19. For example, *Business Corporations Act*, SNB 1981, c B-9.1, s 13(3)(d); *Business Corporations Act*, RSO 1990, c B.16, s 3(1).
20. For example, *Public Accountants Act*, RSNS 1989, c 369, s 22A(2).
21. For example, *Partnerships Act*, RSO 1990, c P.5, s 10(2); and *Partnership Act*, RSA 2000, c P-3. See also the *Law Society Act*, RSO 1990, c L.8.
22. Jeff Gray, "Canadian law firms: Time to take stock?", *The Globe and Mail* (18 October 2011), online: Globe and Mail <http://www.theglobeandmail.com/report-on-business/industry-news/the-law-page/canadian-law-firms-time-to-take-stock/article2205447 /> and Matt Laforge, "U.K. taking a 'leap of faith'", *The Lawyers Weekly* (27 April 2012) 24.

the claimant should not contemplate litigation without hiring a lawyer who has the necessary expertise. Where contingency fees are unavailable, the cost associated with hiring such lawyers can effectively prevent many claimants from pursuing litigation.

Governance Structures of Professions
Legislation

Professions are self-regulating—that is, there are provincial statutes that establish the rights of the professions to govern themselves. The acts create the governing body for the profession and specify when individuals may represent themselves as being qualified to practise in that province. The legislation gives autonomy and sometimes a monopoly over specific activities to professional bodies sanctioned by the legislation. For example, the *Legal Profession Act*,[23] which governs the practice of law in British Columbia,

- provides a very detailed definition of the "practice of law"

- defines members of the Law Society as those lawyers who hold a practising certificate for the current year

- states that only members of the Law Society in good standing are allowed to engage in the practice of law

- recognizes that the society is governed by elected members of the profession (benchers)

- states that the benchers govern and administer the affairs of the society, including determining whether or not a person is a member in good standing of the society and establishing and maintaining a system of legal education and training

Each profession is governed by similar legislation in each province. The provincial professional associations are often linked to federal associations.

The self-regulating model has come under attack for its alleged failure to protect the public interest. Critics say that the accountability of professions is sacrificed in favour of self-interest and protection of members. As a result, the legal profession in England and Wales, Australia, and New Zealand has lost much of its autonomy through the legislated imposition of public bodies to oversee the profession's disciplinary process, creating a consumer-oriented model of regulation based on competence and service.[24] These changes have attracted attention in Canada. The governing body in Ontario (Law Society of Upper Canada) has appointed an independent commissioner to oversee the discipline process.[25] The Competition Bureau is engaged in a multi-staged evaluation of the anti-competitive practices of several professions including accountants and lawyers.[26]

The organization of the accounting profession in Canada is more complex than others, since there are three professional accounting bodies: the Certified General Accountants

---

23. SBC 1998, c 9.
24. Alice Woolley, "Canada lags in regulating lawyers", *The Lawyers Weekly* (17 June 2011) 8.
25. Thomas Claridge, "Ontario Law Society watchdog sees more complaints", *The Lawyers Weekly* (5 June 2009) 1.
26. Competition Bureau of Canada, "Competition Bureau releases ex-post assessment of the self-regulated professions study" (2 September 2011), online: Competition Bureau Canada <http://www.competitionbureau.gc.ca/eic/site/cb-bc.nsf/eng/03406.html>.

Association of Canada (CGA–Canada), the Canadian Institute of Chartered Accountants (CICA), and Certified Management Accountants of Canada (CMA Canada). Historically, the key distinction between the associations has been the right to perform the audit as defined by provincial legislation. In recent years, this distinction has been eased in most provinces. For example, Ontario legislation creates a mechanism whereby members of all three accounting bodies can apply for an audit licence if they meet new internationally recognized standards.[27] However, controversy remains.[28]

In the DT organization, Sandra Roberts is described simply as a "professional accountant." In practice, she could be a member of any one of the three professional accounting bodies.

Professional Practice

From a business perspective, the licensing of professionals may seem an issue of little relevance. However, any business operating across several provinces, like DT, may need to seek advice in different jurisdictions. Business has recently been assisted by the removal of many of the interprovincial barriers to professional practice that once existed.[29] Professionals must belong to provincial societies or associations in order to practise within the particular province. They attain the right to practise in different provinces by demonstrating familiarity with local legislation and rules. All professions have firms that operate nationally, with practitioners in different provinces. If DT is sued in another province, for example, Ted can employ the services of a regional or national law firm, or he can ask his existing firm, Holland & Hunt, to hire a local firm in the other jurisdiction on DT's behalf.

Professional firms are finding means of organizing themselves to better meet the needs of clients. Some firms operate internationally. While accounting firms (now often known as "professional service firms") have been the leaders in international practice, other professions are increasingly moving in the same direction. There are networks of law firms that are expanding rapidly in the United Kingdom, the United States, and Canada.[30] Some are linked to the concept of prepaying for services (a form of insurance). From the client's perspective, many of these changes offer increased convenience and better service.

Disciplining Professionals

Each profession in Canada has established rules of professional conduct or codes of ethics that prescribe acceptable behaviour. Each has established mechanisms for enforcing those rules and disciplining any member who violates them.

Professional rules and codes are critical for the protection of the client. Most professional associations or societies now have materials available online[31] outlining the processes for users to follow if they have a complaint. In the disciplinary process itself, clients

---

27. *Public Accounting Act*, 2004, SO *2004*, c 8, as amended by SO 2006, c 19, Schedule B, s 16.
28. Janet McFarland, "Labour mobility at heart of accounting battle", *The Globe and Mail* (1 June 2009) B9, online: Globe Advisor <https://secure.globeadvisor.com/servlet/ArticleNews/story/gam/20090601/RCGA01ART1829>.
29. Michael Rappaport, "Lawyers can now move provinces easily", *The Lawyers Weekly* (18 December 2009) 22.
30. Christopher Guly, "Global law firms look to Canada", *The Lawyers Weekly* (15 July 2011) 21.
31. For example, see the Institute of Chartered Accountants of Nova Scotia, online: http://www.icans.ns.ca/aboutus.asp?cmPageID=101 and The Law Society of Alberta, online: <http://www.lawsociety.ab.ca/lawyer_regulation/complaints/complaints_initiate.aspx>

(complainants) are, however, only witnesses and observers. For damages or other compensation, the client must sue the professional involved. Depending on the nature of the claim, the professional may have insurance coverage. The legal profession also has an indemnification or assurance fund to compensate clients whose money has been stolen by members of the profession, usually from funds held in trust.

To be effective, the investigatory and disciplinary process must protect the rights of complainants and professionals. Any investigation is a serious matter for the professional, who must participate and who will usually need legal representation. If the process proceeds and the professional is found to have violated the rules, the consequences can extend to withdrawal of the right to practise. Although the disciplinary process is formal, there may be alternative dispute resolution options to resolve complaints before formal hearings are held.

Of course, professionals are subject to criminal prosecution if their misconduct violates the law. For example, lawyers have been implicated in cases of fraud in mortgage transactions, both as direct participants in the fraud or for not detecting the fraud committed by others.[32] The corporate counsel of Hollinger was one of those convicted in the Conrad Black fraud trial. He was sentenced to five years' probation along with home detention and community service. He also lost his right to practise law.[33] The following case illustrates the disciplinary process in the accounting profession.

CASE

Barrington v The Institute of Chartered Accountants of Ontario, 2011 ONCA 409

THE BUSINESS CONTEXT: In cases of negligent audits, the focus is often on the potential liability of auditors to investors or other claimants. This case deals with the complex disciplinary process within the professional body and the implications for the members who did the audit.

FACTUAL BACKGROUND: Livent Inc. was a public company that promoted live entertainment and was involved in the construction and management of theatres. Garth Drabinsky and Myron Gottlieb were Livent's major shareholders and senior officers. Deloitte & Touche LLP was Livent's auditor from 1989 to 1997. Power, Russo, and Barrington were senior members of the audit team. In April 1998, Deliotte provided an unqualified audit opinion of Livent's 1997 financial statements. Later in 1998, new management of Livent discovered serious irregularities in Livent's books. The statements for 1996 and 1997 were revised and criminal fraud charges laid against Drabinsky and Gottlieb.[34] The Professional Conduct Committee (PPC) of the Institute of Chartered Accountants of Ontario (ICAO) brought charges

of professional misconduct against the members of the 1997 audit team. They were charged with failure to follow generally accepted accounting standards (GAAP) and auditing standards (GAAS) in their decisions about the recognition of income, the transfer of receivables, and audit evidence and procedures. The ICAO's Discipline Committee (DC) conducted a hearing for 37 days and found all three members guilty. The DC formally reprimanded the members, ordered them to post notices of the decision, fined each of them $100 000 and ordered them collectively to pay the costs of the disciplinary process of $1 251 000. The members appealed to the ICAO's Appeal Committee (AC) who affirmed the decision of the DC. The members then sought review by the Divisional Court where they were partially successful. All parties appealed.

THE LEGAL QUESTION: Were the members treated fairly in the disciplinary process? Did they have adequate notice of the charges? Did the DC provide adequate reasons? Were the penalties authorized by legislation?

(Continued)

---

32. Jeff Gray, "Alleged fraud victims come gunning for the lawyers", *The Globe and Mail* (22 June 2011) B11, online: Globe and Mail <http://www.theglobeandmail.com/report-on-business/industry-news/the-law-page/alleged-fraud-victims-come-looking-for-the-lawyers/article2069873/>.
33. See Paul Paton, "The Company Moral Compass", *In-House Counsel* (Winter 2008) 6.
34. See Janet McFarland, "Drabinsky loses appeal bid", *The Globe and Mail* (29 March 2012), online: Globe and Mail <http://www.theglobeandmail.com/globe-investor/drabinsky-loses-bid-to-appeal-fraud-conviction/article2385423/>.

RESOLUTION: The Court of Appeal restored the decision of the DC in full. The court found that the DC process was procedurally fair. The members had adequate notice of the charges and evidence against them. The DC fairly considered the evidence of experts regarding accounting and auditing standards and the DC gave adequate reasons for its decision. Justice Karakatsanis made this comment on the process:

> This case is important to the ICAO and the self-regulation of the accounting profession. . . . The hearing was the longest in the history of the Institute. More significantly, the issues of audit process and opinion go to the heart of the integrity of our commercial system. The public,

shareholders, investors, lenders, and business partners of public companies depend upon the objectivity and professionalism of the auditors of financial statements.

> Obviously, this is also an important case for the professional members who have had successful and even distinguished careers. . . . While the ICAO did not revoke their professional designations, it reprimanded and fined them. They have a right to natural justice and procedural fairness in the defence of their reputations and to know the reasons for any finding of misconduct.

CRITICAL ANALYSIS: Does this process provide adequate protection of the public? Is it fair to the auditors?

Business Law in Practice Revisited

1. Did the professionals fulfill their obligations to DT?

DT is concerned with the quality of accounting and legal services received from employees—Sandra Roberts and Bill Caton—and the firms they have retained—Asher & Breem and Holland & Hunt, along with the consulting services provided by DRC Consulting. The obligations of Sandra and Bill to DT are largely a function of their employment—to perform their defined duties according to defined or reasonable standards. The outside firms have obligations to DT based on contract, tort, and fiduciary relationships. Contractual obligations are found in the express terms of the contract or implied as obligations to provide the services requested to the standard of a reasonably competent professional. The duties of the firms in tort are similarly based. Fiduciary obligations relate to the avoidance of conflicts of interest and placing DT's interests first. Their advice should not be based on what is in the business interest of the firm in terms of retaining DT as a client or generating fees.

2. Can creditors and investors in DT recover their losses from the professionals?

Provincial Bank and the investors can sue only for negligence, and their principal obstacle will be establishing that a duty of care was owed to them. The bank and investors were foreseeable users of the consulting report and audited financial statements, but they must establish that no policy considerations exist to limit this duty. This issue will depend on the stated purpose of the consulting and the audit which will depend on what Ted told Asher & Breem at the time the engagement contract for auditing was formed. Since DRC was told that its consulting report would be important for financing purposes, the limited group of third-party users would be owed a duty of care. If Ted failed to be this explicit, then a court, applying a policy analysis, would not likely find that a duty of care was owed.

Claimants will need to prove the other elements of negligent misrepresentation. The standard of care issues are equivalent to those in DT's claims. More critical will be the need to prove that claimants relied on the reports and that this reliance caused their loss. Since the financiers had no other known source of information about the financial state of DT, these last elements in this particular case should be reasonably easy to prove. If the claim is successful, damages will include the amount lost on the loan and the investments.

The law firm, on the other hand, is unlikely to suffer any third-party liability. Its opinion was provided only to DT and not relied upon by any third parties.

3. Did the professionals act consistently with their obligations to their professional bodies?

The accountants, consultants, and lawyers must act in accordance with the professional and ethical standards of their professional bodies. The in-house professionals must avoid conflicts between their professional and ethical duties and the wishes of their employer. Sandra is facing the classic conflict between ethical obligations owed to the employer and to the profession, as well as possible conflicts with her own personal values. Professional obligations must prevail, even if that requires her to leave DT. There may be legitimate alternatives she can present to Ted that at least partially meet his objectives. Sandra cannot engage in any practices that violate the rules of professional conduct. To do so would be ethically wrong, would expose her to professional discipline, and create serious risk for herself, the company, and Ted.

Chapter Summary

Professionals owe a range of duties to their clients. Professionals are governed by contract and tort law. They must deliver services as contracted for and in accordance with the requisite professional expertise. If they are negligent in performing their responsibilities, they will likely be responsible for damages. In addition, professionals are in a fiduciary relationship with their clients if the elements of trust and confidence and the reliance on skill, knowledge, and advice are present. Because of inherent vulnerability or dependency, the client is owed this duty of loyalty and trust. Professionals also owe duties to those who are not clients but who rely on their work and advice. Whether a duty is owed in a particular situation depends on foreseeability and the need to impose reasonable limits on potential liability.

Professional service providers manage risk for the same reasons as businesses in general. Insurance is critical, and many professions make such coverage obligatory. Professionals can consider organizing their practices as limited liability partnerships or corporations. New forms of practice, such as national and international firms, offer benefits for users.

The professions are governed by legislation that establishes them as self-regulating bodies. The professions create codes of conduct or rules of practice. These determine the standards that their members must meet, as well as providing a measure of the expected standard of care in contracts, torts, and fiduciary obligations.

The professional bodies have created dispute resolution services or complaint procedures to assist clients. They also maintain a discipline process that provides assurance to users that professionals violating professional rules will be disciplined or even expelled.

Chapter Study

Key Terms and Concepts

duty of confidentiality (p. 557)

privilege (p. 557)

professional (p. 548)

retainer (p. 550)

Questions for Review

1. Who is a professional?

2. What is the meaning of "fiduciary" in the context of professional–client relationships?

3. How may professionals be in a conflict of interest?

4. What should a professional services contract contain?

5. What are the options for setting professional fees?

6. What is a retainer?

7. What is the basis for determining the cost of professional services if there is no formal contractual term addressing the issue?

8. What are the three types of professional responsibility?

9. Why were accountants traditionally protected from third-party claims?

10. How did the Supreme Court of Canada limit the duty of care for negligent misstatements in the *Hercules* decision?

11. What is the meaning of "self-regulating profession"?

12. What is the key role of the bodies created to oversee the professions?

13. During a disciplinary process, why is it important to protect the rights of the professional against whom a complaint has been made?

14. What are LLPs?

15. What rules establish who can be a member of a particular profession?

16. If a conflict between a professional's ethical obligations to the profession and those to the client cannot be resolved, what must the professional do?

17. What is a professional's duty of confidentiality?

18. Why did the accounting firm Arthur Andersen disappear after the Enron collapse and KPMG survive its tax-shelter prosecution?

Questions for Critical Thinking

1. The following is an excerpt from an auditor's report:

   An audit involves performing procedures to obtain audit evidence about the amounts and disclosures in the financial statements. The procedures selected depend on the auditor's judgment, including the assessment of the risks of material misstatement of the financial statements, whether due to fraud or error. In making those risk assessments, the auditor considers internal control relevant to the entity's preparation and fair presentation of the financial statements in order to design audit procedures that are appropriate in the circumstances, but not for the purpose of expressing an opinion on the effectiveness of the entity's internal control. An audit also includes evaluating the appropriateness of accounting policies used and the reasonableness of accounting estimates made by management, as well as evaluating the overall presentation of the financial statements.[35]

   Is this description of an audit adequate for clients? Could it be written in such a way as to make the extent of their responsibilities clearer to users?

2. If you are the manager in an organization responsible for finalizing contracts with professional service providers, what factors would you consider in deciding between fees based on an hourly basis versus a per-job basis? What protection might you try to build into the contracts?

3. The *Hercules* decision was heavily criticized by some members of the business press as too lenient on auditors, but was received with great relief by auditors. Did the Supreme Court of Canada define the purpose of the audit too narrowly? What is the appropriate balance between fairly compensating those who suffer

---

35. Chartered Accountants of Canada, "General Purpose-Fair Presentation Framework-Canadian GAAP", online: Chartered Accountants of Canada <http://www.cica.ca/cas/site-utilities/item36473.pdf>.

loss and discouraging professionals from providing needed services?

4. In an economic downturn, investors often look to their investment advisors to explain their losses. Investors may claim that their advisors were more interested in their own fees and commissions than their clients' portfolios or that their advisors failed to fully explain the degree of risk in their investments. Are investment advisors "professionals"? Do they owe their clients fiduciary duties? What standards should advisors be required to meet?

5. Most professionals are required to maintain a minimum level of liability insurance in the event that claims are brought against them by those who rely on their advice. However, the cost of this insurance is passed on to clients through the fees they pay for services received. Does this system encourage professional responsibility? Is there a more effective method?

6. Professional organizations are authorized by legislation to regulate their own members in terms of controlling permission to practice, setting standards, and imposing discipline. Can the public expect to receive fair treatment from professional organizations that have a vested interest in protecting their own members?

Situations for Discussion

1. Over the years of running a small business, Lan had acquired sizable savings. She wanted to get the best return on this money and discussed this with her lawyer, Harvey. He advised her that this was an excellent time to get into real estate; he had many clients who required financing. Lan could provide either first or second mortgages, depending on her desired level of risk and return. Harvey said he had some clients involved in a large townhouse development. Lan trusted him implicitly, as he had been her lawyer since she had first started her business. Thus, she lent the bulk of her savings—$200 000—as a second mortgage, which would earn interest at 19 percent per annum over five years.

Within eight months the real estate market collapsed. The mortgagees defaulted on payment, and once the holders of the first mortgage had foreclosed, there was nothing left for Lan. When she complained

to Harvey, he said that investments of any sort carry inherent risk. His personal investment company, for example, had been one of the partners in the townhouse development, and he too had lost his entire investment.

Lan seeks advice about what she can do to recoup her losses. Identify Lan's options.

2. Good Property engaged the services of a professional real estate appraisal firm, McGee and McGee, prior to purchasing a large tract of property on the outskirts of town. When Dan, the CFO of Good Property, first discussed the appraisal with Andy McGee, he said the appraisal was required by 10 January. Andy said this was impossible owing to other commitments and proposed 26 January. It was agreed that Andy would be the appraiser. Dan said he would get back to Andy about the date.

The project was more complex than either Good Property or the appraisers expected. The local water conservation authority was about to issue a report that seriously affected the land, so Andy waited for it. The appraisal was not handed to Good Property until 29 January. By this time, another purchaser had acquired the property. When Dan was handed the sizable invoice for the work, he claimed that Andy had breached the contract by finishing the work late and had caused Dan to lose out on being able to buy the land. Furthermore, the invoice was far more than he expected to pay. How are these matters likely to be resolved? What arguments can Good Property and McGee raise? What would happen if McGee had not waited for the water report and Good Property had bought the land, which was later devalued by the report?

3. Midor was a lawyer with a busy real estate practice focused on mortgages. For a time, Midor's practice prospered. He became wealthy and invested in several highly speculative ventures that failed. Midor found himself in serious financial difficulty and under severe stress. He devised a scheme where he would purchase pieces of real estate using straw buyers. They would allow their names to appear on transfer and mortgage documents in return for a fee. The straw buyers were never the real owners or borrowers. Through successive transfers of these properties, Midor was able to inflate their apparent value and give fraudulent mortgages to a variety of banks at values well in excess of the properties' actual value. When the fraudulent

scheme was eventually discovered, the banks were left with largely worthless mortgages and the straw buyers appeared to owe large sums to the banks based on properties they never owned.[36] Since Midor has lost all of the ill-gotten funds, who is responsible for compensating the banks and the buyers? What consequences does Midor face?

4. Sino-Forest Corp. is an international forestry company. Between 2007 and 2011, the company raised $2.7 billion in the capital markets. In June 2011, allegations were made that Sino-Forest's forest holdings in China and other countries were grossly and fraudulently overstated. The share price plummeted from $26 to $1 before stabilizing at $5. Two pension funds have filed a class action suit against the company, its executives and directors, auditors Ernst & Young, and a number of investment banks. The allegations against Ernst & Young consist of negligence in the audits which should have detected the overstatement of holdings and objections to the presence on the Sino-Forest board of directors of former Ernst & Young partners.[37]

   What must the claimants prove in order to establish Ernst & Young's liability? If the forest holdings were overstated as alleged, should the audits have revealed the problem?

5. Big Cleanups was a public company that had developed products used to address environmental cleanups. Its market performance attracted considerable investor attention. One investor, Max Find, acquired a significant holding in Big Cleanups over a five-year period. He tracked all performance announcements closely and increased his holdings with each favourable announcement.

   Late in 2011, there were rumours of some underlying problems with Big Cleanups' technology. Max therefore paid particularly close attention to the 2011 annual report. Surprisingly, the report indicated further strong performance, and Max, on the basis of the report, increased his holdings in Big Cleanups.

   In the fall of 2012, the results for the second-quarter of 2012 were released. They showed unexpected losses, and the share price precipitously

declined. The auditor withdrew the 2011 audited statements and later issued new statements, which showed a large loss. Max claims that his losses are due to the allegedly misleading audit report. If he had known the true state of affairs he would have reduced, not increased, his holdings in the company. The auditor claims that the audit was prepared according to generally accepted principles and that the firm was not responsible for this turn of events.

   Outline the primary arguments for Max and the auditors.

6. Yul is a CGA working as comptroller for Jones Manufacturing. He is concerned about the cash flow position of the company. Customers have placed large orders, but Andrew (the CEO) has insisted on an aggressive pricing policy, and prices charged do not cover costs.

   Yul approaches Andrew with his concerns, but Andrew will not listen. Andrew is a high-profile member of the local community; the success of the company means that it can hire a large number of people in this economically depressed area, and it is inconceivable to him that booming sales could translate into losses. Yul explains that the auditors will be coming soon and, if he doesn't expose the current position, they will uncover it anyway. Andrew tells him that he understands, but that he wants Yul to do whatever it takes to get through this audit. Afterward, prices can be raised, since by then the company will be in a strong position in the marketplace and this temporary hurdle will have been overcome.

   Yul is trying to devise a strategy to reconcile his professional responsibilities and the survival of this company. It would be devastating to see the company close if he is unable to find a way of presenting the information to satisfy the auditors.

   Discuss the pressures Yul faces. What should he do now?

7. Environmental Consultants Ltd. (ECL) was hired by Crass Developments Ltd. (CD) to evaluate a prospective development site for signs of pollution. The site had previously been used for a variety of industrial purposes, but was then vacant. CD was considering

36. Based in part on Karen Kleiss, "Record fraud draws jail", *The Edmonton Journal* (15 January 2008) 1, online: Canada.com <http://www.canada.com/edmontonjournal/news/story.html?id=05b3f8cc-1a18-4e9f-82f2-74caf8571ba6>.

37. Based in part on Vanessa Lu, "Pension funds sue Sino-Forest for $6.5B", *Toronto Star* (1 September 2011) B1, online: The Star <http://www.thestar.com/business/article/1047653—pension-funds-sue-sino-forest-for-6-5b> and Jeff Gray and Andy Hoffman, "Report alleges possibility Sino-Forest 'accounting fiction'", *The Globe and Mail* (16 April 2012), online: The Globe and Mail <http://www.theglobeandmail.com/globe-investor/report-alleges-possibility-sino-forest-an-accounting-fiction/article2403034>.

a number of possible sites and wanted to choose the one with the lowest environmental risk. At the time, ECL had plenty of work and wished to complete the evaluation for CD as quickly as possible. The senior partner at ECL assigned two junior employees to the CD job—one with two years' experience and the other just recently hired. They did a site inspection and conducted a few soil tests that were appropriate for a "clean" site, but not for one that had been used previously. They produced a positive report. The senior partner was out of the office for a few days, so the report was sent to CD without his approval. CD bought the land; a year later, signs of pollution began to emerge and CD was responsible for an expensive cleanup effort. To what degree are ECL and the three employees responsible for CD's cleanup costs?

8. The B.C. government (BC) embarked on an ambitious building program to replace 50 aging schools. In an attempt to lower construction costs, the government decided to build a few variations of the same model. BC hired ABC Architects to design the basic model and variations, DEF Engineering to oversee the construction, and GHI Construction to actually do the building. The project took three years to complete. Five years later, serious problems began to emerge in the schools. Cracks appeared in the walls, many of the windows leaked, and mould was found in the walls. What responsibility do the architects, engineers, and builders have for these problems? What forms of risk management are relevant?

For more study tools, visit http://www.NELSONbrain.com.

Sales and Marketing

In marketing, the law can be seen as a set of barriers for creative activity, but its objective is fairness. The law seeks to ensure that customers' needs are met and that transactions are conducted according to terms that are generally fair to both parties. Marketing law is the regulatory tool that requires fair competition and ensures that all market participants operate according to the same principles.

Chapter 23 begins with the contract of sale. The remainder of the two chapters deals with competition law and the four key components of marketing strategy, commonly called the marketing mix—product, promotion, price, and place or distribution—along with management of the legal risks in marketing.

RTIMAGES/SHUTTERSTOCK

Sales and Marketing: The Contract, Product, and Promotion

Objectives

After studying this chapter, you should have an understanding of

- the scope of marketing law

- the rights and obligations in a contract of sale

- the scope of competition law

- the legal obligations associated with the product component of marketing

- the legal obligations associated with the promotion component of marketing

TIM BOYLE/GETTY IMAGES

Business Law in Practice

Pacific Play Centres Inc. (PPC), based in Prince George, British Columbia, specializes in children's play equipment for parks and schools. PPC's current products are made from metal and plastic for durability, but the company is developing a new product—smaller equipment sets made from wood and designed for residential backyards. Lisa Patel, the CEO of PPC, believes there is demand for a wood product for home purchases. She thinks that upscale homeowners and parents are more interested in a natural-looking alternative in their backyards than in the greater durability of metal or plastic.

Lisa intends to promote, distribute, and sell the new products nationally. The equipment will be sold partially assembled and will be boxed with pictures of the product on the outside. Assembly instructions and all required parts will be included in the packaging. Initially, products will be designed for relatively young children (under the age of eight), although the strategy is to have the equipment grow with the children, with add-ons becoming available over time. The marketing theme will stress the environmental friendliness of the product, the creativity of the design, and safety. Promotion will be done primarily through in-store displays and print media, with a special focus on advertising in parenting magazines.

The premium pricing will reflect the strategy of selling to affluent parents who are eager to ensure that their children have access to products that maximize play value. The products will be sold through national home improvement and toy retail chains, and directly by PPC on the Internet.

Lisa is aware that her company is moving into a new market and that there are many regulations and legal concerns she will need to address. In light of growing public concern about playground safety, Lisa understands that risk management is critical in this business.

(Continued on the next page)

1. How does the law affect PPC's marketing strategy?
2. What are the key aspects of PPC's contracts with its customers?
3. What impact does the law have on PPC's product?
4. What impact does the law have on the promotion of PPC's product?

Overview of Marketing Law

Marketing practices, like other aspects of business, are directed and influenced by laws and regulations. The fundamental laws affecting the marketing process are the common law principles explained in Parts Two and Three of this text. Marketing is also regulated by all three levels of government: federal, provincial, and municipal. The main objectives of these laws are

- to protect consumers from physical harm
- to foster fair competition
- to protect consumers from unfair selling practices

These objectives give rise to laws regulating a multitude of issues, including implied conditions and warranties for the sale of goods and services, product safety standards, disclosure on packaging, standards for honest promotion, anticompetitive practices, and distribution of products.

If a business sells its products internationally, the marketing practices of that business are subject to the laws and regulations of other countries as well.

Marketing law includes the traditional business law topics of the contract of sale and many pieces of federal and provincial legislation relating to consumer protection and competition. The key aspects of this legislation are presented below and are revisited over the next two chapters where appropriate in terms of the four aspects or "Ps" of the marketing function or mix: product, promotion, price, and place or distribution. This chapter considers the product and promotion components, and Chapter 24 addresses price, place, and risk management.

Marketing law
All areas of law that influence and direct the creation, promotion, pricing, and distribution of goods, services, or ideas.

Contract of Sale

The contract of sale is the essence of marketing and the earliest application of the law to marketing. There are several key aspects of the contract that are the focus of legal rules and therefore worthy of particular attention—the terms of the contract relating to the sale, delivery of the product, the transfer of ownership of the product, and the remedies for breach of the contract terms.[1]

---

1. The assistance of Dion Legge (LLB), now a lawyer with MacLeod Dixon LLP, in researching and writing an earlier draft of this section of the book is gratefully acknowledged.

The Common Law

When customers make a purchase, they have expectations concerning the product's attributes and characteristics. Purchasers of PPC's outdoor play equipment will assume, for example, that the material used to build the equipment is sound and that children will be safe playing on it.

Whether such expectations are protected from a legal perspective is a different matter. The foundation of the common law concerning the product—such as playground equipment or the provision of a service—is contained in the Latin phrase **caveat emptor**. *Caveat emptor* means "let the buyer beware" or "let the buyer take care." The common law requires prospective purchasers to take care of themselves, to be aware of what they are purchasing, and to make appropriate investigations before buying. If the purchaser wants the product to exhibit certain characteristics, the common law requires that expectation to be contained in the contract. Otherwise, the purchaser can be left without a remedy if the product should prove to be deficient.[2]

Because an unwavering application of the doctrine of *caveat emptor* can produce unfair results, judges began to create principles that would provide a measure of protection for the purchaser of goods.

Caveat emptor
"Let the buyer beware" or "let the buyer take care."

Sale of Goods Legislation

Beginning in the 1800s, English judges generated the basic principles that inform the modern law concerning the sale of goods. In response to the harshness of *caveat emptor*, they began to evolve common law rules that, among other matters, implied specific terms into contracts for the sale of goods, whether the parties had expressly agreed to those terms or not. "Goods" means personal property in its tangible, portable form as well as items attached to land that can be severed. "Goods" includes the playground equipment retailed by PPC but does not apply to the sale of land or the provision of services, for example. The various kinds of personal property are discussed in Chapter 17. On this basis, a reasonably predictable set of exceptions to the doctrine of *caveat emptor* was developed. For example, at common law, a contract for the sale of goods ordinarily is understood to contain a term that the item sold is fit—or appropriate—for the purpose sold and is of merchantable—or reasonable—quality.

In 1893, the English Parliament enacted the *Sale of Goods Act*,[3] an influential piece of legislation based on such common law principles. In this way, the Act summarizes—rather than reforms—the case law of the time. This historic legislation protected buyers because, echoing the common law, it implied a set of terms into a sales transaction unless this would be contrary to the parties' intentions. The legislation also provided remedies to the buyer should these statutory terms be breached. Of course, terms prescribed by the statute were in addition to any express terms or representations made by the seller at the time of contracting.

---

2. See Chapter 8 for a discussion of the law concerning mistake as well as negligent and fraudulent misrepresentation.
3. *Sale of Goods Act*, 1893, (56 & 57 Vict) c 71(a). The Act has been repealed and replaced by the *Sale of Goods Act 1979* (UK), c 54.

England's 1893 *Sale of Goods Act* forms the cornerstone of modern sale of goods legislation everywhere in Canada except Quebec.[4] The law governing the sale of goods is a specialized branch of contract law. This means that it is governed by legislation and, where the legislation is not relevant, by the common law rules of contract. Unless the parties expressly agree to the contrary or are otherwise able to exclude the operation of the *Sale of Goods Act*, a number of terms are automatically implied into their contract. In addition to implying terms, the legislation classifies them as either conditions or warranties.[5] The conditions and warranties that the legislation implies into a sales transaction are described below.

Conditions

Conditions are terms that are important or essential to the purpose of the contract. In every contract of sale, it is implied:

- that the seller has the right to sell the goods.

- that the goods will be reasonably fit for the intended purpose where the buyer, expressly or by implication, makes it known what the intended purpose of the goods will be, in such a way as to show that he is relying on the skill and judgment of the seller. Note that a buyer does not have to make his intended purpose known when goods are used for their ordinary purpose.

- that the goods will be of merchantable quality, where the goods are bought by description. Merchantable quality means that the goods are of reasonable quality considering the price paid. The essence of a sale by description is the reliance by the buyer on some description by the seller and, accordingly, there may be reliance even where the buyer has seen or inspected the goods.

- that, where the goods are sold by sample, the goods will correspond to the sample and that the buyer will have a reasonable opportunity to compare the goods with the sample.

- that, where goods are sold by description, the goods will correspond with the description.

Warranties

Though warranties are classically understood as being minor or collateral terms, they can also be important. In this area of law, they are best understood as terms that are not conditions. In every contract of sale, it is implied:

- that the buyer will have and enjoy quiet possession of the goods, which generally means that third parties will not claim rights against them.

- that the goods are free from liens and encumbrances in favour of third parties that were not declared or known to the buyer at the time the contract was made.

---

4. For example, *Sale of Goods Act*, RSO 1990, c S.1; *Sale of Goods Act*, RSA 2000, c S-2. Articles 1726–31 of Quebec's *Civil Code* contain warranties implied in sales transactions.
5. This common law distinction, along with innominate terms that cannot be easily classified, is discussed in Chapter 9.

In order to understand how the Act might apply to business transactions, consider the following problems that PPC might encounter concerning its online ordering system.

Example 1   A building supply store relied on one of PPC's online advisors in order to purchase, over a six-month period, equipment suitable for older children. When the customer received its first shipment, it discovered that the recommended equipment was so small and low to the ground that it could provide entertainment only for children under five.

Sale of Goods Act Violation: PPC has violated a condition implied by the *Sale of Goods Act*, namely that the goods are suitable for the purpose sold. The scenario fits all the requirements of the section in question: the customer made its purpose known by telling the PPC advisor that the equipment was for older children. The customer relied on PPC's advice in selecting the product. The product proved unsuitable for this purpose since it is geared toward significantly younger children.

Example 2   A homeowner purchased an expensive play set through PPC's website. Within one year, the equipment was falling apart.

Sale of Goods Act Violation: Since the play equipment has been sold by description and is not of reasonable quality, PPC has violated the condition of merchantability implied by the *Sale of Goods Act*.

Delivery of Goods

Business has developed standardized terms that describe documentation in contracts of sale. For illustration of these terms, assume that PPC contracts to sell $10 000 worth of play sets to Lumiere, a Montreal-based retailer, and the goods will be shipped through a carrier called Custom Trucking.

Bill of Lading

Bill of lading
A shipping document that serves as a contract between the seller and the carrier.

The **bill of lading**, generically known as a "shipping document," is the contract between the seller (PPC) and the carrier (Custom Trucking). It specifies to whom the goods must be delivered and provides evidence that the goods have been transferred from the seller to the carrier.

The time it takes for goods to reach their destination can be significant, particularly in foreign trade. What happens when, one day after shipping, PPC learns that Lumiere is insolvent? At this time, PPC has the right to exercise **stoppage in transit**. It can direct the carrier to return the goods, even though title may have moved to Lumiere. Provided Custom Trucking receives this direction before it has delivered the goods to Lumiere, it must return them (at PPC's expense) to PPC.

Stoppage in transit
The right of a seller to demand that goods be returned by a shipper to the seller, provided the buyer is insolvent.

Cost, Insurance, and Freight

c.i.f.
A contractual term making the seller responsible for insurance and shipping.

The initials **c.i.f.** stand for "cost, insurance, freight." In a c.i.f. contract, the seller is responsible for arranging the insurance (in the buyer's name) and shipping. The purchase price includes the cost of the goods, insurance, and shipping. The seller must deliver the goods to the carrier and send copies of all documentation and a full statement of costs to the buyer. If the contract between PPC and Lumiere is "c.i.f. Montreal," PPC must arrange shipping and insurance and will not have fulfilled its contractual obligations to deliver to Lumiere until it has transferred the goods to the shipper and provided Lumiere with all necessary documentation.

Free on Board

The initials **f.o.b.** stand for "free on board." In an f.o.b. contract, the buyer specifies the type of transportation to be used, and the seller arranges this and delivers the goods to that shipper. The seller's responsibilities are over when the goods are delivered to the shipper. The seller incurs the cost of delivering the goods to the shipper, and generally the buyer pays for shipping and insurance. So if the contract is "f.o.b. Mississauga," Lumiere will advise how the goods are to be transported, and PPC will arrange for that transportation and ensure that the goods are delivered to the relevant carrier.

Cash on Delivery

A **c.o.d.** or "cash on delivery" contract was once common with consumer orders, particularly before credit cards existed. The purchaser is obliged to pay for the goods upon delivery.

f.o.b.
A contractual term whereby the buyer specifies the type of transportation and the seller arranges that transportation and delivery of goods to the shipper at the buyer's expense.

c.o.d.
A contractual term requiring the purchaser to pay the shipper cash on delivery of goods.

PART SEVEN

INTERNATIONAL PERSPECTIVE

Contracts for the International Sale of Goods

In international trade it is important that shipping terms be standardized to ensure that there is a common understanding between jurisdictions. The International Chamber of Commerce has published a set of definitions for trade terms, known as INCOTERMS. These definitions do not have the force of law but are often adopted by contracting parties. They may differ from the terms outlined above. Businesspeople need to be familiar with the appropriate terms applying to their specific transaction.[6]

In 1980 the United Nations Commission on International Trade Law (UNCITRAL) produced a treaty, the *Convention on the International Sale of Goods (CISG)*. The treaty went into force in 1988 and has been ratified by more than 30 countries, including Canada and the United States. The goal of the convention is to create a uniform body of international commercial law. The *CISG* applies to business-to-business contracts for the sale of goods. The convention automatically applies to the contract if the parties are from ratifying countries, unless they contract out of its provisions. It does not apply to contracts for services and technology, leases and licences, or goods bought for personal, family, or household use.

The convention provides a uniform set of rules for forming contracts and establishes the obligations of the buyer and seller. It addresses in a comprehensive manner such issues as the requirement of writing; offer and acceptance; implied terms; performance of the contract, including the buyer's and

seller's obligations; and breach of contract. Because the rules constitute a compromise among differing rules in the various legal systems, Canadian buyers and sellers need to be aware of significant differences between the *CISG* and Canadian rules. For example, under Canadian law, contracts for the sale of goods worth more than a minimum amount must be in writing in order to be enforceable. The *CISG* states that such contracts need not be in writing or in any particular form.

Reservations have been expressed about the *CISG*,

> The crux of the problem with the *CISG* is its contradictions, its lack of rules around the validity of the contract …, the lack of its widespread use, and the domestic gloss it has been given by various courts, including those of Canada. All of these factors combine to suggest that despite the laudable objectives of the drafters of the convention itself, businesses may favour the continued use of tried and tested national sales laws.

Critical Analysis: The *CISG* is a compromise agreed to by many nations and encompassing aspects of many different legal systems. How useful is this convention to Canadian business?

Sources: *United Nations Convention on Contracts for the International Sale of Goods* (1980) [*CISG*], online: Pace Law School <http://www.cisg.law.pace.edu/cisg/text/treaty.html>; and Sheerin Kalia, *International Business Law for Canadians: A Practical Guide* (Toronto: LexisNexis Canada, 2010) at 109, 126 and 131.

---

6. International Chamber of Commerce, "INCOTERMS 2010", online: International Chamber of Commerce <http://www.iccwbo.org/incoterms/>.

Risk of Loss and Transfer of Title

The concept of ownership of personal property in the form of goods is discussed in detail in Chapter 17. Ownership entails control of the property but also involves the risk of loss from damage or destruction. Transfer of title or ownership of goods from the seller to the buyer is fundamental to the sales transaction and has an impact on a number of business concerns, especially the transfer of risk. Consider these examples:

- If a truckload of goods is destroyed by fire in mid-delivery, who owns them and who bears the loss if they are destroyed?

- If goods are to be paid for within 30 days of sale, does the 30 days begin upon delivery of the goods or at some earlier point?

- Who owns a completed custom-built machine that has yet to be delivered?

At the heart of the transfer of title issue is the notion that possession and ownership of goods can be held by different parties. Possessing goods without owning them (i.e., without having title) confers certain obligations and rights, which were discussed in Chapter 17. Ownership confers additional rights.

The best way for parties to ensure clarity is to write the contract in a way that specifies delivery terms and clearly indicates when and how ownership moves from the seller to the buyer. The parties then know when responsibility shifts and how insurance coverage should be structured. If they fail to do so, there are statutory provisions that resolve the issue.

The provincial *Sale of Goods Act*s set out a series of rules[7] that determine when title changes in the absence of terms in a contract. The rules are stated below, along with an example of each. In broad terms, the acts address two contrasting sets of circumstances. In most contracts for sale, goods are already in existence and can be clearly identified when the contract is formed (Rules 1 through 4 below). These are known as **specific goods.** However, sometimes goods either are yet to be set aside and identified as being the subject of the contract or have not yet been produced. In this scenario, described in Rule 5, goods are said to be **unascertained**.

Specific goods
Goods that are identified and agreed on at the time a contract of sale is made.

Unascertained goods
Goods not yet set aside and identifiable as the subject of the contract at the time the contract is formed.

Rule 1

Where there is an unconditional contract for the sale of specific goods in a deliverable state, the property in the goods passes to the buyer when the contract is made, and it is immaterial whether the time of payment or the time of delivery or both is postponed.

Example   Pacific Play Centres has an inventory surplus at the end of its prime season and offers special discounts off wholesale prices. ABC Discounter goes to PPC's warehouse and orders and pays on the spot for all the remaining equipment, which is immediately set aside in the loading dock for pickup the next day. There is a major fire at the warehouse that night, and all the equipment is destroyed. The destroyed goods belonged to ABC. Title shifted when the contract was made, since the goods were ready for delivery at that time.

---

7. For example, *Sale of Goods Act*, RSO 1990, c S.1, s 19.

Rule 2

Where there is a contract for the sale of specific goods and the seller is bound to do something to the goods for the purpose of putting them in a deliverable state, the property does not pass until the thing is done and the buyer has received notice.

Example   XYZ Discounter places an order for play centres at the spring trade show in Toronto. The sale specifies that PPC will pack the equipment in boxes carrying the XYZ name and logo. In this case, XYZ does not become owner of (acquire title to) these goods until PPC has notified it that the goods have been packed in the appropriate boxes. If the warehouse burns either before the goods are packed in the XYZ boxes or before XYZ is told the goods are ready, PPC remains the owner and incurs the loss. Title does not change until the goods have been put in a deliverable state and XYZ has been notified.

Rule 3

Where there is a contract for the sale of specific goods in a deliverable state but the seller is bound to weigh, measure, test, or do some other act or thing with reference to the goods for the purpose of ascertaining their price, the property does not pass until such act or thing is done and the buyer has received notice.

Example   PPC buys the hardware components for its equipment offshore. Although there are many different components, the contract specifies that price is determined by weight. The metal components have already been manufactured and counted to fill PPC's order, but they have not been weighed. The manufacturer decides to fill another customer's order with the components made for PPC. Until the goods have been weighed, title has not passed. There is an act or event that must take place in order to determine price, and until that act or event has taken place, PPC does not acquire title.

Rule 4

Where goods are delivered to the buyer on approval or on "sale or return" or other similar terms, the property passes to the buyer

a. when she signifies her approval or acceptance to the seller or does any other act adopting the transaction, or
b. if she does not signify her approval or acceptance to the seller but retains the goods without giving notice of rejection, when a time that has been fixed for the return of the goods expires, and if no time has been fixed, on the expiration of a reasonable time.

Example   PPC has a standing contract with ABC Discounter that it will ship out play sets at specified times and in set quantities to the ABC warehouse, and that ABC can return these goods if they are not sold. PPC ships 50 play sets to the ABC Discounter's warehouse in compliance with this agreement. After three weeks, there is severe water damage in the ABC warehouse and the sets in storage are destroyed. ABC did not signify acceptance and there is no fixed time for return. Therefore, title will change after a reasonable time, which will depend on the circumstances and prior practices between PPC and ABC.

Rule 5

Where there is a contract for the sale of unascertained or future goods by description and goods of that description and in a deliverable state are unconditionally appropriated to the contract, either by the seller with the assent of the buyer or by the buyer with the assent of the seller, the property passes to the buyer, and such assent may be express or implied and may be given either before or after the appropriation is made.

Example   XYZ places an order with PPC for 50 play sets. The operator of the forklift truck in the PPC warehouse accidentally drops some boxes that could have been sent to XYZ. Since the order is generic or unascertained (there is no way of knowing which boxes in the warehouse will be used to fill XYZ's order), title changes only when the goods are unconditionally appropriated to the contract. Here, title has not shifted, as boxes for XYZ are still mixed in with general inventory. If, however, the forklift had dropped XYZ's order as it was loading it onto the truck or the truck was involved in an accident en route to XYZ and the order was destroyed, XYZ would have title and incur the risk.

Although the *Sale of Goods Act* rules are important, they are complex. In practice, it is always preferable to avoid potential misunderstandings by drafting contracts that set out clearly when title and the corresponding risk shift from the seller to the buyer.

What are the legal issues created by the shipping of goods?

STEVE COLE/VETTA/GETTY IMAGES

Remedies

The rules determining when title to goods shifts also affect the compensation the seller is entitled to in the event of breach by the buyer. For example, if the buyer commits breach by cancelling an order, the seller is entitled to damages for breach. If title has not shifted according to these rules, the seller still owns the goods. The seller is therefore entitled to the normal measure of **damages for non-acceptance,** recognizing that the seller has an obligation to mitigate the loss. If title has shifted, the buyer owns the goods and must pay the full amount of its obligation under the contract. The seller's claim is known as **action for the price.**

Generally, when a term of a contract of sale is breached, classification of the relevant term of the contract is essential to determining the remedy that a court is entitled to give the disappointed purchaser. As already discussed in Chapter 9, breach of a condition—whether in a sale of goods contract or not—may give the innocent party the right not only to claim damages but also to reject the goods and treat the contract as ended. This is known as the right of repudiation and means that the balance of the contract and further obligations under it can be dismissed, if the non-defaulting party so chooses. For example, the building supply store that received play equipment that was not suitable for the purpose sold is not obligated to accept further shipments from PPC. The customer can bring its contract with PPC to an end, return the equipment, and find another supplier.

However, when a warranty is breached, the sale of goods legislation only permits the buyer to maintain an action for damages or ask the court to reduce the purchase price due to the breach. The buyer cannot return the goods and is obligated to continue with the contract in question and comply with any outstanding terms. If the buyer refuses to perform after breach of warranty, the buyer will also be in breach of contract. The following case demonstrates the importance of these rules in commercial transactions.

Damages for non-acceptance
Damages to which a seller is entitled if a buyer refuses to accept goods prior to the title shifting.

Action for the price
The seller's claim when title to the goods has shifted to the buyer.

CASE	**Chalmers Suspensions International Ltd v B&B Automation Equipment Inc, [2008] OJ No 1394 (Sup Ct J), aff'd 2009 ONCA 360**

THE BUSINESS CONTEXT: Two corporations dealing with highly technical equipment on relatively equal terms need to be aware of the implications of contract terms implied by the applicable *Sale of Goods Act.*

FACTUAL BACKGROUND: Chalmers manufactured automotive suspensions for large vehicles. In 2000 Chalmers converted from manual to robotic welding for its truck suspensions. B&B agreed to design and manufacture a robotic welding machine for Chalmers, to be delivered in 16 to 18 weeks, with payment of $198 000 in three installments. The machine was to complete the welding for each frame in 10 minutes. B&B completed the machine, but after repeated testing and inspection, it could not do welds of acceptable CSA quality within the specified time cycle. Negotiation and consultation went on at length, but eventually Chalmers declared the machine unacceptable and claimed the return of payments made. B&B counterclaimed for the balance plus additional costs and storage fees, alleging that the machine was fully operational and that the problem was with Chalmers' parts.

THE LEGAL QUESTION: Was there a condition implied in the contract that the robotic machine be suitable for the purpose specified by Chalmers? If so, was the condition breached? If the condition was breached, what was Chalmers' remedy?

RESOLUTION: Chalmers received the refund of payments made. B&B's counterclaim was dismissed. The court found that the condition was implied because B&B had previously designed and manufactured equipment for Chalmers and was therefore aware of Chalmers' business; B&B admitted that this type of contract was within its course of business; B&B had complete knowledge of Chalmers' intended purpose for the machine; Chalmers had relied on B&B's expertise in the past; and a reasonable person would have realized Chalmers' reliance in this contract. Expert evidence established that the machine failed to fit Chalmers' process and the welds failed to meet CSA standards. B&B's breach of the implied condition went to the root of the contract, justifying Chalmers' rejection of the machine and its claim for return of payments.

CRITICAL ANALYSIS: Commercial parties such as Chalmers and B&B are able to agree on their own terms and conditions by modifying or excluding the application of the applicable *Sale of Goods Act.* Why did B&B not transfer the risks to Chalmers in the contract?

Limitations of Sale of Goods Legislation

While sale of goods legislation provides helpful inroads on the doctrine of *caveat emptor*, it has limitations. For example, the legislation

- applies only to sales of goods, not land or services

- requires that there be privity of contract between the customer and the "offending" party; breach of warranties by the manufacturer, for example, are not covered

- permits contracting out of the implied terms (the buyer and seller can agree that some or all of the terms will not apply)

- does not address pre-contractual representations made by the vendor

All provinces recognized the need to address these limitations as they affect consumers. This recognition arises from the assumption that consumers are at a disadvantage compared to businesses and therefore require legislative protection. The concept of protecting the consumer implicitly assumes that the commercial purchaser is better able to take care of itself and does not require special safeguards.

Consumer Protection Legislation

All provinces have supplemented the traditional *Sale of Goods Act* with legislation that effectively prevents the express exclusion of implied conditions and warranties in consumer transactions. Generally, these statutes apply only when goods are purchased for personal use. The adopted approach in some provinces[8] has been to imply certain conditions and warranties similar to those contained in the *Sale of Goods Act* into all retail sales of consumer products and to prevent their exclusion. Others[9] have adopted an approach that prevents the exclusion of the *Sale of Goods Act* conditions and warranties in consumer transactions.

All provinces[10] have gone further and enacted broader consumer protection legislation. For example, Ontario has enacted a comprehensive act that consolidates several existing pieces of legislation and addresses consumer rights, unfair trade practices (such as false, misleading, and unconscionable representations), particular consumer agreements (including direct sales and online agreements), credit agreements, and leases, along with remedies and enforcement.

In particular, provinces have legislated to address selling practices that generally can be described as unfair, usually because they prey on ill-informed consumers.[11] Unfairness typically arises in the context of unequal bargaining power. **Unfair practices** arise, for example, when the business intentionally

- targets customers with physical infirmity, ignorance, illiteracy, inability to understand the language or the agreement, or other similar factors and who are therefore unable to understand the serious nature of the agreement

Unfair practices
Illegal business practices that exploit the unequal bargaining position of consumers.

---

8. *Consumer Protection Act*, CCSM c C200, s 58; *Consumer Protection Act*, RSNS 1989, c 92, ss 26, 28; *Consumer Protection Act*, RSNWT 1988, c C-17, s 70; *Consumer Protection Act*, RSY 2002, c 40, s 58.

9. *Sale of Goods Act*, RSBC 1996, c 410, s 20.

10. *Consumer Protection Act*, SS 1996, c C-30.1, ss 39–75; *Consumer Product Warranty and Liability Act*, SNB 1978, c C-18.1; *Consumer Protection Act*, 2002, SO 2002, c 30, Schedule A.

11. *For example, Business Practices and Consumer Protection Act*, SBC 2004, c 2; *Consumer Protection and Business Practices Act*, SNL 2009, c C-31.1; *Consumer Protection Act*, 2002, SO 2002, c 30, Schedule A; *Business Practices Act*, RSPEI 1988, c B-7; *Consumer Protection Act*, RSQ c P-40.1.

- sells at a price that grossly exceeds the price at which similar goods or services are readily available to like consumers

- engages in a calculated and cynical marketing scheme that is subjecting the consumer to undue pressure to enter into the transaction

- persuades a customer to buy where there is no reasonable probability of payment of the obligation in full by the consumer

- imposes terms and conditions of the proposed transaction which are so adverse to the consumer as to be inequitable

While there are some differences in the approach in the various provinces, overall the consumer statutes are quite similar. As a starting point, this model of legislation has a broader scope in that it applies to all forms of transactions for consumer products, not just sales. Protected transactions include contracts of lease, conditional sales, and contracts for services, or for labour and materials, if supplied along with a consumer product. It is also no longer possible to exclude the operation of the implied terms. In many provinces, privity of contract cannot be raised as a defence against the ultimate consumer.

The legislation also eliminates the sometimes artificial distinction between warranties and conditions by implying warranties into protected transactions and providing specific remedies in the event of a breach of an implied warranty. The remedies available generally depend on the seriousness of the breach. Under the New Brunswick statute, for example, if the problem is relatively minor and repairable, the onus is typically upon the consumer to attempt to have the problem corrected and to allow the party at fault a reasonable time to correct the defect. If that does not occur, the consumer is entitled to compensation. If the problem is major or more serious, the consumer is entitled to end the contract and receive compensation where relevant. In either case, the onus is on the consumer to act quickly. The Act also permits recovery of any reasonably foreseeable damages.

While the implied warranties under the legislation are similar to those provided for under sale of goods statutes, greater protection is afforded to consumers by virtue of

- stronger warranties with respect to quality and fitness for purpose

- a warranty of durability to ensure that the goods are merchantable and fit for a reasonable amount of time (what is reasonable depends, generally, on the nature of the goods, the intended purpose, and the price paid)

- a warranty of reasonably acceptable quality of services

- a provision that makes all representations designed to induce a consumer into a transaction, whether written, oral, or otherwise, into express warranties given by the seller to the buyer

Should a vendor's actions be unfair, the consumer is typically entitled to rescission or to a return of money paid. The relevant government agency may also choose to prosecute the seller when a complaint is made. Judges apply the provisions of the legislation in a pragmatic way and tend to recognize that such legislation is endeavouring to balance consumer expectations with practical business concerns.

Before considering the legal issues relating to the four components of marketing—product, promotion, price, and distribution, it is necessary to provide an overview of competition law.

Competition Law

The primary source of competition law in Canada is the federal *Competition Act*[12] which has its origins in antitrust legislation passed first in 1889.[13] Its primary purposes are to promote the efficiency and adaptability of the Canadian economy; to ensure that smaller businesses have an equitable opportunity to participate in the Canadian economy; and to provide consumers with competitive prices and product choices.

The Commissioner of Competition, an independent official, is responsible for enforcing and administering the Act, and in particular, for the conduct of examinations and inquiries under the Act. For administrative purposes, the commissioner is the head of the Competition Bureau, which is part of Industry Canada. The commissioner publishes a wide range of bulletins and guidelines, along with an annual report that describes the bureau's activities. The commissioner is also responsible for administering and enforcing the *Consumer Packaging and Labelling Act*[14], the *Textile Labelling Act*[15], and the *Precious Metals Marking Act*.[16]

Marketing practices that are regulated by the *Competition Act* are either criminal or civil in nature. Criminal matters are of a more serious nature than civil reviewable matters. Examples of criminal offences are materially false or misleading representations made knowingly or recklessly, price fixing, and deceptive telemarketing. Under the criminal process, alleged offences are investigated by the bureau, and evidence obtained in criminal matters can be referred by the commissioner to the attorney general of Canada, who will, in turn, decide whether to proceed to prosecution, as is the normal practice with criminal matters. The accused may also consent to a course of action to avoid prosecution.

Examples of civil reviewable matters are misleading advertising, discriminatory practices, and abuse of dominant position. The civil process was developed to address concerns about the time required for and the difficulty of proving criminal cases. The primary purpose of the civil process is to stop the anticompetitive activity. The Competition Bureau will typically seek an order prohibiting the reviewable activity. Those found responsible may also be ordered to publish an information notice and pay an administrative penalty. Any violation of an order may itself be a criminal offence. While the penalties are not as severe as in the criminal provisions, the cases are easier to resolve since proof of criminal intent is not necessary.

Criminal and reviewable practices such as those listed above are discussed in detail later in this chapter and the next. A key part of the Act that supersedes marketing plans deals with mergers, acquisitions, and takeovers. In Canada it is recognized that there is a fine line between allowing business to expand through merger, acquisition, or takeover in

---

12. *Competition Act*, RSC 1985, c C-34.13.
13. *Act for the Prevention and Suppression of Combinations Formed in the Restraint of Trade*, SC 1889, c 41.
14. RSC 1985, c C-38.
15. RSC 1985, c T-10.
16. RSC 1985, c P-19.

order to operate profitably in what is a relatively small but geographically dispersed market and avoiding the negative consequences of what might through these processes become harmful, monopolistic behaviour. The *Competition Act* sets out the conditions under which the bureau can seek an order ending a proposed or actual merger. A merger is the union of two or more companies to form one larger company. The critical question in each case is whether a merger or proposed merger prevents or lessens, or is likely to prevent or lessen, competition substantially. What is considered "substantial" by the bureau is described in its guidelines[17] as the result of material increase in prices that is not likely to be offset by increased efficiency in the market.

The Act now provides for a two-step merger review process. If the size of the proposed merger exceeds the pre-notification threshold,[18] the businesses proposing the merger must notify the commissioner of their intentions prior to the merger. If the commissioner has concerns about the merger, the parties can be ordered to provide further information. When that information is complete, then within a specified time the parties will be provided with a determination as to whether the commissioner considers that the merger will substantially prevent or lessen competition. The commissioner will then decide whether the merger can proceed as notified, only on specified conditions, or not at all.[19]

Two key developments have affected the bureau's approach to enforcement of the Act. Significant amendments to the Act were passed as part of the *Budget Implementation Act, 2009*[20] and a new commissioner was appointed. In a speech,[21] the commissioner outlined the current priorities and highlighted recent enforcement activity. She stated "In the last 2 years, we have brought forward a number of important cases and demonstrated that, where there is a clear violation of the law, we will not hesitate to use the tools available to us to investigate and prosecute the offenders. To my mind, a consistent, principled enforcement strategy is the best deterrent of all—bar none." The commissioner mentioned recent enforcement activities:

- challenges to mergers in the hazardous waste industry and a joint venture between Air Canada and United Continental

- civil actions involving real estate agents and credit card companies

- criminal charges regarding the fixing of gas prices and rigging bids in residential construction in Quebec

- action for misleading representations by Bell Canada, Rogers, and Nivea.

Several of these cases are discussed in the context of the four components of marketing, beginning with the product.

---

17. Competition Bureau of Canada, "Merger Enforcement Guidelines" (6 October 2011), online: Competition Bureau Canada <http://www.competitionbureau.gc.ca/eic/site/cb-bc.nsf/eng/03420.html>.
18. See Competition Bureau of Canada, "2012 Pre-Merger Notification Transaction Size-Threshold" (7 February 2012), online: Competition Bureau Canada <http://www.competitionbureau.gc.ca/eic/site/cb-bc.nsf/eng/03040.html>.
19. For an example of a ruling on a takeover, see Competition Bureau of Canada, "Competition Bureau Statement on Bell and Rogers' Acquisition of Maple Leaf Sports & Entertainment" (2 May 2012), online: Competition Bureau Canada <http://www.competitionbureau.gc.ca/eic/site/cb-bc.nsf/eng/03464.html>.
20. SC 2009, c 2.
21. Melanie L Aitkin, "Remarks by Melanie L. Aitkin, Commissioner of Competition: Keynote Speech at the Canadian Bar Association 2011 Fall Conference" (6 October 2011), online: Competition Bureau Canada <http://www.competitionbureau.gc.ca/eic/site/cb-bc.nsf/eng/03424.html>. On 28 June 2012, Commissioner Aitken announced her resignation, effective 21 September 2012.

The Product
Basic Principles

Traditionally, the word "product" meant tangible goods, and this was the focus of early regulation. Today, the word and the regulations that apply to it are far broader in scope. A product is anything a business sells. It may include goods, services, or information.

PPC is developing a product that involves inherent and practically unavoidable risks that need to be managed. Children may fall off the best-designed climbing frames and be injured. However, provided the climbing frame is properly designed and built with its users in mind, PPC will have managed the risk and may avoid legal responsibility for such incidents.

In essence, doing the right thing in terms of a safe product coincides with what the law demands from business enterprises. PPC is required by the law of negligence to avoid causing harm that is reasonably foreseeable. PPC is required by contract law to supply the product it has promised. PPC is also required to meet regulatory standards designed to protect the public. In addition, businesses follow voluntary industry codes. If PPC engages in effective risk management in relation to product design, manufacture, packaging, and labelling, legal problems should be minimal. Regulatory standards regarding product elements are discussed below.

Design and Manufacture

Governments establish standards for protection of patents and product design. For example, if another person or company has registered a particular industrial design, PPC cannot produce or sell playground equipment based on that design unless PPC obtains explicit permission in a licence from the registered owner.

In addition, organizations such as the Canadian Standards Association develop voluntary guidelines for use by both producers and users of goods. Guidelines are developed with the assistance of a broad range of experts, including representatives from industry.[22] These guidelines may be adopted by regulators as mandatory standards, and they will typically represent the measure of the standard of care for tort liability.

All businesses should be familiar with voluntary guidelines that apply to their goods and services and must become familiar with the mandatory standards in their field of operation. Governments, through legislation, impose minimum standards for many goods and services where they consider it to be in the public interest to reduce the risk of harm. Examples include the following:

- Some industries must comply with specific legislation. The *Motor Vehicle Safety Act* "regulate[s] the manufacture and importation of motor vehicles and motor vehicle equipment to reduce the risk of death, injury and damage to property and the environment."[23]

22. *The Standards Council of Canada Act,* RSC 1985, c S-16, s 3 creates a Standards Council, which, in turn, accredits bodies, including the Canadian Standards Association , online:<http://www.scc.ca> that create different standards. The Canadian Standards Association also provides testing and certification of products under its brand name CSA International. The international standards-setting body is the International Organization for Standardization (ISO).
23. SC 1993, c 16.

- Broad categories of products such as food and drugs cannot be sold if they are unsafe or fail to meet approved standards.[24]

- The sale or distribution of some products or substances is restricted or prohibited. For example, if PPC sold painted playground equipment, the paint could not contain lead.

MAS KIKUTA

What legal challenges are presented by the design of this product?

Producers of goods and services may consider regulations and voluntary guidelines to be impediments to their development of an effective marketing plan. They are better viewed, however, as the collective opinion of specialists in risk assessment. For example, the voluntary standards on children's playspaces and equipment[25] developed by the Canadian Standards Association represent the consensus of qualified experts, including industry participants, as to what is reasonable to maintain child safety. Viewed in this light, they are a valuable resource for producers like PPC. Ignoring the standards would seriously compromise PPC's marketplace reputation and significantly increase its exposure to legal liability.

Product suitability and quality were addressed in the previous section dealing with the contract of sale.

Packaging and Labelling

Marketing concerns the design of product packaging as well as the creation of the product itself. While package design is used to attract customers, it must also comply with laws concerning safety and accuracy. Information on the package, the labels, instructions, and warnings are crucial in terms of the standard of care in a claim for negligence.

---

24. *Food and Drugs Act*, RSC 1985, c F-27 (*FDA*).
25. Canadian Standards Association International, *A Guideline on Children's Playspaces and Equipment*, Doc No CSA Z614-98 (Toronto: CSA International, 1998).

Labelling and packaging legislation complements common law. Its focus is the imposition of standards in order to prevent harm. Trademark law (see Chapter 18) also affects package design.[26] Most packaging and labelling legislation is federal and therefore applies throughout the country.[27] Some legislation is industry specific—for example, the *Food and Drugs Act* (food, drugs, cosmetics, and other therapeutic devices), the *Textile Labelling Act*,[28] and the *Tobacco Act*.[29] Other legislation regulates consumer products generally.

The *Consumer Packaging and Labelling Act* (*CPLA*)[30] sets out minimum packaging and labelling requirements for all prepackaged goods sold in Canada, other than drugs, cosmetics, and medical devices. The Act encourages fair competition between manufacturers and other sellers by ensuring that consumers can compare the price and quantity of products. It is enforced by Health Canada and the Canada Food Inspection Agency for food products and by the Competition Bureau for non-food products.

The *CPLA* requires manufacturers to

- provide the consumer with certain essential information; specifically, the generic description, net quantity, and identity of manufacturer or importer.

- eliminate any misleading information about the nature or quantity of the product that might flow either from statements made on the container or from the shape or size of the container. For example, goods cannot be labelled "Made in Canada" or "Product of Canada" unless they meet specific requirements.[31]

The regulations are intended to provide customers with the product information required to make purchasing decisions. PPC proposes to sell its playground equipment partially assembled, in boxes. If PPC prints only its name and a graphic on the packaging, purchasers will not know the size of the equipment, whether all the parts are included and holes are pre-drilled, whether the wood requires a sealant, and who should be contacted if there are any questions or parts are missing. Failure to provide this information may confuse consumers and may also violate the *CPLA*.

Much of the information required by law must be disclosed in both French and English. In addition, the regulations can be very specific. For example, wrapping paper, aluminum foil, and paper towel (bi-dimensional products) must be described in appropriate units—square metres, or dimensions of roll, ply, and the number of perforated individual units for paper towels. All information must be prominently and clearly presented. Without this information, the prospective purchaser would have to guess about the quantity being purchased, and a manufacturer might be tempted to make the product look bigger than it is.

26. See Canadian Food Inspection Agency, "The Use of Trade-Marks in Labelling of Foods Sold in Canada" (27 April 2012), online: Canadian Food Inspection Agency <http://inspection.gc.ca/food/labelling/other-requirements/trade-marks/eng/1335544176482/1335544253720>.
27. The principal exception to this is the Quebec language legislation, most importantly that found in s 51 of the *Charter of the French Language*, RSQ c C-11. Otherwise, provincial legislation tends to apply to specialized industries such as alcohol, milk, and margarine.
28. RSC 1985, c T-10. See Competition Bureau of Canada, *Guide to the Textile Labelling and Advertising Regulations* (September 2000), online: <http://www.competitionbureau.gc.ca/eic/site/cb-bc.nsf/eng/01249.html>.
29. SC 1997, c 13.
30. RSC 1985, c C-38. See also Competition Bureau of Canada, *Guide to the Consumer Products Labelling Act and Regulations: Enforcement Guidelines* (October 1999), online: Competition Bureau Canada <http://www.competitionbureau.gc.ca/eic/site/cb-bc.nsf/eng/01248.html>.
31. These requirements were recently tightened. New guidelines for food products came into effect on 31 December 2008. See Canadian Food Inspection Agency, *Guidelines for Product of Canada and Made in Canada Claims*, online: Canadian Food Inspection Agency <http://www.inspection.gc.ca/food/labelling/other-requirements/origin-claims/product-of-canada/guidelines/eng/1333457811817/13334 58040733l>. For non-food products, see Competition Bureau of Canada, "Competition Bureau confirms enforcement approach to new guidelines on "Made in Canada" and "Product of Canada" claims" (14 May 2010), online: Competition Bureau Canada <http://www .competitionbureau.gc.ca/eic/site/cb-bc.nsf/eng/03230.html>.

Some products are inherently hazardous, so the information related to the product should include sufficient warning of any hazards, special instructions for handling or using the product, and critical information about what to do if the product causes harm to the user. Examples of potentially hazardous or dangerous products are chemicals such as household cleaners or petroleum distillates and a wide range of goods, such as pressurized metal cans, flammable carpets, baby cribs, car seats, tents, cigarette lighters, and children's sleepwear. The danger to children of these products has major implications for packaging and labeling. Containers should be child-proof or child-resistant and be clearly labeled to warn adults of the dangers to children.

PHOTOGRAPHED WITH PERMISSION BY BIO-LAB CANADA, INC.

What is the purpose of the information on this container?

There is significant new legislation regarding product safety.

BUSINESS AND LEGISLATION

Federal Consumer Product Safety Legislation

Consumer confidence in protection from the regulatory system has been shaken by significant problems with several products in recent years. These products include children's toys painted with lead-based paint, prescription drugs with serious side effects, contaminated spinach and tomatoes, tainted pet food, suspect plastic bottles, and tainted processed meat.

As the various problem product situations unfolded, consumers became aware that both preventive and reactive regulatory measures were quite different and less effective than they had believed. There were standards for product safety, but manufacturers were left to monitor their own products. Importers were responsible for determining the safety and quality of the products they imported. Information provided to consumers through labels, warnings, or advertising claims was not vetted in advance, but merely subject to complaints of inaccuracy by consumers or competitors.

In terms of reactive measures, regulators had questionable authority to remove products from the market or issue recalls. Violators were rarely caught. The penalties resulting from serious violations were seldom levied.

The federal government reacted to public concerns in 2008 by introducing two bills under the umbrella of the Food and Consumer Safety Action Plan. The bills[32] made major amendments to the *Food and Drugs Act* and proposed the new *Consumer Product Safety Act*, to replace Part 1 of the *Hazardous Products Act*. The bills died on the order paper when the 2008 election was called, but the *Consumer Product Safety Act*[33] (CPSA) was reintroduced and passed. It came into force on 20 June 2011.

The *CPSA* creates a new system to regulate consumer products that might pose a danger to human health and safety. Its purpose is to protect the public by addressing or preventing dangers to human health and safety posed by

(Continued)

---

32. 2nd Session, 39th Parliament.
33. *Canada Consumer Product Safety Act*, SC 2010, c 21.

consumer products, whether domestic or imported. Key provisions

• prohibit the manufacture, importation, advertisement, or sale of consumer products that constitute danger to human health or safety

• prohibit misleading claims on packages, labels, or advertising as they relate to health or safety

• provide authority to order testing and evaluation of consumer products to verify compliance

• require manufacturers, importers, and sellers to report dangerous incidents, product defects, inadequate labels, and product recalls

• authorize entrance to private property, inspection and seizure of products to verify compliance or noncompliance

• enable government to institute and enforce corrective measures, including product recalls

• provide for criminal penalties up to $5 million and administrative penalties up to $25 000.

Now that the *CPSA* is in force, several criteria can be used to measure its effectiveness:

• Is it comprehensible to the consumers who are meant to be protected, the businesses who are meant to comply with the rules, and the regulators who are meant to enforce them?

• Will businesses see sufficient benefit in compliance and perceive a reasonable probability of being caught for failure to comply?

• Will government devote adequate resources to enforcement?

• Will consumer complaints be investigated and disposed of in a timely and adequate fashion?

• Will the increased penalties be imposed upon violators so that they act as an effective deterrent?

Critical Analysis: How effective can the law be in dealing with dangerous and unsafe products? How does the growth of global trade make the problem more challenging?

Sources: Health Canada, *Canada Consumer Product Safety Act Quick Reference Guide* (2011), online: Health Canada <http://www.hc-sc.gc.ca/cps-spc/pubs/indust/ccpsa_ref-lcspc/index-eng.php#a8> and Luis Millan, "The new consumer safety law", *The Lawyers Weekly* (19 August 2011) 14.

The remainder of this chapter is devoted to the promotion component of marketing.

Promotion

A leading marketing text defines promotion as the "communications link between buyers and sellers [with the] function of informing, persuading, and influencing a consumer's purchase decision."[34] Influencing the customer is achieved through an optimal mix of the key elements of promotion—advertising, public relations, personal selling, and sales promotion. For both sellers and buyers, promotion is the most visible component of the marketing mix. As with design and production, promotion is governed by both voluntary industry standards and legislation. To avoid legal problems related to promotion, marketers need only follow the advice of the Commissioner of Competition regarding misleading representations, "It's very simple—don't mislead the public by hiding charges or conditions in fine print, or by making claims you can't back up."[35]

Industry Standards

The most important voluntary standards are those of Advertising Standards Canada (ASC), an organization established by the advertising community to promote public confidence in its products and services, and those of the Canadian Broadcast Standards Council (CBSC), a council supported by the Canadian Association of Broadcasters (CAB) with the approval of the Canadian Radio-television and Telecommunications Commission (CRTC).

The ASC addresses advertising in general and has a detailed code of industry guidelines. It provides a mechanism for public complaints concerning violations of that code, as well

---

34. LE Boone *et al, Contemporary Marketing,* 3rd Can ed (Toronto: Nelson, 2013) at 45.
35. *Supra* note 21.

as business-to-business complaints. Complaints are investigated and, if found to be valid, result in a finding that the advertiser should change or remove the offending promotion. Since this is a voluntary process, enforcement relies on moral suasion. However, findings are publicized, and members of the advertising community can ill afford to ignore a ruling made against them by their peers. For example, in 2011 the ASC ruled on a complaint concerning a billboard advertisement for a radio morning show that featured a close-up of a woman wearing a tight T-shirt. Printed across the chest of her T-shirt were the words "Pray For More Rain." The Council found "that this advertisement demeaned and denigrated women and encouraged, gratuitously and without merit, attitudes that offended standards of decency among a significant segment of the population."[36]

The CBSC has an equivalent code of ethics and complaints process, dealing specifically with promotion in broadcast media. In addition, it has developed more specialized codes, such as those related to sexual stereotyping and violence. The Television Bureau of Canada (TBC) must approve all television commercials before broadcast.

Legislation

The promotion of goods is regulated by legislation, primarily the federal *Competition Act*.[37] If sellers are tempted to mislead customers or make claims they cannot support, they may be engaging in the following prohibited practices.

Misleading Advertising and Representations

The most important provisions relating to **false or misleading advertising** are found in the Act[38] which defines false or misleading advertising as arising where

> [a] person who, for the purpose of promoting, directly or indirectly, the supply or use of a product or for the purpose of promoting, directly or indirectly, any business interest, by any means whatever, makes a representation to the public that is false or misleading in a material respect.

This provision is stated in broad terms so as to capture not only those who deliberately make false statements, but also those who push the limits of truth—intentionally or otherwise—in the impressions given to buyers.

Falsity is judged by an objective test. Whether or not a statement is misleading is measured by the impression that might be formed by the average member of the group of persons to whom the statement is directed. What is important is the impression created by the advertisement in its entirety, including illustrations and disclaimers.[39] The misrepresentation must be "material"—that is, it must apply to statements that entice prospective

False or misleading advertising
Promotional statements that either are false or have the ability to mislead a consumer as to their truth.

---

36. Advertising Standards Council, "Recent Complaint Case Summaries", online: Advertising Standards Canada <http://www.adstandards.com/en/standards/adComplaintsreportscurrent.asp>.
37. RSC 1985, c C-34.
38. *Ibid, ss* 52, 74.01. Other legislation tends to focus on specific issues. For example, the *Consumer Packaging and Labelling Act, supra* note 30, prohibits misleading advertising, specifically in the context of prepackaged goods; it would be misleading to describe the product box as "full" or "large" if this is not the case.
39. For example, a Vancouver career management company made representations to prospective clients that created the false impression that they had an extensive network of personal contacts in the corporate world. See Competition Bureau of Canada, "Federal Court of Appeal rules that career management firm misled vulnerable job seekers" (16 October 2009), online: Competition Bureau Canada <http://www.competitionbureau.gc.ca/eic/site/cb-bc.nsf/eng/03144.html>.

purchasers to the place of business or that influence the customer's decision to purchase the particular item. For example, a fitness company admitted that by failing to disclose additional mandatory fees in its advertising of membership offers in newspapers, billboards, and storefront signs, it had led consumers to believe that the price of memberships was significantly less than the actual price.[40]

There are more specific guidelines for particular types of advertising. One example is environmental or "green" advertising.

ETHICAL CONSIDERATIONS

Environmental Claims in Advertising

Consumers are becoming increasingly aware of the environmental consequences of their consumption of products. Accordingly, they are attracted to environmentally friendly products and producers. Marketers are keen to cater to this development in the marketplace and may be tempted to overstate the environmental features of their products.

In 2000 the Canadian Standards Association (CSA) adopted international standards on environmental labelling. To assist business in interpreting this standard, the CSA and the Competition Bureau developed a best practices guide *Environmental Claims: A Guide for Industry and Advertisers*.[41] It contains detailed advice regarding three aspects of environmental claims:

- Claims that imply general environmental improvement are insufficient and should be avoided.
- Claims should be clear, specific, accurate, and contain no misleading information.
- Claims must be verified and substantiated with supporting data that is accurate and available for scrutiny.

In terms of sustainability in the context of wood, for example, the statement "This wood comes from a forest that is certified to a sustainable forest management standard published by CSA" is preferred. The statement "This wood is sustainable" is discouraged.

Although the guide is not law, following its advice will help businesses to avoid making misleading claims and the bureau will use the guide to assess environmental advertising. Potential penalties are those for contravention of the misleading advertising provisions of the *Competition Act* under the criminal and civil regimes.

Applying the guidelines, the bureau has taken action against a large number of hot tub and spa retailers regarding claims that their products were eligible for ENERGY STAR certification, an international standard. In fact, no products of this type for sale in Canada are eligible for this certification. Two retailers have recently signed a consent agreement, in which they agree to cease the misleading misrepresentations, pay an administrative penalty of $130 000, publish corrective notices, and develop a corporate compliance program.

PPC must be careful about claims such as "Our environmentally friendly harvesting of woods enhances regeneration of local forests." They must be clear, specific, accurate, and not misleading.

Critical Analysis: Will business use these guidelines to improve the quality of environmental advertising? Are consumers likely to receive the information they need to make environmentally sensitive buying choices?

Sources: Competition Bureau of Canada, "What does green really mean?" (25 June 2008), online: Competition Bureau Canada <http://www.competitionbureau.gc.ca/eic/site/cb-bc.nsf/eng/02700.html> and Competition Bureau of Canada, "Spa retailers required to stop making false ENERGY STAR claims" (17 January 2011), online: Competition Bureau Canada <http://www.competitionbureau.gc.ca/eic/site/cb-bc.nsf/eng/03342.html>.

Complaints and Defences

If a business is suspected of false or misleading advertising of goods or services, officers of the Competition Bureau will conduct an investigation. If the misrepresentation is sufficiently serious, criminal charges under the *Competition Act* may be laid, in which case the prosecutor will need to prove that the misrepresentation was made "knowingly and

---

40. Competition Bureau of Canada, "Premier Fitness undisclosed fees investigation successfully concluded" (27 November 2007), online: Competition Bureau Canada <http://www.competitionbureau.gc.ca/eic/site/cb-bc.nsf/eng/02518.html>.
41. Competition Bureau of Canada, (25 June 2008), online: Competition Bureau Canada <http://www.competitionbureau.gc.ca/eic/site/cb-bc.nsf/eng/02701.html>.

recklessly." More frequently, a complaint of false or misleading advertising will be pursued through the civil regime, which is normally faster and can result in an order to halt the deceptive practice and/or an administrative penalty.

A recent example of a settlement concerned misrepresentations by Bell Canada about the prices offered for services. The bureau found that for several years, Bell had charged higher prices than advertised for home phone, Internet, TV, and wireless by hiding additional mandatory fees in fine print disclaimers. Bell agreed to modify its non-compliant ads and pay the maximum administrative penalty of $10 million.[42]

The best defence to allegations of misleading advertising is that the elements of the offence have not been proven, but reviewable matters have an additional defence, namely that of **due diligence**:

> … consideration of what a reasonable man would have done in the circumstances. The defence will be available if the accused reasonably believed in a mistaken set of facts which, if true, would render the act or omission innocent, or if he took all reasonable steps to avoid the particular event.[43]

The onus is on the accused to demonstrate due diligence. Consider the following examples of the application of due diligence in the context of potentially misleading representations.

Example 1   PPC imports products from overseas. It is advised by the exporter that the goods meet CSA standards, and thus, PPC makes this statement in its promotional materials. In fact, the goods meet some lesser standards, and there has been no attempt by the exporter or PPC to establish that Canadian standards have been met. PPC will fail to prove due diligence. As a seller in Canada, PPC should have exercised reasonable care; failing to make any checks is inadequate.

Example 2   PPC publishes and distributes the *PPC Children's Play Catalogue*, a biannual publication. The catalogue lists 250 items, and it is found to have a high incidence of errors in their descriptions. PPC's defence is that it spot-checks every tenth product listed for accuracy. The sampling is unlikely to be considered adequate for this type of catalogue. Reasonableness may not involve the checking of each individual description, but it certainly involves more than 1 in 10.

The Competition Bureau will be influenced by whether or not the advertiser has sought to correct errors. Speedy retraction may also be evidence of due diligence. A pattern of similar errors corrected repeatedly, however, may suggest both a cynical marketing strategy and a lack of due diligence. The retailer using materials provided by the producer (or another party in the distribution chain) does not face liability unless it has transformed the representation made by the manufacturer into its own advertisement and promoted the product itself.

Due diligence
A defence based on adopting reasonable steps to avoid the violation of a legal duty.

---

42. Competition Bureau of Canada, "Competition Bureau reaches agreement with Bell Canada" (28 June 2011) online: Competition Bureau Canada <http://www.competitionbureau.gc.ca/eic/site/cb-bc.nsf/eng/03388.html>.

43. *R v Sault Ste Marie (City)*, [1978] 2 SCR 1299 at para 60.

Performance Claims

Statements about the performance of a product or service may fall within the general provisions described earlier under misleading advertising.

The *Competition Act* also has a specific provision directed to performance claims. It is reviewable conduct to make a representation about the quality of a product that is not based on an "adequate and proper test."[44] A statement such as "the PPC climber develops your child's gross motor skills better than any other play equipment on the market" must be true. PPC must establish that, before making such a claim, there was appropriate testing of its accuracy.

Performance claims are a frequent source of complaint to the Competition Bureau.

BUSINESS APPLICATION OF THE LAW

Unjustified Performance Claims

Optimistic claims about the performance of products are common, but the manufacturer cannot make claims about their effectiveness without proof of their truth. Here are three cases that involved claims relating to stress reduction, cancer treatment, and body slimming.

Lululemon Athletica, a manufacturer of yoga wear, claimed that its seaweed-based clothing would, upon contact with moisture, release minerals and vitamins into the skin to produce effects such as enhancing the blood supply to the skin, promoting skin cell regeneration, and reducing stress. Following complaints and investigation by the bureau, Lululemon agreed to remove all claims alleging therapeutic benefits from its VitaSea line of clothing. The agreement included clothing tags, the company website, and information provided by store managers and employees. Lululemon also agreed to conduct a review of all of its promotional and marketing materials to ensure compliance with legal requirements.

In 2009 the bureau took action against a number of advertisers as part of its education and enforcement initiative, Project False Hope, to target cancer-related health fraud online. Bionergy Wellness Inc. was an Edmonton company that made claims online about magnetic pulse devices and infrared sauna treatments for cancer patients. The claims were not based on adequate and proper tests. The company and its director

agreed to stop making the claims, offer refunds to customers, and post corrective notices.

Beiersdorf Canada is the Canadian distributor of Nivea products. The company misled consumers by claiming that its "My Silhouette" product would slim and reshape the body, causing a reduction of up to 3 centimetres on targeted body parts, and that use of the product would make skin more toned and elastic. Following investigation by the bureau, Beiersdorf agreed to remove the product from stores, provide refunds to customers, pay an administrative penalty, and publish corrective notices. In the notice, Beiersdorf stated that "performance claims and testing related to Nivea 'My Silhouette' are supported by independent research, which has always complied with Canadian requirements and guidelines." The bureau objected to this statement as a violation of the agreement and it was removed.

Critical Analysis: Why are sellers tempted to make claims that they cannot support?

Sources: Competition Bureau of Canada, "Competition Bureau takes action against unproven cancer treatment sold online" (19 February 2009), online: Competition Bureau Canada <http://www.competitionbureau.gc.ca/eic/site/cb-bc.nsf/eng/02988.html>; Competition Bureau of Canada, "Competition Bureau requires maker of Nivea to correct inaccurate public statements related to Nivea consent agreement" (22 September 2011), online: Competition Bureau Canada <http://www.competitionbureau.gc.ca/eic/site/cb-bc.nsf/eng/03413.html>; and Competition Bureau of Canada, "Lululemon VitaSea Clothing" (16 November 2007), online: Competition Bureau Canada <http://www.competitionbureau.gc.ca/eic/site/cb-bc.nsf/eng/02517.html>.

Litigation

The *Competition Act* also allows for civil actions to be brought by individuals or commercial complainants who are harmed by the actions of competitors, particularly in the context of comparative advertising.[45] Since stopping the advertising campaign is of primary importance, the complainant may seek an injunction, as well as pursue claims for damages if the loss is quantifiable. The *Mead Johnson Canada* case, discussed in Chapter 12, was the first case in which an injunction was allowed. The first case in Canada to award damages for

---

44. *Supra* note 37 at s 74.01(1)(b).
45. *Supra* note 37 at s 36.

misleading advertising[46] involved claims by Go Travel that misled the public by suggesting that Maritime Travel's prices were overall more expensive than their's because Maritime was a travel agent. Damages of $216 842 were awarded for commissions lost due to the misleading representation. There has recently been a flurry of litigation among telecommunications companies around claims about the speed and reliability of cellphone and Internet networks and services.[47] In addition, since 2009 the commissioner may request the court to order restitution to those affected by false and misleading representations.[48]

In a recent case expected to influence the interpretation of consumer protection legislation and the *Competition Act*, the Supreme Court awarded damages in a claim based on a misleading magazine subscription contest.[49]

Tests and Testimonials

Advertisers often promote products and services either by presenting supportive test results or by using the assurances of convincing spokespersons, either real or hypothetical. Tests must be carried out prior to the promotion. If conducted by a third party, there must be permission to draw from the tests or they must already be in the public domain.

PPC may claim to have tested its products on a sample of nursery schools in the Prince George area. Provided PPC quotes accurately from these tests and they are fairly presented, this is in compliance with the Act. Alternatively, suppose *Consumer Reports* or *Today's Parent* has published surveys of different play equipment, and PPC wishes to quote from these surveys in promotional material. If copyright approval is required and received, and the quotes are accurately represented, this form of promotion is acceptable.

PPC may also wish to use testimonials, for example, from a childcare professional, an expert in child development, or a parent. These testimonials will be acceptable provided they are accurately stated and current, and provided the persons providing the testimonials have actually used or evaluated the product. Using a well-known personality to provide the desired testimonial will attract close scrutiny. If, however, PPC is using an actor to represent, say, a hypothetical parent, the statements will be measured by the provisions for false and misleading advertising in general.

Bait and Switch

An unscrupulous promotional practice is **bait and switch**. The product is advertised at a very low price (the bait) but the supply is insufficient to meet expected demand. When consumers take the bait, they are informed that this product is "not in stock," "of poor quality," or "inferior to Product B." They are then persuaded to purchase the higher-priced Product B (the switch). It is, of course, Product B that the promoter intended to sell all along, usually because it has better profit margins. This a reviewable practice.

Bait and switch
Advertising a product at a very low price to attract customers, then encouraging them to buy another product that is more expensive.

---

46. *Go Travel Direct.Com Inc v Maritime Travel Inc*, 2009 NSCA 42.

47. See Iain Marlow, "Bell Aliant sues Rogers over Internet ads", *The Globe and Mail* (15 February 2010), online: Globe and Mail <http://www.theglobeandmail.com/news/technology/bell-aliant-sues-rogers-over-internet-ads/article1468899/> ; Simon Houpt, "Rogers ditching 'most-reliable' claim", *The Globe and Mail* (30 November 2009), online: Globe and Mail <http://www.theglobeandmail.com/globe-investor/rogers-ditching-most-reliable-claim/article1383253/>; and Bertrand Marotte and Simon Houpt, "Bell takes Videotron to court over 'fastest' claim", *The Globe and Mail* (30 April 2010), online: Globe and Mail <http://www.theglobeandmail.com/report-on-business/bell-takes-vidotron-to-court-over-fastest-claim/article1552315/>.

48. *Supra* note 37 at s 74.10.

49. *Richard v Time Inc*, 2012 SCC 8 and see Cristin Schmitz, "Caveat venditor for advertisers", *The Lawyers Weekly* (9 March 2012) 2.

Business Law in Practice Revisited

1. How does the law affect PPC's marketing strategy?

PPC's marketing strategy covers the four aspects of the marketing mix: the product, its promotion, its price, and the way it reaches the consumer (distribution or place). Even though the industry in which PPC operates is not highly regulated, both common law and statute law affect every aspect of the marketing mix.

PPC must meet CSA safety standards which also provide guidance for the minimum standard of care in tort and contract. The goods must comply with the *Consumer Packaging and Labelling Act* (*CPLA*). PPC is promoting mainly through the print media and in-store displays. It must be familiar with the provisions related to false and misleading advertising and to tests and testimonials. Any claims of environmental benefits must be supported by evidence.

2. What are the key aspects of PPC's contracts with its customers?

The producer must perform the terms of its contract of sale; otherwise, the purchasers may claim that a breach has occurred. PPC should be aware of how the implied conditions and warranties of the *Sale of Goods Act* affect its contractual obligations regarding the quality of the product. In particular, the goods must match the description PPC provides on the box and be of merchantable quality. Additionally, the goods must be fit for the purpose for which they are sold. PPC also needs to comply with consumer protection legislation that supplements the *Sale of Goods Act,* especially for its online sales. In addition, PPC must be aware of terms relating to the transfer of title and delivery of goods.

3. What impact does the law have on PPC's product?

Under tort law, and the law of negligence and product liability in particular, PPC should take steps to avoid any reasonably foreseeable harm to users of its products that might arise from design, manufacture, or packaging. The federal *CPLA* will govern how PPC packages the goods by providing minimum disclosure requirements. Since PPC's marketing campaign is national in scope, information must be in both official languages. It should limit any potential liability through warnings. PPC must also consider the full range of voluntary guidelines that affect the products, since these, in practice, will define the standard of care in negligence.

4. What impact does the law have on the promotion of PPC's product?

Representations must be truthful—neither false nor misleading. They will be evaluated in their entirety. Where the due diligence defence applies, PPC must establish both that it had a reasonable belief in the accuracy of any representations and that it took reasonable steps to avoid any inaccuracies. PPC must be careful if it makes claims about the performance capabilities of its products. All such claims must be backed by testing. If PPC uses testimonials, these must be given by real people who are familiar with the products, or by people identified as actors. Tests must be current, used with permission if appropriate, and accurately stated. Any environmental claims must be justified.

Chapter Summary

Compliance with the relevant laws coincides, for the most part, with good marketing practice. Providing reliable and safe products and ensuring that consumers are accurately and fully informed goes a long way toward achieving the key feature of effective marketing policy—meeting customer expectations.

Inevitably, however, some market participants disregard these basic principles and attempt to profit at the customers' expense. If there were no regulations in place, such practices would clearly place "good" producers at a distinct disadvantage. Legislation is therefore intended to ensure fair competition.

All sellers must be aware of the implied conditions and warranties of the *Sale of Goods Act*s and other consumer protection legislation. The rules for establishing when title to goods shifts are set out in the *Sale of Goods Act*s unless otherwise provided by contract. Sellers require knowledge of the meaning of a series of standard terms used in shipping of goods, such as c.i.f. and f.o.b.

Regulation relating to the product component addresses the product (or service) itself and its packaging and labelling. The producer must be familiar with voluntary and statutory guidelines for product design and standards. Product labelling regulation is important where the customer cannot see the goods, and there are explicit requirements for disclosure. In promoting goods, the most important regulation is the false and misleading advertising provision of the *Competition Act*. More specific legislative provisions also apply—for example, to tests, testimonials, and performance claims. Any practices that induce purchases through unfair or improper means will come under scrutiny.

Chapter Study

Key Terms and Concepts

action for the price (p. 579)

bait and switch (p. 593)

bill of lading (p. 574)

caveat emptor (p. 572)

c.i.f. (p. 574)

c.o.d. (p. 575)

damages for non-acceptance (p. 579)

due diligence (p. 591)

false or misleading advertising (p. 589)

f.o.b. (p. 575)

marketing law (p. 571)

specific goods (p. 576)

stoppage in transit (p. 574)

unascertained goods (p. 576)

unfair practices (p. 580)

Questions for Review

1. What is the relationship between voluntary standards such as those created by the Canadian Standards Association and common law obligations in tort and contract?

2. What are the key provisions of the *Consumer Products Safety Act*?

3. How did sale of goods legislation originate?

4. What is the difference between an implied condition and a warranty in the *Sale of Goods Act*?

5. What is an example of a condition implied by the *Sale of Goods Act* into a contract of sale?

6. What is an example of a way in which *Sale of Goods Act* provisions have been adapted to consumer contracts of sale?

7. What are "specific" goods?

8. What rules decide when title to goods passes from the seller to the buyer?

9. What is a bill of lading?

10. What is the purpose of the *Consumer Packaging and Labelling Act*?

11. How does the *Competition Act* classify the marketing practices that it regulates?

12. How does the law ensure the safety of consumer products?

13. What is misleading advertising?

14. How can a business defend itself from an accusation of misleading advertising?

15. What is the due diligence defence?

16. How can a corporation use the misleading advertising provisions of the *Competition Act* against a competitor?

17. If a business is investigated for an improper performance claim about its products, what is its best defence?

18. What is the selling practice known as "bait and switch"?

Questions for Critical Thinking

1. If consumer protection legislation equates to good marketing practices, why do we have so much legislation? Would market forces not sort these issues out without state intervention?

2. Why do businesses need to be familiar with the law relating to competition and consumer protection? How does this law relate to marketing practices?

3. The standards relating to children's playground equipment are controversial. Some see them as being too cautious and as imposing undue burdens on service providers such as parks and schools that might have to replace all equipment. Why has this controversy arisen? What interests need to be balanced?

4. The new *Consumer Products Safety Act* is a major federal legislative initiative to force sellers to provide safe products and increase consumer confidence. Such legislation is normally reviewed every five years. When the *CPSA* is revisited in 2016, what criteria should be used to measure its effectiveness?

5. Why does the *Competition Act* focus on regulating the behaviour of business rather than providing remedies directly to consumers? Does provincial legislation serve consumers more effectively?

6. Compare the criminal and civil approaches relating to deceptive marketing practices in the *Competition Act*. What are the advantages of the civil process?

Situations for Discussion

1. Senior management of Superior Chemicals Ltd. has decided to revamp the marketing program for the company's line of household products, which includes kitchen, bathroom, furniture, flooring, and all-purpose cleaners. They wish to promote these products as more environmentally friendly than those of their competitors. The marketing department has developed a large number of possible messages such as "natural," "nature clean," "renewable ingredients," "biodegradable," "the environmental choice," "the responsible choice," and "We care about the earth." Management is aware of the rules regarding misleading advertising and the new guide for environmental claims.[50] What should management consider in developing the advertising campaign for their cleaning products? Which claims are appropriate? How must Superior be able to support its claims?

2. Hammer and Nails Hardware, a nationwide chain, has devised a new product line. It has discerned a growing niche in the market among older "empty nesters" who are moving from houses into apartments or condominiums. It has devised a "We meet all your basic needs" campaign that prepackages tools, home repair products, and decorating products. It intends to introduce a series of 10 different lines over a six-month period. They will be boxed in an attractive, uniform style of packaging that includes "how-to" books. The packages will include the basic items needed for particular household tasks.

   What must Hammer and Nails consider in terms of its choice of package contents, packaging, labelling, instructions, and promotion in order to comply with legal requirements and avoid creating inflated expectations from customers?

3. Outdoor World sells new and used snowmobiles. It makes most of its money from new products, and it attempts to move secondhand ones quickly, particularly since the season is short and it does not want to be caught with expensive storage costs throughout the summer. Each January it has a major "blowout" sale that is heavily promoted and provides genuine savings.

   Morley is in the market for a used snowmobile. He tells the salesperson he wants a basic machine, "no hassles," and as good a deal as he can get. The salesperson shows him three; he starts each one and says that they are roughly equivalent. Morley takes a quick look and picks one basically on colour, since he knows little about snowmobiles. The listed price was $3500, but because Outdoors is anxious to clear the line and Morley is extremely price-sensitive, he is able to bargain down the price to $2000.

   Two days later there is a good snowfall and Morley takes the machine out for a run. Five kilometres from home, the snowmobile splutters to a stop. Morley cannot get the machine started. In the end, a friend rescues him, and Morley gets the machine towed straight back to Outdoor World.

   What are Morley's rights under the common law? Do the *Sale of Goods Act* warranties and conditions help? Do Morley's rights vary according to the province in which the sale occurred?

4. McAsphalt Industries Ltd. is a supplier of asphalt and cement for use in road paving work. Chapman Bros. Ltd. is a road paving company. Chapman ordered some modified asphalt cement from McAsphalt who assured Chapman that the material could be used with its conventional equipment. When Chapman used the material, it broke into chunks, requiring the removal of a filter and the alteration of its equipment. Much of the paving had to be redone. Chapman refused to pay McAsphalt for the material and claimed compensation for the cost of repaving and profit lost on other jobs.[51] Who is responsible for the quality of the material and its suitability for Chapman's equipment? How will the conflicting claims be resolved?

5. Softest Diapers is one of two leading producers of diapers for infants. It has spent several years researching and testing a new brand of super-absorbent diaper. It is now devising an advertising campaign that will make direct comparison with its competitor's products. The marketing team has spent months comparing the two lines of products and genuinely believes that the

50. *Supra* note 41.
51. Based on *McAsphalt Industries Ltd v Chapman Bros Ltd*, 2008 NSSC 324.

new Softest diapers absorb significantly more moisture than do the equivalently priced products of the competitor. The team has asked the scientists to confirm their results, and after several months of testing, the scientists report that there is, on average, a 10 percent increase in absorbency.

The campaign is an immediate success. The competitor, recognizing the threat, immediately seeks an injunction to stop this campaign under section 36 of the *Competition Act*. What provisions of the Act and what arguments will the competitor rely upon? What will Softest use in its defence? What are the possible outcomes?

6. Shopic Inc. imports a wide range of consumer goods, largely from China. One of its products is compact fluorescent bulbs. In recent discussions with its Chinese supplier, Shopic has discovered that one shipment of bulbs was inadvertently shipped to Canada before quality inspection and therefore may not be compliant with CSA standards. Shopic has already sold the bulbs to its customers and no complaints have been received. However, there is a potential safety hazard.[52] What are the relevant rules for the import and sale of the bulbs? What is Shopic's potential legal liability? What should Shopic do about these bulbs?

7. In 1996, Shawna and Jim bought a new Dodge truck from Dodge City Auto. The truck was manufactured by Chrysler Canada. When the truck was a year old and had traveled 30 000 kilometres, it burst into flames and was destroyed. When Shawna approached the dealer and the manufacturer, they refused to assist her in any way and referred her to her insurance company as her only remedy. Shawna later learned that two other 1996 Dodge trucks self-incinerated in her province. She also learned that the cause of the fires was a defective daytime running light module, of which Chrysler was aware.[53] Comment on Shawna's remedies arising from her purchase of the truck. How would you evaluate Chrysler's marketing strategy relating to its product?

8. Loyalist Foods Ltd. processes and sells a wide variety of canned food. It follows industry practice in its use of bisphenol A (known as BPA), a chemical used in plastic bottles and the epoxy resin lining the inside of cans. BPA prevents contamination and lengthens the shelf life of products, but it also mimics estrogen and disrupts biological processes. Since small amounts can seep from the lining into the contents of the containers, the use of BPA has become controversial. Health Canada has banned BPA from plastic baby bottles and has added BPA to its list of toxic substances. Consumers have reacted to the publicity surrounding BPA by essentially abandoning plastic water bottles.

Loyalist is concerned about the future use of BPA. A recent study has suggested there may be danger from consuming a lot of canned food. Loyalist fears that consumers may start avoiding cans containing BPA and wonders what Health Canada may do next.[54] What legal risks does Loyalist face regarding BPA? What changes to its marketing program should Loyalist consider?

For more study tools, visit http://www.NELSONbrain.com.

---

52. Based in part on a Health Canada recall notice – Health Canada, "Consumer Product Recalls" (9 December 2011), online: Health Canada <http://cpsr-rspc.hc-sc.gc.ca/PR-RP/recall-retrait-eng.jsp?re_id=1480>.

53. Based on *Prebushewski v Dodge City Auto (1984) Ltd*, 2005 SCC 28.

54. Based in part on Paul Taylor, "BPA being absorbed from canned food: study", *The Globe and Mail* (24 November 2011), online: Globe and Mail <http://www.theglobeandmail.com/life/health/new-health/paul-taylor/bpa-being-absorbed-from-canned-food-study/article2248262/>.

CHAPTER 24

Sales and Marketing: Price, Distribution, and Risk Management

Objectives

After studying this chapter, you should have an understanding of

- the legal obligations associated with the price component of marketing

- the legal obligations associated with the distribution (place) component of marketing

- the role of ethics, risk management, and corporate compliance in marketing

Business Law in Practice

Pacific Play Centres Inc. (PPC), introduced in the previous chapter, is continuing to develop its marketing strategy for its new line of wooden backyard play centres for children. The preliminary marketing plan included a premium pricing strategy of selling to affluent parents who want attractive and high-quality play equipment for their children. The plan also included distribution through national hardware and toy retail chains, and directly by PPC online. Steve Martin, the head of sales, has concerns about several aspects of pricing and distribution of the new product line. Some retailers are aggressive in negotiations, and he is worried that PPC is being urged to engage in legally suspect practices. In particular, there is a new market participant insisting on preferential terms (higher discounts and longer payment terms) that would give it a distinct advantage over other competitors.

To support the premium pricing strategy, Steve is exploring ways of discouraging distributors and retailers from selling PPC products at discount prices and proposes to place a "recommended retail price" sticker on the packaging. Steve thinks that arranging for exclusive dealerships in different regions of the country might be the best way to promote the high-quality image of the new products. Steve is interested in promoting and selling the new products through PPC's website, but he wants to proceed cautiously. In general, Steve and Lisa Patel, the CEO, wish to develop and implement a marketing plan that incorporates management of legal risks.

1. How does the law affect PPC's pricing strategy?
2. How does the law affect PPC's distribution strategy?
3. How can PPC effectively manage its exposure to legal risk in the context of marketing?

Introduction

The previous chapter covered two elements of marketing strategy—the product and promotion. This chapter continues with the remaining two elements—price and distribution. Key legislation in this chapter is the *Competition Act*,[1] introduced in Chapter 23. It is important to remember the distinction between criminal offences and civil reviewable matters. In broad terms, criminal offences are more serious. They are referred to the attorney general for prosecution, and are difficult to prove because of the higher burden of proof. Reviewable matters are civil in nature, and if not resolved by voluntary agreement, may result in a remedial order from a judge or the Competition Tribunal.

Price

Generally, price is freely negotiated when forming a contract, although prices in a few industries in Canada continue to be regulated by government agencies or are subject to regulatory bodies that set prices between producers/growers and users—for example, utilities and agricultural marketing boards. For the most part, the legal regulation of price is directed against pricing practices that will create an unfair or uneven playing field between market participants, thus harming competition, or that treat consumer purchasers unfairly. Regulations aim to protect the right to negotiate prices. In reviewing the relevant issues surrounding pricing, it is useful to separate pricing between producer and commercial purchaser from pricing between seller and consumer.

Pricing Practices between Producer and Commercial Purchaser

Producers may consider many pricing options to improve their competitive position. They may collude with competitors, take advantage of their strength in the market, or attempt to control prices at the retail level. The *Competition Act* prohibits certain unfair pricing practices, including those involving the producer and its commercial customers. The objective of the legislation is to promote a level playing field with respect to pricing—that is, that prices are freely negotiated at all levels of distribution. To this end, the Act includes the criminal offences of price fixing and bid rigging, along with abuse of dominant position and price maintenance as reviewable activities.

Pricing Conspiracies

One way for business to manipulate a market is through conspiring with direct competitors to control prices. For example, assume there are only three suppliers of the wood that PPC requires for its play sets. PPC observes that all three suppliers quote equivalent prices for equivalent orders. Each supplier likely faces similar costs, and all three may have similar profit expectations. It could be, however, that this is part of a conspiracy to control the cost of wood to major buyers such as PPC. If this can be proven, the wood suppliers will be guilty of a criminal offence under section 45 of the *Competition Act*, a broad provision that addresses more than pricing conspiracies. It proscribes the practices that were the original

---

1. RSC 1985, c C-34.

focus of antitrust legislation in Canada and elsewhere. The pricing conspiracy offence is defined in these terms:

> Every person commits an offence who, with a competitor of that person with respect to a product, conspires, agrees or arranges (a) to fix, maintain, increase or control the price for the supply of the product.

The penalties for conviction under section 45 were increased in 2010 to a maximum of 14 years imprisonment and/or a fine of $25 million.

For a criminal offence to be proven, it must be established not only that there was an agreement or a conspiracy to set prices, but also that the agreement lessened competition.[2] This latter requirement relates to the market structure (factors such as number of competitors and barriers to entry) and the behaviour of the parties (implementation of their agreement combined with market power).[3] There is also now provision for a reviewable practice of anticompetitive agreements.

Convictions under section 45 have occurred mostly as a consequence of guilty pleas. Although the following cases were resolved after the 2010 increase in penalties, the criminal activity occurred before 2010, so the lower penalties apply:

- Korean Air Lines was fined $5.5 million for its role in an air cargo cartel affecting Canada between 2002 and 2006. The company admitted to participation in a conspiracy to fix air cargo fuel surcharges. Previously, six other international airlines (including Air France, KLM, and British Airways) entered guilty pleas and were fined. Total fines in the bureau's investigation were more than $22 million.[4]

- Twenty-seven individuals and seven companies pleaded guilty to fixing the price of gasoline at the pumps in several Quebec towns. Fines have totaled $3 million and six individuals have been sentenced to a total of 54 months imprisonment. A total of 38 individuals and 14 companies were charged in the largest criminal investigation in the history of the bureau. Investigators seized over 100 000 records, searched 90 locations and intercepted thousands of phone conversations.[5]

Higher penalties in future cases are indicated by the first conviction under the amended law. Two companies pleaded guilty to conspiring with competitors to fix the price of polyurethane over an eleven-year period. They were fined a total of $12.5 million.[6]

In connection with price fixing and other anticompetitive conduct, there is a growing volume of litigation in the form of private competition class actions by the consumers who

---

2. The 2009 amendment to s 45 (in force March 2010) lowered the standard of proof by removing the requirement for "undue" lessening of competition.
3. *R. v Nova Scotia Pharmaceutical Society et al*, [1992] 2 SCR 606.
4. Competition Bureau of Canada, "Cargolux pleads guilty in air cargo price-fixing conspiracy" (28 October 2010), online: Competition Bureau Canada <http://www.competitionbureau.gc.ca/eic/site/cb-bc.nsf/eng/03304.html> and Competition Bureau of Canada, "Korean Air pleads guilty to price-fixing conspiracy" (19 July 2012), online: Competition Bureau Canada <http://www.competitionbureau.gc.ca/eic/site/cb-bc.nsf/eng/03482.html>.
5. Competition Bureau of Canada, "Six guilty pleas for fixing gas prices in Victoriaville" (13 April 2012), online: Competition Bureau Canada <http://www.competitionbureau.gc.ca/eic/site/cb-bc.nsf/eng/03459.html>.
6. Competition Bureau of Canada, "Competition Bureau sends signal to price-fixers with $12.5 million fine" (6 January 2012), online: Competition Bureau Canada <http://www.competitionbureau.gc.ca/eic/site/cb-bc.nsf/eng/01353.html>.

purchased products for the "fixed" prices. Even indirect purchasers—those who did not buy directly from co-conspirators are having some success.[7]

Bid Rigging

Bid rigging is a specialized form of conspiracy by producers/suppliers to manipulate a market through price. **Bid rigging** occurs when suppliers conspire to fix the bidding process in a manner that suits their collective needs or wishes. No market impact need to be proven. It is a serious criminal offence, since it attacks the heart of the competitive process. Penalties include fines and/or imprisonment. Bid rigging can take many forms, such as agreements to submit bids on a rotating basis or to split a market geographically.

Bid-rigging investigations are not uncommon. For example, an Ottawa-based consulting company pleaded guilty to rigging bids for the supply of real estate consultants and experts for the federal government. Similar bids were submitted by related firms.[8] A Quebec company admitted to its role in rigging bids for private sector ventilation contracts for residential high-rise buildings in Montreal.[9]

Abuse of Dominant Position

There is no law prohibiting a business from becoming dominant in its industry, but the law is concerned if that dominant position is achieved or maintained through activities that stifle competition in the industry.

Abuse of dominant position is reviewable conduct consisting of anticompetitive acts by a dominant company or group of companies that substantially prevents or lessens competition. Anticompetitive acts include buying up products to prevent the erosion of price levels, requiring suppliers to sell only to certain customers, and selling products below acquisition cost in order to discipline or eliminate competitors.

Two pricing activities that until 2009 were considered criminal are now subject to review as anticompetitive behaviour under the abuse of dominance provisions.[10]

Price discrimination is the practice whereby a seller provides different pricing terms and conditions to competing customers for equivalent volume sales at an equivalent time. This situation may arise either because a producer offers discriminatory prices, or, more commonly, because the producer responds to a customer's pressure tactics. The producer may see this as the only way of maintaining its dominant position in the market. Differential discounts are permitted provided it can be shown that customers who were prepared to purchase under equivalent conditions were offered the same terms. Any difference must be a direct reflection of cost differentials—say, in terms of volume or delivery.

Predatory pricing occurs when the seller sets prices unreasonably low with the intent of driving out its competition. This activity can occur at different levels of the distribution chain.

Bid rigging
Conspiring to fix the bidding process to suit the collective needs of those submitting bids.

Abuse of dominant position
Conduct that is reviewable under the *Competition Act* because a dominant company or group of companies have engaged in anticompetitive behaviour that unduly prevents or lessens competition.

---

7. See Mark Katz, "Competition class actions", *The Lawyers Weekly* (15 July 2011) 9 and Canadian Press, "Class-action lawsuit filed against gas stations", *The Chronicle Herald* (11 April 2012), online: The Chronicle Herald <http://thechronicleherald.ca/business/83358-class-action-lawsuit-filed-against-gas-stations>.
8. Competition Bureau of Canada, "Company pleads guilty to bid-rigging of federal government contracts" (30 July 2012), online: Competition Bureau Canada <http://www.competitionbureau.gc.ca/eic/site/cb-bc.nsf/eng/03484.html>.
9. Competition Bureau of Canada, "Guilty plea and $425,000 fine for bid-rigging in Montreal" (19 July 2011), online: Competition Bureau Canada <http://www.competitionbureau.gc.ca/eic/site/cb-bc.nsf/eng/03391.html>.
10. *Supra* note 1at ss 78-79. Section 50 dealing with price discrimination and predatory pricing was repealed by SC 2009, c 2.

What amounts to unreasonably low prices and predatory effect is seldom clear-cut. Most intervention by the Competition Bureau follows complaints made by competitors or concerned suppliers. Instead of criminal prosecution, the Competition Bureau can now refer complaints to the Competition Tribunal.

In order to take action for abuse of dominant position, the Competition Tribunal must find that the company or group of companies substantially controls the market under investigation, that those under investigation have engaged in a practice of anticompetitive acts, and that the practice has the effect of preventing or lessening competition in the market substantially. The tribunal applies the civil burden of proof and has the authority to make orders stopping the particular behaviour. Should such orders be ignored, penalties can be imposed. The threat of the civil regime may lead to a voluntary agreement between the offending party and the bureau. Otherwise, the tribunal may order the offenders to take corrective action and may impose administrative penalties up to $10 million.[11]

Two recent high profile cases involved real estate agents and listings. The first case involved the Canadian Real Estate Association (CREA) and its restrictions on the use of the Multiple Listing Service (MLS) system. After several years of negotiation, the commissioner challenged CREA's anticompetitive rules before the Competition Tribunal. The challenge alleged that the CREA rules imposed exclusionary restrictions that enabled it to maintain substantial control of the market, denying consumers the ability to choose their desired real estate services. Following the application, CREA and the bureau reached a ten-year agreement, by which CREA would eliminate its ability to adopt anticompetitive rules that discriminate against agents who want to offer less than full service.[12] In a related case, the bureau filed a similar application against the Toronto Real Estate Board (TREB) and its restrictions on the use of information from the Toronto MLS system.[13]

Price Maintenance

A producer can engage in reviewable conduct known as **price maintenance**[14] by attempting to drive upward the final retail price at which its goods are sold to the public. The producer might do this by exerting pressure on the retailer or by placing notice on the goods themselves.

For example, because of its increasing concern that widely advertised low prices for its products will damage product image, PPC may instruct sales staff to advise retailers to cease dropping prices, and to monitor their compliance. PPC might also print on the packaging the "recommended retail price" and refuse to sell to any retailer selling below this price.

Two aspects of this strategy are reviewable: the attempt to influence the final retail price upward and the recriminations against noncompliant retailers. Both attempt to prevent competition and to discipline the marketplace. PPC can use the words "recommended retail price," provided this statement determines only maximum and not minimum prices.

Price maintenance
The attempt to drive the final retail price of goods upward and the imposition of recriminations upon noncompliant retailers.

---

11. *Supra* note 1 at ss 78, 79. See also Competition Bureau of Canada, *The Abuse of Dominance Provisions: Enforcement Guidelines* (20 September 2012), online: Competition Bureau Canada <http://www.competitionbureau.gc.ca/eic/site/cb-bc.nsf/eng/03497.html>.
12. See Luis Millan, "Competition Bureau resolves MLS dispute", *The Lawyers Weekly* (24 December 2010) S8.
13. Competition Bureau of Canada, "Competition Bureau's case against Canada's largest real estate board: hearing starts today" (10 September 2012), online: Competition Bureau Canada<http://www.competitionbureau.gc.ca/eic/site/cb-bc.nsf/eng/03495.html>.
14. *Supra* note 1 at s 76.

There are some circumstances that justify price maintenance. PPC can refuse to sell to retailers that are selling at unreasonably low prices, provided it can show that the retailers were using its products in any of the following ways:

- as loss leaders (typically, below cost price)

- for bait and switch selling

- in misleading advertising

- in sales where they fail to provide a reasonable level of service

Price maintenance ceased to be a criminal offence in 2009. Under the new section 76, it is now a reviewable practice that enables the tribunal to prohibit activities that have an adverse effect on competition. In addition, there are no longer criminal or administrative penalties attached to the review, so that cases decided under the old law involving significant fines are no longer relevant.[15]

A recent case under the price maintenance provisions involves Visa and MasterCard. In response to complaints from retail merchants, the bureau launched an inquiry and in 2010 filed an application with the tribunal regarding restrictive and anticompetitive rules.[16] The rules under challenge prohibit merchants from encouraging customers to consider lower fee payment options, require merchants to accept all cards from a company, and prohibit merchants from applying surcharges on purchases made with high-cost cards. Visa and MasterCard control 90 percent of credit card transactions in Canada which has among the highest credit card fees in the world. The hearing before the Competition Tribunal began in May 2012.

Pricing Practices between Seller and Consumer

In consumer sales, retailers may wish to make their prices as attractive as possible by persuading consumers as if they are being offered a bargain. Sellers may also be careless in the prices they charge compared to those communicated to buyers through various means. The broad protection for consumers is through the civil and criminal misleading advertising provisions that are considered under "Promotion" in Chapter 23. This section addresses more specific provisions.

Sale or Bargain Prices

It is a reviewable offence for the seller to state that a price is less than the ordinary price ("on sale," "reduced," "clearance") when it is not.[17] An advertiser may legitimately claim a price to be the ordinary price if

---

15. See for example, Competition Bureau of Canada, "Competition Bureau settles price maintenance and misleading advertising case regarding the Access Toyota Program" (28 March 2003), online: Competition Bureau Canada <http://www.competitionbureau.gc.ca/eic/site/cb-bc.nsf/eng/00300.html> and Competition Bureau of Canada, "Labatt pleads guilty and pays $250,000 fine following a Competition Bureau investigation" (23 November 2005), online: Competition Bureau Canada <http://www.competitionbureau.gc.ca/eic/site/cb-bc.nsf/eng/02003.html>.
16. Competition Bureau of Canada, "Competition Bureau challenges Visa and MasterCard's anti-competitive rules" (15 December 2010), online: Competition Bureau Canada <http://www.competitionbureau.gc.ca/eic/site/cb-bc.nsf/eng/03325.html>.
17. *Supra* note 1 at ss 74.01(2), 74.01(3), and 74.1(1); Director of Investigation and Research, Bureau of Competition Policy, Consumer and Corporate Affairs Canada, *Ordinary Price Claims, Subsections 74.01(2) and 74.01(3) of the Competition Act: Enforcement Guidelines* (22 September 1999), online: Competition Bureau Canada <http://www.competitionbureau.gc.ca/eic/site/cb-bc.nsf/eng/01227.html>.

[it] reflects the price at which suppliers generally in the relevant market area have either

- sold a substantial volume of the product within a reasonable period of time before or after making the representation (volume test) or

- offered the product for sale in good faith for a substantial period of time recently before or immediately after making the representation (time test)

Both the volume test and the time test are applied according to specific guidelines established by the Competition Bureau. Placing a restriction to the promise in small print on the advertisement is no protection if the overall impression remains misleading.

Stating that prices are "subject to error" provides protection only in the context of catalogue sales, since catalogues are not printed regularly and some protection is reasonable for the seller. Because this is reviewable activity, the due diligence defence applies, and the promoter should correct errors quickly and in a manner consistent with the original promotion.

Complaints regarding inflated "regular" prices have been common in recent years and have generated activity at the bureau. The *Sears* case was the first contested proceeding.

CASE · Canada (Commissioner of Competition) v Sears Canada Inc (2005), 37 CPR (4th) 65 (Competition Tribunal)

THE BUSINESS CONTEXT: Consumers are attracted by bargains. Retailers may be tempted to make their bargains appear as attractive as possible as they compete for consumer sales. The challenge for retailers is to fairly present the bargain price in comparison with the regular or ordinary price.

FACTUAL BACKGROUND: In 1999 Sears advertised five lines of all-season tires. The ads contained claims such as "save 40%" and "1/2 price" and drew comparisons between Sears' ordinary prices and its sale prices. During a lengthy investigation and hearing, Sears admitted that it failed to meet the volume test.

THE LEGAL QUESTION: Did Sears satisfy the time test in terms of good faith and substantial period of time?

RESOLUTION: The tribunal concluded that good faith should be determined on a subjective basis—did Sears truly believe that its ordinary prices were genuine and *bona fide* prices, set with the expectation that the market would validate the prices as ordinary? Sears' claims of good faith were rejected based on its admission that it expected only 5 to 10 percent of the tires to be sold at the ordinary price; Sears' ordinary price was not competitive in the market; and Sears could not track the number of tires sold at the ordinary price. In terms of substantial period of time, the tribunal concluded that if a product is on sale more than half the time, then it has not been offered at its ordinary price for a substantial period of time.

Following the tribunal's decision, Sears reached a settlement with the bureau regarding penalty. Sears agreed to pay $100 000 as an administrative penalty and $387 000 toward the bureau's legal costs.

What must this retailer ensure to avoid complaints about this sale?

CRITICAL ANALYSIS: In other cases, prominent retailers agreed to pay substantial penalties, some in excess of $1 million. Have these high-profile cases altered the behaviour of retailers? Do consumers have greater confidence in advertised bargain prices?

Sale above Advertised Price

A civil provision of the Act prohibits the sale of a product at a price higher than that advertised, unless the price was a mistake which was immediately corrected. Otherwise, the seller faces a penalty of up to $200 000.

Double Ticketing

Double ticketing
The offence of failing to sell at the lower of the two or more prices marked on or otherwise appearing with regard to a product.

Sellers can commit pricing offences in their direct contact with the customer. For example, if there are two or more prices on goods, the product must be sold at the lower of those prices. To do otherwise amounts to the criminal offence of **double ticketing**. Obligations extend to in-store promotions and displays, as well as prices listed in store computers. However, if consumers intentionally move the goods (or change pricing labels), they are committing fraud.

The Competition Bureau is particularly concerned about differentials between prices posted on store shelves and those stored in automatic price-scanning systems, since it is easy for customers to fail to notice an increased price at the checkout counter.

BUSINESS APPLICATION OF THE LAW

Scanner Price Accuracy Voluntary Code

In 2002, several Canadian retail associations launched this code to demonstrate their commitment to accurate scanner pricing. The associations involved are the Retail Council of Canada, the Canadian Association of Chain Drug Stores, the Canadian Association of Independent Grocers, and the Canadian Council of Grocery Distributors. The code acknowledges that incorrect prices can harm customer relations and attract legal sanctions. Its purposes are to demonstrate retailer commitment to scanner accuracy, provide retailers with a national framework, and provide a mechanism for consumer complaints. The code has been endorsed by the Competition Bureau. Over 5000 retailers are voluntary participants.

Key aspects of the code are the following:

• The Item Free Scanner Policy, which states that, for claims that a scanned price exceeds the advertised or display price, the customer is entitled to the product free of charge where the correct price is less than $10; where the correct price is greater than $10, the customer is entitled to $10 off the correct price.

• Retailers should correct errors as quickly as possible.

• Retailers must establish appropriate internal policies, procedures, and training programs.

• Clear and legible labels must be affixed to the shelf next to the product.

• Clear and complete receipts must be provided to customers.

• A Scanner Price Accuracy Committee is established to oversee the code.

• There is a multi-step consumer complaint process that culminates in arbitration.

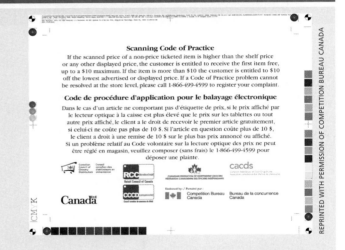

There has been some criticism of the absence of accountability in the code. There is no effective way to discipline retailers that fail to follow the code and no independent review of how the code is working.

Critical Analysis: Do voluntary codes such as this one provide helpful strength to the provisions of the *Competition Act?* Can voluntary codes replace regulation and enforcement? Are you aware of this code?

Sources: Competition Bureau of Canada, "Consumers to be compensated for overcharged scanned purchases" (11 June 2002), online: Competition Bureau Canada <http://www.competitionbureau.gc.ca/eic/site/cb-bc.nsf/eng/00415.html> and Shauna Rempel, "Did the store overcharge you? No need to fume" *The Toronto Star* (14 October 2009), online: The Star <http://www.thestar.com/living/shopping/article/709716—did-the-store-overcharge-you-no-need-to-fume>

Distribution (Place)

Distribution is defined in a leading marketing text as "the movement of goods and services from producers to customers."[18] Distribution includes the process of ensuring that goods get into the customers' hands—that is, shipping and transportation. The contract of sale involves several distribution issues, in particular the transfer of title and delivery of goods. These issues are discussed in detail as part of the "Contract of Sale" section at the beginning of Chapter 23. That material should be reviewed at this point.

Distribution decisions determine whether products will be sold through retailers, wholesalers, a multi-level organization, employed salespeople, door-to-door sales people, telemarketers, or online sales. Whatever structure or channels sellers choose, they should observe two key principles in order to avoid legal difficulties. First, they must resist the temptation to control their distribution scheme to the extent that competition for their products is adversely affected. Second, they should aim for full disclosure of terms and conditions at each selling stage. The material in this section is presented in three sections: restrictive distribution practices, multi-level marketing, and direct marketing.

Restrictive Distribution Practices

Sellers may discriminate unfairly between customers through distribution policies as well as pricing practices. They may refuse to deal with some customers or impose various restrictions on their customers' businesses. The consequence in either case is the same: the practice reduces or eliminates competition.

Most practices that impose these restrictions are reviewable matters. The Competition Bureau will investigate the activity and, if it finds that an offence is being committed, seek a remedial order. These offences are best illustrated through practical examples.

- PPC's playground slides have become one of the dominant brands. All major discount retailers are using these as a means of attracting customers. XYZ finds that PPC will not supply it with the slides, even though XYZ is willing and able to meet the same conditions of sale as ABC. This practice likely falls within the definition of **refusal to deal** and will be reviewable provided that it is substantially affecting XYZ, that XYZ is willing to meet the usual trade terms offered to ABC, and that PPC has an adequate supply of the slides that it refuses to provide.

- PPC tells its distributors that it will continue to supply them with PPC equipment only if they buy from no other suppliers of play equipment. If this practice lessens competition substantially, it falls within the definition of **exclusive dealing** and is therefore reviewable.

- PPC advises XYZ that it will supply the "hottest" play set product of the spring season only if XYZ also buys a number of less popular products and refrains from buying from any competitor. This practice may be **tied selling** and is reviewable provided, again, that the action lessens competition substantially.

Refusal to deal
When a seller refuses to sell to a purchaser on the same terms as those that are offered to the purchaser's competitors.

Exclusive dealing
When a seller agrees to sell to the purchaser only if the purchaser buys from it exclusively.

Tied selling
When a seller will sell to the purchaser only if the purchaser buys other, less desirable goods as well.

---

18. LE Boone *et al*, *Contemporary Marketing*, 3rd Cdn ed (Toronto: Nelson, 2013) at 326.

Multi-level Marketing

Multi-level marketing
A scheme for distributing products or services that involves participants recruiting others to become involved in distribution.

Typically, businesses are free to structure themselves in the manner they consider most effective for organizing their distribution channels to market their products. **Multi-level marketing** plans arise through distributorships. Income is earned through commissions to distributors, and fees are paid upward through the various levels of the sales structure.

Multi-level marketing or selling is not inherently illegal.[19] The legitimacy of the activity is determined by such factors as whether there is a genuine selling opportunity for those buying distributorships in the plan and whether there is a realistic opportunity for distributorships to expand. If a genuine business activity is not obvious, the multi-level selling scheme is likely illegal. Such schemes are unstable, and inevitably those joining at the late stages receive little or no value as the scheme collapses for lack of new participants.

Pyramid selling
A form of multi-level selling that is illegal under the *Competition Act.*

Pyramid selling is the form of multi-level marketing that is illegal. It is a criminal act under the provisions of the *Competition Act* if

- participants pay money for the right to receive compensation for recruiting new participants;

- a participant is required to buy a specific quantity of products, other than at cost price, for the purpose of advertising, before the participant is allowed to join the plan or advance within the plan;

- participants are knowingly sold commercially unreasonable quantities of the product or products (this practice is called inventory loading); or

- participants are not allowed to return products on reasonable commercial terms.[20]

Multi-level selling schemes are the subject of regulation, in particular, relating to disclosure. There must be "fair, reasonable and timely disclosure" of earnings or expected earnings. Complaints and investigations tend to focus on this requirement. For example, the bureau investigated a company operating a multi-level marketing plan known as the Cocooning Club to promote and sell computer software on nutrition and other subjects. The investigation found that the company and participants in the plan made representations on a website and a television infomercial that exaggerated income expectations without disclosing the income of a typical participant in the plan. The company was fined $75 000 and its vice president was given a conditional jail sentence.[21]

Direct Marketing

Direct marketing is "a broad concept that includes direct mail, direct selling, direct-response retailing, telemarketing, Internet retailing, and automatic merchandising."[22]

Regulators traditionally focused on door-to-door sellers but, over time, developed protection for consumers in other types of sales. The *Competition Act* now addresses

19. *Supra* note 1 at ss 55, 55.1. Also *Franchises Act,* RSA 2000, c F-23; *Criminal Code of Canada,* RSC 1985, c C-46, s 206(1)(e).
20. Competition Bureau of Canada, *Information Bulletin: Multi-level Marketing Plans and Schemes of Pyramid Selling* (29 April 2009), online: Competition Bureau Canada <http://www.competitionbureau.gc.ca/eic/site/cb-bc.nsf/eng/03035.html>.
21. Competition Bureau of Canada, "Multi-level marketing firm pleads guilty to misleading participants" (11 March 2005), online: Competition Bureau Canada <http://www.competitionbureau.gc.ca/eic/site/cb-bc.nsf/eng/00190.html>.
22. *Supra* note 18 at 373.

telemarketing specifically. Online shopping is regulated by more general provisions in the *Competition Act*, such as those related to promotion and pricing, and a variety of provincial legislation.

Door-to-Door Selling

Regulation in the area of **door-to-door selling** focuses on protecting consumers from untoward pressure and allowing them the chance to reconsider and the opportunity to cancel the sale. This form of selling is regulated under provincial consumer protection legislation that typically requires

- those selling door-to-door to be licensed

- contracts in excess of a certain dollar figure to be in writing and to disclose specific matters

- consumers who sign a contract to be allowed a "cooling-off" period[23] during which they may cancel the contract

Door-to-door selling
The act of selling in person directly, at a customer's residence.

Telemarketing

Marketers define **telemarketing** as including both inbound sales calls, where the retailer advertises a product and makes it available through telephone orders, and outbound calls, where the focus is on unsolicited calls to consumers in their homes. The regulations[24] apply to any "interactive telephone communication" but do not extend to fax, Internet communications, or automated, prerecorded messages. Regulation is similar to that which governs door-to-door sellers. It protects the consumer from high-pressure tactics. Basic information about the vendor and the product must be disclosed.

Telemarketing
The use of the telephone to communicate product and organizational information to customers.

Deceptive telemarketing is a criminal offence, and many offenders have been successfully prosecuted, often for fraud involving business directories. For example, five Alberta individuals received significant prison sentences for their involvement in a deceptive scheme promoting business directories. Over three years, telemarketers used an "assumed sale" technique—convincing victims that they had already made a purchase and were obligated to pay. They defrauded as many as 10 000 business and organizations of an estimated $3.75 million. Charges were laid under the *Competition Act* and the *Criminal Code*. Sentences ranged from probation to two years in prison.[25]

In another case, three individuals received significant prison sentences (15–23 years) from a U.S. court for their role in a Toronto-based scheme in which 40 000 Americans with poor credit ratings were persuaded to pay processing fees for credit cards that they never received.[26] The Deputy Commissioner of Competition commented that "the severity of

23. For example, *Fair Trading Act*, RSA 2000, c F-2; *Direct Sellers' Regulation Act*, RSNS 1989, c 129. In Alberta and Nova Scotia, the cooling-off period is 10 days.
24. Competition Bureau of Canada, "What you should know about telemarketing" (16 October 2009), online: Competition Bureau Canada <http://www.competitionbureau.gc.ca/eic/site/cb-bc.nsf/eng/03127.html>.
25. Competition Bureau of Canada, "Five Alberta individuals sentenced in deceptive telemarketing scheme" (30 August 2011), online: Competition Bureau Canada <http://www.competitionbureau.gc.ca/eic/site/cb-bc.nsf/eng/03402.html>.
26. Competition Bureau of Canada, "15 Years in jail for Canadian extradited to U.S. in deceptive telemarketing case" (18 December 2008), online: Competition Bureau Canada <http://www.competitionbureau.gc.ca/eic/site/cb-bc.nsf/eng/02867.html>.

PART SEVEN

What are the legal parameters
of telemarketing?

these sentences should serve as a warning that deceptive telemarketing is treated seriously on both sides of the border."

Online Retailing

Selling directly to consumers over the Internet is the fastest-growing area of retailing, even during economic downturns. However, there are continuing matters of concern to both buyers and sellers:

- *Identity of the business*. Websites come and go, and the physical location of the vendor is often unknown. Consumers tend to trust well-known brands and companies at the expense of smaller, less-familiar businesses.

- *Privacy and personal information*. Private information supplied by consumers may become a resource that other marketers use and abuse.

- *Security*. How effective are the current encryption devices in protecting personal and financial information, especially credit card information? Many consumers are still reluctant to provide credit card information online. Is there risk of fraud or identity theft? Internet scams are on the rise.

- *Resolution of disputes*. What happens if something goes wrong? Which laws apply? What court will have jurisdiction?

The challenge is to provide sufficient security and regulation of online transactions without stifling the commercial potential of the Internet. Regulation has moved beyond the general marketing practice provisions in the *Competition Act* and provincial consumer protection provisions that affect all sales of goods and services. Marketers and their industry organizations are instituting various means of gaining the trust of prospective purchasers. Governments and business have addressed the issues through various means, including the following:

- *Establishing principles for protecting e-commerce customers.* For example, industry groups, consumers, and government created the *Canadian Code of Practice for Consumer Protection in Electronic Commerce,* which sets out good business practices for merchants conducting online commercial activities. The Canadian Marketing Association has amended its codes of ethics and standards of practice to address issues of consumer consent, and the Canadian Association of Internet Providers (CAIP) has a voluntary code of conduct. There are third-party seal programs, such as the CA WebTrust program created by the Canadian Institute of Chartered Accountants and the American Institute of Public Accountants.

- *Applying provisions of the* Competition Act. The provisions concerning anticompetitive practices apply to websites, cybermalls, electronic bulletin boards where advertisements may be posted, banner ads in browser programs and search engines, and the use of email. Section 52(1), which deals with representations, applies to third parties such as webpage designers, proprietors of cybermalls, proprietors of electronic bulletin boards, and Internet service providers. The bureau issued an information bulletin titled "Application of the *Competition Act* to Representations on the Internet"[27] and initiated Project FairWeb, an Internet surveillance and enforcement program to combat misleading and deceptive advertising on the Internet. The Competition Bureau also participates in international Internet sweeps targeting bogus product claims and other scams.

- *Applying privacy legislation.* As outlined in Chapters 1 (Knowledge of Law as a Business Asset) and 20 (The Employment Relationship), the *Personal Information Protection* and *Electronic Documents Act* is federal legislation which requires all organizations to obtain consent for the collection, use, or disclosure of personal information. The Act applies provincially in the absence of similar provincial law. It requires marketers to obtain consent for the use or disclosure of personal information for any purpose, including direct or targeted marketing or even market research.

- *Expanding consumer protection legislation.* All provinces have endorsed the *Internet Sales Contract Harmonization Template* (see Chapter 8). For example, Ontario's *Consumer Protection Act*[28] has special provisions for Internet agreements that require disclosure of specified information about the goods or services, dispute resolution limits, full disclosure of contract terms, an express opportunity to accept or decline the contract, a copy of the contract in written or electronic form, the right to cancel the contract within a specified time, and the right to refunds from sellers and credit card companies.

---

27. Competition Bureau of Canada (18 February 2003), online: Competition Bureau Canada <http://www.competitionbureau.gc.ca/eic/site/cb-bc.nsf/eng/01213.html>.
28. *Consumer Protection Act, 2002*, SO 2002, c 30, Schedule A. See Eva Chan, "*Consumer Protection Act* creates a major increase in consumer rights", The *Lawyers Weekly* (2 June 2006) 9.

The following box presents some of the most recent developments.

TECHNOLOGY AND THE LAW

Developments in Online Marketing and Sales

There is new federal legislation to combat identity theft (see Chapter 25). Consumer protection legislation continues to evolve in piecemeal fashion. For example, several provinces now prohibit contract clauses that impose mandatory arbitration for the resolution of disputes arising from online contracts. The enforcement of such clauses was recently considered by the Supreme Court in cases[29] where consumers were attempting to proceed with class actions rather than individual arbitration claims.

On the privacy front, consumers, organizations, and the Privacy Commissioner are becoming more aggressive in the protection of consumer information. The legislation allows organizations to collect only the personal information necessary for the purposes identified by the collector and to use that information only with the consent of the individual who provides it. Online consumers can refuse requests for information that is not necessary to complete the transaction. Collecting organizations cannot provide consumer information to others for secondary marketing purposes without consent. A related and controversial practice is online behavioural advertising resulting from the tracking of consumers' Internet activity. The Privacy Commissioner has published *Guidelines for Privacy and Online Behavioural Advertising*[30] that require transparency and provide the opportunity to opt out of the tracking.

A prominent development in online marketing was the advent of Canada's National Do Not Call List, which began operating 30 September 2008. Pursuant to legislation, the CRTC (Canadian Radio-television and Telecommunications Commission) regulates unsolicited telemarketing communication. The CRTC has developed a set of rules and established the National Do Not Call List. Consumers may register their phone numbers with a registry maintained by Bell Canada. Businesses who conduct telemarketing must subscribe to the list and refrain from calling the registered numbers. Consumers who have registered and continue to receive calls may file a complaint, and there are significant penalties for failure to honour the list. Notable fines imposed include $1.3 million on Bell Canada and $500 000 on Xentel DM. The list has been criticized on many grounds, especially for its broad list of exemptions, which includes calls from charities and businesses who have existing relationships with those being called. It is also alleged that the availability of the list to all telemarketers has resulted in more calls to those on the list, raising the issue of enforcement.

A major concern relating to e-business is the dramatic and continuing increase in spam—bulk, unsolicited, "junk" email. Several countries have legislation[31] directed at spam, but in Canada, only recently has legislation been passed.[32] See Business Application of the Law: *Spamming* in Chapter 6 for details. It is expected that the law will come into force in 2013. It will apply to email and other forms of commercial electronic communication such as instant messaging. Businesses will need to review their communication practices to ensure compliance. The law is intended to combat Canada's reputation as a haven for spammers.

Critical Analysis: Are there persistent barriers to the growth of online business? Will regulators and industry effectively deal with these barriers?

Sources: Iain Marlow, "Bell fined $1.3 million for violating do not call rules", *The Globe and Mail* (20 December 2010), online: Globe and Mail <http://www.theglobeandmail.com/globe-investor/bell-fined-1.3-million-for-violating-do-not-call-rules/article1844965/>; Simon Houpt, "Privacy watchdog takes aim at online consumer 'profiling'", *The Globe and Mail* (6 December 2011), online: Globe and Mail <http://www.theglobeandmail.com/report-on-business/industry-news/marketing/adhocracy/privacy-watchdog-takes-aim-at-online-consumer-profiling/article2262372/>; and Michael Fekete, Patricia Wilson, & Nicole Kutlesa, "Canada's anti-spam law coming into force", *Osler Update* (5 July 2011), online: Osler, Hoskin & Harcourt LLP <http://www.osler.com/NewsResources/Details.aspx?id=3614>.

Ethical Issues in Marketing Law

The nature of marketing and the law that applies to it raise a number of ethical issues.

ETHICAL CONSIDERATIONS

Marketing Law and Ethics

The relationship between the law and ethics was introduced in Chapter 1. Business law is a set of established rules governing commercial relationships, including the enforcement of rights.

Business ethics concern moral principles and values that relate to right and wrong in business. It is generally accepted that ethical standards exceed legal requirements and entail principles of commercial morality, fairness, and honesty. Marketing is especially

---

29. See *Dell Computer Corp v Union des consommateurs*, 2007 SCC 34 and *Seidel v TELUS Communications Inc*, 2011 SCC 15.
30. Office of the Privacy Commissioner of Canada, (December 2011), online: Office of the Privacy Commissioner of Canada <http://www.priv.gc.ca/information/guide/2011/gl_ba_1112_e.cfm#contenttop>.
31. See the *International Perspective: US Spam Laws* in Chapter 1.
32. *An Act to promote the efficiency and adaptability of the Canadian economy by regulating certain activities that discourage reliance on electronic means of carrying on our commercial activities*, SC 2010, c 23, commonly known as Canada's Anti-Spam Law or CASL.

challenging in the context of law and ethics because it involves the cultivation of relationships on the basis of persuasion and trust.

Chapters 23 and 24 demonstrate that the law is highly relevant to all aspects of marketing, including the four aspects of product, promotion, price, and distribution. The key issue is whether observing the law is sufficient. Can society rely on the law to deal with matters such as product safety, truth in advertising, fair prices, and unrestricted distribution of products? Ethics in marketing is commonly considered in the consumer context. The new *Consumer Product Safety Act* is meant to increase consumer confidence by imposing requirements on producers, sellers, and importers of consumer products, but cases have shown that enforcement is not perfect. We must therefore rely on the willingness of businesses to comply with the law on a voluntary basis, perhaps in fear of detection or because they realize that obeying the law and doing what is right are good for business and the bottom line.

Ethical standards are less often considered in business-to-business or competitive relationships. We think less of competitor protection than we do of consumer protection, but competition law is primarily about the promotion of competition which requires the regulation of competitive relationships. As the Commissioner of Competition has recognized, questionable behaviour toward consumers affects the competitive landscape as well: "Companies that make false representations inhibit consumers' ability to make informed purchasing decisions and put rivals at a competitive disadvantage."[33] The line between

ethics and the law is blurred in the competitive context as well. For example, buying smaller competitors may not violate the *Competition Act*, but if done to shut down those competitors with the resulting consequences for employees and the community, there is an ethical issue. The line between cooperation among competitors and criminal conspiracies may be vague. The very term "abuse of dominant position" invites subjective analysis. Comparative advertising is generally meant to portray competitors in an unfavourable light.

The legal system deals with law and ethics indirectly. For example, the Competition Bureau applies its enforcement continuum by providing extensive guidance to business through bulletins and other publications and dealing with complaints on a review basis where it can investigate and then negotiate an arrangement with business to vary the questionable business practices involved. Similarly, the federal private sector privacy legislation *(PIPEDA)* requires businesses to develop and apply privacy policies that are consistent with the principles in the Act—a much different approach than a complex set of rules. It can be argued that these approaches seek to implement and enforce the law in a way that encourages business to evaluate its own practices and standards. *Critical Analysis:* Does the law promote ethical behaviour? Is it in the interest of business to act ethically?

Sources: LE Boone et al, *Contemporary Marketing*, 3rd Cdn ed (Toronto: Nelson, 2013); Canadian Marketing Association, *Code of Ethics and Standards of Practice*, online: <http://www.the-cma.org/regulatory/code-of-ethics>; and Brenda Pritchard and Susan Vogt, *Advertising and Marketing Law in Canada* (3rd), (Toronto: LexisNexis, 2009).

Risk Management in Marketing

Risk management in marketing requires consideration of the four-step legal risk management model presented in Chapter 3 and the business risks discussed in contracts and torts in Parts Two and Three of this text. The products and services must perform as intended, the design of any products must be fundamentally sound and address all reasonably foreseeable risks, and promises must not exceed what it is possible to deliver.

Figure 24.1 (on the next page) is a compilation of the issues and concerns addressed in these two marketing chapters that may create risks that require management.

Here are the basic practices that a business such as PPC should adopt in order to minimize its risk exposure:

- PPC must establish a climate in which maximizing safety of the product is paramount. For any business producing goods or services for children, this is especially important. Product designers must be familiar with all relevant design regulations. Senior management should support this approach to design, even when faced with competing demands for resources or pressure for sales and profits.

---

33. Competition Bureau of Canada, "Spa retailers required to stop making false ENERGY STAR claims" (17 January 2011), online: Competition Bureau Canada <http://www.competitionbureau.gc.ca/eic/site/cb-bc.nsf/eng/03342.html>.

FIGURE 24.1

Sources of Legal Risks in Marketing

The Contract of Sale
- Terms: express and implied
- Contracting out of express terms vs. implied terms
- Commercial vs. consumer sales
- Transfer of title rules
- Delivery terms

Product
- Design
- Quality
- Packaging
- Labelling
- Warnings

Promotion
- False, misleading, or deceptive advertising or claims
- Environmental claims
- Performance claims
- Tests and testimonials
- Deceptive selling practices such as bait and switch

Price
- Conspiracies to fix prices or rig bids
- Abuse of dominant position in the market
- Attempts to control retail prices (price maintenance)
- Misleading sale prices
- Double ticketing and inaccurate price scanning

Distribution
- Restrictive practices (exclusive dealing or tied selling)
- Multi-level selling
- Deceptive telemarketing
- Inadequate disclosure of terms and cancellation for online sales

- The organization should acquire, through its trade association and specialized professional advisors such as lawyers and industrial engineers, knowledge of the standards that must be met for both the production and the labelling of the goods. Information concerning use and suitability must be effectively communicated on product labelling. If the goods come partially assembled, as is the case with PPC, information must be provided so that prospective purchasers can visualize the assembled product.

- PPC should follow the basic guidelines for promotion—that is, ensure that statements and promises are both truthful and clear. Those responsible for advertising must be well versed in the properties of the product or service. Those directly responsible for creating in-store promotions and for explaining products or services to customers must be well educated in the qualities of a product, even when they are not the producer's employees.

- PPC must recognize that it cannot use pricing policies to manipulate the market or try to drive out competitors. Manufacturers such as PPC are not permitted to dictate the retail prices for sales to the consumer. Apart from these limitations, PPC can charge its customers whatever prices it wishes, as long as all customers in the same market are treated the same.

- In terms of distribution, PPC must avoid structuring distribution channels or making agreements with competitors or distributors that substantially interfere with competition. What is most efficient and profitable for PPC may not be acceptable under competition law. Since PPC has chosen to engage in direct marketing through the Internet, the prime considerations are ensuring clear disclosure to buyers and refraining from pressure selling.

- PPC should ensure that those negotiating the sale of products on its behalf are well-versed in the rules of contract law, the sale of goods, and consumer protection.

- PPC should also provide information about all aspects of shipping the goods. It will have standard practices that transfer title or risk. Employees should know the significance of these practices to the risk of the business. Also, basic shipping terminology should be defined so that employees understand the implications of contractual terms.

- Guidelines for sales and shipping staff should set out all pricing and distribution practices that PPC might be tempted or pressured to participate in and all those that are prohibited. Both the nature of the practices and the penalties imposed for engaging in them should be described.

- A clear protocol must be established for decision making and for addressing questionable practices. The Competition Bureau has an Immunity Program to encourage early and complete disclosure of anticompetitive criminal activity.[34]

- Since much of the regulation of marketing activities is found in the *Competition Act*, Lisa and Steve can turn to the compliance program materials provided by the Competition Bureau for guidance. The goal of the bureau is compliance before harm. It promotes a sequence of enforcement activities known as the "Conformity Continuum"; thus, it has devised guidelines[35] for a credible and effective corporate compliance program, including the involvement and support of senior management; development of relevant policies and procedures; ongoing education of management and employees; monitoring, auditing, and reporting mechanisms; and internal disciplinary procedures.

- PPC should establish an informed and properly responsive customer relations process. This is the primary line of communication between the producer and the customer. It can ward off serious problems, reassure customers, and reduce the potential for subsequent complaints and claims. It can also be an early warning system for the need to reconsider design or production techniques.

---

34. Competition Bureau of Canada, "Immunity Program under the *Competition Act*" (7 June 2010), online: Competition Bureau Canada <http://www.competitionbureau.gc.ca/eic/site/cb-bc.nsf/eng/03248.html>.
35. Competition Bureau of Canada, "Bulletin on Corporate Compliance Programs" (27 September 2010), online: Competition Bureau Canada <http://www.competitionbureau.gc.ca/eic/site/cb-bc.nsf/eng/03280.html>. See also Competition Bureau of Canada, "Conformity Continuum" (18 June 2000), online: Competition Bureau Canada <http://www.competitionbureau.gc.ca/eic/site/cb-bc.nsf/eng/01750.html>.

- Since no organization can prevent all untoward events, PPC must have adequate insurance coverage to address expected risk. It must have access to professional advisors who understand the business, including specialized insurance brokers and lawyers.

Business Law in Practice Revisited

1. How does the law affect PPC's pricing strategy?

Generally, the law requires PPC to treat all of its customers equally when they are purchasing under similar conditions. The practices that retailers are pressuring PPC to partake in may violate the provisions of the *Competition Act* and PPC may become the subject of an investigation. If the retailer insists that PPC sell to the competitor under less favourable purchasing terms, PPC may be accused of abuse of dominance through price discrimination. PPC has limited ability to control the final price at which its goods are sold. Directives can only be toward providing a maximum selling price, not a minimum. The exception is where PPC seeks to prevent a retailer, for example, from using its products as loss leaders. PPC must also ensure that accurate prices are posted and sales are not exaggerated.

2. How does the law affect PPC's distribution strategy?

PPC is anxious to promote and maintain the high quality and premium price of its products. PPC is considering imposing terms on customers that may violate the law. It cannot, for example, insist that customers purchase less-popular goods along with popular items, and it must not differentiate between comparable customers that are willing and able to purchase under similar conditions. If a dominant retailer insists that PPC stop selling to a major competitor, PPC may be the subject of investigation for refusing to deal. If PPC sells directly to consumers online, Steve must ensure that all rules governing such transactions are followed.

3. How can PPC effectively manage its exposure to legal risk in the context of marketing?

PPC is making and selling goods that have significant legal risk exposure, as they are designed for children. PPC must ensure that it maintains a "safety-first" strategy, with all employees buying into this fundamental notion. Likewise, all promotion must be truthful. Maximizing safety and honesty will minimize risk. Guidelines for sales and shipping staff can clarify PPC's policies and indicate practices that are illegal. Finally, PPC should ensure that it has full insurance coverage.

Chapter Summary

Price and distribution are two of the four components of the marketing mix. Pricing regulation is designed to protect consumers, but there is also strong public interest in ensuring that businesses compete fairly. If unfair practices are permitted, honest businesses will find themselves at a competitive disadvantage or will be squeezed out of the marketplace. While it is perhaps thought that anything goes in competition between businesses, the regulations outlined in this chapter related to business-to-business dealings show that this assumption is incorrect. Businesses may have to become dominant in the marketplace to achieve economies of scale. Nonetheless, such market dominance cannot be allowed to lead to unfair or discriminatory practices.

Distribution covers a range of activities and practices. Distribution practices that discriminate between customers and thereby substantially reduce competition are reviewable by the Competition Bureau. Direct-marketing practices are regulated both provincially and federally.

Risk management in marketing entails paying close attention to all aspects of a marketing plan to identify risks relating to the business and its customers. A plan should set clear guidelines for staff and ensure awareness of marketing activities that are not permitted. A corporate compliance program is a critical factor in any investigation by the Competition Bureau. More importantly, it positions the business so that compliance with all legislation is a fundamental principle by which it operates.

Chapter Study

Key Terms and Concepts

abuse of dominant position (p. 602)

bid rigging (p. 602)

door-to-door selling (p. 609)

double ticketing (p. 606)

exclusive dealing (p. 607)

multi-level marketing (p. 608)

price maintenance (p. 603)

pyramid selling (p. 608)

refusal to deal (p. 607)

telemarketing (p. 609)

tied selling (p. 607)

Questions for Review

1. Who decides the price in a commercial sale?

2. What are two examples of anticompetitive behaviour?

3. What is a conspiracy to fix prices?

4. What is abuse of dominant position?

5. Under what conditions is it acceptable to state "recommended retail price" on a product?

6. What are two situations where it is legitimate for a seller to refuse to supply to a retailer?

7. What is bid rigging?

8. What is the meaning of "ordinary price" in evaluating the promotion of goods?

9. How did Sears' tire advertising break the law?

10. What is double ticketing?

11. What is the difference between legal multi-level selling and pyramid selling?

12. What must be disclosed to potential participants in a multi-level marketing plan?

13. How are door-to-door sellers regulated?

14. What are two primary concerns of consumers buying online?

15. What are key features of legislation governing online contracts?

16. What is a corporate compliance program in relation to marketing regulations?

17. How is privacy law relevant to marketing?

18. How does a do not call list limit marketing strategy?

Questions for Critical Thinking

1. The prohibition of various unfair pricing practices by the *Competition Act* is intended to promote a level playing field and prevent pricing policies that limit competition. Why are market forces not able to eliminate unfair competitors? Why are customers not able to distinguish the fair competitors from the unscrupulous?

2. A manufacturer that wishes to market a product at a premium price cannot attempt to influence the resale price of its product by distributors without fear of review. How then can manufacturers protect the premium image of their products and discourage discount prices?

3. It has been said that Canada's anti-spam law is long overdue and will finally cure Canada's reputation as a haven for spammers. Will the new law deter spammers? How will we know if it is working?

4. Internet shopping opens up a broad range of risks to consumers. What recommendations would you have for federal and provincial governments moving to improve regulation to enhance consumer confidence?

5. Canadian car drivers are often disgruntled when gasoline prices change. It seems that whether the price goes up or down, every gas station in town adjusts its price at the same time. Is this an indication of a price conspiracy by the oil companies? What do the recent Competition Bureau investigation and prosecutions reveal about gas prices?

6. As a new marketing manager in a fast-moving consumer products business, you are concerned because the firm encourages managers to operate quickly, independently, and aggressively. You are aware of the advisability of a risk management plan and a corporate compliance program under the *Competition Act.* How could you persuade management to adopt this approach given the existing corporate culture?

Situations for Discussion

1. Mega Goods Inc. is a major discount retailer operating throughout Canada. The Home Co-op is also a nation-wide chain, but it is a cooperative buying group of smaller retailers that band together in order to achieve buying power. Both retailers buy large volumes of plastic food containers from the major manufacturer (PFC Inc.) in the market. The product line is an important customer draw and is often used in special promotions.

   Mega Goods is eager to increase its market share, particularly with the entry of a multinational, U.S.-based discounter into the Canadian market. It decides to attempt to eliminate the direct competition from Home Co-op in smaller centres. Mega Goods approaches PFC and requests changed conditions of purchase. Specifically, it asks for a significant drop in price in return for a reduced payment period. This change will place it at a distinct advantage over Home Co-op, as Home Co-op cannot pay quickly because of its membership structure. Mega Goods intends to approach all other major suppliers if this proposal works.

   PFC management is quite concerned, as Home Co-op is a long-standing customer. Would supplying on Mega Goods' terms be legal? Is it a wise business practice?

2. There are three major suppliers of highly specialized industrial chemicals in Canada. They have all operated for many years, and they respect each other and the quality of their products. They recognize that the market, while profitable, is finite, and that for each to survive, none can assume a greater market portion than currently held. For many years, it has been accepted that when calls for supplies are made by various industries, Company A will respond for Western Canada, Company B for Ontario, and Company C for Quebec and the Maritimes.

   Recently, purchasers from these suppliers have been questioning why, of all supplies purchased, these chemicals are subject to the least price fluctuation. They have learned from employees of A, B, and C of the arrangement. What are the implications for A, B, and C, their employees, and their customers?

3. Miguel and Marta are the owners of Universal Suppliers Ltd. They have been reasonably successful in selling printer cartridges and paper to a variety of local customers, but they wish to expand their business. They have decided to begin selling their products by telephone in order to reach potential customers across Canada and in the United States. They hired a number of phone sellers and have given them a free hand in communicating with customers. Some of these sellers have gone to considerable lengths to get orders, including suggestions that potential customers have purchased from Universal in the past and can continue to pay deep discount prices. Does this sales campaign raise any legal issues? What is the potential liability of Universal, Miguel, Marta, and the phone sellers? Should those contacted by telephone be expected to protect themselves? Is contact by telephone more problematic than contact in person, by mail, or by email?

4. Textiles Inc. is a major chain of fabric sellers. In this market, there are a few high-end sellers of fashion designer fabrics, some small independents, and three chains, with Textiles being the largest and most profitable. Textiles thrives on its ability to attract customers, often through discount pricing.

   Every few weeks Textiles has a major promotion, with certain materials being sold at a reduced cost. The business sells both regular fabrics and fashion fabrics. Textiles tends to discount the regular fabrics while the prices of fashion fabrics retain their high markup. After a while, even though advertisements state that fabric prices are reduced by 30 percent and even 50 percent, regular customers have become so accustomed to these reductions that they seldom expect to pay the full price.

   These practices are attracting the attention of competitors, who have notified the Competition Bureau. Why is the bureau likely to be interested in Textiles' pricing practices?

5. Air Canada controls 70 percent of the domestic passenger market in Canada and 20 percent of international air travel through Canadian airports. The airline has been in bankruptcy protection several times and is slowly regaining profitability, although costs for employees, fuel, and airports are rising. It is a challenge to maintain a full Canadian network along with international routes. Canadian competitors have begun to erode Air Canada's market share, particularly on its more profitable routes. Senior management is considering several options to combat the competitive threats, including lowering fares below the competition, boosting loyalty rewards for customers, taking

over the smaller airlines, starting their own smaller airlines to compete on certain routes, abandoning less profitable routes, forming an alliance with several of their largest competitors, or using their bargaining power to negotiate favourable deals with suppliers. Management is concerned about the legal ramifications of the various options. Are any of the possibilities illegal? What are the relevant factors?

6. Two companies (WSI and CA) dominated the commercial waste collection service industry on Vancouver Island. Their customers were restaurants, schools, office complexes, and condominium developments. They jointly engaged in certain business practices to preserve their dominant position and discourage other small and medium-sized waste collection companies. These practices included the use of long-term contracts that locked in customers and contained highly restrictive terms such as automatic renewal clauses and significant penalties for early contract termination. One small competitor (UP) was frustrated by its difficulty in finding customers because it provided prices and services that were competitive with the two major players. UP eventually discovered the terms of the contracts used by WSI and CA. UP considered filing a complaint with the Competition Bureau.[36] How would such a complaint be dealt with?

7. The Rolling Stones produced a new four-disc DVD called *Four Flicks*. TGA Entertainment, the band's management company, made an agreement with Future Shop (FS) granting FS the exclusive right to sell the DVD set to consumers. In return, the Stones received a larger portion of profits from the DVD than they would have through normal distribution. The music retailer HMV Canada anticipates huge demand for the DVD and wants to be able to sell it through its outlets. TGA refuses to sell to HMV because of the agreement with FS.[37] Is this agreement valid under marketing law? Explain.

8. Merck & Co. is the fourth largest pharmaceutical company in the world. It developed and tested an effective painkiller called Vioxx that was particularly helpful to those suffering from arthritis. The drug was approved by the regulatory authorities and put on the market in 1999. Over the next five years it was taken by 20 million patients, generating $2.5 billion in sales and 11 percent of Merck's revenue each year. In 2004, a report was released indicating an elevated risk of heart attack and stroke among those who took Vioxx for 18 months or longer. Merck decided to withdraw Vioxx from the market. Subsequently Merck was named as defendant in over 27 000 lawsuits involving Vioxx. Twenty of the cases went to trial, most of which were won by Merck, but Merck's legal costs exceeded $1 billion. In 2007, Merck negotiated a settlement of all lawsuits totaling $4.85 billion. The total represented less than Merck's annual profit and provided claimants an average of $100 000. Meanwhile, Merck's competitors continue to sell similar drugs with severe warnings on the packages regarding possible health risks. In 2011 Merck agreed to pay $950 million to settle criminal charges related to the marketing of Vioxx.[38] Should Merck have put Vioxx on the market? Should it have been withdrawn from the market in 2004? Why did Merck fight every case for three years and then decide to settle? Why did the criminal process take seven years? What broader marketing law and consumer protection issues does this situation raise?

For more study tools, visit http://www.NELSONbrain.com.

36. Based in part on Competition Bureau of Canada, "Competition Bureau cracks down on joint abuse of dominance by waste companies" (16 June 2009), online: Competition Bureau Canada <http://www.competitionbureau.gc.ca/eic/site/cb-bc.nsf/eng/03081.html>.

37. Based on The Canadian Press, "Music retailers seek satisfaction", *The Chronicle Herald* (14 November 2003) C2.

38. Based, in part, on Alex Berenson, "Merck agrees to settle Vioxx suits for $4.85 billion", *The New York Times* (9 November 2007), online: New York Times <http://www.nytimes.com /2007/11/09/business/09merck.html> and Duff Wilson, "Merck to pay $950 million over Vioxx", *The New York Times* (22 November 2011), online: New York Times <http://www.nytimes.com /2011/11/23/business/merck-agrees-to-pay-950-million-in-vioxx-case.html?nl=todaysheadlines&emc=tha25>.

Financing the Business

The decisions related to financing a business range from paying a supplier to financing an expansion of operations and dealing with financial difficulties. Virtually all financial aspects of starting, operating, and terminating a business have legal implications. As with other sectors of a business, an understanding of the legal aspects of finance can be used to structure activities in a way that minimizes unfavourable legal consequences. Part Eight presents the various aspects of financing a business not simply as a list of legal topics, but rather as a businessperson might encounter them. The major chapter topics are dealing with banks, obtaining credit, and coping with business failure.

ADAM RADOSAVLJEVIC/SHUTTERSTOCK

CHAPTER 25

Business and Banking

Objectives

After studying this chapter, you should have an understanding of

- the relationship between a business and its bank

- the legal issues involved in electronic banking

- the legal challenges involved in the various methods of payment

- the legal framework of negotiable instruments

- the rights and obligations of those connected with negotiable instruments

COURTESY OF DARCY SAGE

Business Law in Practice

Bill Ikeda and Martha Wong operate a building supply outlet in Timmins, Ontario. They also sell hardware, plumbing, and electrical supplies. Their customers are retail and commercial. They operate the business through a corporation, Hometown Hardware Ltd. (Hometown). Bill is the CEO and majority owner. He conducts most of the business apart from the operation of the store. Martha is the vice president and owns the remaining shares. She manages the store. The business has dealt with the local branch of the same bank for many years—the Full Service Bank (FSB). Both Bill and Martha have signing authority.

Bill and Martha have recently begun to reconsider their relationship with FSB. The branch has a new manager. There have been other personnel changes, as well, so that Hometown's accounts and loans are now handled by unfamiliar employees who seem uninterested in Hometown's business and have recently been unhelpful. Bill is also not sure that he has the appropriate types of accounts. He is concerned about high service fees on his accounts and rising interest rates on his loans. He wonders whether he should consider moving his business to another bank. Martha has been advised by business acquaintances that banks are offering a vast array of financial services and that Hometown's banking can be done more easily and cheaper online.

Bill is also concerned about the growing number of cheques being returned to him by the bank because customers have insufficient funds in their accounts to cover them. He currently accepts payment by cash, cheque, debit card, and credit card. Hometown also extends credit to some commercial customers. Bill is interested in the cost and risk of various payment options.

1. What do Bill and Martha need to know about the legal aspects of the relationship between their business and a bank?

2. What are the risks and benefits of various payment options and doing banking electronically?

3. What are the risks and benefits of using cheques to pay bills and allowing customers to pay by cheque?

When operating a building supply store, what financial decisions with legal consequences must the owners make?

BORIS SPREMO/THE CANADIAN PRESS

Business and Banking

This chapter describes the relationship that a business has with its bank, including the financial services the bank provides and the agreements and duties involved in the relationship. Various forms of payment and the related risks are explored—traditional paper-based payments and the growing number of electronic options. The chapter begins with a brief look at the banking system.

The Regulation of Banks

Traditionally, the Canadian financial services industry had four distinct sectors: banks, trust companies, stockbrokerages, and insurance companies. To ensure stability within each sector and to avoid conflicts of interest resulting from institutions providing services from several sectors, each was separately regulated, and institutions in one sector were prohibited from conducting business beyond that sector.

The internationalization of the financial services industry in the 1980s placed pressure on governments to deregulate and relax the strict separation of the four sectors. In 1987, Canadian legislation[1] allowed banks to go beyond traditional banking and participate in other sectors in their branches or through subsidiary firms. Banks have become financial marketplaces, offering services in cash management, payment services, investment advice, and business financing. Subsequent legislation[2] further blurred the distinctions between different types of financial institutions by allowing greater structural flexibility. Among many other changes, it provided for liberalized ownership rules for banks. The key

---

1. The *Office of the Superintendent of Financial Institutions Act*, RSC 1985, c 18 (3rd Supp) Part 1 created a single federal regulator (OSFI).
2. *Financial Consumer Agency of Canada Act*, SC 2001, c 9.

remaining limit on banks' business is the prohibition against selling or promoting insurance products in their branches. Banks have responded by opening separate insurance branches and attempting to conduct insurance business online.[3] The financial sector legislation is reviewed every five years.[4] Bank regulation has become a topic of great interest since the world financial crisis began in 2008.

Banks are increasingly offering international banking services, such as letters of credit, cross-border transfers, and accounts in different currencies. These services are governed largely by voluntary rules created by international bodies, such as the Bank for International Settlements and the International Chamber of Commerce. Parties involved in international transactions frequently incorporate these rules into their agreements.

In Canada, banks are under federal jurisdiction and are regulated through the federal *Bank Act*.[5] The main purposes of the Act are to ensure the stability and liquidity of banks and to identify and regulate the types of business they are permitted to conduct. The relationship between a bank and its individual customers is not a primary concern of the Act. The terms and conditions of that relationship are, instead, found primarily in the agreements made between the bank and its customers, which are influenced by banking practice and common law rules. Contract law is the prime source of guidance in interpreting and enforcing the rights and obligations of the parties in this relationship.

The Bank–Customer Relationship

In its simplest form, the relationship between a business and its bank consists of one bank account into which the business deposits its cash receipts from customers and from which it makes payments to suppliers, employees, government, and owners. As a result of regulatory changes and decisions by banks to broaden their range of services, the relationship is now more comprehensive. It is a challenge for businesspeople like Bill and Martha to decide what banking services they need, which services they can afford, and who will do the best job of providing them.

The legal nature of the relationship is clear. In terms of the customer's money on deposit with the bank, the relationship is that of the bank as debtor and the customer as creditor. Normally, the bank is not obligated to give advice or to look out for the best interest of the customer, unless, for example, the bank provides services such as financial advice, which are outside the normal scope of traditional banking services. In that situation, a fiduciary relationship may exist, and the bank has several additional onerous duties, including

- to provide advice with care and skill
- to disclose any actual or potential conflicts of interest
- to consider the interests of the customer ahead of those of the bank[6]

---

3. See *Regulations Amending the Insurance Business (Banks and Bank Holding Companies) Regulations*, SOR/2011-183, online: Canada Gazette <http://gazette.gc.ca/rp-pr/p2/2011/2011-10-12/html/sor-dors183-eng.html>.
4. The latest review culminated in the *Financial System Review Act*, SC 2012, c 5 which contains relatively minor changes. See Bill Curry and Tara Perkins, "New bill would increase minister's power over banks", *The Globe and Mail* (23 November 2011), online: Globe and Mail <http://www.theglobeandmail.com/report-on-business/new-bill-would-increase-finance-ministers-power-over-banks/article2246925/>.
5. SC 1991, c 46.
6. Alison R Manzer & Jordan S Bernamoff, *The Corporate Counsel Guide to Banking and Credit Relationships* (Aurora, ON: Canada Law Book, 1999) at 36.

For example, if Bill has sought and received advice from his banker as to the amount and structure of the financing he needs for Hometown, he can expect to receive competent advice from the bank and should be encouraged to seek an independent opinion before agreeing to a financing arrangement operating heavily in the bank's favour.

The practical advice for customers is to appreciate the basic nature of the relationship and to understand that banks generally have no obligation to look beyond their own self-interest. However, banks are beginning to broaden their roles to remain competitive.[7] They are also under pressure to deal fairly with customers and to refrain from strict enforcement of agreements that are onerous for their customers. For example, financial services legislation[8] established the Financial Consumer Agency of Canada (FCAC)[9] to protect and educate consumers through the monitoring of institutions' business practices regarding such matters as account fees and credit card rates. In addition, the financial services industry, in cooperation with the federal government, has created the Centre for the Financial Services OmbudsNetwork (CFSON)[10] to provide a one-stop complaint procedure covering brokers, banks, insurance companies, and sellers of mutual funds in order to ensure fair and impartial complaint resolution for consumers.

Duties of the Bank and the Customer

The common law and banking practice imply legal duties on both parties in the banking relationship. For example, the bank must

- honour payment instructions and repay deposits

- collect payments for the customer

- provide account information to the customer on a regular basis

- maintain secrecy of the customer's affairs.[11] This duty is qualified by legislation.

Money laundering
The false reporting of income from criminal activity as income from legitimate business.

PART EIGHT

BUSINESS APPLICATION OF THE LAW

Client Information and Money Laundering

The bank's duty to maintain secrecy of customer information is subject to the law concerning **money laundering**—that is, the false reporting of income obtained through criminal activity as income gained through legitimate business enterprises. Since 1991, banks have been urged to verify the identity of individual and corporate customers and the validity of their business activities, and to determine the source of transfers exceeding $10 000.[12]

Legislation passed in 2000[13] was meant to enable Canada to meet its international obligations in combating money laundering. The legislation created a mandatory reporting system in which banks, trust companies, insurance companies, and professionals must report to a new independent body—the Financial Transactions and Reports Analysis Centre (FINTRAC)—suspicious financial transactions and large cross-border currency transfers. Suspicious transactions are not defined in the act, but FINTRAC provides guidelines under headings such

(Continued)

---

7. See Tara Perkins, "Bankers evolve into advisory roles", *The Globe and Mail* (19 October 2010), online: Globe and Mail <http://www.theglobeandmail.com/report-on-business/small-business/sb-marketing/customer-service/bankers-evolve-into-advisory-roles/article1762494/>.
8. *Supra* note 2.
9. See Financial Consumer Agency of Canada, online: <http://www.fcac-acfc.gc.ca>.
10. See Financial Services OmbudsNetwork, online: <http://www.fson.org> and the Ombudsman for Banking Services and Investments (OBSI), online: <http://www.obsi.ca>. However, some banks have opted out of the OBSI process. See Grant Robertson, "TD quits external banking ombudsman", *The Globe and Mail* (26 October 2011), online: CTV News <http://www.ctv.ca/generic/generated/static/business/article2214604.html>. See also Department of Finance Canada, "Harper government imposes tough new pro-consumer oversight on banking complaints" (6 July 2012), online: Department of Finance Canada<http://www.fin.gc.ca/n12/12-079-eng.asp>.
11. *Supra* note 6 at 14.
12. *Proceeds of Crime (Money Laundering) Act*, SC 1991, c 26.
13. *Proceeds of Crime (Money Laundering) and Terrorist Financing Act*, SC 2000, c 17. See also SC 2006, c 12.

as "economic purpose" of the transaction. For example, if a transaction seems to be inconsistent with the client's apparent financial standing or usual pattern of activities, does not appear to be driven by normal commercial considerations, or is unnecessarily complex for its stated purpose, it should be considered suspicious.

FINTRAC is responsible for managing the information reported by the various organizations affected by the Act and deciding which transactions to refer to law enforcement agencies for investigation.

Subsequent regulatory changes have tightened the requirements by broadening the applicability and expanding the obligations of record keeping, reporting, and registration;

increasing client identification requirements; requiring compliance regimes, employee training, and education; and establishing federal registration for money service and foreign exchange businesses. The legislation is undergoing its five-year mandatory review.

Critical Analysis: To what extent should the confidentiality of individual client accounts be compromised to combat money laundering by a minority of clients? How is the effectiveness of this regime measured? Is the regulatory burden justified?

Sources: Department of Finance Canada, "Minister of Finance launches consultation to update anti-money laundering and anti-terrorist financing regime" (21 December 2011), online: Department of Finance Canada <http://www.fin.gc.ca/n11/11-142-eng.asp> and Christine Duhaime, "Push to expand money laundering law", *The Lawyers Weekly* (9 March 2012) 11.

Customers also have implied duties to the bank. They must

- take reasonable steps to provide documentation as to who is authorized to give instructions to the bank, in order to prevent fraud and forgery

- keep authorizations current

- notify the bank of any suspected problems

- provide safeguards for electronic communications[14]

The Bank–Customer Agreement

Standard banking documents are designed primarily to protect the bank, not the customer. Large customers may have some bargaining power, but small businesses such as Hometown have little. Understanding the terms and conditions in the agreement will enable Bill to identify risks arising from the banking aspects of his business. He can then establish practices to avoid incidents resulting in loss for which the banking agreement would make him responsible.

Banking contract

A contract that specifies the rights and obligations of a bank and a customer.

The purpose of the **banking contract** is twofold:

- to specify who has the authority to issue instructions to the bank on behalf of the customer

- to allocate the risk of loss resulting from problems with verifying the customer's authority and carrying out the customer's instructions

The customer designates those with authority to issue instructions to the bank through such means as signing cheques. At this time, Bill and Martha are the only persons with that authority at Hometown.

The second focus of the banking contract—namely, the allocation of loss—is of greater significance. Bill must be cautious in his dealings because the bank–customer contract is drafted by the bank to limit its duties and liabilities. For example, a verification clause commonly found in banking contracts gives the customer 30 days to detect and report any

---

14. *Supra* note 6 at 15.

unauthorized payments that the bank makes from the customer's account. Beyond that period, the customer absorbs the loss. Normally, the bank also has flexibility in dealing with all of the customer's accounts. For example, the bank can transfer funds from an account with a positive balance to one that is overdrawn.

The key document involved in a banking contract is the account agreement, sometimes broadened into a financial services agreement. It includes provisions dealing with issues such as

- the bank's ability to apply charges to the customer's accounts (commonly known as service charges)

- arrangements concerning instructions for payment by the customer, especially the issue of cheques

- confirmations and stop payments on cheques

- release of information by the bank about the customer.

Traditional banking transactions are increasingly done online.

Electronic Banking

Electronic banking includes a growing range and variety of transactions that previously required formal documentation. A wide variety of technological developments are changing the ways that businesses deal with banks, customers, and other businesses. Banks are encouraging customers to conduct their banking business through ATMs, telephone, or online, rather than through in-person transactions in bank branches. These methods can be more convenient for customers and significantly less expensive for the banks. Some new banks have no physical branches at all and conduct all their business online.

Electronic banking
Financial transactions carried out through the use of computers, telephones, or other electronic means.

There are several legal issues arising from electronic transactions. Electronic storage means that data are subject to system crashes or hackers. Fraud has become a significant concern. Other potential problems are transmission failures or system crashes. As business comes to rely increasingly on instant payments, possibly at the last minute, the potential loss from a failed or delayed transfer is significant.

Most of the legal uncertainty surrounding electronic banking is the result of the irrelevance of existing legislation to a paperless environment. The process and timing of electronic transactions do not fit with existing rules related to risk allocation for authentication, verification, and finalization of payments in paper-based transactions.

The gap in the rules governing electronic banking is being filled in several ways. First, banking contracts now include an agreement for electronic financial services and access. Banks may be tempted to limit their liability through their agreements with customers, but they are also interested in reassuring customers by assuming responsibility themselves. Agreements make provision for risks that specify the customer's duties to report problems to the bank and the bank's responsibility for electronic failures. Customers are also required to choose personal identification numbers (PINs) that are not obvious, to change PINs regularly, and to safeguard those PINs from unauthorized use. If they fail to meet these requirements, customers are liable for any losses that result. Banks are also placing daily and weekly monetary limits on transactions in order to control the losses in the event of fraud. Second, industry codes have been created to provide guidance. The *Code of Conduct for Credit and Debit Card Industry* was revised in 2010[15] and the Minister of Finance has formed a working group to develop a voluntary code for electronic funds transfers and electronic banking. Third, there are international rules, such as the UNCITRAL *Model Law on International Credit Transfers,*[16] since electronic transfers are completed as easily across the world as within the local community. If the sending and receiving banks are in different countries, these international rules deal with the obligations of the parties, timing for payment, consequences for technical problems, and liability and damages.

What rules govern ATM transactions?

EDYTA PAWLOWSKA/SHUTTERSTOCK

Identity theft
The fraudulent use of others' personal information to create a false identity.

BUSINESS AND LEGISLATION

Identity Theft

The Internet has increased the potential for fraudulent activities. In particular, **identity theft** has become a serious problem. Identity theft involves obtaining others' personal information through various means and using that information for fraudulent purposes such as accessing bank accounts or obtaining credit cards, loans, mortgages, or title to property. The victims can be individuals or businesses. Their entire financial situation is compromised. One method for initiating identity theft is through "phishing," whereby fraudsters send email messages that appear to be from reputable companies, such as banks,

and direct recipients to websites that appear genuine, where victims are urged to disclose personal information in order to verify their accounts and ensure their continued access. Simply visiting one of these websites may enable fraudsters to extract valuable information. The information is then used to steal the victim's identity. The danger of identity theft has increased with the advent of wireless technology, to the extent that identity theft has become an organized criminal activity.

To combat this increase in identity theft, the federal government passed legislation[17] to create several new criminal offences, including

15. (18 May 2010), online: Department of Finance Canada <http://www.fin.gc.ca/n10/data/10-049_1-eng.asp>.
16. *UNCITRAL Model Law on International Credit Transfers* (1992), 32 ILM 587, online: UNCITRAL <http://www.uncitral.org/uncitral/en/uncitral_texts/payments/1992Model_credit_transfers.html>.
17. *An Act to Amend the Criminal Code (Identity Theft and Related Misconduct),* SC 2009, c 28 (in force 8 January 2010).

• obtaining or possessing identity information with the intent to commit certain crimes

• trafficking in identity information with knowledge of or recklessness as to its intended use, and

• unlawfully possessing or trafficking in government-issued identity documents.

Identity information is broadly defined to include anything that is commonly used alone or in combination with other information to identify an individual, such as name, address,

fingerprints, date of birth, signature, bank account number, and passport number. Penalties for violation of the law include imprisonment for five years. The challenge with such a law is to address the criminal activity without unduly restricting legitimate business.

Sources: Sharda Prashad, "Identity theft strikes small businesses", *The Globe and Mail* (18 January 2010), online: Globe and Mail <http://www.theglobeandmail.com/report-on-business/small-business/start/legal/identity-theft-strikes-small-businesses/article1433204/>; Christopher Guly, "Identity theft may target innocent acts", *The Lawyers Weekly* (18 December 2009) 17; and Eva Hoare, "Bank staff thwart identity thefts", *The Chronicle Herald* (20 March 2010) A3.

Although fraud and data security breaches are matters of concern, there is little evidence yet of significant legal problems arising from electronic transfers. Business customers of banks are interested in security, convenience, and low costs in terms of banking services. As long as banks can demonstrate to customers that their needs are being met without significant risks, the volume of electronic banking will increase.

Methods of Payment

When Bill and Martha pay an account with one of Hometown's suppliers, they have several options. They can use cash, with the inconvenience and risk of keeping adequate cash on hand to pay bills. Other options are to pay by **cheque** (a written order to the bank) or by electronic funds transfer (a paperless transaction). Electronic payments are expanding in terms of scope and volume.

Cheque
A written order to a bank to pay money to a specified person.

TECHNOLOGY AND THE LAW

Developments in Electronic Payments Systems

Customers are offered a range of electronic options by their banks. Some examples are automatic payments from chequing accounts, direct deposit of cheques, automatic teller machines (ATMs), payment by telephone or computer, and point-of-sale transfers. Banks now offer smart phone apps for access to their accounts. ATMs are available for deposits, withdrawals, transfers between accounts, and bill payments. Telephone banking and online banking can be used for everything other than cash transactions, including applications for mortgages and loans.

There are many models for cashless transactions. Debit cards allow buyers to purchase goods and services and to transfer payment directly from a bank account to the seller. Money cards carry a computer chip that enables virtual money to be loaded on the card and transferred directly from the card to the seller. Electronic money or digital cash takes no physical form, but instead is loaded onto computer hard drives or electronic wallets, enabling payment to be made as easily as sending email. "Smart cards" can now combine all of the above features.

Cellphones are gaining wide use in online banking. They can also be used as virtual wallets by those without bank accounts, who can have cash loaded onto them for transfer by cellphone. This practice is growing for transfers to other countries. Phones with virtual embedded credit cards can also be used to make contactless payments. Customers can now use their cellphone cameras to photograph cheques to be cashed and send the digital image to the bank. Payments can also be made through secure online commercial intermediaries such as PayPal.

Credit card transactions are processed electronically as well. Credit cards have evolved from manual processing to networks accessed with magnetic stripes, then to embedded microchips and PINs, and now to contactless payments using microchips and radio frequencies where the card is simply waved at a reader. They involve three contracts—one between the card issuer and the user, the second between the credit card company and the merchant, and the basic contract of sale between the user (buyer) and the merchant. The second contract has become contentious since merchants are largely at the mercy of card companies in terms of acceptance of cards from buyers

(Continued)

and the associated fees. This imbalance of power has attracted the attention of the Competition Bureau.

Critical Analysis: The range of electronic payment mechanisms is continually expanding. Are the risks associated with these methods outweighed by the low cost, convenience, and customer demand? Can the developers of such methods and the lawmakers stay ahead of those who seek to breach security?

Sources: Ivor Tossell, "Enter the digital wallet", *The Globe and Mail* (7 November 2011), online: Globe and Mail <http://www.theglobeandmail.com/report-on-business/small-business/enter-the-digital-wallet/article2226181/>; Tara S Bernard and Claire C Miller, "Swiping is the easy part", *The New York Times* (23 March 2011), online: New York Times <http://www.nytimes.com/2011/03/24/technology/24wallet.html>; Grant Robertson, "Say cheese! Photo chequing on its way to Canada", *The Globe and Mail* (26 March 2012), online: Globe and Mail <http://www.theglobeandmail.com/globe-investor/say-cheese-photo-chequing-on-its-way-to-canada/article2381965/>; and Competition Bureau of Canada, "Competition Bureau challenges Visa and Mastercard's Anti-competitive rules" (15 December 2010), online: Competition Bureau Canada <http://www.competitionbureau.gc.ca/eic/site/cb-bc.nsf/eng/03325.html>.

Do the same rules apply to various payment choices?

IGOR VLADIMIROVICH ZHOROV/SHUTTERSTOCK

RYAN MCVAY/GETTY IMAGES/JUPITER IMAGES

The rules governing payment by cheque are well defined and are part of the law of negotiable instruments.

Negotiable Instruments

A cheque is the most common example of a **negotiable instrument**, but the rules also apply to other documents, such as promissory notes and bills of exchange. A **promissory note** is a written promise by one person to pay a specified amount on a certain date or on demand to another person. A **bill of exchange** is an order to someone else to pay funds to another person. A cheque is a special type of bill of exchange, which is payable on demand and where the party instructed to pay is a bank. These instruments are federally regulated by the *Bills of Exchange Act*.[18] The rules in this legislation focus on the attributes and transferability of pieces of paper called negotiable instruments.

There are several technical requirements for an instrument (a document) to become negotiable or transferable without the need to investigate its validity through reference to the circumstances of its creation or other documents. The essence of the requirements is that the instrument must be a self-contained obligation. It must be in written form and signed by the person making the promise or authorizing the payment. It must specify an amount of money to be paid on a specified date or on demand, and the obligation must be unconditional. For example, if a promise is made to pay "the balance due" on a construction contract, the promise cannot be a negotiable instrument because the balance can be determined only by consulting the original contract and investigating the work done and payments already made. A negotiable instrument must be for a specific sum without conditions. When Bill issues a cheque (on behalf of Hometown) to a supplier of goods or services, he gives a written order to his bank to pay a specified sum to the supplier. The cheque is a negotiable instrument.

As indicated in Figure 25.1 below, Bill is the creator of the instrument. The supplier is the payee (the business entitled to payment). Bill is formally known as the drawer because

Negotiable instrument
A written contract containing an unconditional promise or order to pay a specific sum on demand or on a specified date to a specific person or bearer.

Promissory note
A written promise to another person to pay a specified amount.

Bill of exchange
A written order to a person to pay a specified amount to another person.

PART EIGHT

FIGURE 25.1

An Annotated Cheque

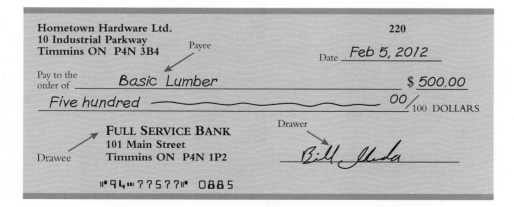

---

18. RSC 1985, c B-4.

he is ordering his bank ("drawing an order") to pay the supplier. The bank, as the recipient of Bill's instructions, is known as the drawee.

Bill's instructions to his bank in the form of a cheque and the bank's actions to carry out his instructions by paying money from the Hometown account to the designated supplier are at the centre of the bank–customer contract. The written agreement addresses these transactions in some detail and a number of duties are imposed through the common law. For example, the customer must keep adequate funds in his accounts to pay any cheques that are issued, and he must provide clear and unambiguous instructions to the bank concerning payment. The bank must take reasonable care in honouring instructions to pay out the money.[19]

Bill's supplier will likely take the cheque to its own bank for deposit. Through the centralized clearing process, the cheque will find its way from the supplier's bank to Hometown's bank, and the specified sum will be taken from Hometown's account (see Figure 25.2 below).

As long as there are adequate funds in Hometown's account and there is no defect in the cheque, it will proceed smoothly through the steps. If Bill accepts cheques as payment from his customers, the customer is the drawer and Hometown is the payee, in relation to the steps in Figure 25.2. The following sections describe the potential problems and risks for the participants if difficulties arise in the circulation or cashing of the cheque.

Implications of Creating a Cheque

When Bill chooses to pay a supplier by cheque, he is discharging a debt that Hometown owes as debtor to the supplier as creditor. That debt has arisen through the contract between Hometown and the supplier for the provision of goods or services. Assuming

FIGURE 25.2

Steps in the Cheque Circulation Process

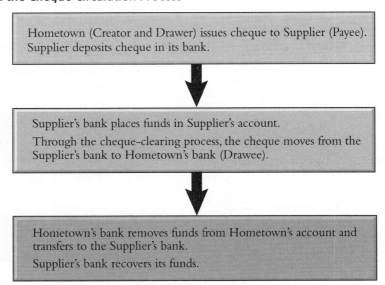

---

19. *Supra* note 6 at 30.

that Bill buys his building supplies from a number of suppliers, he will have regular payment obligations arising from his contractual arrangements with those suppliers. If he encounters problems with the supplies, he will have a valid complaint against the supplier (subject to their contract). He can pursue that complaint as he would any breach of contract.

However, his claim on the contract is a totally different matter from his obligation to pay the cheque. By issuing the cheque, he has made an unconditional promise to pay the specified sum not just to the supplier, but potentially to anyone (known as a **holder**) who presents the cheque to Hometown's bank for payment. The special status of the cheque and the holder are created by legislation[20] that deliberately places the holder in a strong position in terms of collecting on the cheque. If the holder has acted in good faith (meaning she has no reason to doubt the validity of the cheque), that person acquires the status of a **holder in due course**. There are limited arguments (for example, a forged signature or an alteration of the cheque) that Hometown can use to justify refusing payment to a holder in due course. The rights of such a holder are not affected by any terms of Hometown's contract with the supplier. Hometown's bank will pay out the cheque to the holder. Hometown can then seek compensation separately from the supplier.

A cheque involves a markedly different situation from an ordinary assignment of contractual rights, where there can be any number of defences against paying. For example, if Hometown owes money to a supplier, that supplier can assign the right to collect to someone else (known as an assignee). In the absence of a negotiable instrument, the assignee's right to collect from Hometown is subject to any problems with the contract between Hometown and the supplier. Thus, if Bill has a valid reason for refusing to pay the supplier's claim, he can use the same reason to avoid paying the assignee. In law, this idea is captured in the expression "an assignee can have no better rights than the assignor."[21]

This important distinction between an assignment and a negotiable instrument is illustrated by the former practice in some consumer sales (in which the buyer is the final user of the goods for a non-commercial purpose) where the separation of obligations arising from the negotiable instrument and the contract of sale was abused. If a consumer bought something on credit and signed a negotiable instrument such as a promissory note in favour of the seller, that seller could sell the note to another party (such as a finance company). The legal result of the transfer of the note was that the financier became a holder in due course. The buyer's obligation to pay the financier was then nearly absolute and independent of problems with the quality and performance of the purchased goods. Such problems could be pursued against the seller based on the contract of sale, but they did not affect the consumer's continuing obligation to make payments to the holder of the note. These rules enabled collusion between unscrupulous sellers and financiers to sell substandard goods to consumers and require them to make all payments, even when the goods were defective or worthless.

Holder
A person who has possession of a negotiable instrument.

Holder in due course
A holder in good faith without notice of defects, who acquires greater rights than the parties who dealt directly with each other as the drawer and payee.

PART EIGHT

---

20. *Supra* note 18 at s 55.
21. See Chapter 9 for a more complete discussion of assignments.

Consumer note
A negotiable instrument signed by a consumer to buy on credit.

Legislation now[22] classifies promissory notes arising from consumer credit sales as **consumer notes**. The holder of a consumer note is not accorded the special status of a holder in due course and is subject to claims arising from the original contract of sale. The consumer's obligation to pay the note is subject to remedies against the seller if the goods are defective. Note that the special status of promissory notes is preserved in such transactions that are commercial in nature.

FIGURE 25.3

Comparison of Payment and Collection Arrangements

Type of arrangement	Parties involved	Enforcement rights
Contract	Buyer (debtor) Seller (creditor)	Seller can collect subject to performance of its obligations.
Assignment of contractual right	Debtor Creditor (assignor) Assignee	Assignee's right to collect is subject to the debtor's obligation to pay the assignor.
Negotiable instrument (e.g., a cheque)	Drawer (debtor) Payee (creditor) Holder	Holder in due course's right to collect is not tied to the original contract.
Consumer note	Consumer Seller Financier	Financier does not have the status of a holder in due course—consumer's obligation depends on the original contract.

The essential point for the creator of a cheque is that the cheque is a self-contained obligation, the validity of which does not depend on any circumstances outside the cheque. The creator has issued instructions to the bank to pay the designated payee or a holder in due course. As long as the cheque contains the necessary endorsements (signatures) to confirm the holder's right to possession of the cheque, the bank will pay it. Despite the strong position of a holder in due course, there are certain risks, described below.

Implications of Accepting a Cheque

The major risk involved in accepting a cheque relates to the financial health of the cheque's creator, more than any legal rules. The strong and secure legal position of a holder in due course is of no value if the drawer's account does not contain enough money to cover the cheque when it is presented for payment. The likelihood of that happening is the key consideration in Bill's decision about whether to accept any payments by cheque from customers. Deciding to accept cheques is equivalent to extending credit, since there are several days between handing over goods and receiving payment from a cheque.

Certification
The process whereby a bank guarantees payment of a cheque.

In major transactions, the method of payment that overcomes the above risk is the certified cheque. **Certification** is a process in which the drawer (or sometimes the payee) takes the cheque to the drawer's bank and has the bank certify it for payment. The bank immediately removes the money from the customer's account and holds it in reserve until

---

22. *Supra* note 18 at s 191.

the cheque is presented for payment. This process removes the risk of there being insufficient funds in the drawer's account when the cheque is cashed.

Certification usually prevents the drawer from putting a **stop payment** on the cheque. A stop payment means that the drawer (as the bank's customer) countermands (or cancels) its instructions to pay the cheque and orders the bank to refuse payment when the cheque is presented. These instructions can be issued at any time before a cheque has been charged against the drawer's account. However, the banking contract will likely absolve the bank from responsibility if the cheque is cashed accidentally, despite the stop payment order. The drawer of a cheque may also postdate it, which makes it payable on the future specified date and not on the date of creation. Since the bank must follow the drawer's instructions, it cannot cash the cheque until that future date.

Despite the secure position of holders in due course, those who are called upon to accept the transfer of a cheque may be reluctant to do so without verification of the various endorsements on the cheque and some means of recovering funds advanced on a cheque that turns out to be invalid. Thus, banks are reluctant to cash cheques for those who are not their customers with significant balances on deposit with them. If the cheque comes back to the bank due to a lack of funds in the drawer's account, the amount can be deducted from the customer's account (likely in accordance with the bank–customer contract). The bank, therefore, will not suffer the ultimate loss on the cheque. If the bank cashes a cheque for someone who is not a customer, it will be more difficult to recover the funds if the cheque turns out to be worthless. If Bill accepts cheques from customers in his store, he bears the risk that his bank will deduct the value of worthless cheques from his account.

Endorsement and Transfer of Negotiable Instruments

A cheque normally follows a relatively short route, as shown in Figure 25.2 on page 632, but it may also be transferred many times. Eventually, it is presented by a holder to the drawer's bank for payment. The transfer process is known as **negotiation**—hence the name "negotiable instrument." However, negotiation in this context has a distinct meaning from its more common use as a process for resolving disputes. All that is needed for the negotiation of an instrument is for the current holder to **endorse**, or sign, the instrument over to a new holder, who then becomes entitled to either present the instrument for payment or transfer it to yet another holder.

Although a bank or anyone else who gives money in return for a cheque runs the risk that the drawer is not able or obligated to honour it, anyone who has endorsed the cheque is potentially liable for the amount. This liability is a significant risk for anyone who endorses a negotiable instrument.

A bank's responsibility to carry out the instructions of its customers includes verifying a customer's signature on a cheque. The bank and its customers both have obligations when forgery is involved. The bank has a duty to detect unauthorized instructions (such as a forged signature), and customers must take reasonable steps to prevent forgeries and immediately report any potential problems to the bank (see the case on the next page). If a bank is left with liability for a forged cheque, it can look to prior endorsers of the cheque to recover its money. Therefore, anyone accepting a cheque should verify the authenticity of the endorsements on it.

Stop payment
The process whereby the person who writes a cheque orders the bank not to pay the holder who presents it for payment.

PART EIGHT

Negotiation
The process of transferring negotiable instruments from one person to another.

Endorse
Sign a negotiable instrument in order to enable negotiation.

CASE | *SNS Industrial Products Limited v Bank of Montreal*, 2010 ONCA 500

THE BUSINESS CONTEXT: There are situations where the bank fails to detect forged signatures and the customer does not immediately notice that the forged cheques have been cashed from its account. In these cases, the courts will look to the legislation and the bank–customer agreement.

FACTUAL BACKGROUND: Sanfillippo was the president of SNS Industrial Limited. In 1994, he opened an account at the Bank of Montreal and signed an agreement which included a verification clause: "Upon receipt of the … statement of account, the Corporation will check the debit and credit entries, examine the cheques and vouchers and notify the Bank in writing of any errors, irregularities or omissions. This notice will be provided to the Bank within 30 days …" Over a three-year period from 2003 to 2006, the office manager of SNS forged Sanfillippo's signature on a number of cheques worth $186 488. In May 2006, Sanfillippo noticed considerably less money in his account than he expected and inquired at the bank, where he was advised to begin telephone or online banking so that he could more easily monitor his account balance. At this time he signed a new agreement whose verification clause made explicit reference to forged cheques. Shortly afterward, Sanfillippo discovered the forgeries and claimed the value of the cheques from the bank.

THE LEGAL QUESTION: Who was responsible for detecting the forgeries—the customer or the bank?

RESOLUTION: The Court of Appeal relied primarily on the applicable legislation. The *Bills of Exchange Act* (s 48)[23] states: "where a signature on a bill of exchange is forged, or placed

thereon without the authority of the person whose signature it purports to be, the forged or unauthorized signature is wholly inoperative …" It was open to the bank to transfer the risk to the customer, but in the 1994 agreement,

> the Verification Clause does not refer expressly to forged cheques or otherwise to cheques debited to a customer's account for improper purposes or by illegal means. Further, the terms "error," "irregularity," and "omission" are not defined in the Verification Clause. Nor is their meaning clear on a plain reading of the Verification Clause as a whole. Thus, the meaning of these terms is not apparent on the face of the Verification Clause. Certainly, the scope of these terms would not be self-evident to many, if any, customers of the Bank without clarification or explanation. It is difficult to conceive, therefore, absent evidence to the contrary that does not exist in this case, that both parties intended, when the banking agreement was entered into, that the Verification Clause would extend to forged cheques honoured by the Bank.

> Therefore, the bank remained responsible for honouring a forged cheque.

CRITICAL ANALYSIS: Does the specific reference to forgery in the 2006 contract support the court's conclusion regarding the 1994 clause? The trial judge found that the forger did a good job on Sanfillippo's signature and that Sanfillippo did not have adequate controls in place. Are these findings relevant to the interpretation of the legislation and the agreement?

Endorsement in blank
Signing a cheque without any special instructions.

Restrictive endorsement
Signing a cheque for deposit only to a particular bank account.

Special endorsement
Signing a cheque and making it payable to a specific person.

Those in possession of cheques should take steps to safeguard them and transfer them by endorsing in a way that minimizes the risk that others may illegally obtain and cash them. Simply signing a cheque on the back is known as an **endorsement in blank.** This means that the signatures are complete and that anyone who acquires the cheque can cash it (subject to a bank's willingness to do so). Holders should therefore take care with the form of endorsements. Businesses commonly endorse cheques "for deposit only." These are known as **restrictive endorsements** and mean that the cheques can be deposited only in the account of that business. Restrictive endorsements stop the circulation of cheques and remove the risk of anyone else acquiring and cashing them. If Bill accepts cheques from customers, he should routinely endorse them in this manner as soon as possible. If a cheque received by a payee is to be transferred to someone other than a bank, it is wise to endorse it directly to that person (for example, "Pay to Desmond Chu/signed Bill Ikeda"). This is known as a **special endorsement**; it ensures that only the designated person is able to deal with the cheque further.

---

23. *Supra* note 18.

Those accepting cheques should realize that there are financial and legal reasons why collection may be a problem. Apart from a certified cheque, there is no guaranteed payment. Bill must understand that if a customer's cheque is returned to him by Hometown's bank because of insufficient funds in the customer's account, he will recover the funds only if he can collect from the customer. If the customer cannot be located or is unable to pay the amount, Bill will ultimately bear the loss. However, if he can locate the customer, the cheque is valuable evidence of the customer's contractual obligation.

The Future of Payments

A negotiable instrument has a life of its own, quite separate from the contract that produced it. Liability for payment is independent of the original debtor–creditor relationship. The result is convenience and dependability in the commercial environment. The tradeoff is that a relatively small but significant number of the instruments must be honoured by their creators in situations where there is a good reason for liability to be borne by another party, such as someone who breached the originating contract through failure to deliver goods or services.

The basis of the well-established and comprehensive set of rules governing negotiable instruments is the instrument itself—the piece of paper. The information it contains and where it goes are the key features of any dispute. Electronic transfers present several challenges in relation to this set of rules. First, since there is no key piece of paper that circulates through the system, there is no paper trail in the event of a dispute. Second, electronic transfers are instantaneous, so there is no opportunity to change the instructions for payment (for example, by issuing a stop payment). There is no need for the certification process because the transfer is unlikely to be effective unless the account from which the transfer is made has sufficient funds. Electronic deposits may result in problems if no one verifies the validity of the instruments being deposited. For example, if there is a serious defect in a cheque deposited electronically, the amount will initially be added to the customer's balance, but it will be deducted later when the defect is discovered. By this time, the customer may have already spent the money.

Electronic transfers are cheap and efficient. There is no paper to track or store. Instructions can be issued by the customer to the bank instantly, and the funds are transferred to the recipient immediately. However, safeguarding the authority for such transfers becomes a major challenge for customers. Rather than verifying signatures on cheques, banks are looking for the necessary authorization codes in electronic messages. Potential methods for forgery and fraud are changed and expanded. Tracing the cause of an electronic loss may be difficult. Someone must bear that loss, but in terms of the public good, the reliability and convenience of the transfer system may be more important than identifying the one responsible. The convenience and volume of electronic transactions outweigh the occasional injustice resulting from a defective transaction.

Commercial and consumer transactions are increasingly being conducted online. The volume of cheques is declining. Traditional paper cheques are converted to digital images for processing. In practical and legal terms, the focus is shifting to electronic banking, although not without challenges in the transition.[24]

---

24. See Enza Uda, "Banks lost millions on digital cheque project", *CBC News* (24 November 2009), online: The National <http://www.cbc.ca /thenational/indepthanalysis/gopublic/2009/11/banks-lost-millions-on-digital-cheque-project.html>. Also Department of Finance Canada, "Minister of Finance welcomes findings of the Task Force for the Payments Review System" (23 March 2012), online: Department of Finance Canada <http://www.fin.gc.ca/n12/12-030-eng.asp>.

Risk Management

The factors in Bill's decision about the methods of payment he will accept from his customers relate to marketing and finance, as well as to legal risks. He must be responsive to the needs and demands of his customers and sensitive to the cost of various payment options.

Making and accepting payments by cheque involve major risks. Payment by cheque creates an unconditional obligation independent of the purchase Bill has made. Accepting cheques as payment requires careful endorsement to maximize security and creates the risk that there will not be sufficient funds in the customers' accounts.

As long as Bill and Martha are the only ones with signing authority at the bank, authorization should not be a problem. When they reach the point at which they need to share that responsibility, they must make the terms of the arrangement clear to the persons receiving the authority and to the bank. Bill and Martha must also familiarize themselves with the practices of their bank related to authorization by phone, fax, or computer if they choose to use them.

Regarding debit cards and credit cards, Bill needs to understand the implications of the agreements he has with those service providers. By accepting the cards, Bill will pay a portion of the proceeds of those sales to the card providers. In return, he gets immediate payment for debit card sales and a guarantee of payment on credit card sales, as long as he complies with the requirements in his agreements, such as verification of signatures.

Bill and Martha need to ask their bank what happens if an electronic transfer does not happen or the bank transfers funds without proper authorization. They need to ensure that the bank has anticipated potential problems and has a reasonable way of dealing with them. In risk management terms, they need to evaluate the risks against the potential benefits of electronic banking.

Figure 25.4 summarizes the comparative risks of the various payment methods. The possibility of extending credit to customers is the subject of Chapter 26.

FIGURE 25.4

Comparative Risks of Methods of Accepting Payment

Form of Payment	*Nature of Payment*	*Risk for Person Accepting Payment*
Cash	Immediate	The money may be counterfeit or the proceeds of a crime.
Cheque	Deposited	There may be insufficient funds in the account on which the cheque was drawn; the signature may be forged.
Credit card	Guaranteed	Risk is borne largely by the card provider.
Debit card Electronic Transfer	Immediate transfer	Risk is borne largely by the payments system.
Credit	Payment at a later date	The debtor may be unable or unwilling to pay.

Business Law in Practice Revisited

1. What do Bill and Martha need to know about the legal aspects of the relationship between their business and a bank?

Bill and Martha need to appreciate that their basic relationship with the bank is one in which the bank must safeguard their money and follow their payment instructions, but is otherwise not responsible for their interests, unless the bank is engaged to provide expert advice. Bill and Martha need to appreciate the importance of the contract with the bank and become familiar with its basic rights and obligations. They should understand that the contract is written largely to protect the bank and that their bargaining power is limited. Bill and Martha should, however, seek a level of service and comfort that meets their needs and allays their concerns with their current bank.

2. What are the risks and benefits of various payment options and doing banking electronically?

If Bill engages in electronic banking, it will be cheaper and faster, but he risks having transmission problems, he cannot easily cancel e-transactions because they are instantaneous, and he is left with no paper trail to follow the transaction. Bill needs to thoroughly discuss these risks with his bank so that he feels comfortable with his banking arrangements. Since Bill accepts payments by credit card and debit card, he needs to negotiate with the providers of those services and be prepared to pay their fees. Such arrangements are not part of his package of basic banking services.

3. What are the risks and benefits of using cheques to pay bills and allowing customers to pay by cheque?

The risk of paying by cheque is that Bill cannot avoid his obligation to honour the cheque (apart from stopping payment) if he has a problem with the goods or services for which he paid using the cheque. The risk of allowing customers to pay by cheque is that they may have insufficient funds in their accounts, they may be engaged in fraud or forgery, they might issue a stop payment, or there may be a technical defect in the cheque.

The legal benefits of paying by cheque are the relative security compared with cash, the paper trail provided by the cheque, and the ability to issue a stop payment before the cheque is cashed. Accepting payments by cheque is more risky than taking only cash, but it is safer than credit.

Chapter Summary

Customers should be wary of their relationships with their banks, not because banks attempt to take advantage of them, but because the relationship is a contractual one. The rights and obligations are found in the contract, and because the banks write the contracts, the language tends to favour the banks' interests more than those of their customers. The major effect of a banking contract is to transfer risk from the bank to the customer.

The instantaneous nature of electronic transactions greatly improves efficiency, but it also makes the transfers irrevocable. The absence of paper and the inapplicability of the rules that govern paper transactions create major challenges for security and liability.

PART EIGHT

The established system for negotiable instruments focuses on the commercial convenience of instruments circulating freely, with little need for the various holders to be concerned about their validity as long as the requirements for negotiability are met. It is a paper-based system that places prime importance on the piece of paper and the secure status of those in possession of it.

The primary right is the ability of a holder in due course to collect from the creator of the instrument—the person whose promise to pay originated the transaction. The main obligation is that of the creator or drawer of the instrument to pay, regardless of events that preceded or followed the creation of the instrument.

Chapter Study

Key Terms and Concepts

banking contract (p. 626)

bill of exchange (p. 631)

certification (p. 634)

cheque (p. 629)

consumer note (p. 634)

electronic banking (p. 627)

endorse (p. 635)

endorsement in blank (p. 636)

holder (p. 633)

holder in due course (p. 633)

identity theft (p. 628)

money laundering (p. 625)

negotiable instrument (p. 631)

negotiation (p. 635)

promissory note (p. 631)

restrictive endorsement (p. 636)

special endorsement (p. 636)

stop payment (p. 635)

Questions for Review

1. What is the basic nature of the bank–customer relationship?

2. How are banks regulated?

3. What are the key issues addressed in a banking contract?

4. What are the key duties of the customer and the bank?

5. What are the requirements for an instrument to be negotiable?

6. What is a cheque?

7. Why is the volume of cheques declining?

8. Why are electronic transfers not subject to the same regulations as paper transactions?

9. When a business issues a cheque to a supplier, who is the drawer, who is the drawee, and who is the payee of the cheque?

10. What is an electronic financial services agreement?

11. What are the key risks for a business in creating cheques for suppliers and accepting cheques from customers?

12. Why is the holder in due course in a stronger position to collect on a negotiable instrument than the assignee is to collect a debt?

13. What are the banks' obligations regarding suspected money laundering?

14. What is identity theft?

15. What are the benefits of electronic banking?

16. What are the legal uncertainties in electronic banking?

17. How can cellphones be used for banking?

18. What is "phishing"?

Questions for Critical Thinking

1. In banking relationships, customers are expected to take care of themselves and to negotiate and be aware of their rights and obligations. In practice, the terms of banking contracts are dictated by the banks and found in standard form agreements that are not open to negotiation. Should banking contracts be regulated to ensure a basic level of fairness for customers?

2. Retail merchants are caught between their customers and the credit card companies. Customers want their cards to be accepted, especially those offering attractive rewards to card users. Meanwhile, the card companies require merchants to accept all cards and pay whatever fees the companies choose to impose. How can merchants deal with this dilemma?

3. Electronic banking presents a regulatory challenge in that paper-based rules do not apply and the nature of electronic transactions produces a new set of potential problems. What are some of those problems? Are the regulations likely to be outpaced by developments in technology?

4. The regulatory divisions among the four types of financial services (banks, trust companies, insurance companies, and investment brokerages) have disappeared. Now, banks are able to provide all financial services in some form. Who benefits most from this relaxation—clients or banks? Can this relaxation

contribute to a financial crisis and lead to demand for stricter national and international regulation?

5. Considering the number of negotiable instruments and electronic transfers, there are relatively few legal disputes arising from them. Does that mean the system is working well? What criteria might be used to measure the effectiveness of the system?

6. Electronic transactions can result in the creation and combination of databases containing sensitive business and personal information. Those who provide this information are naturally concerned about its security and their privacy. One way to deal with such concerns is to enable anonymous transactions through such means as encryption, which in turn creates concern for illicit activities such as money laundering. Which is more important—providing security or preventing fraud or crime?

Situations for Discussion

1. Grenville agreed to facilitate transfers of funds for a Taiwanese businessman whom he did not know. Grenville was to deposit cheques in his account and forward the funds to Asian accounts in exchange for a five percent commission. Without Grenville's knowledge, the first cheque (in the amount of $10 000) that he deposited in his credit union account had been altered and forged. Several months after the cheque cleared, the defects in the cheque were discovered. Grenville's credit union took the full balance in Grenville's account ($6000) and sued him for the remaining $4000.[25] Is the credit union entitled to recover the $10 000 from Grenville? What are the relevant rules?

2. Ken needed $100 000 to start his restaurant. He sought advice from W Bank. Pamela, the loans officer at the bank, suggested a working capital loan on certain specified terms. She assured Ken that he should have no problem being approved if he decided to apply for a loan. The approval process took longer than usual, but Ken went ahead and signed a lease for space for his restaurant and a contract for renovation of the space. Eventually, W Bank rejected Ken's application. Based on recent experience, the bank decided that restaurants are too risky since most do not last beyond six months. Ken was unable to arrange alternative financing in time and suffered a large loss in his business.[26] Is this a typical banking relationship where Ken must look out for himself, or does the bank have some responsibility for his plight? What should Ken and the bank have done differently?

3. Ratty Publications wrote a cheque payable to LePage on its account at CIBC in payment for the first month's rent on an office lease. Ratty changed its mind about the lease and instructed CIBC to stop payment on the cheque. The following day, LePage got the cheque certified at another branch of CIBC and deposited the cheque in its account at TD Bank. When TD presented the cheque to CIBC for payment, CIBC refused to honour it.[27] Which prevails—the stop payment or the certification? Does the validity of the cheque depend on the lease agreement between Ratty and LePage? Which of the four parties should bear the loss?

4. Harvey's Car Lot bought a used car from Luke. When Luke delivered the car, Harvey gave him a cheque for $5000. Luke cashed the cheque immediately. When Harvey put the car in the garage, he discovered that the bottom was severely rusted and the engine was shot.[28] What can Harvey do about the cheque? How should Harvey change his purchasing practices? How would the outcome be different if instead of giving Luke a cheque, Harvey had promised to pay Luke when Harvey resold the car?

5. Ravanello is a computer hacker. He is motivated primarily by the challenge of breaching systems, but he figures he might as well make some money at the same time. After many months of dedicated effort, he penetrated the electronic customer files of EZ Bank. Not wanting to appear greedy or be caught, Ravenello devised a system to skim $10 from random accounts every month. He began to accumulate money in his account faster than he could spend it. It was nine months before a customer of EZ convinced the bank that his account was short by three $10 withdrawals and the bank was able to trace the reason.

25. Based on *Meridian Credit Union Limited v Grenville-Wood Estate*, 2011 ONCA 512 (leave to appeal to SCC dismissed 8 March 2012).
26. Based on *Royal Bank of Canada v Woloszyn* (1998), 170 NSR (2d) 122 (SC).
27. Based on *A.E. LePage Real Estate Services Ltd v Rattray Publications Ltd* (1994), 21 OR (3d) 164 (CA).
28. Based on *William Ciurluini v Royal Bank of Canada* (1972), 26 DLR (3d) 552 (Ont HC).

What does this scenario reveal about the perils of electronic banking? Do you think this scenario could really happen? Is such a risk likely to be prevented by banking practices, contracts, or the law? Who is responsible for the losses?

6. Rubin and Russell were partners in RRP Associates. They did their personal and business banking with Colossal Bank, where they arranged their accounts so that transfers from one to the other could be made by either partner online, by phone, or in person. Although the business prospered, Rubin and Russell had difficulty working together. Following a serious disagreement, Russell went online and transferred $50 000 from the RRP account to his personal account. When Rubin discovered this transaction, he complained to the bank and was told that the transfer was done in accordance with the agreement between RRP and the bank. How can partners best balance the risks arising from banking arrangements with the need for convenient banking? What action can Rubin take now?

7. Bob was the sole officer, director, and shareholder of 545012 Ltd. Bank of Montreal issued a bank card to Bob for the company's account. Bob entrusted an employee, Paul, with the corporate card and its PIN. Paul forged cheques payable to the company, deposited them in the corporate account, and then used the corporate card to withdraw cash and make point-of-sale purchases, creating an overdraft of $60 000 on the corporate account. The bank sued 545012 Ltd.

and Bob for the amount of the overdraft.[29] Who is responsible for the overdraft? On what will the answer depend?

8. BMP Global Inc. (BMP) was a distributor of nonstick bake ware in British Columbia. BMP was a customer of the Bank of Nova Scotia (BNS) in Vancouver. Hashka and Backman were the two owners of BMP and had personal accounts in the same branch of BNS. BMP received a cheque for $902 563 drawn by First National Financial Corp. on the Royal Bank of Canada (RBC) in Toronto. Hashka deposited the cheque in the BMP account and informed the manager, Richards, that the cheque was a down payment on a distributorship contract with an American company. Richards placed a hold on the cheque for seven days. The cheque cleared and was paid by RBC to BNS and released to BMP. Hashka and Backman paid several creditors and transferred funds to their personal accounts. Ten days later RBC notified Richards that the signatures on the $902 563 cheque were forged. Richards froze the three accounts in his branch and returned the combined balance of $776 000 to RBC.[30] Was Richards justified in freezing and seizing the accounts of BMP, Hashka, and Backman? Can they take action against Richards and BNS? Is RBC responsible for accepting the cheque with the forged signatures?

For more study tools, visit http://www.NELSONbrain.com.

29. Based on *Bank of Montreal v 545012 Ontario Limited*, 2009 CanLII 55127 (Ont Sup Ct J).
30. Based on *BMP Global Distribution Inc v Bank of Nova Scotia*, 2009 SCC 15.

PART EIGHT

CHAPTER 26

The Legal Aspects of Credit

Objectives

After studying this chapter, you should have an understanding of

- the legal significance of credit transactions in business

- methods used by creditors to reduce risk

- the difference between secured and unsecured creditors

- the ways that lenders and borrowers are protected

- the implications of guaranteeing a debt

LIQUIDLIBRARY/JUPITER IMAGES

Business Law in Practice

Hometown Hardware Ltd. (Hometown) and its owners, Bill Ikeda and Martha Wong, were introduced in Chapter 25. They operate a building supply store in Timmins, Ontario. Bill has become concerned about rumours that a big-box store will soon be arriving in Timmins. Bill is worried about the impact on Hometown and has decided that the only way Hometown can remain competitive is to expand and offer a broader range of supplies. Bill is confident that his customers will remain loyal to Hometown if they can obtain the same range of products from Hometown as will be available from the new big-box store. At the same time, Bill is concerned about the recent slowdown in housing construction.

In order to finance the planned expansion, Bill figures that Hometown needs $400 000. Two of Bill's business acquaintances who are now retired have shown interest in investing in Hometown. Bill and Martha have decided to issue new shares of Hometown to each investor for $100 000. Bill and Martha hope to have Hometown borrow the remaining $200 000 from the bank.

1. What is the bank likely to require before agreeing to loan money to Hometown?
2. What will the terms of the loan be?
3. What are the risks for Hometown in borrowing the money?
4. Will Bill, Martha, and the two new shareholders be personally liable for the loan?

Introduction to Debt and Credit

A business participates on a daily basis in a variety of transactions that involve credit. Some credit arrangements are formal and deliberate, with carefully negotiated terms, while others are an incidental feature of routine transactions. A business like Hometown will be both a borrower, or debtor, and a lender, or creditor. When Hometown orders lumber from its suppliers, it is required to pay the invoice within 30 days, making it a debtor. When Hometown sells the lumber to its commercial customers, those customers are probably expected to pay on similar terms, making it a creditor. Retail customers are likely expected to pay immediately, although Hometown may offer financing terms to some retail customers on large purchases.

Credit is a contractual relationship, with the lender agreeing to lend money in exchange for a promise by the borrower to repay the loan, usually with interest and within a certain time frame. There may be other terms and conditions which are agreed to by the parties. Since credit is a contractual relationship, all the fundamental principles of contract law apply. As well, there are legal regulations and principles which are specific to credit. The law of credit forms part of what is known as debtor and creditor law.

Credit can be either secured or unsecured. **Secured credit** means the creditor has an interest in all or some of the property of the debtor in order to secure payment of the debt. If the debtor defaults in repaying the loan, the secured creditor can seize the secured property and sell it to pay down the debt. **Unsecured credit** means that the creditor has only a contractual right to receive payment from the debtor. The unsecured creditor does not have an interest in the property of the debtor that it can enforce in the event of default by the debtor. If the debtor defaults, a secured creditor is in a much better position than an unsecured creditor, as will be explained on the next page.

Secured credit
A debt where the creditor has an interest in the debtor's property to secure payment.

Unsecured credit
A debt where the creditor has only a contractual right to be repaid.

What legal risks arise in financing the expansion of a business?

COBALT88/SHUTTERSTOCK

When Hometown agrees to pay its suppliers within 30 days, or when Hometown's commercial customers agree to pay Hometown on similar terms, that is known as trade credit. Trade credit is usually unsecured. In most cases, payment is made within the designated time period and collection remedies are not needed. However, since these transactions are unsecured, if a debtor fails to pay on time, the creditor may have to sue the debtor, obtain judgment, and then enforce that judgment. If the debtor has limited financial resources, the creditor may end up not being paid. For this reason, it is very important for creditors to exercise good judgment when deciding whether to extend credit. Trade credit can be very risky if the parties have not dealt with each other before, especially if the supplier and the customer are located in different countries. The following International Perspective box provides an example.

INTERNATIONAL PERSPECTIVE

Credit Risk in International Trade

Canadian companies import products from countries around the world to sell in Canada. For example, an international trade relationship might originate with a visit by representatives of the Canadian government and importers to a country that is identified as a potential source of trade. Assume that Star Clothing, based in Toronto, participates in such a trip to China and identifies a manufacturer, Beijing Clothing, which can supply high-quality clothing at a lower cost than Star's current supplier in Canada. Representatives of Star negotiate with their counterparts in the Chinese company and eventually agree upon a contract worth $50 000 for clothing to be delivered in time for the spring fashion season in Canada. The contract includes terms dealing with quantity, price, delivery dates, and terms regarding shipment of the goods from China to Canada.

Since these companies are dealing with each other for the first time, they are sensitive to the risks involved. Beijing wants payment before the goods are shipped because there is significant risk for Beijing if it ships the clothing to Canada with no means of ensuring payment. Beijing appreciates the difficulties involved in suing a Canadian company when they are located in China. Star, on the other hand, is reluctant to pay for the clothing until it knows that the agreed upon quality and quantity of clothing has been manufactured and shipped to Canada. Star knows that suing a Chinese company for breach of contract will be difficult and expensive.

Letters of credit issued by international banks are a common means of dealing with these risks. A **letter of credit** is a written promise made by the importer's bank (on the importer's instructions) and given to the exporter's bank to make payment to the exporter when specified conditions are met. These conditions relate to the exporter's delivery of documents, such as an invoice, shipping receipt, proof of insurance, and customs declaration. These documents are presented and payment is made once the goods have been shipped, but before the importer receives the goods. The exporter ships the goods knowing that payment will be made upon presentation of the documents confirming shipment, and the importer allows payment to be made knowing the goods have been shipped and with confidence that the goods will arrive. In this way, both parties reduce some of the risks to which they are exposed. *Critical Analysis:* Is the letter of credit a device that could be used to manage risk in domestic as well as international transactions? Can it take the place of reputation and experience in commercial dealings?

Source: Mary Jo Nicholson, *Legal Aspects of International Business: A Canadian Perspective*, 2d ed (Toronto: Emond Montgomery, 2007) at 236.

Letter of credit
A written promise by a buyer's bank to a seller's bank to pay the seller when specified conditions are met.

A business may also decide to raise a significant amount of capital by borrowing. These credit arrangements tend to be more formal and provide more security to the lender. Borrowing a large amount of money to purchase a major asset or to finance an expansion, as Hometown is planning to do, is an example of a credit transaction in which the rights and obligations of the parties are carefully negotiated. When Hometown applies to the bank for a loan of $200 000, the bank will probably require extensive documentation to support the loan application, such as a business plan and cash-flow projections.

The bank will then consider two major criteria in evaluating the loan application. First, the bank will focus on Hometown's financial health—in particular, the likelihood that the expansion plans will succeed and Hometown will be able to repay the loan within a reasonable time period. Second, the bank will investigate the security that Hometown can provide—if Hometown cannot repay the loan, the lender will want to ensure that it can seize Hometown's property and sell it for enough money to pay the outstanding loan. In this way, the lender ensures that it will be repaid, whether Hometown's business succeeds or fails.

In addition to the ability of the debtor to repay the loan and the value of the security that the debtor can provide, a lender will also consider the state of the economy, the particular industry in which the debtor carries on business, whether personal guarantees are available, and the state of the credit markets generally. Based on all of these considerations, the lender will decide whether to grant the loan and, if so, on what terms. The lender will set the interest rate at a level that corresponds to the riskiness of the loan from the lender's perspective.

If the borrower and the lender are able to agree on the terms of the loan, they will enter into a credit or loan agreement. The terms of this agreement are negotiated by the parties, and may include many different terms and conditions, including repayment terms, interest, security, fees and **events of default.** In most cases, however, these terms are largely dictated by the lender. Normally, both the borrower and the lender will have their own lawyers to advise them on the credit agreement. In many cases, however, the legal and other fees of the lender must be paid by the borrower.

Events of default
Failure by the debtor to make required payments on a loan or to fulfill its other obligations under the credit agreement.

Methods Used to Reduce Risk in Credit Transactions

There are several ways that creditors can reduce the risk of non-payment by debtors.

First, creditors should employ good credit policies and procedures. This involves steps such as having debtors fill out credit applications and checking debtors' credit references. The easiest way to minimize the risk of default is by not lending money to people who will not pay it back. Although this is a relatively easy and inexpensive strategy, it is often overlooked.

Second, creditors may be able to change the structure of a transaction so that it is not a credit arrangement at all. For example, a supplier of equipment may choose to lease the equipment rather than sell it, so that the supplier retains ownership of the equipment. In the event of default, the lessor can usually repossess the equipment.

Third, creditors may insist on security, or **collateral**, to back up the borrower's promise to pay. If a creditor is able to seize property of the debtor and sell it to pay down the debt, the risk to the creditor is reduced.

Collateral
Property in which a creditor takes an interest as security for a borrower's promise to repay a loan.

Fourth, creditors may ask for assurances from other people that the debt will be repaid. If a creditor is able to obtain a guarantee of the debt from another creditworthy person, then the risk is lessened.

Finally, creditors often include terms in credit agreements which require debtors to carry on business in accordance with specific requirements. For example, a credit agreement may require the debtor to refrain from making significant capital expenditures or allowing certain financial ratios to fall below defined limits.

It is important for businesspeople to think of themselves as creditors any time they are extending credit. In many cases, suppliers will extend credit to customers but fail to take any measures to reduce the risk of not being paid. Banks and other sophisticated creditors employ the techniques described above in order to reduce their risk—businesspeople who extend credit would be wise to think along similar lines.

The Credit or Loan Agreement

In the case of trade credit, the agreement between the debtor and the creditor is usually informal and may even be verbal. If the terms of trade credit are written down, they will often be on a standard form document such as a purchase order or a standard form set of terms and conditions provided by the supplier.

In the case of a large debt financing, however, the credit agreement is typically called a loan agreement and is much more comprehensive and carefully negotiated by the parties. The process of applying for a loan and formulating the terms of credit is much the same as for the negotiation of any other contract. Hometown's need for $200 000 is major in terms of its expansion plans, but it is a routine transaction for a large commercial lender such as a bank. When Hometown applies for the loan, the bank will demand whatever information it deems necessary in order to assess the risk and determine how much, if anything, it is prepared to lend to Hometown and on what terms. If the bank decides to grant the loan, it will usually provide a **letter of commitment** to Hometown, which will set out in a summary manner the basic terms on which the lender is prepared to make the loan. These terms may include

Letter of commitment
A document that is provided by a lender to a borrower and sets out the terms of a loan.

- amount of the loan and how it will be disbursed

- rate of interest, and whether it is floating or fixed

- repayment terms, including the amount and frequency of payments

- term of the loan and conditions for renewal (if the entire loan will not be paid out during the term)

- conditions that must be satisfied before the loan is made (e.g., guarantees, appraisals)

- security or collateral required by the lender

- requirements for maintenance of the borrower's financial position

- events that constitute default and the lender's remedies

- fees to be paid by the borrower

The borrower is free to try and negotiate the terms set out in the letter of commitment, or to try to negotiate with other potential lenders, but the final say over whether the loan will be made is that of the lender. Once the letter of commitment is signed by the borrower, the lender will prepare a more formal and comprehensive loan agreement. The loan agreement will cover all of the terms and conditions set out in the letter of commitment and will often be accompanied by other agreements, such as a mortgage, security agreement or personal guarantee.

Security

In order to reduce the risk of non-payment, a lender may require that the borrower provide security or collateral. Collateral can be either real property, in which case it is accomplished through a mortgage (as discussed in Chapter 19), or personal property discussed on the next page. While the loan obligation is evidenced by the credit or loan agreement, the taking of security is normally covered by a separate security agreement.

Lenders will often try to match their security to the use of the loan proceeds. For example, if Hometown borrows money in order to buy a new piece of equipment, the security for the loan may be the equipment itself. Similarly, if Hometown negotiates a line of credit for working capital, the lender may take security in Hometown's inventory and accounts receivable. Generally, the most attractive collateral to a lender is that which is most liquid (i.e., can most easily be converted into cash).

If the bank decides to lend money to Hometown to fund its planned expansion, the bank will likely require a **general security agreement**, which will include as collateral all the personal property assets currently held by Hometown, as well as all **after-acquired property**, which are assets that are acquired by Hometown during the term of the loan. Hometown is free to carry on business and use its assets as long as it makes the required payments on the loan and complies with its other obligations under the loan agreement. However, if Hometown defaults on the loan, the bank's security will include all of the assets held by Hometown at the time of default.

Some assets used as collateral are intended to be retained by the debtor. For example, if Hometown buys a fork lift for use in its warehouse, the fork lift is available as security for its entire useful life. Other assets, such as inventory and accounts receivable, are meant to circulate through the business on a regular basis. The security in those assets is their value at any given time. The security agreement will allow Hometown to sell inventory in the ordinary course of its business, but will probably prohibit Hometown from selling the fork lift while the loan is outstanding. In addition, the security agreement will likely require Hometown to maintain adequate insurance on the fork lift and its other assets, in order to protect the value of those assets as collateral.

The type and extent of security that a lender requires will depend on several factors, including the risk of default and the market value of the collateral. If Hometown borrows money to buy a piece of equipment and then defaults on the loan, the lender's security is a used piece of equipment. The lender knows that the proceeds from a quick sale of used equipment are likely to be much less than the original purchase price or its value to Hometown in its ongoing business. Similarly, if Hometown gives a general security agreement to the lender, the value of all of Hometown's assets in the event of the business failing is much less than it may have been when the loan was originally made. For these reasons, the lender will typically require security in an amount that exceeds the amount borrowed. Credit insurance may be available to lenders as an additional source of protection against the risk of uncollectible accounts.

General security agreement
A security agreement that includes all of the debtor's personal property assets as collateral.

After-acquired property
Collateral that includes personal property acquired by the debtor during the term of the loan.

PART EIGHT

ENVIRONMENTAL PERSPECTIVE

Credit and Environmental Risk

The value of land as security for credit depends on a variety of factors, including the health of the real estate market and the nature and location of the specific piece of land. Lenders want to minimize the risk of the land being worth less than the outstanding loan should the borrower default. In some cases, a lender, especially one who ends up in possession of the land, may be liable for environmental damage or costs. Financial institutions that engage in commercial lending with real property as security generally require environmental assurance as part of the credit documentation. This assurance consists of representations and warranties by the borrower regarding the environmental status of the property, supplemented by surveys and questionnaires. In addition, lenders are likely to require more detailed environmental reviews and investigations from the borrower or third parties.

These reviews are known as environmental due diligence or site assessment. This is usually a three-phase process, consisting of a historical review of the land's past uses, followed by testing on soil, groundwater, and drilled core samples. The final stage is remediation or cleanup, which may involve considerable expense.

JOSTEIN HAUGE/SHUTTERSTOCK

What environmental hazards could affect the value of the security interest in this property?

Critical Analysis: What previous uses of land would be problematic in the historical assessment stage? What problems might the testing stage reveal? Are these extensive environmental reviews more appropriate for certain types of land?

Source: Pamela Young, "Caveat developer: What lies beneath", *The Globe and Mail* (16 January 2007) at B8.

Personal Property Security Legislation

When considering whether to grant secured credit, lenders must be confident as to their position with respect to the collateral. Every province and territory has legislation in place to provide an orderly system for recognizing interests in personal property collateral and setting out rules to determine priority disputes amongst competing claims to the same collateral. The personal property security systems allow lenders to grant credit, knowing where they will stand with respect to the collateral in the event of default by the debtor. The legislation in each province and territory (except Quebec) is called the *Personal Property Security Act* (*PPSA*).[1] Although the legislation varies somewhat by province and territory, there are a few basic concepts that are common to all the provinces and territories: attachment, perfection, registration, priorities, and remedies. These concepts are discussed on the next page.

Security interest

An interest in personal property that is intended to secure payment or performance of an obligation (usually a debt).

The *PPSA* applies to every transaction that in substance creates a **security interest**. Even if the transaction is called something else (e.g., a lease or a conditional sale), if its real purpose is to create an interest in personal property to secure payment or performance of an obligation (normally a debt), the transaction is a security interest and the *PPSA* applies. The *PPSA* also applies to some transactions that are not intended as security, such as leases for a term of more than one year, commercial consignments (except in Ontario), and absolute assignments (transfers) of accounts.

---

1. See, for example, *Personal Property Security Act*, RSO 1990, c P-10; and *Personal Property Security Act*, SNS 1995–96, c 13.

Attachment

Attachment occurs when three conditions are satisfied:

- the debtor has rights in the collateral (e.g., ownership)

- the secured party has provided value (e.g., granted a loan or extended credit)

- the debtor has signed a written security agreement

Once attachment has occurred, the security interest is enforceable against the debtor and third parties. If Hometown grants a security interest to a lender over a piece of equipment and the three conditions necessary for attachment have been satisfied, then the lender can seize the equipment and sell it if Hometown defaults on the loan.

Perfection

Perfection is the combination of (a) attachment, and (b) **registration** or possession of the collateral.[2] Once a security interest has been perfected, the secured party will have priority over security interests that have not been perfected, as well as judgment creditors and a trustee in bankruptcy. If the security interest in Hometown's equipment is perfected, then on default by Hometown the lender can seize the equipment, sell it, and apply the proceeds of the sale to the debt owed, even if Hometown has become bankrupt, a process which is discussed in the next chapter.

Registration involves filing a form called a **financing statement**. The financing statement discloses the name of the debtor and the type of collateral secured. The *PPSA* registration system is computerized and public and can be searched either by debtor name or, in the case of motor vehicles, by serial number.

Possession, for the purposes of perfection, occurs when the secured party physically takes possession of the collateral for the purposes of holding it as security. For example, if Hometown wanted to pledge a gold bar as security, the lender might take physical possession of the gold bar until the loan is repaid. In that case, assuming attachment has occurred, the lender will have a security interest perfected by possession.

The most common form of perfection is by registration. When a person searches the *PPSA* register and discovers a financing statement of interest to them, they can find out the details of the security interest to which that financing statement relates by making an inquiry to the secured party.

It is important to note that perfection is not "perfect" in the sense that it confers the best possible interest one can have in the collateral—it does not. The term "perfection" is simply a defined term in the *PPSA* and it has only the specific meaning given to it within that legislation.

It is also important to note that perfection may occur even if attachment occurs after registration (except when dealing with consumer goods). When Hometown applies for the loan, the bank may register a financing statement under the *PPSA*. If the loan has not yet been granted, there has been no attachment. However, once the conditions for attachment

Registration
The registration of a financing statement to record a security interest.

Financing statement
The document registered as evidence of a security interest.

PART EIGHT

---

2. In the case of investment property, a security interest may also be perfected in some provinces by "control."

have been met, the security interest will immediately be perfected, because registration has already occurred. This concept becomes very important when we discover that, in a contest between two perfected security interests in the same collateral, the first to register—not the first to perfect—has priority.

Priority among Creditors

One of the most important functions of the *PPSA* is to determine who has priority when there are competing interests in the same collateral. The *PPSA* has rules to resolve such conflicts. The general policy behind the priority rules is that a security interest that has been made public (e.g., by registration) should have priority over a subsequent interest in the same collateral, except where specific policy objectives warrant a different outcome. The priority rules produce predictable outcomes, which promotes the extension of credit generally:

- When there are two unperfected security interests that have both attached, the first to attach has priority.

- When there is one unperfected security interest and one perfected security interest, the perfected security interest has priority.

- When there are two security interests perfected by registration, the first to register (not the first to perfect) has priority.

There are other priority rules dealing with specific types of collateral and security interests perfected otherwise than by registration.

Purchase-money security interest (PMSI)
A security interest that enables the debtor to acquire assets and gives the secured party priority over existing perfected security interests.

The **purchase-money security interest (PMSI)** is a special type of security interest that gives the secured party priority over existing perfected security interests. In order to qualify for this "super priority," two conditions must be met: first, the credit advanced must allow the debtor to acquire the assets in which the security interest is taken; and second, the security interest must be registered within a specific period of time.[3] If these conditions are met, the PMSI holder will have priority over an existing perfected security interest in the collateral that was financed. Suppose Hometown has given a general security agreement to its bank securing all of its assets including after-acquired property, and the bank registers its security interest. Then, Hometown borrows $40 000 from a truck dealer to finance the purchase of a truck, and the dealer takes a security interest in the truck to secure repayment of the loan. If the dealer meets the PMSI conditions, the dealer will have priority over the bank with respect to the truck, even though the bank registered its security interest first. The purpose of the PMSI rule is to enable debtors to obtain financing after they have entered into a security agreement which confers an interest in after-acquired property. Without the PMSI rule, the truck dealer would not have priority over the bank and presumably would not extend the credit required by Hometown to purchase the truck.

---

3. For example, in Ontario, within 10 days of the debtor obtaining the collateral for non-inventory collateral, and before the debtor obtains the collateral for collateral which is inventory.

Transfers of Collateral

Generally, security interests follow the collateral and take priority over subsequent purchasers of the collateral. Why then is it not necessary to conduct a *PPSA* search every time an item is bought in a retail store? The reason is: the exemption for goods sold in the ordinary course of business. The *PPSA* contains a provision which gives priority to a buyer who buys goods in the ordinary course of the seller's business. If Hometown buys a car from a car dealer, it does not have to worry about a security interest in the car given by the car dealer (e.g., to its supplier). However, if Hometown buys a car from a person who does not sell cars in the ordinary course of its business, then the onus is on Hometown to conduct a *PPSA* search prior to purchasing the car, or Hometown will take the car subject to any existing perfected security interest given by the seller of the car.

The computerized and centralized system associated with the *PPSA* is a vast improvement over the earlier patchwork of different statutes and rules within each province dealing with personal property security interests. However, there remain inconsistencies among the various provincial statutes, and there is always the practical problem that personal property is portable and may be moved from one province to another. There are rules in the *PPSA* to deal with the relocation of collateral, but they are complicated and vary by jurisdiction. Lenders and borrowers must both be informed of the rules that apply in the jurisdictions in which they carry on business and in which collateral may be, or end up being, located.

The *PPSA* system provides potential creditors and buyers with a high level of protection. A lender can search the *PPSA* registry before granting credit to determine whether there are existing registrations against the borrower. The creditor can even register a financing statement in advance of granting credit, to ensure that its priority position will be undisturbed when it eventually grants the loan. Purchasers of goods can search the *PPSA* registry to determine whether the goods are subject to a security interest that would take priority over them. This knowledge allows creditors and buyers to make informed business decisions with the confidence of knowing where they will stand in the event of default by the debtor. The same assets can provide security for more than one credit arrangement, but the claims of competing lenders are subject to the priority rules described above. A lender may decide to grant a loan, even with the knowledge that there is one or more existing security interests in the same collateral, but presumably the lender will tailor the terms of the loan, and in particular the interest rate, to suit the particular circumstances.

Other Security Legislation

The federal *Bank Act*[4] permits banks to take security in the inventory and other assets of certain business borrowers. *Bank Act* security is only available to banks that are regulated by the *Bank Act*. *Bank Act* security is registered, but the registration system is quite different than that of the *PPSA* system. Priority disputes between *Bank Act* security and *PPSA* security are complicated and have resulted in a great deal of litigation. Recently, the federal government introduced legislation which is intended to resolve some of these priority disputes.

---

4. SC 1991, c 46, s 427.

Each province and territory has legislation which allows suppliers, building subcontractors, and workers to place liens on real property if they are not paid for work done, or materials supplied, to the property.[5] These liens are called construction or builders' liens and they remain in place until the supplier, subcontractor, or worker has been paid in full. The legislation requires property owners who enter into contracts with builders to holdback a portion of the contract price until the lien period has expired (usually between 30 and 60 days after the contract work is completed). This mechanism provides an incentive for contractors to pay their suppliers and subcontractors in a timely manner.

Remedies

A creditor's remedies in the event of the borrower's failure to pay are largely determined by whether the creditor is secured or unsecured. Unsecured creditors have the right to sue the debtor for the unpaid debt and may, at the end of that litigation process, obtain a judgment against the debtor. In most cases, the unsecured creditor will then be able to enforce its judgment against the assets of the debtor that are not already claimed by secured creditors. Secured creditors also have the right to sue the debtor but, in addition, they can immediately seize the collateral and sell it to pay down the debt owed. The ability to seize the personal property of the debtor without having to commence litigation places the secured creditor in a much better position than the unsecured creditor. Furthermore, if the debtor ends up bankrupt, the secured creditor will still be able to claim its collateral, while the unsecured creditor will have no remedy except under the bankruptcy proceedings (see Chapter 27).

Lenders' Remedies

If the borrower defaults on the loan, secured parties have a variety of remedies from two sources: the security agreement and the *PPSA*. The remedies provided for in security agreements are often broader than those permitted by the *PPSA*, in which case the secured party is generally limited to the remedies permitted by the *PPSA*.

Acceleration clause
A term of a loan agreement that makes the entire loan due if one payment is missed.

Credit agreements normally contain an **acceleration clause**, which permits the creditor to call the entire loan if the debtor misses one payment. This gives the debtor an incentive to make timely payments and allows the creditor to sue for the entire debt immediately upon any default by the debtor.

A secured party can enter the borrower's premises and seize the collateral immediately upon default by the debtor, although the secured party must not break the law and is generally required to provide advance notice to the debtor. The secured party can then dispose of the collateral (or collect collateral such as accounts receivable). The proceeds are applied first to the expenses of the secured party in enforcing its security and then to the unpaid debt. The fees and expenses of the secured party in seizing and selling collateral can often be considerable.

If the amount received by the secured party in disposing of the collateral (less its costs) exceeds the amount owed by the debtor, the surplus must be paid to the next secured party in line, if there is one, and then to the debtor. If, on the other hand, the net proceeds are

---

5. See, for example, *Builders' Lien Act*, RSA 2000, c B-7.

insufficient to pay the outstanding debt, then the secured party becomes an unsecured creditor for the **deficiency**, which is the balance still owing, and has the rights only of an unsecured creditor in respect to the deficiency.

If the security agreement permits, the secured party may appoint a **receiver** or receiver-manager to take possession of the collateral and manage the business of the debtor while a sale of the collateral can be arranged. If the security agreement is silent on whether or not a receiver may be appointed, the secured party can apply to a court for an order appointing a receiver or receiver-manager.

In some cases, the secured party may keep the collateral in satisfaction of the debt owed, however in most provinces doing so will extinguish any deficiency.

Limits on Lenders' Remedies

When enforcing its security, the secured party must act in a commercially reasonable manner in every respect.[6] What is commercially reasonable will depend on the particular circumstances, but the secured party must take reasonable care of the collateral and obtain a reasonable price when disposing of the collateral. Creditors are not expected to obtain the highest possible price, but they must act reasonably. Creditors must also avoid conflicts of interest created by buying collateral themselves or selling to related businesses at a price less than fair market value. Typically, lenders will have the collateral valued by an independent appraiser to ensure that the price is reasonable, or they will sell the collateral at public auction, where the price is set by the highest bidder.

The courts have held that secured parties must generally give the debtor reasonable notice before calling a loan or enforcing their security, even if the credit agreement does not require notice. What is reasonable will depend on the particular circumstances, including the type of collateral and whether it is perishable, the relationship between the debtor and the creditor, and any industry norms or standards. In addition, the *PPSA* requires that debtors be notified of any intended sale of collateral and have the opportunity to pay off the debt and reclaim the collateral prior to the sale. This way, the debtor can monitor any sale and, if possible, bring the debt into good standing and avoid the sale of its assets.

If a secured party is enforcing a security interest against all or substantially all of the inventory, accounts receivable or other assets of a business debtor, the *Bankruptcy and Insolvency Act*[7] requires that the secured party provide the debtor with 10 days' notice of its intention to enforce it security. The notice is in a prescribed form and is commonly known as a "Section 244 Notice." During the 10-day period, the secured party cannot take any steps to enforce its security.

The *PPSA* and other legislation provide special protection for consumer debtors. When dealing with consumer purchases, secured parties may be prohibited from seizing collateral if the debtor has already paid two-thirds of the loan.[8] In some provinces creditors are limited to the proceeds from the seized assets and may not sue the debtor for any deficiency.[9]

Deficiency
The shortfall if collateral is sold for less than the amount of the outstanding debt.

Receiver
A person appointed by the secured party or by the court to seize, and usually sell, collateral.

---

6. For example, *Personal Property Security Act,* SNS 1995–96, c 13, s 66(2).
7. RSC 1985, c B-3.
8. This limitation applies, for example, in British Columbia, New Brunswick, and Nova Scotia.
9. This limitation applies, for example, in British Columbia and Alberta.

Personal Guarantees

If the bank agrees to lend Hometown the money for its expansion, the bank will likely require personal guarantees from at least some of Hometown's shareholders. Guarantees reduce the bank's risk because the personal assets of the shareholders will ultimately be available to the bank if Hometown defaults on the loan. The shareholders of Hometown are not normally liable for Hometown's debt, because as shareholders they enjoy limited liability. However, if the shareholders personally agree to guarantee the loan, then they lose their limited liability protection with respect to that debt. In such a case, the personal liability of the shareholders to the bank arises not from their position as shareholders of Hometown, but because they have agreed to be personally responsible for the debt. The scope of their personal liability will be determined by the guarantee contract. The relationship amongst the borrower, the lender, and the guarantor is shown in Figure 26.1.

Guarantee
A conditional promise to a creditor to pay a debt if the debtor defaults.

A **guarantee** is a contract between a creditor and a **guarantor**. The terms and conditions of the guarantee are set out in the guarantee contract. Since a guarantee is a contractual relationship, the fundamental principles of contract law apply. The essence of the guarantee is a promise by the guarantor to pay the debt if the debtor defaults. The guarantee promise is conditional or secondary to the primary obligation of the debtor. A guarantee must be distinguished from a contract of **indemnity**, in which the indemnifier is primarily and not conditionally liable for the obligation of the debtor.

Guarantor
A person who guarantees a debt.

Indemnity
A primary obligation to pay a debt owed by another person.

The implications for those who give personal guarantees are significant. Guarantors lose their limited liability to the extent of their promises to the creditor and thereby put their personal assets at risk. If the debtor defaults, the creditor can pursue the guarantors for payment immediately and without the need to take any further legal action.

A continuing guarantee is one where the guarantor is liable for any past, present, and future obligations of the debtor. Bank guarantees usually apply to the total debt owed to the bank at any given time. When the initial loan is granted by the bank, Bill and Martha may be confident in Hometown's future and comfortable with the amount of the loan. As time passes, however, the amount of debt may increase, and Hometown's financial situation may deteriorate. The guarantees, however, are continuing. If Hometown eventually defaults, the guarantors will be required to pay the balance owing, whatever that might be at the time of default. If the guarantors are unable to pay, they may be forced into personal bankruptcy.

FIGURE 26.1
Relationships in Personal Guarantees

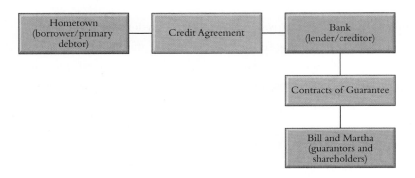

The Guarantee Agreement

A guarantee is one of few contracts that must be in writing and be signed by the guarantor in order to be enforceable.[10]

The guarantee is normally one component of a larger credit arrangement. The lender will require that the guarantor sign the lender's standard form guarantee agreement, which is designed to severely limit ways that the guarantors may avoid liability and provide the lender with maximum flexibility in dealing with the debtor. Guarantees may be required in order for Hometown to obtain the loan, but the shareholders of Hometown must consider these guarantees as an important factor in their decision to seek debt financing on behalf of Hometown.

The guarantee agreement is entered into between the guarantor and the creditor—not between guarantor and debtor—because the creditor wants to be able to enforce the contract without the cooperation of the debtor. If the guarantee contract was entered into between the guarantor and the debtor, privity of contract would prevent the creditor from enforcing the contract against the guarantor.

Consideration can be an issue with guarantee contracts. If Bill and Martha promise to guarantee Hometown's debt to the bank, it is not obvious that they are receiving anything of value in exchange. In order for there to be a valid contract, consideration must be exchanged. Therefore, guarantee contracts normally include language which describes the benefit that the guarantors will receive, even if that benefit is indirect.

The following are typical terms in a guarantee contract:

- Guarantors are jointly liable for the entire debt. If Bill and Martha guarantee the $200 000 loan, they are each liable for the full $200 000 and the bank can recover that amount from either of them.

- The guarantee applies to all credit extended to the debtor while the guarantee is in force. Any limitation must be clearly stated in the guarantee contract.

- The guarantee is in force for an unlimited period. This may become a problem if one of the guarantors decides to sell its shares and leave the business—the creditor may not agree to release the guarantor.

- Guarantees normally exclude any terms, conditions, statements, or representations that are not in the written agreement. Guarantors should ensure that any material assurances or assumptions are clearly stated in the guarantee contract.

- Bank guarantees usually provide that the bank may deal with the debtor and the debt without affecting the guarantee (e.g., increasing the amount of the loan). This is a direct reversal of the common law rule that terminates the guarantee if the terms of the debt are changed without the guarantors' consent.

If the guarantors are required to honour their guarantees and pay the debt, they have a right of **subrogation** against the debtor. If Hometown defaults on its loan and the shareholders are required to pay the bank, they have the right to recover their payment

Subrogation
The right of a guarantor to recover from the debtor any payments made to the creditor.

---

10. The in-writing requirement is in place in all provinces except Manitoba, generally in the *Statute of Frauds*.

from Hometown. Of course, if the guarantors are called upon to pay, it is unlikely that Hometown will be able to repay them. Still, the right of subrogation extends to any rights that the creditor has against the debtor. For example, if the bank had a security interest or a judgment against Hometown, and the shareholders of Hometown have paid Hometown's debt to the bank, then the shareholders would become entitled to the benefit of the bank's security interest or judgment against Hometown.

Defences Available to Guarantors

Guarantors have some common law defences available to them. First, the guarantee obligation is limited to the terms of the debt guaranteed. If the terms of that debt are changed in a way that increases the risk to the guarantors, the guarantee is terminated unless the guarantors have agreed to the changes. Such changes may include increasing the amount of the loan or the interest rate, extending the time for payment, or altering the collateral the debtor has provided. However, standard guarantee contracts usually eliminate this defence by authorizing the creditor to deal with the debtor and the debt in any manner the creditor sees fit without the consent of the guarantor.

Guarantors may argue they did not understand the terms of the guarantee contract or the risk of giving the guarantee. Spouses, friends, or other relatives of the debtor with little or no involvement in the debtor's business may sign guarantees under pressure. Sometimes, a court will relieve a guarantor from liability if it is satisfied that the guarantor did not appreciate the nature and consequences of the guarantee. For this reason, when guarantors are individuals who are not directly involved in the debtor's business, it is customary for them to obtain independent legal advice before signing the guarantee contract. If the bank requires Bill and Martha's spouses to also sign guarantees, the bank will likely insist that they receive independent legal advice before the bank will extend the loan. The bank does not want the guarantors to be able to avoid their obligations using such defences.

The written guarantee contract will normally take precedence over verbal reassurances or statements that contradict or modify its terms. However, courts tend to interpret guarantee terms strictly against the creditor who is relying on the guarantee. For example, if the guarantee contract provides a blanket authorization for the creditor to alter the debt contract without the guarantor's consent, that intention must be clearly stated in the guarantee contract. If there is doubt or ambiguity about the meaning or scope of language in the guarantee contract, that doubt or ambiguity will generally be resolved in favour of the guarantor.

Apart from the requirement that guarantees be in writing, the only regulation of guarantees in Canada is in Alberta.[11] The Alberta statute provides that, for a guarantee to be valid, a notary public must certify that the guarantors were aware of and understood the contents of the guarantee. The statute does not, however, place any limit on the actual content of the guarantee.

It has been argued that the terms of standard form guarantee contracts are so one-sided that banks should be strongly encouraged or forced to change the language.

---

11. *Guarantees Acknowledgment Act,* RSA 2000, c G-11.

ETHICAL CONSIDERATIONS

Banks' Standard Form Guarantees

Since the language of guarantees is dictated by banks, it includes broad terms intended to give banks maximum discretion in dealing with the borrower, the security for the loan, and the terms of the lending agreement without affecting the guarantors' liability to the bank. For example, common terms are "the bank may deal with the security as it sees fit" and "the bank may vary the terms of the loan as it sees fit." Banks maintain that these clauses allow them to release other guarantors or sell security in any way they choose or to raise interest rates or lend more money, all without disturbing the obligation of the guarantors. Guarantors who wish to challenge the banks' interpretation of such language may do so in the courts; however, court decisions have been mixed in such cases. Some take a straightforward approach and rely primarily on the written terms of the guarantee. For example, in a recent case, the judge considered a standard form of guarantee containing complex language and concluded:

> I am in agreement with counsel for [the bank] that the exemption clause is clear. The guarantors have contracted out of any potential defence relating to the way the bank dealt with its client's credit facility.

Others take a more contextual approach and question whether the meaning of the language would be plain and obvious to guarantors or whether the language is specific and clear enough for guarantors to understand that the contract gives the bank such wide powers.

Jan Weir is a civil litigation lawyer who sees the law of guarantees as a real concern for those in small business who are required to sign such agreements. These people understand interest rates and repayment terms, but not the language of standard form agreements and its consequences: "It would probably take a law professor with a large magnifying glass several hours to review and explain the usual bank guarantee form to a layperson."

He further argues that there is no real competition among banks relating to these terms and therefore no real equality of bargaining power between banks and guarantors:

> In my view, the banks have used a statutorily sanctioned monopoly position to use one-sided agreements that often deprive unsuspecting and unrepresented small businesspeople of protections and fair principles that judges have developed.

Weir suggests that we need small business lobby groups to develop fair standard form guarantees.

Critical Analysis: Do you agree with Weir's analysis? Is it ethical for banks to impose these one-sided terms on small businesspeople?

Sources: Jan Weir, "Banks vs. small business: An unequal match", *The Lawyers Weekly* (9 February 2001) at 9; and *Royal Bank of Canada v Speight*, 2006 NSSC 151.

PART EIGHT

Regulation of Credit

Government regulation of credit is largely restricted to **consumer debt**, where the borrower is a consumer rather than a business. Each province has legislation which attempts to protect consumers from the potentially unfair bargaining advantage that lenders enjoy. People with poor credit records are especially vulnerable, and their need for credit may be greater than those on more solid financial footing. However, if consumers are not aware of their legal rights or the legal processes by which they may enforce those rights, the legislative protection is of little practical value. This is a problem that some governments have addressed by providing consumer information and debt counselling.[12]

Within each province and territory, forms of protection are often scattered throughout a number of statutes, but generally they seek to regulate the provision of credit by licensing certain activities, prohibiting other activities, and requiring disclosure regarding the terms of credit transactions. As a result, there are many different rules that businesses must follow when extending credit to consumers.

Consumer debt
A loan to an individual for a non-commercial purpose.

---

12. For example, in Nova Scotia, through Service Nova Scotia and Municipal Relations.

The provincial and territorial legislation

- enables the courts to review and reverse transactions where "the cost of the loan is excessive and the transaction is harsh and unconscionable."[13]

- prohibits credit transactions where there is "no reasonable probability of making payment in full" or where there is no substantial benefit to the consumer.[14]

- prohibits lenders from making misleading statements in advertising dealing with credit transactions and during the loan application and negotiation process.[15]

- requires lenders to provide detailed disclosure regarding credit transactions, including the true cost of borrowing, the annual effective interest rate, and any other charges (such as registration fees or insurance) that the borrower must pay, and the total amount of the loan.[16]

If a lender fails to comply with these regulations, the borrower can file a complaint against the lender with a regulatory body, which may lead to fines, licence suspension or revocation, or orders prohibiting further violations. The borrower can also apply to the courts to have the terms of the loan adjusted or, in some cases, to obtain damages. However, in the case of consumer disputes, the courts are often not a realistic choice for consumers, due to factors such as cost, inconvenience, and the length of time it takes the courts to resolve disputes.

Credit bureau
An agency that compiles credit information on borrowers.

Credit bureaus provide a service to lenders by compiling credit information on consumers and reporting on their credit history. Lenders use this information to evaluate loan applications. There are licensing regulations to ensure the respectability of credit bureaus, and to ensure the accuracy of the information that is compiled. Consumers have access to their credit reports and the opportunity to correct errors.[17]

Collection agency
An agency that assists lenders in obtaining payment on outstanding loans.

Collection agencies assist lenders who have difficulty recovering loans. These agencies are subject to licensing regulations and cannot harass, threaten, or exert undue pressure on defaulting borrowers. They are also prohibited from contacting anyone other than the borrower (such as a family member or business associate) even when the debtor is bankrupt or deceased.[18] Agencies that go beyond the permitted methods of collection risk the revocation of their operating licences.

In addition to the provincial legislation, there are also federal laws dealing with the regulation of credit.

The federal government recently passed regulations that apply to credit cards issued by federally regulated financial institutions,[19] in order "to make financial products more transparent for consumers" and to "protect Canadians and their families from unexpected costs and provide clear information to help them make better financial decisions."[20]

---

13. *Unconscionable Transactions Relief Act*, RSNS 1989, c 481, s 3.
14. *Consumer Protection Act*, 2002, SO 2002, c 30, Schedule A, s 15. See also Chapter 24.
15. *Fair Trading Act*, RSA 2000, c F-2.
16. *Business Practices and Consumer Protection Act*, SBC 2004, c 2.
17. See, for example, *Consumer Reporting Act*, RSO 1990, c C-33, s 12.
18. *Collection Agencies Act*, RSO 1990, c C-14.
19. *Credit Business Practices*, SOR/2009-257.
20. Flaherty, Jim (Minister of Finance), News Release, Ottawa, "Regulations Come into Force to Protect Canadian Credit Card Users" (1 September 2010).

The new regulations require

- a summary box on credit applications and contracts clearly indicating key features, such as interest rates and fees

- express consent for credit limit increases

- restrictions on debt collection practices used by financial institutions

- disclosure of the time to pay off the balance by making only minimum payments

- notice of any interest rate increases

- mandatory 21-day, interest-free grace period for new purchases

- allocation of payments to the balance with the highest interest rate first

In addition, the federal *Criminal Code*[21] prohibits lending at a rate of interest above 60 percent on an annual basis, although this provision has recently been amended to exclude most **payday loans**. Loans with an interest rate in excess of 60 percent are illegal and, as such, are generally unenforceable. In addition, lenders who receive such interest may be subject to fines and imprisonment.

The average payday loan is for $280 and is outstanding for 10 days.[22] Payday lenders typically extend credit until the borrower's next payday. The borrower provides the lender with a post-dated cheque or a pre-authorized withdrawal from a bank account for the amount of the loan plus interest and fees. In many cases, the annual effective interest rate exceeds 60 percent, and can be as high as 1200 percent![23]

Proponents of the payday loan industry argue that the loans fulfill an unmet need for short-term credit and convenience. Critics argue that the industry is rife with unscrupulous and abusive business practices (such as misleading advertising and hidden fees) and exploits people who are already financially vulnerable. Until recently, payday loans were largely unregulated in Canada.

The *Criminal Code* now excludes payday loans from its limitation on the rate of interest that may be charged, provided the loan is for $1500 or less, the term of the loan is for 62 days or less, and the province in which the loan is made has provincial regulations dealing with payday loans. The goal of the new federal legislation is to encourage the provinces to enact legislation which will protect borrowers and limit the total cost of borrowing. Most provinces have passed, or are in the process of passing, payday loan legislation.[24] Critics of the new regulations argue that delegating responsibility to the provincial governments will lead to a lack of consistency in the regulations and their enforcement.[25]

Provincial payday loan legislation generally prohibits a variety of unfair business practices (such as misleading advertising and "rollover" loans), imposes a limit on the total cost of borrowing, provides the borrower with a two-day "cooling off" period, and limits various collection practices.[26] In Ontario, for example, payday loan borrowers may not be charged

Payday loan
A short-term loan for a relatively small amount of money, provided by a non-traditional lender to an individual.

PART EIGHT

---

21. RSC 1985, c C-46, s 347.
22. Whitelaw, Bob, "$280 till payday: The short-term loan industry says it provides a service the (average) Canadian needs, wants and appreciates", *Vancouver Sun* (8 June 2005), A21.
23. Kitching, Andrew and Starky, Sheena, "Payday Loan Companies in Canada: Determining the Public Interest", PRB 05-81E, Parliamentary Information and Research Service, Library of Parliament, Ottawa (26 January 2006).
24. See, for example, *Payday Loans Act,* 2008, SO 2008, c 9.
25. Ziegel, Jacob, "Pass the buck: Ottawa has paramount jurisdiction over interest rate regulation", *Financial Post* (10 November 2006) online: Financial Post <http://www.canada.com/nationalpost/news/story.html?id=b3efb360-60fc-4c86-8818-b579b31fcd63>.
26. *Supra* note 24.

more than $21 for each $100 borrowed. In Alberta, British Columbia, and Saskatchewan, the maximum charge is $23 for each $100 borrowed. Accordingly, in Alberta, a loan of $300 for 14 days, which is a typical payday loan, will require the borrower to repay a total of $369, for an annual effective interest rate of 599.64 percent.

New regulations in place for payday loans.

© ASHLEY COOPER/CORBIS

ETHICAL CONSIDERATIONS

The "No Interest" Offer

The local electronics store flyer advertises "No Interest for 24 Months on all Purchases!" The offer is attractive, especially when the item being considered is a luxury item, such as a giant computer monitor for $299—something Susan would like to have, but does not really need. In Ontario, Susan would have to pay $337.87 including taxes to buy the monitor if she pays cash at the time of purchase. Instead, Susan is enticed by the offer of 24 equal payments without interest, or only $12.46 per month!

The problem is in the fine print. If Susan reads the fine print tucked away inside the flyer, she will see that there are terms and conditions attached to the "No Interest" offer. First, there is an "administration fee" of $49.95, which must be paid at the time of purchase. Second, the sales taxes applicable to both the monitor and the administration fee must also be paid at the time of purchase. Finally, "Interest is charged on all accounts at the annual rate of 28.8 percent. Interest will be waived only if the customer makes all payments on or before the due date, failing which this offer will not apply."

Suppose Susan buys the monitor and makes all 24 payments when due. In that case, she pays $95.31 at the time of purchase (administration fee plus sales taxes on the monitor and the administration fee). She pays $12.46 per month for

24 months for a total of $299. Accordingly, Susan pays a total of $394.31, compared to the $337.87 that she would have paid if she had bought the monitor for cash. Some deal!

But things get worse—much worse—if Susan is late making a payment. Suppose now that Susan buys the monitor with the "No Interest" offer, but because she goes away for a few days during spring break, she is late making one of the 24 monthly payments. Susan makes the other 23 payments on time. Unfortunately for Susan, the terms of the offer no longer apply because she did not comply with the conditions of the offer, which were clearly stated. Interest is now charged on the entire amount for the whole two-year period, even though Susan made 23 out of 24 payments on time. Susan now pays $95.31 at the time of purchase plus $12.46 per month for 24 months, as before, but now Susan also pays interest at the rate of 28.8 percent for two years, amounting to an additional $130.23. Susan now pays a total of $524.54 for her $299 monitor! The total cost of borrowing is $186.67, or 62 percent of the original purchase price.

Critical Analysis: Is this type of credit offer fair? Should consumers be bound by such terms and conditions? Should the "administration fee" be included in the calculation of interest, with the result that the offer would violate the *Criminal Code?*

Business Law in Practice Revisited

1. What is the bank likely to require before agreeing to loan money to Hometown?

Hometown will be asked to provide detailed financial statements and a business plan to justify the expansion and the loan.

2. What will the terms of the loan be?

The bank will require Hometown to provide collateral with sufficient value to cover the loan. The interest rate on the loan will accord with the risk perceived by the bank. Hometown will be required to maintain minimum levels of accounts receivable and inventory, to stay within a specified debt/equity ratio, and to provide financial information to the lender at specified intervals. Hometown will need the lender's permission to deal with secured assets other than inventory, and will be required to maintain appropriate insurance coverage on the collateral.

3. What are the risks for Hometown in borrowing the money?

The major risk is the possibility that the business will be less profitable than anticipated and that Hometown will be unable to repay the loan. If Hometown fails to repay the loan, the collateral can be seized and sold by the bank. In many cases, this will mean the end of the business.

4. Will Bill, Martha, and the two new shareholders be personally liable for the loan?

Bill and Martha will likely be required to personally guarantee the loan. The new shareholders may also be asked to guarantee the loan. If Hometown defaults, their personal assets will ultimately be available to the bank. Since the guarantees are probably unlimited in scope, the failure of Hometown to repay the loan could eventually result in personal bankruptcy for the guarantors.

Chapter Summary

Credit transactions are an important and normal part of every business. A business can be a debtor or a creditor, depending on the transaction. Some arrangements are continuous and informal, such as between a customer and supplier. Others are major individual transactions and involve a formal credit agreement specifying the rights and obligations of the borrower and the lender. Unsecured creditors have a right to be repaid and can sue the debtor in the event of non-payment. Secured creditors have, in addition, the right to seize and sell the collateral to pay down the debt owed. When a debtor defaults, secured creditors are in a much better position than unsecured creditors.

Personal property security is mostly governed by the *PPSA* in each province. The important concepts of the *PPSA* are attachment, perfection, priorities, and lenders' remedies. Lenders and borrowers are protected by credit agreements and by the PPSA and other legislation.

Guarantors place their personal assets at risk when they provide a guarantee. Guarantors should be aware of the onerous terms in most guarantees and ensure that they understand their obligations under standard form guarantee contracts.

Chapter Study

Key Terms and Concepts

acceleration clause (p. 654)

after-acquired property (p. 649)

collateral (p. 647)

collection agency (p. 660)

consumer debt (p. 659)

credit bureau (p. 660)

deficiency (p. 655)

events of default (p. 647)

financing statement (p. 651)

general security agreement (p. 649)

guarantee (p. 656)

guarantor (p. 656)

indemnity (p. 656)

letter of commitment (p. 648)

letter of credit (p. 646)

payday loan (p. 661)

purchase-money security interest (PMSI) (p. 652)

receiver (p. 655)

registration (p. 651)

secured credit (p. 645)

security interest (p. 650)

subrogation (p. 657)

unsecured credit (p. 645)

Questions for Review

1. What are some examples of credit transactions?

2. What are some of the methods that creditors use to reduce risk in credit transactions?

3. What are the rights of an unsecured creditor on default by the debtor?

4. What are the key aspects of personal property security legislation?

5. What are the disclosure requirements for a consumer loan?

6. What is a criminal rate of interest?

7. What are some problems with payday loans?

8. What is a general security agreement?

9. What is the role of a financing statement?

10. How are lenders' remedies limited by law?

11. What is a purchase-money security interest?

12. What is the difference between a perfected and an unperfected security interest?

13. What is the role of a receiver or receiver-manager?

14. What is a deficiency?

15. Who are the parties in a guarantee contract?

16. What are the issues with standard form guarantee contracts?

17. How does a guarantee affect the limited liability of a shareholder?

Questions for Critical Thinking

1. When a business fails, most of the assets may be claimed by secured creditors. Unsecured creditors may receive very little, if anything, and shareholders may be left with nothing. Is the protection accorded to secured creditors justified?

2. There is a complex web of rules governing consumer credit. Should commercial credit be regulated the way consumer credit is now or left to the lender and borrower to negotiate?

3. What factors affect the ability of a borrower to finance their business using debt? How does an economic downturn or credit freeze affect the ability of a business to borrow? How do these developments affect existing credit agreements?

4. Creditors holding general security agreements are required to give the borrower reasonable notice before appointing a receiver to take possession of the assets of the business. How should a secured creditor decide how much time to give a debtor?

5. The Canadian Constitution gives the provinces control over property and civil rights, which includes the regulation of credit and registration of property as security for credit. Do the benefits to the provinces of autonomy outweigh the burden on business of dealing with so many sets of rules?

PART EIGHT

6. In light of this chapter, what factors would you advise Bill and Martha to consider in financing Hometown's expansion? Did they make the right decision in issuing shares? When Hometown borrows, how should they try to structure the terms of the loan to minimize the risk to Hometown and to themselves?

Situations for Discussion

1. Douglas Pools Inc. operates a pool company in Toronto. In order to finance the business, Douglas Pools negotiated a line of credit with the Bank of Montreal to a maximum indebtedness of $300 000. The line of credit was secured by a general security agreement in favour of the bank, in which the collateral is described as "all assets of Douglas Pools, all after-acquired property and proceeds thereof." The Bank registered its security interest under the *PPSA* on 10 January 2011. On 30 March 2011, Douglas Pools bought a 2009 Dodge Ram pick-up truck from London Dodge for $15 000. London Dodge agreed to accept payment for the truck over three years, with interest at 6 percent per year, and took a security interest in the truck in order to secure payment of the purchase price. London Dodge registered its security interest under the *PPSA* on 4 April 2011. On 11 November 2011, Douglas Pools sold the truck to Fisher & Co. (a company owned by the same person that owns Douglas Pools) for $1.00. Douglas Pools defaulted on its obligations to both the bank and London Dodge and, on 28 November 2011, declared bankruptcy. At the time of the bankruptcy, Douglas Pools owed the Bank $240 000 and London Dodge $12 000. Now, the bank, London Dodge, the Trustee in Bankruptcy, and Fisher & Co. all claim the truck. Whose claim to the truck has first priority? Whose claim has second priority?

2. The Weiss Brothers operated a successful business in Montreal for 30 years. They bought a bankrupt hardware business in Ottawa, even though they had no experience selling hardware. Their bank, TD, got nervous about their financial stability and suggested they seek financing elsewhere. The brothers contacted a former employee of TD who was with Aetna Financial Services and negotiated a new line of credit for up to $1 million. Security for the line was a general security

agreement, pledge of accounts receivable, mortgage on land, and guarantees by the brothers. Six months later, the brothers defaulted on the line. Aetna demanded payment in full and appointed a receiver, who seized all the assets three hours later.[27] What can the Weiss Brothers do to save the business and their personal assets? What could they have done to prevent this disaster? Why did Aetna grant credit after TD had become reluctant to continue?

3. The bank agreed to lend money to Wilder Enterprises Ltd. and, in order to secure repayment of the loan, the company granted the bank a security interest in all of its assets. The loan was also personally guaranteed by members of the Wilder family, who owned the company. Periodically, the bank increased the company's credit limit as the company expanded its business. When the company experienced financial difficulty, however, the bank dishonoured two of the company's cheques. That prompted a meeting between the bank and the Wilders, the result of which was that the bank agreed to loan additional funds to the company, and refrain from demanding payment on its loan, in exchange for additional guarantees from members of the Wilder family. Despite the agreement, and without warning, the bank stopped honouring the company's cheques and demanded payment of the loan in full. When the company was unable to pay, the bank appointed a receiver-manager and took control of the company. The receiver-manager refused the company's request to complete the projects that the company then had underway and, as a result, the company went bankrupt. The bank sued the Wilders for payment pursuant to the guarantees that the bank had, all of which permitted the bank to "deal with the customer as the bank may see fit."[28] Will the Wilders be obligated on their guarantees? How sympathetic are the courts likely to be? Could the Wilders have structured their affairs differently to avoid high personal risk for the escalating debts of their failing business?

4. Kyle owned and operated a retail sporting goods shop. A new ski resort was built in the area and, to take advantage of increased activity, Kyle decided to expand his shop. He borrowed money from the bank, who took a security interest in his present inventory and any after-acquired inventory. One year later, an

27. Based on *Kavcar Investments v Aetna Financial Services* (1989), 62 DLR (4th) 277 (Ont CA).
28. Based on *Bank of Montreal v Wilder* (1986), 32 DLR (4th) 9 (SCC).

avalanche destroyed the ski lodge. Kyle's business suffered, and he was left with twice as much inventory as he had when he first obtained the loan. When he defaulted on the loan payments, the bank seized all his inventory. Kyle claims the bank is entitled only to the value of the inventory at the time of the loan. How much inventory can the bank claim? Could Kyle have negotiated better terms at the outset?

5. Nicola applied for a personal loan from ABC Bank. She provided all of the personal and financial information requested by the bank. When she inquired about her application, the bank's credit officer told her that her application had been denied. When Nicola sought an explanation for the refusal, she was told that her "credit score" was not high enough. The bank refused to provide any information concerning her score or the formula used to calculate the score, claiming this was confidential commercial information. What can Nicola do now?

6. King Tire Shop agreed to buy a vacant building supply outlet to expand its tire business. To finance the purchase, King negotiated a loan from its bank, with the land and building as security. As part of the loan documentation, the bank required a report stating that the property was not environmentally contaminated in any way. King engaged a local environmental consulting firm to investigate and prepare the report for the bank. The firm gave the property a clean bill of health, and the loan was granted. Two years later, it was discovered that the adjacent property, which was formerly a gas station, had seriously contaminated the soil, and pollution was leaching into the soil of King's property. The cleanup cost is significant, and King cannot afford it. As a result, King's property is seriously devalued and the bank is concerned about the value of its security, especially since King's business is not doing well. Who is responsible for this environmental damage? What are the bank's options? What are King's options?

7. New Solutions Financial loaned Transport Express, a transport trucking company, $500 000 under a commercial lending agreement. The interest rate was 4 percent per month calculated daily and payable monthly. This arrangement produced an effective annual rate of 60.1 percent. Other clauses in the agreement specified other charges, including legal fees, a monitoring fee, a standby fee, royalty payments, and a commitment fee totalling 30.8 percent for a total effective annual rate of 90.9 percent. Transport Express found the terms of the agreement too onerous and refused to make the agreed payments.[29] Is this agreement enforceable? Why or why not? Should a commercial arrangement like this be treated differently from a payday loan?

8. RST Ltd. is an independent printing company in a medium-sized town in Saskatchewan. It was established 15 years ago by Ron, Sandra, and Tara, who each own one-third of the shares in the company. Last year, RST revenues were $4 million, mainly from local contracts for such items as customized office stationery, business cards, advertising posters, calendars, and entertainment programs. Because the business is prospering, the owners are planning to expand their printing and sales space. They know that significant financing is required for the expanded facilities and the increased business. The current capital structure of RST is 60 percent owners' equity and 40 percent debt. Rather than issue shares to other investors, the owners are prepared to put more equity into the business by purchasing additional shares in order to maintain their debt/equity ratio. The expansion project will cost $1 million, so they need to borrow $400 000. Do you agree with the owners' financing decisions? What are the risks? How can the owners plan for uncertainty in their industry and the economy in general?

For more study tools, visit http://www.NELSONbrain.com.

---

29. Based on *Transport North American Express Inc v New Solutions Financial Corp*, [2004] 1 SCR 249.

CHAPTER 27

Bankruptcy and Insolvency

Objectives

After studying this chapter, you should have an understanding of

- the legal aspects of business failure
- the rights and obligations of debtors and creditors when a business fails
- alternatives to bankruptcy
- the stages in the bankruptcy process

© NAJLAH FEANNY/CORBIS

Business Law in Practice

Hometown Hardware Ltd. (Hometown) and its owners, Bill Ikeda and Martha Wong, were introduced in Chapters 25 and 26. They have successfully operated a building supply outlet in Timmins, Ontario, for the past 35 years. Eighteen months ago, Bill and Martha became concerned about the imminent arrival of a big-box building supply store. They decided to expand Hometown's business in order to respond to the competitive threat. To finance the expansion, Hometown issued $200 000 worth of shares and borrowed another $200 000 from its bank. The loan was structured as a mortgage of $100 000 on Hometown's land and buildings, and a line of credit for up to $100 000 secured by Hometown's inventory and accounts receivable. Bill and Martha personally guaranteed the line of credit. The expansion strategy failed. Just after the large competitor opened, the housing market collapsed. Hometown experienced a 30 percent drop in sales and Bill does not expect the situation to improve.

When the big-box store first opened, Bill reacted with a costly promotional campaign. To cover this extra expense, Bill borrowed $10 000 from his brother, George. More recently, he was under pressure from a major supplier, Good Lumber, to pay Hometown's overdue account. Bill sold land that the company owned adjacent to the store. With the proceeds, Bill paid $20 000 to Good Lumber and repaid George.

Hometown's assets consist of the land and buildings (subject to the mortgage) on which the business is located, inventory, accounts receivable, and a few pieces of equipment. Hometown's liabilities include the mortgage, the line of credit, accounts payable, and property taxes. Hometown is also late in remitting its employee source deductions to the government.

Bill wants to keep Hometown in business as long as possible, but he fears that the store may no longer be viable and he is wondering what he should do.

(Continued on the next page)

Bill would like to continue to draw his regular salary for as long as possible, and he would also like to continue to pay Martha, the store manager. He is concerned that if Hometown stops making payments to the bank or suppliers, they will take some kind of legal action. He is also concerned about the personal guarantees that he and Martha have given to the bank.

1. What options does Hometown have in dealing with this financial crisis?
2. What rights do Hometown's creditors have?
3. What will happen to Hometown, its owners, its creditors, Bill, and Martha if Hometown goes bankrupt?

Business Failure

Business failure is often overlooked in the study of business, which tends to emphasize success and entrepreneurship. Even when the economy is strong, businesses fail or falter because of poor management, lack of adequate financing, death or illness of a principal, fraud, and other reasons. When an industry or the overall economy experiences a downturn, even strong businesses may run into financial difficulty. Hometown is caught in a declining economy, an industry collapse, and a changing market in which local stores are threatened by big-box retailers. Hometown must deal with cash-flow problems, persistent and competing creditors, and possible legal action. The manner in which Hometown responds to these threats affects many people in addition to the business owners. If Hometown fails, customers, suppliers, and employees will be harmed, and the local economy may suffer. How the law addresses the respective interests of creditors and others is of critical importance to a wide and diverse group of stakeholders.

In an attempt to ensure that all stakeholders are treated fairly, a body of law, generically called bankruptcy and insolvency law, has evolved. The two primary pieces of legislation that govern insolvency law in Canada are the *Bankruptcy and Insolvency Act*[1] *(BIA)* and the *Companies' Creditors Arrangement Act*[2] *(CCAA)*. In addition, there are a number of other statutes and common law rules that affect bankruptcy and insolvency.

If a business such as Hometown is no longer able to cope with a specific debt or its financial obligations in general, there are several options available, ranging from informal negotiations to bankruptcy.

Informal Steps

Before contemplating bankruptcy, Hometown may first try to solve its financial problems by way of a negotiated settlement. If Bill can convince Hometown's creditors that the business can be salvaged, they may be willing to make concessions in terms of payment. Bill can deal with creditors individually or as a group. A settlement can be more or less formal,

---

1. RSC 1985, c B-3.
2. RSC 1985, c C-36.

depending on the circumstances. Creditors may agree to meet with Bill and, possibly using the services of a professional facilitator (an accountant, a lawyer, or a debt counsellor), they may be able to reach an agreement that is acceptable to all of them and either allows Hometown to continue operating or wind up its affairs without the need for expensive legal proceedings. In practice, the more creditors that Hometown has, the less likely it is that they will be able to reach such an agreement.

The key to negotiated settlements is ensuring that all creditors are in agreement. Creditors will agree to a settlement if they believe that it will likely produce better results for them in the long run than legal proceedings or bankruptcy. One possible danger is that some creditors will attempt to push through an agreement that is unfair to others or that simply ignores them. The value of using facilitators with appropriate expertise is that they are trained to identify these risks and deal with them. Furthermore, the parties themselves may not recognize alternatives that would result in a better overall outcome. A skilled facilitator will raise these alternatives for consideration.

In some cases, especially when the business is in serious financial trouble, negotiations may not be a viable option or may fail after a reasonable attempt. Creditors may refuse to participate in negotiations, or they may decide that it is not in their best interests to facilitate the debtor continuing to carry on business. In that case, the debtor must look to other options.

Proceedings before Bankruptcy

If informal negotiations fail to produce a settlement with Hometown's creditors, and Hometown's financial situation does not improve, Bill will likely explore more formal proceedings. He should seek advice from a lawyer or accountant with insolvency expertise so that he understands all the available options. If Bill decides that bankruptcy is the best or only option, he will need the services of a **trustee in bankruptcy.**

Trustees in bankruptcy are professionals who are licensed by the Office of the Superintendent of Bankruptcy and have legal authority to administer the bankruptcy process. A trustee in bankruptcy will usually agree to take on a matter if there is no conflict of interest present and the debtor has sufficient assets to pay for the trustee's services. Sometimes the debtor is not able to pay for the trustee and, in that case, it may be very difficult for the debtor to find a trustee willing to assist.

When Bill and the trustee first meet, the trustee will explain the options available to Hometown, the bankruptcy process, and the role of the trustee. The trustee will also begin to assess the **estate** and prepare a preliminary statement of assets and liabilities. Often, in the case of small businesses, this assessment requires the untangling of business and personal affairs. In Hometown's case, the pending bankruptcy is that of Hometown Hardware Ltd., since it is the legal entity that carries on the business. However, it is possible that Bill and Martha may also become bankrupt, or make a proposal to their creditors, as a result of their personal guarantees.

PART EIGHT

Trustee in bankruptcy
The person who has legal responsibility under the *BIA* for administering bankruptcies and proposals.

Estate
The collective term for the assets of a bankrupt individual or corporation.

Following consultation with Bill, the trustee will prepare a statement such as the one shown in Figure 27.1.

FIGURE 27.1

Preliminary Statement of Assets and Liabilities for Hometown Hardware Ltd.

Assets* at estimated cash value

Cash	$ 1 000
Accounts receivable	11 000
Inventory of plumbing supplies	27 000
Land and building	105 000
Equipment	30 000
	$ 174 000

Liabilities

Unremitted payroll deductions (due to Canada Revenue Agency)	$ 24 000
Accounts payable to suppliers	94 000
Mortgage on land and building	97 000
Line of credit at bank (secured by inventory and accounts receivable)	85 000
Municipal property taxes	10 000
	$ 310 000

*Leased property is not an asset of the estate but will revert to the lessors upon default.

Insolvent

Unable to meet financial obligations as they become due or having insufficient assets, if liquidated, to meet financial obligations.

From this initial assessment, it is apparent that Hometown is **insolvent** as that term is defined in the *BIA*.[3] That is, Hometown owes more than $1000 and

- is unable to meet its obligations as they become due, or

- has ceased paying its obligations as they become due, or

- has assets with a fair market value less than its liabilities

It is important to note that insolvency and bankruptcy are not the same, although the two terms are often, incorrectly, used interchangeably. Insolvency is a factual matter relating to a person's assets and liabilities or his ability to pay his debts. Bankruptcy is a legal mechanism whereby the assets of an insolvent person are transferred to a trustee, liquidated, and the net proceeds are distributed to creditors in a manner determined by the *BIA*.

Proposals and Arrangements

It may be possible for an insolvent debtor to avoid bankruptcy by making a proposal or entering into an arrangement with creditors. The general assumption that underlies proposals and arrangements is that a business is worth more to all of its varied

---

3. *Supra* note 1, s 2.

stakeholders (e.g., creditors, employees, suppliers, customers, government, etc.) as a going concern than if it is forced to liquidate all of its assets. If Bill wants to keep the business of Hometown going, he should consider making a proposal to Hometown's creditors.

Proposals under the *BIA*

A proposal is a procedure governed by the *BIA* that allows a debtor to restructure its debt in order to avoid bankruptcy. When a debtor makes a proposal, the debtor offers creditors a percentage of what is owed to them, or to extend the time for payment of debts, or some combination of the two. The goal is to restructure the debts owed by the debtor so that the debtor is able to pay them. In many cases, creditors prefer that a debtor avoid bankruptcy, especially if it means that the creditor will receive more money than if the debtor were to become bankrupt.

There are two types of proposal under the *BIA*:

- Division I proposals[4] are available to individuals and corporations with no limit on the total amount of debt that is owed.

- Division II proposals[5] are available to individuals with total debts less than $250 000 (not including a mortgage on a principal residence). Division II proposals are known as "consumer proposals."

In either case, the debtor works with a trustee in bankruptcy to develop a proposal which is first filed with the Office of the Superintendent of Bankruptcy and is then sent to the creditors of the debtor. Once the proposal is filed, the debtor stops making payments to its unsecured creditors, salary garnishments stop, and lawsuits against the debtor by creditors are stayed (stopped). In the case of a Division I proposal, there will be a meeting of creditors to consider and vote on the proposal, at which time the trustee will provide an estimate to the creditors of the amount they are expected to receive under the proposal compared to the amount they could expect to receive under a bankruptcy. In the case of a Division II proposal, there may or may not be a meeting of creditors, depending on whether they request one.

Creditors vote on whether to accept or reject the proposal. With a Division I proposal, the proposal is approved if creditors representing two-thirds of the total amount owed and a majority in number vote to accept it. In addition, a Division I proposal must be approved by the court. With a Division II proposal, the proposal is approved if creditors representing a majority of the total amount owed vote to accept it. If the proposal is approved by the creditors in this manner, then it is legally binding on all unsecured creditors, whether they voted for or against it.

If the proposal is approved, the debtor will make payments as provided in the proposal and, if the debtor makes all the payments and complies with any other conditions

---

4. *Supra* note 1, s 50.
5. *Supra* note 1, s 66.11.

in the proposal, then the debtor is released from those debts. With Division I proposals, this gives a business the opportunity to remain in business and ultimately be successful. With Division II proposals, the debtor must also attend two mandatory financial counselling sessions, and the proposal will be recorded on the debtor's credit record for several years. If the debtor does not make the payments set out in the proposal, or fails to comply with conditions contained in it, then the trustee or any creditor can apply to have the proposal annulled.

However, if the proposal is not approved by the creditors, the debtor is deemed to be bankrupt under a Division I proposal as of the date of the first meeting of creditors.[6] In the case of a corporation, this usually means that the corporation will cease to exist as of that date. In a Division II proposal, the debtor is free to resubmit an amended proposal, consider other options, or make an assignment into bankruptcy. There is no automatic bankruptcy when a Division II proposal is rejected, unlike the result when a Division I proposal is rejected.

Generally, secured creditors are not bound by *BIA* proposals, unless they elect to participate. Secured creditors can realize on their security before or after the debtor has filed a proposal, even if the unsecured creditors have voted to accept the proposal. For this reason, it may be very difficult for a business to make a viable Division I proposal if the business has a large amount of secured debt. In that case, the secured creditors can be expected to appoint a receiver to seize their collateral and, if the collateral constitutes a majority of the assets used to operate the business, then the business will be effectively shut down.

Bill and the trustee may meet to discuss the possibility of Hometown submitting a Division I proposal to its creditors. The trustee will explain to Bill that as soon as the proposal is filed, the bank can be expected to realize on its security, including the land and buildings, inventory, and accounts receivable. That will leave Hometown with insufficient assets to carry on its business. For that reason, a proposal under the *BIA* is not a viable option for Hometown.

Arrangements under the *CCAA*

Another option for an insolvent business to avoid bankruptcy is an arrangement under the *CCAA*. The *CCAA* may be used by corporations that have total debt exceeding $5 million. The *CCAA* is a federal statute that allows an insolvent company to obtain protection from its creditors while it tries to reorganize its financial affairs. Similar to the situation with a proposal under the *BIA*, once a company obtains a court order under the *CCAA*, the company's creditors are prevented from taking any action to collect money that is owed to them. Unlike the *BIA*, however, the protection afforded by the *CCAA* applies to secured as well as unsecured creditors, and even to lessors and critical suppliers. After the initial court order is obtained, the company continues to operate while attempting to negotiate an arrangement with its creditors. Canadian companies that have reorganized under the *CCAA* include Air Canada, AbitibiBowater, Canwest, Nortel, QuebecorWorld, and Stelco.

---

6. *Supra* note 1, s 57.

When the court grants the initial *CCAA* order staying the creditors, it will also appoint a monitor, usually a major accounting firm, that will oversee the operations of the company while it attempts to reorganize. The monitor reports to the court on any major events that might impact the viability of the company, assists the company with the preparation of its reorganization plan, and tabulates the votes at meetings of creditors.

There are no restrictions on what may be contained in a *CCAA* arrangement. Indeed, one of the most attractive features of the *CCAA* for large companies is its flexibility. Arrangements will often involve companies paying a percentage of the debt owed to creditors, either in a lump sum or over time, or exchanging specific debt for debt with higher interest and longer repayment terms. Sometimes, shares will be offered to creditors in place of existing debt, or a combination of cash and shares.

Eventually, the arrangement will be voted on by creditors, who are grouped together by class for voting purposes. If the arrangement is approved by creditors of a class representing two-thirds of the total amount owed and a majority in number, then the arrangement is binding on that class of creditors. Once all the classes of creditors have approved the arrangement, court approval is required.

If a *CCAA* plan of arrangement is not approved by the creditors, then the company is not automatically bankrupt, as is the case with a Division I proposal under the *BIA*, but the court ordered stay of creditors is lifted. At that point, creditors are free to pursue their claims and it is likely that the company will be pushed into receivership or bankruptcy.

While a company is reorganizing under the *BIA* or the *CCAA*, it will need to fund its business operations. This may be difficult, because the reorganization proceedings are obvious evidence of insolvency and creditors will be reluctant to lend money in such circumstances. However, creditors may be willing to provide funding if the debtor has sufficient assets to provide as collateral and the creditors are given priority over existing creditors. This type of financing is called **debtor in possession (DIP)** or interim financing. DIP financing places existing secured creditors behind new lenders, which can be controversial. Accordingly, when approving DIP financing and giving priority to new lenders over existing secured creditors, courts are careful to balance the competing interests of existing secured creditors, the company in need of funds, and other creditors as well as employees and other stakeholders. The *BIA* was recently amended to allow for DIP financing in connection with a Division I proposal,[7] however, DIP financing is very difficult for smaller companies to find when making a *BIA* proposal.

The *CCAA* is often preferred over the proposal mechanism of the *BIA* because of its flexibility, the fact that it binds secured creditors, and the availability of DIP financing. However, the minimum debt threshold of $5 000 000 and the very high costs associated with a *CCAA* reorganization make it a viable option only for very large companies.

Debtor in possession (DIP) financing
Secured credit provided to companies during the reorganization process with priority over existing secured creditors.

PART EIGHT

---

7. *Supra* note 1, s 50.6.

BUSINESS APPLICATION OF THE LAW

Bankruptcy Protection and Corporate Reorganization

In 2010, Blockbuster Inc., the U.S. video rental company, filed for bankruptcy protection in the United States. The success of video streaming and video-on-demand services such as Netflix proved to be insurmountable competition for Blockbuster's traditional video rental business. Blockbuster announced that its goal was to reduce its $1 billion in debt to approximately $100 million and that its senior secured debtholders would receive equity in exchange for their debt. Blockbuster obtained $70 million in DIP financing from major Hollywood studios, including Warner Bros., Twentieth Century Fox, and Sony Pictures. It was essential for Blockbuster to have the major studios on side during their reorganization to ensure that Blockbuster could continue to provide customers with new releases on the first day of their release. The collateral provided for the DIP financing was the assets of Blockbuster's profitable Canadian operation, Blockbuster Canada.

In 2011, Blockbuster Inc. announced that it would not emerge from bankruptcy protection. The U.S. bankruptcy court ordered the company to be liquidated and, in a court ordered auction, satellite television provider Dish Network Corp. purchased the assets of the company for $320 million, with the result that the DIP loans went into default. Shortly after, on application from the movie studio DIP lenders, an Ontario court appointed accounting firm Grant Thornton as the receiver for Blockbuster Canada giving them the power to "take possession of and exercise control over" Blockbuster's

What happens when a business is no longer viable?

400 retail stores in Canada. By the end of 2011, all Blockbuster stores in Canada had been closed and all the employees were terminated.

Critical Analysis: Were the interests of stakeholders, including the public, adequately protected by the process described above? Should the bankruptcy process work differently when there is an economic downturn?

Sources: Steve Ladurantaye, "Receiver to close up to 140 Blockbuster Canada Outlets" *The Globe and Mail* (25 May 2011) at B10; Jameson Berkow, "Blockbuster Canadian unit seeks bankruptcy protection" *Financial Post* (5 May 2011) online: Financial Post<http://business.financialpost.com/2011/05/05blockbuster-canada-co-has-finally-gone-bust/>; Marina Strauss and Iain Marlow, "Blockbuster to pull plug in Canada" *The Globe and Mail* (31 August 2011) online: Globe and Mail <http://www.theglobeandmail.com/report-on-business/blockbuster-to-pull-plug-in-canada/article592808>.

Remedies for Creditors

A creditor whose payments are overdue has several options. The first step is to determine the reason for the debtor's failure to pay. If the default is temporary, the creditor may decide to continue doing business with the debtor. However, if the debtor is in serious financial difficulty, then the creditor will want to take action before it is too late. The creditor often has a difficult choice to make between allowing the debtor additional time to pay or taking legal action for the recovery of the debt.

A secured creditor can seize its collateral and sell it to pay down its debt, or appoint a receiver to take control of the debtor's business, as discussed in Chapter 26. An unsecured creditor can sue the debtor and try to obtain judgment, which can then be enforced against the debtor. A creditor with a guarantee can pursue the guarantor for payment upon default by the primary debtor. A supplier can threaten to discontinue selling to the debtor, as Good Lumber did with Hometown. Any creditor can threaten to commence legal action in the hope that the threat will persuade the debtor to bring the debt into good standing.

If the business is in serious financial jeopardy and is unable to make a proposal or reach an arrangement with its creditors, bankruptcy may be the only remaining option.

Bankruptcy

Bankruptcy is the legal process by which the assets of the **bankrupt** are automatically transferred to a trustee in bankruptcy for liquidation and distribution to creditors. The bankruptcy process is governed by the *BIA*. The purposes of the *BIA* are

- to preserve the assets of the bankrupt for the benefit of creditors

- to ensure a fair and equitable distribution of the assets to creditors

- in the case of personal bankruptcies, to allow the debtor a fresh financial start

There are three methods by which a person may become bankrupt. An **assignment in bankruptcy** occurs when a person voluntarily assigns her assets to a trustee in bankruptcy. Creditors can also apply to the court for a **bankruptcy order** which, if granted, results in a person being declared bankrupt. The bankruptcy order will normally be granted if the creditor is owed at least $1000 and the debtor has committed an **act of bankruptcy**. Acts of bankruptcy include: defaulting on a proposal, making a fraudulent transfer of property, preferring one creditor over another, trying to avoid or deceive creditors, admitting insolvency or not meeting financial obligations as they come due.[8] Lastly, bankruptcy occurs automatically if the creditors reject a proposal, or if the creditors accept a proposal but the court rejects it. Regardless of the method by which a person becomes bankrupt, the result is the same.

If Hometown makes an assignment in bankruptcy, Hometown will be bankrupt as of the date of the assignment to the trustee in bankruptcy. If creditors of Hometown decide to apply to the court for a bankruptcy order against Hometown, they will probably obtain the order, as Hometown has likely engaged in at least one act of bankruptcy and owes several creditors more than $1 000.

Bankrupt
The legal status of a debtor who has made an assignment or against whom a bankruptcy order has been issued (also used to describe a debtor who is bankrupt).

Assignment in bankruptcy
The debtor's voluntary assignment to the trustee in bankruptcy of legal title to the debtor's property for the benefit of creditors.

Bankruptcy order
An order of the court resulting in a person being declared bankrupt.

Act of bankruptcy
One of a list of specified acts that the debtor must commit before the court will grant a bankruptcy order.

PART EIGHT

BUSINESS AND LEGISLATION

Origins and Purposes of Bankruptcy Legislation

The most famous observer of the miseries of insolvency was Charles Dickens. In the early 19th century, debtors' prisons still existed in most countries. The dubious logic of imprisoning debtors for failing to pay their debts was not lost on Dickens, whose own father was imprisoned in the Marshalsea Prison when Charles was 12.

Dickens' writings made a powerful impact on the reading public throughout the English-speaking world. Largely as a result of Dickens' writings, bankruptcy legislation was introduced in England and elsewhere. Canadian bankruptcy legislation tries to balance the interests of a diverse group of stakeholders when debtors are unable to pay their debts. On one hand, the legislation enables honest but unfortunate debtors to free themselves of their crushing debts and obtain a fresh start. On the other hand, the law establishes priorities between creditors so that assets are distributed fairly and equitably. In the case of dishonest debtors, the law imposes punishment for those who commit bankruptcy offences. Finally, the legislation creates a framework under which potentially viable, but insolvent, businesses may be reorganized so they can continue operating for the benefit of creditors, suppliers, customers, employees, and the broader communities in which they carry on business.

There have been many attempts to revise and update bankruptcy legislation in Canada over the years. It has, however, proven very difficult to achieve consensus on how best to accomplish that goal, in large part due to the diverse group of stakeholders affected by the legislation. In 2009, the *BIA* and the *CCAA* were amended to facilitate DIP financing, deal

(Continued)

---

8. *Supra* note 1, s 42.

with collective bargaining agreements, create a process for appointing a national receiver where appropriate, and give the courts authority to remove obstructive corporate directors, among other things. In addition, the 2009 amendments revised the rules regarding preferences and replaced the rules regarding settlements and reviewable transactions with comprehensive new "transfers at undervalue" rules (discussed later in this chapter).

Marshalsea Prison, the debtors' prison where Charles Dickens' father was incarcerated.

The Bankruptcy Process

Once a person is bankrupt, the assets of the person are transferred to the trustee in bankruptcy, who holds those assets in trust for the benefit of creditors. The trustee has legal authority and responsibility to deal with the assets in a manner which preserves their value. Ultimately, the trustee will dispose of the assets and distribute the proceeds to creditors of the bankrupt in the manner required by the *BIA*. Creditors may appoint an **inspector** to act on their behalf and supervise the actions of the trustee.[9]

Inspector
A person appointed by creditors to act on their behalf and supervise the actions of the trustee in bankruptcy.

Protection of Assets

Following an assignment in bankruptcy or bankruptcy order, the trustee gives public notice of the bankruptcy in order to identify and protect the assets of the estate and to identify all liabilities. Typically, the trustee will

- secure the business premises and storage facilities

- conduct a detailed examination of assets

- prepare the appropriate statements

- ensure that assets are adequately protected, including insurance coverage

- establish appropriate books and accounts

- sell any perishable goods immediately

In exceptional circumstances, the trustee may continue running the business for a period of time in order to perform the duties above.

The protection of assets requires a review not only of assets in possession of the debtor at the time of bankruptcy, but also of assets that were transferred by the debtor prior to bankruptcy. If the debtor made payments to creditors in the ordinary course of business, they will not be challenged. However, if payments were made to favour one creditor over another, assets were transferred for less than their fair value, or transactions have taken place with related parties, then the trustee will review those

---

9. *Supra* note 1, s 116.

transactions to ensure that creditors are treated equitably and according to the priorities set out in the *BIA*. The 2009 amendments to the *BIA* revised the rules regarding preferences and removed the concepts of settlements and reviewable transactions and replaced them with new **transfers at undervalue** rules.[10] The simultaneous *CCAA* amendments incorporated identical rules.[11]

Transfers at Undervalue

A transfer at undervalue occurs when assets are transferred, a payment is made, or services are provided for conspicuously less than their fair market value. Where a transfer at undervalue is found, the court can declare the transfer to be void or can order that the other party to the transaction pay the bankrupt estate the amount by which the consideration for the transaction was less than fair market value.

In order for a transfer at undervalue to be found, specific conditions must be satisfied and the conditions differ depending on whether or not the transaction was at arm's length. Parties are at **arm's length** when they are independent and not related (there are extensive rules in the *BIA* to determine when parties are related[12]).

If the parties to the transaction are at arm's length, then a transaction is a transfer at undervalue if: (a) it took place within one year prior to bankruptcy; (b) the debtor is insolvent (or was rendered insolvent by the transaction); and (c) the debtor intended to defraud, defeat, or delay the interests of a creditor.

If the parties to the transaction are not at arm's length, then a transaction is a transfer at undervalue if it took place within one year prior to bankruptcy. In that case, there are no solvency or intent criteria. If a non-arm's length transaction took place within five years prior to bankruptcy, it is a transfer at undervalue if the solvency and intent criteria in (b) and (c) above are satisfied.

For example, if Hometown transferred its inventory to Bill six months before bankruptcy, the transfer would be a transfer at undervalue and would be void.

There are no cases yet that illustrate the approach the courts will take in determining whether a party intended to defraud, defeat, or delay creditors pursuant to the new *BIA* rules. However, there are cases dealing with similar language in other statutes which suggest that the courts will look primarily to the value of the consideration for which property was transferred in determining intent. If a debtor transfers property to a third party and receives nothing or significantly less than its fair market value in consideration, there will be a presumption of fraudulent intent on the part of the debtor. The presumption will be stronger where the transfer was made in secret or in contemplation of impending bankruptcy or litigation. There may even be fraudulent intent where property is transferred for fair value, if the court finds that the intention of the debtor was fraudulent and the recipient of the property knew of the debtor's intention. The issue of fraudulent intent is always highly specific to the facts of each case.[13]

Transfers at undervalue
Transfers of property or provision of services for less than fair market value.

Arm's length
People who are independent of each other and not related.

PART EIGHT

---

10. *Supra* note 1, s 96.
11. *Supra* note 2, s 36.1.
12. *Supra* note 1, s 4.
13. For example, see *Abakhan & Associates Inc v Braydon*, (2009) BCCA 521, leave to appeal to SCC refused [2010] SCCA No 26 (June 24, 2010).

Preferences

A preference is a payment that benefits one creditor over another. With solvent companies, this is a common occurrence and not a concern. However, when a company is insolvent, the preference may result in the other creditor not being paid at all. One of the purposes of the *BIA* is to ensure that creditors are treated fairly and equitably. This means that ordinary unsecured creditors should be treated equally. When one such creditor receives payment and another does not, this goal is not achieved. If a payment is found to be a preference, the court can rule the payment void, meaning that the creditor in receipt of the payment would have to repay that amount to the bankrupt estate.

As with transfers at undervalue, there is a distinction with respect to preferences depending on whether the parties are dealing at arm's length.

If the parties are dealing at arm's length, a payment is a preference if it is made within three months prior to bankruptcy and it is made with the intention of preferring one creditor over another.

If the parties are not dealing at arm's length, then a payment is a preference if it is made within one year prior to bankruptcy and it has the effect of preferring one creditor over another. In this case, it need only be shown that the effect of the payment was to prefer one creditor over another. The intention of the debtor is irrelevant.

It may be difficult to determine whether the debtor intended to prefer one creditor over another when making a payment. However, the courts have held that there is a rebuttable presumption of that intent if the result of the payment is that one creditor gets paid and another does not. This presumption can be rebutted if it can be shown, for example, that the payment was made in the ordinary course of business, or was made to take advantage of favourable payment terms or to secure the continued supply of goods or services needed for the debtor to remain in business.

Suppose Hometown has made an assignment in bankruptcy. If Hometown's payment to Good Lumber was made within three months of bankruptcy, and the effect of the payment was that Good Lumber received payment while other creditors did not, then the payment is likely a preference, and Good Lumber will have to return the payment to the trustee. Good Lumber is only entitled to the same proportion of their debt as other unsecured creditors. Similarly, the payment to George will be a preference if it was made within one year of bankruptcy, since George is not at arm's length to Hometown. Provided the salaries paid to Bill and Martha were genuine payments for services given, and were paid in the ordinary course of business, they will probably not be considered preferences. Regular payments made to trade creditors that were made in the normal course of business would also not be considered preferences.

Hometown could argue that the payment to Good Lumber was made in good faith and was therefore not a preference. If the payment was made for goods supplied to Hometown, and was made with the intention of obtaining a continued supply of lumber so Hometown could remain in business, then the payment should be allowed to stand.

Fraudulent Conveyances

In addition to the *BIA* provisions dealing with preferences and transfers at undervalue, there are provincial laws dealing with similar situations where creditors are unfairly prejudiced.

In Ontario, the *Fraudulent Conveyances Act*[14] provides that every transfer of property that is made with the intent to defeat, hinder, delay, or defraud creditors is void. This provision may be used by creditors outside of a bankruptcy situation, or may be used by a trustee in a bankruptcy situation. Whether the debtor intended to defeat, hinder, delay, or defraud creditors is highly fact specific and will depend on the circumstances of each case.

Bankruptcy Offences

For the *BIA* to be respected, it must provide penalties for those who violate its provisions. These violations are known as **bankruptcy offences**. They are criminal acts and can be committed by any of the key participants, including debtors, creditors, and trustees.

Bankruptcy offences
Criminal acts defined by the *BIA* in relation to the bankruptcy process.

The *BIA* contains an extensive list of bankruptcy offences.[15] The most common bankruptcy offences include: fraudulently transferring property before or after bankruptcy, refusing to answer questions truthfully, providing false information, hiding, falsifying, or destroying records, hiding or concealing assets, and obtaining credit through false representations.

Penalties for bankruptcy offences range from conditional discharges to fines up to $10 000 and prison terms up to three years.

Identification of Debts

Creditors find out about the bankruptcy through a notice sent by the trustee in bankruptcy. Details of the bankrupt estate are provided at the first meeting of creditors.

Each creditor must file a **proof of claim** in respect to the amount that it is owed. The trustee examines each proof of claim and either accepts or rejects the claim. The trustee rejects claims of unsecured creditors if there is inadequate evidence of the debt. The trustee rejects claims of secured creditors if the security interest is not perfected. Creditors whose claims are rejected have the option to challenge the rejection in court.

Proof of claim
A formal notice provided by the creditor to the trustee of the amount owed and the nature of the debt.

INTERNATIONAL PERSPECTIVE

International Insolvencies

Part XIII of the *Bankruptcy and Insolvency Act (BIA)* and Part IV of the *Companies' Creditors Arrangement Act (CCAA)* deal with international insolvencies. Generally, these provisions address two questions: What happens when a Canadian company in bankruptcy proceedings in Canada has assets in a foreign jurisdiction? And what happens when a foreign creditor wishes to seize assets that are located in Canada pursuant to a foreign bankruptcy proceeding? There are a number of important public interests at stake. Given the importance of international trade to the Canadian economy, it is critical that participants in both Canada and abroad feel confident that the bankruptcy laws of all countries will be respected and, in the event of a bankruptcy order by a court of competent jurisdiction, that assets will be accessible wherever they are located. Furthermore, it would be offensive if a Canadian bankrupt could shield assets from Canadian creditors by locating those assets outside of Canada. It is also important that only foreign orders that generally equate to similar provisions in Canadian law be capable of enforcement in Canada.

In 2009, the *BIA* and *CCAA* were amended to address these issues by repealing the existing provisions dealing with international insolvencies and adopting a modified version of the *UNCITRAL Model Law on Cross-Border Insolvency*. The new provisions give Canadian courts the authority and broad discretion to make orders and grant relief as the courts consider appropriate, and provide a more comprehensive framework for the coordination of cross-border insolvency proceedings in Canada.

(Continued)

---

14. RSO 1990, c F-29.
15. *Supra* note 1, Part VIII.

Generally, a foreign creditor can gain access to a debtor's assets located in Canada pursuant to a legitimate foreign court order. Furthermore, Canadian creditors can gain access to assets located outside of Canada. Note, however, that such actions are subject to international treaties. Should a Canadian bankrupt have assets in a foreign country where reciprocity does not exist, and should that same bankrupt choose to relocate to that country, Canadian creditors will likely have no chance of recovery.

Insolvencies across the Canada–U.S. border have become both common and complicated, with the huge growth in trade and the economic downturn affecting businesses in both countries. The recent amendments provide a code for the recognition of foreign insolvency proceedings, in line with international standards.

Critical Analysis: In practice, to what extent might these provisions be avoided by debtors who are determined to keep their assets from creditors?

Source: Office of the Superintendent of Bankruptcy Canada, "Summary of Legislative Changes" online:<http://www.ic.gc.ca/eic/site/bsf-osb.nsf/eng/br01782.html>.

Distribution to Creditors

Once the trustee has liquidated the assets and determined the debts of the bankrupt estate, the trustee will turn to the distribution of the proceeds to creditors. The *BIA* contains a comprehensive set of priority rules that determine the order of payment. The three broad categories of creditors are: secured, preferred, and unsecured. In addition, unpaid suppliers have a right of repossession under the *BIA* and certain government debts are deemed to be statutory trusts and thus are paid before any creditors.

Unpaid Suppliers

Unpaid suppliers are given special protection under the *BIA*. They are allowed to recover any goods shipped in the past 30 days which were not paid for, provided the debtor is bankrupt and the goods are in the same condition as when shipped.

Deemed Statutory Trusts

The federal government has passed legislation which deems property to be held in trust in regard to unremitted payroll deductions[16] and GST/HST which has been collected but not remitted.[17] These amounts are considered not to be part of the bankrupt estate and as such are payable ahead of all creditors.

Secured Creditors

Secured creditors with properly perfected security interests are entitled to take possession of their collateral and dispose of it, regardless of bankruptcy. If there is a deficiency still owed to the secured creditor, after payment of the secured creditor's expenses and application of the proceeds of sale to the debt, then the secured creditor becomes an ordinary unsecured creditor for the deficiency. A secured creditor can waive its security and elect to proceed as an unsecured creditor for the entire debt owed—this is sometimes done if the collateral is of little value or if it would require undue effort or expense to seize and dispose of the collateral.

Preferred creditors
Certain unsecured creditors who are given priority over other unsecured creditors in the bankruptcy distribution.

Preferred Creditors

Preferred creditors are paid after secured creditors and before other unsecured creditors, in strict order of priority as set out in section 136 of the *BIA*. The list of preferred creditors

---

16. *Income Tax Act*, RSC 1985, c 1, s 227(4).
17. *Excise Tax Act*, RSC 1985, c E-15, s 222(3).

reflects the legislative intent as to the creditors who should be paid first. Preferred creditors, in order of priority, include

- funeral expenses
- trustee fees and expenses, including legal fees
- arrears in wages (up to $2000 per employee for the previous six months)[18]
- municipal taxes
- arrears of rent and accelerated rent, in each case up to three months

Preferred creditors are paid in full before anything is paid to other unsecured creditors.

Unsecured Creditors

The remaining funds in the bankrupt estate, if any, are paid to the ordinary unsecured creditors in proportion to the amounts they are owed. Secured creditors with deficiencies are unsecured creditors to the extent of those deficiencies. Good Lumber and George, to the extent that the payments to them by Hometown are found to be preferences and repaid to the trustee, are unsecured creditors for those amounts (see Figure 27.2).

Employees

Employees who are owed wages are deemed to be secured creditors, with a first charge on the current assets of their employer, for up to $2000 per employee. In addition, the *Wage Earner Protection Program* allows employees to recover some unpaid wages when their employment is terminated as a result of bankruptcy or receivership. These provisions are intended to protect employees, who are particularly vulnerable in the event of business failure due to bankruptcy or insolvency.

FIGURE 27.2
Revised Statement of Assets and Liabilities for Hometown Hardware Ltd.

Assets at estimated cash value

Cash	$ 31 000*
Accounts receivable	11 000
Inventory	20 000**
Land and building	105 000
Equipment	30 000
Cash available for distribution	$197 000

Liabilities at estimated cash value

CRA payroll deductions	$ 24 000
Mortgage on land and building	97 000
Trustee's fees and expenses	4 000
Municipal property taxes	10 000
Accounts payable to suppliers	87 000
Amount owed Good Lumber	20 000
Amount owed George	10 000
Line of credit at bank	85 000***
	$337 000

*　Includes original balance ($1000) plus monies recovered from George and GL ($10 000 + $20 000).
**　Portion ($7000) of original was taken back by suppliers (reducing accounts payable from $94 000 to $87 000).
*** Since Bill Ikeda and Martha Wong have provided personal guarantees for the line of credit, they will be personally liable for any outstanding balance, after distribution.

18. This amount is secured by a first charge on the employer's current assets pursuant to s 81.3 of the *BIA*.

FIGURE 27.3

Final Distribution of Assets of Hometown Hardware Ltd. by Class of Creditor

Schedule 1: Distribution of cash to secured and preferred creditors

Opening balance available	$197 000
Pay CRA the payroll deductions	24 000
	173 000
Secured creditors	
Pay mortgage on land and building	97 000
Pay bank from inventory and accounts receivable	31 000
	$ 45 000
Preferred creditors	
Trustee's fees and expenses	$ 4 000
Pay municipal taxes	10 000
Balance available for unsecured creditors	$ 31 000

Schedule 2: Distribution of cash to unsecured creditors

Balance available for unsecured creditors	$ 31 000
Balance due to unsecured creditors:	
Accounts payable to suppliers	87 000
Amount owed George	10 000
Amount owed Good Lumber	20 000
Line of credit at bank	54 000
	$171 000

Proportion of amount to be paid per dollar of unsecured debt: $31 000/171 000 = 0.18129

Payments to unsecured creditors (rounded)	
Accounts payable to suppliers	$ 15 772
Payment to George	1 813
Payment to Good Lumber	3 626
Line of credit at bank	9 789
Total payments to unsecured creditors	$ 31 000
Balance	0

Bill Ikeda and Martha Wong personally owe the bank the unpaid balance of the line of credit since they have guaranteed the debt: ($85 000 − (31 000 + 9789) = $44 211).

In the final distribution of assets (see Figure 27.3),

- CRA is paid in full for the unremitted payroll deductions

- the bank is paid in full under its mortgage as a secured creditor

- the trustee's fees and municipal taxes are paid in full as preferred creditors

- the remaining claims of unsecured creditors are paid at the rate of $0.18129 for each dollar owed

Since Bill and Martha personally guaranteed the line of credit to the bank, they are personally liable to pay $44 211—the amount remaining on that debt—to the bank. If they cannot pay, they may have to explore their own options regarding insolvency or bankruptcy.

A discharge from bankruptcy is not available to a bankrupt corporation unless it has paid its debts in full. Hometown no longer exists as a corporation as of the date of its assignment in bankruptcy. It is the end of the road for Hometown.

Personal Bankruptcy

Personal bankruptcy is the last remaining option when an individual is unable to pay her debts and there are no alternatives to bankruptcy. People become insolvent for a wide variety of reasons, including loss of employment, medical or other expenses beyond their control, bad business investments, or poor financial planning. Personal bankruptcies differ from corporate bankruptcies in a number of important respects.

People in financial difficulty may attempt informal measures to address their financial situation, including altering their budget, consolidating their debts into a single loan with lower interest and easier payments, or negotiating directly with their creditors for lower payments or more time to pay.

Division II (consumer) proposals are available to individuals with debts (other than those secured by a principal residence) under $250 000, as discussed above. Some provinces[19] have systems for the "orderly payment of debts," which involve a consolidation of debts under the supervision of the courts.

If no other options are available, individuals may be forced into personal bankruptcy. The process of bankruptcy is the same as discussed above and involves the assets of the bankrupt being assigned to a trustee in bankruptcy who holds those assets, and ultimately disposes of them, for the benefit of creditors. Personal bankruptcy can be voluntary, with the debtor making an assignment in bankruptcy, or involuntary, as the result of an application to the court by a creditor for a bankruptcy order.

In a personal bankruptcy, a debtor is entitled to retain certain assets to support themselves and their families, along with any registered retirement savings (except deposits within one year of bankruptcy). The *BIA* provides that the property of the bankrupt transferred to the trustee excludes any property that would be exempt from seizure under provincial law. Accordingly, the property that will be exempt will vary by province. In Ontario, the *Execution Act* provides exemptions for items such as clothing up to $5650 in value, household furniture and utensils up to $11 300, tools of a trade up to $11 300, and one motor vehicle up to $5650.[20]

During the bankruptcy process, the debtor will usually be required to make payments to the trustee for the benefit of creditors. The amounts of the payments are determined by the trustee, taking into account the debtor's total income and living expenses. The bankrupt will also be examined under oath in regard to her assets and liabilities, the causes of bankruptcy, and the disposition of any property. The debtor must also attend two mandatory financial counselling sessions.

Provided the bankrupt has completed all of the steps described earlier, has not committed a bankruptcy offence, and is not required to make additional payments, a first time bankrupt will receive an automatic **discharge of bankruptcy** nine months following bankruptcy. For a second bankruptcy, automatic discharge takes place 24 months following bankruptcy. If an automatic discharge is not available for any reason, the bankrupt must apply to the court for a discharge and the court will conduct a hearing.

Discharge of bankruptcy
An order releasing the debtor from bankrupt status and from most remaining debts.

Once discharged, a bankrupt is released from most of her debts. Not all debts are released by the discharge. Fines, penalties, alimony and support payments, debts arising from fraud, and to some extent student loans[21] survive the discharge. Corporations are not discharged from bankruptcy unless they have paid their debts in full.

---

19. For example, Alberta, Saskatchewan, and Nova Scotia.
20. *Execution Act* RSO 1998, c E-24.
21. If it is less than seven years after ceasing to be a student. However, application may be made for release on the basis of hardship after five years.

Following discharge from bankruptcy, a first bankruptcy remains on a person's credit record for six years. A second bankruptcy remains on the record for 14 years and a consumer proposal remains on the record for three years.

The discharge may be opposed, by the Superintendent of Bankruptcy, the trustee, or a creditor, if a bankruptcy offence has been committed or where there is evidence of extravagance prior to the bankruptcy.

CASE

Southwick-Trask (Re), 2003 NSSC 160

THE BUSINESS CONTEXT: Personal bankruptcy of those involved in a business can follow the insolvency of that business. The individuals are eligible for discharge of the unpaid debts at the end of the process, but the discharge may be conditional. Those conditions can be a matter of dispute between the individuals, creditors, and trustee.

FACTUAL BACKGROUND: Trask (T) was president, CEO, director, and shareholder of RDI Group, a company that operated call centres in Halifax for 15 years and employed up to 150 people. Southwick-Trask (ST) was married to T. She was a director of RDI and operated her own business in strategic management consulting. In 2001, a large account receivable of RDI fell past due and had to be written off. This resulted in the insolvency of RDI. At the time, RDI owed TD Bank $525 000 on a revolving line of credit secured by accounts receivable and guaranteed by T and ST. They attempted to negotiate a settlement with the bank and presented a proposal, but the attempts were unsuccessful. The bank petitioned both T and ST into bankruptcy. At the time, their total debt was in excess of $2 million, of which $573 000 was owed to the bank. The trustee recommended they be discharged, subject to payments of $18 000 by T and $36 000 by ST. T and ST disputed the amount of these payments.

THE LEGAL QUESTION: Are T and ST eligible for discharge from bankruptcy and, if so, on what terms?

RESOLUTION: The judge found that the bankruptcies of T and ST resulted from misfortune in business. He reviewed general principles:

The act permits an honest debtor, who has been unfortunate in business, to secure a discharge so that he or she can make a fresh start and resume his or her place in the business community. The conditional discharge, that is most frequently a result of proving that the value of assets was less than half the liabilities, may also address the purpose of fair distribution. Aside from cases where the conduct of the bankrupt has been reprehensible, setting a condition for discharge requires a balance of rehabilitating the bankrupt and providing the creditors with some dividend.

The judge went on to consider specific factors—RRSPs held by the couple, transfers of their residence and cottage to a family trust, debts for income tax, T's earning capacity, ST's drawings from her business, and household expenses.

Based on the cause of the bankruptcies (misfortune in business), the significant value of assets in the estate, and the absence of any misconduct, the judge ordered that T be discharged without condition and that ST be discharged subject to the payment of $750 per month for 24 months or an equivalent lump-sum payment.

CRITICAL ANALYSIS: Does this case preserve the integrity of the bankruptcy regime? Did the court adequately balance the interests of the debtor, creditors, and the public?

Business Law in Practice Revisited

1. What options does Hometown have in dealing with this financial crisis?
Hometown can seek a voluntary negotiated settlement with creditors in order to continue the business or bring it to an end. Hometown can make a Division I proposal to creditors under the *BIA* that would allow the business to continue. As a last resort, Hometown can make an assignment in bankruptcy.

2. What rights do Hometown's creditors have?
Creditors can exert pressure on Hometown or threaten legal action in an attempt to persuade Hometown to pay. Secured creditors can seize and dispose of their collateral.

Unsecured creditors can sue Hometown and try to obtain judgment. Finally, creditors can apply to a court for a bankruptcy order against Hometown.

3. What will happen to Hometown, its owners, its creditors, Bill, and Martha if Hometown goes bankrupt?

Bankruptcy will result in the transfer of all of Hometown's assets to the trustee, including payments made which constitute preferences. The trustee will dispose of the assets and distribute the proceeds to creditors. Secured creditors will likely realize on their security, leaving only the unsecured assets to be dealt with by the trustee. Preferred creditors will be paid in full before other unsecured creditors receive any payment. Any unpaid debts that Bill and Martha have guaranteed will become their personal responsibility and may result in their personal bankruptcies. Hometown will cease to exist, but Bill and Martha may be discharged from bankruptcy if they satisfy the statutory requirements.

Chapter Summary

The *BIA* and *CCAA* govern situations where debtors become insolvent. The purposes of the legislation are to ensure that all stakeholders are treated fairly, including debtors, creditors, employees, government, and the broader community. It is, however, a very difficult task to try and reconcile all of these different interests.

Prior to bankruptcy, debtors may be able to take informal steps to address their financial situation. Creditors will usually be willing to negotiate if they believe that they will fare better through an informal process than through a formal process such as a proposal or bankruptcy.

If informal steps are not an option, an insolvent debtor can make a proposal to creditors under the *BIA*. Individuals with less than $250 000 in debt can make consumer proposals. Large companies with more than $5 000 000 in debt can reorganize under the *CCAA*. In order to be successful, the debtor will have to submit a plan of reorganization that creditors will approve.

Secured creditors are in a much better position than unsecured creditors in the event of insolvency or bankruptcy, because they can generally enforce their security regardless of bankruptcy proceedings. Secured creditors become unsecured creditors for any deficiency owed.

Bankruptcy is usually a last resort. Bankruptcy is the formal legal process by which the assets of the debtor are transferred to a trustee in bankruptcy for the benefit of creditors. Bankruptcy can be either voluntary, by the debtor, or involuntary, on an application by creditors. The *BIA* contains rules to ensure that creditors are treated fairly and that debtors conduct themselves appropriately both before and during the bankruptcy process. In a bankruptcy situation, secured creditors will usually realize on their security first, leaving only unsecured assets for the trustee to deal with. The trustee will dispose of the remaining assets and distribute the proceeds to creditors in the specific manner and order of priority set out in the *BIA*. Personal bankruptcy differs from business bankruptcy in a number of important respects, including the ability of the bankrupt to be discharged from most debts after a period of time.

Chapter Study

Key Terms and Concepts

act of bankruptcy (p. 675)

arm's length (p. 677)

assignment in bankruptcy (p. 675)

bankrupt (p. 675)

bankruptcy offences (p. 679)

bankruptcy order (p. 675)

debtor in possession (DIP) financing (p. 673)

discharge of bankruptcy (p. 683)

estate (p. 669)

insolvent (p. 670)

inspector (p. 676)

preferred creditors (p. 680)

proof of claim (p. 679)

transfers at undervalue (p. 677)

trustee in bankruptcy (p. 669)

Questions for Review

1. How can negotiated settlements be used when a business is in financial difficulty?

2. What is the difference between insolvency and bankruptcy?

3. What are the purposes of bankruptcy legislation?

4. What is the difference between an assignment in bankruptcy and a bankruptcy order?

5. What are two examples of an act of bankruptcy?

6. What is a preference?

7. Who investigates preferences and transfers at undervalue?

8. Who are preferred creditors?

9. How are preferred creditors treated differently from secured and unsecured creditors?

10. How are employees protected in the bankruptcy of their employer?

11. Under what circumstances will a bankrupt likely not be discharged automatically from bankruptcy?

12. What are the duties of the trustee in bankruptcy?

13. What debts are not released in a discharge?

14. What is the purpose of a proposal?

15. What is the difference between a Division I proposal and a consumer proposal?

16. Why might a large company prefer reorganizing under the *CCAA* rather than making a proposal under the *BIA*?

17. What happens if unsecured creditors do not vote to approve a proposal?

18. What are the differences between an individual being bankrupt and a corporation being bankrupt?

Questions for Critical Thinking

1. Business decisions made prior to bankruptcy can be challenged by the trustee if they are found to be preferences or transfers at undervalue. What is the rationale for giving the trustee this authority? How does it relate to the purposes of bankruptcy legislation?

2. Current bankruptcy law bars graduates from being discharged from their outstanding student loans for seven years after the completion of their studies or five years in cases of hardship. Why does the law deal with student loans in this way? Is it fair to treat student loans differently from other debts?

3. In late 2008, the North American auto industry was in serious financial difficulty. General Motors and Chrysler sought large bailout packages from both the American and Canadian governments. It was speculated that the ripple effects on the economy would be far reaching if these companies failed. Other commentators suggested that bankruptcy protection would be a positive step for the companies. They would be able to sharply reduce their excessive costs by negotiating deals with creditors, dealers, and the unions, and emerge in a stronger position to compete with automakers from other countries. In 2009, both companies went through an expedited process supported by government. Is bankruptcy protection an appropriate process in a potential industry failure of this magnitude?

4. Proposals are an important part of the bankruptcy and insolvency legislation. However, despite the controls that exist, they can have the effect of delaying legal actions by creditors to protect their interests. Does the

PART EIGHT

potential benefit of proposals in salvaging troubled businesses outweigh the potential losses to creditors?

5. The category of preferred creditor is not found in the bankruptcy legislation of many countries. What is the rationale for the protection afforded preferred creditors in Canadian law? Is this special treatment appropriate considering the interests of all creditors?

6. Why does the bankruptcy legislation treat individuals differently from corporations regarding a discharge from bankruptcy? Is this treatment appropriate?

Situations for Discussion

1. Before creditors can petition a debtor into bankruptcy, they must be able to show that at least one act of bankruptcy has been committed by the debtor. Review the events in the Hometown situation and identify any possible acts of bankruptcy. Do the various acts of bankruptcy have a common theme? Should it be obvious to a debtor such as Hometown that such conduct is inadvisable? When the debtor has committed an act of bankruptcy, at what point should the creditors act upon it?

2. Ontario Realty (OR) is a major property developer based in Toronto. It is in the business of building office towers and other commercial premises. In the past year, the Ontario economy has been weak and commercial properties are difficult to sell. OR now finds itself with several significant properties for which there is little chance of development until the economy recovers. OR's debts are $150 million and its assets at today's values are worth $80 million. Two banks hold security for 90 percent of the debt. The balance of the debt is unsecured. The company is unable to make regular payments on its loans.

   John, the CEO of the company, has weathered this kind of crisis before. He believes an economic recovery will begin within a year. His discussions with the two major creditors suggest that only one would be prepared to negotiate a more favourable payment scheme until the market recovers. John seeks advice from an insolvency practitioner about the pros and cons of making a proposal.

   What advice is John likely to receive? What factors will the creditors consider in responding to OR's situation? What are John's options?

3. Designer Shirts is a supplier to Classic Stores (Classic), a major national retail outlet. There are rumours that Classic is in trouble, but the company has been in trouble before and has managed to recover. Industry analysts say that there is too much at stake to allow the company to fail.

   Classic has recently announced an infusion of cash from a major investor. On the strength of this news, Designer Shirts agrees to make deliveries, although it insists on a shorter payment period than normal. Designer makes the first delivery of summer stock at the end of March. It receives its payment within the specified 20 days. It then makes a second delivery, but this time payment is not forthcoming in 20 days. Based on further promises that the payment will be made within two days, Designer makes a third shipment. Within 10 days there is an announcement that Classic has made an assignment in bankruptcy. Designer has received payment for neither the second nor the third shipment and is owed $1.5 million.

   What are Designer's options? Could Designer have better managed its risk in this situation?

4. Falcon Gypsum Ltd. is in the business of manufacturing wallboard, largely for the U.S. housing market, which has been growing for many years. In recent months, several developments have caused Falcon management to become concerned. The U.S. housing industry has slowed considerably. This has caused wallboard prices to fall sharply. In addition, the Canadian dollar has risen in relation to the U.S. dollar, making Canadian manufacturers such as Falcon less competitive in export sales. Falcon currently employs 40 workers. The company owes $32 million to 90 different creditors. The major creditors are the bank and the provincial government, who hold secured loans. Management's strategy is to attempt to wait out the current adverse conditions and hopefully return to prosperity. In order to do that, Falcon needs some breathing room from creditors and some additional bridge financing.[22] What are Falcon's options? What should Falcon do? If Falcon makes a proposal, are creditors likely to approve the proposal?

5. Kim owns a family business that is experiencing serious difficulties because of changing economic circumstances. It operates as a sole proprietorship and

---

22. Based on Bruce Erskine, "Plant shuts down for a bit", *The Chronicle Herald* (13 June 2008) at C1.

has borrowed from a number of sources (originally commercial, but lately from friends and family) over the last three years to keep the business afloat. There are three employees, without whose services Kim could no longer run the business. He is beginning to feel overwhelmed and needs some basic advice as to what he can and cannot do. For example, should he create a corporation and sell the business assets to that corporation? Should he consolidate his loans and pay off as many as he can now by extending his borrowing with the bank? If he repays his friends and family, is there any risk in doing so? What should Kim do?

6. The Great Big Bank has recently conducted a review of its small-business loan failure rates and is concerned about the results. There is strong evidence that failures are increasing disproportionately to loans made and that amounts recovered are decreasing. Interviews of local loans managers suggest a good deal of confusion about how to assess risk, when the bank should call a loan, and what mechanism best meets the bank's needs after the loan has been called. In addition, the credit market is tight and the bank's senior management has ordered that lending requirements be strengthened. Based on all of this information, the bank is redesigning its basic training manual. The primary focus now is on the section entitled "The loan has gone bad. Now what do you do?" Develop guidelines that would offer practical advice and basic information for loans officers. Identify the options and the circumstances under which each might be appropriate.

7. Gaklis was the sole director, officer and shareholder of Christy Crops Ltd. He controlled the company and

made all major decisions. The company had financial difficulty and was placed in receivership. Gaklis had guaranteed substantial debts of the company and was unable to respond to demands for payment. He was forced into bankruptcy and eventually applied for discharge. The trustee and the creditors opposed his application for a discharge based on his conduct: Gaklis had disposed of land belonging to the company. He had given a security interest for $60 000 on an airplane and transferred ownership to his father. He had failed to cooperate with the trustee by refusing to disclose particulars of bank accounts and insurance policies.[23]

Should Gaklis be discharged from bankruptcy and released from his unpaid debts? If so, on what terms?

8. Gregor Grant was the president and sole shareholder of Grant's Contracting Ltd. On application by a major creditor, an order of bankruptcy was issued against the company. In the course of investigating the company's affairs prior to bankruptcy, the trustee discovered that a cheque received in payment from a supplier had not been deposited in the company's account but had been diverted to another company owned by Gregor's brother, Harper. Harper had kept some of the money for himself and returned the remainder in smaller amounts to Gregor.[24] What, if anything, can the trustee do about this situation? What could the impact be on the two companies, the two brothers, and the customer who sent the cheque?

For more study tools, visit http://www.NELSONbrain.com.

---

23. Based on *Re Gaklis* (1984), 62 NSR (2d) 52 (SCTD).
24. Based on *Grant Bros Contracting Ltd v Grant*, 2005 NSSC 358.

PART NINE

Transference of Risk

CHAPTER 28
Insurance

Risk management is the process of establishing and maintaining procedures for identifying risks and reducing, avoiding, or retaining their consequences. Throughout the preceding chapters, the focus has been on identifying legal risks and the means for minimizing them through risk reduction strategies.

This part of the text explores the transference of risk through the use of various insurance products. It explores the general principles of a contract of insurance and discusses how insurance can protect against contractual, tortious, environmental, and other business and legal risks.

ARKADY/SHUTTERSTOCK

Insurance

Objectives

After studying this chapter, you should have an understanding of

- the role of insurance in risk management

- the nature of an insurance contract, including the rights and obligations of the insurer and the insured

- the various kinds of insurance

QMI AGENCY

Business Law in Practice

Wire Experts and Company Ltd. (WEC) is a small business owned and operated by three shareholders. It produces wires used in the manufacture of tires. It buys metal, formulates the alloys, extrudes the necessary wires, and then sells them to tire manufacturers both in Canada and abroad. The manufacture of the wire creates some contaminated waste products that require special storage and disposal. WEC's business office is on the first floor of its manufacturing plant. Suppliers, sales personnel, and representatives of various purchasers are frequent visitors. WEC also owns several trucks, which its delivery personnel use to deliver wires to customers.

As there are considerable risks associated with its business, WEC has purchased a full range of insurance products, including comprehensive general liability, automobile, property, occupier's liability, errors and omissions, directors and officers, and business interruption insurance.

In 2005, WEC moved its operations to Alberta to be closer to its customer base. WEC closed its manufacturing plant in New Brunswick and opened a new facility in Red Deer. Three months later, the vacant plant was destroyed by fire. WEC brought a claim under its fire insurance policy. The insurance company denied the claim on the basis that WEC failed to inform it that the plant was vacant. Furthermore, the insurance company alleged that the fire was suspicious and that perhaps WEC was involved in the plant's destruction.

1. Was WEC under a duty to disclose the plant's vacancy to the insurance company? If so, what is the effect of a failure to disclose?
2. What risk does the insurance company run by making allegations of arson?

Introduction

A cornerstone of an effective risk management program is insurance coverage. As discussed in Chapter 3, insurance is the primary means of transferring the risk of various kinds of losses. It permits a business to shift the risk, because through an **insurance policy**, the **insurer** promises to compensate the person or business (known as the **insured**) should the contemplated loss actually occur. The insurer provides this protection in exchange for payment, known as an insurance **premium**, from the insured (see Figure 28.1 below).

Insurance is not, however, a panacea for all risks, as insurance can be costly and is not always available (or is available only at an exorbitant cost). For example, in the wake of high-profile liability cases involving the directors of Enron and WorldCom, directors' and officers' liability insurance premiums have skyrocketed[1]; for many public companies, the premiums have tripled. For some companies, this has meant that the insurance is so expensive that it is essentially unobtainable. It is also important to remember that insurance does not prevent a loss from occurring, nor does it prevent the potential adverse publicity associated with a loss.

Insurance policy
A contract of insurance.

Insurer
A company that sells insurance coverage.

Insured
One who buys insurance coverage.

Premium
The price paid for insurance coverage.

FIGURE 28.1

The Insurance Relationship

INSURER
(provides protection against a specified loss)

INSURED
(purchases protection against a specified loss)

An insurance policy is a contract. By the terms of the contract, the parties agree to what kind of loss is covered, in what amount, under what circumstances, and at what cost. Insurance policies are also regulated by legislation in each of the provinces.

Insurance legislation serves a number of significant purposes, including the following:

- mandating the terms that must be found in insurance contracts

- regulating the insurance industry generally by setting out licensing requirements for insurance companies, insurance brokers, and insurance adjusters

- putting in place a system for monitoring insurance companies, particularly with respect to their financial operation

The main goal of insurance legislation is to protect the public from unscrupulous, financially unstable, and otherwise problematic insurance companies. It also provides working rules that create stability within the industry at large.

---

1. In 2004, directors of both WorldCom and Enron made large payments out of their own pockets to settle with shareholders. See: Janet McFarland, "The soaring cost of a boardroom safety net", *The Globe and Mail* (23 February 2006) B12.

The three basic kinds of insurance are as follows:

- *Life and disability insurance*: provides payments on the death or disability of the insured.

- *Property insurance (also known as fire insurance)*: provides payment when property of the insured is damaged or destroyed through accidents. It also can cover the costs of machine breakdown.

- *Liability insurance (also known as casualty insurance)*: provides payment in circumstances where the insured is held legally responsible for causing loss or damage to another, known as the third party.[2]

Deductible
The part of a loss for which the insured is responsible.

With the exception of life insurance contracts, insurance policies can be written so that the insured pays a **deductible**. This means that the insured is responsible for the first part of the loss, and the insurer has liability for the balance. Agreeing to a deductible generally reduces the premiums that the insured must pay for the coverage. For example, WEC agreed to a $100 deductible for windshield replacement on its delivery trucks. If a WEC vehicle windshield requires replacement and the cost is $600, WEC's insurers will pay $500. The $100 deductible is WEC's responsibility, and to that extent, WEC is self-insured.

The Insurance Contract
Duty to Disclose

Duty to disclose
The obligation of the insured to provide to the insurer all information that relates to the risk being insured.

Insurance contracts are of a special nature. They are known as contracts of utmost good faith. A key consequence is that the insured has a **duty to disclose** to the insurer all information relevant to the risk; if the insured fails in that duty, the insurer may choose not to honour the policy. For example, assume that WEC wants to change insurers in an effort to save on premiums. Max, one of WEC's employees, fills in an application for fire insurance. In response to the question, "Have you ever experienced a fire?" Max writes, "Yes—in 2001." Max does not mention that WEC also had a fire in 2000, because he is convinced that WEC will end up paying an outrageously high premium. Max has failed to disclose a fact that is germane to the insurer's decision to insure and relevant to what the premiums should be in light of the risk. For this reason, if WEC tries to claim for fire loss should another fire occur at the plant, the insurer could refuse to honour the policy based on Max's non-disclosure.

An insurance company can deny coverage for non-disclosure even if the loss has nothing to do with the matter that was left undisclosed. For example, since WEC has failed to disclose a previous fire loss, the insurer can deny a vandalism claim that WEC might make some time in the future.

The law places a duty of disclosure on the insured for a straightforward reason: the insurer has to be in a position to fully assess the risk against which the insured wants protection. The only way the insurer can properly assess risk is if the insured is candid and forthcoming. In short, the insured is usually in the best position to provide the insurer with the information needed.

---

2. The person who is injured or otherwise suffers loss is the third party in relation to the contract of insurance. In the contract of insurance, the insurer and insured are the first and second parties.

However, The duty to disclose is not all encompassing. The law expects the insurer to be "worldly wise" and to show "personal judgment."[3] For this reason, there is no onus on the insured to inform the insurer of matters "not personal to the applicant." For example, assume that in the application for fire insurance Max notes that some welding occurs on the premises, but he does not go on to observe that welding causes sparks, which, in turn, can cause a fire. This is not a failure to disclose—after all, the insurer is expected to be worldly wise. That said, the insured is much better to err on the side of disclosure, since a miscalculation on the insured's part can lead to the policy being void.

A duty to disclose exists not just at the time of applying for the insurance—it is an ongoing duty. The insurer must be notified about any change material to the risk. For example, if WEC decides to stop producing wire and turn its attention instead to manufacturing plastic cable, the insurer should be advised, in writing, of this change. In the same vein, when WEC leaves a building vacant, the insurer should be contacted so that necessary adjustments to the policy can be made.

© PATRICK BENNETT/CORBIS

When does an insured have a duty to disclose?

PART NINE

CASE | ***Marche v Halifax Insurance Co, 2005 SCC 6, [2005] 1 SCR 47***

THE BUSINESS CONTEXT: The duty of an insured to report material changes to the risk in a fire insurance policy is currently prescribed by statutory conditions in all Canadian common law provinces. This case concerns the ability of an insurance company to deny coverage on the basis of the insured's alleged breach of the statutory condition requiring an insured to report a material change.[4]

FACTUAL BACKGROUND: Theresa March and Gary Fitzgerald (the insureds) purchased a house, converted it into apartments, and insured it under a fire insurance policy issued by the Halifax Insurance Co. In September 1998, the insureds left Cape Breton Island to find work in British Columbia. The house remained vacant from September to early December, when Danny, a brother of one of the insured's, moved in. Danny fell behind in the rent

(Continued)

---

3. C Brown & J Menezes, *Insurance Law in Canada*, loose-leaf, (Scarborough: Carswell, 2008), at 5-6.1 [Brown & Menezes].
4. See also *Royal Bank of Canada v State Farm Fire and Casualty Co*, 2005 SCC 34, [2005] 1 SCR 779. This case deals with the statutory condition requiring reporting of a material change in relation to an insurance policy's standard mortgage clause.

but refused to vacate the premises. In an effort to induce Danny to move out, the insureds had the water and electrical power disconnected. On 7 February 1999, the house was destroyed by fire. At this time, Danny's possessions were still in the house.

Halifax denied liability on the grounds that the insureds had failed to notify Halifax of the vacancy between September and December 1998. The insurer alleged that this was a breach of Statutory Condition 4 of Part VII of Nova Scotia's *Insurance Act* that provides, in part, "Any change material to the risk and within the control and knowledge of the insured shall avoid the contract as to the part affected thereby, unless the change is promptly notified in writing to the insurer."

The insured argued that, if their failure to report the vacancy constituted a breach, they should be relieved from the consequences of the breach by s 171(b) of the *Insurance Act* that provides in part, "Where a contract … contains any stipulation, condition or warranty that is or may be material to the risk … the exclusion, stipulation, condition or warranty shall not be binding on the insured if it is held to be unjust or unreasonable."

THE LEGAL QUESTION: Does s 171 (b) of the Nova Scotia *Insurance Act* apply to statutory conditions? Was there a breach of Statutory Condition 4?

RESOLUTION: The Supreme Court of Canada held that s 171(b) applies to both contractual and statutory conditions. In coming

to this conclusion, the majority rejected the notion that statutory conditions by definition cannot be unnecessary or unjust. The court noted that as the purpose of s 171(b) is to provide relief from unjust or unreasonable insurance policy conditions, it should be given a broad interpretation. The word "condition" in s 171 (b) is not qualified by a restrictive adjective and further, a reading of the entire Act does not support the contention that "condition" in s.171 (b) refers only to contractual conditions. The court stated that s 171 (b) authorizes the court to not only relieve against conditions that are *prima facie* unjust but also to relieve against conditions that in their application lead to unjust or unreasonable results.

The court noted that while the insured had failed to report the vacancy, it is unclear whether the failure constituted a breach of Statutory Condition 4 as the vacancy had been rectified prior to the loss occurring. In any event, if the insureds were in breach, s 171(b) should be applied to relieve the insureds from the consequences of this breach. It would be unjust to void the insurance policy when the vacancy had been rectified prior to the loss occurring and was not causally related to the loss.

CRITICAL ANALYSIS: The court rejected the insurance company's attempt to deny coverage based on an alleged breach of Statutory Condition 4. What is the uncertainty created by the decision for insurers?

Insurable Interest

Insurable interest
A financial stake in what is being insured.

The special nature of the insurance contract also means that its validity is contingent on the insured having an **insurable interest** in the thing insured.[5] The test for whether the insured has an insurable interest is whether he benefits from its existence and would be prejudiced from its destruction.[6] The rationale behind this rule is that allowing people to insure property they have no real interest in may, for example, lead them to intentionally destroy the property in order to make an insurance claim. If WEC's bank holds a mortgage on the WEC production plant, it can purchase insurance on the plant because the bank has an insurable interest in property that is being used as security for a loan. The bank benefits from the continued existence of the plant and would be prejudiced by its destruction. Once the mortgage is paid off, the insurable interest of the bank no longer exists, and the bank cannot file a claim.

Indemnity

Indemnity
The obligation on the insurer to make good the loss.

With the exception of life insurance contracts, insurance contracts are contracts of **indemnity**. This means that the insured is not supposed to profit from the happening of the insured-against event, but at most will come out even. For example, if WEC insured its

---

5. *Supra* note 3 at 4.1. Note that the ordinary insurable interest test is typically altered by statute for life insurance. In life insurance, the statutes generally provide that certain dependants have an insurable interest in the life insured, as does anyone else who gets the written consent of the person whose life is being insured.
6. *Lucena v Craufurd* (1806), 2 Bos & Pul (NR) 269 at 301, 127 ER 630 (HL). Discussed in Brown & Menezes, *supra* note 3 at 66–67.

manufacturing plant against the risk of fire with two different insurance companies, WEC, in the event of a loss, is entitled to collect only the amount of the loss. WEC cannot collect the loss from both insurance companies. However, WEC would be entitled to select the policy under which it will claim indemnity (subject to any conditions to the contrary). The insurer, in turn, would be entitled to contribution from the other insurer on a prorated basis.

Some policies, such as fire insurance policies, require the insured to have coverage for a specified minimum portion of the value of the property in order to fully recover from the insurer in the event of a fire. This requirement takes the form of a coinsurance clause, which is intended to discourage the insured from insuring the property for less than its value on the gamble that any loss is likely to be less than total. If such a clause is in place, and the insured carries less insurance then the amount specified in the clause, the insurer will pay only a specified portion of the loss, and the insured must absorb the remainder. In essence, the insured becomes a coinsurer for the amount of the deficiency (see Figure 28.2).

FIGURE 28.2

Example of the Application of a Coinsurance Clause

Building value	$500 000
Actual insurance coverage	$300 000
Amount of loss	$100 000
Coinsurance clause	80%

$$\frac{\text{Amount of insurance coverage purchased}}{\text{Minimum required under coinsurance clause}} \times \text{Actual loss} = \text{Insurer's liability*}$$

$$\frac{\$300\,000}{(\$500\,000 \times 80\%)} \times \$100\,000 = \$75\,000 \text{ (amount the insurer must pay)}$$

*Subject to policy limits

Subrogation

The insurer also has what is called a right of **subrogation**. This right means that when an insurer compensates the insured, it has the right to sue a third party—the wrongdoer—who caused the loss and to recover from that party what it has already paid out to its insured. In this sense, the right of subrogation permits the insurer to "step into the shoes" of the insured and sue the wrongdoer. Because of the insurer's right of subrogation, WEC must act carefully in the face of a loss. For example, it should not admit liability for any accident that has occurred, since doing so might jeopardize any future action the insurer might commence against the wrongdoer. Instead, WEC should immediately contact its insurer, as well as its legal counsel, for advice on how to proceed.

In addition to the right of subrogation, the insurance company will also have the right to rebuild, repair, or replace what is damaged so as to minimize its costs. It will also have the right of salvage. If, for example, stolen goods are recovered, the insurer can sell the goods to recover its costs.

An insured is also not permitted to profit from his willful misconduct. If he deliberately causes a loss, the **forfeiture rule** will prevent him from collecting on his insurance. For example, if an insured deliberately sets fire to his business, he cannot collect on his fire insurance.

Subrogation
The right of the insurer to recover the amount paid on a claim from a third party that caused the loss.

Forfeiture rule
A rule that provides that a criminal should not be permitted to profit from a crime.

The Policy

Rider
A clause altering or adding coverage to a standard insurance policy.

Endorsement
Written evidence of a change to an existing insurance policy.

Insurance contracts are particularly technical documents. Their content is settled to some extent by legislation, which requires standard form policies for some types of insurance. Changes in standard policy terms take the form of riders and endorsements. A **rider** adds to or alters the standard coverage and is part of the policy from the outset. An **endorsement** is an alteration to the coverage at some point during the time in which the policy is in force. Policies generally contain a number of exclusion clauses that exclude coverage for certain situations, occurrences, or persons for which there would otherwise be protection. For example, the standard fire policy excludes coverage when the insured building has been left unoccupied for more than 30 consecutive days. If a loss occurs after this point, the policy does not cover it. Other common exclusions in property insurance include damage caused by wear and tear or mould, and vandalism or malicious acts caused by the insured.

DILBERT © SCOTT ADAMS. USED BY PERMISSION OF UNIVERSAL UCLICK. ALL RIGHTS RESERVED.

CASE | ***Canadian National Railway v Royal and Sun Alliance Insurance Co of Canada*, 2008 SCC 66, [2008] 3 SCR 453**

THE BUSINESS CONTEXT: Exclusions are common in insurance policies. For example, in standard property insurance policies, common exclusions include damage that arises from external sources such as pollution, arson, mould, vandalism, temperature changes, settlement, and earth movement. Property insurance policies also contain exclusions that preclude coverage from internal defects such as faulty materials, workmanship, or design. The following decision addresses the "faulty or improper design" exclusion in "all-risks" property policies. Prior to this decision, there were two competing standards for interpreting "faulty or improper design." One standard held that a design was faulty if it simply failed to work for its intended purpose. The second standard held that a design was faulty if it failed to provide for, and withstand, all foreseeable risks.

FACTUAL BACKGROUND: In the early 1990s, Canadian National Railway (CNR) undertook to build a rail tunnel under the St. Clair River from Sarnia, Ontario to Port Huron, Michigan. To do so, it commissioned the design of the world's largest tunnel boring machine (TBM). Prior to undertaking the project and in recognition of the risks inherent in developing such a machine, CNR purchased an all-risks insurance policy from Royal

and Sun Alliance Insurance Co. of Canada (Royal). The policy insured all risks of direct physical loss or damage to all real and personal property including the TBM. There was also an exclusionary provision that stated "this Policy does not insure the cost of making good faulty or improper design."

The TBM, constructed in 1993 was 10 metres in diameter, 85 metres long and designed to withstand 6000 metric tonnes of pressure from soil and water. A system of 26 independent lubricated seals prevented excavated material from getting into the main bearing. However, after two months of excavating with only 14 percent of the tunnel complete, dirt penetrated through to the bearing. During design, the engineers realized that dirt could penetrate and bypass the seals if the differential between key components was more or less than 3 mm, but were satisfied that the differential could be kept within the range. In operation, however, this was not possible and the sealing system failed. The project had to be stopped and after a delay of 229 days and a cost of more than $20 million, the boring was restarted and completed. CNR attempted to collect on its insurance policy with Royal but it denied coverage based on the clause in the policy that excluded damages caused by "faulty or improper design."

THE LEGAL QUESTION: Did the design of the TBM fall within the "faulty or improper design" exclusion in the all-risks insurance policy?

RESOLUTION: In a 4 to 3 decision, the Supreme Court of Canada adopted a narrow interpretation of the "faulty or improper design" exclusion and found in favour of CNR. Binnie J. writing for the majority stated that, "the policy did not exclude all loss attributable to 'the design' but only loss attributable to a 'faulty or improper design.'" Simply because a design fails to achieve its intended purpose is not sufficient evidence that it is a "faulty or improper design." The term "faulty or improper design" implied a comparative standard and that the appropriate standard was the state of the art. If a design met the highest standards of the day and failure occurred simply because engineering knowledge was inadequate to the task, the design is not faulty or improper. As the TBM had been designed to state of the art specifications at the time, Royal was not entitled to the benefit of the exclusion simply because the state of the art fell short of perfection and omniscience. The damages caused by the design failure were, therefore, properly covered by the insurance policy.

CRITICAL ANALYSIS: How does this decision affect policyholders who suffer a loss that the insurer attributes to a failed design?

Insurance Products

Insurance is broadly divisible into three categories—life, property, and liability. However, there are many specialized insurance policies or products available to meet the risk management needs of business. In order to secure optimal coverage, a businessperson should assess the business operation and identify the kinds of legal risks it may encounter. For example, in its business, WEC faces a number of possible kinds of liabilities and losses, including the following:

- *Injury and property damage* related to the operation of WEC's delivery trucks. If WEC's delivery personnel drive negligently, they may be involved in traffic accidents that cause injury to other people, as well as property damage to other vehicles. Additionally, such negligence may cause injury to the WEC drivers themselves and damage to WEC vehicles.

- *Personal injury* to suppliers, sales personnel, and purchasers who visit the manufacturing plant floor. Since WEC's business office is located in its manufacturing plant, many people who are not directly involved in production may visit the plant on business. Injuries—from tripping on a carpet to being burned by the extrusion process—can result. As well, WEC employees who work in the manufacturing process and elsewhere face the risk of being hurt on the job.

- *Financial loss and injury* to others caused by defective wire that WEC produced. If WEC delivers defective wires that are later incorporated into tires produced by WEC customers, those tires may fail while being used or repaired, potentially causing both physical injury and financial loss to those involved.

- *Financial loss and injury* caused by employees giving negligent advice to WEC customers concerning their wire needs. If an employee provides bad advice to WEC customers, they may end up with wire that is not appropriate for its intended use. This problem, in turn, may lead to physical injury and financial loss to WEC customers and to the ultimate consumers of the tires produced by WEC customers.

- *Injury and property damage* caused by a fire or other disaster in the manufacturing plant. If WEC experiences a fire in its plant, there can be a significant financial loss, since the building, as well as the equipment and machinery, will have to be repaired or replaced before company operations can resume.

- *Loss of profit* owing to business interruption as a result of a fire or other causes of a plant shutdown. In the event of a fire or other disaster, WEC may have to suspend business operations while it rebuilds. This loss of profit could cripple the company financially and even cause its demise.

- *Environmental damage* caused by improper storage or disposal of waste products. Environmental protection legislation in all jurisdictions prohibits businesses from discharging or spilling contaminants into the environment. Legislation may also permit the government to order the party responsible to clean up or otherwise repair the environmental damage that the contaminant caused.

  This cleanup can be costly for the company involved. As well, WEC can face civil actions by those who are injured or who suffer loss because WEC has improperly stored or disposed of its waste products. Since WEC produces fabricated metal products—a process that is likely to have significant environmental implications—it needs to pay particular attention to this kind of potentially catastrophic liability.

- *Death* of one of the shareholders in WEC. Should one of the WEC shareholders die, the others will likely want to buy out that person's shares. Financing the buyout will be a challenge for WEC.

In order to address these risks, WEC has in place the following policies.

Auto Insurance

An automobile owner is required by law to have insurance for liability arising from its ownership, use, and operation. While each jurisdiction has its own scheme in place, a common aim of these schemes is to ensure that owners are financially responsible for the liabilities that arise through use of their vehicles. Most people do not have the assets on hand to pay off a large judgment against them; insurance provides the funds to fulfill that financial responsibility, should it arise.

There are several types of auto insurance coverage. In Alberta, for example, the Standard Automobile Policy provides the insured with coverage against liability for the injury or death of someone else (third-party liability) caused by the operation of the insured vehicle. It also provides benefits to the insured for injury or death caused by an accident arising from the use or operation of the insured automobile, as well as compensation for loss or damage to the insured automobile itself. The latter is known as collision coverage.

Some people decide not to get collision coverage because the car itself is not worth very much. Third-party liability insurance, however, is not an option, and its purchase is required by law. Since a car accident causing paraplegia, for example, can result in millions of dollars of damages, owners should not be content with purchasing the minimum amount required by law. The minimum amount is simply not enough to cover a catastrophic accident. If there is a deficiency between the amount of insurance coverage and the actual damages sustained by the plaintiff, the insured will be personally responsible for the difference.

Each province specifies through legislation the minimum amount of coverage an owner must obtain for third-party liability. In Ontario, for example, the statutory minimum is $200 000.[7] Since this amount is insufficient to pay damages to another who has been seriously injured, the owner should purchase additional coverage.

GEOSTOCK/PHOTODISC

What are the advantages and disadvantages of no-fault automobile insurance systems?

BUSINESS APPLICATION OF THE LAW

No-Fault Insurance Systems

Automobile insurance systems vary significantly from province to province. A major distinguishing feature is the extent to which they rely on either a tort-based liability system or a "no-fault" system for compensating claims for bodily injury or death. A no-fault system involves the diminution of the ability to sue a tort-feasor for compensation. In this system, the emphasis is on providing accident benefits without regard to the victim's fault. This is a marked departure from the traditional tort system with its emphasis on fault-based liability.

Quebec was the first Canadian jurisdiction to adopt a no-fault system. Automobile accident victims have lost the right to sue in return for a form of income replacement benefit, medical and funeral expenses, and a modest award for pain and suffering depending on the extent of the injury. Manitoba has adopted no-fault legislation similar to Quebec's. Manitoba has eliminated all tort actions for bodily injury or death resulting from automobile accidents. Victims are restricted to recovery of no-fault benefits provided by a universal bodily injury compensation scheme. Saskatchewan consumers can choose between no-fault (or tort-restricted) auto insurance and a tort option. The tort option provides reduced accident benefits, but claimants can sue to recover general damages for their non-economic losses. The no-fault option eliminates the right to sue to recover damages for pain and suffering.

Ontario has adopted a threshold no-fault scheme. Under this scheme, a person who is injured in an automobile accident is entitled to statutory accident benefits (e.g., income replacement, medical benefits, rehabilitation benefits, attendant care benefits, death and funeral benefits), regardless of

(Continued)

PART NINE

---

7. *Insurance Act*, RSO 1990, c I-8, s 251(1) provides: "Every contract evidenced by a motor vehicle liability policy insures, in respect of any one accident, to the limit of at least $200,000 exclusive of interest and costs, against liability resulting from bodily injury to or the death of one or more persons and loss of or damage to property."

fault. In order to make a claim for general damages caused by another, however, the injured person must have sustained injuries in excess of the threshold, which is defined as death, permanent serious disfigurement, permanent serious physical impairment, or impairment of important psychological and mental functions. If an accident victim is entitled to receive general damages, then a $30 000 deductible will be applied unless the general damages awarded are $100 000 or more. Also, an injured person may sue for economic losses, such as lost wages and medical expenses, and no threshold is applied to such a claim.

In the other provinces and territories, the automobile insurance systems are based on the tort-liability model. In Newfoundland, because accident benefits under automobile policies are optional, some accident victims have no choice but to rely on tort law for recovery of their bodily injury or death claims. New Brunswick and British Columbia have undergone significant reforms to their tort-based models that have enhanced the level of accident benefits that claimants are entitled to receive. Also, in New Brunswick, Nova Scotia, Prince Edward Island, and Alberta, legislation has been passed to cap awards for pain and suffering related to minor injuries (usually defined as a strain, sprain, or whiplash injury that leaves no long term impairment or pain). The cap in Nova Scotia is $7500,[8] and it is $2500 in New Brunswick and Prince Edward Island, and approximately $4500 in Alberta.[9] The caps have been unsuccessfully challenged on constitutional grounds in both Nova Scotia[10] and Alberta[11] and the Supreme Court of Canada has refused to hear an appeal in both the cases.[12]

Critical Analysis: What is the purpose of "pain and suffering" caps for minor injuries? Do you see any problems with imposing caps? What is the likely effect on the insurance industry if the caps are removed?

Sources: C Brown et al, *Insurance Law in Canada*, vol 2 loose-leaf, (Scarborough, ON: Carswell, 2005), at 17 1(i)–17 2(a); Donna Ford, "Commentary: Has Ontario's no-fault system lost its way?", *The Lawyers Weekly* (12 January 2007) 7; and Dean Jobb, "Nova Scotia triples auto insurance cap", *The Lawyers Weekly* (25 June 2010) 9.

Employees injured in car accidents on the job may have coverage through workers' compensation legislation. Under such legislation, which is in place in every Canadian province, participating employers pay premiums into a fund administered by a tribunal. Employees who are injured in the workplace or who, for example, suffer from a disease as a result of exposure to a pollutant in the workplace, can then make a claim for benefits from this fund. When an employer participates in a workers' compensation board (WCB) plan, payment from the fund is usually the only compensation the employee is entitled to receive. The legislation makes participation mandatory for most industries and business activities[13] and prevents employees from suing the employer for losses that occur in the course of employment.

Occupiers' Liability Insurance

WEC, as a building owner and occupier, is liable for injuries suffered to people on its premises if the injuries are due to WEC's failure to ensure that the premises are safe. WEC's occupiers' liability insurance will compensate the injured person on behalf of WEC if unsafe conditions, such as improperly installed carpet, uneven walkways, wet floors, or the like, caused the injury. Although WEC has a program in place to prevent such accidents, the insurance will fill the gap when and if the system fails.

Comprehensive General Liability Insurance

The purpose of comprehensive general liability insurance (also known as CGL insurance) is to compensate enterprises like WEC, in a comprehensive way, for any liabilities they incur

---

8. The cap was raised to $7500 from $2500 in 2009.
9. The caps in both Alberta and Nova Scotia are indexed to inflation and in New Brunswick, the provincial government has recommended an increase to $7500.
10. *Hartling v Nova Scotia* (*Attorney General*), 2009 NSCA 130, 286 NSR (2d) 219, leave to appeal ref'd 2010 CanLII 28780 (SCC)
11. *Morrow v Zhang*, 2009 ABCA 215, 454 AR 221, leave to appeal ref'd 2009 CanLII 71477 (SCC)
12. 2010 CanLII 28780 (SCC); 2009 CanLII 71477 (SCC).
13. Participation is non-mandatory for some businesses. For example, in Ontario participation is optional for law offices, insurance companies, and call offices.

during the course of their business. For example, an important general risk faced by WEC is that its wires may fail in use and lead to some kind of loss. WEC's CGL insurance will respond by compensating WEC for property damages, personal injury, loss of profit, and related losses suffered by a third party when WEC is legally responsible for such losses.[14]

The CGL does not respond, however, to losses directly suffered by WEC itself. For this latter type of loss, WEC would need warranty insurance. The following examples reveal the important difference between these two kinds of insurance:

Example 1   WEC produces wire that is seriously defective. When the customer incorporates that wire into its tire-manufacturing process, the tires fail and must be discarded. The customer loses about $50 000 in materials, time, and profit—all of which is attributable to WEC's defective product. WEC's CGL insurance policy will cover this loss.

Example 2   WEC produces wire that the customer notices is defective as soon as WEC attempts to deliver the shipment. Accordingly, the customer refuses to accept delivery, and WEC loses $50 000 in revenue. CGL insurance does not cover this loss because it is not a loss sustained by a WEC customer or other third party—it is a loss suffered directly by WEC itself. For coverage in this situation, WEC would need a warranty policy. Since its cost is so high, WEC has not purchased warranty insurance. From a business perspective, WEC has determined that it is better off establishing an effective quality assurance and testing program, thereby dealing with such risks in-house rather than looking to an insurance company for coverage.

Errors and Omissions Insurance

When WEC's engineers provide professional engineering advice to WEC customers, they are promising that they meet the standard of the reasonably competent person engaged in such activity. Although this implied promise does not amount to a guarantee of perfection, they will be responsible for losses resulting from negligent advice. Through errors and omissions insurance (also known as E&O insurance),[15] the insurer promises to pay on the engineers' behalf all the sums they are legally obligated to pay as damages resulting from the performance of their professional services. Investigation costs and legal expenses will also usually be covered by the policy. However, there may be limits. For example, the policy may only cover defence costs for actions brought in Canada.[16] Like all insurance policies, the engineers' coverage is subject to a number of conditions, such as the requirement that they give immediate notice to the insurer of a claim or potential claim. This notice allows the insurance company to carry out an investigation and otherwise gather facts associated with the alleged negligence. Failure to give prompt notice or to comply with any other condition can result in the insurance company successfully denying coverage.

Corporate directors and officers also face liability for their errors and omissions related to operating their company. This risk can be insured against through directors and officers (D&O) liability insurance described below.

---

14. Note that coverage generally extends only to unintentional torts, rather than intentional acts.
15. See Scott J Hammel, "Insurance Pitfalls: Your errors and omission coverage may surprise you", *Canadian Consulting Engineer* (December 2004) online: Canadian Consulting Engineer <http://www.canadianconsultingengineer.com/news/insurance-pitfalls/1000191738/>.
16. *Ibid.*

BUSINESS APPLICATION OF THE LAW

Directors and Officers (D&O) Liability Insurance: The Basics

The U.S. Securities and Exchange Commission, the Ontario Securities Commission, and Nortel Networks are suing Frank Dunn, the former chief executive officer of Nortel, and Douglas Beatty, Nortel's former chief financial officer. It is alleged that Dunn and Beatty, along with other former executives, engaged in accounting fraud from 2000 to 2004 at Toronto-based Nortel, which at the time was North America's biggest maker of telephone equipment. In 2004, Nortel was required to restate its earnings going back to 1999 after investigations by regulators indicated that executives had incorrectly booked revenue, thereby inflating sales figures by 3.4 billion. Nortel fired Dunn, Beatty, and other executives.

Chubb Insurance Company, Nortel's provider of directors and officers (D&O) liability insurance, refused to pay the full defence costs of Dunn and Beatty, claiming some of their alleged wrongful conduct occurred after the policy had lapsed. Dunn and Beatty sued Chubb. The Ontario Court of Appeal,[17] applying a special endorsement in one of the insurance policies, ordered Chubb to pay 90 percent of the defence costs up to the policy limits. Although Dunn and Beatty have been successful in having most of their legal costs covered by D&O liability insurance, this situation raises questions about the protection offered by this insurance and the basis upon which an insurer can deny coverage.

Purpose: D&O liability insurance provides protection over and above indemnification by the corporation. Indemnification by the corporation does not provide complete protection, as the corporation may become insolvent or have insufficient funds to pay losses and expenses; or the board, in cases where indemnification is discretionary, may refuse to indemnify the officers and directors; or the claim, as a matter of law, may not be indemnifiable. For example, indemnification for a derivative action must be approved by the court, and, when approval is obtained, typically only defence costs are indemnified.

For these reasons, D&O liability insurance is needed to fill the gap between liabilities imposed on directors and officers and indemnification by the corporation.

Basic Features: Generally, there are three types of D&O coverage available:

- Side A coverage, which provides coverage for individual directors and officers against specified losses and where indemnification is not provided
- Side B coverage, which reimburses the corporation for amounts paid to indemnify directors and officers

INGRID BULMER/HALIFAX CHRONICLE-HERALD/THE CANADIAN PRESS

Frank Dunn

- Side C coverage, which extends coverage to include the corporation's liability with respect to securities claims

These three types of coverage are usually obtained from the same insurer under the same policy.

The insurance policy is generally sold for one-year period on a "claims made," rather than a "claims incurred" basis. This means that only those claims that are made during the term of the policy are insured, regardless of when the events giving rise to the claims occurred. Thus, if a policy is in force in year one and a claim is made in year two with regard to the directors' and officers' activities in year one, the year one insurance policy would not be responsible.

Potential Problems: Despite the presence of D&O liability insurance, directors and officers may end up having to make payments out of their own pockets. Such an occurrence may be due to coverage limits being exhausted or coverage being excluded for a number of reasons:

- *Rescission.* A policy may be rescinded by the insurer on the basis of a misrepresentation in the policy application. Where the same policy of insurance is provided to both the directors and officers and the corporation, the directors and officers run the risk that the policy will be rescinded against all insureds, even those that did not participate in the misstatement. This problem can be addressed by a well-drafted severability clause.

---

17. *Dunn v Chubb Insurance*, 2011 ONCA 36, 105 OR (3d) 63.

• *Cancellation*. Insurers and insureds generally have the right to cancel the policy of insurance during the term of the policy by giving notice. This possibility makes directors and officers vulnerable, and it is particularly problematic for directors and officers who have left the board or the corporation. D&O liability insurance is on a "claims made" basis, which means that after the currency of this year's policy, claims made in the future are only insured if insurance is in place. If the corporation does not maintain insurance, retired directors and officers may be without protection. The problem of insurers cancelling a policy can be solved by negotiating a non-cancellation clause. The retired-directors-and-officers problem can be addressed by directors and officers negotiating with the corporation to maintain coverage for a particular period of time.

• *Exclusions*. The insurance policy may exclude coverage either because the matter is insured elsewhere, because the matter is uninsurable by law, or because the matter is outside the intent of the policy. The most common example of this last category is the "insured versus insured" exclusion. This exclusion excludes coverage when one insured makes a claim against another insured—for example, when the corporation makes a claim against the directors.

• *Exhausting coverage*. The policy limits in the coverage provided to both the corporation and the directors and officers may be exhausted by the corporation before the directors' and officers' claims are covered. This problem may be addressed by directors and officers obtaining separate coverage or obtaining a further layer of insurance coverage that is not shared with the corporation.

D&O liability insurance is an important aspect of a corporation's risk management plan. It can respond where an indemnity cannot, and it can provide benefits where the corporation is obligated to indemnify the directors and officers. D&O policies are complex documents and, without proper care, directors and officers may end up with inadequate protection.

Critical Analysis: How much D&O liability insurance is appropriate? What internal and external factors should be considered in making this decision?

Sources: Jacquie McNish & Catherine McLean, "Executives left to foot their own legal bills", *The Globe and Mail* (28 November 2007) B16; Joe Schneider, "Ex-Nortel CEO Dunn seeks payments for legal expenses from Chubb", *Bloomberg* (21 January 2008) online: Bloomberg <http://www.bloomberg.com/apps/news?pid=newsarchive&sid=aTfNpxBawUWM>; Barry Reiter & Aaron Ames, "Protecting Yourself Using Directors' and Officers' Insurance: Part 1", *Lexpert* (May 2006) 98; Barry Reiter & Aaron Ames, "Protecting Yourself Using Directors' and Officers' Insurance: Part 2", *Lexpert* (June 2006) 104; "D&O: An Overview for Public Companies", *Marsh Canada FINPRO* (18 March 2008) 1; and Christina Medland, Tara Sastri & Stacey Parker-Yull, "Executive Compensation", *Lexpert/CCCA Corporate Counsel Directory and Yearbook*, 7th ed (Thomson: 2008/2009), online: Mondaq <http://www.mondaq.com/canada/article.asp?articleid=66234>.

Property Insurance

WEC has insured its manufacturing plant and equipment in order to fund any rebuilding or replacement that a fire or other disaster might occasion. One of the key choices WEC made was whether to insure for the replacement value of its property or for the property's actual cash value.

If WEC had chosen the second option, it would receive from the insurance company only the value of the property at the time it was destroyed; that is, not enough to purchase a replacement. WEC chose the first option; therefore, it will receive a higher level of compensation from the insurer—and also pay a higher premium—but the insurer has the right to require WEC to actually rebuild or otherwise replace its property before it will pay out on the claim. WEC also chose coverage for a number of losses, including loss caused by fire, falling aircraft, earthquake, hail, water damage, malicious damage, smoke damage, and impact by vehicles. Not surprisingly, the more perils WEC insures against, the higher the premiums it must pay.

Business Interruption Loss Insurance

This kind of coverage—often contained in what is called an "all-risk" policy—provides WEC with financial compensation should it have to temporarily shutdown because of a fire or other insured peril. There are two basic forms of business interruption insurance: earnings and profits. The earnings form provides compensation to a business for loss of earnings from the time of a loss until it reopens for business to the extent of the limits of the policy. The profits model provides compensation from the date of the loss to the time the business returns to normal profitability, or until the indemnity period (usually 12 months) expires.

Environmental Impairment Insurance

Not only may WEC face substantial fines for failing to comply with environmental protection legislation and for any cleanup costs associated with a spill or other accident, it can also be sued by its neighbours for polluting the soil or ground water. Furthermore, if a subsequent owner of WEC's plant can trace pollutants back to WEC, it has civil liability for the cleanup and other associated costs, even though it no longer owns the land.

The extensive nature of this type of liability explains why comprehensive general liability insurance policies usually contain pollution exclusion clauses[18] and why environmental impairment liability policies are very expensive. A more viable—though not foolproof—alternative is for WEC to ensure that it has an operational management policy in place to prevent environmental accidents from happening in the first place.[19]

ENVIRONMENTAL PERSPECTIVE

The Pollution Exclusion in Commercial General Liability Policies

The cost of environmental cleanup can be enormous. Beginning in the 1970s, in an attempt to limit its exposure, the insurance industry started including a pollution exclusion clause in commercial general liability (CGL) policies. The wording of these clauses has changed considerably in response to court decisions that tended to limit their effect. By the mid-1980s, the "absolute pollution exclusion" became the standard used in most CLG policies. The clause is very broad and attempts to exclude from coverage all losses arising out of the discharge or escape of pollutants into the environment.

Interpreting the Pollution Exclusion: The effect and scope of absolute pollution exclusion clauses has also been the subject of much litigation. In *Zurich Insurance Co v 686234 Ontario Ltd*,[20] the Ontario Court of Appeal concluded that the exclusion clause did not apply to the escape of carbon monoxide from a negligently installed furnace in a high-rise apartment building. In reaching its decision, the court emphasized that insurance coverage should be interpreted broadly in favour of the insured and exclusion clauses strictly and narrowly construed against the insurer.

More recently, in *ING Insurance Company of Canada v Miracle (Mohawk Imperial Sales and Mohawk Liquidate)*,[21] the Ontario Court of Appeal appears to have taken a more

RAY FAHEY/CAPE BRETON POST/THE CANADIAN PRESS

Cleanup of Sydney tar sands is estimated to be $400 million.

expansive approach to pollution exclusion clauses. The court held that a pollution exclusion clause applied to a liability claim for the escape of gasoline from a service station.

Reconciling the Decisions: In *Zurich*, the Court found that although carbon monoxide was a pollutant within the meaning of the exclusion, the history of exclusion clauses shows that their purpose was to bar coverage for damages arising from environmental pollution, not damages where faulty equipment caused pollution. The pollution exclusion clause was meant to apply only to an insured whose regular business activities placed it in the category of an active industrial polluter of the

---

18. Jonathan LS Hodes, "Pollution Exclusion Clauses in the CGL Policy", *Clark Wilson LLP* (February, 2009), online: Clark Wilson LLP <http://www.cwilson.com/publications/insurance/pollution-exclusion-clauses.pdf>.
19. See Chapter 3.
20. (2002), 62 OR (3d) 447, 222 DLR (4th) 655 (Ont CA).
21. 2011 ONCA 321, 105 OR (3d) 241.

natural environment. It was not intended to apply to a case where faulty equipment caused the pollution. Therefore, an improperly operating furnace that produced carbon monoxide in a residential building fell outside of the exclusion.

In *Miracle*, the court noted that the insured was engaged in an activity that carries an obvious and well-known risk of pollution and environmental damage. The business of the insured, the running of a gas station, and the storing of gasoline in the ground for resale at the gas bar, was precisely the kind of activity that the exclusion was intended to address. The court stated that the phrase "active industrial polluter of the natural environment" should not be read to restrict the pollution exclusion clauses to situations where the insured is engaged in an activity that necessarily results in pollution. The exclusion was found to apply to activities that carry a known risk of pollution and environmental harm such as storing gasoline in the ground for resale.

The Ontario Court of Appeal's decision in *Miracle* appears to have clarified the scope of its decision in *Zurich*. An exclusion clause's actual wording and its historical roots are important factors determining its effect and scope. However, an exclusion clause's application is also dependent on the nature of the business and the actual business activities of the insured.

Critical Analysis: Does giving effect to the pollution exclusion clause virtually nullify the insured's coverage? What are public policy considerations in upholding absolute pollution clauses?

Sources: Douglas McInnis & Aleksandra Zivanovic, "Clarifying pollution exclusions in commercial insurance policies", *The Lawyer's Weekly* (19 August 2011), online: *McCague Borlack LLP* <http://www.mccagueborlack.com/emails/articles/pollution_exclusions.html>; Daniel Kirby, John MacDonald & Dave Mollica, "Ontario Court of Appeal clarifies application of pollution exclusion clauses in commercial general liability policies", (5 July 2011) online: Mondaq <http://www.mondaq.com/canada/x/137682/Insurance/Ontario+Court+Of+Appeal+Clarifies+Application+Of+Pollution+Exclusion+Clauses+In+Commercial+General+Liability+Policies>.

Key-Person Life Insurance

The partners in a firm or the shareholders of a small corporation likely wish their business to continue to be operated by the surviving owners if one of them dies. Their partnership agreement or shareholders' agreement will specify that the surviving owners have the right to buy the shares of the deceased owner. The effective exercise of that right requires a means of valuing the business and the shares of the deceased, as well as a means of financing the purchase of the shares by the survivors. Insurance on the lives of the owners is a means of financing the buyout. The owners need to agree on a method of evaluating the business when the insurance is purchased and at the time of death. They must then agree on how much insurance to purchase on the life of each key person. Key factors in this decision are the age of the key people, the extent of their ownership, and the payment method each prefers for their survivors.

The amount of life insurance purchased by the business for each key person will depend on the affordability of the premium, which will be higher for older owners. Because of their age or medical condition, key people may find that insurance is unobtainable. The owners must also decide whether to purchase enough coverage to provide a lump sum large enough to buy the shares of the deceased outright, or whether the insurance should provide a portion of the buyout price, with the remainder paid to the heirs by the business over a period of time.

Since WEC is owned by three shareholders, it would be prudent for there to be life insurance policies on each one of them. However, as this proved to be uneconomic for some of the shareholders, an agreement between them addresses how the deceased's shares will be purchased.

It may also be prudent for the main stakeholders in WEC to secure disability insurance, so that if one of them is unable to work—owing to serious illness, for example—insurance will fund at least part of that person's salary or other remuneration.

Remedies of the Insured
Against the Broker

It was crucial for WEC to establish a solid working relationship with an insurance broker[22] in order to secure proper advice as to what kind of insurance it required. The term "insurance broker" refers to the middle person between the insurance companies and the insured. As the party who sought insurance, WEC needed the assistance of the broker in reviewing its business operations, assessing the risks it faces, and understanding the coverages available and the policy costs. If WEC did not spend sufficient time with the broker or if it chose a broker who was simply not up to the job, WEC may have ended up with the wrong coverage—or not enough coverage—and face a loss against which it has not been properly insured.

Should WEC face such a situation, it may have an action against its broker for negligence. If WEC is successful in its action, the broker will be required to reimburse WEC for any of its underinsured or uninsured losses or liabilities.

The term "insurance agent" usually refers to someone who acts on behalf of an insurer to sell insurance. An agent acting in that capacity is primarily obligated to the insurer as principal, and not to the third-party insured.

TECHNOLOGY AND THE LAW

Social Networking Sites and Insurance

Nathalie Blanchard, a 29-year-old from Granby, Quebec, believes she lost her disability benefits because of pictures on her Facebook page. In 2008, Blanchard took a medical leave for depression from her job as an IBM technician. Shortly thereafter, she began receiving monthly disability benefits from her insurer, Manulife Financial Corp. A year later, and without warning, the payments ceased. When Blanchard called Manulife to find out why her benefits were discontinued, she says she was told that her Facebook photos showed she was able to work. Investigators had discovered several pictures Blanchard posted on Facebook, including ones showing her drinking at a Chippendales bar show, at her birthday party, and frolicking on the beach during a sun holiday. Blanchard is suing to have her benefits reinstated. Manulife would not comment on Blanchard's case but confirmed that it uses the popular social networking site to investigate clients. It also stated to CBC news: "We would not deny or terminate a valid claim solely based on information published on websites such as Facebook."

Critical Analysis: Do insurers' use of social networks to check on people impinge on privacy rights? Should insurance companies be able to use information culled from sites such as Facebook to deny or terminate an insurance claim or to investigate fraud?

How may social networking activities affect a person's insurance?

BLANCHE/SHUTTERSTOCK

Sources: "Depressed woman loses benefits over Facebook photos", *CBC News* (21 November 2009) online: CBC News <http://www.cbc.ca/news/canada/montreal/story/2009/11/19/quebec-facebook-sick-leave-benefits.html>; Jeff Gray, "Facebook pokes the limits of personal-injury law", *The Globe and Mail* (3 March 2010) B9.

---

22. See Chapter 13 for further discussion of insurance brokers and insurance agents.

Against the Insurance Company

When an insured makes a claim under its policy, an **insurance adjuster** will likely investigate the events and evaluate the loss. On the adjuster's advice, the insurer will offer to settle the claim. There may be disagreements between the insured and the insurer as to the nature or amount of coverage. Should they be unable to resolve these differences, the insured may have to sue the insurer for breach of contract. The claim will be that the insurer has failed to honour its obligations under the policy.

Insurance adjuster
One who investigates and evaluates insurance claims.

In addition to the obligations specified in the insurance policy, an insurer owes the insured a duty of good faith, including a duty to deal with an insured's claim in good faith. Factors considered in determining whether an insurer has fulfilled its obligation to act in good faith include whether the insurer carried out an adequate investigation of a claim, whether the insurer properly evaluated the claim, whether the insurer fairly interpreted the policy, and whether the insurer handled and paid the claim in a timely manner.[23] When the duty of good faith has been breached, the court may award punitive damages, as was done in *Whiten v Pilot Insurance Co* discussed below.

CASE | ## *Whiten v Pilot Insurance Co*, 2002 SCC 18, [2002] 1 SCR 595

THE BUSINESS CONTEXT: An insurer's bad-faith conduct—alleging fraud when none exists or refusing to pay out under a policy, for example—can have a devastating effect on the insured. This kind of reprehensible conduct by the insurer can be addressed by an award of punitive damages. Prior to this decision, the highest punitive damage award handed down by a Canadian court against an insurance company had been $15 000.

FACTUAL BACKGROUND: In January 1994, the Whitens' family home burned down in the middle of the night, destroying all their possessions and three family cats. Knowing that the family was in poor financial shape, the insurer, Pilot Insurance, made a single $5000 payment for living expenses and covered the rent on a cottage for a couple of months. Pilot then cut off the rent without telling the family, and thereafter it pursued a confrontational policy that ultimately led to a protracted trial. Pilot maintained that the Whitens had burned down the house, even though it had opinions from its adjuster, its expert engineer, an investigative agency retained by it, and the fire chief that the fire was accidental. After receiving a strong recommendation from its adjuster that the claim be paid, Pilot replaced the adjuster. Counsel for Pilot pressured its experts to provide opinions supporting an arson defence, deliberately withheld relevant information from the experts, and provided them with misleading information to obtain opinions favourable to an arson theory.

Pilot's position was wholly discredited at trial. The jury awarded compensatory damages and $1 million in punitive damages. The majority of the Court of Appeal allowed the appeal in part and reduced the punitive damages award to $100 000.

THE LEGAL QUESTION: Should the jury's punitive damages award be restored?

RESOLUTION: The court held that, although the jury's award of punitive damages was high, it was reasonable. Pilot's conduct had been exceptionally reprehensible. Its actions, which continued for over two years, were designed to force the Whitens to make an unfair settlement for less than what they were entitled to receive. The jury believed that Pilot knew its allegations of arson were not sustainable and yet it persisted. Insurance contracts are purchased for peace of mind. The more devastating the loss, the more the insured is at the financial mercy of the insurer, and the more difficult it may be to challenge a wrongful refusal to pay.

The jury decided that a strong message of denunciation, retribution, and deterrence needed to be sent to Pilot. The obligation of good-faith dealing requires that the insurer must respect the insured's vulnerability and reliance on the insurer. It was this relationship that was outrageously exploited by Pilot.

An award of punitive damages in a contract case is permissible if there is a separate actionable wrong. In addition to the contractual requirement to pay the claim, Pilot was under an

(Continued)

---

23. *Adams v Confederation Life Insurance*, 152 AR 121, [1994] 6 WWR 662 (Alta QB).

PART NINE

obligation to deal with the insured in good faith. The breach of this separate obligation supports a claim for the punitive damages. The award of $1 million in punitive damages was more than the court would have awarded but was still within the high end of the range where juries are free to make their assessment.

CRITICAL ANALYSIS: The Insurance Council of Canada was an intervenor at the Supreme Court. It submitted that there should be a judicially imposed cap of $25 000 on punitive damages awards. What are the arguments for such a cap? What are the arguments against such a cap?

Since *Whiten*, it is invariably the case that litigation against an insurer will include allegations of bad faith and a claim for punitive damages. Appellate courts, however, following the Supreme Court of Canada decision in *Fidler v Sun Life Assurance Company of Canada*,[24] have exercised restraint and have only awarded punitive damages in exceptional cases. In Fidler, the court stated that the duty of good faith requires an insurer to deal with the insured's claim fairly in both the manner of investigating and the decision whether to pay. An insurer must not deny coverage or delay payment in order to take advantage of an insured's economic vulnerability or to gain bargaining leverage in negotiating a settlement. However, a finding of lack of good faith does not lead inexorably to an award of punitive damages. While a lack of good faith is a precondition, a court will only award punitive damages if there has been malicious, oppressive, or high-handed misconduct that offends the court's sense of decency.

Business Law in Practice Revisited

1. Was WEC under a duty to disclose the plant's vacancy to the insurance company? If so, what is the effect of a failure to disclose?

A contract of insurance is a contract of good faith. This means that the insured has a duty to disclose all material facts to the insurer concerning the subject matter to be insured. Good faith on the part of the applicant is necessary for insurance firms to effectively assess risks and set premiums. The duty to disclose not only arises at the time of applying for insurance but also is a continuing obligation of disclosure. Leaving a building vacant for a period of time, particularly in excess of 30 days, would constitute a breach of the obligation to disclose. The effect of the breach would make the insurance contract null and void with respect to the loss suffered by WEC. In addition, it is probable that WEC's insurance policy contains a clause excluding coverage when the insured building has been left vacant for more than 30 consecutive days.

2. What risk does the insurance company run by making allegations of arson?

The insurer has a duty to deal with an insured's claim in good faith. An insurer's duty to act in good faith developed as a counterweight to the immense power that an insurer has over the insured during the claims process. An insurer may be in breach of its duty of good faith if, for example, it does not properly investigate a claim, does not properly evaluate the claim, and does not handle the claim in a timely manner. Making unfounded allegations of fraud and arson is a breach of the duty of good faith and could result in an award of punitive damages if the dispute between WEC and the insurer ends up in litigation.

---

24. 2006 SCC 30, [2006] 2 SCR 3.

Chapter Summary

Insurance is one of the simplest and most cost-effective ways of managing risk in a business environment. It permits the business to shift such risks as fire, automobile accidents, and liability for defective products onto an insurance company in exchange for the payment of premiums by the business.

An insurance contract is a contract of utmost good faith. This means that the insured must make full disclosure at the time of applying for insurance, as well as during the life of the policy. Failure to do so may permit the insurer to deny coverage when a loss has occurred.

The insured must have an insurable interest in the item insured to prevent moral hazards. The test for insurable interest is whether the insured benefits from the existence of the thing insured and would be prejudiced from its destruction.

Insurance contracts are not intended to improve the position of the insured should the loss occur. Rather, they are contracts of indemnity and are intended to compensate the insured only up to the amount of the loss suffered.

When the insurer pays out under an insurance policy, it has the right of subrogation. This right permits the insurer to sue the wrongdoer as if it were the party that had been directly injured or otherwise sustained the loss.

A business needs to communicate effectively with its insurance broker, as well as its insurance company, in order to assess the kinds of risks its operation faces and the types of insurance coverage that can be purchased to address those risks. Though insurance policies can take a variety of forms, there are three basic kinds: life and disability insurance, property insurance, and liability insurance. More specific insurance policies are simply a variation on one of these types.

Insurance policies are technically worded and often contain exclusion clauses. These clauses identify circumstances or events for which coverage is denied. They may also identify people for whom coverage is denied.

If the insured ends up with insurance of the wrong type or in an inadequate amount, it may have an action against its broker for breach of contract and/or negligence. If the insurance company wrongly refuses to honour the policy, the insured may have to sue the insurer to obtain compensation for its losses.

Chapter Study

Key Terms and Concepts

deductible (p. 692)

duty to disclose (p. 692)

endorsement (p. 696)

forfeiture rule (p. 695)

indemnity (p. 694)

insurable interest (p. 694)

insurance adjuster (p. 707)

insurance policy (p. 691)

insured (p. 691)

insurer (p. 691)

premium (p. 691)

rider (p. 696)

subrogation (p. 695)

Questions for Review

1. What is the purpose of an insurance contract?

2. What is a premium?

3. Every province has enacted insurance legislation. What are the purposes of insurance legislation?

4. What are the three main types of insurance?

5. What is a deductible? What effect does it have on insurance premiums?

6. What does it mean to say that an insured has a duty to disclose? What happens if the insured fails in this duty?

7. What is an insurable interest? Why is it important?

8. Why are contracts of insurance known as contracts of indemnity?

9. What is a coinsurance clause? What is its purpose?

10. What is the right of subrogation? When does the right of subrogation arise?

11. What is the difference between a rider and an endorsement in an insurance policy?

12. How do "no-fault" liability systems differ from tort-based liability systems?

13. Describe comprehensive general liability insurance. How does it differ from warranty insurance?

14. What is the purpose of errors and omissions insurance?

15. When should a business consider buying key-person life insurance?

16. What does an insurance broker do?

17. What is the purpose of an insurance adjuster?

18. Does the insurer have a duty of good faith? Explain.

Questions for Critical Thinking

1. A manufacturing business is in the process of applying for property insurance. What kind of information must the business disclose to the insurance company? Why can insurance companies deny coverage on the basis of non-disclosure or misrepresentation of information?

2. What does it take to establish an insurable interest? For example, does an employer have an insurable interest in an employee's life? A retired executive's life? Does a creditor have an insurable interest in a debtor's life? The owner of property has an insurable interest in the property. Do mortgagees and lien holders have an insurable interest in property? Does a tenant have an insurable interest in the landlord's property? Does a thief have an insurable interest in stolen property?

3. In many regions of the world, kidnapping for ransom has become a thriving business. The victims of this crime have included not only journalists, diplomats, and aid workers, but also business executives. What role, if any, should insurance play in addressing the risk of being kidnapped in a foreign country? Do you think that the presence of insurance might exacerbate the risk? Aside from having money to pay a ransom demand, what are the other advantages of having kidnapping insurance?

4. Fraudulent insurance claims are a problem faced by the insurance industry. Common examples involve inflated property values, exaggerated personal injuries, arson and other deliberate acts of sabotage, and "insider theft." Insurance companies are entitled to question the authenticity of all claims. How far should the insurance company be able to go in obtaining

evidence of fraud? On what basis should the insurance company be entitled to deny a claim? For example, should an unusual pattern of claims be a basis for denial?

5. In *Whiten v Pilot*, the court upheld an award of punitive damages against an insurer for breach of the insurer's duty of good faith. Should the courts award punitive damages against claimants who make fraudulent insurance claims? For example, there have been instances where a group of individuals have conspired to stage motor vehicle accidents and then submitted false property damage and personal injury claims.[25] What factors should the courts consider in awarding damages for insurance fraud?

6. Between April 17 and April 19, 2011, hackers accessed Sony's online gaming service, PlayStation Network (see Technology and the Law: Business' Liability in Contract and Tort for the Consequences of Online Hacking, Chapter 11, page 246, for a detailed account). The names, birth dates, addresses, email addresses, phone numbers and passwords of millions of people who entered contests promoted by Sony were stolen. Credit card information may also have been compromised.[26] What are the potential costs to Sony as a result of this hacking incident? What are the insurance issues?

Situations for Discussion

1. Athena Aristotel operates a retail clothing store in West Vancouver. The store is located on the bottom floor of a building owned by Athena. One of Athena's friends rents the top floor for a residence. Recently, Athena suffered major property damage when a three-alarm fire destroyed her building. The cause of the fire is not known, although faulty wiring is suspected. As a result of the fire, Athena was required to temporarily move her retail operations to a nearby location. Her friend had to find a new place to live.[27] What type of insurance coverage will respond to Athena's loss? Assume that Athena discovers that she is not covered for the full extent of her losses. Must Athena absorb the uninsured portion of the loss, or does Athena have any other options? Explain. What

steps should Athena take to ensure that she has optimal insurance coverage?

2. In an increasing number of residential communities, dwellings are being used for marijuana grow operations. In many instances, a rented house is converted to a hot house to cultivate the plants. The conversion causes extensive structural damage, a compromised electrical system, excessive condensation and mould and it is unlikely that the damage is covered under the homeowner's insurance policy. This is because it is common practice in the insurance industry to include a clause that excludes damage that results from illegal activity, whether the homeowner is aware of the illegal activity or not, and a clause that specifically excludes damage that arises from marijuana growing operations. How can a business that rents out real estate manage the risk posed by marijuana grow operations? What steps should the business take prior to renting out its property? What steps should the business take after the property has been rented out?

3. Dorothy is a sole proprietor who recently incorporated her business in order to take the benefits of limited liability. As part of this change, she transferred all her business assets over to her corporation, Dorothy Ltd. Unfortunately, she forgot to change her insurance policies to name the company as the new insured. The property remains insured in Dorothy's name. Soon after the transfer, there was a break-in at Dorothy Ltd.'s corporate offices, and much of the company's expensive computer equipment was stolen. Dorothy made a claim on her policy, but the insurance company took the position that she did not have an insurable interest in the corporate property.[28]

Explain why the insurance company refused Dorothy's claim. What can she do now? What arguments can she make in support of her claim? What practical advice would Dorothy now give to other small-business owners?

4. Twelve-year-old Aaliyah Braybrook was babysitting two boys, aged three and five, when a fire broke out in their home. Braybrook was able to get the boys and the family pet out but the fire destroyed the home and damaged two neighbouring homes. It is alleged

---

25. Tara Perkins & Grant Robertson, "Staged car accidents on rise, insurers say", *The Globe and Mail* (27 November 2010) A17.
26. Gordon Hilliker, "Cyber risks & liability insurance", *The Lawyers Weekly* (19 August 2011) 9.
27. Based, in part, on Denise Deveau, "Lost: A workplace, and a living", *The Edmonton Journal* (6 October 2008) A14.
28. Based on *Kosmopoulos v Constitution Insurance Co of Canada*, [1987] 1 SCR 2, 34 DLR (4th) 208.

the fire was started by the five-year-old playing with a lighter in the bathroom. TD Insurance, the insurance company for the owners of one of the damaged neighbouring homes, filed on their behalf a $350 000 lawsuit against Braybrook and the father of the boys, who was the owner of the destroyed home. After a public outcry, including a speech by the local Member of Parliament in the House of Commons, TD Insurance dropped the suit against Braybrook.[29] What was the likely basis of the lawsuit by the neighbours against Braybrook? On what basis could TD Insurance sue Braybrook on behalf of the neighbours? What do you think was the reason for TD Insurance naming Braybrook in the lawsuit? What was the risk to TD Insurance in naming Braybrook in the lawsuit?

5. Precision Machine Ltd. manufactures pistons and rings for draglines and excavators that are used in oil sands exploration. Demand for these components is unpredictable but critical, as machines cannot operate without them. In an effort to ensure that customers are satisfied, Precision keeps about $100 000 worth of components in inventory at all times. The value of the inventory is covered by property insurance from SPADE Insurance Ltd. The policy contains a coinsurance clause that requires Precision to hold 80 percent coverage. Precision, however, only carries $60 000 worth of coverage. An electrical fire destroys some of Precision's inventory and precision makes a claim of $30 000 on its policy. How much of the claim is Precision entitled to receive from SPADE? Why would Precision underinsure its inventory? How much is Precision entitled to receive from SPADE if its loss is $40 000?

6. On 12 April 2001, portions of the retractable roof of the Toronto SkyDome collided when it was being opened. Pieces of the roof fell onto the playing field, making the SkyDome unsafe for use. The regularly scheduled Major League Baseball game between the Toronto Blue Jays and the Kansas City Royals was postponed. The Blue Jays sued Sportsco, the owner/operator of the SkyDome, for damages in the amount of $1 million, alleging a loss of revenues from the loss of use of the building on 12 April 2001. Sportsco made a claim under its comprehensive general liability policy with ING Insurance for a defence to the Blue Jays' claim. ING denied coverage and brought an

application seeking a declaration that it did not owe Sportsco a defence (an insurer has a duty to defend the insured only when allegations fall within the coverage of the policy).[30] Who has the onus of proving whether a claim falls within an insurance policy? On what basis may an insurance company like ING Insurance deny coverage to an insured?

7. Greenhouse Inc. owns and operates a greenhouse in rural Nova Scotia. On a busy Saturday in early spring, customer Xavier Donnelly trips over some bags of potting soil and falls onto a table used for repotting large plants and shrubs. Xavier suffers a severe gash to his right arm and a large bruise on his forehead. The way in which accidents and other incidents are handled can have a significant impact on the ultimate cost of a claim. How should the employees of Greenhouse handle Xavier's accident? Outline the steps that they should take in this situation.

8. In 1999, John Jacks signed a long-term car lease agreement, which was assigned by the dealership to GMAC Leaseco. On the same day, Jacks contacted a representative of the Wawanesa Mutual Insurance Company to insure the vehicle. The representative asked Jacks a few questions related to driving. In particular, the representative asked Jacks how many accidents he had had in the previous six years, whether he had ever been convicted of impaired driving, and whether his driver's licence had ever been revoked or suspended.

In 2002, Jacks had an accident and his car was destroyed. In response to his claim for compensation, Wawanesa conducted an investigation and discovered that the insured had been convicted of several crimes between 1980 and 1991, including break and enter, theft, possession of property obtained by crime, abetting in fraud, identity theft, fraud, and possession of drugs. Wawanesa refused to pay compensation on the basis that Jacks had failed in his duty to inform.[31] What is the purpose of the insured's duty to disclose? What is the content of the duty to disclose? Who has the onus of proving whether the duty to disclose has been fulfilled? Did Jacks fulfill the duty to disclose? Discuss.

For more study tools, visit
http://www.NELSONbrain.com.

---

29. Florence Loyie, "'Hero' babysitter sued over fire", *Edmonton Journal* (6 May 2010) A12; Karen Kleiss, "Insurer drops lawsuit against hero babysitter", *Edmonton Journal* (8 May 2010) A3.
30. Based on *ING Insurance Co of Canada v Sportsco International LP*, [2004] OJ No 2254, 12 CCLI (4th) 86 (Ont Sup Ct).
31. Based on *Compagnie mutuelle d'assurances Wawanesa v GMAC location ltée*, [2005] RRA 25 (Que CA).

Glossary

absolute privilege A defence to defamation in relation to parliamentary or judicial proceedings. (p. 275)

abuse of dominant position Conduct that is reviewable under the *Competition Act* because a dominant company or group of companies have engaged in anticompetitive behaviour that unduly prevents or lessens competition. (p. 602)

acceleration clause A term of a loan agreement that makes the entire loan due if one payment is missed. (p. 654)

acceptance An unqualified willingness to enter into a contract on the terms in the offer. (p. 122)

act of bankruptcy One of a list of specified acts that the debtor must commit before the court will grant a bankruptcy order. (p. 675)

action for the price The seller's claim when title to the goods has shifted to the buyer. (p. 579)

actual authority The power of an agent that derives from either express or implied agreement. (p. 290)

administrative law Rules created and applied by those having governmental powers. (p. 42)

adverse effects discrimination Discrimination that occurs as a result of a rule that appears neutral but in its effects is discriminatory. (p. 495)

after-acquired property Collateral that includes personal property acquired by the debtor during the term of the loan. (p. 649)

age of majority The age at which a person becomes an adult for legal purposes. In Canada, this ranges from 18 to 19 years of age, depending on the province. (p. 10)

agency A relationship that exists when one party represents another party in the formation of legal relations. (p. 287)

agency by estoppel An agency relationship created when the principal acts such that third parties reasonably conclude that an agency relationship exists. (p. 293)

agency by ratification An agency relationship created when one party adopts a contract entered into on his behalf by another who at the time acted without authority. (p. 295)

agent A person who is authorized to act on behalf of another. (p. 287)

aggravated damages Compensation for intangible injuries such as distress and humiliation caused by the defendant's reprehensible conduct. (p. 232)

alternative dispute resolution (ADR) A range of options for resolving disputes as an alternative to litigation. (p. 74)

anticipatory breach A breach that occurs before the date for performance. (p. 205)

Anton Pillar order A pretrial order allowing the seizure of material, including material that infringes intellectual property rights. (p. 450)

apparent authority The power that an agent appears to have to an outsider because of conduct or statements of the principal. (p. 292)

appeal The process of arguing to a higher court that a court decision is wrong. (p. 89)

appellant The party who begins or files an appeal. (p. 89)

arbitration A process through which a neutral party makes a decision (usually binding) that resolves a dispute. (p. 12)

arbitrator A person who listens to the parties to a dispute and makes a ruling that is usually binding on the parties. (p. 80)

arm's length People who are independent of each other and not related. (p. 677)

articles of incorporation The document that defines the basic characteristics of corporations incorporated in Newfoundland, New Brunswick, Ontario, Manitoba, Saskatchewan, Alberta, and the federal jurisdiction. (p. 352)

assault The threat of imminent physical harm. (p. 224)

assignment The transfer of a right by an assignor to an assignee. (p. 197)

assignment in bankruptcy The debtor's voluntary assignment to the trustee in bankruptcy of legal title to the debtor's property for the benefit of creditors. (p. 675)

bailee The person who receives possession in a bailment. (p. 405)

bailment Temporary transfer of possession of personal property from one person to another. (p. 405)

bailment for value Bailment involving payment for use of property or a service. (p. 405)

bailor The owner of property who transfers possession in a bailment. (p. 405)

bait and switch Advertising a product at a very low price to attract customers, then encouraging them to buy another product that is more expensive. (p. 593)

balance of probabilities Proof that there is a better than 50 percent chance that the circumstances of the contract are as the plaintiff contends. (p. 200)

banking contract A contract that specifies the rights and obligations of a bank and a customer. (p. 626)

bankrupt The legal status of a debtor who has made an assignment or against whom a bankruptcy order has been issued (also used to describe a debtor who is bankrupt). (p. 675)

bankruptcy offences Criminal acts defined by the *BIA* in relation to the bankruptcy process. (p. 679)

bankruptcy order An order of the court resulting in a person being declared bankrupt. (p. 675)

battery Intentional infliction of harmful or offensive physical contact. (p. 224)

bid rigging Conspiring to fix the bidding process to suit the collective needs of those submitting bids. (p. 602)

bill Proposed legislation. (p. 36)

bill of exchange A written order to a person to pay a specified amount to another person. (p. 631)

bill of lading A shipping document that serves as a contract between the seller and the carrier. (p. 574)

binding Final and enforceable in the courts. (p. 81)

bona fide occupational requirement (BFOR) A defence that excuses discrimination on a prohibited ground when it is done in good faith and for a legitimate business reason. (p. 495)

bond A document evidencing a debt owed by the corporation, often used to refer to a secured debt. (p. 354)

breach of contract Failure to comply with a contractual promise. (p. 8)

burden of proof The obligation of the plaintiff to prove its case. (p. 86)

business ethics Moral principles and values that seek to determine right and wrong in the business world. (p. 15)

business law A set of established rules governing commercial relationships, including the enforcement of rights. (p. 4)

bylaws Laws made by the municipal level of government; also rules specifying the day-to-day operating procedures of a corporation. (p. 29)

cabinet A body composed of all ministers heading government departments, as well as the prime minister or premier. (p. 30)

Canadian Charter of Rights and Freedoms A guarantee of specific rights and freedoms enshrined in the Constitution and enforceable by the judiciary. (p. 32)

Canadian legal system The machinery that comprises and governs the legislative, executive, and judicial branches of government. (p. 24)

carrier A bailee who transports personal property. (p. 408)

causation The relationship that exists between the defendant's conduct and the plaintiff's loss or injury. (p. 242)

caveat emptor "Let the buyer beware" or "let the buyer take care." (p. 572)

certification The process by which a union is recognized as a bargaining agent for a group of employees; also the process whereby a bank guarantees payment of a cheque. (p. 634)

chattel lease A contract where a lessee pays for the use of a lessor's tangible personal property. (p. 412)

cheque A written order to a bank to pay money to a specified person. (p. 629)

c.i.f. A contractual term making the seller responsible for insurance and shipping. (p. 574)

citizen's arrest See **legal authority**.

Civil Code of Quebec The rules of private law that govern Quebec. (p. 41)

claim The formal document that initiates litigation by setting out the plaintiff's allegations against the defendant. (p. 85)

claims The exclusive rights of the patent holder. (p. 430)

class action A lawsuit launched by one person who represents a class of persons having similar claims against the same defendant. (p. 83)

closely held corporation A corporation that does not sell its shares to the public. (p. 347)

closing The final stage of a real estate transaction when final documentation and payment are exchanged. (p. 469)

c.o.d. A contractual term requiring the purchaser to pay the shipper cash on delivery of goods. (p. 575)

collateral Property in which a creditor takes an interest as security for a borrower's promise to repay a loan. (p. 647)

collection agency An agency that assists lenders in obtaining payment on outstanding loans. (p. 660)

collective agreement The employment agreement reached between the union and employer setting out the bargaining unit employees' terms and conditions of employment. (p. 514)

collective bargaining A mechanism by which parties enter a collective agreement or contract. (p. 514)

common law Rules that are formulated in judgments. (p. 38)

common mistake Both parties to the agreement share the same fundamental mistake. (p. 178)

common share A share that generally has a right to vote, share in dividends, and share in proceeds on dissolution. (p. 385)

concurrent jurisdiction Jurisdiction that is shared between levels of government. (p. 27)

condition An important term that, if breached, gives the innocent party the right to terminate the contract and claim damages. (p. 203)

condition precedent An event or circumstance that, until it occurs, suspends the parties' obligations to perform their contractual obligations. (p. 153)

condition subsequent An event or circumstance that, when it occurs, brings an existing contract to an end. (p. 153)

condonation Employer behaviour that indicates to the employee that misconduct is being overlooked. (p. 523)

conduct incompatible Personal behaviour that is irreconcilable with employment duties or prejudicial to the employer's business. (p. 524)

confidential business information Information that provides a business advantage as a result of the fact that it is kept secret. (p. 445)

consideration The price paid for a promise. (p. 128)

constitutional conventions Important rules that are not enforceable by a court of law but that practically determine how a given power is exercised by government. (p. 25)

constitutional law The supreme law of Canada that constrains and controls how the branches of government exercise power. (p. 23)

constructive dismissal Employer conduct that amounts to a breach of a fundamental term of the employment contract. (p. 530)

consumer debt A loan to an individual for a non-commercial purpose. (p. 659)

consumer note A negotiable instrument signed by a consumer to buy on credit. (p. 634)

contingency fee A fee based on a percentage of the judgment awarded, and paid by the client to the lawyer only if the action is successful. (p. 90)

contract An agreement between two parties that is enforceable in a court of law. (p. 101)

contract law Rules that make agreements binding and therefore facilitate planning and the enforcement of expectations. (p. 10)

contractual entrant Any person who has paid (contracted) for the right to enter the premises. (p. 262)

contractual *quantum meruit* Awarding one party a reasonable sum for the goods or services provided under a contract. (p. 148)

contributory negligence A defence claiming that the plaintiff is at least partially responsible for the harm that has occurred. (p. 228)

conversion right The right to convert one type of security into another type. (p. 355)

copyright The right to prevent others from copying or modifying certain works. (p. 439)

corporate opportunity A business opportunity in which the corporation has an interest. (p. 375)

costs Legal expenses that a judge orders the loser to pay the winner. (p. 87)

counterclaim A claim by the defendant against the plaintiff. (p. 85)

counteroffer The rejection of one offer and proposal of a new one. (p. 122)

credit bureau An agency that compiles credit information on borrowers. (p. 660)

cyber-squatting The bad-faith practice of registering trademarks or trade names of others as domain names for the purpose of selling the domain name to the rightful owner or preventing the rightful owner from obtaining the domain name. (p. 435)

damages Monetary compensation for breach of contract or other actionable wrong. (p. 206)

damages for non-acceptance Damages to which a seller is entitled if a buyer refuses to accept goods prior to the title shifting. (p. 579)

debenture A document evidencing a debt owed by the corporation, often used to refer to an unsecured debt. (p. 354)

debtor in possession (DIP) financing Secured credit provided to companies during the reorganization process with priority over existing secured creditors. (p. 673)

deceit or fraud A false representation intentionally or recklessly made by one person to another that causes damage or loss. (p. 221)

decision The judgment of the court that specifies which party is successful and why. (p. 87)

deductible The part of a loss for which the insured is responsible. (p. 692)

defamation The public utterance of a false statement of fact or opinion that harms another's reputation. (p. 274)

defence The defendant's formal response to the plaintiff's allegations. (p. 85)

defendant The party being sued. (p. 82)

deficiency The shortfall between the outstanding mortgage balance and the proceeds from sale of the land; also the shortfall if collateral is sold for less than the amount of the outstanding debt. (p. 475)

derivative action A suit by a shareholder on behalf of the corporation to enforce a corporate cause of action. (p. 387)

director A person elected by shareholders to manage a corporation. (p. 327)

discharge of bankruptcy An order releasing the debtor from bankrupt status and from most remaining debts. (p. 683)

discovery The process of disclosing evidence to support the claims in a lawsuit. (p. 85)

discrimination The act of treating someone differently on the basis of a prohibited ground. (p. 495)

dissent and appraisal right The right of shareholders who dissent from certain fundamental changes to the corporation to have their shares purchased by the corporation at a fair price. (p. 387)

distinguishing guise A shaping of wares or their container, or a mode of wrapping or packaging wares. (p. 434)

distress The right of a commercial landlord to seize the tenant's personal property for non-payment of rent. (p. 479)

distributorship A contractual relationship where one business agrees to sell another's products. (p. 335)

dividend A division of profits payable to shareholders. (p. 328)

domain name The unique address of a website. (p. 435)

domestic law The internal law of a given country, which includes both statute and case law. (p. 40)

door-to-door selling The act of selling in person directly, at a customer's residence. (p. 609)

double ticketing The offence of failing to sell at the lower of the two or more prices marked on or otherwise appearing with regard to a product. (p. 606)

due diligence A defence based on adopting reasonable steps to avoid the violation of a legal duty. (p. 591)

duty of care The responsibility owed to avoid carelessness that causes harm to others. (p. 240)

duty of confidentiality The obligation of a professional not to disclose any information provided by the client without the client's consent. (p. 557)

duty to accommodate The duty of an employer to modify work rules, practices, and requirements to meet the needs of individuals who would otherwise be subjected to unlawful discrimination. (p. 496)

duty to disclose The obligation of the insured to provide to the insurer all information that relates to the risk being insured. (p. 692)

duty to mitigate The obligation to take reasonable steps to minimize the losses resulting from a breach of contract or other wrong. (p. 209)

easement The right to use the land of another for a particular purpose only. (p. 461)

economic duress The threat of economic harm that coerces the will of the other party and results in a contract. (p. 169)

electronic banking Financial transactions carried out through the use of computers, telephones, or other electronic means. (p. 627)

employment equity legislation Laws designed to improve the status of certain designated groups. (p. 498)

employment relationship A contractual relationship whereby an employer provides remuneration to an employee in exchange for work or services. (p. 489)

employment standards legislation Laws that specify minimum standards in the workplace. (p. 503)

endorse Sign a negotiable instrument in order to enable negotiation. (p. 635)

endorsement Written evidence of a change to an existing insurance policy; also, the signature on a negotiable instrument. (p. 635)

endorsement in blank Signing a cheque without any special instructions. (p. 636)

entire contract clause A term in a contract in which the parties agree that their contract is complete as written. (p. 148)

equal bargaining power The legal assumption that parties to a contract are able to look out for their own interests. (p. 107)

equity Rules that focus on what would be fair given the specific circumstances of the case, as opposed to what the strict rules of common law might dictate. (p. 39)

equity of redemption The right to regain legal title to mortgaged land upon repayment of the debt. (p. 472)

estate The property of a deceased person; also an interest in land (p. 459); also the collective term for the assets of a bankrupt individual or corporation. (p. 669)

events of default Failure by the debtor to make required payments on a loan or to fulfill its other obligations under the credit agreement. (p. 647)

evidence Proof presented in court to support a claim. (p. 86)

exclusive dealing When a seller agrees to sell to the purchaser only if the purchaser buys from it exclusively. (p. 607)

exclusive jurisdiction Jurisdiction that one level of government holds entirely on its own and not on a shared basis with another level. (p. 27)

exclusive possession The tenant's right to control land during the term of a lease. (p. 476)

exemption clause A term of a contract that identifies events causing loss for which there is no liability. (p. 155)

expectation damages Damages which provide the plaintiff with the monetary equivalent of contractual performance. (p. 206)

express term A provision of a contract that states a promise explicitly. (p. 142)

fair comment A defence to defamation that is established when the plaintiff cannot show malice and the defendant can show that the comment concerned a matter of public interest, was factually based, and expressed a view that could honestly be held by anyone. (p. 274)

fair dealing A defence to copyright infringement that permits the copying of works for limited purposes. (p. 444)

false imprisonment Unlawful detention or physical restraint or coercion by psychological means. (p. 269)

false or misleading advertising Promotional statements that either are false or have the ability to mislead a consumer as to their truth. (p. 589)

Federal Court of Canada The court that deals with some types of litigation involving the federal government. (p. 32)

fee simple The legal interest in real property that is closest to full ownership. (p. 459)

fiduciary A person who has a duty of good faith toward another because of their relationship. (p. 297)

fiduciary duty A duty imposed on a person who has a special relationship of trust with another. (p. 297)

financing lease A lease that enables the lessee to finance the acquisition of tangible personal property. (p. 412)

financing statement The document registered as evidence of a security interest. (p. 651)

fixed- or definite-term contract A contract for a specified period of time, which automatically ends on the expiry date. (p. 501)

fixtures Tangible personal property that is attached to land, buildings, or other fixtures. (p. 459)

f.o.b. A contractual term whereby the buyer specifies the type of transportation and the seller arranges that transportation and delivery of goods to the shipper at the buyer's expense. (p. 575)

foreclosure The mortgagee's remedy to terminate the mortgagor's interest in the land. (p. 475)

forfeiture rule A rule that provides that a criminal should not be permitted to profit from a crime. (p. 695)

formal executive The branch of government responsible for the ceremonial features of government. (p. 29)

franchise An agreement whereby an owner of a trademark or trade name permits another to sell a product or service under that trademark or name. (p. 331)

frustration Termination of a contract by an unexpected event or change that makes performance functionally impossible or illegal. (p. 198)

fundamental breach A breach of contract that affects the foundation of the contract. (p. 204)

fundamental term A term that is considered to be essential to the contract. (p. 530)

general security agreement A security agreement that includes all of the debtor's personal property assets as collateral. (p. 649)

government policy The central ideas or principles that guide government in its work, including the kind of laws it passes. (p. 23)

gratuitous bailment Bailment that involves no payment. (p. 406)

gratuitous promise A promise for which no consideration is given. (p. 128)

grievance process A procedure for resolving disputes contained in union contracts. (p. 539)

guarantee A conditional promise to a creditor to pay a debt if the debtor defaults. (p. 656)

guarantor A person who guarantees a debt. (p. 656)

habitual neglect of duty Persistent failure to perform employment duties. (p. 523)

holder A person who has possession of a negotiable instrument. (p. 633)

holder in due course A holder in good faith without notice of defects, who acquires greater rights than the parties who dealt directly with each other as the drawer and payee. (p. 633)

human rights commission An administrative body that oversees the implementation and enforcement of human rights legislation. (p. 493)

identification theory A theory specifying that a corporation is liable when the person committing the wrong is the corporation's directing mind. (p. 367)

identity theft The fraudulent use of others' personal information to create a false identity. (p. 628)

illegal contract A contract that cannot be enforced because it is contrary to legislation or public policy. (p. 180)

implied term A provision that is not expressly included in a contract but that is necessary to give effect to the parties' intentions. (p. 144)

incompetence Lack of ability, knowledge, or qualification to perform employment obligations. (p. 523)

incorporator The person who sets the incorporation process in motion. (p. 352)

indefinite-term contract A contract for no fixed period, which can end on giving reasonable notice. (p. 501)

indemnification Reimbursement or compensation for damages, losses or expenses; also the corporate practice of paying the litigation expenses of officers and directors for lawsuits related to corporate affairs. (p. 382)

indemnity A primary obligation to pay a debt owed by another person; also the obligation on the insurer to make good the loss. (p. 656)

independent contractor A person who is in a working relationship that does not meet the criteria of employment. (p. 489)

industrial design The visual features of shape, configuration, pattern, ornamentation, or any combination of these applied to a finished article of manufacture. (p. 432)

inferior court A court with limited financial jurisdiction whose judges are appointed by the provincial government. (p. 31)

injurious or malicious falsehood The utterance of a false statement about another's goods or services that is harmful to the reputation of those goods or services. (p. 276)

innkeeper Someone who offers lodging to the public. (p. 408)

innominate term A term that cannot easily be classified as either a condition or a warranty. (p. 203)

insider A person whose relationship with the issuer of securities is such that he is likely to have access to relevant material information concerning the issuer that is not known to the public. (p. 358)

insider trading Transactions in securities of a corporation by or on behalf of an insider on the basis of relevant material information concerning the corporation that is not known to the general public. (p. 358)

insolvent Unable to meet financial obligations as they become due or having insufficient assets, if liquidated, to meet financial obligations. (p. 670)

inspector A person appointed by creditors to act on their behalf and supervise the actions of the trustee in bankruptcy. (p. 676)

insurable interest A financial stake in what is being insured. (p. 694)

insurance adjuster One who investigates and evaluates insurance claims. (p. 707)

insurance broker One who provides advice and assistance to those acquiring insurance. (p. 300)

insurance policy A contract of insurance. (p. 691)

insured One who buys insurance coverage. (p. 691)

insurer A company that sells insurance coverage. (p. 691)

intangible property Personal property, the value of which comes from legal rights. (p. 401)

intellectual property The results of the creative process, such as ideas, the expression of ideas, formulas, schemes, trademarks, and the like; also refers to the protection attached to ideas through patent, copyright, trademark, industrial design, and other similar laws. (p. 424)

intentional tort A harmful act that is committed on purpose. (p. 224)

interference with contractual relations Incitement to break the contractual obligations of another. (p. 273)

interlocutory injunction An order to refrain from doing something for a limited period of time. (p. 211)

international law Law that governs relations between states and other entities with international legal status. (p. 40)

invitation to treat An expression of willingness to do business. (p. 115)

invitee Any person who comes onto the property to provide the occupier with a benefit. (p. 262)

joint and several liability Individual and collective liability for a debt. Each liable party is individually responsible for the entire debt as well as being collectively liable for the entire debt. (p. 321)

joint liability Liability shared by two or more parties where each is personally liable for the full amount of the obligation. (p. 316)

joint tenancy Co-ownership whereby the survivor inherits the undivided interest of the deceased. (p. 460)

joint tort-feasors Two or more persons whom a court has held to be jointly responsible for the plaintiff's loss or injuries. (p. 227)

joint venture A grouping of two or more businesses to undertake a particular project. (p. 334)

judges Those appointed by federal and provincial governments to adjudicate on a variety of disputes, as well as to preside over criminal proceedings. (p. 30)

judgment debtor The party ordered by the court to pay a specified amount to the winner of a lawsuit. (p. 89)

judiciary A collective reference to judges. (p. 30)

jurisdiction The power that a given level of government has to enact laws. (p. 26)

just cause Employee conduct that amounts to a fundamental breach of the employment contract. (p. 521)

justification A defence to defamation based on the defamatory statement being substantially true. (p. 274)

labour relations board A body that administers labour relations legislation. (p. 514)

land titles system The system of land registration whereby the administrators guarantee the title to land. (p. 462)

landlord The owner of land who grants possession to the tenant. (p. 476)

lapse The expiration of an offer after a specified or reasonable period. (p. 121)

law The set of rules and principles guiding conduct in society. (p. 5)

law firm A partnership formed by lawyers. (p. 64)

law of agency The law governing the relationship where one party, the agent, acts on behalf of another, the principal. (p. 289)

lawyer A person who is legally qualified to practise law. (p. 64)

lease A contract that transfers possession of land from the landlord to the tenant in exchange for the payment of rent; also refers to the tenant's interest in land (p. 476); also refers to a contract that transfers possession of personal property in exchange for a fee (p. 411)

legal authority The authority by law to detain under section 494 of the *Criminal Code*. (p. 269)

legal capacity The ability to make binding contracts. (p. 167)

legal risk A business risk with legal implications. (p. 50)

legal risk management plan A comprehensive action plan for dealing with the legal risks involved in operating a business. (p. 50)

legislative branch The branch of government that creates statute law. (p. 25)

letter of commitment A document that is provided by a lender to a borrower and sets out the terms of a loan. (p. 648)

letter of credit A written promise by a buyer's bank to a seller's bank to pay the seller when specified conditions are met. (p. 646)

liability Legal responsibility for the event or loss that has occurred. (p. 12)

liberalism A political philosophy that emphasizes individual freedom as its key organizing value. (p. 23)

licence Consent given by the owner of rights to someone to do something that only the owner can do. (p. 448)

licensee Any person whose presence is not a benefit to the occupier but to which the occupier has no objection. (p. 263)

lien The right to retain possession of personal property until payment for service is received. (p. 415)

lifting the corporate veil Determining that the corporation is not a separate legal entity from its shareholders. (p. 383)

limitation of liability clause A term of a contract that limits liability for breach to something less than would otherwise be recoverable. (p. 155)

limitation period The time period specified by legislation for commencing legal action. (p. 82)

limited liability Responsibility for obligations restricted to the amount of investment. (p. 328)

limited liability partnership (LLP) A partnership in which the partners have unlimited liability for their own malpractice but limited liability for other partners' malpractice. (p. 326)

limited partnership A partnership in which the liability of some partners is limited to their capital contribution. (p. 325)

liquidated damages clause A term of a contract that specifies how much one party must pay to the other in the event of breach. (p. 158)

litigation The process involved when one person sues another. (p. 11)

marketing law All areas of law that influence and direct the creation, promotion, pricing, and distribution of goods, services, or ideas. (p. 571)

mediation A process through which the parties to a dispute endeavour to reach a resolution with the assistance of a neutral person. (p. 12)

mediator A person who helps the parties resolve their dispute. (p. 78)

misrepresentation A false statement of fact that causes someone to enter a contract. (p. 175)

mistake An error made by one or both parties that seriously undermines a contract. (p. 177)

money laundering The false reporting of income from criminal activity as income from legitimate business. (p. 625)

moral rights The author's rights to have work properly attributed and not prejudicially modified or associated with products. (p. 443)

mortgage A credit arrangement where title to land is security for the loan. (p. 471)

mortgagee The party who lends the money and receives the signed mortgage as security for repayment. (p. 472)

mortgagor The party who borrows the money and signs the mortgage promising to repay the loan. (p. 472)

multi-level marketing A scheme for distributing products or services that involves participants recruiting others to become involved in distribution. (p. 608)

negligence Unreasonable conduct, including a careless act or omission, that causes harm to another. (p. 221)

negligent misstatement or negligent misrepresentation An incorrect statement made carelessly. (p. 248)

negotiable instrument A written contract containing an unconditional promise or order to pay a specific sum on demand or on a specified date to a specific person or bearer. (p. 631)

negotiation A process of deliberation and discussion intended to reach a mutually acceptable resolution to a dispute; also the process of transferring negotiable instruments from one person to another. (p. 635)

neighbour Anyone who might reasonably be affected by another's conduct. (p. 240)

non-competition clause A clause forbidding competition for a certain period of time. (p. 182)

non-pecuniary damages Compensation for pain and suffering, loss of enjoyment of life, and loss of life expectancy. (p. 229)

non-solicitation clause A clause forbidding contact with the business' customers. (p. 182)

novation The substitution of parties in a contract or the replacement of one contract with another. (p. 196)

NUANS Report A document that shows the result of a search for business names. (p. 351)

nuisance Any activity on an occupier's property that unreasonably and substantially interferes with the neighbour's rights to enjoyment of the neighbour's own property. (p. 266)

objective standard test The test based on how a "reasonable person" would view the matter. (p. 106)

occupier Someone who has some degree of control over land or buildings on that land. (p. 262)

offer A promise to perform specified acts on certain terms. (p. 114)

offeree The person to whom an offer is made. (p. 118)

offeror The person who makes an offer. (p. 118)

operating lease A lease where the property is returned to the lessor when the term is up. (p. 412)

oppression remedy A statutory remedy available to shareholders and other stakeholders to protect their corporate interests. (p. 388)

option agreement An agreement where, in exchange for payment, an offeror is obligated to keep an offer open for a specified time. (p. 120)

outsider The party with whom the agent does business on behalf of the principal. (p. 289)

paralegal One who performs legal work under the supervision of a practising lawyer. (p. 462)

paramountcy A doctrine that provides that federal laws prevail when there are conflicting or inconsistent federal and provincial laws. (p. 28)

parol evidence rule A rule that limits the evidence a party can introduce concerning the contents of the contract. (p. 148)

partnership A business carried on by two or more persons with the intention of making a profit. (p. 315)

passing off Presenting another's goods or services as one's own. (p. 271)

patent A monopoly to make, use, or sell an invention. (p. 425)

patent agent A professional trained in patent law and practice who can assist in the preparation of a patent application. (p. 430)

pay equity Provisions designed to ensure that female and male employees receive the same compensation for performing similar or substantially similar work. (p. 509)

payday loans A short-term loan for a relatively small amount of money, provided by a non-traditional lender to an individual. (p. 661)

pecuniary damages Compensation for out-of-pocket expenses, loss of future income, and cost of future care. (p. 229)

periodic tenancy A lease that is automatically renewed unless one party gives proper notice to terminate. (p. 480)

personal property All property, other than land and what is attached to it. (p. 401)

plaintiff The party that initiates a lawsuit against another party. (p. 82)

pleadings The formal documents concerning the basis for a lawsuit. (p. 85)

political executive The branch of government responsible for day-to-day operations, including formulating and executing government policy, as well as administering all departments of government. (p. 29)

precedent An earlier case used to resolve a current case because of its similarity. (p. 38)

pre-emptive right A shareholder's right to maintain a proportionate share of ownership by purchasing a proportionate share of any new stock issue. (p. 386)

pre-existing legal duty A legal obligation that a person already owes. (p. 130)

preferred creditors Certain unsecured creditors who are given priority over other unsecured creditors in the bankruptcy distribution. (p. 680)

preferred share A share or stock that has a preference in the distribution of dividends and the proceeds on dissolution. (p. 385)

premium The price paid for insurance coverage. (p. 691)

price maintenance The attempt to drive the final retail price of goods upward and the imposition of recriminations upon noncompliant retailers. (p. 603)

prima facie At first sight or on first appearances. (p. 241)

principal A person who has permitted another to act on her behalf. (p. 287)

private law Areas of law that concern dealings between persons. (p. 41)

privilege The professional's right not to divulge a client's confidential information to third parties. (p. 557)

procedural law The law governing the procedure to enforce rights, duties, and liabilities. (p. 40)

product liability Liability relating to the design, manufacture, or sale of the product. (p. 250)

product licensing An arrangement whereby the owner of a trademark or other proprietary right grants to another the right to manufacture or distribute products associated with the trademark or other proprietary right. (p. 336)

professional Someone engaged in an occupation, usually governed by a professional body, requiring the exercise of specialized knowledge, education, and skill. (p. 249)

progressive discipline policy A system that follows a sequence of employee discipline from less to more severe punishment. (p. 522)

promissory estoppel A doctrine whereby someone who relies on a gratuitous promise may be able to enforce it. (p. 132)

promissory note A written promise to another person to pay a specified amount. (p. 631)

proof of claim A formal notice provided by the creditor to the trustee of the amount owed and the nature of the debt. (p. 679)

prospectus The document a corporation must publish when offering securities to the public. (p. 357)

proxy A person who is authorized to exercise a shareholder's voting rights. (p. 385)

public law Areas of the law that relate to or regulate the relationship between persons and government at all levels. (p. 40)

public policy The community's common sense and common conscience. (p. 181)

punitive damages An award to the plaintiff to punish the defendant for malicious, oppressive, and high-handed conduct. (p. 206)

purchase-money security interest (PMSI) A security interest that enables the debtor to acquire assets and gives the secured party priority over existing perfected security interests. (p. 652)

pure economic loss Financial loss that results from a negligent act where there has been no accompanying property or personal injury damage to the person claiming the loss. (p. 245)

pyramid selling A form of multi-level selling that is illegal under the *Competition Act*. (p. 608)

qualified privilege A defence to defamation based on the defamatory statement being relevant, without malice, and communicated only to a party who has a legitimate interest in receiving it. (p. 274)

ratify To authorize or approve. (p. 29)

real property Land or real estate, including buildings, fixtures, and the associated legal rights. (p. 459)

reasonable care The care a reasonable person would exhibit in a similar situation. (p. 239)

reasonable notice A period of time for an employee to find alternative employment prior to dismissal. (p. 526)

reasonable person The standard used to judge whether a person's conduct in a particular situation is negligent. (p. 242)

rebuttable presumption A legal presumption in favour of one party that the other side can seek to rebut or dislodge by leading evidence to the contrary. (p. 135)

receiver A person appointed by the secured party or by the court to seize, and usually sell, collateral. (p. 655)

refusal to deal When a seller refuses to sell to a purchaser on the same terms as those that are offered to the purchaser's competitors. (p. 607)

registration The recording of a name or event in a list, book or register (p. 461); also the registration of a financing statement to record a security interest. (p. 651)

registry system The system of land registration whereby the records are available to be examined and evaluated by interested parties. (p. 462)

regulations Rules created by the political executive that have the force of law. (p. 30)

regulatory offence An offence contrary to the public interest. (p. 371)

rejection The refusal to accept an offer. (p. 122)

release A written or oral statement discharging another from an existing duty. (p. 539)

remoteness of damage The absence of a sufficiently close relationship between the defendant's action and the plaintiff's injury. (p. 244)

rescission The remedy that results in the parties being returned to their pre-contractual positions. (p. 175)

respondent The party against whom an appeal is filed. (p. 89)

responsible communication on matters of public interest Defense that applies where some facts are incorrectly reported but (1) the publication is on a matter of 'public interest' and (2) the publisher was diligent in trying to verify the allegation. (p. 274)

restitutionary *quantum meruit* An amount that is reasonable given the benefit the plaintiff has conferred. (p. 212)

restrictive covenant A restriction on the use of land as specified in the title document. (p. 461)

restrictive endorsement Signing a cheque for deposit only to a particular bank account. (p. 636)

retainer An advance payment requested by a professional from a client to fund services to be provided to the client. (p. 550)

revocation The withdrawal of an offer. (p. 118)

rider A clause altering or adding coverage to a standard insurance policy. (p. 696)

risk avoidance Ceasing a business activity because the legal risk is too great. (p. 56)

risk reduction Implementing practices in a business to lower the probability of loss and its severity. (p. 56)

risk retention Absorbing the loss if a legal risk materializes. (p. 57)

risk transference Shifting the risk to someone else through a contract. (p. 57)

royal prerogative Historical rights and privileges of the Crown, including the right to conduct foreign affairs and to declare war. (p. 38)

rules of construction Guiding principles for interpreting or "constructing" the terms of a contract. (p. 143)

sales agency An agreement in which a manufacturer or distributor allows another to sell products on its behalf. (p. 336)

secured credit A debt where the creditor has an interest in the debtor's property to secure payment. (p. 645)

securities Shares and bonds issued by a corporation. (p. 354)

securities legislation Laws designed to regulate transactions involving shares and bonds of a corporation. (p. 347)

security interest An interest in personal property that is intended to secure payment or performance of an obligation (usually a debt).(p. 650)

self-dealing contract A contract in which a fiduciary has a conflict of interest. (p. 374)

serious misconduct Intentional, harmful conduct of the employee that permits the employer to dismiss without notice. (p. 522)

severance pay An amount owed to a terminated employee under employment standards legislation. (p. 538)

share structure The shares that a corporation is permitted to issue by its constitution. (p. 346)

shareholder A person who has an ownership interest in a corporation. (p. 327)

shareholders' agreement An agreement that defines the relationship among people who have an ownership interest in a corporation. (p. 390)

shelf company A company that does not engage in active business. (p. 352)

small claims court A court that deals with claims up to a specified amount. (p. 31)

sole proprietorship An unincorporated business organization that has only one owner. (p. 312)

special endorsement Signing a cheque and making it payable to a specific person. (p. 636)

specific goods Goods that are identified and agreed on at the time a contract of sale is made. (p. 576)

specifications The description of an invention contained in a patent. (p. 430)

stakeholder One who has an interest in a corporation. (p. 344)

standard form contract A "take it or leave it" contract, where the customer agrees to a standard set of terms that favours the other side. (p. 116)

statute law Formal, written laws created or enacted by the legislative branch of government. (p. 25)

stop payment The process whereby the person who writes a cheque orders the bank not to pay the holder who presents it for payment. (p. 635)

stoppage in transit The right of a seller to demand that goods be returned by a shipper to the seller, provided the buyer is insolvent. (p. 574)

strategic alliance An arrangement whereby two or more businesses agree to cooperate for some purpose. (p. 335)

strict liability The principle that liability will be imposed irrespective of proof of negligence. (p. 252)

subrogation The right of a guarantor to recover from the debtor any payments made to the creditor; also the right of the insurer to recover the amount paid on a claim from a third party that caused the loss. (p. 657)

substantive law Law that defines rights, duties, and liabilities. (p. 40)

superior court A court with unlimited financial jurisdiction whose judges are appointed by the federal government. (p. 31)

Supreme Court of Canada The final court for appeals in the country. (p. 31)

systemic discrimination Discrimination that results from the combined effects of many rules, practices, and policies. (p. 495)

tangible property Personal property which is mobile, the value of which comes from its physical form. (p. 401)

telemarketing The use of the telephone to communicate product and organizational information to customers. (p. 609)

tenancy in common Co-ownership whereby each owner of an undivided interest can dispose of that interest. (p. 459)

tenant The party in possession of land that is leased. (p. 476)

thin skull rule The principle that a defendant is liable for the full extent of a plaintiff's injury even where a prior vulnerability makes the harm more serious than it otherwise might be. (p. 244)

third party One who is not a party to an agreement. (p. 249)

tied selling When a seller will sell to the purchaser only if the purchaser buys other, less desirable goods as well. (p. 607)

tippee A person who acquires material information about an issuer of securities from an insider. (p. 358)

title search Investigation of the registered ownership of land in a registry system. (p. 467)

tort A harm caused by one person to another, other than through breach of contract, and for which the law provides a remedy. (p. 221)

tort-feasor Person who commits a tort. (p. 222)

trade name The name under which a sole proprietorship, a partnership, or a corporation does business. (p. 434)

trademark A word, symbol, design, or any combination of these used to distinguish the source of goods or services. (p. 433)

transfers at undervalue Transfers of property or provision of services for less than fair market value. (p. 677)

treaty An agreement between two or more states that is governed by international law. (p. 29)

trespass to land Wrongful interference with someone's possession of land. (p. 221)

trespasser Any person who is not invited onto the property and whose presence is either unknown to the occupier or is objected to by the occupier. (p. 263)

trial A formal hearing before a judge that results in a binding decision. (p. 86)

trustee in bankruptcy The person who has legal responsibility under the *BIA* for administering bankruptcies and proposals. (p. 669)

unanimous shareholders' agreement (USA) An agreement among all shareholders that restricts the powers of the directors to manage the corporation. (p. 390)

unascertained goods Goods not yet set aside and identifiable as the subject of the contract at the time the contract is formed. (p. 576)

unconscionable contract An unfair contract formed when one party takes advantage of the weakness of another. (p. 172)

undisclosed principal A principal whose identity is unknown to a third party who has no knowledge that the agent is acting in an agency capacity. (p. 301)

undue influence Unfair manipulation that compromises someone's free will. (p. 170)

unfair practices Illegal business practices that exploit the unequal bargaining position of consumers. (p. 580)

unjust enrichment Occurs when one party has undeservedly or unjustly secured a benefit at the other party's expense. (p. 212)

unlimited liability Unrestricted legal responsibility for obligations. (p. 312)

unsecured credit A debt where the creditor has only a contractual right to be repaid. (p. 645)

vicarious liability The liability that an employer has for the tortious acts of an employee committed in the ordinary course or scope of employment. (p. 226)

vicarious performance Performance of contractual obligations through others. (p. 196)

void contract A contract involving a defect so substantial that it is of no force or effect. (p. 167)

voidable contract A contract that, in certain circumstances, an aggrieved party can choose to keep in force or bring to an end. (p. 167)

voluntary assumption of risk The defence that no liability exists as the plaintiff agreed to accept the risk inherent in the activity. (p. 247)

warehouseman A bailee who stores personal property. (p. 407)

warranty A minor term that, if breached, gives the innocent party the right to claim damages only. (p. 203)

warranty of authority A representation of authority by a person who purports to be an agent. (p. 301)

widely held corporation A corporation whose shares are normally traded on a stock exchange. (p. 347)

willful disobedience Deliberate failure to carry out lawful and reasonable orders. (p. 525)

winding up The process of dissolving a corporation. (p. 392)

workers' compensation legislation Legislation that provides no-fault compensation for injured employees in lieu of their right to sue in tort. (p. 228)

Index

How to Read a Citation

Citation for a Civil Case

Canadian Civil Liberties Assn	v	*Toronto Dominion Bank*	(1998),	163	DLR	(4th)	193	(FCA)
plaintiff	versus (Latin, "against")	defendant	year of decision	volume number	report listing case	series	page number	court

Citation for a Criminal Case

R	v	*Fuel Base Industries Inc*	(1992),	44	C.P.R.	(3d)	184	(Alta Prov Ct)
Rex or Regina (Latin, "King" or "Queen")	versus (Latin, "against")	defendant or accused	year of decision	volume number	report listing case	series	page number	court

Abbreviations

References to the decisions of the courts, to statutes, and to legal periodicals are abbreviated throughout the text in case citations and footnotes. The list below shows the abbreviations for frequently cited source material.

Jurisdictions

Canada

Alta	Alberta
BC	British Columbia
Man	Manitoba
NB	New Brunswick
NS	Nova Scotia
NWT	Northwest Territories
Nfld	Newfoundland
Ont	Ontario
PEI	Prince Edward Island
Qc	Quebec
Sask	Saskatchewan
Y	Yukon Territory

United Kingdom

E	England

United States

Ohio	Ohio
Minn	Minnesota

Courts

Canada

CA	Court of Appeal
Co Ct	County Court
CS	Cour Supérieure
Cty Ct	County Court
Div Ct	Divisional Court
FCA	Federal Court of Appeal
FCTD	Federal Court (Trial Division)
HC	High Court
H Ct J	High Court of Justice
Gen Div	General Division
Prov Ct	Provincial Court
Prov Div	Provincial Division
QB	Court of Queen's Bench
SC	Supreme Court
SC (AD)	Supreme Court (Appellate Division)
SC (TD)	Supreme Court (Trial Division)
SCC	Supreme Court of Canada

United Kingdom

CA	Court of Appeal
Ch	Chancery Court
ChD	High Court: Chancery Division
HL	House of Lords
KB	Court of King's Bench
PC	Judicial Committee of the Privy Council
QB	Court of Queen's Bench